Makers of Modern Strategy

from Machiavelli to the Nuclear Age

The Editors and Publisher wish to acknowledge the cooperation of the Institute for Advanced Study in the publication of this volume, the successor to the first *Makers of Modern Strategy*, which originated in a seminar in American foreign policy and security issues at the Institute and Princeton University in 1941.

Makers of Modern Strategy

from Machiavelli to the Nuclear Age

edited by PETER PARET

with the collaboration of

GORDON A. CRAIG *and* FELIX GILBERT

Princeton University Press, Princeton, New Jersey

This is a sequel to *Makers of Modern Strategy*, copyright 1943, © 1971 by Princeton University Press. The essays by Henry Guerlac, R. R. Palmer, and Edward Mead Earle are reprinted without significant change. Those by Felix Gilbert on Machiavelli and by Sigmund Neumann on Engels and Marx have been rewritten; the essays by Gordon A. Craig on Delbrück and by Hajo Holborn on the Prusso-German School have been revised. The remaining twenty-two essays are new. Michael Howard's essay "Men against Fire: The Doctrine of the Offensive in 1914" appeared in a slightly different form in *International Security*, Summer 1984 (Vol. 9, No. 1).

Published by Princeton University Press, 41 William Street, Princeton, New Jersey 08540

Library of Congress Cataloging-in-Publication Data

Main entry under title:
Makers of modern strategy

Bibliography: p.
Includes index.

1. Strategy—Addresses, essays, lectures. 2. Military art and science—Addresses, essays, lectures. 3. Military history, Modern—Addresses, essays, lectures. I. Paret, Peter. II. Craig, Gordon Alexander, 1913- . III. Gilbert, Felix, 1905- .

U162.M25   1986   355´.02   85-17029
ISBN 0-691-09235-4   ISBN 0-691-02764-1 (pbk.)

This book has been composed in Linotron Sabon type

Princeton University Press books are printed on acid-free paper and meet the guidelines for permanence and durability of the Committee on Production Guidelines for book Longevity of the Council on Library Resources

Printed in the United States of America

18 19 20 21 22

ISBN-13: 978-0-691-02764-7 (pbk.)

Contents

PART FOUR. FROM THE FIRST TO THE SECOND WORLD WAR

PART FIVE. SINCE 1945

Acknowledgments

THE EDITORS owe a debt of gratitude to the authors of this volume, who have made our task an unusually pleasant one. We also want to express our appreciation to Michael Howard, John Shy, and Russell Weigley for their advice in planning the book, to James E. King, whose criticism has been pertinent as always, and to Donald Abenheim for his assistance with the bibliographies. Loren Hoekzema, Elizabeth Gretz, and Susan Bishop of Princeton University Press saw the book through publication with exemplary intelligence and care. Rosalie West once again produced an index that is useful rather than impenetrable. To Herbert S. Bailey, Jr., Director of Princeton University Press, whose belief in the importance of the subject helped make the volume possible, go our special thanks.

Makers of Modern Strategy

from Machiavelli to the Nuclear Age

Introduction

PETER PARET

C ARL VON CLAUSEWITZ defined strategy as the use of combat, or the threat of combat, for the purpose of the war in which it takes place. This formulation, which a modern historian has characterized as both revolutionary and defiantly simplistic, can be amended or expanded without difficulty.[1] Clausewitz himself, setting no great store in absolute definitions, varied the meaning of strategy according to the matter at hand. Strategy is the use of armed force to achieve the military objectives and, by extension, the political purpose of the war. To those engaged in the direction and conduct of war, strategy has often appeared more simply, in Moltke's phrase, as a system of expedients. But strategy is also based on, and may include, the development, intellectual mastery, and utilization of all of the state's resources for the purpose of implementing its policy in war. It is in both of these senses—the narrower, operational meaning, and its broadly inclusive implications—that the term is used in this volume.

Strategic thought is inevitably highly pragmatic. It is dependent on the realities of geography, society, economics, and politics, as well as on other, often fleeting factors that give rise to the issues and conflicts war is meant to resolve. The historian of strategy cannot ignore these forces. He must analyze the varied context of strategy, and the manner in which context and ideas act on each other, while he traces the development from idea to doctrine to implementation, a progression that in turn will give rise to further ideas. The history of strategic thought is a history not of pure but of applied reason. Consequently the essays in this volume go far beyond theory and touch on many of the military and nonmilitary factors that help shape war. In a variety of ways they demonstrate the close interaction of peace with war, the links between society and its military institutions and policies; but the thread of strategic thought runs through them all. The essays explore ideas of soldiers and civilians since

---

[1] Michael Howard, "The Forgotten Dimensions of Strategy," *Foreign Affairs* (Summer 1979); reprinted in Michael Howard, *The Causes of War*, 2d ed. (Cambridge, Mass., 1984), 101.

the Renaissance on the most effective application of their society's military resources: how can the fighting power available, or potentially available, be used to best purpose? Having addressed these ideas, the essays turn to the further issue: what impact did strategic theory have on wars and on the periods of peace that followed?

I

The concept of this volume, and some of its substance, derive from an earlier work. In 1941 Edward Mead Earle organized a seminar on American foreign policy and security issues for faculty of the Institute for Advanced Study and Princeton University. The seminar led to a collection of twenty-one essays on "military thought from Machiavelli to Hitler," which Earle, assisted by Gordon A. Craig and Felix Gilbert, brought out two years later under the title *Makers of Modern Strategy*. One of the striking features of this book was the confidence of its editors and authors that in the midst of a world war the *history* of strategic thought deserved serious and wide attention. In their eyes, the trials of the present did not diminish the significance of the past. On the contrary, history now seemed particularly relevant. In his introduction, Earle declared that it was the purpose of the book "to explain the manner in which the strategy of modern war developed, in the conviction that a knowledge of the best military thought will enable . . . readers to comprehend the causes of war and the fundamental principles which govern the conduct of war." He added, "we believe that eternal vigilance in such matters is the price of liberty. We believe, too, that if we are to have a durable peace we must have a clear understanding of the role which armed force plays in international society. And we have not always had this understanding."[2]

The impact on these words of the condition in which they were written is apparent. A society that until recently had paid little attention to events beyond its borders was now fighting in the greatest war of all time. A new interest in learning about war, about matters that had been ignored but that now dominated public life, even an interest in gaining some kind of historical perspective not only on the political and ideological but also on the military elements of the conflict, might be expected. And as much a part of the atmosphere in which the essays were written was the belief not alone in the need but also in the possibility of a citizenry that understood the determining realities of war. *Makers of Modern Strategy* was a scholarly contribution from the arsenal of democracy in

[2] Edward Mead Earle, "Introduction," in *Makers of Modern Strategy*, ed. Edward Mead Earle (Princeton, 1943), viii.

the best sense of that contemporary term; a serious and fundamentally optimistic response to important intellectual needs of America at war and at the threshold of world power.

It was a further remarkable aspect of the book that its wartime origin and mission did not compromise its scholarly objectivity. Its contents varied in quality, although the general level was very high, but none of the essays was marred by chauvinism or denigrated current enemies; even essays on "Japanese Naval Strategy" and "The Nazi Concept of War" maintained an exemplarly intellectual honesty. No doubt that is one reason for the collection's continued success, decades after the war ended. The book has now provided two generations of readers with a rich fund of knowledge and insight; for some, very likely, it has been their only encounter with the sophisticated study of war, as opposed to its drum-and-bugle variety.

Makers of Modern Strategy became a modern classic. That the essays dealing with the Second World War were soon overtaken by events did not weaken its overall impact. No book of this kind can remain up to date; more important was the fact that it defined and interpreted crucial episodes in earlier phases of strategic thought, showed their connection with general history, which even many historians tend to ignore, and placed some continuing issues of war and peace in broad historical perspective. But, inevitably, over time the volume as a whole became less satisfactory. Since the defeat of Germany and Japan and the advent of the nuclear age strategic analysis has moved in new directions, while historical research has continued to change and deepen our understanding of the more remote past. A replacement for *Makers of Modern Strategy* has now become desirable.

In preparing the new volume, the editors have had no wish to discard the model of the old. Neither comprehensiveness nor interpretive uniformity is aimed for. Contributors were not asked to employ a particular theoretical scheme; each approaches the subject from his or her point of view. As in the earlier work, too, significant figures and episodes in the history of strategy have had to be excluded if the volume, already large, was to be kept to reasonable size. Nevertheless, collectively the essays—linked chronologically and often thematically—offer the reader a guide to strategic theory and to ideas on the use of organized violence from the time Machiavelli wrote his *Arte della guerra* to the present.

The new *Makers of Modern Strategy* contains eight more essays than did its predecessor. A few essays have been taken over from the earlier work; most were not.[3] Three essays of the 1943 edition remain unchanged

---

[3] Of the essays that were not retained, several did not fit into the new distribution of

except for some corrections and stylistic alterations: Henry Guerlac on Vauban and the impact of science on war in the seventeenth century, Robert R. Palmer on Frederick the Great and the change from dynastic to national war, and Edward Mead Earle on the economic foundations of military power. More might certainly be said about these figures and issues, but each essay retains a strong voice in the continuing scholarly discourse. The bibliographical notes of these essays have been updated. Two further essays have been very extensively rewritten, and two others revised.[4] The remaining twenty-two essays in the present volume are new.

To conclude this brief comparison of the two books, it may be appropriate to note some of the more significant thematic differences between them. The new volume has far more to say about American strategy than did its predecessor. It also contains four essays on the period since 1945, which still lay in the future for Earle and his collaborators. More generally, the new *Makers of Modern Strategy* takes a somewhat broader view of its subject. Earle would have preferred to limit himself and his collaborators to the analysis of major theorists, although the nature of the subject compelled him to look further. Because the United States had "not produced a Clausewitz or a Vauban," the only American soldiers discussed in the earlier volume were Mahan and Mitchell. Other American and European figures were not included "either because they were more tacticians than strategists or because they bequeathed to posterity no coherent statement of strategical doctrine." This last consideration also explains the absence of an essay on Napoleon. In his introduction, Earle wrote that Napoleon "recorded his strategy on the battlefield (if we exclude his trite maxims); hence he is represented here by his interpreters Clausewitz and Jomini."[5] This seems too exclusive a point of view. The difference between strategy and tactics is worth preserving; but strategy is not exclusively—or even mainly—the work of great minds, interested in spelling out their theories. Although Napoleon did not write a comprehensive treatise on his ideas on war and strategy, they deserve to be studied, and not only through the intervening screen of Clausewitz's and Jomini's interpretations. An essay on Napoleon will

---

topics—e.g., Derwent Whittlesey's study of geopolitics and Theodore Ropp's sketch of Continental doctrines of sea power. Others were written before adequate documentation on their subject was available or, although advancing scholarship at the time, have now been superseded. One or two—e.g., the essay on Maginot and Liddell Hart by the author who used the pseudonym Irving M. Gibson—did not achieve the quality of the rest.

[4] Felix Gilbert has rewritten his essay on Machiavelli, as has Mark von Hagen the essay on Marx and Engels by Sigmund Neumann. Gordon Craig has made some changes in his essay on Delbrück, and Peter Paret has revised the first part of Hajo Holborn's essay on Moltke, the second part of which has been replaced by a new essay.

[5] Earle, "Introduction," ix.

6

therefore be found in the present volume. But it must also be recognized that Napoleonic strategy was not created by the emperor alone. It was made possible because he had the genius and the compulsion to combine and exploit the ideas and policies of others. Some of these men, and even such forces as conscription, which cannot be identified with any particular individual, also belong to the history of strategy and are discussed here. As a contributor has commented, because of its broader historical focus, the new volume might be more appropriately titled *The Making of Modern Strategy*.

II

The problems and conflicts of the times in which the new *Makers of Modern Strategy from Machiavelli to the Nuclear Age* appears are very different from those that gave rise to the earlier work. The need to understand war is, if possible, even greater now than it was in 1943. But the enormity of the issues has inhibited as much as it has encouraged their study. Many people have reacted to the destructive power of nuclear weapons by rejecting the concept of war in general, and consequently feel that the nature of war itself no longer requires investigation. It is even claimed that nuclear weapons have made all wars irrational and impossible, a denial of reality that is a measure of the special anxiety that has become a part of contemporary life. Until today the nuclear age has accommodated every conceivable kind of war waged with non-nuclear weapons, from terror and guerrilla operations to large-scale air strikes and armored campaigns. War has not been excluded, it has merely become more dangerous. And even in the realm of the unthinkable—as theories of nuclear deterrence show—strategy and the need to study it have not disappeared.

A continuum—intermittent and dialectical though it may be—runs from the strategies before 1945 to the strategies of conventional war since then. The link is less apparent, more ambiguous, between the prenuclear age and nuclear strategy. It has been argued that at least so far as nuclear conflict is concerned, everything on this side of the nuclear divide is new. The technology is certainly new; but man and his social and political ideas and structures have changed very little. Governments and armed services that dispose over nuclear arsenals are made up of men and women who are not yet so very different from their parents and grandparents.

Under these conditions of crisis and partial discontinuity, in which so many of our earlier experiences seem to be beside the point, the new *Makers of Modern Strategy* raises the question of relevance even more forcefully than did its predecessor. Edward Mead Earle had no doubt that an understanding of war in history would help the reader deal more intelligently with war in the present. Not everyone—certainly not every historian—would fully share his faith in the contemporary relevance of history. Not only is every age unique in its combination of conditions, issues, and personalities; occasionally a profound revolution in technologies, beliefs, or in social and political organization seems to sever us from history, and in the view of some reduces its relevance to an absurd fiction. Much depends, however, on what is meant by relevance. The past—even if we could be confident of interpreting it with high accuracy—rarely offers direct lessons. To claim that kind of relevance is to deceive oneself. But history as the educated memory of what has gone before is a resource not to be abandoned lightly. In the affairs of a nation and in the relations between states, as in the life of the individual, the present always has a past dimension, which it is better to acknowledge than to ignore or deny. And even if we can see the present only in its own surface terms, we still have available to us what may be the greatest value history has to offer: its ability, by clarifying and making some sense of the past, to help us think about the present and future.

The phenomenon of war can be better understood by studying its past. That is one message of this book. But the history of war should also be studied in order to understand the past itself. Historians have sometimes been reluctant to acknowledge this necessity. Although they can hardly deny that war has been a fundamental reality of social and political existence from the earliest stage of political organization to our own day, war is so tragic and intellectually and emotionally so disturbing that they have tended to sidestep it in their research. In the training of historians and the teaching of history, particularly in the United States, war has never been a favorite subject. One result has been to leave far too much scope for a popular, essentially romantic literature on war, which explains nothing, but crudely responds to the fascination that war past and present exerts on our imagination and on our wish to understand. This volume tries to suggest the usefulness of integrating the history of military thought and policy with general history.

The essays that follow have as their common subject the role of force in the relations between states. All recognize that war never has been, and is not today, a unitary or even a wholly military phenomenon, but a compound of many elements, ranging from politics to technology to human emotions under extreme stress. Strategy is merely one of these elements—if a large one at times. Twenty-four of the essays trace the ideas and actions of former generations, as they used and misused war; the remaining four analyze military thought and policy in the very recent past and the present. The book is largely historical; but it also addresses and—as was its predecessor—is dedicated to the timeless cause of "a broader understanding of war and peace."

PART ONE

The Origins of Modern War

1. Machiavelli: The Renaissance of the Art of War

Felix Gilbert

I F THE VARIOUS campaigns and uprisings which have taken place in Italy have given the appearance that military ability has become extinct, the true reason is that the old methods of warfare were not good and no one has been able to find new ones. A man newly risen to power cannot acquire greater reputation than by discovering new rules and methods." With these words from the famous last chapter of *The Prince*—"The exhortation to free Italy from the barbarians"—Machiavelli expressed an idea that recurs frequently in his writings: new military institutions and new processes in warfare are the most urgent and the most fundamental requirement of his time. Machiavelli is usually held to have introduced a new era, the modern era, in the development of political thought; his conviction that the military organization of contemporary Italian states needed changing was a driving force, a central concern behind all his reflections on the world of politics. It hardly goes too far to say that Machiavelli became a political thinker because he was a military thinker. His view of the military problems of his time patterned his entire political outlook.

I

Machiavelli occupies a unique position in the field of military thought because his ideas are based on a recognition of the link between the changes that occurred in military organization and the revolutionary developments that took place in the social and political sphere. To the ordinary observer, the connection between cause and effect in military developments seemed obvious. The discovery of gunpowder and the invention of firearms and artillery suggested that the armor of the knight was doomed and the collapse of the military organization of the Middle Ages, in which knights played the decisive role, had become inevitable. In his epic *Orlando Furioso* (1516), Ariosto, Machiavelli's contemporary and Italian compatriot, narrates how Orlando, his hero and the embodiment of all knightly virtues, was forced to face an enemy with a firearm:

11

> At once the lightning flashes, shakes the ground,
> The trembling bulwarks echo to the sound.
> The pest, that never spends in vain its force,
> But shatters all that dares oppose its course,
> Whizzing impetus flies along the wind.

When the invincible Orlando succeeded in overcoming this redoubtable enemy and could choose from the rich booty:

> ... nothing would the champion bear away
> From all the spoils of that victorious day
> Save that device, whose unresisted force
> Resembled thunder in its rapid course.

Then he sailed out on the ocean, plunging the weapon into the sea and exclaiming:

> O! curs'd device! base implement of death!
> Fram'd in the black Tartarean realms beneath!
> By Beelzebub's malicious art design'd
> To ruin all the race of human kind. ...
> That ne'er again a knight by thee may dare,
> Or dastard cowards, by thy help in war,
> With vantage base, assault a nobler foe,
> Here lie for ever in th' abyss below![1]

In short, if firearms had not been invented or could now be banished, the world of the knights would live on forever in all its splendor.

This dramatic explanation of the decline of the power of the knights hardly corresponds with reality. The history of military institutions cannot be separated from the general history of a period. The military organization of the Middle Ages formed an integral part of the medieval world, and declined when the medieval social structure disintegrated. Spiritually as well as economically the knight was a characteristic product of the Middle Ages. In a society in which God was envisaged as the head of a hierarchy, all secular activity had been given a religious meaning. The particular task of chivalry was to protect and defend the people of the country; in waging war the knight served God. He placed his military services at the disposal of his overlord, to whom the supervision of secular activities was entrusted by the church. Apart from its spiritual-religious side, however, the military bond between vassal and overlord also had its legal and economic aspects. The knight's land, the fief, was given to

---

[1] Lodovico Ariosto, *Orlando Furioso*, trans. John Hoole (London, 1783; Philadelphia, 1816), bk. 1, canto 9.

him by the overlord, and in accepting it, the knight assumed the obligation of military service to the overlord in wartime. It was an exchange of goods against services as was fitting to the agricultural structure and manorial system of the Middle Ages.

A religious concept of war as an act of rendering justice, the restriction of military service to the class of landholding knights and their retainers, and a moral-legal code which operated as the main bond holding the army together—these are the factors that determined the forms of military organization as well as the methods of war in the Middle Ages. The medieval army could be assembled only when a definite issue had arisen; it was ordered out for the purposes of a definite campaign and could be kept together only as long as this campaign lasted. The purely temporary character of military service as well as the equality of standing of the noble fighters made strict discipline difficult if not impossible. A battle frequently developed into fights between individual knights, and the outcome of such single combats between the leaders was decisive. Because warfare represented the fulfillment of a religious and moral duty, there was a strong inclination to conduct war and battles according to fixed rules and a settled code.

This military organization was a typical product of the whole social system of the Middle Ages, and any change in the foundations of the system had inevitable repercussions in the military field. When rapid expansion of a money economy shook the agricultural basis of medieval society the effects of this development on military institutions were immediate. In the military field those who were the protagonists of the new economic developments—the cities and the wealthy overlords—could make great use of the new opportunities: namely, to accept money payments instead of services, or to secure services by money rewards and salaries. The overlord could accept money payments from those who did not wish to fulfill their military obligations and, on the other hand, he could retain those knights who remained in his army beyond the period of war and for longer stretches of time by promises of regular payments. Thus he was able to lay the foundations of a permanent and professional army and to free himself from dependence on his vassals. This transformation of the feudal army into a professional army, of the feudal state into the bureaucratic and absolutist state, was a very slow process and reached its climax only in the eighteenth century, but the true knightly spirit of the feudal armies died early and quickly. We possess an illustration of this change in a fifteenth-century ballad, describing life in the army of Charles the Bold of Burgundy.[2] In the fifteenth century Burgundy

[2] Ballad by Emile Deschamps, "Quand viendra le trésorier?" in E. Deschamps, *Oeuvres complètes*, ed. Saint Hilaire (Paris, 1884), 4:289.

was a very recent political formation and the older powers considered it as a kind of parvenu; therefore, Charles the Bold was particularly eager to legitimize the existence of his state by strict observance of old traditions and customs, and became in effect the leader of a kind of romantic revival of chivalry. It is the more revealing, therefore, that in this ballad, "knight, squire, sergeant and vassal" have only one thought, namely, "when will the paymaster come?" Here, behind the glittering façade of chivalry, is disclosed the prosaic reality of material interests.

In the armies of the greater powers, France, Aragon, or England, old and modern elements, feudal levy and professionalism, were mixed; but the great money powers of the period, the Italian cities, came to rely entirely on professional soldiers. Since the fourteenth century, Italy had been the "promised land" of all knights to whom war was chiefly a means of making money. The single groups, the *compagnie di ventura*, were supplied and paid by their leaders, the *condottieri*, who offered their services to every power willing to pay their price. Thus, in Italy soldiering became a profession of its own, entirely separated from any other civilian activity.

The impact of the money economy provided a broader opportunity for recruiting armies. New classes of men, free from the preceding military traditions, were attracted into the services by money, and with this in-filtration of new men, new weapons and new forms of fighting could be introduced and developed. Archers and infantry made their appearance in the French and English armies during the Hundred Years' War. This tendency toward experimentation in new military methods received a further strong impetus from the defeats that the armies of Charles the Bold suffered at the hands of the Swiss near the end of the fifteenth century. In the battles of Morat and Nancy (1476), the knights of Charles the Bold, unable to break up the squares of Swiss foot soldiers and to penetrate into the forest of their pikes, were thoroughly defeated. This event was a European sensation. Infantry had won its place in the military organization of the period.

The importance of the invention of gunpowder has to be evaluated against the background of these general developments: first, the rise of a money economy; second, the attempt of the feudal overlord to free himself from dependence on his vassals and to establish a reliable foun-dation of power; and third, the trend toward experimentation in military organization resulting from the weakening of feudal bonds.

Firearms and artillery were not the cause of these developments but they were an important contributory factor, accelerating the tempo of the evolution. First of all, they strengthened the position of the overlord in relation to his vassals. The employment of artillery in a campaign was a cumbersome task; many wagons were needed for transportation of the heavy cannon and for their equipment, mechanics and engineers became necessary, and the whole procedure was extremely expensive. The accounts of military expenditures for this period show that the expenses for artillery constituted a disproportionately large part of the total.[3] Only the very wealthy rulers were able to afford artillery. Also, the principal military effect of the invention of artillery worked in favor of the great powers and against the smaller states and local centers of independence. In the Middle Ages, the final sanction of the position of the knight had been that, in his castle, he was relatively immune from attack. The art of fortification was much cultivated in this period.[4] Small states protected themselves by establishing at their frontiers a line of fortresses that enabled them to hold out even against superior forces. These medieval fortifications were vulnerable, however, to artillery fire. Thus, the military balance became heavily weighed in favor of the offensive. Francesco di Giorgio Martini, one of the great Italian architects of the fifteenth century, who was in charge of the building of the fortresses for the Duke of Urbino, complained in his treatise on military architecture that "the man who would be able to balance defense against attack, would be more a god than a human being."[5]

These changes in the composition of armies and in military technique also transformed the spirit of military organization.[6] The moral code, traditions, and customs, which feudalism had evolved, had lost control over the human material from which the armies were now recruited. Adventurers and ruffians who wanted wealth and plunder, men who had nothing to lose and everything to gain through war, made up the main body of the armies. As a result of a situation in which war was no longer undertaken as a religious duty, the purpose of military service became financial gain. The moral problem arose whether it was a sin to follow a profession that aimed at the killing of other people. In the most civilized parts of Europe, such as Italy, people looked with contempt on soldiers and soldiering.

[3] Cf. for instance "Ordine dell'Esercito Ducale Sforzesco, 1472-1474," *Archivio storico Lombardo*, ser.1, vol. 3 (1876), 448-513.

[4] Cf. Charles Oman, *A History of the Art of War in the Middle Ages* (London, 1924), 1:358.

[5] Francesco di Giorgio Martini, *Trattato di architettura civile e militare*, ed. Carlo Promis (Torino, 1841), 131.

[6] In general, see Piero Pieri, *Il Rinascimento e la crisi militare italiana* (Torino, 1952), and see also the chapters "Military Development and Fighting Potential" and "Soldiers and the State" in M. E. Mallett and J. R. Hale, *The Military Organization of a Renaissance State* (Cambridge, 1984), 65-100, 181-98.

II

The circumstances of Machiavelli's personal life were a crucial factor in his becoming aware of the situation and the problems that had emerged in his time.

Machiavelli's career as a political writer began when the Medici returned to Florence in 1512 and ousted him from the Florentine Chancellery, where he had served the Florentine republic for fourteen years. His writings, as many have said, beginning with Machiavelli himself, present the lessons that he had drawn from his "long experience of the affairs of his time."[7] They reduce to prescripts, rules, and laws his observations of the political scene made in the course of his work in the Florentine Chancellery.

In the Italian cities of the Renaissance, chancellery officials usually were somewhat bloodless civil servants who wrote down and carried out the measures on which the ruling circle had decided. Machiavelli was an exception; he was a person of political importance in the Florentine republic between 1498 and 1512. As Guicciardini wrote to him teasingly in the years of his disgrace, when he had accepted a minor, almost ridiculous mission to a chapter of the Franciscan Order—"in other times [you] negotiated with many kings, dukes and princes."[8]

There were several reasons why Machiavelli had played a greater political role before 1512 than Chancellery bureaucrats usually did. The Machiavelli were an old, highly regarded family with twelve Gonfalonieri and sixty-six high magistrates among them. Niccolò Machiavelli was descended from an illegitimate branch of this family and could not be a member of the ruling councils or of the policy-making magistrates, but his name and his friendship with Niccolò di Alessandro Machiavelli, a leading politician, set him apart from other Chancellery officials.[9]

The principal reason, however, for Machiavelli's prominence was his close relation to Piero Soderini, the lifetime Gonfaloniere.[10] The office of a lifetime Gonfaloniere had been created in 1502 by a group of Florentine patricians who had hoped that the Gonfaloniere would restrict and reduce the influence of the Great Council in which the middle classes had the upper hand. But Soderini disappointed the patricians because he viewed his election as a mandate to maintain and stabilize the popular

---

[7] From Machiavelli's dedication of *The Prince* to Lorenzo de' Medici: "lunga esperienza delle cose moderne."

[8] Francesco Guicciardini to Niccolò Machiavelli, May 18, 1521.

[9] See Roberto Ridolfi, *The Life of Niccolò Machiavelli*, trans. Cecil Grayson (London, 1963), 29; this is the best recent work on the facts of Machiavelli's life.

[10] On Machiavelli's position in the times of Soderini, see my *Machiavelli and Guicciardini* (Princeton, 1965; pbk., New York, 1984), particularly ch. 2.

regime embodied in the Great Council. Soderini favored Machiavelli and used him in a variety of governmental tasks and missions, knowing that in his struggle with his aristocratic opponents it was useful to have the services of a man who was entirely dependent on him.

Beyond that, however, Machiavelli was a remarkable personality, and this was certainly the crucial factor in extending his activities and responsibilities beyond the scope of an average government official. Contemporary portraits of Machiavelli do not exist. The pictures and busts that are supposed to represent him and show a face of foxlike cleverness with an ambiguous smile were made in the later part of the sixteenth century when Machiavelli had become the personification of calculating amorality and evil. But Machiavelli was not just an embodiment of rationality and intelligence. He could be emotional, and in the storms of passion could throw all caution to the wind. He loved to make fun of himself and of others. The chief bond between Machiavelli and the leading Florentine statesmen—Guicciardini, Filippo Strozzi, Francesco Vettori—was a common interest in the political developments of their time, and certainly these Florentines found Machiavelli's analysis of the contemporary situation fascinating. But Machiavelli served them also in many other functions: he could eagerly embark on excogitating marriage proposals for the daughters of his friend Guicciardini, or organize a sumptuous meal for Filippo Strozzi. Machiavelli knew that acting as a *maître de plaisir* helped him retain the friendship of these great men, who kept in touch with the goings on in the world. His outlook and approach were formed by this situation: being kept in a dependent, outsider position, but feeling equal and even superior in his grasp of the political world to those who had the right and the power to make decisions. Machiavelli was deeply involved in the political world, yet he also looked upon it from a distance. None of his contemporaries had to the same degree a view that combined both sharpness and perspective, and that moved continuously between what is and what ought to be.[11] Machiavelli was aware of the tension inherent in the ambiguity of his position. In the prologue of his *Mandragola*, he says of the author that "in the whole Italian world he acknowledges no one to be his superior, but he will cringe before anyone who can afford better clothes."[12]

One of Machiavelli's functions in the Chancellery was to serve as a secretary of the Office of Ten, the government committee in charge of war and military affairs.[13] Thus, Machiavelli became intimately involved

---

[11] On Machiavelli's concern with this issue, see *The Prince* ch. 15.

[12] ". . . in ogni parte del mondo ove e sì sona, non istima persona, ancor che facci e sergieri a colui che può portar miglior mantel di lui."

[13] For Machiavelli's activities in the Chancellery, see Jean-Jacques Marchand, *Niccolò*

in the Florentine efforts to regain possession of Pisa, and the war against Pisa remained his continuous preoccupation for the next ten years—until Pisa finally surrendered in 1509. In his first government mission outside Florence, he negotiated the salary of a condottiere whose demands the Florentine government found excessive. Then Machiavelli was drawn into the discussions concerning the fate of Paolo Vitelli, one of the condottieri whom Florence had hired. Vitelli's troops had taken one of the bulwarks of the defense of Pisa and the city lay open before them, but Vitelli hesitated to order his troops to advance and so this opportunity was lost. Vitelli's exaggerated caution raised the suspicion of treason. He was deposed, brought to Florence, imprisoned, and finally decapitated. Much of the correspondence on this affair was in Machiavelli's hands. Doubts about the usefulness of relying on the services of a condottiere, which the Vitelli affair must have raised in Machiavelli's mind, were certainly reinforced when, on a mission to the Florentine camp before Pisa, he witnessed the behavior of the lansquenets and Gascons whom the French king, the ally of Florence, had sent in fulfillment of his promise to restore Florentine rule over Pisa; they refused to advance against the city, complained about their pay and their food, mutinied, and disappeared from the camp.

Machiavelli's most famous and most discussed official mission was that to Cesare Borgia in the last months of 1502; he was present at Sinigaglia when Cesare Borgia had persuaded a number of hostile condottieri to meet with him and then ordered his men to slay them. The stupidity with which the condottieri had fallen into Cesare's trap further justified for Machiavelli the contempt he felt for the condottieri system. Their shortsightedness, indecisiveness, and timidity struck him particularly because at the same time he had encountered in Cesare Borgia a man who seemed to him to have all the qualities of a great captain: ambition, insistence on supreme command, capacity for detailed planning, secrecy, decisiveness, quickness of action, and, if needed, ruthlessness. Although Machiavelli's view of Cesare underwent changes in the course of years, the experience of Sinigaglia was crucial for his recognition of the need for a new type of military leadership.

The most important official reflection of Machiavelli's thought on military affairs is the law of December 1505, which ordered the organization of a Florentine militia.[14] It was drafted by Machiavelli, and its

---

Machiavelli: I primi scritti politici (1499-1512) (Padua, 1975), which reproduces most of the official documents written by Machiavelli as a Chancellery official, and analyzes them.
[14] See Marchand, *Niccolò Machiavelli*, 450-61. The "militia" was not a new idea in Florence, but had a long tradition; see Charles Calvert Bayley, *War and Society in Renaissance Florence* (Toronto, 1961), particularly the chapter "The Survival of the Militia Tradition from Bruni to Machiavelli."

introduction immediately enunciated some of Machiavelli's favorite ideas: the foundation of a republic is "justice and arms," and long experience, great financial expenses, and dangers have shown us that mercenary armies are of questionable usefulness. The law, called the Ordinanza, provided for the formation of a militia of 10,000 who were to be selected by a government committee from males between eighteen and fifty years, living in the rural districts of Tuscany under Florentine rule. The militia was to be divided into companies of three hundred men, who were to be drilled—in the pattern of German lansquenets—on festival days. Conscription was limited to rural districts because arming the inhabitants of the towns in the Florentine territory would have made it easier for these towns to revolt. It was not expected that the citizens of Florence could be persuaded to accept for themselves the burden of some military service, although Machiavelli hoped that at some future time this would come about. He considered the Ordinanza merely a beginning. He worked—without success—toward adding a levy of horsemen to the levy of foot soldiers. His final aim was an army composed of men from the city of Florence, the towns of the territory, and the rural districts, under a unified command.

The unreliability of the condottieri and of mercenaries was only one reason for Machiavelli's passionate interest in the creation of a conscript army. He expected it would have important consequences for Florentine foreign and domestic policy: greater independence in foreign affairs and stabilization of the domestic situation. Machiavelli had learned on several of his diplomatic missions that the necessity of relying on mercenaries or foreign troops limited freedom of action and created dependence on other powers. He had been forced to ask other Italian rulers to allow Florence to engage the services of their condottieri and mercenaries; on a mission to France his task was to implore the French king to send French troops who would help to reestablish Florentine authority in areas that had revolted. The dangers arising from military weakness loomed particularly large in the first decades of the sixteenth century. The overthrow of the Italian balance of power by the French invasion in 1494, followed by the rise of Cesare Borgia supported by the pope and the French king had brought about an unstable and fluid situation in which every larger power believed it might be able to expand and to absorb its weaker neighbors by the use of force. In Machiavelli's first political memorandum, written soon after he became a member of the Chancellery, he stated that a state had two ways only to attain its goal: "o la forze o lo amore,"[15] and he immediately explained that negotiations and agree-

---

[15] Marchand, *Niccolò Machiavelli*, 403.

ments—and that is what he understood by "amore"—would never lead to the desired goals; governments had to rely on force.

Furthermore he knew only too well that the hiring of a condottiere, the determination of his salary, and the calculations about the number of troops needed for a particular military operation always increased internal tension. The required sums were provided primarily through loans and taxes imposed on the wealthier citizens; accordingly the upper classes tried to keep these extraordinary expenses to a minimum. In a memorandum to the Gonfaloniere, Machiavelli bitterly attacked the wealthy citizens who always raised difficulties when they were expected to make sacrifices.[16] In his draft for the Ordinanza, Machiavelli gave much attention to the financial aspects of this law. He discussed the administrative apparatus that ought to be established to secure regular payments; because the conscripted men needed to come together for a few hours of military training only once or twice a month, and otherwise had to be paid only in wartime when they were absent from home, the expenses of the Ordinanza seemed to him forseeable and could be provided from regular taxes. The concrete result would be a diminution of the influence of the wealthy elites, hostile to Soderini, and a shift away from their domination over foreign policy. At the outset, the Florentines, Machiavelli among them, limited conscription to the peasants, who were suppressed by the towns and looked to Florence for recourse and accordingly were loyal. That a militia would fight willingly, perhaps even enthusiastically, only if its members were well treated by the state in which they lived was evident to Machiavelli. Machiavelli expected—or at least hoped—that, after the militia had stood its first tests, the advantages of a conscript army would become clear and the resistance to the extension of the Ordinanza to the city of Florence could be overcome. With arms in the hands of the people, the influence of the wealthy upper classes would be diminished and the popular regime would be stabilized.

Machiavelli took an intense interest in the formation of the militia. In some districts he himself selected the men who were to serve in the militia, and supervised their drill. He arranged for a parade of the militia on the Piazza della Signoria in Florence. Machiavelli was in actual command of the various militia companies when they were employed before Pisa in the last stages of the siege. The surrender of the city confirmed him in his conviction of the correctness of his military ideas. Even the return of the Medici, after a disastrous defeat of the militia before Prato, did not shake him in these convictions.

In his *Florentine History* Machiavelli took particular pleasure in

[16] Ibid., 412-16.

describing the battles fought by the condottieri on Italian soil in the fifteenth century. In 1423, in the battle of Zagonara, a victory "famous throughout all Italy, none was killed except Lodovico degli Obizzi and he, together with two of his men, was thrown from his horse and suffocated in the mud." In the battle of Anghiari "lasting from the 20th to the 24th hour, only one man was killed and he was not wounded or struck down by a valiant blow but fell from his horse and was trampled to death." This contemptuous and derisive picture of the Italian condottieri is obviously unfair; some of them were competent soldiers, courageous, with a strong feeling for honor and reputation.[17] But Machiavelli's aim was not historical truth and objectivity. During his years in office three battles had been fought that had aroused wonder and fear all over Italy: Cerignola, where Gonsalvo da Cordoba's superbly drilled Spaniards defeated the French and drove them out of Naples, the French victory of Agnadello where the discord of their condottieri cost the Venetians their *terra ferma*, and Ravenna, where the tempestuous attack of Gaston de Foix brought the French victory over the Spanish and papal troops and which is believed to have been the bloodiest battle of the entire century. Machiavelli made it evident to his contemporaries, to whom these battles were a subject of much discussion, that a new era of war had opened.

III

In *The Prince* Machiavelli promised fame to a new ruler who would introduce new laws of warfare; the reader can have little doubt that Machiavelli was the man who knew what these new rules were. And it is also clear that the new revolutionary doctrine will be presented in his book *The Art of War*. But the student of this book will be astonished and perhaps disappointed because he will find in this book something very different from a "new" modern theory. The problem lies in the word "new." In our illusionistic belief that the future must be better than the past and the present, "new" seems to us the opposite of "old." But before the idea of progress had taken hold over the European mind people saw what happened mainly as a decline from a high point that lay in the past. The situation at the beginning set the ideal norm for humanists of the Renaissance: a perfect world had existed in classical times.

Machiavelli was a humanistically educated man: it was particularly Rome that demonstrated to him the possibility of the rise of a city-republic to world power, and therefore was for him the embodiment of an ideal

---

[17] Battle of Zagonara: *Florentine History*, bk. 4, ch. 6; battle of Anghiari: ibid., bk. 5, ch. 33. For a more positive evaluation of the condottieri see Michael E. Mallett, *Mercenaries and Their Masters* (London, 1974).

republic. A characteristic example of the extent to which he modelled his views in accordance with those that he believed the Romans had held is a memorandum he wrote as Secretary of the Office of Ten in answer to the question how the people of Arezzo, who had revolted against Florence, ought to be treated after Florentine rule had been restored. The memorandum began by explaining what, according to Livy, Lucio Furio Camillo had done after the people of Latium had rebelled.[18]

The *new* laws of warfare therefore, which Machiavelli wanted to see introduced in Italy, were the *old* laws of the Roman military order. To a large extent his true principles of military warfare are attempts to show on the basis of ancient sources how the Romans conducted war. However, it ought always to be kept in mind that Machiavelli's aim was not a historically correct reconstruction of facts. He wanted to deduce the laws and principles that stood behind the facts of Roman military history, and show their applicability to the present. Certainly Machiavelli's idea of Rome is a utopia and he used facts to build up the picture that was already in his mind. But in his steady striving for discovering the general rule behind a particular event or an individual action, he penetrates to the basic issues of war and military order.

Of Machiavelli's political writings, only *The Art of War* was published during his lifetime. In all likelihood Machiavelli wrote this book with its impact on the public of his time in mind. It fit the literary and scholarly conventions of the time.[19] His ideas are presented in the form of a dialogue among Florentine patricians and the condottiere, Fabrizio Colonna.[20] The organization of the Roman army and the Roman methods of warfare are described on the basis of ancient sources, particularly Vegetius, Frontinus, and Polybius, from whose works sometimes lengthy passages are translated.[21] According to Machiavelli or, perhaps more precisely, according to Fabrizio Colonna, the main speaker of the dialogue, the Roman armies were a carefully selected militia whose soldiers came from rural areas. The Roman armies were of moderate size, and foot soldiers were their backbone; the value of the cavalry in a battle

[18] Marchand, *Niccolò Machiavelli*, 427.

[19] For recent discussions of Machiavelli's indebtedness to humanist notions, see J. G. A. Pocock, *The Machiavellian Moment* (Princeton, 1975) and Quentin Skinner, *The Foundations of Modern Political Thought*, vol. 1 (Cambridge, 1978).

[20] An English translation of Machiavelli's *Arte della guerra*—with the title *The Art of War*—has been published in the Library of Liberal Arts by the Bobbs-Merrill Company (Indianapolis, 1965). The translation is the revised text of an eighteenth-century translation and is not always correct. The edition has an excellent introduction by Neal Wood and contains a useful selected bibliography.

[21] For a special investigation of Machiavelli's dependence on these sources, see L. Arthur Bird, "Le fonti letterarie di Machiavelli nell'Arte della Guerra," *Atti della Academia dei Lincei*, series 5, vol. 4 (1896), pt. 1, pp. 187-261.

was very limited, although they were useful in reconnoitering and in preventing supplies reaching the enemy. Machiavelli's emphasis on the infantry as the core of the Roman army implies criticism and rejection of the condottieri, the core of whose armies was formed by heavy cavalry; moreover, because, as the Ordinanza had proved, Italian cities could organize a militia, imitation of the Roman example was in the realm of possibility. For Machiavelli this possibility of resurrecting the Roman military system justified a very detailed description of Roman army practice. He described the different units into which the army was divided, the chain of command, the drawing up of the army in battle order and its operations during the battle, the selection of campsites, and the attack and defense of fortified places. Machiavelli clearly delighted in establishing with precision how the Romans proceeded, and the Renaissance admiration for everything that came from the classical world might have enabled his sixteenth-century readers to take interest in all these details. For today's student of Machiavelli, *The Art of War* is not his most exciting work.

It could not be entirely limited to an explanation of the Roman military system because Machiavelli had to discuss an obvious objection to the applicability of the Roman model to his own times: the invention of artillery, which had introduced an element in warfare that seemed to make the Roman methods obsolete. Fabrizio's answer to this objection is brief because, as he explains, this issue had been discussed at length at other places—an allusion to the seventeenth chapter of the second book of Machiavelli's *Discourses*.

Fabrizio's chief argument was that artillery is inaccurate; its shots are frequently too high or too low. Moreover artillery is slow and difficult to move: in a battle it would be easy to take the artillery by storm; a battle is decided in hand-to-hand fighting in which there is no room for action by artillery. Finally, artillery is of greater use to the attacker than to the defender, particularly in the siege of a town, and since the great strength of the Roman army was its capacity for attack, artillery might be used to reinforce the Roman methods of warfare. It does not invalidate them.[22]

But the discussion or—more correctly—the refutation of the revolutionary significance of the invention of gunpowder does not entirely remove the modern world from encroaching upon Machiavelli's ideal Rome. Machiavelli states that the aim of war must be to face an enemy in the field and to defeat him there; this is the only way "to bring a war to a happy conclusion."[23]

[22] This discussion follows the description of a battle in book 3 of *The Art of War*.
[23] ". . . non condurrà mai una guerra a onore," from book 1.

Machiavelli's *Art of War* is divided into seven books and a good part of the third book, which is in the center, is taken up with the destruction of an imaginary battle. Moreover this fictitious battle is placed in the present and is reported from the point of view of an eyewitness. " 'Do you not hear our artillery. . . . See with what virtù our men charge. . . . See how our general encourages his men and assures them of victory. . . . Behold what havoc our men wreak among the enemy; see with what virtù, confidence and coolness they press upon the enemies. . . . What carnage! How many wounded men! They are beginning to flee. . . . The battle is over; we have won a glorious victory.' "[24] Although the rest of *The Art of War* is concerned with the technical aspects of military organization—weaponry, marching order, line of command, fortifications—the section on the battle concentrates on the human qualities needed in war: courage, obedience, enthusiasm, and ferocity.

We have said that in *The Art of War* Machiavelli makes compromises with convention. In the preface of the book he wrote that the rulers of ancient times took care to inspire all their subjects, and particularly their soldiers, with fidelity, love of peace, and fear of God. "Who ought to be fonder of peace than soldiers whose life is placed in jeopardy by war?"[25] Readers of *The Prince* and the *Discorsi* will doubt that these sentences reflect Machiavelli's true sentiments. *The Prince* and the *Discorsi* are books on political rules and behavior and not on military organization and war, but when we want to enter into Machiavelli's ideas about war, we must study them. We find nothing about the desirability of peace; in *The Prince* and the *Discorsi* war appears as an inescapable, grandiose, and terrifying force. In these works the world appears in permanent flux. Machiavelli does not share the widespread belief of his time that man is entirely in the hands of Fortuna, but he acknowledges Fortuna's power; only when people and states make themselves as strong and powerful as possible can they resist becoming a helpless toy in her hands. It is very natural, therefore, for states and their rulers to wish to expand and to conquer. War is the most essential activity of political life.

The continued existence of struggles and uncertainties patterns the character and the methods of war: there is no safe course. Risks must be taken in these surroundings of uncertainties and dangers, wars ought to be ended as quickly as possible with the attainment of a definite result: the complete defeat of the enemy. Wars ought to be "short and sharp."[26] A quick decision, however, can be reached only in a battle. Because

---

[24] From book 3; in the English translation pp. 92-94 (see note 20).

[25] "In quale debbe essere più amore di pace, che in quello che solo dalla guerra puote essere offeso?"

[26] "Fare le guerre, come dicano i Franciosi, corte e grosse," *Discorsi*, II, 6.

everything depends on the outcome of the battle, you ought to do everything to make sure of victory; you should use your full forces even if the enemy seems of inferior strength. Decision by battle is the aim of every military campaign, which must be a planned and coordinated operation. Command, therefore, must be in the hands of one man. If the state is a monarchy, the ruler himself ought to be the commanding general. But republics too should entrust their army in wartime to one commander who should have unlimited authority; that is what the Romans had done who had left all the details of a campaign "to the discretion and authority of the consul."[27]

Machiavelli fully recognized that the "short and sharp" war that he envisaged demanded involvement of the soldiers' passions, and would be a ferocious war. For Machiavelli the brutality inherent in war had its ambiguous consequences. It had dangers but also possibilities. The dangers were that the great masses of soldiers, when the struggle became confused and vehement, would no longer obey but think only of their own salvation. They might start looting, hoping to exploit the struggle for their personal advantage. The army would disintegrate. The importance of discipline and training is emphasized again and again in *The Prince* and the *Discorsi*. Military success depends on order and discipline. Natural courage is not enough. Machiavelli observed with approval that the German cities "hold military exercise in high repute and have many regulations for maintaining them."[28] Training is never finished or completed. A wise leader should keep the necessity of training always in mind and insist on it in peacetime as well as in wartime. But even the bonds that training and discipline create cannot guarantee obedience. They must be reinforced by fear of harsh punishment. Severity and harshness are needed to hold a political body together.[29] "A prince must not mind incurring the charge of cruelty for the purpose of keeping his subjects united and faithful"; "it is much safer to be feared than loved." According to Machiavelli this general political rule was particularly appropriate to the command of an army. Hannibal's "inhuman cruelty" was necessary to keep his forces, "composed of men of all nations and fighting in foreign countries," united; writers who admire Hannibal as a mighty hero and blame him for his cruelty are thoughtless; his cruelty was a principal cause of his success.

Coercion, however, needs to be supplemented by measures of a very different character. A spiritual bond that will inspire heroic action must

---

[27] *Discorsi*, II, 33.

[28] *The Prince*, ch. 10.

[29] For this and the following, see the famous chapter 17 of *The Prince*: "An sit melius amari quam timeri, vel e contra."

be created among the soldiers of an army. Such a bond is most directly produced by necessity; even if a situation is not hopeless, a general ought to emphasize that the dangers of defeat are great, so that the soldiers fight with the courage of desperation. The strongest incitement to courage and enthusiasm, however, is aroused by a feeling of personal involvement and moral obligation. War service must be considered fulfillment of a religious duty.[30] Machiavelli believed that in the ancient world the pomp and show of religious ceremonies—"the ferocious and bloody nature of the sacrifice by the slaughter of many animals and the familiarity with this terrible sight"—intoxicated men with bellicose zeal. The Christian religion has created difficulties to the development of warlike virtues because it "places the supreme happiness in humility, lowliness and a contempt for worldly objects"; it has made men feeble. However, even if the relationship between religion and martial courage that existed in the ancient world cannot be revived, religion is compatible with love for one's country in Christianity, and sacrificing one's life for one's *patria* has been compared to the martyrdom of saints. In Machiavelli's thought the appeal to patriotism could be and was one of the most powerful forces in inspiring an army to heroic deeds.

However, patriotic enthusiasm could be expected only of an army composed by men fighting for their native land. Machiavelli's most fundamental thesis, emphasized in all his writings, is that the military forces of a ruler or of a republic must be composed by the inhabitants of the state that the army is expected to defend. "The present ruin of Italy is the result of nothing else than reliance upon mercenaries."[31] "They are disunited, ambitious, without discipline, disloyal, overbearing among friends, cowardly among enemies; there is no fear of God, no loyalty to men." The necessary prerequisite of success in war—confidence and discipline—"can exist only where the troops are natives of the same country and have lived together for some time." Thus, the first crucial step in military reform which Machiavelli envisages is that the state forms an army composed of its own inhabitants, that a state has its *"proprie armi."*[32]

Machiavelli is convinced, however, that citizens will be willing to fight and die for their ruler or government only when they are content in the society in which they live. "There is a great difference between an army that is well content and fights for its own reputation and one that is ill disposed and has to fight only for the interests of others." This thesis

[30] *Discorsi*, II, 2; for patriotism as religious duty also in Christianity, see Ernst Kantorowicz, "Pro Patria Mori in Medieval Political Thought" in his *Selected Studies* (New York, 1965), 308-24.
[31] For this and the following, see particularly *The Prince*, ch. 12.
[32] *Discorsi*, I, 43.

of the close connection and interrelationship between political and military institutions is the most important and also the most revolutionary argument of Machiavelli's notions.[33] From the draft of the law for the establishment of a Florentine *Ordinanza* on, the statement that "la justitia et le armi" belong together can be found in almost all his writings. In *The Prince* he wrote that "there must be good laws where there are good arms, and where there are good arms there must be good laws,"[34] and at the end of the *Discorsi* he gave this notion of the interdependence of military and political organization its most categorical formulation: "Although I have elsewhere maintained that the foundation of states is a good military organization, yet it seems to me not superfluous to report here that without such a military organization there can neither be good laws nor anything else good."[35]

IV

Machiavelli's *Art of War* was a successful book: in the course of the sixteenth century twenty-one editions appeared and it was translated into French, English, German, and Latin.[36] Montaigne named Machiavelli next to Caesar, Polybius, and Commynes as an authority on military affairs.[37] Although in the seventeenth century changing military methods brought other writers to the fore, Machiavelli was still frequently quoted. In the eighteenth century, the Marshal de Saxe leaned heavily on him when he composed his *Reveries upon the Art of War* (1757), and Algarotti—though without much basis—saw in Machiavelli the master who had taught Frederick the Great the tactics by which he astounded Europe.[38] Like most people concerned with military matters, Jefferson had Machiavelli's *Art of War* in his library,[39] and when the War of 1812 increased American interest in problems of war, *The Art of War* was brought out in a special American edition.[40]

[33] Ibid. Sometimes it is difficult for Machiavelli to separate the usefulness of military measures from their impact on domestic policy. Machiavelli is very skeptical about the value of fortresses, but the question whether they serve to strengthen or to undermine a regime plays a crucial role in these discussions; see "To Fortify or Not to Fortify? Machiavelli's Contribution to a Renaissance Debate" in J. R. Hale, *Renaissance War Studies* (London, 1983), 189-209.

[34] *The Prince*, ch. 12.

[35] *Discorsi*, III, 31.

[36] See Sergio Bertelli and Piero Innocenti, *Bibliografia Machiavelliana* (Verona, 1979).

[37] Montaigne, *Essais*, bk. 2, ch. 34: "Observations sur les moyens de faire la guerre de Julius Caesar."

[38] Francesco Algarotti, lettres 8 and 9 of his work *Scienza militare del Segretario Fiorentino*, in F. Algarotti, *Opere*, vol. 5 (Venice, 1791).

[39] Catalogue of the Library of Congress 1815, i.e., Thomas Jefferson's library.

[40] *The Art of War in Seven Books Written by Nicholas Machiavel . . . to Which Is Added Hints Relative to Warfare by a Gentleman of the State of New York* (Albany, 1815).

This continued interest in Machiavelli as a military thinker was not only caused by the fame of his name; some of the recommendations made in *The Art of War*—those on training, discipline, and classification, for instance—gained increasing practical importance in early modern Europe when armies came to be composed of professionals coming from the most different social strata. This does not mean that the progress of military art in the sixteenth century—in drilling, in dividing an army into distinct units, in planning and organizing campaigns—was due to the influence of Machiavelli. Instead, the military innovators of the time were pleased to find a work in which aspects of their practice were explained and justified. Moreover, in the sixteenth century, with its wide knowledge of ancient literature and its deep respect for classical wisdom, it was commonly held that the Romans owed their military triumphs to their emphasis on discipline and training. Machiavelli's attempt to present Roman military organization as the model for the armies of his time was therefore not regarded as extravagant. At the end of the sixteenth century, for instance, Justus Lipsius, in his influential writings on military affairs, also treated the Roman military order as a permanently valid model.

However, it ought also to be admitted that in several respects Machiavelli misjudged what was possible and feasible in his own day.

In the past, and sometimes still in our time, Machiavelli has been assigned a prominent place in the development of military thought because of his advocacy of conscription: his military thought was of a seminal character; he was able to foresee what would happen in the future. Although the assumption of the prophetic character of Machiavelli's military ideas might be pleasing to students and admirers of Machiavelli, it would be a mistake to attribute great importance to his advocacy of conscription. His idea of a conscript army was that of a city-state militia, a part-time military service patterned on the model of the ancient city-republics, but hardly suited for the army of a territorial state. Moreover, the future, at least in the two or three centuries following Machiavelli, did not belong to conscript armies but to that kind of soldier whom Machiavelli despised and ridiculed: the mercenary, the professional.

A factor that Machiavelli clearly misjudged in its importance contributed decisively to this development: the equipment of soldiers with firearms, and the increased role of artillery. As a result, specialized personnel and permanent military establishments formed the necessary core of any army. Expenses, particularly expenses for artillery, grew. Although Machiavelli was aware of the financial needs of any military organization, he certainly had not taken fully into account the growing costs of military equipment with guns and rifles, the interrelationship between economic strength and military strength. Only rulers of larger territories could afford an army, and with its help force the estates or their smaller neighbors under their control. Absolutism had to rely on standing armies; each was dependent upon the other.

But Machiavelli's influence on military thought reached far beyond the technical-military sphere. If his view of the exemplary character of the Roman military organization might have misled him in underestimating the impact of new weapons and of the economy on military developments, his admiration for Rome was crucial in opening his eyes to the role of war in modern times. In the centuries of the Middle Ages, the conduct of war had been the function of a particular class of society and had been shaped by its values and code of honor. The first and crucial lesson that Machiavelli drew from his study of the ancient world was that defense of a state was the task not of a special privileged group but should be the concern of all those who live in the same society.

It was of even greater importance that the study of Roman historians helped him to understand the international system of his time: states were steadily growing and expanding; they were permanently involved in war, seeking to extend their power and territories, and fighting for their existence in fending off others trying to subdue them. Machiavelli was one of the first to grasp the competitive nature of the modern state system—that as his reluctant follower, Frederick II of Prussia, wrote: "s'agrandir" is the "principe permanent" of the policy of a state—and to conclude that the existence of a state depends on its capacity for war.

Because the life of the state depends on the excellence of its army, the political institutions must be organized in such a manner that they create favorable preconditions for the functioning of the military organization. That is one thesis that permeates all of Machiavelli's military discussions—in *The Art of War*, *The Prince* and the *Discourses*. The other thesis is that the aim of war is to subject the enemy to your will; a military campaign therefore must be a planned operation, under a unified command, culminating in a battle of decision. What the appropriate means are—what the correct strategy is—to carry out this aim will depend on the particular circumstances under which a campaign is conducted.

Machiavelli's insight into the nature of war and the role of the military establishment in the structure of society is the foundation of his military thought; the problems that these questions raise are not bound to a particular historical period. Thus, even when, with the French Revolution and the rise of Napoleon, military organization and the conduct of war had assumed new forms, Machiavelli's ideas retained their vitality.

To a surprising degree, military thought since the sixteenth century has proceeded on the foundations that Machiavelli laid. This is not to say that Machiavelli's recommendations were accepted as final truth. Yet further discussion did not develop in opposition to his view, but rather as an expansion and enlargement of his ideas. For instance, however important Machiavelli's idea of the decisiveness of battle was, it soon became clear that there was a real need for a much more thorough analysis of its consequences. Military theory could not stop with making rules for the formation of the correct battle order; it had also to scrutinize the course of events during the combat action. On the other hand, if a battle constituted the climax of war, it is clear that the whole campaign had to be planned and analyzed in respect to the decisive battle. Such considerations show that the role which theoretical preparation and planned direction of military action played in modern war was much greater than Machiavelli had envisaged. He had made a perfunctory acknowledgment of the importance of the role of the general, but in reality he had hardly said more than that a general should know history and geography. Later, the question of planning in military leadership and of the intellectual training of the general became central problems in military thought. In developing these problems, military thought advanced far beyond Machiavelli, yet these more modern conclusions were a logical continuation of the inquiry that he had started.

Nevertheless, there is one aspect in modern military thought that not only cannot be connected with Machiavelli's thought, but is in sharp contrast to it. Machiavelli was mainly concerned with a general norm, valid for the military organizations of all states and times; modern military thought emphasizes that actions under different historical circumstances must differ and that military institutions will be satisfactory only when they are fitted to the particular constitution and conditions of an individual state. Moreover, Machiavelli's emphasis on the establishment of military institutions and conduct of war according to rational and generally valid rules gave great weight to the rational factor in military matters. Although Machiavelli began as a vehement critic of the chesslike wars of the fifteenth century, eighteenth-century generals returned to some extent to wars of maneuvering, and this development is not entirely against the line of thought in military science that Machiavelli had started. When war is seen as determined by rational laws, it is only logical to leave nothing to chance and to expect that the adversary will throw his hand in when he has been brought into position where the game is rationally lost. The result of considering war as a mere science or at least of overvaluing the rational element in military affairs leads easily to the view that war can be decided quite as well on paper as on the battlefield.

It has since been realized that war is not only a science but also an art. With the end of the eighteenth century and of the Age of Reason, there was a sudden recognition of the importance of other than rational factors. Not the general element, but the individual and unique feature of a phenomenon was considered as of supreme importance; the imponderables were seen as no less influential than the rational and calculable elements.

The introduction of these new intellectual trends—of the realization of the importance of uniqueness and individuality, of the recognition of the creative and intuitive element aside from the scientific—into military theory is connected with the name of Clausewitz. It is remarkable, however, that Clausewitz, who usually is extremely critical and contemptuous of other military writers, is not only very careful in examining suggestions made by Machiavelli but concedes that Machiavelli had "a very sound judgment in military matters."[41] This is an indication that, despite the new features which Clausewitz introduced into military theory and which are outside the framework of Machiavelli's thought, he agreed with Machiavelli in his basic point of departure. Like Machiavelli he was convinced that the validity of any special analysis of military problems depended on a general perception, on a correct concept of the nature of war. All doctrines of Clausewitz have their origin in an analysis of the general nature of war. Thus, even this great revolutionary among the military thinkers of the nineteenth century did not overthrow Machiavelli's fundamental thesis but incorporated it in his own.

[41] Carl von Clausewitz, *Strategie*, ed. Eberhard Kessel (Hamburg, 1937), 41. See also the discussion of Clausewitz's response to Fichte's essay on Machiavelli in Peter Paret, *Clausewitz and the State* (Oxford and New York, 1976; repr. Princeton, 1985), 169-79.

2. Maurice of Nassau, Gustavus Adolphus, Raimondo Montecuccoli, and the "Military Revolution" of the Seventeenth Century

GUNTHER E. ROTHENBERG

THE CONCEPT of a "military revolution" in Europe during the early modern era has come to be generally accepted. There is, however, disagreement about the exact time frame of this development. Traditionally historians have regarded the army that Charles VIII took to Italy in 1496 as the first modern army, "not fundamentally different in composition to that which Napoleon was to lead to the same battlefields three hundred years later."[1] On the other hand, while agreeing that many of the elements of the military revolution, including the rise of infantry, the widespread adoption of firearms, and the rapid evolution of fortifications capable of withstanding the new artillery, had already made their appearance by the end of the fifteenth century, other historians have argued that the most important component of this revolution, the emergence of professional standing armies, took place later, between 1560 and 1660.[2]

Before this period, they would maintain, warfare in western and central Europe—matters admittedly were somewhat different in the eastern fringe areas—had become increasingly static and indecisive. Tactically, the lethal combination of missile fire and rapidity of movement, demonstrated perhaps most effectively at Agincourt, had been replaced by massive formations of musket and pike. And although these formations forced cavalry to abandon charges against formed and unshaken infantry, the deep order of battle, with men ranged in twelve lines or more, also inhibited offensive action. Tactical sluggishness was reinforced by logistic and strategic factors. Few areas could sustain armies for prolonged periods, and with poor communications, troops were dependent

---

[1] Michael Howard, *War in European History* (London, 1976), 19-20; Geoffrey Parker, "The 'Military Revolution, 1560-1600'—A Myth?" in *Spain and the Netherlands: Ten Studies* (London, 1979), 90, 92. Cf. Charles Oman, *A History of the Art of War in the Sixteenth Century* (London, 1937), 6.

[2] Michael Roberts, *The Military Revolution, 1560-1600* (Belfast, 1956) reprinted with slight changes in his *Essays in Swedish History* (Minneapolis, 1967), 195-225.

for supply on fixed points, usually magazines located in fortresses. But these vital points, their works now constructed on the multibastioned design, the so-called Italian trace, no longer could be rapidly reduced by artillery. They had to be formally besieged, a lengthy process requiring heavy artillery, much ammunition, and stores. Whole campaigns came to revolve around sieges, considered more important than battles in the field and now also far more numerous, even in the records of commanders wishing to fight in the open. In this military environment the "art of war was stiffening into immobility," with an "almost total lack of an abstract conception of 'strategy' as a way of looking at a military enterprise."[3]

It should not be assumed, however, that this development was entirely due to contemporary problems of logistics and siege warfare. Perhaps the greatest obstacle to the conduct of consistent military operations could be found in the social characteristics of most armies. Although by the sixteenth century there existed some permanently embodied units, these were inadequate to provide strong field armies, which had to be constituted from other sources. And although most countries retained relics of obsolete medieval institutions, feudal knight service and militia levies, these normally were inefficient and the great bulk of armies everywhere was composed of mercenaries.[4] Mercenaries were competent enough in combat, but at the same time unreliable and often dangerous to their employers. Unless promptly paid and supplied, something early modern states found difficult, they might mutiny, desert, or defect, paralyzing operations.[5] Altogether, the ascendancy of the tactical defense, the strength of the new fortifications, and the mercenary character of the troops explain why warfare in Europe had become so drawn out and indecisive.

The problem of how to raise an effective army, capable of serving as a reliable instrument of state policy, was recognized as early as the late fifteenth century, and soon the revival of interest in classical civilization had a distinct impact on military theory and practice. The study of Roman military methods especially became a source of inspiration for reformers, and Machiavelli's *Arte della guerra* ranks only as the most famous in a long line of treatises that rediscovered the virtues of the Graeco-Roman military system and recommended its revival. Although frequently scorned as impractical amateurs, these "neoclassicists" ac-

[3] Roberts, *Essays in Swedish History*, 59-60; J. R. Hale, "Armies, Navies, and the Art of War," in *The New Cambridge Modern History* (Cambridge, 1968), 3:200-201.
[4] André Corvisier, *Armies and Societies in Europe 1494-1789* (Bloomington, 1979), 27-40.
[5] Geoffrey Parker, "Mutiny and Discontent in the Spanish Army of Flanders, 1572-1607," in *Spain and the Netherlands*, 106-21.

33

tually included some experienced soldiers like Lazarus von Schwendi and the Huguenot captain La Noue, and even if their suggestions on weapons and tactics often proved impractical and many classically inspired reforms were short-lived or quickly changed beyond recognition, Machiavelli and other humanists were right in their central idea—the need for discipline and the notion that society had a military obligation. Beginning with the Florentine, many of these writers suggested that native troops were superior and more reliable than mercenaries. Rulers, however, hesitated to arm their subjects and, perhaps more importantly, believed that only experienced mercenaries could master the intricacies of contemporary weapons and tactics. Indeed, in both western and central Europe, the performance of part-time militia troops left much to be desired. Slow to muster and clumsy in the field, they were primarily useful in the defense of their own towns, but inadequate for complex and prolonged operations.[6]

Even so, Machiavelli's emphasis on discipline based on a hierarchical chain of command, functional assignments, and military competence achieved by constant drill and training, all implicit in his advocacy of the Roman legion system, had considerable influence on the emergence of combat-effective but also controlled forces during the Eighty Years' War in the Netherlands. Here the ruling Dutch oligarchy was prepared to entrust its commanders, princes of the House of Orange-Nassau, with the organization of a new model army. Like other cultured soldiers of the age, the Orangist princes were acquainted with the military texts of the ancients, but they also recognized that obtaining the greatest possible benefits from the tactical mix of musket and pike required a new degree of control, combined with a new style of combat leadership and more training. To achieve the highest degree of fire and mobility, infantry no longer could be deployed in large mass-formations, but instead was increasingly strung out in smaller units, requiring officers and men to display a greater degree of personal initiative and tactical skills, while at the same time conforming to an overall battle plan. A purely mechanistic imitation of Roman tactical models was not enough; it had to be supplemented by a new military ethos, different from the reckless individual courage of the feudal knights and the selfish drive for personal enrichment of the mercenaries. Resolving this problem, the Orangist reformers created a new type of professional soldier and combat leader, combining martial expertise with specific social and spiritual values.

Inspiration for this owed much to Justus Lipsius, a neo-Stoic phi-

[6] Hale, "Armies, Navies, and the Art of War," 181-82; Helmut Schnitter, *Volk und Landesdefension* (E. Berlin, 1977), passim; Eugen v. Frauenholz, *Lazarus von Schwendi* (Hamburg, 1939), 16-21.

losopher, polyhistorian, and philologist at the University of Leiden between 1571 and 1591, who had a direct influence on Maurice of Nassau.
In his lectures and writings, Lipsius, an admirer of Machiavelli, whom
he ranked with Plato and Aristotle, stressed the doctrines of obedience,
loyalty, and service to the state. His *Politicorum libri six*, published in
1589, a copy of which he presented to his sometime student Maurice,
has been described as the intellectual basis of the Dutch reforms. War,
Lipsius argued, was not an act of uncontrolled violence, but rather the
orderly application of force, directed by a competent and legitimate authority, in the interest of the state. His ideal officer was not motivated
by the quest for individual glory, but, having learned to command as
well as to obey, would consider himself first and foremost as a professional serving his community. Patient and sober, with no act of common
violence besmirching his standing, such an officer not only would provide
an example for his men, but through constant drill and training, turn his
troops into effective and disciplined fighters. These qualities, Lipsius
maintained, had been the main factors enabling Roman citizen-soldiers
to overcome superior numbers of less disciplined foes.[7]

Discipline then became the key element, and even though circumstances compelled the Orangist reformers to discard the concept of a
citizen army for a long-service professional mercenary force, they retained
an emphasis on discipline, achieved by professional officers, drill, and
training. It was enough to transform the relationship between the soldier
and the state and to increase greatly the combat capabilities of the Dutch
army. "It was discipline and not gunpowder," Max Weber concluded,
"which initiated the transformation," and "gunpowder and all the war
techniques associated with it became significant only with the existence
of discipline."[8] Social and moral dimensions, rather than technology,
provided the fundamental parameters for the new military establishments
of the early modern era, and the methods practiced by Maurice and his
cousins became the normative standards for all later European armies.
Although when measured against the standards set by Lipsius, the professional forces that came to predominate in Europe retained grave deficiencies, compared to the mercenaries of the preceeding period they were
reasonably efficient instruments of state policy, responding in a predict-

---

[7] Gerhard Oestreich, "Justus Lipsius als Theoretiker des neuzeitlichen Machtstaates,"
Historische Zeitschrift 181 (1956), 66-67; David C. Rapoport, "Military and Civil Societies:
The Contemporary Significance of a Traditional Subject in Political Theory," *Political
Studies* 13 (1964), 178-83; and G. Martin, "Moritz von Oranien," in *Grosse Soldaten der
europäischen Geschichte*, ed. Wolfgang v. Groote (Frankfurt a.M., 1961), 37-62.

[8] *From Max Weber: Essays in Sociology*, trans. and ed. Hans H. Gerth and C. Wright
Mills (New York, 1946), 256-57.

able pattern of obedience to the orders of a defined political-military chain of command.

These developments had a substantial influence on strategy and tactics. Although both continued to suffer from poor communications and an environment dominated by fortresses, and although the lines between strategy and tactics continued to be blurred into the late eighteenth century, disciplined standing armies enabled commanders to plan and carry out sustained operations. Also, even though their forces differed in many aspects from those of Maurice, there was substantial continuity. Both Gustavus Adolphus and Montecuccoli were "disciples of the Netherlandish reformers," especially in their conviction that well-regulated troops were a basic requirement of modern war.[9] Still, it should be noted that the evolution of standing European armies came from two independent lines of development. The Dutch model, undoubtedly, was the more widely imitated, but there also existed an "imperial" model, derived from the long wars against the Turks. In the Holy Roman Empire, humanists like Aventinus and commanders like Fronsperger and Schwendi had come to admire the military establishment of the Ottoman Empire and repeatedly urged the introduction of a similar system.[10] With experience in fighting both the Swedes and the Turks, Montecuccoli eventually fused these two lines in his writings, the first systematic attempt in early modern times to address the phenomenon of war in all its strategic, tactical, administrative, political, and social dimensions. And it was in this form that the Dutch, Swedish, and Austrian heritage was transmitted to Eugene, Marlborough, Frederick the Great, and ultimately to the age of the French Revolution. Scharnhorst, Clausewitz's mentor, greatly admired Montecuccoli and considered him an indispensable guide to the eternal nature of war.[11]

If, then, the term "military revolution" is taken to mean more than the adoption of new weapons and tactical formations and is designed to embrace a complete and fundamental shift in the nature of armies and warfare, such a shift took place only after 1560, that is, in the era of Maurice, Gustavus Adolphus, and Montecuccoli. It was only then that

[9] Werner Hahlweg, "Aspekte and Probleme der Reform des niederländischen Kriegswesens unter Prinz Moritz von Oranien," *Bijdragen en mededeelingen betreffende de geschiedenis der Nederlande* 86 (1971), 164, 176.

[10] Gunther E. Rothenberg, "Aventinus and the Defense of the Empire against the Turks," *Studies in the Renaissance* 10 (1961), 60-67; Hans Schnitter, "Johann Jacobi von Wallhausen: Ein fortschrittlicher deutscher Militärtheoretiker des 17. Jahrhunderts," *Militärgeschichte* 6 (1980), 709-12; Hans Helfritz, *Geschichte der preussischen Heeresverwaltung* (Berlin, 1938), 41-42.

[11] Rudolf Stadelmann, *Scharnhorst: Schicksal und geistige Welt* (Wiesbaden, 1952), 92-95.

modern armies, founded on the principle of hierarchical subordination, discipline, and social obligation, took the shape they have retained to the present day. This transformation, accomplished in large part by the efforts, practices, and theories of these three commanders, does indeed constitute a true "military revolution."

I

The name of Maurice of Nassau, the second son of William the Silent, is associated above all with the organization of the Dutch professional army. Although a distinguished administrator, tactician, and master of siege warfare, Maurice can not be ranked as a truly great strategist. Exceedingly cautious, he avoided placing his army at risk and fought only one major battle in twenty years. He achieved his strategic objective, securing the independence of the United Netherlands, but his caution sometimes placed him at a disadvantage against more combative and less methodical adversaries.[12] Even so, his success in transforming a motley crowd of unreliable mercenaries and part-time militias was enough to win him a lasting place in the evolution of modern war.

Of course, the actual implementation of military reforms in the years 1589 to 1609 was the product of collaboration. In building the overall framework of the army and in finances, Maurice had the support of Johan van Oldenbaarneveldt, the *landsadvocaat* of Holland and for three decades the most important official in the States General, the assembly of the Seven Provinces forming the United Netherlands. In administrative and tactical matters Maurice was assisted by his two cousins, William Louis and Johann of Nassau-Siegen.[13] Finally, in siege warfare and military technology, Maurice relied on the advice of Simon Stevin, his tutor in mathematics and siege techniques, who became chief engineer of the army, directed many of the major sieges, and helped establish the corps of military engineers.[14]

Maurice's cautious and deliberate strategy also derived from his unique position, reflecting the complex political and military conditions of the Dutch Republic. Unlike a Gustavus Adolphus, Frederick the Great, or Napoleon, he was not a sovereign warlord but always subject to a substantial degree of civilian control. In 1588, then twenty-one years old, Maurice was appointed "Admiral-General of the United Netherlands"

---

[12] Jan W. Wijn, *Het krijgswezen in den tijd van Prins Maurits* (Utrecht, 1934), 538-41; Pieter Geyl, *The Revolt of the Netherlands, 1555-1609* (London, 1962), 244.

[13] Jan W. Wijn, "Johann der Mittlere von Nassau-Siegen," in *Klassiker der Kriegskunst*, ed. Werner Hahlweg (Darmstadt, 1960), 119-24.

[14] Christopher Duffy, *Siege Warfare* (London, 1979), 81-82; Wijn, *Krijgswezen*, 28-32, 376-88.

as well as "Captain-General of the Troops in Brabant and Flanders," the main field army of the provinces. In addition, Maurice already held office as *stadtholder*, representative of the sovereign, in two of the provinces, Holland and Zeeland, and after 1591 also in Gelderland, Overijsel, and Utrecht. At the same time his cousin William Louis was *stadtholder* of Friesland and from 1594 on of Groningen and Drenthe.[15] But the many offices did not mean power. As naval commander, Maurice was answerable to five different provincial admiralty boards and though often called "General of the Armies" by the States, he never commanded all Dutch land forces. Provincial particularism inhibited force development and sometimes operations, while at all times a special committee of the States General, the Council of State, coordinated military affairs and watched over operations through special field deputies. One historian has described Maurice's position as that of a "technical expert, operational manager, and military advisor to the States."[16]

Despite the potential conflict inherent in this arrangement, for a long time it worked well enough. Maurice had limited political ambitions, while the ruling merchant oligarchs lacked martial traditions and a taste for military careers and were content to leave details of army management to the *stadtholders*. Still, conflict could not be avoided entirely. When political pressures compelled Maurice to undertake an ambitious campaign into Flanders in 1600, senior officers grumbled about the "long coats," the politicians, for needlessly hazarding the army.[17] And ultimately, when during a sectarian-political conflict Oldenbaarneveldt tried to reduce the role of the army by raising city-paid forces, Maurice had him arrested, tried, and executed in 1619. But even this unhappy event, a deadly quarrel among longtime friends, did not shake civil control over the army.

All this still lay in the future when Maurice was appointed commander in chief in 1588. At that time politicians and soldiers were united by the need to transform the ineffective mix of mercenaries and militias into a force capable of repelling the veteran Spanish Army of Flanders, then led by the able Alexander Farnese, Duke of Parma, and poised to complete its reconquest of the northern Netherlands. That year, as it had been from the outset of the Dutch revolt, the struggle was asymmetrical. The long conflict in the Low Countries had been as much a civil war as a war of national liberation, and the Dutch, facing the leading military power of the time, had survived not only because of their extraordinary efforts but also because of their geography and the difficulties the Spanish

---

[15] Geoffrey Parker, *The Dutch Revolt* (Ithaca, 1977), 241-43.
[16] Wijn, *Krijgswezen*, 533.
[17] Parker, *The Dutch Revolt*, 234.

experienced in mounting large-scale operations for extended periods of time.

At the outset of the revolt in 1566, the Spanish Netherlands consisted of seventeen provinces with about three million inhabitants. The Rhine, Maas, and Scheldt river systems divided the ten southern provinces, open, prosperous farming country that also included the major cities, from the poorer, more sparsely inhabited north. The South had been the original focus of the revolt, but by 1579, following repeated defeats of the improvised insurgent field armies and a split between the aristocratic leaders and their increasingly radicalized urban supporters, the southern provinces had returned to Spanish rule. Forming their own union at this time, the seven northern provinces tried to succor the places continuing to resist in the south, but after William the Silent, the one insurgent leader respected by North and South, was assassinated in 1584 their military effort faltered. Divided by factional and local rivalries, the northern provinces would not make a joint effort, while their unpaid mercenaries demanded "money when they were ordered to fight."[18] Without relief, town after town fell to Parma's troops. Some, above all Antwerp, offered protracted resistance, but many surrendered or were delivered by treachery. As Parma continued north across the river barriers, he opened a second front in the east, moving through Friesland, Groningen, and Gelderland against the Ijsel river, threatening Utrecht, Holland, and Zeeland. Fear of a Spanish victory compelled Elizabeth of England, already providing indirect support to the insurgents, to intervene directly with troops and subsidies. In the event, the English intervention proved ineffective. The commander, the Earl of Leicester, quarrelled with the States and some of his lieutenants sold important strongholds entrusted to them to Parma. In 1587, the crisis of the revolt was at hand. Parma's eastern offensive reached the Zuider Zee and linked up with his southern front, reducing the area still in arms to Holland, Zeeland, Utrecht, a few isolated places in Overijsel, Gelderland, and Friesland, with Ostend and Bergen-op-Zoom south of the great rivers. If Parma did not complete his undertaking in 1587-1588, it was because English intervention had angered King Philip enough for him to send the "Invincible Armada" against the island, and Parma was ordered to Dunkirk to prepare to embark his army. After the enterprise failed and he was ready to move again the following year, he was diverted to support the Catholic side in the French religious wars.[19]

These diversions provided the time for Maurice to rebuild the army, recover much of the northeastern area, and bolster defenses. Retention

[18] Geyl, *The Revolt of the Netherlands*, 188.
[19] Parker, *The Dutch Revolt*, 208-24; Charles Wilson, *Queen Elizabeth and the Revolt of the Netherlands* (Berkeley, 1970), passim.

of the strategic redoubt area, the *Vesting Holland* as the Dutch would call it (which held against the French in 1672, but fell to the Germans in 1940), was a crucial asset. Protected north and west by the North Sea and the Zuider Zee, in the south by the rivers, and in the east by the Ijsel and marshlands, it consisted mainly of low-lying terrain, cut up by canals, dikes, estuaries, and bogs and studded with small fortified towns.[20] By cutting dikes, the defenders could inundate vast stretches, a measure already employed in 1572-1574 to halt a Spanish penetration. Moreover, since that time, the Dutch usually maintained control over the inshore and inland waters. If Spain could have concentrated a superior fleet, it still might have gained victory, but its intervention in France, its Mediterranean commitments, and the security needs of its overseas empire dissipated resources. And finally, Spanish financial difficulties provoked frequent mutinies in the Army of Flanders, while with control of the Channel in doubt, reinforcements for the army had to come over the long and circuitous land route from Italy, the Spanish Road.[21]

By contrast, mastery of the sea and inland waters enabled the Dutch to shift their forces rapidly on the great rivers and mount short stabs into Brabant and Flanders. Moreover, with growing, though not yet undisputed, control of the sea approaches, the Dutch rapidly expanded their maritime commerce, and their economy prospered. "Whereas," commented the mayor of Amsterdam, "it generally is the nature of war to ruin land and people, these countries have been noticeably improved thereby."[22] Financial strength provided the Orangist reformers with the resources to pay a standing professional army, conduct large-scale siege warfare, and construct new fortified lines along their fronts.

II

Inspiration for army reforms was derived from classical models as well as from the practical necessities of sixteenth-century warfare.[23] Although recent events had demonstrated that mercenary forces were not totally reliable, and although Lipsius had advocated the use of loyal citizen-soldiers, the reformers were forced to use hired professionals. Though they served with distinction at sea, it "was only rarely that the Dutch themselves bore arms against the enemy . . . fighting was left largely

[20] Duffy, *Siege Warfare*, 58-61.
[21] Geoffrey Parker, *The Army of Flanders and the Spanish Road, 1567-1659* (Cambridge, 1972), 80-101, 188-202.
[22] Geyl, *The Revolt of the Netherlands*, 233.
[23] Maury D. Feld, "Middle-Class Society and the Rise of Military Professionalism: The Dutch Army 1589-1609," *Armed Forces and Society* 1 (1975), 428-29, 437-38. The standard treatment remains Werner Hahlweg, *Die Heeresreform der Oranier und die Antike* (Berlin, 1941), 20-23, 191-96.

to the troops recruited from abroad." This was not just a dislike of combat. During the earlier sieges in the Low Countries Dutch burgher militias had fought well enough, but maritime trade and the growing navies had first call on native manpower. Therefore, although for local defense and garrison duties the old militia companies, supplemented by paid garrison troops, the *waardgelder*, were retained, the *stadtholders*, always realists rather than doctrinaire neoclassicists, recruited a disciplined mercenary field army, in Michelet's words "not many men, but well chosen, well fed, and very well paid."[24]

The distinguishing characteristics of the new force were intelligent leadership, unquestioning obedience, loyalty to the unit, and improvements in tactical deployment and movement. Reform began with a reduction in numbers, bringing troop strength into line with reduced finances. Up to 1600, the Dutch field forces rarely exceeded twelve thousand men, about two thousand horse and ten thousand foot, supported by a relatively powerful artillery train, forty-two pieces in 1595, but only six field guns.[25] The majority of the rank and file were foreigners, French, German, English, and Scotch, with a few Swiss and Danes. With year-round employment and prompt payment, these men accepted discipline. Although Maurice enforced a stern code of conduct, he also rediscovered drill as a method to instill discipline. Following the suggestion of William Louis, the men were drilled daily with routines taken directly from the Roman models as described by Aelian and Leo, with the commands translated into Dutch, English, and German.[26] Of course, armies always had trained soldiers to handle weapons, but here the objective transcended the achievement of individual or unit proficiency. Proper execution of the manual of arms became the outward manifestation of discipline, with exercises designed to teach instant obedience to commands and to build unit cohesion. The reintroduction of drill into the army was an essential element of the Orangist reforms and a basic contribution to the modern military system.[27]

A corollary of drill and unit cohesion was improved combat effectiveness. "Nature," Lipsius wrote, "brings forth some valiant men, but good order through industry makes more."[28] Daily exercises under arms permitted more precise evolutions, improved coordination of shot and

---

[24] Johan H. Huizinga, *Dutch Civilization in the Seventeenth Century* (London, 1968), 34-35; Geyl, *The Revolt of the Netherlands*, 235; Wijn, *Krijgswezen*, 9-10, 19-21.

[25] Wijn, *Krijgswezen*, 40-43, 62-64; F. J. G. ten Raa and François de Bas, *Het Staatsche Leger 1568-1795* (Breda, 1913), 2:35.

[26] Hahlweg, *Heeresreform*, 31, 39, 48, 255-64; Wijn, *Krijgswezen*, 480-81.

[27] William H. McNeill, *The Pursuit of Power* (Chicago, 1982), 128-33.

[28] Justus Lipsius, *Six Bookes of Politickes or Civil Doctrine*, trans. William Jones (London, 1594), bk. 5, p. 13.

pike, and increased the rate of fire by the adoption of a new form of the countermarch, the so-called choric method, recommended to Maurice by William Louis in 1594.[29] Conforming to the general tendency toward smaller units, even the Spanish *tercios* were reduced to about 1,500 men after 1584, and Maurice cut down companies to 130 of all ranks, raised the ratio of shot to pike, and formed his units first ten and later six deep. He did not establish permanent major tactical formations, but for battle the companies were combined into battalions, initially 800, and later 550, strong, arrayed in a linear checkerboard pattern similar to the Roman legionary deployment.[30]

Constant training as well as the more independent combat roles assumed by subunits in the Dutch tactical system required better-educated and a larger number of junior officers, and Maurice has been described as the progenitor of the modern European officer corps. More importantly, he changed the basic ethos of the profession. Influenced by his Calvinist upbringing and neoclassical teachings, he regarded command as a public trust, with authority derived not from noble birth but from a commission awarded by the state. Combined with the concept of unconditional obedience within an established hierarchy of ranks, this provided the foundations of the modern command structure. In practice, of course, things were different. Most senior positions in the Dutch service were held by relatives of the *stadtholders* and nobles predominated in the upper grades. Many foreigners were also employed as senior officers because they alone had the necessary expertise, and it was not until 1618 that fixed promotion criteria were introduced.[31]

The new tactical system has sometimes been criticized. One prominent historian has claimed that the new order failed "to restore, both to horse and foot, the capacity for a battle-winning tactical offensive." The new combat formations were too rigid, too small for decisive assaults, and generally suitable only for the defensive.[32] But this assertion is not borne out by the facts. In the broken terrain of the Low Countries the Dutch did well enough in their only two major actions, the encounter at Tournhout in 1597 and the battle of Nieupoort in 1600. At Tournhout the cavalry drove the Spanish horse off the field and then shattered the infantry; at Nieupoort the Dutch mounted charge first defeated the ene-

---

[29] Hahlweg, *Heeresreform*, 61-68, 70-78. The choric countermarch is described by James Turner, *Pallas Armate: Military Essayes of the Ancient Grecian, Roman, and Modern Art of War* (London, 1683; repr. New York, 1968), 9-11.

[30] Ten Raa and de Bas, *Staatsche Leger*, 2:332-35; Wijn, *Krijgswezen*, 32-33.

[31] Wijn, *Krijgswesen*, 32-33. The introduction of the concept of professional officership is sometimes ascribed to Wallenstein. See Francis Watson, *Wallenstein: Soldier under Saturn* (London, 1938), 161.

[32] Roberts, *Essays in Swedish History*, 61-62.

my horse and then, supported by advancing infantry, broke the Spanish front.[33]

Maurice's contributions to siege warfare are undisputed. He increased his siege train and began to assign a permanent role in his army to artillery, engineers, and supply, and he made siege operations more efficient by introducing the use of troop labor.[34] Until this time, soldiers had considered digging to be below their dignity and armies had had to rely on hired or impressed labor for such work. Aware that this was a poor practice, some commanders had taken up pick and shovel themselves to shame their men into following their example. Lipsius had recommended that "officers carry boards and planks . . . to teach them and not command them."[35] Maurice went further. He made shovels part of the standard infantry equipment and detailed men for work as needed. Extra pay, up to several times the normal rate, provided the incentive. During the long siege of Gertruidenberg in 1593, "three thousand pioneers worked night and day," but, so it is reported, "the soldiers liked the business, for every man so employed received his ten stivers a day additional wages, punctually paid."[36] With reliable manpower at hand, Maurice was able to establish his siege lines rapidly or to throw up field works when necessary.

As for strategy, Maurice, following the wishes of the States General and his own inclinations, sought limited objectives, basically the recovery of the territory of the Seven Provinces. Moreover, he sought to achieve this objective primarily by positional warfare and did not look to defeat the enemy's main force. Between 1589 and 1609 he captured more than twenty-nine fortresses and relieved three sieges, but fought only one battle, Nieupoort, and that reluctantly. He made use of the interior lines of the great rivers to shift his army between the southern and eastern fronts, which gave his small army a far greater striking force than its size warranted. Away from water transport, he found the going much more difficult as was demonstrated in his abortive campaign into Brabant in 1602. Finally, the scope of his enterprises was further restricted by the perennial particularism of the provinces and the reluctance of the States General to maintain a larger force than absolutely necessary.

Operations during the years 1590 to 1594 illustrate Maurice's style of war. The diversion of Spanish forces against England and France provided an opportunity and the Council of State declared that it was a

[33] Oman, *A History of the Art of War in the Sixteenth Century*, 578-83, 587-603.
[34] Wijn, *Krijgswezen*, 319-28, 376-88.
[35] Cited in Rapoport, "Military and Civil Societies," 186.
[36] John L. Motley, *History of the United Netherlands from the Death of William the Silent to the Twelve Years' Truce—1609* (New York, 1886), 3:74.

"good occasion . . . for doing the enemy an injury." The States General, however, opposed offensive action. It was better, they maintained, to use the quiet period to strengthen defenses; offensive action "would arouse the sleeping dog and bring the war, now averted, upon themselves again."[37] In the end, Maurice was authorized to undertake limited operations to recover the key towns seized by Parma in the north. In 1590, beginning with a coup against Breda, the Army of the States eliminated Spanish footholds north of the great rivers and then crossed the Waal to reduce a chain of small forts in Brabant and Flanders. The next year Maurice conducted a remarkable offensive, capturing four major fortresses during the campaign season from May to October. Beginning in the east, he took Zutphen and Deventer on the Ijsel line in two weeks in May and June 1591; next he shifted his forces by barge to capture Hulst near Antwerp in five days in September, and then he doubled back to Dordrecht and marched overland to Nijmegen, which fell after a six-day siege in October. These spectacular results were achieved by surprise and by rapid siege operations, aided by favorable terms offered to the enemy garrisons.

In 1592, Maurice continued operations in the northeast, quickly seizing Steenwijk and Coevorden. Then provincial particularism asserted itself. Friesland had supported the campaign in Overijsel and Gelderland, but when pressure from Zeeland compelled Maurice to turn against Gertruidenberg in the southeast, the States of Friesland forbade William Louis and his troops to participate in the operation. After considerable delay and a long siege, Gertruidenberg fell in June 1593, and the following year Maurice returned east and conquered Groningen in July 1594. After that, with the immediate objectives achieved, the provinces scaled down their contributions to the army, forcing a partial suspension of operations.[38]

During the pause, Maurice reorganized and in 1597, with Spain once again heavily committed in France, he took a number of fortresses, severing communications between the eastern and southern Spanish fronts. In 1598, however, peace between Spain and France changed the situation. Reinforced, a Spanish army pushed across the river lines on the southeastern flank of the Dutch redoubt, but was repulsed early in 1599. At that, the Spanish troops mutinied once again, and emboldened by success, the States General prevailed on Maurice to advance down the Flemish coast against the privateer bases at Nieupoort and Dunkirk. On July 2, 1600, he defeated a hastily mustered Spanish army near

[37] Geyl, *The Revolt of the Netherlands*, 220.
[38] Summary of operations in Oman, *A History of the Art of War in the Sixteenth Century*, 569-603.

Nieupoort, a tactical but not a strategic victory because, unequal to either of the proposed sieges, the Dutch army had to be evacuated by sea in early August.

After that, Archduke Albrecht, the Spanish commander, decided to take Ostend. Maurice tried to lift the siege by his most ambitious operation ever. With an army increased to 5,442 horse and almost 19,000 foot, he planned to penetrate into Brabant, and then swing into Flanders to defeat the Spaniards. The operation failed when, after crossing the Maas, the Dutch could not find enough fodder for their horses, and Maurice was compelled to fall back across the river.[39] He was ordered by the States General to assume the defensive; the initiative now passed to Spain and to the newly arrived Ambrogio Spinola, by far the best Spanish general in the long war. While the siege of Ostend, a powerful fortress supplied from the sea, dragged on for three years, the States began to construct an extensive line of earthworks to bolster the vulnerable eastern front. Even so, when Spinola managed to transfer his main army there in 1609, he made progress in Overijsel and Gelderland before heavy autumn rains stopped his advance. At this point Spinola, aware of Spain's near catastrophic financial condition, advocated an end to hostilities and a truce was concluded in April 1607 with a term of twelve years dating from the end of 1608. It was the end of the solitary struggle for the Dutch Republic. When fighting was renewed in 1621, it was subsumed in the greater conflict then being waged in Germany.[40]

III

After the battle of Nieupoort, the Dutch tactical system attracted wide attention. The Army of the States was now considered the finest in Europe and "for good or ill," one writer observed, the Low Countries became "the Military Schools where most of the Youth of Europe did learn their Military Exercises."[41] In general, the Orangist reforms were most readily accepted by the Protestant states. In Sweden, Gustavus Adolphus "established the methods of Prince Maurice from the outset," but with modifications that added to their offensive capabilities.[42] Gustavus was the first soldier to fully understand the value of combining shock and fire, and he increased the effects of both by new fighting methods and improved weapons. Administratively, the king revived the national conscript army, though he fought his great campaigns mostly with mercenaries whom he disciplined and taught his tactics. In all this he was

---

[39] Martin Van Creveld, *Supplying War* (Cambridge, 1977), 11-12.
[40] Duffy, *Siege Warfare*, 85-88; Parker, *The Dutch Revolt*, 237-39.
[41] Turner, *Pallas Armate*, 360.
[42] Michael Roberts, *Gustavus Adolphus*, 2 vols. (London, 1953-58), 2:188-89.

assisted by officers who had learned their profession in the Netherlands, including Jacob de La Gardie who has been described as being to Gustavus "what Schwerin was to Frederick or Parmenio to Alexander."[43]

Although much more inclined to give battle, Gustavus like Maurice owes his place in history above all to his tactical and administrative innovations. In his strategic concepts he could not escape the limitations of his time. Although as a sovereign he was able to make plans on a far grander scale than was Maurice, he also was a careful general who "secured each step and risked nothing unnecessarily," a "solid, methodical strategist."[44] His famous campaigns in Germany took place in a fortress environment and, his great plans notwithstanding, his actual operations generally were determined by his ability to seize and hold strong places controlling communications and supply areas. Of course, this limited his capability to achieve a rapid decision, and, like Maurice, he has been regarded as an exponent of positional and maneuver warfare, a precursor of the eighteenth-century strategists. Reacting against this trend, Clausewitz judged Gustavus harshly. He was not, Clausewitz wrote, a "bold conqueror," but rather a "learned commander full of careful combinations," much too concerned with an "artificial, maneuvering, systematic style of warfare."[45]

When Gustavus Adolphus, barely seventeen years old, ascended the Swedish throne in 1611, he found an "ill-trained, undisciplined," and poorly organized military establishment.[46] Its origins dated back some fifty years to Gustavus Vasa and Erik XIV, who, anticipating the Dutch reforms, had converted the late feudal host and the hired foreign mercenaries of the crown into a standing national army. Originally well organized in small battalions with a good mix of pike and shot, these innovations had occurred too far from the European mainstream to have much influence, and in any case most had been short-lived. Under the succeeding rulers the army had declined during the intermittent wars against Denmark, Poland, and Russia. Johann of Nassau-Siegen who observed it in Poland in 1605 had been greatly disappointed. It was not an instrument equal to the ambitions of the young king. Although Gustavus had only a sketchy military education, including an acquaintance with the classical literature and some of the more recent humanist writings, he had knowledge of the Dutch reforms and had served an ap-

---

[43] Theodore A. Dodge, *Gustavus Adolphus* (Boston and New York, 1895), 77.

[44] Roberts, *Gustavus*, 2:297.

[45] Carl von Clausewitz, *Strategische Beleuchtung mehrerer Feldzüge*, in *Hinterlassene Werke*, 10 vols. (Berlin, 1832-37), 9:29, 47.

[46] Roberts, *Gustavus*, 1:33.

prenticeship under La Gardie. He clearly recognized the army's deficiencies, and rebuilding the force became his major priority.[47]

Immediately he concluded an armistice with Poland and in 1613 settled the war with Denmark, albeit on most unsatisfactory terms. Then, with La Gardie as his second in command, he campaigned in Finland, managing to gain a favorable peace from Russia in 1617. Three years later, with his forces much improved, he invaded Poland, then at war with the Ottoman Empire and Russia. But his expectations of a short and easy campaign did not materialize. Instead, it became a long war of attrition in which the young king learned useful lessons in logistics, mobility, cavalry shock, and siege warfare.[48] Interrupted only by a two years truce in 1622, the war continued until 1629, when it was halted by another armistice. By that time, realizing that the greater conflict in Germany represented a threat as well as an opportunity for Sweden, Gustavus, had made major changes in his military establishment.

He began, in 1625, by overhauling the method of recruitment. A cantonal system was introduced in which the local clergy kept registers of men between the ages of eighteen and forty. Service was set at twenty years, but normally only one man in ten was called and there were family and occupational exemptions. Unpaid while on home service, foot soldiers were supported by land allotments; cavalry was recruited from the nobility and the wealthier farmers. Townspeople served in the expanded navy. Taxes levied on the rest of the population provided equipment. The system produced a substantial long-service national army, up to forty thousand men, the first such in Europe.[49]

Perhaps too much has been made of the national army. The system was designed primarily for home defense. Campaigns abroad, above all the king's war in Germany, could not be sustained by a population base of some one and a half million, and mercenaries retained a prominent place. Although his 1627 statutes averred that the "state is best defended by its natives" and he described foreign mercenaries as "faithless, dangerous, and expensive," Gustavus started recruiting English, Scotch, and German regiments even before sailing for Pomerania. By 1631, foreign troops constituted the bulk of his army and did most of the fighting. It was a deliberate policy so that even if the army was badly hurt, the Swedish units would be safe to defend the homeland.[50] Therefore they normally were kept in strategic reserve, guarding the lines of commu-

[47] Ibid., 2:191-99.
[48] Dodge, *Gustavus Adolphus*, 61-62, 141-42.
[49] Roberts, *Essays in Swedish History*, 64-65.
[50] Roberts, *Gustavus*, 2:205-206; Theodore Lorentzen, *Die schwedische Armee im Dreissigjährigen Kriege* (Leipzig, 1894), 8-9.

nications. Montecuccoli observed that "all seaports are protected by Swedish commandants and garrisons; they trust neither the Finns, Livonians, or the Germans."[51] By the time Gustavus was killed in 1632, of the 120,000 men under his command, only one-tenth were Swedes. The remainder were foreign troops, including those of allies and paid associates such as Bernhard of Saxe-Weimar and other German princes. Most of the foreign units were trained in and adopted Swedish tactics, first tested on a large scale in the battle of Breitenfeld in 1631, "a victory of mobility and firepower over numbers and the push of the pike," which forced virtually all other European armies to revise their fighting methods.[52]

The tactical system of Gustavus stressed offensive action by combined arms although, because of frequent improvisations, there was "no moment . . . when any method universally obtained."[53] Infantry regiments, two squadrons or eight companies, were the basic administrative and tactical unit, combined for combat into brigades of two or three regiments. Each regiment numbered about eight hundred men with an additional ninety-four musketeers for detached duties. Normally deployed in a shallow formation six ranks deep for both shot and pike, the brigades continued to advance even during the countermarch, with the pikes, considered an offensive weapon by Gustavus, contributing to the final impact.[54] At close range the rolling fire of the countermarch was replaced by a heavy volley, delivered simultaneously by three ranks of closed-up musketeers, "one long and continuated crack of Thunder . . . more terrible and dreadful to mortals than ten interrupted and several ones."[55] The cavalry, trained to charge at the gallop, and supported by the commanded musketeers, usually was used against the enemy flanks, while artillery opened the attack with fire from fixed gun lines. After Breitenfeld, the introduction of a light mobile four-pound regimental piece provided direct fire support for the foot. Reserves, horse and foot, were withheld for use as needed. It was an effective, if complicated, system and even Gustavus, a great combat commander with drive, willpower, decisiveness, and originality, found it hard to control such a battle. Nevertheless, the Swedish pattern became the standard for all commanders of the next century.

The new Swedish army was much less effective as a strategic in-

---

[51] "Relation ueber die Art der Kriegsfuehrung der Schweden," *Ausgewählte Schriften des Raimund Fürsten Montecuccoli*, 4 vols., ed. A. Veltzé (Vienna and Leipzig, 1899-1900), 2:9.

[52] J. F. C. Fuller, *Decisive Battles* (New York, 1940), 340.

[53] Dodge, *Gustavus Adolphus*, 51.

[54] Roberts, *Gustavus*, 2:258-60.

[55] Turner, *Pallas Armate*, 237.

strument. Gustavus recognized that battlefield mobility was founded upon discipline and discipline upon effective administration, but this aspect of Swedish military affairs remained shaky. Training reached a high standard in most Swedish units and was acceptable in the mercenary regiments, but this was not always the case in the allied and associated contingents. As for discipline, the king had introduced a strict code in 1621, backed up by army chaplains, daily prayers, and other moral sanctions. Even so, as early as 1630, discipline began to erode. This was not merely due to the predominance of hard-bitten mercenaries, although the Swedish conscripts remained somewhat better controlled, but to the inability to sustain the army properly. Although Gustavus had made elaborate logistic preparations, Swedish resources could not supply the growing army in Germany. As one Swedish diplomat put it, "others nations went to war because they were rich, Sweden because she was poor."[56] French and Dutch subsidies could not change this. Moreover, when funds were available, there remained the difficulties in procuring and transporting supplies. By the spring of 1631 Swedish troops looted Protestant towns, and that summer Gustavus complained that his unpaid and hungry forces were stripping his regional supply base.[57] Although combat discipline was maintained to the end, the Swedish army, as any other army of that time, had to live off the land. By exhausting even rich areas, the "need to feed men and horses," rather than operational considerations, dictated its movements, with the result that the king's "great strategic schemes were but paper schemes."[58]

IV

When Gustavus landed at the mouth of the Oder River in the summer of 1630, the Thirty Years' War, originating both as a conflict between Catholics and Protestants but also as a conflict over the issue of imperial authority in Germany, had already become internationalized. After initial Hapsburg victories, a loose coalition of France, England, Denmark, and some lesser German Protestant princes had formed to oppose the imperial resurgence. But this ill-assorted array soon was shattered by imperial forces under Albrecht von Wallenstein, the formidable military entrepreneur, and Johann Tilly, a highly competent general commanding the forces of the Catholic League. By 1627 the emperor had regained control of most of the southern shore of the Baltic. Only a few ports, above all Stralsund, reinforced by Danish and Swedish troops, had managed to hold out. Even so, the prospect of an imperial hegemony on the Baltic

[56] Lorentzen, *Schwedische Armee*, 3.
[57] Ibid., 23-24; Roberts, *Gustavus*, 2:204-205.
[58] Van Creveld, *Supplying War*, 16-17.

disturbed the king and he told his *Riksdag* that he was going to Germany not only because the fate of Protestantism was in the scales, but also because it would be better to fight abroad than at home. By 1629 preparations for a full-scale intervention in Germany were under way.

The strategic situation appeared favorable. Believing the war in Germany as good as over, Emperor Ferdinand II turned to fight the French in Italy, dismissed Wallenstein, and left Tilly with only a few scattered garrisons in the north. Still, Gustavus took a gamble. His expeditionary force could muster but thirteen thousand, though recruiting agents in Scotland and Denmark were gathering more men and the king expected important aid from the German princes. But he was wrong in his expectations. The two major Protestant rulers in North Germany, the electors of Brandenburg and Saxony, were determined to remain neutral, and so from the outset Gustavus was forced to adopt a strategy that would produce a protracted war. Logistics and the need to guard communications with the homeland, together with misgivings about potential threats from Denmark and Russia, imposed severe restrictions on his strategy. The first consideration compelled him to follow rivers and to secure the strong places along their courses; the second compelled him to establish and hold fortified base areas in northern Germany into which his army could withdraw and to retain the major part of his native troops for home defense.[59]

Gustavus opened his campaign not from Stralsund (the city did not lie on a river), but from further east along the mouth of the Oder. Here he found a good strategic location flanking Tilly's garrisons in Mecklenburg and western Pomerania, and from here he might be able to pressure Brandenburg and Saxony into an alliance. After an unopposed landing he entered Stettin, forty miles up the Oder, in early July and then spent the remainder of 1630 slowly expanding his base, reducing some small towns and gathering troops. Although this was necessary, it also was self-defeating. As he gradually enlarged the area under his control, he dispersed his field army, and the slow progress failed to move the two electors from their cautious neutrality. Perhaps Gustavus missed an opportunity. Though his army still was small, his opponent, Tilly, also had few forces and moreover was facing a revolt in Magdeburg, a rich and strategic city on the middle Elbe. If Gustavus had advanced swiftly to the Elbe, he might have compelled Tilly into battle before the imperial forces were concentrated, and an early victory might have rallied Protestant support. Instead, in October the Swedes went into winter quarters in Pomerania and Mecklenburg.

[59] Roberts, *Gustavus*, 2:26.

About this time, Gustavus conceived a grand strategic design for the following year. It envisaged five armies, over 100,000 men, converging in a more or less concentric advance along the rivers into central Germany. Although one admiring biographer has described it as a plan of "Napoleonic breadth and grandeur," it lacked substance. The king did not have the strategic position or the necessary troops. He vastly overestimated his ability to raise new forces and failed to understand the relationship between distances, communications, supply, and the operational range of his army.[60]

For that matter, when lack of supplies forced him to emerge early from winter quarters, he again failed to engage Tilly's main army. Instead, hoping perhaps to maneuver Tilly away from his investment of Magdeburg, he conducted minor operations along the Oder and in western Mecklenburg. In early March 1631, Tilly moved to fight him there with twelve thousand men, but Gustavus with eighteen thousand declined to accept battle. It was "one of the most conspicuous blunders" of his military career, an example of what Clausewitz scornfully described the "new method of attempting to win a war by strategic maneuver."[61] Gustavus continued up the Oder, capturing some small towns, and stormed Frankfurt on the Oder on April 3, massacring the garrison and plundering the Protestant citizens. While Gustavus still was moving cautiously, clearly concerned about a safe line of retreat, the imperial army took Magdeburg on May 20. The sack that followed became famous even in the seventeenth century; some twenty-five thousand people were butchered and every building, except the cathedral, was burned. It was a great setback to Gustavus's claim to be the protector of the German Protestants, and forced him into action. He finally coerced the elector of Brandenburg to place two key fortresses, Küstrin and Spandau, at his disposal and then, with the lower Oder firmly garrisoned, the king swung west to the Elbe. But he still moved cautiously, building entrenched camps as he went. The next was at Werben, between the Havel and the Elbe, a strong position which Tilly unsuccessfully tested in July. It was, however, not a major action. The Imperial forces were expecting reinforcements from Italy and when these arrived they entered Saxony and demanded that the Elector John George declare himself. This, at long last, compelled the Elector to support Gustavus.

Now a decision was near. Gustavus marched to join the Saxons and on September 17, 1631, the main armies collided at Breitenfeld. Although the Saxon contingent fled soon after the battle opened, Gustavus won a

---

[60] Ibid., 450, 470-72; Dodge, *Gustavus Adolphus*, 177-78.
[61] Roberts, *Gustavus*, 2:478-79; Clausewitz, *Strategische*, 29.

signal victory in five hours of hard fighting. But the victory was not exploited. There was no immediate pursuit as the remnants of Tilly's army withdrew. Instead, one week after the battle a council of war at Halle debated available options. Pursuit was ruled out, and the discussion then turned on whether to push across the Bohemian mountains against Vienna or whether to turn southwest into the Lower Palatinate and the Rhineland. A move on Vienna would have struck at the heart of imperial power, but Gustavus considered it too risky with winter approaching and with only the weak Saxons guarding his rear. Therefore he opted to march southwest, placing his army in a rich area that also provided a good strategic position between the Bavarians to the east and possible Hapsburg reinforcements from the west. To secure his lines north, strong Swedish detachments were placed near Magdeburg and at Erfurt, the center of the German road network, while John George moved an army of observation into Bohemia and Silesia.[62]

Some critics have blamed Gustavus for not exploiting his victory. Tilly's army, rather than the Rhine or even Vienna, was the real objective. As it was, Tilly and his chief lieutenant, Pappenheim, were able to raise new forces during the winter while a chastened emperor hastily struck a deal with Wallenstein to form a new army in Bohemia. But Gustavus was interested in establishing a secure base. Marching to the Rhine, and evicting the small Hapsburg, Bavarian, and Spanish garrisons, he soon had the Rhineland under control. His progress was fast and his siege methods a remarkable mixture of bluff and rapid assault, with little sapping and bombardment. By late October 1631, he was again making an ambitious plan for the coming year. This time he planned to make a grand envelopment, "conceived as one huge operation, in which seven armies acted in coordination on a sickle-shaped front extending from the Vistula to the Brenner, from Glogau to Lake Constance."[63] The main army, led by the king, was to invade Bavaria and follow the Danube to Vienna, while the Saxons in Bohemia and Silesia were to provide the hinge of the movement. Other substantial detachments would contain imperial forces in northwestern Germany and others still would protect his lines of communication with Sweden. Discounting the Saxons, the king expected to have some 120,000 men at his disposal and by intense recruiting intended to bring this number up to 170,000 by the late spring. Meanwhile, always cautious, he intended to turn the entire region between the Danube to the north, the Lech to the east, and the alpine

[62] Roberts, *Gustavus*, 2:539, 543-44.
[63] Roberts, *Essays in Swedish History*, 72-73.

foothills to the south into an offensive-defensive base, a *sedem belli*, in case his grand design met with a reverse.[64]

In March 1632, the king took the field again, storming Donauwörth, the most westerly Bavarian fortress on April 10 and five days later making a spectacular opposed river crossing of the Lech, a tactical masterpiece. But again, it decided little. Although Tilly was mortally wounded, the Bavarians merely retreated downstream and when Gustavus appeared before Ingolstadt, a strong fortress, he found that he could not take it with his usual methods. Turning aside, Gustavus made lesser conquests in Bavaria and Swabia, but lost the strategic initiative.

The main reason was that he lacked the strength to continue his advance on Vienna. He still had very substantial numbers, but his recruiting drive had failed and his armies were too dispersed for effective coordination. His failure to crush Tilly after Breitenfeld had allowed the enemy to recover and the Swedes now were facing new armies, especially the powerful force that Wallenstein was mustering with surprising speed in Moravia. Moreover, the king's ultimate ambitions alarmed his allies. His actions on the Rhine had put him at odds with France, his chief financial backer since January 1631, while his attempts to control the alpine passes had estranged the Swiss cantons. Moreover, the electors of Brandenburg and Saxony were wavering as Wallenstein quietly suggested to them that perhaps the major objective on which all sides could agree was to get the foreign invader out of Germany.

While Gustavus tried to force Wallenstein into Bavaria by devastating its northern region, his adversary understood perfectly the main weakness in the Swedish situation. It lay in the Saxon alliance. If Saxony were lost, Gustavus would be cut off from his communications with Sweden and this he could not permit. Therefore, Wallenstein moved into Bohemia, easily drove the Saxons out, and then, moving with surprising speed, turned south and linked up with the Bavarians near Eger. From Sweden, Chancellor Oxenstierna tried to persuade the king to continue along the Danube, cutting loose from his communications, if necessary. It did not matter, he argued, if northern Germany was lost as long as the advance on Vienna continued. Once again, however, Gustavus would not take the risk.[65] Having failed to prevent the linkup between the Bavarians and Wallenstein he took position near Nuremberg, establishing an entrenched camp. Wallenstein followed and set up a camp nearby, intending to wait out the king. He had analyzed the Swedish operational methods and realized that their tactical system depended on mobility in

[64] Roberts, *Gustavus*, 2:676-78.
[65] Ibid., 743-44.

the field and their strategic system on fighting battles while maintaining secure bases and communications. Unable to meet Gustavus on equal terms in battle, Wallenstein intended to see who could stand the deadlock longer. After the armies faced each other for six weeks, both sides going hungry and being decimated by illness, Gustavus was compelled on September 3-4 to make a desperate assault against Wallenstein's lines and failed with heavy losses.

Now the king's situation became critical. Wallenstein was dangerously close to Protestant territory and in order to draw him south, Gustavus commenced another drive toward Vienna. Wallenstein ignored him, marched into Saxony, took Leipzig, and then began to despoil the country. It was a clever move, a fine example of the strategy of the indirect approach.[66] Because the imperial forces could spare Vienna far better than Gustavus could risk a Saxon defection, he hurried north, covering 270 miles in twenty days. It was a remarkable feat, but Gustavus could bring only some eighteen thousand men. Difficulties of supply and the need for garrisons against imperial raids had reduced his strength. He was joined by a contingent under Duke Bernard of Saxe-Weimar, his most loyal German ally, but the elector of Saxony had withdrawn his substantial army to Torgau and ignored all pleas to join the Swedes. By this time it was already November, and Wallenstein intended to disperse his troops for the winter. When he realized this, Gustavus decided to attack. "Now in the very truth," he declared, "I believe that God has delivered him into my hands."[67] On November 6, 1632, unsupported by his Saxon allies, he fought his last battle at Lützen, southwest of Leipzig. It was a desperate affair. Even though Wallenstein was reinforced during the fighting, Gustavus defeated the Catholic host, but was killed charging with his cavalry.

It was a fitting end to a spectacular martial career, although when he fell at the age of thirty-seven, Gustavus had already passed the peak of his success. When the king died on the field at Lützen his great scheme to control and exploit Germany as a base of operations had failed. Even had he survived and managed to retain the loyalty of his allies, one more victory would not have ended the war. The state of communications and the agricultural resources of central Europe made theater-wide operations such as Gustavus had contemplated impossible. Unless supplies were laid down in advance or were transported in boats, few areas could sustain large armies over extended periods and movement was dictated more by logistic than by strategic considerations. Moreover, all moves were slow,

[66] Basil H. Liddell Hart, *Strategy* (New York, 1962), 85.
[67] Roberts, *Gustavus*, 2:747-48.

especially if heavy equipment had to be shifted by land rather than by water. Even Marlborough, over a generation later, could not finish his wars in one major operation; great victories such as Blenheim or Ramillies were followed by another campaign the next year. And although Gustavus sometimes tried to ignore these constraints in his multi-army schemes of 1630 and 1631, in practice he had to conform and his strategy "typified rather than transcended that of the age."[68]

Even so, he was the outstanding commander of the Thirty Years' War. His strategy of position and maneuver, backed by his willingness to risk battle under the right conditions, prevailed until the French Revolution and Napoleon. Given the objective conditions, Gustavus achieved much. He greatly expanded the operational range of his army and although outmaneuvered by Wallenstein in 1632, he was never defeated in the field. His administrative, tactical, and operational practices were widely imitated and more than any other general of his age, he mastered the various elements that comprise leadership in combat. He was a great captain of men, imposing his will and determination on the army, which he infused with the sense that there was nothing it could not do. Despite his mistakes he was a great commander, a practitioner of war rather than a theorist, the "military ancestor" of Turenne and Montecuccoli, of Eugene of Savoy and Marlborough. Napoleon recognized his merits when he included Gustavus on his very short list of great generals.[69]

V

Raimondo Montecuccoli, lieutenant general and field marshal of the army of the Austrian Hapsburgs, victor at the battle of St. Gotthard in 1664, master of maneuver warfare who outgeneralled Turenne in 1673, able administrator with claims to be one of the founders of the Hapsburg standing army, is perhaps known best as a military intellectual. His major victory at St. Gotthard was surpassed by the defeat of the Turks before Vienna in 1683 and his success against Turenne was not repeated during his somewhat lackluster campaign two years later. For that matter, the impact of his innovations in administration, technology, and tactics was limited. As an administrator Montecuccoli could never overcome the innate sluggishness of the Hapsburg bureaucracy; his tactics, like those of all other western European armies of the time, were adopted from the Swedish model. His real importance and his great contribution to the development of strategic thought lie in his writings. He was the first modern theorist to attempt a comprehensive analysis of war in all of its

[68] Van Creveld, *Supplying War*, 16-17.
[69] Roberts, *Essays in Swedish History*, 74.

aspects. Reflecting the prevailing importance of the ideas of "law" and "system" in his writings, Montecuccoli searched for a universal paradigm, an integration of all knowledge, scientific, military, and political, derived from experience, yet firmly within the framework of the Catholic Church of which he always remained a faithful son. If properly applied, he hoped that his axioms would make the conduct of operations predictable while reducing casualties and costs. This, of course, proved impossible, and his concepts tended toward a rigid dogmatism that was not so much innovative as, in the words of one admiring historian, "an effort to extract the utmost from a once glorious but now passing art of war."[70] Even so, his writings, published only after his death and then only in part, became the most widely read treatise on military matters between the time of Machiavelli and that of the French Revolution and Napoleon, cited with approval by Frederick, Scharnhorst, and even the great emperor himself.[71]

Montecuccoli's writings were so widely accepted because of his reputation as one of the foremost practitioners of maneuver warfare. His campaigns against Turenne were greatly admired. Even Clausewitz, not a proponent of maneuver strategy, conceded that occasionally it was necessary and that Montecuccoli's actions in 1673 and 1675 were among "the most brilliant examples of this form."[72] In his own time Montecuccoli was sometimes attacked as a timid commander, a "Fabius Cunctator," but such charges did not disturb him. "Everybody," he once wrote, "wants to be a commander and a military critic," but good generals would not be dictated by fickle mass opinion. On the contrary, he advised that "one ought to study the dictator Fabius to learn that after a series of defeats it is necessary to change one's fighting methods and meanwhile to adopt a strategy of attrition."[73] Attrition, however, was not his only strategic mode. Under favorable conditions, he was quite willing to fight. "There are those," he wrote, "who deceive themselves that war can be waged without battle. But conquests and decisions can only be achieved by combat and battle and to believe otherwise is a delusion." Moreover, he was writing about pitched field battles and not skirmishes. Raids, incursions, ambushes, and the like, much favored by the Hungarian leaders with whom he bitterly quarreled during the campaign against the Turks, never were decisive. He warned that "if someone wants to make war in this fashion he is grasping at shadows and misses

[70] Piero Pieri, "Raimondo Montecuccoli," *Klassiker,* ed. Hahlweg, 141-43.

[71] Thomas M. Barker, *The Military Intellectual and Battle* (Albany, 1975), 1-5.

[72] Carl von Clausewitz, *On War,* trans. and ed. Michael Howard and Peter Paret, rev. ed. (Princeton, 1984), bk. 7, ch. 13, p. 542.

[73] Raimondo Montecuccoli, "Della guerra col Turco in Ungheria," in *Ausgewählte Schriften,* ed. Veltzé, 2:257-59, 485-86.

the substance." But because battles were decisive, "handing down non-appealable judgments between princes, ending wars, and making commanders immortal," they should not be accepted lightly.[74] Montecuccoli recognized that war had two opposite poles, later described by Delbrück as attrition and annihilation, and he tried to encompass both in his theories.

Montecuccoli was born in 1609, the son of a minor noble family of Modena in the Emilia Romagna. He began his military career as a simple soldier at the age of sixteen and advanced to lieutenant colonel of horse by 1632 and to colonel by 1635. By the end of the Thirty Years' War he had attained the rank of general. A participant in most major battles, he was wounded at Breitenfeld and taken prisoner; released six months later, he distinguished himself at Nördlingen in 1632 and again in covering the retreat after the imperial army suffered defeat at Wittstock in 1636. Wounded in the rearguard action following the battle of Melnik in 1639, he was captured and spent three years as a Swedish prisoner in Stettin. He had a good fundamental education and continued his studies during this period, producing two of his earliest works. Following his release he was promoted to *Generalfeldwachtmeister*, but at his own request, released from the imperial service to become the Modenese commander in the duchy's conflict with the papal states. He returned to the imperial army in 1643 and distinguished himself as a cavalry leader during the waning years of the war. Following the Peace of Westphalia, he carried out a series of diplomatic missions and then commanded the Austrian auxiliary corps assisting Poland against Sweden in the Nordic War (1656-1658). Thereafter, he held a number of posts in Hungary, and when the Turks assumed the offensive in 1663, took command of a combined Austrian, imperial, and French army, defeating a superior enemy in the battle of St. Gotthard on August 1, 1664. A grateful emperor appointed him lieutenant general, then the highest rank in the army; in 1668 he also was named president of the *Hofkriegsrat*, thus holding the two highest military offices in the state. During the war against France from 1672 to 1678 he conducted a model campaign against Turenne in 1673 and again held field command in 1675, though this time with somewhat less success. Thereafter, wounded by criticism and in failing health, he returned to Austria and died in 1680.[75]

Montecuccoli's style of war changed during his career. Up to 1648 he was a dashing cavalry combat leader, modeling himself on Baner and Torstensson. As he obtained independent command he became more

[74] Ibid., 522-23, 343-44.
[75] H. Kaufmann, "Raimondo Montecuccoli, 1609-1680" (Diss., Free Univ. Berlin, 1974), 8-28.

cautious. Fully aware that the Austrian standing army comprised but nine regiments of foot and ten of horse, with trained replacements difficult to obtain, he husbanded his strength at all times. He did so during the Nordic War and again in Hungary where, moreover, he also had to contend with the command difficulties inherent in an allied force. Moreover, his relations with the Hungarians, especially self-willed magnates like Miklos Zrinyi, were strained. Writing about the difficulties of governing Hungary, Montecuccoli concluded that the Magyars were "unstable, stubborn, ungrateful, undisciplined, and tumultuous," and required a firm hand.[76] This earned him the lasting dislike of Hungarian patriots and nineteenth-century historians who denigrated his generalship and even coined a derogatory term, *metodizmus*, for his maneuver strategy.[77]

But it was this strategy that brought him success in his campaign against Turenne, often considered the greatest of French generals before Napoleon. In 1673 Turenne's mission was to keep the imperial army from crossing the Rhine and invading Alsace, and to keep Montecuccoli from moving north to link up with the Dutch army in the Low Countries. Montecuccoli's objective was to join the Dutch. Seeking to preempt him, Turenne crossed the Rhine and moved to Würzburg, where Montecuccoli deceived him by first offering battle and then slipping away. He moved along the Main to the Rhine, captured Turenne's supplies, and by feinting a push across the Rhine, forced the French to hasten to the defense of Alsace, only to find that the imperial army had embarked on river barges and floated down the Rhine to join the Dutch. The combined allied armies then forced the French out of Holland, while Turenne still was trying to organize in Alsace. By contrast, in 1675, Turenne, despite some brilliant moves by Montecuccoli, generally managed to hold the upper hand, although in the end his death in battle nullified most of the French advantage.

From 1675 on, Montecuccoli's position became more difficult. As president of the *Hofkriegsrat* he had to deal with an entrenched court bureaucracy and its endless paper shuffling. "It took these men," he wrote, "a year for what should and could have been done in one hour."[78] He continually was compelled to fight for funds to maintain the small permanent military establishment and to introduce new weapons, regimental guns, and even experimental flintlock muskets. A standing army

[76] Raimondo Montecuccoli, "L'Ungheria nell'anno 1677," in *Ausgewählte Schriften*, ed. Veltzé, 3:423-24, 450.

[77] Thomas M. Barker, "Montecuccoli as an Opponent of the Hungarians," in *Armi Antiche*, special issue of *Bolletino dell'Academia di S. Marciano* (1972), 207-21.

[78] Kaufmann, "Raimondo Montecuccoli," 30.

he considered the only guarantor of the state; under its protection "arts and commerce flourished, while if arms decayed, there is no security, no strength, no honor." And this was particularly important for Austria because "no other part of Europe faces as many enemies."[79] Montecuccoli opposed the practice of maintaining the standing regiments as cadre formations, hastily completed when hostilities opened. Veteran troops, "trained and never disbanded," he noted, constituted a reliable instrument, whereas freshly raised units were "nothing but a despicable rabble, inexperienced and indisciplined, an army in name only."[80] His recommendations were not heeded. After the Treaty of Nijmwegen in 1679, the Austrians disbanded their forces and in 1683, despite their clear tactical inferiority, the Turks were able to brush aside the weak imperial army in Hungary and advance to besiege Vienna.[81] Laying siege to a major fortified town, albeit not a great fortress, proved to be a strategic mistake. Operating at the extreme end of their logistic capability, the Turks were too weak to take the town, and in the end Vienna managed to hold out until relieved by an international force.[82] During the siege, the regulars had provided the backbone of the defense, and it was regulars who spearheaded the Austrian drive to expel the Turks from Hungary after 1683. Montecuccoli had been right, but despite his best efforts, the permanent military establishment of the Hapsburgs did not appreciably increase. His major legacy was in the example he set for his successors, Francis of Lorraine, Rüdiger of Starhemberg, Louis of Baden, and perhaps Eugene of Savoy, and above all in his writings.

VI

Montecuccoli's literary work spanned thirty years and can be divided into three main periods: the first from 1640 to 1642, the second from 1649 to 1654, and the last from 1665 to 1670. During the first period he wrote the *Sulle battaglie* (On battle), and the *Trattato della guerra* (Treatise on war). During the second, he completed the compendium *Dell'arte militare* (On the art of war), devoted to mathematics, logistics, organization, and fortification, and produced a second version of *Sulle battaglie*. His most famous work, *Della guerra col Turco in Ungheria* (On war against the Turks in Hungary), better known under the title *Aforismi dell'arte bellica* (Aphorism on the art of war), containing his ideas for a future campaign against that enemy, was finished in 1670.

[79] Montecuccoli, "Della guerra col Turco," 459, 467.
[80] Ibid., 456-57.
[81] Walter Leitsch, "Il dolce suono della pace: Der Kaiser als Vertragspartner des Königs von Polen im Jahre 1683," *Studie Austro-Polonica* 3 (1983), 163-67.
[82] Thomas M. Barker, *Double Eagle and Crescent* (Albany, 1967), 228-35.

Although Montecuccoli's writings appear to have circulated in manuscript among the upper political and military echelons in Vienna, nothing was published in his lifetime. During the early eighteenth century, however, the *Della guerra col Turco in Ungheria*, sometimes augmented with excerpts from his other works, appeared in seven Italian, two Latin, two Spanish, six French, one Russian, and two German editions, establishing his reputation as a military theorist.[83]

Montecuccoli's approach was inductive. "I have," he declared in the preface to the *Trattato della guerra*, "found much pleasure in following the methods of Lipsius" and "have carefully read the major ancient historians as well as the best of modern authors. To these I have added examples derived from my experience of fifteen years of unbroken service." No listing of authors was provided, but the carefully footnoted *Della guerra col Turco in Ungheria* indicates that his sources included fifteen ancient, five late-medieval and Renaissance, and twenty-two contemporary or near-contemporary authors. The ancients included both Greeks and Romans, Aeneas Tacticus, Herodotus, Thucydides, and Xenophon, as well as Caesar, Aelian, Frontinus, Polybius, and Vegetius. Medieval writers like Commines and Froissart contributed only some historical detail, but Machiavelli's writings clearly influenced his thinking on the political side of war. Naturally, modern authors and examples are cited frequently, but from the outset, Montecuccoli was at pains to claim that he was more practical and comprehensive than his predecessors. "Many ancients and moderns," he wrote in the *Trattato della guerra*, "have written about war. Most, however, have not trascended the limits of theory. Although some, like Basta, Melzi, Rohan, La Noue, and others, have combined practice with speculation, they have cultivated but part of a very large field or have restricted themselves to generalities without immersing themselves in details of the specific acts. Knowledge of the latter is what makes an accomplished commander. After all, it is impossible to understand the whole, if one does not understand its constituent parts."[84] He maintained this approach throughout, and at the same time was remarkably consistent in all of his writing so that they can be considered as one body.

His view of the world, politics, and war was realistic. War, he conceded, was a great evil, but it was part of the natural order: "Philosophers may debate whether a permanent state of war exists in nature, but states-

---

[83] Kurt Peball, "Raimund Fürst Montecuccoli 1609-1680," *Österreichische Militärische Zeitschrift* 2 (1964), 303. Max Jähns, *Geschichte der Kriegswissenschaften* (Munich and Leipzig, 1890), 2:1162-1171 provides summaries of the writings and Veltzé, 1:xli-xc (see note 51) gives a complete bibliography.

[84] Montecuccoli, *Ausgewählte Schriften*, ed. Veltzé, 1:5-8.

men cannot doubt that there can be no real peace between powerful competing states; one must suppress or be suppressed, one must either kill or perish."[85] There were, however, different levels of conflict. In the *Trattato della guerra*, he already differentiated between foreign and civil wars, aggressive or defensive wars, and hostilities conducted by indirect means. A state, he warned, could be subverted, and he advised that sociopolitical solutions were preferable to military action. "If a prince is not a tyrant, he is safe from treason and conspiracies." And in a formulation that may seem to foreshadow Clausewitz, Montecuccoli defined war as "the use of force or arms against a foreign prince or people" and the art of war as the "ability to fight well and to win," requiring advance preparation and, repeating an earlier statement made by Gian-Jacopo Trivulzio to Louis XII of France, he declared that "money, money, and again money" was the "very nerve of war." Commanders should be selected on the basis of their position as well as their qualifications, which should include inspiring leadership and the ability to make rapid decisions. Because war was a matter of life or death for the state, he urged that "princes and republics should give their commanders the necessary latitude to act rapidly and to exploit opportunities."[86]

Montecuccoli's most often quoted statements appear in the *Guerra col Turco in Ungheria* where, in the form of aphorisms, they repeat earlier views. War, he held, is an "activity in which the adversaries try to inflict damage on each other by all possible means; the objective of war is victory." Whatever the nature and level of war, victory will depend on preparation, plans, and operations. Preparations included manpower, matériel, and finances. Planning depended on the strength ratios between opposing forces, the theater of war, and the overall objectives. Under all circumstances, operations were to be conducted with secrecy, dispatch, and resolution.[87] Montecuccoli elaborated his operational maxims, the "order of things," as he called them, in formulations later taken up by Frederick, Clausewitz, and Moltke. Before entering into an action, he advised that "one should weigh matters carefully and then execute them rapidly." Even so, a modification from his attempt to achieve a high degree of predictability, he noted that it was impossible to calculate all factors in advance and some matters "should be left to fortune," because "he who worries about everything achieves nothing; he who worries about too little deceives himself."[88] Montecuccoli's ideal commander was

---

[85] Montecuccoli, "Della guerra col Turco," 459-60.

[86] Raimondo Montecuccoli, "Trattato della guerra," in *Ausgewählte Schriften*, ed. Veltzé, 1:21, 47, 76, 89-90.

[87] Montecuccoli, "Della guerra col Turco," 206-207.

[88] Ibid., 253-54.

warlike, in good health, and of martial stature. He should possess moral strength, prudence, and above all have "force," a quality embracing courage, fortitude, energy, and determination, similar to the *virtù* demanded by Machiavelli and the *constantia* praised by Lipsius.

Montecuccoli did not clearly distinguish between strategy, operations, and tactics, all of which he regarded as an indivisible entity. His basic principle was always to retain a reserve because "whoever at the end disposes of more intact forces wins the battle." In his battle dispositions, he adopted the system of combined arms developed by Gustavus, but proposed to use the main strength only for a decisive counterattack after an active defense had weakened the enemy, and insisted on an immediate pursuit. "The remnants of the routed army must be hunted and annihilated."[89] He realized that the size of an army was limited by what one man could conveniently command and what the logistic system could sustain. Although the size of armies was increasing rapidly—Louis XIV deployed 100,000 men against the Dutch in 1672—Montecuccoli recommended an upper limit of 50,000 for a field army.[90] In regard to the composition of the ideal army, primarily the proportion of horse to foot, his views changed, showing a steady increase in cavalry strength. Following the Swedish model, he favored cavalry charging home, while the infantry's combat potential was to be raised with improved muskets, light regimental guns, and an increased proportion of pikes.[91] Such ideas, of course, were hardly unique and basically reflected the contemporary state of military thought in western and central Europe.

Montecuccoli made his mark as a field commander and a military administrator, although it might be argued that he was too cautious and prudent, perhaps because he was only too well aware of the limited resources at his disposal, to rank among the truly great. Even so, his generalship was well regarded by Folard, de Saxe, and Frederick the Great; Napoleon considered his 1673 campaign a masterpiece of maneuver strategy.[92] Montecuccoli's most important contribution, however, was in the realm of military thought. Although his ideas often were presented in didactic form, he was not primarily a teacher of strategy. He held that the art of command could only be acquired by practice, "under arms, in the field, sweating and freezing."[93] A devout and observant Catholic, Montecuccoli nonetheless was a rationalist trying to

[89] Barker, *Military Intellectual*, 153-54, 162-63; Pieri, "Raimondo Montecuccoli," 140-41.
[90] Montecuccoli, "Della guerra col Turco," 497-99.
[91] Pieri, "Raimondo Montecuccoli," 139-40.
[92] Kaufmann, "Raimondo Montecuccoli," 75-76.
[93] Montecuccoli, "Della guerra col Turco," 482.

discover by empirical inquiry constant principles, which, if correctly applied, would make war a scientific progress with predictable results. In his introduction to *Dell'arte militare*, he wrote that "I have attempted within this concise framework, to encompass the vast areas of the only science vital for the monarch, and I have done my utmost to discover basic rules on which every science is based ... and, having considered the entire range of world history, I dare to say that I have not found a single notable military exploit which would not fit in with these rules."[94] His investigation, moreover, was not limited to purely mechanistic aspects of the art of war, but included moral, psychological, social, and economic considerations.

Montecuccoli's approach then was both scientific and humanistic, with the additional advantage that he brought to his writings the experience and the concise style of a veteran soldier. If his attempt to define and delineate war as a scientific enterprise in the end was futile, and he himself chose to designate it as the "*art* of war," it nonetheless was a major intellectual undertaking. One German historian, highly critical of Montecuccoli as a commander, described him as "towering above all military thinkers of the second half of the seventeenth century," and another asserted that "what Bodin represented for the science of politics or Bacon for philosophy, Montecuccoli represented for the science of war."[95] Perhaps this is claiming too much. Still, Montecuccoli was both an impressive practitioner and an imaginative theorist of war. He integrated his own experience with the ideas of Machiavelli and Lipsius, as adapted by Maurice and further developed by Gustavus Adolphus, into a comprehensive intellectual structure. By synthesizing the many different parts of the military revolution and transmitting its major concepts to the next century, his writings form a significant link in the evolution of modern strategy.

[94] Raimondo Montecuccoli, "Dell'arte militare," in *Ausgewählte Schriften*, ed. Veltzé, 1:xlvi-xlvii.
[95] Jähns, *Geschichte*, 2:1162; Stadelmann, *Scharnhorst*, 95-96.

3. Vauban: The Impact of Science on War

HENRY GUERLAC

AN ALMOST uninterrupted state of war existed in Europe from the time of Machiavelli to the close of the War of the Spanish Succession. The French invasion of Italy which had so roused Machiavelli proved to be but a prelude to two centuries of bitter international rivalry, of Valois and Bourbon against Hapsburg. For a good part of this period epidemic civil wars cut across the dynastic struggle, never quite arresting it, and often fusing with it to produce conflicts of unbridled bitterness. Toward the end of the seventeenth century, when civil strife had abated and the chief states of Europe were at last consolidated, the old struggle was resumed as part of Louis XIV's bid for European supremacy, but with a difference: for now the newly risen merchant powers, Holland and England, which had aided France in bringing the Spanish dominion to an end, were arrayed against it. The Peace of Utrecht (1713) was an English peace. It set the stage for England's control of the seas, but by the same token it did not weaken France as much as its Continental rivals had fervently desired. It left France's most important conquests virtually intact; it scarcely altered the instrument of Westphalia that was its charter of security; and above all it left its army—the first great national army of Europe—weakened but still formidable, and its prestige as the leading military power of the Continent virtually undiminished.

The military progress of two hundred years was embodied in that army. And this progress had been considerable.[1] In the first place armies were larger. Impressed as we are by the first appearance of mass armies during the Wars of the French Revolution, we are prone to forget the steady increase in size of European armies that took place during the sixteenth and seventeenth centuries. When Richelieu, for example, built up France's military establishment to about 100,000 men in 1635, he had a force nearly double that of the later Valois kings; yet this force was only a quarter as large as that which Louvois raised for Louis XIV.

[1] In this and the following section I have relied heavily upon Edgard Boutaric, *Institutions militaires de la France avant les armées permanentes* (Paris, 1863); Camille Rousset, *Histoire de Louvois et de son administration politique et militaire*, 4 vols. (Paris, 1862-64); and General Susane, *Histoire de l'ancienne infanterie française* (Paris, 1849), *Histoire de la cavalerie française* (Paris, 1874), and *Histoire de l'artillerie française* (Paris, 1874). Louis André, *Michel Le Tellier et l'organization de l'armée monarchique* (Paris, 1906) proved the most valuable single work concerned with army reform in the seventeenth century.

This expansion of the military establishment was primarily due to the growing importance of the infantry arm, which was only twice as numerous as the cavalry in the army with which Charles VIII invaded Italy, but five times as great by the end of the seventeenth century. The customary explanation for this new importance of infantry is that it resulted from the improvement in firearms; and it is true that the invention of the musket, its evolution into the flintlock, and the invention of the bayonet, all led to a pronounced increase in infantry firepower, and hence to an extension of foot soldiery. But this is only part of the story. The steadily mounting importance of siege warfare also had its effects, for here—both as a besieging force and in the defense of permanent fortifications—infantry performed functions impossible to cavalry.

European armies in the seventeenth century were bands of professionals, many of them foreigners, recruited by voluntary enlistment. Except for infrequent recourse to the *arrière-ban*, a feudal relic more often ridiculed than employed, and except for the experiment of a revived militia late in the reign of Louis XIV, there was nothing in France resembling universal service. In still another respect this "national" army seems, at first glance, hardly to have been representative of the nation. Whereas the nobility competed for admission into the elite corps of the cavalry and provided officers for the infantry, and whereas the common infantryman was drawn from the lowest level of society—though not always or preponderantly from the moral dregs as is sometimes implied—the prosperous peasant freeholder and the members of the bourgeoisie escaped ordinary military service whether by enlistment, which they avoided, or through the revived militia, from which they were exempt.

Did one whole segment of society, then, fail to contribute to the armed strength of the country? By no means. The bourgeoisie made important contributions to French military strength, even though they did not serve in the infantry or the cavalry. Their notable contributions fell into two main categories. First, they were important in the technical services, that is to say in artillery and engineering and in the application of science to warfare; and second, they were prominent in the civilian administration of the army that developed so strikingly during the seventeenth century, and to which many other advances and reforms are attributable. These technical and organizational developments are perhaps the most important aspects of the progress that has been noted above. In both, the French army led the way.

I

The army that Louis XIV passed on to his successors bore little resemblance to that of the Valois kings. The improvement in organization, discipline, and equipment was due chiefly to the development of the

civilian administration at the hands of a succession of great planners—
Richelieu, Le Tellier, Louvois, and Vauban—whose careers span the seventeenth century.

Until the seventeenth century army affairs were almost exclusively administered by the military themselves, and there was very little central control. The various infantry companies, which had at first been virtually independent under their respective captains, had, it is true, been coordinated to some extent by uniting them into regiments, each commanded by a *mestre de camp*, subject to the orders of a powerful officer, the *colonel général de l'infanterie*. But the prestige and independence of this high office was such as to weaken, rather than to strengthen, the hold of the crown over the newly regimented infantry. The cavalry, in the sixteenth century, had likewise been only imperfectly subjected to the royal will. By virtue of their prestige and tradition, the cavalry companies resisted incorporation into regiments until the seventeenth century. The elite corps of the gendarmerie, representing the oldest cavalry units, were controlled only by their captains and by a superior officer of the crown, the constable, who was more often than not virtually independent of the royal will. The light cavalry, after the reign of Henry II, was placed under a *colonel général* like that of the infantry. Only the artillery provided something of an exception. Here bourgeois influence was strong, a tradition dating back to the days of the Bureau brothers, and the effective direction was in the hands of a *commissaire général d'artillerie*, usually a man of the middle class. But even here the titular head was the grand master of artillery who, since the beginning of the sixteenth century, was invariably a person of high station. Thus, the army manifested a striking lack of integration. Other than the person of the king, there was no central authority. And except in the artillery there were no important civilian officials.

Richelieu laid the foundations of the civil administration of the army by extending to it his well-known policy of relying upon middle-class agents as the best means of strengthening the power of the crown. He created a number of *intendants d'armée* who were usually provincial intendants selected for special duty in time of war, one to each field army. Responsible to the intendants were a number of *commissaires* who were to see to the payment of troops, the storage of equipment, and other similar matters. Finally it was under Richelieu that the important post of minister of war was to all intents and purposes created. Under two great ministers, Michel Le Tellier (1643-1668) and his son, the Marquis de Louvois (1668-1691), the prestige of this office and the complexity of the civilian administration associated with it increased mightily. Around the person of the minister there grew up a genuine departmentalized government office complete with archives. By 1680 five separate bureaus had been created, each headed by a *chef de bureau* provided with numerous assistants. It was to these bureaus that the intendents, the commissioners, and even commanding officers sent their reports and their requests. From them emanated the orders of the minister of war; for only persons of great importance dealt directly with the minister, who had thus become, in all that pertained to important military decisions, the king's confidential advisor.

Judged by modern, or even Napoleonic, standards, the French army of Louis XIV was by no means symmetrically organized. There were gross defects of all sorts, anomalies of organization and administration, vices of recruitment and officering. But this army was no longer an anarchic collection of separate units, knowing no real master but the captain or colonel who recruited them. If it possessed a clearly defined military hierarchy with clearly defined powers, and if the royal authority could no longer with impunity be evaded by underlings or challenged by rebellious commanders—this was made possible by the painstaking work of the civilian administration during the seventeenth century. The great, semi-independent offices of the crown were abolished or brought to heel. Reforms were effected within the hierarchy of general officers to make powers more clear-cut and to eliminate vagueness of function and incessant rivalry among the numerous marshals and lieutenant generals. The principle of seniority was introduced. Unity of command was possible by creating the temporary and exceptional rank of *maréchal général des armées*, held for the first time by Turenne in 1660. A host of minor reforms were also put through during this creative period, touching such diverse matters as the evil of plurality of office within the army, which was severely checked, venality of office, which proved ineradicable, the introduction of uniform dress and discipline, and improvements in the mode of recruiting, housing, and paying the troops.

Doubtless this sustained effort to systematize and order the structure of the army reflected what was taking place in other spheres. Throughout French political life traditional rights and confusions sanctified by long usage were being attacked in the interest of strengthening the central power. This cult of reason and order was not merely an authoritarian expedient, nor just an aesthetic ideal imposed by the prevailing classicism. Impatience with senseless disorder, wherever encountered, was one expression, and not the least significant expression, of the mathematical neorationalism of Descartes, of the *esprit géométrique* detected and recorded by Pascal. It was the form in which the scientific revolution, with its attendant mechanical philosophy, first manifested itself in France. And it resulted in the adoption of the machine—where each part fulfilled its prescribed function, with no waste motion and no supernumerary cogs—as the primordial analogy, the model not only of man's rational construction, but of God's universe. In this universe the cogs were Gassendi's atoms or Descartes' vortices, while the *primum mobile* was Fontenelle's divine watchmaker. We often speak as though the eighteenth or the nineteenth century discovered the worship of the machine, but this is a half-truth. It was the seventeenth century that discovered the machine, its intricate precision, its revelation—as for example in the calculating machines of Pascal and Leibnitz—of mathematical reason in action. The eighteenth century merely gave this notion a Newtonian twist, whereas the nineteenth century worshiped not the machine but power. So in the age of Richelieu and Louis XIV the reformers were guided by the spirit of the age, by the impact of scientific rationalism, in their efforts to modernize both the army and the civilian bureaucracy, and to give to the state and to the army some of the qualities of a well-designed machine. Science, however, was exerting other and more direct effects upon military affairs, and to these we must now turn.

II

Science and warfare have always been intimately connected. In antiquity this alliance became strikingly evident in the Hellenistic and Roman periods. Archimedes' contribution to the defense of Syracuse immediately springs to mind as the classic illustration. The cultural and economic rebirth of western Europe after the twelfth century shows that this association was not fortuitous, for the revival of the ancient art of war was closely linked with the recovery and development of ancient scientific and technical knowledge.[2] Few of the early European scientists were soldiers, but many of them in this and later centuries served as consulting technicians or even as technical auxiliaries of the army. A number of military surgeons have their place in the annals of medical or anatomical science; while still more numerous were the engineers, literally the masters of the engines, whose combined skill in military architecture, in ancient and modern artillery, and in the use of a wide variety of machines served equally to advance the art of war and to contribute to theoretical science. Leonardo da Vinci, the first great original mind encountered in the history of modern science, was neither the first nor the last of these versatile military engineers, although he is probably the greatest.

Throughout the sixteenth century and most of the seventeenth, be-

---

[2] In this section I have relied chiefly upon my own unpublished doctoral dissertation, "Science and War in the Old Régime" (Harvard University, 1941).

fore the technical corps of the army had really developed, a number of the greatest scientists of Italy, France, and England turned their attention to problems bearing upon the technical side of warfare. By the year 1600 it was generally realized that the service of outside specialists must be supplemented by some sort of technical training among the officers themselves. All the abortive projects for systematic military education, such as the early plans of Henry IV and of Richelieu, gave some place to elementary scientific training.[3] The great Galileo outlines in a little-known document a rather formidable program of mathematical and physical studies for the future officer. Although organized military education, to say nothing of technical education, had to await the eighteenth century, nearly every officer of any merit by the time of Vauban had some smattering of technical knowledge, or regretted that he had not. The developments of science that brought this about are best described by a brief survey of the changes in military architecture and in artillery.

The art or science of military architecture suffered a violent revolution in the century following the Italian wars of Machiavelli's time. The French artillery—using the first really effective siege cannon—had battered down with ridiculous ease the high-walled medieval fortifications of the Italian towns. The Italians' reply was the invention of a new model enceinte—the main enclosure of a fortress—which, improved by a host of later modifications, was that which prevailed in Europe until the early nineteenth century. It was characterized primarily by its outline or trace: that of a polygon, usually regular, with bastions projecting from each angle, in such a manner as to subject the attacker to an effective cross fire. As it was perfected by the later Italian engineers this enceinte consisted of three main divisions: a thick low rampart, with parapet; a broad ditch; and an outer rampart, the glacis, which sloped gently down to the level of the surrounding countryside.

Designing these fortresses became a learned art, involving a fair amount of mathematical and architectural knowledge. A number of scientists of the first rank were experts in this new field of applied science. The Italian mathematician Niccolò Tartaglia, and the great Dutch scientist, Simon Stevin, were as famous in their own day as engineers as they are in ours for their contributions to mathematics and mechanics. Even Galileo taught fortification at Padua.[4]

Francis I of France, aware of the skill of the Italian engineers, took a number of them into his service, using them in his pioneer efforts to fortify his northern and eastern frontiers against the threat of Charles V.

---

[3] F. Artz, *Les débuts de l'éducation technique en France, 1500-1700* (Paris, 1938).

[4] J. J. Fahie, "The Scientific Works of Galileo," in *Studies in the History and Method of Science*, ed. Charles Singer (Oxford, 1921; repr. New York, 1975), 2:217.

This first burst of building activity lasted throughout the reign of Henry II, only to be brought to a halt by the civil wars. When the work was resumed under Henry IV and Sully, the Dutch were beginning to contest the primacy of the Italians in this field, and French engineers like Errard de Bar-le-Duc were available to replace the foreigners.[5]

Errard is the titular founder of the French school of fortification, which may be said to date from the publication of his *Fortification ré-duicte en art* (1594). In the course of the seventeenth century there appeared a number of able engineers, some of them soldiers, others civilian scientists of considerable distinction. Among the men in the latter category can be mentioned Gerard Desargues, the great mathematician, Pierre Petit, a versatile scientist of the second rank, and Jean Richer, astronomer and physicist. In the development of the theory of fortification the great precursor of Vauban, one might almost say his master, was the Count de Pagan.

Blaise de Pagan (1604-1665) was a theorist, not a practical engineer. So far as is known he never actually directed any important construction. In engineering, as in science where he fancied himself more than the dilettante that he really was, his contributions were made from the armchair. He succeeded, however, in reforming in several important respects the type of fortresses built by the French in the later seventeenth century. Vauban's famous "first system" was in reality nothing but Pagan's style, executed with minor improvements and flexibly adapted to differences in terrain. Pagan's main ideas were embodied in his treatise *Les fortifications du comte de Pagan* (1645). They all sprang from a single primary consideration: the increased effectiveness of cannon, both for offense and in defense. To Pagan the bastions were the supremely important part of the outline, and their position and shape were determined by the help of simple geometrical rules that he formulated, with respect to the outside, rather than the inside, of the enceinte.

In the development of artillery there was the same interplay of scientific skill and military needs during the sixteenth and seventeenth centuries. Biringuccio's *De la pirotechnia* (1540), now recognized as one of the classics in the history of chemistry, was for long the authoritative handbook of military pyrotechnics, the preparation of gunpowder, and the metallurgy of cannon. The theory of exterior ballistics similarly was worked out by two of the founders of modern dynamics, Tartaglia and Galileo. Perhaps it would not be too much to assert that the foundations of modern physics were a by-product of solving the fundamental ballistical problem. Tartaglia was led to his criticisms of Aristotelian dy-

---

[5] Lt. Col. Antoine Augoyat, *Aperçu historique sur les fortifications*, I:13-21.

namics by experiments—perhaps the earliest dynamical experiments ever performed—on the relation between the angle of fire and the range of a projectile. His results, embodying the discovery that the angle of maximum range is forty-five degrees, brought about the widespread use of the artillerist's square or quadrant. But to Galileo is due the fundamental discovery that the trajectory of a projectile, for the ideal case that neglects such disturbing factors as air resistance, must be parabolic. This was made possible only by his three chief dynamical discoveries, the principle of inertia, the law of freely falling bodies, and the principle of the composition of velocities. Upon these discoveries, worked out as steps in his ballistic investigation, later hands erected the structure of classical physics.

By the end of the seventeenth century the progress of the "New Learning" had become compelling enough to bring about the first experiments in technical military education and the patronage of science by the governments of England and France. The Royal Society of London received its charter at the hands of Charles II in 1662, while four years later, with the encouragement of Colbert, the French *Académie Royale des sciences* was born. In both of these organizations, dedicated as they were at their foundation to "useful knowledge," many investigations were undertaken of immediate or potential value to the army and navy. Ballistic investigations, studies on impact phenomena and recoil, researches on improved gunpowder and the properties of saltpeter, the quest for a satisfactory means of determining longitude at sea: these, and many other subjects, preoccupied the members of both academies. In both countries able navy and army men are found among the diligent members. In France especially the scientists were frequently called upon for their advice in technical matters pertaining to the armed forces. Under Colbert's supervision scientists of the *Académie des sciences* carried out a detailed coast and geodetic survey as part of Colbert's great program of naval expansion, and what is perhaps more important, they laid the foundations for modern scientific cartography so that in the following century, with the completion of the famous Cassini map of France, an army was for the first time equipped with an accurate topographic map of the country it was charged to defend.

III

If we ask how these developments are reflected in the military literature of the sixteenth and seventeenth centuries, the answer is simple enough: the volume is, on the average, greater than the quality. Antiquity was still the great teacher in all that concerned the broader aspects of military theory and the secrets of military genius. Vegetius and Frontinus

71

were deemed indispensable; and the most popular book of the century, Henri de Rohan's *Parfait capitaine*, was an adaptation of Caesar's *Gallic Wars*. Without doubt the most important writing concerned with the art of war fell into two classes: the pioneer works in the field of international law; and the pioneer works of military technology.

Machiavelli had been the theorist for the age of unregulated warfare, but his influence was waning by the turn of the seventeenth century. Francis Bacon was perhaps his last illustrious disciple; for it is hard to find until our own day such unabashed advocacy of unrestricted war as can be found in certain of the *Essays*. But by Bacon's time the reaction had set in. Men like Grotius were leading the attack against international anarchy and against a war of unlimited destructiveness. These founding fathers of international law announced that they had found in the law of nature the precepts for a law of nations, and their central principle, as Talleyrand put it once in a strongly worded reminder to Napoleon, was that nations ought to do one another in peace, the most good, in war, the least possible evil.

It is easy to underestimate the influence of these generous theories upon the actual realities of warfare, and to cite Albert Sorel's black picture of international morals and conduct in the period of the Old Regime. Actually the axioms of international law exerted an undeniable influence on the mode and manner of warfare before the close of the seventeenth century.[6] If they did not put an end to political amoralism, they at least hedged in the conduct of war with a host of minor prescriptions and prohibitions that contributed to making eighteenth-century warfare a relatively humane and well-regulated enterprise. These rules were known to contending commanders and were quite generally followed. Such, for example, were the instructions concerning the treatment and exchange of prisoners; the condemnation of certain means of destruction, like the use of poison; the rules for the treatment of noncombatants and for arranging parleys, truces, and safe-conducts; or those concerned with despoiling or levying exactions upon conquered territory and with the mode of terminating sieges. The whole tendency was to protect private persons and private rights in time of war, and hence to mitigate the evils.

In the second class, that of books on military technology, no works had greater influence or enjoyed greater prestige than those of Sébastien Le Prestre de Vauban, the great military engineer of the reign of Louis XIV. His authority in the eighteenth century was immense, nor had it

---

[6] The notion has been stressed by Hoffman Nickerson, *The Armed Horde, 1793-1939* (New York, 1940), 34-40.

appreciably dimmed after the time of Napoleon.[7] And yet Vauban's literary legacy to the eighteenth century was scanty and highly specialized, consisting almost solely of a treatise on siegecraft, a work on the defense of fortresses, and a short work on mines.[8] He published nothing on military architecture, and made no systematic contribution to strategy or the art of war in general; yet his influence in all these departments is undeniable. It was exerted subtly and indirectly through the memory of his career and of his example, and by the exertions and writings of a number of his disciples. But by this process many of his contributions and ideas were misunderstood and perverted, and much that he accomplished was for a long time lost to view. Thanks to the work of scholars of the nineteenth and twentieth centuries, who have been able to publish an appreciable portion of Vauban's letters and manuscripts, and to peruse and analyze the rest, we have a clearer understanding of Vauban's career and of his ideas than was possible to his eighteenth-century admirers. He has increased in stature, rather than diminished, in the light of modern studies. We have seen the Vauban legend clarified and documented; we have seen it emended in many important points; but we have not seen it exploded.

The Vauban legend requires some explanation. Why was a simple engineer, however skillful and devoted to his task, raised so swiftly to the rank of a national idol? Why were his specialized publications on siegecraft and the defense of fortresses sufficient to rank him as one of the most influential military writers?

The answers are not far to seek: these works of Vauban were the authoritative texts in what was to the eighteenth century a most important, if not the supremely important, aspect of warfare. In the late seventeenth century and throughout the eighteenth century, warfare often appears to us as nothing but an interminable succession of sieges. Almost always they were the focal operations of a campaign: when the reduction of an enemy fortress was not the principal objective, as it often was, a

---

[7] An eighteenth-century writer on the education of the nobility suggests that the five most important authors a student should study are Rohan, Santa Cruz, Feuquières, Montecuccoli, and Vauban. Cf. Chevalier de Brucourt, *Essai sur l'éducation de la noblesse, nouvelle édition corrigée et augmentée* (Paris, 1748), 2:262-63.

[8] The works published in his lifetime were two: a work on administrative problems, called the *Directeur général des fortifications* (The Hague, 1685, reprinted in Paris, 1725), and his *Dixme Royale* (The Hague [?], 1707). A number of spurious works, however, had appeared before his death, purporting to expound his methods of fortification. His three treatises best known to the eighteenth century were printed for the first time in a slovenly combined edition titled *Traité de l'attaque et de la défense des places suivi d'un traité des mines* (The Hague, 1737). This was reprinted in 1742 and again in 1771. The *Traité de la défense des places* was published separately by Jombert in Paris in 1769. No carefully prepared editions were published until 1795.

siege was the inevitable preliminary to an invasion of enemy territory. Sieges were far more frequent than pitched battles and were begun as readily as battles were avoided. When they did occur, battles were likely to be dictated by the need to bring about, or to ward off, the relief of a besieged fortress. The strategic imagination of all but a few exceptional commanders was walled in by the accepted axioms of a war of siege. In an age that accepted unconditionally this doctrine of the strategic primacy of the siege, Vauban's treatises were deemed indispensable and his name was necessarily a name to conjure with.

Yet only a part of the aura and prestige that surrounded Vauban's name arose from these technical writings. He has appealed to the imagination because of his personal character, his long career as an enlightened servant of the state, his manifold contributions to military progress outside of his chosen speciality, and his liberal and humanitarian interest in the public weal. From the beginning it was Vauban the public servant who aroused the greatest admiration. With his modest origin, his diligence and honesty, his personal courage, and his loyalty to the state, he seemed the reincarnation of some servitor of the Roman Republic. Indeed, Fontenelle, in his famous *éloge*, describes him as a "Roman, whom the century of Louis XIV seems almost to have stolen from the happiest days of the Republic." To Voltaire he was "the finest of citizens." Saint-Simon, not content with dubbing him a Roman, applied to him, for the first time with its modern meaning, the word *patriote*.[9] In Vauban, respected public servant, organizational genius, enlightened reformer, seemed to be embodied all the traits which had combined, through the efforts of countless lesser persons, to forge the new national state.

Still more felicitously did Vauban's technical knowledge, his skill in applied mathematics, his love of precision and order, and his membership in the *Académie des sciences*, symbolize the new importance of scientific knowledge for the welfare of the state. Cartesian reason, the role of applied science in society both for war and peace, the *esprit géométrique* of the age: all these were incarnated in the man, visible in the massive outline of the fortresses he designed.

V

Vauban's career was both too long and too active for anything but a summary account in an essay of this sort. Scarcely any other of Louis XIV's ministers or warriors had as long an active career. He entered the royal service under Mazarin when he was in his early twenties and was

---

[9] Sébastien Le Prestre de Vauban, *Lettres intimes inédites adressées au Marquis de Puyzieulx (1699-1705). Introduction et notes de Hyrvoix de Landosle* (Paris, 1924), 16-17.

still active in the field only a few months before his death at the age of seventy-three. During this half century of ceaseless effort he conducted nearly fifty sieges and drew the plans for well over a hundred fortresses and harbor installations.

He came from the indeterminate fringe between the bourgeoisie and the lower nobility, being the descendant of a prosperous notary of Bazoches in the Morvan who in the mid-sixteenth century had acquired a small neighborhood fief. He was born at Saint-Léger in 1633, received his imperfect education—a smattering of history, mathematics, and drawing—in nearby Semur-en-Auxois; and in 1651, at the age of seventeen enlisted as a cadet with the troops of Condé, then in rebellion against the king. Sharing in Condé's pardon, he entered the royal service in 1653 where he served with distinction under the Chevalier de Clerville, a man of mediocre talents who was regarded as the leading military engineer of France. Two years later he earned the brevet of *ingénieur ordinaire du roi*; and soon after acquired as a sinecure the captaincy of an infantry company in the regiment of the Maréchal de La Ferté.

During the interval between the cessation of hostilities with Spain in 1659 and Louis XIV's first war of conquest in 1667, Vauban was hard at work repairing and improving the fortifications of the kingdom under the direction of Clerville.

In 1667 Louis XIV attacked the Low Countries. In this brief War of Devolution Vauban so distinguished himself as a master of siegecraft and the other branches of his trade that Louvois noticed his distinct superiority to Clerville and made him the virtual director, as *commissaire général*, of all the engineering work in his department. The acquisitions of the War of Devolution launched Vauban on his great building program. Important towns in Hainaut and Flanders were acquired, the outposts of the great expansion: Bergues, Furnes, Tournai, and Lille. These and many other important positions were fortified according to the so-called first system of Vauban, which will be discussed below.

This, then, was to be the ceaseless rhythm of Vauban's life in the service of Louis XIV: constant supervision, repairs, and new construction in time of peace; in time of war, renewed sieges and further acquisitions; then more feverish construction during the ensuing interval of peace. In the performance of these duties Vauban was constantly on the move until the year of his death, traveling from one end of France to the other on horseback or, later in life, in a famous sedan chair borne by horses. There seem to have been few intervals of leisure. He devoted little time to his wife and to the country estate he acquired in 1675, and he sedulously avoided the court, making his stays at Paris and Versailles as short as possible. The greatest number of his days and nights were spent in the inns of frontier villages and in the execution of his innumerable tasks, far from the centers of culture and excitement. Such free moments as he was able to snatch in the course of his engineering work he devoted to his official correspondence and to other writing. He kept in constant touch with Louvois, whom he peppered with letters and reports written in a pungent and undoctored prose. As though this were not enough Vauban interested himself in a host of diverse civil and military problems only indirectly related to his own specialty. Some of these subjects he discussed in his correspondence, while he dealt with others in long memoirs which make up the twelve manuscript volumes of his *Oisivetés*.

These memoirs treat the most diverse subjects. Some are technical, others are not. But in nearly all of them he answers to Voltaire's description of him as "un homme toujours occupé de sujets les uns utiles, les autres peu practicables et tous singuliers."[10] Besides discussing military and naval problems, or reporting on inland waterways and the interocean Canal of Languedoc, he writes on the need for a program of reforestation, the possible methods of improving the state of the French colonies in America, the evil consequences of the revocation of the Edict of Nantes, and—in a manner that foreshadowed Napoleon's creation of the Legion of Honor—the advantages of instituting an aristocracy of merit open to all classes, in place of the senseless and archaic nobility of birth and privilege.

The *Oisivetés* reveal their origin and belie their name. They were written at odd times, in strange places and at various dates. They are often little more than notes and observations collected in the course of his travels over the length and breadth of France; at other times they are extended treatises. What gives the writings a certain unity is the humanitarian interest that pervades them all and the scientific spirit which they reveal. The writings and the career of Vauban illustrate the thesis suggested earlier in this paper that in the seventeenth century scientific rationalism was the wellspring of reform. Vauban's proposals were based on first-hand experience and observation. His incessant traveling in the performance of his professional duties gave him an unparalleled opportunity to know his own country and its needs. His wide curiosity and his alert mind led him to amass facts, with the pertinacity known only to collectors, about the economic and social conditions of the areas where he worked; and his scientific turn of mind led him to throw his observations, where possible, into quantitative form.

These considerations help us to answer the question whether Vauban deserves, in any fundamental sense, the label of scientist, or whether he

---

[10] Voltaire, *Le siècle de Louis XIV*, ch. 21.

was merely a soldier and builder with a smattering of mathematics and mechanical knowledge. Was membership in the *Académie des sciences* accorded him in 1699 solely to honor a public servant and was Fontenelle thus obliged to devote to him one of his immortal *éloges* of men of science?

Vauban's achievements are in applied science and simple applied mathematics. He was not a distinguished mathematician and physicist like the later French military engineer, Lazare Carnot. He made no great theoretical contributions to mechanical engineering, as did Carnot's contemporary, Coulomb. He invented no steam chariot like Cugnot. Aside from the design of fortresses, scarcely a matter of pure science, his only contribution to engineering was an empirical study of the proper proportions of retaining walls.[11] Vauban's chief claim to scientific originality is that he sought to extend the quantitative method into fields where, except for his English contemporaries, no one had yet seriously ventured. He is, in fact, one of the founders of systematic meteorology, an honor that he shares with Robert Hooke, and one of the pioneers in the field of statistics, where the only other contenders were John Graunt and Sir William Petty.[12] His statistical habit is evident in many of his military and engineering reports. Many of these are filled with apparently irrelevant detail about the wealth, population, and resources of various regions of France.

From his harried underlings he exacted the same sort of painstaking survey. In a letter to Hue de Caligny, who was for a time director of fortifications for the northwest frontier from Dunkirk to Ypres, he expressed annoyance at the incomplete information he received in reports about that region. He urged Caligny to supply a map, to describe in detail the waterways, the wood supply with the date of cutting, and to provide him with detailed statistical information on population, broken down according to age, sex, profession, and rank. In addition Caligny was to give all the facts he could mass about the economic life of the region.[13] It was by information of this sort, painstakingly acquired as a byproduct of his work as an army engineer, that Vauban sought to extend into civilian affairs the same spirit of critical appraisal, the same love of logic, order, and efficiency, that he brought to bear on military problems.

[11] Abraham Wolf, *History of Science, Technology and Philosophy in the Eighteenth Century* (New York, 1939), 531-32; Bernard Forest de Bélidor, *La science des ingénieurs* (1739), bk. 1, 67-79.

[12] His right to pioneer status in meteorology rests upon a memoir on rainfall that he submitted to the *Académie des sciences*. Cf. Bélidor, *La science des ingénieurs*, bk. 4, 87-88.

[13] Georges Michel, *Histoire de Vauban* (Paris, 1879), 447-51.

VI

Vauban was one of the most persistent of the military reformers of the century. His letters and his *Oisivetés* are filled with his proposals. There were few aspects of military life or of the burning problems of military organization and military technology where Vauban did not intervene with fertile suggestions or projects for overall reorganization.[14]

The incorporation of his engineers into a regularly constituted arm of the service, possessed of its own officers and troops and its distinctive uniform, was something for which he struggled, though with little success, throughout his career.[15] His recommendations, however, bore fruit in the following century, as did also his efforts in the matter of scientific education for the technical corps. He enthusiastically praised the earliest artillery schools which were created toward the end of the reign of Louis XIV; and though he never succeeded in creating similar schools for the engineers, he established a system of regular examinations to test the preparation of candidates for the royal brevet, and took some steps to see that they were adequately prepared by special instructors.

Improvement of the artillery arm was a matter in which, as an expert on siegecraft, he was deeply interested. His studies and innovations in this field were numerous. He experimented with sledges for use in transporting heavy cannon. He found fault with the bronze cannon then in use, and tried to persuade the army to emulate the navy in the use of iron. He made numerous, but unsatisfactory, experiments on a new stone-throwing mortar. And finally he invented ricochet fire, first used at the siege of Philipsbourg, where the propelling charge was greatly reduced so that the ball would rebound this way and that after striking the target area, a peril to any man or machine in the near vicinity.

Vauban found space in his correspondence and in the *Oisivetés* to suggest numerous fundamental reforms for the infantry and for the army as a whole. He was one of the most tireless advocates of the flintlock musket for the infantry and was the inventor of the first satisfactory bayonet. As early as 1669 he wrote to Louvois strongly urging the general use of flintlocks and the abolition of the pike; and shortly thereafter he specifically proposed to substitute for the pike the familiar bayonet with a sleeve or socket that held the blade at the side of the barrel, permitting the piece to be fired with bayonet fixed.

He was preoccupied with the condition and welfare of the men as well as with their equipment. He sought to improve still further the mode

---

[14] Pierre Elizier Lazard, *Vauban, 1633-1707* (Paris, 1934), 445-500.

[15] H. Chotard, "Louis XIV, Louvois, Vauban et les fortifications du nord de la France, d'après les lettres inédites de Louvois adressées à M. de Chazerat, Gentilhomme d'Auvergne," *Annales du Comité Flamand de France* 18 (1889-90), 16-20.

of recruiting and paying the troops. To him is due in part the limitation of the practice of quartering soldiers on the civilian population which, after the peace of Aix-la-Chapelle, was supplemented by the creation of *casernes*.[16] These special barracks, many of them designed and built by Vauban, were chiefly used in frontier regions and recently conquered territory.

Vauban made no systematic study of naval construction, and what he knew seems to have been learned from Clerville who was skilled in this sort of work.[17] His first effort was at Toulon, where he improved the harbor installations, but his masterpiece was the port of Dunkirk. He devoted an interesting study to the naval role of galleys, in which he envisaged extending their use from the Mediterranean to the Atlantic coast, where they could serve as patrol vessels, as a mobile screen for heavier ships close to shore, or for swift harassing descents upon the Orkneys, or even upon the English coast. Closely related to these studies was his advocacy of the *guerre de course*, which he deemed the only feasible strategy after the collapse of the French naval power painstakingly built up by Colbert.

VII

Vauban's most significant contributions to the art of war were made, as was to be expected, within his own specialties: siegecraft and the science of fortification. It was characteristic of Vauban's dislike of unnecessary bloodshed, as much as of the new spirit of moderation in warfare that was beginning to prevail in his day, that his innovations in siegecraft were designed to regularize the taking of fortresses and above all to cut down the losses of the besieging force. Before his perfection of the system of parallels, which he probably did not invent, attacks on well-defended permanent fortifications took place only at a considerable cost to the attackers.[18] Trenches and gabions were employed without system, and as often as not the infantry was thrown against a presumed weak point in a manner that left them exposed to murderous fire.

Vauban's system of attack, which was followed with but little variation during the eighteenth century, was a highly formalized and leisurely procedure. The assailants gathered their men and stores at a point beyond the range of the defending fire and adequately concealed by natural or artificial cover. At this point the sappers would begin digging a trench

[16] Bélidor, *La science de ingénieurs*, bk. 4, 73.

[17] Lazard, *Vauban*, 501-24; La Roncière, *Histoire de la marine française* (1932), 6:164-69.

[18] For a description of early methods, cf. Gaston Zeller, *L'organisation défensive des frontières du nord et de l'est au XVIIᵉ siècle* (1928), 54-55.

that moved slowly toward the fortress. After this had progressed some distance, a deep trench paralleling the point of future attack was flung out at right angles to the trench of approach. This so-called first parallel was filled with men and equipment to constitute a *place d'armes*. From it, the trench of approach was moved forward again, zigzagging as it approached the fortress. After it had progressed the desired distance, the second parallel was constructed, and the trench was moved forward once more, until a third and usually final parallel was constructed only a short distance from the foot of the glacis. The trench was pushed ahead still further, the sappers timing their progress so as to reach the foot of the glacis just as the third parallel was occupied by the troops. The perilous task of advancing up the glacis, exposed to the enemy's raking fire from their covered way, was accomplished with the aid of temporary structures called *cavaliers de tranchées*, which were high earthworks, provided with a parapet, from which the besiegers could fire upon the defenders of the covered way. This outer line of defense could be cleared *par industrie*, that is, by subjecting the defenders to the effects of a ricochet bombardment, or by sending up grenadiers to take the position by assault under cover of a protecting fire from the *cavaliers*. Once the enemy's covered way was seized, siege batteries were erected and an effort was made to breach the main defenses.

The essential feature of Vauban's system of siegecraft, then, was the use he made of temporary fortifications, trenches, and earthworks in protecting the advancing troops. His parallels were first tried out at the siege of Maestricht in 1673, and the *cavaliers de tranchées* at the siege of Luxembourg in 1684. The perfected system is described at length in his *Traité des sièges*, written for the Duc de Bourgogne in 1705.

Vauban's work in military architecture has been the subject of considerable dispute, first as to whether the style of his fortresses showed great originality, second as to whether in placing them he was guided by any master plan for the defense of France.

Until very recently even Vauban's most fervent admirers have agreed that he showed little originality as a military architect and added almost nothing to the design of fortresses he inherited from Pagan. Lazare Carnot admired Vauban in the manner characteristic of other eighteenth-century engineers, yet he could find few signs of originality. "The fortification of Vauban reveals to the eye only a succession of works known before his time, whereas to the mind of the good observer it offers sublime results, brilliant combinations, and masterpieces of industry."[19] Allent echoes

[19] Didot-Hoefer, *Nouvelle Biographie Générale* (Paris, 1870), s.v. "Vauban, Sébastien Le Prestre."

him: "A better cross section, a simpler outline, outworks that are bigger and better placed: these are the only modifications that he brought to the system then in use."[20] This judgment remained in vogue until very recent times. The most recent serious study, that of Lieutenant Colonel Lazard, has modified in Vauban's favor this somewhat unfavorable opinion.[21]

Lazard has made important changes in our interpretation of Vauban's methods of fortification. Whereas earlier writers have had the habit of referring to Vauban's three systems, Lazard points out that, strictly speaking, Vauban did not have sharply defined systems; rather, he had periods in which he favored distinctly different designs, all modifications of the bastioned trace discussed above. With this restriction in mind, it is convenient to retain the old classification.

Vauban's first system, according to which he built the great majority of his fortified places, consisted in using Pagan's trace almost without modification. The outlines of these forts were, whenever possible, regular polygons: octagonal, quadrangular, even roughly triangular, as at La Kenoque. The bastions were still the key to the defensive system, though they tended to be smaller than those of Vauban's predecessors. Except for improvements of detail and the greater use of detached exterior defenses (such as the *tenailles* and the *demi-lune*, and other items in Uncle Toby's lexicon), little had altered since the days of Pagan. Since, therefore, most of Vauban's structures were built according to this conservative design, and since this was taken as characteristic of Vauban's work, it is not to be wondered at that later critics could find there little or no originality. The originality, according to Lazard, is evident rather in those other two styles that had little influence on Vauban's successors and that were exemplified in only a few samples of his work.

The second system, used for the first time at Belfort and Besançon, was an outgrowth of that previously used. The polygonal structure was retained, but the curtains (the region between the bastions) were lengthened, and the bastions themselves were replaced by a small work or tower at the angles, these being covered by so-called detached bastions constructed in the ditch.

The so-called third system is only a modification of the second. It was used for only a single work, the great masterpiece of Vauban at Neuf-Brisach. In this scheme the curtain is modified in shape to permit an increased use of cannon in defense, and the towers, the detached bastions, and demi-lunes are all increased in size.

[20] Ibid., but cf. A. Allent, *Histoire du Corps Impériale du Génie* (1805), 1:209-10 (only one volume published).
[21] Lazard, *Vauban*, 377-94.

It is the second system that deserves our attention. Here, although his contemporaries could not see it, Vauban had made an important, even revolutionary improvement: he had freed himself from reliance on the main enceinte and taken the first steps toward a defense in depth. He had gained a new flexibility in adapting his design to the terrain without imperiling the main line of defense. In all previous cases adaptation had been through projecting crown works or horn works that were merely spectacular appendages to the primary enceinte; and when these were taken the main line was directly affected. The second system was rejected by Cormontaigne and later by the staff of the Ecole de Mézières, whose ideas dominated the eighteenth century, and whose schemes of fortification were based squarely upon Vauban's first system. To them this second system seemed only a crude return to medieval methods. Only late in the eighteenth century do we find a revival of Vauban's second system: the revolt of Montalembert, which the Germans accepted long before the French, consisted chiefly in substituting small detached forts in place of the conventional projecting outworks, in reality part of the main enceinte.[22] Montalembert's great revolution, like the later advocacy of fortification in depth, was implicit in Vauban's second system, though whether Montalembert was inspired by it may well be doubted.

The confusion about his ideas that has existed until recently results from the fact that Vauban never wrote a treatise on the art of permanent fortification, never expounded it systematically as he did his theories of the art of attack and of defense. All the books that appeared in his own lifetime and thereafter, purporting to summarize his secrets, were the baldest counterfeits. Only the great work of Bélidor, which treated not of basic design or the problems of military disposition, but only of constructional problems and administrative detail, was directly inspired by Vauban.[23] There are, however, two treatises remaining in manuscript that deal with basic principles of fortification and that were directly inspired by him. One of these was written by Sauveur, the mathematician whom Vauban chose to instruct and to examine the engineer candidates; the other by his secretary, Thomassin. These are the best sources, aside from the works themselves, for learning Vauban's general principles of fortification. It is possible to speak only of general principles, not of a dogmatic system, and these principles are exemplified equally well by all three of the Vauban styles. They are few enough and quite general. First of all, every part of the fort must be as secure as every other, with security provided both through sturdy construction of the exposed points (bas-

[22] Lazard, *Vauban*, 389-90; A. de Zastrow, *Histoire de la fortification permanente* (3d ed., 1856), 2:62-208 (trans. from the German by Ed. de La Barre Du Parcq).
[23] Bélidor, *La science des ingénieurs*, bk. 3, 29-34, 35-43, 90-96.

tions) and by adequate coverage of the curtains. In general these conditions will be provided for if (1) there is no part of the enceinte not flanked by strong points, (2) these strong points are as large as possible, and (3) they are separated by musket range or a little less. These strong points should be so designed that the parts which flank should always confront as directly as possible the parts they are protecting; conversely, the flanking parts should be visible only from the protected parts. A little thought will show that these basic principles are applicable to all of Vauban's schemes. The actual problem of building a permanent fortification consisted in so adapting the bastioned trace (or the polygonal trace with detached bastions) to the exigencies of a particular terrain that none of the basic principles was violated. Clearly this left the engineer a wide range of freedom and an admirable flexibility. It was by this method of work that the second style was developed, for Vauban himself tells us that it was not arrived at as a result of theoretical considerations but was forced on him by the terrain conditions at Belfort.[24]

VIII

To what extent was the military building program of Louis XIV guided by some unifying strategic conception; and what is the evidence that his conception, if in truth there was such a thing, was due to the genius of Vauban? These are two of the most important questions, but they are not the easiest to answer.

The earlier biographers of Vauban, with characteristic impetuosity on behalf of their hero, leave us sometimes with the distinct impression that before Vauban France had no system of fortification worthy of the name, and that the ring of fortresses girding the kingdom by the end of his career represented the execution of some cleverly conceived master plan sprung from the mind of the great engineer. To these writers it was just as incredible that anyone besides Vauban could have had a hand in organizing this defensive system as it was that this system itself might have been the result of a slow historical growth.

Of late we have drifted perhaps too far in the other direction. Although, as we have seen, Vauban's technical reputation as a military architect has been enhanced by recent studies, there has been a simultaneous tendency on the part of certain writers to reduce him to the level of a great craftsman devoid of strategic imagination. He has been represented as a brilliant technician, executing blindly the tasks dictated by historical necessity or by the orders of superiors who alone did all the strategic thinking.

[24] Letter to Louvois, October 7, 1687, cited by Zeller, *L'organisation défensive*, 144.

Who was there who was capable of challenging Vauban's authority in the field of his speciality? The answer is, the king himself. Louis XIV, it has been shown, was more than decently proficient in the art of fortification. He had studied it in his youth, and, during the early part of the reign, he had profited by the advice and instruction of Turenne, Villeroi, and Condé. Throughout his career he showed a constant interest in the most humble details connected with the art of fortification and on a number of occasions he resolutely opposed insistent recommendations of Vauban. Two important forts, Fort Louis and Mont-Royal, were created on the initiative of the king, and one at least of these was against the express advice of Vauban.[25] To one author, Louis the Diligent was in everything, even in these technical matters, the unquestioned master. Louvois was only an "excellent servant, not to say clerk," while Vauban in his turn "was never anything but the executor of his orders, albeit . . . an excellent one."[26] Another writer describes Vauban as "the chief workman of a great undertaking, the direction of which was never fully entrusted to him."[27] This interpretation is in fact inescapable. Vauban drew or corrected all plans for fortresses that had been decided upon; he submitted technical memoirs and recommendations; he gave his opinion on crucial matters when asked and sometimes when he was not asked. But his presence was not deemed necessary when the decisions were being debated. He was not a policy maker; his was only a consultative voice.

This should not lead us to underestimate his influence upon the royal decisions. Yet even if Vauban had had a master plan for the defense of France, it could only have been imperfectly executed. Many recommendations dear to Vauban's heart were rejected; many of his schemes were shattered by the realities of war and diplomacy. The Peace of Ryswick in 1697, for example, marked Louis XIV's first withdrawal from the high watermark of conquest. To Vauban, who was not directly consulted about its terms, this treaty, though not as bad as he feared, was a great deception. Much work had to be done over to make up for the loss of Luxembourg—which he considered one of the strongest places in Europe—and of Brisach, Fribourg, and Nancy.[28]

Did Vauban in reality have a master plan? On this question there is almost complete disagreement. The writers of the last century took it for granted that Vauban had a strategic pattern for his fortresses, though they were not altogether certain in what it consisted. One writer described

[25] Chotard, "Louis XIV, Louvois, Vauban," 30-35; Zeller, *L'organisation défensive*, 96-117; Lazard, *Vauban*, 49-50, 202-204.

[26] Chotard, "Louis XIV, Louvois, Vauban," 36.

[27] Zeller, *L'organisation défensive*, 118.

[28] Ibid., 103-104; Th. Lavallée, *Les frontières de France* (Paris, 1864), 83-85.

it as "an assemblage of works sufficiently close to one another so that the intervals between them are not unprotected. Each of these works is strong enough and well provisioned enough to impose upon the enemy the obligation of a siege, yet small enough to demand only a small number of defenders."[29] With this interpretation Gaston Zeller is in categorical disagreement. He points out that Louis XIV and Vauban did not start work with a clean canvas, that neither of these men could have imposed a doctrinaire plan of defense without reference to the work that had gone before; and he indicates that many of the characteristics of the defense system were due to Francis I, Sully, Richelieu, and Mazarin, to their building programs and their treaties. Just as the actual frontier of the France of Louis XIV was the culmination of a long-sustained national policy, just so the disposition of the fortress towns was "the resultant of a long succession of efforts to adapt the defensive organization of the kingdom to the changing outline of the frontier."[30] In support of Zeller's contention that the fortress system was the work of historical evolution, not the work of a single man, is the evidence from the career of Vauban himself. The greatest number of strongholds that we associate with him were not *places neuves* but older fortresses, some dating back to Errard or his Italian predecessors, that Vauban modernized and strengthened. The fortresses did not in any sense constitute a system as Vauban found them; they were important only as separate units. There was no liaison between them and they were almost always too far apart. Each situation, moreover, had been chosen for its local importance: to guard a bridge, a crossroads, or the confluence of two rivers. Their total value depended not on their relative positions but rather upon their number.[31] Zeller and Lazard both agreed that Vauban's general scheme resulted from a process of selection from among these fortresses. He made order out of prevailing chaos by choosing certain forts whose positions made them worth retaining and strengthening, and by suggesting that others be razed. His strategic vision could not work with complete freedom; he was limited—largely for reasons of public economy—to working with what France already possessed. It is easy to discover the principles that guided his process of selection and thus to find the key to his strategic thinking. To Zeller there is nothing outstanding about these principles; the "order" that Vauban effected fell far short of a great strategic conception. But Lazard is much more flattering. He takes the view that Vauban was the first man in history to have an overall notion of the strategic role of fortresses. He was not only an engineer but a *stratège*, and one with ideas

[29] Hennebert, cited by Chotard, "Louis XIV, Louvois, Vauban," 42.
[30] Zeller, *L'organisation défensive*, 2.
[31] Ibid., 123.

far in advance of his own day.[32] Only Vauban's own writings can allow the reader to decide between these two interpretations.

It should be remembered that as a result of the War of Devolution against Spain, his first war of conquest, Louis XIV extended his holdings along the northwest frontier deep into Spanish-held Flanders. The new positions—from Furnes near the coast eastward through Bergues and Courtrai to Charleroi—gave France a number of strong points scattered among the Spanish garrisons. Vauban's first great task was to strengthen and refortify these new acquisitions, and this occupied most of his time during the peaceful years from 1668 to 1672. In the spring of 1672, however, Louis launched his war against the Dutch. Vauban took the opportunity to raise for the first time the question of the general organization of the frontier. In a letter to Louvois, dated January 20, 1673, he wrote: "Seriously, my lord, the king should think seriously about rounding out his domain [*songer à faire son pré carré*]. This confusion of friendly and enemy fortresses mixed up pell-mell with one another does not please me at all. You are obliged to maintain three in the place of one."[33]

In 1675, a year that saw him busy consolidating French conquests in Franche Comté and elsewhere, Vauban made more specific suggestions. In September of that year he proposed the sieges of Condé, Bouchain, Valenciennes, and Cambrai. The capture and retention of these places would, he said, assure Louis's conquests and produce the *pré carré* that was so desirable. These towns were accordingly taken: Condé and Bouchain in 1676, Valenciennes and Cambrai in 1677. The Peace of Nimwegen, signed in August of the following year, gave France a frontier approximating the *pré carré*. France gave up some Flemish holdings but acquired instead Saint-Omer, Cassel, Aire, Ypres, and a half-dozen other important strongholds. To the eastward were gained Nancy in Lorraine and Fribourg across the Rhine. But Vauban was not satisfied with the western end of the frontier; he felt that the recent peace had disrupted it and left it open toward the Lowlands. In November 1678, three months after Nimwegen, he wrote the first of a series of important general statements on the organization of the northern frontier from the Channel to the Meuse.[34]

Vauban opens by discussing the purposes of a fortified frontier: it should close to the enemy all the points of entry into the kingdom and

[32] Lazard, *Vauban*, 408-21.

[33] Ibid., 155; Albert de Rochas d'Aiglun, *Vauban, sa famille et ses écrits, ses oisivetés, et sa correspondance*, 2 vols. (Paris, 1910), 2:89.

[34] Lazard, *Vauban*, 409-14; Zeller, *L'organisation défensive*, 96-98. This important memoir is printed *in extenso* in Rochas *Vauban, sa famille et ses écrits*, 1:189f.

at the same time facilitate an attack upon enemy territory. Vauban never thought that fortresses were important solely for defense; he was careful to stress their importance as bases for offensive operations against the enemy. The fortified places should be situated so as to command the means of communication within one's own territory and to provide access to enemy soil by controlling important roads or bridgeheads. They should be large enough to hold not only the supplies necessary for their defense, but the stores required to support and sustain an offensive based upon them. These ideas, enunciated tersely in this memoir, were later elaborated and systematized by one of Vauban's eighteenth-century disciples, the engineer and adventurer Maigret, whom Voltaire mentions in his *Charles XII* and whose *Treatise on Preserving the Security of States by Means of Fortresses* became the standard work dealing with the strategic significance of fortifications. This book, all too little known, was used by the famous French school of military engineering, the Ecole de Mézières. In this work Maigret writes that "the best kind of fortresses are those that forbid access to one's country while at the same time giving an opportunity to attack the enemy in his own territory."[35] He lists the characteristics that give value and importance to fortresses: control of key routes into the kingdom, such as a mountain gorge or pass; control of the bridgeheads on great rivers, a condition eminently fulfilled by Strasbourg, for example; control of important communication lines within the state, as for example, Luxembourg, which secured the emperor's communications with the Lowlands.

There were still other factors that might make a fort important. It might be a base of supplies for offensive action, or a refuge for the people of the surrounding countryside; perhaps it could dominate trade and commerce, exacting tolls from the foreigner; or perhaps it might be a fortified seaport with a good and safe harbor; a great frontier city with wealth, more than able to contribute the cost of fortification and sustaining the garrison; or a city capable of serving the king as a place to store his treasure against internal and external enemies.[36] The value of a fortress depends in large part, of course, upon the nature of its local situation. Art or science may make up for certain defects in the terrain but they can do little with respect to the matter of communication. Thus certain fortresses are advantageously situated because the defenders have the communications leading to them well under their control, whereas

[35] *Traité de la sureté et conservation des états, par le moyen les forteresses. Par M. Maigret, Ingénieur en Chef, Chevalier de l'ordre Royal et Militaire de Saint Louis* (Paris, 1725), 149.
[36] Ibid., 129-48.

the enemy, in consequence, will have difficulty in bringing up the supplies necessary for a sustained siege.[37]

These criteria make it possible to select certain fortresses in preference to others but there still remains the question of their relation one to the other, of liaison. Vauban, in the memoir of 1678, concluded that the frontier would be adequately fortified if the strongholds were limited to two lines, each composed of about thirteen places, stretched across the northern frontier in imitation of infantry battle order.[38] This first line could be further strengthened and unified by the use of a waterline stretching from the sea to the Scheldt. Canals or canalized streams or rivers would link one fort with another, and the canals themselves would be protected at regular intervals by redoubts. This scheme was not original with Vauban; in fact it was in operation over part of the frontier even as he wrote. He was under no illusions as to the strength of the waterlines, for he saw that their chief purpose was to ward off the harassing raids by which small enemy detachments plagued the countryside. Should an enemy decide to attack the lines with an army, then the lines must be defended with an army.[39]

Such a project would of course necessitate new construction, but Vauban was careful to point out that it would also mean the elimination of numerous ancient strongholds, and he accordingly urged the razing of all fortresses remote from the frontier and not included in the two lines. This would not only be a saving for the treasury but, he urged, also a saving in manpower: with the elimination of their garrisons, ten fewer strongholds would mean about thirty thousand soldiers free for duty elsewhere.

This famous memoir of 1678 also embodied a consideration of possible future conquests and these indicate that, so far as the northern and eastern frontiers were concerned, Vauban was willing to pave the way for something more ambitious than a mere local rectification of a line. In the event of a future war, he said, certain enemy fortresses should be immediately seized. Dixmude, Courtrai, and Charlemont would open up the Lowlands, while to the east, Strasbourg and Luxembourg were the supremely important cities to acquire. Not only did these fortresses have the most admirable features of size, wealth, and situation—in these matters they were the best in Europe—but they were the keys to France's

[37] Ibid., 152f., 221-22.

[38] The first line: Dunkirk, Bergues, Furnes, Fort de La Kenoque, Ypres, Menin, Lille, Tournai, Fort de Mortagne, Condé, Valenciennes, Le Quesnoy, Maubeuge, Philippeville, and Dinant. The second line: Gravelines, Saint-Omer, Aire, Béthune, Arras, Douai, Bouchain, Cambrai, Landrecies, Avesnes, Marienbourg, Rocroi, and Charleville.

[39] Lazard, *Vauban*, 282-84; Augoyat, *Aperçu historique*, 1:229.

expansion to its natural boundaries. Vauban would not have been Frenchman and patriot had he not accepted the familiar and tempting principle that France's natural frontier to the north and east was the Rhine. We know that he held this view and we can suspect that it was already clearly formulated in his mind early in his career. It certainly was later. Just before the Peace of Ryswick, when he was terrified for fear France was about to lose both Strasbourg and Luxembourg, he wrote: "If we do not take them again we shall lose forever the chance of having the Rhine for our boundary."[40]

It is not easy to say with certainty whether this memoir of 1678 represents Vauban's mature and final view on the matter of permanent fortification. Vauban's later memoirs leave much to be desired as examples of strategic thinking about the role of fortresses. Except for a memoir on the fortification of Paris, in which he discusses at length the strategic importance of a nation's capital, most of the later studies are lacking in genuine strategic interest. They are concerned chiefly with detailed recommendations as to which fortresses should be condemned and which enlarged or rebuilt.

Despite these handicaps it is not hard to detect a series of changes in Vauban's opinions, due partly to a gradual evolution of his ideas, but chiefly to the changed conditions under which he was obliged to work in the later years of the reign. Increasing financial stringency and a growing drain on the manpower supply encouraged Vauban to stress the razing of fortifications as much if not more than new construction.[41] This led him to urge the destruction of many of the places that had been listed in his second line of defense in the memoir of 1678. At the same time the armies of Louis XIV were being thrown more and more on the defensive and Vauban adapted himself increasingly to defensive thinking. He followed the trend that was becoming evident at the close of the century toward still greater reliance upon a continuous waterline along the northern frontier. But he was aware of the peculiar weakness of this sort of defense. In 1696 he wrote a memoir in which he urged the creation of *camps retranchés*, fortified encampments to supplement the fortresses and to strengthen the waterline. The purpose of these encampments was either to guard the waterline in the interval between the fortresses or to strengthen the forts themselves by producing a veritable external defense. With a small army—smaller than the ordinary field army—camped beyond the outworks of a fortress and protected by elaborate earthworks it was possible either to interfere with any besieging forces unwise enough

[40] Lavallée, *Les frontières de France*, 83-85.
[41] Zeller, *L'organisation défensive*, 98-107.

to tackle the fortress directly or to impose upon them a wider perimeter to be invested.

Taken together these two factors—first, the stress upon the continuous line supplemented by the fortified encampments; and second, the willingness to sacrifice the second line of forts he had favored in 1678—do not offer support to Lazard's assertion that Vauban was a pioneer advocate of the "fortified zone" that modern strategy has adopted. Quite the contrary, Vauban's thinking seems to have evolved in the direction of favoring a thinner and thinner line. He simplified that disorganized parody on a fortified zone that he had inherited from his predecessors. At first he reduced it to a double line of fortifications, a palpable imitation of the familiar infantry line, and then proceeded to simplify this still further into a single cordon, based on strong points linked by a continuous waterline and supported by troops. Perhaps it is not too far-fetched to see in this a sign that the great engineer, toward the close of his career, was led gradually to lay more emphasis upon armies and less upon fortification. He seems almost to have come closer to the idea of Guibert that the true defense of a country is its army, not its fortifications; that the fortified points are merely the bastions of that greater fortress of which the army forms a living and flexible curtain.

4. Frederick the Great, Guibert, Bülow: From Dynastic to National War

R. R. PALMER

T HE PERIOD from 1740 to 1815, opening with the accession of Frederick the Great as king of Prussia, and closing with the dethronement of Napoleon as emperor of the French, saw both the perfection of the older style of warfare and the launching of a newer style which in many ways we still follow. The contrast between the two styles is the main subject of this chapter. Much of the old, however, was continued in the new. The underlying ideas sketched in the three preceding chapters were not outdated and they remain today essential to the theory of war. Machiavelli had made the study of war a social science. He had dissociated it from considerations of ethical purpose and closely related it to constitutional, economic, and political speculation. He had tried, in military matters, to enlarge the field of human planning and to reduce the field of chance. Vauban had opened up to military men the resources of natural science and technology. The seventeenth century, while enlarging armies beyond precedent, had advanced the principles of orderly administration and control. It had put a new emphasis on discipline, created a more complex hierarchy of tactical units, clarified the chains of command, turned army leaders into public officials, and made armed force into a servant of government. All these developments were accelerated and elaborated in the period of change with which this essay deals.

The significant innovations concerned the constitution and the utilization of armies, i.e., manpower and strategy. Citizen armies replaced professional armies. Aggressive, mobile, combative strategy replaced the slow strategy of siegecraft. Both had been anticipated by Machiavelli, but neither had been realized on a large scale since 1500. Together, after 1792, they revolutionized warfare, replacing the "limited" war of the Old Regime with the "unlimited" war of subsequent times. This transition came with the shift from the dynastic to the national form of state, and was a consequence of the French Revolution. War before the French Revolution was essentially a clash between rulers. Since that event it has become increasingly a clash between peoples, and hence has become increasingly "total."[1]

The dynastic form of state set definite limits to what was possible in the constitution of armies. The king, however absolute in theory, was in fact in a disadvantageous position. Every dynastic state stood by a precarious balance betwen the ruling house and the aristocracy. The privileges of the nobility limited the freedom of government action. These privileges included the right not to pay certain taxes and the right almost to monopolize the commissioned grades in the army. Governments, with their taxing power restricted, could not draw on the full material resources of their countries. Nor could they draw on their full human resources. Officers must come from a hereditary class that rarely exceeded two percent of the population. Between populations as a whole and their governments little feeling existed. The tie between sovereign and subject was bureaucratic, administrative, and fiscal, an external mechanical connection of ruler and ruled, strongly in contrast to the principle brought in by the Revolution, which, in its doctrine of responsible citizenship and sovereignty of the people, effected an almost religious fusion of the government with the governed. A good government of the Old Regime was one that demanded little of its subjects, which regarded them as useful, worthy, and productive assets to the state, and which in wartime interfered as little as possible with civilian life. A "good people" was one that obeyed the laws, paid its taxes, and was loyal to the reigning house; it need have no sense of its own identity as a people, or unity as a nation, or responsibility for public affairs, or obligation to put forth a supreme effort in war.

The army reflected the state. It was divided internally into classes without common spirit, into officers whose incentive was honor, class consciousness, glory, or ambition, and soldiers enlisted for long terms who fought as a business for a living, who were thought incapable of higher sentiments, and whose strongest attachment was usually a kind of naive pride in their regiments. The armies of Russia, Austria, and Prussia were composed largely of serfs. Prussia also used large numbers of foreigners, as did England. The Austrian forces were linguistically heterogeneous. In all countries the tendency was to recruit men who were economically the most useless, which is to say the most degraded elements in the population. Civilians everywhere kept soldiers at a distance. Even in France, which already had the most national of the large armies of

---

[1] For the contemporary literature of the subject see Max Jähns, *Geschichte der Kriegswissenschaften vornehmlich in Deutschland*, 3 vols. (Munich and Leipzig, 1889-91).

92

Europe, cafés and other public places put up signs reading, "No dogs, lackeys, prostitutes or soldiers."[2]

To make armies of such motley hosts, of soldiers who were almost social outcasts and of officers who were often only youthful aristocrats, some kind of common purpose had to be created. For this end the troops had few moral or psychological resources in themselves. Governments believed, with good reason in the circumstances, that order could be imposed only from outside and from above. The horrors of an ungoverned soldiery were remembered, especially in Germany after the Thirty Years' War. The enlightened monarchies of the eighteenth century tried to spare their civilian populations, both for humane reasons and as sources of revenue. To promote civil order, and to build morale among troops who could not be appealed to on a level of ideas, governments increasingly took good physical care of their men, quartered them in barracks, provided them with doctors and hospitals, fed them liberally, and established great fixed permanent magazines for their supply. It was feared that soldiers would desert if left to forage in small parties or if not furnished with a tolerable standard of living, since to make a living, not to fight or die for a cause, was the chief aim of the professional soldier. And in truth, in the eighteenth century, both officers and men passed from one army to another, in war or in peace, with a facility inconceivable after the French Revolution.

Along with good care went a strict attention to discipline and training, also handed down from above. Only iron rule could make into a unified force men who had no cohesion in themselves. Rulers and aristocrats scarcely expected to find moral qualities in the lower classes who made up the soldiery—neither courage, nor loyalty, nor group spirit, nor sacrifice, nor self-reliance. Nor were these qualities in fact developed in the troops of the time, who, like the peoples in general of the dynastic states, felt little sense of participation in the issues of war. Soldiers could not be trusted as individuals, or in detached parties, or out of sight of their officers. Technical considerations also discouraged individuality. The poor state of communications and low quality of scouting (due in turn to the ignorance and unreliability of individual soldiers) made it more than ordinarily hazardous to divide an army in the field. The inaccuracy and short range of muskets made individual firing relatively harmless. As a result the ideal of military training was to shape a spiritless raw material into machinelike battalions. When engaged with the enemy each battalion stood close to the next in a solid line, the men being almost elbow to elbow, usually three ranks deep, and each battalion constituting

[2] M. Weygand, *Histoire de l'armée française* (Paris, 1938), 173.

93

a kind of firing machine, delivering a volley at the word of command. To achieve tactical alertness, long and intensive training was necessary. Two years were considered scarcely sufficient to turn a ragamuffin into a good professional soldier.

The constitution of armies strongly affected their utilization. For the governments of the Old Regime, with their limited resources, the professional armies were expensive. Each soldier represented a heavy investment in time and money. Trained troops lost in action could not easily be replaced. The great magazines of munitions and foodstuffs, which, in the poor state of transportation, had to be kept near the expected scenes of action, needed protection. In addition, in the latter part of the seventeenth century scientific progress improved the art of fortification, and a great revulsion spread through France and Germany against the chaotic and roving warfare of the so-called wars of religion, by which productive civilian life had been much impaired. The net result was to concentrate armies in chains of heavily fortified positions. Armies, and fragments of armies, were immobilized near their bases, from which they were not supposed to depart by more than five days' march. Even with magazines close behind them, they carried long baggage trains, so that a day's march was very short. Nor could the baggage trains be easily reduced: in most armies the aristocratic officers traveled in style, and the troops, fighting without political passion, would lose morale if their food supply became uncertain or if operations became distastefully strenuous.

A large-scale pitched battle between complete armies was in these circumstances a rare occurrence. It was not easy for a commander to establish contact with an unwilling enemy. Even with two armies face to face, to draw up a battle line took time, and if one side chose to depart while the other formed, no complete engagements would ensue. Battle was a tremendous risk. A margin of advantage gained on the battlefield could not easily be widened, because the technique of destructive pursuit was undeveloped. Military thinkers held that a state might suffer almost as much by victory as by defeat. Quick and decisive political results were in any case not expected from battle. Here the contrast between eighteenth-century and Napoleonic battles is especially clear. After Blenheim, Malplaquet, Fontenoy, or Rossbach, the war dragged on for years. After Marengo, Austerlitz, Jena, Wagram, or Leipzig, peace overtures began in a few months.

To sum up, many factors combined before the French Revolution to produce a limited warfare, fought with limited means for limited objectives. Wars were long, but not intense; battles were destructive (for the battalion volleys were deadly), but for that reason not eagerly sought. Operations turned by preference against fortresses, magazines, supply lines, and key positions, producing a learned warfare in which ingenuity in maneuver was more prized than impetuosity in combat. War of position prevailed over war of movement, and a strategy of small successive advantages over a strategy of annihilation.

All this was changed in the upheaval that shook Europe after 1789. The "world war" of 1792-1815 was, except in the earliest years, and except for the struggle between France and Great Britain, a series of short wars each of which was promptly decided on the battlefield and concluded by the imposition of peace. Authorities agree that these wars marked a major turning point, closing a period which had begun about 1500, and opening a period from which we have not yet clearly emerged. Most writers attribute the change to the French Revolution, with the consequent nationalizing of public opinion and closer relations between governments and governed. This interpretation was established half a century ago by Max Jähns and Hans Delbrück. There has been some evidence of a "revisionist" tendency, as in the writings of Jean Colin, who looked for a more material or at least technical explanation, and found it in the great improvements in the latter half of the eighteenth century in artillery, army organization, road building, and cartography. The burden of informed opinion, while recognizing the importance of technical progress, still considers the effects of the political revolution to have been more profound. As Delbrück said, the new *politisches Weltbild* of the French Revolution produced "a new constitution of the army, which first brought forth a new tactics, and from which a new strategy would then grow."[3]

The transition is evident in the works of the three writers treated below. Each of the three represents a significant stage in the history of military thinking. Frederick the Great embodied the utmost in military achievement that was possible in Europe in the conditions prevailing before the French Revolution. Guibert was a conscious disciple of Frederick, but he forecast more clearly than Frederick some of the transformations that were to come. Bülow, a contemporary of the Revolutionary and Napoleonic Wars, gradually perceived many of the lessons that they offered. Of the three, only Frederick was an experienced practical commander. His writings describe the actual warfare of the day. Guibert and Bülow, though army officers by training, commanded no armies; they were notable as critics, prophets, and reformers. Frederick reveals a mind completely master of its subject. Guibert and Bülow, writing less from experience, aiming to go beyond existing conditions, were much less

---

[3] Hans Delbrück, *Geschichte der Kriegskunst*, 7 vols. (Berlin, 1900-1936), 4:363, 426; Jean Colin, *L'éducation militaire de Napoléon* (Paris, 1900).

steady in their grasp. With their fluctuating and partial insights they may be taken to illustrate the difficulty, familiar in all ages, with which military theory adjusts itself to shifting realities in the world of fact.

Frederick the Great, invading Silesia without warning in 1740, gave Europe a taste of what later was to be called blitzkrieg. In three Silesian wars he managed to retain the coveted province, whose acquisitions almost doubled the size of his small kingdom, and he proved himself, fighting at times against incredible odds, to be incomparably superior as a general to any of his opponents. His Prussia, in addition, possessed to the point of exaggeration the main features of the dynastic state. Of the chief states of Europe Prussia was the most mechanically put together, the most ruled from above, the least animated by the spirit in its people, and the poorest in both material and human resources. Frederick was also a voluminous and gifted writer. In the writings of such a king of such a kingdom, the generalities outlined in the section above take on definite and concrete form.

Frederick's first military work of importance was his *Principes généraux de la guerre*, written in 1746, and embodying the experience of the first two Silesian wars. It was circulated confidentially among his generals. The capture of one of these generals by the French in 1760 led to its publication. The king further developed his ideas in a *Testament politique* composed in 1752 for the private use of his successors to the throne. To this testament the *Principes généraux* was attached as an appendix. In 1768, when his wars were over and his ideas somewhat modified, he drew up a *Testament militaire* for his successors. To his generals in 1771 he issued his *Eléments de castramétrie et de tactique*. Continuously throughout his reign he composed special instructions for various branches of the army, which were brought together and published with his other writings in 1846. Among works that he made public are a didactic poem, *L'art de la guerre*, a number of political essays that touch on military questions, and the various histories and memoirs of his reign, together with their prefaces. In these writings contemporaries tried to discover the secrets of his generalship. He wrote most of his theoretical works in French, but many of the tactical and technical instructions are in German. His literary career reached over more than forty years. In general he adhered to the same ideas in army organization and tactics, but in the strategy and politics of war he moved from the sharp aggressiveness of 1740 to a philosophy of relative inactivity.

The organization of the army was an old concern of the rulers of Prussia. In 1640, exactly a century before Frederick's accession, his great-grandfather, the Great Elector, came to the throne in the full fury of the Thirty Years' War. There was then no kingdom of Prussia, only parcels of territories along the flat north German plain, swarmed over and ravaged by the brutal mercenaries of every contending power. The Great Elector founded an army. To support this army he virtually founded a new polity and a new economy. With his reign began the distinctive features of Prussia. First, Prussia owed its existence and its very identity to its army. Second, military science, politics, and economics merged inseparably into a great science of statecraft. Third, Prussia, made by the Hohenzollern dynasty, was a triumph of careful planning. By the time of Frederick's father, Frederick William I, the king of Prussia was commonly considered one of the hardest-working men in Europe. He directed the state in person, all threads came together in his hand, and the only center of unity was his own mind. Order, in Prussia, had not come from free discussion and collaboration. As Frederick the Great once observed, if Newton had had to consult with Descartes and Leibnitz, he would never have created his philosophical system.

A king of Prussia, in Frederick's view, must, to have an army, hold a firm balance between classes in the state and between economic production and military power. He must preserve the nobility by prohibiting the sale of noble lands to peasants or townsmen. Peasants were clearly too ignorant to become officers;[4] to have bourgeois officers would be "the first step toward the decline and fall of the army."[5] Rigid class structure—with noble persons and inalienably "noble" land—was necessary to the army and to the state. A brave colonel, says Frederick, makes a brave battalion; and a colonel's decision in a moment of crisis may sway the destiny of the kingdom. But the king must make sure (so new, disjointed, and artificial was the state) that these aristocrats have the desired spirit. In his first political testament Frederick confides to his successors that, during the first Silesian wars, he had made a special effort to impress upon his officers the idea of fighting for the kingdom of Prussia.[6]

For common soldiers Frederick often expressed a rough respect, as for men who risked their lives in his service, but his real interest in them rested almost entirely on disciplinary and material questions. The peasant families (i.e., serfs, east of the Elbe) must be protected; their lands must not be absorbed by bourgeois or nobles; only those not indispensable in agriculture, such as younger sons, should be recruited. By and large, the

---

[4] *Politisches Testament von 1752*, in *Die Werke Friedrichs des Grossen*, 10 vols. (Berlin, 1912-14), 7:164. *Die Werke Friedrichs des Grossen* hereafter cited as *Werke*.

[5] *Exposé du gouvernement prussien, des principes sur lequels il roule* (1775), in *Oeuvres de Frédéric le Grand*, 30 vols. (Berlin, 1846-56), 9:186. *Oeuvres de Frédéric le Grand* hereafter cited as *Oeuvres*.

[6] *Pol. Test. 1752* in *Werke*, 7:146; *Oeuvres*, 29:58.

peasants and townsmen are most useful as producers. "Useful hard-working people should be guarded as the apple of one's eye, and in wartime recruits should be levied in one's own country only when the bitterest necessity compels."[7] Half the army or more might be filled with non-Prussian professionals, with prisoners of war or with deserters from foreign armies. Frederick praises the Prussian canton system, by which, to equalize the burden of recruiting, specific districts were assigned to specific regiments as sources of manpower. By this system (and by the use of foreigners), he observed with satisfaction in 1768 that only five thousand natives of Prussia needed to be conscripted each year. Yet he was aware of the value of patriotic citizen forces, which he thought that the cantons produced by putting neighbors beside each other in war. Our troops, he wrote in 1746, recruited from "citizens," fight with honor and courage. "With such troops one would defeat the whole world, were victories not as fatal to them as to their enemies." Later on Frederick, like other *philosophes*, placed even higher theoretical value on patriotism. But he never did anything about it, nor could he, without revolutionizing his kingdom. In practice he assumed that common soldiers were without honor, and he died in the belief that to use foreigners to do one's fighting was only sensible statecraft.[8]

Frederick's soldiers felt no great inward attachment to him. Desertion was the nightmare of all eighteenth-century commanders, especially in politically fragmented Germany, where men of the same language could be found on both sides in every war. In 1744, Frederick had to stop his advance in Bohemia because his army began to melt away. He drew up elaborate rules to prevent desertion: the troops should not camp near large woods, their rear and flanks should be watched by hussars, they should avoid night marches except when rigorously necessary, they should be led in ranks by an officer when going to forage or to bathe.[9]

Working with untrustworthy material Frederick insisted on exact discipline, to which the Prussian armies had been habituated by his father. "The slightest loosening of discipline," he said, "would lead to barbarization."[10] Here again the army reflected the state. The aim of discipline was partly paternalistic, to make the soldier a rational being by authority, through preventing such offenses as drunkenness and theft. But the prin-

---

[7] *Militärisches Testament von 1768*, in *Werke*, 6:226-27.

[8] *Principes généraux de la guerre* (1746) in *Oeuvres*, 28:7; *Lettres sur l'amour de la patrie* (1779), in *Oeuvres*, 9:211-44.

[9] *Prin. gén.* (1746), in *Oeuvres*, 28:5-6; *Ordres für die sämmtlichen Generale von der Infanterie und Cavalerie, wie auch Huzzaren, desgleichen für die Stabsofficiere und Commandeurs der Bataillons* (1744), in *Oeuvres*, 30:119-23; *Règles de ce qu'on exige d'un bon commandeur de bataillon en temps de guerre* (1773), in *Oeuvres*, 29:57-65.

[10] *Pol. Test.* 1752, in *Werke*, 7:172.

cipal aim was to turn the army into an instrument of a single mind and will. Officers and men must understand that every act "is the work of a single man." Or again: "No one reasons, everyone executes"; that is, the thinking is done centrally, in the mind of the king. All that can be done with soldiers, he said, is to give them *Korpsgeist*, to fuse their personalities into their regiments. As he grew older and more cynical, he observed that good will affected common men much less than intimidation. Officers must lead men into danger; "therefore (since honor has no effect on them) they must fear their officers more than any danger." But he added that humanity demanded good medical care.[11]

Made amenable by discipline the troops were to be put through careful training. Prussia was famous for its drillfields, where, to the admiration of foreign observers, battalions and squadrons performed intricate evolutions with high precision. The aim was to achieve tactical mobility, skill in shifting from marching order to battle order, steadiness under fire, and complete responsiveness to command. An army so trained, Frederick repeatedly said, allowed full scope to the art of generalship. The commander could form his conceptions in the knowledge that they would be realized. With all else shaped to his hand, his presiding intelligence would be free. Frederick therefore never tired of urging his generals to ceaseless vigilance over drill, in war and in peace. "Unless every man is trained beforehand in peacetime for that which he will have to accomplish in war, one has nothing but people who bear the name of a business without knowing how to practise it."[12]

Battle, with troops so spiritually mechanized, was a methodical affair. Opposing armies were arrayed according to pattern, almost as regularly as chessmen at the beginning of a game: on each wing cavalry, artillery fairly evenly distributed along the rear, infantry battalions drawn up in two parallel solid lines, one a few hundred yards behind the other, and each line, or at least the first, composed of three ranks, each rank firing at a single command while the other two reloaded. Frederick never departed from the essentials of this battle formation, though like all good generals he allowed himself liberty in adapting it to specific purposes. Battle order tended to determine marching order: troops should march, according to Frederick, in columns so arranged that by a quick turn the columns presented themselves as firing lines with cavalry on the flanks. Battle order was also the end object of severe discipline. It was not easy to hold men in the lines, standing in plain sight, elbow to elbow, against an enemy only a few hundred yards away. But orders were strict. "If a

<hr>

[11] *Mil. Test. 1768*, in *Werke*, 6:233, 237; *Oeuvres*, 28:5.
[12] *Pol. Test 1752*, in *Werke*, 7:173-75; *Prin. gén.* (1746), in *Oeuvres*, 28:7.

soldier during an action looks about as if to flee, or so much as sets foot outside the line, the non-commissioned officer standing behind him will run him through with his bayonet and kill him on the spot."[13] If the enemy fled, the victorious line must remain in position. Plundering the dead or wounded was forbidden on pain of death.

Frederick set a great value on cavalry, which constituted about a fourth of his army, but he used it in general only for shock action in solid tactical units. His scouting service was therefore poor; in 1744, with twenty thousand cavalry, he could not locate the Austrians. Nor was he successful in the use of light infantry for skirmishing and patrolling. The Austrians had many light troops, mounted and foot, in their Croatians and Pandours; the French were to make use of light infantry in the untrained levies of the Revolution. Frederick hardly knew what to do with such troops, which, dispersed and individualistic, could not be extensions of his own mind.[14]

The middle years of the eighteenth century saw a more rapid increase in the use of artillery, in proportion to other arms, than any other period from the sixteenth century to the twentieth.[15] The Austrians, after their humiliating loss of Silesia, turned especially to artillery to meet the menace

[13] *Disposition, wie es bei vorgehender Bataille bei seiner königlichen Majestät in Preussen Armée unveränderlich soll gehalten werden* (1745), in *Oeuvres*, 30:146.

[14] Delbrück, *Geschichte der Kriegskunst*, 4:327-28.

[15] Cf. column II of the following table, which, compiled from data in G. Bodart, *Militärhistorisches Kriegslexikon* (Vienna, 1908), 612, 784-85, 816-17, shows the mounting intensity of war since 1600.

	I	II	III	IV
Thirty Years' War	19,000	1.5	1	.24
Wars of Louis XIV	40,000	1.75	7	
Spanish Succession				.77
Wars of Frederick II	47,000	3.33	12	
Austrian Succession				.82
Seven Years War				1.40
Wars of French Revolution	45,000	—	12	
First Coalition				3.0
Second Coalition				4.4
Wars of Napoleon	84,000	3.5	37	
Third Coalition				7.0
War of 1809				11.0
War of 1812				5.2
American Civil War	54,000	3.0	18	1.0
War of 1870	70,000	3.3	12	9.0
Russo-Japanese War	110,000	3.75	3	1.0

Explanation of columns:

I. Average size of an army in battle, computed where possible from thirty battles in each war.

II. Number of cannon per 1,000 combatants.

III. Number of battles in which the opposing armies together numbered over 100,000.

IV. Average number of battles per month.

of Frederick's mobile columns. The French were the most progressive artillerists of Europe. Frederick often bemoaned this development, for Prussia of all major states could least afford an artillery race. The new vogue for artillery, observed the king in 1768, was a veritable abyss to the state's finances. Yet he joined the scramble; it was Frederick, with his appreciation of speedy movement, who introduced horse-drawn field artillery for shift of position during battle. He continued to insist that artillery was not an "arm" but only an "auxiliary," inferior to infantry and cavalry, but he gave increasing thought to its use, and one of his last writings, an *Instruction* of 1782, seems to show the influence of the French artillery theorists from whom Bonaparte was to learn. Frederick here orders his artillery officers to avoid firing simply to satisfy the infantry or cavalry, to educate themselves in the discriminate use of ball and canister, and to concentrate their opening fire on the enemy's infantry in order to smash a hole in the enemy line and help their own infantry to break through.[16]

The use of the long unbroken battle array, since a frontal clash of two such solid lines would be butchery, caused Frederick to prize the flank attack, for which he designed his famous "oblique order," the advance of one wing by echelons with refusal of the other. Omitting tactical details, it may simply be said that Frederick's purpose in favoring this type of battle was, in case of success, to gain a quick victory by rolling up the enemy's line, and, in case of failure, to minimize losses, since the refused wing maneuvered to cover the withdrawal of the wing engaged. Frederick's superior mobility and coordination gave a special effectiveness to these flanking movements, which in themselves were of course among the oldest expedients of war.[17]

On these matters of army organization and tactics Frederick never seriously altered his opinions. He changed his mind on the larger issues of strategy. At first he seemed to introduce a new spirit, but in the end he accepted the limitations imposed by the political order on questions of under what circumstances wars should be fought, and where and when battle should be joined.

His lightning attack on Silesia startled Europe. This first Silesian war (1740-1742) was a desperate gamble, played for what to a king of Prussia were very high stakes. In the second Silesian war (1744-1745, forming like the first a part of the War of the Austrian Succession) he aspired for

---

[16] *Mil. Test. 1768*, in *Werke*, 6:228ff.; *Mémoires depuis la paix de Hubertsbourg*, in *Oeuvres*, 6:97; *Eléments de castramétrie et de tactique* (1771), in *Oeuvres*, 29:42; *Oeuvres*, 30:139-41, 391-96.

[17] *Eléments de castramétrie*, in *Oeuvres*, 29:25; Delbrück, *Geschichte der Kriegskunst*, 4:314-22.

a while even to the total destruction of the Hapsburg monarchy. The project failed, but Frederick retained Silesia. Thereafter his war policy became less ambitious. In the Seven Years' War (1756-1763), after the battles of Rossbach and Leuthen, which probably saved Prussia from extinction, he was reduced to maintaining a brilliant defensive against the combined powers of France, Austria, and Russia, each of which had a population at least four times his own. Frederick's last war, that of the Bavarian Succession (1778-1779), dragged itself out in bloodless military demonstrations and promenades.

In the *Principes généraux de la guerre*, we find him calling for a strategy of blitzkrieg, though he did not use that term. The wars of Prussia, he says, should be "short and lively"; Prussian generals should seek a speedy decision.[18] These were in fact the principles on which he at first acted. It is notable, however, that the reasons given for these dashing operations were much the same as those which in later years made him increasingly cautious. A long war, he said, would exhaust the resources of Prussia and break down the "admirable discipline" of the Prussian troops. From preferring a short quick war it was no great distance to preferring either no war at all, or a longer war of low intensity in expenditure of men and material. In any case the governing conditions were the same: the limited resources of the state, the dependence of armies on fixed magazines prepared beforehand, and the use of soldiers who, however well drilled, had no inward conviction to sustain them in times of trouble.

None of these conditions could Frederick overcome. He could not make Prussia a wealthy state; he could only economize its resources. He could not, like the governments of the French Revolution, let his armies live on occupied countries, although he recommended this procedure. His armies would melt away if dispersed to seek subsistence, and lose morale if they were not regularly supplied. Nor could he count on any welcome in occupied territories. His efforts to build a "fifth column" in Bohemia repeatedly failed. And he could not communicate moral enthusiasm to his troops without changing his whole system and view of life.

In addition, when the Austrians strengthened their artillery and their fortifications after the loss of Silesia, they added technical hindrances to the development of aggressive strategy by Frederick. The old king, in his last years, repeatedly observed that conditions had changed since his youth—that henceforth Prussia could fight only a war of position. He himself, with his great permanent magazines and vulnerable frontiers, set a high value on fixed fortifications. Forts, he observed, were "mighty

[18] *Prin. gén.* (1746), in *Oeuvres*, 28:84.

nails which hold a ruler's provinces together." To besiege and overwhelm such fortresses became a main object of warfare. The conduct of sieges had been a science since Vauban. Frederick carried on in this tradition. Even his concept of battle was colored by it. "We should draw our dispositions for battle from the rules of besieging positions." The two lines of infantry in battle order, he said in 1770, corresponded to the parallels formed by a besieging force. Even in occupying villages these principles should not be lost from mind. Nothing could be further from the direction in which military practice was to move. Napoleon was to conduct only two sieges in his whole career.[19]

Again unlike Napoleon, Frederick, though a successful battle general, was not fond of full-size battles, that is, showdown clashes between the main forces of the belligerents. To his mind the outcome of battle depended too much upon chance and chance was the opposite of rational calculation. The supreme planning intelligence, the power of command to elicit obedience, which to Frederick were the first premises of scientific war, could not be relied on in the heat of a major engagement. "It is to be remarked in addition that most generals in love with battle resort to this expedient for want of other resources. Far from being considered a merit in them, this is usually thought a sign of the sterility of their talents."[20]

To annihilate the enemy's main combat force was thus not Frederick's usual strategic objective. He indeed realized that, if battle is fought, the winner should attempt a destructive pursuit of the enemy. But destructive pursuit was not easy to a Frederician army: the cavalry, trained for shock action in solid units, inclined to desert if scattered, fired neither by the half-barbaric ferocity of Croatian irregulars, nor by the political passion of more modern troops, was not suited to pursue a fugitive and broken army. Nothing like Napoleon's cavalry action after the battle of Jena would have been possible to Frederick. In effect for Frederick the purpose of battle was to force an enemy to move. "To win a battle means to compel your opponent to yield you his position."[21]

So Frederician war became increasingly a war of position, the war of complex maneuver and subtle accumulation of small gains; leisurely and slow in its main outlines (though never in tactics), and quite different from the short sharp warfare recommended in 1746. "To gain many small successes," he wrote in 1768, "means gradually to heap up a

---

[19] *Mil. Test.* 1768, in *Werke*, 6:247, 257; *Pol. Test.* 1752, in *Werke*, 7:176; *Eléments de castramétrie*, in *Oeuvres*, 29:4, 21, 38.

[20] *Réflexions sur Charles XII* (1759), in *Oeuvres*, 7:81; *Essai sur les formes du gouvernement* (1777), in *Oeuvres*, 9:203.

[21] *Mil. Test.* 1768, 6:246-49; *Pol. Test.* 1752, in *Werke*, 7:174.

treasure." "All maneuvers in war," he added in 1770, "turn upon the positions which a general may occupy with advantage, and positions which he may attack with the least loss." He concluded also, from unfortunate experiences in Bohemia, that an army could not successfully operate far beyond its own frontiers. "I observe," he wrote in 1775, "that all wars carried far from the frontiers of those who undertake them have less success than those fought within reach of one's own country. Would this not be because of a natural sentiment in man, who feels it to be more just to defend himself than to despoil his neighbor? But perhaps the physical reason outweighs the moral, because of the difficulty in providing food supplies at points distant from the frontier, and in furnishing quickly enough the new recruits, new horses, clothing and munitions of war." Bonaparte, who could win battles in places as far from France as Austerlitz and Friedland, would have smiled at such maxims of caution, though Borodino came to remind him of their force. For Frederick the rule held good.[22]

But although Frederick's strategic thinking remained within the old limits of the war of position, and although he remained disinclined to serious battle (it was his advisors who pressed for action in the year of Rossbach and Leuthen), he never favored passivity in operations. He continued to insist on the importance of surprise. He was prepared, in the years of peace after the Seven Years' War, to spring at a moment's notice into Saxony or Bohemia, equipped with detailed maps and exact information, and with new ten-pound howitzers and new kinds of cavalry charges kept as a state secret. He favored offensive strategy in the field, as permitting more freedom of initiative; but would willingly fight on the defensive, as he often had to, when less strong than his enemy or when expecting to gain an advantage by time. It must however be an active and challenging defensive, which, while based on fixed fortifications, freely assaulted enemy positions and detachments. A commander, he said, "deceives himself who thinks he is conducting well a defensive war when he takes no initiative, and remains inactive during the whole campaign. Such a defensive would end with the whole army being driven from the country that the general meant to protect."[23]

Of the gains to be expected from war, under conditions then existing, he became increasingly dubious. Having made his debut by achieving the most successful revolution in the balance of power effected on the continent of Europe in his lifetime, he became with the acquisition of Silesia a man of peace, and ended by believing firmly in the value of the European

[22] *Mil. Test.* 1768, in *Werke*, 6:248; *Oeuvres*, 29:3; *Histoire de mon temps*, preface of 1775, in *Oeuvres*, 2:xxviii.

[23] *Mil. Test.* 1768, in *Werke*, 6:253, 260-61; Jähns, *Geschichte*, 3:2027.

balance now that Prussia was one of its main components. For Prussia he envisaged eventual expansion in Poland, Saxony, and Swedish Pomerania; but (except for the first partition of Poland, which was accomplished without war and without disturbance to the balance of power, to the great satisfaction of diplomats) he was willing to leave this eventual expansion to his successors. He was a dynast, not a revolutionary or an adventurer; he could leave something to be done by others than himself. In 1775 he stood for the military status quo. "The ambitious," he wrote, "should consider above all that armaments and military discipline being much the same throughout Europe, and alliances as a rule producing an equality of force between belligerent parties, all that princes can expect from the greatest advantages at present is to acquire, by accumulation of successes, either some small city on the frontier, or some territory which will not pay interest on the expenses of the war, and whose population does not even approach the number of citizens who perished in the campaigns." Nor did he fear being crushed by his huge neighbors. "I perceive that small states [meaning Prussia, with its five million inhabitants] can maintain themselves against the greatest monarchies [meaning France, Austria, and Russia with some twenty million each], when these states put industry and a great deal of order into their affairs. I find that the great empires are full of abuses and confusion; that they maintain themselves only by their vast resources and by the intrinsic force of their mass. The intrigues of these courts would ruin less powerful princes; they are always harmful, but do not prevent the keeping of numerous armies on foot." He seems never to have considered what would happen to the "equilibrium of Europe," should the greatest of the monarchies throw off its abuses and confusion, break down the limits set by the dynastic-aristocratic regime, and introduce into its affairs some of the attention to business already familiar in Prussia. He did not foresee the French Revolution.[24]

II

In France, however, the foundations of Napoleonic warfare were already being laid. The humiliating peace of 1763, by which France lost its empire overseas and its prestige in Europe, was followed by serious military thinking. Gribeauval revolutionized artillery by introducing the principle of interchangeable parts, improving the accuracy of fire, and heightening the mobility of guns through reducing weight. His reforms created the types that remained standard until the 1820s. The marshal

[24] *Pol. Test. 1752*, in *Werke*, 7:158; *Histoire de mon temps*, preface of 1775, in *Oeuvres*, 2:xxviii-xxx.

de Broglie and the duke de Choiseul, in the 1760s, introduced a new and larger unit of army organization, the division. Developed gradually, the division came to be defined as a distinct, permanent, more or less equal part of an army, commanded by a general officer, and strong enough to engage the enemy successfully until other divisions reached the scene of action. Large armies ceased to be a single mass forming an unbroken front in battle; they became articulated wholes, with detachable and independently maneuverable members. Great new strategic and tactical possibilities were opened for a commander in chief, and at the same time, as divisional commanders, subordinate generals achieved an importance never enjoyed under Frederick. The Revolutionary Wars were the first in which the division was important. Napoleon and his marshals were the outcome.[25]

Along with practical innovations, after 1763, went a great deal of theoretical writing. Among the theorists was a young nobleman, the count de Guibert, who in 1772 published his *Essai général de tactique*. He was only twenty-nine, but his book made him a celebrity at once. He became a lion of the salons, fell in love with Mlle. de Lespinasse, wrote three tragedies in verse, served for a while in the War Office, and in 1789, at one of the district assemblies called to elect members to the Estates-General, he was liquidated from the incipient revolution by a combination of the reactionary, the disgruntled, and the jealous. He died in 1790, crying on his deathbed: "I shall be known! I shall receive justice!"[26]

Guibert was an unstable person, vain, unpredictable, and brilliant, a *littérateur* and a *philosophe*, regarded by contemporaries as the embodiment of genius. He was inconsistent, overemphatic, swayed by the enthusiasm of the moment. When he wrote the *Essai* he had served as an officer in Germany and Corsica. Like other *philosophes* he warmly admired Frederick, who stood in their eyes for modernity and enlightenment. The great Frederick, according to rumor, was so annoyed to find his secrets divined by this impertinent youngster, that reading the *Essai* threw him into fits of rage. Whether the book divined old Fritz's secrets we cannot know; that it sometimes went beyond Frederician warfare is certain.

[25] E. Picard, *L'artillerie française au XVIIIe siècle* (Paris, 1906); J. Campana, *L'artillerie de campagne, 1792-1901* (Paris, 1901); Weygand, *Histoire de l'armée française*, 192; Colin, *Education militaire*, 1-85.

[26] Editor's introduction, written in 1790, to Guibert, *Journal d'un voyage en Allemagne* (Paris, 1803); P. de Ségur, "Un grand homme des salons: Le comte de Guibert, 1743-1790," *Revue de Paris* 2 (1902), 701-36; P. Vignié, "Un Montalbanais célèbre; le comte de Guibert," *Bulletin archéologique de Tarn-el-Garonne* 52 (1924), 22-43; Guibert, *Précis de ce qui s'est passé à mon égard à l'Assemblée de Berry* (Paris, 1789); Jähns, *Geschichte*, 3:2059-72.

Two themes pervaded the *Essai général de tactique*. One demanded a patriot or citizen army. The other sounded the call for a war of movement. Both fell within Guibert's conception of *tactique*. The word at this time usually meant the maneuvering of troops, including under "grand tactics" what we call strategy, and under "elementary tactics" what we call tactics. This meaning Guibert rejected as too narrow. Tactics to him meant virtually all military science. It had two parts: first, the raising and training of armies; second, the art of the general, or what people then called tactics, and what we call tactics and strategy. Tactics, in his own enlarged sense, the young author wished to raise to the level of universal truth. "It becomes," he said, "the science of all times, all places and all arms . . . in a word the result of everything good which the military ages have thought, and of what our own age has been able to add."[27]

The theme of the citizen army was a common doctrine in *philosophe* circles. Montesquieu, Rousseau, Mably, and the host of lesser figures who by the 1770s made up liberal opinion maintained that, as a safeguard against tyranny, the citizens of a country must be trained to arms. A contributor to Diderot's *Encyclopédie*, J. Servan, who became war minister during the Revolution, published in 1780 a book on the citizen soldier. Guibert was riding the crest of a mighty wave. His *Essai*, dedicated "à ma patrie," proposing "to erect both a military and a political constitution" in which all Frenchmen, noble and commoner, king and subject, should glory in the title of "citizen," can be regarded as the leading work on military science by a *philosophe*.

The present governments of Europe, Guibert begins, are all despotic machines. All peoples would overthrow them if they could. No people will fight for them. No government is really interested in military science. Even in Prussia discipline is purely external, the inhabitants are mostly unmilitary, and youth is not trained to warlike and Spartan habits. In France, where the king is not a soldier, conditions are even more relaxed. Peoples are indifferent to the fortunes of war, because prisoners are no longer slaughtered in cold blood, and the civilians of a conquered province suffer no inconvenience except to pay a tribute often no heavier than their old taxes. In short, all the peoples of Europe are soft, and all the governments are weak. "But suppose," he says, "that a people should arise in Europe vigorous in spirit, in government, in the means at its disposal, a people who with hardy qualities should combine a national army and a settled plan of aggrandizement. We should see such a people

---

[27] *Essai général de tactique* (1772) in *Oeuvres militaires du comte de Guibert*, 5 vols. (Paris, 1803), 1:136-41. In his *Défense du système de guerre moderne* (1779), in ibid., vols. 3 and 4, Guibert introduces the term *la Stratégique*.

subjugate its neighbors and overwhelm our weak constitutions like the north wind bending reeds."[28]

This remark has often been quoted out of context as a prophecy of the Revolutionary and Napoleonic Wars. It was no such thing. No such vigorous people, says Guibert, will arise. Russia under Peter might have become such at the beginning of the century, but even Russia is now too westernized, too habituated to "luxury" and the refinements of civilization. But though Guibert expects no change adequate to his theories, he observes that, in so effete a world, the country that reforms itself only slightly will have a great advantage over others. This much he hopes for France.

By introducing the vigor of its people into its army. France may develop a more decisive, swifter, and more crushing kind of war. But even this much, though he hopes for it, he scarcely expects. The "vices" of modern warfare, he says, are incorrigible without political revolution. Revolution is out of the question—Guibert, like other *philosophes*, had little notion that revolutionary thinking might be followed by revolutionary behavior. What we must do, he says, "since we cannot have citizen troops and perfect troops, is to have our troops at least disciplined and trained." So, after the fanfare of general principles, as he works into his subject, Guibert arrives about where the great Frederick had started, at the idea, expressed by Frederick in 1746, that citizen-soldiers were indeed the best, but that since most soldiers were not citizens they must be rigidly disciplined and trained.[29]

The second theme of the *Essai*, the demand for a war of movement, is accordingly far more developed than the theme of a citizen army. Through this second theme, as through the first, runs the same strain of primitivism, the same feeling that the culture of the eighteenth century is too complex and sophisticated, the same idealizing of rude and Spartan virtues. Guibert hopes to make war more mobile and decisive by simplifying its elements. He thinks the armies of his day too big, artillery overvalued, fortifications and magazines overgrown, the study of topography overdone. The European peoples, in his opinion, having no force of spirit, proliferate themselves in material objects and empty numbers. Lacking valor, they rely on money.

In his views on the size of armies and quantity of artillery, both of which were in the ascendant, reaching at Leipzig in 1813 the highest point attained in battle until the twentieth century, Guibert saw no further than his master Frederick, and remained within the school of limited

---

[28] *Essai général*, in *Oeuvres militaires du comte de Guibert*, 1:1-23.
[29] Ibid., 1:1-151.

war. However partial to citizen troops, he was no prophet of mass armies. Huge armies he regarded as signs of the ineptitude of men in authority. A good general, he said, would be encumbered by an operating force of more than seventy thousand. On the contemporary artillery race he echoed Frederick's lamentations. Like Frederick, he regarded artillery only as an auxiliary, not as an "arm." The technical innovations of Gribeauval had, as usual, produced a wide split among experts. In a smaller way artillery was then in somewhat the position of aviation in our time. Guibert took a middle ground, favorable to Gribeauval, but he never fully appreciated the work of contemporary artillery theorists, such as Du Teil, who were using the new mobility of guns to achieve heavy concentration of fire, and whose teaching shaped the mind of that most successful of all artillery officers, Napoleon Bonaparte.[30]

Guibert departed further from Frederick, and approached nearer to the practice of the world war that was soon to come, in his low opinion of fortifications and magazines. Armies, he thought, should live by requisitions on the countries they occupied. War must support war, as in the best days of Rome; troops should be frugal, have few needs, carry short baggage trains, endure scarcity and hardship without complaint. The present French system, he says, by which civilians accompany an army to supervise its provisioning, is ruinous, for military decisions come to depend on the consent of civil officials who care more about protecting supplies than about fighting the enemy. An army that travels light, living on the country, will gain new mobility, range of action, and power of surprise.[31]

The art of fortification, Guibert thought, had been greatly overvalued since Vauban. Fortresses would become less necessary with the abolition of the large magazines which it was one of their functions to protect. Building chains of forts made war more costly than necessary. Dispersing the troops in garrisons made armies larger than necessary. The turning of military operations into a series of sieges made wars needlessly long. Nor would Guibert admit that fortified points had any real defensive value against a highly mobile army of the kind he envisaged. "As if," he wrote, "bastions alone could defend the cities which they surround, as if the destiny of these cities does not depend on the quality and vigor of the troops which defend and support them; as if, in short, fortresses poorly defended would not turn to the exhaustion, disgrace and certain enslavement of the conquered peoples who were their builders and mas-

[30] Ibid., 1:97, 445-72.
[31] Ibid., 2:254-307.

ters." Forts, he concluded, should be few, very strong, and entirely auxiliary to strategic movement.[32]

To accelerate movement Guibert had available the recent invention
of the division. The divisional principle had not been carried very far in
1772, and Guibert failed to distinguish clearly between the new divisions
in the French army and the temporary division of forces practiced by
Frederick the Great. His doctrine, however, is clear, and marks an advance beyond Frederick. Frederick's usual aim was to divide his army
on the march in such a way that, upon reaching the enemy, the parts
would fall into place in a battle line planned in advance. The army
marched as it intended to fight. Guibert emancipated marching order
from this dependency on battle order. In marching, according to Guibert's
conception, each division constitutes a column. These columns, in separating on the march, move more rapidly, cover a wider theater, and
force the enemy to turn in a desired direction; for battle they concentrate,
never having lost the higher unity that makes them a single army. The
commander in chief, going ahead, surveys the field of prospective battle,
determines his battle tactics in the light of what he sees, and arranges
the placing of his divisions as they arrive upon the field. Battle becomes
more flexible than before, more exactly adapted to terrain and circumstance, more susceptible to guidance by the commanding general after
the armies are committed. Guibert credits Frederick with having used
such a system at Hohenfriedberg, but in truth the idea was more Napoleonic than Frederician.[33]

The net message of the *Essai général de tactique*, in a sentence, was
to call for a new kind of army, ideally a people's army, but in any case
an army made more mobile by living on the country, more free to act
because released from fortified points, more readily maneuverable because organized in divisions. With such an army the old war of position
would yield to a war of movement. "In proportion as we fought more
a war of movements, we should get away from the present routine, return
to smaller and less overburdened armies, and seek less for what are called
'positions,' for positions should never be anything but a last resource for
a mobile and well commanded army. When an army knows how to
maneuver, and wants to fight, there are few positions that it cannot attack
from the rear or cause to be evacuated by the enemy. Positions, in a
word, are good to take only when one has reason not to try to act." And
he sketches the lightning war that Bonaparte was to practice. A good
general, he says, will ignore "positions" in the old-fashioned sense. "I

[32] Ibid., 2:208-20.
[33] Ibid., 2:15-88.

say that a general who, in this matter, shakes off established prejudices will throw his enemy into consternation, stun him, give him no chance to breathe, force him to fight or to retreat continuously before him. But such a general would need an army differently constituted from our armies today, an army which, formed by himself, was prepared for the new kind of operations which he would require it to perform."[34] The Revolution was to produce this new kind of army.

Unfortunately for his reputation as a prophet, Guibert's second important work on military science, the *Défense du système de guerre moderne*, published in 1779, explicitly repudiated the main ideas of the *Essai*. "When I wrote that book," he said, "I was ten years younger. The vapors of modern philosophy heated my head and clouded my judgment."[35] In addition, after becoming famous by the *Essai*, he had met Frederick, traveled through Germany, broken into society, been hailed as an expert, and become more contented with the world.

The "modern system" that the *Défense* tries to vindicate is simply the warfare of the day as contrasted with the warfare of classical antiquity. It is the conservative military technique of 1779. The body of the book deals with only one aspect of this "modern" war: the relative merits, debated for a generation, of column and line in the combat tactics of infantry. Guibert took the conservative side, defending the line, or principle of firepower, against the column, or principle of shock assault. To the body of this discussion Guibert added a final chapter, "The present system of war examined in relation to politics and administration." Here came the great recantation.

He will now have none of the idea of a citizen army. Citizen forces, while Guibert wrote, were fighting British and Hessian professionals in America. Many European officers watched the spectacle with interest; Lafayette, Berthier, Jourdan, and Gneisenau were to bring back from America some favorable ideas on patriot-soldiers and open fighting formations. Guibert insists that ex-civilians can never stand against professionals, and attributes the success of the Americans entirely to the incompetence of the British. No modern state, he says, could possibly take the risk of using citizen levies, which were all very well for the ancients, among whom maneuvers were simple and firearms unknown, but which every nation of Europe has outgrown and discarded, except Turkey and Poland—and Poland is in ruins. In these contexts the word "citizen" meant hardly more than "inhabitant."[36]

[34] Ibid., 2:249-54.
[35] *Défense du systéme de guerre moderne*, in *Oeuvres militaires du comte de Guibert*, 4:212.
[36] Ibid., 4:219-31.

Guibert also praises "modern," that is professional, war for the mild and even innocuous character which in the *Essai* was a main charge against it. Nowadays, he observes, a conquered country escapes the horrors of revenge and destruction, but "any country defended by its inhabitants must inevitably experience this kind of calamity." It is more humane for peoples to remain spectators to warlike violence. The emphasis on fortified positions, with all the subtleties of formalized maneuver, "may be an abuse . . . but certainly results advantageously for the tranquillity of nations and security of empires." The relative equality of training, discipline, resources, and talent among the military powers creates a salutary balance. So much the less, therefore, "will wars be decisive and consequently disastrous to the nations; the less possibility will there be of conquest, the fewer subjects of temptation for ambitious rulers, and the fewer revolutions of empires." Thus ends the thought of the *Défense*. It is scarcely distinguishable from that of Frederick the Great.[37]

Guibert, in both his books, glimpsed the difference between limited and unlimited war, or between the clashes of professional soldiers and the destructive struggles of peoples. He saw the close relation between warfare and the structure of government. His inconsistency was not logical but moral, an inconsistency of attitude, not of analysis. At twenty-nine, he looked upon the ideas of national armies and blitzkrieg strategy with favor. At thirty-five he looked upon these same ideas with disapproval. At neither time did he show much practical foresight, as distinguished from lucky predictions, or any sense that the ideas that he favored in 1772 and rejected in 1779 would become realities for the generation then alive.

Before concluding the *Défense* Guibert took a parting shot at the *philosophes*, who sometimes showed pacifist inclinations, or at least objected to the wars fought by governments then existing. "To declaim against war," he said, ". . . is to beat the air with vain sounds, for ambitious, unjust or powerful rulers will certainly not be restrained by such means. But what may result, and what must necessarily result, is to extinguish little by little the military spirit, to make the government less interested in this important branch of administration, and some day to deliver up one's own nation, softened and disarmed—or, what amounts to the same thing, badly armed and not knowing how to use arms—to the yoke of warlike nations which may be less civilized but which have more judgment and prudence."[38] Here too was a prophecy for France.

[37] Ibid., 4:263-75.
[38] Ibid., 4:213.

112

It was a warning not needed in the eighteenth century, however, for of the ideas of the *philosophes* it was not pacifism that was to prevail.

III

In 1793 the revolutionary French Republic faced a coalition of Great Britain, Holland, Prussia, Austria, Sardinia, and Spain. Of peoples living under one government the French were the most numerous and perhaps the most wealthy. A Committee of Public Safety, to meet the crisis, exploited their military potentialities in a way never possible under the Old Regime. Freed from the old special rights, local and class privileges, internal barriers and exclusive monopolies that had encumbered the monarchy, the Committee created a war economy by dictatorial methods, stimulated the national self-consciousness of the population, and introduced the principle of universal military service in the *levée en masse*. In this, the political side of warfare, the revolutionists were conscious of bringing about a new military order. They were less conscious of innovating in technical and strategic matters. Carnot's strategic ideas were rather old-fashioned.[39] Yet in leaving their armies to be supplied by requisitions rather than magazines the Republicans effected a revolution in logistics, and in throwing their half-trained troops into battle in rushing columns or in fanned-out lines of *tirailleurs*, men who fought, fired, and took cover as individuals, they broke away from the Frederician system of solid battalions, and gave impetus to a revolution in tactics.

By 1794 the French took the offensive. In 1795 Prussia, Holland, and Spain withdrew from the war. In 1796 Bonaparte dropped into Italy out of the mountains. By 1797 the continent was at peace, and England negotiated. In 1798 war was resumed with the Second Coalition. In 1799 Bonaparte became autocrat of France. In 1800 he destroyed the Second Coalition, winning, again by lightning operations in Italy, the first of his great, quick, decisive "Napoleonic" battles—Marengo.

A revolution had occurred in the art of war. Its significance dawned only gradually on observers. Certain civilians, Mallet du Pan and Gentz, for example, perceived some of the deeper causes sooner than professional soldiers. This is because the most fundamental change was in the political premises of military organization, in that new *Weltbild* whose coming, according to Delbrück, was necessary to the revolutionizing of warfare. In France the professional soldiers in these years were too busy in action to write treatises on what they were doing. In Germany Scharnhorst edited a journal and published piecemeal studies of events, and Gneisenau

---

[39] R. Warschauer, *Studien zur Entwicklung der Gedanken Lazare Carnots über Kriegführung* (Berlin, 1937).

in a Silesian garrison town attempted to train his company according to more realistic, less mechanical principles; both were reeducating themselves in their profession, and both came forward after 1806 to rebuild the Prussian army. The military writers most in the public eye, in the years just before and just after 1800—Behrenhorst, Bülow, Hoyer, Venturini—seemed for a while to learn nothing from the facts before them. It is most instructive to dwell upon Bülow.[40]

Freiherr Heinrich Dietrich von Bülow, like the count de Guibert, was a minor aristocrat with a modicum of experience in the army. To earn a living he wrote books on many subjects. He proved to be as erratic as Guibert, and even more pathologically egotistical. He repelled everyone by his claims to unrecognized wisdom, offended the Russians during the period of the Prusso-Russian alliance, was adjudged insane, and died in 1807 in confinement at Riga. He has since been called everything from a conceited crank to the founder of modern military science.[41]

His first military treatise, the *Geist des neuern Kriegssystems*, appeared in 1799, won great favor, and was soon translated into French and English. Geopoliticists today see in it a step in the development of their subject. Bülow concluded his book with reflections on political "space." He declared (contrary to Frederick) that, because of the modern military system, the age of small states was over. He held that state power tended to fill a certain area, and beyond that area to be ineffective; hence each power had natural frontiers; the attainment of these frontiers would produce a political balance and lasting peace, since each power would then have reached the natural limits of its action. There would be, he said, about a dozen states in Europe: the British Isles; France extending to the Meuse; a North Germany gathered around Prussia, reaching from the Meuse to Memel; a South Germany looking to Austria, which in turn would extend its borders down the Danube perhaps to the Black Sea; a united Italy; a united Iberian peninsula; Switzerland; Turkey; Russia; Sweden; and probably, though not necessarily, an independent Holland and an independent Denmark.[42]

This was a surprisingly good anticipation of the map of Europe as it came to be by 1870. It was scarcely grounded on an accurate perception of the military situation in 1799. *Der Geist des neuern Kriegssystems* showed no real understanding of the wars of the Revolution. Only in

[40] J. Mallet Du Pan, *Considérations sur la nature de la révolution de France* (London, 1793); F. Gentz, *Von dem politischen Zustande von Europa vor und nach der französischen Revolution* (1801); and see Jähns, *Geschichte*, under the names cited.

[41] Jähns, *Geschichte*, 3:2133-45.

[42] R. Strausz-Hupé, *Geopolitics: The Struggle for Space and Power* (New York, 1942), 14-21; H. D. v. Bülow, *The Spirit of the Modern System of War* (London, 1806), 187-285.

the new open formation of *tirailleurs*, that is, only in infantry tactics, did Bülow find any significant innovation.[43] He is credited with clarifying terminology, by giving currency, as words of distinct meaning, to the terms "strategy," "tactics," and "base of operations," though his definitions were not generally accepted. But the thesis of his book was a codification of obsolescent ideas.

Bülow's "modern system," like Guibert's, was simply the system developed since the seventeenth century. He claimed, however, to have discovered the true key to this system in the concept of the base of operations. He held also (as if they were new) to old notions of the geometry of war. The "base of operations" in his system must be a fortified line of prepared magazines; the two "lines of operations" projected from the ends of this base must converge upon the point under attack at an angle of at least ninety degrees. The attacking army must not move by more than three days' march from its magazines. The general should have as his principal objective, not attack on the enemy force, but the security of his own service of supply; and in offensive operations he should concentrate not against the enemy army, but against the enemy's supplies. Fighting should be avoided. A victorious general should refrain from pushing his advantage, "stopping judiciously in the midst of triumphs." Modern battles decide nothing; an enemy defeated on the battlefield can always attack again in a few days.[44]

The unreality of these conceptions had been shown as early as 1794, when the French cavalry rode into Amsterdam on the ice. The battles of Hohenlinden and Marengo, a few months after the publication of Bülow's book, came as an answer to his "system." This campaign opened his eyes. He wrote a book on it, perversely insisting that the French victories gave proof of his doctrine but in reality contradicting much of what he had said before. He learned, but he learned very reluctantly.

Marengo, said Bülow, in less than a month "has decided the destiny of the French Revolution and hence of humanity in Europe." Mobility is the secret of French success. Before a mobile army most fortifications are shown to be useless. Mobility and audacity are made possible by reduction of baggage trains and emancipation from magazines. Bonaparte, he observes, crossed the Alps with no food but biscuit, a compact, durable, portable nutriment that needs no cooking; and he arrived in Italy with a hungry army, planning to live on the country. How all this harmonized with the theory of the "base of operations" with its comfortable ninety-degree angle, Bülow failed to make clear, though he ar-

[43] Bülow, *Spirit of the Modern System*, 109ff.
[44] Ibid., passim, but see pp. 1-25, 81-82, 108, 183-84.

gued the matter at great length. He noted, as a source of the new boldness of action, the new type of personnel in the French army. The Austrian officers, he said, owe their positions to seniority. Their talents are average. "With the fermentation inseparable from revolution there have appeared in France men who in time of calm would not even have suspected what they were capable of. This sudden deployment of transcendent abilities is one of the first causes to which the marked superiority of the French in this war must be ascribed."[45]

Even with these explanations Bülow could not understand a blitzkrieg that astounded Europe. He called the French victory a portent, a miracle, a message from Providence. He became Bonapartist and pro-French. This made his position increasingly awkward as the national movement swept over Germany, and no doubt accentuated his paranoid inclinations.

Then came the campaign of 1805. In that year Austria and Russia joined with Great Britain in the Third Coalition. The two Continental powers moved large armies westward. In these armies centered the highest hopes of aristocratic Europe. Seldom has disappointment been so swift. Bonaparte in a few days marched several army corps from coastal points to South Germany. There, at Ulm, he forced General Mack, reputed to be a master strategist, to surrender thirty thousand men without serious fighting. Moving on to Vienna and into Moravia, he found the combined Austro-Russian forces eager to attack. He routed them at the village of Austerlitz.

Bülow immediately wrote a two-volume work on the campaign, published in the anxious months after Austerlitz, during which the Prussian state, having conducted a two-faced diplomacy, moved as if hypnotized toward the disaster of Jena. Bülow had to publish this work privately. It was too dangerous for anyone to touch but himself and it led to his ruin. A strange and contradictory book, it reflected both his own mental unbalance and the general bewilderment of Europe. He wrote as one convinced that he alone saw the truth, that ignored though he was he must in duty give everyone advice, impelled by Kant's categorical imperative—metaphysics and military thought have gone together in Germany. He announced that he was destined to create a new theory of war, to be known as *Bülowisch*, by which all future officers would be formed. He berated Frederick the Great and the Frederician system, demanding the kind of regeneration that until Jena Prussia was not willing to undergo. Yet he said, too, that reform was hopeless, that Napoleon was

[45] H. D. v. Bülow, *Histoire de la campagne de 1800 en Allemagne et en Italie* (Paris, 1804), 4-5, 16, 90, 92, 142ff., 183.

about to unify Europe by war, and that the Continental powers should accept his supremacy. Austerlitz, said Bülow, was the modern Actium.[46]

Bülow saw in the French victory of 1805 a proof of the doctrine of Guibert. He used a metaphor from business. The great art in war, he said, is to get the most out of one's capital, not to scatter an army in garrisons but to keep the whole of it constantly in circulation. Napoleon, more than others, "keeps his capital active." This was to recognize the obsolescence of the old war of position. At Ulm Mack had a strong army in a powerful position. Napoleon nevertheless forced him to surrender. He did it by applying Guibert's principles: skillful manipulation of the divisions (facilitated by the Napoleonic innovation of the army corps); physical dispersal of these divisions for speed in marching, and to cover a larger theater of action, without loss of unity of conception; simultaneous reconcentration at the objective with adoption of battle positions in the light of concrete local conditions. The result, according to Bülow, was "the most perfect manifestation of the superiority of strategy over tactics in modern war."[47]

As more depended on strategy and comparatively less on tactics, the problems of supreme command took on a hitherto unknown complexity and scope. Battle lost some of the element of pure chance that Frederick had feared in it, and that before the Revolution had served as a deterrent to aggressive operations. It became rather the test of elaborate preparations made long beforehand. Planning became more fruitful, prediction somewhat more possible, warfare more of a "science." Military command shaded into diplomatic relations on the one hand, and into domestic policy and constitutional practice on the other. On these matters Bülow had much to say.

Bülow, like Frederick, insisted on the need of a single unifying intelligence at the head of a state. He held that under modern conditions of strategy there could be no separation between politics and war—great soldiers must understand foreign affairs, as successful diplomats must understand military action. Of the advantage of uniting foreign policy and military responsibility in one mind Napoleon's career was an example and the fumbling of the Allied governments a kind of negative demonstration. A firm guiding intelligence also became more necessary with modern conditions of technology. The supreme command must rise above the specialists and the experts. The technique of fortification, the theory of artillery fire, military medicine, logistics, said Bülow, are only "preparatory sciences." "The science of employing all these things fittingly

---

[46] H. D. v. Bülow, *Der Feldzug von 1805, militärisch-politisch betrachtet*, 2 vols. (auf Kosten des Verfassers [Leipzig], 1806), 1:i-lxxvi; 2:158.
[47] Ibid., 1:lviii-lix; 2:xxxiv, 109.

for the strengthening and defense of society is true military science." This is the real business of generalship. "Hear this plainly: when a chief of state is obliged to leave the guidance of the state's energies in war to a squad of mere specialists trained in the preparatory sciences, the inevitable outcome will be fragmentation and cross-purposes, of which the first result will be weakness—a stable full of calves and donkeys—and the end result dissolution; because the binding power of intelligence is missing, which unites the materials in one building, or in one purpose." Here again the lesson was driven home by the contrast between Napoleon and every other ruler of Europe.[48]

On manpower, or the constitution of armies, Bülow had views not at all flattering to contemporary Prussia. He upbraided the Prussian government for blindly maintaining the Frederician system, of which he said even Frederick saw the weaknesses before his death—a system that left the common people demoralized and uneducated, subject to a discipline that violated the rights of man. He recommended the French system of universal conscription with its nationalistic effect on morale. "Even if we take a purely utilitarian view, an army could be regarded as the most general educational establishment for youth." Military science must face "a weighty matter of internal administration, the inspiring and rewarding of virtues and talents." Prussia, he observes, has produced few men of genius; yet resources are wasted unless able men control them. So Bülow calls for a policy of careers open to talent, and offers Napoleon's Legion of Honor as a model. He proposed a *Bund der Tugend*, in which men should be graded by intelligence, judgment and utility to the state, and which, at least ideally, should efface the old aristocratic distinctions.[49]

All these ideas remained unassembled in Bülow's mind. He never attained that firmness of grasp and singleness of purpose that he recognized as essential to leadership. It is impossible to say what he felt his own aims to be. He seemed to favor the French Revolution, and spoke well of the rights of man; yet he was less a liberal than Gneisenau, to name another professional soldier for comparison. He called himself a Prussian patriot, but he despised Frederick, and said that Prussia by its very existence had ended the national existence of Germany. Sometimes he spoke as a German nationalist, but he remained stubbornly pro-French. Sometimes he favored a balance of power; again, he professed not to care whether the sovereigns of Europe maintained their independence. He certainly was a crusader, to what end is not clear. He was a vehement reformer but held reform to be a chimera. He was a kind of

[48] Ibid., 1:5-20.
[49] Ibid., 2:xviii-xxxii, 131-136; H. D. v. Bülow, *Neue Taktik der Neuern* (Leipzig, 1805), 48.

transcendental philosopher in military science, enjoying a sense of duty for its own sake without specifying its object. On the practical level, he advised Prussia, and all Europe, to come to terms with Napoleon after Austerlitz; he said that a Fourth Coalition would be useless and urged the Continent to join with the French emperor for the humiliation of England. His attitude after Jena was simply, "I told you so."

Bülow by 1807 had given cause to the Prussian government to regard him as a madman, or at least as a nuisance in time of public disaster. He seemed to write for no purpose except to air his own views and the worst that can be said of the officials who sent him to prison, given the catastrophic conditions of 1807, is that in perceiving his faults they failed to recognize his merits. He was too irresponsible, vain, and vague to collaborate in the practical work of reconstruction. The world lost no Scharnhorst with his death.

As a theorist, he had the merit of sensing, though slowly and confusedly, the nature of the military revolution of his time. This revolution was not based on technology, despite important improvements in artillery; nor was it primarily a revolution of strategy in the strict sense, despite the heightened mobility and striking power of an army emancipated from magazines and organized in divisions. The military revolution was at bottom a political revolution. The driving force of the French was their new *politisches Weltbild*. This consisted in the fusion of government and people which the Revolution had effected. On the one hand the people, in a way not possible before 1789, felt that they participated in the state, that they derived great advantages from their government, and therefore should fight for it loyally and with passion. On the other hand the government, ruling by the authority of the nation and invoking its sovereign power, could draw upon human and material resources in a way not dreamed of by Frederick the Great. More temporary advantages of the French were revolutionary fanaticism and missionary zeal. The net result was that, after 1793, the wealth, manpower and intelligence of France were hurled against Europe with an effectiveness that for a time was irresistible. During the nineteenth century the fundamental principle, the fusion of government and people, which may or may not be democratic, was built into the political system of most European states. The wars of kings were over; the wars of peoples had begun.

The Expansion of War

5. Napoleon and the Revolution in War

PETER PARET

I N T H E L A T E summer of 1805 the further expansion of France appeared to have been checked. The failure of the French navy to control the Channel even for a few days rendered England secure from invasion. Austria was concentrating substantial forces north of Venice, in the Tyrol, and in southern Germany to block any French threat to central Europe, perhaps even to take the offensive itself to regain northern Italy. From Poland the first Russian divisions were moving to Austria's assistance, and in the north, Prussia—courted by the czar, although still neutral—was mobilizing. The combined strength of the Third Coalition, if not yet wholly operational, promised to create the basis for a new European balance of power.

On August 23, Napoleon changed his military objective. The 176,000 men of the *Grande Armée* left the Channel coast, crossed the Rhine in the last week of September, advanced on the Danube, their way through southern Germany smoothed by alliances hurriedly negotiated, and threatened the Austrian lines of communication to Vienna and to the Russian army in Moravia. The Austrian forward position at Ulm was enveloped; on October 19, 33,000 men surrendered. Without fighting a major battle, the Grande Armée entered Vienna on November 13, and continued beyond the city to reach the now united Austrians and Russians before reinforcements would make them too strong to attack. On December 2, Napoleon destroyed the Allied army at Austerlitz. Three weeks later the Peace of Pressburg detached Austria from the Third Coalition, ceded Venetia to France, and made France dominant in central Europe.

These events had no parallel in earlier wars. The magnitude of the opposing armies was merely unusual; but the speed and sweep of French operations were unique, as was the emperor's handling of diplomacy and force to destroy within a matter of months the traditional checks and balances on the Continent. The shock to governments and soldiers was profound; its effect can still be traced in the discouragement and confusions of the following year, which contributed to the destruction of the Prussian army at Jena and Auerstedt, and helped carry French power to the borders of Russia.

Subsequent observers found the outcome of the campaign of 1805 less surprising. In *On War*, Clausewitz took note of the "flimsy web of scientific but extremely feeble strategic schemes," which radiated from the Austrian position at Ulm, and commented that such a net might have caught generals schooled in the cautious maneuvers of the eighteenth century; "but it was not strong enough for Bonaparte, Emperor of the Revolution."[1] These words reveal the ultimate sources of the shock that had stunned Europe: the genius of one man, who also, as "Emperor of the Revolution," personified, and profited from, the unique fusion of social, political, and military elements brought about by the overthrow of the Old Regime in France.

I

The French Revolution coincided with a revolution in war that had been under way through the last decades of the monarchy. Soon the two meshed. Profound changes in military institutions and practice, some already firmly established under the Old Regime, others still tentative and experimental, were adopted by the Revolution, and developed further. By infusing them with its dynamic, and linking them with its frequently violent domestic and foreign policies, the Revolution expanded the scope of these innovations. The army, its requirements and values, gained new importance in French life, which eventually was reflected in the rise to supreme political power of a soldier; but already under the Convention and the Directory domestic policy and foreign expansion went hand in hand. At the same time the military revolution ceased to be a purely French phenomenon. The wars waged by a succession of French governments from 1792 on ensured that not only political and social change, but military change as well, spread across Europe.

The most important of these innovations, whose French antecedents lay less in the practices of the monarchy than in the military and political literature of the late Enlightenment, was the gradual adoption by the Convention of a policy that at least in theory approached universal conscription. It produced a great increase in the number of soldiers, which lent new weight to French foreign policy, and enabled French commanders to fight more aggressive and costly campaigns, and to fight more of them. The expanding and increasingly sophisticated military administration of the last decades of the monarchy was available to equip, train, and maintain the new forces. The outcome of the intense debate on infantry tactics since the Seven Years' War, the "mixed" system of skirmishers, march and attack columns, and linear formations, was found

---

[1] Carl von Clausewitz, *On War*, trans. and ed. Michael Howard and Peter Paret, rev. ed. (Princeton, 1984), bk. 6, ch. 30, p. 518.

by trial and error to suit the Revolutionary armies best. The reform of the royal artillery by Gribeauval, Du Teil, and others from the 1760s on gave Revolutionary France the most efficient and mobile artillery in the world. For the first time infantry could be closely supported by field guns in all phases of combat, which significantly increased the striking power of the French armies. Supplying the now very large number of troops in the field was made possible in part by the only break with eighteenth-century practice for which the Revolution was responsible: compelling the soldier to requisition, on the principle that *la guerre nourrit la guerre.* "To know . . . how to draw supplies of all kinds from the country you occupy," Napoleon wrote at the apex of his success, "makes up a large part of the art of war."[2]

The system of living off the country was facilitated by the institutionalization of a development that reached back to the Seven Years' War, and was to be fundamental to Napoleon's strategy and his conduct of battle: the breaking up of the formerly unitary army into permanent divisions and corps, combining infantry, cavalry, artillery, and support services. On campaign these large subunits usually moved on separate roads, each responsible for its own area, but capable of mutual support. The extended army covered much ground, which made it easier to maintain, but also, and primarily, enabled its component parts to move more rapidly, gave them greater flexibility, and multiplied the commander in chief's operational choices. The expansion of his staff, and the proliferation of subordinate staffs, already under way in the last campaigns of the Old Regime, made possible the control of constantly larger and more widely dispersed forces. These and other innovations broke with the assumptions, techniques, and practices of generations of European soldiers. They radically changed the conduct of war between 1792 and 1815, and established patterns that remained influential throughout the nineteenth century, and beyond.

But although the effect of the revolution in war on the Wars of the Revolution was dramatic, it was not as immediately conclusive as might be assumed. Against opponents who mobilized only a segment of their forces and who, after the failure of the Duke of Brunswick's politico-military expedition at Valmy in 1792, fought merely for limited aims, the new France more than held its own. Soon French armies had overrun the Austrian Netherlands and pushed far into the Rhineland. But since they suffered almost as many defeats as they gained victories, it cannot

[2] *Correspondance de Napoléon Ier* (Paris, 1857-70), vol. 12, no. 9944, to Joseph Bonaparte, March 8, 1806. The formulation "war feeds [or 'must feed'] war," used frequently during the Revolution, can also be found in Napoleon's writings; for instance, "Mémoire sur l'armée d'Italie" (July 1795), *Correspondance*, vol. 1, no. 49.

be said that the military results clearly favored the new methods. In part this was because the political events since 1789 had seriously disorganized the country's military institutions. It was difficult to expand the royal army quickly, and to transform it into a force that was both efficient and loyal to the new government. Much trial and error was needed to master the various elements of the military revolution and to learn how to integrate them in the field. In the meantime the performance of the French armies was uneven. It Italy in 1796 the new system for the first time scored a decisive and seemingly irreversible success. By then universal conscription had made the French army by far the largest in Europe and also the easiest to keep up to strength, and many of its officers and rank and file had become accustomed to the new organization, administration, and tactics. Yet even now the revolution in war did not sweep all before it. The War of the Second Coalition, which in the Mediterranean opened with Napoleon's evasion of the British fleet and his landing in Egypt, began on the European continent with a sequence of French defeats. By the summer of 1799 Napoleon's conquests of 1796 had been lost; all of Italy except the Riviera was again in Allied hands, and the Austrians again controlled southern Germany. If in the end the French triumphed, it was only after very hard fighting. Their conduct of war was undoubtedly superior to the old system; but even with the experience of a dozen campaigns it was a qualified, not an absolute, superiority.

The ambiguous efforts of the revolution in war justify our asking what might have been the course of subsequent events had Napoleon not assumed power. No doubt such speculations are of limited value, but weighing alternatives that did not come to pass may on occasion help us see the historical reality more clearly. All that we know of Napoleon's most competent colleagues and rivals—such men as Carnot, Jourdan, Hoche, Masséna, and Moreau—suggests that had Napoleon been killed before Toulon or captured off the coast of Crete on his way to Egypt, France would have ceased or at least slowed its efforts to destroy the European balance of power. Without his insistence on the immense exertions demanded by Europe-wide wars, the government would probably have been content with securing France's "natural" frontiers—in itself a very considerable expansion of French territory. Had further wars been waged—particularly if the fighting had taken place far from France—the record of the senior French commanders indicates that they would have been defeated as often as not. The Revolution and the transformation of war would still have left France the most powerful country in Europe, but a country integrated in the political community, rather than dominating and, indeed, almost abolishing it.

Instead Napoleon recognized the full potential of the revolution in war, discovered how its components could be made to work together—

in Clausewitz's words, he corrected the technical imperfections of the innovations that until then had limited their effectiveness—and by placing the resources of France in the service of the new system for a time gave it absolute superiority.[3]

II

Napoleon, the scion of a minor noble family who rose in the army of the Republic, personifies the military revolution, with its roots in the Old Regime, and its intensification by the events after 1789. Not a reformer himself, he made use of the work of reformers that the new leaders had not completely understood or had not been able to exploit fully. To give two examples: from the Consulate on, conscription was applied more regularly and broadly than in the earlier 1790s. The separation of the army into largely self-sufficient commands, which in the Revolutionary Wars often meant the fragmentation of effort, was continued by Napoleon; but he imposed much firmer central control on the dispersed commands, and infused them with his faith in rapid movement and the offensive. The result was a new mobility, which made possible the concentration of superior force at the decisive point.[4]

If Napoleon used existing institutions and methods, his strategy also, in one sense, owed much to others. In the words of the most knowledgeable and profound student of Napoleonic war, Jean Colin, whose analyses still directly or indirectly inform all serious work in the field: "If we take Napoleon's most brilliant projects, and compare them with the corresponding plans of his opponents, we shall hardly perceive a difference." And again: "Napoleon's contemporaries understood as well as he did the advantage of turning or outflanking the opponent"[5] At times it was not so much what Napoleon did or tried to do in a campaign or battle that made the difference, as how he did it, and how he used battle as the focus and climax of the simple but far-reaching strategic schemes that the revolution in war enabled him to carry out. "The art of war is simple," he still believed at the end of his life; "everything is a matter of execution."[6]

Napoleon never wrote a comprehensive account of his ideas on war.

---

[3] Clausewitz, On War, bk. 8, ch. 3B, p. 592.

[4] On St. Helena, criticizing the actions of a French general during the 1799 campaign in Switzerland, Napoleon condemned the dispersal of forces as a vicious habit that made it impossible to achieve important results. He added, "But that was the fashion in those days: always [fight] in little packets" (Charles Tristan de Montholon, Récits de la captivité de l'empereur Napoléon [Paris, 1847], 2:432-33).

[5] Jean Colin, The Transformations of War, trans. L. H. R. Pope-Hennessy (London, 1912) 253, 290. I have retranslated the quoted passages, since the original English version is both stilted and inexact.

[6] "Oeuvres de Sainte-Hélène, Événements des six premiers mois de 1799," Correspondance, 30:263. See also ibid., 289.

To learn his thoughts on the organization and administration of armies, on the conduct of campaigns, and on the function of war in the relation between states, we must look to other kinds of evidence: his policies and actions, and his extensive if diverse writings, ranging from memoranda, orders, and official correspondence to retrospective appraisals, historical discussions, and the various memoirs he dictated on St. Helena to justify himself in the eyes of his contemporaries and of future generations. His evaluation of events and individuals could change markedly as he transformed his recollections into legend, but his views of war itself varied little after his first campaign. This consistency did not always extend to his choice of words. He might speak of first principles or of fundamental elements of war—though these themselves could differ according to the occasion; but by "principle" or "rule" he did not mean exactly defined elements in a systematic theory, the validity of which he denied in any case. Rather such terms as *un principe général* or *une grande règle de la guerre* simply lent added authority to a recognition arrived at by experience and inspired common sense. The one concept that invariably dominated his actions was to be as strong for battle as possible, even if this meant leaving secondary bases and his communications unguarded. Inevitably he often misinterpreted enemy intentions or actions in particular situations, misjudged the possibilities of his own troops, and especially in later years could be deceived by his hopes and gigantic ambition. But these errors and weaknesses did nothing to limit or blur his understanding of war, which was always distinguished by a profound and brutal appreciation of its reality.

An attempt to draw the salient characteristics of Napoleon's conduct of war from his actions and reflections may appropriately begin with the political context and purpose, proceed to strategy and battle, and conclude with some comments on Napoleon's personal qualities of leadership.

The fact that all wars result from political decisions and express a political intent—whether or not the politics are realistic and may be regarded as desirable—does not mean that any particular war is necessarily appropriate for implementing the policy it serves. Historically, governments and their military advisors and commanders have found it difficult and often impossible to decide on such aspects of the relationship between foreign policy and war as the proportion of resources to be mobilized, or the manner in which they should be employed. Even as a junior officer these fundamental issues occupied Napoleon far more than did such purely military matters as the training of soldiers or their tactical employment. The German historian Hans Delbrück believed that despite Napoleon's strategic vision and his genius in the conduct of battles, his innate talents were those of a statesman even more than of a soldier.[7] But his statesmanship was of an unusually aggressive, warlike kind. He did not regard war as an emergency measure, a measure of last resort with which to repair the failures of diplomacy; instead it was the central element of his foreign policy.

Unless compelled by circumstance, Napoleon never pursued major policy goals with inadequate military resources. He refused to fall into the error the Austrians committed against him in Italy in 1796 and 1797, mobilizing only a segment of the forces available, mobilizing, a second segment after the first had been defeated, and then a third. Had they operated in force from the beginning, they might have overpowered even him. On the contrary, he believed in the fullest employment of all means available. Major goals, and resources mobilized to achieve them, were always as well balanced as was possible. His political and military strategy suffered from a different weakness. He found it difficult to fight limited wars with limited means; a war such as that between Austria and Prussia in 1778, in which not a single battle was fought, went against his nature. In his hands all conflicts tended to become unlimited, because openly or by implication they threatened the continued independent existence of his antagonists.

That for fifteen years he was both head of state and supreme commander, with few if any restrictions placed on his freedom of action, was certainly conducive to the closest integration of policy and war. The unity of political and military authority eliminated the friction at the top that otherwise was inevitable. Above all it facilitated quick decisions and their rapid implementation, and made possible the startling flexibility with which he adjusted his diplomacy to the shifting military situation, increasing his demands or showing a willingness to compromise as he saw fit. Unity of command did not, of course, guarantee sound policy. In Napoleon's later years the absence of checks and balances in his one-man rule led to critical errors, and in the end brought down the Empire. But until the invasion of Russia, the emperor's comprehensive authority gave him an advantage over opponents who could not develop a system of politico-military command capable of matching the quickening pace of modern war.

Nowhere was Napoleon's integration of diplomacy and violence more effective than in the manner in which he pursued the traditional goal of politically isolating a prospective opponent. Even if he could not prevent the formation of alliances against France—largely because his ultimate intentions were too transparent—he still played on the special

[7] Hans Delbrück, *Geschichte der Kriegskunst*, new ed. (Berlin, 1962), 4:494.

interests of one or the other partner in order to delay the linkup of Allied forces in the field. In 1805 diplomatic representatives coupled with the astonishingly rapid advance of the Grande Armée from France to Bavaria enabled him to capture an Austrian army while Russian troops were still hundreds of miles to the east. In December of that year, having seduced Prussia into neutrality, he defeated the Austrians and Russians. In 1806 England and Russia watched as the Prussian army was destroyed. The following spring he defeated the Prussian remnants and their Russian allies while Austria was still arming; and in 1809 Austria was once more defeated while potential supporters were still debating whether to come to its aid.

If it proved impossible for Napoleon to prevent the appearance of the forces of two or more allies in the same theater of operations, their point of junction or possible junction still afforded valuable opportunities to his recognition of political and military interaction. The presence of armies of different states raised all the political and operational difficulties of divided command. "One bad general would be better than two good ones," he wrote to Carnot during the first Italian campaign, an opinion he reiterated in nearly identical words on St. Helena.[8] In 1796 he opened the campaign that was to make his reputation with a deep strategic penetration, interposing his forces between the Sardinian and Austrian armies, and preventing their junction; this was followed by what some analysts have called a strategy of the central position, first knocking the Sardinians out of the war, and then turning on the Austrians. He adopted the same strategy in the Hundred Days, operating on interior lines between Blücher and Wellington to eliminate the Prussians before attacking the Anglo-Dutch army as soon as he believed it had been isolated. At Waterloo, as at Dego and Mondovi twenty years earlier, the political factor of the opposing alliance became an operational opportunity.

A complex variant of playing on the inherent difficulties of an allied force may be found in the Austerlitz campaign. By exploiting the Austrians' wish to reoccupy Vienna, Napoleon induced the main Austro-Russian army, its command structure and units too poorly integrated for effective cooperation, not to wait for the Russian and Austrian reinforcements that were approaching from north to south, but to launch a premature offensive, the direction of which, designed to cut off Napoleon from Vienna, reflected political rather than military considerations.

His own strategy always had a clear political purpose, but at least until the final years of his rule considerations of policy were not permitted

[8] *Correspondance*, vol. 1, no. 421, to Carnot, May 14, 1796; "Oeuvres de Sainte-Hélène, Campagnes d'Italie," ibid., 29:107.

to inhibit the most effective threat or application of force. On the contrary, Napoleon believed that the best method of reaching whatever political goal he sought was to reduce his opponent's power of resistance to the greatest extent possible. That meant above all to defeat the major enemy armies. The capture of fortresses, the occupation of terrain or of capitals only rarely had the same impact on the enemy's war-making potential as did the defeat of his field army. A severe defeat created a new situation—militarily by leading to further losses, withdrawals, and capitulations; politically, by maneuvering or forcing the opposing government into negotiations under newly unfavorable circumstances.

Napoleon's strategic plans—or more correctly, since he disliked the term's implications of a fixed, unchanging design, his strategic preparations—aimed at an overwhelming tactical decision, the major battle or battles that eliminated the opposing field army. In his greatest campaigns the climactic battle emerges naturally from long and rapid advances deep into enemy territory; but the advances were never directed at a particular location, a geographic objective. Rather they pushed a strong army so far forward that it could not be ignored but had to be fought. The aim of Napoleonic strategy was to bring about the threat or reality of the decisive battle. The campaign itself might either be launched from, or occupy, a central, interior position that would permit the piecemeal defeat of the opposing forces, or it took the form of a maneuver against the rear that enveloped the enemy's position and threatened his lines of communication.

An example of the daring and consequentiality with which the emperor pursued the decisive battle is the brief campaign of 1806, which proved to be a strategic triumph despite the fact that until nearly the end Napoleon remained uncertain of the Prussian army's position and intentions. That the two climactic battles of Jena and Auerstedt were fought on mistaken assumptions and could be won only by tactical improvisation underscores the strength of the basic concept.

Napoleon did not want to fight Prussia. The war came about because after its victories in 1805 France had achieved such dominance in central Europe that the existence of another major power in the area was no longer a practical possibility. When the Prussians mobilized and advanced south through Saxony to the Thuringian Forest, the major part of the French army was stationed along the Rhine and in southern Germany. In the first days of October Napoleon concentrated his forces between Bamberg and Würzburg, and began to move north, incidentally leaving his lines of communication to the Rhine almost unprotected. Essentially his plan of campaign consisted of mobilizing the greatest force possible, and then creating an opportunity for its exploitation by advancing on

131

Berlin. Should the Prussians take the offensive, they would be diverted by the need, or wish, to defend their capital, and once the armies met, French numerical superiority and greater mobility should decide the issue. Considering his far greater strength, an offensive from any direction promised success. But an advance from the west would have pushed the Prussians back on Berlin and toward possible Russian assistance, while an offensive from the south could be launched more rapidly and stood the chance of separating the main Prussian forces from their capital, supply bases, and the Russian frontier.

The Grande Armée, some 180,000 men, divided into three columns of two corps each, advanced on a front of thirty to forty miles, the columns near enough to support each other should the need arise. By October 12, this gigantic "battalion square," the name Napoleon employed to emphasize the ideal of coordination and mutual support that inspired the formation, had moved around and beyond the left flank of the Prussians, now slowly withdrawing north between Weimar and Jena, and cut the Prussian lines of communication to Leipzig, Halle, and Berlin. On the 13th Napoleon wheeled the greater part of his forces west against what he believed to be the main Prussian army, stationed on the heights beyond Jena, while ordering Davout, already some fifteen miles further north, to support the main French assault by striking at the enemy's rear. On the following day the two battles were fought with the fronts reversed, the French advancing from east to west. Contrary to his assumptions, Napoleon faced only a small part of the Prussian army, which he outnumbered almost two to one, while Davout, far from carrying out an enveloping attack, was himself attacked by the far stronger Prussian main army, which was trying to regain its lines of communication by forcing its way through the French. When Davout's 26,000 men held, the Prussians withdrew west, away from Berlin. They crossed the line of retreat of their other army, which had been defeated at Jena, and a very energetic French pursuit completed their disorganization and virtual destruction.

The enormous military power that Napoleon placed near the center of the Prussian state created a threat to which the Prussians had to respond. The result was a victory of exceptional magnitude. That after such a disaster Prussia nevertheless continued to fight for another eight months indicates both the expansion in warfare that the revolution in war had brought about, and one of its new limitations. The mobilization by the Republic and Empire of national resources and energies for war was beginning to evoke countermeasures of similar dimensions and intensity.

Strategy in the Napoleonic Era even more than today meant thinking and acting in an uncertain realm, in which the only ultimately reliable points of reference were the commander's understanding of the potentials and limitations of armed force and of national power. Napoleonic battle was also filled with uncertainty; but the commander possessed a surer knowledge than is possible in strategy of many of its components— terrain, strength, and position of his troops and the enemy's, often even the intentions of the other side. He also had direct and more comprehensive control over his forces than was possible during an advance of hundreds of miles by widely dispersed corps against an opponent whose position was known only in general terms. Napoleon lived near the end of the very long period in history in which during battle the commander might actually see most of his troops, as well as many of the enemy's. With the industrial revolution the character of battle changed: the battlefield expanded, the troops took to the ground, and the degree of visual control over their armies that Napoleon and Wellington still took for granted is exerted today at most by a sergeant over his few men.

If his opponent was markedly superior in numbers, Napoleon waged a frontal battle, if possible on terrain divided by such natural obstacles as streams that would inhibit the enemy's lateral movements, while his own forces were placed in a strong defensive position, with as many troops as could be spared kept in reserve. Once the enemy was committed along the entire front, the reserves, now the *masse de rupture*, would attack one part of the front, and having broken through move against the flanks and rear of the other sectors. If his forces were equal or superior to those of the enemy, he would attempt to outflank him by extending his front, or launch a flank attack with a separate corps. The latter, because of its deeper penetration, promised greater results, but was more difficult to achieve since communication and coordination between units separated by more than a few miles was unreliable. Outflanking movements were nothing unusual in the warfare of that time—or, indeed, of any time. Napoleon's opponents were as aware of their effectiveness as he was. But what proved the norm for him was more rarely attempted by them: a frontal encounter was technically easier to control, and offered less scope for the unforeseen. In this regard, as in many others, the real difference between Napoleon and the generals opposing him tended to be one of emphasis and psychological attitude.

Although Napleon sometimes stayed on the defensive until his opponent had committed and overextended himself, he preferred the attack. He disliked purely defensive battles; he knew the value of the initiative, and feared losing it. But whether offensive, defensive-offensive, or defensive—all battles posed complex problems of the use of time and space, and of the expenditure of force; of the morale, different resources, and conflicting missions of the opposing sides; and of the character and will

133

of the commanders. In the early nineteenth century these problems were still resolved not only by analyzing the secondary evidence—reading reports and studying maps—but by intervening in the directly perceived reality, by maneuvering the tens of thousands of men in one's field of vision. The concrete tasks of deploying these units of military energy, and of overcoming and destroying his opponents, whom he could see through the smoke of cannons and muskets, stimulated Napoleon's deepest concerns, and evoked his strongest psychic and intellectual responses. It was his sense of political and military conflict as another form of mechanics that could be mastered intellectually—"in war, time . . . is the great element between weight and force"—combined with his recognition and exploitation of the human emotions involved, that made him the greatest soldier of the age.[9]

The impact of his charisma and the belief in his absolute superiority extended from his troops and their officers and generals to his opponents. Wellington thought his presence was the equal of forty thousand soldiers. French troops miles from where he might be were ordered to shout *Vive l'Empereur!* to make the enemy believe he was facing them. In the fall of 1813 the war plan for the various allied armies in central Europe bluntly advised the withdrawal of any army against which he advanced. Clausewitz, who was convinced that no theory of war could be taken seriously unless it included the psychology of commanders and soldiers and their relations to one another, went so far as to state that not a victorious battle or successful campaign but restoring the morale of the army in Italy in 1796 was Napoleon's greatest achievement.[10]

III

Among the reasons for Napoleon's long run of victories was the difficulty his opponents experienced in understanding his way of fighting and in devising effective responses. Their uncertain perception is in large part explained by the nature of the revolution in war.[11] In most of its significant aspects this revolution, as we know, consisted not in sudden innovation but in the more general and forceful employment of institutions and methods that had existed for decades or had been extensively

[9] Napoleon's comparison of war and mechanics occurs in "Notes sur la défense de l'Italie" (January 14, 1809), ibid., vol. 28, no. 14707.
[10] Carl von Clausewitz, *Der Feldzug von 1796 in Italien* in *Hinterlassene Werke*, 10 vols. (Berlin 1832-37), 4:15.
[11] On the problem of perception, see this author's "Revolutions in Warfare: An Earlier Generation of Interpreters," in *National Security and International Stability*, ed. Bernard Brodie, Michael D. Intriligator, and Roman Kolkowicz (Cambridge, Mass., 1983); and "Napoleon as Enemy," *Proceedings of the Thirteenth Consortium on Revolutionary Europe*, ed. Clarence B. Davis (Athens, Ga., 1985).

discussed in the literature. In the long run this led to differences in substance, to a new kind of war; but at first it was not unreasonable to think that whatever changes were taking place were merely the expansion of the already familiar, and therefore would not demand radical adjustments in one's thought and actions. Two facts reinforced this outlook: the French were often defeated, consequently it was not self-evident that they should be copied. And some of their methods—universal conscription, open access to commissions, even systematically living off the land—could scarcely coexist with the values and conditions of the Old Regime. An objective military analysis of these methods was made much more difficult by the belief that to adopt them meant changing one's social and political system.

To the observant soldier it nevertheless became apparent that at least in some major respects warfare was changing. In the Wars of the First and Second Coalition the French employed new techniques on a grand scale, although for a time it remained unclear whether these were improvisations caused by the country's political turmoil, which would give way to traditional methods once conditions returned to normal. Other countries, too, were experimenting—with various forms of corps organization, for example, with enlarged and reorganized general staffs, with new systems of officer education; a vogue for light infantry swept much of military Europe. In this general turbulence, Napoleon did not at first stand apart. In the 1790s he could still be seen as an energetic, competent, and lucky general, whose manner of fighting did not significantly differ from that of other able commanders. It was not until Ulm and Austerlitz, a decade after his first appearance as a commanding general, that the essentials of his system were sufficiently documented and analyzed to become generally recognized.

In reaction to his success, but even more so in the train of nearly constant warfare since 1792, military institutions in much of Europe modernized to varying degrees. Some closely followed the French pattern—the armies of the new Confederation of the Rhine, and of the satellite kingdoms of Holland and Naples—others built on native traditions, stimulated and influenced by the French challenge—in particular the armies of the Hapsburg Empire and of Prussia. These innovations necessarily implied some degree of change in society and civil administration. But both the Napoleonic Empire and, after 1807, Prussia revealed that the most radical military innovations need not be backed by a social and political revolution as they had been in France in the early 1790s; they could be imposed and maintained by stable, highly authoritarian governments. The main exception to this process of modernization was the British army. Despite numerous organizational changes, it remained essentially an eighteenth-century force, a condition made possible by its small size, its reliance on allies and on the British navy, and—except in Spain—its generally restricted operational assignments.

If institutional and tactical modernization spread to armies far beyond France, though never without intense conflict between innovators and traditionalists, changes in strategic concepts and operational leadership were slower in coming. No one emerged to equal Napoleon in his mastery of operational techniques and his passion for the physical annihilation of the opponent. But everywhere men became more proficient in using the new or refurbished military instrument, and in Prussia the introduction of a new type of general staff, whose members, assigned to various units, acted with a measure of independence in the service of a comprehensive strategic design, constituted an early, still primitive solution to the problem of coordinating the movement and combat of large armies dispersed beyond the reach of quick, constant communication. The result of these developments was that by the time Napoleon decided on the invasion of Russia, his potential and actual opponents had begun to benefit from the revolution in war. The absolute superiority Napoleon had enjoyed for some years imperceptibly declined.

A point of view that earlier had helped him now began to work to his disadvantage. As a young man he had perceived the effectiveness of striking at the core of his opponent's power. Once the enemy's main armies were defeated, and perhaps also once his administrative and economic centers were occupied, all else was likely to follow. Napoleon recognized as well that the surest means to reach these goals was to raise the strongest force possible and concentrate it on the essential objectives— two recognitions that accurately identified some aspects of political and military reality, while—not incidentally—reflecting Napoleon's own intense psychological need for conquest and absolute domination.

But these insights unrealistically narrowed the range of his wars to conflicts waged with the greatest possible force for the greatest possible ends. It is rare that a state's foreign policy stands in need only of major wars, yet Napoleon excluded limited wars for circumscribed goals from his political and military system. In this way he not only reduced his options, he was driven into wars that were beyond the resources even of the Empire, that stimulated his opponents to extraordinary efforts, and that in the end could be won neither tactically, strategically, nor politically.

On the strategic level, Napoleon's tendency toward gigantism created two serious flaws beyond the basic defect of insufficient power: the command system that had functioned well in northern Italy and central Europe began to falter under the burden of the wars in Spain and Russia, and of the campaigns against the reconstituted and increasingly powerful coalition from 1813 on. In turn, these strains and defeats threw the relationship between military and political decisions and measures out of balance.

Because Napoleon insisted not only on one-man rule but also on one-man command, the operational core of his staff was never more than an organization for assembling information he required and for transmitting reports and orders. The staff neither generated strategic plans, nor developed an institutional capacity for independent decision making within the context of his strategic and operational intentions. As long as the army, though divided into corps, fought in the same general area this caused little harm; but as the size of the armies increased and as they were committed in widely separated theaters of war, Napoleon's strategic control broke down. Neither in Russia nor in the spring and fall campaigns of 1813 in Germany could his marshals be counted on to interpret his orders in accord with the constantly changing situation. He would never have tolerated the peculiar combination of independence and subordination on the part of separate army commands that might have successfully directed hundreds of thousands of troops against strong opposition over vast distances. Even such a system, to be sure, would have been handicapped by the crude means of communication of the time. The large armies of Napoleon's last years, and the missions he gave them, strained the technological capacity of the early nineteenth century to its limits.

As his victories became more equivocal, the unity of military and political authority in his person led to disastrous policies, which a division of responsibilities among two or more individuals, or at least the existence of advisors who would be heard, might have avoided. Other rulers, most recently Frederick the Great, had assumed absolute authority without ruining the state. But Frederick, though prepared to take great risks, could limit his ambition. Napoleon's invasion of Russia went beyond the bounds of reason; at best it was a desperate and unnecessary gamble, as was the decision to advance on Moscow even though the Russian field army had not been destroyed. To stay in Moscow until the middle of October meant sacrificing the Grande Armée to the vain hope that Alexander would, after all, negotiate. The refusal to make a compromise peace in the summer of 1813 imposed on the French a fall campaign against very unfavorable odds. On a lower, operational level, not to give up Dresden in October for the sake of the Saxon alliance removed St. Cyr's corps from the battle of Leipzig where it was urgently needed, and failed to preserve the Saxon alliance anyway. "Policy intervened before the decisive battle, and lost all."[12] The campaign of 1814, generally extolled as one of Napoleon's masterpieces, was, while brilliant, a pointless bloodletting, because the fighting occurred in a political vacuum. Before the Allies crossed into France Napoleon had rejected a further chance to divide them politically and negotiate a tolerable peace, despite the fact that the military odds now favored the Allies by two or three to one. The talks at Châtillon, opened when Blücher was nearly halfway to Paris, were not pressed by the French representatives with the urgency and determination the situation seemed to demand. The entire campaign reveals not the grandeur but the misery of the unity of political and military command. It is not too much to say that in their absence of a rational political purpose, Napoleon's operations in the first months of 1814 are reminiscent of Hitler's insistence after Rundstedt's offensive had failed, to continue defending western Germany in the hopeless situation of spring 1945.

IV

Until Napoleon's last campaigns, politics that stood in some reasonable relationship to French power were an integral part of his strategy, but the analyses of his wars by contemporaries and by the following generations focused almost entirely on their purely military aspects. The great majority of soldiers who studied his campaigns regarded them as the acme of modern war; they tried to discover the secrets of the emperor's strategic thought and operational technique, less to understand what he had done than to prepare themselves for future wars. The impact on Europe of his reign and his wars had been so broad and deep that the sequence of defeats in his last years did little to reduce his stature. The fact that in the end they had beaten him might even have helped his former enemies to acknowledge his greatness more freely. A Napoleonic tradition or school developed, which emphasized numerical strength, deep strategic penetration, and rapid concentration of force on the decisive point. In the 1790s these had still been alien concepts and practices; in the gathering industrial revolution they made sense.

In the thinking of many soldiers, Napoleon as the exponent of mass and mobility assumed a timeless, paradigmatic quality, which in its essentials was not affected by technological development. On the contrary, it could appear that such innovations as railroads, the telegraph, or breechloading rifles at last made feasible the emperor's most daring projects, which at their conception might have been ahead of their time. In the same manner, the full-blown nationalism of the late nineteenth cen-

---

[12] Colin, *Transformations of War*, 264.

tury at last provided the new mass armies with a reliable motivating force, which the emperor had known only in rudimentary form.

To indicate the strength and duration of the impact of Napoleonic war on military thought, it may suffice to quote from three works that appeared on the eve of the First World War, and from one that was written in its aftermath. In 1910 a German colonel who rose to senior command during the war published a book entitled *Napoleon's Generalship and Its Significance for Our Time*, declaring in the introduction that "while much from the Napoleonic Era is now outdated, the study of his wars remains of the greatest value to us, because the lessons of these wars form the basis of military thought today."[13] Two years later the head of the historical section of the German general staff stated that Napoleon's orders and official correspondence during the fall campaign of 1813 remain "even today . . . an inexhaustible source of insights into every kind of military activity, one of the foundations for the military theories of the nineteenth century."[14] That the campaign ended in an unmitigated disaster for Napoleon makes General Friederich's appraisal only more noteworthy, although it is most unlikely that many of his readers were surprised by it. In France at the same time, Jean Colin, in a comparison of Napoleonic flank attacks with similar operations in the Russo-Japanese War, wrote: "While we cannot copy Napoleon's actual maneuver, we should nevertheless be inspired by it." He went on to say that "for those who know better than to copy forms slavishly, it will still be Napoleonic war that offers models to inspire, subjects to reflect on, ideas to be applied to the twentieth century."[15]

The stalemate on the western front during the First World War made a literal interpretation of this last assertion absurd to many; indeed, blaming a fixation on "Napoleonic" mobility for the blindness of commanders on both sides to the realities of trench warfare was not uncommon in the recriminations after 1918. In defense of the now classic ideal, the French general staff officer and historian General Hubert Camon published a reaffirmation of the continuing validity of Napoleonic strategy, and—what was more—insisted that it had directly influenced the most successful operations of the war: "Trench warfare did not become dominant until the initial German maneuver [the invasion of northern France through Belgium] had been checked, a maneuver that was inspired by Napoleon's initial operations in 1812. If this maneuver was blocked

[13] Hugo von Freytag-Loringhoven, *Die Heerführung Napoleons in ihrer Bedeutung für unsere Zeit* (Berlin, 1910), v. The work was dedicated to Schlieffen, "the patron of warfare conducted according to Napoleon and Moltke."

[14] Rudolf Friederich, *Die Befreiungskriege 1813-1815* (Berlin, 1911-13), 2:413.

[15] Colin, *Transformations of War*, 167, 226.

it was not that the means available in 1914 rendered the system of Napoleonic maneuver out of date, but because it was poorly executed."[16] Ludendorff's operations on the eastern front, Camon continues, were "Napoleonic maneuvers." If, on the other hand, the Germans failed to gain total victory in Russia, it was because "Falkenhayn, insufficiently familiar with the Napoleonic pattern, did not believe in the possibility of its success." Ludendorff's "offensive in March 1918 was undoubtedly inspired by the opening phase of Napoleon's campaign in Belgium in 1815." Finally, "if we move from strategic maneuvers to battle, we recognize that the Battle of the Marne was a neo-Napoleonic battle. The only thing missing [on the French side] was the ultimate element: the *masse de rupture*."[17]

These and many other works of similar cast make it apparent that a century after Waterloo Napoleon remained a force in military thought. But what did this force actually consist of? As the quoted passages suggest, we should distinguish between inspiration and influence. Inspiration derives from the suggestive quality of the past, which may stimulate, strengthen, and extend our thinking about the present. Influence, on the other hand, if it is to mean anything at all, must connote a degree of specificity, in this case a link between Napoleon's strategy and the strategies of later generations. To demonstrate conclusively the existence of such connections over fifty or a hundred years would be difficult, probably impossible, in a field such as war, in which plans and decisions are fed by many sources, and must take account of the greatest variety of factors in a constantly changing, unforgiving context. To revert to one of General Camon's examples: undoubtedly Schlieffen studied certain Napoleonic campaigns in great detail—for example, Napoleon's invasion of central Germany in 1806, which might be called a Schlieffen plan in reverse; but he studied Hannibal's wars even more closely, and it would require a peculiarly romantic boldness to hold that the German offensive in 1914 was influenced by Carthaginian operations in Apulia some two thousand years earlier. What Schlieffen did—and it may not even be relevant that most of his historical studies date from the years after he retired—was to put himself as best he could in the position of soldiers of another age, and to work through the problems they faced and the solutions they reached. These intellectual and psychological exercises probably afforded him some distance from the strategic problems and solutions of his own time, which he might even have come to see in a

---

[16] Hubert Camon, *Le système de guerre de Napoléon* (Paris, 1923), 1-2. Camon's numerous studies on Napoleonic warfare were widely read both before and after the First World War.

[17] Ibid., 3.

somewhat different perspective: by being for a time diverted to the past, his mind might have recognized new possibilities in the present, or found confirmation for ideas already held. But that is very different from the crude cause and effect, and the repetition of strategic patterns, asserted—almost taken for granted—by General Camon.

Actually, even the most extreme claims of influence, when seriously pursued, almost always reveal themselves to be something far less specific: the claim that Napoleon had uncovered certain permanent values in war, which his campaigns and writings transmitted to the modern soldier. Napoleon is seen as the inspired interpreter of eternal verities, conveying to us in especially clear form insights and understandings that other men might also have had. In the nineteenth century, and even in 1914, this belief could be facilitated by a certain contemporaneity the Napoleonic Era still possessed; compared to Frederick or Gustavus Adolphus, Napoleon stood at the beginning of what men then regarded to be the modern age. To our own day, the conditions in which he lived and fought are as remote as those of the seventeenth and eighteenth centuries. But even this view of Napoleon is justified only if we interpret the timeless verities in the most general sense: the desirability (usually) of the concentration of force, the advantage of economy of effort, the importance of morale—largely common-sense observations, which the Napoleonic and post-Napoleonic Age turned into varying checklists, called "principles of war." In practice these principles often clash, and with changing circumstances tend to assume new, sometimes very surprising forms.

Each age has its own strategy. The strategies of 1806, of 1870, of 1914 were the products of their own times, certainly paying some attention to history, but primarily attempting with varying degrees of success to use and respond to the economic, social, technological, and political conditions of their day. Often—as in significant phases of the First World War—a strategy lags behind contemporary reality. Napoleon, by contrast, developed strategies that were attuned to the possibilities of his age, and for some years succeeded in exploiting them fully. As the conditions that he understood and had mastered began to change, sometimes in response to his own actions, his strategic concepts, too, had to change or become outdated. It is not so much the elusive influence he exerted on the strategic and operational thought of later generations that is of real interest, as the fact that so many soldiers throughout the nineteenth century and later believed in this influence. Napoleon's true impact may be elsewhere. His trust in the massive accumulation and use of force, his insistence on absolute victory, his rejection of limited wars for limited goals—these ideas and policies seem to have added a measure of historical authority and confirmation to attitudes that were in any case rapidly

141

emerging throughout the Western world. Here may be an unacknowl-edged reason for the claims that he is the master of modern war. But these are speculations.

What can be determined with certainty is not the impact Napoleon might have had on later generations, but what he achieved and failed to achieve in his lifetime. As a soldier of the Old Regime who survived and rose in the Revolution, he reflects in his education and experience the revolution in war, with its mixture of innovation and continuity. More accurately than others he recognized the military potential of the changes taking place, and brought them together into a system of unexcelled destructive power. For a time he rose above events, shaping and driving them forward, until in his later years he sank back again into the stream of general historical development and the long-range tendencies of West-ern civilization toward the further expansion of war.

6. Jomini

JOHN SHY

THREE NAMES stand out in the formative period of modern military thought: Napoleon, Clausewitz, and Jomini. Napoleon and Clausewitz are names known even to those ignorant of history, but Jomini is familiar only to military specialists, although his influence on both military theory and popular conceptions of warfare has been enormous. No book-length study of his ideas and their influence, no adequate biography based on his unpublished papers, has rescued him from the obscurity into which his reputation has slowly sunk.[1] The great disparity between his influence and our general unawareness of it is one key to understanding his important place in Western history since the French Revolution.[2]

Like his contemporaries Napoleon and Clausewitz, Antoine-Henri Jomini was a product of the great Revolution that shook France and the whole Western world from 1789 on. He was Swiss, born in 1779. At nineteen he was clearly—if reluctantly—headed for a career in banking or commerce. But from the age of ten he had been excited by news of the French Revolution. As a banker's apprentice of seventeen in Basel, on the French frontier, he had seen French troops at close range. During the next two years, in Paris, he had witnessed the *coup d'état* of Fructidor and had studied reports from Italy of General Bonaparte's spectacular military victories. Then, in 1798, the Swiss had their own revolution, assisted by French military intervention, and young Jomini gave up what might have been a brilliant career in banking to devote the next seventy years of his life to war and its study.

War and revolution were closely connected in the great upheaval of 1789-1815; the nature of the French Revolution powerfully shaped its

NOTE: In preparing this essay, I have had the valuable criticism of John Bowditch, Robert Cummins, Jonathan Marwil, and members of the Military Studies Group at the University of Michigan.

[1] The most valuable account of Jomini remains the essay by Crane Brinton, Gordon A. Craig, and Felix Gilbert published more than forty years ago in the original *Makers of Modern Strategy*. More recent essays on Jomini are listed in the bibliographical note.

[2] The basic biography remains that of Jomini's disciple, Ferdinand Lecomte, who drew on long conversations with Jomini as well as his voluminous papers: *Le général Jomini, sa vie at ses écrits* (Paris, 1860; 3d ed., Lausanne, 1888).

Napoleonic sequel. But it would be Jomini's life work, begun when still in his teens, to divorce Western theories of warfare, so strongly shaped by the Napoleonic experience, from the actual historical situations in which those theories operate. In the name of making warfare "scientific," he reduced its study to a preoccupation with "strategy"—a set of prescriptive techniques for military analysis and planning that has continued to dominate thinking on the subject, and he did it by effectively breaking the obvious link between Napoleon and the French Revolution. Many of Jomini's specific ideas—on "interior lines" of operation, for example—are now of only historical interest, but his general approach to the problem of war, abstracting it from its political and social context, emphasizing decision-making rules and operational results, turning warfare into a huge game of chess, has been surprisingly durable. Jomini, more than Clausewitz, deserves the dubious title of founder of modern strategy.

Historians are in general agreement that the remarkable success of Revolutionary armies against the allied forces of much of the rest of Europe during the later 1790s depended on the equally remarkable mobilization of French society. Growing resistance to the Revolution after 1789 by the royal court, by most aristocrats and churchmen, and by many ordinary people in large areas of southern and western France brought with it efforts to gain foreign support for a counterrevolution. By 1792 there was open war. In the eyes of the Revolutionary leadership, war soon became a desperate, ideological struggle for survival, and their efforts to fight it almost inevitably led to the overthrow of the monarchy, the execution of the royal family, and the Reign of Terror against "internal enemies." War also brought military chaos. Entire regiments defected to the enemy and many royal officers—nobles and therefore suspected of treason—emigrated. Successive calls from Paris for volunteers to defend the Revolution were partially obeyed, but the Allied advance continued and the Revolution turned to conscription.[3] The famous *levée en masse* of August 1793 simply dramatized a move already well under way:

> From this moment until our enemies have been driven from the territory of the Republic, all Frenchmen are permanently requisitioned for military service.
>
> Young men will go forth to battle; married men will forge weapons and transport munitions; women will make tents and clothing; children will make bandages from old linen; and old men will

[3] The effects of the Revolution on the army are described in Louis Hartmann, *Les officiers de l'armée royale et la Révolution* (Paris, 1910). R. R. Palmer, *Twelve Who Ruled* (Princeton, 1941) contains a graphic account of the Revolution at war.

be brought to the public squares to arouse the courage of the soldiers, while preaching the unity of the Republic and hatred against kings.[4]

Not all Frenchmen sprang to arms, of course, but within a year French armies of more than a million men (in a population of about twenty-five million), an armed force of unprecedented size, had stopped the counter-Revolutionary coalition and had gone over to the offensive.

Within this gigantic mass of improvised military power, there was also a solid core of military professionalism represented by men like Lazare Carnot, Alexander Berthier, and Napoleon Bonaparte—the military legacy of the Old Regime. Historians still disagree about the relative importance to French survival and eventual victory of this professional legacy on the one hand, and about the sheer size and enthusiasm of the new Revolutionary army on the other. From the old army most junior and noncommissioned officers joined the Revolution, as did much of the rank and file; support from the "technical" arms—engineers and artillery—was especially important. But only a great rise in numbers and new levels of motivation, both results of the Revolution, can fully explain the amazing military results.[5] What is not disputed is that the French achieved a breakthrough in warfare; using their new forces with daring and increasing skill, French generals repeatedly left their enemies beaten and demoralized. From 1794 on, in the years when the adolescent Jomini was seeking a career, French armies shattered the anti-French coalition, began to transform the political structure of Europe, and brought to supreme power in France itself one of their own leaders—Napoleon Bonaparte.

How had they done it? Answering this question, persuasively and influentially, would be Jomini's great achievement. The wars of the French Revolution and Napoleon generated a vast, receptive audience for the kind of clear, simple, reassuring explanation that he would offer. Drawing overtly on the prestige of "science" and yet almost religious in its insistent evangelical appeal to timeless verities, Jomini's answer to this troubling question seemed to dispel the confusion and allay much of the fear created by French military victories. After Waterloo, Napoleon defeated and the military power of the Revolution humbled, his answer was all the more persuasive, confirmed by the self-evident historical outcome. And the underlying premise of his answer changed little through the decades; he claimed that it had come to him when he was eighteen, and he died at

---

[4] *Archives Parlementaires de 1787 à 1860*, 1st ser., LXXII (Paris, 1907), 688-90.
[5] Samuel F. Scott, *The Response of the Royal Army to the French Revolution* (Oxford, 1978) and Jean-Paul Bertaud, *La Révolution armée* (Paris, 1979).

ninety insisting on the validity of the same basic ideas, first set down in 1803:

That strategy is the key to warfare;

That all strategy is controlled by invariable scientific principles; and

That these principles prescribe *offensive action* to *mass forces* against weaker enemy forces at some *decisive point* if strategy is to lead to victory.[6]

Jomini's answer, then, was that for almost two decades Napoleon and the French had grasped and applied these principles better than had their opponents. This was the core of Jomini's theory of warfare. To understand the ramifications and influence of these deceptively simple ideas, we can begin by examining how they were formulated and promulgated.

I

The Jominis were an old Swiss family, closely tied by marriage to other old families, important people in a small place: the town of Payerne in the *pays* of Vaud, between Geneva and Berne.[7] The Vaud is French-speaking, but before 1798 it was constitutionally subordinated to the German-speaking canton of Berne, which had led the fourteenth-century "liberation" of the Vaud from Burgundian rule. During the 1790s the Vaud was understandably pro-French, but it was also for the Revolution in its desire to end its "feudal" relationship with Berne. Jomini's father, Benjamin, like his father before him, had served as mayor of Payerne. In the Swiss Revolution of 1798 Benjamin Jomini became a deputy in the provincial assembly of the Vaud, and later served on the Grand Council of the new Helvetian Republic. But Jomini's maternal grandfather, who had important financial ties to Berne, strongly opposed the Swiss "patriot movement." Although this political split in the family foreshadows later aspects of Jomini's life, in 1798 he himself was an eager revolutionary. In Paris he associated with émigré Swiss radicals, notably LaHarpe, and when news arrived of the Swiss Revolution he hurried home to find employment in the new regime. For about three years he served as secretary to the Swiss minister of war, acquired the military rank of captain

---

[6] Antoine-Henri Jomini, *Traité des grandes opérations militaires, contenant l'histoire des campagnes de Frédéric II, comparées à celles de l'empereur Napoléon; avec un recueil des principes généraux de l'art de la guerre*, 2d ed., 4 vols. (Paris, 1811), 2:312n. This is the first complete edition, and will be cited throughout as *Traité*. Jomini did not always give the same date for the writing of his first essay on principles, but 1803 seems best supported by other evidence.

[7] Jean-Pierre Chuard, "Les années d'enfance et de jeunesse," in *Le général Antoine-Henri Jomini (1779-1869): Contributions à sa biographie*, Bibliothèque Historique Vaudoise, no. 41 (Lausanne, 1969), 11-24; R. R. Palmer, *Age of the Democratic Revolution, 1760-1800*, 2 vols. (Princeton, 1959, 1964), 1:358-64, 2:395-421.

and later *chef de bataillon*, survived several political coups, and in 1802 returned to Paris, presumably to seek wider scope for his talent and ambition.

The surviving evidence for these early years evokes a superheated political atmosphere and a youthful intoxication with revolutionary excitement not unlike that described by Stendhal in his autobiography; there is the same boyish fear felt by Henry "Brulard" in Grenoble that a "golden moment in the great world" will have passed before he can escape his provincial prison.[8] Late in life, Jomini would remember the story his own way. He claimed to have been one of the first, despite his youth, to have signed LaHarpe's petition in 1798 to the French Directory, which called for a French guarantee of the rights of the Vaud against Bernese oppression. In fact his signature is not on the petition. Again, Jomini seems to have forgotten that it was in the aftermath of scandal, arising from his request for a bribe from a military supplier to pay his gambling debts in Berne, that he resigned from the Swiss war ministry and returned to Paris. But he could not conceal his petition in 1804 to Napoleon for outright French annexation of Switzerland. A furious Swiss government demanded the expulsion of Jomini—described as a "rogue" and a "notorious Jacobin." Talleyrand, the French foreign minister, did nothing—perhaps because Jomini, at twenty-five already reputed to be a slippery and presumptuous character, had been taken under the protective wing of General Ney, commander of the Sixth Corps.[9]

In 1803 Ney subsidized publication of Jomini's first book. Soon to be legendary as "the bravest of the brave," Ney was hardly a bookish soldier, but he had been French viceroy in Switzerland during the anti-French uprising of 1802, when the Vaud had solidly supported France, and it was this Swiss connection that brought the bright, diligent, ambitious young man to Ney's attention. Jomini remembered that it was the exploits of the French Army of Italy under General Bonaparte in 1796-1797 that had made him a military theorist. In a single year, Bonaparte had forced Piedmont to make peace, driven the Austrians out of the Po Valley, held the rest of Italy to ransom, defeated four massive Austrian counteroffensives, and ended by advancing through the mountain passes on Vienna itself. In this case, there is no reason to question Jomini's memory, because somehow in the five or six years before 1803

[8] Stendhal, four years younger than Jomini, remembered hearing of Bonaparte's victories at Lodi and Arcola in 1796 and of his return from Egypt in 1799, and hoping that the handsome young general would make himself king of France (*Vie de Henry Brulard*, ed. Henri Martineau, 2 vols. [Paris, 1949]), 1:388-89.

[9] Jean-Charles Biaudet, "Jomini et la Suisse," in *Le général Antoine-Henri Jomini (1779-1869): Contributions à sa biographie*, Bibliothèque Historique Vaudoise, no. 41 (Lausanne, 1969), 25-52.

he had found time to read and write a great deal about war. Not only was he obsessed by visions of military glory, with himself imitating the incredible rise of Bonaparte who was only ten years his senior, but in a telling phrase Jomini remembered being possessed, even then, by *"le sentiment des principes"*—the Platonic faith that reality lies beneath the superficial chaos of the historical moment in enduring and invariable principles, like those of gravitation and probability.[10] To grasp those principles, as well as to satisfy the more primitive emotional needs of ambition and youthful impatience, was what impelled him to the study of war. Voracious reading of military history and theorizing from it would reveal the secret of French victory.

According to Jomini, he owed his greatest intellectual debt to General Henry Lloyd.[11] A Welshman, Lloyd had been implicated in the 1745 Rebellion, fled England, and served in several armies on the Continent before making peace with the British government sometime before his death in 1783. He may, indeed, have been a British spy or a double agent. He held an important field command in the Austrian army during the Seven Years' War and he wrote, among other works, a history of the German campaigns of that war. His criticism of Frederick II as a strategist excited considerable interest, as did his so-called *Military Memoirs*, published in 1781, in which he offered a systematic discussion of warfare and its underlying principles.[12] These memoirs were translated into French and republished in Basel in 1798. Almost certainly it was in this form that they made their strong impression on the young Jomini. Lloyd provided both a model and a challenge in the young man's efforts to reduce the fantastic world of war at the end of the eighteenth century to some kind of intellectual order.

The art of war is founded on "certain and fixed principles, which are by their nature invariable. . . ."[13] The words are Lloyd's, but words like them were repeated again and again by Jomini and his disciples. When we turn to Lloyd's books for the specific content of these "invariable principles," there is surprisingly little. It all seems to come down

[10] Antoine-Henri Jomini, *Tableau analytique des principales combinaisons de la guerre* (Paris, 1830), vii.

[11] Michael Howard (see n. 37) first emphasized the influence of Lloyd on Jomini; see "Jomini and the Classical Tradition." The fullest account of Lloyd, based on much new evidence, is Franco Venturi, "Le avventure del Generale Henry Lloyd," *Rivista storica italiana* 91 (1979), 369-433. Max Jähns, *Geschichte der Kriegswissenschaften*, 3 vols. (Munich, 1889-91), 3:2102-2114, is also valuable for Lloyd's military writing.

[12] What is often cited as Lloyd's *Military Memoirs* was published originally as *Continuation of the History of the Late War in Germany . . .* (London, 1781). It purported to be Part II of *The History of the Late War in Germany*, but is in fact an essay of about two hundred pages on "the General Principles of War" (vi).

[13] Lloyd, *Continuation of the History of the Late War in Germany*, vi.

to a single point: only an undivided army, moving on a single line of operations kept as short and safe as possible, can hope to avoid defeat. It can win, of course, only if the enemy is rash enough to divide his forces and extend them on a long and vulnerable line. Lloyd, in his search for principles, produced a rationalization—almost a parody—of the cautious, defensive-minded maneuver strategy that characterized much of European warfare before the French Revolution. Jomini found in Lloyd the clear expression of his own still inchoate "ideal" of war as a science, but he could have found little or nothing to explain how the Army of Italy, at the end of a long and vulnerable line of operations, had not only won victories but had upset the military balance of Europe. Lloyd's appeal to the Enlightenment is easy to see; his science of war, if understood and observed by all, made battle virtually impossible and even promised an end to war. But it is more difficult to see how Lloyd could offer anything to an age of revolution and dramatic military innovation. Napoleon himself read and annotated Lloyd; his marginalia deserve to be quoted: "Ignorance . . . Ignorance . . . Absurd . . . Absurd . . . Impossible . . . False . . . Bad . . . Very Bad . . . How absurd . . . What absurdity!"[14] And yet it was in the intellectual mold created by Lloyd that Jomini would recast, more or less definitively, the military legend of Napoleon.

There is an obvious contradiction: Jomini admired Lloyd for his work as a military critic and theorist, and used Lloyd as a model for his own work on Revolutionary and Napoleonic warfare; but Napoleon clearly regarded Lloyd's theorizing as a pathetic joke, and indeed nothing in Lloyd's critical study of the Seven Years' War suggests that anything like the French military breakthrough of the 1790s is possible. It is too easy simply to say that Jomini used the military categories of the Old Regime in his interpretation of Napoleon; too many intelligent and ex-perienced soldiers, including Napoleon himself, admired Jomini's work, which in fact repeatedly emphasized the profound differences between European warfare before and after 1789.[15] More is involved here than an intellectual puzzle. By resolving the apparent contradiction we can take an important step toward understanding exactly what Jomini was saying and why, then and later, his message was influential.

Lloyd's search for principles of war was inextricably linked to his

[14] *Notes inédites de l'Empereur Napoleon Ier sur les mémoires militaires du Général Lloyd*, ed. Ariste Ducaunnès-Duval (Bordeaux, 1901).

[15] "In the last analysis, the great wars for a man like Jomini were those of the eighteenth century . . ." (Brinton et al., "Jomini," 92) is fairly typical of historical judgments that stress his empathy with the Old Regime. Writing this essay has persuaded me that this emphasis is one-sided and neglects the degree to which he himself was a product of the Revolution, a fervent admirer of Napoleon, and an experienced veteran of the Napoleonic Wars.

history of the Seven Years' War and to his critique of Frederick as a commander; his criticism was purportedly based on the application of scientific principles to the historical event. Before Lloyd, almost all serious writing on war during the Enlightenment was in French or German—the English had contributed virtually nothing of value to the discussion. Not only was Lloyd's work in that sense novel, but his criticism of Frederick produced an extended German rebuttal by Colonel Georg Friedrich Tempelhof of the Prussian army.[16] Their controversy aroused interest in France, where the bitter lessons of the Seven Years' War were a subject of intense debate, and thus Lloyd's work came to be widely known in Europe. When the young Jomini began his military studies to find the secret of how the Revolution waged war, the works of Lloyd and Tempelhof came readily to hand. They were recent, detailed, and controversial accounts of the most relevant military experience by two veteran officers. He also found in both Lloyd and his chief critic the faith in "general principles" that attracted him so strongly. And, finally, in their debate on the strategic possibilities of 1756-1762, neither Lloyd nor Tempelhof had imagined anything like the astonishing military events of 1793-1801. Standing on the shoulders of Lloyd and Tempelhof, Jomini could extend their limited vision of the true nature of warfare.

A single case can serve to illustrate his method. Jomini discussed the campaign of 1756 at length in his first book, the *Treatise on Major Military Operations of the Seven Years' War*, whose first two volumes appeared in 1805.[17] He summarized Lloyd's account of each operation and Tempelhof's response to provide a basis for his own version of the Seven Years' War, as well as for his own vision of the timeless principles of war and their correct application. Of course the campaigns of 1756-1762—like all warfare—revealed these principles, but Jomini also drew on the campaigns of the French Revolutionary Wars to correct the imperfect efforts of Lloyd and Tempelhof to discern and apply the principles correctly. For the campaign of 1756, Lloyd had approved of Frederick's invasion of Saxony as a prudent operation to protect his flank at the outset of a war with Austria. But Lloyd had also suggested that an invasion of Bohemia or Moravia, which would have threatened Vienna directly, might have been even better as long as Frederick had detached a force to cover his Saxon flank. Tempelhof had criticized this idea by calculating its logistical requirements, which he argued would have made it impossible. Furthermore, Tempelhof added, the risky direct move

[16] Jähns, *Geschichte der Kriegswissenschaften*, 3:1873-75.
[17] *Traité*, 1:i-v, 24-43, and 85. The original edition of the first two volumes appeared under the title *Traité de grande tactique . . .* (Paris, 1805).

would have violated the basic principle of keeping the line of operations short and safe.

The young Jomini criticized both his predecessors for their timidity. Lloyd had a good idea in moving directly against Vienna, but weakened it by his concern for the Saxon threat. Rather than alienate the Saxons by invading their country, as Frederick had actually done, or weakening the main army by detaching a force to cover Saxony, as Lloyd had proposed, Jomini argued that a united Prussian army should have driven at maximum speed for Olmütz on the road to Vienna. The Saxons, relieved at being spared the horrors of Prussian invasion, would have been too frightened to move. Clearly, Jomini argued, this is what Napoleon would have done in 1756, as he had repeatedly done in Italy forty years later. As for Tempelhof's critique, based on logistical calculations and the principles of war, Jomini was scathing. The habit of tying all military plans and operations to supply trains and fortified magazines simply proved that during the eighteenth century "the art of war had taken a step backwards." Caesar had said that war could feed war, and he was right. The eight to ten million people of Bohemia and Moravia could have easily supplied a Prussian army of ninety thousand men. In the 1811 edition of the *Treatise*, Jomini cited the "immortal campaign of the Emperor Napoleon in 1809" as positive proof that it might have been done in 1756 and that Napoleon was a better strategist than Frederick. In response to Tempelhof's invocation of the principle of keeping the line of operations short and safe, Jomini called for better judgment and more daring. Tempelhof's literal-minded application of the principle would mean that no army would ever cross its own frontier. "In all military operations," Jomini wrote, "there is always some imperfection or weak point; but in judging operations we must apply principles with the objective in mind, and ask whether a given operation offers the best chance for victory."[18]

Nothing in Jomini's first book, which was quickly translated and widely discussed, suggests that he failed to recognize the new face of warfare in the 1790s or that by some sleight of hand he was conflating the campaigns of Frederick and Napoleon into an undifferentiated art of war. On the contrary, he saw and vastly admired the new style of warfare, reckless of manpower and the constraints of supply, all energies focused on the sole aim of victory. He used the hesitations and limitations of Frederician warfare as a background to set off the brilliance of Bona-

---

[18] *Traité*, 1:35. In this edition, published in 1811, he was more critical of Tempelhof than he had been in the 1805 edition. In the former, he asked (40n) the indulgence of his readers for erring in his "first essay," when he had had less experience with war.

parte, much as he used the labored partisanship of Lloyd and Tempelhof to display his own clear-sighted universalism.

In chapters 7, 14, 34, and 35 of the *Treatise* (the last two chapters first appearing in 1809, in Volume IV), Jomini moved from the particulars of military history to the general truth of warfare. His introductory language was very like that of Lloyd: "The idea of reducing the system of war to its fundamental combination, on which all else depends, and which will provide the basis for a simple and accurate theory, offers numerous advantages: it will make instruction easier, operational judgment sounder, and mistakes less frequent. I believe that commanders cannot do enough to absorb this concept, and that it ought to guide all their plans and actions."[19] When he turned to more specific conclusions from the historical evidence, Jomini seemed still to be following Lloyd: a single unified line of operations is best.[20] But beyond this point, Jomini appears as a man of the French Revolution, offering a new, radical theory of warfare: all strategic "combinations" are faulty (*vicieuses*) if they do not conform to the basic principle "of operating with the greatest possible force in a combined effort against the decisive point."[21] Deciding how to attack—frontally or on the flank—will depend on the specific situation, but attack itself is essential; the initiative must not be left to the enemy. Once committed to action, the commander must not hesitate. He and his officers must, by their boldness and courage, inspire their troops to the greatest possible effort. If beaten, the enemy must be pursued relentlessly. If victory for some reason should elude the commander, he must not expect it from any other system, but must try again, using sound principles—massing, attacking, persisting. Jomini's picture of warfare could hardly differ more from the cautious, limited-war strategies of the Old Regime. His closing words can stand without translation: "*Voilà la science de la guerre en peu de mots.*" Ignoring these principles led to the defeats of the Austrians in 1793-1800 and again in 1805, to the French loss of Belgium in 1793, and to French failures in Germany (1796) and in Italy and Swabia (1799). By contrast, "*Le système de l'Empereur Napoléon présente une application constante de ces principes invariables.*"[22]

Jomini continued to write and publish while on active service from 1805, when he joined Ney's staff, to 1813, when he left the French army to join the Russians. By 1811 he had carried his *Treatise* to six volumes, from the Seven Years' War through the first two years of the Revolu-

[19] *Traité*, 1:288.
[20] Ibid., 2:271.
[21] Ibid., 4:275.
[22] Ibid., 4:286.

tionary Wars. He had completed the next two volumes, on the campaigns of 1794-1797, and would publish them in 1816. He had also published a number of articles and pamphlets, three of which distilled his ideas on the principles of war.[23] As an officer on the staff of Ney and of Napoleon himself, he had risen to the rank of *général de brigade* and had served in the Ulm, Jena, Eylau, Spanish, and Russian campaigns. At the battle of Bautzen in 1813, he had distinguished himself. When he left French service shortly after Bautzen, at the age of thirty-four, he had achieved an international reputation as the preeminent historian and theorist of modern warfare, although the book for which he is best known still lay years in the future. It is only a slight exaggeration to say that his rapid rise, by sheer energy and determination plus a little luck within the somewhat constricted world of military studies, had been Napoleonic.

From 1813 until his death in 1869 as a Russian general, Jomini continued to write and publish, defending and elaborating his military theory, and enhancing his considerable reputation.[24] He served as advisor to the czar at the Congresses of Vienna, Aix-la-Chapelle, and Verona, as well as during the Russo-Turkish War of 1828-1829 and the Crimean War. He took part in establishing a new Russian military academy and served as tutor to the future Alexander II. But in the last fifty-six years of his life there is surprisingly little intellectual development. Living mostly in Paris, he completed his history of the French Revolutionary Wars, published separately from the *Treatise*, in fifteen volumes. He devoted four more volumes to a military biography of Napoleon. In 1830, at the suggestion of Czar Nicholas I, he hastily combined his various chapters and essays on the principles of war into a *Synoptic Analysis of the Art of War*. An expanded two-volume edition, published in 1837-1838 as the *Summary of the Art of War*, was his most famous book. The *Summary* shows that he had read the posthumously published *On War* of Clausewitz and had been moved by it, in late middle age, to reconsider some of his own ideas. But the new material incorporated into the *Summary*, which has since been translated into many languages, was stillborn in terms of its influence. Jomini's audience had received his basic message long before, and no new subjects or chapters, unless accompanied by a radical change of emphasis, or perhaps even a virtual abandonment of his stress on prescriptive principles, could have shifted the

[23] The invaluable pamphlet by John I. Alger, *Antoine-Henri Jomini: A Bibliographical Survey* (West Point, N.Y., 1975), clarifies an often confusing list of publications.

[24] Three bundles of papers from his later years are in the British Library (Egerton MSS. 3166-3168). A perceptive account of his Russian service is Daniel Reichel, "La position du général Jomini en tant qu'expert militaire à la cour de Russie," *Actes du Symposium 1982*, Service historique, Travaux d'histoire militaire et de polémologie, vol. 1 (Lausanne, 1982), 59-75.

direction of his influence on the military profession and on students of warfare.

The most mature and influential expression of his ideas, in the *Summary*, elaborates without altering the basic points made in his earliest published work. The title tells the reader that his subject is not "war," but "the art of war." For this art there are timeless principles, as valid for Caesar as for Napoleon. In searching for the secret of these principles, Jomini had failed to find them in the theoretical "systems" of earlier writers but had discovered them in the military history of Frederick II. Frederick had won by throwing the mass of his army against only a part of the enemy army. That technique, raised to the highest level of war making, was in essence the secret of strategy from which all other principles derived. Critics like Clausewitz, who doubted the validity of any theory of war, failed to distinguish between a theory of *systems* and a theory of *principles*. Principles were guides to action, not infallible mathematical calculations. The specific application of principles would vary with the thousand changing physical and psychological factors that made war "a great drama." Genius would defeat the military pedant, just as talent and experience would outdo the bumbling novice. But the principles themselves, whose truth is demonstrated by all military experience, could not be ignored without peril and, when followed, had "almost invariably" (*presque en tout temps*) brought victory.

The principle of maneuvering the mass of an army so as to threaten the "decisive points" in a theater of war and then to hurl all available forces against a fraction of the enemy force defending those points is, Jomini admitted, very simple. But what, his critics had asked, is a "decisive point"? It is a point, answered Jomini, whose attack or capture would imperil or seriously weaken the enemy. It could be a road junction, a river crossing, a mountain pass, a supply base, or an open flank of the enemy army itself. The great merit of Napoleon as a strategist lay in not simply maneuvering for some limited advantage, but in identifying those points that, if lost, would "dislocate and ruin" the enemy. Informing himself fully, moving his forces quickly to converge on the decisive point, and pursuing a beaten foe *à outrance*, the young Bonaparte had established his reputation. In a larger theater or in a war with different aims, the principle might be applied differently, perhaps more cautiously. But the basic principle never changed. Almost without exception the enemy flanks and supply line would define the decisive points for attack; an army could not survive without supply and to threaten its base would compel it to fight, no matter how unfavorable the circumstances. Although acknowledging the special nature of Napoleonic warfare, Jomini, by a variety of illustrative historical cases deployed throughout his theoretical discussion in the *Summary*, stressed that beneath the chaotic changes in modern warfare lay strategic universality.[25]

II

How did this man of the Revolution disconnect the French break-through in warfare from its Revolutionary roots? We have already seen that he was fully aware of the dramatic differences between the old and the new ways of waging war and that his views were fully developed while serving in the very midst of Napoleonic campaigns. Jomini was no armchair strategist of the Restoration, spinning out untested theories in his library, but a veteran of many campaigns, remarkably well placed to observe a decade of intense warfare across the face of Europe. Understanding how he came, in his work and still more in his influence, to abstract his conception of warfare from the environment in which wars take place requires consideration at several different levels.

Jomini's own personality and career offer the most accessible level at which to consider the peculiar direction taken by his mind and work. As a boy he was troublesome, bright but obnoxious, and he never changed. He was always embroiled with someone about something, and he was too sensitive ever to pass up the chance to quarrel. His portrait as a young officer in the *Grande Armée* is all arrogance, and the old man looks out from his photograph like an angry hawk. That he remained a quarrelsome, tactless personality is confirmed by all who knew him, even his admirers.[26] Nothing expresses his character better than his own words, disguised as the words of Napoleon. In his *Life of Napoleon . . . as told by himself*, published anonymously in 1827, Jomini was able to describe his own role as Ney's chief of staff in the campaign of 1813. Napoleon is made to say that Jomini was responsible at the battle of Bautzen for a "perfect" manuever of "incalculable" benefit, and that his subsequent departure for Russian service (in fact, Napoleon at the time had called it "desertion") was a serious loss "because he was one of the officers who understood best my system of war." Jomini's vanity in these remarks is breathtaking but perfectly in character. More revealing are Napoleon's purported words excusing his defection to the enemy: "Jomini was a

---

[25] Antoine-Henri Jomini, *Précis de l'art de la guerre*, new ed., 2 vols. (Paris, 1855; repr. Osnabrück, 1973, with an introduction in German by H. R. Kurz) is the ultimate statement. See 1:5-10, 16, 21-22, 27, 159, 191-205, et passim. (Hereafter cited as *Précis*.)

[26] The language of this judgment may seem harsh, but it is readily confirmed by the admiring biography of Lecomte, who was close to Jomini for many years. *Général Antoine-Henri Jomini, 1779-1869* (Payerne, 1969) is a catalogue of an exhibition of Jomini memorabilia on the centenary of his death, and includes reproductions of his portraiture. General George B. McClellan visited Jomini in 1868; he described his face as "much like that of an old worn-out eagle" (*The Galaxy* 7 [June, 1869], 887).

sensitive man, violent, quick-tempered [*mauvaise tête*], but too honest [*franc*] to have been part of a premeditated intrigue."²⁷ Thus by his own account, written and published in his forties, Jomini was irascible, vain, and sensitive to a fault.

Behind the sensitivity and irascibility lay the deeper sources of personality—ambition, frustration, insecurity, and possibly depression. As an adolescent, Jomini had been stunned and thrilled by the rise of Bonaparte, and he had set out himself, at nineteen, to find glory, fame, and power. By attaching himself to Ney and for a while even gaining the favorable attention of Napoleon himself, he had risen fast, but not far enough. He had never been trusted with the command of troops and his presumptuous intellectuality had grated on some of the hard-bitten generals with whom he had served. If Ney and Napoleon were his lodestars, Berthier, Napoleon's chief of staff, was his *bête noire*. Berthier had blocked him more than once, and when Ney recommended him for promotion after Bautzen, Berthier ordered his arrest for failing to submit his periodic report as Ney's chief of staff.²⁸ It was this incident that led to his joining the Russian army at what, in retrospect, appears an opportune moment, just before the death struggle of the Napoleonic regime.

In the Russian service he had attached himself as military advisor to Alexander I, and after his death in 1825 to Nicholas I. But the Russian court was too complex and too involuted for Jomini ever to penetrate very far or very securely; always there was the same quest for a patron—Alexander himself for a while, then Nicholas, and at the end the reformist minister Miliutin—but there was also always a Berthier, some villain blocking his proposals.²⁹

The evidence suggests a man who, for all his reputation, was hanging on desperately—to his irregular position on Ney's staff, to his personal

²⁷ [Antoine-Henri Jomini], *Vie politique et militaire de Napoléon*, racontée par lui-même, au tribunal de César, d'Alexandre et de Frédéric, 4 vols. (Paris, 1827), 4:305, 368-70.

²⁸ Jomini's version of his action, which he never ceased trying to justify, is in ibid., 370n. Less sympathetic versions abound; a recent one is François-Guy Hourtoulle, *Ney, les braves des braves* (Paris, 1981), 140-43, which includes the suggestion by another member of Ney's staff that Jomini's claim to exemplary conduct at Bautzen was unfounded, and that his extravagant behavior subsequently may have been induced by medicinal drugs. A detailed account of the affair, sympathetic to Jomini, appeared in *Revue historique vaudoise* 1 (1893), 65-80, prompted by the publication in 1890 of the memoirs of General Marbot, who accused Jomini of betraying Napoleon's plans to the Allies.

²⁹ In letters written in old age to his son Alexander, who had risen high in the Russian foreign ministry, Jomini claimed to have given crucial advice to the czar in 1813-1814 and later in the war with Turkey, but that a "plot" led by Chernyshev had ruined his plan for a Russian military academy and that in the Crimea he had been no more than "a prompter at the play" (*un souffleur de comédie*). Jomini to Alexander, April 30, 1867, Egerton MSS. 3167, ff. 78-79, British Library. Earlier letters, written in 1864, tell the story of the military academy (Egerton MSS. 3166, ff. 91-93, 112, 115, 122, and 126). On Jomini's situation in Russia, see Reichel, "La position du général Jomini."

relationship with the emperor or the czar, to his rank and pay as a Russian general. He had quarrelled with his brother and sister over the family inheritance, and his expressed financial fears, despite the continued sale of his books, seem genuine.[30] The evidence also suggests a man who felt, deeply, that he had failed. He had never held military command, and could never find complete satisfaction in writing books about war. Soldiers might praise him and even pay court to him, but he was too much the soldier himself not to know what the profession thought of those who only wrote about war. Too vain to admit it freely, too intelligent not to know it, Jomini in his own eyes seems to have been a failure. And his self-absorption, the deep sense of his own precarious and ultimately unsatisfactory place in a harsh world, a sense arising from the exciting but troubling experiences of his early years and reinforced by the rest of his life, shaped his thinking about war itself.

War, at least the only part of it that truly interested him concerned the supreme commander, the Frederick or Napoleon who played the great bloody game, who by sheer intellect and will dominated the men who served him and used them to defeat his enemies. This was war—and life—as experienced by Jomini, the headquarters staff officer. At general headquarters, the play of personality often seems overwhelming, success or failure appearing to depend on the abilities and quirks of a few men—the commander and his staff—who are under great pressure. Perspective on the larger, impersonal forces shaping events is notoriously easy to lose in just those circumstances under which Jomini had experienced war.

There is no need to exaggerate the psychological element in Jomini's work to see how naturally his thinking reflected his own personal experience. From early on, his life had been a frantic scramble to succeed by making an impression on some key man—the new Swiss war minister, Ney, Napoleon, the czar, or at the end of his life Miliutin—and at the same time to out-do some rival and enemy—Berthier, Chernyshev, Clausewitz, or whoever might be blocking his way.[31] Jomini had operated as a young upstart in a competitive jungle, and was always something

---

[30] There are glimpses of great anger and unhappiness in published extracts from his personal papers, most of which are still held privately. Returning to Payerne in 1823, he wrote of it as "this nasty hovel" (*cette horrible bicoque*). He threatened to send his teenage son Henry into the navy as a common seaman for his "perseverance in the vice which will destroy him." (Henri Perrochon, "Jomini écrivain," in *Le général Antoine-Henri Jomini [1779-1869]: Contributions à sa biographie*, Bibliothèque Historique Vaudoise, no. 41 [Lausanne, 1969], 73-87.)

[31] In drafts of long private letters to Russian minister of war Miliutin in 1864 concerning the reform of military education, he told the story of how his earlier plans for a Russian military academy were ruined by Chernyshev (Egerton MSS. 3168, ff. 43-57). He also crossed out passages in which he had praised the French system of education and had defended the Ecole Polytechnique against allegations of being a nest of sedition.

of an outsider. His world was less one of great forces clashing than of the constant collision of ambitious men.

It is instructive to compare Jomini in this respect with Clausewitz. Born a year later, Clausewitz rose in Prussian service from modest origins to high rank, partly through talent and ambition, partly through the patronage of Scharnhorst. But beyond this similarity there were great differences—between Prussia and France, Scharnhorst and Ney as patrons, Clausewitz and Jomini themselves—that marked each man's perception of modern war. Clausewitz and Prussia knew adversity, defeat, and humiliation; only after major reforms carried out in the aftermath of the military catastrophe of Jena in 1806 did the Prussian military system find means to cope with the power of Napoleonic France. Captured in the Jena campaign, Clausewitz was a junior member of the reform group. After Waterloo, Napoleon safely exiled, Clausewitz and the other Prussian reformers fell under a cloud of suspicion. A conservative monarchy and aristocracy never forgot or forgave their demands for liberalizing changes after 1806, and by the 1820s Clausewitz could hardly doubt that he had been relegated to the professional shelf as administrator of the Berlin War College. Clausewitz knew failure; Jomini might suspect it, but spent a long life proclaiming the success of his own ideas. A stronger, stabler person, Clausewitz wrote on war to satisfy himself and perhaps the ghost of Scharnhorst, killed in 1813, who had set he highest standard of personal and intellectual integrity for his young protégés. Ney, by contrast, had given Jomini a job, money, and valuable but sporadic support, abandoning the young man when he tired of his obstreperous personality. Jomini wrote to publish, and he published to impress, for only by impressing could he hope to move up or hang on. From the perspective of their contrasting psychologies, it should not be surprising that Clausewitz approached war as a complex totality, seeing it in what may be called tragic terms, always threatening to escape human control, and that Jomini saw war largely in personal, heroic terms, controlled by the masterful commander.

How far his quest for a science of commanding generalship could carry Jomini is exemplified by the campaigns of 1793-1794. This was the Year of the Terror, when French forces in the north and east finally turned defeat into victory. While being rebuilt, the French army fought an all-out war on several fronts. Mutinies were frequent, and the heads of defeated French generals literally rolled. It was a time of frenzied effort and desperate innovation. From this period Jomini chose the campaign of 1794 to illustrate his theory of "lines of operation" in the famous fourteenth chapter of his *Treatise*. He said little about political, emotional, and organizational conditions, but dwelt instead on the similarities between 1757 and 1794. In both campaigns two separate armies moved "concentrically" on a single objective—Frederick in 1757 invading Bohemia from Saxony and Silesia, French armies in the 1794 advancing on Brussels from Flanders and the Meuse Valley. Jomini was well aware that others saw the 1794 operations in a different light. "But there has been exaggeration in presenting [the campaign of 1794] as a new military system, as some kind of miracle unprecedented in the annals of warfare. French armies do not need exaggeration, which only obscures the true nature of their victory."[32] The true nature of French victory lay, according to Jomini, in strategic maneuver, which on the French side might have been improved to secure a still more decisive victory, and which on the Austrian side was a classic case of the failure to exploit "interior lines," of not concentrating all forces first against one French army, then against the other (just as the Austrians had failed to do against Frederick in 1757). This Austrian failure to maneuver according to the principles of war was the proximate cause of French victory in 1794.

But the operations that led to the French conquest of Belgium in 1794 were in fact far more complex than a set of game-like moves at which the Austrians were simply outplayed. Virtually every account, contemporary or modern, stresses the relentless character of the French offensive, supported by a stream of reinforcements to replace heavy losses and whipped on by the personal presence of Carnot and Saint-Just.[33] The historical evidence points clearly to the decisive importance of both the *quantity* and the *qualities* of the French forces engaged in the campaign. That Jomini would choose to emphasize the Austrian failure to exploit the supposed advantage of an "interior line of operations" against the French "concentric lines of operations" is at best a simplification. That he would go further by explicitly denying the explanatory value of institutional, political, and psychological factors in this campaign seems bizarre and barely credible. But however questionable his use of the specific example to illustrate his general point may be, the influence of his theoretical method, like the general acceptance of his version of military history, can hardly be denied.

The overwhelmingly positive response of Jomini's readers is what gives his work its importance. Without that response, he would have become little more than a historical curiosity, like his contemporary

---

[32] *Traité*, 2:305.

[33] "Observations sur l'armée française de 1792 à 1808," published anonymously in 1808, reprinted in *Spectateur militaire*, 5th series, vol. 47 (1902), 25-34, 93-103, exemplifies contemporary views of the campaign; Steven T. Ross, *Quest for Victory: French Military Strategy 1792-1799* (New York, 1973), 58-87, is a fair example of modern scholarship on the subject.

Bülow. But students of warfare during and after the Napoleonic epoch found what they were seeking in the *Treatise*, in his history of the Revolutionary Wars, in his life of Napoleon, and above all in his *Summary of the Art of War*. Jomini had given his audience what it obviously wanted.

His books, in both their narrative and theoretical aspects, conformed to an ancient tradition of military historiography: Joshua, Caesar, Alexander, Frederick, Napoleon—the saga of the warrior-king who, possessed of superhuman qualities, leads his people to victory. The story is as old as literature. Jomini fit comfortably into this tradition, in which armies are faceless masses, armed and fed in mysterious ways, whose behavior in battle appears to reflect the ascribed character of their race, their nation, and their commander. In the end, judgment is traditionally passed on the performance of the Great Captain and his enemies.[34] Although the best of Jomini's analytical writing rises above this kind of military historiography, most of his published work is campaign narrative, focused on command decisions. Even today these narratives offer clear, fairly detailed, and—within their didactic limits—reliable accounts of military operations in Europe from 1756 to 1815. But they also powerfully reinforced the traditional way of seeing warfare, with all its judgmental and ahistorical tendencies.

Other more active, historically specific forces also helped bring Jomini and his audience together. During Jomini's own lifetime the modern military profession emerged in Western societies, with rationalized recruitment, education, promotion, retirement, staff systems—all the features of a separate, specialized priesthood of technicians, increasingly distinct both from the civilian world that it presumably served and from the traditional identification of the military role with the aristocracy and gentry. To this emergent profession, whose growth and confidence were greatly stimulated by the long wars of 1792-1815, Jomini gave the prestige of science as well as a rationale for the professional claim to autonomy. The desire of the new military profession to make its expertise "scientific" is merely one chapter in the larger story of nineteenth-century professionalism, in which every profession was seeking to define and defend its own special "science." But the military faced another problem: its relationship to power and authority. As long as officers were aristocrats or gentlemen, the relationship was implicitly defined by their social origins. When democracy, bureaucracy, and meritocracy began to transform the military—as was perceptibly happening almost everywhere by

---

[34] John Keegan, *The Face of Battle* (London, 1976), ch. 1, is a good discussion of traditions in military historiography.

1800—the political relationship became problematical.[35] No longer a part of the contract by which monarchy and aristocracy shared authority, was the military to be simply a subordinate part of the state apparatus?

The military coup that brought Napoleon to power in 1799, the politically motivated defection of Prussian officers in the crisis of 1812, and the Decembrist revolt of 1825 led by Russian officers were major incidents that made this political question more than academic. Conservatives no less than liberals feared a military so professionalized that it would be alienated from state and society, and the military in turn sought means to avoid the external controls that these fears might impose. In Jomini, soldiers found just what they wanted: good arguments against strict subordination to political authority. He focused his studies on Frederick and Napoleon, who combined political and military authority in their own persons. These were unique cases, irrelevant even to the most autocratic states where never again would the reigning monarch actually take the field as generalissimo, but Jomini did not explicitly confront the problem. Instead he chose to dwell on the opposite case of Austria, which had lost so many of the major campaigns from 1756 to 1815, and thereby he conveyed a strong message on this subject of the political-military relationship. Austrian military commanders, wrote Jomini, were frequently crippled by "interference" from the "Aulic Council," whose strategic naiveté and supreme political power had often led the house of Hapsburg to military disaster.[36]

The lesson was clear: a government should choose its ablest military commander, then leave him free to wage war according to scientific principles. Governments should not neglect their armed forces, but they must not meddle in matters that only educated and experienced officers understand. The military profession, naturally, took this lesson to heart, taught it to their recruits, invoked it whenever threatened by political "interference," and—following Jomini, their mentor—never felt much need to explore the difficulties such a simplistic formulation created. These difficulties were a central theme of *On War*, but soldiers managed to read even Clausewitz in ways that twisted his meaning back into the comfortable Jominian formula.[37]

Still broader currents of opinion and feeling helped create a receptive

[35] Among numerous works on the military profession in the eighteenth and nineteenth centuries, outstanding are Samuel P. Huntington, *The Soldier and the State* (Cambridge, Mass., 1957); Gordon A. Craig, *The Politics of the Prussian Army, 1640-1945* (New York, 1964); and Raoul Girardet, *La société militaire dans la France contemporaine, 1815-1939* (Paris, 1953).

[36] *Précis*, 1:135-136.

[37] Peter Paret, "Clausewitz and the Nineteenth Century," in *The Theory and Practice of War*, ed. Michael Howard (London and New York, 1965), 21-41.

audience for Jomini's work. He wrote for a Europe shaken by the Revolution and Napoleon, and yet also fascinated by that experience. A generation of upheaval and the remarkable impact of the French Empire on the Western world could not be ignored. At the same time the desire was widespread to bring this disturbing epoch into some kind of intellectual order, to normalize it by somehow returning the French genie to its bottle. Jomini, with his emphasis on strategy, biography, and science, responded to this desire.

The greatness of Napoleon, said Jomini, lay not in exploiting the energies of the Revolution for military ends, but in discerning and applying the scientific truths of warfare. In that sense, Napoleon had not been an unprecedented revolutionary force, but a supreme modern case of a recurrent phenomenon—the leader of genius. The French Revolution had made possible his rapid rise, but it had not been the source of his power; that had come from his powerful intellect and will, which first had to stop the destructive, centrifugal effects of the Revolution before building the Empire. Jomini never lost his youthful admiration for Napoleon, and this gave his theoretical and historical work an ambiguity that was an important part of its appeal in post-Waterloo Europe. Conservatives found in Jomini a skillful disconnecting of the political and social upheaval of the Revolution from the causes and consequences of Napoleonic military victories; they were able to think about warfare without being troubled by its possible relationship to revolution. Jomini's own politics support such a reading of his work; after being embarrassed by criticism of the favorable treatment he had given to Napoleon in his four-volume biography published in 1827, Jomini used the occasion of a book-length "supplement and rectification" of the biography's brief account of the 1815 campaign to preach the virtues of divine-right monarchy.[38] He had come a long way from the Jacobinism of his youth, but he had done so without any perceptible shift in his approach to the study of war.

There is in Jomini, not surprisingly, an important element of pure salesmanship; he knew what his readers wanted, and he gave it to them. In some of his published work, there are revealing digressions on the technical problem of persuading the reader to accept his argument. If in his earliest book he had stood on the shoulders of Lloyd and Tempelhof, from this position he had opened fire on the hapless Heinrich Dietrich von Bülow, whose work is discussed in an earlier essay in this volume. Bülow, he was sure, had made himself incomprehensible to all but math-

---

[38] *Précis politique et militaire de la campagne de 1815*, "par le général J***" (Paris, 1839), 3, 15-41, 88ff. Jomini claimed that in writing his original biography of Napoleon, the manuscript for 1815 had been mislaid (ibid., 1-4).

ematicians, which was a mistake no matter what the merits of his theory might be. At first Jomini had tried to use a running critique of the studies by Lloyd and Tempelhof to elucidate the principles of war, but gave up when he saw that this method would produce a long, boring work. Tedious, obscure, pessimistic—these were also the great faults of Clausewitz in Jomini's view, although he admitted that there were some good ideas buried in *On War*.[39] The problem, then, lay less in being right than in finding the format that would attract and persuade.

Jomini seems all too modern in his confidence that discovering the truth is a less demanding task than packaging and marketing it. Never shaken in his faith that he had a firm grip on the only truth that mattered to soldiers and strategists, he worked hardest at making his versions of military history and his formulation of military theory as attractive as possible. He kept the message clear, simple, and repetitive. He stayed well within the established canon of military historiography. Although telling soldiers and conservatives what they wanted to hear, he escaped any charge of bias by making his own contribution to the growing Napoleonic legend. For variety and a touch of scientific patina, he introduced schematic diagrams and a little mathematics, but not too much, avoiding Bülow's mistake.[40]

In essence, Jomini fused two of the great cultural currents of the early nineteenth century: a boundless romantic sensibility and an obsession with the power of science, reduced to formulaic statements and prescriptive injunctions. Jomini's Napoleon, prefigured by Frederick, was a military genius whose transcendent mind and will grasped, as in religious revelation, the beauty and power of science—the romance of science. Jomini's influence must be understood in the context of influential contemporaries who saw reality in much the same way, however their specific conclusions or programs might diverge: Bentham, Comte, Marx, and the now-forgotten popularizer Victor Cousin, to choose only a few examples. Like Cousin, but unlike Bentham and Marx, Jomini was not absorbed by the solution of his chosen intellectual problem as such; he had solved that satisfactorily as a very young man.[41] Rather, he wanted to be heard, to convince, to establish the way that men think about war; and to this task he devoted his long life and restless energy. And in this

[39] *Traité*, 1:iii-vi; *Précis*, 1:17-18, 21-22.
[40] See *Précis*, 1:180, 183, where he used an ABCD rectangle to explain his ideas about the "base of operations," or 2:25 (plate), diagramming his twelve offensive and defensive orders of battle.
[41] D. G. Charlton, *Secular Religion in France, 1815-1870* (London, 1963), ch. 3, "The Cult of Science."

163

task, whatever secret feelings of failure and futility he may have had, he was uniquely successful.

III

His actual ideas, particularly when seen through the monstrous prism of twentieth-century warfare, lend themselves readily to parody and ridicule. A host of antiwar novelists, and some historians as well, have put Jominian banalities into the mouths of modern military commanders, who are variously depicted as stupid, sadistic, or both. His insistence that not even the most radical changes in military technology can alter the principles of war seems to explain a mentality that could order cavalry to attack machine guns or describe nuclear energy as "just another weapon." Equally dismaying is his contribution to the lamentable gulf between the military profession and political authority that appears to be a chronic malady of the modern world. By isolating strategy from its political and social context, Jomini helped to foster a mode of thinking about war that continues to haunt us. But we would be mistaken to blame him for our subsequent military troubles. Like any set of powerfully influential ideas, his gave clear expression to thoughts, attitudes, and feelings already prevalent, in his case during and after the Napoleonic wars. We can understand more if, mustering all possible sympathy, we take these ideas seriously.

Today Jomini is known chiefly through his *Summary of the Art of War*, translated into many languages and often abridged, extracted, and plagiarized. This is as he hoped. Describing himself as the Copernicus or the Columbus of military theory, he liked to say that all his books, including some thirty volumes of military history, were less valuable than his single short essay on the principles of war, written by 1804 and published in 1807.[42] This essay, expanded and elaborated, was the core of the *Summary*. Critics of Jomini from Clausewitz in his time to Bernard Brodie in ours have complained that he tried to reduce warfare to a simple set of rules.[43] On this point, he could claim no misunderstanding. But his very didactic emphasis, whose aim so exasperates his critics, may have obscured other important aspects of his work.

His military historiography deserves more than a passing glance. The earliest work, on the Seven Years' War, was a serious attempt to transcend the evident partisanship that consistently afflicted the genre.

---

[42] *Tableau analytique*, vii; Lecomte, *La général Jomini*, 3rd ed., xxxi.

[43] Peter Paret, *Clausewitz and the State* (New York, 1976; repr. Princeton, 1985), 152-53 and passim; Bernard Brodie, "Strategy as a Science," *World Politics* 1 (1949), 467-88, and more briefly in the *Encyclopedia of the Social Sciences* (New York, 1968), 15:281-88.

Military history was used so often to celebrate a leader or a people as an adjunct of monarchical power or an expression of national pride, that Jomini's quest for a less partial, more critical account of warfare is impressive. Even his mentors Lloyd and Tempelhof were obvious partisans; Lloyd had served as a general on the Austrian side, and Tempelhof was encouraged by Frederick to refute Lloyd's criticisms. Jomini's bias, of course, lay in believing that principles of war actually existed and that their operation could be discerned in the actual conduct of warfare. But at least he exemplified a new standard, in which praise and blame were less important than establishing, on some realistic basis, the range of historical possibilities. His later work on the Revolutionary and Napoleonic Wars has surely been underrated. Jomini had some access to French, Russian, and Austrian archives, he took a personal part in many campaigns, and after 1815 he questioned senior commanders—the Duke of Wellington at the Congress of Verona, for example. Any historian concerned with the military history of the period will find these volumes still valuable for their detail, clarity, and general accuracy. By trying to explore the actions of each belligerent, he tried to escape from the one-sided research that still plagues the writing of military history.[44] All this said, our attention must shift to what he himself insisted was the more important part of his work, the theory of strategy.

Central to Jomini's argument that there are immutable "principles" of war, as valid for Caesar and Alexander as for Frederick and Napoleon, is his emphasis on "lines of operations."[45] For modern critics of Jomini, who deplore his long-term influence on Western military thought, these "lines of operations" are simply reflections of the pseudoscientific nature of his theorizing; at best they are narrowly technical, certainly obsolete terms that might have meant something in premodern warfare but are of no serious interest except as they apply to a particular historical form of warfare. To see "lines of operations" in this way is to miss a vital part of what Jomini was attempting to say.

Jomini inherited the term *lignes d'opérations* from Lloyd and Tempelhof, to whom he gave credit for the origins of his own serious thinking about warfare. But he also saw that the term had been used by his

[44] Examples of good modern historians strongly influenced by what might be called the Jominian conception of military historiography are David G. Chandler, *The Campaigns of Napoleon* (New York, 1966) and Hew Strachan, *European Armies and the Conduct of War* (London and Boston, 1983).

[45] The title of chapter 14 of the *Traité* (2:269-328) is "Observations générales sur les lignes d'opérations. Maximes sur cette branche importante de l'art de la guerre." In a note to the chapter title Jomini said that he had been uncertain where to place this key chapter, finally deciding against leaving to the end of the work his statement of the ideas on which all his historical judgments were based.

predecessors in a confusing, unclear way and that it needed elaboration and clarification. Perhaps he made a mistake in not dropping the term altogether at some early stage, because it led him, his readers, and his critics to new levels of confusion, to sterile polemics, and—eventually, even before his death—to ridicule. Instead of beginning afresh, he took obvious delight, as a brash young staff officer in French service, in correcting the errors of Lloyd, Tempelhof, and Bülow in their misunderstanding of this centrally important concept. And once committed to the published word, by 1805, he was caught for the rest of his life by his own combative nature in an intellectual trap of his own design.

The trap, once built and sprung on himself by the ambitious youth, never changed. If *lignes d'opérations* are understood to mean *where* an armed force fights, for what *objective*, and in *what force* relative to the total available military power of the state, then Jomini insists that a fundamental distinction must be made; there are, he argued, two kinds of *lignes d'opérations*. First is the "natural" kind—the rivers, mountains, seacoasts, oceans, deserts, and sheer distances through, over, and around which military operations must be conducted. But there is more: the fairly permanent, man-made environment constricting warfare is also part of the "natural," or available, *lignes d'opérations*—fortifications, political boundaries, naval bases, and road networks. His point may seem banal, but insofar as military historians and theorists had blurred the distinction between what in warfare was environmentally possible and what was actually done, the point was worth making. The second kind of *lignes d'opérations*, once the environmentally constricting factors are recognized and set apart, is concerned exclusively with strategic choice; within the range of choice allowed by the prewar environment, where to fight? To what purpose? In what force? These, today as in the Napoleonic Wars, are not trivial or easy questions.

Jomini unhappily began by using different words to make the distinction: the natural or environmental constriction of strategic choice was categorized as "territorial" lines of operations and the actual strategic choices became "maneuver" lines of operations. When the more detailed, historical discussion inevitably mixed these categories with references to "bases" and "zones" or "theaters" of operations, confusion was not eliminated but compounded. Generations of impatient soldiers and unsympathetic critics have been puzzled and exasperated by what seems an elusive, abstract use of these neologisms, whose essential—and important—meaning is much less comprehensible than it might have been from an author who claimed to be above all realistic, direct, simple, and clear.

Jomini compounded the chances for misunderstanding when he further divided "maneuver" *lignes d'opérations* into no fewer than ten subcategories, ending with the implausible category of "accidental." But even the term "accidental line of operations" contains a vital point: in warfare the unexpected must be expected—rapidly changing circumstances might require a new line of operations. We must return to some of these sub-categories later in the discussion, but here it is enough to recognize that a very young Jomini—ambitious, sensitive, and brash—rushed the first full statement of his "*principes généraux de l'art de guerre*" into print at Glogau, of all places, during a lull when Ney's Sixth Corps was gar-risoned in Silesia, sending most of the five hundred copies off to book-sellers in Berlin and Breslau, the rest to Napoleon and others he hoped to impress. The chief result was to freeze prematurely, in misleading and obscurantist language, his valuable thought on a vital aspect of all warfare.[46]

Strategic choice, regarded in time and space, remains a basic problem even in an age of microelectronics, nuclear energy, and the exploitation of "space" itself for military purposes. This was the problem that Jomini saw at the heart of Napoleonic success, the less spectacular victories of Frederick II, and the outcome of all warfare past and future. He tried to distinguish "territorial" lines of operations, or warfare as it can be planned on a map, in order to set it aside and allow himself to focus more clearly on strategy itself. Similarly, as he elaborated his ideas, he recognized that the highest and lowest levels of military action, where values and emotions, and weapons and techniques, came into play, levels that he called "political and moral" and "tactical," respectively, were important factors in military results. But these "political" and "tactical" levels were qualitatively different, he argued, from the "strategic"; po-litical systems and emotional climates varied greatly, while tactics were narrowly determined by existing—and changing—weaponry. Neither was subject to underlying, unchanging principles; the only aspect of warfare susceptible to scientific analysis is strategy.[47] The long-term effect of his work, then, although he repeatedly denied any such intention, was to reduce the problem of war to the professional concerns of the wartime commander.

His "principles" of war were, and still are in their various modern versions, prescriptions for making strategic choices. "Strategy," as he used the term, applied to all levels of military action below the political

[46] Alger, *Antoine-Henri Jomini*, 22 n. 20, indicates that no copy of the original 1807 pamphlet has been found. But the essay was reprinted in the journal *Pallas* 1 (1808), 31-40. It appears as chapter 35 of the *Traité*, 4:275-86.

[47] The point is implicit in his treatment of both politics and tactics in the *Précis*, 1:42-147 and 2:195-97, but as pointed out below he often ignored his own categorical distinctions.

decision to wage war against certain enemies down to, but not including, combat itself. At every level the commander must decide where, when, and how to move his forces in order to carry out his mission and to fight under the best conditions. In Jomini's judgment, which he claimed to have reached when still in his teens by considering Bonaparte's Italian campaign of 1796-1797, most commanders made the wrong choices because they did not understand the principles of strategy. Those principles can be summarized in the fewest words as bringing superior force to bear on a point where the enemy is both weaker and liable to crippling damage.

Again, Jomini seems banal if we fail to see why he emphasizes the point: most commanders make bad strategic choices because they are misled by "common sense" (a phrase not used by Jomini, but strongly implied by his endless discussions of historical cases). Attempting to defend territory or a weaker army, they let the enemy decide where, when, and how to attack. Uncertain how to protect or exploit several "natural" lines of operations, they hedge their bets by dispersing force among several possibilities. The uncommon sense of Napoleon and usually of Frederick and of all victorious commanders had always been—says Jomini—to attack with massed forces against some enemy point judged to be "decisive." Properly understood, the apparent recklessness of such strategy, which leaves some areas weakened or vulnerable, is actually prudence. Aggressive, offensive action deprives the enemy of time to think and act, while superior force at the time and place of battle is the best guarantee of ultimate victory. Any other approach to strategy is, in one of Jomini's favorite words, "*vicieuse*." As simple as these formulations may seem, he reiterated them throughout his writings because in the actual conduct of warfare they were so often ignored, with disastrous consequences.

History for Jomini was both the source of his own grasp of these principles, and their confirmation and elucidation in the real world of military action. A question arises about the degree to which Jomini's historical accounts were simply shaped to reflect his theoretical preconceptions. Clausewitz, for one, disagreed sharply with a number of Jomini's specific historical judgments, and charged him with both faults—theoretical bias and inadequate knowledge.[48] But the enormous difficulty in making the right strategic choices within the various military coalitions against Revolutionary and Napoleonic France, as against Prussia during the Seven Years' War, is clearly beyond the slightest doubt.

A recent study, for example, of British strategy at the end of the

---

[48] Paret, *Clausewitz and the State*, 148-49.

Second Coalition (1799-1802), based on exhaustive research in British archives, shows a war cabinet with vast naval and financial powers and a considerable land force at its disposal completely unable to decide where or whether to attack—in the Mediterranean? in America? against France itself, somewhere between Flanders and the Bay of Biscay? Had men less capable than William Pitt, Henry Dundas, and Lord Grenville been involved in this gross strategic failure, we might think them the fools that Jomini, in his more unqualified accounts of military defeat, suggests losers usually are.[49] The difficulty of making and implementing strategic choices, however simple and limited they may appear in retrospect, is confirmed in war after war, down to the present. And the core of the difficulty is as Jomini defined it, in correctly weighing risks, benefits, and probabilities, and in reaching some conclusion firm enough to be carried out. Whether massed offensive action is always or usually the right prescription is an altogether different question, but at least we must credit Jomini for giving the problem of strategic decision making the attention its history and consequences deserve.

The strategic concept that received most attention in his analysis is that of the "inner" or "interior" line of operations. It refers to the simple idea that one side may have a position between—"inside"—separated enemy forces. With such an "interior" position, it is possible to strike first one part of the enemy force, then the other, defeating each in turn, although the enemy—if united—might be the stronger side. Jomini never tired of demonstrating how a smaller army commanded by a Frederick or a Napoleon could defeat a larger, presumably stronger army by operating on a "single" or united line of operation when the enemy was operating on "multiple" or "concentric" lines of operation. A skillful commander, like Bonaparte in 1796, by rapid maneuver could exploit enemy dispersion, achieve an "interior" line of operation against the "exterior" lines of his opponent, and win a decisive victory.

Jomini claimed that the idea had first struck him in studying Frederick's victory of 1757 at Leuthen. There Frederick had managed to bring the mass of his army to bear against a single Austrian flank. Jomini saw that Bonaparte had done the same thing on a much larger strategic scale in Italy, to be repeated, in one form or another, in his later campaigns. At Waterloo, nothing but Prussian refusal to play the game kept Napoleon from using the victorious formula once again. Separated from the British army under Wellington, the Prussians had been defeated at Ligny, but they had painfully learned never to give Napoleon the time and space

[49] Piers G. Mackesy, *War Without Victory: The Downfall of Pitt, 1799-1802* (Oxford, 1984).

needed to defeat their ally. At the critical moment at Waterloo, the Prussians, instead of retreating along their own line of operation, returned to the fighting zone, crushed the French right flank, and changed a drawn battle into a decisive Allied victory.

The "interior" line of operation was the most specific, practical form given by Jomini to his general principle of massing force against some vulnerable part of the enemy force. As such, it aroused much interest among soldiers seeking useful strategic ideas. Of course its application depended, as it had at Waterloo, on exact calculations of time and space as well as on enemy behavior. If the enemy kept his own forces united or left too little time and space for his divided forces to be attacked and defeated, then victory might not be possible. Jomini did not deal with this problem except to say that a Great Captain would induce his opponent, by confusing and deceiving him, to divide his forces, as had been done to the Austrians in 1805 and to the Prussians in 1806. In that respect Jomini conceded that the science of war would always be an art.

In his mature writing on strategy, Jomini admitted one great exception to the fundamental principle of massed, offensive action against a single point. The exception he variously called civil, religious, or national war, or wars of opinion. These were armed struggles not with regular armies on both sides, but wars in which an entire people was aroused and active. The most intense phase of the Wars of the French Revolution, at the time of the *levée en masse* and the Reign of Terror, had been of this nature. Jomini himself had taken part in two other such wars: the French invasions of Spain and Russia. In these campaigns it was literally pointless to mass forces because there was no decisive point to attack; the enemy was everywhere, usually concealed behind a screen of popular hostility that blinded the invader. Jomini remembered a horrible night in northwestern Spain, with no Spanish troops reported within sixty miles, when an entire artillery company of Ney's corps had been wiped out. The sole survivor said that the attack had come from peasants led by priests. All the gold in Mexico, Jomini wrote, could not buy the combat intelligence needed by French forces in Spain.[50] Similarly Jomini, who had lost all his papers at the desperate crossing of the Beresina River in 1812, remembered how Russian partisans had harrassed the retreating French columns. Wars like these, in his view, were "dangerous and deplorable"—"they always arouse violent passions that make them spiteful, cruel, terrible." Any soldier prefers warfare *"loyale et chevaleresque"* to the "organized assassination" of civil, national, and ideological wars.[51]

[50] *Précis*, 1:77-78.
[51] Ibid., 1:83.

He had little to say about the principles, if any, that informed the correct strategy for such "dangerous and deplorable" wars. Conquering a people in arms inevitably meant dividing forces; massing troops for battle would always run the risk of losing control in weakened areas to insurgent forces like Spanish peasants and Russian partisans. The only answer seemed to be in having both a mobile field army and separate territorial "divisions" to garrison and control each conquered district. The commanders of these divisions would need to be intelligent and experienced (*instruit*) because their political role would be as important as armed force in securing victory.[52] That this pragmatic advice, which claimed no scientific authority, meant ignoring his fundamental prescription of massed offensive action against one point, does not appear to have troubled him, his audience, or even his critics. Instead, he left a strong suggestion that the whole subject sickened him, and the clear implication that any military power would do well to avoid involving itself in national or civil wars.

Viewed either as a military problem or as a means of defense, people's war was too destructive, too costly and uncontrollable to be part of any scientific study of strategy. To the suggestion that future wars would— or should—be "national wars," as in 1793-1794, Jomini replied that strategy, like politics, must find some "*juste milieu*" between wars of the past fought by professional armies and the new yet old barbaric warfare unleashed by the Revolution. The middle way, he argued, lay in channeling popular passions into a trained, organized military reserve that could quickly join the regular army in time of war.[53] To that extent, his prescription proved to be prophetic. But in the end he wavered, using a hypothetical scenario. If France should invade Belgium and in retaliation German troops occupied Rhenish territory to prevent French annexation of Flanders, should the French government unleash a *levée en masse* to defend its eastern frontier? No, of course not; clearly, aims on both sides were limited and not worth the horrors of popular war. But if German forces achieved victory in the east, what could stop a euphoric decision to annex the occupied French territory? How might the risk of such escalation alter the original French calculation? It was, he admitted, a difficult question; and there ended the discussion.[54]

As he grew older, Jomini seemed more concerned with the political and psychological aspects of war that his own theorizing had pushed into the background. In his early work discussion of political factors, as such, was sporadic and infrequent. The hastily compiled *Synoptic Analysis* of

[52] This specific bit of advice appeared in his work very early; see *Traité*, 4:284-85n.
[53] *Précis*, 1:81-82.
[54] Ibid., 1:80-81.

171

1830 has about fifty pages on the diplomacy of warfare (*politique de la guerre*) and the political aspects of strategy (*politique militaire*). The *Summary*, published seven years later, has much longer, more carefully considered sections on the political dimension of warfare. It seems likely that reading *On War*, the unfinished masterpiece of Clausewitz, who had criticized Jomini as narrow, simplistic, and superficial and who himself had stressed the need to see war as an extension of politics, was an important factor in this expanded treatment of the subject in 1837. It was here that Jomini added a long chapter on "wars of opinion" as well as new sections on supreme command and morale. But in giving these subjects fuller treatment, he could not break out of his established mode of discourse. At every point he described good and bad results, exhorted his readers to pursue the good and avoid the bad, and offered various techniques for doing so. For example, it was ideal if a supreme commander, like Frederick or Napoleon, combined political and military power. But if the monarch had to appoint a supreme commander, then the problem was one of avoiding friction and intrigue and of giving the supreme commander all possible political support in carrying out his strategic plans.[55] There is little attention to the question of why friction arises between political authority and military command, except as a symptom of human weakness. Similarly, national military spirit is reckoned to be a good thing; but there is no analysis of the phenomenon, simply a call for the military to be honored and respected.

Although Jomini did not claim to base his discussion of politics on any scientific principles, there is the same stultifying emphasis on prescription rather than analysis. His description of the ideal supreme commander epitomizes his entire treatment of nonstrategic matters in the *Summary*: he should be a man of great moral and physical courage, but not necessarily of great learning; "he must know a few things very well [*il faut savoir peu mais bien*] especially the regulating principles."[56] Even as Jomini tried to broaden his approach to war, he failed to escape his obsession with strategy and its principles.

The basic criticism of Jomini is obvious, that he was committed to reductionism and prescription. But his response to this criticism would be, "Exactly!" To reduce the complexity of warfare to the smallest number of crucial factors and to prescribe those lines of action that make victory most likely were his consistently held intentions.[57] He would ask his critics whether they think that warfare cannot be simplified by analysis

[55] Ibid., 1:121-36. In this section he also deplored the baneful effects of "councils of war."
[56] Ibid., 1:128.
[57] He was most explicit about this aim in his attacks on Clausewitz; see *Précis*, 1:21ff.

or that analysis cannot identify the probable outcomes of various options. Criticism of Jomini must do more than insist that he ought to have approached his subject in another way; it must take him on his own terms and then ask where the work falls short of its own aims.

Four such internal weaknesses suggest themselves. One is that he failed to test, as a good scientist should, the "null hypothesis"—the historical cases in which actual military experience did not conform to prediction based on his principles. Indeed he discussed such cases—the campaign of 1794 was one of them, when the French won despite dividing their forces and giving the Austrians the potential advantage of "interior lines"—but Jomini was too evidently concerned to explain such cases away, too little interested in the ways that they might have broadened or enriched his theory. These cases were, in short, treated as a threat to his position, and he discussed them only to preempt doubts and criticism.

A second weakness is closely related to his reductionist method. To reduce relevant factors in his analysis, he made the assumption that military units of equivalent size were essentially equal—equally well armed, trained, disciplined, supplied, and motivated.[58] Only differences at the top, in the capacity of commanders and the quality of their strategic decisions, were of interest. Like chess players or war gamers, commanders play with units of force whose "values" are more or less known, not variables as Clausewitz would suggest, but constants in the equation of warfare. This assumption facilitates analysis within its own limits of validity but beyond these limits becomes a crippling impediment to further analysis. It was not unreasonable of Jomini to assume that an important class of wars were fought between states whose armed forces were modern and of roughly equal strength. Too much inequality, and the weaker side would not risk war. European warfare after 1815 fit this model neatly, as it had before 1789, so that Jominian assumptions seemed realistic within the international system of nineteenth-century Europe.

But there was another class of wars, whose importance was growing in Jomini's own lifetime, in which the asymmetrical character of the armed forces in conflict is critical to any adequate analysis. It is this assumption of symmetrical forces that causes Jomini to flounder in his treatment of popular wars, like those in Spain and Russia, and virtually to ignore the inherent problems of coalition strategy, as in the campaigns against Napoleon, when the conflicting aims of allied states simply could not be reconciled even in the fact of a united and dangerous enemy. It is this same assumption that makes Jominian theory dogmatically insen-

[58] His assumptions of symmetry and equivalence appear clearly in his essay, "Sur la formation des troupes pour le combat," published as the second appendix to the *Précis*, 2:375-401, in which he attempts to assess the impact on tactics of rifled infantry weapons.

sitive to the kinds of technological and organizational changes that brought Prussian victories in 1866 and 1870, European disaster in 1914-1918 and 1939-1945, and some spectacular results outside Europe from modern wars of liberation and revolution. All of these wars have hinged on imbalances or changes in the *qualities* of the armed forces engaged; but Jominian theory is peculiarly unsuited to qualitative analysis—except of strategic decision making.

The third weakness is related to the second; Jomini himself had stated that neither the political realm in which wars take place nor the military technique with which wars are fought is susceptible to the kind of scientific analysis that he brought to strategy and strategic decision making. Politics depend too much on varying conditions and on the ever-changing relationship between political leaders and political forces. Similarly, the details of military tactics depend on changing weaponry and other factors that readily escape the operation of fixed principles. But in his own mature work, notably in the main part of his *Summary*, Jomini is very careless about the location and importance of this distinction between what is and what is not susceptible to scientific analysis. Often acknowledged as the inventor of the modern concept of "strategy" (as distinct from "politics" and "tactics"), he wanders freely up into the one and down into the other, citing principles and prescribing action as if he himself had forgotten that all three zones were regulated by different laws. The worst faults are in the tactical zone, where most of his professional readers would naturally have sought useful instruction. He had based his earliest theorizing on the battle of Leuthen, and the battlefield—where "timeless principles" did not apply—always attracted his interest.[59] He developed schematic options for battle, invoking wherever possible the principle of massed force against a single point, noting the value of "interior lines," warning against the danger of exposing one's rear while attacking that of the enemy. The effect was to blur the vital distinction between levels of military operation—to confuse hopelessly the situation in which a subordinate unit may, quite reasonably, defend passively, divide its forces, or expose its rear while operating as part of a larger, well-founded strategic plan.

A final weakness of his work, judged on its own terms, is illustrated by his vagueness about where the principles of war do and do not apply. The weakness lies in a pervasive ambiguity that leaves readers, including scholarly commentators, to understand the work in quite different, sometimes contradictory ways.[60] Clausewitz is also full of ambiguity, but *On*

[59] *Précis*, 1:16.
[60] For example, in John Gooch, "Clio and Mars: The Use and Abuse of History," *Journal of Strategic Studies* 3, no. 3 (1980), 26, the following statement appears: "Jomini did not

War is consciously provocative, reflecting the author's own perception of war—complex, dynamic, often ambiguous. Jomini sought simplicity and clarity, but when read carefully and not hastily or selectively, the Jominian message is ambiguous. At one time victory depends on strict adherence to strategic principles, at another the genius of the commander in applying them (or in knowing when he can safely ignore them) is the crucial element. Warfare is, or can be made, scientific; yet war is a chaotic drama, full of chance and irrational forces. The varying emphasis often seems to follow the shifting line of Jomini's polemical attack, whether he is disparaging the extreme scientism of Bülow and all those who would make warfare a mechanical operation or refuting Clausewitz and others who questioned the value of prescriptive operational principles. To this extent his ambiguity is neither surprising nor especially troubling. But in the critical area of strategic decision, ambiguity seriously blunts the point of his argument. Attacking the enemy armed force is the essence of strategy, but to what end? Despite his emphasis on relentless pursuit of a beaten foe, there is much in Jomini to indicate that territorial control is the true objective of armed conflict. Unlike Clausewitz, Jomini conceived of warfare in largely spatial terms, and this predilection grew more pronounced in his later, more influential work. Closely related to his ambiguity, whether the control of territory or the destruction of enemy power should be the aim of strategic action, is an ambiguity about the competing demands of aggressiveness and security. He left no doubt that only offensive action could bring victory, but he also insisted that this action must be taken without exposing friendly forces to counteroffensive action. In the real world of warfare, as Jomini well knew, it is rarely possible to attack without risk of counterattack, but once again he did not directly confront the issue. The competing principles of "offensive" and "security" were left without satisfactory resolution, their ambiguous relationship exacerbated by uncertainty about the operational meaning of a third principle, that of the "objective."

In reviewing these criticisms, which are internal to his own approach to warfare and thus are not an attack on the approach itself, we might conclude that Jomini had a shallow or undisciplined mind or was psychologically incapable of controlling the reach of his basic intellectual position, which in turn he seemed unable to expand or modify. All of this seems true enough if not pressed too far. Although his irascible, narcissistic personality makes it easy to turn the man and his work into caricature, Jomini by every account and on the evidence of his own

intend his work to be regarded in a normative light." Surely, Gooch or I must be mistaken. But the more important point is that Jomini is easily misread.

writing had a quick, penetrating mind. Buried in the repetitive polemics of his books are valuable observations, stimulating ideas, and a single argument about strategy that, at least within the hazy limits of its applicability, is surely correct.

In one of his last published essays, on the Austro-Prussian war of 1866, he pondered the new technique of railway transport.[61] He wondered whether the constricting effect of prewar rail networks on strategic choice—of the new "territorial" lines of operation on maneuver lines of operation, to use his own terminology—might actually increase the role of chance in determining victory or defeat in the future. But this interesting speculation quickly gave way to a predictable insistence that neither steam power nor anything else could change the principles of strategy, "which remain immutable."[62] He simply would not, probably could not, give up the pattern in which his mind had worked for decades. But that pattern was more than a personal quirk; it appealed deeply to generations of soldiers. They belonged to a profession, conservative by nature, whose commitment to the values of loyalty, obedience, and order responded strongly to Jomini's insistence on an unchanging truth, essentially simple, and—once grasped—of great utility. His view of military reality enabled them and other students of warfare to stifle doubts provoked by experiences like that of 1866 and to fend off unwelcome criticism of military policy. This continuing appeal of Jominian thought requires some further discussion.

IV

Evidence of Jomini's influence during the nineteenth century and after is impressive. As early as 1808 his commentary on Lloyd and Tempelhof was translated into English and his essay on the principles of war was published and favorably received in Germany.[63] By 1811 the entire *Treatise* was being published in German and Russian. After Waterloo his reputation grew, enhanced by the regular appearance of each new volume on the campaigns of the Revolution and by a widespread belief

---

[61] "Questions stratégiques relatives aux événements de la guerre de Bohême," *Revue militaire suisse* 11 (1866), 577-86, signed by "Un invalide quasi nonagénaire."

[62] Ibid., 580. He repeated the point to his son Alexander, in response to Miliutin's thanks for a copy of the essay (October 4, [1866], Egerton MSS. 3167, ff. 54-55).

[63] The noted military writer Berenhorst, although critical of Jomini's published account of the battle of Jena, commented favorably on his essay on the principles of war published in *Pallas* in 1808 (*Aus dem Nachlasse von Georg Heinrich von Berenhorst*, ed. Eduard von Bülow, part 2 [Dessau, 1847]), 286. Captain Charles Hamilton Smith of the British army translated *The History of the Seven Years War in Germany by Generals Lloyd and Tempelhof, with Observations and Maxims Extracted from the Treatise of Great Military Operations of General Jomini*, vol. 1 (London, n.d. [c. 1808]). A note on page 81 says that the rest of Jomini's *Traité* deserves translation.

that his advice had been crucially important in the Allied campaign of 1813 against Napoleon. After Napoleon's death in 1821, his comments on Jomini's account of the Italian campaign of 1796-1797 were published; the exiled emperor praised the work, absolved Jomini of treason in 1813 (he was, after all, Swiss, not French), and offered new information only on a few matters of fact concerning the campaign, "for a new edition." On another occasion during his exile Napoleon mused that in a future regime he would put Jomini in charge of military education.[64]

Although Jomini betrayed throughout his life a certain Anglophobia, English writers were no less admiring. William Napier, leading historian of the Peninsular campaigns, was an avowed Jominian.[65] In 1825 Lieutenant J. A. Gilbert of the Royal Artillery published *An Exposition of Grand Military Combinations and Movements compiled from . . . Jomini.* Even across the Atlantic, Jomini was the leading interpreter of Napoleon and the dean of military theorists. In the tiny American military academy at West Point, where the emphasis was on the training of technicians—artillerists and engineers—cadets used a translation of Gay de Vernon's *Treatise on the Science of War and Fortification.* But added to it was an appendix on the principles of war drawn chiefly from Jomini, whose work was praised by the American editor as "a master-piece, and as the highest authority. Indeed no man should pretend to be capable of commanding any considerable body of troops, unless he have studied and meditated on the principles laid down by Jomini."[66] These characteristic judgments of Jomini appeared before he publication of the *Synoptic Analysis* (1830) and the *Summary of the Art of War* (1837-1838). The younger, post-Napoleonic generation of officers was as impressed as its seniors by the value of reducing warfare to a handful of strategic maxims. The chief effect of the later works, then, was to etch the Jominian message in granite.

If there can be such a thing as a joke in military history, surely a small one is the belief that with the posthumous publication of Clausewitz in the 1830s, *On War* became the bible of the Prussian army, the source of their great victories of 1866 and 1870, and soon thereafter the chief military theory of the Western world. The truth is that most German students of war found Clausewitz no less difficult, obscure, and of doubtful utility than did non-Germans, most of whom read Clausewitz in poor

[64] Comte de Montholon, *Mémoire pour servir à l'histoire de France sous Napoléon,* 6 vols. (Paris, 1832), 1:1.

[65] Jay Luvaas, *The Education of an Army: British Military Thought, 1815-1940* (London, 1964), 25-28.

[66] Simon François Gay de Vernon, *A Treatise on the Science of War and Fortification* . . . , trans. John Michael O'Connor, 2 vols. (New York, 1817), 1:v. Vol. 2, p. 386, also praises Jomini for having "transcended all writers on war."

translations. Willisen, a leading German military writer who published his own *Theory of Great War* in 1840, described himself as an "ardent pupil" of Jomini. A younger Prussian officer and military theorist, Friedrich Wilhelm Rüstow, was an extreme case who tests the generalization that the influence of Jomini was pervasive. Rüstow was a political radical who fled Prussia after the Revolution of 1848, served as Garibaldi's chief of staff, was well known to Marx and Engels, and might be expected to attack Jomini as a "bourgeois" theorist. But he did not. Like Willisen, Rüstow is described as "really a staunch adherent" of Jomini, and his own studies of strategy published in 1857 and 1872 reiterated the dogma that new weapons can never change the principles of strategy. A number of lesser German writers took the same position.[67]

After the Franco-Prussian War, when French and British students of warfare were "discovering" Clausewitz as one of the secret weapons in the Prussian arsenal, influential German writers kept the Jominian faith. In 1880, Albrecht von Boguslawski of the Prussian army carefully reedited and translated Jomini's *Summary*. Explaining the relationship of Jomini to Clausewitz, Boguslawski asserted that he saw no reason whatsoever for setting the theories and conceptions of war of these two "erudite thinkers" in opposition to one another, a judgment that would have startled both men.[68] At the end of the century, another Prussian officer, Yorck von Wartenburg, published his biographical *Napoleon as a General*; its message is pure Jomini, and in translation was still being used as the basic text at West Point in the 1950s. Although there was lively debate over military theory in the Prussian and German armies, the evidence confirms the judgment of Peter Paret on the "discovery" of Clausewitz by Victorian, Wilhelmine, and *fin-de-siècle* students of warfare: "Essentially it was a Jominian rather than a Clausewitzian attitude that dominated military thinking, and in the intensely empirical atmosphere of the times, *On War* could hardly avoid being considered as a kind of operational manual."[69]

Considered as an operational manual, *On War* simply reinforced Jomini's emphasis on the massive, aggressive use of force. But the enormous difference between the two theories lay in Clausewitz's insistence that war was extremely complex in reality (however simple ideally); that theory could only illuminate this complexity, identifying and clarifying relationships (but not prescribe action); and that warfare was intrinsically

[67] Rudolph von Caemmerer, *The Development of Strategical Science during the 19th Century* (London, 1905), 135, 142-143, and 221.

[68] Antoine-Henri Jomini, *Abriss der Kriegskunst*, ed. and trans. Albrecht von Boguslawski (Berlin, 1881), iv.

[69] Paret, "Clausewitz and the Nineteenth Century," 31.

political and must be approached as such (and was not an autonomous activity occurring within more or less fixed political boundaries). As the name of Clausewitz, after 1870, became a universally known symbol of German military prowess, Jomini had already won their personal duel, in effect desensitizing their audience to the vital parts of Clausewitz's message.

The list of Jomini's disciples and admirers is very long, and even his few nineteenth-century critics accepted his basic approach to the study of war. But about 1890 his general influence made a quantum leap upward through the work of Alfred Thayer Mahan.[70] Unlike Clausewitz, Jomini had given some attention to the specifically maritime dimension of warfare, although chiefly as a medium for colonial and amphibious operations. Both Clausewitz and Jomini were primarily concerned with the classic European problem posed by several great military powers coexisting in a constricted space. Mahan was an American naval officer. His father, Dennis Hart Mahan, taught "military art (or science)" at West Point for many years and was arguably the leading American exponent and purveyor of Jominian ideas.[71] When the younger Mahan, bored in the 1880s by the peacetime routine of naval service, turned to scholarship, he consciously decided to do for "sea power" what Jomini had done for land warfare. The resulting *Influence of Sea Power upon History, 1660-1783*, published in 1890, left a deep mark on the modern world, on modern imperialist doctrine as much as on naval policy and strategy. Mahan is treated elsewhere in this volume; here it is enough to note how his use of six "principles" to frame his analysis and his reiterated stress on the need to command the sea through offensive, concentrated naval action make him a maritime counterpart of Jomini—a description that Mahan himself would have accepted with pleasure.

Simplifying, reducing, prescribing—these had become the inescapably dominant qualities of Western military thought at the turn of the century. And, almost invariably, these qualities combined to extol the Napoleonic model of massing, attacking, and quickly winning decisive victories. Anything less or different was reckoned as failure. Defensive, attritional, protracted, and limited warfare were among those non-Napoleonic, non-Jominian forms of military action that were condemned in principle, doomed in practice. An alternative approach, represented by Clausewitz, who was more aware of complexity and variety, insistent on the dynamic character of violence, and less concerned with prescription

[70] Russell F. Weigley, *The American Way of War: A History of United States Military Strategy and Policy* (New York and London, 1973), 173-91.

[71] Stephen E. Ambrose, *Duty, Honor, Country: A History of West Point* (Baltimore, 1966), 99-102.

than with analysis, lay at hand but went largely unheeded. Similarly, the reading of Jomini's own work was highly selective; few noticed that "wars of opinion" stood outside his fundamental principles of strategy. The emphasis might shift, as it did in the work of Foch and other French military writers, from the physical and mechanical aspects of warfare to the psychological, but the shift took place within the framework of Jominian orthodoxy.[72]

Before tracing his influence beyond the bloody divide of 1914, we can summarize what lay behind Jomini's enduring appeal. Nothing could match the Napoleonic Wars in their traumatic effect on subsequent Western thinking about war—its nature, its potential, and its method. Jomini had established himself almost instantly as the authoritative interpreter of Napoleonic warfare. Not only was his version of the Napoleonic experience persuasive, it was—within its limits—perceptive and sound, not to be brushed aside by those who found fault with it, and in that respect quite unlike Bülow. Napoleon, said Jomini, had won quick, decisive victories by the ferocious application of concentrated military force against weak, sensitive points. The most serious criticism of Jomini was not that what he said was wrong, but that by omission and exaggeration he had produced a grotesquely simple account of what happened from 1796 to 1815 and thereby a grossly inadequate theory, whose consequences were potentially disastrous. But this criticism, before 1914, rested on speculation about future war. For a long century Western military experience was limited, and the potential weaknesses of his theory went unrealized. The quick victories of 1859, 1866, and 1870, as well as the protracted American Civil War and the debacle of the Crimean War could be readily explained in terms of lines of operation, of he need to concentrate force and use it offensively, and of the dangers of dividing forces and defending passively. If the Russian army bogged down in attritional, trench warfare in 1905 against the Japanese, the explanation lay in Russian ignorance and inefficiency. "Colonial" military operations, so different in so many ways from the classical European military problem, could be safely ignored. After Waterloo little or nothing happened to shake the paradigm of Jominian theory until 1914.

The Great War shattered many things, and none more than military theory. After the horrors and fiascos of trench warfare, the very idea of "military science" seemed laughable. On all sides military commanders had vocally defended their own apparent ineptitude with simple strategic maxims drawn from Jomini, whose reputation began a steep decline from

---

[72] Ferdinand Foch, *Des principes de la guerre* (Paris, 1903), 3-4. Foch took Jomini's description of war as a great "drama" as the point of departure for his work on the "principles of war."

which it has never recovered. Modern weapons, the total mobilization of economies and societies, and attritional warfare with its revolutionary consequences seemed to make nonsense of his preoccupation with lines of operations and little diagrams of strategic maneuvers.

But out of the Great War also came new military developments, at least two of which had the effect of recasting and thus perpetuating the Jominian vision of warfare. No military critic of wartime strategy was more articulate and influential than the Englishman, Captain B. H. Liddell Hart. He spoke directly to all those who were horrified by the pointless carnage of the western front, and who were determined that never again would Europeans fight in this way. No pacifist, and pessimistic about the chances for permanent peace, Liddell Hart identified the central problem of modern war as the suicidal obsession with the Great Battle, the direct clash of main armies or fleets with victory defined as physical survival. He blamed the obsession not on Jomini but on Clausewitz. Blind admiration and imitation of the German military after 1870 and particularly the influence of its Prussian prophet, "the Mahdi of Mass" as Liddell Hart called Clausewitz, lay behind the terrible degeneration of the theory and practice of European warfare.

Against a Clausewitzian conception of warfare—the collision of mass armies, the outcome decided by sheer numbers and will power, but the human cost higher than any imaginable "victory" could justify— Liddell Hart called for renewed emphasis on mobility, audacity, and skill. His strategy of the indirect approach, elaborated in a series of historical and theoretical books and articles, advocated the war of maneuver to out-think and out-flank the enemy, psychologically as well as geographically, at minimum risk and minimum cost. It was strategy that called less for a nation in arms than for a fairly small, highly professional force equipped with the latest technology. Although hardly proclaiming himself a Jominian, Liddell Hart, by his caricature of Jomini's sharpest critic and his own emphasis on strategy as a set of techniques, in effect revived the didactic, prescriptive, reductionist approach that characterized Jomini's work.[73] Without exaggerating the influence of Liddell Hart himself, we find that ideas like his resonate during the interwar decades in the military thinking of important contemporaries: J. F. C. Fuller, Charles de Gaulle, the young George Patton, and above all young German officers, like Heinz Guderian, who developed techniques for quick, limited victories— the blitzkrieg.[74]

Of still greater long-term significance than the strategies of indirect

[73] Brian Bond, *Liddell Hart: A Study of His Military Thought* (London and New Brunswick, N.J., 1977), 80.
[74] See the essays on the twentieth century in this volume.

181

approach and blitzkrieg was the emerging concept of strategic bombing. Here too there was a clear link with the Jominian tradition. In the 1920s Giulio Douhet and other early theorists of "air power" did for the airplane what Mahan in the 1890s had done for the warship; they developed a doctrine for its optimal strategic employment that closely resembled the Jominian version of Napoleonic warfare.[75] Airplanes, like warships and armies, should be massed against the decisive point. That point was located not in the armed force of the enemy, but in his economic and administrative centers, which were so vulnerable to aerial attack.

In this definition of "decisive point," strategic-bombing doctrine seems to diverge from the older orthodoxies of Jomini and Alfred Thayer Mahan, who had stressed the army-to-army and fleet-to-fleet confrontation. Closer examination, however, shows less divergence than there might seem. Both Jomini and Mahan had stressed what may be called the military economy of the target. For armies, it was the vital zone behind the fighting front, where supply and communications were centered. For navies, it was the ports and trade that gave sea power its rationale. To strike at or even to threaten these centers would force the enemy to defend them, often under unfavorable conditions. Strategic bombing used new technology to attack targets at once more vital and more vulnerable than those described by Jomini and Mahan, and in that sense air power promised to be the ultimate form of strategy; but conceptually the three sets of military ideas were much alike.

In all three there is a common emphasis on using armed force to attack the nervous and circulatory systems of enemy strength. By assuming that these systems consist of people who are not primarily fighters and are thus fairly helpless in the face of violence, all three theories reflect the classic Western distinction between soldier and civilian. A hard shell of soldiers defends, while being supported by a soft nucleus of civilians; breaking the shell thus produces victory, because nonsoldiers are assumed to have little or no capacity for military resistance. But even armies have fighting fronts and weak, vulnerable rear areas manned by civilianized soldiers. Presented as a straightforward, self-evident description of reality, this dichotomy is better seen as a metaphor, unexamined and behavioristic in nature. A great deal of historical experience, as well as an alternative line of thought from Clausewitz through Marx to contemporary theories of revolution, supports the opposite idea: that ordinary people, "civilians," even in complex societies can display great resilience and toughness in the face of violence. Once again, the Jominian approach

[75] Brodie, *Strategy in the Missile Age*, 71-106.

forecloses the question; the results of strategic bombing in 1940-1945 indicate some of the possible consequences.[76]

Tracing the Jominian line beyond 1945 becomes more difficult and debatable, but the effort to do so has value. "Principles of War" continue to be part of the official statements of military doctrine in virtually every modern armed force, including those in the Soviet bloc.[77] Although a question naturally arises as to the actual influence and function of this ritualistic assertion of doctrine, which is possibly no more profound in effect than teaching soldiers to march in step, there is no doubt that these principles, although varying slightly from one armed force to another, derive directly from Jomini.

More important, and much less simple, is the nature of military thought since 1945.[78] It would be foolish to claim direct links; contemporary strategy is not the product of some genealogical chain of military theory. The social scientists who have dominated modern strategic studies do not read Jomini, except perhaps as a historical curiosity, and none would admit to being influenced by work so obviously antiquated. The persistence of the Jominian approach after 1945, however, is most visible in *criticism* of contemporary strategic thought. Those critics who do not reject war as an instrument of policy repeatedly make points about current thinking that are very like the standard critique of Jomini. The criticism is that strategists in the nuclear age employ abstract methods like model building and systems analysis that reduce war to an operational exercise, transforming it thereby into an unrealistic but extremely dangerous game. The danger, argue the critics, lies not only in death and destruction, which modern weaponry has raised to fantastic levels, but in the method, which lifts "strategy" out of its real-world context, demonstrably increasing the risk of major miscalculation. The increased risk is inherent in the method: time, space, force levels and capabilities, plus some general description of national "interests" and "objectives" are taken to be the crucial variables for strategic analysis, with all other factors or possibilities relegated to the background, available of course for further consideration but essentially regarded as negligible in the business of using and controlling violence. Analysis of this small number of selected variables will yield a small set of available strategic options, which are then evaluated in terms of costs, benefits, and probabilities.

[76] Ibid., 107-144, as well as Kent Roberts Greenfield, *American Strategy in World War II: A Reconsideration* (Baltimore, 1963), 85-121.

[77] John I. Alger, *The Quest for Victory: The History of the Principles of War* (Westport, Conn., 1982) includes a remarkable compendium (pp. 195-270).

[78] Useful accounts are Laurence Martin, ed., *Strategic Thought in the Nuclear Age* (Baltimore, 1979) and John Baylis et al., *Contemporary Strategy* (London, 1975).

Even when the conclusions reached by contemporary strategists are less rigidly prescriptive than Jomini himself tended to be, there is a fundamental similarity in the two intellectual processes. In defending themselves against this criticism, contemporary strategists echo Jomini (in his defense against Clausewitz) by insisting that the critics fail to meet the urgent demand of strategy itself for clarity, rigor, and utility. The question here is not one of who, in this argument, has the better position, but of how and why a way of thinking about warfare that emerged with Jomini's account of Napoleon did not wither away with the appearance of railroads, machine guns, and aerial bombardment. It did not disappear because it remained responsive to a pressing, inescapable need.

One of the most powerful forces changing the modern world has been the idea that underlying the apparent disorder of existence are laws regulating the universe, principles that can be discovered and understood. In virtually every sector of human activity the quest for regulating principles, which once discovered offer new means to control and shape existence, is endless. The growing excitement of this quest is the distinguishing characteristic of the eighteenth-century Enlightenment (and certainly its most appealing feature), as the undoubted discoveries of laws regulating the action of the natural world convinced many that comparable laws must govern all human activities. War was among the last of these activities to be touched by the idea of regulating laws. Soldiers had long known of various military "maxims"—useful advice based on personal experience—but not until the later eighteenth century did a serious search for the laws or principles of war begin. Doubts that violence, seemingly so antithetical to the idea of a rational world, could be governed by laws gave way when confronted by the impressive military feats of Frederick II of Prussia, and yielded completely as French armies swept through Europe at the end of the century. Converted to the faith just as he reached manhood in 1800, Jomini joined and would soon lead thousands of others who saw war in the same new, exciting way. Every Napoleonic victory hardened the dogma of this faith, and by the third and fourth decades of the nineteenth century only an occasional heretic, like Clausewitz, could imagine another, less prescriptive and instrumental, way of seeing the subject. That the most vocal critics of the dogma have not been dissenting military theorists, but pacifists and others who oppose war on moral grounds, indicates how securely Jomini and his followers had established the unassailable tenets of their science.

No final word on a mode of thinking about warfare that has proved so durable, despite its flaws and momentous changes in the nature of war, seems possible. It has become, during almost two centuries, so deeply imbedded in Western consciousness that many adherents refuse to accept it as a "mode" of thinking at all, but insist that—correctly understood—Jomini and latter-day Jominians simply offer the Truth about war, or at least about strategy. The man himself and his published work may have receded into the shadows of academic scholarship, but his basic ideas, though seldom acknowledged, have survived. Perhaps there is no more appropriate way to end a study of Jomini than in recognizing the continued existence and remarkable tenacity of this Jominian faith.

7. Clausewitz

PETER PARET

THE QUESTIONS that Clausewitz ultimately sought to answer in his writings—How can we analyze war? What is war?—have come to assume greater importance in the nuclear age than they possessed for his generation. From 1792 to 1815 waves of violence swept across Europe, brought death or suffering to millions, shifted frontiers, but also changed and opened societies. But when the flood receded, no urgent desire to study and explain the cataclysm was left behind. As after every war, men wrote about their experiences and drew what they took to be the lessons for the future; but there was little interest in delving beneath the surface of tactics and strategy to explore the phenomenon of war itself, to study its structure, its internal dynamic, its links with other elements of social existence that might be its causes and that were altered or destroyed under its impact. War continued to be accepted as a permanent force in human existence, whose technical aspects might change over time, but could always be mastered. Clausewitz, too, proceeded on his unusually innovative course of inquiry without a sense of cultural or historical crisis. Today, in the shadow of nuclear proliferation, we cannot escape that sense, and the awareness of the crisis in which we live affects not only our thinking about war in the future but also about war in history. It intensifies our interest in early attempts to understand the nature of violence between states. Clausewitz's most important theoretical work, *On War*, is read more widely today than at any time since it was first published in the 1830s. Probably that is so not only because the book has gradually acquired the aura of a classic, a unique achievement that combines intellectual and aesthetic attributes of the age of Goethe with an uncompromising realism that might be termed modern if such realism were not rare even now; the book is also read because we hope to find its ideas useful.

Whether war can be understood and, by implication, intellectually mastered and controlled, is merely one of several related questions we might ask. Others are: Is war an ethical instrument of foreign policy? Can war be limited, even eliminated? Or, on the other hand, how can war be waged most effectively? In *On War* Clausewitz scarcely addresses the first two of these questions. He was conscious of the ethical problem, but dealt with it differently than we would. He regarded war as an extreme but natural expression of policy, and never regretted that he himself had fought in seven campaigns. His first war, against the French Republic, he thought a justified if politically and strategically inept defense of Prussian and German interests. The others, against Napoleon, he believed passionately to have been not merely justified but an ethical imperative. On the third question—how to fight effectively—he had a great deal to say, much of it no longer relevant, at least not directly so. But after the Napoleonic threat receded, he regarded prescription as secondary to analysis. To devise effective strategic schemes and tactical measures mattered far less to him than to identify the permanent elements of war and come to understand how they function. It is for this reason that *On War* may still be relevant to issues of war and peace facing readers who are separated from the author by the industrial revolution and the military cataclysms of the twentieth century.

The work's relevance is, however, of a particular kind, to be expected of theories that were formulated under conditions very different from our own. Clausewitz liked to compare the study of war with the study of painting; both concern activities that demand specific technical expertise, but whose processes and outcome are not predictable, and cannot be mechanically pursued if we strive for important results. Few artists today would read an early nineteenth-century treatise on painting to help them practice their art, or even to gain a theoretical understanding of it. An artist interested in the history and theory of painting may nevertheless read the treatise for its observations and concepts, some perhaps of permanent validity, which he can use to construct his own theories, and which might even influence the application of his ideas.

A further example may clarify the point. Some years after the Napoleonic Wars had ended, Clausewitz began work on a manuscript on strategy. "My original intention," he commented later, "was to set down my conclusions on the principal elements of this topic in short, precise, compact statements, without concern for system or formal connection. The manner in which Montesquieu dealt with his subject was vaguely in my mind. . . ."[1] When he realized that this approach did not suit his tendency of systematic and expansive analysis, he revised the manuscript; when it still left him dissatisfied he abandoned it, and used parts as building blocks for a new, longer work, *On War*. But his choice of Montesquieu as a model tells us something of his intentions, and also raises a question about the intentions and expectations of his readers. Is

---

[1] Carl von Clausewitz, "Author's Comment" [1818?], *On War*, trans. and ed. Michael Howard and Peter Paret, rev. ed. (Princeton, 1984), 63.

it not the case that today we read *The Spirit of the Laws* not with the hope of encountering a comprehensive theory of government that we can make our own, but for different, less immediately utilitarian reasons? On the one hand, we want to become acquainted with a work that has held the interest of readers for more than two centuries; on the other, we read it to advance our thinking on basic issues of politics, to be stimulated by Montesquieu's ideas and arguments. In the sphere of war, *On War* calls for a similar approach.

Like *The Spirit of the Laws*, Clausewitz's work is a highly personal, in some respects almost autobiographical document, a characteristic that removes it even further from modern varieties of theory. The two books reflect their authors' antecedents, their position in society, their professions, such turning points in their lives as Montesquieu's sojourn in England and Clausewitz's in France, their views of history, their political beliefs. Both men develop the generalizations, the high levels of abstraction that give their works lasting value, by pondering and reacting to the specifics of their condition and experience, specifics that are clearly apparent in their work. It will help our understanding of Clausewitz's ideas if we remain alert to his historical environment and to his personal fate.

I

Carl von Clausewitz was born in 1780 in the small town of Burg, seventy miles southwest of Berlin, the fourth and youngest son of bourgeois parents, who claimed nobility on the strength of family tradition. His father, a retired lieutenant who served in the local tax office, was the son of a professor of theology, himself son and grandson of Lutheran pastors; his mother's father managed a royal farm. It was only after the death of Frederick the Great, who in his later years took great pains to keep his officer corps free of commoners, that the army accepted Clausewitz and two of his brothers as officer cadets. All became generals, and in 1827 their noble status was at last attested to by royal order. Together with many other families during this period, the Clausewitzes entered the nobility by way of the Church and service in the army or bureaucracy of the expanding Prussian state.

Clausewitz first saw combat as a twelve-year-old, in the campaign that drove the French out of the Rhineland in the winter and spring of 1793. After Mainz had been recaptured in July, his regiment marched south to the Vosges Mountains, where it fought a war primarily of detachments, raids, and ambushes. When the army was demobilized in 1795, Clausewitz returned to Prussia with some understanding of skirmishing and small-unit tactics, in contrast to the majority of infantry officers whose main, almost sole duty in combat was to maintain the

188

close alignment and rapid volleys of their men. Imperceptibly at first, his career began to take a somewhat atypical course. For the next few years he was stationed in a small garrison, a post that nevertheless provided some unusual advantages. His regimental commander was a pioneer of military education in Prussia, who organized schools for the children of the rank and file and for the noncommissioned officers and ensigns of his regiment, and who encouraged his junior officers to study professional subjects, literature, and history. In this supportive if provincial environment, Clausewitz progressed sufficiently to apply for admission to the military school in Berlin, and in the summer of 1801, soon after his twenty-first birthday, was accepted to the three-year course.

The school had recently been reorganized by a newcomer to the army, Gerhard von Scharnhorst, who was to play a major role in the history of Prussia and in Clausewitz's life. Scharnhorst, the son of a retired cavalry sergeant, had been a soldier since his sixteenth year, first in a small German principality, then in the Hanoverian army, where he made a name for himself as a gunnery officer and writer on military affairs. After Hanover entered the war against France in 1793, Scharnhorst revealed himself to be an exceptionally enterprising fighting soldier as well. His reputation led to an offer from Prussia of a colonelcy and a patent of nobility, and he transferred to the Prussian service in 1801. Among numerous other duties, he assumed the directorship of the military school in Berlin, soon turning it into one of several channels through which he hoped to introduce modern ideas on war to the Prussian army. Scharnhorst was among the first anywhere to recognize and analyze objectively the interdependence of military innovation and social and political change in the Revolutionary Wars. As he saw it, the problem facing the central European powers, far weaker than France, was how to appropriate essential components of modernization in time to prevent being overrun by the Republic, and he had the self-confidence to believe that he could make the difference in Prussia. No one could have been a better teacher for Clausewitz than this scholarly soldier, who encouraged the young man's theoretical interests while reinforcing his dissatisfaction with the traditionalism of the Prussian army.

In 1804 Clausewitz graduated at the top of his class, and was appointed adjutant to Prince August of Prussia. His social and professional horizons expanded. He was frequently at court, where he met Countess Marie Brühl, lady-in-waiting to the Queen Mother, whom he was to marry some years later. Scharnhorst recommended him to the editor of the most important military journal in Germany, which in 1805 published his first article, a lengthy refutation of the strategic theories of Heinrich

Dietrich von Bülow, in those years the most widely read German interpreter of Napoleonic warfare.

Bülow had the great merit of recognizing that the recent changes in
war constituted a revolution. But he failed to understand the nature of
this revolution; in particular, he could not grasp the new importance of
battle. He refused to dismiss the new ways as temporary expedients or
anarchy, as some other writers did; instead he searched for mathematical
principles that would reveal the rational structure beneath the seemingly
chaotic surface. Typical of this effort was his assertion that the appro-
priateness of a military operation was largely determined by the geometric
relationship between its geographic objective and its base. Clausewitz
saw war very differently. His article raised three main criticisms, which
are worth noting for the light they throw on the distance that separates
even the work of an unusually gifted late-Enlightenment theorist like
Bülow, who wanted to turn war into a kind of applied mathematics,
from the realistic, yet methodologically rigorous approach that Clausewitz was trying to develop.

Above all, Clausewitz objected, Bülow's method was flawed. For
example, Bülow defined strategy as "all military movements out of the
enemy's cannon range or range of vision," and tactics as "all movements
within this range." Clausewitz rejected this distinction as superficial,
timebound—because it would be affected by technological change—and
irrelevant, because the purpose of the two concepts was left unstated.
Instead he proposed definitions that were functional and applied to every
war, past, present, and future: "Tactics constitute the theory of the use
of armed forces in battle; strategy forms the theory of using battle for
the purposes of the war."[2] It hardly needs adding that for Clausewitz
the term "use" also meant "threat of use."

Second, Clausewitz considered Bülow's view of war unrealistic. By
basing his analysis on geography and mathematics, Bülow ignored the
actions of the enemy and the physical and psychological effects of the
fighting. "Strategy, however, is nothing without battle, for battle is the
raw material with which it works, the means it employs."[3]

Finally, Clausewitz insisted that any meaningful theory should be
able to accommodate—as Bülow's does not—all elements pertaining to
its subject. In his urge to understand the use of violence, turn it into a
science, and make it predictable, Bülow excluded essential parts of war.
A theory of war must address not only elements "that are susceptible to

[2] [Carl von Clausewitz], "Bemerkungen über die reine und angewandte Strategie des
Herrn von Bülow," Neue Bellona 9, no. 3 (1805), 271.
[3] Ibid.

mathematical analysis," distances and angles of approach, for instance, but also such imponderables as the soldiers' morale and the commanders' psychology.[4]

Although Clausewitz, eager to make a name for himself, was not reluctant to show up Bülow's confusions and errors, his major concern was to construct a reliable method with which to test Bülow's and other men's theories, and with which he himself could develop an analysis of war that was intellectually defensible. Underlying his arguments even at this early stage is the interplay between the observable present and hypotheses concerning timeless phenomena of war, which are discovered by historical study, common sense, and logic. He agreed that Bülow's idea of the significance of the geometric relationship between the base of operations and its objective was interesting, and might even help explain this or that Napoleonic campaign. But if history demonstrated that campaigns had been won from bases that Bülow thought inadequate, and lost with bases that met his requirements, and if logic and common sense as well as history and contemporary reality suggested that an objective need not be stationary, but might be the enemy army, then Bülow's idea could not stand.

Clausewitz welcomed war in 1806 as the only means to check Napoleon's drive to dominate Europe; but he was not confident of victory. The Prussian army was outnumbered, its leadership too divided for Scharnhorst—now chief of staff of the main force—to impose his views; and its organization, administration, and supply, as well as its tactical doctrine, precluded rapid operations. At the battle of Auerstedt, Prince August, in command of a grenadier battalion, and Clausewitz tried to oppose the flexibility of the French with similar tactics, Clausewitz turning one-third of the rank and file into skirmishers. After the battle was lost, the battalion formed part of the rear guard of the retreating army, until it ran out of ammunition and surrendered. As a nephew of the king, Prince August was of some value to Napoleon. The prince and his adjutant were ordered to France, where they were given relative freedom of movement; but it was not until the fall of 1807 that they received permission to return to Prussia.

Apart from his stay in Russia in 1812, these ten months were the only long period in his life that Clausewitz spent outside Germany. It gave him some direct knowledge of French society and culture, and the opportunity to see conditions in Prussia from a new intellectual and emotional perspective. His criticism of the attitudes and policies that he blamed for the defeat was harsh: the government had not used war as

---

[4] Ibid., 276.

an instrument of foreign policy, but allowed itself to be isolated from prospective allies, and then gave its soldiers an impossible task. The army, although antiquated and inefficient, might have achieved more if its leaders had sought battle instead of relying far too long on the efficacy of maneuvering into and out of strong positions. Above all, Prussian society had been inert; the country regarded the war as a matter for the army alone. Because the government had kept society in a condition of passivity and total obedience, it could not tap the population's potential energy and idealism when the crisis came. Only revolutionary changes could now save the state.[5]

During the later phases of the war, Scharnhorst had again demonstrated his worth as a fighting soldier and strategic planner, and he became an obvious choice to head a commission to draft plans for the reorganization of the army when the fighting ended. Scharnhorst soon made the commission the center of a new campaign to modernize the country's military institutions, from its manpower policies to the design of muskets and the development of up-to-date operational and tactical doctrines. Opposition was immediate and powerful. Reforms as far-reaching as those Scharnhorst proposed would not only transform the army but affect the country's society and economy, break the nobility's near monopoly on officer positions, and release the rank and file from the bondage of the old, often inhumane system of drill and discipline. The conflict over reform, which really was a struggle over the character of the Prussian state, raged for the next five years. When in the spring of 1808 Clausewitz left occupied Berlin for Königsberg, the temporary seat of the Prussian government, he was soon drawn into the inner circle of reformers, and among conservatives acquired a reputation of possibly dangerous radicalism, which he was to retain for the rest of his life.

At first Scharnhorst employed Clausewitz as a personal assistant. He helped organize secret rearmament measures, and wrote articles to explain and defend such socially sensitive innovations as competitive examinations in the selection and promotion of junior officers. When the government returned to Berlin, Clausewitz became the head of Scharnhorst's office, a position that placed him at the center of the reform movement. Through Scharnhorst's influence he was appointed to the general staff and to the faculty of the new war college, where he lectured on strategy and on partisan warfare. In October 1810 he became military

---

[5] See especially Clausewitz's letters to his fiancée between December 1806 and October 1807, in *Karl und Marie von Clausewitz: Ein Lebensbild in Briefen und Tagebuchblättern*, ed. Karl Linnebach (Berlin, 1917), 67-149, and his later history of Prussia during this period, *Nachrichten über Preussen in seiner grossen Katastrophe*, vol. 10 of the German general staff series *Kriegsgeschichtliche Einzelschriften* (Berlin, 1888).

tutor to the crown prince, and a few months later joined the commission that drafted new operational and tactical regulations for the infantry and cavalry. The range of his duties over these years gave Clausewitz a rare opportunity to come to know the intellectual, technical, organizational, and political problems of rebuilding an army almost from the ground up.

These new responsibilities did not lessen his earlier interest in the scientific analysis of war. In essays and notes during these years he clarified his ideas on the appropriate goals and procedures of a theory that deals with a complex activity such as war. He distinguished between the cognitive, pedagogic, and utilitarian potential of theory. In the first instance, the function of theory is to structure past and present reality intellectually, to show "how one thing is related to another, and keep the important and unimportant separate"; to reach the irreducible elements of the phenomenon of war, and to discover the logical and dynamic links that bind them into comprehensible structures. A theory that is logically and historically defensible, and that reflects present reality, has the pedagogic function of helping the student organize and develop his ideas on war, which he draws from experience, study, and from history—the exploration of the past extends the reality that any one individual can experience. Theory can never lead to complete understanding, which is an impossibility, but it can strengthen and refine judgment. It is not the primary task of theory to generate doctrine, rules, or laws of action. Knowledge and performance are different; but utilitarian benefits may flow from valid theories.

Theory must be comprehensive, that is, it must be able to accommodate all aspects of its subject, whether of the present or of other times. It must be based on the constants or absolutes of its subject, not on phenomena that may be temporary, even if currently these phenomena seem to dominate war. Napoleonic warfare is a temporary phenomenon. Examples of absolutes are the social and political nature of war, and the psychology of the commander. Absolutes serve as the organizing principles of theory. All other phenomena depend on them, and are linked—often indirectly—to each other, links that theory must reveal. Clausewitz noted in 1808 that the opposite of such an intellectual structure, in which a logical place is left for every current or subsequent observation and insight, is the practice of writers like Bülow or Jomini to construct definitive doctrines around thoughts and recognitions haphazardly arrived at—to generalize from ideas that have only limited or temporary validity.

Theory must constantly pass the test of reality. In the name of logic it cannot insist on something that is disproved by reality. At any given moment, reality appears narrower than theory; eighteenth-century war-

193

fare, for example, does not exhaust all possibilities of war, nor do the campaigns of Napoleon. On the other hand, since reality constantly changes and is marked by imponderables and the unforeseen, no theory can ever completely reflect, let alone explain it. Theory must be sufficiently flexible and open to take account of imponderables, and it must have the potential for further development.[6]

Many of these ideas were borrowed from the philosophy of German Idealism and from the scientific thought of the time, which is not to say that Clausewitz was deeply versed in philosophy. As a young officer he attended introductory lectures on logic and ethics by Johann Gottfried Kiesewetter, a popularizer of Kant, and then and later read books and articles on mathematics, philosophy, and on aesthetic theory, which he came to believe had some relevance to the analysis of war—for instance in its treatment of talent and genius. Above all he drew ideas at second and third hand from his cultural environment: his use of the concept of polarity, for instance—the separation and connection of active and passive, positive and negative, which he employed to analyze the relationship of attack and defense—and his dialectical development of ideas through thesis and antithesis were the common property of educated Germans at the time. But if the components of the theoretical system he formulated during the years of reform were derivative, he was unique in systematically applying these ideas to phenomena that transcendental philosophy would not have regarded as "real," or real only in a naive sense. The reality that Clausewitz wanted to understand was not the abstract reality of pure reason but the actual physical, intellectual, and psychological components of political and military existence.[7]

The outbreak of war between France and Austria in 1809 raised Clausewitz's hopes that Napoleon had at last overreached himself. He applied for an Austrian commission, and only the sudden armistice after the French victory at Wagram kept him in Prussia. Throughout the next

[6] This summary is drawn from such writings during the Reform Era as Clausewitz's additions of 1808 and 1809 to an essay on strategy originally written in 1804, published by Eberhard Kessel under the title *Strategie* (Hamburg, 1937); and the essay "Über den Zustand der Theorie der Kriegskunst," published by Walter Schering in his collection of Clausewitz's writings *Geist und Tat* (Stuttgart, 1941). Subsequent restatements and developments of these ideas can be found throughout *On War*, particularly in books 1, 2, and 8. Note also such passages as: "Our aim is not to provide new principles and methods of conducting war; rather we are concerned with examining the essential content of what has long existed, and to trace it back to its basic elements" (bk. 6, ch. 8, p. 562); or "We cannot formulate principles, rules, or methods. . . . [Nevertheless] while history may yield no formulae, it does provide an *exercise for judgment*, here as everywhere else" (bk. 6, ch. 30, p. 756).

[7] The relationship between Clausewitz's ideas and German philosophy is discussed in my *Clausewitz and the State* (Oxford and New York, 1976; repr. Princeton, 1985), see particularly pp. 147-208.

194

years he never entirely renounced the possibility of armed insurrection in Germany. When at the end of 1811 Napoleon forced Prussia to make its territory available to him as a staging area for the invasion of Russia, and to contribute twenty thousand men to the *Grande Armée*, Clausewitz was among the most outspoken opponents of what he called a surrender that was both unheroic and politically unwise, and with some thirty other officers resigned his commission, a step that confirmed his reputation as a man who put his own values above the policies of the king.

During the war of 1812 he served as a Russian colonel in various staff positions, little more than an observer because he hardly spoke the language. Toward the end of the campaign, however, he grasped the opportunity to strike a blow against the French by helping to persuade the commander of the Prussian auxiliary corps, General von Yorck, to defect from the Grande Armée and neutralize his force. The so-called Convention of Tauroggen that Yorck concluded with the Russian Count Wittgenstein on whose staff Clausewitz served not only prevented the French from regrouping at the Russian border but carried the revolutionary message that under certain conditions a Prussian officer's conscience or political judgment took precedence over his oath of obedience.

Clausewitz returned with Yorck to East Prussia, where he drew up a plan for raising the provincial militia—a further act of potential revolutionary import, because twenty thousand men were armed without the king's permission. When Prussia at last joined the war against France in March 1813, Frederick William III repaid Clausewitz for his independence by turning down his request to reenter the Prussian service. Still in Russian uniform, he acted unofficially as Scharnhorst's assistant, until Scharnhorst was fatally wounded in the battle of Grossgörschen. In the fall of 1813 he served as chief of staff of a small international force that cleared the French from the Baltic coast. After being at last readmitted to the Prussian army, he was appointed chief of staff of the third corps during the Hundred Days, which by tying down Grouchy's corps at the battle of Wavre prevented it from reinforcing Napoleon at Waterloo.

The suspicion in which Clausewitz was held by conservatives at court and in the army undoubtedly kept him from the more important assignments in which his friends wanted to place him; nevertheless as the Napoleonic Wars drew to a close, few officers his age could look back on experiences as varied as his, ranging from combat and staff duties to strategic planning and participation in politico-military decisions of the highest significance. The reform movement of which he had been an active though not leading member had succeeded in a few years in revitalizing the Prussian army from one of the more cumbersome military organizations of the Old Regime to a force that in many respects now was superior to that of the French. Social change was linked to the innovations, but it did not go as far as the reformers had hoped. As Prussia returned to an increasingly rigid conservatism, Clausewitz reacted to his personal and political disappointments by renouncing the excessive expectations he had once placed in the idealized reformed state. The intense if often critical patriotism of his twenties and early thirties gave way to a more balanced view of his country—as early as 1814 he disagreed with a friend who called for a vindictive peace. France, he argued, should not be weakened beyond a certain measure because it was needed to maintain the balance of power in Europe. In politics, too, he was becoming more of a theorist than a partisan.

During the first years of peace, Clausewitz served as chief of staff of the Prussian forces in the Rhineland. In 1818, at the age of thirty-eight, he was offered the directorship of the war college in Berlin, an administrative position he accepted without enthusiasm, and promoted to the rank of major general. For a time he sought the appointment of ambassador to the Court of St. James, but once again his reputation for independence and political unreliability ruined his chances. In 1816 he had returned to the intensive study of military history and theory, which the climactic struggle against Napoleon had interrupted. In the remaining fifteen years of his life he wrote numerous histories of wars and campaigns, but also a biographical study of Scharnhorst, subsequently published by Ranke, some political essays of exceptional originality, and a history of Prussia before and during the defeat of 1806, which remains one of the notable interpretations of these years. In 1819 he began the writing of *On War*, and in the next eight years completed the first six of eight planned parts, as well as drafts of Books VII and VIII. But by 1827 he had come to realize that the manuscript did not bring out with sufficient clarity two constants that he had first identified in his early twenties and that were key elements in his theory: the political nature of war, and the two basic forms that war assumes. In a note explaining the need for extensive revisions, he wrote:

> I regard the first six books, which are already in a clean copy, merely as a rather formless mass that must be thoroughly reworked once more. The revision will bring out the two types of war with greater clarity at every point. . . .
>
> War can be of two kinds, in the sense that either the objective is to *overthrow the enemy*—to render him politically helpless or militarily impotent, thus forcing him to sign whatever peace we please; or *merely to occupy some of his frontier-districts* so that we

can annex them or use them for bargaining at the peace negotiations. Transitions from one type to the other will of course recur in my treatment; but the fact that the aims of the two types are quite different must be clear at all times, and their points of irreconcilability brought out.

This distinction between the two kinds of war is an actual fact. But no less practical is the importance of another point that must be made absolutely clear, namely that *war is nothing but the continuation of policy with other means.* If this is firmly kept in mind throughout, it will greatly facilitate the study of the subject and the whole will be easier to analyze.[8]

Before beginning the changes, Clausewitz wrote histories of Napoleon's Italian campaigns and of the Waterloo campaign, to understand more clearly how his ideas of the dual form of war and of the political character of war worked in reality. Consequently he could revise only a few chapters before he received a new assignment in the artillery inspectorate in 1830, and was forced to put the manuscript of *On War* aside. Later that year when the French Revolution and the Polish revolt against Russia raised the possibility of a European war, Prussia mobilized part of its army, and Clausewitz was appointed its chief of staff. The great cholera epidemic of 1831, which spread from Russia to Poland and then to central and western Europe, caused his death at the age of fifty-one in November 1831.

II

On War is divided into 128 chapters and sections, grouped into eight books.[9] The first, "On the Nature of War," defines the general characteristics of war in the social and political world, and identifies elements that are always present in the conduct of war: danger, physical and mental effort, psychological factors, and the many impediments to carrying out one's intentions, which Clausewitz collected under the concept of "friction." Book II, "On the Theory of War," outlines the possibilities and limitations of theory. Book III, "On Strategy in General," includes not only chapters on force, time, and space, but also a more detailed treatment of psychological elements—all, according to Clausewitz, "the operative elements in war."[10] Book IV, "The Engagement," discusses "the essential military activity, fighting, which by its material and psychological effect

---

[8] Clausewitz, "Note of 10 July 1827," *On War*, 69. Emphasis in original.
[9] The following analysis relies in part on my discussion of *On War* in *Clausewitz and the State*, especially pp. 356-81.
[10] Clausewitz, *On War*, bk. 4, ch. 1, p. 225.

comprises in simple or compound form the overall object of the war."[11] Book V, "Military Forces," Book VI, "Defense," and Book VII, "The Attack"—the three most conventionally military parts of the work— illustrate and elaborate earlier arguments. Finally, Book VIII, "War Plans," again takes up the most important themes of the first book, explores the relationship between "absolute" war in theory and real war, and in a sweep of theoretical and historical essays of great originality analyzes the political character of war and the interaction of politics and strategy.

Except perhaps for Book V, "Military Forces," for which no completely satisfactory place exists in the sequence, the material is arranged logically, beginning with a survey of the whole in the opening chapter, proceeding to the nature of war and to the purpose and difficulties of theory. Books III through VII discuss strategy and the conduct of military operations. The work ends with an analysis of the most important functions of political and military leadership in war, and more fully integrates war into social and political intercourse.

Even this brief outline will indicate that Clausewitz set himself two primary goals: one, to penetrate by means of logical analysis to the essence of absolute war, "ideal" war in the language of the philosophy of the time; the other, to understand war in the various forms it actually takes, as a social and political phenomenon, and in its strategic, operational, and tactical aspects. But the philosophic, scholarly aim meant far more to him than an intellectual exercise, a play with abstractions that had little bearing on reality. Theoretical analysis alone, Clausewitz was convinced, could provide the means by which actual war in its incredible variety might be understood. In turn, the analysis of real war continually tests the validity of theory. According to Clausewitz's simile: "Just as some plants bear fruit only if they don't shoot up too high, so . . . the leaves and flowers of theory must be pruned and the plant kept close to its proper soil—experience."[12]

The organization of the work into eight main parts does not, however, constitute a sure guide for the reader. The distinctions between the parts are less important than is the network of themes and arguments that links them. An idea is defined with extreme, one-sided clarity, to be varied, sometimes chapters later, and given a new dimension as it blends with other propositions and observations. Thesis is followed by antithesis; the characteristics of one phenomenon are ultimately fixed by analyzing its opposite. Discussions of the nature of war in the abstract al-

---

[11] Ibid.
[12] Clausewitz, "Author's Preface," *On War*, 61.

198

ternate with the application to real war of such analytic devices as the theory of purpose and means, of the major concepts of friction and genius, of propositions of lesser magnitude such as those concerning the relationship of attack to defense, and with detailed operational and tactical observations—all embedded in historical evidence.[13] The text is characterized by movement, cross-references, and allusions, not only to other parts of the book, but also to the experiences of the author and of his generation. Through the entire work, creating an internal unity surpassing that of its external design, run two dialectical relationships, both introduced in the opening chapter: the relationship between war in theory and real war; and the relationship between the three factors that together make up war—violence, the play of chance and probability, and reason.

Organized mass violence is the only feature that distinguishes war from all other human activities. War is "an act of force, and there is no logical limit to the application of that force." It is not "the action of a living force upon a lifeless mass (total nonresistance would be no war at all), but always the collision of two living forces." Neither side is wholly in control of its action, and each opponent dictates to the other; consequently as they seek to outdo each other, their efforts escalate. "A clash of forces freely operating and obedient to no law but their own," eventually reaches the extreme—absolute war, that is, absolute violence ending in the total destruction of one side by the other.[14]

The thesis of total war as the ideal war is followed by the antithesis that war, even in theory, is always influenced by forces external to it. War is affected by the specific characteristics of the states in conflict, and by the general characteristics of the time—its political, economic, technological, and social elements. These may inhibit the escalation to total violence. Furthermore, if a particular war does not seek the enemy's total defeat but a lesser goal, then even theory does not demand escalation toward extremes. Violence continues to be the essence, the regulative idea, even of limited wars fought for limited ends, but in such cases the essence does not require its fullest expression. The concept of absolute war and the concept of limited war together form the dual nature of war.

In the real world, the absolute is always modified, although sometimes it is closely approached, as in certain Napoleonic campaigns or in the attempt of one primitive tribe to exterminate another. War is never

---

[13] Clausewitz defines the four theoretical functions of historical examples: "A historical example may simply be used as an *explanation* of an idea. . . . Second, it may serve to show the *application* of an idea. . . . Third, one can appeal to historical fact to support a statement . . . to prove the *possibility* of some phenomenon or effect." Finally, a tenet or proposition may be derived from the detailed, circumstantial treatment of a historical event. (*On War*, bk. 2, ch. 6, p. 171.)

[14] Ibid., bk. 1, ch. 1, pp. 77-78. See also bk. 1, ch. 2.

an isolated act, but the result of other forces, which affect it and may modify its violence. Nor does it consist of a single, decisive act, or of a set of simultaneous acts. If war were one short, uninterrupted blow, preparations for it would tend toward totality, because "no omission could ever be rectified." But in reality war is always a longer or shorter succession of violent acts, interrupted by pauses for planning, the concentration of effort, the recovery of energy—all on the part of two or more antagonists, who interact. A variety of elements within the opposing societies, the "free will" of the leadership, which may or may not conform to the objective realities, and the political motives of the war, will determine the military objective and the amount of effort to be expended. "War is merely the continuation of policy by other means."[15]

Clausewitz's thesis of the dual nature of war creates a basis for the analysis of all acts of organized mass violence, from wars of annihilation to armed demonstrations that differ from other diplomatic maneuvers solely by their direct threat of violence. The thesis makes it impossible to consider any one type of war as the norm that should determine policy, the standard by which all wars are measured.

Clausewitz's recognition of the political character of war reinforces the point expressed in the dual nature of war that war is not an autonomous or isolated act. The defeat of the enemy's armed power and of his will to use it is not an end in itself but a means to achieve political goals. Violence should express the political purpose, and express it in a rational, utilitarian manner; it should not take the place of the political purpose, nor obliterate it.

Consequently the political leadership should ultimately control and direct the conduct of war. That is not to say that it should displace soldiers in the planning and conduct of operations. It should take care not to ask the impossible, and collaborate with the senior commanders in developing overall policy; but the armed forces do not exist for their own sake. They are an instrument to be used. In demanding the subordination of the military to the political leadership, Clausewitz was far from expressing an ideological preference; he merely drew the logical conclusion from his analysis of the political nature and purpose of war.

Because war is the continuation of policy, "there can be no question of a *purely military* evaluation of a great strategic issue, nor of a purely military scheme to solve it."[16] If the political purpose demands it, the armed forces must be content with the partial mobilization of resources,

---

[15] Ibid., 87.

[16] Carl von Clausewitz, *Two Letters on Strategy*, trans. and ed. Peter Paret and Daniel Moran (Carlisle, Penn., 1984), 9. Emphasis in the original. Compare also *On War*, bk. 8, ch. 6B, p. 607.

and with limited achievements; or, on the other hand, they must be prepared to sacrifice themselves, and neither society nor government should regard this sacrifice, if it is an expression of rational policy, as beyond their mission.

These are some of the more significant implications of Clausewitz's theory of the dual nature of war and of the political nature of war for war in reality. The second major dialectical relationship that runs through the eight books of *On War* is encompassed in the assertion that real war is a composite of three elements. Its dominant tendencies, Clausewitz declared, "always make war a remarkable trinity," composed of violence and passion; uncertainty, chance, and probability; and political purpose and effect.[17]

To analyze war in general or to understand a particular war, but also to plan and conduct a war, requires the study or the exploitation of all three of these elements. A theory or policy would be flawed if it ignored any one of them, or paid attention only to some of their component parts—for instance, only to the military aspect of the second element: how planning, leadership, and effort might succeed in the uncertain process of defeating the enemy. Equally inadequate would be a view that had regard primarily to the political aspects of the war, or to the emotions that were expressed in the war, or were caused by it.

Theory and leadership must remain suspended, to use Clausewitz's metaphor, between the three magnets of violence, chance, and politics, which interact in every war.

Having identified the three areas that together make up war, Clausewitz assigned each as the main field for action to a different segment of society. On the whole, he thought, the first element, violence and passion, concerns mainly the people. The second, uncertainty and chance, provides scope primarily to the courage, determination, and talent of the commander and his forces. The third, politics, "is the business of government alone."[18]

These assumptions—probably made in the interest of theoretical neatness—are, of course, highly subjective. They reveal the author of *On War* in his historical posture, a soldier who regards himself as the servant of the Prussian state and the protector of a society whose raw emotions must be exploited but also controlled. In his view it was the task of the political leadership to abstract the energies of society without succumbing to their irrational power: a government channels psychic energy into rational policy, which the army helps carry out.

[17] Clausewitz, *On War*, bk. 1, ch. 1, p. 89.
[18] Ibid.

Even in Clausewitz's somewhat tentative formulations, these affinities—hatred and violence mainly identified with the people; chance and probability with the army and its commander; rational policy with the government—are of questionable validity. In the Napoleonic Wars, to draw on Clausewitz's favorite pool of examples, the passion and violence of the emperor certainly carried more weight than whatever hatred the French population might have felt toward the rest of Europe; and at least in the final years of the Empire, common sense, that particularly impressive form of rationality, rested more with the war-weary people than it did with Napoleon. But the affinities Clausewitz suggests—obviously the product of personal experience acting on his psychology and his intellectual and political outlook—do not diminish the validity and analytic power of the tripartite definition: war is composed of, and exists in, the realms of violence, chance, and politics.

III

The trinity of violence, chance, and politics encompasses the progression of violence between states, from the preparation and beginning of hostilities to the conclusion of a peace and beyond. Within each of the three parameters, and often in all of them, the actions and occurrences that make up war find their place. But in order to render them susceptible to analysis, recognize their links, and prevent them from overwhelming the analytic framework, the mass of practical detail must be grouped and abstracted. For this purpose Clausewitz developed concepts ranging in magnitude from general significance to specific operational characteristics. Of these the most comprehensive are the concepts of friction and of genius.

Friction refers to uncertainties, errors, accidents, technical difficulties, the unforeseen, and to their effect on decisions, morale, and actions:

> Friction is the only concept that more or less corresponds to the factors that distinguish real war from war on paper. The military machine . . . is basically very simple and therefore easy to manage. But we should bear in mind that none of its components is of one piece: each part is composed of individuals, every one of whom retains his potential of friction. . . . A battalion is made up of individuals, the least important of whom may chance to delay things or somehow make them go wrong. The dangers inseparable from war and the physical exertions [that] war demands . . . aggravate the problem. . . .
>
> This tremendous friction, which cannot, as in mechanics, be reduced to a few points, is everywhere in contact with chance, and

brings about effects that cannot be measured. . . . One, for example, is the weather. Fog can prevent the enemy from being seen in time, a gun from firing when it should, a report from reaching the commanding officer. Rain can prevent a battalion from arriving, make another late by keeping it not three but eight hours on the march, ruin a cavalry charge by bogging the horses down in mud, etc.

Action in war is like movement in a resistant element. Just as the simplest and most natural of movements, walking, cannot easily be performed in water, so in war it is difficult for normal efforts to achieve even moderate results.

Friction, as we choose to call it, is the force that makes the apparently easy so difficult.[19]

This passage, which in its shuttling between the abstract and the specific is characteristic of Clausewitz's manner of thinking and expression, outlines some of the many psychological as well as impersonal possibilities of friction. In one form or another, friction is always present. Friction would dominate war if it were not countered by the creative employment of intellectual and emotional energy. To a degree at least, intelligence and determination can overcome friction, and beyond that exploit chance, and transform the unpredictable into an asset. In turn, these forces should be subject to analysis. Just as theory must not ignore imponderables and the singularity of events, "which distinguish real war from war on paper," so theory must address the often unquantifiable forces that combat friction: the intellectual and psychological strengths of the commander and of his subordinates; the morale, spirit, and self-confidence of the army; and certain temporary and permanent traits of society as reflected in its soldiers—enthusiasm for the war, political loyalty, energy.

On War examines these qualities directly, as "moral or psychological elements," and indirectly through the medium of "genius." The use of genius in this context would make little sense unless we recognize that for Clausewitz the term applies not only to the exceptional individual, but also to abilities and feelings on which the behavior of ordinary men is based: "We cannot restrict our discussion to genius proper, as a superlative degree of talent. . . . What we must do is to survey all those gifts of mind and temperament that in combination bear on military activity. These, taken together, constitute the essence of military genius."[20] Originality and creativity raised to the highest power—which is how the late Enlightenment and idealist philosophy defined genius—were

---

[19] Ibid., bk. 1, ch. 7, pp. 119-21.
[20] Ibid., bk. 1, ch. 3, p. 100.

thus used by Clausewitz to identify and interpret general intellectual and psychological qualities, just as they represented and helped explain the freedom of will and action that was potentially present in every human being. The psychological configuration of the great man, "genius," is meant to clarify the emotions of all men, much as the concept of absolute war illuminates all wars.

This manner of conceptualizing and discussing psychological qualities may appear needlessly complex. Clausewitz was driven to it by the primitive state of the discipline of psychology in his day. In the chapter "On Military Genius" in *On War* he refers to psychology as an "obscure field," and in a subsequent chapter regrets that psychological elements will not yield to academic wisdom. They cannot be classified or counted. They have to be seen or felt.[21] But although good reasons exist for his approach, in some respects it is bound to be unsatisfactory. His enumeration of psychological traits remains conventional; his speculations on their relevance to war, although full of common sense and marked by flashes of brilliance, suffer, as he himself admits, from the same impressionistic defect that he condemns in the writings of other theorists.[22] The psychological characteristics of the great leader are the prism through which Clausewitz interprets the feelings and abilities of the average man; but in his fascination with a Napoleon or Frederick, who alone are capable of supreme achievements, his analysis usually limits itself to exploring their exceptional talents.

This one-sidedness, however, does not diminish the significance of the fact that Clausewitz incorporated psychology as a major component in his theory. Since antiquity writers had stressed the importance of emotion in war; but beyond listing desirable and undesirable characteristics, they had done little with the subject. More recently, in the train of the Revolutionary Wars, some authors had emphasized the importance of the irrational, linked it with the power of chance, and concluded either that the psychology of the soldier was too obscure or that war was too anarchic to be subject to scientific analysis. Clausewitz took the decisive step of placing the analysis of psychological forces at the very center of the study of war. In accord with Kantian philosophy he acknowledged that some things could not be fully understood; but that did not mean that they should be ignored. *On War* made the psychology of the soldier, his commander, and the society they served an essential part of the theory of war. As more comprehensive and dynamic theories of human behavior were developed at the beginning of the twentieth century, the psycho-

[21] Ibid., 106; ibid., bk. 3, ch. 3, p. 184.
[22] Ibid., 185.

logical content of Clausewitz's theoretical structure could be strengthened without doing damage to his tripartite definition of war, or to the dialectical relationship that he posited between "genius"—the psychological roots of initiative and other kinds of military creativity—on the one hand, and "friction" on the other.

Their interaction defines every clash between the antagonists, every incident of fighting, large or small, that occurs in the course of the war. Clausewitz categorized and conceptualized these constituent parts in a series of propositions, which despite their importance are of more limited relevance than are the concepts of friction and genius. The two theses, already mentioned, of the reciprocal relationship of the antagonists and of the tendency of their efforts to escalate, give rise to the thesis of the interdependence of attack and defense in strategy and tactics. Another proposition holds that for reasons of time, space, and energy the offensive gradually weakens until a "culminating point" is reached—the stage beyond which the attacker can no longer easily defend himself against a counterattack. A third argues that the defensive consists of counterattacks as well as of resistance, just as the offensive is made up of attack, pause, and resistance.

From analyzing the nature of war as a whole, Clausewitz has moved to the study of the various forms in which a conflict is waged. This secondary class of propositions continues to apply to all wars in history—the culminating point of an attack may be present in a fight between two tribes just as it was in the German advance on the Marne in September 1914 or in the North Korean invasion of the South in June 1950. But Clausewitz's discussion of these principles reflects the specific experiences of his generation far more directly than do his thoughts on the basic nature of war. Because it concerns the action of forces in the field, his analysis is couched largely in terms of the Revolutionary and Napoleonic Era—the most recent significant incidents of large-scale warfare—while to illustrate the character of raids and of other small-unit operations, Clausewitz often refers to his first years as a soldier, in the Allied campaigns against France in the 1790s.

These propositions and the discussion of detailed topics that grows from them constitute the immediate reality that provided much of the raw material for Clausewitz's theories. They also had another function that went to the core of his entire theoretical effort. They demonstrated that although the higher reaches of war, where reason, emotion, and the play of imponderables resolve the fate of states and societies, posed tremendous difficulties for theory, large if relatively subordinate areas of war were readily susceptible to analysis, and thus proved that a theory of war was in fact possible. As he wrote toward the end of his life:

It is a very difficult task to construct a scientific theory for the art of war, and so many attempts have failed that most people say it is impossible, since it deals with matters that no permanent law can provide for. One would agree and abandon the attempt, were it not for the obvious fact that a whole range of propositions can be demonstrated without difficulty: that defense is the stronger form of fighting with the negative purpose, attack the weaker form with the positive purpose; that major successes help bring about minor ones, so that strategic results can be traced back to certain turning-points; that a demonstration is a weaker use of force than a real attack, and that it must therefore be clearly justified; that victory consists not only in the occupation of the battlefield but in the destruction of the enemy's physical and psychic forces . . . that success is always greatest at the point where the victory was gained . . . that a turning movement can only be justified by general superiority or by having better lines of communication or retreat than the enemy's; that flank positions are governed by the same consideration; that every attack loses impetus as it progresses.[23]

Many of these propositions were not, in fact, as self-evident as Clausewitz hoped his readers would find them. For instance, his statement that defense was the stronger form of fighting was misunderstood and rejected by several generations of German soldiers, whose analytic capacities were dimmed by their country's geopolitical situation. But for Clausewitz the dialectical logic of action and reaction, which no ideological preconception prevented him from following to its necessary conclusion, provided the assurance that his pronounced pragmatic outlook craved: violence on the tactical and operation level, and therefore violence on all levels, could be analyzed and mastered intellectually.

To conclude this summary of the principal themes of *On War*, we must revert to Clausewitz's ideas on the function and relationship of purpose, objective, and means, which run through the entire work. The political purpose for which a war is fought should determine the means that are employed and the kind and degree of effort required. The political purpose should also determine the military objective. Sometimes the two are identical—Clausewitz gives the example of a war fought in order to conquer a particular territory. In other cases, "the political objective will not provide a suitable military objective. In that event, another military objective must be adopted that will serve the political purpose. . . ."[24] To destroy the political system of an antagonist, it may become necessary

[23] Ibid., "Unfinished Note, Presumably Written in 1830," 71.
[24] Ibid., bk. 1, ch. 1, p. 81.

to destroy his armed forces, or to occupy his political and economic centers, or both. To defend oneself against attack, it may be sufficient to ward off the attacking force. Or it is possible that its bases will have to be destroyed, or it may become necessary in other ways to raise the price of further hostilities to such an extent that the opponent will desist.

The military objective is dependent on the political purpose, but also on the enemy's political and military policies, and on the conditions and resources of the two antagonists, and should be proportionate to these factors.[25] The means of war consist in the application of force, or the threat of force. Force, too, should be suitable and proportionate to the military objective and the political purpose.

The relationship between purpose, objective, and means exists in tactics and operations no less than it does in strategy and the overall conduct of the war.

> If a battalion is ordered to drive the enemy from a hill, a bridge, etc., the true purpose is normally to occupy that point. Destruction of the enemy's force is only a means to an end, a secondary matter. If a mere demonstration is enough to cause the enemy to abandon his position, the objective has been achieved; but as a rule the hill or bridge is captured only so that even more damage can be inflicted on the enemy. If this is the case on the battlefield, it will be even more so in the theater of operations, where it is not merely two armies that are facing each other, but two states, two peoples, two nations. . . . The gradation of objects at various levels of command will further separate the first means from the ultimate objective.[26]

On the tactical and operational levels, the political element is usually remote, but it will always be potentially present. Furthermore, any particular military act may have immediate or indirect political implications. From the struggle of a few soldiers to the clash of armies and the intellectual and emotional battlefields of grand strategy and ultimate political decisions, the network of purpose, objective, and means determines events, and should guide the thinking and behavior of the antagonists.

IV

Much of *On War* may on closer reading appear to be mere common sense. Even highly abstract passages, when dissected, generally point to self-evident facts, or reveal implications that almost necessarily follow from them. The close focus on the familiar was, of course, in accord with Clausewitz's purpose in writing the book. The problems he studied were

[25] Ibid., bk. 8, ch. 3B, pp. 585-86.
[26] Ibid., bk. 1, ch. 2, p. 96.

not new, and he was not interested in suggesting new solutions for them. What he wanted was to clarify well-known phenomena, and restate them in such a way that theory could deal with them, while in turn the conceptualized phenomena contributed to the overall theoretical structure. The invention of "friction" is an example. Everyone knows that unexpected changes in weather, misunderstood orders, and accidents may affect events. By grouping such occurrences under the concept of friction, Clausewitz turned them from ideas of haphazard familiarity into a firm component of an analytic description that seeks to explain its subject.

His description, it should be noted, is incomplete, and not only because the manuscript is unfinished. On War contains a comprehensive analysis of the strategy, operations, and tactics of Napoleonic war, and of their eighteenth-century background. Left out of account are most technological, administrative, and organizational factors; characteristically, even the institution of conscription, the major lever in the new machinery for generating military energy, is not thoroughly studied, even though it is often referred to and its share in making war more dynamic and destructive is emphasized. On War deals almost entirely with the ultimate issues, as Clausewitz saw them: political and strategic planning, and the conduct of hostilities.

The theory of war that emerges from, and accompanies, this partial view may seem equally incomplete. Not only does it not directly address the roles of administrative and institutional elements in war, technological change, or the fundamental significance of economics; barring a reference or two to amphibious operations, On War ignores naval warfare. Clausewitz has often been criticized for his inability to transcend his experiences as a soldier of a land-locked monarchy, and to recognize the other half of war of his time. But this criticism confuses his theory with the experiences from which it sprang. It is possible to develop and analyze a concept without illustrating it exhaustively. Friction, escalation, the interaction of attack and defense exist in war on and under the sea—and in the air—as much as they do on land. It is fallacious to consider the theoretical structure of On War incomplete on the ground that its illustrations are drawn only from the types of conflict that Clausewitz knew best and that interested him most.

Much the same may be said about the absence of systematic treatments of the role of technology and of economics in war. Clausewitz took it as a matter of course that technological development, brought about by economic, social, and political change, constantly affects tactics and strategy. On War contains numerous references to this basic fact. Nor did he ignore the dependence of military institutions and of warfare as such on economic resources and policies, although he was too knowledgeable to equate mere wealth with military strength. The history of Prussia sufficed to indicate how many other factors might be at work.[27] A state's economic resources, together with its geography and its social and political conditions, according to Clausewitz, determine, or should determine, its military policies. As long as theory accommodates this truth and provides an appropriate place for it in its dynamic representation of war, a comprehensive treatment of economics is not necessary. If subsequently the relationship of economics to war is fully explored, the analysis can be fitted into the already existing theoretical scheme. Theories concerning the motives and behavior of individuals and of groups and societies need not, and indeed never can, address every variable of their subject; it is enough that the theory has the capacity to incorporate the new findings and investigations of new areas as these are developed without its basic hypotheses being proved inadequate or false.

Some readers have criticized Clausewitz for ignoring ethics in *On War*, for not thoroughly discussing the causes of war, and for not questioning the validity of policies that lead to war. These objections raise important issues; once again, however, they seem to derive from a failure to accept Clausewitz's intentions and to acknowledge the logical parameters of his work.

The morality of going to war, Clausewitz thought, was a question of political ethics, not one that concerned the theory of war. War is a social act, and the decision to resort to it lies beyond war itself. That remains true even if the decision is influenced, or wholly determined, by the military leadership, for in that case the soldiers share in, or assume, political authority. They step outside of war.

Ethical justifications for resorting to war may certainly influence the conduct of operations. Insofar as they affect the governments of the warring powers and the international community, these justifications, too, lie outside the theory of war. Their impact, if any, on the soldiers actually engaged in the war is subsumed in Clausewitz's discussions of morale, loyalty, and the psychology of the fighting man.

That is also true of the ethics of behavior in war. Codes of ethics, their observance or transgression, may influence the soldier. They are part of the values of society, which according to Clausewitz always affect war. But *in themselves*, he thought, they have little substance: "Attached to force are certain self-imposed, imperceptible limitations, hardly worth mentioning, known as international law and custom . . . moral force has

---

[27] A good example of Clausewitz's awareness of the role of economic factors in war is his discussion of the nature of eighteenth-century warfare that begins with the sentence, "This military organization was based on money and recruitment" (ibid., bk. 8, ch. 38, pp. 588-89).

no existence save as expressed in the state and the law."[28] In short, the theory concerns itself with ideals only to the extent that these values actually influence behavior. *On War* seeks to understand the reality of war, and to lay bare the logical demands of the forces involved in war; it does not try to adjust this reality to a particular ethical system. Clausewitz, as he himself recognized, is far closer to Machiavelli's position than to that of the Church fathers and of moral philosophers who want to define the just war and just behavior in war.

Policy in *On War*—the German word *Politik* may mean either policy or politics—refers to those political acts that lead to war, determine its purpose, influence its conduct, and bring about its termination. In his historical writings and political essays, Clausewitz frequently analyzed the failings of policy, whether those of Prussia or of other states. In *On War* he set himself a different task. Here the substance of policy is not at issue; what matters is the effectiveness with which the government directs its military resources to achieve the political purpose. That purpose Clausewitz assumes to be in general realistic and responsible. Policy, he wrote in Book VIII, "is nothing in itself; it is simply the trustee for all ... interests [of a particular society, including its "spiritual" values] against the outside world. That it can err, subserve the ambitions, private interests, and vanity of those in power, is neither here nor there. In no sense can the art of war ever be regarded as the preceptor of policy, and here we can only treat policy as representative of all interests of the community."[29] Because the theory of war deals with the use of force against external enemies, Clausewitz was logically correct in not exploring the problems caused by irrational or mistaken policies—questions he left to political theory. In the illustrative, exemplary passages of his work he might, of course, have expanded his brief references to the misguided policies of such men as Napoleon and Charles XII, without doing damage to the theoretical structure. Whether he would have done so, had he lived to complete the revision of his manuscript, it is impossible to say.[30]

V

In the history of ideas it is not unusual for an author's work to be widely discussed and to influence thinking on its subject—private mo-

---

[28] Clausewitz, *On War*, bk. 1, ch. 1, p. 75.

[29] Ibid., bk. 8, ch. 6B, pp. 606-607.

[30] James E. King, in a personal communication, observes that Clausewitz "left the analytic questions as to why and how political values (the objective) control the armed forces and their employment in war (the means) to be answered by a political theory as sophisticated as his theory of war. That task has still not been accomplished."

rality, for example, or forms of government—while the subject itself is hardly affected by the work. Clausewitz is such an author. But perhaps because he wrote in a field in which the theoretical literature was almost entirely utilitarian rather than speculative in a philosophic or scientific sense, there has been no lack of effort to discover the impact his ideas have had on war in reality, on the manner in which wars are actually fought—an odd fate, it may be thought, for a writer who stressed the nonutilitarian nature of his work.

The influence of a theorist whose intentions in his major work are not prescriptive is perhaps especially difficult to determine. It is not surprising that the search for Clausewitz's influence, which began in the second half of the nineteenth century, has been confused and inconclusive. That one or two sentences from *On War* have entered common usage, or that some of its arguments have been misinterpreted to support the military fashions of the day, scarcely proves that the ideas have had a genuine impact. On the contrary, if we examine the conduct of war since Clausewitz wrote, we will find little evidence that soldiers and governments have made use of his theories. Wars have repeatedly demonstrated the relevance of Clausewitz's theories, but nothing has proved more elusive to discover than an application of "lessons" learned from *On War*.

The discussion of Clausewitz's influence may benefit from a temporary separation of two related aspects of the issue: how he has influenced the manner in which people think about war; and how and to what extent he has influenced the actions of soldiers and statesmen. Reading Clausewitz seems, for example, to have helped Marx, Engels, and Lenin to clarify their ideas on the political nature of war; but it is far from certain that their encounters with Clausewitz's work were essential to the development of their thought. Nor is it clear whether other political figures gained insights from *On War* that they might not have acquired elsewhere. Points of view may agree without one having influenced the other. The close interaction of war and politics, to give only the most obvious example, is after all not a program but a piece of reality, a process that in some societies is more readily understood and better managed than in others. Abraham Lincoln or Georges Clemenceau did not need to read Clausewitz to discover the relationship between the military objective and the political purpose of the wars they were fighting. Some people reached conclusions similar to Clausewitz's without reading *On War*; on the other hand, many of his readers either did not understand or did not agree with him.

In his own society it is precisely the political aspects of Clausewitz's theories that were given what was at best an ambiguous reception. Until the 1930s, his most significant German readers were either unwilling or unable to accept his thesis of the close integration of politics and war and of the primacy of political considerations even during the fighting. Instead, throughout the nineteenth and early twentieth centuries the chiefs of staff and commanders in chief of the Prusso-German army thought of war, once it had broken out, as an essentially autonomous activity, and did everything in their power to protect the army, its strategy and its operations, from political interference. Even the close partnership between Bismarck and Moltke was at times shaken by the soldiers' efforts to preserve their autonomy. Hindenburg and Ludendorff finally achieved a very considerable measure of independence during the First World War, until the failure of the spring and summer offensives in 1918 caused them to drop responsibility into the lap of a now helpless government. The instinctual sense of the permanent interaction of politics and war that Clausewitz had developed as a young man, and that guided his thinking throughout life, was no longer as comprehensible to Germans as their society became industrialized and entered the era of imperialism. In a culture increasingly shaped by specialists and technocrats, with an assertive but anxious military unchecked by the political leadership, the universalistic outlook that Clausewitz expressed in *On War* dimmed and was lost.

Perhaps the two most important legacies that German soldiers accepted from Clausewitz, two strands in the army's doctrine well into the twentieth century, were his agreement with Napoleon that a major victory was likely to be more important than many small successes, and his concept of imponderables. Not to be overwhelmed by the unforeseen demanded flexibility in all aspects of war, from grand strategy (though the decision to stay with the Schlieffen plan in 1914 cannot be regarded as an example of flexibility) to tactics. One result was the development of *Auftragstaktik*, the policy of issuing directives stating the overall intentions of the supreme command, while leaving a high degree of initiative and the issuance of specific orders to subordinate commands. Shortly before 1914, the distinguished French officer and historian Jean Colin still found a pronounced utilitarian benefit in this aspect of Clausewitz's writings: Clausewitz had "the incomparable merit of driving formalism out of military education."[31] In Colin's view, the belief that a theory of action should not lay down rules, which Clausewitz first expressed in his

---

[31] Jean Colin, *The Transformation of War* (London, 1912), 298-99. It is characteristic of the search for Clausewitz's influence that even this brilliant historian simply took for granted the impact Clausewitz's ideas had on Prussian strategy in 1866 and 1870 (ibid., 303-304), an assumption that would have puzzled the Prussian general staff and the commanders of the Prussian armies in these conflicts.

criticism of Bülow, was in itself a practical lesson of the greatest significance.

But with such exceptions, Clausewitz's influence on the manner in which wars are prepared for and fought is difficult to discern and even harder to verify. It is easier to see his impact on more theoretical or historical thinking about war; although even among scholars he cannot be said to have founded a school.[32] In many disciplines and fields of study—ethics or political theory may again serve as examples—general analyses of a discursive, speculative nature are not rare; but the subject of war still tends to evoke works that condemn or try to eliminate war, or that seek to improve the effectiveness of the means and strategies of conflict. That war can be studied in a different spirit is perhaps the most important lesson to be drawn from Clausewitz's work. He has given us a base on which to build. But the detached interpretation of organized mass violence continues to pose the greatest difficulties to the modern world.

Clausewitz stands at the beginning of the nonprescriptive, nonjudgmental study of war as a total phenomenon, and *On War* is still the most important work in this tradition. Even Machiavelli, whom he perhaps most resembles in his passionate interest in the actual functioning of politics and war, was more of an advocate. *The Prince* and *The Art of War* are informed by a view of the political conditions of Italy, and Machiavelli's dissatisfaction with them; but *On War* was not written to strengthen the Prussian monarchy. Clausewitz ranges far beyond the parameters of success and failure in which strategic thought moves to explore the ultimate nature and dynamic of war. It would be comforting to believe that this intellectual understanding not only forms the basis for effective strategy, but that it is also conducive to responsible military policy and statecraft. Clausewitz never made that assumption, and history before and since he wrote has demonstrated that the assumption would not invariably be correct. Nevertheless both as an issue that dominates our time and as a still imperfectly understood force in our past, war demands much further exploration. That so few scholars and soldiers have taken it up in something of Clausewitz's spirit of objective inquiry, and with his ability to combine reality and theory, is not the least measure of his achievement.

[32] A historian whose thinking was strongly influenced by Clausewitz, and who tried to apply and develop Clausewitz's ideas in his interpretations of war in history, was Hans Delbrück, whom Gordon Craig discusses in another essay in this volume.

PART THREE

From the Industrial Revolution to the First World War

8. Adam Smith, Alexander Hamilton, Friedrich List: The Economic Foundations of Military Power

EDWARD MEAD EARLE

O NLY IN THE most primitive societies, if at all, is it possible to separate economic power and political power. In modern times—with the rise of the national state, the expansion of European civilization throughout the world, the industrial revolution, and the steady advance of military technology—we have constantly been confronted with the interrelation of commercial, financial, and industrial strength on the one hand, and political and military strength on the other. This interrelationship is one of the most critical and absorbing problems of statesmanship. It involves the security of the nation and, in large measure, determines the extent to which the individual may enjoy life, liberty, property, and happiness.

When the guiding principle of statecraft is mercantilism or totalitarianism, the power of the state becomes an end in itself, and all considerations of national economy and individual welfare are subordinated to the single purpose of developing the potentialities of the nation to prepare for war and to wage war—what the Germans call *Wehrwirtschaft* and *Kriegswirtschaft*. Almost three hundred years ago Colbert epitomized the policy of the rising French monarchy of Louis XIV by saying that "trade is the source of finance and finance is the vital nerve of war." In our day, Goering has indicated that the political economy of the Nazi garrison state was aimed at the production of "guns, not butter." And a favorite device of Soviet preparation for total war was the slogan that it is better to have socialism without milk, than milk without socialism. Democratic peoples, on the other hand, dislike the restraints that are inherent in an economy based upon war and the preparation for war: *Wehrwirtschaft* is something alien to their way of life and beyond the bounds of what they consider necessary to their safety and prosperity. They prefer an economic system that is predicated upon individual welfare rather than upon the overweening power of the state. And they have a deep-rooted suspicion of coordinated military and economic power, as something that constitutes an inherent threat to their long-established liberties.

But whatever the political and economic philosophies that motivate a nation, it can ignore only at dire peril the requirements of military power and national security, which are fundamental to all other problems of government. Alexander Hamilton was enunciating a basic principle of statecraft when he said that safety from external danger is "the most powerful director of national conduct"; even liberty must, if necessary, give way to the dictates of security because, to be more safe, men are willing "to run the risk of being less free."[1] Adam Smith, who believed the material prosperity of the nation to be founded upon a minimum of governmental interference with the freedom of the individual, was willing to concede that this general principle must be compromised when national security is involved, for "defense is of much more importance than opulence."[2] Friedrich List, who disagreed with Smith on most subjects, found himself in perfect accord on this point: "Power is of more importance than wealth . . . because the reverse of power—namely, feebleness—leads to the relinquishment of all that we possess, not of acquired wealth alone, but of our powers of production, of our civilisation, of our freedom, nay, even of our national independence, into the hands of those who surpass us in might. . . ."[3]

For more than two centuries before Adam Smith published *The Wealth of Nations* western Europe was governed by beliefs and practices that, as a whole, are known as mercantilism. The mercantilist system was a system of power politics. In domestic affairs it sought to increase the power of the state against the particularist institutions that survived from the Middle Ages. In foreign affairs it sought to increase the power of the nation as against other nations. In short, the ends of mercantilism were unification of the national state and development of its industrial, commercial, financial, military, and naval resources. To achieve these ends the state intervened in economic affairs, so that the activities of its

[1] *The Federalist* (1787), No. 8 (New York, Modern Library edition, 1937, with an introduction by E. M. Earle), 42. All page references will be to this edition. The full text also is in vols. 11 and 12 of Hamilton's collected *Works*, cited in footnote 30.

[2] Adam Smith, *An Inquiry into the Nature and Causes of the Wealth of Nations*. Originally published in 1776. For convenience I have used the Modern Library edition (introduction by Max Lerner), which is a reprint of the edition of Edwin Cannan (London, 1904). The phrase here used is to be found in bk. 4, ch. 2, p. 431.

[3] Friedrich List, *Das nationale System der politischen Ökonomie* (Stuttgart, 1841) in *Schriften, Reden, Briefe*, 10 vols. (Berlin, 1927-35), vol. 6 (ed. Artur Sommer, Berlin, 1930), 99-100. This is the best edition of List's works, published in cooperation with the *Deutsche Akademie*. The quotation is from the English translation by Sampson S. Lloyd, *The National System of Political Economy* (London, 1885), 37-38. Hereafter cited as *National System* from the English translation.

citizens or subjects might be effectively diverted into such channels as would enhance political and military power. The mercantilist state—like the totalitarian state of our time—was protectionist, autarkic, expansionist, and militaristic.

In modern terminology, we would say that the predominant purpose of mercantilist regulations was to develop the military potential, or war potential. To this end exports and imports were rigidly controlled; stocks of precious metals were built up and conserved; military and naval stores were produced or imported under a system of premiums and bounties; shipping and the fisheries were fostered as a source of naval power; colonies were settled and protected (as well as strictly regulated) as a complement to the wealth and self-sufficiency of the mother country; population growth was encouraged for the purpose of increasing military manpower.[4] These and other measures were designed with the major, if not the single, purpose of adding to the unity and strength of the nation.

War was inherent in the mercantilist system, as it is in any system in which power is an end in itself and economic life is mobilized primarily for political purposes. Representatives of a policy of power believe that their goals can be achieved "as well, if not better, by weakening the economic power of other countries instead of strengthening one's own. If wealth is considered as an aim, this is the height of absurdity, but from the point of view of political power it is quite logical. . . . Any attempt at economic advance by one's own efforts in one country must have appeared pointless, unless it consisted in robbing other countries of part of their possessions. Scarcely any other element in mercantilist philosophy contributed more to the shaping of economic policy, and even of foreign policy as a whole."[5] This logic was remorseless with the mercantilists and in large measure accounts for the almost continuous war—open or concealed—that raged in Europe from the middle of the seventeenth century to the early part of the nineteenth. Napoleon's Continental System and the retaliatory British Orders in Council were simply the culmination of a long series of similar measures.

From the mercantilist wars, England alone emerged triumphant. Achieving national unification earlier than any other European power, and enjoying the security that its insular position afforded, it was better able than the others to put "the might of her fleets and admiralty, the

[4] A typical measure for encouraging population was prohibition of enclosure of pasture lands in favor of the extension of lands under cultivation of foodstuffs. A proclamation of 1548 in England, for example, stated that "the surety . . . of the Realm must be defended against the enemy with force of men, and the multitude of true subjects, not with flocks of sheep and droves of beasts." Cited by Eli Heckscher, *Mercantilism*, trans. M. Shapiro, 2 vols. (London, 1935), 2:44.

[5] Ibid., 2:21, 24.

apparatus of customs and navigation laws, at the service of the economic interests of the nation and the state with rapidity, boldness, and clear purpose," and thereby to gain the lead in the struggle for commercial and political hegemony.[6] By 1763 England had crushed the commercial, colonial, and naval aspirations of Spain, Holland, and France. The resurgent France of the Revolution and Napoleon was crushed again at Waterloo. In 1815, despite the loss of the American colonies, Great Britain seemed to have arrived at world power in a manner and degree reminiscent of the great empires of antiquity. "In all ages there have been cities or countries which have been pre-eminent above all others in industry, commerce, and navigation; but a supremacy such as that [of Britain] which exists in our days, the world has never before witnessed. In all ages, nations and powers have striven to attain to the dominion of the world, but hitherto not one of them has erected its power on so broad a foundation. How vain do the efforts of those appear to us who have striven to found their universal dominion on military power, compared with the attempt of England to raise her entire territory into one immense manufacturing, commercial, and maritime city, and to become among the countries and kingdoms of the earth, that which a great city is in relation to its surrounding territory; to comprise within herself all industries, arts, and sciences; all great commerce and wealth; all navigation and naval power—a world's metropolis. . . ." Thus wrote a German nationalist in 1841, in envy and in admiration.[7]

It was against the background of mercantilism and of a triumphant England that Smith the Briton, Hamilton the American, and List the German outlined economic and political policies for their respective countries. What they had to say concerning the economic foundations of military power can be understood only within the framework of their times and the spirit and special conditions of their respective countries.

I

When *The Wealth of Nations* was published in 1776, the time was ripe in Britain for critical reappraisal of the theories and practices of mercantilism. The revolt of the American colonies had focused attention upon the entire system of trade regulation that was involved in Britain's colonial policy. There was dissatisfaction with the wars that had been going on for over a century and with the mounting burden of war debts.

---

[6] This is a paraphrase, not a quotation, from Gustav Schmoller, *The Mercantile System and Its Historical Significance*, trans. W. J. Ashley (London and New York, 1896), 72. The German text is in *Das Merkantilsystem in seiner historischen Bedeutung*, first published in *Schmollers Jahrbuch* for 1884.

[7] List, *National System*, 293.

Furthermore, after Britain's triumph over France in the Seven Years' War (1756-1763), there remained no serious rival to England in either commercial or naval power. Hence there was increasing skepticism concerning a political and economic philosophy by which "nations have been taught that their interest consisted in beggaring all their neighbors." The feeling began to grow, now that Britain's position as a world power seemed assured, that a more liberal policy might be initiated and that "the wealth of a neighboring nation, however dangerous in war and politics, is certainly advantageous in trade."[8] There was a growing conviction, too, that there had been abuses in the prevailing system, which enabled entrenched privilege to benefit from its association with the real or imagined interests of the nation. It was against these abuses that Smith struck out in attacking the merchant class in general and the chartered companies in particular for monopolistic practices, usurpation of governmental authority, and the fomenting of war.[9] "The capricious ambition of kings and ministers has not, during the present and the preceding century," he said, "been more fatal to the repose of Europe, than the impertinent jealousy of merchants and manufacturers. The violence and injustice of the rulers of mankind is an ancient evil. . . . But the mean rapacity, the monopolizing spirit of merchants and manufacturers, who neither are, nor ought to be, the rulers of mankind . . . may very easily be prevented from disturbing the tranquility of any body but themselves."[10]

Smith's most trenchant criticisms of mercantilism were directed at its monetary theories, including the notion that the state must accumulate great stocks of bullion as a war chest. He admitted that Britain must be prepared to wage war, because "an industrous, and upon that account a wealthy nation, is of all nations the most likely to be attacked." Nor was he unaware that Britain's vast colonial and commercial commitments overseas required the maintenance of a substantial military and naval establishment. But he denied that war chests were essential or even useful to the effective defense of the nation, for "fleets and armies are maintained, not with gold and silver, but with consumable goods. The nation which, from the annual produce of its domestic industry, from the annual revenue arising out of its lands, labour, and consumable stocks, has

---

[8] Smith, *Wealth of Nations*, 460-461. Even before the Seven Years' War, David Hume in an essay on the *Jealousy of Trade* had gone counter to all mercantilist ideas in saying, "not only as a man, but as a British subject, I pray for the flourishing commerce of Germany, Spain, Italy, and even France itself," on the ground that all nations would flourish were their policies toward one another more "enlarged and benevolent." (David Hume, *Essays Moral, Political and Literary*, ed. T. H. Green and T. H. Grose [London, 1898], 1:348.)

[9] On the chartered companies, see Smith, *Wealth of Nations*, 595-606.

[10] Ibid., 460.

wherewithal to purchase those cosumable goods in distant countries, can maintain foreign wars there." This was proved by Britain's experience in defraying "the enormous expence" of the Seven Years' War from the profits of its expanded manufactures and greatly increased foreign trade.[11] In other words, Smith believed that the ability of a nation to wage war is best measured in terms of its productive capacity, as was later to be argued so effectively by Friedrich List. Furthermore, he objected to war chests, as well as to war loans, as the principal means of financing wars. He favored heavy taxes instead. Wars currently paid for "would in general be more speedily concluded, and less wantonly undertaken" by governments, and "the heavy and unavoidable burdens of war would hinder the people from wantonly calling for it when there was no real or solid interest to fight for."[12]

Despite the fact that *The Wealth of Nations* became the bible, and Adam Smith the intellectual progenitor, of the laissez-faire school of nineteenth-century British economic theorists, the truth is that Adam Smith did not really repudiate certain fundamentals of mercantilist doctrine. He rejected some of its means, but he accepted at least one of its ends—the necessity of state intervention in economic matters insofar as it might be essential to the military power of the nation. His followers were more doctrinaire free traders than Smith was himself, and they certainly were more ardent pacifists. "The first duty of the sovereign," he wrote, "that of protecting the society from the violence and invasion of other independent societies, can be performed only by means of a military force." But the methods of preparing this force in time of peace, and of employing it in time of war will vary according to the different states of society. War becomes more complicated and more expensive as societies advance in the mechanical arts; hence the character of the military establishment and the methods of supporting it will be different in a commercial and industrial state from that in a more primitive society.[13]

---

[11] The discussion concerning war chests is in ibid., bk. 4, ch. 1, especially pp. 398-415. The quotations here given are from pp. 399, 409, 679.

[12] Ibid., 878-79. The facts of history hardly support the thesis that governments or peoples carefully calculate the costs of war in advance of hostilites.

[13] Ibid., bk. 5, ch. 1, pt. 1, pp. 653-69. Quotation on p. 653. Heckscher, *Mercantilism*, understood fully the extent to which Smith accepted some of the basic tenets of mercantilism. Smith's admirer William Cunningham in his monumental *Growth of English Industry and Commerce in Modern Times*, 2 vols. (Cambridge, 1882) seems to have missed the whole truth when he said that Smith treated "wealth without direct reference to power"; certainly Smith would not have subscribed to Cunningham's statement that "national rivalries and national power are mean things after all" and that the study of wealth had to be dissociated from these "lower aims" (1:xxix, 593-94, especially note 2, p. 594). Smith, writing shortly after the Seven Years' War and on the eve of the French and American revolutions, was keenly aware of the realities of power politics; Cunningham, writing almost midway in a century of peace, when war seemed remote, saw the situation differently. Smith's bitter

In other words, as Marx and Engels later pointed out, the forms of economic organization in large measure determine what are to be the instruments of war and the character of military operations. It is inevitable, therefore, that military power be built upon economic foundations.

Insofar as Great Britain was concerned, the heart of the mercantilist system—the ark of the covenant—was the Navigation Acts. Mercantilism in its other aspects may have been essential at an earlier period of its development, but by the end of the eighteenth century England was so far advanced industrially that protectionism was of much less importance to it than to France and the German states. The British could have afforded, if necessary, to dispense with duties on most manufactures because they were without serious competition in their domestic and overseas markets. Indeed, Great Britain was later, in self interest, to abandon its earlier restrictive policies because it had learned, as Bismarck said, that "free trade is the weapon of the strongest." But sea power was another matter, and anything related to it had to be judged by different criteria. The safety of the homeland and the empire demanded that Britain have virtually unchallenged control of the ocean highways; any power that thought otherwise was certain to earn implacable hostility. Furthermore, the entire superstructure of British industry, finance, and commerce was founded upon overseas markets and overseas sources of supply. Hence, the merchant marine was both an economic asset and an absolutely indispensable element in military security, especially in an age when merchant vessels were readily converted into privateers or men-of-war. "Your fleet and your Trade," declared Lord Haversham in the House of Lords, "have so near a relation and such mutual influence on each other, they cannot well be separated: your trade is the mother and nurse of your seamen: your seamen are the life of your fleet: and your fleet is the security and protection of your trade: and both together are the wealth, strength, security and glory of Britain."[14]

For these reasons the real test of Adam Smith's view on mercantilism and power politics was his stand on the Navigation Acts and the fisheries. "The defense of Great Britain," he said, "depends very much upon the number of its sailors and shipping. The act of navigation, therefore, very properly endeavours to give the sailors and shipping of Great Britain the monopoly of the trade of their own country." Smith continued:

When the act of navigation was made, though England and Holland were not actually at war, the most violent animosity subsisted be-

---

opponent List missed the truth just as badly as Cunningham; he mistook the views of Smith's followers from those of Smith himself, as will presently be shown.

[14] Cited in G. S. Graham, *Sea Power and British North America* (Cambridge, Mass., 1941), 15. This work should be consulted for an excellent discussion of the place of the Navigation Acts in British statecraft. See especially pp. 7-15.

tween the two nations. It had begun during the government of the long parliament, which first framed this act, and it broke out soon after in the Dutch wars during that of the Protector and of Charles the Second. It is not impossible, therefore, that *some of the regulations of this famous act may have proceeded from national animosity. They are as wise, however, as if they had all been dictated by the most deliberate wisdom. National animosity at that particular time aimed at the very same object which the most deliberate wisdom would have recommended, the diminution of the naval power of Holland*, the only naval power which could endanger the security of England.

The act of navigation is not favourable to foreign commerce, or to the growth of that opulence which can arise from it. . . . As defence, however, is of much more importance than opulence, the act of navigation is, perhaps, the wisest of all the commercial regulations of England.[15]

As regards the fisheries he took essentially the same point of view: "But though the tonnage bounties to those fisheries do not contribute to the opulence of that nation, it may perhaps be thought that they contribute to its defence, by augmenting the number of its sailors and shipping."[16] Smith likewise approved of the laws that authorized the payment of a bounty for the production of naval stores in the American colonies and prohibited their export from America to any country other than Great Britain. This typical mercantilist regulation was justified, in Smith's view, because it would make England independent of Sweden and the other northern countries for the supply of military necessities and thus contribute to the self-sufficiency of the empire.[17]

Furthermore, Smith was not averse to protective duties when they were required for reasons of military security. "It will generally be advantageous to lay some burden upon foreign, for the encouragement of domestic industry," he said, "when some particular industry is necessary for the defense of the country." Such protection was afforded the shipping industry by the Navigation Acts. But Smith was willing to pay bounties or to impose tariffs in the interest of other industries as well for the same public purpose: "It is of importance that the kingdom depend as little as possible upon its neighbours for the manufactures necessary for its defense; and if these cannot be maintained at home, it is reasonable that all other branches of industry be taxed in order to support them." With

[15] Smith, *Wealth of Nations*, bk. 4, ch. 2, pp. 430-31. Italics added.
[16] Ibid., bk. 4, ch. 5, pp. 484-85.
[17] Ibid., 545-46, 609-10. 484, n. 39.

some reluctance he also approved of retaliatory duties and hence of what came to be called "tariff wars."[18]

Adam Smith was a free trader by sincere conviction. He completely demolished some of the theories that underlay mercantilism; and mercantilist practices, as they existed in the British Empire of his day, were repugnant to him. He was suspicious of state interference with private initiative, and he was no worshiper of state power for its own sake. But the critical question in determining his relationship to the mercantilist school is not whether its fiscal and trade theories were sound or unsound but whether, when necessary, the economic power of the nation should be cultivated and used as an instrument of statecraft. The answer of Adam Smith to this question would clearly be "Yes"—that economic power should be so used.

This has not been altogether understood. Smith's followers, particularly in nineteenth-century England, were responsible for presenting him as an uncompromising free trader. Some of his critics, particularly the Germans Schmoller and List, allowed cries of "free trade" to drown out the rest of Smith's teachings which would have been music to their ears. Thus in some quarters Smith has been considered a hypocrite—a British patriot who had seen his country outgrow the mercantilist strategy and tactics by which it rose to unchallenged power, and was then prepared to recommend the discarding of such strategy and tactics by other nations of lesser good fortune. That Smith was a British patriot need hardly be denied, but that he was a hypocrite is emphatically not true. He does not deserve the following withering indictment by List, who was more familiar with what he called "the school" of Smith's followers than with Smith himself:

> It is a very common clever device that when anyone has attained the summit of greatness, he kicks away the ladder by which he has climbed up, in order to deprive others of the means of climbing up after him. In this lies the secret of the cosmopolitical doctrine of Adam Smith, and of the cosmopolitical tendencies of his great contemporary William Pitt, and of all his successors in the British Government administrations.
>
> Any nation which by means of protective duties and restrictions on navigation has raised her manufacturing power and her navigation to such a degree of development that no other nation can sustain free competition with her, can do nothing wiser than to throw away these ladders of her greatness, to preach to other nations the benefits of free trade, and to declare in penitent tones that she has

[18] Ibid., 429, 434, 484-89 (esp. n. 39).

225

hitherto wandered in the paths of error, and has now for the first time succeeded in discovering the truth.[19]

II

More than three hundred years ago, Francis Bacon pointed out that the ability of a nation to defend itself depended less upon its material possessions than upon the spirit of the people, less upon its stocks of gold than upon the iron of determination in the body politic.[20] As a professor of moral philosophy, Adam Smith must have been acquainted with the works of Bacon. In any case, he believed that "The security of every society must always depend, more or less, upon the martial spirit of the great body of the people. . . . Martial spirit alone, and unsupported by a well-disciplined standing army, would not, perhaps, be sufficient for the defence and security of any society. But where every citizen had the spirit of a soldier, a smaller standing army would surely be necessary." And Smith went even further in the belief that "even though the martial spirit of the people were of no use towards the defense of the society, yet to prevent that sort of mental mutilation, deformity, and wretchedness, which cowardice necessarily involves in it, from spreading themselves through the great body of the people, would still deserve the most serious attention of government; in the same manner as it would deserve its most serious attention to prevent a leprosy or any other loathsome and offensive disease, though neither mortal nor dangerous, from spreading itself among them. . . ." Only through "the practice of military exercises," supported by the government, could the martial spirit be effectively maintained.[21] During the nineteenth century many of Smith's followers, notably Cobden and Bright, were convinced pacifists, as well as ardent free traders, and would not have endorsed any such doctrine.

There is a long-standing and deeply rooted Anglo-American prejudice against "standing armies." The insular position of the British Isles made it possible for Parliament to "muddle through" in questions of national defense, and the long contest between Parliament and the Crown (in which the army was an instrument of the Stuarts) fostered the belief that a professional army was dangerous to civil liberty. On the continent of Europe the rivals of Great Britain had resorted to large standing armies

[19] List, *National System,* 295-96. See a similar, but less vindictive, comment by Schmoller, *Mercantile System,* 79-80. A recent Nazi critic is also worth consulting in this same connection: P. F. Schröder, "Wehrwirtschaftliches in Adam Smiths Werk über den Volkwohlstand," *Schmollers Jahrbuch,* 63, no. 3 (1939), 1-16.

[20] Francis Bacon, "Of the True Greatness of Kingdoms and Estates," no. 19 of *Essays Civil and Moral,* in *The Works of Francis Bacon,* ed. James Spedding (Boston, 1840), 7:176 ff.

[21] Smith, *Wealth of Nations,* bk. 5, ch. 1, pp. 738-40.

as the bulwark of their strength, and under professional soldiers had made great progress in military organization and the art of war.[22] Nevertheless, Parliament continued during time of peace to maintain the army at inconsequential strength, persisted in the inefficient and demoralizing system of billeting of troops on the people, and continued its reliance on the militia, which Dryden had so effectively lampooned in *Cymon and Iphigenia*:

> The country rings around with loud alarms,
> And raw in fields the rude militia swarms;
> Mouths without hands, maintained at vast expense,
> In peace a charge, in war a weak defence.
> Stout once a month they march, a blustering band,
> And ever, but in time of need, at hand.

At the end of the seventeenth century, Macaulay wrote, "there was scarcely a public man of note who had not often avowed his conviction that our policy and a standing army could not exist together. The Whigs had been in the constant habit of repeating that standing armies had destroyed the free institutions of the neighboring nations. The Tories had repeated as constantly that, in our own island, a standing army [under Cromwell] had subverted the Church, oppressed the gentry, and murdered the King. No leader of either party could, without laying himself open to the charge of gross inconsistency, propose that such an army should henceforth be one of the permanent establishments of the realm."[23]

This was still the situation when Smith was professor of moral philosophy at Glasgow, 1752-1763, and delivered his famous lectures on justice, police, revenue, and arms.[24] In these lectures Smith broke with his famous teacher Francis Hutcheson, who had opposed a standing army on the ground that "the military arts and virtues are accomplishments highly becoming all honorable citizens" and that "warfare therefore should be no man's perpetual profession; but all should take their turns in such services."[25] This seemed to Smith an utterly impracticable program, and he took a categorical stand in favor of a professional army.

Smith admitted that a standing army might be a menace to liberty—

[22] See the essay by Henry Guerlac, above. For further material on Smith's convictions regarding the standing army, see a particularly valuable article by the late Professor Charles J. Bullock of Harvard, "Adam Smith's Views upon National Defense," *Military Historian and Economist* 1 (1917), 249-57.

[23] Thomas Macaulay, *History of England*, Riverside edition (Boston, n.d.), 4:186-87.

[24] Adam Smith, *Lectures on Justice, Police, Revenue and Arms*, ed. Edwin Cannan (Oxford, 1896; repr. New York, 1956) from notes taken by a student in 1763.

[25] Francis Hutcheson, *A Short Introduction to Moral Philosophy*, 2 vols. (Glasgow, 1764), 2:348-49.

after all, Cromwell had "turned the long parliament out of doors." But he believed that with proper precautions the army could be made to support, rather than undermine, the authority of the constitution. In any case, security demanded a well-trained and well-disciplined armed force; only then could the nation commit its fate to the god of battles. No militia, however trained and disciplined, could take the place of professional soldiers, especially in an age when the development of firearms put a greater premium on organization and order than on individual skill, bravery, and dexterity. The most elementary requirements of military precaution, therefore, demanded that the historic reliance upon the militia, and the traditional suspicion of the professional army, give way to the exigencies of the times. Furthermore, the sound economic principle of the division of labor demanded that war be made a vocation, not an avocation. Smith wrote:

> The art of war, as it is certainly the noblest of all arts, so in the progress of improvement it necessarily becomes one of the most complicated among them. The state of the mechanical, as well as of some other arts, with which it is necessarily connected, determines the degree of perfection to which it is capable of being carried at any particular time. But in order to carry it to this degree of perfection, it is necessary that it should become the sole or principal occupation of a particular class of citizens, and the division of labour is as necessary for the improvement of this, as of every other art. Into other arts the division of labour is naturally introduced by the prudence of individuals, who find that they promote their private interest better by confining themselves to a particular trade, than by exercising a great number. But it is the wisdom of the state only which can render the trade of a soldier a particular trade separate and distinct from all others. A private citizen who, in time of profound peace, and without any particular encouragement from the public, should spend the greater part of his time in military exercises, might, no doubt, both improve himself very much in them, and amuse himself very well; but he would certainly not promote his own interest. It is the wisdom of the state only which can render it for his interest to give the greater part of his time to this peculiar occupation: and states have not always had this wisdom, even when their circumstances had become such that the preservation of their existence required that they should have it.[26]

[26] Smith, *Wealth of Nations*, bk. 5, ch. 1, pp. 658-659. In addition, see *Lectures*, part 4, "Of Arms," of which the foregoing chapter is an elaboration.

It is a coincidence, but a coincidence of significance to the English-speaking peoples, that 1776 was the date of publication of both *The Wealth of Nations* and the Declaration of Independence. Smith dealt at length with the relations of Great Britain with its American colonies, and what he had to say is of moment to any student of American or British history. For our present purposes, however, it is necessary to consider only Smith's attitude toward imperialism. He clearly believed that a colonial policy did not "pay" in the mercantilist sense. And although he thought that the Americans had not suffered, in fact, from the restrictions imposed by the mother country, such restrictions were nevertheless "a manifest violation of the most sacred rights of mankind," as well as "impertinent badges of slavery" imposed upon America by the official and mercantile classes of England. The value of colonies in an imperial system should be measured, in his judgment, by the military forces they provided for imperial defense and by the revenue that they furnished for the general support of the empire. Judged by these criteria, the American colonies were a liability, not an asset, to Great Britain; they not only contributed nothing to imperial defense, but they required British forces to be dispatched to America and they had involved the homeland only recently in a costly war with France.[27] Stated in terms of a commercial and financial balance sheet, England would be better off without the colonies.

This is a parochial view of empire, which will be suggestive of Neville Chamberlain. But Smith did not propose that England accede to the American demand for independence; this would be "to propose such a measure as never was, and never will be adopted, by any nation in the world. No nation ever voluntarily gave up the dominion of any province, how troublesome soever it might be to govern it, and how small soever the revenue which it afforded might be in proportion to the expence which it occasioned. Such sacrifices, though they might frequently be agreeable to the interest, are always mortifying to the pride of every nation, and what is perhaps of still greater consequence, they are always contrary to the private interest of the governing part of it, who would thereby be deprived of the disposal of many places of trust and profit, of many opportunities of acquiring wealth and distinction, which the possession of the most turbulent, and, to the great body of the people, the most unprofitable province seldom fails to afford."[28]

[27] Smith was clearly wrong in saying that the "whole expence" of the Seven Years' War, as well as the cost of the wars which preceded it, should be charged to the colonies. The discussion on colonies is in *Wealth of Nations*, bk. 4, chaps. 7 and 8.

[28] Ibid., 581-82. It is interesting to compare Smith's views on colonies with those of Jeremy Bentham, one of the Smith's most faithful followers. Bentham agreed that the defense

Smith shrewdly foresaw that the American War of Independence would be a long and costly war. He even visualized a possible victory for the embattled colonists, who, from "shopkeepers, tradesmen, and attornies are become statesmen and legislators, and are employed in contriving a new form of government for an extensive empire, which, they flatter themselves, will become, and which, indeed, seems very likely to become, one of the greatest and most formidable that ever was in the world."[29] Smith was right, and among the attorneys who became statesmen was Alexander Hamilton, a giant among that remarkable galaxy of truly great men who brought into being the United States of America.

III

With the exception of two years of travel on the Continent (1764-1766), Adam Smith's life was devoted entirely to academic pursuits. He was a student at Glasgow and Oxford, lectured at Edinburgh, and was successively professor of logic and professor of moral philosophy at Glasgow. After his return from Europe, he devoted himself to his great work, *The Wealth of Nations*, published fourteen years before his death.

Alexander Hamilton, on the other hand, was a man of action from his earliest youth. His life began inauspiciously on the tiny West Indian island of Nevis. His father was impecunious; and after the death of his mother in 1768, when he was only eleven years old, Hamilton had to make his own way in the world. He served as clerk in a general store, but soon went to New York, where he entered Kings College (now Columbia) in 1773. Within a year he became involved in the war of pamphlets that preceded the American Revolution and, while still in his teens, established a reputation as one of the most vigorous writers of his generation. He entered the army early in 1776, received a commission, fought with Washington on Long Island and at White Plains, Trenton, and Princeton. In March 1777, at the age of twenty, he was made military secretary to the commander in chief, with the rank of lieutenant colonel; as such, he was not only a confidant and advisor of Washington, but the author of a series of brilliant reports on army organization and administration.[30] Later he commanded an infantry regiment in Lafayette's corps, distinguishing himself by conspicuous bravery at Yorktown. He continued his military career long after the Revolution when, in 1798,

---

of colonies costs too much, but went farther and advocated the relinquishment by Britain of its existing colonies and the abandonment of all attempts to acquire new ones. *Principles of International Law*, in *Works*, ed. John Bowring (Edinburgh, 1843), vol. 2, essay 4, esp. pp. 548-50.

[29] Smith, *Wealth of Nations*, 587-88.

[30] Hamilton's military papers are to be found in volumes 6 and 7 of his collected *Works*, ed. Henry Cabot Lodge, Federal Edition, 12 vols. (New York and London, 1904).

he was commissioned major general and inspector general of the army, second in command to Washington, for the purpose of preparing for a threatened war with France.

Hamilton's role in bringing into being the Annapolis and Philadelphia conventions and, above all, his brilliant services in securing ratification of the Constitution, are too well known to need extensive comment. Quite aside from his other great state papers, his authorship of more than half of *The Federalist* would alone entitle him to high rank among political writers. He was the most influential single member of Washington's cabinet, roaming far afield from his own duties as secretary of the Treasury. During the years 1789-1797 he probably did more than any other single person to formulate the early national policies of the United States, some of which came to have the binding force of traditon.[31] His tragic death in 1804, when he was only forty-seven, was a national disaster.

For the student of military affairs, Hamilton is a link between Adam Smith and Friedrich List. Hamilton was familiar with *The Wealth of Nations* and had it before him when, with the assistance of Tench Coxe, he wrote his famous "Report on Manufactures."[32] He agreed with Smith on the wisdom and necessity of a professional army, as well as on certain questions of economic policy related to national defense. Hamilton's influence on Friedrich List is evident in much of what the latter wrote. And in view of List's association with the protectionist groups in the United States, including the economist Mathew Carey, there can be little doubt that List considered the "Report on Manufactures" a textbook of political economy. Indeed, he invoked the support of Hamilton from time to time, and there is strong internal evidence throughout List's writings that Hamilton's ideas had a prominent place in his "national system."[33]

William Graham Sumner, an ardent free trader and hence an unsympathetic critic, said that Hamilton's concept of national policy was "the old system of mercantilism of the English school, turned around

[31] See the article by Allan Nevins on Hamilton in the *Dictionary of National Biography*.

[32] This fact is established by W. S. Culbertson's admirable essay *Alexander Hamilton* (New Haven, 1911), pp. 90, 107-108, 127-29. See also Henry Cabot Lodge in *Works*, 3:417, and the article "Alexander Hamilton and Adam Smith," by Edward G. Bourne, *Quarterly Journal of Economics*, 8 (April 1894), 328-44. Concerning the role of Tench Coxe see note 61.

[33] William Notz, "Friedrich List in America," *American Economic Review*, 16 (June 1926), 240-65. Dr. Notz was one of the editors of the above-mentioned edition of the works of List (see note 3). His admirable introductory essay to vol. 2 (Berlin, 1931), pp. 3-61, is the best account of List's years in America and their significance to List's career as a whole. For estimates of Hamilton's influence on List see C. Meitzel, article on Hamilton in *Handwörterbuch der Staatswissenschaften*, (1923), 4:21, and M. E. Hirst, *Life of Friedrich List* (London, 1909), 112-18.

and adjusted to the situation of the United States."[34] There is some merit to the statement but not in the sense that Hamilton was a blind follower or admirer of mercantilist doctrines. As has been indicated above, European mercantilists were concerned with two distinct but closely related things: national unification, as opposed to particularism; development of the resources of the nation, with special reference to its military potential.[35] Hamilton was certainly a nationalist and he certainly believed in using economic policy as an instrument of both national unification and national power. Almost everything he said and believed can be related, in some manner, to this central theme. His advocacy of a well-rounded national economy which would include manufactures, his recommendations as regards the public debt (particularly the assumption of the debts of the states), his belief in a national bank, his concepts of foreign policy and security, his doctrine of the "implied powers" of the federal government, his conviction that the manufacture of munitions of war should be encouraged and if necessary controlled by the nation, his reports on military policy, his ardent espousal of the navy, even his attitude toward democratic government—all these can best be understood in relation first to his passion for national unity and second his jealous regard for the political and economic power of the nation.

On the other hand, it is doubtful if even Adam Smith could have written a fairer or more eloquent summary of the case for free trade than that which appears in Hamilton's "Report on Manufactures," submitted to the Congress December 5, 1791.[36] Furthermore, if a system of industrial and commercial liberty, said Hamilton, "had governed the conduct of nations more generally than it has done, there is room to suppose that it might have carried them faster to prosperity and greatness than they have attained by the pursuit of maxims too widely opposite." There then would and could be a genuine international division of labor to the benefit of all. But liberty of trade and exchange has not prevailed; in fact, precisely the opposite is the case, and the nations of Europe, particularly those that had developed manufactures, "sacrifice the interests of a mutually beneficial intercourse to the vain project of selling everything and buying nothing." As a result, "the United States are, to a certain extent, in the situation of a country precluded from foreign commerce" and rendered impotent to trade with Europe on equal terms. This statement of the facts, continued Hamilton, is "not made in a spirit of complaint.

[34] W. G. Sumner, *Alexander Hamilton* (New York, 1890), 175.

[35] See introductory section of this essay.

[36] Hamilton, "Report on Manufactures," in *Works*, 4:70-198, esp. pp. 71-73, 100-101. The report also is included in an admirably edited volume by Samuel McKee, Jr., *Papers on Public Credit, Commerce, and Finance by Alexander Hamilton* (New York, 1934).

It is for the nations whose regulations are alluded to, to judge for themselves, whether, by aiming at too much, they do not lose more than they gain. It is for the United States to consider by what means they can render themselves least dependent on the combinations, right or wrong, of foreign policy" of other states.[37]

The program set forth in his "Report on Manufactures" stamps Hamilton as an economic nationalist. His aim, he said, was to promote such manufactures "as will tend to render the United States independent of foreign nations for military and other essential supplies."[38] He believed that

> not only the wealth but the independence and security of a country appear to be materially connected with the prosperity of manufactures. Every nation, with a view to those great objects, ought to endeavor to possess within itself, all the essentials of national supply. These comprise the means of subsistence, habitation, clothing, and defense.
>
> The possession of these is necessary to the perfection of the body politic; to the safety as well as to the welfare of the society. The want of either is the want of an important organ of political life and motion; and in the various crises which await a state, it must severely feel the effects of any such deficiency. The extreme embarrassments of the United States during the late war, from an incapacity of supplying themselves, are still matter of keen recollection; a future war might be expected again to exemplify the mischiefs and dangers of a situation to which that incapacity is still, in too great a degree, applicable, unless changed by timely and vigorous exertion. To effect this change, as fast as shall be prudent, merits all the attention and all the zeal of our public councils: 't is the next great work to be accomplished.
>
> The want of a navy, to protect our external commerce, as long as it shall continue, must render it a peculiarly precarious reliance for the supply of essential articles, and must serve to strengthen prodigiously the arguments in favor of manufactures.[39]

Hamilton believed that a young country like the United States could not compete with countries like Great Britain that had been long estab-

[37] Hamilton, "Report on Manufacturers," 73, 100-102.

[38] Ibid., 70. Compare with the statement in Washington's first annual message to Congress in 1790 that "the safety and interest [of a free people] require that they should promote such manufactories as tend to render them independent of others for essential, particularly military supplies."

[39] Hamilton, "Report on Manufacturers," 135-36.

lished in manufacturing. "To maintain, between the recent establishments of one country, and the long-matured establishments of another country, a competition upon equal terms ... is in most cases, impracticable." Hence the industries of the newer country should enjoy the "extraordinary aid and protection of the government."[40] This aid and protection should be extended in the form of import duties (to the point of prohibition in some instances), restraints on export of raw materials, pecuniary bounties and premiums, drawbacks exemption of certain essential raw materials from import tariffs, and other devices. This is the "infant industry" argument, but it also is the characteristic mercantilist case for autarky.

In determining the commodities on which duties are to be levied, and the amount of such duties, for the purpose of encouraging domestic manufactures, important and perhaps primary consideration should be given to "the great [factor] of national defense." Thus:

> Fire-arms and other military weapons may, it is conceived, be placed without inconvenience, in the class of articles rated at fifteen per cent. There are already manufactories of these articles, which only require the stimulus of a certain demand to render them adequate to the supply of the United States.
>
> It would also be a material aid to manufactures of this nature, as well as a means of public security, if provision should be made for an annual purchase of military weapons, of home manufacture, to a certain determinate extent, in order to [assure] the formation of arsenals; and to replace, from time to time, such as should be drawn for use, so as always to have in store the quantity of each kind which should be deemed a competent supply.
>
> But it may, hereafter, deserve legislative consideration, whether manufactories of all the necessary weapons of war ought not to be established on account of the government itself. Such establishments are agreeable to the usual practice of nations, and that practice seems founded on sufficient reason.
>
> There appears to be an improvidence in leaving these essential implements of national defence to the casual speculations of individual adventure—a resource which can less be relied upon, in this case, than in most others; the articles in question not being objects of ordinary and indispensable private consumption or use. As a general rule, manufactories on the immediate account of government

[40] Ibid., 105-106.

are to be avoided; but this seems to be one of the few exceptions which that rule admits, depending on very special reasons."[41]

The "Report on Manufactures" also emphasizes the idea—to be developed at great length by Friedrich List—that a country with a diversified economy, including agriculture, manufactures, and commerce, will be more unified at home and stronger in its relations with other powers than it otherwise would be. But Hamilton made his best statement of this thesis in his first draft of Washington's "Farewell Address," which he wrote during the summer of 1796.[42] Hamilton visualized a nation in which sectional economies would interweave themselves into a common national economy and interest. The agricultural South would not merely contribute its own share to the national wealth but would share in the benefits of the industrial strength of the North. The West, especially after the development of adequate transportation, would offer a market for the manufactures and foreign commerce of the East and, in turn, would profit from the development of the "weight, influence, and maritime resources of the Atlantic States." Furthermore, "where every part finds a particular interest in the Union, all parts of our Country will find greater independence from [i.e., by reason of] the superior abundance and variety of production incident to the diversity of soil and climate." The aggregate strength of a nation thus united by a common economic interest would be increased in every essential respect. The United States, by developing a diversified economy, would enjoy enhanced "security from external danger, less frequent interruption of their peace with foreign nations, and, what is more valuable, an exemption from those broils and wars between the [several] parts, if disunited, which their own rivalships, fomented by foreign intrigue ... would inevitably produce." In consequence, the nation would profit from "exemption from the necessity of those military establishments upon a large scale which bear in every country so menacing an aspect towards Liberty." Thus did Hamilton link his economic system with national security.

Hamilton's argument for an American navy and merchant marine was a similar amalgam of politics and economics. He was convinced that the United States was destined to become a great maritime power. The

---

[41] Ibid., 167-68. This is not the first occasion on which Hamilton made such a proposal as regards munitions. As chairman of a special committee of Congress he suggested in 1783 that "it ought to be made a serious object of policy, to be able to supply ourselves with all the articles of first necessity in war" and that to this end public manufactories of arms and munitions should be constructed (ibid., 467, 475).

[42] For the text and all other details see Victor H. Paltsits, *Washington's Farewell Address* (New York, 1935), esp. pp. 184-85. The extent to which Washington adopted Hamilton's argument in this respect will be evident by comparing the foregoing draft with the final manuscript (ibid., 143-44). For clarity, I have supplied punctuation in the text.

adventurous voyages of Americans to all quarters of the earth—"that unequalled spirit of enterprise . . . which is in itself an inexhaustible mine of national wealth"—had already "excited uneasy sensations" among Europeans, who "seem to be apprehensive of our too great interference in that carrying trade, which is the support of their navigation and the foundation of their naval strength." Some European states, by restrictive legislation, were resolved upon "clipping the wings by which we might soar to a dangerous greatness." But by a firm union, a flourishing merchant marine, prosperous fisheries (as a nursery of seamen), appropriate retaliatory navigation acts, and a navy "we might defy the little arts of the little politicians to control or vary the irresistible and unchangeable course of nature." The navy of the United States might not "vie with those of the great maritime powers." but it would at least "be of respectable weight if thrown into the scale of either of two contending parties," particularly in the West Indies. Our position, even with a few ships of the line, is therefore "a most commanding one," which would enable us to "bargain to great advantage for commercial privileges." Furthermore, "a price would be set on our neutrality and our friendship" in the event of a war between foreign powers. Hence, "by a steady adherence to the Union, we may hope, ere long, to become the arbiter of Europe in America, and to be able to incline the balance of power in this part of the world as our interest may dictate."[43] Surely, this is *Realpolitik* of a high order and shows that a strategy for America in world politics was evolved by the fathers of the republic.

It is imperative, Hamilton claimed, that the United States have an integrated national economy. To this great object, a navy would contribute, just as political and economic union would contribute to the growth of the navy:

> A navy of the United States, as it would embrace the resources of all, is an object far less remote than a navy of any single State or partial confederacy, which would only embrace the resources of a single part. It happens, indeed, that different portions of confederated America possess each some peculiar advantage for this essential establishment. The more southern States furnish in greater abundance certain kinds of naval stores—tar, pitch, and turpentine. Their wood for the construction of ships is also of a more solid and lasting texture. The difference in the duration of the ships of which the navy might be composed, if chiefly constructed of Southern wood,

[43] All quotations in the preceding paragraph and the one that follows are from *The Federalist*, No. 11. It should be noted that Hamilton did not wish us to pursue a balance-of-power policy in Europe. See, e.g., *Works*, 9:327; 10:397.

would be of signal importance, either in the view of naval strength or of national economy. Some of the Southern and of the Middle States yield a greater plenty of iron ore, and of better quality. Seamen must chiefly be drawn from the Northern hive. The necessity of naval protection to external or maritime commerce does not require a particular elucidation, no more than the conduciveness of that species of commerce to the prosperity of a navy.[44]

Hamilton's fiscal policy likewise had its political connotations. By funding the public debt, assuming the debts of the states, and founding a national bank, he hoped to link "the interest of the State in an intimate connection with those of the rich individuals belonging to it" and to turn "the wealth and influence of both into a commercial channel, for mutual benefit." Hence, a national debt might be a "national blessing" since it would be "a powerful cement to our Union."[45] He wanted the support of the merchant and propertied classes because he knew how they had been able to influence the government in England in the enactment of mercantilist legislation, and he believed that the economic motivation of politics was inherent in almost any society.[46] Furthermore, the establishment of the national credit on a firm basis was essential "as long as nations in general continue to use it as a resource in war. It is impossible for a country to contend, on equal terms, or to be secure against the enterprises of other nations, without being able equally with them to avail itself of this important resource; and to a very young country, with moderate pecuniary capital, and a not very various industry, it is still more necessary than to countries more advanced in both." One "cannot but conclude that war, without credit, would be more than a great calamity—would be ruin." Although admitting the legality of sequestration of private property in wartime, he opposed it on grounds, among other valid reasons, that it would discourage foreign investment in American securities.[47] In short, he recommended that we "cherish credit as a means of strength and security."[48]

[44] Compare this with the following statement which Theodore Roosevelt (who was a great admirer of Hamilton) made to a midwestern audience in 1910: "Friends, the Navy is not an affair of the seacoast only. There is not a man who lives in the grass country, in the cattle country, or among the Great Lakes, or alongside the Missouri who is not just as keenly interested in the Navy as if he dwelt on the New England Coast, or on the Gulf Coast, or on Puget Sound (speech at Omaha, Sept. 2, repr. in *The New Nationalism* [New York, 1910], 147).

[45] Alexander Hamilton, letter to Robert Morris, 1780, in *Works*, 3:338, 387.

[46] On this point see also *The Federalist*, No. 10, written by Madison.

[47] Alexander Hamilton, "Second Report on the Public Credit" (December 1794), in *Works*, 3:199-300. Quotations are from pp. 295-96.

[48] Hamilton's draft for Washington's "Farewell Address." Paltsits, *Washington's Farewell Address*, 193.

IV

National security was a problem of absorbing interest to Hamilton, and he had a realistic appreciation of the factors that were pertinent to it. He understood that the distance of the United States from Europe and the vast extent of our territory were great assets to us, since they would make conquest by a foreign power difficult if not impossible. But he knew also that we were a young, undeveloped, and politically immature country, needing time to consolidate our position. Hence his reiterated emphasis upon national unity, his strictures against factionalism and sectionalism, his injunctions against "passionate attachment" or "rooted prejudice" as regards other nations, and his advice against political commitments abroad. Hence also his belief that "if we remain a united people under an efficient government the period is not distant when we may defy material injury from external annoyance."[49] But security is not possible without power, for "a nation, despicable by its weakness, forfeits even the privilege of being neutral."[50] Only if we are strong can we "choose peace or war as our interest guided by justice shall dictate."[51] But strength depends on union and, as Jay said, "on government, the arms, and the resources of the country."[52]

Hamilton saw clearly, too, that we would never be altogether secure while European powers had substantial territories on this continent. He was opposed to transfers of American territory from one non-American power to another; consequently, he favored the purchase of Louisiana, even though it was effected by his opponent Jefferson. He even seems to have visualized the policy that came to be known as the Monroe Doctrine.[53] He was an Anglophile, not only because he detested the radical principles of Revolutionary France, but also because he believed that we were too weak for a definitive test of arms with Great Britain, as well as too dependent upon British toleration of our growing commercial stength.

Hamilton agreed with the preamble of the Constitution that a more perfect union, the common defense, the general welfare, and the pres-

---

[49] Ibid., 193-96.

[50] *The Federalist*, No. 11, p. 65.

[51] This famous phrase was Hamilton's, not Washington's (Paltsits, *Washington's Farewell Address*, 196). Washington changed "dictate" to "counsel."

[52] *The Federalist*, No. 4, p. 65.

[53] For the nontransfer principle see Alexander Hamilton, "Answer to Questions Proposed by the President of the United States," September 15, 1790, in *Works*, 4:338. Regarding the menace of European territories in America, see *The Federalist*, No. 24, pp. 150-51. The elimination of European influence on this continent is a fairly constant factor in American foreign policy; cf. E. M. Earle, "National Security and Foreign Policy," *Yale Review* 29 (1940), 444-60. *The Federalist*, No. 11, p. 69, indicates that, had he lived, Hamilton would have supported the Monroe Doctrine.

ervation of liberty were inextricably interwoven. In No. 8 of *The Federalist* he wrote at length and with keen understanding on the delicate problem of reconciling military power with basic political liberties—a paper that shows striking resemblances to some of Adam Smith's ideas on the same subject. He pointed out also that it was not enough for a government to have authority to raise armies in time of war; it must maintain adequate forces in time of peace. Otherwise "we must expose our property and liberty to the mercy of foreign invaders . . . because we are afraid that rulers, created by our choice, dependent on our will, might endanger that liberty, by an abuse of the means necessary to its preservation."[54] In time of war, furthermore, the power of the executive must be adequate for "the direction of the common strength" despite the traditional fear of Americans for centralized authority.[55]

Like Adam Smith, Hamilton believed that the professional army should be the basis of national defense. As he wrote in *The Federalist*: "The steady operations of war against a regular and disciplined army can only be successfully conducted by a force of the same kind. Considerations of economy, not less than of stability and vigor, confirm this position. The American militia, in the course of the late war, have, by their valor on numerous occasions, erected eternal monuments to their fame; but the bravest of them feel and know that the liberty of their country could not have been established by their efforts alone, however great and valuable they were. War, like most other things, is a science to be acquired and perfected by diligence, by perseverance, by time, and by practice."[56]

During the latter part of the eighteenth century there was a widespread belief that parliamentary governments, especially those dominated by a commercial class, were less likely to be involved in war than monarchies. Hamilton thought any such opinion contrary to the dictates of common sense and the known facts of history. He was persuaded that popular assemblies were just as subject as other forms of government

---

[54] *The Federalist*, No. 25, p. 156. On this same point see ibid., No. 4 (by Jay), No. 23 (by Hamilton), and No. 41 (by Madison). *The Federalist*, in these and other numbers, is a textbook for students of military policy and national security.

[55] Ibid. No. 74, p. 48.

[56] *The Federalist*, No. 25, p. 157. Even earlier, Hamilton had given serious thought to a military policy for the United States. See a letter to James Duane in 1780 and Hamilton's report on behalf of a special committee of the Congress in 1783, in *Works*, 1:215-16; 6:463-83. He believed that the army should be national in organization and loyalty; that a system of defenses should be built without reference to state lines; that the militia should be under national supervision as regards uniformity of service, training, and equipment; that there should be a national military academy; and that the manufacture of munitions should be encouraged and perhaps owned by the federal government. Hamilton also believed in the principle of universal liability to military service. (Ibid., 7:47.)

(perhaps more so) to "the impulses of rage, resentment, jealousy, avarice, and other irregular and violent propensities." He also disagreed with the view of the physiocrats that—to quote Montesquieu—"the natural result of commerce is to promote peace." On the contrary, in his judgment, commerce was more likely to be a cause of recurring wars. "Has commerce hitherto done anything more than change the objects of war? Is not the love of wealth as domineering and enterprising a passion as that of power or glory? Have there not been as many wars founded upon commercial motives since that has become the prevailing system of nations, as were before occasioned by the cupidity of territory or dominion? Has not the spirit of commerce, in many instances, administered new incentives to the appetite, both for the one and for the other?" He thought the answer to these questions clearly to be in the affirmative. War was too deeply rooted in human society, however changing its forms, to warrant belief in undisturbed peace and security.[57]

Surprisingly enough, Thomas Jefferson agreed with Hamilton that commerce was a potential cause of war. "Our people are decided in the opinion," he wrote John Jay from Paris in August 1785, "that it is necessary for us to take a share in the occupation of the ocean, and their established habits induce them to require that the sea be kept open to them, and that that line of policy be pursued, which will render the use of that element to them as great as possible. I think it a duty in those entrusted with the administration of their affairs, to conform themselves to the decided choice of their constituents; and that therefore, we should, in every instance, [even at the cost of almost certain war] preserve an equality of right to them in the transportation of commodities, in the right of fishing, and in the other uses of the sea."[58] And Jefferson gave practical effect to this belief when, as President, he waged war against the Barbary pirates, his pacifist convictions to the contrary notwithstanding.

Indeed, some measure of Hamilton's stature may be taken by observing further the extent to which Jefferson—his most bitter opponent—came to agree with him as regards economics and national defense. Jefferson was a free trader and an avowed enemy of manufactures. He

---

[57] *The Federalist*, No. 6, discusses the causes of war at length. Quotations are from p. 30. Concerning the view of the physiocrats and others that the influence of commerce was in the direction of promoting international peace see Edmond Silberner, *La guerre dans la pensée économique du xvie au xviiie siècle* (Paris, 1939). In Nos. 3, 4, and 5 of *The Federalist* John Jay also discusses the causes of war and makes the remarkable forecast (in No. 4) that the growing trade with China would involve the United States in international conflict in the Far East.

[58] *Writings of Thomas Jefferson* (Memorial Edition), ed. Andrew A. Lipscomb, 20 vols. (Washington, D.C., 1903-1904), 5:94.

detested Hamilton's protectionist program. But after his own experiences with the embargo and after observing the consequences of the War of 1812 with Great Britain, he reluctantly came to the conclusion that the realities of power politics might require a change in the views which he had previously held. As he wrote the French economist and free trader Jean Baptiste Say in March 1815:

> ... I had then [earlier] persuaded myself that a nation, distant as we are from the contentions of Europe, avoiding all offences to other powers, and not over-hasty in resenting offence from them, doing justice to all, faithfully fulfilling the duties of neutrality, performing all offices of amity, and administering to their interests by the benefits of our commerce, that such a nation, I say, might expect to live in peace, and consider itself merely as a member of the the great family of mankind; that in such case it might devote itself to whatever it could best produce, secure of a peaceable exchange of surplus for what could be more advantageously furnished by others, as takes place between one county and another of France. But experience has shown that continued peace depends not merely on our own justice and prudence, but on that of others also; that when forced into war, the interception of exchanges which must be made across a wide ocean, becomes a powerful weapon in the hands of an enemy domineering over that element, and to the other distresses of war adds the want of all those necessaries for which we have permitted ourselves to be dependent on others, even arms and clothing. *This fact, therefore, solves the question by reducing it to its ultimate form, whether profit or preservation is the first interest of a State?* We are consequently become manufacturers to a degree incredible to those who do not see it, and who only consider the short period of time during which we have been driven to them by the suicidal policy of England. The prohibiting duties we lay on all articles of foreign manufacture which prudence requires us to establish at home, with the patriotic determination of every good citizen to use no foreign article which can be made within ourselves, without regard to difference of price, secures us against a relapse into foreign dependency.[59]

And although Jefferson never quite came to support Hamilton's views concerning a standing army, he did come around to believe that much more thought must be given to the maintenance of a military establishment based upon universal liability to service. Commenting on

---

[59] Ibid., 14:258-60. Emphasis added.

a memoir of the secretary of war, he wrote James Monroe in 1813: "It is more a subject of joy that we have so few of the desperate characters which compose modern regular armies. But it proves more forcibly the necessity of obliging every citizen to be a soldier; this was the case with the Greeks and Romans, and must be that of every free State. . . . We must train and classify the whole of our male citizens and make military instruction a regular part of collegiate education. We can not be safe till this is done."[60]

Alexander Hamilton can hardly be rated high as an economist, except, perhaps, in one respect—his effective statement of the "infant industry" argument for the protection of manufactures, in which he said with great effectiveness virtually all that can be said. In the formulation of this part of his famous report he had the active collaboration of Tench Coxe, his assistant secretary of the Treasury and one of the Philadelphia school of protectionists who had so marked an influence on Hamilton. But the historical significance of his plea for the development of American industry is greater than its inherent worth, for upon what he wrote was built the structure of American economic policy. As one who combines economics with politics and statecraft, however, Hamilton ranks with the great statesmen of modern times. He is, in fact, an American Colbert or Pitt or Bismarck. The power and effect of his ideas was indelibly impressed upon succeeding generations of Americans, so that in the realm of government and industry his influence is more marked than that of any of his contemporaries except Jefferson.[61]

V

It is one of the ironies of history that Hamilton's political opponents Jefferson and Madison did more than Hamilton himself to give effect to his protectionist and nationalist views of economic policy. The embargo, which Jefferson initiated in December 1807, the Non-Intercourse Act, and the succeeding war with Great Britain, upon which Madison reluc-

---

[60] Ibid., 13:261.

[61] Mr. Julian Boyd, librarian of Princeton University, has had the privilege of examining correspondence and manuscripts of Tench Coxe which indicate that the latter had an active part in the formulation and drafting of the "Report on Manufactures." The actual extent of Coxe's contribution to the final document must await release and publication of the Coxe papers by the Coxe family. For a very critical analysis of the report, pointing out certain inconsistencies and contradictions in the document, see Frank A. Fetter, in L. S. Lyon and V. Abramson, *Government and Economic Life*, 2 vols. (Washington, D.C., 1940), 2:536-40. A longer treatment of the same subject, less unfavorable to Hamilton, is E. C. Lunt, "Hamilton as a Political Economist," *Journal of Political Economy* (1895), 289-310. For the influence of the Philadelphia School see a paper by Professor Fetter, "The Early History of Political Economy in the United States," *Proceedings of the American Philosophical Society* 87 (1943), 51-60.

tantly embarked, had the practical result of closing virtually all avenues of foreign trade and making the United States dependent upon its own resources for manufactures and munitions of war. The industries that were born under the stress and necessity of the years 1808 to 1815 were the infants to which the nation gave protection in 1816 and in a succession of tariff acts thereafter.

While Americans were still smarting from the indignities inflicted upon the United States by Napoleonic France and Great Britain, there seemed to be substantial agreement upon governmental protection of manufactures. Madison and Jefferson, on the one hand, and the "war hawks" of 1812, Clay and Calhoun, on the other, found themselves in the same camp. Jefferson in January 1816 wrote an exceedingly bitter denunciation of those who cited his former free-trade views as "a stalking horse, to cover their disloyal propensities to keep us in eternal vassalage to a foreign and unfriendly people [the British]." He called upon all Americans to "keep pace with me in purchasing nothing foreign where an equivalent of domestic fabric can be obtained, without regard to difference of price," for "experience has taught me that manufactures are now as necessary to our independence as to our comfort." For the sake of securing independence from others, "we must now place the manufacturer by the side of the agriculturist."[62] Hamilton himself could not have said more.

But as time went on, the old cleavages reappeared, and a bitter struggle over protectionism raged until the Walker Tariff of 1846 temporarily settled the issue. It was as a participant in this debate that Friedrich List made his appearance on the American scene and formulated the economic theories that were to have influence not only in the United States but, even more, in Germany. List was born in Württemberg in 1789, studied at the University of Tübingen (where he later served briefly as professor of politics), and entered public life as an ardent exponent of the *Zollverein*. His liberal and nationalist ideas kept him in constant hot water with the reactionary government of his native state, leading finally to his exile in 1825, when he came to America and settled among the Pennsylvania Germans of Reading. He became the editor of the Reading *Adler*, a German-American weekly with an influential voice in the affairs of Pennsylvania. His interest in commercial policy soon brought him into contact with the Pennsylvania Society for the Encouragement of Manufactures and the Mechanic Arts, which was under the vigorous and able leadership of Mathew Carey, Charles Jared Ingersoll, and Pierre

---

[62] *Writings of Thomas Jefferson*, 14:389-93. Letter to Benjamin Austin.

du Ponceau, among others.[63] Although Mathew Carey was the more effective pamphleteer, List was able to write with a wider experience of economics and politics and became the foremost literary and scholarly propagandist of protectionism during his residence in America. He was lionized by Pennsylvania industrialists, met most of the prominent American statesmen of the day, was offered the presidency of Lafayette College, and, when he finally returned to Germany in 1832, did so as a naturalized citizen and as a member of the consular service of the United States by appointment of Andrew Jackson. He was consul at Baden-Baden until 1834, at Leipzig (1834-1837), and at Stuttgart (1837-1845). He died by his own hand in 1846, after illness had terminated his public service.

List's intellectual history is fairly easy to trace. In his youth, "seeing to what a low ebb the well-being of Germany had sunk," he decided to study political economy and also to teach his fellow citizens the means, in terms of national policy, by which "the welfare, the culture, and the power of Germany might be promoted." He came to the conclusion that the key to the solution of Germany's problems was the principle of nationality. "I saw clearly that free competition between two nations which are highly civilized can only be mutually beneficial in case both of them are in a nearly equal position of industrial development, and that any nation which owing to misfortunes is behind others in industry, commerce, and navigation . . . must first of all strengthen her own individual powers, in order to fit herself to enter into free competition with more advanced nations. In a word, I perceived the distinction between *cosmopolitical*[64] and *political* economy. I felt that Germany must abolish her internal tariffs, and by the adoption of a common uniform commercial policy towards foreigners, strive to attain to the same degree of commercial and industrial development to which other nations have attained by means of their commercial policy."

[63] This society seems to have been inspired by the earlier Philadelphia Society for Promotion of Domestic Industries, founded by Hamilton. The Pennsylvania Society published and distributed several editions of the "Report on Manufactures," as well as pamphlets by Mathew Carey, who did more than any other American except Hamilton to bring about the so-called American System. It sponsored the famous Harrisburg Convention of 1827, memorializing Congress in favor of higher tariffs (which materialized in the "Tariff of Abominations" of 1828), attracted nationwide attention by its effective propaganda, and in general served to put the state of Pennsylvania permanently in the protectionist camp in American politics.

[64] "Cosmopolitical" was the term by which List described the writings of Adam Smith, J. B. Say, and others of their "school." That he frequently misrepresented Smith's views must be apparent to any reader of *The Wealth of Nations* and *The National System of Political Economy*. List hopelessly confused *Smithianismus*—which was what anybody said Smith had said—with Smith's own ideas. On this point see the admirable introduction by Professor J. S. Nicholson to the 1904 edition of Lloyd's translation of *The National System* (cited in note 3 above).

244

The similarity of the foregoing views to the central themes of mercantilism—national unification and the development of national power through economic policy—is obvious.

"When afterwards I visited the United States," continued List, "I cast all books aside—they would only have tended to deceive me. The best work on political economy which one can read in that modern land is actual life. There one may see wilderness grow into rich and mighty States; and progress which requires centuries in Europe, goes on there before one's eyes. . . . That book of actual life, I have earnestly and diligently studied, and compared with my previous studies, experience, and reflections. And the result has been (as I hope) the propounding of a system which . . . is not founded upon bottomless cosmopolitanism, but on the nature of things, on the lessons of history, and on the requirements of the nations."[65]

There is reason to believe that List formulated his views on politics and economics not, as he said, while a young man in Germany but only after his arrival in the United States. Certainly his *Outlines of American Political Economy* (a series of letters written to Charles Jared Ingersoll during the summer of 1827, subsequently printed in pamphlet form and widely distributed by the Pennsylvania protectionists) contains all the essential ideas elaborated in *The National System of Political Economy*, which appeared fourteen years later. The *Outlines* so clearly show the influence of Hamilton and Mathew Carey that there can be little reasonable doubt that American conditions and ideas were predominant, if not decisive, in the development of List's economic theories.[66]

Nevertheless, List was first, last, and above all a German. He was always an unhappy exile in America and acquired American nationality partly to avoid the petty persecutions that had been his previous lot in his native land. He admired and envied the vast undeveloped resources of the United States, the youthful vigor of the country, its success in achieving political unification, the *Realpolitik* of Hamilton, the lusty nationalism of Jackson, the American enthusiasm for railways and canals, and the seemingly unlimited possibilities for the future of the United

[65] Author's preface to *That National System*, xl, xlii. List always denied that he was a mercantilist, although he admitted that he had taken over "the valuable parts of that much-decried system" (ibid., xliii).

[66] This question has been debated with much heat. See Professor K. T. Eheberg's historical and critical introduction to the seventh edition of *The National System* (Stuttgart, 1853) for the viewpoint that Hamilton had little or no influence on List. *Contra* see Hirst, *Life*, 111-18 and, more especially, Ugo Rabbeno, *American Commercial Policy* (London, 1893), an English translation of *Protezionismo americano: Saggi storizi di politico commerciale* (Milan, 1893). Essay 3, chapters 2 (on Hamilton) and 2 (on List), of Rabbeno's work is perhaps the fairest summary of the question.

States as a world power.[67] But all of these things he related to his hopes and aspirations for his own country, then so tragically disunited. The Germany of his day might well have frustrated the determination of even a Colbert. Prussia, the dominant North German state, had more than sixty-seven different tariffs within its own territories, with almost three thousand articles subject to duties, to be collected by an army of customs officials; it had boundaries meandering almost a thousand miles through the rest of Germany, touching twenty-eight different states. Notwithstanding the seemingly insuperable difficulties, List dreamed dreams and saw visions of a new and greater Germany, unified by internal free trade, external protection, and a national system of posts and railways; and, finally, rising to the stature of a great European power. He lived to see only part of his program realized. The *Zollverein*, which destroyed more obstacles to internal commerce and political unity "than had been swept away by the political whirlwinds of the American and French Revolutions," was partly the result of his untiring efforts. His ceaseless propaganda for railways had some material results before it wore him out and hastened his death. He did not live to see the revolutions of 1848, the successes of Bismarck, and the final creation of a German empire. But that he is one of the makers of modern Germany has come to be more and more appreciated with the passage of time. And he is also, alas, one of the earlier exponents of that Greater Germany which has become the nightmare of the civilized world.[68]

VI

The primary concern of List's policies, both political and economic, was power, even though he linked power with welfare. In this respect, despite all his denials to the contrary, he was reverting to mercantilism. "A nation," he wrote, "is a separate society of individuals, who, possessing common government, common laws, rights, institutions, interests, common history, and glory, common defense and security of their rights, riches and lives, constitute one body, free and independent, following

[67] List firmly believed that the United States would, within a century, surpass Britain in industry, wealth, commerce, and naval power (*National System*, 40, 77-86, 339).

[68] List has been adopted by the expansionists, the Pan-Germans, and even the Nazis as a patron saint. For a characteristic pamphlet of the First World War see Karl Kumpmann, *Friedrich List als Prophet des neuen Deutschland* (Tübingen, 1915). For the present day see the best-selling novel *Ein Deutscher ohne Deutschland: Ein Friedrich List Roman*, by Walter von Molo (Berlin, Vienna, Leipzig, 1931 and subsequent editions). This novel is valuable not as historical fiction but as an example of the Pan-German and Nazi mentality— bitterly hostile to Britain and France, patronizing toward the United States (whose independence is accredited to the military genius of Steuben), contemptuous of Austria. Von Molo makes many unsupported assertions, some of them inherently improbable, concerning the influence of List on Andrew Jackson, von Moltke, and others.

only the dictates of its interest, as regards other independent bodies, and possessing power to regulate the interests of the individuals, constituting that body, in order to create the greatest quantity of common welfare in the interior and the greatest quantity of security as regards other nations.

"The object of the economy of this body," he continued, "is not only wealth as in individual and cosmopolitical economy, but power and wealth, because national wealth is increased and secured by national power, as national power is increased and secured by national wealth. Its leading principles are therefore not only economical, but political too. The individuals may be very wealthy; but if the nation possesses no power to protect them, it and they may lose in one day the wealth they gathered during ages, and their rights, freedom, and independence too."

Furthermore, "as power secures wealth, and wealth increases power, so are power and wealth, in equal parts, benefited by a harmonious state of agriculture, commerce and manufactures within the limits of the country. In the absence of this harmony, a nation is never powerful or wealthy." Hence productive power is the key to national security. "Government, sir has not only the right, but it is its duty, to promote every thing which may increase the wealth and power of the nation, if this object cannot be effected by individuals. So it is its duty to guard commerce by a navy, because the merchants cannot protect themselves; so it is its duty to protect the carrying trade by navigation laws, because carrying trade supports naval power, as naval power protects carrying trade; so the shipping interest and commerce must be supported by breakwaters—agriculture and every other industry by turnpikes, bridges, canals and rail-roads—new inventions by patent laws—so manufactures must be raised by protecting duties, if foreign capital and skill prevent individuals from undertaking them."[69]

Wealth is of no avail without the "unity and power of the nation." Thus modern Germany, failing to achieve either political unification or a "vigorous and united commercial policy," was for many generations unable to maintain the position among the nations to which its civilization entitled it and was "made a convenience of (like a colony)." Germany was several times "brought to the brink of ruin by free competition with foreigners, and thereby admonished of the fact that under the present conditions of the world every great nation must seek the guarantees of

[69] Friedrich List, *Outlines of American Political Economy*, in *Schriften, Reden, Briefe* (Berlin, 1927-35), 2:105-106 (hereafter cited as *Works*). The similarity of the idea of harmonious interests to Hamilton's views on the same subject is obvious. See also ibid., p. 374n, in which the editor, Dr. Notz, relates List's doctrine not only to Hamilton but also to Daniel Raymond, Mathew Carey, and John C. Calhoun.

its continued prosperity and independence, before all other things, in the independent and uniform development of its own powers and resources."

Tariffs and other restrictive devices designed to develop such powers and resources" are not so much the inventions of mere speculative minds, as the natural consequence of the diversity of interests, and of the strivings of nations after independence or overpowering ascendancy"—in other words, the war system. "War or the very possibility of war makes the establishment of a manufacturing power an indispensable requirement for any nation of first rank." Just as it would be the height of folly for a state to "disband its armies, destroy its fleets, and demolish its fortresses" in the modern world, so it would be ruinous for a nation to base its economic policy on an unwarranted assumption of a state of perpetual peace and world federation that exists only in the minds of the free-trade school.[70] The ability of a nation to wage war is measured in terms of its power to produce wealth, and it is the greatest possible development of productive power that is the goal of national unification and protectionism. Protectionist policies may for a time—but only for a time—result in a lower standard of living, because tariffs necessarily involve higher prices. But those who argue that cheapness of consumers' goods is a major consideration in weighing the advantages of foreign commerce "trouble themselves but little about the power, the honour, or the glory of the nation." They must realize that the protected industries are an organic part of the German people. "And who would be consoled for the loss of an arm by knowing that he had nevertheless bought his shirts forty per cent cheaper?"[71]

The greater the productive power, the greater the strength of the nation in its foreign relations and the greater its independence in time of war. Economic principles, therefore, cannot be divorced from their political implications: "At a time where technical and mechanical science exercise such immense influence on the methods of warfare, where all warlike operations depend so much on the condition of the national revenue, where successful defence greatly depends on the questions, whether the mass of the nation is rich or poor, intelligent or stupid,

[70] Friedrich List, *Le système naturel d'économie politique* (1837), ch. 2, in *Works*, 4:186. *The National System*, 87, 91-92, 102-107. The reader need not be reminded that Adam Smith did not base his system upon any assumption of universal peace or a federation of the world. List himself, on some occasions, said that the ultimate goal of all society was a world state, although he was too much of a nationalist to be an evangelist for the idea.

[71] List, *The National System*, 119, 140. Compare List's idea of productive power with Adam Smith's statement that the power to wage war is measured by "the annual produce of [a nation's] industry, from the annual revenue arising out of its lands, labour, and consumable goods. Above, section I. See also Jefferson as regards price, section IV, and Hamilton as regards self-sufficiency in war time, section III above.

energetic or sunk in apathy; whether its sympathies are given exclusively to the fatherland or partly to foreign countries; whether it can muster many or but few defenders of the country—at such a time, more than ever before, must the value of manufactures be estimated from a political point of view."[72]

List had a keen appreciation of the factors that enter into the military potential. "The present state of the nations," he wrote, "is the result of the accumulation of all discoveries, inventions, improvements, perfections, and exertions of all generations which have lived before us; ... and every separate nation is productive only in the proportion in which it has known how to appropriate these attainments of former generations and to increase them by its own acquirements, in which the natural capabilities of its territory, its extent and geographical position, its population and political power, have been able to develop as completely and symmetrically as possible all sources of wealth within its boundaries, and to extend its moral, intellectual, commercial, and political influence over less advanced nations and especially over the affairs of the world."[73]

From any such beliefs it is an easy step toward a policy of territorial expansion on the continent of Europe and colonial expansion overseas, and List did not hesitate to take the step. He wanted a unified Germany to hold sway from the Rhine to the Vistula and from the Balkans to the Baltic. He believed that "a large population and an extensive territory endowed with diversified natural resources are essential requirements of normal nationality; they are the fundamentals of the spiritual structure of a people, as well as of its material development and political power. ... A nation restricted in population and territory, especially if it has its distinctive language, can possess only a crippled literature, only crippled institutions for promoting the arts and sciences. A small state can never bring to the fullest state of development its diversified productive resources." Hence small nations will maintain their independence with the greatest difficulty and can exist only by tolerance of larger states and by alliances that involve a fundamental sacrifice of national sovereignty.[74]

The foregoing is not very different from present-day German definitions of *Lebensraum*, as will be obvious from List's program for a Greater Germany. He advocated the inclusion in a unified Germany of Denmark, the Netherlands, Switzerland, and Belgium—the first three on grounds of race and language, as well as on grounds of economics and strategy. As regards Denmark, Belgium, and the Netherlands, they were

---

[72] List, *The National System*, 168-69; also 118-19.
[73] Ibid., 113-14.
[74] Ibid., 142. In this instance Lloyd's translation seems unsatisfactory and I have rephrased it in certain essential respects. For the German original see *Works*, 6:210-11.

required because it was essential that Germany control the mouths of German rivers, plus the entire seacoast from the mouth of the Rhine to East Prussia, thus assuring the German nation "what it is now in need of, namely fisheries and naval power, maritime commerce and colonies." The acquisition of these three countries, together with Switzerland, furthermore, would assure Germany the natural boundaries of seas and mountains that are essential on both economic and military grounds.[75] Germany should likewise begin peaceful penetration of the Danubian territories and European Turkey. These areas were Germany's natural frontier, or *Hinterland,* and it had "an immeasurable interest that security and order should be firmly established" there.[76]

A nation should "possess the power of beneficially affecting the civilisation of less advanced nations, and by means of its own surplus population and of its mental and material capital to found colonies and beget new nations." When a nation cannot establish colonies, "all surplus population, mental and material means, which flows from such a nation to uncultivated countries, is lost to its own literature, civilisation, and industry, and goes to the benefit of other nationalities." This is notoriously true as regards German emigration to the United States. "What good is it if the emigrants to North America become ever so prosperous? In their personal relation they are lost ever to German nationality, and also from their material production Germany can expect only unimportant fruits. It is a pure delusion if people think that the German language can be maintained by the Germans who live in the interior of the United States, or that after a time it may be possible to establish German states there." Hence the conclusion is inescapable that Germany must have colonies of its own, in southeastern Europe and in Central and South America. And such colonies should be supported by all the resources of the nation, including state-sponsored colonization companies and "a vigorous German consular and diplomatic system."[77]

List knew full well that his program for Continental expansion and overseas colonies could not, in all probability, be realized without war. The advocates of a national system for Germany were aware, he wrote in a bitter polemic against the *Times* of London, that the future might bring national wars but they were therefore the more determined to mobilize the moral and material resources of the German nation in support of a national economy.[78]

---

[75] List, *The National System,* 142-43, 216, 327, 332, 346-47. For some unexplained reason List was unimpressed by rivers as natural boundaries.

[76] Ibid., 347. List said that it was better for Germans to emigrate to the Danube than to the shores of Lake Erie. For the frontier quotation see *Works,* 5:499-500.

[77] List, *The National System,* 142, 216-17, 345-47.

[78] Friedrich List, "Die Times und das deutsche Schutzsystem," *Zollvereinsblatt,* 4 (1846), 693-94.

It was England, of course, which stood in the way of German ambitions. It was the leading exponent of the balance-of-power policy that mobilized "the less powerful to impose a check on the encroachments of the more powerful." England stood virtually unchallenged in its position as an imperial power, which it had achieved by the development of manufactures. Hence, "if the other European nations wish also to partake of the profitable business of cultivating waste territories and civilising barbarous nations, or nations once civilised but which are again sunk in barbarism, they must commence with the development of their own internal manufacturing powers, of their mercantile marine, and of their naval power. And should they be hindered in these endeavours by England's manufacturing, commercial, and naval supremacy, in the union of their powers lies the only means of reducing such unreasonable pretensions to reasonable ones."[79]

It was England, also, which stood like a colossus astride the sea lanes of the world, making it difficult for any other nation to achieve the sea power that was necessary to the fulfillment of its destiny. In a statement on British control of the seas which would do credit to Admiral Mahan, List wrote:

> England has got into her possession the keys of every sea, and placed a sentry over every nation: over the Germans, Heligoland; over the French, Guernsey and Jersey; over the inhabitants of North America, Nova Scotia and the Bermudas; over Central America, the island of Jamaica; over all countries bordering on the Mediterranean, Gibralter, Malta, and the Ionian Islands. She possesses every important strategical position on both the routes to India with the exception of the Isthmus of Suez, which she is striving to acquire; she dominates the Mediterranean by means of Gibraltar, the Red Sea by Aden, and the Persian Gulf by Bushire and Karachi. She needs only the further acquisition of the Dardanelles, the Sound, and the Isthmuses of Suez and Panama, in order to be able to open and close at her pleasure every sea and every maritime highway.[80]

In view of Great Britain's overwhelming naval, commercial, and colonial strength, no single nation could successfully challenge it without powerful assistance from others. "The nations which are less powerful at sea can only match England at sea by uniting their own naval power"; hence every such nation "has an interest in the maintenance and pros-

---

[79] List, *The National System*, 216-17, 330.

[80] Ibid., 38. As regards Panama, for the possession of which Britain was then contending with the United States, List proposed an internationalized waterway under German entrepreneurs: "Der Kanal durch die Landenge von Panama, ein Unternehmen für die Hansestädte, in *Works*, 7:234-36.

perity of the naval power of all other nations"; and, together, they should "constitute themselves into one united naval power" for the purpose, among other things, of preventing undisputed control by Great Britain of the sea lanes of the world (especially those of the Mediterranean).[81] The part of wisdom would be for the Continental nations to form a European bloc to check British power: "If we only consider the enormous interests which the nations of the Continent have in common, as opposed to the English maritime supremacy, we shall be led to the conviction that nothing is so necessary to these nations as union, and nothing is so ruinous to them as Continental wars. The history of the last century also teaches us that every war which the powers of the Continent have waged against one another has had for its invariable result to increase the industry, the wealth, the navigation, the colonial possessions, and the power of the insular supremacy [of Britain]."[82]

But List's strategical thinking never had parochial, or even continental, limits. Gazing far into the future, he saw the day when the Stars and Stripes, not the Union Jack, would wave over the seas, and when effective measures would have to be taken by the other nations of the earth to curb the power of the United States.

> The same causes which have raised Great Britain to her present exalted position, will (probably in the course of the next century) raise the United States of America to a degree of industry, wealth, and power, which will surpass the position in which England stands, as far as at present England excels little Holland. In the natural course of things the United States will increase their population within that period to hundreds of millions of souls; they will diffuse their population, their institutions, their civilisation, and their spirit over the whole of Central and South America, just as they have recently diffused them over the neighboring Mexican province. The Federal Union will comprise all these immense territories, a population of several hundred millions of people will develop the resources of a continent which infinitely exceeds the continent of Europe in extent and in natural wealth. The naval power of the western world will surpass that of Great Britain, as greatly as its coasts and rivers exceed those of Britain in extent and magnitude.
>
> Thus in a not very distant future the natural necessity which now imposes on the French and Germans the necessity of establishing a Continental alliance against the British supremacy, will impose on the British the necessity of establishing a European coalition against

---

[81] List, *The National System*, 332, 337.
[82] Ibid., 338.

the supremacy of America. Then will Great Britain be compelled to seek and to find in the leadership of the united powers of Europe protection, security, and compensation against the predominance of America, and an equivalent for her lost supremacy.

It is therefore good for England that she should practise resignation betimes, that she should by timely renunciations gain the friendship of European Continental powers, that she should accustom herself betimes to the idea of being only the first among equals.[83]

Friedrich List's views on England are an interesting study in psychology, perhaps more especially of German psychology. List enormously admired and envied Britian and British liberal institutions, and few men of any nationality have ever paid Britain more eloquent tributes. On the other hand, he feared and even hated Britain. He himself suffered from a persecution complex—arising out of petty ways in which he was harassed by official Germany—and it was therefore not suprising that he believed that Britain was actively engaged in frustrating the *Zollverein* and other steps toward German unification. Always cantankerous, he became involved in particularly vitriolic controversies with Englishmen—especially, of course, with the long-deceased Adam Smith and his living followers. At the very end of his life, on the other hand, he went to England in the vain hope of paving the way for an Anglo-German alliance. He prepared an elaborate memorandum on the subject which he submitted to Prince Albert, Sir Robert Peel (the prime minister), Lord Clarendon (the foreign secretary), and the King of Prussia. He had encouragement from de Bunsen, the Prussian ambassador in London, and from some British sources. But Peel could not accede to the plan, and List returned to Germany in the autumn broken in health and in spirit—on the verge of the suicide that occurred November 30, 1846.[84]

There are some fantasies in List's memorandum on the value and the conditions of an Anglo-German alliance, but it nevertheless reveals an acute appreciation of some of the strategic realities facing both countries in the middle of the nineteenth century. To begin with, List foresaw what Sir Halford Mackinder was to elucidate more than half a century later, that there was nothing eternal about British maritime supremacy. The development of steam railways and steam navigation, he thought, might give the Continental powers advantages in relation to the British

---

[83] Ibid., 339-40. The same theme is developed at some length in a remarkable document written shortly before List's death in 1846: "Über den Wert und die Bedingungen einer Allianz zwischen Grossbritannien und Deutschland," *Works*, 7:267-98. See also "Die vorige und die gegenwärtige Regierung von Nordamerika," *Staatslexikon* (1841), 219ff.

[84] For the English mission see Hirst, *Life*, 97-106. For the memorandum on the proposed alliance, to be discussed in the next paragraph, see note 83.

Isles that they did not then possess. The rising power of other nations, especially the United States, held the possibility that control of the seas might be threatened; without control of the seas, the unique advantages that Britain enjoyed from its insular position would become serious liabilities. List foresaw also the union of the Latin and Slavic races, through a Franco-Russian alliance, and believed that Britian and Germany should counterbalance any such combination by taking the lead of the Germanic peoples. He was convinced that Franco-Russian power would not only threaten Britain's interests in Europe and the east but would almost certainly crush Germany. Britain could use the help of a Continental land power and Germany would welcome reinforcement from an insular sea power. All that Germany asked of Britain was sympathetic understanding and support for a moderate protective tariff in unified Germany, which seemed to List a small price for Britain to pay for German friendship. Any such concession, List foresaw, would be resisted by the vested interests of British industry but, against these, Britain must set the fact that its position as a world power would be fortified and even extended.

List failed, as so many others have failed, to find a formula that would lead to Anglo-German solidarity because, for better or worse, there has never been any agreement between the two nations on what constitutes a true community of interest and because so many moral and psychological factors have stood in the way of mutual understanding. He failed, also, because he could not undo in a few months the harm that he had done over the years by strident anti-British propaganda.

VII

The greatest single contribution that List made to modern strategy was his elaborate discussion of the influence of railways upon the shifting balance of military power. He first became interested in railways during his residence in America, when he was one of the promoters of the Schuylkill Navigation, Railroad and Coal Company, a forerunner of the present Reading System. Thereafter, railways were one of the passions of his life. His writings on railways fill two complete volumes and almost two pages of the index volume of his collected works. During the years 1835 and 1836 he published *Das Eisenbahn Journal*, a magazine devoted to forwarding railway construction in Germany. To no other single cause did he give more devotion or more energy, for he saw, correctly, that a network of railways, ultimately incorporated in a truly national system, would be one of the forces that would cement German unification.

His interest in the economic effects of railways was to be expected, although he was much more foresighted than most of his contemporaries. But his understanding of the strategic implications to Germany of steam

254

transportation is surprising and by any objective standards quite re-markable. Before the advent of the railway the strategic position of Ger-many was the weakest in Europe, with the result that it was the traditional battleground of the entire Continent. List saw sooner than anyone else that the railway would make the geographical situation of Germany a source of great strength, instead of one of the primary causes of its military weakness. With political unification fortified by a nation-wide link of railway communications, Germany could be made into a defensive bas-tion in the very heart of Europe. Speed of mobilization, the rapidity with which troops could be moved from the center of the country to its pe-riphery, and the other obvious advantages of "interior lines" of rail transport would be of greater relative advantage to Germany than to any other European country. In a word, List wrote, a perfect railway system would transform the whole territory of the nation into one great fortress, which could be readily defended by its entire combatant manpower, with a minimum of expenditure and with the least disorganization of the economic life of the country. And after the conclusion of the war, the return of the troops to their homes could be brought about with equal facility and expedition. For all of these reasons, and others, List foresaw that the network of railway lines that he visualized for Germany in 1833—which is substantially that of the present *Reichsbahnen*—would enable the army of a unified Germany, in the event of invasion, to move troops from any point in the country to the frontiers in such a way as to multiply many fold its defensive potential and thus prevent the re-current invasions that had been going on for over two hundred years. Ten times stronger on the defense, Germany also would be ten times stronger on the attack, should it undertake offensive war—which List thought unlikely.[85]

There was a note of urgency in List's pleas for railway construction in Germany. "Every mile of railway which a neighboring nation finishes sooner than we, each mile more of railway it possesses, gives it an ad-vantage over us," he wrote. Hence "it is just as little left in our hands to determine whether we shall make use of the new defensive weapons given us by the march of progress, as it was left to our forefathers to determine whether they should shoulder the rifle instead of the bow and arrow."[86] When it is considered that all of the foregoing was written before the

[85] For the 1833 plan see Friedrich List, "Über ein sächsisches Eisenbahnsystem als Grund-lage eines allgemeinen deutschen Eisenbahnsystems," in *Works*, vol. 3, pt. 1, pp. 155-95. For the general strategic theory of railways see "Deutschlands Eisenbahnsystem in mili-tärischer Beziehung," in ibid., 260-70, the latter written in 1834-1836.
[86] List, "Deutschlands Eisenbahnsystem," 266-68.

LIST'S PROPOSED RAILWAY AND STEAMSHIP LINES, 1820–1844

American Civil War gave the first definitive proof of the military value of railways, it shows truly remarkable prescience.

List was wrong in thinking that railways would enable European states to reduce the size of their armies; on the contrary, as the Franco-Prussian War subsequently showed, the railway simplified logistical problems and permitted the movement of larger armies, together with their astronomical quantities of munitions and supplies, than anyone had theretofore believed possible. List was also wrong in thinking that the construction of railways might render attack so costly to the attacker that the danger of war would be mitigated. But he was right in asserting that railway trackage and right of way were relatively less vulnerable to military destruction than many other permanent installations—a fact that has most recently been demonstrated in the German bombings of England and in Anglo-American aerial attacks on the Continent.[87]

Even before Germany itself had a railway system, List's dreams went far beyond its borders into the rest of Europe and into Asia. In fact, he seems to have been the originator of the Baghdad Railway idea. In his project for an Anglo-German alliance he proposed that British communications with India and the Far East should be improved by railway lines extending from the English Channel to the Arabian Sea. The Nile and the Red Sea, he wrote, should be brought as close to the British Isles as the Rhine and Elbe were at the time of Napoleon; Bombay and Calcutta should be made as accessible as Lisbon and Cadiz. This could be accomplished by the extension of the projected Belgian-German railway systems to Venice, thence via the Balkans and Anatolia to the Euphrates Valley and the Persian Gulf and, finally, to Bombay. A Syrian spur would link the main line with Cairo and the Sudan. A telegraph line would parallel the railway, so that Downing Street would be in as easy touch with the East Indies as with Jersey and Guernsey. List also visualized a transcontinental line from Moscow to China.[88] None of these projects seemed to him any more ambitious or daring than the plans then being discussed in America for railways from the Atlantic to the Pacific.

To ensure political security for the territories through which the proposed railways would pass, Germany and Great Britain should enter into an effective alliance defining their respective spheres of interest. The expansion of German rule over all of European Turkey would prevent interference by any power hostile to the British Empire—speaking in hyperbole, as he so often did, List said that "seventy or eighty millions"

[87] In addition to the foregoing see Friedrich List, "Über ein allgemeines Eisenbahnsystem in Frankreich," in *Works*, vol. 3, pt. 2, pp. 564-73.
[88] See map, which is from Friedrich Lenz, *Friedrich List: Der Mann und das Werk* (Munich and Berlin, 1936).

257

of Germans would constitute the guarantee that the situation required. Great Britain, on the other hand, should control all of Asia Minor, Egypt, Central Asia, and India—a vast territory that would more than compensate for the threat of a nascent American world power.[89]

List's proposal concerning German control of European Turkey was, of course, closely connected with his desire to see large-scale emigration to the Danubian region and the Balkans. Indeed, all of his plans for railway construction were in some way linked with his passion for a unified and greater Germany. "A German railway system and the *Zollverein*," he wrote, "are Siamese twins. Born at the same time, physically knit together, of one spirit and one soul, they support each other and strive for the same great aim: the unification of the German tribes into one great, cultivated, wealthy, powerful, and inviolable German nation. Without the *Zollverein* no German railway system would ever have been even discussed, let alone constructed. Only with the aid of a German railway system is it possible for the social economy of the Germans to rise to national greatness, and only through such national greatness can a system of railways realize its full poentialities."[90]

VIII

When List died in 1846, few of the causes to which he devoted his life were within reasonable hope of success. In 1846 Britain repealed the Corn Laws and the United States adopted the Walker Tariff, which seriously compromised the principles of autarky and protectionism and were, indeed, a step in the direction of free trade. Industrialization had proceeded but slowly in Germany and a German railway system existed only in blueprints. Conservatism and separatism continued to rule east of the Rhine, with the result that German national unification was not quite within reach. To be sure, List carried with him into another world the comfort of the *Zollverein*, a solid achievement for which he could justly claim a large share of credit. But it remained for historians to appreciate fully the importance of the *Zollverein* in the creation of the later German Empire.

Nevertheless, List's soul went marching on. Two years after his tragic death revolutionary movements swept Germany, giving birth to the hope

[89] For discussion of the railway to India see List, "Über . . . einer Allianz zwischen Grossbrittannien und Deutschland" cited in footnote 83. For details concerning the route of the Constantinople-Baghdad-Basra-Bombay line see *Works*. vol. 3, pt. 2, p. 679. The population of the German Empire did not approach seventy million until the eve of the First World War.

[90] Friedrich List, "Das deutsche Eisenbahnsystem," in *Works*, vol. 3, pt. 1, p. 347. Concerning railway expansion in the Danubian area: "Die Transportverbesserung in Ungarn," in ibid., pp. 434-60.

that the German people would become a national state under liberal auspices—an event that List would have welcomed with all his heart, for he was an ardent believer in liberal, middle-class, constitutional government with adequate guarantees of individual liberty. But the liberal revolutions of 1848 failed and gave way to the policy of blood and iron. "German nationalists of conservative and traditionalist stamp could and did accept the economic teachings of List, while rejecting his political counsels [of liberalism and individual rights]; and an increasing number of German industrialists, regardless of nationalist or political bias, foresaw delightful solace for the woes of British competition in List's national programme. Even liberal nationalists of an ensuing generation, growing more in the grace of nationalism than in that of liberalism, came gradually to agree with List's contentions. By 1880 the German national state, under Bismarck's nominal guidance, was actually treading the economic path which had been blazed by Friedrich List."[91]

In fact, Bismarck and his successors went even farther than List would have gone in the direction of economic nationalism and autarky. List had always opposed import duties upon foodstuffs. But the German tariff system as it developed under the empire was an all-inclusive plan giving protection both to the Junkers and to the industrialists, who were thus drawn together in support of economic nationalism, militarism, navalism, and colonialism. Whatever List might have thought of tariffs on grain, he could hardly have objected to the spirit and purposes of chancellor Caprivi's statement to the Reichstag, December 10, 1891: "The existence of the State is at stake when it is not in a position to depend upon its own sources of supply. It is my conviction that we cannot afford to dispense with such a production of corn as would be sufficient in an emergency to feed our increasing population . . . in the event of war. . . . I regard it as the better policy that Germany should rely upon its own agriculture than that it should trust to the uncertain calculation of help from a third party in the event of war. *It is my unshakable conviction that in a future war the feeding of the army and the country may play an absolutely decisive part.*"[92]

Much of the economic policy of the Second Reich was based upon the assumption that sooner or later Germany would be involved in a war to defend the realm and to win a recognized place in the sun. In preparation for such an eventuality German statesmen believed that they should depend upon Germany's inherent strength rather than upon the

---

[91] C. J. H. Hayes, *The Historical Evolution of Modern Nationalism* (New York, 1931), 272-73.

[92] Quoted by W. H. Dawson, *The Evolution of Modern Germany* (New York, 1908), 248. Emphasis added.

good will of neighbors or the uncertainty of overseas communications. The Kaiser's statesmen may have been guilty of some distortion of List's ideas, but had List lived he would have understood full well the language that they spoke. And he also would have understood the autarkical motivation of the *Wehrwirtschaft* of the Nazis, however much he would have disapproved of Hitler's racial ideas and Himmler's disregard of individual rights.

List also, unhappily, laid the foundation for certain other basic concepts of Pan-Germanism and National Socialism, such as *Lebensraum*, the *Drang nach Osten*, naval and colonial expansion, the impermanency of frontiers, the permanent allegiance of the *Auslanddeutsche* to the fatherland, and the desirability of a Continental bloc against Anglo-American power.

List, like Hamilton, was a leading figure in the revival of mercantilism in the modern world. Whatever may have been the virtues of mercantilism in the seventeenth and eighteenth centuries, its modern counterpart has been an incendiary force in a highly inflammable and explosive world. The new mercantilism is the more dangerous because it operates in our highly organized and closely integrated society. It is warp and woof with the war system. To a degree that would have shamed the mercantilists of old, it has enlisted the power of the state for the further enhancement of state power. All of the old, familiar devices have been reinforced by a host of new ones in the form of quotas, boycotts, exchange controls, rationing, stockpiles, and subsidies. Out of the economic nationalism of the fifty years beginning in 1870 have come totalitarian economics, the totalitarian state, and totalitarian war, which are so inextricably interconnected that it has become impossible to tell which is cause and which is effect. In the name of national security, political authority has been extended into almost every domain of human activity.[93]

As an almost inescapable consequence of all this came the explosions of 1914 and 1939. One can understand them only with reference to the power concepts of nineteenth-century Europe. The thinking of Adam Smith, Alexander Hamilton, and Friedrich List was conditioned by the fact that they were, respectively, British, American, and German. But in certain fundamentals of statecraft their views were suprisingly alike. They all understood that military power is built upon economic foundations and each of them advocated a national system of economics that would

[93] For further development of these ideas see E. M. Earle, "The New Mercantilism," *Political Science Quarterly* 40 (1925), 594-600. Also, with particular reference to totalitarian economics, A. T. Lauterbach, *Economics in Uniform: Military Economy and Social Structure* (Princeton, 1943), especially chap. 1-4.

best meet the needs of his own country. That the world has come to grief as a result of neomercantilism is not necessarily their fault. For so long as nations continue to place their faith in unbridled nationalism and unrestricted sovereignty they will continue to rely upon whatever measures will, in their judgment, best guarantee independence and security.

9. Engels and Marx on Revolution, War, and the Army in Society

SIGMUND NEUMANN AND MARK VON HAGEN

T HE PHILOSOPHERS have only *interpreted* the world in various ways; the point, however, is to *change* it." This credo of Karl Marx in his *Theses on Feuerbach*, at the beginning of his literary career, provides a key to an understanding of the dynamics of Marxian theory. It is primarily directed toward action; theoretical analysis becomes nothing but spadework and preparation for the final revolutionary assault. To make the proletarian revolution a reality, Marx and Engels gave unremitting attention to tactical problems and military considerations in their writings.

This crucial side of their studies was long neglected in the literature on Marxism. The omission derived partly from the fact that the immense amount of material bearing upon military problems is scattered throughout their writings and is not easily available in one monumental work as is the case with *Capital*, the basic study of Marxian economic theory. Of special importance for a comprehensive analysis of Marx and Engels as military thinkers, apart from their pertinent historical sketches, are the Marx-Engels correspondence and their extensive journalistic writings.

Basic misconceptions regarding the teachings of Marx and Engels are also in part responsible for the lack of attention to their military concerns. Concepts of military strategy and tactics may seem alien to the spirit of these radical thinkers, whose declared policy was one of enmity toward the military machine, the military caste, and the military state; whose anticipated socialist order merged with the pacifist millennium; and whose position as "outsiders of the state" would hardly suggest a realistic consideration of military power and the planning of specific campaigns. Moreover, in Engels's later writings, he expressed increasing revulsion at the prospect of a future world war, which threatened to destroy all the advances made not only by the working class and by socialist movements, but by Western civilization itself. He saw greater possibilities ahead for the triumph of socialism through the ballot, rather

NOTE: Mark von Hagen has substantially revised the essay by Sigmund Neumann that appeared in the original *Makers of Modern Strategy*.

than through violent upheavals. And yet it would be utterly misleading to view the protagonists of the international class struggle as pacifists.

Marxism superseded the earlier utopianism of the 1820s and 1830s not only in a new "scientific" approach to social development, but also in a more realistic evaluation of political forces. The new analysis was meant to be eminently practical, an "applied science." Strategic considerations were the core of their political theory. Although succeeding generations were above all impressed by the theoretical edifice that Karl Marx and Friedrich Engels left behind, specific historical problems and their analysis seem to have been of equal interest to them. And it is in their more concrete analyses that the two worked out their understanding of war and the problems of military organization.

The writings of Marx and Engels gained in significance and perspective as the patterns and problems of twentieth-century warfare became clear and fully developed. Marx and Engels can rightly be classed among the ancestors of modern total war. The proud discovery of National-Socialist ideologues, that modern warfare is of a fourfold nature—diplomatic, economic, psychological, and only as a last resort military—was common knowledge to Engels and Marx. They were fully aware the campaigns could be lost long before the first shot was fired, that they would in fact be decided beforehand on the battlefronts of economic and psychological warfare. During the "promising" crisis of 1857, Engels wrote to Marx: "A continuing economic depression could be used by astute revolutionary strategy as a useful weapon for a chronic pressure . . . in order to warm up the people . . . just as a cavalry attack has greater *élan* if the horses trot five hundred paces before coming within charging distance of the enemy." To Marx and Engels war was fought with different means in different fields. In the words of the militant syndicalist Georges Sorel, a general strike could become a "Napoleonic battle," just as the Crimean War could be regarded as a prelude to great international civil strife. Marx's and Engels's dialectical approach to historical phenomena is nothing but this all-inclusive and dynamic view of the sociopolitical forces at work in the modern world. This perspective gave them an insight far superior to that of their forerunners into military affairs as they affected the character of modern revolutions.

Even more significant for the development of revolutionary politics was the turning of the fathers of socialism toward the study of international affairs in general. They soon began to realize that the German revolution of 1848 had failed to a large extent because of its international implications. In fact, from the early days of the *Neue Rheinische Zeitung*, to which Marx was called as editor "to produce the most radical, the most spirited, and the most individual journalistic enterprise of the first

German revolution," the two friends had realized how closely foreign policy, war, and internal affairs were connected. They also saw that the future of the European revolution would not be determined by the efforts of one country alone. This realization directed their attention to a serious consideration of the relationships between socialism, military policy, and foreign affairs, because without an understanding of these relationships a realistic revolutionary strategy could not be possible. It is a major contribution of Marx and Engels, often overlooked by their interpreters, that they raised the question of social change in their time beyond the insurrectionary stage of the isolated *Putsch* to the plane of world politics. War and revolution—unmistakably established as twin movements in our time—were at that early period seen in their fundamental and continuous interrelationship by these still obscure theorists of world revolution.

I

If one recognizes the essentially militant and activist nature of modern socialism, the roles of its leaders somewhat change in significance, and Friedrich Engels gains in stature as compared with his friend and partner, Karl Marx. Not only did Engels actually write a good part of the historical studies once attributed to Marx, but the "Carnot of the future revolution" also had a much clearer understanding of the impact of military developments on history. Engels foresaw important future trends, not only in peacetime but in war as well, and in this way contributed, if only indirectly, to concepts and techniques of military strategy in decades to come.

In many respects the very opposite in character and temperament, Marx and Engels exemplify a friendship of almost classic nature. For a span of nearly forty years, the literary work of one complemented that of the other. Theirs was a natural division of labor. Marx, revealing in his profound and searching work the stern intellectual tradition of his forebears, was clearly the more systematic thinker. Without him, Engels's writings would have lacked direction and power of synthesis. Marx was probably also the better political strategist, with a certain gift for sizing up a situation, especially in revolutionary moments—a quality that often kept his lifelong collaborator from hasty conclusions. Nevertheless the somber Marx, who "struggled with the spirit of his time as Jacob wrestled with the angel and whose work came slowly to fruition," admired Engels's power. "He can work at any hour of the day, fed or fasting; he writes and composes with incomparable fluency."

Although the genuinely modest Engels readily consented to play second fiddle, his contribution was no less significant to their work as a whole. With his early studies in England, and especially his groundbreaking book *The Condition of the Working Class in England*, he had helped to lay the foundations of socialist theory. All his life he brought together valuable material, selecting and combining it with a sure hand and a wealth of common sense. He had a feeling for what was in the air and for what promised results. His was a practical mind. Son of a Rhenish industrialist, and for a good part of his life an entrepreneur in his own right (though against his own inclination) in the teeming city of Manchester, he knew firsthand the nature of the rising factory system, but was above all a man of action.

Engels said of his own style that, as with artillery, "each article struck and burst like a shell." His militant vocabulary was no mere play on words. Even in his most abstract writings, Engels made ample use of military terms and experiences, because he regarded himself as by nature a soldier and warrior. Proud of his early service in the Prussian army, and especially of his active role in the Baden insurrection of 1849, he turned his attention to the study of military science during his many years of exile in England, in order to prepare himself for the coming revolution.

Engels's writings in the field of military affairs are more extensive than the rest of his literary work. He wrote careful treatises on campaigns, detailed studies on weapons and tactics, thumbnail biographical sketches of military leaders, and authoritative and often cutting reviews of books on war and military institutions. Throughout his work he shows a striking familiarity with the actions and writings of the great commanders in history. At the same time his independent and original judgment is surprising. In his analyses of specific campaigns or technical developments he was often more farseeing than recognized military experts, and his newspaper and periodical articles on military topics are still of value. Even his contemporary adversaries among military critics respected his judgments. His articles on the Crimean War in the *New York Tribune* were attributed to General Winfield Scott, who, at the time, was running for the American Presidency. His pamphlet *Po and Rhine* was long considered to be the work of the Prussian General von Pfuel.

One may say of his military writings what a commentator once said about Clausewitz: "He is a genius in criticism. His judgments are as clear and weighty as gold. He shows how greatness in strategic thought consists in simplicity." Clausewitz, in fact, greatly impressed Engels, who wrote Marx in September 1857: "Among other things I am now reading Clausewitz' *On War*. A strange way of philosophizing but very good on his subject. To the question whether war should be called an art or a science, the answer given is that war is most like trade. Fighting is to war what cash payment is to trade, for however rarely it may be necessary for it actually to occur, everything is directed towards it, and eventually it must take place all the same and must be decisive."

Clausewitz's emphasis on decisive action and on the tactical offensive even in the strategic defensive became the stock-in-trade of revolutionary strategy. Militancy and preparedness for offensive action remained axiomatic for Engels and, under his influence, also for Marx. Beyond these fundamental concepts, however, their military thought clearly changed— a development that led them to an increasingly more realistic, more circumspect, but also more dynamic interpretation of the military and political events of their time.

II

The revolutions of 1848, as is so often the case with lost causes in history, have been misjudged and underestimated in their spirit and performance. The radicalism of 1848 was eminently militant. It was an echo, often self-consciously so, of the great tradition of 1793. On the Continent, to be sure, the movements of 1848 ended in defeat. After a successful beginning hopeless disagreements soon split the revolutionary forces, and the politically immature middle classes succumbed to an experienced ruling caste. The revolutionary momentum faded away without visible result. And yet this civil war in Europe was a military event of great import. It was fought on the barricades, and in Germany and Austria also on the battlefield. The rebels were often led by trained officers who had gone over to the revolutionaries, for the Prussian and Austrian armies were not free from what in the twentieth century would have been called "Bolshevik" influences.

Among these military pioneers of the revolution were colorful soldiers like the adventurer Otto von Corvin. George Weydemeyer, one of the first followers of Marx and Engels, had been a Prussian artillery officer and, after his emigration to the United States, distinguished himself as a colonel in the Union army during the Civil War. Friedrich Wilhelm Rüstow, a Prussian officer turned revolutionary, won an international reputation as a military historian, critic, and teacher, and as chief of staff to Garibaldi in the conquest of Sicily and the march on Naples. In fact, official military circles, the contemporary military literature shows, looked upon the fighters of the barricades, however small their number, as a significant and dangerous power, as puzzling to the military professional as were the Riffs to the colonial armies of twentieth-century Europe. Cavaignac, who first succeeded at Paris, in June 1848, in breaking the myth of the barricades, was celebrated as a military genius. Over 53,000 Prussian troops were thought necessary to defeat the Baden insurrectionists in a field campaign.

266

The revolutions of 1848, in spite or because of their failure, became the starting point of scientific socialism. The inquiry into their meaning—their historical background and military strategy—was the central theme of the writings of Marx and Engels during the first years of their exile. The lessons of defeat revealed the laws of a future strategy of insurrection. These laws were first elaborated in the brilliant analyses of the revolutions of 1848-1849 in central Europe, written by Engels and edited by Marx, under whose name a series of articles on the subject was published in the *New York Tribune* in 1851-1852. "Insurrection is an art as much as war . . . and subject to certain rules of procedure. . . . Firstly, never play with insurrection unless you are fully prepared to face the consequences of your play. . . . Secondly, the insurrectionary career once entered upon, act with the greatest determination and on the offensive. The defensive is the death of every armed rising. . . . Surprise your antagonist. . . . Keep up the moral ascendancy which the first successful rising has given you. . . . In the words of Danton, the greatest master of revolutionary policy yet known, 'De l'audace, de l'audace, encore de l'audace!' "

Once the revolutionary situation had passed, Marx and Engels vigorously pointed out, any attempt at playing at revolution was futile and dangerous. They opposed Schapper and Wilrich, who in the early 1850s were agitating for renewed violence, and cautioned the workers against attempting a *Putsch*, which would only benefit reactionary interests. Until conditions became favorable, they insisted on a strategy of preparation for the eventual struggle. However impatiently Engels awaited the time when he could saddle up again for "that great duel to the death between bourgeoisie and proletariat," he knew too well that the greatest danger for such an enterprise lay in the rash desire for action. Patience and timing became the main requisites of sound strategy.

The implications of Marx's and Engels's concepts of revolutionary tactics can be better understood against the background of their philosophic system, based upon the materialistic interpretation of history, and its emphasis on the prevailing economic conditions as a key to an understanding of sociopolitical dynamics. In the *Communist Manifesto* this theory had been applied in rough outline to all of modern history. It was also drawn on in their numerous essays dealing with contemporary affairs. According to the theory, the rise and fall of the popular movements of 1848 were in the last analysis determined and conditioned by economic causes. As Engels wrote in his introduction to a reprint in 1895 of Marx's *The Class Struggles in France 1848-50*: "The world commercial crisis of 1847 was the real cause of the February and March revolutions, and the industrial prosperity which arrived gradually in the middle of 1848, coming to full bloom in 1849 and 1850, was the vitalizing fact of the renascent European reaction. This was decisive." By the same token, he stated, "A new revolution is possible only as a consequence of a new crisis, and it is also as certain as the latter."

The approach of a new economic crisis was for Marx and Engels the clarion call of the revolution. Thus the depression of 1857 raised their hopes that the European reaction would give way to a new revolutionary situation. Engels was delighted by the thought that he might soon be able to leave business for the battlefield and his office stool for a horse. "Now our time is coming—this time it is coming in full measure: a life-and-death struggle. My military studies will at once become more practical. I am throwing myself immediately into the tactics and organization of the Prussian, Austrian, Bavarian and French armies. And apart from that I do nothing but ride, that is hunt; for hunting is a real cavalry school." But the "chronic crisis" led to neither revolution nor war.

Sometimes with difficulty, Marx and Engels guarded themselves against the characteristic pitfalls of an émigré existence, and instead turned their exile into a challenging and productive experience. The first decade of their London exile became a period of *weltpolitische Lehrjahre* as they entered the larger world of nineteenth-century middle-class society and culture. Separated now from the local, particularistic, and limited world of politically fragmented Germany and from French party politics, the two could gaze upon a broader vista. "Nothing but an objective account of the totality of all mutual relationships of all the classes of a given society ... can serve as the basis for the correct tactics of the advanced class."

Such an "objective account" of social forces Marx offers in his masterful study *The Eighteenth Brumaire*. The tactical lesson of this great defeat of the second French Revolution at the hands of "Napoleon the Little" is seen by him in the need for developing the "democratic energy" of the peasantry. "The whole thing in Germany will depend on the possibility of backing the proletarian revolution by some second edition of the Peasant War," Marx stated in a letter to Engels. Engels came to the same conclusion in his study of the *German Peasant War*. From now on the peasantry as a possible ally or driving force in the coming social revolution played a major part in their considerations. Especially the prospects for revolution in Russia were almost exclusively measured in terms of the fate of the peasantry. They hailed the emancipation of the serfs as a turning point in political history that would contribute to a new lineup of revolutionary forces. "At the next revolution," Marx wrote, as commander in chief of the world revolution, issuing Napoleonic commands from his wretched home in London, "Russia will kindly join the rebels." Henceforth a Russian revolution became a permanent factor in their political speculations.

The most profound conclusions Marx and Engels were to draw from their studies of the revolutions of 1848 were grounded in another fundamental Marxian hypothesis—that world history is the history of class struggle. Every society exists in a state of only relative civil peace. The mask of civil peace conceals both a constant class struggle and the fact that the ruling class maintains its temporary monopoly on power by means of physical, economic, and ideological coercion of the oppressed classes. During any crisis this tenuous and seeming social cohesion could rapidly deteriorate into a state of civil war, as the oppressed classes rise up against their oppressors. Thus the boundaries separating civil peace from civil war are illusory.

From this perspective, the class struggles in any society can be projected onto the international arena when ruling classes declare war on one another. War is in the interests of those ruling classes until it places too much strain on the fragile social fabric that supports it. At this point war could be a catalyst for revolution. Engels, in his first writings in the revolutionary years, looked to the model of France in 1793. Not only would war feed the revolution, but the revolution would also force the rest of Europe into war. Engels hoped that the revolution would provide the moral as well as physical force necessary to carry the embattled people through to victory. Though the 1848-1849 revolutions proved the failure of the legend of 1793, the lesson that war and peace, civil war and social peace, existed along a gradual continuum remained a central tenet in Marxian analysis.

III

It is in the years of their exile that the expatriates also discover their own national ties. Engels, no doubt, is more outspoken in his expression of deeper loyalties and of sincere patriotism; but even Marx, often unconsciously, reveals definite national biases in his attacks on his political adversaries. What is more significant, the socialist leaders now begin to take full stock of national individuality and its growing importance in international affairs. They carefully note the awakening nationalism in central and eastern Europe and, in fact, expect from these independence movements a renewal of revolutionary impulses that would destroy the political apathy which had followed the collapse of the revolutions of 1848. Typical of such hopes were Engels's great expectations for the Hungarian revolution under the leadership of Louis Kossuth, whom at that time, in contrast to his later opinion, he regarded as "a combination of Danton and Carnot." It has been suggested that the daily reports of

269

the military campaign in Hungary that Engels wrote for the *Neue Rhein-ische Zeitung* awakened in him his lifelong interest in the tasks of the general staff officer.

Internationalists as they claimed to be, Marx and Engels began to think in terms of international power politics long before the spokesmen of the middle-class parties emancipated themselves from their purely national outlook. Every political action in whatever country it might occur was viewed in terms of the larger European issues. This interna-tional orientation, to be sure, was at first dogmatic and only a rough approach to reality. Political divisions were simply drawn according to the formula of the two Europes: reaction versus revolution, czarism versus the progressive West. For a long time France continued to be regarded as the revolutionary homeland. An alliance of the Western powers to fight Russia, a war between Jacobin France and the Holy Alliance—that was the international policy which Marx and Engels had strongly rec-ommended in 1848. When the expected clash between East and West finally came in the Crimea, it was, however, a conflict between the czar and the usurper Napoleon, with Britain supporting France. Still, they were hopeful that in time the war would release the forces of revolution.

The Crimean War provided the first occasion for Engels to analyze in detail the military problems of the time. He even tried to become a professional military analyst, but failed to find a desired position with the London *Daily News*. The only outlet for Engels's extraordinary knowledge became the articles that regularly appeared under Karl Marx's name in the *New York Tribune*. They showed a mastery of technical material and keen strategic judgment, and were well received by their American readers.

At the beginning of the war, Engels expressed great hopes for quick and energetic action on the part of the Allied forces in the Black Sea and, in combination with Sweden and Denmark, in the Baltic, which would lead to the destruction of Russia's navy and the capture of its coastal fortifications. "The giant without eyes" would thus be forced to his knees by a great pincer movement, and an impending internal revolution would soon bring down the Romanov dynasty. But the undecided attitude of Prussia and Austria created difficulties for the Allies. Eventually, Austria's mobilization neutralized a substantial part of the Russian army, but the hope for active Hapsburg participation delayed any major Allied action for five months. Engels regarded such a delay as a tactical blunder but, with Marx, also suspected Palmerston to be a secret ally of "his friend Czar Nicholas," following in this respect the lead of the much-talked-about Scottish monomaniac David Urquhart.

A careful analysis of the organization and tactical characteristics of

270

the opposing armies, however, left Engels in no doubt about the superiority of the Allied powers. By the time the battle of Inkerman was fought, the supremacy of their artillery and cavalry had been proved. The Russian infantry, effective though it had been against Turks and Polish insurgents, showed its inability to cope with modern military techniques and the tactics of small detachments. Many years later, Engels characterized the Crimean War to the Russian economist Danielson as "a hopeless struggle between a nation with primitive techniques of production and others which were up-to-date." Confidence to an Allied victory did not, however, prevent Engels from sharply criticizing the organization of the English army, and especially the scandalous lack of food, clothing, and medical care, which had also aroused the anger of the British public.

An important feature of the Crimean War was the role played by fortifications and siege warfare. To a superficial observer this fact might have indicated a change in the art of war, "slipping back" from the age of Napoleon to the seventeenth century. "Nothing could be less true," Engels concluded after the fall of Sebastopol. "Today fortifications have no other importance than to be concentrated points in support of the movements of a field army. Their value is relative. They are no longer independent factors in military campaigns, but valuable positions which it might or might not be wise to defend to the last." For this reason, he concluded, the Russians had been equally right in avoiding an open battle and in considering the safety of their army more important than the abstract value of a fortress. On the eve of the Crimean War, Engels had not only read the writings of the major military theorists since Napoleon, but had also closely studied Napoleon's campaign in Russia. He could predict how difficult it might be for the Allied forces after conquering Crimea to come to grips with Russia. The problems of logistics in this vast country seemed insurmountable, and the Allied desire for an early end of the war was understandable.

To such an impasse Engels's answer, however, was an appeal to revolutionary strategy. "A war of principle" seemed to him the solution for both the Allies and Russia, appealing on one hand to the revolutionary forces of rising nationalism in Germany, Poland, Finland, Hungary, and Italy; and on the other, to Pan-Slavism. These possibilities of ideological warfare were certainly considered by some of the protagonists in the Crimean War. Napoleon III himself later confessed to Queen Victoria that a continuation of the war would have forced him to call to arms the peoples striving for independence. Much as Engels would have welcomed such a turn, however, neither Nicholas nor Napoleon was prepared to unloose the frightening potential of nationalist movements that became decisive in twentieth-century conflicts. The end of the Crimean War in 1856 shattered Engels's hopes for greater revolutionary upheavals. It also hardened the opinions of both Marx and Engels in respect to the danger of Bonapartism. Bonapartism and Pan-Slavism now became major themes in their analyses of European affairs.

Their fear of the rising expansion and national ambitions of Russia was, of course, inextricably mixed with undiminished hatred for its reactionary absolutism, whose military intervention had helped destroy the revolutions of 1848. The bitter and intensely personal nature of the controversy between Marx and Karl Vogt, a quarrel that occupied Marx's energies for eighteen months, also showed to what extent thoughts of Germany's security were at the base of Marx's and Engels's fight against this "Pan-Slavist." Vogt had been a leader of the left wing in the Frankfurt Assembly, who, after its dissolution, emigrated to Switzerland. The immediate cause of the controversy was an article Vogt wrote in his émigré newspaper during the Franco-Austrian War of 1859. He argued that Austria's defeat would benefit Germany; therefore, German diplomatic efforts should support Bonaparte. Marx publicized a rumor that Bonaparte was subsidizing Vogt's newspaper and that Vogt himself had entered into secret negotiations with Prince Jerome Bonaparte to advance the French plan to place the Russian czar's brother on the throne of Hungary. Marx charged that Vogt would not care if "Bohemia, right in the heart of Germany, should become a Russian province." Engels too joined in the fray. A German renunciation of Bohemia, he contended, would mean the end of German national existence, for the direct way from Berlin to Vienna would thus run through Russia. Strategic, cultural, and economic considerations now convinced Engels that all those territories in eastern and southeastern Europe that in the past had been won by Germany should remain German. He vigorously opposed the dissolution of the great cultural nations and the creation of splinter states incapable of an independent national existence—and all that in the name of national self-determination.

Bonapartism posed different analytical problems to Engels. Its real strength and danger, he rightly recognized, were its demagogic appeal to the latent economic expansionism of a dissatisfied middle class and to the "patriotism" of the revolutionary masses. Engels carefully scrutinized the military implications of Napoleon's ambitions in two authoritative pamphlets *Po and Rhine* and *Savoy, Nice and the Rhine*. In the first essay, he attacked the popular thesis of his day, as it prevailed among military experts like General von Willisen in his *Italian Campaign of the Year 1848*, that the Rhine should be defended on the Po, which thus was regarded as an integral part of Germany. In an analysis of the courses of the upper Italian rivers and of the strategic position of the Italian fortifications Engels proved that control of the Po Valley was not required for the defense of Germany's southern frontier. Moreover, he suggested that, hidden behind so-called military arguments, the real motivations for such strategies were political ambitions for a renewal of the Holy Roman Empire and a German claim to become the arbiter of Europe. He specifically warned against an annexationist policy of a greater Germany, whose "liberation" of weak neighbors would make it the most hated nation in Europe.

Even more interesting was Engels's discussion of the possible strategy of a western campaign. Here he tried to prove that France, having fortified Paris, could now abandon its traditional claim to the left bank of the Rhine. Again, as in the case of German-Austrian claims in northern Italy, Engels disproved, exclusively in terms of military evidence, the validity of the French plea for "a natural frontier." The strategy of French campaigns was directed primarily toward the defense of Paris, and justifiably so because the centralization of France made Paris the key to the country's survival. The surrender of the capital would mean national defeat. With the recent fortification of Paris, however, Vauban's threefold ring of fortifications was superfluous and meant only a useless diversion of military forces. The real danger to French security Engels considered to be its weak Belgian frontier, because in spite of European treaties, "history has yet to show that in case of war Belgium's neutrality is more than a scrap of paper." On the basis of such a realistic evaluation Engels elaborated his plan for a successful military campaign. With Paris fortified, France could defend itself offensively on the Belgian frontier. "If this offensive is repulsed the army must make a final stand on the Oise-Aisne line; it would be useless for the enemy to advance farther, since the army invading from Belgium would be too weak to act against Paris alone. Behind the Aisne, in unchallengeable communication with Paris—or at the worst behind the Marne with its left wing on Paris—the French northern army could take the offensive and wait for the arrival of the other forces." Fifty-five years later Galliéni's counterattack fulfilled Engels's prophetic prediction of the miracle of the Marne.

During the Franco-Prussian War, Engels once again demonstrated his analytic mastery of strategic developments. In a series of articles written for the London *Pall Mall Gazette* he suggested the sudden shift of the Prussian army marching on Châlons toward the Belgian frontier, and thus was among the few European observers to predict the moves that led to Moltke's decisive victory at Sedan.

Savoy, Nice and the Rhine pointed to another element of military strategy, the full meaning of which was not realized until the First World

War: the specter of a two-front war resulting from a Franco-Russian alliance. "Has the Rhineland no other calling," Engels exclaimed, "but to be cursed by a war in order to give Russia a free hand on the Vistula and the Danube?" Russia remained the main threat to European liberty, though Engels now harbored the vain hope that this danger would soon be checked by a new ally of the revolution, the liberated serfs. "The struggle that has now broken out in Russia between the ruling classes of the rural population and the ruled is already undermining the whole system of Russian foreign policy. The system was possible only so long as Russia had no internal political development; but that time is past."

The plans of Napoleon III, on the contrary, were not so easy to dismiss. Engels explored in some detail the prospect of a French invasion of England and the defense of the British Isles. In this connection he published in two journals specializing in military affairs (the *Darmstädter Allgemeine Zeitung* and the *Volunteer Journal of Lancashire and Cheshire*) a number of articles dealing especially with the volunteer riflemen. Some of these articles were brought out in 1861 in pamphlet form: *Essays Addressed to Volunteers*. Despite his sympathy for the riflemen and their less rigid system of drill, Engels concluded that they were no match for the newly enlarged French army, which he called the "best military organization in Europe."

The great military event of the following years was the American Civil War. Contrary to most European soldiers, who at the time showed little interest in this long, bitter struggle—Moltke is said to have stated that he did not care to study the "movements of armed mobs"—Engels regarded it as a "drama without parallel in the annals of military history." It was a revolutionary war not only in its first strategic use of railways and armored ships over a vast area of operations, but also in its "world-transforming abolition of slavery." In the preface of the first edition of *Capital* Marx wrote: "As in the eighteenth century the American War of Independence sounded the tocsin for the European middle class, so in the nineteenth century the American Civil War sounded it for the European working class."

Although Engels's sympathies were on the side of the North, he was appalled by its "slack management" as contrasted with the deadly earnestness of the South. In a letter to Marx of November 5, 1862, he said that he could not "work up any enthusiasm for a people which on such a colossal issue allows itself to be continuously beaten by a fourth of its own population." He was even doubtful about the outcome of the war. It was Marx who warned him not to be misled by a one-sided attention to military aspects. Only when Lee, whose superior strategy he had admired, was surrounded and Grant, like Napoleon, delivered his battle of

"Jena" by capturing the whole of the enemy's army, did Engels recognize the remarkable discipline and morale of the northerners, who had entered the war "sleepily and reluctantly."

The rise of Prussia under Bismarck's leadership turned Engels's thoughts once again to European battlegrounds. The short Danish war proved to Engels that, as he had expected, the German infantry was superior to the Danish and that "Prussian firearms, both rifles and artillery, were the best in the world." Still, he underestimated the military striking power of Prussia. Indeed, in an article in the *Manchester Guardian* written on the eve of the battle of Königgrätz, he went so far as to predict Prussia's defeat in the war. He sharply attacked Moltke's plan for the campaign, only to admit the following day that the Prussians, "in spite of their sins against the higher laws of warfare, had not done badly." Engels's grave miscalculation was largely derived from his erroneous appraisal of Prussia's internal situation. The bitter constitutional struggle over the army reforms in the early 1860s had been mistaken by him, as by so many socialists, for a disintegration of the army and a prelude to revolution. "If this chance passes without being used . . . then we can pack up our revolutionary bags and turn to studying pure theory," he confessed. Indeed, another revolutionary situation had passed, and the day after Königgrätz Engels was quick to recognize the fact.

With his unqualified respect for the Prussian army he also accepted the political consequences of its victory. "The simple fact is this," he wrote to Marx, "Prussia has five hundred thousand needle guns and the rest of the world has not five hundred. No army can be equipped with breech loaders in less than two or three, or perhaps five, years. Until then Prussia is on top. Do you suppoose that Bismarck will not use this moment? Of course he will." Engels now recognized in Bismarck the real Bonapartist, more dangerous than Napoleon III, and he regretted that German unification had been "temporarily flooded with Prussianism"; but he equally rejected the unrealistic refusal of socialist leaders like Wilhelm Liebknecht "to look at the facts." Instead, Engels renewed the struggle with Bismarck upon the very basis created by the Prussian successes.

The analytic power of the historical dialectics of Marx and Engels now faced a test. In the hard school of their exile they had learned to see the particular developments of classes and nations in their greater European context and to base their own revolutionary strategies on an "account of the objective state of social development." The outcomes of the European conflicts, the Sepoy rebellion, and the American Civil War did not encourage belief in an early outbreak of the long-awaited revolution. Marx, and more particularly Engels, were coming to the conclusion that limited wars were not the harbingers they had counted on; in fact, the short-term effect of these conflicts could be reactionary, as Marx characterized the Italian War of 1859. As the armies of the major European powers gained in strength and technological capabilities, Engels began to consider the alarming prospect that only a large-scale world war would bring about the desired revolution. But such an Armageddon was not an outcome Engels could welcome.

Even the Franco-Prussian War left the revolutionaries with a dilemma. France and Germany were the two countries with the largest working-class movements in Europe. War now carried with it too many risks for the socialist movement. By 1888 Engels warned that the destruction of a future world war "will eat all Europe more bare than any swarm of locusts" and make the devastation of the Thirty Years' War pale in comparison. War was ruled out as a desired means to the revolutionary end, but now the revolutionary movement was left without a revolutionary strategy.

IV

Faced with these quandaries about the future of the revolutionary movement, Engels turned to other aspects of the relationship between the military and society, among them the role of the military in a revolutionary state. The contours of the future revolutionary state as visualized by Engels remained only fragmentary, to be sure. Moreover, his concepts were given a tepid welcome, and were even opposed by the leadership of the socialist parties. Still, the direction of his many and diverse proposals became clear at this stage, crowning a lifelong study of war and shaping the future development of radicalism in Europe. Engels's military policy now was based on the doctrine of the democratic army, the nation in arms, and the belief in its progressive realization. Indeed, in Engels's pamphlet *The Military Question and the German Working Class* this vision had already appeared. It became his guiding principle during the next thirty years.

The study of the military question in Prussia, published at the height of the constitutional conflict between the Prussian conservatives and the rising liberal bourgeoisie, was above all intended as a primer for the workers' party. Engels's advice to the proletariat, fighting for its own political emancipation, was to support the bourgeoisie against the forces of reaction (now fashioned in the new type of Bonapartist state in which every vestige of political power was withdrawn from both workers and capitalists alike). What gave this essay its special significance was not only its shrewd appraisal of the strength and weaknesses of the middle-class opposition and its command of technical details concerning the history of Prussian army organization since the Napoleonic Wars, but also its realistic support of the army reforms in view of Prussia's increase in population and wealth, and especially in view of its neighbors' military potential. In fact, Engels's attack was directed in large part against the bourgeoisie, which had lost its political advantage and had failed to win over the army during these critical years. This fundamental failure, Engels later claimed, was above all responsible for the stagnation of democratic development in Germany after 1870. The development of the army, in his judgment, was an integral part of social growth.

In earlier studies, such as the articles written for the *New American Cyclopaedia*, Marx and Engels had emphasized the social basis and preconditions for military organization, past and present. Now they realized that the army itself could serve as a social agency of the first order; in fact, it could serve as the major channel through which a democratic society might emerge. The formula was simple and it followed the historical trends introduced by the French Revolution. The emancipation of the bourgeoisie and peasantry had opened the way for the modern mass army. General conscription, if practiced consistently, guaranteed the strongest and most efficient army for defense of the nation against the outside world. By the same token, it necessarily transformed the character of the armed forces, changing them from a force of long-serving professionals or mercenaries into a people's army. Proudly Engels could exclaim in 1891: "Contrary to appearance, compulsory military service surpasses general franchise as a democratic agency. The real strength of German social democracy does not rest in the number of its voters but in its soldiers. One becomes a voter at twenty-five, a soldier at twenty; and it is youth above all from which the party recruits its followers. By 1900, the army, once the most Prussian, the most reactionary element of the country, will be socialist in its majority as inescapably as fate."

Obviously, Engels miscalculated the staying power and inner dynamics of established institutions; no less did he mistake the tempo of great historical transformations. Yet his view was part of his optimistic belief in the final confluence of democracy and the socialist state. Engels's advocacy of the militia army associated him with many nineteenth-century liberals. They as well as Engels proposed the militia as an alternative to standing armies—the professional mercenary armies of eighteenth-century absolutism. Behind Engels's defense of the militia lay his wish to deprofessionalize the army and render it a truly democratic and democratizing institution.

This conviction, however, did not lead Engels to underestimate the military needs of the capitalist state, especially in view of a constantly threatening world war of "unexampled violence and universality." The final decision in such a general European war, he surmised, would rest with England because it could blockade either France or Germany and so starve one or the other into submission. "We cannot demand that the existing military organization [of Germany] should be completely altered while the danger of war exists," he wrote to August Bebel in October 1891. In a series of articles entitled *Can Europe Disarm?* he suggested, as a means of preventing war, the "gradual diminution of the term of military service by international agreement," such service at first to be for two years. Yet consistent with his basic conviction, he stated that "I limit myself to such proposals as any existing government can accept without endangering the security of its country"; and although he regarded the militia system as a final goal, he hastened to caution Marx that "only a communist society could get really near the full *Miliz* and even that approach would only be asymptotic."

Whether the final stage of Engels's thought on war and revolution contradicted the revolutionary appeals of his early days is an open question. Both evolutionary and revolutionary socialists, twin brothers in conflict, can claim him as their master. Fighter and soldier that he was, Engels found it difficult to reconcile himself to slow and tedious reforms. At the same time, he was too astute not to recognize that every conflict was dependent on the weapons available, and that every society and every historical period would demand different methods and strategies. Engels viewed armies as forms of social organization. Armies, just as forms of economic production, were subject to laws of change. And much as Marx related changes in modes of production to transformations in social relations, so Engels investigated the impact of technological change on military organization. Above all in his pamphlet *Anti-Dühring*, Engels applied the principles of materialist history to military questions. Even if Engels's writings had little impact on the development of nineteenth-century military thinking itself, his comprehensive approach to military questions as a subspecies of economic and social investigations has left its mark on subsequent military thought. "It is not the 'free creations of the mind' of generals of genius that have revolutionized war," he wrote in *Anti-Dühring*, "but the inventions of better weapons and changes in the human material, the soldiers; at the very most the part played by generals of genius is limited to adapting methods of fighting to the new weapons and combatants." Changes in society and in military technology altered warfare, and beyond that demanded changes in revolutionary strategy.

Even at the end of his life Engels did not abandon all hopes for a revolution. He paid attention to the necessary changes in revolutionary strategy in the introduction of the newly edited *Class Struggles in France*

278

1848-1850. "The fighting methods of 1848," he stated, "are obsolete today in every respect." Gone was the day of the barricades, of street-corner revolutions. In fact, Engels pointed out, "even during the classic period of street battles, the barricade had a moral rather than a material effect." If the barricade held until it had shaken the self-confidence of the military, the victory was won; if not, it meant defeat. But already by 1849 the chances of success had diminished. "The barricade had lost its charm; the soldier saw behind it no longer the people but rebels . . . the officer in the course of time had become familiar with the tactical forms of street battles. No longer did he march in direct line and without cover upon improvised breastworks, but outflanked them through gardens, courts, and houses." Since then much more had changed, all in favor of the military, while for the insurgents conditions had become worse. Modern armaments, the products of advanced technology and heavy industry, could no longer be improvised. The newly built quarters of the large cities erected since 1848 had been laid out in long, straight, and wide streets as though made to order for the effective use of the new cannon and rifles. But the ruling classes should not expect the revolutionary to build barricades in these new working-class districts. "They might as well ask of their enemies in the next war to face them in the linear formation of Frederick the Second or in the columns of whole divisions à la Wagram and Waterloo. The time is past for revolutions carried through by small minorities at the head of unconscious masses. When it gets to be a matter of the complete transformation of the social organization, the masses themselves must participate, must understand what is at stake; that much the history of the last fifty years has taught us."

Now the legal conquest of the state was the order of the day. There was but one means by which the steady growth of the militant socialist forces could for the moment be stemmed—a collision on a large scale with the military, a bloodletting like that of 1871 in the short-lived Paris Commune. This first attempt at a "Socialist Republic" has often been praised as the great object lesson for the European revolutionaries of the following decades. Marx himself had analyzed it carefully in his *Civil War in France*. Yet these studies of the Commune contributed almost nothing to the development of Engels's thinking about the military aspects of revolutionary strategy. In fact, a renewal of a Paris Commune, though it might be provoked by a threatening *coup d'état* of reactionary forces, did not accord with his theories. In this last stage of his long career, he expected the triumph of socialism to come about through the democratic processes of the franchise, as he visualized the victory of democracy through the channels of universal military service.

"The nation in arms" had become the declared military ideal of

Engels. He regarded as futile the campaign to destroy militarism in nineteenth-century European society. Instead, he advocated eradicating its feudal traditions and awakening its democratic tendencies by means of universal compulsory military service. It is interesting to see how his ideas coincided with those of his enemies, the ministers of war and the general staffs of the European powers, who also put their faith in the nation in arms, but always feared its susceptibility to socialist contamination.

No doubt, Engels would have fully agreed with one of his outstanding disciples, the French socialist Jean Jaurès, who in his *Armée Nouvelle* stated: "Governments will be far less ready to dream of adventurous policies if the mobilization of the army is the mobilization of the nation itself. . . . If a nation that wants peace is assailed by predatory and adventurous governments in quest of some colossal plunder or some startling diversion from their domestic difficulties, then we shall have a truly national war . . . the 'nation in arms' represents the system best calculated to realize national defense in its supreme and fullest form. The nation in arms is necessarily a nation motivated by justice. It will bring to Europe a new era, it will bring hopes of justice and peace."

History was to prove that ideal terribly wrong. But if Engels exaggerated the power of socialist ideology over the European masses, he more accurately understood the dynamic of conscription and mass armies. And far better than his conservative and liberal contemporaries, he recognized the interpenetration of political and military factors and of the civilian and military spheres, a recognition that continues to guide revolutionary thinking and strategy in the last decades of the twentieth century.

280

10. The Prusso-German School: Moltke and the Rise of the General Staff

HAJO HOLBORN

FOR HALF a century after the Peace of Vienna, Prussia abstained from active participation in European wars. When the Prussian army emerged in the 1860s as the most powerful force on the Continent, it had had for almost two generations no practical experiences of war. It had undertaken some insignificant campaigns during the revolution of 1848-1849 and had been mobilized repeatedly between 1830-1859 in anticipation of conflicts that did not materialize. In the same period the Russian, Austrian, French, and British armies had been fighting wars. The superiority of the Prussian army in the 1860s was made possible only by its organization, by its peacetime training, and by the theoretical study of war that had been brought to perfection in the half-century before Königgrätz and Sedan.

The Prussian army of the nineteenth century was created by four men: Frederick the Great, Napoleon, Scharnhorst, and Gneisenau. Frederick bequeathed precious memories of victory and endurance in adversity, which are so essential for the pride and self-reliance of an army. In addition, he impressed upon his military successors the knowledge that even the peacetime life of an army consists of hard labor and that battles are won first on the training ground. There was undoubtedly in the Prussian army an overemphasis on the minutiae of military life, which was originally counterbalanced by the strategic genius of the king. He did not train younger strategists, however, and it was a foreign conqueror who reminded the Prussians of the role that strategy plays in warfare, and two young officers, both non-Prussian by birth, had to remold the Prussian army, which they did largely along the modern French pattern. Thus Napoleon became the second taskmaster of the Prussian army,

NOTE: This text constitutes the first half, somewhat revised by the editor, of Hajo Holborn's essay "Moltke and Schlieffen: The Prussian-German School" from the original *Makers of Modern Strategy*. The second half has been replaced by a new essay by Gunther Rothenberg, which takes account of the more recent scholarly literature and of important documentation, particularly on the Schlieffen plan, that has become available since the Second World War.

and—after Jena—Scharnhorst and Gneisenau adapted the Prussian army to the new type of warfare.

The Prussian military reformers knew that new methods of war were an expression of the profound social and political changes that the French Revolution had produced. The army of Frederick the Great had been a force of mercenaries isolated from civilian society. Only the noble-born officer's sense of honor and loyalty was glorified while the rank and file were kept together by brutal discipline. The Prussian military reformers undertook to transform the army of the age of despotism into a national army. To this end they introduced universal conscription of a more radical type than had ever been attempted before. Napoleon's Treaty of Tilsit hampered the immediate realization of Scharnhorst's ideas, but in the Prussian military law of 1814, drafted by his pupil, Boyen, his plan became the permanent order of Prussia's military system.

Conscription became the rule in practically all countries on the Continent, but outside of Prussia it amounted merely to the conscription of the poor, since the well-to-do were allowed to make money payments or purchase substitutes. In Prussia, all groups of the population actually served. In this respect, the Prussian army was more clearly a citizens' army than that of any other country. Unfortunately, the Prussians were not democratic citizens, but remained subjects of a bureaucratic absolutism. There was also a recrudescence of the privileged position of the Prussian gentry in government and army, and the Junker class continued to monopolize the officers' positions. National service, the logical outcome of national and liberal thought in America and France, became in Prussia a device for strengthening the power of an absolutist state.

The dream of the Prussian military reformers of creating a true citizens' army was frustrated by the political reaction after 1815. The legacy of their strategic and tactical knowledge fared better, though even here the old school scored certain successes. Still Scharnhorst's and Gneisenau's strategic ideas were not forgotten in the Prussian army.

Among their contemporaries, these two officers from Hanoverian and Saxon families were the only equals to Napoleon in the art of war. An early death in the summer of 1813 kept Scharnhorst from ever assuming high command in the field. Gneisenau, as the chief of staff of the Prussian army from the fall of 1813 to the summer of 1815, was destined to prove that the new Prussian school of military thought could produce not merely a new philosophy, but also men able to translate their insight into action.

There has been much controversy about which of the two was the greater general. Clausewitz, friend and pupil of both, gave the crown to Scharnhorst because he combined a profound contemplative mind with a deep passion for action. Schlieffen found Gneisenau superior because he seemed to have higher perspicacity and determination on the battle-field. From a historical point of view, however, what matters is to realize that both, the calm and self-possessed Scharnhorst and the impetuous and generous Gneisenau, represented a new type of general. Both were born leaders of men, the one possibly greater in educating them for war, the other in directing them on the battlefield, but both these children of Germany's philosophical age, of the epoch of Kant and Goethe, believed that thought should lend wings to action.

The new Prussian strategy sprang from an original interpretation of Napoleon's art of war. To most nineteenth-century students of war before Königgrätz and Sedan, Jomini's writings seemed the last word on Napoleonic strategy. Had not Napoleon himself said that this man from Switzerland had betrayed the innermost secrets of his strategy? Napoleon, however, though admiring Jomini, had also remarked that he set down chiefly principles, whereas genius worked according to intuition.[1] Jomini's cold rationalism was not capable of doing justice to the spontaneity that was the hidden strength of Napoleon's actions. The interpretation of Napoleon's strategy, which Scharnhorst developed and which animated Gneisenau's conduct of the campaigns of 1813-1815, was based on a historical and inductive method that gave full credit to the creative imagination of the commander and the moral energy of his troops. In Clausewitz's work *On War*, the new philosophy found its classic literary expression.

The new Prussian school of strategy created its own organ in the Prussian general staff, which became the brains and nerve center of the army. The origins of the general staff go back to the years before 1806, but not before Scharnhorst's time did it receive its characteristic position. When, in 1809, Scharnhorst reorganized the War Ministry, he created a special division that was charged with the plans for organization and mobilization and with the peacetime training and education of the army. Under the jurisdiction of this section came also the preparation of military operations by intelligence and topographical studies, and finally the preparation and direction of tactics and strategy. As minister of war, Scharnhorst retained the direction of this section and exercised a strong influence on the tactical and strategical thought of the officers in it by training them in war games and staff maneuvers. It became customary to assign these officers as adjutants to the various army units, which went far to extend the influence of the chief of staff over all generals.

Under Scharnhorst, the general staff was still a section of the War

---

[1] Gen. Baron Gourgaud, *Sainte Hélène, Journal inédit, 1815 à 1818* (Paris, 1899), 2:20.

Ministry, under which it would have remained if Prussia had received a parliament. The absolutist structure of the Prussian government, however, made it possible to divide military responsibility under the supreme command of the king. In 1821, the chief of the general staff was made the highest advisor of the king in matters of warfare, while the War Ministry was restricted to the political and administrative control of the army. This decision was of far-reaching consequence, since it enabled the general staff gradually to take a leading hand in military affairs, not merely after the outbreak of war, but also in the preparation and initial phase of a war.

I

Moltke was destined to take full advantage of the traditional ideas and institutions that were created during the wars of liberation. Like Scharnhorst and Gneisenau, he was not a Prussian by birth, but came from neighboring Mecklenburg. His father was an officer of the king of Denmark, who, as the Duke of Schleswig and Holstein, was then still a German prince. Moltke was brought up as a Danish cadet, becoming a lieutenant in 1819. His experiences at school had been unhappy, however; his relations with his father were not close; nor did service in the Danish army hold out great prospects. In 1822, Moltke applied for a commission in the Prussian army in which his father had started his military career before transferring to the Danish army.

The Prussians put the young lieutenant through a stiff examination and made him begin at the very bottom of the military ladder again. His promise soon became apparent; in 1823 he passed the entrance examination to the War College, at that time under Clausewitz's direction. Clausewitz gave no lectures, however, and Moltke did not become acquainted with his ideas until Clausewitz's work was posthumously published. From his studies at the War College, Moltke gained his lasting interest in geography, physics, and military history, which were well represented at the school. In 1826 Moltke returned to his regiment, but after two years he was already assigned and then permanently transferred to the general staff, with which he was to be associated for more than sixty years.

With the exception of five years as a lieutenant in the Danish and Prussian armies, Moltke never served with the troops. He had never commanded a company or any larger unit when, at the age of sixty-five, he took virtual command of the Prussian armies in the war against Austria. But the years from 1835 to 1839, which he spent in Turkey as a military advisor of the Sublime Porte, gave him some actual war experiences in the futile campaign against Mehemet Ali of Egypt. The Turkish commander threw the good advice of the young captain to the winds, and Moltke saw war at its worst among defeated troops.

When he returned to Berlin from Turkey, the hardest period of his life was over. As a lieutenant he never had an extra penny to spend. Dire need compelled him to write short novels, which appeared in installments in a popular journal. In order to purchase mounts, without which he could not serve on the general staff, he translated six volumes of Gibbon's *Decline and Fall*. It is impressive to see the young Moltke wrestle with the problems of genteel poverty and yet acquire an Attic education in the Spartan setting of Berlin.

In his first years of service with the general staff his main duties concerned preparing an up-to-date map of Silesia, but he soon went beyond topography to other aspects of geography, and penetrated deeply into history as well. As his education matured, so did his power of expression. Moltke became an excellent writer of German prose, whose letters from Turkey are still read as literature.

He did not, however, become an original political thinker or a statesman. Scharnhorst and Gneisenau had been politicians as much as generals, and their military reforms aimed directly at a reform of the whole life of the nation. This had made them suspect in the conservative atmosphere of the Prussian or, for that matter, of the Austrian and Russian courts. Almost as soon as the French Revolution and Napoleon were defeated, Gneisenau and the younger reformers were neutralized. Moltke was conscious of the natural interrelationship of generalship and statesmanship, and took a lively personal interest in politics. He abstained from active participation in political affairs, however, and rarely questioned the powers that be. He was convinced of the superiority of monarchical government and found its special justification in the fact that it allowed officers to manage army affairs without interference from nonprofessional elements. The defeats of German liberalism in the revolution of 1848-1849, and again in the 1860s, were highly gratifying to him.

An officer of his quiet manner, conforming political views, and wide learning was well received at court. In 1855, Frederick William IV made him aide-de-camp to his nephew, Prince Frederick William, the future emperor Frederick III. This appointment brought Moltke into contact with the prince's father, known as the Soldier-Prince, the future William I, who apparently discovered in Moltke talents that seemed to recommend him for the position of chief of the general staff.

One of William's first actions when in 1857 he became regent of Prussia was to appoint Moltke to that post. Still William I was immediately more interested in the political and technical reorganization of the army, and the figure of the minister of war, Roon, overshadowed the

285

silent chief of staff in the councils of state. What Roon and William proposed was a decided improvement in the efficiency of the army, but it meant at the same time the ultimate abolition of those militialike sections of the army in which a more liberal spirit had survived. The popular *Landwehr* (territorials or national guard) was curtailed in favor of a greatly expanded standing army. This gave the professional royalist officer corps unchallenged control over all military institutions of the nation. The Prussian parliament fought this measure, but the reorganization became effective under Bismarck even without parliamentary consent. The ensuing constitutional conflict was still raging when the battle of Königgrätz was fought. The parliamentary opposition, however, broke down when the Bismarckian policy and Moltke's victories fulfilled the longing for German national unity. Moltke's successful strategy, therefore, decided two issues: first, the rise of a unified Germany among and over the nations of Europe; second, the victory of the Prussian crown over the liberal and democratic opposition in Germany through the maintenance of the authoritarian structure of the Prussian army.

The role that Roon, as minister of war, played in the years of political conflict made him the most influential figure in the army before 1866. William I was so used to taking military advice from him that the chief of the general staff was almost forgotten. The unpretentious Moltke was little known in the army, and even during the battle of Königgrätz, when an officer brought an order from him to the commander of a division, the latter replied, "This is all very well, but who is General Moltke?" Moltke's rise to prominence among the advisors of the king was sudden and unexpected, though it was the logical outcome of Prussian military history since the days of Scharnhorst and Gneisenau.

His aloofness from the political scene in the years from 1857 to 1866 allowed him to give his undivided attention to the preparation of future military operations. The revolutions of 1848-1849, the rise of the Second Empire in France, and the Crimean War had already shown that a new epoch of European history had opened in which military power was freely used. Moltke began at once to overhaul the plans that the Prussian general staff had drawn up. His predecessor, General Reyher, incidentally one of the few Prussian generals who had come up from the ranks, had been a man of great vision and a remarkable teacher of strategy. Molkte could count on the ability of the Prussian officer to find original solutions for the tactical problems of war. In fact, the officers silently dropped the official and overly conservative service regulations of 1847 as soon as they crossed the Bohemian frontier in 1866 and followed largely their own ideas.

The peacetime formation of the Prussian army was a more highly developed system than that of any country. With the exception of the guard troops, the regiments drew their recruits and reservists from their local districts. The Hapsburg Empire with its nationality problems could not use such a system. Moreover, after 1815, the Prussian army had retained the division of the army into army corps that Napoleon had created during his campaigns, but which had been given up by France under the Bourbons. Except in Prussia, army corps were formed on the eve of war, which again acted as a brake upon rapid mobilization and upon the capacity of troops and leaders in the performance of large-scale operations.

Rapid as the mobilization of the Prussian army was, comparatively, Moltke accelerated it still further. The unhappy geographical structure of the Prussian monarchy of this period, with its far-flung east-west extension from Aix-la-Chapelle to Tilsit severed by Hanover, aggravated Prussia's military problems. The railroad age offered a remedy that Moltke exploited to the full. Moltke had begun to study railroads before a single line had been built in Germany. He apparently believed in their future, for when in the early 1840s railroad building got under way, he even risked his savings by investing in the Berlin-Hamburg railroad. His speculative interest was enhanced by his matrimonial concern, namely to cut down the distance that separated him from his young bride in Holstein! But his military thinking was always awake. In 1847-1850, troops of various nations were for the first time moved by rail. In 1859, when Prussian mobilization was pending during the Italian war, Moltke could test the facilities for the rail transportation of the whole army and could introduce important improvements.

The railroads offered new strategic opportunities. Troops could be transported six times as fast as the armies of Napoleon had marched, and the fundamentals of all strategy—time and space—appeared in a new light. A country that had a highly developed system of rail communications gained important and possibly decisive advantages in warfare. The speed of the mobilization and of the concentration of armies became an essential factor in strategic calculations. In fact, the timetable of mobilization and assemblage, together with the first marching orders, formed in the future the very core of the strategic plans drawn up by military staffs in expectation of war.

In addition to making use of railroads, Moltke proposed to employ the dense road system that had come into being in the course of the industrial revolution. Napoleon had already pointed the way by dividing his army on marches and in the campaign of 1805 that led to the surrender of the Austrian army at Ulm had set a classic example for the strategic use of advancing in separate columns. An army column is, however, not

287

ready for battle, and it takes a full day to deploy a corps of thirty thousand. The changeover from marching to battle formation was accordingly a time-consuming process, and armies had, therefore, to be massed days before the battle. After 1815, road conditions improved greatly and new tactics became possible. In 1865, Moltke wrote: "The difficulties in mobility grow with the size of military units; one cannot transport more than one army corps on one road on the same day. They also grow, however, the closer one gets to the goal since this limits the number of available roads. It follows that the normal state of an army is its separation into corps and that the massing together of these corps without a very definite aim is a mistake. A continuous massing becomes, if merely on account of provisioning, embarrassing and often impossible. It makes a battle imperative and consequently should not take place if the moment for such a decision has not arrived. A massed army can no longer march, it can only be moved over the fields. In order to march, the army has first to be broken up, which is dangerous in the face of the enemy. Since, however, the concentration of all troops is absolutely necessary for battle, the essence of strategy consists in the organization of separate marches, but so as to provide for concentration at the right moment."

It is probable that Moltke already envisaged operations in which the concentration of the army would take place on the battlefield itself, thus discarding the Napoleonic principle that the army should be concentrated well before the start of a battle. Still, Moltke's direction of operations in the weeks before Königgrätz did not disregard the Napoleonic rule from the very beginning. He could have drawn the armies together before the battle but he decided at a late date to continue their separation and to achieve their union on the battlefield. After Königgrätz, he summed up his ideas thus: "It is even better if the forces can be moved on the day of battle from separate points against the battlefield itself. In other words, if the operations can be directed in such a manner that a last brief march from different directions leads to the front and into the flank of the enemy, then the strategy has achieved the best that it is able to achieve, and great results must follow. No foresight can guarantee such a final result of operations with separate armies. This depends, not merely on calculable factors, space and time, but also often on the outcome of previous minor battles, on the weather, on false news; in brief, on all that is called chance and luck in human life. Great successes in war are not achieved, however, without great risks."

The last remarks permit a glimpse at Moltke's philosophy of war. Naturally Moltke was eager to extend the control of reason over warfare as far as possible. But in agreement with Clausewitz he recognized that the political and military problems of war cannot be totally mastered by calculation. War is an instrument of policy and, though Moltke maintained that a commander should be free in the actual direction of military operations, he admitted that fluctuating political aims and circumstances were bound to modify strategy at all times.

While the impact of politics on strategy confronted a general with an element of uncertainty, Moltke felt that the mobilization and initial concentration of the army was calculable since it could be prepared a long time before the outbreak. "An error," he said, "in the original concentration of armies can hardly be corrected during the whole course of a campaign." The necessary orders, however, can be deliberated long before and, assuming that the troops are ready for war and transportation is properly organized, they will inevitably lead to the desired results.

Beyond this stage, war becomes a combination of daring and calculation. After actual operations have begun, "our will soon meets the independent will of the enemy. To be sure, we can limit the enemy's will if we are ready and determined to take the initiative, but we cannot break it by any other means than tactics, in other words, through battle. The material and moral consequences of any larger encounter are, however, so far-reaching that through them a completely different situation is created, which then becomes the basis for new measures. No plan of operations can look with any certainty beyond the first meeting with the major forces of the enemy. . . . The commander is compelled during the whole campaign to reach decisions on the basis of situations that cannot be predicted. All consecutive acts of war are, therefore, not executions of a premeditated plan, but spontaneous actions, directed by military tact. The problem is to grasp in innumerable special cases the actual situation that is covered by the mist of uncertainty, to appraise the facts correctly and to guess the unknown elements, to reach a decision quickly and then to carry it out forcefully and relentlessly. . . . It is obvious that theoretical knowledge will not suffice, but that here the qualities of mind and character come to a free, practical, and artistic expression, although schooled by military training and led by experiences from military history or from life itself."

Moltke denied that strategy was a science and that general principles could be established from which plans of operations could be logically derived. Even such rules as the advantages of the inner line of operation or of flank protection seemed to him merely of relative validity. Each situation called for a definition in terms of its own circumstances, and for a solution in which training and knowledge were combined with vision and courage. In Moltke's opinion, this was the chief lesson to be derived from history. Historical study was also of the greatest usefulness

289

in acquainting a future commander with the complexity of the circumstances under which military actions could take place. He believed that no staff or army maneuvers, indispensable as they were for the training of staff officers, could put before their eyes as realistic a picture of the significant aspects of war as history was able to do.

The study of military history was made one of the central responsibilities of the Prussian general staff and not left to a subordinate section. Moltke set the style by his classic monograph on the Italian war of 1859, first published in 1862, which aimed at an objective description of the events in order to draw from them valid practical conclusions. The histories of the wars of 1866 and 1870-1871 were later written in a similar manner under his direction.

Moltke took the view that strategy could benefit greatly from history, provided it was studied with the right sense of perspective. His own practice exemplifies the benefits that he derived from historical study. He knew, of course, of Napoleon's occasional use of detached corps for attacks against the flank or rear of the enemy. These operations with detached units, however, had not diminished Napoleon's belief in the value of concentrating one's forces and in the power of a well-timed frontal attack. The advantages of such a strategy had been great in the Age of Napoleon, but they had not shielded him against ultimate defeat. The battle of Leipzig had shown the possibilities of concentric movements of individual armies, which Scharnhorst had predicted in his advice that one should never keep an army aimlessly massed, but always fight with concentrated forces. In Moltke's opinion, the progress of technology and transportation made it possible to plan concentric operations on a much larger scale than had been used half a century before.

Important as history was for the officer, Moltke pointed out that it was not identical with strategy. "Strategy is a system of *ad hoc* expedients; it is more than knowledge, it is the application of knowledge to practical life, the development of an original idea in accordance with continually changing circumstances. It is the art of action under the pressure of the most difficult conditions."

Accordingly, the organization of command held a prominent place in Moltke's ideas on war. He treated the subject with great clarity in his history of the Italian campaign. No war council could direct an army, and the chief of staff should be the only advisor of the commander with regard to the plan of operations. Even a faulty plan, provided it was executed firmly, was preferable to a synthetic product. On the other hand, not even the best plan of operations could anticipate the vicissitudes of war, and individual tactical decisions that must be made on the spot. In Moltke's view, a dogmatic enforcement of the plan of operations was a deadly sin and great care was taken to encourage initiative on the part of all commanders, high or low. Much in contrast to the vaunted Prussian discipline, a premium was placed upon independent judgment of all officers.

Moltke refrained from issuing any but the most essential orders. "An order shall contain everything that a commander cannot do by himself, but nothing else." This meant that the commander in chief should hardly ever interfere with tactical arrangements. But Moltke went beyond this. He was ready to condone deviations from his plan of operations if the subordinate general could gain important tactical successes, for, as he expressed it, "in the case of a tactical victory, strategy submits." He remained unmoved when certain generals in the first weeks of the Franco-Prussian War by foolhardy, though gainful enterprises, wrecked much of his plan of operations.

Moltke did not wish to paralyze the fighting spirit of the army or to cripple the spontaneity of action and reaction on the part of subordinate commanders. Modern developments had placed a greater responsibility upon them than was the case in former ages. One of the chief reasons why Napoleon kept his army close together was his wish to keep all troops within the reach of his direct orders. Moltke's system of disposition in breadth made the central direction of the battle itself extremely difficult, although the marches prior to the battle could be easily arranged by telegraph. Moltke directed most movements in the war of 1866 from his office in Berlin, and arrived at the theater of war just four days before the battle of Königgrätz. He confined himself very wisely to general strategic orders. To ensure an adequate, and this meant free, execution of strategic ideas, army commands were created while the authority in tactical questions rested with the commanders of corps and divisions.

Moltke's strategic thought and practice met its test in the Austrian campaign of 1866. His role in the war that Austria and Prussia conducted against Denmark in 1864 had been modest. In the latest phase of the war he had quickly stopped the bungling that characterized the regime of the old field marshal Wrangel, and his critical counsel established him in the eyes of William as a prudent strategist. In the discussion of war plans against Austria he became increasingly prominent so that William I, on June 2, 1866, directed that all orders to the army should be issued through him. Since the king henceforth accepted Moltke's advice almost unconditionally, the sixty-five-year-old general, who had thought of retirement, found himself the virtual commander in chief of the Prussian army.

The first test of his generalship was at the same time the greatest one in his career. The forces were more evenly matched than later in the

Franco-Prussian War, and Moltke had to overcome more obstinate geographical and political problems. The war of 1866 and particularly the Bohemian campaign also illustrate the strategic side of war in a much clearer form than the Franco-Prussian or for that matter most other wars.

William I wished to avoid the war with Austria into which Bismarck ultimately pushed him. The Prussians thus began their mobilization much later than the Austrians and even then it remained doubtful whether the king could be persuaded to declare war, thereby enabling the army to take the offensive. The original strategic problems were accordingly very delicate. From Bohemia and Moravia the Austrians could have operated against either Upper or Central Silesia or marched into Saxony to threaten Berlin, possibly after effecting a union with the Bavarian army in Northern Bohemia or Saxony. Whether one or the other of these possibilities could be realized depended entirely upon the date of the actual opening of war. Naturally enough, Moltke supported Bismarck in urging the king to act soon, but he avoided prejudicing the political issue by military measures—in contrast to his nephew, who as chief of staff had to inform William II in August 1914 that the strategic plans of the general staff had deprived the government of its freedom of action.

The elder Moltke's moves were aimed in the first place at making up for the delay caused by the belated start of the Prussian mobilization. In addition, he wished to cope with a possible Austrian advance against Saxony and Berlin or against Breslau in Central Silesia while Upper Silesia remained originally unprotected. Whereas the Austrians could employ only one railroad line for their mobilization in Moravia, Moltke used five to transport the Prussian troops from all over Prussia to the neighborhood of the theater of war. As a consequence, on June 5, 1866, the Prussian armies were spread over a half-circle of 275 miles from Halle and Torgau to Görlitz and Landeshut. The original placement of the Prussian troops was safe as long as the Austrian forces were far to the south. In point of fact, they were not even in Bohemia, as Moltke assumed, but still in Moravia.

Moltke, of course, never planned to leave his troops at their points of disembarkation but began at once to draw them closer toward the center around Görlitz. At all times he refused, however, to order a full concentration in a small area as was advocated by most Prussian generals and even by members of his own staff. On the other hand, he too felt somewhat worried when he ultimately learned that the main Austrian forces were assembling in Moravia and not in Bohemia, a fact that seemed to point to a contemplated Austrian offensive toward Upper Silesia. Reluctantly he allowed the left wing to extend toward the Neisse River, thus again spreading the Prussian armies over a distance of more than

270 miles from Torgau to Neisse. His hesitation was chiefly caused by uncertainty about the policy of William I and not by military considerations. In Moltke's opinion, everything would be well if he did not miss the opportunity of achieving the ultimate concentration of the Prussian armies along the shortest route, which meant by a forward move into Bohemia.

Moltke had chosen Gitschin as the point for such a concentration—not because it offered important strategic advantages of itself, but merely on account of distances. It was about equally close to the two main Prussian armies, the Second Army under the crown prince, Friedrich Wilhelm, which formed the left wing in Silesia, and the First Army under Prince Friedrich Karl, which had its base around Görlitz. At the same time, Gitschin was equally distant from Torgau and Olmütz, that is, from the Prussian Elbe Army and from the Austrian main army. Provided the Prussian armies could begin marching on the same day on which the Austrian army left Moravia their concentration should have been completed before the Austrians arrived at Gitschin.

It was not before the twenty-second of June that officers of the Prussian vanguard handed Austrian officers notification of the Prussian declaration of war, but Prussia had opened hostilities against other German states on June 16. Thus the Elbe Army began to occupy Saxony on the same day on which the Austrian army started its march from Olmütz to Josephstadt at the upper Elbe.

The Austrian army was worthy of the best traditions of Austrian military history. Its morale and enthusiasm were high; its officers, among them some of the best generals of the period, had great ability and practical experience. Certain branches of the services, namely cavalry and artillery, were definitely superior to those of the Prussian army. The strength of the latter was in its infantry, which excelled both in tactics and arms. The Prussian needle-gun by itself, however, could not have achieved victory, as was proved in the war against France where the Prussians fought against an infantry armed with superior rifles. It was the outmoded shock tactics of the Austrian infantry together with its old-fashioned weapons that put the Austrians at a decided disadvantage.

The scales were turned, however, by the lesser strategic ability of the Austrian High Command. Benedek was a fine soldier with a distinguished record of service to the Hapsburg Empire. He was at his best in battle; fearlessly and correctly he directed even the retreat of his beaten army on the battlefield of Königgrätz. But he had grown up in the classic school of strategic thought and his chief strategic advisor, General Krismanic, whom he had not selected, lived largely in the operational thought of the eighteenth century. These elements determined the strategic conduct of the war by the Austrian High Command. They meant formation in depth and emphasis upon the maintenance of naturally strong positions. Moltke, on his part, showed that space could be conquered by time.

The Austrian army moved from Moravia in three parallel columns. Though the strain of such marching arrangements was considerable, the Austrians reached their goal quickly and in good order. But after the arrival of the vanguards in Josephstadt on June 26, at least three days were needed to mass the army again. This loss of time probably saved the Prussian armies.

In spite of Moltke's continuous warnings, the Prussian First Army had made slow progress, since Prince Friedrich Karl wanted to wait for the Elbe Army, which, after occupying Saxony, was to be joined to his command. This gave Benedek an opportunity to use the inner line of operations. Which of the two about equally strong Prussian armies Benedek should have attacked has been an interesting controversy among students of military history. Probably Benedek's judgment was right when he considered chiefly an attack on the First Army. He failed, however, to recognize in time that he had only one or possibly two days in which he could have taken the offensive against one of the Prussian armies without having to fear the other in his rear. Since the Austrian High Command believed rather in the tactical advantage of strong positions than in the priceless value of time, and since the early concentration of the army hindered its mobility, the opportunity slipped by. When Benedek discovered the mistake, it was even too late to retreat behind the Elbe at Josephstadt and Königgrätz, and he had to accept battle with the river at his rear.

The danger of an Austrian attack against one of the two Prussian armies having passed, Moltke began to delay the concentration of the armies, keeping them at one day's distance from each other in order to achieve their union on the battlefield. During the night of July 2, the last orders were given. They were actually bolder than their execution made them appear. According to Moltke, the left wing of the Second and the right wing of the First Army were supposed to operate not merely against the flanks but also against the rear of the enemy. Moltke conceived of Königgrätz as a battle of encirclement. But the Prussian generals did not follow him and the Austrian army got away—though losing a fourth of its strength. An immediate pursuit was impossible since the troops of the Second Army had run into the front of the First, thus causing a mix-up of all army units, which could not be easily disentangled. Four years later, the battle of Sedan proved that the Prussians had learned their lesson.

It has been suggested that Moltke's success reflected the superior military strength which Prussia enjoyed at that time, but such a statement is true only within certain limitations. In 1866, Moltke had to create the slight superiority of the Prussian armies in Bohemia, which, incidentally, was not to be found in overall manpower. He took the risk of denuding all Prussian provinces of troops and of leaving only an extremely small army to deal with Austria's German allies. If the Bohemian campaign had dragged on or turned into a deadlock, Napoleon III could have used the chance to take the Rhineland and to settle the fate of the Continent. Nor were possibilities of foreign intervention entirely lacking during the war of 1870-1871.

Moltke's strategy in 1866 showed that the much-vaunted inner line of operations were merely of relative significance. He summed up his experiences in these words: "The unquestionable advantages of the inner line of operations are valid only as long as you retain enough space to advance against one enemy by a number of marches, thus gaining time to beat and to pursue him, and then to turn against the other who is in the meantime merely watched. If this space, however, is narrowed down to the extent that you cannot attack one enemy without running the risk of meeting the other who attacks you from the flank or rear, then the strategic advantage of the inner line of operations turns into the tactical disadvantage of encirclement during the battle."

These sentences have often been interpreted as a definite condemnation of operations along the inner line and a recommendation of concentric maneuvers. This was not Moltke's opinion. During the Franco-Prussian War of 1870-1871, he used both concepts freely and successfully, depending chiefly upon the actions of the enemy. Moltke's strategy was characterized by his openness of mind and by the elastic changes from one device to the other.

11. Moltke, Schlieffen, and the Doctrine of Strategic Envelopment

GUNTHER E. ROTHENBERG

TWO GREAT SOLDIERS, Helmuth von Moltke the Elder and Alfred von Schlieffen dominated Prusso-German military thinking from the mid-nineteenth century into the First World War and beyond. They taught and practiced a mode of offensive warfare that adapted to the industrial age Napoleon's precept to seek prompt decision by battle and in battle seek to destroy the enemy. Confronted with the deadlock imposed by new weapons and extended frontages, Moltke, chief of the general staff from 1857 to 1887, developed the concept of out-flanking the enemy in one continuous strategic-operational sequence combining mobilization, concentration, movement, and fighting. By seizing the initiative from the outset, he intended to drive his opponent into a partial or complete envelopment, destroying his army in a great and decisive battle of annihilation or encirclement, the *Vernichtungs-* or *Kes-selschlacht*. To control the execution of this sequence, Moltke built on earlier developments to create the modern general staff system and in-troduced the *Auftragstaktik*, mission tactics, a command method stress-ing decentralized initiative within an overall strategic design.

Although Moltke had demonstrated the potential of his new methods in 1866 and 1870, Schlieffen, his eventual successor from 1891 to 1906, never commanded armies in battle. Nevertheless, he became historically significant as a teacher and an exponent of stragegic envelopment, which he described and glorified as the Cannae concept and came to regard as the only really effective method of waging war. His great project for gaining a rapid and decisive victory against France came close to success in 1914, although it ultimately failed, while on the eastern front the concept produced a number of spectacular victories. Schlieffen's ideas influenced another generation of German strategists who updated the strategic envelopment concept and applied it with striking success during the blitzkrieg phase of the Second World War. General Hans von Seeckt, the head of the *Heeresleitung* and a formative influence on the German army between 1919 and 1926, believed that Schlieffen's teaching had continued relevance, because with a small professional army Germany's only chance of success lay in rapid and decisive victories at the very outset of a war. The tactical framework for this strategic conception was refined by Ludwig Beck, chief of the general staff from 1933 to 1938, and cast in its armored-mechanized form by General Heinz Guderian and others. Spearheaded by such forces, supported by tactical airpower, strategic envelopment achieved rapid victory in the Polish and French campaigns, and the new combination of firepower and maneuver enabled Germany to destroy a succession of Russian armies in 1941. But then the blitzkrieg began to falter. Effective against poorly prepared and often poorly commanded adversaries and within a limited theater of operations, it could not be sustained over longer distances or bring final victory against an enemy who could trade space for time and disposed of ample reserves. In the latter part of the war, from 1943 on, the concept of the strategic envelopment began to be used against Germany, though again falling short of total success because of inherent command, control, and logistics problems. Remaining a strategic ideal, it played a role in a number of post–World War II conflicts, but by the second half of the century new technical, political, and social developments combined to deprive it of its ability to achieve fast and decisive results.

I

Moltke may be considered the most incisive and important European military writer between the Napoleonic Era and the First World War. Clausewitz was a more profound thinker, and equal claims to greatness as tacticians and combat leaders could be advanced for a number of other commanders, but Moltke excelled not only in organization and strategic planning but also in operational command, abilities he combined with an acute awareness of what was and was not possible in war. Moltke had broad cultural interests and has been pictured as "essentially a humanist of the post-Goethe era."[1] Perhaps too much has been made of this. Moltke did indeed share many of the intellectual characteristics of German classicism, but above all he was a soldier and what truly mattered to him was the controlled application of force in the service of the Prussian monarchy.

Like many Prussian soldiers, he attributed some of his ideas to Clausewitz and described himself as his disciple. Yet Clausewitz's actual contribution to Prussian military doctrine and practice is hard to estimate. In Moltke's case there may be some convergence with Clausewitz on the relationship of the state and the army, but much less agreement on or-

---

[1] Gerhard Ritter, *The Sword and the Scepter*, 4 vols. (Coral Gables, Fla., 1969-73), 1:189.

ganizational and operational matters. Where Clausewitz was ever the philosopher, seeking to discover the universal nature of war and using specific examples primarily as illustrations, Moltke was essentially a grammarian of war who engaged in very little abstract speculation. In common with most soldiers of his generation, he regarded war as inevitable, an essential element in the divinely ordained order and he looked, above all, for ways to conduct war successfully. Therefore he always was concerned with the specifics of the actual political-military situation rather than the general aspects of war.

Not a great theorist, Moltke never produced a single comprehensive system of either war or strategy in his prolific writings; it is necessary to study his ideas through his correspondence, instructions, and memoranda. His fullest statement on policy, war, and strategy can be found in his "Instructions for the Senior Troop Commanders" of 1869 and in his essay "On Strategy" dated 1871.[2] In these general areas, Moltke followed Clausewitz closely and in some key statements he paraphrased the master. The "Instructions" declared that the "objective of war is to implement the government's policy by force." Although Clausewitz always stressed the subordination of strategy to policy even in war, he also emphasized the need of policy to be realistic: "The first duty and the right of the art of war is to keep policy from demanding things that go against the nature of war."[3] With this statement, too, Moltke agreed completely. But he went much further than Clausewitz in his interpretation of what was or was not in accord with the nature of war. In "On Strategy," completed soon after his confrontation with Bismarck concerning the shelling of Paris, he argued that once the army had been committed to war, the direction of the military effort should be defined by the soldiers alone. "Political considerations," he wrote, "can be taken into account only as long as they do not make demands that are militarily improper or impossible."[4] Moltke has been accused of advancing a perilous doctrine when he excluded policy from any meaningful role in the actual conduct of war. Yet insistence on pursuing victory, which he defined as the "highest goal attainable with available means," by military means alone was not so automatically censurable as many later writers have suggested. Moltke considered the army as an instrument of the sovereign, who to him represented the state. The king's two principal

[2] Excerpts in Gerhard Papke, "Helmuth von Moltke," in *Klassiker der Kriegskunst*, ed. Werner Hahlweg (Darmstadt, 1960), 311-16.

[3] Peter Paret, *Clausewitz and the State* (New York and London, 1976; repr. Princeton, 1985), 369.

[4] Papke, "Helmuth von Moltke," 316. Cf. *Moltke: Ausgewählte Werke*, ed. Ferdinand v. Schmerfeld (Berlin, 1925), 1:35.

advisors, the chief of the general staff in the military and the chancellor in the political sphere, were coequal within their respective jurisdictions, though obliged to keep each other informed.[5] If in later years a fatal overvaluation of the purely technical aspects of the military and its needs inhibited responsible political and diplomatic policies, this was as much due to civilian weakness as to military presumption.[6]

Moltke also endorsed Clausewitz's contention that the objective of war was the achievement of a satisfactory political result and that this required flexibile and adaptive strategy. Rigid systems were anathema to Moltke, who held that nothing in war was certain. Therefore he believed that it was impossible to lay down any firm rules. "In war as in art," he stated, there "exist no general rules; in neither can talent be replaced by precept," and given the uncertainties of war, he concluded that strategy could be no more than a "system of expedients."[7] The basic elements of strategy, he thought, hardly went beyond the propositions of common sense, but their correct execution required strength of character and the ability to make rapid decisions under stress. Frederick the Great and Gneisenau were his ideal models, though interestingly enough, Moltke also included George Washington, not a notably successful field commander, but resolute in adversity and with a profound sense of the political and psychological dimensions of war, among the "world's greatest strategists."[8]

In the more restricted sphere of operations, Moltke was at his best in recognizing that the changes brought about by vastly improved firearms, transportation, and communications, together with the ability of states to raise and maintain ever larger armies, required corresponding changes in strategy, tactics, command, and organization. The American Civil War had demonstrated that these new factors could create a tactical and operational deadlock, and Prussia, always facing a potential multifront conflict, could not afford a protracted war. But rapid decision required an aggressive offensive to destroy hostile forces, while the great increase in killing power derived from rifled firearms had made frontal attacks prohibitively costly and extended frontages made tactical outflanking impossible. Moltke's solution, the "strategic envelopment" mounted directly from the initial concentration, fused operational and tactical requirements. Aware that "no plan of operations survives the

---

[5] A different view is presented in Gordon A. Craig, *The Politics of the Prussian Army 1640-1945* (New York, 1964), 214-16.

[6] Ritter, *Sword and Scepter*, 1:196; Eberhard Kessel, *Moltke* (Stuttgart, 1957), 508-509.

[7] Oberkommando des Heeres, *Gedanken von Moltke* (Berlin, 1941), 13; *Moltke's militärische Werke*, in *Kriegslehren*, ed. Grosser Generalstab, Abteilung für Kriegsgeschichte (Berlin, 1892-1912), 3:1. (Hereafter cited as *Kriegslehren*.)

[8] Kessel, *Moltke*, 507.

first collision with the main enemy body," he nonetheless was determined to seize and retain the initiative and to structure the decisive battle by combining strategy and operations into one sequence.[9] Technical advances, he realized, not only strengthened the defensive but also helped to implement a large offensive scheme. His flexible "strategy of expedients," using exterior lines in 1866 and interior lines during the first phase of war in 1870, made every effort to concentrate numerically superior forces more rapidly than the enemy. Once that was achieved and his armies were within supporting distance of each other, they had the strength necessary to simultaneously engage the front and the flanks of the adversary and destroy him by envelopment.[10] This interaction of movement and combat, culminating in several armies converging for the decisive battle, became the hallmark of Moltke's wars.

Within this strategic-operational sequence, the most difficult elements were the initial concentration and deployment (the *Aufmarsch*), and the control of the different armies converging over separate routes for the decisive battle. Other problems, such as logistics, an almost intractable subject in the age of horse-drawn operational transport, held a much lower priority in Moltke's operational scheme.[11] Planning and preparation, railroads and telegraph could accelerate mobilization, but the initial concentration and deployment of the field armies was critical. "A mistake in the original concentration of the army," Moltke wrote, "can hardly be rectified during the entire course of the campaign."[12] The apparent dilemma was that initial concentration required highly centralized control, while the movements of the separate armies in the field required decentralized command. Moltke's approach to directing modern war, reinforced by his study of the 1859 campaign in northern Italy, was that the High Command, in this case the chief of the general staff, should limit itself to issuing general instructions to the senior subordinate commanders outlining the general objective and specific missions, and allow the subordinates to handle the details. "War," he observed, "cannot be conducted from a green table."[13]

Some writers have condemned Moltke's command system. J. F. C. Fuller, for instance, stated that whereas Napoleon led and controlled, "Moltke brought his armies to their starting point and then abdicated

[9] *Kriegslehren*, 3:3.

[10] Kessel, *Moltke*, 514.

[11] Martin Van Creveld, *Supplying War: Logistics from Wallenstein to Patton* (Cambridge, 1977), 79-82, 91-96, 103-08.

[12] Cited in Papke, "Helmuth von Moltke," 316.

[13] *Kriegslehren*, 3:42-3.

his command and unleashed them."[14] On the face of it, the charge appears to have some validity. The loose system of command required subordinate commanders of high quality, and both in 1866 and in 1870, Prussian generals revealed a deplorable propensity to blunder into frontal attacks, a procedure encouraged by their cavalry's failure to provide accurate intelligence. But given the Prussian military framework, with the king acting as commander in chief and with princes acting as army commanders, Moltke's powers of command could hardly be compared with those held by Napoleon. Often Moltke had to extemporize after orders had been issued that interfered with his overall scheme. Moreover the forces Moltke directed were much larger than the Napoleonic armies and more widely dispersed, and although the electric telegraph provided an instrument of strategic direction, it was not flexible enough for operational control.

To offset the evident constraints of the command system as he found it, Moltke transformed the Prussian general staff into a unique instrument combining flexibility and initiative at the local level with conformity to a common operational doctrine and to the intentions of the high command. This development, not completed until 1873, ushered in the modern era of staff work and organization. The reformed Prussian general staff, named the Great General Staff after 1871 to distinguish it from the Bavarian, Saxon, and Württemberg staffs, which continued to exist, performed both collective and decentralized functions. In its central role it was the brains of the army developing strategic plans and operational methods. Its decentralized functions were handled by the staff officers, the *Truppen Generalstab*, assigned at the division, corps, and army levels. Although in other contemporary armies these men were mere technical advisors, in Germany they became junior partners in command. The commander retained ultimate authority, but was expected to make operational decisions jointly with his chief of staff, who had the right, indeed the duty, to protest what he regarded as unsound operational judgments. At its best, the Prussian general staff system institutionalized combat efficiency by ensuring that in a given situation different staff officers, educated to a common fighting doctrine, would arrive at approximately the same solution for making the most effective employment of available forces.[15]

Transformation of the Prussian general staff, still a subordinate department of the War Ministry in 1857, into the most important command agency of the army required general recognition of Moltke's central role

[14] J. F. C. Fuller, *A Military History of the Western World*, 3 vols. (New York, 1954), 3:134.
[15] Theodore Ropp, *War in the Western World* (Durham, 1959), 137-39.

as well as new indoctrination and training of staff officers. At that, considering the scope of its duties, the size of the staff remained modest. Never comprising more than a few hundred officers in all of its branches and departments, the German general staff constituted a highly selected, self-conscious elite, distinguished by outstanding intellectual capacity, hard work, and dedication. Next to the excellence of its personnel, the new command-and-control system depended on conformity to a common fighting doctrine and common operational procedures. These were imparted through education at the War Academy, a prerequisite for subsequent selection to the staff, and continued training, alternating with assignments to command positions. Aware that few soldiers ever have the opportunity to experience a wide range of operational situations, Moltke stressed military history as a tool to forearm staff officers against the many possible contingencies. Together with a thorough grounding in the practical aspects of their work, the didactic study of history became one of the hallmarks of the preparation of German general staff officers. By 1870-1871 Moltke's system was already widely recognized for both its spectacular performance in the field and its impressive professionalism. Within the next three decades, albeit with important modifications, it was adopted by all major armies.

II

The campaign of 1866 in many ways represented the Moltkean ideal of war. The decisive battle was fought within weeks after the outbreak of hostilities, and its outcome deprived the adversary of the means and the will to fight further. Even so, Moltke regarded the war against Austria as a regrettable, if unavoidable, fratricidal conflict. By contrast, he desired war against France, a country he distrusted deeply and considered "not only the most dangerous but also the best prepared enemy."[16] Still widely believed to be the best in Europe, the army of Napoleon III was a professional veteran force, combat experienced, with modern weapons and seasoned commanders. Soon after becoming chief of the Prussian general staff, Moltke prepared his first war plan against France, a defensive deployment along the Main, flanking a French drive into either northern or southern Germany. He adopted a defensive posture because at the time the Prussian army was still weak; but as army reform progressed, concentration of the field forces was advanced to the Rhine, and he began to speculate about a possible envelopment of the enemy in that region. The Austro-Prussian War transformed his outlook. Prussian successes coupled with the strength of the new North German Confederation, and

[16] Kessel, *Moltke*, 536.

after 1867 the expectations of South German support, provided him with a mobilized strength of twelve seasoned North German corps, some 740,000 combatants, backed by over 200,000 second-line *Landwehr* troops and some 80,000 South Germans, against which the professional French army could at best muster some 350,000 men.[17] From 1867 on Moltke prepared for offensive war against France, and even considered a preemptive strike. His basic scheme was simple. He intended to seek out and destroy the enemy with the numerically superior forces made available by mobilizing national manpower, careful planning, and a highly developed railroad system. "The plan of operations against France," he wrote in 1868, "simply consists of locating the main enemy army and attacking it wherever it is found. The only difficulty is how to execute this simple plan with very large masses."[18]

France, however, did possess one significant advantage. In theory at least, its professional army would be ready sooner than Prussia's conscript-reservist troops, and Moltke worried about a French spoiling attack across the Rhine. But even in this eventuality he would dispose of larger forces. He calculated that during the initial stages of the war the French could not muster more than 250,000 men against his 380,000, and with conscription Prussian reserves in time would triple available numbers. A study of the French railroad network revealed that to assemble rapidly, the enemy would have to concentrate in two areas divided by the Vosges Mountains, one group in Metz and the other at Strasbourg. To guard against a French spoiling offensive, Moltke massed his three armies on the Rhine between Trier in the north and Landau to the south, so that if the French did attack, the three armies holding the central position could reinforce each other more rapidly than could the separated French commands in Lorraine and Alsace. Speed of mobilization was all-important and when, on the night of July 15, 1870, the king ordered his army on a war footing, the Prussian general staff proved that it had mastered the problems of mass organization and movement. After mobilization was complete, the Prussian army would have over a million men; meanwhile in eighteen days six trunk lines and three additional lines for the South Germans transported 426,000 men, ten corps, to the frontier. War was declared on July 19, but the French were unable to assemble their forces in time and only launched a minor attack in the Saar on August 4 when German concentration was nearly complete.[19]

Combat revealed that weaknesses remained in Moltke's partially implemented command system. Disregarding instructions to lure the

[17] Ibid., 534-38.
[18] *Kriegslehren*, 1:98-99, 106-107.
[19] The classic account is Michael Howard, *The Franco-Prussian War* (New York, 1961).

French into positions where they could be enveloped, his subordinates reacted too soon and too vigorously, pushing the enemy back into Lorraine. A German advance followed, during which "few commanders can have fought more battles they did not intend to fight, or did not mean to fight in the way or at the time the battles occurred."[20] Reconnaissance, once again, was poor and generals insisted on rushing into frontal assaults. Still, the mission tactics proved effective. Marching to the sound of the guns, neighboring formations converged on the scene of action without waiting for orders, and provided the numbers needed to outflank French positions. By August 18, one of the two main French armies had been pushed into Metz, where it capitulated after a long siege, while the second, attempting to relieve the fortress, was intercepted, driven against the Belgian frontier at Sedan, and forced to surrender on September 1. Together with Napoleon III, who had accompanied this army, 104,000 men became prisoners of war. Superior staff work, speedy mobilization, and despite some blundering, efficient and aggressive operational leadership exploiting the advantages of larger battalions had crushed the French imperial army. Difficulties in controlling subordinate commanders had compelled the High Command on several occasions to assume direct control, and logistic problems caused by the swift advance had been made good by improvisation. On the French side overconfidence, lack of planning, and an obsolete organization all contributed to the disaster.

It was a spectacular victory, achieved less than seven weeks after the French declaration of war, but it took five more months to break the French will to resist. When news of Sedan reached Paris, a provisional government of national defense was established, which managed to raise four armies in the provinces and one in the capital, supported by numerous irregular forces. The Germans invested Paris on September 18, while the French tried to raise the siege and interrupt their communications. The Germans held only a narrow corridor leading to Paris. The French still had significant resources, and their command of the sea enabled them to bring in supplies from abroad. What they needed was time, which Bismarck, alarmed about sinking German morale and the possibility of foreign intervention, wanted to deny them. He demanded an immediate bombardment of the city, and a major clash with Moltke erupted on this issue. Since the outset of the war Bismarck had resented Moltke's failure to keep him fully informed of the progress of operations, and only after the king insisted had the chief of the general staff agreed to do so. Even so, he still refused to include the chancellor in planning

[20] Cyril Falls, *The Art of War from the Age of Napoleon to the Present* (New York, 1961), 78.

of future operations. Thus the question of the bombardment assumed greater importance; it highlighted civil-military tensions within the Prussian headquarters.[21]

The soldiers regarded Bismarck as an interloper and his claim to be included in operational planning as merely a screen for designs to gain influence in the military. Moltke held that he lacked sufficient guns for an effective bombardment of Paris and that a weak effort would merely stiffen resistance. But with the supply situation still critical, he considered it counterproductive to overload the railroads with the transport of the heavy siege trains. Therefore, Bismarck was asking for something that was "militarily improper or impossible." In the end, the king once again sided with the chancellor, though by this time the conflict had resolved itself. In December the supply situation eased and heavy artillery began to arrive. The bombardment opened on January 5, 1871. In the meantime, the French repeatedly had mounted attacks against the German lines but, badly trained, lacking equipment and leaders, their improvised forces were no match for the Germans and none of these efforts succeeded. Armistice negotiations opened on January 23, five days after a new *Reich* had been proclaimed at Versailles, and Paris surrendered on January 28, 1871.

The unexpected popular resistance in France was an unsettling experience for Moltke, who always had envisioned war as a contest between conventional forces. He was appalled by improvised armies, irregular elements, and appeals to popular passion, which he described as a "return to barbarism." Futher perturbed by the bloody spectacle of the Paris Commune, he was at pains to distinguish the French "nation-in-arms" from the Prussian system of conscription. By indiscriminately arming the population, the former raised the specter of social revolution. "Rifles," he observed, "are distributed quickly, but are difficult to withdraw." The Prussian system, by contrast, instilled "discipline as well as proper military virtues."[22] Popular war and revolution made a lasting impression on Moltke, leaving him in a quandary. On the one hand, when after 1871 the other powers followed Prussia's lead and introduced conscription, he worried that Germany would lose its manpower advantage and noted that "lasting success can only be achieved when one enters the war from the outset with superior numbers." On the other hand, as a staunch conservative, he feared that socialism was undermining the allegiance of the industrial workers. Therefore he opposed major increases in the annual recruit quotas unless adequate regular training cadres were made

---

[21] Howard, *Franco-Prussian War*, 325-26.
[22] *Letters of Field-Marshal Helmuth von Moltke*, ed. and trans. Clara Bell and Henry W. Fischer (New York, 1892), 204, 209.

available.[23] His views were widely shared within the military and social elites, with the result that until two years before the outbreak of war in 1914, Germany called only about half of its eligible men to the colors.

III

Prussia had always dreaded a multifront war and this possibility continued to preoccupy Moltke. Soon after he was named chief of the general staff he had speculated about a combination of the "Slav East and the Latin West against the centre of Europe." Such reflections were among the main reasons of his search for a short and decisive war, and had been a major concern during the first weeks of the 1870 campaign. Even at the height of victory this potential danger continued to worry him and within three months after the fall of Paris he described a Franco-Russian alliance as the "most dangerous threat to the new German Empire" and made detailed plans to meet it.[24] He recognized that political differences made such an alliance rather unlikely, but considered it his duty to prepare for all possible contingencies. Until 1879, the general staff also prepared plans for war against an even less likely Franco-Russian-Austrian coalition.[25]

The war in France also modified Moltke's strategic expectations. In his first war plan against France and Russia, prepared in April 1871, he already warned that rapid victory had become unlikely. "Germany cannot hope to rid itself of one enemy by a quick victory in the west in order then to turn against the other. We have just seen how difficult it is to bring even the victorious war against France to an end." Understanding the power of the defensive and realistic enough to recognize that the search for total victory would provoke prolonged resistance, he now advocated a strategy based on defensive-offensive operations. No longer seeking a rapid decision marked by decisive battles, he planned to operate offensively, moving into enemy territory west and east to disrupt mobilization and occupy easily defensible lines, and then have the enemy suffer heavy casualties in futile attacks against German defensive firepower. To achieve this he intended to allocate approximately equal forces to the two fronts.[26] He neither expected total victory nor favored additional territorial acquisitions, but counted on diplomacy to bring the conflict to an acceptable conclusion.

Basically, all of Moltke's later plans derived from these defensive-

[23] *Kriegslehren*, 3:25-26; Kessel, *Moltke*, 741-47.
[24] Gerhard Ritter, *The Schlieffen Plan* (London, 1958), 18; Ferdinand v. Schmerfeld, *Die deutschen Aufmarschpläne 1871-1890* (Berlin, 1928).
[25] Schmerfeld, *Aufmarschpläne*, 62-67; Kessel, *Moltke*, 649-50.
[26] Ritter, *Schlieffen Plan*, 18.

offensive assumptions, though developments soon invalidated his roughly equal deployment of forces east and west. To be sure, after 1873, Bismarck's League of the Three Emperors reaffirmed monarchical solidarity against republican France, and temporarily at least decreased the danger of a two-front war. But even the chancellor's immense diplomatic skill could not banish the danger inherent in Germany's geographic position. The surprisingly rapid French military recovery increased Moltke's concern. In 1872, France introduced universal service, training almost four-fifths of all eligibles, at the same time developing an efficient staff and mobilization system. By 1873 Moltke declared it "imperative to accelerate our mobilization process," and decided to increase troop strength in the West at the expense of the East.[27] He now envisaged the possibility that the Germans might be driven back by a more rapidly mobilized French army. In that eventuality, he intended to regroup on the Rhine and then, with the French again expected to mass in two groups, counterattack through their center, driving the northern group toward Paris and the southern to the Loire. If the plan succeeded, France would be offered generous terms, and even if these were refused, France would be so weakened that major forces could be returned to the East.[28] At that, the proposed allocation of forces still was not heavily weighted toward the West and, as late as 1877, Moltke expected that in the event of a two-front war, a decisive battle would be fought in Lorraine in the third week after mobilization. Once again, however, he did not look for a complete victory, emphasizing that "we cannot extend our pursuit to Paris. It must be left to diplomacy to see if it can achieve a peace settlement on this front."[29]

Another reason for his limited expectations for war against France was that Russia's improved military capabilities, demonstrated during the Russo-Turkish War of 1877-78, coupled with the near completion of a strong French frontier fortification belt, made defensive operations in the West and offensive operations in the East more promising and necessary. "If we must fight a two-front war," Moltke observed, ". . . we should exploit the defensive advantage of the Rhine and of our strong fortifications, and employ all forces not absolutely indispensable [in the west] for an imposing offensive against the east."[30] By this he did not mean that Germany should be passive in the West. The proposed distribution of forces was fairly balanced, 360,000 against Russia and 300,000 against France, and Moltke decided that an effort should be

[27] Schmerfeld, *Aufmarschpläne*, p. 19; Ritter, *Sword and Scepter*, 1:227.
[28] Schmerfeld *Aufmarschpläne*, 21, 29, 38, 52-55.
[29] Ibid., 64-66; Ritter, *Schlieffen Plan*, 19.
[30] Schmerfeld, *Aufmarschpläne*, 77; Craig, *Politics of the Prussian Army*, 274-75.

made to defeat the French offensive from forward positions in Lorraine and on the Saar. A retreat to the Rhine without a major fight would endanger morale and create a difficult strategic situation. "I am of the opinion," he concluded, "that even facing superior numbers, we must risk a battle in front of the Rhine before withdrawing beyond it."[31] On the Russian front he intended to conduct a limited offensive on interior lines, driving between the western Russian armies assembling at Kovno and Warsaw to disrupt their mobilization. Combined with a systematic effort to promote insurrections among the subject peoples, the plan was designed to throw Russia off balance and induce the Czarist government to negotiate with Germany on reasonable terms. In addition, since 1871, Moltke occasionally speculated on the possibility of Austro-Hungarian support against Russia, and the Dual Alliance, signed in October 1879, created prospects for a complementary offensive north from Austrian Galicia into central Poland. But from the military point of view the treaty of 1879 had one major weakness. It lacked specific military commitments. Bismarck had designed it primarily to meet Austria-Hungary's need for reassurance against Russia, and had given it a purely defensive character. The treaty promised mutual support in the event that either of the partners was attacked by Russia, but it did not provide any mechanism for planning coalition warfare. In any case, Moltke remained skeptical about making advance commitments. "It is useless," he wrote, "to stipulate common operations in advance, because in practice they will not be carried out."[32] Basically, he doubted that the Austro-Hungarian army, relatively weak and slow to mobilize was really prepared to undertake major offensive operations.

Staff talks nonetheless were initiated in 1882 and continued on and off for over a decade at the instance of Moltke's newly appointed first deputy, Oberquartiermeister Count Alfred von Waldersee. Moltke had asked to retire in 1881, but Emperor William I had persuaded him to stay on with a younger man to share his burdens. An ambitious and restless officer, Waldersee, who in 1888 became Moltke's successor, never formed a consistent strategic policy and spent much of his effort in intrigues that ran counter to Bismarck's avowed purpose to stay on good terms with both Austria-Hungary and Russia. In 1882, following repeated suggestions by Baron Friedrich Beck, the new Austro-Hungarian chief of staff, the two men met and Waldersee promised that in case of a two-front war, Germany was prepared to assist Austria-Hungary with

[31] Kessel, *Moltke*, 651-52, 672-75; Schmerfeld, *Moltke*, 1:250.
[32] Schmerfeld, *Moltke*, 1:44. Cf. the excellent survey by Dennis E. Showalter, "The Eastern Front and German Military Planning, 1871-1914—Some Observations," *East European Quarterly* 15 (1981), 163-80.

some twenty active and six reserve divisions to carry out a double envelopment of the Russian armies in the Polish salient. Beck was disappointed with the proposed forces, especially because his own army would
be ready only two weeks later than the German and he had counted on
his ally to assume a major share of the initial fighting. Additional conversations between Moltke and Beck produced little change. Waldersee
and Moltke were about to shift the main German strength against France
and when Beck asked for clarification at the end of 1886, Moltke told
him that in the event of war, a distinct possibility at that point, Germany
would engage only one-third of its army in the East. And Moltke's final
plan, going into effect on April 1, 1888, expected that the repulse of the
initial French offensive would be followed by a strong counterattack with
two-thirds of the German army. Only eighteen divisions were to remain
in the East.[33] The tilt towards an offensive in the West, though not yet
in the all-out manner later envisaged by Schlieffen, already was apparent
in 1887-1888.

This shift in priorities also reflected Bismarck's views. The chancellor
always considered France rather than Russia to be the greater danger
and, in response to inquiries from Vienna early in 1887, had stated that
although Germany would stand by its alliance, Austria-Hungary should
refrain from provoking Russia and that if it came to a two-front war,
Germany would seek a decision against France first. Bismarck's secret
negotiations with Russia, leading to the Reinsurance Treaty, about which
Moltke was informed only after it had been signed, contributed to further
estrangement between the two allies. Even so, when Waldersee succeeded
Moltke in 1888, negotiations between the Austro-Hungarian and German staffs continued, but although the new chief of the general staff had
favored a preemptive strike against Russia in 1887, he now proposed
making the main effort in the West. Considering Russia's growing
strength, German troops assigned to the eastern front were clearly inadequate even for limited offensives, and Schlieffen, who in 1891 replaced
Waldersee, merely was candid when he informed Beck in 1895 that
Germany had abandoned the projected joint offensive into Poland. Instead, Schlieffen advised that Austria-Hungary undertake an independent
thrust in the general direction of Warsaw, a proposal clearly exceding
Austrian capabilities and confirming still lingering suspicions about German intentions in Vienna. On this note, staff talks lapsed in 1896 and
were not resumed until 1908. Even then they achieved no clear agreement
concerning the vital initial dispositions.[34]

[33] Ritter, *Sword and Scepter*, 1:232-34; Schmerfeld, *Aufmarschpläne*, 144-45; Kessel,
Moltke, 708-09.
[34] Gunther E. Rothenberg, *The Army of Francis Joseph* (W. Lafayette, 1976), 112-17,

The fluid, even confused, relationship between the two allied general staffs reflected, at least in part, a mounting operational quandary. During his last years in office, the octogenarian Moltke no longer was able to find a solution for Germany's basic strategic-operational dilemma. He had been flexible enough to realize the mounting odds against offensive warfare, and after 1871 developed his concept for a defensive-offensive posture looking toward limited victories and a strategic standoff. But as both the French and Russian armies became more powerful, the need to attain an early victory against one adversary once again became apparent. Yet Moltke no longer saw a possible way to achieve this goal and to avoid a long and destructive war of exhaustion. In 1890, making his last public statement, he warned the Reichstag that with popular passions aroused, future conflicts could last "seven and perhaps thirty years" and shatter the established social order.[35]

Moltke was prophetic, of course, but he could provide no guidance to prevent war from deteriorating into a lengthy and bloody stalemate. For that matter, none of the German military thinkers after 1871 could resolve the conflict between the requirement for offensive action and the capacity of entrenched infantry with modern weapons to inflict unsupportable casualties on the attacking forces. The experiences of 1870 were reinforced by those of the Russo-Turkish War and the wars in the Balkans and in South Africa. There was agreement among writers like Generals Wilhelm von Blume, Prince Kraft zu Hohenlohe-Ingelfingen, and Colmar von der Goltz that an attack could only succeed if increased infantry firepower was neutralized by improved artillery, including mobile heavy artillery to accompany the field forces. At the same time, these younger men did not fully accept Moltke's pessimistic views about the future of war. Without becoming rigidly dogmatic in their operational doctrines, all held that the offensive remained the superior mode of war, though they conceded that it might have to be combined with a preliminary defense to weaken the adversary. They felt that even under modern conditions strategic envelopment, especially in the restricted spaces of western Europe, still offered the best prospects for a major victory, though perhaps not on the scale of Sedan. Finally, they shared the conviction that numbers were of the utmost importance and advocated greater exploitation of German manpower reserves.[36] All these concepts, with par-

---

155; Gordon A. Craig, "The Military Cohesion of the Austro-German Alliance, 1914-18," in his *War, Politics, and Diplomacy* (New York, 1966), 47-51.

[35] Kessel, *Moltke*, 747-48; *Kriegslehren*, 1:7.

[36] Heinz-Ludger Borgert, "Grundzüge der Landkriegsführung von Schlieffen bis Guderian," in Militärgeschichtliches Forschungsamt, *Handbuch zur deutschen Militärgeschichte* (Munich, 1979), 9:435-37, 462-66. (Hereafter cited as *Handbuch*.) Cf. Jay Luvaas, "European Military Thought and Doctrine," in *The Theory and Practice of War*, ed.

ticular emphasis on the search for a rapid decision, were shared by Alfred von Schlieffen, who took office as chief of the general staff on February 7, 1891.

IV

The descendant of an old Prussian family, Schlieffen was born in Berlin on February 28, 1833. Educated in the spirit of Protestant pietism, he was graduated from the Joachimsthaler Gymnasium in that city and in 1853 reported to the 2nd Guard Uhlans as a one-year volunteer. He transferred to the regular service within a year and was commissioned in December 1854. Selected early to attend the War Academy, he joined the general staff in 1865, and served in various staff and line assignments, including command of the 1st Guard Uhlans from 1876 to 1884. That year he returned to general-staff duty and after heading several sections became Waldersee's first deputy in 1889. When Waldersee was compelled to step down as the result of his attempts to meddle in politics, Schlieffen became his successor until he in turn handed over to Helmuth von Moltke the Younger on January 1, 1906. In retirement Schlieffen continued to perfect his great plan for a decisive western envelopment, but he no longer influenced policy. He died on January 4, 1913, nineteen months before the outbreak of the First World War.[37]

Schlieffen became the best-known and most controversial strategist of his time. He represented a new generation of professional military leadership, combining first-rate administrative talents with a solid education, though he lacked the broader cultural interests of Moltke. He was a specialist who favored concrete calculations over abstract speculations, an austere, solitary man who after the death of his wife devoted himself exclusively to his profession. General Erich Ludendorff called him "one of the greatest soldiers ever," and his many disciples were convinced that he had found an answer to Germany's strategic dilemma that would have brought an early victory in the First World War.[38] His critics have faulted him for his "narrow-minded military scholasticism" and reckless disregard of wider political ramifications. Schlieffen, they claim, "seems to have taken the technician's view that his duty was fulfilled when he did his utmost with the means available, and 'made the best of a bad job' in compliance with the customs and rules of his profes-

Michael Howard (London and New York, 1965), 73-76, and Hermann Teske, *Colmar Freiherr von der Goltz* (Göttingen, 1958), 32-56 passim.

[37] Friedrich v. Boetticher, *Schlieffen* (Göttingen, 1957).

[38] Erich Ludendorff, *My War Memories 1914-1918* (London, 1920), 24; Wilhelm Groener, *Lebenserinnerungen* (Osnabrück, 1972), 85-91.

sion."[39] His reliance on purely military plans, and flawed ones at that, was "nothing less than the beginning of Germany's and Europe's misfortunes."[40] Critics and admirers alike agree that Schlieffen's strategic practices, if not his basic concepts, were a break in continuity from Clausewitz and Moltke. An admirer, General Wilhelm Groener, noted with approval that his writings, unlike those of Clausewitz, were free from "verbose theoretical speculations . . . but reflected life and reality," while Schlieffen's efforts to remove the element of "friction" from operations had been called an "antithesis to Clausewitz."[41] Schlieffen also differed from Moltke in the last stage of his career both in his resolve to command rather than to direct the armies in war and in his determined search to develop a strategy for an early and decisive victory over one enemy in a two-front war.[42]

The main reason behind this renewed search for a rapid victory was the changed political-military situation. A few months after Schlieffen assumed his post, the hypothetical two-front war bcame much more likely. Between 1891 and 1894, a number of Franco-Russian staff talks, agreements, and treaties shifted the manpower balance in Europe. Popular belief regarded Germany as an armed camp; but France trained more men annually, while the Russian army, already very large, continued to expand. The military strength of the Dual Entente, actual or projected, clearly outnumbered that of the Dual Alliance. Numbers were considered all-important. "Our past victories," Schlieffen wrote in 1891, "were gained with superior numbers." The "essential element of the art of strategy," he continued, is "to bring superior numbers into action. This is relatively easy when one is stronger from the outset, more difficult when one is weaker, and probably impossible when the numerical imbalance is very great."[43] Therefore, he rejected the strategy of attrition implied in the defensive-offensive war plans. If adopted, the "German forces will have to shuttle between the fronts, pushing back the enemy here and there . . . [while] the war drags on with growing disadvantages and debilitation of our forces."[44] Time was not on Germany's side in a two-front war, and it was essential to destroy one enemy at the outset. This could not be achieved by a frontal assault, which at best produced

[39] Ritter, *Schlieffen Plan*, v, vii.

[40] Ibid., p. 88; Jehuda L. Wallach, *Das Dogma der Vernichtungsschlacht* (Frankfurt a.M., 1967), 55-56.

[41] Wilhelm Groener, *Das Testament des Grafen Schlieffen* (Berlin, 1927), 11; Werner Hahlweg, *Clausewitz* (Göttingen, 1957), 95.

[42] Ritter, *Sword and Scepter*, 2:198.

[43] Alfred v. Schlieffen, *Briefe*, ed. Eberhard Kessel (Göttingen, 1958), 296-97.

[44] Generalstab des Heeres, *Dienstschriften des Chefs des Generalstabes der Armee General Feldmarschall Grafen von Schlieffen*, 2 vols. (Berlin, 1937-38), 1:86-87.

an "ordinary" victory followed by a protracted war. A battle of annihilation was required. "A Solferino would not help us; it has to be a
Sedan or at least a Königgrätz."[45]

The chief of the general staff might have looked to diplomacy to
reduce the military odds against Germany, but Schlieffen rigidly observed
the by now traditional separation of jurisdictions. The example of Waldersee, who had ventured into policy questions, and cautioned the emperor that the German naval buildup was unsound and merely antagonized Great Britain, and who consequently had been forced from office,
may have stood as a warning. In any case, Schlieffen confined himself to
his own professional sphere. In 1904-1905, "when temptation was greatest for Germany to . . . disrupt the Franco-Russian alliance by a preemptive strike," he abstained from pressing his case.[46] And even on such
matters as increasing the size of the army by raising the annual recruit
quota, he refused to enter into a political fight. When his proposals
encountered opposition from the War Ministry, the legally responsible
agency, he gave way. In Schlieffen's view, the proper role of the chief of
the general staff in peacetime was restricted to planning, improving combat doctrine and capabilities, and offering advice when asked.

V

Schlieffen devoted considerable effort to making existing forces more
effective. At the close of the century improvements in firepower, machine
guns, quick-firing field artillery, and smokeless powder as well as new
developments in communications, radio, and telephone were changing
the nature of land warfare, though armies everywhere did not yet fully
understand these innovations. Cavalry still favored mounted combat,
infantry tactics retained too much emphasis on shock, and field artillery
lacked striking power. The need for heavy mobile artillery, the central
and perhaps the decisive weapon of the coming war, had been perceived,
but Schlieffen had to push through the introduction of heavier matériel
against the opposition of old-line gunners. As Waldersee's deputy he
already had strongly supported adoption of new infantry regulations in
1888, formally recognizing the mission tactics, and in his new post he
tried to improve cavalry reconnaissance capabilities. In addition, he increased the number of technical units and backed the introduction of
machine guns, modern signal equipment, and motorized vehicles. Within
the general staff, he paid special attention to preparing junior officers for

---

[45] Ibid., 2:222-23.

[46] Ritter, *Sword and Scepter*, 2:194; L. F. C. Turner, "The Schlieffen Plan," in *The War
Plans of the Great Powers, 1880-1914*, ed. Paul M. Kennedy (London, 1979), 207-10. But
compare Craig, *Politics of the Prussian Army*, 283-85.

independent command. Overall, his efforts contributed substantially to the performance of the German army in the years to come.[47]

All of this was meant to make a decisive battle possible. Schlieffen believed that certain basic principles of war, above all the offensive, maneuver, mass, and economy of force, applied equally to large and small actions. Like Napoleon and Moltke before him, he held that to avoid prohibitive losses one had to outflank the enemy and that the objective of operations was to destroy the opposing forces. His study of military history convinced him that even a weaker army could achieve this by concentrating against one or both flanks of the adversary. Hannibal, Frederick the Great, Napoleon, and Moltke had demonstrated this in battle as well as in entire campaigns, Sedan being the most recent example. Schlieffen, however, feared that under stress, army commanders might lose sight of the central objective. After all, he claimed, these generals had failed to fully implement "Moltke's simple and grand plan for a complete encirclement and annihilation of the enemy," and he doubted that since 1870 their understanding and self-control had improved. The "strategy of expedients" had been part of the problem. He reproached Moltke for thinking that the chief of the general staff "could direct rather than command."[48] Going well beyond Clausewitz and Moltke, who recognized the unpredictable effects of "friction" and the enemy's "independent will," Schlieffen maintained that one could compel the opponent to conform substantially to one's own operational design. By taking the offensive, he planned to seize the initiative, and by massing against the enemy's flanks, he intended not only to throw him off balance but deprive him of viable strategic options. The scheme required close integration of the entire sequence from mobilization through the climactic battle, including rigid adherence to schedules and set operational objectives. He allowed for some unexpected developments, but his controlled system of strategy, the *manoeuvre a priori*, sought to exclude them as far as possible by preplanning and centralized command.[49] Schlieffen recognized that modern armies might become too large to be controlled by a single man, but looked to technology to provide the answer. A "modern Alexander," he wrote in 1909, ought to make fullest use of the new means of communications, "telegraph, wireless, telephones . . . automobiles and motorcycles," to command from a distant headquarters.[50]

Critics of Schlieffen's approach were not lacking both within the

---

[47] Boetticher, *Schlieffen*, 57-60; *Handbuch*, 9:427-34.

[48] Alfred v. Schlieffen, *Gesammelte Schriften*, 2 vols. (Berlin, 1913), 1:163-84; Schlieffen, *Briefe*, 312.

[49] Wallach, *Dogma*, 90; *Handbuch*, 9:444.

[50] Schlieffen, *Schriften*, 1:15-16.

general staff and among senior commanders. General von Schlichting, chief of staff of the Guard Corps until 1896, published several attacks against set-piece operations and the concept of the offensive at all costs, and strongly defended the right and duty of Prussian officers to act on their own initiative, accepting personal responsibility for their actions.[51] Another influential writer, General von Bernhardi, the head of the military history section in the Great General Staff at that time, also opposed the *manoeuvre a priori* concept. Such a depersonalized, mechanistic approach, he complained, reduced the art of war to little more than a trade and the strategist to a mere technician. He questioned the emphasis on mass, and insisted that the quality of leadership and of troops counted as much. Moreover, instead of relying on envelopment alone, he claimed that breakthroughs, if not tactical then operational, still were possible and effective. General von Bülow, one of Schlieffen's deputies, and General von der Goltz, then commanding in East Prussia, also opposed Schlieffen's ideas.[52] But Schlieffen shrugged off his critics. As time went on, he became more and more convinced that Germany would have to win the initial battle at any price, and pushed aside all considerations that might interfere with the execution of the project that alone, he thought, could lead to victory.

VI

His grand scheme was the rapid and total overthrow of the French army, as outlined in the memorandum, usually called the "Schlieffen Plan," that the recently retired chief of the general staff delivered to his successor in February 1906. It was only the latest in a series of strategic plans drawn up by Schlieffen. Each year the Great General Staff developed different contingency plans which, if adopted after being tested in staff rides and war games, became effective on April 1 the following year. During his term in office, Schlieffen formulated a total of sixteen plans against France, fourteen against Russia, and nineteen for a two-front war, which now was a near certainty.[53] The most pressing issues were to decide against which enemy to launch the main strength and what force would be adequate to defend the other frontier. Interior lines facilitated redeployment, but it was recognized that once put in motion, the initial *Aufmarsch* was difficult, probably impossible, to change. Military decisions therefore had enormous political consequences and se-

[51] Summaries in Rudolph v. Caemmerer, *The Development of Strategic Science during the 19th Century* (London, 1905), 248-67; Herbert Rosinski, *The German Army* (New York, 1966), 135-56.

[52] *Handbuch*, 9:465-66; Ritter, *Schlieffen Plan*, 51-52.

[53] Boetticher, *Schlieffen*, 61.

verely restricted diplomatic options. The persistent impression that in the years before 1914 the soldiers imposed their schemes on the civilian authorities is, however, incorrect. Schlieffen maintained close ties with Friedrich von Holstein, a very influential senior official at the Foreign Ministry, and both Chancellors Bülow and Bethmann Hollweg were informed of the general features of the war plans. Even so, they were not aware of some specific and crucial details, such as the *coup de main* planned against Liège from 1912 on. Unlike Bismarck, these men made no effort to be informed, and because there existed no formal mechanism to coordinate strategic planning and foreign policy, the division of jurisdictions resulted in a serious, possibly fatal, overreliance on military schemes alone.

On assuming the post of chief of the general staff, Schlieffen inherited plans drafted by Moltke and only slightly modified by Waldersee. However, he was not satisfied with the underlying assumptions of Moltke's defensive-offensive scheme for a two-front war. Above all he feared that Germany could not afford to ride out a French offensive before counterattacking. At the same time, he questioned the prospects of the proposed limited spoiling attack into Russia's western provinces. In 1894 he made a fundamental change. To retain the initiative and to forestall the French offensive, he decided to move the initial German concentration further west, even at the risk of an encounter battle. If the French decided to remain on the defense, he intended to rupture their frontier fortifications by an attack against the advanced Frouard-Nancy-St. Vincent position leading to seizure of the Nancy plateau.[54] It was not, he soon recognized, a satisfactory plan. Even if successful, a breakthrough here neither eliminated the French army nor permitted the transfer of major elements to the East. It required lengthy follow-up operations, giving Russia the time needed to complete mobilization. Nor did the plan hold out the promise of surprise; an attack here was anticipated by the French general staff.[55]

But Schlieffen remained convinced that France was the major threat that had to be eliminated by a crushing offensive, and therefore he discontinued further planning for joint operations with Austria-Hungary against Russia. By 1897 he contemplated, and then discarded, a breakthrough immediately north of Verdun. He decided that the strategic envelopment had to have more space to unfold. "An offensive that seeks to wheel around Verdun," he concluded, "must not shrink from violating the neutrality of Belgium as well as that of Luxembourg."[56] This new

[54] *Handbuch*, 9:447-48; Ritter, *Schlieffen Plan*, 38.
[55] Ritter, *Schlieffen Plan*, 38.
[56] *Ibid.*, 41.

direction was spelled out in an 1899 memorandum that, until 1904-1905, remained the basis for the offensive in the West in case of a two-front war. A total of seven armies, three in Lorraine and two on each wing, were to assemble between Aachen and Basel. Assuming that the French would be ready to advance first, either through Belgium or against Lorraine, Schlieffen intended to counter with an attack against their left wing. "If this succeeds, " he noted, "it will enable us to drive the entire French army away from its fortifications toward the Upper Rhine." If the French stood on the defensive, he planned to pin them down by a frontal attack in the Belfort-Verdun sector and defeat them by an out-flanking thrust through Belgium. No great difficulties were expected here. "Luxembourg," he observed, "has no army, and the relatively weak Belgian army will want to withdraw into its fortresses."[57] Although during the next years Schlieffen repeatedly examined alternative options, he always returned to the wheel through Belgium.[58] The need for speed and concentration demanded keeping the wheel tight, and at first he envisaged a sweep restricted to the area south of the Meuse. But he questioned whether such a limited maneuver would be enough to drive the French out of their fortifications. Moreover, the 1904 staff ride revealed that the right wing was too weak, while the center of the planned German deployment was too strong. In the late summer, moreover, Russian defeats in Manchuria for the time being eliminated any major threat from the East. Accordingly, Schlieffen further downgraded the eastern front and decided to assign 75 percent of the then-available mobilized field strength to an extended envelopment on the line Verdun-Lille.[59]

The 1905 revolution in Russia reinforced his decision to allocate the bulk of the German army to the marching wing pivoting north of Metz. Lecturing to his staff in October 1905, Schlieffen recalled Napoleon's "battalion square" and declared that his projected envelopment would follow the same pattern, "only in a more concentrated, massive, and powerful form."[60] He elaborated on this in his final critique of the 1905 war games. A situation like the stalemate in Manchuria, he argued, could be avoided by a far-reaching, massive envelopment coupled with a frontal attack, followed by relentless pursuit. He did not, however, disregard the eastern front completely and cautioned that the "idea that on the morning following a decisive battle we can entrain the army for the east is not realistic. Sedan was such a decisive battle, but who can claim that

[57] *Handbuch*, 9:449-51.
[58] Boetticher, *Schlieffen*, 63-65.
[59] Ritter, *Schlieffen Plan*, 44-45.
[60] Hans Meier-Welcker, "Graf Alfred von Schlieffen," in *Klassiker*, ed. Hahlweg, 335-36.

on 2nd September the bulk of the German army could have been transported to the east?"[61] His last official war plan, going into effect on April 1, 1906, provided three corps for the eastern front, with the expectation that despite the absence of any firm agreement, an Austro-Hungarian offensive north from Galicia would offer additional relief. Still, with strength massively deployed on the right wing in the West, this plan contained the essentials of the famous memorandum dated December 31, 1905 (but not transmitted to his successor until the following February).

Conscious since late 1903 of his imminent retirement, Schlieffen composed the memorandum entitled "War against France" as his strategic testament. It was not a complete war plan, but rather a detailed exposition and a guide for his successor. Omitting all political considerations and ignoring Russia, it focused on operational aspects. These embodied Schlieffen's determination to establish the feasibility of a decisive offensive war against the increasing power of the defense. This determination to seek the offensive, rather than the much-debated question whether the hypothetical plan could have succeeded if carried out in its original form, is the real issue and Schlieffen's most important legacy to the development of strategic thought.[62]

The memorandum described France as a great fortress with almost impregnable lines covering the 150-mile-long frontier with Germany. To outflank these positions, Schlieffen wanted the German right wing, thirty-five corps divided among five armies, to sweep on a broad front extending as far as Dunkirk, through Belgium and southern Holland. Dropping off troops to mask Antwerp, the wheel was to pass Amiens, cross the Somme at Abbeville and the Seine west of Paris, and then swing southwest to drive the French against the Vosges and the Swiss frontier. It envisaged a Cannae on a gigantic scale, with a neutral frontier and mountain ranges replacing the second envelopment wing. Conforming to the Cannae model, the weak left wing, five corps only, was supposed to lure the French eastwards toward the Rhine. One military writer compared the scheme to a revolving door: the more a man pushed on one side, the harder it would spring around to strike him in the back.[63]

Uninterrupted momentum on the right wing was all-important, and Schlieffen did not foresee an easy victory. All depended on improvements in Germany's military posture. The fortress of Metz, the anchor, had to be strengthened, more mobile heavy artillery was needed to smash forts encountered on the march, and above all the army had to have more

[61] Ibid.; *Handbuch*, 9:451-53.
[62] Ritter, *Schlieffen Plan*, 134-60.
[63] Basil H. Liddell Hart, *A History of the World War 1914-18* (London, 1934), 68-69.

men. He was uneasy about the troops required to invest the "gigantic fortress of Paris" and noted the lessons of the past that offensive war "calls for much strength and also consumes much." The attacker's strength, he wrote, "dwindles constantly as the defender's increases." At least eight additional corps were needed, otherwise the German army was "too weak for this enterprise." On the other hand, he was confident that an intervention by a British expeditionary force could be brushed aside and, somewhat surprisingly, he was sanguine concerning the problems of troop fatigue and supply. He conceded that the extreme right wing would "have to make great exertions," but apparently he expected that the Belgium and French railroads would fall substantially intact into German hands. And even though the distances at which troops could operate away from their railheads had almost been halved since 1870, he assumed that operational supply could be improvised. "The logistic side of his intentions," one analyst has observed, "appears to have rested on singularly shaky foundations."[64]

Out of office, Schlieffen busied himself with revisions of his memorandum, making the document ever more rigid. There was little or no margin for "friction," and the whole operation became virtually one enormous *manoeuvre a priori*. Convinced that the great battle in Belgium and France was all that mattered, Schlieffen disregarded Russia's military recovery and declared that the fate of the eastern provinces would be decided on the Seine and not on the Vistula. In his last revision, dated 1912, Schlieffen proposed expanding the scope of operations to include the occupation of all of Holland, while the march around Paris changed from a dangerous necessity to part of an inflexible timetable. He was compounding risks and, even worse, underestimating his adversaries. The success of the strategic envelopment depended almost as much on the enemy as on the Germans. Competent adversaries, who kept their heads and could commit reserves, would place the enterprise in grave jeopardy. The victories of 1866 and 1870, the models for Schlieffen's concept, were achieved against opponents with poor command systems, inadequate organization, and inferior numbers. This time the enemy's command system was much improved, its organization was equal to the German, and even with the additional eight corps available after passage of the 1912 army law, the Imperial Army enjoyed no decisive numerical advantage in the West. Liddell Hart was correct when he called the plan a "conception of Napoleonic boldness," but noted that although it would have been feasible in the emperor's time, by 1914 the speed of marching

[64] Larry H. Addington, *The Blitzkrieg Era and the German General Staff, 1865-1914* (New Brunswick, N.J., 1971), 19-20; Van Creveld, *Supplying War*, 113, 118.

German infantry could be countered by more rapid French rail movement. "The plan," he concluded, "would again become possible in the next generation—when air-power could paralyse the defending side's attempt to switch its forces, while the development of mechanised forces greatly accelerated the speed of encircling moves, and extended their range. But Schlieffen's plan had a very poor chance of success at the time it was conceived."[65]

Of course, all military operations involve risks; nevertheless, assertions that the plan was the "work of a genius, an infallible formula for victory which unfortunately fell into the hands of an inadequate successor," are off the mark.[66] Essentially these claims rest on the assumption of German martial superiority, the "immense advantages of training and leadership," and the "excellence of the Imperial Army of 1914."[67] But if these advantages did, in fact, exist and though the German army did come close to success, they were not sufficient to overcome logistic and numerical weakness and the determined resistance of a battered but unbroken enemy. Moreover, even if the initial offensive had succeeded, it seems unlikely that France, England, and Russia would have given up the fight. German soldiers continued to wrestle with the basic problem presented by the problem of a two-front war, the need to overthrow one enemy rapidly, and this induced its leading generals to assert that the Schlieffen Plan could have won the war. As late as the 1940s as sober a strategist as Field Marshal von Rundstedt held that the great battle was lost because the original design had been "watered down," and General Ludwig Beck agreed that the decision to seek a speedy victory in the West had been correct. He did, however, blame Schlieffen for thinking in purely military terms, neglecting overall political and economic considerations.[68]

VII

Frequently dismissed as an inept and timid commander who failed to execute Schlieffen's grand scheme properly, General Helmuth von Moltke, the nephew of the great field marshal, actually was an able and conscientious soldier. He had served with distinction in 1870, was graduated from the War Academy with high marks, and held a number of staff and command positions. Although on familiar terms with the court

[65] Ritter, *Schlieffen Plan*, vi-vii.
[66] Ibid., p. 48.
[67] Rosinski, *German Army*, 138; Walter Goerlitz, *History of the German General Staff 1657-1945* (New York, 1966), 135.
[68] Günther v. Blumentritt, *Von Rundstedt: The Soldier and the Man* (London, 1952), 22; Ludwig Beck, *Studien*, ed. H. Speidel (Berlin, 1955), 63, 106-107.

elite in Berlin, he was prepared to assert his prerogatives as chief of the general staff; however, he lacked the strength of character, self-assurance, and robust health needed to stand the stress of high command in war.

In peacetime the younger Moltke was a competent administrator, who did much to upgrade the combat capabilities of the army. Above all, breaking with the precedent set by Schlieffen, he actively promoted the May 1912 service law, which increased the active army from 624,000 to 650,000 men. He was faced with a worsening military situation, England joining the Entente and Russia making a rapid recovery, and it was his right and duty to modify the war plans left behind by his predecessor. Certainly he was not bound by the concepts of the December 1905 memorandum.

Moltke had a good grasp of the major strategic problems and he was more aware than Schlieffen of the wider ramifications of Germany's position. Perhaps the type of general who in Napoleon's words "saw too much," he was unwilling to gamble everything on one card, and tried to keep his options open. Convinced that Germany's security in the East required an active Austro-Hungarian effort, he welcomed an initiative by Franz Baron Conrad von Hötzendorf to reopen staff contacts and, after some hesitation, promised that the Eighth Army in East Prussia, some ten to twelve divisions strong, would actively support an Austrian offensive from Galicia. In addition, he indicated that within a "reasonable time" after France was eliminated, strong forces would be switched to the East, a statement that Conrad chose to interpret as meaning between four and six weeks. Nevertheless, the renewed German-Austro-Hungarian military contacts did not really clarify mutual obligations or coordinate plans at the highest level.[69]

Moltke was aware of the great odds against Germany's plans to mount a lightning campaign to drive France out of the war and to make the best of a bad situation he introduced certain changes in the operational design. Following his uncle's example, he favored an open system of strategy and was prepared to direct rather than to command. As Schlieffen's deputy from 1903 to 1905, he had opposed his chief's insistence on rigid adherence to preplanned operations and had differed with him about the effectiveness of the expected French and Belgian railroad demolitions.[70] In fact, Moltke believed that the logistic underpinnings for the western campaign were inadequate. After he became chief of the general

[69] Rothenberg, *Army of Francis Joseph*, 157-58; Norman Stone, "Moltke and Conrad: Relationships between the Austro-Hungarian and German General Staffs, 1909-1914," in *War Plans*, ed. Kennedy, 225-28. Compare, however, Showalter, "Eastern Front," 173-74.

[70] *Handbuch*, 9:467-68.

staff he ordered a number of logistics and communication exercises, which confirmed his view. From then on, in contrast to Schlieffen, he paid considerable attention to logistic arrangements, and in 1914 his preparations helped to make the advance to the Marne possible.[71]

Moltke followed both his uncle and Schlieffen in the belief that Germany's optimal strategy was to seek a decision during the early stages of a war. The battle of annihilation remained his primary obejctive, but he was willing to be more flexible about the way to achieve it. "The march through Belgium," he declared, "is not an end in itself, but only the means to an end." He emphasized that the French retained the option of standing on the defensive or attacking. Therefore, the advance into Belgium merely constituted the opening move in his strategic design, placing the German armies in a position either to continue with the wide envelopment or to fall on the flank and rear of the French armies attacking in Lorraine. "There is no point," he explained, "in continuing the march through Belgium when the main French army is in Lorraine. Then only one idea can be considered: to fall on the French army with all possible strength and strike it wherever it is found." He elaborated this concept during the 1912 staff ride. As soon as it was evident, he stated, that the mass of the French army was engaged in an offensive between Metz and the Vosges, no further strategic purpose was served by a continued German advance in Belgium. Instead, "while the German left wing maintains the defensive . . . all forces not required to contain the Belgians and the British should march southwest to attack on a line passing through Metz to the west."[72]

To support this shortened wheel, Moltke and the head of the operations section of the general staff, Colonel Erich Ludendorff, planned to make the center strong enough both to pin down the enemy and to counterattack, creating the potential for a double envelopment. At the same time, reinforcing the center removed the unacceptable threat of a deep French penetration against the industrial Rhine region and the rear of the right wing in Belgium. The revised distribution of forces, the alleged "watering down" of Schlieffen's scheme, did not actually remove any troops already allocated to the right wing, which remained fifty-four divisions strong, but it augmented the center and left as new formations became available.[73] Moreover, Moltke made the task of the right wing easier when, for economic as well as strategic reasons, he abandoned the

[71] Van Creveld, *Supplying War*, 119-21; Helmut Haeussler, *General William Groener and the Imperial Army* (Madison, 1962), 34-36.

[72] Wolfgang Foerster, *Aus der Gedankenwerkstatt des deutschen Generalstabes* (Berlin, 1931), 38, 66; *Handbuch*, 9:470-73.

[73] Wallach, *Dogma*, 113, 136-37.

march through southern Holland, thereby removing the Dutch army, sometimes considered more effective than the Belgian, from the growing list of adversaries.

Narrowing the initial frontage of the advance to the Liège sector created new logistic problems, but these were not insurmountable, provided a surprise attack on the Liège fortified region succeeded in securing the rail lines intact. Altogether, the changes made by Moltke and Ludendorff, above all the option of cutting the northern outflanking movement short and enveloping the French army in a double pincer operation near the German border, were promising. The result was a new war plan, admittedly incorporating major elements of Schlieffen's earlier schemes, but nonetheless Moltke's plan and not merely a version of the former.[74]

When war came in August 1914, Moltke's plan failed, even though it did not fall completely short of success. The failure was the result of the intrinsic problems of speed, endurance, and logistics, as well as of Moltke's inability to find a balance between command and control. During the first phase, the French were completely outmaneuvered, and the British Expeditionary Force was driven back, though not destroyed. By the first week of September, however, the extreme right wing of the German advance, the First Army under General von Kluck, found itself in danger of becoming in turn enveloped by the French, who, making good use of the railroads radiating out from Paris, threw a hastily assembled army against his flank, which by then was only in loose contact with von Bülow's neighboring army. By this time, in his distant general headquarters in Luxembourg, Moltke had lost effective communications with his right wing, and no longer was able to coordinate operations. Out of touch with the High Command, his troops exhausted and short of supplies, von Kluck was halted and then, making his own decision in accordance with German operational command doctrine, withdrew to escape the threatening envelopment. Although he did not suffer a serious tactical defeat, the reverse was the end of Moltke's plan, and after some months of unsuccessfully trying to outmaneuver each other, the armies of both sides stabilized their front lines from the Channel to the Swiss Alps.[75]

To be sure, the failure of Moltke's plan was in part a question of operational and technical detail and did not necessarily demonstrate a basic flaw in the strategy of envelopment. In fact, operations in the East showed that the concept was sound. The Eighth Army in East Prussia, acting with secrecy and speed, was able to envelop and destroy one

[74] *Handbuch*, 9:474.
[75] There is a good summary in Addington, *Blitzkrieg Era*, 17-22.

Russian army at Tannenberg in late August. In the larger perspective, however, fundamental shortcomings characterized the classic German strategy, deriving from the belief that a growing political-military threat could be removed by military means alone. For all their differences, the two Moltkes and Schlieffen shared the assumption that Germany's geo-strategic position demanded a rapid decision, and they looked to operations culminating in a battle of annihilation to provide the answer. Even the elder Moltke's defensive-offensive posture adopted after 1870 had not abandoned this premise, but merely modified it. By the early twentieth century, however, the outcome of war no longer could be predicted by calculations based on manpower, railroads, and operational design. Instead, the technologically determined impossibility of a rapid victory caused war to be increasingly dominated by such forces as national morale, social stability, and economic resources. Although it was not widely recognized, least of all by the military, the nature of war had changed. Even if by some masterpiece of operational planning a field army was destroyed, as happened at Sedan and at Tannenberg, a resolute government with untapped resources at its disposal normally could raise other forces and continue to fight. Any war plan based on military considerations alone had become inadequate, and political-military cooperation of the highest order was now essential.

In the past, great commanders like Gustavus Adolphus, Frederick the Great, and Napoleon had coordinated policy and strategy by combining all power in a single hand, but this had become impossible by the middle of the nineteenth century. An exceptional statesman like Bismarck, enjoying the full confidence and support of the ruler, and a soldier of the calibre of the elder Moltke still could arrive, albeit grudgingly, at a common understanding of what was necesssary, desirable, and possible in war. But once these men were gone, strategic planning in Germany, and for that matter in most European states, was dominated by military appreciations alone and no longer was subject to any serious political appraisal and review. It has been suggested that Clausewitz's demand that governments should not ask their soldiers to do the impossible in turn required soldiers to inform their governments of the limitations of military actions. Therefore, so the argument continues, the German general staff would have served its nation better had it acknowledged after 1894 that the situation no longer could be solved by military means and that diplomacy would have to find at least a partial remedy for the mounting strategic dilemma. These suggestions make a valid point, but give too little attention to the prevailing circumstances of the period. Such admissions not only would have conflicted with the basic perceptions of the army's role held by leading general staff officers, but also would have required a major shift in Germany's foreign and domestic policies. Under these circumstances, though increasingly pessimistic about the chances of ultimate success, the German general staff continued to perfect its strategic envelopment concept and eventually launched its desperate gamble in 1914.

12. Delbrück: The Military Historian

GORDON A. CRAIG

H ANS DELBRÜCK, whose active life coincided almost exactly with that of the Second German Empire, was at once military historian, interpreter of military affairs to the German people, and civilian critic of the general staff. In each of these roles his contribution to modern military thought was noteworthy. His *History of the Art of War* was not only a monument to German scholarship but also a mine of valuable information for the military theorists of his day. His commentaries on military affairs, written in the pages of the *Preussische Jahrbücher*, contributed to the military education of the German public and, during the First World War especially, helped them comprehend the underlying strategic problems that confronted the general staff. His criticisms of the High Command, written during the war and in the period following it, did much to stimulate a reappraisal of the type of strategical thinking that had ruled the German army since the days of Moltke.

The military leaders of Germany have always placed great emphasis upon the lessons that can be drawn from military history. This was especially true in the nineteenth century. It had been Clausewitz's ideal to teach war from purely historical examples; and both Moltke and Schlieffen had made the study of military history one of the responsibilities of the general staff. But if history was to serve the soldier, it was necessary that the military record be an accurate one and that past military events be divested of the misconceptions and myths that had grown up around them. Throughout the nineteenth century, thanks to the influence of Leopold von Ranke, German scholars were engaged in the task of clearing away the underbrush of legend that obscured historical truth. But it was not until Delbrück had written his *History of the Art of War* that the new scientific method was applied to the military records of the past, and it is this that constitutes Delbrück's major contribution to military thought.

It was not, however, his sole contribution. In the course of the nineteenth century the basis of government was broadened and in the Western world generally the voice of the people was felt increasingly in every branch of governmental administration. The control of military affairs could no longer remain the prerogative of a small ruling class. In

326

Prussia, the embittered struggle over the military budget in 1862 was an indication that the wishes of the people and their representatives with regard to matters of military administration would have to be given serious consideration in the future. It seemed important therefore for the safety of the state and the maintenance of its military institutions that the general public should be educated to a proper appreciation of military problems. The military publications of the general staff were designed not only for use in the army but also for more general consumption. But the writings of professional soldiers, devoted as they were to accounts of single wars and campaigns, were generally too technical to fulfill the latter function. There was a need for instruction in the elements of military affairs on a popular level, and Delbrück undertook to supply it.[1] In all of his writings, he thought of himself as a kind of military preceptor to the German people. This was most marked during the First World War, when in the pages of the *Preussische Jahrbücher*, he wrote monthly commentaries on the course of the war, explaining on the basis of available materials the strategy of the High Command and of Germany's opponents.

Finally, especially in his later years, Delbrück became a valuable critic of the military institutions and the strategical thinking of his time. His study of the military institutions of the past had shown him, in every age, the intimate relationship of war and politics, and had taught him that military and political strategy must go hand in hand. Clausewitz had already asserted that truth in his statement that "war admittedly has its own grammar, but not its own logic" and in his insistence that war is "the continuation of state policy by other means." But Clausewitz's dictum was too often forgotten by men who misinterpreted Clausewitz as having argued for the freedom of military leadership from political restrictions.[2] Delbrück returned to the Clausewitz doctrine and argued that the conduct of war and the planning of strategy must be conditioned by the aims of state policy and that once strategical thinking becomes inflexible and self-sufficient even the most brilliant tactical successes may lead to political disaster. In Delbrück's writings in the war years, the critic outgrew the historian. When he became convinced that the strategical thinking of the High Command had become antithetical to the political needs of the state, he became one of the foremost advocates of a negotiated peace. After the war, when the Reichstag undertook to investigate the causes of the German collapse in 1918, Delbrück was the

[1] See Hans Delbrück, "Etwas Kriegsgeschichtliches," *Preussische Jahrbücher* 60 (1887), 607.
[2] See the essays on Clausewitz and Moltke, above.

most cogent critic of Ludendorff's strategy, and his criticism grew naturally from the precepts that he had drawn from history.

I

The details of Delbrück's life may be passed over quickly.[3] He himself summed them up tersely in 1920 with the words: "I derived from official and scholarly circles, on my mother's side from a Berlin family; I had war service and was a reserve officer; for five years I lived at the court of Emperor Frederick, when he was Crown Prince. I was a parliamentarian; as editor of the *Preussische Jahrbücher*, I belonged to the press; I became an academic teacher."

Delbrück was born in November 1848 in Bergen. His father was a district judge; his mother, the daughter of a professor of philosophy at the University of Berlin. Among his ancestors were theologians, jurists, and academicians. He received his education at a preparatory school in Greifswald and later at the universities of Heidelberg, Greifswald, and Bonn, showing an early interest in history and attending the lectures of Noorden, Schäfer, and Sybel, all men deeply inspired by the new scientific tendency that was Ranke's contribution to scholarship. As a twenty-two-year-old Bonn student, he fought in the war against France, being invalided out as a result of an attack of typhus. After his recovery, he returned to the university and, in 1873, took his doctoral degree under Sybel with a dissertation on Lambert von Hersfeld, a German chronicler of the eleventh century, whose writings he subjected to a penetrating appraisal that revealed for the first time the critical acumen that was to distinguish all of his historical work.[4]

In 1874, with the assistance of the Badenese minister Franz von Roggenbach, Delbrück was appointed as tutor of Prince Waldemar of Prussia, the son of the crown prince, and his five years in this post not only gave him an insight into the political problems of his time but helped to turn his attention to military affairs. While he was performing his annual duties as a reserve officer, during the spring maneuvers in Württemberg in 1874, he read the *History of the Infantry* by Friedrich Wilhelm Rüstow, a former Prussian officer who had been forced to flee the country to escape punishment for political activity in 1848-1849, had served as

---

[3] Delbrück himself has written brief autobiographical sketches in *Geschichte der Kriegskunst im Rahmen der politischen Geschichte* (Berlin, 1900-20), 1:vii f., and *Krieg und Politik* (Berlin, 1918-19), 3:225ff. See also J. Ziekursch in *Deutsches biographisches Jahrbuch* (1929). An excellent account of Delbrück's life is given in Richard H. Bauer's article on Delbrück in *Some Historians of Modern Europe*, ed. Bernadotte Schmitt (Chicago, 1942), 100-27.

[4] Hans Delbrück, *Über die Glaubwürdigkeit Lamberts von Hersfeld* (Bonn, 1873). See Richard H. Bauer in *Some Historians of Modern Europe*, ed. Schmitt, 101f.

Garibaldi's chief of staff in Sicily in 1860, and was one of the founders of the Swiss general staff system.[5] Delbrück later said that his reading of Rüstow had determined his choice of career, although it was not, in fact, until 1877, when he was given the opportunity to complete the edition of Gneisenau's memoirs and papers that had been begun by Georg Heinrich Pertz, that he began the study of war in a serious way. As he immersed himself in the history of the War of Liberation he was struck by what seemed to be a fundamental difference in the strategical thinking of Napoleon and Gneisenau on the one hand and Archduke Charles, Wellington, and Schwarzenberg on the other. As he carried his investigations further in the biography of Gneisenau with which he followed his editorial task,[6] the difference seemed more marked, and he sensed that nineteenth-century strategy in general was markedly different from that of the previous century. He read Clausewitz for the first time and held long conversations with the officers attached to Frederick's court. While he did so, his interest was heightened and he determined to seek the basic and determining elements of strategy and of military operations.

After the death of Prince Waldemar in 1879, Delbrück embarked upon his academic career, although not without difficulty. His *Habilitation* took place in 1881, but his first lectures in Berlin, on the campaign of 1866, aroused the objections of the university dean because of the contemporary nature of the theme and because Delbrück had not been authorized to teach military history. The young scholar persisted but shifted his attention to more remote periods of history, lecturing first on the history of the art of war from the beginning of the feudal system, and then pushing his researches even further back into the period between the Persian Wars and the decline of Rome. He began a systematic study of the sources in the ancient and medieval periods and published short studies of the Persian Wars, the strategy of Pericles and Cleon, the tactics of the Roman maniple, the military institutions of the early Germans, the wars between the Swiss and the Burgundians, and the strategy of Frederick the Great and Napoleon. Meanwhile, he encouraged his students to make equally detailed studies of special periods. Out of these lectures and monographs grew Delbrück's *History of the Art of War in the Framework of Political History*, the first volume of which appeared in 1900.[7]

[5] On Rüstow, see *Allgemeine Deutsche Biographie*, 30:34ff.; Marcel Herwegh, *Guillaume Rüstow* (Paris, 1935); and Georges Rapp, Viktor Hofer, and Rudolf Jaun, *Der schweizerische Generalstab*, 3 vols. (Basel, 1983), esp. vol. 3.

[6] Hans Delbrück, *Das Leben des Feldmarschalls Grafen Neidhardt von Gneisenau* (Berlin, 1882).

[7] *Geschichte der Kriegskunst im Rahmen der politischen Geschichte* (Berlin, 1900). The work is in seven volumes but only the first four can be considered Delbrück's own. The

Delbrück's preoccupation with a subject that was not highly regarded in academic circles, and his political and publicistic activities (from 1882 to 1885 he was a Free Conservative deputy in the Prussian Landtag and from 1884 to 1890 in the German Reichstag, and he was a member of the editorial board of the *Preussische Jahrbücher* from 1883 to 1890 and sole editor thereafter), which were often highly critical of imperial policy,[8] robbed him of much of the recognition that his scholarship normally would have received. He did not become a professor until 1895, when the official in charge of university matters in the Prussian Kultusministerium, Friedrich Althoff, appointed him to a newly created *ausserordentliche Professur* at the University of Berlin. A year later he became *Ordinarius* when he succeeded Heinrich von Treitschke as Professor of Universal and World History, but he never became *Rektor* of his university and was never elected to the Prussian Academy of Sciences, although these distinctions fell to colleagues who never wrote or did anything comparable to the work for which he is chiefly remembered.[9]

II

From the date of the publication of the first volume, the *History of the Art of War* was the butt of angry critics. Classical scholars resented the way in which Delbrück manhandled Herodotus; medievalists attacked Delbrück's section on the origin of the feudal system; patriotic English scholars were furious at his slighting of the Wars of the Roses. Many of the resultant controversies have been written into the footnotes of the later editions of the work, where the fires of academic wrath still smolder. But in its main outlines the book stands unaffected by the attacks of the specialists and it has received its meed of praise from such widely separated readers as General Wilhelm Groener, Reichswehr minister under the Weimar Republic, and Franz Mehring, the great socialist publicist. The former referred to it as "simply unique";[10] the latter as "the most significant work produced by the historical writing of bourgeois Germany

---

fifth volume (1928) and the sixth (1932) were written by Emil Daniels; a seventh volume (1936) was written by Daniels and Otto Haintz. The first four volumes will be treated here. All citations will be made from the first edition. A second edition of the first two volumes appeared in 1908 and a third edition of the first volume in 1920. None of the changes in these later editions made essential differences in the original work. The first four volumes were also repeated in 1962-64 (Berlin).

[8] See especially Annelise Thimme, *Hans Delbrück als Kritiker der Wilhelminischen Epoche* (Düsseldorf, 1955).

[9] Andreas Hillgruber, "Hans Delbrück," in *Deutsche Historiker*, ed. Hans-Ulrich Wehler (Göttingen, 1972), 4:42.

[10] Wilhelm Groener, "Delbrück und die Kriegswissenschaften," in *Am Webstuhl der Zeit, eine Erinnerungsgabe Hans Delbrück dem Achtzigjährigen ... dargebracht*, ed. Emil Daniels and Paul Rühlmann (Berlin, 1928), 35.

in the new century," a comment repeated with less qualification ("by far the greatest work in this field in view not only of the colossal scope of the materials used but also of the seriousness of the undertaking") by K. Bocarov in his introduction to the first volume of the Soviet Defense Ministry's complete edition of the work in translation.[11]

Of the four volumes written by Delbrück, the first discusses the art of war from the period of the Persian Wars to the high point of Roman warfare under Julius Caesar. The second volume, which is largely concerned with the early Germans, treats also the decline of Roman military institutions, the military organization of the Byzantine Empire, and the origins of the feudal system. The third volume is devoted to the decline and near disappearance of tactics and strategy in the Middle Ages and concludes with an account of the revival of tactical bodies in the Swiss-Burgundian Wars. The fourth volume carries the story of the development of tactical methods and strategic thinking to the age of Napoleon.

In Proust's novel *The Guermantes Way*, a young officer remarks that "in the narrative of a military historian, the smallest facts, the most trivial happenings, are only the outward signs of an idea which has to be analyzed and which often brings to light other ideas, like a palimpsest." These words are a reasonably accurate description of Delbrück's conception of military history. He was interested in general ideas and tendencies rather than in the minutiae that had crowded the pages of earlier military histories. In his introduction to the first volume of his work, he specifically disclaimed any intention of writing a completely comprehensive history of the art of war. Such a work, he pointed out, would necessarily include such things as "details of drill with its commands, the technique of weapons and of the care of horses, and finally the whole subject of naval affairs—matters on which I have either nothing new to say or which I don't for a moment comprehend." The purpose of the history was stated in its title; it was to be a history of the art of war in the framework of political history.[12]

In the introduction to his fourth volume, Delbrück explained this in greater detail. The basic purpose of the work was to establish the connection between the constitution of the state, and tactics and strategy. "The recognition of the interrelationship between tactics, strategy, the constitution of the state and policy reflects upon the relationship [between military history and] world history and has brought to light much that

---

[11] Franz Mehring, "Eine Geschichte der Kriegskunst," *Die Neue Zeit* (Ergänzungsheft, no. 4, October 1908), 2, and *Gesammelte Schriften*, vol. 1 (Berlin, 1959). On the Soviet edition of the *Geschichte der Kriegskunst*, see Otto Haintz, introduction to the first four volumes of the 1962 edition of the Delbrück work, p. 6.

[12] *Geschichte der Kriegskunst*, 1:xi.

until now has been hidden in darkness or left without recognition. This work has been written not for the sake of the art of war, but for the sake of world history. If military men read it and are stimulated by it, I am pleased and regard that as an honor; but it was written for friends of history by a historian."[13]

At the same time, however, Delbrück realized that, before any general conclusions could be drawn from the wars of the past, the historian must determine as accurately as possible how those wars had been fought. It was precisely because he was intent on finding general ideas that would be of interest to other historians that Delbrück was forced to grapple with the "trivial happenings," "the smallest facts" of past campaigns; and, despite his own disclaimer, his reappraisal of those facts was of great value not to historians alone but to soldiers as well.

The "facts" were to be found in the great volume of source material that had been handed down by the past. But many of the sources of military history were obviously unreliable and were no better than "washroom prattle and adjutants' gossip."[14] How was the modern historian to check these ancient records?

Delbrück believed that this could be done in several ways. Provided the historian knew the terrain in which past battles were fought, he could use all the resources of modern geographical science to check the reports that were handed down. Provided he knew the type of weapons and equipment used, he could reconstruct the tactics of the battle in a logical manner, since the laws of tactics for every kind of weapon could be ascertained. A study of modern warfare would supply the historian with further tools, for in modern campaigns he could judge the marching powers of the average soldier, the weight-carrying capacity of the average horse, the maneuverability of large masses of men. Finally, it was often possible to discover campaigns or battles, for which reliable reports existed, in which the conditions of earlier battles were reproduced almost exactly. Both the battles of the Swiss-Burgundian Wars, for which accurate records exist, and the battle of Marathon, for which Herodotus was the only source, were fought between mounted knights and bowmen on the one side and foot soldiers armed with weapons for hand-to-hand fighting on the other; in both cases, the foot soldiers were victorious. It should be possible, therefore, to draw conclusions from the battles of Granson, Murten, and Nancy that could be applied to the battle of

[13] Ibid., 4:preface.
[14] Ibid., 1:377.

Marathon.[15] The combination of all of these methods, Delbrück called *Sachkritik*.[16]

Only a few applications of the *Sachkritik* need be mentioned. Delbrück's most startling results were attained by his investigations of the numbers of troops engaged in the wars of the past. According to Herodotus, the Persian army that Xerxes, son of Darius, led against Greece in 480 B.C. numbered 2,641,610 fighting men and at least as many crew members, servants, and camp followers.[17] Delbrück pointed out that this could not be considered reliable. "According to the German order of march, an army corps, that is 30,000 men, occupies about three miles, without the baggage trains. The marching column of the Persians would therefore have been 420 miles long and as the first troops were arriving before Thermopylae the last would have just marched out of Susa on the other side of the Tigris."[18]

Even if this awkward fact could be explained away, none of the fields on which battles were fought was big enough to hold armies as large as those in Herodotus' accounts. The plain of Marathon, for instance, "is so small that some fifty years ago a Prussian staff officer who visited it wrote with some astonishment that a Prussian brigade would scarcely have room enough there for its exercises."[19] On the basis of modern studies of the population of ancient Greece, Delbrück estimated the size of the Greek army that faced the Persians under Datis at Marathon in 490 B.C. at about 12,000. Since Herodotus claimed that it was outnumbered (and, although not giving the size of the opposing army, estimated Persian casualties at 6,400),[20] this would mean that total troops engaged far exceeded the limits set by the Prussian observer.

Nor were these the only reasons for believing that Herodotus tended always to inflate Persian troop strength. The Greek army at Marathon was a citizen army trained to fight in a rude phalanx but incapable of tactical maneuver. The Persian army was a professional army, and the bravery of its soldiers was admitted even in the Greek account. "If both things were true, the size (of the Persian army) as well as its military bravery, then the ever-repeated victory of the Greeks would remain inexplicable. Only one of the two things can be true; hence, it is clear that

---

[15] Delbrück used this last method in his first account of the Persian Wars, *Die Perserkriege und die Burgunderkriege: Zwei kombinierte kriegsgeschichtliche Studien* (Berlin, 1887).
[16] *Geschichte der Kriegskunst*, 1:introduction.
[17] Herodotus, 7:184-87.
[18] *Geschichte der Kriegskunst*, 1:10.
[19] Hans Delbrück, *Numbers in History: Two Lectures Delivered before the University of London* (London, 1913), 24.
[20] Herodotus, 6:109-16.

the advantage of the Persians is to be sought not in numbers but in quality."[21] Delbrück concludes that, far from having the mass army described by Herodotus, the Persians were actually inferior in numbers to the Greeks throughout the Persian Wars.

The account of Herodotus had long been suspect, and Delbrück's criticism was by no means wholly original. But his real contribution lay in the fact that he applied the same systematic methods to the numerical records of every war from the Persian Wars to those of Napoleon. Thus, in his discussion of Caesar's campaigns in Gaul, he clearly demonstrated that Caesar's estimates of the forces pitted against him were, for political reasons, grossly exaggerated. According to Caesar, the Helvetians, in their great trek, numbered 368,000 persons and carried three months' provisions with them. To Delbrück the numerical estimate smacked of the fabulous; but it was Caesar's remarks on the Helvetian food supply that enabled him to prove it so. He pointed out that some 8,500 wagons would be required to carry such provisions and, in the condition of roads in Caesar's time, it would be quite impossible for such a column to move.[22] Again, in his discussion of the invasion of Europe by the Huns, Delbrück effectively disposed of the belief that Attila had an army of 700,000 men, by describing the difficulties that Moltke experienced in maneuvering an army of 500,000 men in the campaign of 1870. "To direct such a mass unitedly is, even with railroads, roads, telegraphs and a general staff an exceedingly difficult task. . . . How could Attila have led 700,000 men from Germany over the Rhine into France to the Plain of Chalons, if Moltke moved 500,000 with such difficulty over the same road? The one number acts as a check on the other."[23]

Delbrück's investigations of numbers have more than a mere antiquarian interest. At a time when the German army was being taught to seek lessons in history, the destroyer of myths helped it avoid the drawing of false conclusions. In war and the study of war, numbers were of the highest importance.[24] Delbrück himself pointed out that "a movement that a troop of 1,000 men executes without difficulty is a hard task for 10,000 men, a work of art for 50,000, an impossibility for 100,000."[25] No lessons can be drawn from past campaigns unless an accurate statement of the numbers involved is available.

Sachkritik had other uses. By means of it, Delbrück was able to

---

[21] *Geschichte der Kriegskunst,* 1:39.

[22] Ibid., 1:427.

[23] Delbrück, *Numbers in History,* 18.

[24] General Groener made explicit acknowledgment of Delbrück's contribution. See "Delbrück und die Kriegswissenschaften," 38.

[25] *Geschichte der Kriegskunst,* 1:7.

reconstruct the details of single battles in a logical manner, and his success in doing so made a profound impression upon the historical section of the German general staff. General Groener has attested to the value of Delbrück's investigation of the origins of that oblique battle order that made flanking possible;[26] and it is well known that his scientific description of the encircling movement at Cannae strongly influenced the theories of Count Schlieffen.[27] But it is his account of the battle of Marathon that is perhaps the best example of the skill with which Delbrück reconstructed the details of past battles, the more so because it most clearly illustrates his belief that "if one knows the armament and the manner of fighting of the contending armies, then the terrain is such an important and eloquent authority for the character of a battle, that one may dare, provided there is no doubt as to the outcome, to reconstruct its course in general outline."[28]

The Greek army at Marathon was composed of heavily armed foot soldiers, formed in the primitive phalanx, the maneuverability of which was restricted to slow forward movement. It was opposed by an army inferior in numbers but made up of highly trained bowmen and cavalry. Herodotus had written that the Greeks had won the battle by charging across the plain of Marathon some 5,480 feet and crushing the center of the Persian line. Delbrück pointed out that this was a physical impossibility. According to the modern German drill book, soldiers with full pack could be expected to run for only two minutes, some 1,080 to 1,150 feet. The Athenians were no more lightly armed than the modern German soldier and they suffered from two additional disadvantages. They were not professional soldiers, but civilians, and many of them exceeded the age limit required in modern armies. Moreover, the phalanx was a closely massed body of men that made quick movement of any kind impossible. An attempted charge over such a distance would have reduced the phalanx to a disorganized mob that would have been cut down by the Persian professionals without difficulty.[29]

---

[26] Groener, "Delbrück und die Kriegswissenschaften," 38. The oblique battle order, first used by the Theban Epaminondas, bears a striking resemblance to that used by Frederick the Great at Leuthen in 1757. On Epaminondas, see *Geschichte der Kriegskunst*, 1:130-35.

[27] *Geschichte der Kriegskunst*, 1:281-302. Graf Schlieffen, *Cannae* (Berlin, 1925), 3. See also the essays on Moltke, above.

[28] *Geschichte der Kriegskunst*, 2:80. Delbrück used the method not only for the battle of Marathon but also in his reconstruction of the battle of the Teutoburger Wald.

[29] Delbrück's argument becomes weaker if one assumes that the Greeks would begin their charge only when they came within arrow range, but Herodotus says explicitly (6:115) that they "advanced at a run towards the enemy, not less than a mile away." Ulrich von Wilamowitz defended Herodotus by arguing that the goddess Artemis gave the Greeks sufficient strength to make the charge and criticized the kind of scholarship that under-

The tactics described by Herodotus were obviously impossible, the more so because the Greek phalanx was weak on the flanks and, in any encounter on an open field, could have been surrounded by Persian cavalry. It seemed obvious to Delbrück that the battle was not fought on the plain of Marathon proper but in a small valley to the southeast where the Greeks were protected by mountains and forest from any flanking movement. The fact that Herodotus speaks of the opposing armies delaying the engagement for days shows that Miltiades, the Athenian commander, had chosen a strong position; given the tactical form of the Greek army, the position in the Brana Valley was the only one possible. Moreover, that position dominated the only road to Athens. To reach the city, the Persians were forced to dispose of Miltiades' army, or give up the whole campaign, and they chose the former alternative. The only logical explanation of the battle, then, is that the Persians, despite their numerical inferiority and inability to use flanking tactics, made the initial attack; and Miltiades, shifting at the crucial moment from the defensive to the offensive, crushed the Persian center and swept the field.[30]

To the casual reader, the *History of the Art of War*, like many a work before it, is a mere collection of such battle pieces. But the care with which Delbrück reconstructed battles was necessary to his main purpose. He felt that by the study of key battles the student could acquire a picture of the tactics of an age and from that could proceed to the investigation of broader problems.[31] For the key battles are important not only as typical manifestations of their age but as mileposts in the progressive development of military science. In a sense, Delbrück, like Proust's young officer, believed that past battles were "the literature, the learning, the etymology, the aristocracy of the battles of today." By reconstructing single battles he sought continuity in military history, and thus his *Sachkritik* enabled him to develop the three major themes which give his work a meaning and a unity found in no previous book on the subject: namely, the evolution of tactical forms from the Persians to Napoleon, the interrelationship of war and politics throughout history, and the division of all strategy into two basic forms.

Delbrück's description of the evolution of tactical bodies has been called one of his most significant contributions to military thought.[32]

---

estimated the importance of divine, and other forms of, inspiration. He was supported by J. Kromayer, with whom Delbrück argued the point in the *Historische Zeitschrift* (95:1ff., 514f.) and the *Preussische Jahrbücher* (121:158f.).

[30] *Geschichte der Kriegskunst*, 1:41-59.

[31] Ibid., 1:417.

[32] F. J. Schmidt, Konrad Molinski, and Siegfried Mette, *Hans Delbrück: Der Historiker und Politiker* (Berlin, 1928), 96. Eugen von Frauenholz, *Entwicklungsgeschichte des deutschen Heerwesens* (Munich, 1940), 2:vii.

Convinced by his researches that the military supremacy of the Romans was the direct result of the flexibility and articulated movement that resulted from the tactical organization of their forces, he went on to argue that it was the gradual evolution of the primitive Greek phalanx into the skillfully coordinated tactical formations used by the Romans that comprised "the essential meaning of the ancient art of war,"[33] and that the revival of such formations in the Swiss-Burgundian Wars of the fifteenth century and their improvement and perfection in the period that ended with Napoleon's mastery of Europe was the salient development of modern military history.

The turning point in the history of ancient warfare was the battle of Cannae,[34] where the Carthaginians under Hannibal overwhelmed the Romans in the most perfect tactical battle ever fought. How were the Romans able to recover from that disaster, to defeat the Carthaginians and eventually to exercise military supremacy over the whole of the ancient world? The answer is to be found in the evolution of the phalanx. At Cannae the Roman infantry was ordered as the Greeks had been at Marathon, and this delivered them into Hannibal's arms, for their exposed flanks and the inability of their rear to maneuver independently of the mass of the army made it impossible for them to prevent the encircling tactics employed by the Carthaginian cavalry. But in the years following Cannae, striking changes were introduced into the Roman battle form. "The Romans first articulated the phalanx, then divided it into columns [*Treffen*] and finally split it up into a great number of small tactical bodies that were capable, now of closing together in a compact impenetrable union, now of changing the pattern with consummate flexibility, of separating one from the other and of turning in this or that direction."[35] To modern students of warfare this development seems so natural as to be hardly worthy of notice. To accomplish it, however, was extremely difficult and only the Romans, of all the ancient peoples, succeeded. In their case it was made possible only by a hundred years of experimentation—in the course of which the army changed from a civilian to a professional army—and by the emphasis upon military discipline that characterized the Roman system.[36]

The Romans conquered the world, then, not because their troops "were braver than all their opponents, but because, thanks to their dis-

---

[33] *Geschichte der Kriegskunst*, 2:43.
[34] Ibid., 1:330ff.
[35] Ibid., 1:380.
[36] Ibid., 1:381. See also 1:253. "The meaning and power of discipline was first fully recognized and realized by the Romans."

cipline, they had stronger tactical bodies."[37] The only people who successfully avoided conquest by the Romans were the Germans, and their resistance was made possible by a natural discipline inherent in their political institutions, and by the fact that the German fighting column, the *Gevierthaufe*, was a tactical formation of great effectiveness.[38] Indeed, in the course of their wars with the Romans, the Germans learned to imitate the articulation of the Roman legion, maneuvering their *Gevierthaufen* independently or in union as the occasion required.[39]

With the decline of the Roman state and the barbarization of the Empire, the tactical progress that had been made since the days of Miltiades came to an end. The political disorders of the age following the reign of the Severi weakened the discipline of the Roman army, and gradually undermined the excellence of its tactical forms.[40] At the same time, as large numbers of barbarians were admitted into the ranks, it was impossible to cling to the highly integrated battle order that had been devised over the course of centuries. History had shown that infantry was superior to cavalry only if the foot soldiers were organized in strong tactical bodies. Now, with the decline of the state and the consequent degeneration of tactics, there was a growing tendency, in the new barbarian empires of the west and in Justinian's army as well, to replace infantry with heavily armed mounted soldiers.[41] As that tendency gained the upper hand, the days when battles were decided by infantry tactics died away and Europe entered a long period in which military history was dominated by the figure of the armed knight.[42]

Delbrück has been accused of maintaining that the development of military science stops with the decline of Rome and starts again with the Renaissance,[43] and the accusation is justified. The essential element in all warfare from the days of Charlemagne to the emergence of the Swiss infantry in the Burgundian Wars was the feudal army. This, in Delbrück's opinion, was no tactical body. It depended upon the fighting quality of the single warrior; there was no discipline, no unity of command, no effective differentiation of arms. In this whole period, no tactical progress was made, and Delbrück seems inclined to agree with Mark Twain's Connecticut Yankee, that "when you come to figure up results, you can't tell one fight from another, nor who whipped." It is true that at Crécy,

---

[37] Ibid., 2:43.
[38] Ibid., 2:45ff.
[39] Ibid., 2:52f.
[40] Ibid., 2:205ff. This chapter, entitled "Niedergang und Auflösung des römischen Kriegswesens," is the key chapter of the second volume.
[41] Ibid., 2:424ff.
[42] Ibid., 2:433.
[43] T. F. Tout in *English Historical Review* 22 (1907), 344-48.

the English knights dismounted and fought a defensive battle on foot and that, at Agincourt, dismounted knights actually took the offensive; but these were mere episodes and cannot be considered as forecasts of the development of modern infantry.[44]

It was among the Swiss in the fifteenth century that the independent infantry was reborn. "With the battles of Laupen and Sempach, Granson, Murten and Nancy we have again a foot soldiery comparable to the phalanx and the legions."[45] The Swiss pikemen formed themselves in bodies similar to the German *Gevierthaufe*;[46] and, in the course of their wars against the Burgundians, they perfected the articulated tactics used by the Roman legions. At Sempach, for instance, the Swiss infantry was divided into two bodies, one holding a defensive position against the mounted enemy, the other delivering a decisive blow on the enemy's flank.[47]

The revival of tactical bodies was a military revolution comparable to that which followed Cannae. It was this revival, rather than the introduction of firearms, that brought feudal warfare to an end. At Murten, Granson, and Nancy the new weapons were employed by the knights, but had no effect upon the outcome of the battle.[48] With the restoration of the tactical body of infantry as the decisive one in warfare, the mounted soldiers became a mere cavalry, a highly useful but supplementary part of the army. In his fourth volume, Delbrück discussed this development and the evolution of the modern infantry to the age of the standing army and concluded with an account of the revolution in tactics made possible by the French Revolution.[49]

The attention that Delbrück pays to the emergence of tactical bodies serves not only to give a sense of continuity to his military history but also to illustrate the theme that he considered basic to his book, namely, the interrelationship of politics and war. In every period of history, he pointed out, the development of politics and the evolution of tactics were closely related. "The Hopliten-Phalanx developed in quite a different manner under the Macedonian kings than it did in the aristocratic Roman *Beamten-Republik*, and the tactics of the cohort were developed only in relationship with constitutional change. Again, according to their nature, the German *hunderts* fought quite differently from the Roman cohorts."[50]

---

[44] *Geschichte der Kriegskunst*, 3:483. For a penetrating criticism of Delbrück's discussion of medieval warfare, see Tout, cited in note 43.

[45] *Geschichte der Kriegskunst*, 3:661. See essay on Machiavelli, above.

[46] Ibid., 3:609ff.

[47] Ibid., 3:594.

[48] Ibid., 4:55.

[49] See the essay on Frederick the Great, Guibert, and Bülow, above.

[50] *Geschichte der Kriegskunst*, 2:424.

The Roman army at Cannae, for example, was defeated because of the weakness of its tactics. But contributory to that weakness was the fact that the army was composed of untrained civilians rather than professional soldiers and the constitution of the state required that the high command alternate between the two consuls.[51] In the years following Cannae the necessity of a unified command was generally recognized. After various political experiments were tried, P. C. Scipio was in the year 211 B.C. made general in chief of the Roman armies in Africa and assured of continued tenure for the duration of the war. The appointment was in direct violation of the state constitution and it marked the beginning of the decline of republican institutions. The interrelationship of politics and warfare is in this case apparent. "The importance of the Second Punic War in world history," Delbrück writes, "is that Rome effected an internal transformation that increased her military potentiality enormously,"[52] but at the same time changed the whole character of the state.

Just as the political element was predominant in the perfection of Roman tactics, so also the breakdown of tactical forms can be explained only by a careful study of the political institutions of the later Empire. The political and economic disorders of the third century had a direct effect upon Roman military institutions. "Permanent civil war destroyed the cement that till now had held the strong walls of the Roman army together, the discipline that constituted the military worth of the legions."[53]

In no part of the *History of the Art of War* does Delbrück include a general discussion of the relationship of politics and war. But, as he moves from one historical epoch to another, he fits the purely military into its general background, illustrating the close connection of political and military institutions and showing how changes in one sphere led of necessity to corresponding reactions in the other. He shows that the German *Gevierthaufe* was the military expression of the village organization of the German tribes and demonstrated the way in which the dissolution of German communal life led to the disappearance of the *Gevierthaufe* as a tactical body.[54] He shows how the victories of the Swiss in the fifteenth century were made possible by the fusion of the democratic and aristocratic elements in the various cantons, and the union of the urban nobility with the peasant masses.[55] And in the period of the French

---

[51] Ibid., 1:305.
[52] Ibid., 1:333.
[53] Ibid., 2:209.
[54] Ibid., 2:25-38, 424ff.
[55] Ibid., 3:614f.

340

Revolution he describes the way in which the political factor, in this case "the new idea of defending the fatherland, inspired the mass [of the soldiers] with such an improved will, that new tactics could be developed."[56]

The most striking of all of Delbrück's military theories was that which held that all military strategy can be divided into two basic forms. This theory, formulated long before the publication of the *History of the Art of War*, is conveniently summarized in the first and fourth volumes of that work.[57]

The great majority of military thinkers in Delbrück's day believed the aim of war to be the annihilation of the enemy's forces and that, consequently, the battle that accomplishes this is the end of all strategy. Often they selectively cited Clausewitz to support their claim. Delbrück's first researches in military history convinced him that this type of strategical thinking had not always been generally accepted; and that there were long periods in history in which a completely different strategy ruled the field. He discovered, moreover, that Clausewitz himself had asserted the existence throughout history of more than one strategical system, suggesting in a note written in 1827 that there were two sharply distinct methods of conducting war: one which was bent solely on the annihilation of the enemy; the other, a limited warfare, in which such annihilation was impossible, either because the political aims or political tensions involved in the war were small or because the military means were inadequate to accomplish annihilation.[58]

Clausewitz began to revise *On War*, but died before he could complete his intended comprehensive analysis of the two forms. Delbrück determined to accept the distinction and expound the principles inherent in each. The first form of warfare he named *Niederwerfungsstrategie* (the strategy of annihilation). Its sole aim was the decisive battle, and the commanding general was called upon only to estimate the possibility of fighting such a battle in a given situation.

The second type of strategy Delbrück called variously *Ermattungsstrategie* (the strategy of exhaustion) and two-pole strategy. It was distinguished from the strategy of annihilation by the fact "that the *Niederwerfungsstrategie* has only one pole, the battle, whereas the *Ermattungsstrategie* has two poles, battle and maneuver, between which the decisions of the general move." In *Ermattungsstrategie*, the battle is merely one of several equally effective means of attaining the political ends of the war and is essentially no more important than the occupation

[56] Ibid., 4:474.
[57] Ibid., 1:100ff.; 4:333-63, 426-44.
[58] See the essay on Clausewitz, above.

of territory, the destruction of crops or commerce, and the blockade. This second form of strategy is neither a mere variation of the first nor an inferior form. In certain periods of history, because of political factors or the smallness of armies, it has been the only form of strategy that could be employed. The task it imposes on the commander is quite as difficult as that required of the exponent of the strategy of annihilation. With limited resources at his disposal, the *Ermattungsstratege* must decide which of several means of conducting war will best suit his purpose, when to fight and when to maneuver, when to obey the law of "daring" and when to obey that of "economy of forces." "The decision is therefore a subjective one, the more so because at no time are all circumstances and conditions, especially what is going on in the enemy camp, known completely and authoritatively. After a careful consideration of all circumstances—the aim of the war, the combat forces, the political repercussions, the individuality of the enemy commander, and of the government and people of the enemy, as well as his own—the general must decide whether a battle is advisable or not. He can reach the conclusion that any greater actions must be avoided at all cost; he can also determine to seek [battle] on every occasion so that there is no essential difference between his conduct and that of one-pole strategy."[59]

Among the great commanders of the past who had been strategists of annihilation were Alexander, Caesar, and Napoleon. But equally great generals had been exponents of *Ermattungsstrategie*. Among them, Delbrück listed Pericles, Belisarius, Wallenstein, Gustavus Adolphus, and Frederick the Great. The inclusion of the last name brought down upon the historian a flood of angry criticism. The most vocal of his critics were the historians of the general staff who, convinced that the strategy of annihilation was the only correct strategy, insisted that Frederick was a precursor of Napoleon. Delbrück answered that to hold this view was to do Frederick a grave disservice. If Frederick was a strategist of annihilation, how was one to explain away the fact that in 1741, with 60,000 men under his command, he refused to attack an already beaten army of only 25,000, or that, in 1745, after his great victory at Hohenfriedberg, he preferred to resort again to a war of maneuver?[60] If the principles of *Niederwerfungsstrategie* were to be considered the sole criteria in judging the qualities of a general, Frederick would cut a very poor figure.[61] Yet

[59] Hans Delbrück, *Die Strategie des Perikles erläutert durch die Strategie Friedrichs des Grossen* (Berlin, 1890), 27-28. This work is Delbrück's most systematic exposition of the two forms of strategy.

[60] *Preussische Jahrbücher*, 115 (1904), 348f.

[61] In the *Strategie des Perikles*, Delbrück wrote a parody that showed that the application of such criteria to Frederick's campaigns would prove him a third-rate general. For this Delbrück was accused in the Prussian Landtag of maligning a national hero.

Frederick's greatness lay in the fact that although he realized that his resources were not great enough to enable him to seek battle on every occasion he was nevertheless able to make effective use of other strategical principles in order to win his wars.

Delbrück's arguments did not convince his critics. Both Colmar von der Goltz and Friedrich von Bernhardi entered the lists against him, and a paper warfare ensued that lasted for over twenty years.[62] Delbrück, who loved controversy, was indefatigable in answering refutations of his theory. But his concept of *Ermattungsstrategie* was rejected by an officer corps trained in the tradition of Napoleon and Moltke and convinced of the feasibility of the short, decisive war.

Yet the military critics completely missed the deeper significance of Delbrück's strategic theory. History showed that there could be no single theory of strategy, correct for every age. Like all phases of warfare, strategy was intimately connected with politics, with the life and the strength of the state. In the Peloponnesian War, the political weakness of Athens in comparison with that of the League that faced it determined the kind of strategy which Pericles followed. Had he attempted to follow the principles of *Niederwerfungsstrategie*, as Cleon did later, disaster would have followed automatically.[63] The strategy of Belisarius' wars in Italy was determined by the uneasy political relations between the Byzantine Empire and the Persians. "Here as always it was politics that determined the administration of the war and that prescribed to strategy its course."[64] Again, "the strategy of the Thirty Years' War was determined by the extremely complicated, repeatedly changing political relationships," and generals like Gustavus Adolphus, whose personal bravery and inclination toward battle were unquestioned, were nevertheless compelled to make limited war.[65] It was not the battles won by Frederick the Great that made him a great general, but rather his political acumen and the conformity of his strategy with political reality. No strategic

---

[62] A full account of the controversy, with bibliography, appears in *Geschichte der Kriegskunst*, 4:439-44. See also Friedrich von Bernhardi, *Denkwürdigkeiten aus meinem Leben* (Berlin, 1927), 126, 133, 143. The most thorough and judicious criticism of Delbrück's strategical theory is that of Otto Hintze, "Delbrück, Clausewitz und die Strategie Friedrichs des Grossen," *Forschungen zur Brandenburgischen und Preussischen Geschichte* 33 (1920), 131-77. Hintze objects to the sharp distinction that Delbrück draws between the strategy of Frederick's age and that of Napoleon and insists that Frederick was at once a *Niederwerfung* and an *Ermattung*-strategist. He also questions Delbrück's interpretation of Clausewitz's intentions, as does H. Rosinski in *Historische Zeitschrift* 151 (1938). See Delbrück's answer to Hintze, *Forschungen zur Brandenburgischen und Preussischen Geschichte* 33 (1920), 412-17.

[63] *Geschichte der Kriegskunst*, 1:101f.

[64] Ibid., 2:394.

[65] Ibid., 4:341.

system can become self-sufficient; once an attempt is made to make it so, to divorce it from its political context, the strategist becomes a menace to the state.

The transition from dynastic to national war, the victories of 1864, 1866, and 1870, the immense increase in the war potential of the nation seemed to prove that *Niederwerfungsstrategie* was the natural form of war for the modern age. As late as 1890, Delbrück himself, despite his insistence on the relativity of strategy, seems to have believed that this was true.[66] Yet in the last years of the nineteenth century, the mass army of the 1860s was being transformed to the *Millionenheer* which fought in the First World War. Might not that transformation make impossible the application of the strategy of annihilation and herald a return to the principles of Pericles and Frederick? Was not the state in grave danger as long as the general staff refused to admit the existence of alternate systems of strategy? These questions, implicit in all of Delbrück's military writings, were constantly on his lips as Germany entered the First World War.

III

Since Delbrück was Germany's leading civilian expert on military affairs, his writings in the war years, 1914-1918, are of considerable interest. As a military commentator, his sources of information were in no way superior to those of other members of the newspaper and periodical press. Like them he was forced to rely on the communiqués issued by the general staff, the stories that appeared in the daily press, and reports from neutral countries. If his accounts of the war were distinguished by a breadth of vision and understanding not usually found in the lucubrations of civilian commentators, it was due to his technical knowledge of modern war and the sense of perspective he had gained from his study of history. In his monthly commentaries in the *Preussische Jahrbücher* one can find a further exposition of the principles delineated in his historical works and especially of his theory of strategy and his emphasis upon the interrelationship of war and politics.[67]

In accordance with the Schlieffen strategy, the German army swept into Belgium in 1914 with the purpose of crushing French resistance in

---

[66] *Strategie des Perikles*, ch. 1.

[67] The articles that Delbrück wrote in the *Preussische Jahrbücher* are collected in the three-volume work called *Krieg und Politik* (Berlin, 1918-19). To the articles as they originally appeared Delbrück has added occasional explanatory notes and a highly interesting summary statement. The best article on Delbrück's war writings is that by General Ernst Buchfinck, "Delbrücks Lehre, das Heer und der Weltkrieg," in *Am Webstuhl der Zeit*, ed. Schmitt, 41-49. See also Martin Hobohm, "Delbrück, Clausewitz und die Kritik des Weltkrieges," *Preussische Jahrbücher*, 181 (1920), 203-32.

short order and then bringing the full weight of its power against Russia. This was *Niederwerfungsstrategie* in its ultimate form, and Delbrück himself, in the first month of the war, felt that it was justified. Like most of his fellows, he had little fear of effective French opposition. The instability of French politics could not but have a deleterious effect upon France's military institutions. "It is impossible that an army that has had forty-two war ministers in forty-three years will be capable of an effectively functioning organization."[68] Nor did he feel that England was capable of continued resistance. Its past political development, he believed, would make it impossible for it to raise more than a token force. England had always relied on small professional armies; the institution of universal conscription would be psychologically and politically impossible. "Every people is the child of its history, its past, and can no more break away from it than a man can separate himself from his youth."[69]

When the first great German drive fell short of its goal, however, and the long period of trench warfare set in, Delbrück sensed a strategical revolution of the first importance. As the stalemate in the West continued, and especially after the failure of the Verdun offensive, he became increasingly convinced that the strategical thinking of the High Command would have to be modified. In the West at least, defensive warfare was the order of the day, a fact "the more significant since, before the war, the preeminence of the offensive was always proclaimed and expounded with quite exceptional partiality in the theory of strategy fostered in Germany."[70] Now, it was apparent that conditions on the western front approximated those of the age of *Ermattungsstrategie*. "Although this war has already brought us much that is new, nevertheless it is possible to find in it certain historical analogies: for example, the Frederician strategy with its impregnable positions, its increasingly strengthened artillery, its field fortifications, its infrequent tactical decisions and its consequent long withdrawals presents unmistakable similarities with today's war of position and exhaustion (*Stellungs- und Ermattungskrieg*)."[71] In the West, reliance upon the decisive battle was no longer possible. Germany would have to find other means of imposing its will upon the enemy.

By December 1916 Delbrück was pointing out that "however favorable our military position is, the continuation of the war will scarcely

---

[68] *Krieg und Politik*, 1:35.

[69] Delbrück's views on England's weakness as a military power were most clearly developed in an article in April 1916. See *Krieg und Politik*, 1:243ff.

[70] Ibid., 2:242.

[71] Ibid., 2:164. See also 2:17.

bring us so far that we can simply dictate the peace."[72] A complete and crushing victory of German arms was unlikely, if not impossible. That did not mean, however, that Germany could not "win the war." Its inner position not only separated its opponents but enabled it to retain the initiative. Its strength was so formidable that it should not be difficult to convince its opponents that Germany could not be defeated. While a firm defensive in the West was sapping the will of Allied troops, the High Command would be well advised to throw its strongest forces against the weakest links in the Allied coalition—against Russia and Italy. A concentrated offensive against Russia would complete the demoralization of the armies of the czar and might very well precipitate a revolution in St. Petersburg. A successful Austro-German offensive against Italy would not only have a tremendous moral effect in England and France but would threaten France's communications with North Africa.[73]

In Delbrück's opinion, then, Germany's strategy must be directed toward the destruction of the enemy coalition and the consequent isolation of England and France. In this connection, it was equally important that no measures be adopted that might bring new allies to the Western powers. Delbrück was always firmly opposed to the submarine campaign, which he rightly feared would bring the United States into the war.[74]

But in the last analysis, if the war was to be won by Germany, the government would have to show a clear comprehension of the political realities implicit in the conflict. Since the war in the West had become an *Ermattungskrieg*, the political aspect of the conflict had increased in importance. "Politics is the ruling and limiting factor; military operations is only one of its means."[75] A political strategy must be devised to weaken the will of the people of France and England.

In the political field, Delbrück had felt from the beginning of the war that Germany suffered from a very real strategical weakness. "Because of our narrow policy of Germanization in the Polish and Danish districts of Prussia, we have given ourselves the reputation in the world of being not the protectors but the oppressors of small nationalities."[76] If this reputation were confirmed in the course of the war, it would give moral encouragement to Germany's enemies and would jeopardize the hope of ultimate victory. Turning to history, Delbrück argued that the example of Napoleon should serve as a warning to Germany's political leaders. The emperor's most overwhelming victories had served only to strengthen the will of his opponents and to pave the way for his ultimate

[72] Ibid., 2:97.
[73] Buchfinck, "Delbrücks Lehre, das Heer und der Weltkrieg," 48.
[74] *Krieg und Politik*, 1:90, 227ff., 261.
[75] Ibid., 2:95.
[76] Ibid., 1:3f.

defeat. "May God forbid that Germany enter upon the path of Napoleonic policy. . . . Europe stands united in this one conviction: it will never submit to a hegemony enforced upon it by a single state."[77]

Delbrück believed that the invasion of Belgium had been a strategical necessity;[78] but it was nonetheless an unfortunate move, for it seemed to confirm the suspicion that Germany was bent upon the subjugation and annexation of small states. From September 1914 until the end of the war, Delbrück continued to insist that the German government must issue a categorical disclaimer of any intention of annexing Belgium at the conclusion of hostilities. England, he argued, would never make peace as long as there was danger of German retention of the Flanders coast. The first step in weakening the resistance of Western powers was to state clearly that Germany had no territorial desires in the West and that its war aims would "prejudice in no way the freedom and honor of other peoples."[79]

Perhaps the best way to convince the Western powers that Germany was not seeking world domination was to make it apparent that Germany had no objection to a negotiated peace. Delbrück had favored such a peace ever since the successful Allied counteroffensive on the Marne in September 1914. He firmly believed that the war had been caused by Russian aggression and saw no reason why England and France should continue to fight the one power that was "guarding Europe and Asia from the domination of *Moskowitertum*."[80] As the war was prolonged, he was strengthened in his conviction that a sincere willingness to negotiate would win for Germany a victory that arms alone would be powerless to effect; and after the entrance of the United States into the war he openly predicted defeat unless Germany's leaders used that weapon. He was, therefore, enthusiastic about the passage by the Reichstag of the Peace Resolution of July 1917,[81] for he felt that it would do

[77] See ibid., 1:59, and the article entitled "Das Beispiel Napoleons," in ibid., 2:122ff.
[78] *Krieg und Politik*, 1:33.
[79] Ibid., 2:97.
[80] Ibid., 1:18.
[81] The Peace Resolution, passed by the Reichstag by 212 votes to 126, stated in part: "The Reichstag strives for a peace of understanding and a lasting reconciliation among peoples. Violations of territory and political, economic and financial persecutions are incompatible with such a peace. The Reichstag rejects every scheme which has for its purpose the imposition of economic barriers or the perpetuation of national hatreds after the war. The freedom of the seas must be secured. Economic peace alone will prepare the ground for the friendly association of the peoples. The Reichstag will actively promote the creation of international organizations of justice. But so long as the enemy governments dissociate themselves from such a peace, so long as they threaten Germany and her allies with conquest and domination, then so long will the German people stand united and unshaken, and fight till their right and the right of their allies to live and grow is made secure. United thus, the German people is unconquerable."

more to weaken the resistance of the Western powers than any possible new offensive upon the western front.

Delbrück never for a moment wavered in his belief that the German army was the best in the world, but he saw that that best was not good enough. Throughout 1917 he hammered away at one constant theme: "We must look the facts in the face—that we have in a sense the whole world leagued against us—and we must not conceal from ourselves the fact that, if we try to penetrate to the basic reasons for this world coalition, we will ever and again stumble over the motive of fear of German world hegemony. . . . Fear of German despotism is one of the weightiest facts with which we have to reckon, one of the strongest factors in the enemy's power."[82] Until that fear was overcome, the war would continue. It could be overcome only by a political strategy based upon a disclaimer of territorial ambitions in the West and a willingness to negotiate.

Just as the conditions of the present war were, to Delbrück, comparable in some ways to those of the eighteenth century, so was this heightened emphasis upon the political aspects of the war in full accordance with the principles of *Ermattungsstrategie* as practiced by Frederick the Great. When the German army had taken the field in 1914 it had staked all on the decisive battle and had failed. Delbrück would now relegate military operations to a subordinate position. The battle was no longer an end in itself but a means. If Germany's political professions failed at first to convince the Western powers that peace was desirable, a new military offensive could be undertaken and would serve to break down that hesitation. But only such a coordination of the military effort with the political program would bring the war to a successful issue.

In his desire for a political strategy that would be effective in weakening the resistance of the enemy, Delbrück was bitterly disappointed. It became apparent as early as 1915 that strong sections of German public opinion regarded the war as a means of acquiring new territory not only in the East but in the West. When Delbrück called for a declaration of willingness to evacuate Belgium, he was greeted with abuse and was accused by the *Deutsche Tageszeitung* of being "subservient to our enemies in foreign countries."[83] The changing fortunes of war did not diminish the desire for booty and the powerful *Vaterlandspartei*, the most important of the annexationist groups, exercised a strong influence on national policy. Not only did the German government not make any declaration concerning Belgium but it never made its position clear on the question of a negotiated peace. When the Peace Resolution was being

[82] *Krieg und Politik*, 2:187.
[83] See R. H. Lutz, ed., *Fall of the German Empire*, Hoover War Library Publications, no. 1 (Stanford, Ca., 1932), 307.

debated in 1917, Hindenburg and Ludendorff threatened to resign if the Reichstag adopted the measure. After the passage of the resolution, the influence of the High Command was exerted so effectively that the government did not dare to make the resolution the keystone of its policy. As a result of the so-called crisis of July 1917, the Western powers were encouraged to believe that the Reichstag's professions were insincere and that Germany's leaders were still bent on world domination.

To Delbrück the crisis of July had a deeper significance. It showed within the government a dearth of political leadership and a growing tendency on the part of the military to dominate the formulation of policy. Germany's military leaders had never been known for their political acumen, but in the past they had followed the advice of the political head of the state. Gneisenau had willingly subordinated his views to those of Hardenberg; Moltke—although at times reluctantly—had bowed to Bismarck's political judgment. Now, in the time of Germany's greatest crisis, the military were taking over completely and there was among them no man with a proper appreciation of the political necessities of the day. For all their military gifts, Hindenburg and Ludendorff still thought solely in terms of a decisive military victory over the Western powers, a *Niederwerfung* that would deliver western Europe into their hands. It was with a growing sense of despair that Delbrück wrote: "Athens went to her doom in the Peloponnesian War because Pericles had no successor. We have fiery Cleons enough in Germany. Whoever believes in the German people will be confident that it has not only great strategists among its sons but also that gifted statesman in whose hands the necessity of the time will place the reins for the direction of foreign policy."[84] But that gifted statesman never appeared; and the fiery Cleons prevailed.

It was, consequently, with little confidence that Delbrück watched the opening of the German offensive of 1918. "It is obvious," he wrote, "that no change can be made in the principles I have expounded here since the beginning of the war, and the dissension with regard to our western war aims remains."[85] Strategy, he insisted, is not something in the abstract; it cannot be divorced from political considerations. "The great strategical offensive should have been accompanied and reinforced by a similar political offensive, which would have worked upon the home front of our enemies in the same way as Hindenburg and the men in field gray worked upon the front lines." If only the German government had announced, fourteen days before the opening of the offensive, that they firmly desired a negotiated peace and that, after such peace, Belgium

[84] *Krieg und Politik*, 3:123.
[85] Ibid., 3:63.

would be evacuated, what would the result have been? Lloyd George and Clemenceau might have regarded these claims as signs of German weakness. But now, as the offensive rolled forward, "would Lloyd George and Clemenceau still be at the helm? I doubt it very much. We might even now be sitting at the conference table."[86]

Because of the failure to coordinate the military and political aspects of the war, Delbrück felt that the offensive, at most, would lead to mere tactical successes and would have no great strategical importance. But even he did not suspect that this was the last gamble of the strategists of annihilation, and the suddenness and completeness of the German collapse surprised him completely. In the November 1918 issue of the *Preussische Jahrbücher* he made a curious and revealing apology to his readers. "How greatly I have erred," he wrote. "However bad things looked four weeks ago, I still would not give up the hope that the front, however wavering, would hold and would force the enemy to an armistice that would protect our boundaries." In a sentence that illustrates the responsibility that he felt as a military commentator to the German people, he added, "I admit that I often expressed myself more confidently than I felt at heart. On more than one occasion, I allowed myself to be deceived by the confident tone of the announcements and reports of the army and the navy." But despite these mistakes in judgment, he could, he said, be proud of the fact that he had always insisted that the German people had a right to hear the truth even when it was bad and, in his constant preaching of political moderation, he had tried to show them the road to victory.[87]

It was in this spirit also that Delbrück made his most complete review and most searching criticism of the military operations of the last phase of the war. This was in the two reports which he made in 1922 before the Fourth Subcommittee of the commission set up by the Reichstag after the war to investigate the causes of the German collapse in 1918. In his testimony before the subcommittee, Delbrück repeated the arguments that he had made in the pages of the *Preussische Jahrbücher*, but the removal of censorship restrictions enabled him to give a much more detailed criticism of the military aspect of the 1918 offensive than had been possible during the war.[88]

---

[86] Ibid., 3:73.

[87] Ibid., 3:203-206.

[88] Delbrück's testimony is reproduced completely in *Das Werk des Untersuchungsausschusses der Deutschen Verfassunggebenden Nationalversammlung und des Deutschen Reichstages 1919-1926. Die Ursachen des Deutschen Zusammenbruches im Jahre 1918* (Vierte Reihe im Werk des Untersuchungsausschusses), (Berlin, 1920-29), 3:239-73. Selections from the Commission's report, but only a very small portion of the Delbrück testimony, may be found in *The Causes of the German Collapse in 1918*, ed. R. H. Lutz, Hoover War Library Publications, no. 4 (Stanford, 1934).

The main weight of Delbrück's criticism was directed against Lu-dendorff, who conceived and directed the 1918 offensive. In only one respect, he felt, had the general shown even military proficiency. He had "prepared the attack, as regards both the previous training of the troops and the moment for taking the enemy by surprise, in a masterly manner with the greatest energy and circumspection."[89] But the advantages of this preliminary preparation were outweighed by several fundamental weaknesses and by gross mistakes in strategical thinking. In the first place, the German army on the eve of the offensive was in no position to strike a knockout blow against the enemy. Its numerical superiority was slight and, in reserves, it was vastly inferior to the enemy. Its equipment was in many respects equally inferior, and it was greatly handicapped by a faulty supply system and by insufficient stocks of fuel for its motorized units. These disadvantages were apparent before the opening of the offensive but were disregarded by the High Command.[90]

Ludendorff was sufficiently aware of these weaknesses, however, to admit the impossibility of striking the enemy at that point where the greatest strategical success could have been won. In his own words, "tactics were to be valued more than pure strategy." That meant, in effect, that he attacked at those points where it was easiest to break through and not at those points where the announced aim of the offensive could best be served. The strategical goal of the campaign was the annihilation of the enemy. "In order to attain the strategical goal—the separation of the English army from the French and the consequent rolling-up of the former—the attack would have best been arranged so that it followed the course of the Somme. Ludendorff, however, had stretched the offensive front some four miles further to the south because the enemy seemed especially weak there."[91] The defensive wing of the army under Hutier broke through at this point, but its very success handicapped the development of the offensive, for its advance outpaced the real offensive wing under Below which was operating against Arras. When Below's forces were checked "we were forced with a certain amount of compulsion to follow the line of [Hutier's] success . . . thereby the idea of the offensive was altered and the danger of dispersing our forces evoked."[92]

In short, by following the tactical line of least resistance Ludendorff began a disastrous policy of improvisation, violating the first principle of that *Niederwerfungsstrategie* that he professed to be following. "A

[89] *Die Ursachen des Deutschen Zusammenbruches*, 3:345. Lutz, ed., *Causes of the German Collapse*, 90.
[90] *Die Ursachen des Deutschen Zusammenbruches*, 3:246.
[91] Ibid., 3:247.
[92] Ibid., 3:346.

strategy that is not predicated upon an absolute decision, upon the annihilation of the enemy, but is satisfied with single blows, may execute these now in this place, now in that. But a strategy which intends to force the decision, must do it where the first successful blow was struck." Far from obeying this precept, Ludendorff and Hindenburg operated on the principle that, when difficulties developed in one sector, new blows could be struck in another.[93] As a result, the grand offensive degenerated into a series of separate thrusts, uncoordinated and unproductive.

The cardinal fault was the failure of the High Command to see clearly what could be accomplished by the Germany army in 1918 and the failure to adapt its strategy to its potentialities. Here Delbrück returned to the major theme of all his work as historian and publicist. The relative strength of the opposing forces was such that the High Command should have realized that annihilation of the enemy was no longer possible. The aim of the 1918 offensive, therefore, should have been to make the enemy so tired that he would be willing to negotiate a peace. This in itself would have been possible only if the German government had expressed its own willingness to make such a peace. But once this declaration had been clearly made, the German army in opening its offensive would have won a great strategical advantage. Its offensive could now be geared to the strength at its disposal. It could safely attack at the points of tactical advantage—that is, where success was easiest—since even minor victories would now have a redoubled moral effect in the enemy capitals.[94] The High Command had failed in 1918 and had lost the war because it had disregarded the most important lesson of history, the interrelationship of politics and war. "To come back once more to that fundamental sentence of Clausewitz, no strategical idea can be considered completely without considering the political goal."[95]

IV

The military historian has generally been a kind of misfit, regarded with suspicion both by his professional colleagues and by the military men whose activities he seeks to portray. The suspicion of the military is not difficult to explain. It springs in large part from the natural scorn of the professional for the amateur. But the distrust with which academicians have looked on the military historians in their midst has deeper roots. In democratic countries especially, it arises from the belief that war is an aberration in the historical process and that, consequently, the study of war is neither fruitful nor seemly. It is significant that in his

---

[93] Ibid., 3:250-51.
[94] Ibid., 3:253f.
[95] Ibid., 3:253.

general work *On the Writing of History*, the dean of military historians in the early twentieth century, Sir Charles Oman, should entitle the chapter dealing with his own field "A Plea for Military History." Sir Charles remarks that the civilian historian dabbling in military affairs has been an exceptional phenomenon, and he explains this by writing: "Both the medieval monastic chroniclers and the modern liberal historiographers had often no closer notion of the meaning of war than that it involves various horrors and is attended by a lamentable loss of life. Both classes strove to disguise their personal ignorance or dislike of military matters by deprecating their importance and significance in history."[96]

The prejudice that Oman resented was felt equally keenly, throughout his life, by Hans Delbrück. When, as a relatively young man, he turned his talents to the study of military history, he found that the members of his discipline regarded his specialty as not worth the energy he expended upon it. Ranke himself, when he learned after Delbrück's *Habilitation* that the young man intended to write a history of the art of war, expressed his disapproval of the project, and Theodor Mommsen, when Delbrück presented him with the first volume of the work, said rather ungraciously that "his time would hardly permit him to read this book."[97] Few academic historians heeded Delbrück's plea in 1887 that there was a crying need for scholars "to turn not only an incidental but a professional interest to the history of war,"[98] and in his last years he was still complaining, as he did in the pages of his *Weltgeschichte*, about those who persisted in believing that "battles and wars can be regarded as unimportant by-products of world history."[99]

It may be that the passage of time has diminished interest in the discoveries of Delbrück's *Sachkritik* and that even the strategical controversies that he delighted in have become somewhat remote from our present concerns. But there is no doubt that the *History of the Art of War* will remain one of the finest examples of the application of modern science to the heritage of the past, and, however modified in detail, the bulk of the work stands unchallenged. Moreover, in an age in which war has become the concern of every man, the major theme of Delbrück's work as historian and publicist is at once a reminder and a warning. The coordination of politics and war is as important today as it was in the age of Pericles, and strategical thinking that becomes self-sufficient or neglects the political aspect of war can lead only to disaster.

[96] Charles Oman, *On the Writing of History* (New York, n.d.), 159f.
[97] Haintz, introduction to the 1962 edition of *Geschichte der Kriegskunst*, 9.
[98] Delbrück, "Etwas Kriegsgeschichtliches," 610.
[99] Hans Delbrück, *Weltgeschichte* (Berlin, 1924-28), 1:321.

13. Russian Military Thought: The Western Model and the Shadow of Suvorov

WALTER PINTNER

F ROM THE TIME of Peter the Great's victory over the Swedes at
Poltava in 1709, Russia has been a major European power, rising
in the course of the following centuries to become one of the great
powers of the world. Military strength made this ascent possible. But
despite many effective military leaders and despite the development of
an extensive literature on the theory of war in the nineteenth century,
Russia produced no strategic thinkers whose work has had more than a
temporary impact. There are no Russian Mahans, Clausewitzes, or Jominis—even if Jomini ended his career in the Russian service.

This paradox may seem still more surprising when we consider that
until the middle of the nineteenth century service in the army was the
preferred career for educated Russians.[1] The army and military values
played a dominant role in the reigns of Alexander I and Nicholas I. After
1855, as the economy expanded and society became more complex, the
army lost some of its former hold over the lives of the upper classes, but
nothing justifies the suggestion that it became in any sense insignificant.

It cannot be the aim of this essay to explain why literary, musical,
and scientific genius flourished in nineteenth-century Russia and strategic
genius did not. Rather we shall discuss the course of Russian military
thought in the broad context of the country's social and political development. Even if no Russian military thinkers would seem to merit extensive analysis purely for their own sake, Russian ideas on military
service, tactics, and strategy form an interesting and important subject
because they are Russian, and because Russia was and is important in
the real world of politics, diplomacy, and war.

I

In almost every question relating to Russia, one is forced to begin
one's answer by considering the tortured and complex matter of its relationship to the rest of Europe, or as it is usually but somewhat mis-

[1] Walter M. Pintner, "The Burden of Defense in Imperial Russia, 1725-1914," *The
Russian Review* 43, no. 3 (1984), 256-57.

leadingly put, of "Russia and the West." It is misleading to suggest that Russia is somehow beyond the pale of Western civilization; clearly that is not the case. Since the adoption of Christianity in 988 Russia has been more closely related to the Western tradition than to that of any other major civilized society. Whatever the differences, past and present, Russian culture has its roots in the same ultimate sources as the rest of Europe. It is as much the closeness as the differences that have made it difficult for Russians to know where they stand. How much of Western culture in general is "Western European" but not Russian and therefore to be consciously borrowed or rejected? What is uniquely Russian?[2]

Military thinkers shared this central concern of Russian intellectuals. The search for a "Russian art of war" was a central issue in nineteenth-century Russian military writing. Related to, but not the same as, the search for Russianness was the question of backwardness and practical competition with other powers, particularly Western ones. Issues that affected Russia's power and strategic position, however, did not necessarily correspond to issues that aroused the concern of intellectuals who dealt with the problem of Russia and the West.

In particular, the serf system, which enslaved half of the Russian population, increasingly troubled Russian intellectuals from the late eighteenth century onward. They saw it, among other things, as inconsistent with the Western belief in human liberty that they had come to share. Eventually some of them, rejecting what they had begun to see as over-westernization, opposed serfdom because it was to them a distortion of the paternalistic unbureaucratic pre-Petrine society they imagined had once existed. Yet serfdom was an issue for intellectuals for fifty years before it became a military concern. Throughout the eighteenth century and through the end of the Napoleonic Wars the serf system, whatever its moral and other faults, posed no problem for the Russian army; on the contrary, it strengthened the army, and helped make it what it was.

The harsh but effective device of forcibly enrolling a relatively small number of serfs for lifetime (later twenty-five-year) service to maintain a large standing army of professional soldiers was the basis of Russia's remarkable successes from 1709 to the mid-nineteenth century. In the eighteenth century this system was perhaps more satisfactory than the

---

[2] Russian nationalists in the mid-nineteenth century decided, for example, that the Russian peasant village system of repartitional tenure was an ancient national tradition going back to early times and that therefore it demonstrated something about Russian national character. Exactly what it demonstrated depended on the political stance of the writer. Later it was established that the repartitional commune was generally a relatively new institution that developed as a response to changes in the taxation system in the reign of Peter the Great. Jerome Blum, *Lord and Peasant in Russia from the Ninth to the Nineteenth Century* (Princeton, 1961), 504-535.

mixture of conscription and mercenary service that characterized the armies of Old Regime Western Europe. Russian peasant soldiers were paid virtually nothing, and once the trauma of recruitment and transportation to their regiments, during which many fled, was over, desertion was very low in comparison with the high rates reported in the West.[3]

It can be argued that Russian commanders in the eighteenth century were overly impressed by the Frederician model, which they adopted with great success. They failed, however, to take advantage of the potential for tactical innovation that the reliable Russian peasant soldier afforded them.[4] Only very late in the century, under the greatest of all Russian commanders, Alexander Suvorov, were some of the innovations in tactics that came to characterize the Revolutionary Era, such as rapid forced-marches and dispersed order, adopted by Russian forces. Suvorov was above all an inspired leader of men and, aristocrat though he was, clearly recognized the value of the peasant soldier as none of his predecessors had. He was also a sophisticated and well-read man, familiar with the major European languages and aware of the discussions of tactical innovations that were filling the pages of Western, particularly French, military articles and books.[5] Whether Suvorov instinctively sensed that the Russian peasant soldier might be able to fight in a more flexible, modern manner, or self-consciously experimented with techniques described in Western theoretical writing is not particularly significant. He demonstrated that the Russian military system at the end of the eighteenth century was capable of adopting new tactics and of competing with the best the West could offer. Even under able though less-inspired commanders, such as Michael Kutuzov and Michael Barclay de Tolly, who used more traditional methods, the Russian mobilization system and military effort as a whole proved capable of defeating Napoleon's armies in 1812.

Suvorov's example is probably more important than anything he wrote. He was not a systematic strategic or tactical thinker, or at least he did not put his thoughts on that subject down on paper. His most famous work, *The Art of Victory* (1975), is an eight-page pamphlet, a manual of practical advice directed at junior officers and noncommissioned officers. Written in simple language, it emphasizes the importance of the troops' fighting spirit, explains battlefield tactics, and adds instruc-

---

[3] Walter M. Pintner, "Russia's Military Style, Russian Society, and Russian Power in the Eighteenth Century," in *Russia and the West in the Eighteenth Century*, ed. A. G. Cross (Newtonville, Mass., 1983), 262-70. See also Pintner, "Burden," 251.

[4] Pintner, "Russia's Military Style," 262-70.

[5] Philip Longworth, *The Art of Victory: The Life and Achievements of Generalissimo Suvorov, 1729-1800* (New York, 1965), ch. 10.

tion on maintaining health and morale.[6] Whatever Suvorov's achievements as a theorist, his talents as a commander were great, and set a standard against which all subsequent Russian commanders are compared. None, not even Kutuzov, conqueror of Napoleon, ever quite equaled him.

Despite his linguistic skills and sophisticated knowledge of the West, Suvorov came to symbolize the Russian art of war. There were many reasons: he did not get along with Paul I, the arch Prussianizer; although eccentric, his eccentricity had a common touch, and he appealed to the peasant soldier and therefore to later intellectuals of populist-nationalist inclinations; and above all, he won battles over Russia's enemies. Even his final retreat over the Alps was such a spectacular effort that the Russians regarded it as a moral victory, a triumph in the face of Austrian perfidy.

Russians thus entered the nineteenth century with the practical experience of military success, in part because of the backwardness, or at least because of the distinctive characteristics of their social and political order. But nothing in the cultural or intellectual efforts of their country was comparable with their political and military achievements. They were the winners, but they had to look to the West, in a sense to the losers, represented by Clausewitz and Jomini, to instruct them in strategic thought.[7]

In a paradoxical way, the emerging "Russian national school" or the notion of a Russian art of war was greatly influenced by, or was possibly a product of, the Revolutionary Era, which stressed the national element as a force making men fight with loyalty and enthusiasm. This notion and the associated concept of an army based on universal service and a large trained reserve or militia were the most important features of the military thought of the younger generation of progressive military officers, some of whom participated in the unsuccessful attempt at a *coup d'état* in December 1825. That they espoused these military ideas, as well as a long list of other liberal political notions, may have contributed to the conservatism of military thought during the ensuing reign of Nicholas I (1825-1855). Nicholas, above all, wanted to extirpate the subversive

---

[6] The title is often translated as *The Science of Victory*, which distorts the meaning of *nauka* in that context and the actual nature of the work. Perhaps even more accurate, if awkward, would be *Practical Wisdom for Winning*. His other major work was the "Suzdal' Regulations" (1765), a training manual written early in his career. See A. V. Suvorov, *Dokumenty*, ed. G. P. Meshcheriakov (Moscow, 1952), 3:501-508, for *Nauka pobezhdat'*, and A. V. Suvorov, *Polkovoe uchrezhdenie* (Moscow, 1948), for the "Suzdal' Regulations," which are also in *A. V. Suvorov, Dokumenty* (Moscow, 1949), 1:73-168.

[7] Both Clausewitz and Jomini were at times in Russian service, Clausewitz briefly and Jomini for much of his life.

influence of the Decembrists, who had attempted to prevent his accession to the throne, and whatever they advocated was automatically suspect. But the ideal of the national spirit was already too deeply entrenched in the Russian military tradition. Discussion of shifting to a short-term conscript army with a large reserve force ended, however, because it was inevitably linked with major reforms in the serf systems, which although discussed, made no actual progress under Nicholas.[8]

The reign of Nicholas I is usually described as the apogée of Russian militarism, which indeed it was in many respects. Nicholas certainly wished it to be so. Far from unintelligent, and not always opposed to change or experimentation if the risks were not too great, he was profoundly conservative when it came to military matters, his greatest love.[9] A leading military theorist of the second half of the century, G. A. Leer, later wrote of the Nicolaian Era: "It is usually said of Frederician tactics that they were buried . . . at Jena and Auerstedt. Indeed, their outer cover, their forms, were buried, but their spirit continued to live, at least in our army in the 1850's."[10]

Nevertheless, it was during the reign of Nicholas that major changes in the balance between military and civilian society began to take place. Despite the huge standing army that was maintained after the Napoleonic Era, the rapid growth of the civil bureaucracy meant that by the middle of the century civil officials for the first time outnumbered military officers. Furthermore, the civil career had become to a great degree separated from the military, so that by the end of Nicholas's reign the younger generation of top civil officials were mostly men who had spent their entire careers in civil agencies. No longer was the career of the military officer virtually the only reasonable option open to the majority of the nobility.[11] The quantitative expansion of higher and secondary education that began under Alexander I and continued under Nicholas, even though accompanied by increased attempts to control the content of the curric-

---

[8] John L. H. Keep, "The Russian Army's Response to the French Revolution," *Jahrbücher für die Geschichte Osteuropas* 28, no. 4 (1980), 515-16; E. A. Prokof'ev, *Borba Dekabristov za peredovoe russkoe voennoe iskusstvo* (Moscow, 1953), 109-28; Peter H. C. Von Wahlde, "Military Thought in Imperial Russia" (Ph.D. diss., Indiana University, 1966), 47-49.

[9] Nicholas, for example, supported Kiselev's extensive reorganization of the state peasant administration and authorized the building of the first railroads in Russia, despite opposition from his more traditional advisors (Walter M. Pintner, *Russian Economic Policy under Nicholas I* [Ithaca, 1967], 131-52).

[10] G. A. Leer, *Korennye voprosy* (St. Petersburg, 1897), 33, as quoted by Von Wahlde, "Military Thought," 59.

[11] Walter M. Pintner, "The Evolution of Civil Officialdom, 1755-1855," in *Russian Officialdom: The Bureaucratization of Russian Society from the Seventeenth to the Twentieth Century*, ed. Walter M. Pintner and Don Karl Rowney (Chapel Hill, 1980), 209; Pintner, "Burden," 254-57.

ulum, meant that there emerged a significant reading public, which provided a market for the new generation of Russian writers, who included the first really great figures of nineteenth-century Russian literature—Pushkin, Lermontov, and Gogol, to mention only the most well known. Paradoxically the nonmilitary aspects of Russian life were developing more rapidly and more successfully under Nicholas than was the military.

Nevertheless, despite Leer's gloomy observation about the barracks square mentality of the period, some of the issues that later dominated military thought in Russia began to emerge, in the age of Nicholas, even among official writers. General N. V. Medem, writing in 1837, argued that improvements in weapons and techniques of defensive warfare increased the importance of "moral force" in war, anticipating the primary thrust of the nationalist "back to Suvorov" school led by Dragomirov in the late nineteenth century.[12] Dragomirov himself attributed his views to the lectures of another figure of the era, Colonel A. P. Kartsov, professor at the General Staff Academy in the 1850s.[13]

Something of a problem for the nascent nationalist school was the fact that Russia's second great hero, Kutuzov, was most noted for his careful strategic retreat in the face of Napoleon's invading army, a retreat that ultimately included the abandonment and burning of Moscow. M. I. Bogdanovich, who succeeded Medem as professor of strategy at the General Staff Academy, emphasized the importance of defense as a means of weakening the enemy, and the value of a large standing army for that purpose, and praised Kutuzov for avoiding unproductive battles.[14]

Throughout the reign of Nicholas I a very large standing army was maintained on the basis of the traditional system of twenty-five-year terms of service for peasant conscripts. In relatively minor conflicts with Persia and Turkey, and in the suppression of rebellions in Poland and Hungary the army did its job, although with the benefit of hindsight some weaknesses can be discerned. Nothing happened, however, to upset the regime's conviction that all was well and that no substantial changes were needed.[15] Russia's policy was aimed at preserving the European *status quo*, and Nicholas described it in terms that would now be labeled a

[12] N. V. Medem, *Taktika* (St. Petersburg, 1837), 7-8, 32-39, as cited in Von Wahlde, "Military Thought," 37.

[13] G. P. Meshcheriakov, *Russkaia voennaia mysl' v XIX v.* (Moscow, 1973), 94, citing M. I. Dragomirov, *Uchebnik taktiki* (St. Petersburg, 1879), xxv.

[14] M. I. Bogdanovich, *Zapiski o strategii. Pravila vedeniia voiny, isvelechennye iz sochienenii Napoleona, ertsgertsoga Karla, generala Zhomini i drugikh pisatelei* (St. Petersburg, 1847), pt. 2, pp. 324-36, as cited in Von Wahlde, "Military Thought," 72-73.

[15] For a discussion of each campaign see John Shelton Curtiss, *The Russian Army under Nicholas I, 1825-1855* (Durham, 1965), chs. 2, 4, 8, and 15.

policy of deterrence: "Russia is a power mighty and fortunate in its own right; it will never be a threat to its neighbors or to Europe. However, its defensive position must be so impressive as to make any attack impossible."[16]

II

The defeat in the Crimean War and the death of Nicholas marks the beginning of the end of the old regime in the Russian military and much else in Russian society. Russian soldiers fought bravely and well in the Crimea. Despite great difficulties the troops were supplied, and very likely the Allied commanders made as many blunders as their opponents. Nevertheless, the war was lost. The mobilization of 1,742,297 officers and men (plus 787,197 irregulars and militia) proved inadequate to deal with a force of 300,000 French, British, Sardinian, and Turkish troops.[17] Of course, the need to defend the Baltic coast against possible Allied landings and the Austrian frontier against possible intervention dissipated Russian numerical strength, and lacking substantial reserves there was no way to increase rapidly the number of effective troops available.

The Crimean War demonstrated to perceptive Russians that the military balance in Europe had shifted since 1815 and that the advantages Russia had enjoyed and exploited successfully since the time of Peter the Great no longer sufficed to ensure its continued status as a great power, much less as the dominant European land power. Innovations in weapons technology were part of the problem; but if that had been all that was involved, the solution would have been relatively simple. Even at the end of the century, when many of the new weapons had been adopted, military hardware was still a very modest part of the total military budget.[18] New model rifles and artillery could be bought abroad or copied at home.

Far more difficult to deal with were fundamental changes that involved the mobilization, transportation, and organization of men and matériel. European powers were developing the means to mobilize the entire society for war to an unprecedented extent, a process that would culminate in the horrors of the First World War. The Russian autocracy in the eighteenth century had had the advantage of being able to conscript peasants for life, exploiting the tradition of the service state and the serf

---

[16] A. A. Shcherbatov, *General' Feldmarshal Kniaz' Paskevich, Ego zhizn' i deitatel'nost'* (St. Petersburg, 1894), 4:167, 174, quoting a handwritten memorandum of the czar from 1831.

[17] Robert F. Baumann, "The Debate over Universal Military Service in Russia, 1870-1874" (Ph.D. diss., Yale University, 1982), 3, citing an unpublished document from the Central State Military Historical Archive, dated 1870.

[18] Pintner, "Burden," 240-45.

system. By the mid-nineteenth century, modern administrative techniques, mass education, and railroad transport made it possible for Germany, France, and Austria to turn a high proportion of the adult male population into trained soldiers, available on short notice. This was the basic strategic problem that confronted the Russian military in the post-Crimean period.

Fortunately for Russia, a remarkable group of progressive, intelligent, and energetic officials emerged from the bureaucracy of Nicholas I to launch a wide range of major projects, the so-called Era of the Great Reforms, beginning with the accession of Alexander II in 1855. The reforms touched virtually every aspect of Russian life except the central political system, with the emancipation of the serfs as the centerpiece.[19] One of the leading members of the small group of "modernizing bureaucrats," Dmitrii Miliutin, who was minister of war from 1861 to 1881, was largely responsible for the attempt to deal with Russia's basic strategic problem, manpower mobilization and training, that was embodied in the military reform of 1874 and related measures.

Miliutin had served with distinction in the Caucasus, but his main activity, which, perhaps surprisingly, brought him to the attention of the most influential circles, was his work as a military historian and as director of the training section of the Supreme Headquarters for the Institutions of Military Education.[20] There he served directly under the Grand Duke Mikhail Pavlovich, brother of Nicholas I, and General Ia. I. Rostovtsev, who was later to be closely associated with the elaboration of the emancipation. His major historical work, published in five volumes in 1852-1855, was his history of Russia's participation in the Wars of the Second Coalition, primarily Suvorov's famous Italian campaign. Miliutin was a practical modernizer, no romantic who dreamed of a uniquely Russian art of war, but he was clearly struck by Suvorov's emphasis on the crucial importance of moral or spiritual factors in war. There are two sides in military art, he wrote,

> the material and the spiritual. An army is not only a physical power, a mass consisting of weapons of military operations, but it is as well a union of humans endowed with intelligence and heart. Spiritual force plays an important part in all considerations and calculations of the military leader, and consequently for the latter it is insufficient to rule armies as a machine. He must be able to rule the human

---

[19] For an excellent discussion of the origins and development of this remarkable group of reforming bureaucrats see W. Bruce Lincoln, *In the Vanguard of Reform* (De Kalb, Ill., 1983).

[20] Forrestt A. Miller, *Dmitrii Miliutin and the Reform Era in Russia* (Nashville, 1968), 19-20.

being to fasten the army to himself, and with his spiritual power over the army acquire conditional authority.[21]

Miliutin's reform program had three main goals: (1) to improve the administrative structure of the military; (2) to shift to a system of short-term service with a reduced standing army and a large reserve force; and (3) to raise the quality of military education, particularly of officers but of the rank and file as well. All of these efforts and especially the introduction of general conscription and improved education had broad societal implications, far different from hiring a few foreign technicians to build a new weapon. Miliutin recognized that Russian society, not just the Russian army, had to modernize if Russia was to maintain its position among the major powers. Changes in the administrative structure, although opposed by Miliutin's bureaucratic rivals, gave more authority to the minister of war.[22] Of far greater general significance was the shift to the more or less universal conscription and the reserve system, which was impossible to consider seriously prior to the emancipation of the serfs, due to the long-standing tradition that army service ended serf status. Peasant recruits could not be expected to return to the status of serfs after spending several years in the army.[23] For the first time since Peter the Great westernized the upper class to enable him to compete with Western military powers, Russia's military requirements dictated major social changes.

The Miliutin reform not only instituted short-term conscription and a reserve system but went far beyond that to change Russia's traditional system of legally defined social classes. Before the reform only peasants and the lowest levels of urban society were subject to conscription, while since 1762 the nobility had served as officers if they chose to. The reformed system introduced the principle of a universal service obligation, regardless of social status, the one distinction being the length of service, which varied inversely with the amount of education. Totally uneducated peasants served for six years (later reduced to five); at each level of

[21] Dmitrii A. Miliutin, *Istoriia voiny s Frantsieiu v Tsarsvovanie Imperatora Pavla I, v 1799 godu*, 5 vols. (St. Petersburg, 1852-55), 5:115, as cited by Von Wahlde, "Military Thought," 70.

[22] David R. Jones, "Administrative System and Policy-Making Process, Central Military (before 1917)," *The Military-Naval Encyclopedia of Russia and the Soviet Union* (Gulf Breeze, Fla., 1980), 108-30.

[23] Alfred J. Rieber, ed., *The Politics of Autocracy: Letters of Alexander II to Prince A. I. Bariatinskii, 1857-1864* (Paris and The Hague, 1966) and Daniel Field, *The End of Serfdom: Nobility and Bureaucracy in Russia, 1855-1861* (Cambridge, Mass., 1976). Rieber argues on pages 15-58 that the desire to have general conscription and a reserve system was the main reason for emancipation. Field, in the most extensive Western study of the subject, does not accept this position (see ch. 2).

education there was a substantial reduction, with university graduates serving for only six months. Of course nobles generally had more education than non-nobles, but there were significant numbers of non-nobles with primary, secondary, and even university educations. That they should be treated equally with nobles in this area was a major departure in social policy, and one that could not be justified on narrowly military grounds. But in a broad historical sense it was consistent with the Russian state's policy of always leaving the door open to use non-nobles in state service, even at very high levels, when that seemed desirable. Unquestionably, however, an element of idealism permeates the Era of the Great Reforms that was well expressed in the State Council's statement about the old army when it came to discuss the completed reforms proposal: "Not long ago service, virtually for life and accompanied by many deprivations, was not considered honorable and natural for every citizen of the fatherland but a penalty for crime and a depraved life. The conscription of a man into the army was defined in the criminal code as the equivalent of exile to Siberia and detention in a penal brigade; further, society permitted landowners to remove depraved individuals by this means if other methods failed."[24]

The State Council was a high-level advisory body composed of very senior bureaucrats and soldiers. That this body took a firm stand against the old military system that had served for so long is striking evidence that the need for substantial change was recognized by many, not only by the leaders of the reform movement. The compelling example to which the Russian military reformers looked was Prussia before and particularly after its dramatic defeat of France in the Franco-Prussian War. Nevertheless the State Council's statement and similar declarations by Miliutin himself[25] also suggest an attempt to restore what was believed to have been the spirit of the army at an earlier time, the era of Russian triumphs under Suvorov and Kutuzov, when even the oppressive system of recruitment had not, it seemed, destroyed the enthusiasm of the Russian soldier.

The same general goal was involved in Miliutin's attempts to improve officer training. In the old army most of the officers were nobles who served briefly as "Junkers" or officer cadets in regiments and were then promoted with minimal education and were destined, in most cases, to second-class status throughout their careers. A much smaller group (17 percent overall) of nobles attended special state military schools, generally filled the higher ranks, and served in the elite regiments. Miliutin hoped

---

[24] Baumann, "Debate," 134, citing an unpublished document in the Miliutin collection in the manuscript division of the Lenin library in Moscow.
[25] Ibid., 34.

to eliminate what was essentially a two-class system and establish common educational standards for all officers. However, the entrenched political influence of the elite officers enabled them to preserve their special, and for the state very expensive schools, leaving fewer resources to be devoted to the expanded facilities for the mass of the officer corps. Some of Miliutin's measures in this area were even further watered down after his resignation as minister of war in 1881, but by the eve of World War I the educational differences between the various types of officers had been greatly reduced if not eliminated, and many colonels and generals were of humble origin.[26]

In society as a whole, however, the status of the officer corps declined during the last fifty years of the old regime. Officers were very poorly paid and, more importantly, the economy was expanding, creating alternative career opportunities for men with education. Until the 1850s the choice for a young nobleman was usually military service or the civil bureaucracy; now he could consider the professions, teaching, commerce, engineering, and much else. Selecting a career was also a political decision. The military was the bulwark of the regime; after the era of the Great Reforms was succeeded by a new conservatism, a larger and larger segment of educated Russian society, if it did not go into active opposition, at least lost its enthusiasm for the regime. This made the choice of a military career less attractive than it had been, except for men of very humble background who still saw it as a way to rise in society, and for a small elite of wealthy nobles whose families had traditionally served in the famous regiments.

III

Thus by the mid-1870s, Russia had in place the basic structure of a modern continental European military system. The problem now was how to make it work and to develop a force truly comparable to that of the other major Continental powers. Manpower was no longer the issue; Russia had more men available than it could ever afford to train. By means of generous exemptions coupled with a lottery, the new system remained well short of being truly universal. Nor, as mentioned above, did the new military technology that rapidly developed in the decades from the 1870s to 1914 pose insuperable difficulties; Russia introduced

[26] About half of the total officer corps were sons of hereditary nobles, and over one-third sons of "personal nobles," that is, of men who served the state but who had not risen high enough in the table of ranks at the time of their son's birth to confer hereditary status on him. The remainder came from non-noble backgrounds, most commonly sons of soldiers. Curtiss, *The Russian Army*, 176-77, 189-90; Peter Kenez, "A Profile of the Pre-revolutionary Officer Corps," *California Slavic Studies* 7 (1973), 121-45.

weapons comparable to those of its rivals in reasonable quantity. The basic problem was the budget and the size of the army. Even aside from a less than efficient administration, the long frontiers and the less extensive railroad network meant slower mobilization and the need for larger standing forces. It was also believed that illiterate Russian peasants needed longer training than their Western counterparts, another reason for keeping many men under arms. The bulk of the military budget still went for subsistence expenses despite a modest rise in the proportion spent on hardware, so the total size of the army was the crucial factor in determining the military budget.[27] Russia was a poor, relatively underdeveloped country, even after the rapid industrialization of the 1890s, and maintaining forces somewhat larger than those of its neighbors immediately to the West was a great burden. More important than the best way to stop an Austrian or German invasion of Poland, the crucial problem was the failure of the economy to develop rapidly enough to support the necessary military establishment in an era of mass armies and the rapid mobilization and concentration of these forces.

At the end of the century one soldier, Lt. Colonel A. A. Gulevich of the General Staff Academy, recognized the intimate connection of modern war and the national economy. He even foresaw that the next European war would probably be drawn out and exhausting rather than quick and decisive. Optimistically, however, he saw Russia's lower level of economic development and poorer standard of living as better enabling it to stand the strain of such a war. A smaller proportion of Russia's large labor force would be mobilized than in the well-developed industrial economies of France and Germany, which were much more fragile, easily disrupted, and would suffer more because of greater withdrawals of manpower due to mobilization.[28]

Probably the only Russian work on military affairs that had any significant impact outside of Russia in the nineteenth century was not written by a soldier. Jan Bloch's *The Future War in Its Technical, Economic, and Political Aspects* was a massive five-volume study of the impact of industrial and scientific progress on warfare, lavishly illustrated, and filled with innumerable charts and tables. It correctly described the awesome potential of the new technology of warfare that had developed in the last years of the nineteenth century but argued that the modern industrial economy was incapable of sustaining itself long under the stress of war. It was a profoundly pacifist work, determined to demonstrate by weight of numbers that war was simply unacceptable in the modern

[27] Pintner, "Burden," 245-48.
[28] A. A. Gulevich, *Voina i narodnoe khoziaistvo* (St. Petersburg, 1898), 15-16, 23-32.

365

world, but its conclusions were very similar to Gulevich's.[29] Bloch was a Polish Jew, a railroad magnate who collaborated with General A. K. Puzyrevskii and probably many others in putting this huge treatise together. Gulevich may possibly have been involved in or at least aware of the project and of Bloch's earlier publications. Bloch remained a prominent figure in the European antiwar movement before World War I, but his work seems to have been largely ignored by the military, at least in Russia.

Russian military thought in the post-reform era down to the First World War did not focus on the growing problem of modern industrial war. Rather it centered to a surprising degree on what would seem to be a largely irrelevant historical dispute over the Russian art of war. Its exponents were intelligent men with a sense of mission, and a pride in the military achievements of their nation that was stimulated by the general growth of Russian nationalism in the second half of the century. The humiliation of the Crimean War and the less than brilliant showing of Russia against Turkey (1877-1878) caused them to seek solutions in their own tradition, a search that led inevitably back to Peter the Great and Suvorov. A leading exponent of the school was the talented military historian D. A. Maslovskii, who was to hold the first chair of the History of Russian Military Art at the General Staff Academy, established for him in 1890.[30] For Maslovskii, Peter was not a borrower but a transformer:

> The entire mass of original and translated works on the military art and the statutes of Western European armies which were certainly at Peter's disposal in composing the statute [the Military Statute of 1716], only served the great commander as material for the systematic development of what were solely his own views and experience, and only his genius makes it possible to explain how the "barbaric complexity" of European drill and formations were made brilliantly simple in the Russian military art, at the time of the beginning of the development of our regular army.

Like any able commander Peter was aware that he must know his opponents, but that, Maslovskii argued, did not diminish the uniquely Russian nature of his achievement.[31]

[29] Ivan S. Bliokh, *Budushchaia voina v tekhnicheskom, ekonomischeskom i politicheskom otnosheniiakh*, 5 vols. (St. Petersburg, 1898). It was also published in varying numbers of volumes in Polish, French, and German versions, and partially in English. See the discussion of Bloch in essay 18, below.

[30] Von Wahlde, "Military Thought," 104.

[31] D. F. Maslovskii, *Stroevaia i polevaia sluzhba russkikh voisk vremen Imperatora Petra Velikaga i Imperatritsy Elizavety* (St. Petersburg, 1883), 6-7; see also his *Zapiski po istorii voennago iskusstva v Rossii* (St. Petersburg, 1891), 1:4.

Military historians like Maslovskii and the successor to his chair, the somewhat more moderate A. Z. Myshlaevskii, had only an indirect, if at times significant, influence on the strategic thinking of men more immediately involved in military policy. By far the most prominent of these was M. I. Dragomirov, who served with troops in the field, taught tactics, and later was head of the General Staff Academy. His textbook on tactics, published in 1879, was the standard work used by Russian officers for thirty years.[32] Dragomirov is noted for advocating the bayonet in preference to firearms, and stressing the importance of morale. Even the experience of the Russo-Japanese War did not change his position. Citing that war, Dragomirov argued in a work published posthumously in 1906 that "the bullet and the bayonet do not exclude but supplement each other: the first paves the way for the second. This mutual relationship remains the same no matter how far the perfection of firearms is carried."[33] Not as blunt as Suvorov when he supposedly said "The bullet is a fool, but the bayonet is a fine fellow," his basic notion was the same—what really matters in war is the will of men to fight:

> Imagine, for example, contemporary advanced rapid-firing artillery; assume that the officers are skilled in aiming, and those servicing the artillery are superbly trained in the working of these guns; the significance of such artillery will be nevertheless destroyed if the men working it cannot stand the experience of shells exploding over their heads and abandon their wonderful guns.[34]

Even more prominent in Russian military thought in the late nineteenth century was General G. A. Leer, Dragomirov's successor as director of the General Staff Academy. Leer was the foremost of the "academics" who opposed Dragomirov and the "national school" and, except for Dragomirov, the only Russian military writer who was known to any extent outside of Russia.[35] For him the basic elements of strategy were permanent, unchanging, and to be derived from the study of the great commanders and writers of the past in European warfare: Lloyd, Napoleon, Jomini, and Clausewitz. However, it was more in the sources of his inspiration than in the substance of his views that he differed from Dragomirov. Leer, too, emphasized the decisive importance of cold

---

[32] Dragomirov, *Uchebnik taktiki*. Dragomirov was a prolific author of books and articles. Meshcheriakov, in *Russkaia voennaia mysl'*, lists nine monographs and four volumes of collected essays on page 302.

[33] M. I. Dragomirov, *Uchebnik taktiki*, 1906 ed., in *Russkaia voenno-teoreticheskaia mysl' XIX i nachala XX vekov*, ed. L. G. Beskrovnyi (Moscow, 1960), 346.

[34] M. I. Dragomirov, "Podgotovka voisk v mirnoe vremia (vospitanie i obrazovanie)" (Kiev, 1906) in *Izbrannye trudy* (Moscow, 1956), 603.

[35] Between 1868 and 1880 at least four of his works appeared in German and one, in 1894, in French.

steel—firepower was preparatory, the bayonet decisive, and victory depended ultimately on moral force.[36]

Defeat in the Russo-Japanese War and the concomitant near-revolution in Russia produced much discussion within military circles but no consensus beyond the obvious need to strengthen the armed forces. A large-scale, very expensive, and controversial program of naval construction was begun to replace the fleet sunk at the battle of Tsushima. For several years after the war much of the army's attention was diverted to problems of internal security, to the disgust of most military leaders.[37] Not until 1910 was it possible to begin a major program of improvement to prepare the army for the general European war that by then had come to seem likely or even inevitable.

Despite the lessons of the Russo-Japanese War about the importance of modern firepower and the difficulty of attacking entrenched positions, the national school was by no means discredited. Indeed the spirit and enthusiasm of the Japanese troops reinforced the Russian basic belief in the paramount importance of morale, as the comments of Dragomirov cited above suggest.[38] A new group of senior theorists replaced the generation of Dragomirov and Leer on both sides of the fence, with some attempting to straddle it. For a short time there was talk of abolishing the chair of the History of Russian Military Art at the General Staff Academy, traditionally the bastion of the national school, but it did not happen. Myshlaevskii was replaced in 1906 by General A. K. Baiov, an energetic and prolific historian. Perhaps even more important was the presence of General N. P. Mikhnevich, who shared many of the views of the national school, as director of the academy.

Not surprisingly, however, the defeat in the Far East brought forth a wave of self-criticism and for some this meant, as it always had throughout Russian history, looking west for solutions. Foremost among them was Colonel A. A. Neznamov, lecturer on tactics at the General Staff Academy. Although Neznamov was fond of citing the great Russian as well as European commanders and military writers of the past, the primary thrust of his highly polemical writing was that Russia must look forward and be prepared to fight "contemporary war," a phrase he used as the title of one of his major works.[39] As Neznamov put it:

[36] On Leer see Meshcheriakov, *Russkaia voennaia mysl'*, 200-202, 246-47.

[37] William C. Fuller, Jr., *Civil-Military Conflict in Imperial Russia* (Princeton, 1985), chaps. 5-8. See also John S. Bushnell, "Mutineers and Revolutionaries: Military Revolution in Russia, 1905-7" (Ph.D. diss., Indiana University, 1977).

[38] I owe this point to William Fuller.

[39] A. A. Neznamov, *Sovremennaia voina. Deistviia polevoi armii* (St. Petersburg, 1911; 2d ed., 1912).

Merely knowing basic principles, as already mentioned, is not enough; principles are eternal, but the means of battle change and with them, it goes without saying, methods and forms must change too. The task of theory is to show just these contemporary methods and forms and even look forward somewhat into the near future. For ideas there is an inexhaustible source in the best models of *all* of the *most recent* past, that is, those in which contemporary factors were prominent, factors of strategic significance—railroads, the telegraph and mass armies, and of tactical significance—rapid-firing weapons and the telegraph.[40]

Neznamov believed that Russia lost the war with Japan not because of poor communications, lack of popular support, the unfamiliar Manchurian terrain and vegetation, poor generals, or even the "general drift of government policy." All of those factors had also been present in the days of Russia's military glory—was not Northern Italy just as unfamiliar to Suvorov's men as Manchuria's to Kuropatkin's? In the days of modern fire power, Russia still dreamt of thunderous bayonet charges, put its faith in the valor of its soldiers, and expected the war to give birth to a hero-commander.[41] Decisively reversing Suvorov and the long line of his followers, Neznamov firmly asserted: "Fire decides battle."[42]

On the eve of the First World War, Neznamov was probably as up to date as anyone could be. He discussed the problems of dealing with mass armies on extended fronts. The goal of war, he thought, remained the destruction of the enemy army in a quick decisive battle, but he realized that such an outcome was unlikely in the future war he attempted to describe. However, he did not foresee the stalemate of trench warfare, but expected the continued deployment of large forces over wide areas with considerable movement as each side tried to outflank the other, a scenario that presumably could not last for more than some months, so that the war would be short.[43]

As did the members of the national school, Neznamov took Peter the Great as a model, but his interpretation of the czar differed from theirs:

[40] Neznamov, *Sovremennaia voina*, 1911 ed., 9. Emphasis in original.
[41] Ibid., vi.
[42] A. A. Neznamov, *Tekushchie voennye voprosy* (St. Petersburg, 1909), 56, as cited by Von Wahlde, "Military Thought," 321.
[43] Neznamov, "Sovremennaia voina," 1912 ed., in Beskrovnyi, *Russkaia voenno-teoreticheskaia mysl'*, 557-61, 567, 624; Neznamov, "Plan voiny" (St. Petersburg, 1913), in Beskrovnyi, *Russkaia voenno-teoreticheskaia mysl'*, 673-93; see also the discussion of Neznamov in Von Wahlde, "Military Thought," 223-33.

Peter the Great with his genius certainly recognized the boundary between the useful and the damaging in adopting foreign things; he loved Russia more than his own son, whom he sacrificed for its welfare. In his own words he thus described the nature of his "imitations": "Europe is still necessary to us for several decades, after that we will turn our back to it." He dreamed "that we would overtake and outstrip it." In some ways so it was, even if only in military affairs! But then history repeated itself, and Europe overtook us again. And once again we will take up the old method; quickly take what is ready, what is best, and improve upon it at home and then "turn our backs" afterwards.[44]

Clearly Neznamov stood in that long line of Russian thinkers and leaders who believed that Russia could and should borrow from the West without worrying about losing its national identity. Some had been government leaders like Peter I, Count Witte in the late nineteenth century, or Miliutin; others were dissenters like Alexander Radishchev, who took Catherine's Enlightenment rhetoric to heart, Paul Miliukov, the leader of the liberal Cadet party in Neznamov's own day, or Lenin and other Marxists.

Neznamov was a colonel when he published *Sovremennaia voina* in 1911, a professor at the General Staff academy. Although his seniors may have read his works and even approved of them in part, it seems unlikely that he influenced the major strategic decisions that were made in those years, and which affected Russian policy in 1914 and subsequently. He is important and interesting because he represents the extreme "Western" position in the spectrum of military thought.

IV

Among the men who planned, or wished to plan, Russia's strategy on the eve of the First World War a division of opinion existed that very roughly corresponded to the division among theorists between the national school and the academics. Sukhomlinov, the minister of war and a dominant figure in the development of policy was a protégé of Dragomirov, the grand old man of the national school. Arrayed against his views on many matters was a group of officers known as the Young Turks who were convinced that Western technology and military methods were of central importance for the Russian army. This group included General Golovin, whose extensive writing as an émigré after the Revolution made him well known in the West, and General Alekseev, commander of the important Kiev Military District in 1914. The latter's

[44] Neznamov, "Plan voiny," 714.

influence was crucial in determining the plan put into effect, of attacking both Austria and Germany in the early weeks of the war.

This fateful and, in retrospect, clearly mistaken decision was the result of geographical reality and political circumstances, which made it very difficult to attack only one or the other of the Central European powers. The outcome was an unhappy compromise that had the advantages of neither alternative. The western limit of the empire was Russian Poland, bordered by Austria-Hungary on the south and by Germany to the west and north. It was thus an exposed salient, vulnerable to a pincers movement from Austrian Galicia to the south and German East-Prussia to the north. In the years immediately after the Russo-Japanese War and the 1905 revolution when much of the Russian army was diverted to internal security duties, the High Command decided on a strategic defensive that called for abandoning much of Poland and establishing a defensive line further to the east that would not be threatened from either the northern or southern flanks. This was consistent with reality and with some of the ideas of the "national school," which recognized defense in depth as part of the Russian tradition. However, as a defensive plan it went counter to the widespread notion among virtually all strategic theorists of the day that offensive action was normally preferable.

Between 1910 and 1914 as the Russian army increased in strength, the alliance with France became closer, and as Russian confidence in the French and fear of the Germans grew, the plan was revised. Minister of War Sukhomlinov and General Danilov argued for the earliest possible offensive against Germany, while maintaining a defensive stance against Austria. Germany was the main threat and if the Germans succeeded in overwhelming France, Russia's position would be hopeless. Therefore it was essential to do everything possible to divert German pressure from France. But geography made this approach very difficult. An offensive from the western border of Russian Poland against Berlin would be exposed to German flank attacks south from East Prussia that might well cut it off. An offensive against East Prussia was complicated by the impenetrable Masurian Lakes region and the lack of north-south rail lines. The Russians could attack only from the east and march north from Poland while the German forces could be moved east and west by rail to deal with a two-pronged Russian attack. In the event this is what actually happened.

The alternative to mounting an immediate offensive against Germany, advancing south into Austrian Galicia was advocated by General Alekseev. The Austro-Russia frontier was not easily defended, and even if the Russians did not attack, many troops would be needed to guard against an Austrian offensive. Therefore, the argument was, why not move west and south against Austria into territory inhabited by friendly Slavic peoples? An early success there might force Austria out of the war. The plan was consistent with traditional pan-Slav sentiments and anti-Austrian feelings, and for purely geographical reasons seemed to promise much greater prospects of rapid victory. The upshot of the disagreement was an attempt to attack both Austria and Germany quickly, which meant that neither offensive had the resources it needed to achieve a decisive success. Good arguments could be made for each strategy, but no one had sufficient authority to insist on one or the other and the result was a disastrous compromise.[45]

None of the major military writers of the prewar period belonged to the group that was primarily responsible for determining Russia's actual moves at the start of the war. The man who came closest was N. P. Mikhnevich, from 1904 to 1907 director of the General Staff Academy and from 1911 to 1917 chief of the general staff. Mikhnevich's textbook on strategy replaced Leer's as the standard at the beginning of the twentieth century.[46] He was a moderate nationalist, somewhere between the extreme of Neznamov on one side and A. N. Kuropatkin on the other. Kuropatkin, the unsuccessful commander of the Russian armies in the war with Japan, argued in his three-volume history of the Russian army, published in 1910, that since the defeat of Napoleon, Russia had been weakened in both a spiritual and material sense by increased westernization and involvement in European affairs. Although not opposed to adopting modern military technology, Kuropatkin was first and foremost a romantic nationalist who believed that "Russia must belong to the Russians," not to the foreigners or to the non-Russian citizens of the empire.[47]

A sober and systematic writer, familiar with Western military thought, Mikhnevich did not engage in any such nationalistic excesses, but he was nevertheless capable of writing in 1898: "Our military art has almost never lagged behind Europe and quite often advanced ahead of it, giving direction and new ideas in tactics and strategy which Europe acquired from us."[48] Like Kuropatkin, Mikhnevich was well aware that technology was having a major impact on warfare; he published a book

---

[45] See Jack Snyder, The Cult of the Offensive in European War Planning, 1870-1914 (Ithaca, 1984), chs. 6, 7, and Norman Stone, The Eastern Front, 1914-1917 (London and New York, 1975), chs. 1, 2. The principal Russian source on war plans is A. M. Zaionchkovskii, Podgotovka Rossii k imperialisicheskoi voine (Moscow, 1926).

[46] N. P. Mikhnevich, Strategiia, 2 vols. (St. Petersburg, 1899-1901).

[47] A. N. Kuropatkin, Zadachi russkoi armii (St. Petersburg, 1910), 1:i-iii, 3:189.

[48] N. P. Mikhnevich, Osnovy russkogo voennogo iskusstva. Sravnitel'nyi ocherk sostoianiia voennogo iskusstva v Rossii i zapadnoi Evrope v vazhneishie istoricheskie epokhi (St. Petersburg, 1898), 9-10, as quoted in Von Wahlde, "Military Thought," 206.

in 1898 called *The Influence of the Newest Technical Inventions on Army Tactics*.[49] In it he deals carefully with the various new and improved weapons, but concludes that the balance between attack and defense has not really been changed and that all great commanders preferred attack because it confers a moral advantage and permits concentration of effort at a decisive point.[50]

Fifteen years later, in 1913, after the experience of the Russo-Japanese War, Mikhnevich was somewhat less Suvorov-like when he wrote: "Offensive action reaps greater benefits, but can only be undertaken when the army has completed its strategic deployment, and is fully prepared with sufficient forces."[51] Possibly this was a criticism of Russia's war plans at the time, which called for a very rapid move to the offensive in order to support France. Nevertheless, the traditional national-school emphasis on moral force is evident when he argues that superiority of forces is essential to victory not merely in numbers but in moral force as well. He quantifies the relative importance of the two factors, saying that victory depends three-fourths on moral force and one-fourth on material factors. Furthermore, to demonstrate Russia's superior military spirit, Mikhnevich presents tables showing that European armies over the centuries have suffered higher casualty rates fighting Russian soldiers than in fighting other Europeans. Finally, returning to the question of technology, he concludes that an army's weapons must be as good as its enemies', not so much because of the greater effectiveness of superior ones, but because having inferior weapons hurts morale.[52] In contrast to Neznamov and many European writers of the time, Mikhnevich rejected the notion of a "lightning war" and argued that Russia had an advantage over the more developed European industrial states, whose economies would be disrupted by the mobilization of labor: "Thus time is the best ally of our military forces, and for that reason it is not dangerous for us to follow 'a strategy of attrition and exhaustion,' initially avoiding decisive engagements with the enemy on the border when the superiority of forces may be on its side."[53] This opinion, which recalls Gulevich, was something of a departure from the usual national view that discounted economic backwardness as an advantage, despite the possible example of Kutuzov's defeat of Napoleon. The national school had gen-

---

[49] N. P. Mikhnevich, *Vliianie noveishikh tekhnicheskikh izobretenii na taktiku voisk* (St. Petersburg, 1898).

[50] Mikhnevich, "Vliianie" in Beskrovnyi, *Russkaia voenno-teoreticheskaia mysl'*, 415, 426.

[51] N. P. Mikhnevich, "Osnovy strategii" (St. Petersburg, 1913), in Beskrovnyi, *Russkaia voenno-teoreticheskaia mysl'*, 463.

[52] Ibid., 464, 467-69.

[53] Ibid., 461.

erally preferred to emphasize the more positive quality of the spiritual advantage of the Russian soldier. Mikhnevich, of course, was wrong about the vulnerability of advanced industrial economies—but so was almost every other writer, European and Russian, on the eve of World War I.

V

It has not been the purpose of this essay to suggest that the relationship between Russia and the West was the only issue in Russian strategic thought. The men who have been discussed briefly, and others who have not even been mentioned, were well-informed, perceptive professionals and their works dealt with many subjects: mobilization, logistics, the coordination of different types of forces (infantry, artillery, cavalry, etc.), operational and strategic planning, and so forth. However, it is the issue of Russia's special characteristics that separates Russian strategic thinkers from other European writers on the subject and also provides the intellectual link between them and Russian thinkers in other fields. Whether they were eager westernizers or the most ardent believers in Russia's special advantages, all had to grapple with the threefold problem of the glorious Russian military past, the depressing experiences of the nineteenth and twentieth century, and their wish as professionals to hold their heads up in a world where Russian achievements in other fields were gaining worldwide recognition.

It is easy to dismiss the national school as foolish romantics who ignored the technical realities of their own time, yet to do so would be a mistake. The will to fight, to risk death, is essential for any army. Russian soldiers under the worst of commanders, not to mention inspired leaders like Suvorov, had proven repeatedly that they would fight both at home and abroad with impressive tenacity. This was unquestionably an asset that it would have been foolish to ignore. That it dovetailed nicely with the desire of intellectuals to satisfy their own need for confidence relative to Europe is incidental. But the emphasis on the importance of moral force, of spirit, seems not to have penetrated the lower levels of the officer corps, and thus had little effect on the miserable life of the enlisted men and the relationship between them and their officers. That the soldiers at the front remained loyal until after the February 1917 revolution suggests that, nevertheless, the exponents of the national school were to some degree correct about the nature of the Russian peasant soldier.

But the two schools of thought were not fundamentally incompatible; it was after all, a matter of emphasis. "Academics" did not deny the importance of morale and spirit, and nationalists recognized that

374

modern weapons were essential. Perhaps only in Russia, because of the sensitive nature of the broader issue of Russia and Europe, could emphasis on one or the other of these two essential aspects of a military effort have come to be the basis of a division in strategic thought that lasted for generations.

14. Bugeaud, Galliéni, Lyautey: The Development of French Colonial Warfare

Douglas Porch

COLONIAL WARFARE remains one of the more neglected areas of military history. This is particularly strange when it comes to the nineteenth century, because the major military experience of both the British and the French armies between Waterloo and the Marne lay outside of Europe. The British fought only one European opponent between 1815 and 1914—Russia in the Crimea. The French, it is true, played a more active military role on the continent of Europe, especially under Napoleon III. However, between 1830 and 1854, sixty-seven of France's one hundred line infantry regiments saw an average of six years' service in North Africa and most of the senior generals during the Second Empire were "Africains." In the forty-three-year period of peace between the major European powers that preceded the outbreak of the First World War, the colonies were the only place where a French soldier might hear a shot fired in anger. Colonial service offered one of the favored paths of advancement in the French army. It is hardly surprising, therefore, that some of the most influential soldiers in pre-1914 France possessed substantial colonial experience: Joffre and Galliéni, together with a host of lesser-known officers, including Franchet d'Esperey, Mangin, Gouraud, Henrys, and Philipot, who were to rise to high rank in the war. In fact, so conspicuous was the colonial element in the French High Command both in 1870 and in 1914 that the blame for France's poor military performance in both wars has often been based on the misplaced application in Europe of methods of warfare developed in the colonies. Critics especially stressed the link between colonial service and the murderous and futile attacks of the early months of the First World War that was provided by Colonel Louis de Grandmaison, a colonial soldier who, as chief of the 3ᵉ Bureau, inspired the infantry Regulations of 1913, which officially sanctioned the offensive *à outrance*.

The French army abroad prided itself on its ability to adapt to the new conditions of warfare that it met outside of Europe. Almost from the moment they set foot in North Africa in 1830, many soldiers of the *armée d'Afrique* began to exhibit the desire to "go native" that was to characterize the French approach to colonial conquest. The colorful, Africanized uniforms adopted by many soldiers in Algeria simply offered the most visible evidence of their commitment to adapt, chameleon-like, to their new environment. Although the British army abroad recruited among conquered peoples and made some concessions to native tradition, its colonial regiments were essentially cast in a European mold. French soldiers, however, adopted not only the dress but also the tactics they encountered in Africa. Indeed, the strength of their colonial methods in their own judgment lay in their ability to harness the "natural" fighting abilities and styles of warfare of their erstwhile enemies to the juggernaut of French colonial conquest. The French did not seek to Europeanize their native recruits. Rather, they wanted them to practice their traditional methods of warfare, but under the guiding hand, and in the interests, of France.

French strategy and tactics in Africa were not only dictated by the enemy. They were also determined by the nature of the terrain. Campaigning over barren and remote areas, against an often-elusive foe, French soldiers were forced to abandon methods of fighting suitable to Europe. Mobility, small-unit operations, and surprise became more important in Africa than weight of numbers and conventional logistics.

Our received view of the French colonial army, then, is that there existed a "colonial school" of warfare whose main theories were developed by Bugeaud in Algeria and later refined by Galliéni in Tonkin and Lyautey in Morocco. This "colonial school" came into being because of the new conditions that French soldiers met abroad. Isolated in Africa and Indochina, French colonial soldiers lost touch with the realities of European warfare. Encouraged by their successes against poorly armed and organized natives, they transferred their African experience back to Europe and sought to apply it in conditions that were entirely inappropriate. Therefore, a large share of the blame for French military shortcomings in Europe in 1914 has fallen upon the shoulders of these men.

This view needs closer examination. Given the great variety of French military experience abroad, the different levels of sophistication of the opponents French troops encountered, and the extremes of terrain and climate in which they fought, it must have been difficult, if not impossible, to distill a set of tactical principles applicable in all situations. Much has been said about the influence of the colonial experience in France. But how important was the influence of the metropolitan army, of "European" thinking, in the colonies? Also, given the steady deterioration of civil-military relations in France during the nineteenth and twentieth centuries, and the basic indifference, and at times downright hostility, of most Frenchmen to colonialism, might not politics or popular prejudices have had some influence on the development of the French army abroad? In short, did there exist in the French army a "colonial school" of warfare as Lyautey and others suggest,[1] or were colonial methods no more than the product of trial and error and perhaps of factors that were not even African in origin? And lastly, how far did the colonial military experience influence French methods in Europe before 1914?

I

If a "colonial school" of warfare existed in France, its founder was incontestably Marshal Thomas-Robert Bugeaud. A Napoleonic veteran who had seen extensive service in Spain, Bugeaud spent his years of enforced retirement from the army during the Bourbon Restoration pondering France's defeat. When he reentered the army following the July Revolution of 1830, his views on counterinsurgency warfare were already well formed. Although he spent a few months in Algeria in 1836, his outspoken hostility to the Algerian adventure eliminated him from consideration for high command there. However, Bugeaud seems to have undergone a change of heart by 1839, and actively sought the posts of governor general and commander in chief, to which King Louis Philippe appointed him the following year.

When Bugeaud arrived in Algeria in 1840, he was nearly overwhelmed by a sense of *déjà vu*—the French army was repeating all of the mistakes that it had made in Spain. Most of the soldiers were tied down defending fixed points and tormented by the Arabs who raided their supply wagons and destroyed crops and supplies "behind the lines." Attempts to launch reprisal raids faltered in the absence of any clear objectives. Columns of thousands of men, weighted down by artillery and heavy convoys of supplies, toiled over a stark and blistered countryside in search of their foe. The enemy retreated before them, refusing battle but slashing at flanks, supply convoys, and stragglers. After a few weeks of campaigning in this manner, French columns would return to base exhausted, with very little to show for their efforts.

Bugeaud set out to remodel his listless and demoralized command: "We must forget those orchestrated and dramatic battles that civilized peoples fight against one another," he proclaimed to his troops, "and realize that unconventional tactics are the soul of this war." Bugeaud based his reforms on four principles: mobility, morale, leadership, and firepower. In place of fortifications, which had been the principal French method of controlling the countryside, he emphasized the value of scout-

---

[1] Jean Gottman, "Bugeaud, Galliéni, Lyautey: The Development of French Colonial Warfare," in *Makers of Modern Strategy*, ed. Edward Mead Earle (Princeton, 1943).

ing parties and intelligence reports in locating enemy forces against which troops could be rapidly deployed. Mobile columns numbering from a few hundred to a few thousand men, shorn of artillery and heavy wagons, could fan out over the countryside to converge from different directions on a previously selected objective. In this way, Bugeaud was able to penetrate into areas that before had been immune to attack, carry the fight into the very heart of the Kabylia Mountains, and give his enemies no rest.

Such a strategy would have been impossible, however, without appropriate psychological preparation. Demoralized soldiers are seldom offensive-minded, and the morale of Bugeaud's command in 1840 stood at rock bottom. French uniforms and equipment were unsuited to the African climate. Confined to disease-ridden garrisons, continually harassed by Arab raiders, most soldiers preferred a diet of dogs, cats, and roots to the stale bread, poor-quality rice, and salted bacon provided, a diet that often produced violent diarrhea and could lead to death from dehydration. Arrangements for dealing with the sick and wounded were primitive, and assignment to the hospital almost tantamount to a death sentence. Indeed, conditions in military hospitals were so frightful that soldiers would sometimes commit suicide to avoid a lingering and squalid death there.[2]

Bugeaud set out to instill a new sense of optimism. The health of his men improved almost as soon as they were taken out of their pestilential garrisons. New provisions were made for the care of sick and wounded who before, on campaign, had often been abandoned to the mercy of the Arabs. Permanent hospitals replaced wooden sheds that were little more than mortuaries. Equipment was redesigned and the load of the foot soldier considerably lightened; supplies were carried by mules instead of men or wagons. Small mobile columns now moved into the hills, surviving by plundering the grain silos or raiding the flocks of the Arabs. Concern for the welfare of his men combined with their confidence in his talents as a leader to breathe new life into military operations. Bugeaud's example filtered through the officer corps, lending confidence and energy to the entire army. By 1842, he had put the army back on the offensive and could claim with only slight exaggeration that he had made his force "even more Arab than the Arabs."

Bugeaud's thinking about firepower underwent some modifications during his stay in Algeria. Originally, he had criticized the French for forming massive squares of up to three thousand men, several lines deep.

[2] Anthony Thrall Sullivan, *Thomas-Robert Bugeaud, France and Algeria 1784-1849: Politics, Power, and the Good Society* (Hamden, Conn., 1983), 85.

Arabs seldom attempted to overwhelm squares, and the men in the interior ranks were wasted because they were unable to fire. Instead, he advocated a number of small squares with overlapping fields of fire to give mutual support. Volleys should be regular, and firing withheld for as long as possible to allow the enemy to get close enough to do him real damage. After 1836, however, it became apparent that no Arab army existed that was large enough to threaten French squares or posts. Skirmishing, rather than pitched battles, became the rule in Algeria, and the emphasis on squares and fire discipline diminished.[3]

Bugeaud was certainly one of the ablest and most imaginative technicians of war in the nineteenth century. He moulded a force capable of offensive operations, set his objective, and then sought to bring his enemy to battle where the superior discipline and firepower of his troops gave him the advantage. When the Arabs could not be brought to battle, as was increasingly the case after 1836, he operated against their resources. By destroying their livelihoods, Bugeaud forced the Arabs to submit.

The *razzia*, or raid, had long been practiced in Africa. The acquisition of booty rather than the desire to inflict death characterized North African warfare before the arrival of the French. Pitched battles were few, and were usually formless skirmishes in which men sought to overawe with noise rather than to kill large numbers of the enemy.

In 1841, however, Bugeaud elevated the *razzia* to the level of total war. Before this time, the French had only sporadically practiced the burning of crops and cutting down of trees. Bugeaud was frustrated, no doubt, by the Arabs' refusal to stand and fight. Also, despite his much-vaunted claims of French mobility, his troops were often unable to catch their elusive enemy. Therefore, he launched his first campaign of devastation in the upper Cheliff near Miliana. Blackened fields, destroyed fruit orchards, and devastated villages soon marked the passage of French columns everywhere in Algeria. General Castellane, who visited Algeria in this period, defended the *razzia*: "In Europe, once [you are] master of two or three large cities, the entire country is yours," he wrote. "But in Africa, how do you act against a population whose only link with the land is the pegs of their tents? . . . The only way is to take the grain which feeds them, the flocks which clothe them. For this reason, we make war on silos, war on cattle, the *razzia*."[4]

Whatever the military arguments in favor of the *razzia*, its long-term effects were baleful. Discipline was difficult to maintain when soldiers

[3] For Bugeaud's military reforms, see Gottman, "Bugeaud, Galliéni, Lyautey," and Sullivan, *Thomas-Robert Bugeaud*, 77-93.

[4] General le Comte de Castellane, *Souvenirs de la vie militaire en Afrique* (Paris, 1879), 268.

were allowed to burn, pillage, and rape. Soon attitudes hardened, sensibilities were anesthetized, and any political or military goals beyond utter devastation were lost in an orgy of brutality and excess. The growing savagery of the war hit its nadir in June 1845, when Colonel Amable Pelissier trapped a group of Arabs in the caves of Dahra in the coastal mountains north of Cheliff. After desultory negotiations, Pelissier ordered a fire built in the cave mouth. Five hundred Arab men, women, and children were asphyxiated.

When Pelissier's report describing the atrocity in lurid and self-congratulatory prose was released to the Chamber of Peers, a storm of protest broke out in France. But far from condemning his subordinate, Bugeaud praised Pelissier and even suggested that the action might be repeated. In August of that year, Colonel Saint-Arnaud entombed a large number of Arabs who had sought refuge in a cave: "There are five hundred brigands down there who will never again butcher Frenchmen," he trumpeted. Other mass liquidations followed over the next two years.[5]

It must be said that the French behaved with no greater brutality abroad than did other colonial powers—the Russians in the Caucausus, the British during the Indian Mutiny, or the Germans at the turn of the century. But these well-publicized atrocities were to have long-term consequences, the first and most obvious being the continued hostility of the Arabs. Bugeaud saw no need to appease his opponents, arguing that only through the hard hand of war would they "accept the yoke of conquest." For Bugeaud, the Arabs' hostility was unalterable and therefore, they had to be crushed to be controlled.[6] He also attempted to establish villages of retired soldiers in strategic locations to ensure the security of the countryside. But few settlers stepped forward and these plans were abandoned.

With the conquest of Algeria completed, some officers came to see the army as the protector of the Arabs against the French settlers' greed and racism. However, the bad blood and distrust of these years of conquest was never dissipated. Soldiers were always conscious that they stood guard over a sullen and hostile mass of Algerians who might one day rise up and cast them into the sea. Hence their extreme nervousness at the slightest indication of an Islamic religious revival, which they feared might galvanize the Algerians into revolt.

The second consequence of Bugeaud's campaigns was that they outraged Frenchmen. It was only too obvious that Algerian service had distorted the values of French soldiers, and that a gulf had opened be-

[5] Sullivan, *Thomas-Robert Bugeaud*, 127-32.
[6] Ibid., 129.

tween the claims of France to bring civilization and order to Africa and the bitter realities of conquest. In 1846, Alexis de Tocqueville returned from Algeria horrified by the excesses of the military regime there—he later described the officers of the Algerian army as "imbecilic."[7] The atrocities of the French army in Algeria, their flaunting of the most basic notions of liberty even when dealing with European civilians, fed anti-militarism in France that with the Dreyfus affair at the end of the century would become a significant political force.

Finally, Bugeaud's campaigns alienated the army from France. Cast from Europe into an Islamic region, their sense of *dépaysement* was already acute. They consoled themselves with the thought that they were fighting for the greater glory of their country. However, they were per-plexed when their hardships were ignored at home, annoyed when the purpose of their presence in Africa was questioned, and, ultimately, en-raged when their methods of campaigning were condemned. France, they felt, neither understood nor appreciated them: "Here we are in Africa, ruining our health, risking our lives, working for the glory of France, and the most uninformed observer can insult us and slander our inten-tions, imputing to us criminal feelings which are not of this century and which cannot belong to a soldier," Saint-Arnaud bellowed. "Be off with you, public revilers!"[8] This feeling that it had been "wronged and mis-represented" forced the army in Africa to turn in on itself, to seek comfort in the fact that they were a band of brothers, professional military ex-patriates for whom France was increasingly a remote and incomprehen-sible land. They were men trapped between two cultures, unwilling to become African and unable to return home.

The long-term effects of this attitude on civil-military relations in France have frequently been noted. What is interesting within the frame-work of this study is the effect that it had on operations in the colonies. They lost nothing of their brutality. On the contrary, among all but a few officers the feeling that disapproval in France was automatic removed any need to cater to metropolitan sensibilities. It is in this context of the growing unpopularity of the army in France and the discredit that the campaigns of the 1840s and later campaigns in West Africa brought upon the entire colonial enterprise, that the theories of Galliéni and Lyautey must be understood.

II

Galliéni and Lyautey are two names most commonly associated with France's second phase of colonial expansion, which began under the

---

[7] Melvin Richter, "Tocqueville on Algeria," *Review of Politics* 25 (July 1963), 377.
[8] Sullivan, *Thomas-Robert Bugeaud*, 130.

Third Republic. To be sure, French imperial expansion had not come to a halt after Algerian resistance ceased in 1847. The French navy established coastal bases in Vietnam, General Faidherbe extended the French foothold in Senegal, and there was the ill-fated Mexican venture. But these were relatively limited operations. This changed in the 1880s. Almost overnight, French soldiers took on the tasks of digesting an enormous chunk of Africa, invading Madagascar, and extending French power into the Indochinese hinterland.

The situation of colonial soldiers under the Third Republic had altered somewhat since the days of Bugeaud. In the first place, advances in military technology were to give Europeans in Africa enormous advantages over their opponents. When the French invaded Algeria in 1830, the Algerians possessed at least eight thousand muskets, enough to deprive the conquerors of any significant technological advantage. In the field, the long-barrelled *jezail* could actually out-range French muskets, which were designed for volley-firing at close quarters. Discipline, rather than superior weaponry, was the key to conquest. The only advantage in firepower the French possessed—their artillery—was willingly forfeited by Bugeaud because of its weight and immobility.

In the last quarter of the nineteenth century, the availability of bolt-action and magazine-fed rifles gave the French an incontestable technological advantage over opponents who were armed with an assortment of antique or primitive weapons. Even when their opponents did manage to acquire modern rifles, as did Samori and some Moroccan tribes, they seldom had them in sufficient numbers, possessed an adequate supply of ammunition, or developed the fire discipline to use them to full advantage.

French firepower was assisted by the introduction in the 1890s of the Maxim gun, which fired at a rate of eleven shots a second. The kind of artillery that Bugeaud had jettisoned as too heavy was replaced by portable 80-mm, and later 65-mm "mountain guns," which could be broken down and carried on the backs of mules or camels. In Morocco, the French could even use their 75s. Their opponents seldom acquired artillery, and when they did, they were usually museum pieces. These technological advances obviously added muscle to French expeditions. They also allowed smaller numbers of men to campaign, because volume of fire was no longer related absolutely to numbers of soldiers. Smaller expeditions permitted an increase in mobility. Artillery also allowed French to break into the mud- and stone-walled fortresses, called "tatas," which dotted the African landscape. Small numbers of disciplined troops armed with rapid-fire rifles and artillery could now defeat far larger armies armed with old-fashioned weapons. Superior firepower was incontestably the major advantage that the French held over their non-European opponents.

A second way in which the army's situation differed from that under Bugeaud had to do with the creation of regiments tailored for colonial service. As has been noted, the conquest of Algeria was carried out in the main by metropolitan French regiments; but a few imaginative commanders had begun to develop specialized native regiments.

As the century wore on, France increasingly relied on native recruits to do its fighting. In 1857, Faidherbe raised the first regiment of *tirailleurs sénégalais*. Native troops were also raised in Tonkin, Madagascar, Vietnam, and in the Sahara, and henceforth served with the French marines, who also provided most of the officers and NCOs for the native regiments, the Foreign Legion, and the French disciplinary units. By 1900 at the latest, colonial troops made up one-tenth of French army strength.[9]

There are many reasons why the French chose to rely on native troops to bear the brunt of imperial expansion. French officers claimed that these men, recruited in the country, were more resilient and adaptable than whites, who tended to die in large numbers when exposed to the rigors of the African climate. They also argued, mainly for home consumption, that native recruitment was part of a "divide and rule" policy, which helped to split African opposition to French expansion: Frenchmen were not conquering Africans; Africans were conquering Africans for France. In this way, brutalities might be explained as the result of African, rather than of French, excesses.

Another factor that favored native recruitment was cost. Natives were paid next to nothing; often they would sign up for a campaign simply for a new rifle and the prospect of booty. They could live off the land, and so did not require the supply convoys that accompanied French troops.

French colonial soldiers also came to prefer native troops for a reason that was linked to the introduction of universal conscription in France following the Franco-Prussian War. Although colonial soldiers argued

[9] The term "colonial soldier" is perhaps a confusing one, especially within the scope of this essay. France, in effect, possessed two colonial forces. The *armée d'Afrique* was composed of North African soldiers and white regiments raised for service in the Maghreb—the Foreign Legion, *bataillons d'Afrique*, Zouaves, and *chasseurs d'Afrique*. The *armée coloniale* properly speaking grew out of the *infanterie de marine* and *tirailleurs* recruited in sub-Saharan Africa, Indochina, and other colonies. The colonial army formed a branch of the French navy until it was given separate status within the War Ministry in 1900. However, these categories were never watertight. The Foreign Legion was used in the Sudan, Dahomey, Madagascar, and Indochina; Algerian *tirailleurs* fought in Indochina and Madagascar; and marines and Senegalese *tirailleurs* participated in the conquest of Morocco. It was also common for soldiers of the metropolitan army to be seconded to the colonies, as was the case with both Galliéni and Lyautey.

that French conscripts adapted poorly to colonial conditions, their real fear was that citizen-soldiers would bring political influence to bear overseas. The last thing colonial officers desired was parliamentary committees of enquiry criss-crossing the colonies in answer to complaints initiated by disgruntled French conscripts. The poor civil-military relations of the Bugeaud era had taught colonial soldiers the value of a closed professional corps. Their desire to isolate themselves from France and from the French metropolitan army was fully realized in 1900, when the colonial army was given a separate organization and status.

A third factor that influenced colonial operations in the late nineteenth century was the atmosphere of intense international competition that surrounded the race for colonies. The Congo Congress in Berlin of 1884-1885 had established the principle of "effective occupation" as the prerequisite for colonial claims. It also announced that Germany had joined the race for African territory. French colonial soldiers, among whom a buccaneering element predominated, now ranged themselves on the starting blocks for the great African land rush.

The urgency that international competition gave to colonial conquest, especially in the minds of nationalistic and ambitious French soldiers, often led to the most elemental notions of tactical prudence being sacrificed in a headlong rush to stake territorial claims. Bugeaud had disdained supply lines and launched flying columns into the Algerian hinterland. But his experience confirmed that these operations should not be prolonged because they took an excessive toll on men and animals.[10] And Bugeaud's flying columns had had a military rationale. This was often not the case in the Western Sudan. By the 1880s, independent military columns began to venture far beyond the bounds of what even Bugeaud would have thought safe. Usually firepower was sufficient to extricate the French from difficult situtions. But on more than one occasion in West Africa, columns set out over unexplored territory only to run short of supplies. They were then forced to retreat, often after leaving a precarious outpost far too distant to be effectively supported when it was attacked.[11] The French column of eight thousand men that set out from Majunga on the Madagascar coast to march the 350 miles to Tananarive in 1895 suffered horribly in the malarial swamps and almost perished once it reached the arid central plateau. After three months it was still 125 miles from its objective. General Duchesne was forced to

[10] Hew Strachan, *European Armies and the Conduct of War* (London and Boston, 1983), 83.
[11] A. S. Kanya-Forstner, *The Conquest of the Western Sudan* (Cambridge, 1963), 188-89.

select 3,500 of the fittest troops and order them to march to Tananarive or die in the attempt.

The neglect of common sense in colonial warfare became especially apparent in the century's closing years, when the "flying column" entered the realm of the surreal. Marchand's epic march across Africa to Fashoda and the supporting missions of Foureau-Lamy, Voulet-Chanoine, and Emile Gentile, which together composed what is often referred to as the three-pronged "race for Lake Chad," demonstrated how far military planning had been sacrificed to the ambitions of colonial soldiers and their desire to steal a march on international competition. Marchand's three-thousand-mile expedition offered a tremendous demonstration of stamina, an inspiration to French schoolboys. But the military purpose of his expedition has never been clear. Only two things could have happened to him: either the Madhi's forces would wipe him out, or those of Kitchener would. The 250-man column of Foureau and Lamy, which took the desert route from Algiers to Lake Chad, was able to survive only by shooting hostages and surrounding wells to force the thirsty inhabitants to bring them food and pack animals. The notorious Voulet-Chanoine mission soon lost all military cohesion because its troops were unable to feed themselves: they meandered through the countryside east of the Niger River raiding and killing until the two captains perished in a mutiny among their African auxiliary troops. Gentil's route of advance from the south along the Chari River encountered a series of forts constructed by the Sudanese adventurer Rabih. The frequent need to return to Brazzaville for men and supplies meant that his campaign to reach Lake Chad took nearly five years.

A final element that influenced the evolution of French colonial tactics under the Third Republic was the political evolution of the army. The force that emerged from the Napoleonic Wars contained a large number of officers considered left-wing by the standards of the times. The Bourbon Restoration never trusted its soldiers, and the army's lackluster performance in the "trois glorieuses" of 1830 can be attributed in great part to the gulf of confidence that existed between it and the Restoration. The Ecole Polytechnique in the early years of the nineteenth century was a bastion of liberalism. Consequently, the artillery and the engineers especially were regarded as the "republican" arms.

As the century progressed, however, the army's political center of gravity shifted toward the right. This change was due more to the bureaucratization of the army, which gave it an interest in order, rather than to the fact that the conservative classes were attracted in great numbers to the career of arms. Officers like Cavaignac, who had been exiled to Algeria because of his extreme left-wing views, saw no contradiction in 1848 in being both republican and antirevolutionary. However, the army's suppression of the Parisian workers in the June Days of 1848, the association of some officers like Saint-Arnaud with Louis-Napoleon's *coup d'état* of December 2, 1851, and, finally, the violent repression of the Commune in 1871, served notice on the Left that they could no longer hope to find support within the military. The Dreyfus affair was a singular disaster for the army, because it fostered a cynical view of military justice and the military mentality in a broad section of the middle classes. It shattered the understanding among political parties that the army was inviolate. The army, like the Church, was now thrust into the world of politics as never before. Politicians on the Left, who controlled governments from 1899, were now prepared to exploit any military scandal for their own ends. The Right was equally prepared to go very far in the army's defense.

The distinctly military stamp of French imperialism left the colonialists vulnerable to the Left's antimilitarism. Few politicians were seriously interested in military reform, or in halting the race for colonies in Africa. However, colonial operations were now drawn into domestic politics. This was first apparent in 1885, when the Chamber of Deputies used Negrier's defeat at Lang-son in Indochina as an excuse to overthrow the procolonial government of Jules Ferry. Toward the end of the century, the wedding of militarism and colonialism produced even more political offspring. The Right complained loudly over the government's retreat at Fachoda. The news of the Voulet-Chanoine atrocities could not have broken at a worse time for the army and the center-right, in the summer of 1899 in the midst of Captain Dreyfus's politically charged retrial at Rennes. The death of 25,000 camels at the hands of inexperienced French soldiers during the Tuat expedition of 1901-1902, together with the enormous costs of conquering a region whose annual trade "does not equal that of a grocery store in a large town," provoked denunciations of the "Algerian generals" in parliament and the introduction of a bill to bring military operations under the civilian governor general. The conquest of Morocco provided numerous occasions for political denunciations of soldiers and colonialists. The socialist leader Jean Jaurès could always be counted upon to condemn any military excesses in the colonies in ringing terms—for instance, in 1913, over 100,000 mourners were mustered by the Socialists for the funeral of Private Aenoult, who had died in mysterious circumstances in a Tunisian disciplinary battalion.

The growing strength of antimilitarism in France by the 1890s and the consequent vulnerability of the colonialist movement required a new approach to colonial conquest. The strategic theories of Galliéni and Lyautey were the response to the new conditions.

III

In his early years in Africa, there was little to distinguish Joseph-Simon Galliéni from other ambitious and impetuous young officers. However, by 1890, Galliéni seems to have become genuinely concerned about the reckless and ill-prepared French expeditions that had laid waste to great areas of the Western Sudan. He called for a suspension of operations to allow the devastated areas to recover. Galliéni argued that, by catering to the interests of African merchants, France would be able to extend its influence without further recourse to brute force. These views brought Galliéni to the attention of Eugène Etienne, deputy for Oran, undersecretary of state for the colonies, and future leader of the powerful "Colonial Party" in the Chamber of Deputies. It was through his contact with Etienne, and his presence as the military delegate on the 1889 departmental commission set up to advise on the future course of French policy on the Upper Niger—a commission extremely hostile to the French colonial officers—that Galliéni was made aware of the full extent of metropolitan discontent with military brutalities in Africa. Galliéni's views did not prevail, however, and when a rival, Colonel Louis Archinard, was reappointed *commandant supérieur* of the Sudan in 1892, Galliéni moved to Tonkin.

In Indochina, Galliéni was given the tasks of pacifying the extreme north of the country, which was infested by the Black Flags, Chinese "pirates" whom the French had driven from their coastal strongholds. Abandoning concepts of large-scale operations or "front lines," Galliéni put into practice a method he called "progressive occupation." Posts were established around which patrols would circulate, progressively extending the area of control until they touched upon that of an adjacent post. At the same time, the post would become a market that attracted the natives, often by purchasing their goods at prices above the market level. The arrival of the indigenous population allowed the French to make contacts and gather intelligence but, above all, to demonstrate that prosperity would follow cooperation with the French. The natives, grateful for the economic reconstruction of their land via the roads, markets, wells, and other public works projects sponsored by the French, recognized the advantages of colonialism and rallied to the occupying power.

Galliéni's views were codified and elaborated by his enthusiastic subordinate, Hubert Lyautey. At first glance, the two men seemed to have little in common. Galliéni's social origins were modest; Lyautey traced his roots to the great noble families of Normandy and the eastern marches of France, and openly disdained the "mediocrity" of bourgeois France. Galliéni was a hardened *broussard*—a man who had spent the greater part of his career in colonial service—and Lyautey had come to the colonies at the rather advanced age of forty. Until then, his service had been spent in general-staff assignments and in fashionable cavalry regiments; he had influential friends in the political and literary salons of the Faubourg Saint-Germain. Galliéni's devotion to the Third Republic was more than matched by Lyautey's nostalgia for the departed monarchy. Galliéni was cool, austere, aloof. Lyautey was warm, enthusiastic, a man of immense, if slightly brittle, charm.

That the two men were to meet and collaborate in Tonkin and subsequently in Madagascar was a fortuitous event that was to influence French military policy for years to come. How much Lyautey wanted to be assigned to Tonkin is unclear. Despite his obvious promise, or perhaps because of it, Lyautey was not popular in the army. Very ambitious, he quickly came to regret his choice of a military career with its slow promotion and tedious duties, and to despise the lack of imagination and torpor of his colleagues. In 1891, his frustrations found their way into print in an article that appeared in the prestigious *Revue des deux mondes*. "Du rôle social de l'officier dans le service militaire universel" offers a litany of complaints about the failure of the French army in the Third Republic to adapt to universal conscription. Lyautey draws a depressing picture of officers "who know their horses better than their men," of a general staff consumed by ambition, given to an excessively intellectual approach to the study of war, whose members sought to avoid troop command at all costs. Above all, Lyautey decried the failure of the officer corps to enter into the spirit of reformers like Captain Albert de Mun and General Louis Lewal, who saw the army as an institution that could reconcile the political, social, and religious differences that divided Frenchmen, and give them a sense of common purpose and patriotism. "Du rôle social de l'officier" reveals Lyautey as a frustrated idealist, in search of a cause that would forge national unity and lead to the regeneration of France.

In 1894, Lyautey was assigned to Indochina, and there discovered a man and an ideal worth serving. Despite their differences in background and temperament, Galliéni and Lyautey complemented each other perfectly. Galliéni was the quintessential soldier, who saw pacification as basically a military problem, even though he was prepared to employ politics and diplomacy to achieve his military goals. Lyautey absorbed Galliéni's methods but sought to elevate them into a general system, one that would reconcile colonial expansion with his idealism and patriotism. This was not an easy task, for Lyautey recognized that his idealized version of colonialism contained at least two inherent contradictions. First, colonialism meant the domination, and consequently the exploitation, of one race by another. Second, as many critics pointed out, colonial expansion was costly. How was Lyautey to convince them that all those acres of sand, scrub, and jungle that colonial soldiers were winning for France could eventually profit the colonizing power?

The answer is provided in part in a second article published by the *Revue des deux mondes* in January 1900, entitled "Du rôle colonial de l'Armée." The article praised Galliéni's methods in Tonkin. But more, it announced that the social role that metropolitan officers seemed reluctant to take up had, in fact, been adopted by officers in the colonies: "The colonial officer defines himself, above all, by his social role." A colonial soldier was more than a warrior. He was an administrator, farmer, architect, and engineer—in short, he took up any skill required to develop the region in his charge. In the colonies, Lyautey claimed, war was a constructive force, the prelude to the economic revival of lands torn by anarchy or suffering the heavy hand of oriental despotism. The colonial army became "an organization on the march" which employed economic, political, and diplomatic weapons to minimize the violence of conquest. In this way, colonialism was no longer the exploitation of one race by another and the imposition of an alien government. Colonialism led to progress, and therefore was beneficial to conqueror and conquered alike. Peace, stability, and the development of commercial and agricultural resources eventually would mean profits for both France and its colonies. Furthermore, this could be done in "association" with the native elites, through a supple, flexible protectorate that sought to guide the traditional hierarchy rather than supplant it with hidebound French officials who would try to run Tonkin or Madagascar as if they were metropolitan *départements*.

But Lyautey's article had a third dimension that is seldom discussed. In 1900, a bill to remove the colonial army from the custody of the navy and give it an independent status within the War Ministry was before parliament. Lyautey sought to influence the vote on that bill not only by praising the virtues of colonial expansion, but by claiming that the great task of empire building required, "a *colonial army*, that is really a *colonial army* and not only the *army in the colonies*, which is not the same thing." The colonial army needed its "autonomy" lest it be "absorbed, bureaucratized" by the metropolitan army, or flooded with officers who come to the colonies "to refight Austerlitz . . . badly prepared to carry out the patient, ungrateful, obscure work which are the daily tasks, the only profitable ones, of the colonial officer."[12]

[12] Hubert Lyautey, "Du rôle colonial de l'Armée," *Revue des deux mondes* 157 (January 15, 1900), 324-25.

"Du rôle colonial de l'Armée" is important, if for no other reason than that it announced that colonial soldiers were well on their way to acquiring a mentality that set them apart from their metropolitan colleagues, and a sense of mission that included not only the development of the colonies, but also the spiritual reconstruction of France. "It is impossible, as soon as one steps outside of France, not to realize everywhere the fluctuations of our methods and our receding influence," Lyautey wrote. "... This life outside [of France] brings with it our hours of doubt and anguish." However, his pessimism was tempered by the hope of national salvation through colonial action. According to Lyautey, the colonies had witnessed the "continuing, if not growing, worth of *individual* Frenchmen," which offered "an incomparable capital of energy and will which must not be squandered." For Lyautey, the colonial army was to furnish the spark and the cadre that would restore "la race française" to its preemiment place in the world.[13]

On the surface, at least, "Du rôle colonial de l'Armée" offers a sensible and humane approach to the problems of colonial conquest and development. Who could fail to applaud the functionary who castigated the idiocy of bureaucratic practice, the colonial soldier who decried the destructiveness of war, who envisaged a colonial world of happy and prosperous natives guided by enlightened colonial soldiers and administrators? However, the obvious question is, "Did it work?" Was the "rôle colonial" simply a vision of an ideal world, a piece of propaganda designed to ensure the passage of the colonial army law, or was it a realistic description of French colonial methods abroad? The answer is perhaps to be found in the French conquest of Morocco, an event with which Lyautey's name is indelibly linked. In 1903, he was named to command the military district of the South Oranais on the Algerian-Moroccan frontier. The apprentice now became a sorcerer in his own right, with carte blanche to apply the "Galliéni method" in Morocco. The experience was to prove that Lyautey's theories were at once too narrow and too idealistic.

The narrowness followed inevitably from his view of man as essentially an economic animal. In Morocco he told his officers: "The raison d'être of our colonial military operations is always, and above all, economic."[14] Consequently, the military engineers established posts that were to become "centers of attraction," where Moroccans could sell their goats, sheep, camels, and horses at prices far higher than they would fetch in the Tafilalet or Fez. They were also happy to visit army doctors

[13] Ibid., 238.
[14] André Le Révérand, *Lyautey* (Paris, 1983), 283.

391

whom Lyautey imported as part of his "hearts and minds" approach to conquest. But the marketplace never proved to be the "great agent of dissolution of the dissidents" that Lyautey had hoped. The Moroccans saw no contradiction in trading with the French one minute and plundering them the next. By drawing commerce away from the Tafilalet and Fez with his artificially inflated prices, he alienated powerful interests there. In 1906, these people ordered a boycott of French markets. By July, trade in French posts had virtually dried up.[15]

Nor were Moroccans offered many incentives to settle near French posts. French-led troops could behave with great arrogance, riding into a "friendly" douar to demand that a sheep or several chickens be prepared for dinner. The French habit of requisitioning mules and camels for their interminable convoys was not popular. At its worst, to settle near a French post could prove positively dangerous, for French military justice tended to deal with natives en bloc and to punish those nearest at hand.[16] It must come as no surprise, therefore, that by mid-1906 Lyautey's program of "economic penetration" lay in tatters.

Lyautey's military reforms met with little more success than did his economic ones. He was the French army's most prestigious advocate of "going native," of lightening the load of his troops and increasing their mobility. "In Africa, one defends oneself by moving," he was fond of saying. In many respects, this made sense. However, his attempts to create specialized units foundered on the old problem of how to reconcile mobility with solidity. Lyautey relied on units of partisans, or *goumiers*, to provide long-range security for his posts. But he soon discovered that they had their shortcomings. If closely supported by regular troops, they were adequate for *razzias*. In formal combat, they could prove a positive liability: they fired all their ammunition in five minutes and fled if pressed.[17] It was not uncommon for families to place one son in the *goumiers* while the rest of the family joined the dissidents. Not surprisingly, attacks were often not pressed home with the ardor that French officers would have liked. A few officers in charge of *goumiers* died with a bullet in the back, possibly the result of the wild, indiscriminate firing for which native levies were famous. But no one quite trusted *goumiers*. Certainly, their military usefulness was limited. Time and again, French officers found that their partisans were less mobile than the bands of raiders they were set to catch. They were often less well armed, having to content themselves with surplus French arms while their opponents

---

[15] Ross E. Dunn, *Resistance in the Desert* (London, 1977), 116-19.

[16] Hubert Lyautey, *Vers le Maroc* (Paris, 1937), 276.

[17] Charles Kuntz, *Souvenirs de campagne au Maroc* (Paris, 1913), 20-21. See also L. Lehuraux, *Le conquérant des oasis, Colonel Theodore Pein* (Paris, 1935), 87-89.

could purchase the latest models on the open market. Moroccans, operating in small groups, continued to attack supply columns and to plunder the herds of tribes who had "submitted" to the French. Seldom were the *goumiers* able to track the raiders down.[18]

Lyautey's "organization on the march" required a reliable intelligence network. A sound knowledge of the tribes, their divisions, and their principal leaders was essential if the French hoped to minimize resistance. Lyautey detailed the Intelligence Service to study the tribes, send out spies, and bribe those who might use their influence for France. As an academic organization drawing up ethnographic studies, it was a great success. As a spy service, it was largely a failure. Intelligence officers received a poor return on their money. Tribesmen gave them vague or fragmentary information, always holding back something to sell on the next market day.[19] There was no shortage of Moroccans eager to take Lyautey's money. But bribes handed out by French officers who had only a superficial knowledge of Moroccan society almost inevitably went to the wrong people, "small men who had no influence," according to the Moroccan caid Raisuni. "They promised great things, but they had no power to carry them out."[20]

Less mobile than their enemy and inadequately informed, the French fell back upon the only option they saw open to them—the *razzia*. If they could not punish the guilty, they would punish whom they could catch. The "Lyautey method" boiled down in practice to a series of reprisal raids for damage inflicted. The dreadful *razzia* was institutionalized and perpetuated. "Economic penetration," "zone of attraction," "native politics," and "organization on the march" increasingly sounded like so many hollow clichés. To be sure, Lyautey had never ruled out the use of force—occasionally he admitted that "in this country, force alone imposes respect." But if regarded as a philosophical doctrine, Lyautey's "hearts and minds" approach to conquest had a curiously mid-Victorian ring to it. It assumed that all men, even Arabs, could be taught to act in their own interests, as these interests were defined by Europeans; only a few fanatics might require more persuasive methods. This view had been largely discredited in Britain following the Indian Mutiny of 1857-1858. The reason why Lyautey, a man so utterly conservative, steeped in history and in his own brand of tribalism, would preach such a doctrine must be sought in the realm of politics rather than in that of military theory.

In Tonkin, Galliéni had been engaged in frontier pacification. He had no desire to extend French occupation into China, but only to subdue

[18] Douglas Porch, *The Conquest of Morocco* (New York, 1983), 185-86.
[19] Said Guennoun, *La montagne berbere* (Paris, 1929), 107, 137.
[20] Rosita Forbes, *El Raisuni* (London, 1924), 194.

Black Flags operating in the north. More research is needed before we can know the extent of Galliéni's success in Tonkin. He and Lyautey claimed that their peaceful methods had borne fruit. It may have been that hostility between the Vietnamese and the Chinese was so acute that the Vietnamese favored the French over their traditional enemies. Or the Vietnamese may have been so worn down by war that they submitted out of sheer exhaustion.[21] Whatever the case in Tonkin, in Morocco Lyautey's methods enjoyed less than complete success. Despite their tribal rivalries, Moroccans did share a common sense of living in the "Dar al-Islam" and a common loyalty to the sultan. Lyautey's two attempts to advance by setting up posts further into Morocco at Bechar and Ras el-Ain failed in part because they provoked protests in Paris. But more importantly, they worked to galvanize a tribal uprising in eastern Morocco in 1908. The subsequent French invasion allowed the extension of the occupation in the East to the very foothills of the Atlas Mountains. Morocco was not conquered by Lyautey's "organization on the march." On the contrary, every attempt by the French to work through "peaceful penetration," whether diplomatic or military, eventually provoked a reaction that required an invasion by heavy columns of French troops. As a doctrine of frontier pacification, Lyautey's "organization on the march" worked poorly; as a doctrine of conquest, it failed.

Why, then, does the myth still linger that the French relied far more upon persuasion than force to conquer Morocco? Essentially because "hearts and minds" was more a public-relations exercise with the French people than a workable military formula in Morocco. As in all guerrilla wars, the problem for Lyautey was to deprive the determined handful of warriors of the support and sympathies of the noncombatant population. Lyautey's "economic penetration" sought to persuade this soft center that its interests lay in supporting the French. As we have seen, this proved too simplistic an approach and ultimately failed as a military practice.

If Lyautey continued to promote "hearts and minds," it was for reasons connected far more with the political situation in France than in Morocco. Only by claiming that he was "civilizing" Morocco, that the Moroccans actually preferred the French presence to their normal state of anarchy, could he sell colonial expansion to a French public skeptical of its value. "Hearts and minds"—or "native politics," as Lyautey called it—was designed to appeal to Frenchmen who were at best ambivalent about the acres of scrub and desert that their soldiers insisted on bringing

[21] J. Kim Munholland, " 'Collaboration Strategy' and the French Pacification of Tonkin, 1885-1897," *The Historical Journal* 24, no. 3 (1981), 629-50.

under the flag.[22] Imperial expansion through economic penetration and peaceful relations did not work in Africa. Tunisia offers a good example: if modern-day Algeria looks on a map as if it is about to crowd its eastern neighbor out of the Maghreb, it is because French soldiers in Tunisia tried to extend their influence into the Sahara through trade and diplomacy, while those in Algeria adopted a more muscular approach.[23] Armies advanced at the points of their bayonets, not with smiles and trade treaties.

One must be careful not to paint too bleak a picture of Lyautey. He was fundamentally a humane individual whose methods of conquest were far less brutal than those practiced for instance by marine officers in the Sudan. And he was an experienced diplomat who was often able, by sheer force of personality, to tilt the balance between revolt and allegiance in Morocco. Nonetheless, it would have been difficult, if not impossible, to transform Lyautey's personal talents into an effective system of colonial government, especially with the heavy-handed bureaucratic system of the French. Nor was Lyautey's charm, immense as it was, able to prevent the wholesale defection of a number of tribes to Abd el-Krim's Riff rebellion in 1925.

So much for the narrowness of Lyautey's views. But how did his idealism fail him? Lyautey held a vision of colonialism as a "fraternal union between two peoples to vanquish sterility and misery."[24] In practice, however, not even a man as ingenious as Lyautey could make the system live up to its ideal. The Moroccan protectorate stripped the sultan of his powers and Europeans administered in the place of Moroccans, while immigrants dispossessed the natives of their lands. Racism retained all of its vitality despite Lyautey's admonitions that Moroccans were not inferior, only "different." In tribal areas ruled by the army, a system of "indirect administration" under the guiding hand of officers too often meant merciless exploitation by caids who were backed by French power. Perhaps the greatest abuses occurred in the south where Lyautey allowed the "Lords of the Atlas" free rein to govern as they pleased, with the result that Madani el Glaoui virtually ran Marrakech like a Mafia chief, down to the control of the city's 34,000 prostitutes. "You cannot run a colony with virgins," was all that Lyautey could say in his defense. The French certainly brought stability to Morocco, which allowed the economy to develop within narrow limits. However, it was administrators and immigrants, rather than the mass of Moroccans, who benefited.

[22] Porch, *Conquest of Morocco*, 187-88.
[23] Kenneth J. Perkins, *Quaids, Captains, and Colons: French Military Administration in the Colonial Maghrib, 1844-1934* (New York, 1981), 154.
[24] Le Révérand, *Lyautey*, 235.

IV

If Africa was won by French bayonets rather than by "hearts and minds," what were the military lessons that the French drew from their colonial experience and how far did they influence European tactical doctrine before 1914? In discussing a colonial school of warfare it is difficult to distill a set of basic military principles from an experience that was so varied. The form of operations could be dictated by the nature of the enemy, the nature of the terrain, or, lastly, by domestic political pressures.

The first and most obvious influence on French methods was the nature of the enemy. In what amounted to almost a century of extra-European warfare, the French encountered opponents with markedly different levels of organization. Some were well organized and well armed, like the armies of the king of Dahomey, which included the "Amazonian" contingents. These troops were able to fire by ranks, offer covering fire, form extended lines from deep columns, and undertake flanking movements, although, as will be seen, this did not necessarily make them militarily effective.[25] Others were semiorganized: the Arabs of Abd el-Kader, Samori's *sofas*, Rabih's army on Lake Chad, or the Black Flags in Vietnam. They possessed reasonably modern weapons, a rudimentary military organization, and were trained to standards of drill and discipline which, if not up to European norms, at least gave them a marked superiority over any indigenous opponents. A third category had only primitive weapons—the Tuareg, for instance, whose armament consisted of a spear, broadsword, and shield. Many other Africans had at most muskets designed for hunting or keeping animals out of crops rather than for warfare. The French also encountered guerrillas in all theaters of operation. Of course, some of these categories could and did overlap. Algerians, Moroccans, Black Flags, and Samori all fought set-piece battles and resorted to guerrilla tactics of ambush and operations against communications. Given the variety of enemy tactics and weapons that the French encountered abroad, it is hardly surprising that they declined to establish general principles of colonial warfare and instead concluded that the important thing was to adapt to each situation as it arose.

The most important consideration for a commander at the onset of a campaign was to select an objective that matched both the nature of his opposition and the aims of his campaign. The French might be engaged in straight invasion and annexation, or in frontier pacification. In either case, war had to made on that which, in the words of the British General

[25] R. A. Kea, "Firearms and Warfare in the Gold Coasts from the 16th to the 19th Centuries," *Journal of African History* 12 (1971), 185-213.

Sir Garnet Wolseley, the enemy "prized most." A capital or other center of resistance offered the most obvious objective: Tunis, Tananarive, Fez, Marrakech, or Abomey. In this case, a column could be launched and the objective seized. With luck, resistance would then collapse. Fortresses were also targeted. The early stages of the Indochinese campaign were taken up largely in the seizure of river forts by marine amphibious assault. In the Western Sudan, Africans often chose to defend their tatas. These might prove costly to storm, as Emile Gentil discovered on the Chari. However, the mud and stone construction of their walls made them extremely vulnerable to artillery, even the light 80-mm cannon that the French carried on campaign. Once a breach had been made, the better armed and disciplined French usually had little trouble.

By far the least troublesome foes were those whose bravery led them to suicidal attacks on French squares. Such battles forcefully demonstrated the superiority of French firepower and the futility of resistance. It made the subsequent task of pacification much easier. Bugeaud's spectacular victories on the Sikkak River in 1836 and against the Moroccans at Isly in 1844 did not end resistance, but they did prove the value of bringing the enemy to battle. Despite its elaborate organization, indeed because of it, the army of Dahomey was defeated with relative ease. In the Western Sudan, the Tuat, and Morocco, French forces were able to decimate those who attacked them in the open. This helped to sow the seeds of discord in enemy ranks, break up tribal coalitions and allow the conquest to proceed in a piecemeal fashion. Bringing the enemy to battle where the superiority of French firepower would prove decisive removed the need for complicated strategies of maneuver in the Jominian tradition.

Once the enemy had been badly hurt in battle, or his main base had been seized, he might resort to guerrilla operations. Although some guerrilla leaders, like Samori, proved to be extremely resourceful, in the end the superiority of French firepower usually rendered the best-planned ambush a costly undertaking, while French loses remained trifling.

Most "dissidents," recognizing the difficulty of opposing the invaders in battle, withdrew into their territory. The task of the French was to convince them to submit. As the marketplace seldom proved to be the "great agent of dissolution of the dissidents" that Lyautey had hoped, the French usually were forced to resort to *force majeure*. The *razzia* was the preferred method of subduing a territory. It was certainly the most profitable for the soldiers; pillage sustained a column and made it more mobile. But the principal purpose of the *razzia* was to terrorize the enemy and reduce him to starvation. In the Western Sudan, where the French were often short of trained troops, native auxiliaries would lay waste to great areas of the countryside, forcing the survivors to submit from sheer exhaustion. These practices made a mockery of Lyautey's claims that colonial soldiers applied only the minimum of force necessary for victory and never lost sight of the fact that today's enemy was tomorrow's ally. His admonitions that the enemy was to be overawed rather than eliminated usually fell on deaf ears. The *razzia* worked, and so colonial officers, including Lyautey, used it.

The nature of the terrain was a second factor that influenced colonial operations. In a real sense, all colonial campaigns were fought "against nature" as much as, and perhaps even more than, against the enemy. It was often the inaccessibility of the enemy rather than his actual fighting powers that caused the French problems. For instance, according to Captain F. Hellot, the Hovas of Madagascar might have done great damage to the exhausted and overextended French "had the courage of the rebels been as great as their mobility. But the fear of coming into direct contact with the troops, the terror of the bayonet, made them flee as soon as a march was made on them."[26] In Madagascar, as in Tonkin and the Western Sudan, and in the early years in Algeria, however, the difficulties were caused not so much by rebel bullets as by terrain, climate, and especially disease. The need to march through disease-ridden areas quickly, the absence of roads for supply wagons, the lack of food and often water, the difficulties of campaigning in mountainous terrain or in desert conditions, and the sheer vastness of the distances forced the French to tailor operations to the lay of the land. They had to lighten loads, work for mobility, leave their bases far behind, live off the land, and, in the teeth of conventional European military wisdom, be prepared to divide their forces in the presence of the enemy. Bugeaud developed the tactic of converging columns—that is, dividing a force into separate columns which would converge on an objective from several directions—principally to be able to move as many men as possible quickly over a land that could provide only limited supplies. However, the division of forces was not without its dangers. The most famous debacles that occurred as the result of separating one's force on the march were American and British rather than French. Divided forces allowed the enemy to concentrate on the most vulnerable column, as Custer discovered at the Little Big Horn in 1876 and Lord Chelmsford at Isandhlwana in 1879. The French too had their problems with dividing forces—during the Chaouia campaign of 1907-1908 in Morocco, General d'Amade's persistent use of converging columns allowed mobile Moroccan horsemen repeatedly to concentrate on the weakest one.

The nature of the terrain and the availability of water and food

---

[26] Sonia Howe, *The Drama of Madagascar* (London, 1938), 320.

might also determine the line of advance of a force, the numbers of troops committed, and whether artillery might be included. The heavy columns employed by the French in the first decade of the Algerian conquest were forced to follow the valleys, leaving the resistance relatively safe in their hills. Even then, up to 1,500 soldiers in a column of 8,000 or 10,000 men would be employed solely in building a road so that the rest of the column could pass. The Tuareg of the Sahara took so long to defeat not because they were particularly formidable fighters but because they were so difficult to get at. Intelligent insurgent commanders like Samori took care to destroy all available resources in the path of the advancing French. In this way they were able to limit the effectiveness of French incursions and often force them to retire due to lack of supplies. If a column was too heavy, as was that of Voulet and Chanoine, who allowed the men to bring their wives on campaign, it might lose all sight of a military objective and simply wander about looking for sustenance.

The nature of the enemy and the nature of the terrain certainly dictated colonial strategy and tactics to a great degree. Nevertheless, it is surprising, given the long experience of the French army abroad and their claims of adaptability in the face of new and different colonial conditions, how often they opted for military solutions that seemed to owe more to Europe than to Africa. Indeed, the essential problem of the French colonial army was not to decide how much of its colonial military experience was applicable to Europe, but how to keep European military practices out of the colonies.

The most obvious evidence of the encroachment of European campaign methods into the colonies was the persistent use of the heavy column. Colonial soldiers objected to it for a variety of reasons. They claimed it was ineffective: the invasion of Tunisia in 1881 confirmed Bugeaud's view that a column without occupation "is like the wake of a ship upon the sea." The local inhabitants sat still until the column passed, and then revolted anew, requiring a second invasion and a permanent occupation. Second, heavy columns operated often in country that could not support the passage of large numbers of men. The Foureau-Lamy expedition into the Sahara in 1898-1899 almost perished because it outdistanced its supply convoys. The Tuat expedition of 1901-1902 required the requisition of 35,000 camels, virtually the entire camel population of southern Algeria, to support it. As the French soldiers were unable to manage them properly, fully 25,000 of the camels died, which deprived many Arabs in the Saharian regions of their means of a livelihood. "I do not think that there has been a massacre comparable to that of 1901," the Sahara expert E. F. Gautier wrote. "The jackals and the

399

vultures along the way were overwhelmed with the immensity of their task."[27]

A third objection to the column was that, in Lyautey's estimation, it was like using "a hammer to crush a fly."[28] The French could depend on firepower, rather than numbers, to overcome an ill-organized enemy, as Lyautey reminded General Alix during the 1908 invasion of eastern Morocco. Fourth, the column was inefficient: too much precious manpower was expended in convoy duty and in guarding posts on the line of march. In modern military parlance, the ratio of "tail" to "teeth" was excessive. This certainly was the case when General Monier led 7,500 men to relieve Fez in 1911. "When you drag along regular troops, seventy-fives, horses, you have to feed all that lot," Lyautey complained to the future general Georges Catroux. "You need shells, you need bases and men to guard them. That's no way to operate in this country."[29] As usual, Lyautey was being less than frank. The column was used in part because his methods of "peaceful penetration" produced results diametrically opposed to those he had predicted. He was on more solid ground when he objected to the heavy column because it attracted unwanted attention in Europe. Experienced colonial hands were firm believers in advancement through stealth, nibbling away at enemy territory and changing the names of towns to throw Paris off the scent, especially in the delicate period of international relations that preceded the First World War. Therefore, Lyautey's objections to the use of the column were founded principally on political rather than military factors.

Despite the complaints of colonial soldiers, the heavy column survived in the colonies far beyond what they believed should have been its normal lifetime. There were several reasons for this. When a big operation was planned, command might be assigned to a metropolitan officer seconded to the colonies, rather than to a colonial soldier—d'Amade and Monier, for example, were sent out of crucial stages of Morocco operation. As colonial warfare was not taught in the War College, there was no way of passing colonial experience on to new generations of officers. Also, most generals sought safety in numbers, and felt that small columns launched into unmapped country against a foe whose strength was not known was like betting the family estate at Monte Carlo.

But there was a final reason why the heavy column survived, and that was because, in fact, it often did prove effective. Of course there were limits—clever opponents like Samori might blunt it through scorched earth tactics, or by operating against its communications. A

[27] L. Lehuraux, *Les français au desert* (Algiers, n.d.), 102.
[28] Georges Catroux, *Lyautey le marocain* (Paris, 1952), 125.
[29] Ibid.

column might be too large to survive far beyond its base, as was the column that marched on Tananarive. It might be caught off guard and forced to retreat, as was Negrier's column at Lang-son. However, in most cases, the column served its purpose—Africans who attempted a test of arms with the invaders were given hard lessons in the force of modern firepower. General Servière's column, although expensive in camels, ended resistance in the Tuat. General d'Amade's columns, though much criticized by colonial soldiers, crushed the Moroccans in the Chaouia in 1908, as did the column of General Alix across the Atlas in the same year. Even the man whom one thinks of as a colonial soldier par excellence, Charles Mangin, took a heavy column to Marrakech in 1912. A pitched battle might not end resistance. But it certainly fragmented it, forced home the point that the French were strong, and paved the way for piecemeal conquest of the tribes and factions.

Europe intruded into French military methods abroad in other ways. The colonial soldier's knowledge that the government tended to disapprove proposed operations overseas meant that operations were often launched in haste, usually without adequate support or intelligence, in an attempt to present the government with a *fait accompli*. Many of the French setbacks in the colonies, like Bonnier's death near Timbuktu, can be traced to the fact that operations were quickly cobbled together to avoid detection in France and possibly a countermanding order from Paris.

The lack of funds for campaigns, shortage of trained troops, hostility to colonial expansion at home, and political restraints placed on soldiers in the colonies might force them to adopt "African" methods as a last resort. If colonial officers advocated small, light columns, it was often because they had no alternative. For instance, the Saharians, the camel corps that Laperrine founded after 1901 to police the Sahara, came into being after the government refused to provide more than a handful of native infantry to garrison the Tuat. Laperrine was forced to adapt to local conditions or be content to be ambushed in his oasis.

The lack of funds or the refusal to provide troops often was not enough to restrain the young and ambitious officers who sought to make a name for themselves in Africa at any cost. What was needed were explicit orders and senior soldiers, perhaps even seconded from the metropolitan army, to see that they were carried out. In the absence of either, officers recruited inexpensive "auxiliaries" through local chiefs or caids. Porters were kidnapped and chained together by their necks to prevent escape. The result of operations organized in this manner is not difficult to imagine. The Voulet-Chanoine mission offers but the most extreme example of an operation that "went native" with a vengeance. Officers turned to auxiliaries and *goumiers* in Africa, not because they were particularly effective, but because they were cheap and available.

Officers might also fly the banner of scientific research to circumvent restrictions on military operations. Exploration, topographical studies, examination of flora and fauna, or anthropological studies of tribes all served as cover: indeed, some of these mission objectives read more like university research proposals than plans for military operations. They might even disguise their purpose more thoroughly by providing a "military escort" for a scientist. The veteran explorer Ferdinand Foureau was the nominal commander of Lamy's 1898 expedition to Lake Chad. Theodore Pein's 1899 incursion into the Tuat, which touched off a long and costly campaign of conquest, masqueraded as a geological expedition under the leadership of a professor from the Ecole des Hautes Etudes Scientifiques at Algiers. In this way, officers were able to supplement the inadequate resources of the War Ministry with contributions from the Paris Geographical Society, the Ministries of Education or Public Works, or from colonialist groups. Flatters, Lamy, Pein, and Voulet and Chanoine all found nonmilitary financing for their missions.

V

The long years of peace in Europe that preceded the outbreak of the First World War meant that colonial soldiers alone among their colleagues had any experience of combat. However, it proved difficult to translate the lessons of colonial warfare into French military thinking, in great part because those lessons were contradictory. Without rigorous analysis, the colonial experience might confuse rather than enlighten those seeking to develop doctrine. Colonial campaigns emphasized the value of the battle over maneuver. But French staff thinking in 1914 stressed the importance of flanking movements and envelopment. Overseas, infantry attacks against an ill-armed and undisciplined enemy usually brought success. At the same time, colonial operations offered a stunning demonstration of the superiority of firepower over numbers. The square survived precisely because it allowed the French to maximize their defensive firepower.

The shock power of cavalry was not particularly evident in the colonies. The wars in Africa and Indochina were primarily infantry duels. In North Africa, spahis were seldom employed as a unit, but used as flank guards, convoy escorts, in reconnaissance, or to block lines of retreat. Saharians and *goumiers* were used as mounted infantry, the same concept that had inspired the founding of the *chasseurs d'Afrique* in the 1840s. The chasseurs did mount a classic charge against the Moroccans at R'Fakha during the Chaouia campaign of 1908, but the Moroccans

402

lay down and let the charge pass over them.[30] In that same year, a cavalry charge at Bou Denib in eastern Morocco lost its momentum in a palm grove and was forced to retreat.[31]

The development of light artillery made that arm more prominent on the colonial battlefield. If artillery never attained the dominant position overseas that it was to occupy in Europe after 1914, this was in part because colonial opponents, especially swirling horsemen, often offered poor targets. Nor was there much call for artillery support in the raids and counterguerrilla operations that made up much of colonial fighting. But artillery did augment the defensive power of French squares once the enemy was massed. Morocco provided many examples of this. Cannon were also a vital support to the army during fortress assaults.

At least three major factors worked against the importation of colonial tactics into France before 1914. First, there was a strong prejudice against colonial soldiers in the metropolitan army. This stemmed in great part from 1870, when men who had earned brilliant reputations in Algeria, Mexico, and other far-flung battlefields proved inept when faced with a European enemy. The feeling persisted in the metropolitan army that colonial skirmishes provided poor preparation for European warfare and that soldiers who chose exile abroad were lost to the serious business of preparation for war with Germany. Jealousy was also a factor—colonial soldiers had seen action, earned decorations, and often enjoyed accelerated promotion. Snobbery played its part—the colonial army tended to attract officers who lacked the social or professional connections to stake out a satisfactory career in France, whose records at Saint-Cyr or the Ecole Polytechnique had been undistinguished, or adventurers forced abroad because of poor professional prospects or social ostracism. Metropolitan officers condemned their colonial colleagues as "a collection of hooligans," "bachi-bouzouks" engaged in a parody of military life rather than in serious soldiering. Given the gulf of prejudice that separated the two forces and the fundamental differences in temperament between men who had opted for the risks and uncertainties of life abroad and those who selected the safe, formalized existence of an officer in a peacetime army, it is unlikely that soldiers who suggested that methods be adopted in France merely because they worked in the colonies would have been taken seriously.

But few colonial soldiers harbored ambitions to rewrite the strategic and tactical regulations. The difficulties of selecting a set of principles out of the varied colonial military experience were virtually insurmount-

[30] Porch, *Conquest of Morocco*, 175-76.
[31] Ibid., 194.

able. However, far more than this, the entire thrust of the thoughts and writings of Bugeaud, Galliéni, and Lyautey stressed the differences rather than the similarities between colonial conquest and warfare as it was practiced in Europe. Nowhere do they argue for the importation into France of colonial methods, for, by their reckoning, colonial soldiering was essentially a political, rather than a purely military, métier. The colonial soldier's task required imagination, judgment, and special skills, not stiff obedience or Prussian formalism. Adaptability in the face of each new situation, not the application of some pat formula of the Ecole de Guerre, made for success in the colonies. Lyautey argued that each colonial situation was different, and dreamed of the day when, like British India, each French colony would possess its own colonial army, commanded by French officers and NCOs well versed in local dialects and customs, and therefore able to play an effective political role. It was hardly the place of colonial soldiers to lecture the army in France on the finer points of strategy and tactics. After all, methods that succeeded against Black Flags might fail utterly when applied against Moroccans. Nor did approaches that worked against Samori in one campaign necessarily prove successful in the next. Why should Prussians be expected to fight like Africans? Colonial warfare was valuable because it instilled resilience and the ability to react under pressure. When colonial soldiers like Galliéni and Lyautey returned to high command in France, their immediate concern was to be brought up to date on the latest Continental theories.

Indeed, what is most striking about the colonial military experience is how little it influenced metropolitan thinking. This is especially the case when one considers that only a few soldiers or politicians looked to Africa to solve the problem of French numerical inferiority before 1914. Mangin argued in his 1910 book, *La force noire*, that Africa offered an inexhaustable reservoir of manpower to offset German superiority. But his calls for massive enlistment of Africans found little support, even among colonial soldiers. Galliéni and Lyautey were silent on the contributions that the colonies might make to French strength. This silence is all the more astonishing given that the British, who were far less concerned with the problem of numerical inferiority than were the French, used large numbers of colonial troops from the beginning in 1914. Lyautey's concern in 1914 was the remarkably parochial one of saving Morocco, not of sending Moroccans to serve in France. One can only conclude that Mangin's views did not enjoy wide acceptance because French soldiers, even those in the colonies, did not believe that colonial warfare offered any useful lessons for Europe, and because they believed that

404

native troops especially lacked the qualities suitable to warfare in Europe.[32]

Finally, they realized that the political climate in France was unfavorable to the expansion of the colonial army to make up for the shortfall in French conscripts. Colonialism was not popular in France, especially on the Left, where colonial soldiers were regarded as little better than mercenaries. The colonial army was tolerated because it was relatively small and distant. However, to advocate the wholesale expansion of the colonial army and the transfer to France of large numbers of soldiers recruited in Africa and Indochina, answerable only to their officers, would have antagonized a broad section of political opinion and opened the army to charges of Caesarism.

All this is not to say that colonial warfare did not provide some useful indications of the shape of future wars. Colonial operations often obscured the dividing line between political and military considerations. The state of European diplomatic relations and political pressures from Paris or from within the colonies, rather than purely military considerations, often determined the timing and form of an operation, a factor that many future commanders of the First World War might have pondered with profit. Also, the devastation of colonial warfare pointed toward total war, despite the disclaimers from colonial soldiers that its purpose was to subdue the enemy with a minimum of force.

The most damning criticism of colonial soldiers links their facile victories against tribesmen to the futile offensives of the early months of the war. How valid is this view? It must be remembered that for Lyautey colonial expansion offered three advantages. The first two—a "fraternal union of two peoples," and a profitable economic relationship between France and its colonies—have been discussed. The third goal of colonial expansion was equally political: to build up a core of colonial soldiers

---

[32] On this point, colonial officers were quite categorical. It was axiomatic in colonial warfare that native troops, especially irregulars, were liable to cut and run unless backed up by French soldiers. Colonial officers retained a paternal affection for their native levies, but few thought them the equal of European soldiers. Even when colonial troops were transported to France during the First World War, the stereotypes developed over the decades largely determined how they would be employed: Indochinese troops, thought intelligent, were assigned almost exclusively to armaments and aviation factories; Madagascar troops were placed in the ambulance corps, but also in the artillery; North Africans and Senegalese, considered the elite of nonwhite soldiers, were thrown into almost all of the major offensives, but even Mangin divided his black troops into "warrior races"— those from the savannah—and the rest, who were employed as workers or replacements. North Africans were sent to the front in regiments, but the High Command preferred to intersperse battalions of blacks and whites because, until the final offensives of 1918, they continued to suspect the solidity of the Senegalese. See Marc Michel, *L'appel à l'Afrique, contributions et réactions a l'effort de guèrre en AOF, 1914-19* (Paris, Publications de la Sorbonne, 1982).

with energy and a sense of national purpose who would react against the inertia, formalism, and institutional malaise of Republican France. In this, Lyautey was not merely stating some distant hope. Rather, he reflected the view of a growing elite of colonial officers that their mission was the political one of the salvation of France. This was not dissimilar to the attitude of a number of colonial officers in the 1950s who took it upon themselves to protect France, Europe, and Western civilization from the perils of a communist world conspiracy in the form of "la guerre révolutionnaire." To colonial soldiers in the years before 1914, France appeared to be a country hopelessly riven by political and social conflicts, in poor condition to confront a powerful, confident Germany. The confusion, divisions, and institutional malfunctioning in France seemed at their most critical within the army itself. The Dreyfus affair and the subsequent vilification of the army by the Left had savaged morale. Colonial soldiers had been largely immune to this settling of accounts between the Left and the army after 1899—distance and the protection of powerful colonialist politicians had seen to that. However, they returned home to find a demoralized, leaderless, and bureaucratized army which appeared incapable of facing up to the mounting German threat. They sought to revive the spirit of the army, to bolster its confidence and morale. Colonial soldiers were not concerned so much with the mechanics of the offensive, for in this area they knew that they traded in a devalued currency and had little to teach their metropolitan colleagues. Rather they argued for the value of offensive-mindedness. The success of Bugeaud, Galliéni, and Lyautey as commanders lay primarily in their ability to motivate men. Morale, aggressiveness, initiative, the very qualities that had sustained soldiers overseas, seemed to them lacking in the army at home before 1914.

It is therefore more accurate to say that colonial soldiers contributed to the spirit, rather than to the techniques of the offensive. For soldiers abroad, France was a political and spiritual invalid, deprived of unity by self-inflicted divisions that undermined national defense. Colonial soldiers sought to transport the unity of purpose felt in the colonies back to the fatherland, uniting Frenchmen in a common bond of fraternity and national purpose. Lyautey led a chorus of colonial soldiers who believed it their "social duty to tear this county from decomposition and ruin. Not by changing the constitution, an empirical and transitory method, but by a violent reaction upon manners, inertia and worries . . . [we must] react upon metropolitan inertia, establish a continuing and regenerating current of life between France without and France within, which will be a revival for this country."[33]

[33] Hubert Lyautey, *Lettres de Tonkin et de Madagascar, 1894-1899* (Paris, 1942), 489.

The nationalist revival of 1911-1914 offered colonial prophets their chance. Grandmaison, whose attitudes had been formed by service in Tonkin, was largely responsible for drawing up the controversial 1913 regulations, which declared the offensive to be the key to success in war. However, his concern was not to prove that it worked in Tonkin and therefore should work in Europe. For Grandmaison, the offensive was not so much a strategic and tactical doctrine as an expression of the "moral force" unleashed in the colonies, which he hoped would regenerate France and its army. His views struck a responsive cord among officers well aware of their army's weaknesses. "It is far more important to develop a conquering state of mind than to cavil about tactics," Grandmaison concluded.[34] But the state of mind he proclaimed inevitably affected tactics and strategy as the First World War began.

[34] Louis de Grandmaison, *Deux conférences faites aux officiers de l'état major de l'armée* (Paris, 1911), 34.

15. American Strategy from Its Beginnings through the First World War

RUSSELL F. WEIGLEY

WHEN Francis Parkman chronicled the first American wars in some of the earliest volumes of American military history, he drew romantic effects from the contrasts between the ordered ranks of British regulars and the untamed American wilderness in which the redcoats fought to conquer New France. But few of the European regular soldiers discarded their bright coats or their European tactics, notwithstanding the wilderness and the unconventional tactics of the Indians they confronted there. Parkman could not offer a military variant of the Frederick Jackson Turner frontier thesis of American history, which claimed that Europeans discarded both their European vestments and their European thoughts when they arrived in the New World.

Nor could other informed military historians advance a military version of the frontier thesis to claim that American war became uniquely American. Despite a certain tendency to exaggerate the impact of the forest warfare of the Indians upon the soldiers—to suggest, for example, that General Edward Braddock could have averted disaster at the Monongahela if only his redcoats had dispersed to fight from behind trees—military historians have had to recognize that European military discipline and the European art of war generally triumphed over wilderness adversaries. The glorious conquest of New France that formed the climax of Parkman's volumes was a triumph of warfare on the European pattern, symbolized by the classically European-style battle between James Wolfe's redcoats and the Marquis de Montcalm's whitecoats on the Plains of Abraham outside the fortress walls of Québec. The frontier interpretation of American history applies only minimally to war; American ways of war were offshoots of European ways of war, and American strategic thought was therefore a branch of European strategic thought.

Yet the particular emphases that Americans drew from European methods of war making were to help shape American strategy into the twentieth century, when Americans ceased to be simply pupils of Europe and became tutors to the military forces of much of the world, in addition to building a war machine of their own that gave the United States the status of a superpower. From the beginning, one of the American changes of emphasis was toward less restraint in the conduct of war, in both means and ends, than became characteristic of European war after the close of the Wars of Religion and before the Wars of the French Revolution. As Europe after 1648 entered an age of limited war, employing the means of carefully regulated combat among professional armies to achieve ends of limited dynastic advantage, in North America the colonists and the Indians were discovering that their cultures were so incompatible that they could not well endure side by side. Wars between settlers and Indians became—beginning at least with King Philip's War in New England in 1675-1676—struggles aimed at reducing the enemy to military impotence. To this end, the means frequently disregarded European restrictions on attacks against the property and lives of noncombatants. Seventeenth- and eighteenth-century Americans came to conceive of war in more absolute terms than did their European contemporaries.

Eventually, Great Britain's colonists in America applied American conceptions of war against rival European colonizers as well as against the Indians, demanding at the close of the Seven Years' War in 1763 that the peace treaty completely eliminate New France from the North American continent. The British cabinet had misgivings over conditions so extreme by European standards of the day, but in no small part in order to avoid offending the American colonists, the settlement was imposed in the Treaty of Paris of 1763.[1]

Just as the limitations of eighteenth-century European war can be exaggerated, however—testimony about the restrained conduct of troops marching through a district does not often come from inarticulate peasants—so conversely, historians may tend to exaggerate the readiness of early Americans to turn toward absolute war. Colonial American sermons and political tracts reflect an awareness and acceptance of the European conception of the just and therefore limited war, which was becoming increasingly codified in such works as Emerich de Vattel's *Droit des gens* of 1758.[2] On occasion, the standards of *jus ad bellum* and *jus in bello*

---

[1] This view of the beginnings of American attitudes toward war draws heavily on John W. Shy, "The American Military Experience: History and Learning," *The Journal of Interdisciplinary History* 1 (Winter 1971), 205-28; repr. in John W. Shy, *A People Numerous and Armed* (New York, 1976), 225-54. Francis Parkman, *France and England in North America*, 9 vols. (vol. 8, *The History of the Conspiracy of Pontiac*, Boston and London, 1851; remaining vols., Boston, 1865-92; many later editions exist with varying numbers of volumes) remains a foundation for study of the American military past as well as a historical narrative in the grand literary tradition.

[2] Emerich de Vattel, *Le droit des gens* . . . (Leyden, 1758); trans. Charles G. Fenwick as *The Law of Nations* (Washington, D.C., 1916).

were applied even to Indian wars, as when the Connecticut government refused to assist Massachusetts in an Indian conflict that Connecticut judged unjust.[3] If it was much more common to consider the Indians outside the protection of the Christian laws of war, the Americans nevertheless explicitly acknowledged those laws as applicable to their own conflicts with Europeans, even amid the violent emotions of the American Revolution.[4]

I

Foremost among American advocates of transplanting European modes of war to the western shores of the Atlantic was General George Washington. The commander in chief of the Continental Army accepted European tutelage in virtually every aspect of his conduct of the War of Independence, including the tactical training of his troops, respect for the rights of combatants and noncombatants under the international law of war, and most certainly in strategy.

Washington rejected the counsel of Major General Charles Lee, who believed that a war fought to attain revolutionary purposes ought to be waged in a revolutionary manner, by calling on an armed populace to rise in what a later generation would call guerrilla war.[5] Washington eschewed the way of the guerrilla, and where he was in personal command the revolutionaries never resorted in any significant measure to blurring the rules of war, particularly the distinction between combatants and noncombatants. In the "Northern Department," where he was not present to resist Major General (later Lieutenant-General) John Burgoyne's campaign of 1777 up Lake Champlain toward the Hudson River, guerrilla-style hit-and-run harassment of Burgoyne's flanks and line of communications helped force the British to surrender at Saratoga. In the "Southern Department," Major General Nathanael Greene in Washington's absence encouraged "the partisan war" conducted by such leaders of irregulars as Francis Marion, Thomas Sumter, and Andrew Pickens. Greene developed a capacity to weave together guerilla operations and

[3] Reginald C. Stuart, *War and American Thought: From the Revolution to the Monroe Doctrine* (Kent, Ohio, 1982), 9. For a modern explication of the principles of the just war, see Michael Walzer, *Just and Unjust Wars: A Moral Argument with Historical Illustrations* (New York, 1977).

[4] Stuart, *War and American Thought*, 9-35. For the American Revolution, see Charles Royster, *A Revolutionary People at War: The Continental Army and American Character, 1775-1783* (Chapel Hill, 1979), esp. ch. 1.

[5] John W. Shy, "Charles Lee: The Soldier as Radical," in *George Washington's Generals*, ed. George Athan Billias (New York, 1964), 22-53; repr. slightly revised, in Shy, *A People Numerous and Armed*, 133-62.

those of his regular forces with a skill that makes him not unworthy of comparison with Mao Tse-tung and Vo Nguyen Giap.[6]

But the influence of Washington far overshadowed that of Greene and other unconventional warriors in shaping the roots of American strategy and the institutional development of the United States Army, and aborted development of either guerrilla or counterguerrilla methods of war. Whenever after the Revolution the American army had to conduct a counterguerrilla campaign—in the Second Seminole War of 1835-1841, the Filipino Insurrection of 1899-1903, and in Vietnam in 1965-1973—it found itself almost without an institutional memory of such experiences, had to relearn appropriate tactics at exorbitant costs, and yet tended after each episode to regard it as an aberration that need not be repeated.[7]

Washington molded the main Continental Army into as close a facsimile of the rival British army as he could achieve, and with this version of an eighteenth-century professional army he conducted the Revolution as a conventional war, in terms of both tactics and adherence to the international law of war. Because the limited numbers of militarily educated officers and trained noncommissioned officers available as well as the limits of time prevented Washington from bringing his army up to the tactical and disciplinary standards of its adversary—save for a few exceptional units—he found that committing his troops to battle was an invitation to defeat. Therefore as the war went on he fought fewer and fewer battles; after the revolutionaries' unsuccessful defense of New York City in 1776, there was only one more collision between the main bodies of the rival armies, along the Brandywine Creek on September 11, 1777. On that occasion, Washington fought because he believed that for the sake of morale he could not give up the Continental capital, Philadelphia, without a contest. As he might have anticipated, he lost.

[6] See my own *The American Way of War: A History of United States Military Strategy and Policy*, The Macmillan Wars of the United States (New York and London, 1973), ch. 2; and *The Partisan War: The South Carolina Campaign of 1780-1782*, Tricentennial Booklet no. 2 (Columbia, S.C., 1970). Chapter 2 of the former comments on Burgoyne's campaign as well as the campaign in the South. For other modern interpretations of the Southern campaign, see Theodore Thayer, *Nathanael Greene: Strategist of the American Revolution* (New York, 1960), 282-430, and Martin F. Treacy, *Prelude to Yorktown: The Southern Campaign of Nathanael Greene, 1780-1781* (Chapel Hill, 1968).

[7] On the Second Seminole War, see John K. Mahon, *History of the Second Seminole War, 1835-1842* (Gainesville, 1967) and Francis Paul Prucha, *The Sword of the Republic: The United States Army on the Frontier, 1783-1846*, The Macmillan Wars of the United States (New York and London, 1968), ch. 14. On the Filipino Insurrection, see John Morgan Gates, *Schoolbooks and Krags: The United States Army in the Philippines, 1898-1902*, Contributions in Military History, no. 3 (Westport, Conn., and London, 1973) and Russell Roth, *Muddy Glory: America's Indian Wars in the Philippines, 1899-1935* (West Hanover, Mass., 1981).

By this time, Washington's strategy was not to win the war through victory in battle, but to wage what "has even been called a War of Posts. That we should on all Occasions avoid a general Action, or put anything to the Risque, unless compelled by a necessity, into which we ought never to be drawn."[8] Avoiding general actions, Washington could keep the Continental Army alive, and he hoped the Revolution would thus remain alive as well. By combining sheer endurance with raids against the enemy to nourish American morale and undermine the British will to persist, Washington hoped to win the war through what Hans Delbrück would have called a strategy of attrition. With the great good fortune of French assistance and particularly the entrapment of Lieutenant-General Lord Charles Cornwallis by a French fleet at Yorktown in 1781, Washington succeeded.

Washington's insistence on creating a European-style professional army to wage war on the European pattern reflected his apparent fear of the tendency of irregular war, with its violations of the international rules of war, to tear apart the entire social contract, as well as his specific concern to guard the dignity of the American cause as an essential part of the new nation's claim to equality of status among the nations of the world. With independence won, the same concerns guided Washington in shaping the permanent military institutions of the United States. In his "Sentiments on a Peace Establishment," composed at the request of the Confederation Congress in 1784, Washington proposed a small regular army supported by a well-regulated compulsory-service militia. As first President of the United States, he responded to military defeats at the hands of the Northwest Indians soon after he took office by sponsoring and encouraging a vigorous training program, in which Major General Anthony Wayne made the small Regular Army of under four thousand for the first time a miniature version of a European army in discipline and tactical proficiency. Washington also sought to realize his idea of a militia, but he had to settle for the Militia Act of 1792, which imposed a compulsory military obligation without erecting the machinery necessary to make the obligation much more than a theory. He wanted a military academy for the European-style education of officers, but in this, too, he was disappointed. The academy was inaugurated instead, and rather surprisingly, under the antimilitary, states'-rights administration

[8] Washington to the President of Congress, Sept. 8, 1776, in *The Writings of George Washington from the Original Manuscript Sources, 1745-1799*, ed. John C. Fitzpatrick, 39 vols. (Washington, D.C., 1931-44), 6:28. For an interpretation portraying Washington as a more daring strategist, see Dave Richard Palmer, *The Way of the Fox: American Strategy in the War for America, 1775-1783*, Contributions in Military History, no. 8 (Westport, Conn., and London, 1975).

of Thomas Jefferson, who signed the statute creating the United States Military Academy at West Point in 1802.[9]

Unlike Washington, Jefferson professed to favor the citizen-soldiers of the militia over regulars as the backbone of American defense—though he did little to strengthen the militia system. His motives in approving the creation of the Military Academy have therefore remained a subject of controversy. In part he may have expected the graduates of the academy not to remain professional soldiers but to enter civilian life and in time to disseminate their military skills among the militia. In part he may have anticipated that West Point would offer, as it long did, less a military than an engineering curriculum, to provide a nation-building army in the most literal sense, with army engineers mapping the continental domain and building roads, canals, highway improvements, even the United States Capitol. In part Jefferson may have perceived offering a military education at government expense as a means of replacing the existing domination of the officer corps by Federalist partisans with a preponderance of Jeffersonians. Whatever his motives, Jefferson did little to nurture the Military Academy after creating it. Not until after the War of 1812 had demonstrated anew the deficiencies of amateur officers and soldiers did West Point cease to be, as its first superintendent called it, "a foundling, barely existing among the mountains, and nurtured at a distance out of sight, and almost unknown to its legitimate parents." The superintendency of Sylvanus Thayer, beginning in 1817 and lasting until 1833, at length made of West Point what Washington had desired.[10]

II

Thayer's principal coadjutor in this work was Dennis Hart Mahan, the highest-ranking graduate of the class of 1824, for whom Thayer arranged in 1826 a four-year sojourn in France to observe the French army, study at the School of Application for Engineers and Artillery at

---

[9] For Washington's "Sentiments on a Peace Establishment," May 2, 1783, see Fitzgerald, *Writings of Washington*, 26:374-98. On Washington's post-Revolutionary military policies in detail, see Douglas Southall Freeman, *George Washington: A Biography*, 7 vols. (New York, 1948-57), vols. 6 and 7. On Jefferson and the founding of West Point, see Theodore J. Crackel, "The Founding of West Point: Jefferson and the Politics of Security," *Armed Forces and Society: An Interdisciplinary Journal* 7 (Summer 1981), 529-43. For Hans Delbrück on a strategy of attrition, see his *Die Strategie des Perikles erläutert durch die Strategie Friedrichs des Grossen* (Berlin, 1890), 27.

[10] Williams quoted in Stephen E. Ambrose, *Duty, Honor, Country: A History of West Point* (Baltimore, 1966), 34. Crackel, "The Founding of West Point," interprets Jefferson's motivation in terms of ending Federalist predominance in the army; see also the same author's "Jefferson, Politics, and the Army: An Examination of the Military Peace Establishment Act of 1802," *Journal of the Early Republic* 2 (April 1982), 21-38. There are numerous accounts of Sylvanus Thayer as superintendent; see Ambrose, *Duty, Honor, Country*, 4.

Metz, and bring back French instructional materials to the academy. Returning to teaching duties at West Point in 1830, Mahan was from 1832 to 1871 "Professor of Military and Civil Engineering, and of the Science of War." As such, he taught the professional soldiers who became the generals of the American Civil War most of what they knew through systematic study of the conduct of war.[11]

Principally, Mahan transmitted French interpretations of Napoleonic war. So strong was the magnetic attraction of Napoleon to nineteenth-century soldiers that American military experience, including the generalship of Washington, was almost ignored in military studies here. The standard West Point text on the science and art of war for a considerable time was Captain J. M. O'Connor's translation of S. F. Gay de Vernon's *Treatise on the Science of War and Fortification*, which included a summary of the strategic precepts of Antoine-Henri Jomini prepared by O'Connor.[12] Mahan's own teachings on the conduct of war were eventually published in part as *An Elementary Treatise on Advanced-Guard, Out-Post, and Detachment Service of Troops*, a volume that offered more guidance to the higher levels of the direction of war than its title implies, especially in later revised editions.[13]

Mahan published only this one relatively short book on warfare but numerous works on military and civil engineering.[14] His capstone West Point course for first classmen similarly concerned engineering more than other aspects of military studies, and the entire West Point curriculum remained, for various reasons including political ones, more that of an engineering college than of a school for educating military professionals. This technical emphasis has led Samuel P. Huntington to argue that American soldiers of the early and middle nineteenth century were technicists rather than professionals.[15] The engineering emphasis was not without value, however, as preparation for nineteenth-century warfare. It encompassed fortification, of course, including field fortification, and

[11] Thomas E. Griess, "Dennis Hart Mahan: West Point Professor and Advocate of Military Professionalism, 1830-1871" (Ph.D. diss. Duke University, 1969).

[12] Simon François Gay de Vernon, *A Treatise on the Science of War and Fortification . . . to which Is Added a Summary of the Principles and Maxims of Grand Tactics and Operations*, 2 vols. (New York, 1817). The excerpt from Jomini appears in 2:385-490.

[13] Dennis Hart Mahan, *An Elementary Treatise on Advanced-Guard, Out-Post, and Detachment Service of Troops . . .* (New York, 1847; rev. ed. New York, 1864).

[14] Notably *Complete Treatise on Field Fortification . . .* (New York, 1836); *Elementary Course of Civil Engineering . . .* (New York, 1837); *Summary of the Course of Permanent Fortification and of the Attack and Defence of Permanent Works . . .* (West Point, 1850); *Industrial Drawing . . .* (New York, 1852); *Descriptive Geometry as Applied to the Drawing of Fortification and Stereotomy . . .* (New York, 1864); *An Elementary Course of Military Engineering . . . ,* 2 vols. (New York, 1866-67).

[15] Samuel P. Huntington, *The Soldier and the State: The Theory and Politics of Civil-Military Relations* (Cambridge, Mass., 1957), 195-203, 246-53.

thus helped lead to the readiness with which officers during the American Civil War encouraged their soldiers to construct field fortifications when they halted their marches even briefly. This was a most appropriate policy in the face of the destructive firepower displayed; the Civil War was the first war in which rifled shoulder arms were the standard infantry weapon on both sides. It may be significant that General Robert E. Lee, who was relatively slow in recognizing the value of field fortifications against an enemy equipped with rifles, was also the only principal general of the war who had attended West Point too early to study the military art under Dennis Mahan.[16]

But too much should not be made of Mahan's emphasis on the value of fortifications. Although he taught that the spade is as useful in war as the musket,[17] nonetheless he regarded the value of field fortifications ultimately as that of springboards upon which to concentrate strength for launching attacks.[18] He was sufficiently a disciple of Napoleon to believe that defense alone cannot win military campaigns, least of all passive defense, and that seizing the initiative through aggressive action is indispensable to final success. He approached advocating the Austerlitz or Jena-Auerstedt style of offensive battle of annihilation. To Napoleon, he said,

> we owe those grand features of the art, by which an enemy is broken and utterly dispersed by one and the same blow. No futilities of preparation; no uncertain feeling about in search of the key-point; no hesitancy upon the decisive moment; the whole field of view taken in by one eagle glance; what could not be seen divined by an unerring military instinct; clouds of light troops thrown forward to bewilder his foe; a crashing fire of cannon in mass opened upon him; the rush of the impetuous column into the gap made by the artillery; the overwhelming charge of the resistless cuirassier; followed by the lancer and hussar to sweep up the broken dispersed bands; such were the tactical lessons taught in almost every battle of this great military period.[19]

"Vigor on the field and rapidity of pursuit," taught Mahan, "should go hand in hand for great success." "Carrying the war into the heart of the assailant's country, or that of his allies, is the surest plan of making him share its burdens and foiling his plans."[20] The battles of annihilation

---

[16] Lee was a cadet from 1825 to 1829.
[17] William T. Sherman, *Memoirs of General William T. Sherman by Himself*, 2 vols. (New York, 1875; repr., 2 vols. in Bloomington, 1957), 2:396.
[18] D. H. Mahan, *Elementary Treatise*, rev. ed., 185-96.
[19] Ibid., 30.
[20] Ibid., 190, 199.

waged by Ulysses S. Grant and the destructive marches of William T. Sherman, both students of Dennis Mahan, are at least in some measure prefigured in the mentor's dicta.

Mahan's favorite student, however, his special protégé among the many cadets he taught, was a military intellectual who managed to anticipate his tutor in publishing the first major American textbook on the military art. This was Henry Wager Halleck, "Old Brains," as the army came to know him. The book was *Elements of Military Art and Science*, first published in 1846.[21] As the third-ranking graduate of the class of 1831, Halleck was automatically entitled to choose a commission in the Corps of Engineers, as was then the custom for the highest graduates. This preferred status of military engineering emphasizes the preoccupation with fortification in early American military thought, notwithstanding Dennis Mahan's more Napoleonic moods, as do Halleck's writing and much of his military career.[22]

In addition to composing his textbook, Halleck translated Jomini's *Life of Napoleon*, and it was once fashionable to regard him as a mere translator and paraphraser of Jomini.[23] But to dismiss Halleck in this way is to ignore his efforts to deal in his own book with particularly American military issues. His main thrust in this regard was a focus upon military engineering, by reaffirming the value of America's longstanding program of coastal fortification. This was needed, in his judgment, to defend the United States from foreign attack by buying time for the mobilization and training the citizens' militia.[24]

In his more abstract considerations of strategy Halleck similarly emphasized fortification, apparently under the influence of the Archduke Charles of Austria. Halleck cited the archduke's *Principes de la stratégie* ahead of Jomini's *Précis de l'art de la guerre* in the bibliography of his chapter on strategy, calling it "a work of great merit."[25] He quoted

[21] Henry Wager Halleck, *Elements of Military Art and Science* . . . (New York, 1846; 3d ed., *With Critical Notes on the Mexican and Crimean Wars*, New York and London, 1862). All citations are to the third edition.

[22] For the engineering emphasis, see Ambrose, *Duty, Honor, Country*, 87-105. For the status of the highest-ranking graduates, see George W. Cullum, *Biographical Register of the Officers and Graduates of the U.S. Military Academy*, 3 vols. (Boston, 1891), e.g., 1:631.

[23] *Life of Napoleon* by Baron Jomini . . . , trans. H. W. Halleck, 4 vols. (New York and London, 1864).

[24] Halleck, *Elements of Military Art and Science*, esp. ch. 7, pp. 155-209, and on the weakness of American forces at the beginning of a war, pp. 144-54.

[25] Ibid., 59. Thomas Lawrence Connelly and Archer Jones, *The Politics of Command: Factions and Ideas in Confederate Strategy* (Baton Rouge, 1973), 27, called my attention to this point. They discuss the American influence of the Archduke Charles on pp. 27-28, 30, 104, and 176. See the Archduke Charles, *Principes de la stratégie*, . . . rev. ed. (Brussels, 1840).

Charles on the importance of possessing strategic points as "decisive in military operations," and on the consequent necessity to protect one's own strategic points by fortifying them.[26] Jomini in contrast had taken explicit issue with the archduke's fondness for strategic points, arguing that mobile armed forces were both the principal means of waging war and, properly, one's main objective among the enemy's assets. Jomini rejected in particular Charles's claim that France's frontier fortifications played a decisive role in the wars of the eighteenth century and the French Revolution.[27] Yet Halleck not only quoted this claim by the archduke with approval but emphasized it with italics. At the beginning of the French Revolutionary Wars, according to Halleck:

> France . . . was well fortified: and although without armies, and torn in pieces by domestic factions, (we here use the language of the Archduke,) "she sustained herself against all Europe; *and this was because her government, since the reign of Louis XIII, had continually labored to put her frontiers into a defensive condition agreeably to the principles of strategy*; starting from such a system for a basis, she subdued every country on the continent that was not thus fortified; and this reason alone will explain how her generals sometimes succeeded in destroying an army, and even an entire state, merely by a strategic success.[28]

Thus, notwithstanding Mahan's shift from an emphasis on fortification to a call for mobile war, his protégé returned to fortification and therefore to engineering as the foundation of the military profession. Five of the fifteen chapters in Halleck's *Elements* are devoted to fortification; a sixth chapter is given over to the history and importance of military engineers.

The same sort of emphasis, coupled with a more general preoccupation with the technical details of military paraphernalia—cannons, sabers, saddles, and the like—shapes the other major contribution to American military literature in the years before the Civil War. President Franklin Pierce's secretary of war, Jefferson Davis, was a West Point graduate and Mexican War hero. He prided himself on possessing expertise uncommon in a civilian head of the War Department and sought to use it to shape a program of army reforms. Not least, he hoped to restore a close and current acquaintance with European armies and military thought. Thus he arranged for three outstanding officers—Majors Richard Delafield and Alfred Mordecai, and Captain George B. Mc-

[26] Halleck, *Elements of Military Art and Science*, 74.
[27] Connelly and Jones, *The Politics of Command*, 28-29n.
[28] Halleck, *Elements of Military Art and Science*, 77.

Clellan, of the West Point classes of 1818, 1819, and 1846, respectively—to travel to Europe to observe the Crimean War.

The trio arrived in the Crimea in time to witness only the closing incidents of the siege of Sevastopol, but thereafter they toured installations of the principal European armies and gathered impressively careful observations, which were subsequently published in book form. Delafield, superintendent of the Military Academy from 1838 to 1845 and from 1856 to 1861, and chief of engineers late in the Civil War, naturally stressed engineering and fortification in his report. Mordecai focused on artillery, McClellan on cavalry.[29] Their reports remain among the most useful sources on the organization and equipment of mid-nineteenth-century European armies and, together with Dennis Mahan's and Henry Wager Halleck's military works, constitute the beginnings of a professional military literature of a quality surpassing what might have been expected from an army whose day-to-day chores were mainly those of constabulary duty in scattered outposts among the American Indians. At the same time, however, except for certain sections of Mahan's works, these writings mirrored a small and isolated army's lack of self-confidence and the defensive orientation of military engineers building masonry casemates on the seacoast and the Canadian border and trench systems in the field.

III

When the soldiers whose military thought was nurtured by this literature went to war against each other in the 1860s, many of them soon had their troops industriously digging into the ground: McClellan conducting a full-fledged formal siegecraft approach against the Confederate entrenchments around Yorktown, Virginia, in the spring of 1862, Halleck soon thereafter employing his military-engineering knowledge in a cautious and laborious approach to the Confederacy's western fortress city of Corinth, Mississippi. Even Robert E. Lee, less impressed by entrenchments than most of his contemporaries, soon provoked his soldiers to dub him "the King of Spades," because of the use he insisted they make of those implements in guarding the Confederate capital at Richmond.[30]

The Civil War dragged on through four years, and by its latter stages the rival systems of field fortifications, particularly those around such

[29] Richard Delafield, *Report on the Art of War in Europe in 1854, 1855, and 1856* (Washington, D.C., 1860); Alfred Mordecai, *Military Commission to Europe in 1855 and 1856: Report* (Washington, D.C., 1861); George B. McClellan, *The Armies of Europe* (Philadelphia, 1861).

[30] Douglas Southall Freeman, *R. E. Lee: A Biography*, 4 vols. (New York, 1934), 2:86.

418

much-contested strategic points as Petersburg and Atlanta, offered previews of the western front of 1914-1918. Many European military observers of the war found the propensity to entrench to be the most striking feature of combat in America, and tended to attribute the phenomenon to the paucity of trained soldiers in the American war.[31] The Regular Army of the United States, some 16,000 strong, remained almost entirely loyal to the Union except for 313 officers who resigned their commissions, but this force was swamped by a Union war army that reached about 500,000 within four months of the firing on Fort Sumter.[32]

Although it is true that these swarms of volunteers—many of them with a modicum of militia training, but no more—required many months to develop a resemblance to trained soldiers, the digging of field fortifications had a far more profound cause than military inexperience. Indeed, the trenches became more, not less, conspicuous as the soldiers developed into veterans. The true cause of the trench networks was the emergence of the rifled musket as the standard shoulder arm in both armies, and of rifled cannons as about half the artillery pieces on both sides. The rifled musket increased the effective range of the infantryman's weapon from not much over 50 yards to 250 yards, and the extreme range from 250 yards to about half a mile. Against rifled firepower, the only safety was in trenches or behind other kinds of protection. To rise up and deliver a frontal attack became almost always futile against any reasonably steady defenders. Even well-executed flank attacks tended to suffer such heavy casualties as experienced riflemen maneuvered to form new fronts against them that they lost the decisiveness they had enjoyed in the Napoleonic Wars.[33]

The devastating effect of rifled muskets and cannons aggravated the difficulties of developing a workable offensive strategy among soldiers whose military education already favored the defensive. Except during

---

[31] Jay Luvaas, *The Military Legacy of the Civil War: The European Inheritance* (Chicago, London, and Toronto, 1959), esp. pp. 29-30, 46, 54, 64, 66, 68-70, 73-74, 131, 132, 140, 149-50.

[32] Mark Mayo Boatner III, *The Civil War Dictionary* (New York, 1959), 858; Kenneth P. Williams, *Lincoln Finds a General: A Military Study of the Civil War,* 5 vols. (New York, 1950-59), 1:115.

[33] Among many discussions of the impact of the rifle on Civil War tactics, see Stephen E. Ambrose, *Upton and the Army* (Baton Rouge, 1964), 28-34, 56-60; Alfred F. Becke, *An Introduction to the History of Tactics* (London, 1909), 57-108; Bruce Catton, *Mr. Lincoln's Army* (Garden City, N.Y., 1951), 191-99; John K. Mahon, "Civil War Infantry Assault Tactics," *Military Affairs* 25 (Fall 1961), 57-68. An excellent discussion based on the tactical manuals of the time is in Grady McWhiney and Perry D. Jamieson, *Attack and Die: Civil War Military Tactics and the Southern Heritage* (University, Ala., 1982); the student should not be put off by this volume's interspersing of its sound tactical history with its highly dubious thesis that it was their Celtic inheritance that caused the Confederate armies to be consistently on the attack.

the brief war with Mexico, the practical military problems facing American soldiers before the Civil War had been, like their education, primarily matters of defense—protecting the United States from possible incursions by European powers from across the Atlantic or the Caribbean or from Canada. Even on the western frontier, military problems had been essentially defensive; settlers pushed the frontier westward, with the army then engaged in protecting the settlements.[34]

This inheritance of defensive military thought and experience obviously had to be left behind by Union generals whose objective in the Civil War was to destroy the southern states' pretensions to independent sovereignty through offensive action. The inheritance nevertheless bore with special heaviness on Major General McClellan, the careful student of Dennis Mahan. Named general-in-chief of the United States Army in succession to the aged Brevet Lieutenant General Winfield Scott, and charged with inaugurating the first major Union offensive after the improvised march against Bull Run in July 1861, McClellan could not bring himself to assault the field fortifications that the Confederates constructed around the Bull Run battlefield in the late summer and autumn of 1861. Relieved as general-in-chief but retaining field command, McClellan avoided those fortifications by carrying the Union's principal field army in the East, the Army of the Potomac, by sea to the Virginia Peninsula between the York and James rivers. There he stopped short again in front of the field fortifications on the old Revolutionary War battleground of Yorktown. Against entrenchments manned by much weaker forces than his own—albeit he did not acknowledge the enemy's weakness—he resorted to a formal siege straight out of the West Point engineering curriculum. The Confederates retreated when he was about to open his climactic artillery bombardment, but McClellan resumed his advance only to halt abruptly yet again in front of field fortifications outside the Confederate capital at Richmond. He confronted these fortifications through half of May and almost all of June 1862 with little effort to penetrate them, and there is every reason to think he would never have essayed anything more vigorous against them than another formal siege. West Point had taught him the value of fortifications almost too well.[35]

McClellan's dallying before Richmond was interrupted, however, by a Confederate counterstroke, because certain of its leaders believed that the Confederacy's politically defensive purpose in the war—to pro-

---

[34] Prucha, *Sword of the Republic* and Robert M. Utley, *Frontiersmen in Blue: The United States Army and the Indian, 1848-1865*, The Macmillan Wars of the United States (New York and London, 1967) deal best with the pre-Civil War army and the Indian frontier.

[35] For a favorable assessment of McClellan, see Warren W. Hassler, Jr., *General George B. McClellan: Shield of the Union* (Baton Rouge, 1957).

tect its claim to independence—did not necessarily require a defensive strategy. Most notable among the Confederate leaders ready to break loose from the inheritance of defensive military thought were General Robert E. Lee and Major General (later Lieutenant General) Thomas J. "Stonewall" Jackson.

In the spring of 1862, Lee was military advisor to Confederate President Jefferson Davis, Jackson commander of a small Confederate force in the Shenandoah Valley. Jackson was destined to become the subject of a penetrating study of American strategy. Colonel George F. R. Henderson, a major figure in the making of British strategic thought through his teaching at the Staff College, Camberley, made his *Stonewall Jackson and the American Civil War* less a biography than a strategic analysis.[36] In his view, a critical difference between strategy and tactics lay in the capacity of soldiers to master the latter less through intellect and study than through experience and almost intuitive qualities. "The nature of tactics is such that men may win battles and be very poor generals. They may be born leaders of men, and yet absolutely unfitted for independent command."[37] Problems of strategy, in contrast, involve "the movement of large bodies, considerations of time and space, and the thousand and one circumstances, such as food, weather, roads, topography, and *moral*, which a general must always bear in mind, ... composed of so many factors, that only a brain accustomed to hard thinking can deal with them successfully."[38] To these thousand and one factors, and above all to "the grand combinations which prepare and complete success" in achieving the objectives of war as a whole, Lee and Jackson turned their minds while McClellan still laid siege to Yorktown.[39]

Doing so, the two Confederate generals agreed that their armies must grasp the initiative in the war. Notwithstanding the caution with which McClellan limped toward any reasonably strong defenses, his advance up the Peninsula might in time carry him into Richmond through sheer weight of numbers and resources and the inexorability of siegecraft. Other Federal forces were penetrating Virginia from the north to the Rappahannock River and into the Shenandoah Valley and across the Commonwealth's western mountains from the Ohio. Westward beyond Virginia, Union arms had achieved yet more dangerous penetrations of the Confederacy. Aided by naval gunboats on the Mississippi and its tributaries, Union troops had overrun much of the rich agricultural state

---

[36] George F. R. Henderson, *Stonewall Jackson and the American Civil War*, 2 vols. (New York and London, 1898).
[37] Ibid., 1:55.
[38] Ibid.
[39] Ibid., 1:56.

of Tennessee and its industrial area around Nashville. Along the seacoast, the Confederacy's largest city and port, New Orleans, had fallen to Federal naval power, and the Union navy had also captured Port Royal Sound on the South Carolina coast from which to tighten the blockade of Charleston, Savannah, and all the lesser South Atlantic ports.

Lee himself had recently commanded on the South Carolina-Georgia coast and had lacked the strength necessary to halt incursions of the enemy, whom command of the sea enabled to concentrate readily wherever he chose. The experience confirmed for Lee what his military judgment and study already told him: that fortification was not enough—on the seacoast the Union navy found ways to bypass the old permanent fortresses when it could not outgun them; that the Confederacy could not protect itself indefinitely by passive defense; that if the Union were allowed to retain the initiative and the choice of battlegrounds, it could enhance its overall superiority in manpower and resources with still greater superiority at the points of collision; and that if the Confederacy could not wrest the initiative away from the Union along the coast, where it could not counter the navy, at least on land the Confederates might attempt to control the shape of the war. By concentrating their forces at points that they, not the enemy, chose, they rather than the Union might select the sites of collision and achieve at least a measure of parity of strength if not even local superiority at those places.[40] Thus to concentrate at some places would obviously mean running risks by weakening defenses elsewhere. But, said Lee, "we must decide between the positive loss of inactivity and the risk of action." "It is only by concentration of our troops that we can hope to win any decisive advantage."[41]

To Jackson in the Shenandoah Valley, Lee therefore proposed that, reinforced by various detachments from elsewhere around Virginia's periphery, Jackson should take the offensive against the Federals confronting him. If he could sweep them from the Valley, the geography of the region would put him in a position to threaten the Federal capital at Washington. "I have hoped," Lee wrote to Jackson on April 25, 1862, "in the present divided condition of the enemy's forces that a successful blow may be dealt them by a rapid concentration of our troops before they can be strengthened themselves either in position or by reinforcements."[42]

---

[40] For Lee's experiences and the development of his strategic thought to this point, see Freeman, *Lee*, esp. 2:30-40.

[41] Lee made these statements June 8 and November 4, 1863, both to President Jefferson Davis, but they express the basis of his strategy from the Valley campaign onward. *The War of the Rebellion: A Compilation of the Official Records of the Union and Confederate Armies*, 4 series, 70 vols. (Washington, D.C., 1880-1901), ser. 1, vol. 27, pt. 3, p. 868; ibid., vol. 29, pt. 2, p. 819. Hereafter cited as *O.R.*; all citations are of Series One.

[42] Ibid., vol. 12, pt. 3, p. 865.

Jackson had long been proposing similar plans, but no one in Richmond had heeded him before Lee took his place at Jefferson Davis's side. Jackson was if anything even more intent on seizing the initiative than Lee. He had urged an invasion of the North even during the harsh weather of the previous winter. As Henderson summed them up, Jackson's principles of strategy to guide the Confederacy were: "That a concentrated attack on a vital point is a better measure of security than dissemination along a frontier, that the counter-stroke is the soul of the defence, and that the true policy of the State which is compelled to take up arms against a superior foe is to allow that foe no breathing-space. . . ." "The North should be given no leisure," Henderson again summarized his protagonist's ideas, "to reorganize the armies or to train recruits. A swift succession of fierce blows, delivered at a vital point, was the only means of bringing the colossus to its knees, and that vital point was far from Richmond."[43]

Jackson's swift succession of fierce blows against Major General Nathaniel P. Banks's Federal troops in the Valley and then against two additional columns sent to trap him caused Lincoln's government to deny to McClellan in front of Richmond an entire army corps that had been advancing overland across Virginia to meet him. With this corps held back to ensure that Jackson could at least be contained if not punished, any prospect of McClellan's tightening his grip upon Richmond became more remote than ever. But with Union attention thus focused on northern and western Virginia, Jackson moved quickly by railroad to the vicinity of Richmond to reinforce the Confederate field forces already there and together with them to attempt to destroy McClellan's army. This design also was conceived by Lee and Jackson together. Lee had assumed the field command around Richmond, and he directed the Confederate forces there—now named the Army of Northern Virginia—in a series of maneuvers and attacks against McClellan's flank and rear, intended to break the Federal army's line of communications to its maritime base on the York River and thus to expose the Federals to annihilation.

In the resultant combats, called the Seven Days' battles, McClellan fought far more skillfully and bravely on the defensive than his offensive generalship might have suggested he would. Not for nothing had he learned the West Point teachings on field fortifications, which served him especially well at Malvern Hill during the last of the Seven Days. Behind his army's defensive screen, moreover, he changed his base to a better-protected harbor on the James River. The Seven Days' battles drove McClellan back from Richmond, but Lee lamented to President Davis that "under ordinary circumstances the Federal army should have been

[43] Henderson, *Jackson*, 2:131, 397.

destroyed."[44] By "ordinary circumstances," Lee meant division command and staff work up to his own standards of performance. To the lack of them, in a new army with too few professional officers, rather than to McClellan's awakened abilities, Lee attributed his failure to attain his real objective, the destruction of the enemy army.

Lee and Jackson were not so much disciples of Dennis Mahan or Jomini or of other interpreters of Napoleon than of Napoleon himself. From their study of his campaigns they drew more aggressive strategic concepts than had any previous American generals. Jackson had utilized his years of relative leisure between the Mexican and Civil Wars, when he was a professor of mathematics at the Virginia Military Institute, to study thoroughly the campaigns of Napoleon within the context of a wider examination of military history.[45] When Lee was superintendent of West Point from 1852 to 1855, a Napoleon Club flourished at the Military Academy, with Mahan as chairman and commentator. We do not know how much connection with the club Lee had, but we do know that of fifteen books on military subjects that he borrowed from the academy library during his superintendency, no more than seven concerned Napoleon.[46]

More than that, Lee's recorded comments on strategy and war as well as his actions suggest the influence of the emperor. From the Seven Days onward throughout his command of Confederate armies, the hallmark of Lee's generalship, like Napoleon's, was *la manoeuvre sur les derrières*. Lee's objective was to exploit the maneuver against the enemy's rear and flanks to deal psychological and physical blows that would win a victory of annihilation. As long as his own armies' strength permitted him to contemplate the goal with the slightest element of realism, his strategic purpose remained the same, that "the Federal army should [be] destroyed." As late as early June 1864, Lee was still defining his immediate objective by saying: "We must destroy this army of Grant's before he gets to James River."[47]

In the quest to destroy the Federal armies as effective fighting forces, Lee moved closer to what had initially been Jackson's more completely offensive strategy. Before the genesis of the Valley campaign, Lee's response to Jackson's overtures proposing invasion of the North had been noncommittal. After battlefield attacks as part of a strategic defensive failed to destroy the enemy army during the Seven Days, however, and

---

[44] Report dated March 30, 1863, O.R., vol. 11, pt. 2, 497.

[45] Henderson, *Jackson*, 1:43.

[46] Freeman, *Lee*, 1:352-58.

[47] Ibid., 3:398, from James William Jones, *Personal Reminiscences, Anecdotes, and Letters of Gen. Robert E. Lee* (New York, 1874), 40.

424

after a similar combination of the tactical initiative with the strategic defensive bore similar results in the Second Manassas campaign later in the summer of 1862—at Second Manassas, Lee and Jackson fell short of destroying the enemy army despite a *manoeuvre sur les derrières* worthy of Napoleon himself—Lee concluded that the strategic defensive would not suffice. To destroy the Federal army would require carrying the war into the enemy's country and winning an Austerlitz or Jena-Auerstedt victory there. If the Federal forces were resilient enough to survive a Second Manassas on Virginia soil, then to inflict a Napoleonic turning maneuver on them on their own soil might multiply the psychological effects of Confederate victory and Union defeat enough to bring the Federal government into peace negotiations.

Thus, after Second Manassas, Lee and Jackson led the Army of Northern Virginia northward across the Potomac into Maryland. Lack of adequate reinforcement before the beginning of this invasion, the straggling by Confederate soldiers, who could not understand the purpose or logic of the advance, and a complex of logistical difficulties so eroded Lee's strength that in the climax of his strategic offensive he was obliged to fight on the tactical defensive, along Antietam Creek on September 17, 1862. He held his ground on the battlefield, but his losses obliged him to retreat to the south shore of the Potomac. As soon as he was back in Virginia, however, he began planning to invade the North again, and sought from President Davis adequate resources and reinforcements for this purpose. Before the more defensive-minded president supplied the necessary resources, Lee had to respond to another Federal invasion of Virginia, culminating in the battle of Fredericksburg on December 13, 1862. By that time the season was unpropitious for renewed offensive action, and in the spring of 1863 Federal activity in extreme southeastern Virginia obliged Lee to detach Lieutenant General James Longstreet's corps to that area and to postpone a Confederate offensive yet again. But as soon as Longstreet could rejoin him, Lee turned the Army of Northern Virginia toward the Potomac once more for his supreme offensive effort, the invasion of Maryland and Pennsylvania: the Gettysburg campaign.[48]

In the interval between Fredericksburg and Gettysburg, the parrying of still another Federal thrust during Longstreet's absence led Lee to the battle of Chancellorsville on May 2-4, 1863. In the course there of another Napoleonic operation on the lines of communication worthy of ranking with that of Second Manassas, the tragic shooting of Jackson by his own

[48] See O.R., vol. 19, pt. 2, p. 627, for Lee's expression of his desire to march north into Maryland again immediately after his retreat from Antietam. See also Freeman, *Lee*, 2:425.

troops deprived Lee of his skillful and aggressive coadjutor. He was by this time so imbued with Jackson's unalloyed offensive strategy, however, that he proceeded unhesitatingly to the invasion of the North. Yet the death of Jackson was symptomatic of an inherent, and for the Confederacy in time insurmountable, flaw in the Lee-Jackson effort to turn hitherto defensively-oriented American strategic thought to the offensive. Against mid-nineteenth-century military technology—particularly the rifle—the cost of an offensive style of war was immense. In the end, it imposed a mortal toll upon the scarcest of all the Confederacy's scarce resources, its manpower and its military leadership.[49]

As in an earlier conspicuous exception to the defensive focus of American strategic thought—the war with Mexico and particularly Major General Winfield Scott's march from Veracruz to Mexico City—Lee and Jackson sought to sustain the offensive while at the same time minimizing casualties by means of maneuver. In Mexico, Scott had deliberately eschewed battle except on a few occasions when his reading of the nature of the enemy's defenses led him to think combat unavoidable. For the most part, he maneuvered rather than forced the Mexicans out of one stronghold after another until he entered the capital city, whereupon the enemy, beset by numerous internal weaknesses and schisms, gave up the war.[50] It helped keep Scott's casualties low, moreover, that the contestants in the Mexican war were still armed mainly with smoothbore muskets, not rifles. Probably taking his cue from Scott, with whom he had served, as well as from his reading of Napoleon, Stonewall Jackson in his Valley campaign similarly attained his objectives more by maneuvering and marching than by fighting; the battles of the Valley campaign were disproportionately small affairs when set against the strategic impact of the campaign.

To win, however, not merely temporary strategic advantages but Confederate independence against a United States government much firmer of purpose and richer in resources than the Mexican government had been, skillful maneuver proved not enough. One of the differences between Lee and Jackson appears to have been Lee's earlier acceptance of the conclusion that Confederate victory must entail large-scale battles and large casualties. The acceptance of this daunting prospect may help explain Lee's lesser initial exuberance when Jackson was first calling for

[49] The problem of the scarcity of qualified commanders is the theme of Douglas Southall Freeman, *Lee's Lieutenants: A Study in Command*, 3 vols. (New York, 1942-44); see 1:xvii. Yet Freeman did not face squarely the issue of Lee's own contribution to his problem through a strategy that expended officers as well as troops at a rate the Confederacy could not afford.

[50] See my summary in *The American Way of War*, 74-76.

strategic offensives. There is a longstanding temptation in strategic thought to regard maneuver warfare as relatively painless, a means of economizing on both resources and casualties; Basil Liddell Hart sometimes succumbed to this temptation in the twentieth century, and so in the later twentieth century have many of the proponents of maneuver warfare as a remedy for the difficulties of planning the defense of Western Europe against the Soviet Union. But Lee was too realistic to expect war on the scale of the contest between the Union and the Confederacy to be won cheaply. He perceived that against a resolute and resilient opponent, maneuver can achieve the strategic objectives of war only when it culminates in successful battle and in the substantial destruction of the enemy army. "We must destroy this army" was Lee's persistent watchword, and the aim of his maneuvers was always the battle of annihilation.

Seeking battle rather than eschewing it as Scott had done, however, Lee, despite the most skillfully Napoleonic tactical generalship since Napoleon himself, could not avoid suffering heavy casualties in his own ranks in the effort to inflict destructive casualties on the enemy. In the Seven Days' battles, Lee drove McClellan from Richmond but suffered 20,141 casualties in an army of 80,000.[51] At Second Manassas, Lee's defeat of Major General John Pope nearly completed the task of clearing the Federals from Virginia but cost casualties of 9,197 out of 48,527 engaged. At Antietam, a dubious hazard in view of Lee's losses just before and during his invasion of Maryland, he lost 13,724 out of 51,844. As a purely defensive battle, Fredericksburg was relatively uncostly, with Confederate losses of only about 5,300 of 72,500 engaged.[52] But at Chancellorsville, a brilliantly executed envelopment of the Federals by Stonewall Jackson's corps could not prevent Confederate casualties from reaching 12,821 out of 60,892.[53] And Lee's resort to the offensive again in his invasion of Pennsylvania led to the desperate assaults at Gettysburg, in which Confederate casualties were a staggering 28,063 in an army of about 80,000.[54] The total losses were so great that after Gettysburg Lee could no longer contemplate a resumption of the strategic offensive. He might still hope through superior tactics on the battlefield, including local attacks, to realize his continuing aim of destroying the enemy army; but his previous method of warfare had already imposed so heavy a drain upon the strength of his army that the hope was fast becoming chimerical.

[51] Freeman, *Lee*, 2:230, drawing on the calculations of Edward Porter Alexander, *Military Memoirs of a Confederate: A Critical Narrative* (New York, 1907), 171.

[52] Thomas L. Livermore, *Numbers and Losses in the Civil War in America* (Boston and New York, 1901), 88-89, 92-94, 96.

[53] Boatner, *Civil War Dictionary*, 140.

[54] Livermore, *Numbers and Losses*, 103.

Realistic though Lee may have been in believing that no mere maneuver but only destructive battle could break the ability and will of the Union to persist in the struggle against him, he and Jackson as well were probably less than realistic in their initial perceptions of the impact of rifled muskets and artillery. Their experiences of war in Mexico had not prepared them for the rifle. Because of the new effectiveness of infantry fire, closing with the bayonet proved rare in Civil War battles; bayonet and saber wounds combined accounted for only 922 of some 250,000 wounded treated in Union hospitals during the war.[55] Early in the war, nevertheless, Jackson said of his tactical preferences: "But my opinion is that there ought not to be much firing at all. My idea is that the best mode of fighting is to reserve your fire until the enemy get—or you get them—to close quarters. Then deliver one deadly, deliberate fire—and charge [with the bayonet]."[56] As late as the battle of Cedar Mountain, a prelude to Second Manassas fought after the Valley campaign and the Seven Days, Jackson still urged the Light Division under attack to hold their fire and use their bayonets. Lee's penchant for frontal attacks when flanking and enveloping maneuvers failed to secure the results he hoped for—one thinks of Malvern Hill, Pickett's Charge, and the effort to recapture Fort Harrison as late as September 30, 1864—suggests slowness on the part of this otherwise astute and even brilliant commander to appreciate the power of the new weaponry.

Rifled firepower, moreover, permitted enemy forces attacked on flank and rear to form a new front whence they could extract from the enveloping force casualties approximately their own. Second Manassas and Chancellorsville were Lee's and Jackson's supreme efforts in Napoleonic battle, yet the superbly executed Confederate envelopments on those battlefields did not prevent the Federals from inflicting heavy losses on their foe. At Second Manassas, the Confederate casualty rate was about 19 percent; the badly outgeneraled Federals lost 21 percent, 16,054 of 75,696 (largely in missing; in killed and wounded, the Federals lost only 13 percent, while almost all of the Confederates' 19 percent losses were killed and wounded).[57] At Chancellorsville, which has been called Lee's "Absolute Masterpiece," the Confederates actually lost 22 percent to casualties to only 13 percent for the defeated Federals (17,278 of 133,868).[58]

---

[55] William F. Fox, *Regimental Losses in the American Civil War, 1861-1865* . . . (Albany, 1898), 24.

[56] Henderson, *Jackson*, 1:124, no citation given.

[57] Livermore, *Numbers and Losses*, 88-89.

[58] Boatner, *Civil War Dictionary*, 140. Fletcher Pratt, *Ordeal by Fire: An Informal History of the Civil War*, rev. ed. (New York: 1948) calls its chapter 25 on Chancellorsville, "The Absolute Masterpiece."

The most skillful generalship thus could no longer achieve against resolute enemies armed with rifles sufficiently favorable casualty rates and margins of victory in battle to make the results of any one battle decisive. There were no more Austerlitz or Jena-Auerstedt victories to be had. Lee's conviction that in any one battle or campaign "the Federal army should have been destroyed" had in fact become chimerical long before the casualties that he exacted from his own forces stripped them of their offensive power.

Thus the first major effort to move from the previously defensive tenor of American strategic thought toward an effective mode of offensive action ended in failure. Because Lee and Jackson were always handicapped by the limitations of Confederate resources, particularly the scarcity of manpower, it remained to be seen whether the rival Union generals, more richly blessed with men and matériel, might succeed on the offensive where the Confederates had failed.

IV

Among the Union generals McClellan, so altogether lacking in aggressiveness, certainly could not show the way to a successful American strategy of offensive war. Neither could any of the procession of generals who followed rapidly after him in the East, nor most of the Union commanders in the West. McClellan at least possessed a strategic design for winning the war; most of his successors were at best tacticians, whose vision was limited to the immediate problems of the battlefield and would not have been likely to achieve Clausewitz's definition of strategy, the use of battles to attain the object of the war, even if they had been sufficiently capable tacticians to win in battle against the likes of Robert E. Lee. (Major General George G. Meade, the best of them, did outgeneral Lee on the tactical level at Gettysburg.)

In the West, Dennis Mahan's favorite student Halleck, now a major general, received command of the Department of Missouri in November 1861, and the following March became in effect western theater commander as head of the Department of the Mississippi, with several armies operating under him. Halleck partially fulfilled the promise that might have been expected from the first systematic and comprehensive American analyst of strategy. He sponsored and encouraged the operations of Brigadier General Ulysses S. Grant and Flag Officer Andrew H. Foote that captured Forts Henry and Donelson in February 1862 and thereby opened the Tennessee and Cumberland Rivers for Union penetration deep into the state of Tennessee and toward the strategically important Memphis and Charleston Railroad. Halleck's insights into the logistical foundations of strategy proved consistently acute. Throughout the war, he maintained a shrewd eye for logistically viable lines of operation for the Union forces, and he increasingly recognized that one of the most effective weapons of offensive strategy, in an age when battle meant exposure to rifled firepower, was to aim not directly at the enemy armies but at their logistical bases.[59]

On the other hand, Halleck displayed almost McClellan-like diffidence when he personally took the field to conduct the siege of Corinth, Mississippi, on the Memphis and Charleston line, from April 29 to June 10, 1862, and, after he had been rewarded for his western achievements by being named general-in-chief of all the Union armies in July 1862, his diffidence grew into an unwillingness to accept responsibility. He became a useful strategic and logistical advisor to President Abraham Lincoln, Secretary of War Edwin M. Stanton, and Union generals in the field, but little more. Indeed, he came perilously close to fulfilling the soldier of action's worst stereotype of the soldier-scholar: however perceptive his strategic theories, he lacked resolution when he had to apply them to reality.

His subordinate Grant seemed at first glance the opposite type of soldier, a man of action simple and direct, without historical study or theoretical reflectiveness. Although it is true that Grant's limited study of war as a West Point cadet appears to have been buttressed by almost none of the reading in military history of a Stonewall Jackson, Grant soon demonstrated that his capacities reached far beyond a mere intuitive grasp of the battlefield. As a battlefield commander, in fact, he was never to be outstanding, except in the imperturbable courage against adversity with which he saved the day against a powerful enemy counteroffensive at Shiloh. Rather, untutored though he was, Grant rapidly developed into a strategist whose vision of the offensive combining of particular battles and campaigns to achieve the object of the war made him at least Lee's equal in the overall conduct of war. He became the most influential figure in the shaping of American strategic thought for the next hundred years, not always with fortunate results.

Grant's emergence as a strategist began with the Fort Henry-Fort Donelson campaign, which he executed and in whose design he shared with his commanding officer, General Halleck. Like Halleck, he grasped from the beginning of the war the importance of the rivers that penetrated the western Confederacy as logistically workable lines of operation in a

[59] An excellent reappraisal of Halleck together with a stimulating discussion of Civil War strategy in general is to be found in Herman Hattaway and Archer Jones, *How the North Won: A Military History of the Civil War* (Urbana, Chicago, and London, 1983). See for example pp. 54-57, 76-77, 143-50, 205-12, 285-89, and 513-15 on Halleck as a strategist and on his special concern with logistics.

vast area otherwise lacking in such lines, except for a few long and vulnerable railroads. Grant's first major offensive campaign in autonomous command, after Halleck went east to be general-in-chief, was the campaign against the Confederacy's Mississippi River citadel of Vicksburg. The purpose was to open the entire length of the Mississippi to Union navigation and at the same time to impede the flow of agricultural products and European imports coming via Mexico from the Confederate trans-Mississippi area to the East.

Grant's image in military history is principally that of an unsubtle practitioner of attrition warfare designed to destroy the enemy army by means of a brutal day-after-day exchange of casualties. His chief impact on subsequent American strategic thought lay in that direction. During his Vicksburg campaign, nevertheless, his strategy was very different. Drawing on the example of Scott's march from Veracruz to Mexico City—in which Grant, like Lee and Jackson, had served—he employed a strategy of maneuver to turn the enemy out of one defensive position after another and ultimately to trap and force the surrender of the principal opposing army.[60] In the climactic weeks of the campaign, Grant's conduct of maneuver warfare easily matched the achievements of Scott in Mexico or Jackson in the Valley. His troops marched 130 miles, split the Confederate defenders of the state of Mississippi in two, and won five battles—Port Gibson, Raymond, Jackson, Champion's Hill, and Big Black River—with relatively few casualties. When Vicksburg surrendered on July 4, Grant captured 29,491 Confederate officers and men, with 172 artillery pieces and 50,000 to 60,000 muskets and rifles. The earlier phases of the campaign had cost the enemy another 7,000 losses. Meanwhile Grant's own casualties totaled only 8,873: 1,243 killed, 7,095 wounded, 535 missing.[61]

More important than the casualty toll in the Vicksburg campaign was the attainment of the campaign's geographic objectives. But when this campaign and his subsequent lifting of the Confederate siege of Chattanooga brought Grant the command of all the Union armies, his objectives had to expand beyond the capture of strategic places. Charged in March 1864 with winning total military victory in the war—a goal necessary because the Union was bent on forcing the complete surrender of all the Confederacy's claims to sovereignty—Grant felt compelled to

[60] Ulysses S. Grant, *Personal Memoirs of U. S. Grant . . .* , 2 vols. (New York, 1885-86), 1:154, 164-66.
[61] Boatner, *Civil War Dictionary*, 871-77, for summary of the campaign; Grant, *Memoirs*, 1:325-28, 377, for Confederate losses and surrenders; J. F. C. Fuller, *Grant & Lee: A Study in Personality and Generalship*, Civil War Centennial Series (Bloomington and London, 1957), 183, for Union casualties.

modify his strategy and to seek the utter destruction of the Confederacy's capacity to wage war.

After the experience of three years of war, Grant could not share Lee's hope—if he had ever shared it—that the destruction of a major enemy army could be achieved in a single Napoleonic battle. The rival armies of the Civil War were too big, too resilient, too thoroughly sustained by the will of democratic governments for that. Grant hoped, nevertheless, that he might capture or destroy all the Confederate armies by some less appalling means than a brutal exchange of casualties in which the Union would triumph because it had more men to expend. Unlike many admirers and students of Napoleon, he was never infatuated with battle in any form, whether climactic or of prolonged attrition; he thought that even Scott in Mexico had fought battles unnecessarily,[62] and he himself was always a Jominian rather than a Clausewitzian strategist.

Grant assigned Major General William Tecumseh Sherman, long his most trusted subordinate in his western campaigns, to command the Union forces in the West and to eliminate the Confederate armies there, particularly General Joseph E. Johnston's Army of Tennessee. Grant proposed that, leaving Halleck in Washington in the newly created post of army chief of staff to coordinate operations, he himself as general-in-chief would take the field with the principal Union army in the East, the Army of the Potomac, though retaining Major General George G. Meade as its commander. "Lee's army will be your objective point," Grant instructed Meade in perhaps the most famous of American military orders. But in describing in detail how he hoped to eliminate Lee's army, Grant tended to speak less of destroying than of capturing it.[63] Evidently he hoped to outgeneral Lee through a maneuver campaign in Virginia similar to his Vicksburg campaign. The subsequent unfolding of his campaign in Virginia in 1864, as well as his expressions of his intentions and his later reflections, all indicate his hope that by means of turning movements to place the Union forces astride Lee's lines of communications—separating Lee's army from Richmond, or later, separating both Lee's

[62] Grant, *Memoirs*, 1:154, 164-66.

[63] April 9, 1864, ibid., 2:135n; O.R., 33:828. For example, Grant said in his *Memoirs*: "To get possession of Lee's army was the first great object. With the capture of his army Richmond would necessarily follow" (Grant, *Memoirs*, 2:141). "Soon after midnight, May 3d-4th, the Army of the Potomac moved out from its position north of the Rapidan, to start upon that memorable campaign, destined to result in the capture of the Confederate capital and the army defending it" (ibid., 2:177). Rather than using the word "destroy" when instructing Sherman to move against Johnston's army, Grant said: "You I propose to move against Johnston's army, to break it up . . ." (April 4, 1864, ibid., 131n; O.R., vol. 32, pt. 3, p. 246).

army and Richmond from their railroad lines to the deeper South—he might capture the Army of Northern Virginia as he had captured Pemberton's Army of Vicksburg. The means to the destruction of Lee's army was to be its capture, not its attrition and ultimate annihilation.

Unhappily for this design, Lee was not Pemberton. The Confederate master of Napoleonic maneuver was much too wily to be maneuvered into a position where he had to surrender his army, as long as he had an army strong enough to continue the fight. Grant therefore had to settle for the second-best method of accomplishing his objective. He locked Lee's army in battle and held it there day after day, almost every day from his crossing of the Rapidan River on May 3-4, 1864, until the end of the war, trading casualties with Lee in the knowledge that the Union's superior reserves of manpower meant that someday the Union army would remain and Lee's would not. His objects were "not to be accomplished," Grant said,

> ... without as desperate fighting as the world has ever witnessed; not to be consummated in a day, a week, a month, or a single season. The losses inflicted, and endured, were destined to be severe; but the armies now confronting each other had already been in deadly conflict for a period of three years, with immense losses in killed, by death from sickness, captured and wounded, and neither had made any real progress toward accomplishing the final end. . . . The campaign now begun was destined to result in heavier losses, to both armies, in a given time, than any previously suffered; but the carnage was to be limited to a single year, and to accomplish all that had been anticipated or desired at the beginning in that time. We had to have hard fighting to achieve this.[64]

Lee at last surrendered to Grant, but not because he was outmaneuvered. Rather, Lee surrendered on April 9, 1865, because his army no longer existed as an effective fighting force. Only some 26,765 Confederates furled their flags and stacked their arms at Appomattox, the hungry and exhausted shadow of an army that the Confederacy had generally maintained at well over 50,000. Grant's hard fighting had achieved the objective that eluded Lee, the destruction of the enemy army.[65]

It had done so, however, at so high a toll in Union casualties that the outcome of the war was put at risk politically: in 1864, rather than Lincoln, a President might be elected who was committed to a negotiated

[64] Grant, *Memoirs*, 2:177-78.
[65] Boatner, *Civil War Dictionary*, 22.

peace. Not Grant's campaign of attrition in Virginia but fortunately timed victories by Rear Admiral David Glasgow Farragut at Mobile Bay, Sherman at Atlanta, and Major General Philip H. Sheridan in the Shenandoah Valley gave the needed military impetus to Lincoln's prospects at the polling place. The political liabilities of Grant's prolonged exchange of casualties with Lee—and beyond that, of course, the simple hideousness of this new face of war—inevitably prompted a search for less terrible roads to victory, for strategies less calculated to leave the victor almost as battered and bleeding as the vanquished.

Grant himself, driven to his campaign of attrition only when he found no alternative against Lee, continued the search for a more satisfactory strategy against other enemy commanders less deft in riposte than Lee and in theaters of war less geographically constricted and offering more scope for maneuver than Virginia. A hint of the possibilities that he perceived is to be found in the orders he gave his lieutenant in the West, Sherman, for the campaign there to begin simultaneously with Grant's and Meade's assaults upon Lee in the first days of May 1864. Where Meade was ordered to make Lee's army his objective, Grant's instructions to Sherman were somewhat different. The western general was "to move against Johnston's army, [and] to break it up"; but he was also "to get into the interior of the enemy's country as far as you can, inflicting all the damage you can upon their war resources."[66]

Sherman's own predilections helped shape these orders, and so probably did General Halleck's. As the subsequent campaign evolved, Sherman, Halleck, and Grant all contributed to building, upon the foundation of Grant's orders to Sherman to inflict all possible damage upon the enemy's war resources, the design for Sherman's eventual destruction of Atlanta with all its manufacturing and storage capacity, and beyond that the famous marches from Atlanta to the sea and then northward through the Carolinas. In these marches, Sherman's armies destroyed the enemy's war resources across a swath of territory as much as sixty miles wide. As Grant's design matured in Sherman's mind, furthermore, the destructive marches aimed also at breaking the will of the South to persist in the war. Sherman aimed deliberately at terrorizing the people of Georgia and the Carolinas, to "make old and young, rich and poor, feel the hard hand of war, as well as their organized armies."[67] Denied war resources

[66] April 4, 1864, Grant, *Memoirs*, 2:131n; *O.R.*, vol. 32, pt. 3, p. 246.

[67] Dec. 24, 1864, Sherman, *Memoirs*, 2:227. For the development of the ideas for Sherman's strategy among Sherman, Grant, and Halleck, see, e.g., Sherman to Halleck, September 20, 1864, ibid., 117-18; Halleck to Sherman, September 28, 1864, ibid., 128-29; Sherman to Grant, October 9, 1864, ibid., 152, and October 11, 1864, ibid., 153-54; Grant to Sherman, November 1, 1864, ibid., 164; Sherman to Grant, November 2, 1864, ibid., 165; Grant to Sherman, November 3, 1864, ibid., 166.

and the supporting will of the Confederate population, Sherman believed, the organized armies would soon collapse.

British interest in the strategists of the American Civil War, focused in the late nineteenth century under the leadership of G. F. R. Henderson upon the Confederates, shifted in the twentieth century to the Union leaders, who had come to seem more modern than the Confederates, more likely to offer lessons for the era of the world wars. J. F. C. Fuller fixed upon Grant as a general who had foreseen and effectively grappled with the problems of the western front half a century in advance.[68] Liddell Hart in contrast scorned Grant as all too literally a forerunner of the generals of the western front—a prototype of Sir Douglas Haig—but found in Sherman much to admire. Sherman's marches deep behind the enemy armies seemed a magnificent demonstration of Liddell Hart's own favored strategy of the indirect approach. Sherman appealed, unlike Grant, precisely because instead of anticipating the western front he offered a strategic avenue for avoiding it.[69]

Liddell Hart's writings about Sherman display his usual persuasiveness and eloquence, but they tell us less about the real Sherman and his strategy than about how Liddell Hart would have liked to behave had he worn a uniform of Union blue. An examination of Sherman's analyses indicates that he himself saw little divergence between his strategy and Grant's. Not only was the strategy of Sherman's marches developed with the counsel and encouragement of Grant, but in explaining his methods of making war, Sherman like Grant tended to give first priority to disposing of the enemy armies.[70] There was a decidedly fundamental reason for Sherman's thus ordering his priorities, furthermore, apart from any inclination on his part to appear appropriately deferential toward his general-in-chief. Sherman was not able to reach behind the enemy armies to the enemy's war resources and popular will until those armies were first substantially destroyed. Sherman's marches would in time help inspire the twentieth-century prophets of air power, as well as Liddell Hart, because with air power it became possible to leap over hostile armies to

---

[68] Fuller, *Grant & Lee* (orig. pub. London, 1933), and the same author's *The Generalship of Ulysses S. Grant* (New York, 1929).

[69] Basil H. Liddell Hart, *Sherman: Soldier, Realist, American* (New York, 1929). See also, for an analysis praising Sherman but highly critical of Grant, Hart's *Strategy*, 2d rev. ed. (New York, 1967), 149-54.

[70] E.g., Sherman said of his campaign from Chattanooga toward Atlanta: "Neither Atlanta, nor Augusta, nor Savannah, was the objective, but the 'army of Jos. Johnston,' go where it might" (Sherman, *Memoirs*, 2:26). And in discussing with Grant the plan for the march to the sea, Sherman insisted that he could contemplate it only because the rival Confederate army was not strong enough to endanger the force Sherman intended to leave behind (Nov. 2, 1864, ibid., 164-65).

the enemy's economy and people. In the American Civil War, the armies still had to be dealt with first.

Sherman's campaign from Chattanooga to Atlanta almost swept the rival army opposing him from the board before the famous marches began. It did so with considerable assistance from Johnston's successor in command of that army, General John Bell Hood, who mounted a series of assaults against Sherman's forces outside Atlanta in a vain effort to save the city. Hood offered further assistance when after the fall of Atlanta he elected to march northward into Tennessee, hoping to draw Sherman along with him. By that time, however, his army was so weakened that Sherman could counter its maneuver by sending a relatively small part of his force under Major General George H. Thomas back to Tennessee to gather reinforcements there and await Hood. Sherman himself could step off toward the sea with scarcely a shadow of organized resistance remaining before him. But he could adopt the strategy of the indirect approach only after a direct approach had decisively weakened the armed forces initially in front of him.

Altogether, the limitations afflicting Sherman's efforts to find an alternative to Grant's strategy, together with the futility of Lee's Napoleonic strategy and the appalling costs of Grant's method of destroying Lee's army, could well encourage a return to the defensive emphasis that had characterized the beginnings of American strategic thought before the demands of the Civil War imposed a quest for a workable offensive strategy.

V

Such a defensive orientation did return. For the United States Army, the day-to-day realities of existence after the Civil War became again those of patrolling the western frontier. Little strategic thought was given to the most efficacious means of controlling the Indians there. The work was more often that of a constabulary force maintaining the peace between Indians and settlers than that of an army on campaign anyway; spectacular incidents of active warfare like the battle of the Little Big Horn in 1876 were rarities. Perhaps West Point and the postgraduate army schools that developed after the Civil War might profitably have devoted more of their study to the strategic and tactical problems posed by such active Indian warfare as occurred; the Indians were unconventional warriors whose methods more closely resembled those of guerrillas than of conventional European armies, but the American army's schools and thinkers were so much more attracted by the Napoleonic glories of

436

European war than by grubby skirmishes that the army never created a coherent body of guiding principles for Indian war.[71]

After the Civil War, however, there was not much vigor or creativity in the army's contemplation of European-style war either. The late-nineteenth-century army produced no strategic thinker remotely comparable to the navy's Alfred Thayer Mahan. To be sure, there was little stimulus to produce such a thinker; the uninspiring drudgery of duties on the Indian frontier lacked the magnetism to divert American military thought from the contemplation of European wars, but frontier chores occupied the energies of American soldiers too constantly to encourage grand-scale strategic theorizing of the A. T. Mahan variety. The American army fell between two stools, too European an army to be as efficient on the frontier as it might have been, too much a frontier constabulary to be preparing itself effectively for European-style war.

The preparations that did develop turned from the offensive strategies of Lee, Jackson, Grant, and Sherman to the defensive. They might well have done so out of simple discouragement with the Civil War experiments in offensive war, but it was natural, also, that the United States should have conceived of the prospects of war with any European power in defensive terms. Even the naval writings of Alfred Thayer Mahan certainly gave little hint that American expeditionary forces might someday fight on European battlefields. Attention thus returned to the oldest and most continuous of American military policies and strategies, the fortification of the major seaports to prevent their capture by an amphibious *coup de main* and to impose upon any invader from overseas the necessity to land, reinforce, and resupply across open beaches.

Union attacks on coastal fortifications in Confederate hands had demonstrated that rifled artillery rendered obsolete the masonry forts of the post-War of 1812 building program. By firing conical rather than spherical projectiles, rifled cannons could hurl heavier missiles in relation to the diameter of their bore than could the earlier smoothbores. Captain Quincy Adams Gillmore, chief engineer of the Union's amphibious expedition into Port Royal Sound, demonstrated the consequences when he wrecked several of the walls of Fort Pulaski off Savannah, Georgia in 1862. The naval commander of the same expedition, Flag Officer Samuel

---

[71] Robert M. Utley develops this point well in *Frontier Regulars: The United States Army and the Indian, 1866-1891*, The Macmillan Wars of the United States (New York and London, 1975), 44-58, and in "The Contribution of the Frontier to the American Military Tradition," in *The American Military on the Frontier: The Proceedings of the 7th Military History Symposium, United States Air Force Academy 30 September-1 October 1976*, ed. James P. Tate (Washington, D.C., 1978), 3-13.

Francis Du Pont, had already demonstrated when he bombarded his way into the Sound in November 1861 that forts no longer enjoyed the advantages over naval squadrons that they had had in the age of fighting sail, because steamships could maneuver continuously to evade their fire.[72] This combination of developments seemed to require redesigning the coastal forts, and in 1885-1886 much labor was devoted to the task by a Board on Fortifications or Other Defenses, chaired by Secretary of War William C. Endicott.

The Endicott Board projected a new system of forts featuring earthworks bolstered by concrete. The report of the board is a handsome publication with many illustrative plates, and a new generation of coastal defenses followed from it. But by the 1880s the preoccupation with coastal defense was yet another American military activity not quite attuned to reality, because the limited range of steam warships meant that a formidable European naval threat was much less likely than it had been during the Revolution and the War of 1812. Nor did any European power except Great Britain possess sufficient maritime tonnage to transport a formidable army to American shores, and the time when Britain might prove an enemy was passing rapidly if it had not already passed.[73]

In every way, therefore, the experience of the Civil War failed to inspire any impressive flowering of American strategic thought concerning land warfare in the postwar era. At West Point, Dennis Hart Mahan died in 1871, and the Military Academy lapsed into a period of stagnation. The army's principal intellectual of the era, Colonel and Brevet Major General Emory Upton, wrestled with the tactical problems posed by rifled firepower, but rather than moving into strategic studies, he wrote two books about military organization and became obsessed with the impediments that democracy and civilian control put in the way, he thought, of America's ever becoming a mighty military power on the order of Bismarckian Germany. The new professional military journals

---

[72] John D. Hayes, ed., *Samuel Francis Du Pont: A Selection from His Civil War Letters*, 3 vols. (Ithaca, 1969), 1:lxix-lxxi, 301-302, 304-308; 2:33. On the bombardment of Fort Pulaski, see Ralston B. Lattimore, *Fort Pulaski National Monument, Georgia*, National Park Service Historical Handbook Series no. 18 (Washington, D.C., 1954), esp. pp. 23-36.

[73] *Report of the Board on Fortifications or Other Defenses ...* , 49th Cong. 1st sess., House Exec. Doc., vol. 28, no. 49 (serial 2395, 2396); this report has been reprinted as *Report of the Board on Fortifications, 1885 and Plans to Accompany the Report*, U.S. House of Representatives (New York, 1979) in The American Military Experience series, Richard H. Kohn, advisory editor. General Philip H. Sheridan as commanding general of the army commented on the near impossibility of a serious attack by an overseas power in *Report of the Secretary of War, 1884*, p. 49, quoted in John Bigelow, *The Principles of Strategy: Illustrated Mainly from American Campaigns*, The West Point Military Library (New York, 1968; repr. of 2d ed., rev. and enl., Philadelphia, 1894), 35.

of the period, particularly *The Journal of the United States Military Service Institution* and *The United Service*, similarly clung to tactical matters or to the Uptonian dead end of deploring the military deficiencies of democratic government. Newly founded postgraduate schools intended to continue officers' education beyond West Point similarly busied themselves with tactical instruction, and with relatively elementary tactics at that.[74]

Only one American book-length study of strategy worthy of mention came out of the postwar era, an effort to review mainly Jominian principles in the light of specifically American experience. This was Captain John Bigelow's *The Principles of Strategy: Illustrated Mainly from American Campaigns*. Bigelow almost alone, except for an occasional Civil War memoirist, tried to assess the implications of the Civil War for offensive strategy. His focus on American examples obliged him to find a way to fit Sherman's marches into the classical principles of strategy.

Bigelow defined Sherman's incursions through Georgia and the Carolinas, such similar Union campaigns as Sheridan's devastation of the Shenandoah Valley, and to a degree, the naval blockade as "political strategy." He divided political strategy into two subcategories: efforts to make the enemy's government the object of strategy, and efforts to attack the will of the enemy people. Sherman's marches he perceived as aimed at the Confederate government, in the sense of seeking to undermine confidence in its ability to protect its people.[75] Bigelow quoted Grant as saying that the Confederate newspapers long managed to convey to the people of the interior an impression of impenetrable defenses, but when Sherman came, "as the [Union] army was seen marching on triumphantly, . . . the minds of the people became disabused, and they saw the true state of affairs."[76] Sherman's marches also fitted the second subcategory, however, aiming to bring "the war home to the Southern people." "On account of the superiority in republics of the civil over the military power," thought Bigelow, "the people of a republic are a more decisive objective than those of a despotism or absolute monarchy. . . ."[77]

Yet while trying to place Sherman's destructive marches within the principles of strategy, Bigelow seemed more interested in Sherman's ability to break free from his lines of communications than in the uncom-

---

[74] See Emory Upton, *The Armies of Asia and Europe* (New York, 1878) and *The Military Policy of the United States* (Washington, D.C., 1904). The influence of Upton, particularly as reflected in the professional military journals around the turn of the century, is examined at length in Russell F. Weigley, *Towards an American Army: Military Thought from Washington to Marshall* (New York, 1962), 137-61.

[75] Bigelow, *Principles of Strategy*, 224-33, esp. p. 225 on Sherman's marches.

[76] Ibid., 225.

[77] Ibid., 228.

monly broad objectives of the marches.[78] Political strategy, furthermore, remained to Bigelow "often an incident of regular strategy,"[79] the traditional strategy aimed at the enemy's armed forces—but by implication only an incident. Concerning Sherman's attacks upon the enemy people's will to persist in the war, Bigelow expressed doubts of a kind not often expressed in the North in the glow of victory following the war. The doubts remain worth considering when contemplating modern forms of carrying war to civilian populations:

> How far the idea of dispiriting a people may be advantageously carried is a function of most uncertain factors. The infliction of suffering on a people who can stand all that can be inflicted only makes the military problem more difficult by embittering them, and so the infliction of inadequate suffering is a cruel mistake.[80]

In the end, Bigelow returned to the conventional aim of strategy: "As a rule, the primary object of military operations should be to overpower, and, if possible, to capture or destroy the hostile army."[81]

To return to that conclusion was to confirm the ascendancy in American strategic thought of the Ulysses S. Grant of the Virginia campaign of 1864-1865 and of Grant's own *Memoirs*. Bigelow's text concerned itself for the most part with Jominian maneuver, but the American experience on which Bigelow relied for examples tended to undercut confidence that such maneuver could suffice to achieve the object of war, if it had not sufficed for Grant against Lee. Studying strategy from the Grant of the Wilderness, Spotsylvania, Cold Harbor, and Petersburg, American soldiers entered the twentieth century and the time of America's emergence into world power believing that the superior weight of military force that America could bring to bear against almost any rival could be their only sure military reliance.

With no influential American strategic thinkers presenting a persuasive contrary view, it was a strategy based on Grant's in Virginia that shaped the American military participation in the First World War. American reliance on superior numbers and resources prevailed in 1918; the American reinforcement of the Allies on the western front confronted the German army with force beyond its capacity to resist had the war continued into 1919, thereby precipitating the demoralization of the

---

[78] Ibid., 144-47; Sherman's marches are here considered within chapter 10, "Operations Independently of a Base," pp. 132-51.
[79] Ibid., 223.
[80] Ibid., 232.
[81] Ibid., 263.

German high command and its appeal for an armistice. The First World War experience appeared to confirm the inevitability as well as the strength of a strategy derived from Grant in that, as General Tasker H. Bliss commented, "the modern strategist has many limitations upon his freedom in making military combinations," limitations so severe that maneuver and surprise became almost impossible.[82]

Bliss, the American military member of the Allied Supreme War Council, believed that unless at the very outset of war a plan on the order of the Schlieffen plan brought rapid victory to one of the belligerents without the need to engage in frontal assaults—a rapid resolution that the sheer size of modern armies rendered unlikely—then the ensuing struggle would become like the First World War, "rather a test of the courage and endurance of the soldier and of the suffering civil population behind him than of the strategical skills of the general."[83] In his opinion, the First World War signified virtually the end of the age of the strategist, and the confirmation of the arrival instead of the age of war as a mere mechanical trial of the ability of rival coalitions to generate armies and matériel.[84]

Bliss was far from standing alone with such views. Repeatedly, American strategic commentators after the First World War dwelt on the likelihood that political, economic, social, and military endurance based on superior resources had displaced strategy as the foundation of victory in modern war. Here, too, the undercurrent of a Sherman style of war could be heard beneath the insistence on a Grantian destruction of the enemy armed forces. Repeatedly, American military men after 1918 expressed doubt that the most skillful of maneuver could any longer serve decisively in war. Lieutenant Commander (later Commander) Holloway H. Frost of the navy, who before his premature death in 1935 was emerging as the leading American naval writer on strategy after Alfred Thayer Mahan, noted how "our Civil War resulted in another protracted struggle in which economic pressure, exerted through the Navy, greatly assisted our field armies in winning their decisions."[85] Frost believed that in this combination of forces he had found the pattern shaping modern war. By the time of the First World War, he remarked:

[82] Tasker H. Bliss, draft of an article on the strategy of World War I, January 1923[?], p. 1, Bliss Papers, Library of Congress, Box 274.

[83] Ibid., 16.

[84] Ibid., esp. pp. 1-2, 15-16.

[85] Lt. Comdr. Holloway H. Frost, "National Strategy," *United States Naval Institute Proceedings* 51 (August 1925), 1348. For Frost's career, see "A Brief Transcript of His Service Record" in Holloway H. Frost, *The Battle of Jutland* (Annapolis and London, 1936), v-vi.

It was only where a lesser power, Belgium, Serbia, or Rumania, was attacked that a purely military decision could be won, although even here brilliant leadership was usually necessary to supplement superior resources.

From the above facts it may be deduced that when a great power is at war with a small power it will probably still be possible to win a purely military decision by destroying the enemy field armies: but when great nations are at war with approximately equal military forces it will seldom be possible to win a purely military decision.[86]

Colonel W. K. Naylor of the army, offering to an Army War College audience one of the first American expositions of the new post-World-War-I vogue of setting forth succinct lists of the "principles of war," placed more emphasis than Frost on the enemy's armed forces as remaining the major objective in war. But referring to the Civil War experience, he acknowledged the value of economic pressure in the form of the Union naval blockade, and most pertinently he rejected any suggestion that subtleties of maneuver could achieve victory in modern war. Only hard fighting in the manner of Grant could ultimately destroy the enemy armies.

> I wish to stress this point; that warfare means fighting and that war is never won by maneuver, not unless that maneuvering is carried out with the idea of culminating in battle. . . .
>
> Disabuse your mind of the idea that you can place an army in a district so vital to the enemy that he will say "What's the use" and sue for peace. History shows that the surest way to take the fighting spirit out of a country is to defeat its main army. All other means calculated to bring the enemy to his knees are contributory to the main proposition, which is now, as it ever has been, namely, the defeat of his main forces.[87]

In a standard strategic textbook of the post-1918 years, Lieutenant Colonel Oliver Prescott Robinson put the idea still more succinctly: "War means fighting; it has only one aim, to crush the enemy and destroy his will to resist."[88]

Early in the American participation in World War II, on January 22, 1942, a deputy chief of the War Plans Division of the War Department

---

[86] Frost, "National Strategy," 1351-1352.

[87] Col. W. K. Naylor, Inf., "The Principles of War," Command Course no. 12, Army War College, 1922, pt. 1, January 5, 1922, p. 6, copy in Bliss Papers, Library of Congress, Box 277.

[88] Oliver Prescott Robinson, *The Fundamentals of Military Strategy* (Washington, D.C., 1928), 16.

General Staff, charged with Pacific Ocean and Far East concerns but soon to become head of the division, stated the same idea yet more succinctly, and with special reference to the war just commencing: "We've got to go to Europe and fight. . . ."[89] The deputy chief was Brigadier General Dwight D. Eisenhower. In time he would lead the journey to Europe to fight—the cross-Channel invasion that, by directly assailing Germany where it was strongest in the West, confronting its main power and overwhelming it with superior American and Allied power, was the culminating event of the ascendancy of the strategy of Grant in American military thought.

But the undercurrent of the influence of Sherman and his destructive marches also persisted; and while a Grant-style strategy pointed toward Operation Overlord and the great campaign of 1944-1945 across Europe, the memory of Sherman led toward the strategic bombing of Germany and Japan and eventually to Hiroshima and Nagasaki.

[89] Alfred D. Chandler, Jr., ed., *The Papers of Dwight David Eisenhower: The War Years*, 5 vols. (Baltimore and London, 1970), 1:73; "Notes," January 22, 1942.

16. Alfred Thayer Mahan: The Naval Historian

PHILIP A. CROWL

WRITING OF his years in Washington as secretary of war (1940-1945), Henry L. Stimson ruefully recalled "the peculiar psychology of the Navy Department, which frequently seemed to retire from the realm of logic into a dim religious world in which Neptune was God, Mahan his prophet, and the United States Navy the only true Church."[1] The "prophet" alluded to in Stimson's left-handed tribute had then been in his grave for thirty years. He had spent most of his adult life on active duty as a commissioned officer in the United States Navy, retiring as a captain in 1896. Only after the age of fifty did he emerge from the obscurity of an undistinguished naval career to achieve international renown as a historian, strategist, imperialist, and navalist, rubbing shoulders with presidents, prime ministers, and even European royalty, his name venerated in naval circles the world over. His is a remarkable story of the power of the written word.

I

Alfred Thayer Mahan was born on September 27, 1840, at West Point, New York, where his father, Dennis Hart Mahan, was dean of the faculty and professor of civil and military engineering at the United States Military Academy. The elder Mahan was the author of two minor military classics, *Field Fortifications* and *An Elementary Treatise on . . . the Rise and Progress of Tactics*, and was personally responsible for the military indoctrination of hundreds of cadets who would command both Union and Confederate troops in the Civil War. The major source of his writings and teachings was the Swiss strategist, Antoine-Henri, Baron de Jomini, though there is no evidence that he imparted any of this learning to his eldest son who would one day become America's most eminent Jominian. Indeed, there would have been scant opportunity to do so, for at the age of twelve, Alfred was sent off to board at St. James School in Hagerstown, Maryland, and, in 1854, enrolled in Columbia College in

[1] Henry L. Stimson and McGeorge Bundy, *On Active Service* (New York, 1948), 506.

444

New York City, where he lived for two years in the home of his uncle, Milo Mahan, professor of ecclesiastical history at General Theological Seminary. Until his death in 1870, this Anglo-Catholic Episcopal clergyman, church historian, and Christian numerologist served as his nephew's spiritual advisor and was to influence the latter's religious convictions profoundly, especially his view of history as the manifestation of a divinely ordered plan.[2]

After two years at Columbia, the young Mahan, against his father's advice, entered the United States Naval Academy at Annapolis, Maryland, and three years later, in 1859, was graduated second in his class. He made more enemies than friends among his fellow midshipmen, and thus began a lonely career as a Navy misfit, an aloof and solitary figure in a profession that laid much stress on socialization and camaraderie. Annapolis, however, gave him his first joyful experience with sailing ships—a type soon to disappear with the conversion of naval vessels from sail to steam. Of his midshipman cruise aboard USS *Plymouth*, a three-masted square-rigged frigate, he wrote: "In a stiff breeze when the ship is heeling well over there is a wild sort of delight that I never experienced before."[3] Twenty-six years later, aboard the Navy's most up-to-date steam-powered cruiser, USS *Chicago*, he would complain: "I had forgotten what a beastly thing a ship is, and what a fool a man is who frequents one."[4] Later, when he turned his hand to writing naval history, Mahan's early affection for the great square-rigged vessels of his youth would inspire and inform his loving treatment of naval tactics in the age of sail. Likewise, his aversion to the smoky, noisy, unwieldy coal-burners of his manhood made him ever ready to avoid sea duty for the more congenial task of writing books and articles ashore.

Two years after graduation came the Civil War, which for Mahan meant mostly uneventful patrols off the Confederate coasts. An interlude as instructor in seamanship at the Naval Academy (temporarily removed to Newport, Rhode Island) put him briefly under the command of Stephen B. Luce, later to become his mentor and guardian angel. At the war's end, Mahan was twenty-six years old and a lieutenant commander—a rank too high to be lightly given up. So, despite misgivings, he stayed in the Navy, and for the next twenty years, by which time he had achieved the rank of commander, he served in navy yards, on the staff of the Naval Academy (now back in Annapolis), and aboard ship on the Asiatic Station

---

[2] On Milo Mahan's influence, see Robert Seager II, *Alfred Thayer Mahan: The Man and His Letters* (Annapolis, 1977), 10, 39-40, 68-70, 445-52.

[3] Robert Seager II and Doris D. Maguire, eds., *Letters and Papers of Alfred Thayer Mahan*, 3 vols. (Annapolis, 1975), 1:4.

[4] Ibid., 2:114.

and off the west coast of South America. It was while in command of the decrepit, single-screw, schooner-rigged, steam sloop USS *Wachusett* off Peru that he received from Luce, now Commodore, an invitation to join the faculty of the Naval War College, soon to be established under Luce's command, at Newport. Mahan's major qualification for the position was his authorship of a short book on Civil War naval history, *The Gulf and Inland Waters*, published the previous year. He could not have known that he was Luce's third choice for the job when, homesick and sea-weary, he replied on September 4, 1884, "Yes—I should like to come."[5]

After an agonizing delay aboard *Wachusett*, followed by a winter of intense study at libraries in New York City, the novice historian reported for duty at Newport in the summer of 1886. There he discovered that Luce had been ordered back to sea, and that he, a newly promoted captain, was to be both lecturer in naval history and strategy and president of the United States Naval War College. It was the major turning point in his life. The War College was to be the launching pad for a new career as naval historian, strategist, publicist, and world-recognized "evangelist of sea power."[6]

When he took over the former almshouse that had become home to the world's first naval war college, the new president found the quarters bare except for a scattering of borrowed desks and chairs and a wall chart of Trafalgar—scene of his favorite naval battle. The first class consisted of eight naval lieutenants, the following year's of twenty—all assigned to Newport for two or three months' schooling, mostly against their will. Mahan lectured on naval history and strategy (chiefly British); his tiny staff gave instruction in army tactics and strategy, international law, logistics, naval gunnery and tactics, the strategic significance of the Caribbean, and naval hygiene.[7] Much of the new president's energy was spent, however, in foraging for equipment, finding money to pay for coal, and fending off bureaucratic pressures to consolidate the college with the nearby Naval Torpedo Station, or move it to Annapolis, or abolish it altogether. Meanwhile, he was trying to organize his first lectures into book form. The effort paid off with the publication in 1890 of *The Influence of Sea Power upon History, 1660-1783*, but not before the author had narrowly escaped orders from the Bureau of Navigation to return to sea duty. "It is not the business of a naval officer to write books," said the bureau's chief, Commodore Francis M. Ramsay—a

[5] Ibid., 1:578.
[6] The term is Margaret Sprout's. See "Mahan: Evangelist of Sea Power," in *Makers of Modern Strategy*, ed. Edward Mead Earle (Princeton, 1943).
[7] Alfred Thayer Mahan, *Naval Administration and Warfare* (Boston, 1906), 199-213.

truism much ridiculed in later years, but which Mahan himself found "doubtless unassailable" as "my turn for sea service had come."[8] Opposition to the college was strong within the navy—not necessarily because of personal animus against Mahan, as he suspected, or of sheer bureaucratic obtuseness. In an era of rapidly changing technology, many naval officers considered such matters as Lord Nelson's maneuvers at Trafalgar to be archaic irrelevancies. To such as these Mahan's emphasis on history was reactionary, and still worse, impractical. His response was that nothing could be more practical for a naval officer than "the formulation of the principles and methods by which war may be carried on to the best advantage" through the study of history.[9]

For the time being, at least, the issue was resolved in favor of Mahan. He served two terms as president of the Naval War College (1886-1889 and 1892-1893) and by the time he left to take command of USS *Chicago*, his course of instruction at Newport was well established—even to the extent that in his absence his lectures were read aloud to each new class. This curious practice provoked Commodore Ramsay to remark that, although he fully appreciated the value of Captain Mahan's books, "it seems very foolish to send officers . . . [to the Naval War College] to have them read to them."[10] Ramsay's lack of enthusiasm was not shared in Great Britain, where *The Influence of Sea Power upon History, 1660-1783* had received instant acclaim. When Mahan brought *Chicago* into Southampton in late July 1893 he stepped ashore to find himself the lion of the season. Then, and on the ship's return visit the following year, he was entertained by Queen Victoria; her visiting grandson, Kaiser Wilhelm II; the Prince of Wales (later King Edward VII); Prime Minister, Lord Rosebery; Baron Rothschild; and the Royal Navy Club—the first foreigner to be so honored. Oxford and Cambridge universities awarded him honorary degrees, each in the same week; and the *Times* of London proclaimed him to be "the new Copernicus." The British were, of course, gratified that an American author had so fulsomely applauded their country's rise to imperial grandeur, and were to be even more so with the appearance in 1892 of Mahan's second book, *The Influence of Sea Power upon the French Revolution and Empire, 1793-1812*. Of this two-volume work, the naval historian John Knox Laughton wrote that it was "throughout a splendid apotheosis of English courage and English en-

---

[8] Alfred Thayer Mahan, *From Sail to Steam: Recollections of Naval Life* (London and New York, 1907), 311-12.

[9] Mahan, *Naval Administration*, 241.

[10] Ronald Spector, *Professors of War: The Naval War College and the Development of the Naval Profession* (Newport, R.I., 1977), 66.

durance, of English skill, and of English power."[11] Such flattery was balm indeed to a nation already beginning to suffer self-doubt as the era of Pax Britannica was drawing to a close.

Back in the United States, Mahan lectured at the Naval War College in 1895 and again in 1896, in which year he retired from active service. Now he could devote almost full time to his writings, which proved to be voluminous, and for which he was well remunerated. The total *corpus* of his work comes to twenty books and 137 articles, the latter usually written at the request of the editors of such journals as the *Atlantic Monthly, Forum, North American Review,* and *Century Magazine.* Of these, the most important were republished in book form. The other publications included five naval histories, two histories of the Boer War, three biographical studies, one autobiography, and one Christian devotional tract. All the while kudos poured in. Honorary degrees came from Harvard (1896), Yale (1897), Columbia (1900), and McGill (1909) universities, and from Dartmouth College (1903). The American Historical Association elected him its president in 1902. Nor was official recognition lacking. When war with Spain broke out in 1898, Mahan was recalled from an Italian junket to serve on the Naval War Board, newly created to provide strategic advice to the secretary of the navy and the President. In 1899 he was appointed advisor to the American delegation at the first Hague Peace Conference. There, according to the delegation's chairman, Andrew D. White, his views served as "an excellent tonic," preventing "any lapse into sentimentality."[12]

Thereafter, in spite of his growing fame, few calls came for renewed public service. An old friend, President Theodore Roosevelt, appointed him to several committees to promote the reorganization of the Navy Department, but nothing came of the endeavor. In 1906 an Act of Congress advanced all retired navy captains who had served in the Civil War to the rank of rear admiral on the retired list. Mahan accepted the promotion, but kept the title "Captain" as his nom de plume. With the outbreak of World War I, he at once applied his busy pen in the cause of Britain. On August 6, 1914, however, by order of President Woodrow Wilson, all officers, active or retired, were directed to refrain from any public comment on the war. To Secretary of the Navy Josephus Daniels, Mahan objected: "Personally, at the age of seventy-four, I find myself silenced at a moment when the particular pursuits of nearly thirty-five years . . . might be utilized for the public."[13] It was of no use. There was

[11] Quoted in Charles Carlisle Taylor, *The Life of Admiral Mahan* (New York, 1920), 50.
[12] Seager, *Alfred Thayer Mahan*, 411.
[13] Seager and Maguire, *Letters and Papers*, 3:540.

to be no exception to the rule, even for the world's most distinguished naval historian and strategist. Three and a half months later, on December 1, 1914, he died of heart failure at the Naval Hospital in Washington.

II

Mahan's reputation as a historian rests chiefly on his two books, *The Influence of Sea Power upon History, 1660-1783*, and *The Influence of Sea Power upon the French Revolution and Empire, 1793-1812*, published in 1890 and 1892, respectively. Together they come to more than 1,300 pages, devoted chiefly to the naval history of Britain from 1660 through 1812, with the minor omission of the years 1784-1793. The narrative consists mostly of sea battles fought against Dutch, Spanish, Danish, and chiefly French adversaries; the political events leading thereto; and the political, economic, and military consequences thereof. Though these works originated as lectures to be delivered at the Naval War College, there is evidence that Mahan hoped from the beginning to have them published in book form.[14]

The original idea of instructing naval officers in maritime history came from Commodore Luce in his capacity as the first president of the Naval War College. Though missing, the contents of his 1884 letter of invitation to Mahan can be inferred from his article printed in the *United States Naval Institute Proceedings* the previous year. In it Luce asserted that the naval officer should be "led into a philosophic study of naval history, that he may be enabled to examine the great naval battles of the world with the cold eye of professional criticism, and to recognize where the principles of the science have been illustrated, or where a disregard for the accepted rules of the art of war has led to defeat and disaster."[15] Later, in his opening address to the War College students, Luce would elaborate: "Now naval history abounds in materials whereon to erect a science . . . there is no question that the naval battles of the past furnish a mass of facts amply sufficient for the formulation of laws or principles which, once established, would raise maritime war to the level of a science . . . by the comparative method."[16] The "comparative method" to Luce meant drawing analogies between land warfare and war at sea, between military and naval "science," and between past and present. He sought, in short, a usable past: history should teach lessons in the form of fundamental principles.

---

[14] Ltr., Mahan to Luce, May 16, 1885, ibid., 1:606-607.
[15] Stephen B. Luce, "War Schools," *United States Naval Institute Proceedings* 9, no. 5 (1883), 656.
[16] Stephen B. Luce, "On the Study of Naval Warfare as a Science," *United States Naval Institute Proceedings* 12, no. 4 (1886), 531-33.

Such were Mahan's marching orders and such were the constraints that he accepted on agreeing to teach at the Naval War College. His own knowledge of the subject had been derived from a casual reading of the works of John Lothrop Motley, Leopold von Ranke, François Pierre Guillaume Guizot, and Robert Cornelis Napier. While his ship was in Callao harbor in the autumn of 1884, he visited the English club in Lima to find in its library a copy of Theodor Mommsen's *The History of Rome*. Perusing it, he later wrote: "It suddenly struck me . . . how different things might have been could Hannibal have invaded Italy by sea . . . or could he, after arrival, have been in free communication with Carthage by water."[17] Here was the clue to the rise and fall of empires: control of the sea or lack of it. Back home in New York City, the sailor-turned-scholar delved into other secondary works: Royal Navy histories by Sir George Augustus Elliot, Sir John Montague Burgoyne, and Sir Charles Ekins; the *Journal of the Royal United Service Institution*; Leonard L. La Peyrouse Bonfils's *Histoire de la Marine Française*; and Henri Martin's three-volume *A Popular History of France from the First Revolution to the Present Time*.[18] Finally, in late January 1886, six months before his lecture series was to begin, he turned to Baron Jomini.[19] From him he learned "the few, very few" principles of land warfare applicable by analogy to war at sea.[20] But to none of these sources, according to Mahan's own recollection, did he owe his major inspiration. While still serving aboard *Wachusett*, a light had dawned on his "inner consciousness," and "from within" had come the suggestion that "control of the sea was an historic factor which had never been systematically appreciated and expounded." "Once formulated consciously," he declared, "this thought became the nucleus of all my writing for twenty years to come. . . . I owed it to no other man."[21]

Mahan's object was, as he put it in the introduction to his first "Influence" book, to estimate "the effect of sea power upon the course of history and the prosperity of nations."[22] The term "sea power" he claimed to have invented himself, in order, so he later wrote, "to compel

[17] Mahan, *From Sail to Steam*, 277.
[18] Seager and Maguire, *Letters and Papers*, 1:616-19.
[19] On Mahan's preparation for his first lectures, see Mahan, *From Sail to Steam*, 281-82, 384-85; William E. Livezey, *Mahan on Sea Power* (Norman, Okla., 1981), 40-44; William D. Puleston, *Mahan: The Life and Work of Captain Alfred Thayer Mahan, USN* (New Haven, 1939), 74-80; Seager, *Alfred Thayer Mahan*, 164-67.
[20] Mahan, *From Sail to Steam*, 282-83.
[21] Ibid., 275-76.
[22] Alfred Thayer Mahan, *The Influence of Sea Power upon History, 1660-1783* (Boston, 1890), v-vi (hereafter cited as Mahan, *Influence #1*).

attention."[23] Unfortunately, he neglected to define it to any degree of precision. As the term appears throughout his works, two principal meanings emerge: (1) command of the sea through naval superiority; and (2) that combination of maritime commerce, overseas possessions, and privileged access to foreign markets that produces national "wealth and greatness." The two concepts are, of course, overlapping. With the first in mind, Mahan would write of "that overbearing power on the sea which drives the enemy's flag from it, or allows it to appear only as a fugitive." His second meaning was more succinctly stated: "(1) Production; (2) Shipping; (3) Colonies and Markets—in a word, sea power."[24] The reader, however, is frequently left in doubt as to which meaning, if not both, the author has in mind in any given instance. But in still another sense, Mahan, the committed Christian, would write of "this wonderful and mysterious Power" as "a complex organism, endued with a life of its own, receiving and imparting countless impulses, moving in a thousand currents which twine in and around one another in infinite flexibility." Of the power behind that power there was no doubt in the author's mind: it was "the exhibition of a Personal Will, acting through all time, with purpose deliberate and consecutive, to ends not yet discerned," but in the past "tending toward one end—the maritime predominance of Great Britain."[25]

The "maritime predominance of Great Britain," the supreme example of sea power at work, is the subject, then, of Mahan's two major works. Their central theme is simple: in every phase of the prolonged contest between France and England, from 1688 to the fall of Napoleon, command of the sea by naval domination, or lack of it, determined the outcome. Thus, in the War of the League of Augsburg (1688-1697), Louis XIV's failure to provide adequate naval support to the ousted English King James II's invasion of Ireland, coupled with the "gradual disappearance from the ocean of the great French fleets," led to the Peace of Ryswick which "was most disadvantageous to France."[26] The War of the Spanish Succession (1703-1713), though waged mainly by armies on the continent of Europe, ended chiefly to the benefit of England, who had "paid for that continental war and even backed it with her troops, but who meanwhile was building up her navy, strengthening, extending,

[23] Ltr., Mahan to Roy B. Marston, February 19, 1897, Seager and Maguire, *Letters and Papers*, 2:494.

[24] Mahan, *Influence #1*, 138, 71.

[25] Alfred Thayer Mahan, *The Influence of Sea Power upon the French Revolution and Empire, 1793-1812*, 2 vols. (Boston, 1892), 2:372-73 (hereafter cited as Mahan, *Influence #2*); Alfred Thayer Mahan, *The Interest of America in Sea Power, Present and Future* (Boston, 1897), 307-308.

[26] Mahan, *Influence #1*, 179, 180, 185-87, 197.

and protecting her commerce, seizing maritime positions,—in a word, founding and rearing her sea power upon the ruins of that of her rivals."[27] Again, in the Seven Years' War (1756-1763) sea power dictated the outcome, not directly, "but indirectly . . . by the subsidies which the abundant wealth and credit of England enabled her to give Frederick [the Great] . . . and, second, in the embarrassment caused to France by the attacks of England upon her colonies and her own sea-coast, in the destruction of her commerce, and in the money . . . which France was forced to bestow on her navy."[28] As to the American War of Independence, its "successful ending" at Yorktown was due to the control of the sea—to "sea power in the hands of France," foiling, as it had, the Royal Navy's relief of Lord Cornwallis.[29]

The final triumph of sea power, both in the military and economic sense, was the defeat of Napoleon. Here Mahan achieved the height of his not inconsiderable eloquence. Even before Lord Nelson's famous victory at Trafalgar (October 19, 1805), while Bonaparte was assembling an expeditionary force at Boulogne for an amphibious descent on England, the British navy's "far distant, storm-beaten ships, upon which the Grand Army never looked, stood between it and the dominion of the world." After Trafalgar, it was sea power, "that noiseless pressure upon the vitals of France," that cut off French resources and destroyed it, "as a fortress falls by blockade." Specifically, according to Mahan, it was the economic strangulation of France by naval blockade that forced Napoleon to retaliate by barring English goods and ships from European ports; and this "Continental System" in turn caused such privations in Europe as to persuade Czar Alexander I to open his ports in defiance of the French emperor, who thereupon marched into Russia—and so to his downfall. "It was not by attempting great military operations on land, but by controlling the sea, and through the sea the world outside Europe," that English statesmen "ensured the triumph of their country."[30]

Later generations of historians have found considerable fault with this analysis, chiefly on the grounds of oversimplification by omission.[31] First, it is argued, Mahan's general theories about the influence of sea power on history do not account for the rise of such obviously non-maritime empires as Russia, Austro-Hungary, Turkey under the Otto-

[27] Ibid., 222-23.
[28] Ibid., 295.
[29] Ibid., 397.
[30] Mahan, *Influence #2*, 2:118, 108, 184-85, 400-402.
[31] See, for example: Charles A. Beard, *A Foreign Policy for America* (New York, 1940), 75-76; Gerald S. Graham, *The Politics of Naval Supremacy: Studies in British Maritime Ascendancy* (Cambridge, 1965), 6-8, 19-27; Paul M. Kennedy, *The Rise and Fall of British Naval Mastery* (New York, 1976), chs. 3-5, passim.

452

mans, and Germany under Bismarck. More telling, however, is the contention that many factors other than naval superiority must be taken into account to explain Britain's victories over France in the period from 1688 to 1815. Mastery of the seas was no doubt critical, but so were the military (army) operations of England and its allies on the European continent. So too were the diplomatic successes of British statesmen in manipulating the balance of power against France by organizing and sustaining hostile coalitions among its Continental neighbors.

In the War of the League of Augsburg, for example, Britain dispatched a sizeable army across the Channel and subsidized even larger contingents of Dutch and German troops, so that "it was the long-drawn-out bleeding of France's strength on the continent which more than anything else compelled Louis XIV to make peace in 1697."[32] In the War of the Spanish Succession the victorious land campaigns of the Duke of Marlborough and Prince Eugene of Savoy were major factors in determining the outcome. So, too, Frederick the Great's military genius cannot be written off as the byproduct of British subsidies made possible by the profits of maritime supremacy. Nor, according to Gerald S. Graham, "is there any evidence to suggest that the denial of colonial commerce [by the Royal Navy] materially altered the French strategic position on the Continent. . . . Loss of 'command of the sea' diminished but never dangerously reduced French resources and staying power. There was not . . . a 'strangulation' of France by English sea power."[33] In the American War of Independence, notwithstanding the significance of French naval intervention in the Chesapeake Bay off Yorktown, "sea power alone," in the words of Paul M. Kennedy, "was insufficient to crush the American rebellion."[34] Given the nature of the resistance, the size of the country being fought over, its poor communications, the financial burdens imposed upon the mother country, and political opposition to the war at home, it is very doubtful whether Yorktown was the critical factor deciding the Revolution's outcome. More significant perhaps was the absence in this case, as distinct from the other five Anglo-French wars between 1688 and 1815, of any continental enemies to distract France's attention, thus rendering possible the delivery of crucial financial and military, as well as naval, aid to the colonists.

As to the Napoleonic Wars, and the great importance Mahan attached to Trafalgar, it only needs to be pointed out that Bonaparte had abandoned his plans for a cross-Channel attack on England *before* that battle, not afterwards; that his great victories at Ulm, Austerlitz, Jena,

[32] Kennedy, *Rise and Fall*, 76.
[33] Graham, *Politics of Naval Supremacy*, 19.
[34] Kennedy, *Rise and Fall*, 114.

and Wagram took place in the years 1805-1809, when Britain's mastery of the seas was uncontested; and that it was during these same years that the French emperor enjoyed his most unchallenged sway over Europe. Nor was the Continental System solely responsible for the renewal of Franco-Russian hostilities in 1812. Other issues were involved, not mentioned by Mahan at all: the acute Francophobia of most of the Russian aristocracy, Napoleon's resentment at the frustration of his hopes for marriage to the czar's sister, and, most importantly, Franco-Russian rivalry over the disposition of Poland.[35] Finally, by closing his narrative at 1812, Mahan omits consideration altogether of the disastrous failure of Bonaparte's Russian campaign, the "War of Liberation," the battle of Leipzig where the French lost nearly 300,000 troops, and of course the final catastrophe at Waterloo. In these events, it was the clash of armies, not "far distant, storm-beaten ships," that decided the issue.

Mahan, it must be concluded, was consistently guilty of what David Hackett Fischer calls "the reductive fallacy [that] reduces complexity to simplicity, or diversity to uniformity" by confusing *a* necessary cause with *the* sufficient cause.[36] Sea power was a necessary cause—perhaps even the most important cause—of Britain's triumph over France in the seventeenth and eighteenth centuries. It was not, however, the sufficient cause. Mahan's failure as a logician (and therefore as a historian) was the direct result of his methodology: he began his labors with an insight, a light dawning on his "inner consciousness"; the insight hardened into a predetermined conclusion; facts were then mustered as illustration and proof.

There was, it must be said, no pretense on the historian's part to scientific objectivity, nor any claim to having reached his conclusions on the basis of exhaustive research. In his presidential address to the American Historical Association in 1902, Mahan baldly asserted that written history should consist of the "artistic grouping of subordinate details around a central idea"; that some facts were "not really worth the evident trouble" of searching them out; that the scholar's "passion for certainty may lapse into incapacity for decision"; and that "facts must be massed as well as troops" and kept subordinate to the "central feature."[37] This last comes embarrassingly close to Humpty Dumpty's well-known stricture on the proper relationship between words and their user: "The

[35] See Vincent Cronin, *Napoleon Bonaparte: An Intimate Biography* (New York, 1972), 305-310; Andrei A. Lobanov-Rostovsky, *Russia and Europe, 1789-1825* (repr. Westport, Conn., 1968) 152-97.

[36] David Hackett Fischer, *Historians' Fallacies: Toward a Logic of Historical Thought* (New York, Evanston, and London 1970), 172.

[37] Alfred Thayer Mahan, "Subordination in Historical Treatment," in Mahan, *Naval Administration*, 245-72.

question is . . . which is to be master, that's all." In any case it is a far cry from Leopold von Ranke's oft-quoted aspiration "only to show what actually happened."

III

"If navies, as all agree, exist for the protection of commerce, it inevitably follows that in war they must aim at depriving their enemy of that great resource, nor is it easy to conceive what broad military use they can subserve that at all compares with the protection and destruction of trade." Thus wrote Captain Mahan in one of the earliest of the many magazine articles that flowed from his pen after 1890.[38] Though he sometimes adverted to the employment of navies for forward coastal defense, the statement represents the major foundation of Mahan's strategic thought. "The stoppage of commerce," he wrote later, "compels peace." Wars are won by the economic strangulation of the enemy from the sea—by the assertion of that "overbearing power on the sea which drives the enemy's flag from it, or allows it to appear only as a fugitive." They are lost by failure to prevent such strangulation of one's own country. Control of maritime commerce through command of the sea is the primary function of navies.[39]

Such, in Mahan's view, was the major lesson of history as illustrated by England's ultimate triumph over its Continental enemies in a century and a half of intermittent war. But were the strategies pursued by its admirals in the age of sail still applicable to the age of steam? Was "the experience of wooden sailing ships, with their pop-guns, useful in the naval present"?[40] No empirical evidence was available. Except for the uninstructive battle of Lissa fought in July 1866, there had been no recent instance of fleet action between steam-driven ships of war.[41] By default then, as well as by inclination, Mahan was driven to search for analogies that would reveal the unchangeable fundamental truths of warfare, those "teachings in the school of history which remain constant, and being, therefore, of universal application can be elevated to the rank of general principles."[42] Such principles of war, as applied to army operations, had already been elucidated by Jomini. Luce had urged the adoption of the "comparative method"; that is, "resort to the well-known rules of the

[38] Mahan, *Interest of America in Sea Power*, 128.

[39] Alfred Thayer Mahan, *Lessons of the War with Spain and Other Articles* (Boston, 1899), 106; Mahan, *Influence #1*, 138; William Reitzel, "Mahan on the Use of the Sea," *Naval War College Review* (May-June 1973), 73-82.

[40] Ltr., Mahan to William H. Henderson, May 5, 1890, Seager and Maguire, *Letters and Papers*, 2:9.

[41] Seager, *Alfred Thayer Mahan*, 167, 172.

[42] Mahan, *Influence #1*, 2.

military art with a view to their application to the military movements of a fleet."[43] Mahan promised Luce to "keep the analogy between land and naval warfare before my eyes."[44] Accordingly, he turned to Jomini.

The great Swiss strategist's twenty-seven volumes of military history, covering the wars of Frederick the Great and of the French Revolution and Napoleon, would have provided ample data for drawing analogies between military (army) and naval operations. Time, however, would not have allowed even so diligent a worker as Mahan to explore these works to any depth before preparing his War College lectures. In any case, the *Précis de l'art de la guerre (The Art of War)* offered in succinct form the fundamental principles he was seeking. Of these the most fundamental was the principle of concentration, outlined by Jomini in four maxims:

1. Throw by strategic movements the mass of an army successively upon the decisive points of a theater of war, and also upon the communications of the enemy as much as possible without compromising one's own.
2. Maneuver to engage fractions of the hostile army with the bulk of one's own forces.
3. On the battlefield throw the mass of the forces upon the decisive point, or upon that portion of the hostile line which it is of the first importance to overthrow.
4. So arrange that these masses shall not only be thrown upon the decisive point, but that they shall engage at the proper times and with energy.[45]

Although at times stressing the "decisive" character of favorable geographic positions, Jomini, like Clausewitz, viewed the enemy's army as the primary strategic objective of military operations. "The offensive army," he wrote, "should particularly endeavor to cut up the opposing army by skillfully selecting objective points of maneuver; it will then assume, as the objects of its subsequent undertakings, geographical points of more or less importance." A corollary Jominian principle had to do with the choice of the "line of operations" to attain the end of "bringing into action upon the decisive point . . . the greatest possible force." Such choice depended of course on the enemy's dispositions on the field, but

[43] Stephen B. Luce, "On the Study of Naval Warfare as a Science," *United States Naval Institute Proceedings* 12, no. 4 (1886), 534. First delivered in lecture form at the Naval War College in 1885 and 1886, repr. in *The Writings of Stephen B. Luce*, ed. John D. Hayes and John B. Hattendorf (Newport, R.I., 1975), 1:47-68.

[44] Ltr., Mahan to Luce, January 6, 1886, Seager and Maguire, *Letters and Papers*, 1:619.

[45] Antoine-Henri Jomini, *The Art of War* (Philadelphia, 1862; repr. Westport, Conn., 1966), 63.

in the event he had divided his forces, each fraction thereof should be attacked successively by the major portion of one's own army, while a "body of observation" was detached to hold the other fraction in check. Such a maneuver could best be accomplished from a central position along "interior lines."[46]

Finally, although the subject was too complex to be reduced to a simple maxim or principle, Jomini laid great stress on logistics, the all-inclusive term he used to describe a multitude of supportive military functions, including provisioning of troops, supply of munitions, medical services, and securing lines of communication between separate components of a field army and between the army's base of operations and the theater of war.[47]

These three ingredients of Jomini's art of war—the principle of concentration, the strategic value of the central position and interior lines, and the close relationship between logistics and combat—were to be borrowed by Mahan to form the framework of his own system of naval strategy. "System" is too strong a word. Unlike Jomini, Mahan was not systematic. His thoughts on strategy are widely scattered throughout his naval histories, biographies, and magazine articles. To a degree, however, they were brought together in a series of lectures first delivered at the Naval War College in 1887 and thereafter repeated, either by the author himself or else by some other officer reading from Mahan's text. In revised form this series was published in 1911 as a book with the awkward title *Naval Strategy: Compared and Contrasted with the Principles and Practice of Military Operations on Land.*

Borrowing from Jomini, Mahan insisted that concentration was "the predominant principle" of naval warfare. "Like the A, B of the Greeks, which gave its name to the whole of their alphabet and ours, concentration sums up in itself all the other factors, the entire alphabet, of military efficiency in war." This, he said, was true of naval tactics as well as naval strategy. The line between the two he drew at the point of contact between opposing forces; that is, "when the fleets come into collision." In either case, whether engaged in strategic deployment or tactical maneuver, the correct course of action is that "of so distributing your own force as to be superior to the enemy in one quarter, while in the other you hold him in check long enough to permit your main attack to reach its full result." Here lies the main advantage of a central position such as that enjoyed by England vis-à-vis its Continental rivals: it makes possible a naval offensive along interior lines outward from the center and enables the

[46] Ibid., 296, 104, 106.
[47] Ibid., 232-34.

attacker to keep his enemy separated and therefore inferior "by concentrating against one unit while holding the other in check."[48]

But the central position is "contributory, not principal. . . . It is of little use to have a central position if the enemy on both sides is stronger than you. In short, it is power plus position that constitutes an advantage over power without position. . . . The interior position will enable you to get there sooner, but with that its advantage ends." The "only really determining elements in naval war" are fighting fleets.[49]

Whether to build a navy of "a few very big ships, or more numerous medium ships" might be arguable.[50] But there could be no doubt that, to be decisive in war, a navy must be composed primarily of capital ships, which in Mahan's lexicon meant armored battleships.[51] Nor could there be any doubt that "the maximum offensive power *of the fleet* . . . and not the maximum power of the single ship, is the true object of battleship construction."[52] From this proposition followed the much-cited Mahanian dictum: "Never divide the fleet!" If the Naval War College, "had produced no other result than the profound realization by naval officers of the folly of dividing the battle-fleet, in peace or in war, it would by that alone have justified its existence and paid its expenses."[53]

If the concentrated fire of the battle fleet is the principal means by which naval power is to be asserted, the preferred target of such fire is the enemy's fleet. On no point is Mahan more emphatic: the primary mission of a battle fleet is to engage the enemy's fleet. "The one particular result which is the object of all naval action, is the destruction of the enemy's organized force, and the establishment of one's own control of the water." And again, he asserts that "the sound general principle that the enemy's fleet, if it probably can be reached, is the objective paramount to all others; because the control of the sea, by reducing the enemy's navy, is the determining consideration in a naval war."[54]

Hence, both strategically and tactically, navies should be employed offensively. "In naval war," according to Mahan, "coast defence is the

[48] Alfred Thayer Mahan, *Naval Strategy: Compared and Contrasted with the Principles and Practice of Military Operations on Land* (Boston, 1911), 6; Mahan, *Influence #1*, 8-9; Mahan, *Naval Strategy*, 49, 31.

[49] Mahan, *Naval Strategy*, 53, 55; Mahan, *Lessons of the War with Spain*, 262.

[50] Mahan, *Lessons of the War with Spain*, 37.

[51] Ibid., 264; Mahan, *Naval Administration*, 165; Mahan, *The Interest of America in Sea Power*, 198.

[52] Mahan, *Lessons of the War with Spain*, 38-39.

[53] Mahan, *Naval Strategy*, 6.

[54] Alfred Thayer Mahan, *Sea Power in Its Relations to the War of 1812*, 2 vols. (New York, 1903), 2:51; Mahan, *Lessons of the War with Spain*, 167, 137; Mahan, *Naval Strategy*, 189, 199, 254; Mahan, *Influence #1*, 287-88; Mahan, *Influence #2*, 1:155-56; Mahan, *Sea Power in the War of 1812*, 2:52, 301.

defensive factor, the navy the offensive." Quoting Farragut, " 'The best protection against the enemy's fire is a well directed fire from our own guns.' " The great fallacy of the French in the eighteenth century was that they deliberately and constantly "used their fleet for defensive action." Tactically this meant yielding the weather gage to the English; that is, taking position downwind, the better to break off action during a sea fight or avoid it altogether. Strategically, it meant overreliance on *la guerre de course*, defined as "using small ships as commerce destroyers rather than sending large fleets against the enemy,"—a practice that Mahan believed "amounts to abandoning any attempt to control the sea."[55]

Given the importance he attached to maritime commerce, Mahan would have been the last to minimize the value of its denial to the enemy. "The harrassment and distress caused to a country by serious interference with its commerce will be conceded by all." But, he added, "as a primary and fundamental measure, sufficient in itself to crush an enemy, it [commerce destruction] is probably a delusion and a most dangerous delusion." Preying on the enemy's merchant ships was not the way to dry up his resources and effect his economic strangulation. That could only be accomplished by engaging and defeating, or alternatively by immobilizing, his naval forces. Then the sea would become untenable to his merchant shipping. A close blockade, to be sure, might succeed in keeping both merchant and naval vessels bottled up in their own harbors. But when the enemy's warships inevitably escaped to sea, they must be sought out and destroyed. As Jomini said in another connection, the fundamental principle of war was to throw one's forces upon the decisive point of a theater of war and so arrange that "they shall engage at the proper time and with energy."[56]

But Jomini had also laid great stress on logistics. Mahan, for reasons unknown, preferred the word "communications." As in the case of "sea power," he used the term loosely. On the one hand, he defined communications as "a general term, designating the lines of movement by which a military body . . . is kept in living connection with the national power."[57] On the other, he declared that "communications mean essentially, not geographical lines, like the roads an army has to follow, but those necessaries, supplies of which the ships cannot carry in their own

---

[55] Mahan, *Interest of America in Sea Power*, 194; Alfred Thayer Mahan, *Admiral Farragut* (New York, 1892), 218; Mahan, *Naval Administration*, 194; Mahan, *Influence #2*, 1:355.

[56] Mahan, *Influence #1*, 539; Jomini, *The Art of War*, 63.

[57] Alfred Thayer Mahan, *The Major Operations of the Navies in the War of American Independence* (Boston, 1913), 33.

hulls beyond a limited amount." These are, he specified, "first, fuel; second, ammunition; last of all, food."[58] Under either definition, proper naval bases and access to them by the fleet are essential ingredients to a successful maritime strategy. This had become all the more necessary since the advent of steam power, for the obvious reason that no ship could steam for any considerable distance without refueling.

Distant coaling stations, then, were a necessity for a fleet if it were to move very far beyond its home waters, at least in time of war. Mahan, however, though recognizing the necessity for coaling stations, was somewhat leery about their acquisition, except for purposes of hemispheric defense. "Fortified bases of operation," he conceded, "are as needful to a fleet as to an army," but "the number of points to be seriously held must be reduced as much as can be, so as to drain as little as possible the strength of the mother country, and to permit her to concentrate on those of vital importance." Elsewhere, he warned that "the multiplication of such bases, as soon as you pass the limits of reasonable necessity, becomes a source of weakness, multiplying exposed points, and entailing division of force."[59]

Division of naval forces was, of course, anathema to Mahan. Hence, probably, his failure to give more than passing attention to the requirements of amphibious warfare and its place in naval strategy. This neglect is all the more surprising in view of Jomini's having included in *The Art of War* an entire article on what he called military "descents" onto hostile shores.[60] In any case, in treating of "maritime expeditions in remote waters" Mahan was cautionary. He noted that the "peculiar characteristic" of such operations was "the helplessness while afloat of the army contingent embarked." He warned that "you cannot think your conquest secure until you have established your naval superiority," and he advocated the early release of the navy after a landing operation, so that the fleet could take charge of communications "and so of its own element, the sea."[61] If the fleet's role, he warned, is reduced merely to guarding "one or more positions ashore, the navy becomes simply a branch of the army," whereas "the true end of naval war . . . is to preponderate over the enemy's navy and so control the sea" by assailing the enemy's ships and fleets on all occasions.[62]

In truth, Mahan was dubious about any employment of naval forces

[58] Mahan, *Naval Strategy*, 166.
[59] Ibid., 191-92; Alfred Thayer Mahan, *Retrospect and Prospect: Studies in International Relations, Naval and Political* (Boston, 1902), 46.
[60] Jomini, Article 60, *The Art of War*, 226-30.
[61] Mahan, *Naval Strategy*, 205, 213, 218, 243.
[62] Mahan, *Influence #1*, 287-88.

460

against the land. Experience in, and knowledge of, Union ship bombardments of Confederate fortifications during the Civil War had made him skeptical of the effectiveness of naval gunnery against coastal artillery. "A ship can no more stand up against a fort costing the same money," he wrote, "than the fort could run a race with the ship." And again: "Defence on the sea side against direct naval attack is comparatively easy, because . . . ships . . . are at a recognized disadvantage contending against forts."[63]

Power-projection from the sea, a naval mission of growing significance in the twentieth century, was thus mostly disregarded by Mahan. Even more noteworthy is his failure to give much serious attention to the interdependence of armies and navies in wartime. Although devoting about half a page to Sir John Moore's expedition to Spain in 1808,[64] for the most part, throughout his two *Influence* books, he treated the Royal Navy as an autonomous agent acting independently of military operations on the Continent and not much concerned with, or affected by, the outcome of land battles. Coordination between ground and naval forces, to be sure, was not a salient characteristic of warfare in the seventeenth and eighteenth centuries. Nevertheless, in a study devoted to illustrating the fundamental and unchangeable principles of naval warfare, Mahan's general neglect of the utility of naval artillery and of sea-borne infantry assaults against targets ashore stands out as a glaring omission.[65]

But if Mahan overstressed the autonomy of sea power as an instrument of war, he did not fail to remind his readers and listeners that it was indeed an *instrument*. Once again his source was Jomini, who had devoted the first chapter of *The Art of War* to "those considerations from which a statesman concludes whether a war is proper, opportune, or indispensable, and determines the various operations necessary to attain the object of war."[66] It was from Jomini, Mahan testified, that "I imbibed a fixed disbelief in the thoughtlessly accepted maxim that the statesman and general occupy unrelated fields." "For this misconception," he added, "I substituted a tenet of my own, that war is simply a violent political movement."[67] The subordination of strategy to policy was as central to his scheme of thought as it was to that of Carl von Clausewitz whose treatise, *On War*, Mahan did not examine until 1910,

---

[63] Mahan, *Naval Strategy*, 139, 435.

[64] Mahan, *Influence #2*, 2:296.

[65] James A. Barber, "Mahan and Naval Strategy in the Nuclear Age," *Naval War College Review* (March 1972), 83-85.

[66] Jomini, *The Art of War*, 12.

[67] Mahan, *From Sail to Steam*, 283.

and then only in abbreviated form.[68] "War," wrote Mahan in 1896, "is simply a political movement, though violent and exceptional in character." And again: "It is not until this political determination has been reached that the data for even stating the military problem are in hand; for here, as always, the military arm waits upon and is subservient to the political interests and civil power of the state."[69]

In Mahan's view, also, navies were better instruments of national policy than were armies. Less blunt, less symbolic of aggressive intent, more mobile and therefore more responsive to political direction, the influence of a navy could "be felt where the national armies cannot go." This was especially true for the United States, which had "neither the tradition nor the design to act aggressively beyond the seas," but at the same time had "very important transmarine interests which need protection."[70] As he turned his attention to an audience far wider than the student body of the Naval War College, the definition of these "very important transmarine interests" was to become one of Mahan's major preoccupations.

IV

"As far as my own views went," wrote Mahan retrospectively in 1901, "I might say I was up to 1885 traditionally an anti-imperialist; but by 1890 the study of the influence of sea power and its kindred expansive activities upon the destiny of nations had converted me." Aside from an early concern for U.S. interests in the Caribbean and Central America, his memory served him correctly. "I don't know how you feel," he had written to his only close friend, Samuel A. Ashe, in late July 1884, "but to me the very suspicion of an imperial policy is hateful. . . . Though identified, unluckily, with a military profession, I dread outlying colonies or interests, to maintain which large military establishments are necessary." But by 1890 he was changing course, at least to a degree. Readers of his first *Influence* book, published that year, could not have failed to note the author's admiration for the British Empire or to have overlooked the strong suggestion that the United States might look to Britain as a model for emulation. Though most of the pages are devoted to a narrative account of English naval operations, the first chapter is unmistakably didactic. Here, under the guise of discussing "the elements of sea power,"

---

[68] Although an English translation of *On War* was in the library of the Naval War College as early as 1908, it was probably not until two years later that Mahan first made his acquaintance with Clausewitz by way of a commentary written by Major Stewart L. Murray of the Gordon Highlanders, entitled *The Reality of War*. (Puleston, *Mahan*, 293.)

[69] Mahan, *Interest of America in Sea Power*, 177, 180.

[70] Alfred Thayer Mahan, *Armaments and Arbitration, or the Place of Force in the International Relations of States* (New York and London, 1912), 66-67.

the author, extrapolating from the history of Britain in the seventeenth and eighteenth centuries, postulates six "general conditions affecting Sea Power," which, he indicates, are universal and timeless in character. These are: (1) geographical position; (2) physical conformation; (3) extent of territory; (4) number of population; (5) national character; and (6) character and policy of governments.[71]

This section of his book has received far more attention from commentators than it deserves—probably because Mahan is more systematic here than in most of his writings. Actually, the argument is tangential to the main line of his thought, and the outline of six "general conditions" can best be understood simply as an artful device for exposing America's woeful backwardness. Like France, the author argues, the United States has neglected its maritime interests in favor of inland development; its government, being democratic, is less inclined to support military expenditures than was the landed aristocracy of England; its merchant marine has disappeared and its navy has dwindled; not enough of its people follow "callings related to the sea"; it has "no foreign establishments, either colonial or military" and therefore no "resting places" where ships of war can coal and repair. But there is hope. With the impending construction of a canal across the Central American Isthmus, the Caribbean Sea will become "one of the great highways of the world." The position of the United States "will resemble that of England to the Channel." Then the United States will be motivated to build a navy and be compelled to obtain bases in the area which "will enable her fleets to remain as near the scene as any opponent."[72]

Here is the cardinal principle of Mahan's "imperialism." No other prospect of American overseas expansion so engaged his attention or his enthusiasm. As early as 1880, he had written his friend Ashe that an isthmian canal "may bring our interests and those of foreign nations in collision," and therefore "we must without any delay begin to build a navy which will at least equal that of England . . . and must begin to build as soon as the first spadeful of earth is turned at Panama." In the following decade, as the interest of Americans in the Isthmus quickened, so did Mahan's. In his first magazine article, entitled "The United States Looking Outward," published in the August 1890 issue of the *Atlantic Monthly*, he warned of the "many latent and yet unforeseen dangers to the peace of the western hemisphere" attendant upon the opening of a canal through the Central American Isthmus; hinted at the possibility of German intrusion into the area; predicted "a great increase of commercial

[71] Mahan, *Retrospect and Prospect*, 18; ltr., Mahan to Ashe, July 26, 1884, Seager and Maguire, *Letters and Papers*, 1:154; Mahan, *Influence #1*, 29-87.
[72] Ibid., 33-34.

activity and carrying trade throughout the Caribbean Sea"; noted that "the United States is woefully unready . . . to assert in the Caribbean and Central America a weight of influence proportioned to the extent of her interests"; and argued for U.S. naval expansion to meet the threat.[73]

Three years later the same journal published Mahan's "The Isthmus and Sea Power." Enterprising European countries, again chiefly Germany, Mahan argued would undoubtedly aim at naval predominance over such a critical region as the Caribbean; the chief political result of the Canal would be to bring the West Coast closer to the great navies of Europe and therefore "present an element of much weakness from the military point of view"; an artificial waterway across Central America would "enable the Atlantic coast [of the United States] to compete with Europe, on equal terms as to distance, for the markets of eastern Asia; and finally "we must gird ourselves to admit that freedom of interoceanic transit depends upon predominance in . . . the Caribbean Sea," insured primarily by a naval presence.[74]

In 1899, after the war with Spain appeared to have vindicated his preoccupation with the area, Mahan argued that Puerto Rico was to the future Panama Canal and to the West Coast what Malta was to British interests in Egypt and beyond. Nor was that the end of it. As late as 1909, six years after Teddy Roosevelt "took Panama," Mahan would write that the American stake in the Caribbean was "even greater now than it was when I first undertook the strategic study of it, over twenty years ago."[75]

Second in the order of America's overseas interests were the Hawaiian Islands. In 1890 Mahan warned that the opening of the Canal would immediately place the West Coast in jeopardy and that "it should be an inviolable resolution of our national policy, that no foreign state should henceforth acquire a coaling position within three thousand miles of San Francisco,—a distance which includes the Hawaiian and Galapagos islands and the coast of Central America." In January 1893, after American residents in Honolulu had overthrown Queen Liliuokalani and established a republic, he addressed a letter to the *New York Times* advocating U.S. annexation of "the Sandwich Islands" and "a great extension of our naval power" against the day when China "burst her barriers eastward" in "a wave of barbaric invasion."[76]

Subsequently, Walter Hines Page, editor of the *Forum*, asked the

---

[73] Ltr., Mahan to Ashe, March 12, 1880, Seager and Maguire, *Letters and Papers*, 1:482; Mahan, *Interest of America in Sea Power*, 11-15, 20-21.
[74] Mahan, *Interest of America in Sea Power*, 66, 81-87, 100-103.
[75] Mahan, *Lessons of the War with Spain*, 29; Mahan, *Naval Strategy*, 111.
[76] Mahan, *Interest of America in Sea Power*, 26; ibid., 31-32.

letter writer for a full-length article on the subject. He complied with "Hawaii and Our Future Sea Power," published in the March issue. After pausing to note the importance of the islands' position athwart the major trade routes in the Pacific, he again urged immediate annexation on the grounds of the military vulnerability of the West Coast, as well as on America's need to dominate the trade which would ultimately funnel through the Canal. Four years later, in "A Twentieth Century Outlook" appearing in the September 1897 issue of *Harper's Magazine*, he adverted once more to the "Yellow Peril" emanating from China and to the danger implicit in any foreign power's acquiring a coaling station within steaming range of America's west coast.[77]

Thus, before 1898, except for references to unexplained commercial opportunities awaiting Americans in East Asia, Mahan's imperialistic vision went no farther than the Caribbean, the Central American Isthmus, and the Hawaiian Islands. Then on May 1, 1898 Commodore George Dewey steamed boldly into Manila Bay and within twelve hours had destroyed the feeble Spanish squadron lying off Cavite. By the end of July almost eleven thousand American troops had been dispatched to Luzon at Dewey's request. Conquest of the entire archipelago followed. Guam, in the southern Marianas, was picked up by USS *Charleston* en route to Manila. Hawaii was at last annexed; so were the Philippines. Wake Island was occupied with the intention of building a cable station there, although in the event Midway was used instead. All of a sudden the United States had become an empire. As James Field has put it, " 'Imperialism,' we may say, was the product of Dewey's victory."[78]

Mahan's own adjustment to this rapid course of events was slower than one might expect of the prototypical imperialist that some historians have made him out to be.[79] On July 27, 1898, while U.S. Army troops were still outside Manila, he advised Henry Cabot Lodge that, "though rather an expansionist," he himself was "not fully adjusted to the idea" of taking the Philippines and thought it might be a "wise compromise to take only the Ladrones [Marianas] & Luzon, yielding to the 'honor' & exigencies of Spain the Carolines and the rest of the Philippines." Before long, however, adjustment came, and Mahan, like President McKinley, saw annexation as the will of God. Along more worldly lines, he defended American acquisition of the entire group of islands as an

---

[77] Ibid., 32-58, 217-70.

[78] James A. Field, Jr., "American Imperialism: The 'Worst Chapter' in Almost Any Book," *American Historical Review* 83, no. 3 (June 1978), 666.

[79] See, for example, Julius Pratt, *Expansionists of 1898* (Baltimore, 1936), 12-22, 222-83; Walter LaFeber, *The New Empire: An Interpretation of American Expansion, 1860-1898* (Ithaca and London, 1963), 85-101.

expedient backup to the naval base in Manila harbor. But to Mahan, as perhaps to most of his contemporaries, it was the war with Spain that provoked thoughts of American dominion in the Western Pacific, and not vice versa. Up to that time, as he acknowledged, his vision, like that of other sea-power advocates and expansionists "reached not past Hawaii."[80]

But *l'appétit vient en mangeant*, and within a very short time Mahan's thoughts, like others', turned still farther westward to the Asiatic mainland. While Secretary of State John Hay was circulating his Open Door notes and the Boxer Rebellion erupted in China, the now retired but busy Captain wrote four articles, reprinted and published as *The Problem of Asia*. The most pressing "problem," as he saw it, was Russia, whose expansionist aims in eastern Asia had yet to be checkmated by Japan. Conceding Manchuria as already lost to the great Slavic state, Mahan suggested a coalition of sorts among the four "maritime states" of Germany, Japan, Great Britain, and the United States which "by their positions on the eastern side of Asia seriously impede advance from the north." Specifically what he had in mind, as he explained to Vice President Theodore Roosevelt, was the projection of naval power into the Yangtze valley. Looking into the more distant future, Mahan foresaw a danger more ominous even than the Russian threat; that is, China itself. "[I]t is difficult to contemplate with equanimity," he wrote, "such a vast mass as the four hundred millions of China concentrated into one effective political organization, equipped with modern appliances, and cooped within a territory already narrow for it." The answer was for the Western powers to bring the Asian peoples "within the compass of the family of Christian states," not so much by show of military force as by peaceful commercial penetration, in the train of which "we may hope will follow those moral and spiritual ideals, the appropriation of which outweighs material well-being." As to the economic benefits to be derived from such penetration, they "not impossibly may fall very short of the rosy hopes of trade suggested by the mere words 'four hundred millions of people.' "[81]

This last remark raises the question of the economic content of Mahan's thinking about navies, colonies, and imperial expansion. As Kenneth Hagan says, he "was not particularly lucid about what precisely made colonies so valuable to the mother country,"—nor for that matter

---

[80] Ltr., Mahan to Lodge, July 27, 1898, Seager and Maguire, *Letters and Papers*, 2:569; Mahan, *Retrospect and Prospect*, 44-45; Alfred Thayer Mahan, *The Problem of Asia and Its Effects upon International Policies* (Boston, 1900), 7-9.

[81] Mahan, *Problem of Asia*, 67; ltr., Mahan to Roosevelt, March 12, 1901, Seager and Maguire, *Letters and Papers*, 2:707; Mahan, *Problem of Asia*, 88, 154, 163, 34.

about any other economic aspect of imperialism.[82] But the question cannot be dodged, if only because some American historians of the New Left—notably Walter LaFeber—have nominated Mahan to high rank among the late nineteenth-century proponents of something called "the New Empire."[83] Briefly, the argument runs as follows: Mahan believed that American surplus production had to seek new external markets and that the most promising of these were to be found in South America and China, especially in the latter. To exploit these possibilities, he advocated U.S. control of the Panama Canal, Hawaii, and the Philippines as "stepping stones to the two great prizes: the Latin-American and Asian markets." The role of the navy in this scenario was "to provide and protect lines of communication and to settle the conflicts which inevitably erupt from commercial rivalry, thus ensuring access to foreign markets for the surplus goods."[84]

The New Left thesis is doubtless a fine example of Mahanian "subordination in historical treatment." Like Mahan's own scholarship, however, it suffers from overselectivity and errs on the side of omission. That the evangelist of sea power recognized the interdependence of navies, oceanic commerce, and overseas markets is clear enough. As he himself puts it, "political, commercial, and military needs are so intertwined that their mutual interaction constitutes one problem."[85] That his extravagant expectations for a flow of traffic through the Panama Canal, and on past Hawaii to the Orient, presumed a receptive market at the eastern terminus is obvious. But he was less than optimistic about the commercial possibilities of East Asia and, though supportive of the Open Door, was more concerned about the military threat posed by a modernized China than beguiled by the prospect of four hundred million added customers. As for the potential South American market, Mahan was so indifferent that he recommended the exclusion of the entire continent south of the Amazon valley from the operation of the Monroe Doctrine.[86] Finally, his abiding preoccupation with the Caribbean stemmed mostly from his recognition of the area's strategic importance to the security of the United States and the future of the U.S. Navy.

[82] Kenneth J. Hagan, "Alfred Thayer Mahan: Turning America Back to the Sea," in *Makers of American Diplomacy*, ed. Frank J. Merli and Theodore A. Wilson, 2 vols. (New York, 1974), 1:284.

[83] Walter LaFeber, *The New Empire*, passim. Another leading member of this school, however, wisely avoids all but the bare mention of Mahan in this context: see Thomas McCormick, *China Market: America's Quest for Informal Empire, 1893-1901* (Chicago, 1967).

[84] Walter LaFeber, *The New Empire*, 91, 93.

[85] Mahan, *Retrospect and Prospect*, 139-40.

[86] Mahan, *Problem of Asia*, 85-86, 138.

Indeed, as Walter Millis concluded: "It is difficult to resist the impression that Mahan's major impulse was simply to produce an argument for more naval building." Peter Karsten agrees that he was "a simple navalist first and everything else thereafter." William E. Livezey concurs that "for him the navy was central and the advancement of his service was primary." Even his early mentor, Stephen B. Luce, found that by 1897 Mahan had "allowed the views of a naval strategist to dominate those of the political economist." Speaking for himself on the subject of the U.S. Navy, Mahan made his position clear: "Our fleet must be . . . adequate, considering those who might oppose us, whether in the East or in the Caribbean . . . we must be able to exert naval power in both the Pacific and the Atlantic, remembering also that the future canal is . . . open to interruption by force or treachery." Not surprisingly for a naval officer, national defense through command of the sea was his major concern.[87]

Yet there is another dominant theme in Mahan's writings sometimes overlooked by the secular-minded. That is his militant Christianity: his belief in war as a regenerative spiritual force; his view of imperial expansion as a manifestation of the Divine Will; and his conviction that with empire came Christian obligations more weighty than the attendant material rewards. Although not unfamiliar with, or averse to employing the clichés of Social Darwinism, it was not from the likes of Herbert Spencer, but from the Bible that Mahan chiefly drew inspiration for his *Weltanschauung*. Citing the "religion of Christ" as his authority, he could write: "Conflict is the condition of all life, material and spiritual; and it is to the soldier's experience that the spiritual life goes for its most vivid metaphors and its loftiest inspirations." Referring to America's "unwilling acquisition of the Philippines," he writes that "the preparation made for us, rather than by us . . . is so obvious as to embolden even the least presumptuous to see in it the hand of Providence." And from all the territories recently acquired by the United States, an "acreage . . . trivial compared with our previous possessions, or with the annexation by European states within a few years," he doubted whether the material gain would be substantial; but affirmed: "What the nation has gained in expansion is a regenerating idea, an uplifting of the heart, a seed of future beneficent activity, a going out of self into the world to communicate the gift it has so bountifully received."[88]

[87] Walter Millis, *Arms and Men: A Study of American Military History* (New York, 1958), 144; Peter Karsten, *The Naval Aristocracy: The Golden Age of Annapolis and the Emergence of Modern American Navalism* (New York, 1972), 337; Livezey, *Mahan on Sea Power*, 343; John D. Hayes, "The Influence of Modern Sea Power," *United States Naval Institute Proceedings* (May 1971), 279; Mahan, *Problem of Asia*, 198-99.
[88] Mahan, *The Interest of America in Sea Power*, 268; Mahan, *Problem of Asia*, 175; Mahan, *Retrospect and Prospect*, 17.

It is words like these that remind us of how dated Mahan's world view is. What public figure today, after the carnage of two world wars and the eruption of the Third World, would dare to speak in such manner? This is the voice of a pre-Sarajevo man. Yet his reputation for sagacity on naval matters endured well into the twentieth century; and his influence, in naval circles at least, may have been even greater after, than before, his death in 1914.

V

In her essay in the first *Makers of Modern Strategy*, Margaret Sprout stated unequivocally: "No other single person has so directly and profoundly influenced the theory of sea power and naval strategy as Alfred Thayer Mahan. He precipitated and guided a long-pending revolution in American naval policy."[89] On closer examination, it appears that Mahan was not alone in "precipitating" the change of U.S. naval policy in the last decade of the nineteenth century. That this "revolution" was "long-pending," however, is true enough.

In the five years after Lee's surrender at Appomattox, the U.S. Navy shrank in size from 700 vessels aggregating 500,000 tons and mounting almost 5,000 guns to a total of 200 ships displacing 200,000 tons and carrying only 1,300 guns. While European, and even South American countries were building or buying armored, steel-hulled, steam-powered vessels and arming them with rifled, breech-loading guns, the United States retained its prewar wooden cruisers, armed with smooth-bored, muzzle-loading cannon and carrying full sets of sail for auxiliary power. U.S. naval strategy, such as it was, consisted of harbor defense by iron-clad monitors and cruiser deployments in distant waters to show the flag.[90]

Fewer ships meant fewer men. Active duty personnel, numbering about 58,000 officers and men in 1865, declined to a peacetime level of only 9,361.[91] For regular officers this meant an alarming slowdown of promotions, particularly for the younger men who had received their commissions after the war's end. The twelve top graduates of the Naval Academy's class of 1868, for example, were still lieutenants in 1889.[92] To such as these, the only hope for future professional advancement lay in an expanded ship-building program. Mahan, as an 1859 graduate, had of course escaped this logjam. He had been promoted to lieutenant

---

[89] Sprout, "Mahan," 416.
[90] Harold Sprout and Margaret T. Sprout, *The Rise of American Naval Power* (Princeton, 1939), 169-76.
[91] Benjamin Franklin Cooling, *Benjamin Franklin Tracy: Father of the American Fighting Navy* (Hamden, Conn., 1973), 48.
[92] Karsten, *Naval Aristocracy*, 280.

in 1861, to lieutenant commander in 1865, and to commander in 1872.[93] For him the navy had not been a dead end, and his burgeoning navalism of the 1880s cannot be attributed to career anxiety.[94] It may have been otherwise, however, with the younger officers who kindled the fires of a new professionalism centered in the United States Naval Institute founded at Annapolis in 1873.

The Institute held monthly meetings where papers were read, later to be published and circulated among its growing membership—including Mahan, the organization's one-time vice president. Prizes were awarded for the best essays submitted on assigned professional topics. Articles published in the Institute's *Proceedings* expounded on the intimate relationship between oceanic commerce and naval power, explained the historic connection between maritime strength and national greatness, urged the need for more coaling stations for the U.S. Navy, argued for American control of the Central American Isthmus, and advocated prompt construction of capital ships and their integration into fighting fleets. Indeed, all of the major arguments and ideas promulgated by Mahan in his early books were anticipated in the 1880s by the Institute's contributors. And among the most regular of these, though certainly not a junior officer, was Stephen B. Luce. His published pieces (1883-1889) included pleas for advanced education for naval officers, arguments for the reorganization of the Navy Department, and a strong case for building a battleship navy. Clearly the way had been prepared within the navy for Mahan's articulation of his philosophy of sea power. He was not moving into uncharted waters, nor was he without company.[95]

Yet, in the United States, naval officers neither make naval policy nor authorize the construction of new ships. Such responsibilities lie with the Congress and the executive branch of the federal government. The "revolution in American naval policy" was "precipitated" therefore, not by Mahan, but by Benjamin Franklin Tracy, secretary of the navy (1889-1893) and continued by his successor, Hilary A. Herbert (1893-1897). Both, it must be said, were indebted to Mahan for his impressive rationalization of the country's need for battleships. Having restored him to the presidency of the Naval War College in 1889, Tracy consulted with Mahan and may have read the manuscript of his first *Influence* book

[93] Seager and Maguire, *Letters and Papers*, 1:371-72.
[94] For a contrary view, see Karsten, *Naval Aristocracy*, 331.
[95] Robert Seager II, "Ten Years before Mahan; The Unofficial Case for the New Navy, 1880-1890," *Mississippi Valley Historical Review* (December 1953), 491-512; Seager, *Alfred Thayer Mahan*, 199-203; Hagan, "Alfred Thayer Mahan," 1:287-93; Lawrence C. Allin, "The Naval Institute, Mahan, and the Naval Profession," *Naval War College Review* (Summer 1978), 29-48; summaries of Luce's articles appear in *The Writings of Stephen B. Luce*, ed. Hayes and Hattendorf, 191-205.

before submitting his report to President Benjamin Harrison in November of that year, urging the construction of twenty new armored battleships to be organized into two fleets.[96] Harrison asked the Congress for eight and got three—*Indiana, Massachusetts,* and *Oregon*—each displacing more than 10,000 tons and mounting 13-inch and 8-inch rifled guns.

The Naval Act of 1890 had marked the birth of the new Navy.[97] The next administration (Cleveland's second—1893-1897), however, took office prepared to reduce naval expenditures. Hilary Herbert was determined, moreover, to abolish the Naval War College. Providentially, en route to Newport in August of 1893, he was persuaded to read Mahan's second *Influence* book and thereupon changed his mind. Later he read the first of these volumes and decided, as he later explained to the author, "to use in my forthcoming report the information you have therein set forth in my arguments for the building of battleships."[98] Before Cleveland left office, Herbert had persuaded the Congress to supply funds for five more battleships. He was Mahan's first major, and possibly most important, convert.

Theodore Roosevelt and Henry Cabot Lodge needed no conversion to navalism, but were happy nonetheless to have their opinions buttressed by Mahan's seemingly exhaustive scholarship. Lodge had the article "Hawaii and Our Future Sea Power" incorporated into the report of the Senate Committee on Foreign Relations and quoted Mahan frequently on the floor of the Senate. So did other pro-Navy members of Congress, including Senator John T. Morgan and Representative William McAdoo.[99] Among other influential admirers were Albert Shaw, editor of the *Review of Reviews,* and Ambassador and later Secretary of State John Hay, though the latter once remarked that he was "so glad Mahan had been publicly recognized as Theodore would now no longer feel obliged to make [us] all go . . . to hear his lectures."[100]

---

[96] Sprout and Sprout, *Rise of American Naval Power,* 205-213; Richard S. West, Jr., *Admirals of American Empire* (Indianapolis and New York, 1948), 147; Cooling, *Benjamin Franklin Tracy,* 72-74; Walter R. Herrick, Jr., *The American Naval Revolution* (Baton Rouge, 1966), 3-11.

[97] In 1883 three unarmored steel-hulled cruisers, *Atlanta, Boston,* and *Chicago,* plus the dispatch boat *Dolphin* (the "White Squadron") had been authorized, but none exceeded 6,000 tons and all carried auxiliary sail. During the first Cleveland administration (1885-1889), eight more cruisers were ordered, including *Texas* and *Maine* (sometimes called "second-class battleships") and *Charleston,* the first to be free of all canvas. None of these, however, was a true battleship; they were designed mostly for the interdiction or destruction of commercial shipping, not engagements with other fleets.

[98] Seager, *Alfred Thayer Mahan,* 274.

[99] Livezey, *Mahan on Sea Power,* 181; George T. Davis, *A Navy Second to None: The Development of Modern American Naval Policy* (New York, 1940), 75-76.

[100] Peter Karsten, "The Nature of Influence: Roosevelt, Mahan and the Concept of Sea Power," *American Quarterly* 23 (October 1971), 590.

"Theodore" considered Mahan to be his own personal discovery. On first reading *The Influence of Sea Power upon History*, Roosevelt wrote its author: "It is the clearest and most instructive general work of the kind with which I am acquainted. It is a *very* good book—admirable. . . ." His review in the *Atlantic Monthly* for October 1890 was equally laudatory. When he became McKinley's assistant secretary of the navy, Roosevelt pressed Mahan to write him "from time to time." "I wish very much I could get a chance to see you," he added, as "there are a number of things about which I want to get your advice." Specifically, he asked for the latter's comments on the Navy Department's plans for the coming war with Spain, and, on receiving them, advised the sender: "There is no question that you stand head and shoulders above the rest of us! You have given us just the suggestions we wanted." Then, on his departure to join the Rough Riders, Roosevelt saw to it that Mahan replaced him on the Naval War Board.[101]

It is an exaggeration to say, however, that "Mahan's philosophy of sea power entered the White House in the person of Theodore Roosevelt." The President, as in the past, found the Captain a useful authority to cite in arguing the case for naval preparedness. But now his own navalism exceeded that of Mahan. Roosevelt urged the construction of all-big-gun battleships, comparable to the new British *Dreadnoughts*, displacing eighteen thousand tons and mounting single massive batteries of 12-inch guns. Mahan, suspicious as always of new technology, advocated an investment in more ships of smaller size. He debated the issue in the pages of the *Naval Institute Proceedings* with a bright, young lieutenant commander, William S. Sims. Roosevelt sided with the latter. Outdone by his opponent's superior technological knowledge, Mahan retired from the fray. At the age of sixty-seven, the navy's most eminent strategist had to admit: "I am too old and too busy to keep up."[102]

The incident is indicative of Mahan's waning influence within the navy in the final decade before the outbreak of the First World War. Bradley Fiske, who in 1903 had been captivated by Mahan's lectures at Newport, by 1907 considered him to have been "dethroned from his position as the brains of the Navy." Another former supporter, Captain Caspar F. Goodrich, noted that "I used to think with Mahan, but a couple of years ago, I changed my mind." Even Luce broke with his

---

[101] Seager, *Alfred Thayer Mahan*, 209-210; Livezey, *Mahan on Sea Power*, 123-24, 143-44.

[102] Sprout and Sprout, *Rise of American Naval Power*, 20; on Roosevelt's "use" of Mahan and vice versa, see Karsten, "Nature of Influence," 585-600, and Michael Corgan, "Mahan and Theodore Roosevelt: The Assessment of Influence," *Naval War College Review* (November-December 1980), 89-97; Seager, *Alfred Thayer Mahan*, 519-32; ltr., Mahan to Bouverie F. Clark, January 15, 1907, Seager and Maguire, *Letters and Papers*, 3:203.

former disciple on the matter of the all-big-gun ship.[103] And that was not all. When asked in 1911 by Rear Admiral Raymond P. Rodgers to comment on the Naval War College's new strategic plan for the defeat of Japan (Plan Orange), Mahan responded with an elaborate scheme for a naval attack across the northern Pacific from Kiska. This the college rejected as unrealistic. Mahan accepted the rebuff graciously, but his loss of status was obvious.[104]

Abroad, his early books attracted favorable attention, especially in naval and government circles.[105] The acclaim awarded their author in Britain has already been noted. But it cannot be said that his writings affected the course of British naval policy, other than to confirm and popularize decisions already reached. In 1889, a year before the first *Influence* book was published, Parliament had passed the Naval Defence Act establishing the principle that the Royal Navy "should at least be equal to the naval strength of any other two countries." The threat in 1889 was a possible combination of French and Russian fleets in the Mediterranean. By the turn of the century it was Germany.[106]

In that country too Mahan's works had become well known. Emperor Wilhelm II, a naval enthusiast since boyhood, read the first volume of the *Influence* series and was entranced. In May 1894 he cabled Poultney Bigelow of the *New York Herald*: "I am just now, not reading but devouring, Captain Mahan's book; and am trying to learn it by heart. It is a first-class work and classical in all points. It is on board all my ships and constantly quoted by my Captains and officers."[107] The Kaiser, however, must have missed one of the author's major points. Addressing the Kriegsakademie in February 1896, he advocated construction of a new fleet of *cruisers*. Admiral Alfred von Tirpitz, secretary of state of the Imperial Naval Office beginning in June 1897, understood better the requirements of sea power. His first memorandum to the emperor stressed that "the military situation against England demands battleships in as great a number as possible" and that "the proportion of cruisers to battleships should be kept as low as possible."[108] It is doubtful that Tirpitz had read Mahan before forming these opinions. In his memoirs, written

[103] Seager, *Alfred Thayer Mahan*, 532-33.

[104] Ibid., pp. 466-68; ltrs., Mahan to Rodgers, February 22, March 4, 1911, Seager and Maguire, *Letters and Papers*, 3:380-94.

[105] Livezey, *Mahan on Sea Power*, 60-82.

[106] Ronald B. St. John, "European Naval Expansion and Mahan, 1899-1906," *Naval War College Review* (March 1971), 76-78; Arthur J. Marder, *The Anatomy of British Sea Power* (New York, 1940), 24-43.

[107] Taylor, *The Life of Admiral Mahan*, 131.

[108] Jonathon Steinberg, *Yesterday's Deterrent: Tirpitz and the Birth of the German Battle Fleet* (New York, 1965), 72-74, 125-27.

in 1919, he insisted that his tactical doctrine for battleship deployment had been developed independently of Mahan, and that, when he later read the American captain's work, he was struck by the "extraordinary coincidence" of their identical opinions.[109] Nevertheless, the admiral welcomed the German Colonial Society's printing of two thousand copies of *The Influence of Sea Power upon History* as part of his propaganda campaign to persuade the Reichstag to authorize a fleet of battleships. The resultant Navy Law of 1898 was the first of four that kindled the naval race with Britain with all its well-known consequences. Yet Mahan's role in all this was of marginal significance, and Sir Charles Webster's remark (if correctly recalled by Gerald Graham) that " 'Mahan was one of the causes of World War I' " can only be understood as hyperbole.[110]

In his autobiography, Mahan wrote that, so far as he knew, more of his works had been translated into Japanese than into any other language. This may have been so; at least the reception there of his *Influence* books was enthusiastic. In 1897 the Oriental Association of Tokyo advised him that the first of these had been translated by the Club of Naval Officers and circulated among the association's membership, which included 1,800 ministers of state, Diet members, civil and military officers, editors, bankers, and merchants. Copies had been presented to the emperor and the crown prince, and by imperial edict had been placed in every middle, higher middle, and normal school in Japan. Perhaps more importantly, in the light of events to come, *The Influence of Sea Power upon History* was adopted as a text in all Japanese naval and military colleges.[111]

After the end of World War I, Mahan, dead four years, was to become something of a cult hero in U.S. naval circles. At Annapolis a hall was named in his honor, and at the Naval War College, a library. The extent to which his teachings continued to affect naval thinking, however, is another matter, and one not easy to determine. In 1918 Professor Allan Wescott of the Naval Academy published a collection of excerpts from Mahan's works, which for three years was required reading in the course in naval history taken by all midshipmen of the third (Junior) class. After 1922, however, the book was dropped in favor of a conventional textbook coauthored by Professor Wescott.[112]

[109] Gordon A. Craig, *Germany 1866-1945* (Oxford and New York, 1978), 307; Grand Admiral Alfred von Tirpitz, *My Memoirs*, 2 vols. (New York, 1919), 1:72.

[110] Graham, *The Politics of Naval Supremacy*, 5.

[111] Mahan, *From Sail to Steam*, 303; Taylor, *The Life of Admiral Mahan*, 114-15; Livezey, *Mahan on Sea Power*, 76.

[112] Allan Wescott, ed., *Mahan on Naval Warfare* (Boston, 1918); William O. Stevens and Allan Wescott, *A History of Sea Power* (New York, 1920); U.S. Naval Academy Archives, Record Group 5, Division of English and History, Academic Course Materials.

At the Naval War College, the study of history was deemphasized in the 1920s and 1930s. The works of Mahan appeared in the "prescribed reading course," but no more prominently than those of such other naval intellectuals as Sir Julian Corbett, Sir Herbert W. Richmond, and Admiral Raoul Castex. Actually, during the interwar period at Newport, conventional academic studies of any sort yielded precedence to war gaming. Students year after year replayed the battle of Jutland on the gaming board.[113]

Perhaps, in this intense preoccupation with an inconclusive duel of World War I battle fleets, one can detect the lingering ghost of Alfred Thayer Mahan. That was the opinion, anyway, of one disillusioned officer who blamed Mahan's aversion to *la guerre de course* for the U.S. Navy's neglect of the study of submarine warfare despite the bitter lessons of the First World War. "The reason for this obvious lack of appreciation of the commerce raiding loss of World War I," he concluded, "was . . . a material fixation on the capital ship, supported by a strategic doctrine which concentrated on the Mahanian concept of a decisive battle in which the battleship was supreme."[114] The same "fixation" apparently governed the annual playing of "The Game," a simulated war at sea between Blue (the United States) and Orange (Japan). Though the participation of aircraft carriers was assumed, the tactical climax of the simulation was always a fight between fleets of battleships. None of these games envisioned a final invasion or aerial bombardment of Japan; the mission ended with the establishment of an economic blockade by the victorious U.S. Navy.[115] Perhaps these exercises did perpetuate among their participants a Mahanian view of strategy at a time of apparently declining interest in Mahan's writings. This may be why Captain William D. Puleston could confidently assert in 1939 that "today, in the American Navy, every officer who prepares for or discusses war, follows the methods and invokes the ideas of Mahan."[116] Perhaps too it explains the charge leveled against the Navy Department by Secretary of War Stimson, as quoted at the beginning of this essay.

It is surprising, however, that some historians have persisted in describing the United States' victory over the Japanese Empire in World War II as a validation of "the principle of strategy which Mahan had so ably elucidated and popularized," or as "a Mahanian triumph of sea

[113] Michael Vlahos, *The Blue Sword: The Naval War College and the American Mission, 1919-1941* (Newport, R.I., 1980), 72-73; Spector, *Professors of War*, 144-48.

[114] R. A. Bowling, "The Negative Influence of Mahan on Anti-Submarine Warfare," *RUSI (Journal of the Royal United Service Institute for Defense Studies)* (December 1977), 55.

[115] Vlahos, *The Blue Sword*, 146.

[116] Puleston, *Mahan*, 333.

power."[117] Although the wartime chief of naval operations, Fleet Admiral Ernest J. King, might properly be labelled a Mahanian, the war in the Pacific was not conducted entirely according to his wishes.[118] Nor was it conducted entirely according to the strict Mahanian canon, which prescribed a climactic battle between opposing fleets of capital ships. There was no such climactic battle, even between aircraft carriers—not Midway, nor the Philippine Sea, nor Leyte Gulf. Moreover, Mahanian doctrine simply cannot be stretched to include General MacArthur's reconquest of the vast Japanese-held territories in the Southwest Pacific, the successive amphibious assaults in the Central Pacific made possible by prolonged naval gunfire against fortifications ashore, or the B-29 bombing of Japan by the U.S. Army Air Forces, or the highly successful *guerre de course* waged by American submarines against Japanese merchant shipping. Victory in the Pacific was the product of combined arms, not of the autonomous operations of the United States Navy.

Developments since 1945 have further enhanced the interdependence of all armed services and have blurred former distinctions between land-, air-, and sea-based weapons to a degree inconceivable to Mahan. Laurence W. Martin states the matter thus:

> In the second half of the century, developments in naval propulsion, in aircraft, missiles, explosives and techniques of computation, have overthrown completely the context in which fleet actions were the focus of strategy. Submarines, aircraft and missiles have become the dangerous enemies of the larger surface ships while those ships find their prime targets on shore. Bombardment of the land, once one of the most humble naval tasks, has become a dominant concern of the larger navies—strategically with missiles launched from submarines, tactically with aircraft based at sea.[119]

Yet in naval circles Mahan's name, in the decades following World War II, continued to command respect and even veneration. It appeared with some regularity in articles in the *U.S. Naval Institute Proceedings* and the *Naval War College Review*. At Newport, lectures on such subjects as "Mahan in the Nuclear Age" were not uncommon. As late as 1972, at the beginning of his enlightened and innovative presidency of the Naval War College, even Vice Admiral Stansfield Turner bowed to tradition to

---

[117] Livezey, *Mahan on Sea Power*, 313; Russell F. Weigley, *The American Way of War: A History of United States Military Strategy and Policy* (New York and London, 1973), 311.

[118] Thomas B. Buell, *Master of Sea Power: A Biography of Fleet Admiral Ernest J. King* (Boston and Toronto, 1980), 34-35, 51-52.

[119] Laurence W. Martin, *The Sea in Modern Strategy* (New York, 1967), 10.

the extent of announcing: "There may be another Alfred Thayer Mahan in this year's class or the next. We cannot afford to miss him."[120]

Traditionalism aside, however, there is scant indication that the U.S. Navy today holds to the Mahanian view of strategy that exalts sea power over all other forms of military action, claims for navies an autonomous domain in the realm of warfare, and equates command of the sea with victory. "Our maritime strategy," according to the 1984 fiscal year "posture statement" of the chief of naval operations, "relies not only on U.S. naval forces, but also depends on the contributions of other U.S. air and land assets and the forces of our friends and allies."[121] Secretary Stimson would have approved. Mars, not Neptune, is again the god of war.

It must be said, however, that if Mahan's answers are no longer relevant, the questions he raised still are. He consistently asked his listeners and readers to give serious thought to such matters as the meaning of the concept of national interest; the moral dimensions of military force; the responsibilities, as well as the opportunities, of world power; the nature of American dependence on sea-lines of communication; the composition of fleets; the logistical requirements of warfare; and, most importantly, the uses of navies as instruments of national policy. "All the world knows, gentlemen," he announced to the Naval War College class of 1892, "that we are building a new navy. . . . Well, when we get our navy, what are we going to do with it?"[122] That was—and is—the question.

[120] John B. Hattendorf, "Some Concepts in American Naval Strategic Thought, 1940-1970," *The Yankee Mariner & Sea Power*, The Center for Study of the American Experience, Annenberg School of Communications, University of Southern California, Los Angeles, 1981, p. 95; Stansfield Turner, "Challenge!" *Naval War College Review* (September-October 1972), 2.

[121] "A Report by Admiral James D. Watkins, U.S. Navy, Chief of Naval Operations on the Posture of the U.S. Navy," *Department of Navy Fiscal Year 1984 Report to the Congress*, Washington, D.C., 1983, 16.

[122] Mahan, *Naval Administration*, 229.

PART FOUR

From the First to the Second World War

17. The Political Leader as Strategist

Gordon A. Craig

THE PROPER ROLE of the political leader in the direction of a nation's war effort is difficult to establish in theory. Clausewitz's statement that "policy is the guiding intelligence and war only the instrument. . . . No other possibility exists, then, than to subordinate the military point of view to the political," though of great theoretical significance, is of little use to anyone trying to formulate rules for decision making in twentieth-century warfare or to delineate responsibility for the determination of strategy.[1] If, as David Fraser has argued, "the art of strategy is to determine the aim, which is or should be political: to derive from that aim a series of military objectives to be achieved: to assess these objectives as to the military requirements they create, and the pre-conditions which the achievement of each is likely to necessitate: to measure available and potential resources against the requirements and to chart from this process a coherent pattern of priorities and a rational course of action," the difficult question is how much of the deriving and assessing and measuring and charting falls within the political leader's purview and how much of it becomes a military function.[2] It is clear that this cannot be answered by any categorical formulation, even one that is invested with the authority of Clausewitz's name.

Much the same can be said of the relationship between civilian and military authority at that moment in the process of war in which strategy is translated into operations. Sir Edward Spears has written with some asperity:

> The picture . . . of . . . civilians examining plans and maps and work-ing out the meaning of the vast number of orders based on these, issued by Army Groups and Armies to artillery of every description, to the air force, the cavalry, infantry, tanks, etc. is ridiculous. . . . Only one possessed of that most dangerous of disqualifications, an amateur's half-knowledge, would [suggest] that statesmen, innocent of all military training, [were] capable . . . of estimating such things

[1] Carl von Clausewitz, *On War*, ed. and trans. Michael Howard and Peter Paret, rev. ed. (Princeton, 1984), 607.
[2] David Fraser, *Alanbrooke* (London, 1982), 215.

as the firepower on their own side and the power of resistance of the enemy, the weight of the shock of the attacking infantry and its tactical dispositions, without any knowledge of the ground, of assimilating in fact . . . the highly technical staff-work which represented many weeks of study by highly trained professionals."[3]

This is all very well, but one feels that it is overstated. All operations have political consequences. They can increase or diminish a nation's ability to achieve its goals; they can commit it unwisely to new and unforeseen objectives; they can, by failure of calculation or execution, discourage its allies or bring new support to the side of the enemy. If excessive meddling in operational planning and decision making by political leaders can have disruptive consequences, inability or unwillingness on their part to exercise critical control over such plans and decisions runs the risk of placing in military hands powers that can jeopardize the national security for which the political leadership has ultimate responsibility. Here too, then, it is difficult to frame a theoretical definition of appropriate roles that is not so general as to be meaningless.

In practice, these questions have been resolved by the interplay of such factors as the nature of the political system, the efficiency and prestige of the military establishment, and the character and personality of the political leader. In the two world wars of this century, the last of these has been the most important.

I

The case of Germany's first chancellor in the Great War, Theobald von Bethmann Hollweg, may serve as an extreme but by no means unique illustration of the difficulties that confronted the political leaders of all belligerent states in 1914. As soon as hostilities commenced, he found himself in a situation in which nearly all the political parties, the business community, a high proportion of the university professoriate, the bulk of the middle class, and significant portions of the working class were desirous of the most ambitious kind of territorial expansion and were sure that the war would make this possible. Simultaneously, he had to deal with a military establishment that had greater freedom from political control and a higher degree of public veneration than any similar body in the world.

Judged from the standpoint of intelligence and administrative talent, Bethmann was certainly the best of Bismarck's successors, but he was also, as Gerhard Ritter has pointed out, "an intellectual who lacked a wholly secure instinct for power, . . . who did not enjoy possessing it,

---

[3] Edward Spears, *Prelude to Victory* (London, 1939), 377f.

482

and who [held on to office, only because he] regarded this as an iron responsibility in the service of the national state and the traditions of the Prussian-German monarchy."[4] He was not a fighter, the kind of robust man of will who follows his own objectives without scruple or distraction. His natural diffidence disarmed him when he was opposed by arrogance and self-confidence, and in moments of crisis he was apt to be overcome by fatalism.

It is therefore not surprising that in August 1914 Bethmann allowed himself to be overimpressed by the technical arguments of the soldiers and swept into a war that he had, in any case, convinced himself was all but inevitable. He had had no share in devising the strategical plan for the war, and he does not seem to have questioned openly its basic assumptions, that a massive enveloping movement in the West would knock France out of the war in six weeks and discourage the British from further participation, and that the bulk of German forces could then be turned eastward to relieve the Austrian holding operation and destroy the Russian advance.

What has to be said for Bethmann, however, is that, after the strategy of the First High Command had failed and the long stalemate in the trenches began, he strove valiantly to submit the war to rational control and to direct it to achievable ends. For a time it looked as if he might be successful. He denied Chief of Staff Falkenhayn's demands to be consulted on all matters of foreign policy that might conceivably affect operations in the field, a patent attempt to broaden the powers of the military at the expense of the chancellor. He won a signal victory over Tirpitz and the admirals in 1915, preventing the introduction of unlimited submarine warfare at that time. He used all of his persuasive powers to prevent the emperor from falling completely under the sway of the military and, until 1917, was not ineffective in this effort.

He was less effective with respect to the annexationists, whose ambitions he considered to be unrealistic and dangerous, since they threatened to broaden the scope of the war to a point where any peace by negotiation would become impossible. In the end, he became so concerned about this that he resorted to tactics that helped to undermine his own position. He conceived the idea of using the authority of the military against the expansionist lobbies, of finding a general who would support his own moderate course and would be popular enough to force the annexationists into line. He decided that he must persuade the emperor to dismiss Falkenhayn—whose popular support had seeped away during the wasting Verdun campaign—and to bring in Hindenburg, the hero of

---

[4] Gerhard Ritter, *Staatskunst und Kriegshandwerk* (Munich, 1964), 3:586.

Tannenberg, in his place. In an audience with William II in July 1916, he said flatly that Hindenburg must be made supreme commander at once. "This is a matter that involves the fate of the Hohenzollern dynasty. With Hindenburg he could make a compromise peace, without him he could not."[5] A few weeks later, the emperor agreed, and the change was made.

This proved to be a grave miscalculation. Hindenburg did not want a compromise peace, and neither did his first general quartermaster Erich Ludendorff, who proved to be more rabid about territorial acquisition than the annexationists themselves. Moreover, the chiefs of the new Supreme Command were not as easily barred from intervention in political decisions as Falkenhayn had been. Before long, they were claiming and obtaining the right to be heard on all matters of high policy and were themselves urging courses of action that could not help but prolong and broaden the war. In November 1916, Ludendorff successfully defeated the possibility of a negotiated peace with Russia by insisting that military needs required the creation of a satellite Kingdom of Poland out of Russian lands occupied by German troops since 1914, a decision that led to the fall of the peace party in St. Petersburg and kept the Russians in the war for another year. And not content with that, the Supreme Command, in the spring of 1917, called for the immediate inception of unlimited submarine warfare.

Bethmann had fought staunchly against the expansion of submarine operations in 1915. This time his resistance was weaker, and in the end he yielded. His reasons for doing so show the dilemma of the civilian statesman in wartime in all its cruelty. In the crucial Crown Council, Bethmann was surrounded by naval experts who brandished statistical tables and technical charts, all of which proved that to loose the submarines would bring victory in a given number of months. He was not an intellectually arrogant man and, before this massive uniformed assurance, he could not help but doubt his own instincts. He gradually convinced himself that the Admiralty might, after all, be right and gave way. This was doubtless an act of weakness, but Ritter has a point when he writes that it would have taken a person of wholly extraordinary will and self-confidence to oppose a course of action that was demanded by all of the responsible military leaders, as well as by the emperor, the Reichstag majority, and most politically aware Germans, including the Social Democrats.[6]

Bethmann's capitulation on this issue was not enough to satisfy either

[5] Ibid., 241.
[6] Ibid., 383ff.

484

the Supreme Command, who were irritated at the chancellor's presumption in opposing their views on a matter of national security, or the annexationists, who knew that he still hoped for a compromise, and hence a "soft," peace. In the months that followed, these forces allied and launched an elaborate campaign against Bethmann's "flabbiness," insisting that the successful prosecution of the war would be impossible unless he were dropped. Their intrigues were successful, and the man who had striven to keep the war within rational limits was hounded from office. The striking thing about his fall is not the way in which it was accomplished but rather the fact that no voice was raised in his behalf. It was not only the soldiers and the business interests that brought Bethmann down. Such future leaders of Weimar democracy as Matthias Erzberger and Gustav Stresemann actively participated in the dirty maneuvers that effected his dismissal; the Reichstag majority gave its approval, the Socialists were mute, and public opinion in general greeted the event with satisfaction, apparently convinced that Hindenburg and Ludendorff would bring them the total victory that they craved.

In a striking corroboration of Clausewitz's insight that the successful prosecution of war depends upon the proper coordination of political leadership, armed forces, and the passions of the people, it was the disarticulation of these forces that defeated Bethmann. The combination of military self-confidence and public heedlessness nullified all attempts to coordinate Germany's political and military strategies rationally and to direct its operational planning to achievable ends. The result was a stubborn prolongation of the war that caused millions of needless casualties, an ill-conceived offensive in 1918 that the country did not have the resources to support, and, in the end, defeat and revolution.

II

Although the British are supposed to be politically more sophisticated than the Germans and more firmly set against vesting authority in the military, the difference is hardly supported by their experience in the First World War. Indeed, it can be fairly said that the country's first wartime prime minister never tried as hard as Bethmann Hollweg did to see that war was used as an instrument of policy and that the great strategical issues remained under the control of the political leadership.

H. H. Asquith was a gifted parliamentarian and a superb party leader, but he had neither the knowledge nor the energy to be a great war minister. A. J. P. Taylor has said of him that he "did not understand the great issues which the conduct of the war provoked. Though resolved on victory, he supposed that the only contribution that statesmen could make was to keep out of the way, while free enterprise supplied the arms with which generals would win the battles."[7] This was a curious attitude for a British statesman to take, for Great Britain was a sea power and, at war against predominantly land powers, it had strategical options, the choice between which could not, or should not, be made by the military alone. Asquith's diffidence about taking a firm line himself meant that the basic decisions that would affect the nature, locus, length, and financial and human cost of the conflict, and the future of the British Empire, would not be made logically and responsibly. Rather they would be haggled over in various ministries, committees, and staffs; compromise solutions would be found that pleased no one and proved to be ineffective (like the Dardanelles plan, which failed for lack of conviction, energy, and resources), and ultimately the country would drift into a strategical posture from which it was impossible to withdraw, whether it was rationally supportable or not.

This is pretty much what happened under Asquith's lax leadership in the first two years of the war. After much strategical backing and filling, and the unhappy Dardanelles affair, the leadership of the army passed into the firm control of Douglas Haig and William Robertson, a combination that proved to be almost as impervious to civilian supervision as the Hindenburg-Ludendorff team and which imposed a set of strategical concepts upon the country that were very nearly as fatal in their results as those of their German counterparts. Both Haig and Robertson were "westerners"—that is, they believed that the war could be won only by killing Germans in Flanders, and they were prepared to accept the heavy loss in British casualties that this would entail. Under their leadership, the war became not one of movement but of attrition. As Roy Jenkins has written in his biography of Asquith, and his words are a judgment and a criticism of his subject, "In these circumstances, the job of the politician ceased to be that of looking for strategical alternatives and became concentrated upon supplying men and munitions for the slaughter."[8] Unless one regards the bloodletting that went on at the Somme or at Arras as a rational use of war for an intelligible end (and it is difficult to do so), then one is forced to conclude that the prime minister had given up the effort to keep the war within the limits of reason long before Bethmann had done so, and that he had surrendered his proper functions to the soldiers, first to Kitchener, later to the duumvirate Robertson-Haig.

Asquith was a shrewd politician, and it was probably his knowledge of the currents of public opinion, rather than personal lethargy, that

---

[7] A. J. P. Taylor, *Politics in Wartime* (New York, 1965), 21.
[8] Roy Jenkins, *Asquith: Portrait of a Man and an Era* (New York, 1964), 387.

inspired this abdication. A few days before the outbreak of the war, he had written disdainfully in his diary: "There were large crowds perambulating the streets and cheering the King at Buckingham Palace, and one could hear the distant roaring as late as 1 or 1:30 in the morning. War or anything that seems likely to lead to war is always popular with the London mob. . . . How one loathes such levity!"[9]

Once the war had started, the passions of the mob became more inflamed, and Asquith probably felt that any attempt to assert himself in strategical questions would meet with popular disapproval and lead to a governmental crisis. And, in any case, how could one really prove that the soldiers were wrong in their estimates of military possibilities? It was all so difficult to get at! On the first day of the battle of the Somme in July 1916, more than 1,000 officers and 20,000 men were killed, fatally wounded, or reported missing, and over 1,300 officers and 34,000 other ranks were wounded. Before the battle was over, the British had suffered 420,000 casualties. These were impressive and daunting figures. Yet, when the government remonstrated with the commander in chief in France, Haig gave them the kind of answer that has been heard from many commanders on many occasions since 1916 and is always difficult for politicians to deal with. The Somme battle, he pointed out, had relieved pressure on other parts of the Allied line and had diverted enemy resources from other fronts. At the same time, by proving that Britain could mount an offensive in the main theater of war and drive the cream of German troops from their positions, it had had important psychological effects and had fortified the will to victory. Most important, the attacks had used up 30 percent of the enemy's divisions so that, in another six weeks, he "should be hard put to it to find men. . . . The maintenance of a steady offensive pressure will result eventually in his complete overthrow."[10] Who was to deny the validity of these confident assertions? Confronted with them, Asquith simply lapsed into tacit acquiescence.

His successor as prime minister, David Lloyd George, had stronger convictions about strategy and a greater desire to bring logical direction to the war effort, but he suffered from the same fear of public disapproval or disavowal if he were to be too outspoken. He argued with the soldiers. He told Robertson, "I will not drive thousands to slaughter like cattle. For three years we have been promised victory in France and Belgium. What is there to show for this ceaseless battery? We must strike again at a soft front!"[11] When the army command nevertheless planned new offensives in Flanders, he muttered about "wild military speculation,"

---

[9] Ibid., 328.
[10] E. L. Woodward, *Great Britain and the War of 1914-1918* (London, 1967), 148-49.
[11] Quoted by Robert Graves in *The Observer*, March 1, 1959.

"insane enterprises," and "muddy and muddle-headed ventures," but he did not try to forbid the soldiers to go on squandering the nation's resources, nor did he urge their recall. As Leon Wolff has written, he knew all too well that "were Haig to be summarily dismissed, Robertson would quit in sympathy, and the entire country, Parliament, even the War Cabinet would hit the ceiling. Firing Haig would also imply that the Empire was losing the war, would encourage the enemy, and was certain to strike a heavy blow at Allied morale."[12] With these thoughts in mind, and that of his own political future, Lloyd George did not insist too much, and the killing went on.

In these circumstances, the idea of seeking a peace by negotiation got as short shrift in Britain as it did in Germany. In 1916, when Lord Lansdowne sent a memorandum to the cabinet, urging a vigorous search for opportunities for negotiation, Asquith was less interested in following up the idea than he was in preventing it from being leaked to the soldiers or the general public. A year later, Lansdowne took a more direct approach and made his proposal public in a letter to the *Daily Telegraph*. It was received, in the words of his biographer, with "a flood of invective and an incredible mass of abusive correspondence which, though largely incoherent, was marked by a violence rare in English political life."[13] The *Times*, then owned by Lord Northcliffe, denounced Lansdowne with a quite exceptional lack of moderation, and the Rothermere and Hulton press chimed in to castigate his letter as "craven," "inept," and "inopportune." Before this flood of denunciation, neither the Lloyd George government nor the Opposition had any desire to make the cause of negotiation its own. As in Germany, the soldiers, having already smothered the issue of strategical alternatives, were allowed to carry the war in France to the ultimate in irrationality, with consequences hardly less drastic than those suffered by the enemy.

III

The experience of French political leaders came close in the first years of the Great War to duplicating that of their counterparts in Germany and Britain, and in the critical year 1917 France provided a quintessential illustration of civilian diffidence and capitulation before military expert opinion. In the last year of the war, however, the political leadership reasserted its authority, and, as a result, France enjoyed a degree of political-military collaboration in the direction of the war that was achieved in neither Britain nor Germany.

---

[12] Leon Wolff, *In Flanders Fields* (New York, 1958), 184.
[13] Lord Newton, *Lord Lansdowne: A Biography* (London, 1929), 468.

France started the war with what amounted to a military dictatorship, for reasons noted by Jere King:

That France had been no better equipped to meet the problems of a democracy at war was due to a complex of historic circumstances. The great prestige which the military had enjoyed for centuries gave them an advantage over the civilians at the outset of the war. The very idea of the 'sacred union' was chiefly to the benefit of conservatives, of which the military were a most important part. Criticizing the command would have been considered disloyal—if not downright treasonable—during the crucial weeks of August and September 1914. The government and Parliament deferred to the command, thus carrying out popular expectation. A short war was anticipated, and only a temporary overshadowing of the civilian power.[14]

But France also had a revolutionary tradition and an expectation that its generals would be successful or would be replaced. The inconclusive battle of the Marne and the coming of the war of attrition aroused enough doubts about French commanders to prevent the ascendancy of the military chiefs from becoming as pronounced as it was in either Germany or Britain. The emergence of a really successful general, another Napoleon, might have made a difference. Even as late as 1917, the political leaders were cautious in dealing with potential Napoleons, and the generals retained sufficient authority to have their way in operational matters, as was tragically demonstrated in April of that year at a conference in Compiègne. At this meeting the President of the Republic, Raymond Poincaré, the Prime Minister Ribot, and the War Minister Painlevé reviewed the plan of General Nivelle for another great offensive against the German lines. They had no faith in his project. They had the authority to forbid it. Yet they were incapable of pointing out its failings or suggesting alternatives and hence were impotent to block it. Sir Edward Spears has written, "The Cabinet was hobbled by its lack of technical knowledge and fettered by public opinion, which, aware of its ignorance in military matters, would have been intolerant of civil intrusion into the military sphere. [The conference] epitomizes the terrible disability from which democracies, even when fighting for their existence, are unable to free themselves. What this weakness in the supreme direction of the war cost the Allies in lives and money can never be computed."[15]

The disaster that resulted from the conference, however, prevented the French from following the example of the other countries discussed

---

[14] Jere King, *Generals and Politicians* (Berkeley, 1951), 242.
[15] Spears, *Prelude to Victory*, 377.

here. The doubts of the civilians were more than justified. In the first ten days of the Nivelle offensive, 34,000 troops died in the field, 90,000 were wounded, of whom a good percentage died, and 20,000 were missing. Before long the whole French army was wracked with mutiny, and public sympathy had turned decisively against the military establishment. In the resultant shakeup, the man who emerged to direct the war effort was Georges Clemenceau.

This odd mixture of cynical condottiere from the parliamentary wars of the 1880s and 1890s and impassioned patriot was no great admirer of the military. Upon assuming office, he made it clear that he regarded war as too serious a matter to be left in the hands of the generals. While having no compunction about making his own views felt in all fields of military administration and on operational questions as well, he treated military ventures into the political realm with brutality. *"Taisez-vous!"* he snapped at Marshal Foch at a meeting of the Supreme War Council in London in March 1918. "I speak for France here!"[16] Clemenceau had all the political skill necessary to rally parliamentary support behind his sometimes willful self-assertiveness, and he acquired (largely from his military aide General Mordacq) the kind of expertise necessary to enable him to speak with authority on questions of strategical and tactical choice, so impressing Lord Alfred Milner with the clarity and force of his views that in March 1918 the British statesman proposed that Clemenceau be made generalissimo of the Allied armies.[17]

The French premier had perhaps too great a sense of his own limitations to encourage this plan, but this in no wise diminished his paramount authority in the direction of the French war effort in 1918. Among the achievements attributed to him by Mordacq are the reorganization of the War Ministry, the abolition of many military sinecures and useless commissions, the selection of new and energetic troop commanders, the reorganization of the general staff on a logical basis, the revitalization of the French structures of command in Italy and Salonika, and a great expansion of tank and armored car production.[18] More important than any of these, certainly, was his reaction to the shattering impact of the German spring offensive of 1918. The strategical disarray in Allied councils that Ludendorff's hammer blows effected convinced Clemenceau that a continuation of the dual leadership of Pétain and Haig would lead inevitably to the loss of the war. He became the most determined and persuasive advocate of a unified command under Foch, and

[16] C. Bugnet, *Rue St. Dominique et GHQ* (Paris, 1937), 273.

[17] On all of this, see Harvey A. DeWeerd, "Churchill, Lloyd George, Clemenceau," in *Makers of Modern Strategy*, ed. Edward Mead Earle (Princeton, 1943), 303.

[18] General Jean Jules Mordacq, *Le Ministère Clemenceau* (Paris, 1930), 2:363-67.

490

his success in carrying this through and his insistence, once the momentum of the German offensive began to wane, upon coordinated attacks against the German lines of communication were major contributions to the Allied strategic offensive of July-November 1918.[19]

There is no doubt that the enhanced role of the political leader in directing the war in France was influenced by the fact that public opinion was more volatile and critical than in Germany and Britain, and by the additional fact no French general possessed the charisma of Hindenburg or Haig. But greater than these factors was the accident of personality: it was Clemenceau's willpower that impressed itself upon his contemporaries and commanded their cooperation or obedience.

IV

In the final volume of his war memoirs, David Lloyd George, reflecting upon the general course of civil-military relations in the various belligerent nations, wrote: "Looking back on this devastating war and surveying the part played in it by statesmen and soldiers respectively in its direction, I have come definitely to the conclusion that the former showed too much caution in exerting their authority over the military leaders."[20] That this was far less true in the Second World War will become clear from the three examples that follow, in each of which it is again the accident of personality that supplies the explanation, although the constitutional framework in which authority was exercised was not of negligible importance.

Adolf Hitler, to take our first example, was the supreme political authority in his country, by virtue of his double role as chancellor (an office to which the powers of the former Reichspräsident had been added in August 1934) and uncontested leader of Germany's only political party, the others having been eliminated, with all other potentially dissident elements, in the process of *Gleichschaltung* in the years 1933-1934. His authority over the army was firmly established by the oath of allegiance that all officers and other ranks had, ever since August 1934, made to him personally as leader of the German Reich and Volk and supreme commander of the Wehrmacht and by the reorganization of the command of the armed forces in February 1938, which established a Supreme Wehrmacht Command (OKW) under his direct authority. In December 1941, Hitler made his command over army operations even more immediate by dismissing General von Brauchitsch as commander in chief of the army (OKH) and taking over his duties, explaining to the OKH

---

[19] Ibid., esp. pp. 308ff.
[20] David Lloyd George, *War Memoirs* (London, 1933-37), 6:3421.

chief of staff that "the trifles" of operational leadership were something that "anyone could perform."[21]

In these circumstances, there was no possibility of military domination of the strategical decision-making process. The question became rather whether and how far the Führer could concede to his OKW and OKH operations staffs the role of strategical advisor. It rapidly became apparent that he was little inclined to think in terms of a genuine collaboration. General Alfred Jodl, chief of the OKW operations staff said in a memorandum dictated to his wife during the Nuremberg trials:

> Hitler was willing to have a working staff that translated his decisions into orders which he would then issue as Supreme Commander of the Wehrmacht, but nothing more. The fact that even men like Frederick the Great would have their own thoughts and decisions tested and re-examined against the often contradictory ideas of their generals made no difference to Hitler, who resented any form of counsel regarding the major decisions of the war. He did not care to hear any other points of view; if they were even hinted at, he would break into short-tempered fits of enraged agitation.[22]

Already pronounced before the war (it was after the success of his Rhineland coup in March 1936 that he said, "I go my way with the assurance of a sleep-walker"), Hitler's mystical conviction of his infallibility as the leader of his country's march to world power was enhanced by the successes of his strategy in 1939 and 1940. As Jodl testified,

> The man who succeeded in occupying Norway before the very eyes of the British fleet with its maritime supremacy, and who with numerically inferior forces brought down the feared military power of France like a house of cards in a campaign of forty days, was no longer willing, after these successes, to listen to military advisers who had previously warned him against such over-extensions of his military power. From that time on, he required of them nothing more than the technical support necessary to implement his decisions, and the smooth functioning of the military organization to carry them out.[23]

In fact, this self-confidence was nothing more than an advanced form of megalomania. Hitler's strategical gifts, once he turned to actual opera-

[21] Generaloberst Franz Halder, *Kriegstagebuch*, ed. Hans-Adolf Jacobsen (Stuttgart, 1962), 3:354, 356-59; *Hitler als Feldherr* (Munich, 1949), 15, 45.

[22] Percy Ernst Schramm, *Hitler: The Man and the Military Leader*, trans. and ed. Donald S. Detweiler (Chicago, 1971), 198.

[23] Ibid.

tions, were limited and guided by no realistic assessment of capabilities and costs.

Hitler's grand strategical plan for Germany's future has been well described by Andreas Hillgruber.[24] Limned for the first time in the long-unknown book of 1928, Hitler's dream was to make Germany the dominant world power, first, by the conquest and consolidation of Europe and Russia, preferably with the benevolent neutrality of Great Britain, and then at a later date, after colonial bases had been acquired and a powerful navy built, by a war—perhaps in alliance with Great Britain—against the only power that could still threaten Germany, the United States of America.

Toward the completion of the first stage of this ambitious program, Hitler made remarkable progress in the years from 1933 to 1939, initially by means of a dazzling display of diplomatic virtuosity, by which he succeeded in hiding his real objectives from the Western powers while skillfully exploiting all of their differences and distractions, and then, after the spring of 1938, by an adroit combination of military and political pressures. It is by no means certain that he had exhausted the possibilities of this strategy of mixed means by the fall of 1939, when he seems to have decided that victories won without the direct application of German military might were not satisfying enough. It is evident, however, that once he abandoned the political weapon and chose to seek his objectives by the sword alone, his strategical gifts soon proved inadequate to solve the problems he created for himself.

This became abundantly clear as early as June 1940, that is, at the very moment when General Keitel was hailing the victor over Scandinavia, the Low Countries, and France as "the greatest commander of all times." The OKW chief might more accurately have described his Führer as a strategical bankrupt, for the fact that Great Britain refused to surrender as France had done disrupted his grand design, and he had no plan for resolving the difficulties that this posed. Field Marshal Erich von Manstein wrote after the war that Hitler was always so confident that his force of will would be able to overcome any possible obstacle to his desires that he forgot that the enemy possesses a will too.[25] Now this awkward truth confronted him for the first time, adding a dimension to the war that he did not understand and could not master. The effect upon his strategy was disturbing and permanent. From now on, it was marked increasingly by impatience, by plans that were ill-conceived, im-

[24] Andreas Hillgruber, *Hitlers Strategie: Politik und Kriegführung 1940-1941* (Frankfurt am Main, 1965) and "Der Faktor Amerika in Hitlers Strategie 1938-1941," in Hillgruber, *Deutsche Grossmacht-und Weltpolitik im 19, und 20. Jahrhundert* (Düsseldorf, 1977).
[25] Erich von Manstein, *Verlorene Siege* (Bonn, 1955), 305ff.

plemented without conviction, and then abandoned, by profligacy in the use of human and material resources, and by an impulsive willfulness that had disastrous results.[26]

The extraordinary lability of Hitler's thinking in the second half of 1940 is indicative of his lack of a clear sense of direction. The plan for an assault on the British Isles was slipshod in conception and the air offensive upon which it depended ill-designed for the objectives it sought to gain. There are indications that Hitler was never very deeply committed to Operation Sea Lion in any case, since, as early as July, he was letting his highest commanders know that the key to ending Britain's participation in the war was Russia, which might have to be destroyed first. In October, when it was clear that the aerial bombardment of Britain was not sufficiently effective, he was off on another tack and was holding conferences with Mussolini, Pétain and Laval, and Franco in an effort to induce them to join in a series of attacks to cut Britain's Mediterranean line of communications completely; and in the same month he was actually considering trying to talk the Russians into an offensive against British holdings in the Middle East. Hitler's staff planners in the OKH had good reason to be bewildered by their master's continual changes of front, since they had, in the course of five months, been ordered to draw up plans for Sea Lion, the capture of Gibraltar, the Azores, and the Canaries, the defense of the Finnish nickel mines, the support of the Italians in North Africa, and the invasion of Russia.[27]

Clarity came at the end of the year, after Foreign Minister Molotov's visit to Berlin in November convinced Hitler that the Nazi-Soviet Pact had outlived its usefulness and that the time had come for the long-desired assault upon the Soviet Union. As the detailed planning for Operation Barbarossa got under way, however, the more prescient of Hitler's staff had some difficulty in understanding what its strategical purpose was to be, and the OKH chief of staff Halder became increasingly fearful, as his diary reveals, lest military objectives be subordinated to ideological ones, and the destruction of the Bolshevik system and the extermination of the Jews take priority over a Clausewitzian strategy of seeking the most expeditious means of weakening the enemy's will to continue the struggle.[28]

That there was reason for such concern became abundantly clear

---

[26] These sentences repeat what I have said in *Germany, 1866-1945* (Oxford and New York, 1978), 721.

[27] Barry A. Leach, *German Strategy against Russia, 1939-1941* (Oxford, 1973), 78f.

[28] Halder, *Kriegstagebuch*, 2:261, 320, 336. That a large proportion of the army leadership did not worry about such distinctions is shown by Jürgen Förster in his essay in *Das Deutsche Reich und der Zweite Weltkrieg*, ed. Militärgeschichtliches Forschungsamt, vol. 4; *Angriff auf die Sowjetunion* (Stuttgart, 1983).

once the attack was begun in June 1941, and the campaigns of 1941 and 1942 in Russia were marked by bitter but unavailing attempts by the soldiers to persuade Hitler to recognize the importance of coherence and consistency. It has been argued that the German armies failed to take Moscow in 1941 because of the delays caused by the campaigns in Yugoslavia and Greece, which were necessary to eliminate a potential danger to the German right flank; but this overlooks the more serious loss of time that was spent between July and September on debates over the missions of the three German army groups in Russia and the question of priority among them. Both Jodl and Halder favored concentrating upon the capture of Moscow, not only because it was the capital of the Soviet Union but because the Russians would defend it with all of their resources and thus provide an opportunity for the destruction of their military strength. Hitler shied away from this solution, insisting at various times that Leningrad was his chief goal or that it was essential to capture the Donets Basin and immobilize the Crimea and end its threat to the Romanian oil fields. He indignantly rejected a Brauchitsch-Halder memorandum of August 18, 1941, in which they argued for an immediate drive on Moscow before the approaching winter made it impossible, and scathingly described the OKH as being filled with minds that were "fossilized" in obsolete theory,[29] an insult that led Halder to suggest to Brauchitsch that they submit their resignations. It was not until September 30, after the southern armies had taken Kiev, that Hitler authorized the advance upon the Soviet capital, and the long delay proved fatal to the enterprise.

The same kind of nervous vacillation characterized Hitler's conduct of the 1942 campaign. Instead of resuming the attack on Moscow, the Führer declared in April that the principal thrust would be made in the south with the aim of destroying units of the Red Army in the Don Basin and then seizing the oil fields of the Caucasus. Concern over the Reich's shortages of fuel gave some plausibility to this operational plan, but once it was put into effect in late June Hitler again showed his tendency to be diverted by local opportunities and to sacrifice strategical goals for tactical successess. A fateful example of this is provided by his War Directive no. 45 of July 23, which split his southern forces, ordering Army Group B, commanded by General Maximilian von Weichs, to move on the city of Stalingrad, while Army Group A under Field Marshal Wilhelm List—weakened by the loss of two armored divisions that had been detached and sent to Weichs's Sixth Army and most of the Eleventh Army in the Crimea, which had been reassigned to the siege of Leningrad—

[29] Trumbull Higgins, *Hitler and Russia* (New York, 1966), 156.

was expected to cross the lower Don and the Kerch Strait from the Crimea and penetrate the Caucasus.[30]

This was a prescription for disaster. Halder wrote in his diary, "The chronic tendency to underrate enemy capabilities is gradually assuming grotesque proportions and develops into a positive danger. Serious work is becoming impossible here. This so-called leadership is characterized by a pathological reacting to the impressions of the moment."[31] Indeed, Hitler's disposition of his now seriously diminished resources and his choice of objectives were increasingly determined by willfulness and volatility of mood: the names Leningrad and Stalingrad appeared to exercise a baleful attractiveness out of all proportion to their strategical importance; as the Führer's difficulties mounted, his designs became more grandiose and unrealistic; and he became ever more irrational in his reaction to setbacks, squandering resources out of obstinate blindness to facts or for reasons of prestige. The refusal to allow Paulus's Sixth Army to break out of Stalingrad while there was still time to do so and—in another theater of war—the decision to go on reinforcing the bridgehead in Tunisia with troops and equipment long after its fall was predictable were signs of a strategical judgment in disarray.

The decision to declare war upon the United States in December 1941, after the Japanese attack upon Pearl Harbor, is more difficult to explain. A reading of Hitler's speech to the Reichstag on December 10, with its long passages of personal abuse and vituperation of President Franklin Roosevelt, lends some credence to the view that the action was motivated by the Führer's long-bottled-up resentment of Roosevelt's pro-British actions in the Atlantic in 1940 and 1941. A desire to demonstrate solidarity with the Japanese in the hope that they might still be induced to attack the Soviet Far Eastern provinces doubtless played a part also. But it is just as likely that Hitler took this critical step for the sake of the gesture alone and its effect upon the German people and because he knew that it could do no harm: that is, he realized that he must win the war in Russia in 1942, and that if he did so there was nothing that the United States could do to prevent his winning the global mastery that he desired; if he did not, Germany's doom was certain, and deserved.

"Earlier than any other person in the world," Jodl wrote in his Nuremberg memorandum, "Hitler sensed and knew that the war was lost." After the catastrophe at Stalingrad, Rommel's defeat at El Alamein, and the Allied landings at Casablanca, Oran, and Algiers, the momentum of the war had shifted to the enemy's side, and, in Jodl's words, Hitler's

[30] Ibid., 209-210.
[31] Halder, *Kriegstagebuch*, 3:489.

"activity as a strategist was essentially ended. From then on, he intervened more and more frequently in operational decisions, often down to matters of tactical detail, in order to impose with unbending will what he thought the generals simply refused to comprehend: that one had to stand or fall, that each voluntary step backwards was an evil in itself."[32] The war now attained the ultimate in irrationality, with Germany's commanding generals reduced, as one of them said, to the status of "highly paid NCOs" and the Führer giving the orders in every sector of every front and insisting that willpower was enough to triumph over superior numbers and equipment.

It was a kind of warfare best characterized in the words of one of Paulus's subordinates in Stalingrad, who described the orders to fight and die in place as "not only a crime from a military point of view but a criminal act as regards our responsibility to the German nation." But then Hitler, to whom the war had always been a personal drama, had never had a very highly developed sense of that kind of responsibility, and perhaps, at bottom, that was his greatest deficiency as a strategist.

V

One could never say the same of Winston Churchill, whose thinking was deeply influenced, in the first place, by his memory of what the losses of the First World War had meant to his country and a determination that the defeat of Hitler should not be won at the same cost and, in the second, by an awareness of the kind of problems that would have to be faced after victory was achieved. In consequence, his strategical ideas had a more emphatically political cast than was true, as we shall see in due course, in the case of his friend and ally in Washington, Franklin Roosevelt.

Of all the political leaders of the major belligerents in the Second World War, Churchill had the greatest experience in war. Commissioned in the 4th Hussars in 1895, he had within eight years seen fighting in Cuba, the northwest frontier of India, the Sudan, and South Africa, either as a combatant or as a war correspondent. Elected to the House of Commons at the age of twenty-five, he made his name first as a cogent critic of military budgets and later as a vigorous advocate of naval construction, the change of heart coinciding with his translation in 1911 from the post of Home Secretary in Asquith's Liberal cabinet to that of First Lord of the Admiralty. During the Great War, he was an energetic First Lord, boldly resorting in 1914 to the use of Britain's amphibious capability to prevent German capture of the Channel ports and, a year

---

[32] Schramm, *Hitler*, 203f.

later, becoming a powerful champion of the plan to take the Dardanelles and drive Turkey out of the war. When the failure of this operation led to a cabinet shakeup and the loss of his position, he went back to the army and was given command of the 6th Royal Scots Fusiliers, earning the praise of his superiors. He returned reluctantly to Parliament in the spring of 1916 when it became apparent that he could not expect a brigade when Haig became commander in chief.[33] In the last year of the war, Lloyd George appointed him as minister of munitions, over the objections of those who still held him responsible for the failure at the Dardanelles.

This varied experience had two sharply different effects upon Churchill's thinking about war and its management. In the first place, his memory of the unhappy results of the loose and redundant committee system of the Asquith-Kitchener days led him, as soon as he became prime minister in 1940, to introduce structural changes that sharply centralized government operations and had the effect of making him both head of government and supreme commander of the armed forces. Working through a small War Cabinet, he formed under it a Defence Committee (Operations) consisting of the deputy prime minister, the three service ministers and, later, the foreign secretary, with other ministers attending when necessary and the chiefs of staff always present. Within the new Ministry of Defence, whose leadership he also assumed, the chiefs of staff formed a "combined battle headquarters," which met daily in Churchill's presence or that of his deputy defence minister, General Ismay. The minister of defence had direct authority over both the Joint Planning Committee and the Joint Intelligence Committee, as well as over a Joint Planning Staff that was independent of the separate service ministries and met, under Ismay's chairmanship, in the War Cabinet Secretariat. As the war continued, the concentration of power in the hands of Churchill and the chiefs of staff gradually excluded both the War Cabinet and Parliament from any effective role in the formulation of strategy, a fact that occasioned intermittent protests and complaints, which were, however, rendered ineffective by the system's proven efficiency. The coordinated staff planning that it made possible was far superior to anything produced by its American counterpart, as the Americans learned to their discomfiture at the Arcadia, Casablanca, and Trident conferences in 1942 and 1943. Ronald Lewin has written that "the embodiment in Churchill of both political and military authority provided the keystone for a new High Command structure which proved to be the most efficient central

[33] Basil Liddell Hart, "The Military Strategist," in A. J. P. Taylor, Robert Rhodes James, J. H. Plumb, Basil Liddell Hart, and Anthony Shore, *Churchill Revised* (New York, 1962), 197. See also Ronald Lewin, *Churchill as Warlord* (New York, 1973), 13.

system for running a war ever evolved, either in Great Britain or any other country."[34]

For the first two years of Churchill's tenure of power, much of the energies of the chiefs of staff had to be directed toward restraining the impetuosity of the system's creator and toward trying to maintain a tolerable working relationship between him and the commanding generals in the field. For, if the Great War had taught Churchill a good deal about effective organization for the direction of the war effort, it had also left him with a low regard for professional soldiers that comported ill with his boundless confidence in his own military judgment and in his talent for strategical and tactical decisions. Since he was also a robust and combative personality who had no patience with the systematic and unexciting aspects of operational command and was further endowed with a powerful imagination that dismayed practitioners who were forced to have a scrupulous regard for the relationship between means and ends, conflict between him and his commanders was inevitable. Field Marshal Archibald Wavell once said that Churchill "never realized the necessity for full equipment before committing troops to battle. I remember his arguing that, because a comparatively small number of mounted Boers had held up a British division in 1899 and 1900, it was unnecessary for the South African Brigade to have much more equipment than rifles before taking the field in 1940. In fact, I found that Winston's tactical ideals had to some extent crystallized in the South African War. His fertile brain was always inventive or receptive of new tactical ideas and weapons, but I do not think that right up to the end he ever understood the administrative side of war; he always accused commanders of organizing 'all tail and no teeth'."[35]

Because he suspected his generals of lacking enterprise and aggressive spirit, Churchill deluged them with streams of orders, memoranda, and directives on matters that were really their business rather than his own. On August 16, 1940, for instance, to the astonishment of Chief of the Imperial General Staff Sir John Dill and Major-General Sir John Kennedy, director of military operations, he sent a directive for the conduct of the campaign in the Middle East that was virtually an operations order, including detailed tactical instructions, down to the forward and rear distribution of battalions, and giving minutely detailed orders for the employment of forces[36]—the very kind of supersession of the authority of the field commander to which Hitler was prone in the last stages of

---

[34] Gordon Wright, *The Ordeal of Total War* (New York, 1968), 238f.; Lewin, *Churchill*, 32.
[35] John Connell, *Wavell: Soldier and Statesman* (London, 1964), 256.
[36] R. W. Thompson, *Generalissimo Churchill* (New York, 1973), 100.

the war. He was constantly on the watch for signs of faint-heartedness on the part of his generals, and, in April 1941, learning from Kennedy tht Wavell had a plan for withdrawal from Egypt if it should be forced upon him, shouted in rage, "Wavell has 400,000 men! If they lose Egypt, blood will flow! I will have firing parties to shoot the generals!" and—when Kennedy protested that every prudent general must have such a plan—"This comes as a flash of lightning to me. I never heard such ideas! War is a contest of wills! It is pure defeatism to speak as you have done!"[37]

There is no doubt that Great Britain was well served by Winston Churchill's indomitable spirit in the grim years of 1940 and 1941, and that his defiance of odds that would have daunted most men not only sustained the courage of his own countrymen but won the admiration and the material support of the people of the United States as well. Even so, his combativeness exacted a price, and his eagerness to get at the enemy wherever an opportunity to do so presented itself led to a serious muddling of priorities. The decision to go to the aid of Greece in March 1941, without any rational estimation of how gravely this would drain the strength of the Middle East Command and how slight the chances of success, seems in retrospect to have been an almost frivolous exercise in gallantry, and Churchill's responsibility for the resultant debacle is not palliated by the fact that Dill and Wavell, against their better judgment, concurred in the decision. And Churchill's later fascination with Rommel, which was doubtless due to his penchant for seeing the conflict in terms of individual combatants, led him to elevate the position of Egypt in Britain's list of strategic priorities from fourth place (after the security of the home islands, Malaya, and the Cape of Good Hope) to second and to declare, in a directive issued without consulting the chiefs of staff, that its loss would be second only to successful invasion and final conquest, a conclusion with which the DMO Kennedy violently disagreed.[38] Nor was this merely the rhetoric of the moment. It influenced Churchill's views on the allocation of resources; it deprived Malaya, in particular, of needed reinforcement; it led to the fall of Singapore, an event that went a long way toward advancing that dissolution of the British Empire over which Churchill had vowed he would not preside.

After Sir Alan Brooke succeeded Dill as CIGS, Churchill's forays into the operational field were gradually limited, for Brooke was more willing than his predecessor to resist notions that he thought were dangerous and was cunning enough to keep from the prime minister's attention matters that he thought might have an excitable effect upon his

[37] Connell, *Wavell*, 421.
[38] Thompson, *Churchill*, 120f.

stormy temperament. "The more you tell that man about the war," he said to Kennedy after radically reducing a minute to Churchill, "the more you hinder the winning of it."[39] At the same time, the entrance of the United States into the war, which took place in the same month as Brooke's appointment, marked the opening of a new phase in which the most important requirement was effective joint strategical planning, and Churchill's response to this challenge was flawed by none of the impulsiveness and lack of measure that he had shown in 1940 and 1941.

Thanks to the special relationship that the prime minister had established with Franklin Roosevelt from the very beginning of the war, which was fostered at the outset by their common interest in naval affairs,[40] a certain amount of contingency planning had been accomplished even before the United States became a belligerent. Thus, Anglo-American staff talks were held in Washington from January 29 to March 29, 1941 to determine "the best methods by which the armed forces of the United States and the British Commonwealth . . . could defeat Germany and the Powers allied with her, should the United States be compelled to resort to war." These ABC-1 talks had been guided by the conclusions of an earlier American memorandum of chief of naval operations Admiral Harold Stark that, in the event of war, the United States would adopt an offensive posture in the Atlantic as an ally of Great Britain and a defensive one in the Pacific.[41]

The American mood after Pearl Harbor, however, aroused concern in Churchill's mind lest this order of priorities be reversed, and he resolved to go to Washington at once "with the strongest team of expert advisers who could be spared. . . . to persuade the President and the American Service chiefs that the defeat of Japan would not spell the defeat of Hitler, but that the defeat of Hitler made the finishing off of Japan merely a matter of time and trouble."[42] As it happened, his fears were groundless. At the Arcadia Conference in Washington in January 1942, the concept of "Germany first" was reaffirmed, as was the continuation of a bombing campaign, a blockade, and measures of subversion to weaken Germany

---

[39] Major General Sir John Kennedy, *The Business of War* (London, 1957), 108. It should be noted that Churchill continued to be excessively critical of his commanders in the field and that Brooke, after listening to his abuse of Montgomery and Alexander in July 1944, "flared up and asked him if he could not trust his generals for five minutes instead of continuously abusing and belittling them" (Fraser, *Alanbrooke*, 442).

[40] For the full development of this relationship, see *Roosevelt and Churchill: Their Secret Wartime Correspondence*, ed. Francis L. Loewenheim, Harold D. Langley, and Manfred Jonas (New York, 1975). See also *Churchill and Roosevelt, The Complete Correspondence*, ed. Warren F. Kimball, 3 vols. (Princeton, 1984).

[41] See above all Mark S. Watson, *Chief of Staff: Pre-War Plans and Preparations* (Washington, D.C., 1950).

[42] Winston S. Churchill, *The Grand Alliance* (Boston, 1950), 625, 643.

until major landings could take place somewhere in western Europe, presumably in 1943. No positive proposals were made for the Pacific beyond the establishment of a supreme command (ABDA) for all allied forces operating in the area from Burma to the China Sea, a plan that soon proved to be unworkable.

On the voyage to America in *Duke of York*, Churchill composed a series of papers that came close to justifying Ismay's statement that "in his grasp of the broad sweep of strategy [he] stood head and shoulders above his professional advisers," and that embodied what came to be the basic assumptions of British strategy for the next two years.[43] He recognized the limited capabilities of the Allies in the immediate future. "Hitler's failures and losses in Russia are the prime facts in the War at this time." The most favorable areas for Anglo-American action were on the Atlantic sea lanes and in the air, to maintain supply lines and inhibit German production, and in the northern African theater. The main offensive action in 1942 should be "the occupation of the whole of the North and West African possessions of France, . . . further control by Britain of the whole North African shore from Tunis to Egypt, thus giving, if the naval situation allows, free passage through the Mediterranean to the Levant and the Suez Canal." Planning should simultaneously be made for landings, in the summer of 1943, in Sicily and Italy, as well as in Scandinavia, the Low Countries, France, and the Balkans, the actual choice of several specific targets to be deferred until later. He made clear his belief that the war could only be won "through the defeat in Europe of the German armies or through internal convulsions in Germany." He envisaged an invasion army of forty armored divisions, covered by command of the sea and superior air power, with their way prepared by an intensive bombing offensive.[44]

This was, in fact, the strategy that was followed by the Allies in 1942 and 1943, although there were, along the way, stormy scenes with the American chiefs of staff, who, after joint consultation with the British in April, thought that they had persuaded them to agree to a cross-Channel invasion in 1943 (and even in 1942, if the Russians seemed on the point of collapse) and who suspected them of reneging and, indeed, of having no stomach for a Western landing. At such moments, Churchill's friendship with the President proved to be invaluable. It was his eloquence in the Washington conference of June 1942 that persuaded Roosevelt that a delayed Channel crossing was preferable to one that failed; it was his persuasion that edged the President toward the accept-

[43] Lord Ismay, *Memoirs* (London, 1960), 163.
[44] Fraser, *Alanbrooke*, 231-32; Lewin, *Churchill*, 127ff.

ance of a North African invasion as a feasible and profitable alternative; and, at Casablanca, it was his skillful portrayal of the offensive possibilities opened by the North African lodgment that won Roosevelt's support for a landing in Sicily and, by extension, in Italy.[45]

In a real sense, then, Churchill's strategical views were determinant of Allied operations in 1942 and 1943 and had the consequence of preventing the implementation of the Overlord plan until the attrition of German strength and the improvement of the shipping situation made it seem feasible to the British Chiefs of Staff. It was not until the Teheran conference of November 1943 that this ascendancy came to an end, when, with Stalin's strong support, the Americans got a firm date for Overlord and for a supporting invasion of southern France (Anvil). Before agreeing to this, Churchill and Brooke were given a clear understanding that operations in Italy would not be curtailed until the other landings took place, since they were the only means of pinning down German divisions that might otherwise be employed in Russia or France, and that Roosevelt's light-hearted promise to Chiang Kai-shek at the first Cairo conference, to launch an amphibious operation against the Andaman Islands in the next few months—Operation Buccaneer, to which, as Brooke said, the British "had not agreed and of whose merits they were not convinced"—was revoked.[46]

The diminution of Churchill's strategical influence in the subsequent period he bore manfully but with mounting foreboding. However great his admiration of the Americans, he was exasperated by their insensitivity to the fact that wars create as many problems as they solve and that the art of grand strategy is to foresee the outlines of the future and be prepared to deal with it. After Stalingrad, when the momentum in the east shifted to the Soviet side, he began to apprehend an excessively large Soviet pressure in postwar Europe and to consider plans for limiting it by border agreements or mutually recognized spheres of influence. Such suggestions were, however, vigorously resisted by Secretary of State Cordell Hull, who had returned from the Foreign Ministers Conference in Moscow in November 1943 convinced that in the future there would "no longer be any need for spheres of influence, for alliances, for balance of power, or for any other of the special arrangements through which, in the unhappy past, the nations strove to safeguard their security or to promote their interests."[47]

Nor was Hull alone in opposing the intrusion of the concepts of the

---

[45] Liddell Hart, "The Military Strategist," 215; Fraser, *Alanbrooke*, 311ff.

[46] Fraser, *Alanbrooke*, 384-92.

[47] Maurice Matloff and Edwin S. Snell, *Strategic Planning for Coalition Warfare, 1941-1942* (Washington, D.C., 1953), 272-73.

old diplomacy into the pursuit of the war. American soldiers, who were convinced that their preference for the direct rather than the peripheral approach to battle problems showed their adherence to Clausewitz's doctrines, were all too obviously ill-informed about the German theorist's insistence that political considerations can be forgotten in wartime only with peril,[48] as Eisenhower was to prove in April 1945 in refusing to consider an advance on Berlin.[49] As for the President himself—to whom Churchill, in an appeal not to foreclose strategical options, had wired in July 1944, "On a long-term political view, [Stalin] might prefer that the British and Americans should do their share in France in this very hard fighting that is to come, and that East, Middle and Southern Europe should fall naturally into his control"[50]—he was no more open to the idea that strategy had a political side than his secretary of state or his soldiers. In his view, winning the war was the first priority, and politics would come later.

VI

If Franklin D. Roosevelt had been slow in appreciating Hitler's boundless ambitions and if, in consequence, his diplomacy before 1939 had been at best indifferent,[51] his direction of American policy after the outbreak of the European war, while hesitant, tentative, and even contradictory in its tactics, inevitably so in view of his domestic restraints, was masterly in its overall strategy. To the military situation, he responded with vigor and assurance. He had long been interested in naval affairs and geography, and his service as assistant secretary of the navy from 1913 to 1920 had given him confidence in his ability to make decisions about military questions and grand strategy.[52] In July 1939, as the certainty of war became apparent, he had issued a Military Order in his capacity as commander in chief, moving the Joint Board of the Army and Navy, the body that coordinated the strategical plans of the two services, and the Army and Navy Munitions Board, which controlled procurement programs, and the civilian agency in charge of military production into the new Executive Office of the President. This meant

[48] See *On War*, bk. 1, ch. 1 and, especially, bk. 8, ch. 6.

[49] *The Papers of Dwight David Eisenhower: The War Years*, ed. Alfred Chandler, 5 vols. (Baltimore, 1970), 4:2592-95.

[50] *Roosevelt and Churchill*, 548. On the growth of Churchill's fears in this regard, see Herbert Feis, *Churchill, Roosevelt, Stalin: The War They Waged and the Peace They Sought* (Princeton, 1957), 338ff.

[51] See Gordon A. Craig, "Roosevelt and Hitler: The Problem of Perception," in *Deutsche Frage und europäisches Gleichgewicht: Festschrift für Andreas Hillgruber zum 60. Geburtstag*, ed. Klaus Hildebrand and Reiner Pommerin (Cologne and Vienna, 1985).

[52] Robert Dallek, *Franklin D. Roosevelt and American Foreign Policy, 1932-1945* (New York, 1979), 321.

that he intended to keep the military power of the United States under his own control, for as members of the Joint Board the chiefs of staff were now responsible directly to him, and the secretaries of war and the navy, Henry L. Stimson and Frank Knox, were largely excluded from the area of strategic decision.

To the British, this was a system of baffling looseness. Sir John Dill wrote to Brooke on January 3, 1942 that the American chiefs of staff never seemed to have regular meetings and, when they did meet, there was no secretariat to record their proceedings. Unlike the British, they had no joint planners or executive planning staff, and their contacts with the President were intermittent and, again, unrecorded. "It seems to me," Dill wrote, "that the whole organization belongs to the days of George Washington, who was made Commander-in-Chief of all the Forces and just did it. Today the President is Commander-in-Chief of all the Forces, but it is not so easy just to do it."[53] The American system was, in fact, more efficient than Dill supposed, but there is no doubt that it was less coordinated than its British counterpart. Franklin Roosevelt always preferred to keep his options open, his thoughts shrouded, and the right of ultimate decision firmly in his own hands and, although in time he became dependent upon General George Catlett Marshall and relied increasingly upon his military judgments, this was less true in the period between his Military Order of July 1939 and Pearl Harbor, during which, Kent Roberts Greenfield has written, "FDR made all his important decisions regarding the use of American military power either independently of his military chiefs, or against their advice, or over their protests."[54]

Even before the outbreak of hostilities in 1939, the President had come to the conclusion that, if war came, the United States would be forced, in its own interest, to support Great Britain. It was his hope that, if it did so vigorously enough, actual military intervention by the country might not be necessary. This strategical concept was implemented by three decisions. The first was Roosevelt's order in November 1938 for the creation of a plant capacity to produce ten thousand combat planes a year, later stepped up, in May 1940, to fifty thousand, to the indignation of the chiefs, who feared that the rearmament of their services would become hopelessly unbalanced. The second was the decision in May-June 1940 to commit the country to all-out assistance to Great Britain, a step revealed to the public for the first time in the President's Charlottesville speech on June 6 and later put in force by means of the destroyers-bases arrangement and the Lend-Lease legislation. This too the army and navy

[53] Fraser, *Alanbrooke*, 230.
[54] Kent Roberts Greenfield, *American Strategy in World War II: A Reconsideration* (Baltimore, 1963), 52f.

found dangerous, expecting the imminent collapse of Great Britain and preferring a policy of hemispheric defense. The third was the decision in the spring and summer of 1941, against Marshall's strong reservations, to establish garrisons and convoys in the Atlantic and to extend them as far as necessary in order to keep the supply lines to Britain open.[55] These actions and the stubborn refusal on the part of the British government to consider surrender were the crucial factors in disrupting Hitler's grand strategical plan and in forcing him along the desperate course that led to his destruction.

After Pearl Harbor, the President's greatest concern was that popular passions might force a concentration of the American effort upon the war with Japan, thus fatally compromising the strategical assumptions of ABC-1 with which he was in full agreement. This explains the course that he followed in the debates between the American and the British staff planners. Roosevelt was always more skeptical about the possibility of a successful invasion of the European continent from the British Isles in 1943 than he thought it advisable to make clear to his chiefs of staff, and he was, for domestic political reasons, attracted by Churchill's argument about the necessity of engaging the Germans before the end of 1942 and the feasibility of doing so in North Africa. In July 1942, when Marshall, exasperated by what he considered to be British stalling on plans for a cross-Channel operation, joined forces with Admiral Ernest L. King and suggested shifting the major American effort to the Pacific, Roosevelt firmly overruled them, saying tartly that this would be like angry children "picking up their dishes and going home." He ordered Marshall, along with King and his chief civilian advisor Harry Hopkins, to go to London and reach some decision that would bring American ground forces into action against the Germans in 1942, and he gave them a set of orders that allowed them little freedom of action. "Please remember three cardinal principles—speed of decisions on plans, unity of plans, attack combined with defense, but not defense alone. This affects the immediate objective of U.S. ground forces fighting against Germans in 1942. I hope for total agreement within one week of your arrival."[56] Since the British chiefs had already voted firmly against a cross-Channel attempt in 1942, these instructions eventuated in the plan for Operation Torch, the North African landing of November 1942.

Roosevelt's primary motive had been to ensure domestic support for the Allies' grand strategical concept; and this also guided him in two other decisions that were likely, like the support of Torch itself, to post-

[55] Ibid., 53.
[56] Feis, *Churchill, Roosevelt, Stalin*, 54-55.

pone a 1943 cross-Channel invasion. The first, to which the President persuaded the British to agree at the Casablanca Conference, was to authorize Admiral King to go on the offensive in the Pacific as opportunities presented themselves; and the second, activated in 1943, was to follow up the German defeat in Tunisia with an invasion of Sicily and Italy. Superb politician that he was, Roosevelt had a remarkable ability to gauge the public mood, and he was aware by 1943 that, although the danger of a groundswell of opinion, orchestrated by the China lobby, in favor of an exclusive emphasis upon the Pacific war was no longer as great as it had been, it had been replaced by another source of concern. There was a growing tendency in the country to regard the war as all but won and a growing irritation that it wasn't completely won.

This new mood was reflected in such things as the threatened strike of the Railway Brotherhoods in December 1943, the widespread resentment against proposed legislation dealing with civilian manpower, the increased pressure for deferment from the armed services, and a tendency on the part of the press to give prominence to news items that discredited the administration of the services. A major part of George Marshall's time was devoted to attempts to check these tendencies by explaining to Congress, the press, and business, labor, and private groups the enormities of the task ahead and the importance of a truly national effort—an assignment that he performed so ably that, when it came time to choose a commander for Overlord, the President felt that he could not do without Marshall in Washington and selected Eisenhower, although the chief of staff had been considered the obvious choice.[57] Concern over the public mood also influenced Roosevelt's strategical choices, persuading him to support Churchill's Italian proposals so that there would be no slack periods in the European conflict and so that there would be demonstrable daily evidence of progress toward final victory.

It was for the same reason that he was little inclined, in the last two years of the war, to share Churchill's worries about the looming Soviet threat and the necessity of agreements about spheres of influence in southeastern Europe and a firm and united stand against Soviet intentions in Poland. He was well aware that such terms as balance of power and spheres of influence were viewed with distrust by most Americans, and that many of them were uninterested in what went on in other countries and unpersuaded that the domestic problems of other peoples were a legitimate source of concern to the United States. He feared that any intimation of cracks in the Grand Alliance would cause a degree of

[57] On all this, see Forrest G. Pogue, *George C. Marshall: Organizer of Victory, 1943-1945* (New York, 1973).

consternation and indignation at home that would be deleterious to the war effort. He was conscious of the fact also that, after Germany was defeated, there would still be the task of defeating Japan, in which it appeared that the collaboration of the Soviet Union would be necessary. Finally, he recognized the strong sentiment in the United States for a new international system after the war that would secure the hard-won peace. Whether that was to take the form of a Great Power directorate (like the curious Four Policemen plan of which he was so enamored)[58] or would be modeled after the League of Nations, Soviet participation would be indispensable.

In the President's mind, these great goals precluded disputes over boundary lines in Europe or the claims of rival Polish governments. He was, in his airy way, confident that on matters of high import he would be able to handle "Uncle Joe," but he had no intention meanwhile of following the cautionary prescriptions of Winston Churchill. *Realpolitik* must not be allowed to interfere with the winning of the war. The American people would not tolerate that.

VII

These observations began with a quotation from Clausewitz concerning the necessity, in a nation's strategy, of subordinating the military to the political point of view, and it has become clear, from the cases chosen, that the political leaders who were most successful in doing this were Clemenceau, Hitler, Churchill, and Roosevelt. This is such an oddly mixed group that it merely illustrates the fragility of general rules. If we set Clemenceau aside—for he was more an *animateur de la victoire* than one who put any distinctive stamp upon the strategy of the Entente powers—the case of Hitler would seem to prove that the subordination of the military point of view to the political can be just as disastrous in its results as the opposite state of affairs. The case of Franklin Roosevelt, on the other hand, suggests that the legitimate political concerns of the most responsible of war leaders can be contradictory and self-defeating, domestic political considerations making it inexpedient to attend to political issues that have been created by the war itself and that threaten, unless attended to, to render strategy ineffective in the long run.

Even more ambiguous is the example of Winston Churchill, who was both *animateur de la défiance* and a leader with great strategical vision, and who succeeded in mastering his own military establishment

[58] Gordon A. Craig and Alexander L. George, *Force and Statecraft: Diplomatic Problems of Our Time* (New York, 1983), 101ff.

and making it an efficient collaborator in the pursuit of his objectives. This was a notable achievement, but an imperfect one. For Churchill was, after all, forced by circumstances to fight side by side with stronger allies, and, in the end, their conflicting strategies for victory and peace defeated his own.

18. Men against Fire: The Doctrine of the Offensive in 1914

MICHAEL HOWARD

WHEN WAR broke out in Europe in August 1914, every major belligerent power at once took the offensive. The Austro-Hungarian army invaded Poland. The Russians invaded East Prussia. The Germans invaded France through Belgium; and the French tried to reconquer their lost provinces of Alsace and Lorraine. By the end of the year every one of these offensives had been checked or repulsed at a cost of some 900,000 missing, prisoners, wounded, or dead. The attacks continued through 1915, when Italy attacked Austria with equally disastrous results; through 1916, when the Germans assaulted Verdun and the new British armies entered the war with their great offensive on the Somme; and began to falter only in 1917, when after Nivelle's disastrous offensive in April the French troops refused to attack again and the Russian Empire collapsed under the strain of the war. These disasters, compounded by the failure of the four-month British offensive at Passchendaele from August to November 1917, have left a historical image of strategic and tactical blindness virtually unparalleled in history, an image that the successful German offensives on the eastern front and the final Allied attacks on the western front in 1918 have done little to redeem.

Yet the military leaders who planned and the political leaders who sanctioned these operations though they may appear callous by later standards, were neither blind to the likely consequences of their attacks nor ill-informed about the defensive powers of twentieth-century weapons. None of them expected that the war could be won without very heavy losses. "Anyone who should think that great tactical success can be achieved in modern war without staking a great deal of human life is, I believe, very much mistaken" wrote General Friedrich von Bernhardi in 1912. "The dread of losses will always ensure failure, while we can assume with certainty that those troops who are not afraid of losses are bound to maintain an enormous superiority over others who are more

510

sparing of blood."[1] Specialists in other nations thought no differently. "Success in the assault is all a case of how you train your soldiers beforehand 'to know how to die or to avoid dying,' " wrote the British colonel F. N. Maude; "if the latter, then nothing can help you, and it would have been wiser not to go to war at all."[2] And frequently quoted were the somber words of Clausewitz: "The fact that slaughter is a horrifying spectacle must make us take war more seriously and not provide an excuse for gradually blunting our swords in the name of humanity."[3]

I

The growing lethality of weapons had been studied and taken into account by military experts ever since the great slaughters of mid-century on both sides of the Atlantic: Antietam and Fredericksburg in the American Civil War, Gravelotte-St. Privat in the Franco-Prussian War. The problem had been further complicated by the technological developments of the 1880s and 1890s. The substitution of high explosive for gunpowder as the propellant for small-arms and artillery ammunition transformed both the range and accuracy of these weapons. Greater explosive power made possible smaller caliber rifles with a low trajectory and a range of up to 2,000 meters, much more effective not only against assaulting infantry but against the older field guns, which, from a range of 1,000 meters or so, had previously supported those assaults. Small calibers made it possible, further, for the infantryman to carry more ammunition into battle while brass cartridges and magazine-loading made for a more rapid rate of fire.

However the range, weight, and accuracy of artillery was comparably increased. Field artillery extended its range to 6,000 meters, with "recoilless carriages" making possible rapid and continuous fire, and mobile heavy artillery came into service with ranges of 10,000 meters or more. The scale of the battle was thus increased from a few miles to several score and indeed, with the capacity of railways to bring troops to the battlefield, to several hundred; and since the new explosives combusted with virtually no discharge of smoke, the combatants, so long as they remained immobile, remained also very largely invisible.

It was hotly contested, among military experts, whether these developments on the whole favored the attack or the defense. On the one hand it was claimed, with particular strength by Jan Bloch in his multi-

---

[1] Friedrich von Bernhardi, *On War Today* (London, 1912), 2:53.

[2] F. N. Maude, *The Evolution of Infantry Tactics* (London, 1905), 146.

[3] Carl von Clausewitz, *On War*, trans. and ed. Michael Howard and Peter Paret, rev. ed. (Princeton, 1984), bk. 1, ch. 11, p. 260.

volume study *La guerre future*, published in 1898, that frontal assaults would in future be not simply prohibitively expensive, but statistically impossible: "Between the combattants will always be an impassable zone of fire deadly in equal degree to both the foes."[4] But Bloch was a civilian, and the weight of military opinion held that the new technology favored the attack no less than the defense. No assault could succeed, it was agreed, until the attackers had achieved superiority of fire; but the increasing range, power, and accuracy of artillery made this possible; it was the task of the advancing infantry to move under cover from position to position until it could bring its own fire to bear on the defenses and overwhelm them before it attacked. "It is evident," wrote Colonel (later Marshal) Ferdinand Foch in the lectures he delivered at the French Ecole de Guerre in 1900

> ... that today, fire-direction and fire-control have immense importance. Fire is the supreme argument. The most ardent troops, those whose morale has been the most excited, will always wish to seize ground by successive rushes. But they will encounter great difficulties, and suffer heavy casualties, whenever their partial offensive has not been prepared by heavy fire. They will be thrown back on their starting point, with still heavier losses. *The superiority of fire ... becomes the most important element of an infantry's fighting value.*[5]

Nevertheless, the moment always arrived when the attacking infantry could get no further under cover either of their own fire or that of the supporting artillery. "Before it," as Foch wrote, "lies a zone almost impassable; there remain no covered approaches; a hail of lead beats the ground."[6] How, if at all, was this "zone of death" to be crossed?

Traditionally, since the days of the Napoleonic Wars, assaulting infantry always advanced in three waves. First went the skirmishers in loose formation, making use of any cover available, working their way forward to gain firing positions from which to cover the advance of those who came after them. Next came the main body of the infantry in close formation with their officers in front to inspire and their sergeants behind to intimidate them, drums beating, bugles blaring, the regimental colors borne aloft to be planted on the captured positions. Finally came the supports, reserves to be fed in at the discretion of the commander. It was a practical arrangement that proved its worth until 1870, when French rifle fire stopped the attacking German battalions quite literally dead in

---

[4] Jan Bloch, *The Future of War in Its Technical, Economic and Political Relations* (Boston, 1899), xxx. See also the discussion of Bloch in essay 13, above.

[5] Ferdinand Foch, *The Principles of War* (New York, 1918), 362. Emphasis added.

[6] Ibid., 365.

their tracks; the German army never again reverted to the traditional formations. Instead the Germans accepted that the second line was to advance, not in close formation, but in open, like the first; its function became not to assault but to thicken up and extend the firing line, gradually lapping around its opponents' flanks. Only after the defenses had been crushed by fire and surrounded by flanking formations (which was seen increasingly as the role of the cavalry) would their positions be overrun. It was a tactical doctrine that the Schlieffen plan was to extend into strategy.

In the immediate aftermath of 1870 the French had also adopted these procedures. Their Infantry Regulations of 1875 forbade the use of close formations within range of enemy fire, advocated dispersal to take advantage of cover and prescribed the function of the skirmishing line as being not simply to prepare the attack but to conduct it. But it was a doctrine bitterly opposed in the French army as in all others. Not only was there a general feeling that to shrink from a bayonet attack was "unmanly," a view most eloquently expounded by the Russian general Dragomirov. More to the point, there was a well-founded uncertainty whether the infantry, if scattered and left to their own devices, would not seize the occasion to "get lost": go to ground and not get up again. Careful analysis of German operations in 1870 had revealed numerous occasions when this had happened. On the vaster battlefields that the new firearms made possible, and in face of the invisible menace they now posed, such behavior, in armies made up largely of short-service conscripts, seemed likely to become not the exception but the rule.

Colonel Charles-Ardent du Picq, who was killed in action in 1870 and whose *Etudes sur le combat* is one of the few great classics of military literature, had observed this tendency even on the battlefields of his own day, where "the soldier is unknown often to his closest companions. He loses them in the disorienting smoke and confusion of a battle which he is fighting, so to speak, on his own. Cohesion is no longer ensured by mutual observation."[7]

La solidarité n'a plus la sanction d'une surveillance mutuelle: that has been the problem of morale on the battlefield ever since. Du Picq himself believed that to cope with these new conditions it would be necessary to breed a military elite very different from the mass armies that were to develop in the last quarter of the nineteenth century. The military authorities under the Third Republic, however, saw no hope of a solution along these lines. In 1884 they once again prescribed, for an

[7] Charles-Ardent du Picq, *Etudes sur le combat: Combat antique et moderne* (Paris, 1942), 110.

army that still consisted of peasant youths from the provinces, attack formations in the old style, which should march forward "with their head held high, regardless of losses . . . under the most violent fire, even against strongly defended entrenchments, and seize them." Ten years later the notorious regulations of 1894 specifically prescribed that infantry should advance to the attack "elbow to elbow in mass formations, to the sound of bugles and drums." It sounds absurd; but how else were they to get their conscripts to charge forward over that final "zone of death"?[8]

Foch, in his lectures six years later, was to prescribe the same solution to this problem: "The laurels of victory hang on the enemy's bayonets, and have to be plucked from them, by man to man struggle if need be. . . . To flee or charge is all that remains. To charge, but to charge in numbers, as one mass, therein lies safety. For numbers, if we know how to employ them allow us, by the superiority of material placed at our disposal, to overcome the enemy's fire. With more guns we can reduce his to silence, and the same is true of rifles and bayonets, if we know how to use them all."[9] Too much emphasis has been placed on the importance and influence of Foch as a military theorist. He did no more than echo views very generally held, not only in the French army, but in others as well. Colonel G. F. R. Henderson, perhaps the most intelligent and literate theorist in the British army at the end of the century, observed with satisfaction how, in the British Infantry Regulations of 1880, "the bayonet has once more reasserted itself. To the second line, relying on cold steel only, as in the days of the Peninsula, is entrusted the duty of bringing the battle to a speedy conclusion. . . . The confusion of the Prussian battles was in a large degree due to their neglect of the immutable principles of tactics and . . . therefore, in regard to tactics, they are a bad model for us to follow."[10]

The model that Henderson held before his own army was that of the armies in the American Civil War, which had always attacked in massed formations; having learned that "to prevent the battle degenerating into a protracted struggle between two strongly entrenched armies, and to attain a speedy and decisive result, mere development of fire was insufficient."[11] It was true that weapons had changed during the past twenty-five years, but, Henderson asserted confidently, "neither smokeless powder nor the magazine rifle will necessitate any radical change. If the defence has gained, as has been asserted, by these inventions, the plunging fire of rifled howitzers will add a more than proportional

[8] Eugène Carrias, *La pensée militaire française* (Paris, 1960), 275-76.
[9] Foch, *Principles of War*, p. 365.
[10] G. F. R. Henderson, *The Science of War* (London, 1905), 135, 148.
[11] Ibid., 150.

strength to the attack. And if the magazine rifle has introduced a new and formidable element into battle, the moral element remains the same."[12]

The moral element remains the same: this is the theme that we find running through the military literature at the turn of the century, and it was to be sounded ever more strongly in the decade leading up to the First World War. The works of Clausewitz were studied as eagerly in the French and Russian armies as in the German, and the passages most often quoted were those in which he emphasized the overriding importance of moral factors in war, and the relative insignificance of material elements. The briefer, more elegantly expressed works of Ardent du Picq, with their profound insights into military psychology, were gaining popularity in France, and they taught the same lesson. Battles, wrote du Picq, were won not by weapons but by men, and nothing could be effectively planned in an army "without exact knowledge of this primary instrument, man, and his moral condition at the vital moment (*cet instant définitif*) of combat."[13] In battle, argued du Picq,

> two moral activities rather than two material activities confront one another, and the stronger will carry the day. . . . When the confidence one has placed in a superiority of material, incontestable for keeping the enemy at a distance, has been betrayed by the enemy's determination to get to close quarters, braving your superior means of destruction, the enemy's moral effect on you will be increased by all that lost confidence, and his moral activity will overwhelm your own. . . . Hence it follows that the bayonet charge . . . in other words the forward march under fire, will every day have a correspondingly greater effect.[14]

Du Picq went on to qualify this statement in a less frequently quoted passage. "Do not neglect *destructive* action before using *moral* action; so employ fire up till the last possible moment; otherwise, given existing rates of fire, no attack will reach its objective."[15] But this was exactly the point made by Bloch: given existing rates of fire, no attack would, or could succeed.

II

The year after Bloch published *La guerre future*, the Anglo-Boer War in South Africa provided the first test in which the new weapons

---

[12] Ibid., 159.
[13] Du Picq, *Etudes*, 3.
[14] Ibid., 121.
[15] Ibid., 127.

were used on both sides. As we have seen, the British army had come to the conclusion that the advantage that smokeless powder and magazine rifles would bring to the defense would be nullified by the employment of the new quick-firing artillery, whose shrapnel air-bursts would destroy any defenders who were not entrenched and whose plunging high-explosive shells would dig out those who were. In consequence they had reverted to close formations, "the second line, relying on cold steel only, [being] entrusted [with] the duty of bringing the battle to a speedy conclusion."[16] The result was that at the Modder River, Colenso, at Magersfontein, and Spion Kop, British forces were pinned down, decimated, and in places forced to surrender by the fire of Boer defenses they could not even see, let alone get close enough to assault. Continental observers attributed this to the inadequate training of an army unused to fighting "civilized" opponents, and a somewhat chastened Colonel Henderson, who had observed the compaign from Lord Roberts's headquarters, reacted angrily to their criticisms. "It is with something more than surprise," he wrote, "that we note a stubborn refusal to admit that the flat trajectory of the small bore rifle, together with the invisibility of the man who uses it, has wrought a complete revolution in the art of fighting battles."[17] Close formations under fire, he stated, were now impossible. Infantry attacking over open ground now had to move in successive lines of skirmishers at wide intervals; while "cavalry, armed and equipped as the cavalry of the Continent, is as obsolete as the crusaders." As for the argument that close formations were necessary to keep up morale, he pointed out: "When the preponderant mass suffers enormous losses; when they feel, as they will feel, that other and less costly means of achieving the same end might have been adopted, what will become of their morale?"[18] It was a highly prescient observation.

As a result of its wartime experiences, the British army redrafted its infantry regulations along the lines indicated by Henderson. The German army did not need to revise a doctrine that already stressed the advantage of enveloping enemy positions rather than taking them by frontal assault. The French, a little surprisingly, imitated the British. The French Infantry Regulations introduced in December 1904 explicitly abandoned the *coude à coude* formations of 1894 and substituted tactics more in line with those of the skirmishers of the French Revolutionary armies: infantry advancing in small groups, making maximum use of ground, covering each other by fire and movement, with initiative devolved as low as possible in the chain of command. These remarkably liberal reforms,

[16] Henderson, *Science of War*, 135.
[17] Ibid., 371.
[18] Ibid., 372-73.

516

however, seemed to many senior French officers to betray the radical if not socialistic influence of the Dreyfusards who were beginning to take over control of the army in the aftermath of that unhappy affair. General Langlois founded a new journal, the *Revue militaire générale*, very largely to combat "acute transvaalitis," the term he coined to describe "this abnormal dread of losses on the battlefield." Such dispersion, he argued, was alien to the French military tradition, in that it deprived the commander of "the right or even the possibility of securing a decisive result through the combined efforts of material and moral forces at his disposal."[19] But in any case the new regulations seem to have had little impact on the actual practice of a very confused and internally divided army in which consensus about anything was, at this time, painfully absent.

This reaction against "acute transvaalitis" was to be given powerful reinforcement by the lessons of the next major conflict fought with modern weapons, the Russo-Japanese War of 1904-1905. It was a campaign followed with intense interest not only by the naval and military specialists of Europe and the United States but by the governments they served, all of which were deeply concerned with the changes it effected in the power balance of the Far East and its consequent impact on Europe. Newspaper readers in two continents were kept fully informed by their war correspondents, accompanied by photographers and war artists, about the course of this first great war of a new century that no one expected to be very peaceful. The war in South Africa might be dismissed as atypical, fought as it was by an army trained in methods of colonial warfare against an adversary that hardly rated as an organized army at all. But the Russian army was one of the foremost in Europe, and the Japanese army had been trained by German experts as its navy had been by British. Both forces were equipped with all those weapons that Bloch had confidently asserted would henceforth make war impossible, or at least suicidal: small-caliber magazine rifles, quick-firing field artillery, mobile heavy artillery, and machine guns. The Russians fortified their positions at Port Arthur and Mukden with lines of trenches protected by barbed wire and machine-gun redoubts, covering their front with electrically detonated minefields and using searchlights to illuminate them at night. Both armies were equipped with telegraph and field telephones. Indeed the only weapons not available in 1905 that European armies were to possess in 1914 were the primitive aircraft that in the early months

[19] Joseph C. Arnold, "French Tactical Doctrine 1870-1914," *Military Affairs* 42, no. 2 (April 1978).

of the world war were beginning to take over the function of reconnaissance from the cavalry.

The main lesson that European observers deduced from the Russo-Japanese War was that in spite of all the advantages which the new weapons gave the defense, the offensive was still entirely possible. The Japanese sucessfully took the initiative from the very beginning of the war and in a series of set-piece attacks drove Russian forces slightly larger than their own out of southern Manchuria. The cost had been high, but as a result Japan had graduated as a Great Power; and any nation that wished to remain a Great Power, European commentators pointed out, must be prepared to face comparable costs.

The technical lessons were closely studied. Artillery had been used to great effect on both sides, but only with masked batteries using indirect fire. Its shrapnel fire as well as infantry rifle-fire made any movement within sight and range of the enemy out of the question, and put an end to all idea of close formations maneuvering on the battlefield. On well-entrenched infantry, however, field artillery made little impression, and only heavy artillery used in massive concentrations could break their resistance. No infantry attack could hope to succeed unless it was not only prepared but accompanied up until the last moment by artillery barrages; but with adequate preparation Japanese infantry assaults were repeatedly successful. The Japanese showed that the best answer to the invisible defense was the invisible attack. They therefore carried out their advance by night, digging themselves in before dawn and remaining immobile during the day. In the last stages of the advance they sapped their way forward yard by yard, as if conducting a siege. Then they assaulted. Casualties were still terrible: in the assaults on Port Arthur the Japanese lost fifty thousand men, in the ten-day battle of Mukden, seventy thousand. But they showed that by a combination of careful preparation and fanatical courage the problem of the attack on the modern battlefield could be solved.

One British comment written on the eve of the First World War by an influential staff officer, Major-General E. A. Altham, sums up the general European reaction:

> There were those who deduced from the experience in South Africa that the assault, or at least the assault with the bayonet, was a thing of the past, a scrap-heap manoeuvre . . . the Manchurian campaign showed over and over again that the bayonet was in no sense an obsolete weapon and that fire alone could not always suffice to move from a position a determined and well-disciplined enemy. . . . The assault is even of more importance than the attainment of fire mas-

tery which antecedes it. It is the supreme moment of the fight. Upon it the final issue depends.[20]

The real lesson of the Russo-Japanese War was widely seen as being that the truly important element in modern warfare was not technology but *morale*; and the morale, not of the army alone, but of the nation from which it was drawn. This was a matter on which the military leaders of the industrialized nations of western Europe were beginning to feel grave doubts. The German colonel Wilhelm Balck in his massive textbook on tactics warned that

> The steadily improving standards of living tend to increase the instinct of self-preservation and to diminish the spirit of self-sacrifice ... the fast manner of living at the present day tends to undermine the nervous system, the fanaticism and religious and national enthusiasm of a bygone age is lacking, and finally the physical powers of the human species are also partly diminishing. ... We should [therefore] send our soldiers into battle with a reserve of moral courage great enough to prevent the premature moral and mental depreciation of the individual.[21]

Within the German army a reaction set in, spearheaded by the eloquent and influential General von Bernhardi, against the cautious tactics and outflanking strategy of the Schlieffen era, which Bernhardi described as "a declaration of bankruptcy of the art of war." Schlieffen's emphasis on material factors and his reliance on numerical superiority, he maintained, failed to take into account the fact "that those troops will prove superior who can bear the greater losses and advance more vigorously than the others; or that boldness, daring and genius of leadership play any role at all in the war."[22]

In the German army the critics of Schlieffen remained a small if vocal minority. Their opposite numbers in the French army became very powerful indeed when General Joffre was appointed chief of the general staff in 1911. Joffre had spent most of his career in the French colonial army, which saw itself as an adventurous elite, achieving its conquests more through individual initiative and force of character than force of arms. Its officers despised the army of the metropole, which they considered to be lethargic, inefficient, and (in the aftermath of the Dreyfus affair) heavily politicized—typical indeed of France as a whole.[23] Nothing less than a moral crusade, they believed, was needed to restore the greatness

[20] E. A. Altham, *The Principles of War Historically Illustrated* (London, 1914), 295.
[21] William Balck, *Tactics*, 4th ed. (Fort Leavenworth, Kans., 1911), 194.
[22] Bernhardi, *On War Today*, 2:158, 179.
[23] Douglas Porch, *The March to the Marne* (Cambridge, 1981), 151-68.

and spirit of the French army and the French nation on the eve of a confrontation with their old enemy which, from 1911 onward, was widely considered to be inevitable. For this it was necessary, in Joffre's view, "to endow the Army with a clear war doctrine, known to all and unanimously accepted": the doctrine of the offensive.

After the war in South Africa, wrote Joffre,

> A whole series of false doctrines . . . began to undermine even such feeble offensive sentiment as has made its appearance in our war doctrines, to the detriment of the Army's spirit, its confidence in its chiefs and in its regulations. . . . an incomplete study of the events of a single war had led the intellectual élite of our Army to believe that the improvement in firearms and the power of fire action had so increased the strength of the defensive that an offensive opposed to it had lost all virtue. . . . [after the Manchurian campaign] our young intellectual élite finally shook off the malady of this phraseology which had upset the military world and returned to a more healthy conception of the general conditions prevailing in war.[24]

The "more healthy conception" consisted in an emphasis on "the spirit of the offensive." This, Joffre admitted in his memoirs, did assume "a somewhat unreasoning character"; especially as expounded by Colonel de Grandmaison, the director of military operations, in two famous lectures that he delivered in February 1911. He did not call in question the validity of the Infantry Regulations of 1904, with their emphasis on the importance of dispersed formations. These were indeed not only retained but reissued as late as April 1914. But "it is more important," wrote de Grandmaison, "to develop a conquering state of mind than to cavil about tactics," and it was this state of mind that he set himself to develop. "In battle one must always be able to do things which would be quite impossible in cold blood. To take one example: to advance under fire. . . . Nothing is more difficult to conceive of in our state of mind now. . . . We have to train ourselves to do it and train others, cultivating with passion everything that bears the stamp of the offensive spirit. We must take it to excess: perhaps even that will not go far enough."

Two years later de Grandmaison drew up the Regulations for the Conduct of Major Formations of October 1913, which contained the famous words: "The French Army, returning to its traditions, recognizes no law save that of the offensive."[25]

This doctrine suited the mood of the hour. It appealed to the military

---

[24] Joseph Joffre, *The Memoirs of Marshal Joffre* (London, 1932), 1:26-29.
[25] Carrias, *Pensée militaire*, 296; Henri Contamine, *La revanche 1871-1914* (Paris, 1957), 167.

elites who believed, with Ardent du Picq, that this spirit could be cultivated only within the framework of a dedicated professional army; their views were expressed by the novelist Ernest Psichari, whose novel *L'appel aux armes*, preaching the need for "a proud and violent army," enjoyed huge popularity on the eve of the war.[26] But it appealed no less to the radical Left, who had always declared that military morale was a matter of popular patriotic passion and did not require years of service with the colors to produce.[27] And more generally it was echoed in the enormously popular lectures the philosopher Henri Bergson was delivering at the Sorbonne, which were diffusing to a wide audience Nietzschean concepts of the Creative Will in the more elegant formulation of *l'élan vital*.

De Grandmaison, like Foch, has been much pilloried by subsequent historians and critics, but, allowing for a certain Gallic bravura, one finds much the same sentiments expressed by British and German writers of the time. In England, General Sir Ian Hamilton, one of the most sensitive and intelligent as well as influential of Britain's professional soldiers, argued along very much the same lines: "All that trash written by M. de Bloch before 1904 about zones of fire across which no living being could pass, heralded nothing but disaster. War is essentially the triumph, not of a chassepot over a needle-gun, not of a line of men entrenched behind wire entanglements and fire-swept zones over men exposing themselves in the open, but of one will over a weaker will . . . the best defence to a country is an army formed, trained, inspired by the idea of attack."[28]

Nor was there any doubt, in the minds of the soldiers before 1914, about the cost of all this in human lives. "It is always suspicious," wrote Balck, "if troops have become accustomed to consider insignificant losses . . . as indications of good leadership. Great victories are, as a rule, accompanied by great losses."[29] And Maude went even further: "The chances of victory turn entirely on the spirit of self-sacrifice of those who have to be offered up to gain opportunity for the remainder . . . in other words the true strength of an Army lies essentially in the power of each, or any of its constituent fractions to stand up to punishment, even to the verge of annihilation if necessary . . . [W]ith troops trained to judge their

---

[26] Raoul Girardet, *La société militaire dans la France contemporaine* (Paris, 1953), 305.

[27] Douglas Porch, "The French Army and the Spirit of the Offensive 1900-1914," in *War and Society: A Yearbook of Military History*, ed. Brian Bond and Ian Roy (London, 1975).

[28] Ian Hamilton, *Compulsory Service*, 2d ed. (London, 1911), 121. The same view is expressed in the Field Service Regulations of the British army published in 1909: "The success of the decisive battle is not predetermined by material or environmental causes, but by the exercise of human qualities directed by the will-power of individuals" (quoted in T. H. E. Travers, "The Offensive and the Problem of Innovation in British Military Thought 1870-1915," *Journal of Contemporary History* 13, no. 3 (July 1978).

[29] Balck, *Tactics*, 109.

leaders merely by the skill they show in economising their men's lives, what hope of adequate endurance can ever exist?"[30]

The armies and nations of Europe thus went to war in 1914 expecting that there would be heavy losses. The spirit in which their young men were indoctrinated was not simply to fight for their country, but to die for it. The concept of "sacrifice," above all of "the supreme sacrifice," was to dominate the literature, speeches, sermons, and journalism of the belligerent societies during the early years of the war. And the casualty lists that a later generation was to find so horrifying were considered by contemporaries not an indication of military incompetence, but a measure of national resolve, of fitness to rank as a Great Power.

III

In discussing the course of the First World War, European and American historians have tended to focus on the western front, and we shall follow their example here. In the East the losses of the Russian and Austrian armies rapidly mounted into hundreds of thousands, but these were accounted for mainly by sickness, prisoners, and desertion rather than by heroic self-sacrifice on the battlefield. Bloch's expectation of a future war in which armies held one another paralyzed across an intervening "zone of death," was paradoxically to be least applicable to the part of the world with which he was most familiar. In eastern Europe the conflict never bogged down into a war of positions; it remained one of maneuver until the very end.

It was the hope and intention of General von Schlieffen that this would be the case in western Europe as well. The Schlieffen plan, as we have seen, was the extension into strategy of the tactical doctrine that had prevailed in the German army since 1870—the avoidance of frontal attack and the attainment of the objective by envelopment, even if that development demanded armies numbered in millions. So the German armies marched through Belgium and France largely unopposed, and when they encountered opposition they masked it with artillery fire and tried to outflank it. They thus won a great deal of territory very cheaply indeed, but in the long run Schlieffen's critics proved right. His strategy achieved no decision.

In France, however, the high priests of the offensive, the equivalent of Schlieffen's opponents in Germany, were in charge, and it was under their influence that the High Command implemented its famous Plan XVII. The general concept behind this plan, that the French should take the strategic initiative rather than passively await the German assault,

---

[30] Maude, *Evolution of Infantry Tactics*, x.

had much to recommend it. It did after all provide the flexibility that enabled Joffre to recover so rapidly from his initial disasters and redeploy his forces to win the so-called battle of the Marne. The trouble with the French army in 1914 was not so much that it was offensively minded as that it was inefficient. Bureaucratic confusion prevented the main lessons of the Russo-Japanese War from being applied. No provision was made for the supply of heavy artillery, which meant that German guns consistently outranged the French. There was no doctrine for close cooperation between artillery and infantry, and no serious training in fieldcraft was carried out, whatever may have been laid down in the regulations. As a result, when war came French commanders at every level responded instinctively rather than in accordance with any systematic program of training. As one officer put it: "Before being subjected to the actual ordeal of fire, the idea that we were face to face with the enemy threw too many of our officers into a state of wild excitement which anyone who has experienced such moments can well understand. The man who can keep a cool head under such circumstances is a very unusual kind of animal. Much more than a question of doctrine it is a matter of temperament."[31]

In consequence, out of the 1,500,000 French troops who went on campaign at the beginning of August 1914, 385,000, or about one in four, were casualties after six weeks of fighting. Of these, 110,000 were dead.[32]

Most of these losses were suffered, not in set-piece attacks against prepared positions, but in encounter battles when both armies were on the move and the French infantry were caught in the open and destroyed by artillery fire. The second great clash on the western front in 1914, that in November at Ypres when the German and British armies both suffered heavy losses, was also an encounter battle in which each side tried to outflank the other in the so-called race to the sea. Only after that did the Germans begin to fortify the positions they had won, converting the trenches they had hurriedly scratched in the ground into an elaborate system of fortifications, strengthened with barbed wire, and utilizing for the first time large numbers of machine guns in a defensive role.

The strength of these defenses was tested by French and British attacks throughout 1915, and always with the same barren result. It was not that their attacks never succeeded. Often they did. But the bridgeheads thus established in the German defenses could not be held long enough, or reinforced fast enough, to resist the rapid counterattacks that the Germans mounted to regain their lost positions; and usually the Allies

[31] Contamine, *Revanche*, 249.
[32] Ibid., 276.

were driven back to their start-line with heavy losses. The only answer appeared to be attack on a broad enough front to establish a position invulnerable to counterattack, and to do so behind a curtain of artillery fire so heavy that it would destroy the capacity of the defenders to resist at all. The lesson of 1914 had been well learned; infantry would not be committed to action again without massive artillery support.

General Sir Douglas Haig, when asked early in 1915 whether he thought the British people could tolerate the heavy losses that would be involved in breaking the German lines, replied with incautious optimism that such losses would not be necessary; "as soon as we were supplied with ample artillery ammunition . . . [he] thought we could walk through the German lines at several places."[33] But four months later, after the failure of the British assault at Festubert in May 1915, he modified his view. "The defences on our front are so carefully and so strongly made," he noted in his diary, "and mutual support with machine guns is so complete, that in order to demolish them a *long methodical bombardment* will be necessary by heavy artillery . . . before the Infantry is sent forward to the attack."[34] That autumn, in the offensive he launched to relieve pressure on his Russian ally, Joffre attempted to put this doctrine into practice. Some five million artillery rounds were fired in support of the infantry, one million by heavy artillery. That attack also was contained. Nonetheless, sufficient local successes were achieved to encourage the Allies to believe that "it was possible, given some element of surprise, sufficient guns, ammunition and other appliances, and adequately trained troops, to break the enemy's front."[35]

In the spring of 1916 the Germans themselves set a pattern of how this might successfully be done. They launched a limited offensive at Verdun preceded by a bombardment so heavy that all resistance was literally crushed. But instead of then standing on the defensive, as their High Command had intended, and leaving it to the French to break themselves in counterattacks, the German field commanders continued to attack, and suffered punitive losses as a result. Verdun became a nightmare for French and Germans alike. But the German technique of attack under fire so heavy that, in the words of the British official history, "man was not pitted against man, but against material," was taken as a model by the British in planning their own first great offensive on the

[33] Robert Blake, ed., *The Private Papers of Sir Douglas Haig, 1914-1919* (London, 1952), 84.
[34] Ibid., 93.
[35] J. E. Edmonds and G. C. Wynne, *Military Operations France and Belgium 1915* (London, 1927), 2:399.

Somme in the summer of 1916.[36] The whole available work force of British industry, under the energetic direction of Lloyd George at the Ministry of Munitions, was set to produce guns and ammunition on the requisite scale. By the end of June 1,437 guns had been assembled along an eighteen-mile front, and in a week-long bombardment they fired over 1,500,000 shells.[37] General Sir Henry Rawlinson, the commander of the assaulting troops, assured his subordinate commanders that "nothing can exist at the conclusion of the bombardment in the area covered by it and the infantry would only have to walk over and take possession."[38] So the infantry went over the top on July 1 not as an assaulting force, but as a huge carrying party, each man bearing upward of seventy pounds of equipment, expecting at worst to have to mop up a few dazed survivors.

The result was one of the most terrible days in the history of war. The barrage had not been heavy enough to reach the dugouts that the Germans had excavated deep in the chalk hills above the Somme. Appalling as the experience they suffered was, the German infantry were still able to emerge in time to set up their machine guns and mow down the advancing waves of British infantry. German artillery was able to create such havoc in the British lines that it was several days before the High Command understood the scale of the catastrophe they had on their hands. Of the 120,000 men who assaulted, nearly half were casualties, and 20,000 were dead.[39]

The attacks continued until November, by which time the British and French armies engaged had lost nearly 500,000 men. By then, however, the object of the battle had changed. It was no longer to secure ground, but to compel the Germans to commit, and use up, their troops—the original object of the Germans themselves when they attacked at Verdun. "In another six weeks the enemy should be hard put to it to find men," Haig wrote in reply to anxious inquiries from London; ". . . the maintenance of a steady offensive pressure will result eventually in his complete overthrow."[40] The tactical deadlock, in short, was utilized to serve a strategy of attrition, in which the manpower and morale not only of the armies but of the entire nation was put to the test. To those brought up in the atmosphere of Social Darwinism, which dominated the first decade of the century, this came as no surprise. Readiness to suffer huge losses remained the criterion of fitness to survive as a Great

---

[36] Ibid., 357.
[37] James E. Edmonds, *Military Operations France and Belgium 1916* (London, 1932), 1:486.
[38] Ibid., 289.
[39] Ibid., 483.
[40] Blake, *Private Papers*, 157.

Power, and this readiness enabled the most advanced, industrialized, and educated nations of Europe to go on fighting for a further grueling two years.

By the end of the war, the tactics of both sides had been transformed. The British perfected the careful techniques of siege warfare associated with the armies of Plumer and Monash and experimented with armor and close air support. The Germans exploited the new weapons of trench warfare—light machine guns, grenades, gas—to give their infantry a flexibility that enabled them to break through fronts held by weaker and more ponderous adversaries.

It would be a mistake to try to establish too close a connection between the doctrine of the offensive current before 1914 and the terrible losses incurred during the First World War. It is true that, given the strength of the new firepower, heavy losses were accepted as inevitable. It is also true that, in the frenetic atmosphere of 1914, which intellectual historians have so thoroughly analyzed, there was a remarkable public readiness to accept them.[41] But much of the writing before 1914 about the supreme importance of morale in war and the need to maintain an offensive mentality in the face of all obstacles did no more than restate truths that have been valid in all periods of warfare. The influence of firepower on tactics had been exhaustively analyzed by general staffs before 1914, and well-trained regular forces already knew that the best answer to the rifle was the spade. The worst losses were those due not to faulty doctrine but to inefficiency, inexperience, and the sheer organizational problems of combining fire and movement on the requisite scale. From the very first days of the war, the professional soldiers of Europe were trying to adjust themselves to the new realities of the battlefield. It took them a tragically long time to solve the tactical problems that confronted them. Until they did, strategy was crippled by the adverse balance between defensive and offensive power to a degree rare in the history of war.

[41] See in particular Roland N. Stromberg, *Redemption by War: The Intellectuals and 1914* (Lawrence, Kans., 1982), and Robert Wohl, *The Generation of 1914* (Cambridge, Mass., 1979).

19. German Strategy in the Age of Machine Warfare, 1914-1945

MICHAEL GEYER

THE RETREAT behind the Marne in 1914 buried all hope for a quick end to a war that had been begun with such self-assurance. It revealed serious shortcomings in the strategic thought of the prewar years.[1] Even worse, it raised doubts about the principles of war as they had been taught to each new generation of German officers since the rise of a professional education system in the nineteenth century. When victory eluded the general staff, a world of military certainties fell apart.

The knowledge of war and of the military craft fused the geopolitical conditions of Prussia-Germany with military considerations into a self-contained universe. Although this knowledge was expressed primarily in the planning and conduct of military operations, it contained its own internal system of references that encompassed political assumptions about the nature of the national and international order as much as an appreciation of specific weapons. In this sense a good German strategist was always a generalist. Although the German operational outlook may be called "realist," it was embedded in a strategic framework that derived from the idealistic philosophy about war and the state in the early nineteenth century. As such, strategic thinking increasingly came under pressure with the rise of mass armies.[2] However, a comprehensive and holistic approach kept German strategists apart from makers of military doctrine, that is, all those who followed an "empirical" approach to war and developed their notions of the use of force through instrumental reason-

NOTE: I should like to thank John Shy, Charles Bright, and the editors of this volume for their kind advice in the preparation of this essay, which is dedicated to my *Doktorvater*, Prof. Dr. Andreas Hillgruber, on the occasion of his sixtieth birthday.
    [1] Gotthard Jäschke, "Zum Problem der Marneschlacht von 1914," *Historische Zeitschrift* 190 (1960), 311-48; Karl Lange, *Marneschlacht und die Öffentlichkeit 1914-1931: Eine verdrängte Niederlage und ihre Folgen* (Düsseldorf, 1974).
    [2] Rudolf von Caemmerer, *Die Entwicklung der strategischen Wissenschaft im 19. Jahrhundert* (Berlin, 1904); see also the essays by Hajo Holborn and Gunther Rothenberg in this volume.

ing. As opposed to the "professional" strategist in the German idealist tradition, these were military "managers" or "technocrats."

The universalist approach to strategy depended on the autonomy of the military and the maintenance of a dichotomy between military and civilian society. The dualism was not all that far removed from a "liberal" notion of civil-military relations. In a liberal tradition, strategy remained separate from military doctrine, the guideline for the optimal use of weapons and men. The former was considered the domain of politics and the latter the proper realm of military men. The gap between the two was bridged by an elite discourse concerning the commitments of the nations. The German military did not entertain debates about war, strategy, and national defense. It possessed the certain knowledge of war—and this knowledge failed in 1914.

After 1914, we see time and again a tenacious effort to rebuild a semblance of this universalist notion of war in the quest for a coherent military practice that would unify strategy, operations, and tactics and form the intramilitary basis for the autonomy of the profession. Efforts to resynthesize a holistic strategy and to re-create the political conditions for it were made repeatedly between 1914 and 1945. However, once the certitudes of idealistic thinking were destroyed, the German practice of war developed strong centrifugal tendencies. German strategic thinking in the interwar years was propelled by intense struggles between two currents of strategy, one aiming at the reconstruction of unifying principles and the other at a new practice of war. By 1942, a radically different notion of strategy and a transformed officer corps had come into existence.

This development has commonly been identified with the "strategic revolution" of mechanized and armored warfare.[3] However, tank warfare is only a part—though a critical part—of a more encompassing process in which the unified approach to German strategy devolved into two directions, the management of arms on the one hand and ideological "strategy" on the other. The former rested on the maximization of the effectiveness of arms, the latter on the mobilization of society for war. Even though they are normally kept apart as distinct and even irreconcilable features of modern war, they were birds of a feather. Engineers and ideologists of violence always came in pairs. When the capabilities of the two were fused in a single effort between 1938 and 1941, they propelled Germany into World War II.

This assessment runs counter to prevalent interpretations of German

[3] Larry H. Addington, *The Blitzkrieg Era and the German General Staff, 1865-1941* (New Brunswick, N.J., 1971); Charles Messenger, *The Art of Blitzkrieg* (London, 1967).

strategy. The "genius of war"[4] of the German general staff has found both admirers and detractors who have debated for almost a century what one should or should not accept of the Prussian revolution in warfare. They have pointed to the continuity of strategic concepts,[5] their underlying power-politics or "realistic" rationale, and the political benefits as well as dangers of the exclusive military caste behind it. Conversely, they have stressed the increasingly mechanistic underpinnings of strategic idealism that in the nineteenth century had already replaced its philosophical or metaphysical roots, and have focused on the nemesis of a military profession which demanded a leading role in society and politics in the pursuit of "timeless" principles of war that were increasingly propelled by industrial means of warfare.[6] To emphasize these military traditions and continuities is to make a valid point. But traditions never simply exist and continuities do not just roll along. They have to be maintained by continuous renewal in a changing national and international environment, a setting they have influenced in their use of force and preparation for it. This was the precondition for the continuous struggle between the re-creation of a German tradition of strategy and the radical challenge of military technocrats and ideologues. It was a struggle in which idealistic strategy remained remarkably vigorous and attractive for a long time, but which its adherents ultimately lost.

The agonistic quality of German strategic thinking echoed far more dramatic changes nationally and internationally. Between 1914 and 1945 Germany saw the demise of a hybrid form of authoritarian regime, a state of revolution and counterrevolution between 1917 and 1923, the temporary consolidation of a pluralistic republican order and its collapse in the world economic crisis, the emergence and consolidation of an aggressive National Socialist state, and its downfall in six years of war. In the same period German armies occupied the northern parts of France, Belgium, and Luxemburg, eastern Europe deep into Russia, and Romania, lost all this and some of their own territory, only to come back after twenty years to occupy most of Europe deep into the Soviet Union and then saw their country wiped out as an independent nation. It was indeed a period of virtually continuous upheaval.

If we try to discover the deep structure underneath these rapid and violent changes, we invariably encounter: (1) a quest for mass participation in national politics, which undermined both elite politics and the

---

[4] Trevor N. Dupuy, *A Genius for War: The German Army and General Staff, 1807-1945* (Englewood Cliffs, 1977).

[5] Jehuda Wallach, *Das Dogma der Vernichtungsschlacht: Die Lehren von Clausewitz und Schlieffen und ihre Wirkungen in zwei Weltkriegen* (Frankfurt, 1967).

[6] Gordon A. Craig, *The Politics of the Prussian Army* (New York, 1964).

autonomy of the military institution; and (2) the dissolution of the unity of power politics under the impact of new forms of international competition—primarily the rise of popular nationalism and the formation of industrial concentrations of power. Their impact on national and international politics had contradictory effects on Germany. It was propelled into a position as the predominant power on the Continent by virtue of the fact that from the 1890s on it was Europe's most populous and industrialized nation, rather than by virtue of its arms. At the same time, beginning with the interwar years, Germany's position in the world declined together with that of the old core of Europe. This growing asymmetry of the German position in international relations, reinforced by mass demands for the autonomy and welfare of the nation, posed the major challenge to German politics in the first half of the twentieth century. It was by no means self-evident that a military answer to these problems would succeed, and it was even less clear that the military would ever develop a strategy to master the problem. As it is, military solutions prevailed with terrible costs to Germany and the world.

I

Before 1914, military writers and planners had long assumed that if a European conflict could not be brought to a quick solution, war would turn into a monster, devouring ever larger masses of people, ever more resources, and, in due course, the military leaders as well. It would, moreover, affect deeply, if not destroy, the fabric of civil society. Although some, like General Alfred von Schlieffen, considered this to be a major disaster for both civil society and the military, others like the members of the *Deutsche Wehrverein* rejoiced in the idea of an Armageddon for a corrupt, decadent, and materialistic world.[7] The elder Moltke exclaimed in great agitation in the Reichstag: "Gentlemen, it may turn into a seven, even a thirty years' war! Woe betide him who sets Europe ablaze," but others celebrated and hoped for a war as a purge that could not end before the grand national cleansing was completed, the shackles of materialism and corporatism had fallen off, and a new society was forged in the pure spirit of nationalism.[8] Meanwhile Friedrich Engels growled

---

[7] Alfred von Schlieffen, *Gesammelte Schriften* (Berlin, 1913), 1:11-22 ("Vom Krieg der Zukunft"); Roger Chickering, "Der deutsche Wehrverein und die Reform der deutschen Armee, 1912-1914," *Militärgeschichtliche Mitteilungen* 25 (1979), 7-34.

[8] Reichsarchiv, ed., *Kriegsrüstung und Kriegswirtschaft: Die militärische, wirtschaftliche und finanzielle Rüstung Deutschlands, 1871-1914* (Berlin, 1930), Anlagen, 44; Otto Nippold, *Der deutsche Chauvinismus* (Stuttgart, 1912). Compare also the contributions in *Deutsche Wehrzeitung*, 1912ff. On the "cult of violence" see Hans Barth, *Masse und Mythos, die ideologische Krise an der Wende zum 20. Jahrhundert und die Theorie der Gewalt: Georges Sorel* (Hamburg, 1959).

that war would be like an Egyptian plague and the elites of Europe had better take heed before the crowns of Europe rolled into the gutter, governments toppled, and power lay in the street. Yet the overwhelming majority of German socialists opposed revolution through destruction.[9] Whatever their political orientation, almost everyone seemed to agree that a coming war was going to be either short or apocalyptic.

Every age has its own apocalypse. There were indeed visions of the carnage of a potential war. The Hamburg teacher and pacifist Wilhelm Lamszus movingly described the *Menschenschlachthäuser* of future wars in one of the more remarkable treatises of the time. Mostly, though, the public and the military expected a different kind of apocalypse. Much like Engels, they had come to understand that fighting war was an immensely risky social and economic undertaking because of the social mobilization that it required. The apocalyptic quality of a future war consisted less in the utter terror of physical destruction than in the notion that old attitudes and social ties would be dissolved and European society reforged. War would change the mores, the social culture, and the habits of individuals. It would create a "new society" and a "new man."[10]

Military elites in all countries put a premium on limiting and thus controlling war.[11] The Prussian answer to the potential limitlessness of war lay in the war of annihilation (*Vernichtungsschlacht*) or, as Delbrück following Clausewitz called it, *Niederwerfungsstrategie*. What were the proper dimensions of the *Vernichtungsschlacht*? Schlieffen seemed to have found the perfect solution for a professionally autonomous war in which the art of military operations—decision-oriented warfare, the Cannae principle of envelopment—served only one superior rationale: to preserve war as a professional domain. He established a trade-off between civilian society and the military in which the latter fought the war on their own in return for a quick end of military action within the context of a self-contained and militarily defined balance-of-power system. Pol-

[9] Wolfram Wette, *Kriegstheorien deutscher Sozialisten: Marx, Engels, Lasalle, Bernstein, Kautsky, Luxemburg* (Stuttgart, 1971). On the SPD see Friedhelm Boll, "Die deutsche Sozialdemokratie zwischen Resignation und Revolution: Zur Friedensstrategie 1890-1919," in *Frieden, Gewalt, Sozialismus: Studien zur Geschichte der sozialistischen Arbeiterbewegung*, ed. Wolfgang Huber and Joachim Schwertfeger (Stuttgart, 1976), 179-281; Friedhelm Boll, *Frieden ohne Revolution* (Bonn, 1980); Hellmut Bley, *Bebel und die Strategie der Kriegsverhütung* (Göttingen, 1975).

[10] Wilhelm Lamszus, *Das Menschenschlachthaus: Bilder vom kommenden Krieg* (repr. of 1912 ed., Munich, 1980); Carl Bleibtreu, *Das Heer* (Frankfurt, 1910); Nahum Goldman, *Der Geist des Militarismus* (Stuttgart and Berlin, 1915); Friedrich Naumann, *Wie wir uns im Krieg verändert haben* (Vienna, 1916).

[11] Lancelot L. Farrar, Jr., *The Short War Illusion: German Policy, Strategy, and Domestic Affairs, August-December, 1914* (Santa Barbara, Calif., 1973); Jack Snyder, *The Ideology of the Offensive: Military Decision Making and the Disaster of 1914* (Ithaca and London, 1984).

itics abdicated in favor of the mechanics of balance-of-power and operational considerations, but military operations did not interfere with the growth of civilian society and industry.[12] It was crucial for this kind of professional warfare that politics in the sense of societal participation in decisions on war and peace be cut out, but just as a crucial that civilian society exist as a distinct, separate, and equally important "estate."

To this end, Schlieffen resolved the problem of the fluidity of war in an elegant and exemplary fashion. The dynamics of operational movement would create, by this forward thrust, the center of gravity and thus escalate into the annihilation of the enemy forces. Schlieffen called this kind of campaign *Gesamtschlacht*. His notion of the *Gesamtschlacht* is less well known than his operational doctrine, the Cannae principle, even though the former provided the rationale for the latter. The *Gesamtschlacht* was an answer to the expansion of the theater of war and the increasing mobility of troops. Both had led to a growing concern of the general staff over controlling the rules of engagement, without which elite control of the use of force would slip away. The *Gesamtschlacht* combined diverse battlefields and partial battles into an "integral operation," in which military action no longer consisted of maneuvers that narrowed down the space of an operation to the actual battlefield and culminated in a final and decisive battle with the enemy's main forces. The new "integral operation" knew only one joint and continuous movement, whose object was not any specific battlefield or specific concentration of forces at a given place, but the unfolding dynamics of military action against a whole nation or even nations. Schlieffen thus replaced an arithmetical concept of operations, which added up battles into a campaign, with a dynamic one that developed out of deployment and rolled on, self-sustaining and gathering velocity in a grand enveloping action encompassing the whole European theater of war. This drastically altered the relation between individual battles and the military campaign overall. Now there were no individual battles, but only the expanding torrents of a campaign. Integrated and continuous motion was the only way, in Schlieffen's mind, to force a fluid situation with many possible points of concentration toward a decision—a concept that underwrote the original Schlieffen plan, but was abandoned by the younger Moltke. War as uninterrupted movement was Schlieffen's answer to the problem of a two-front war; by defeating France he hoped to contain the global powers, Great Britain and Russia. The proper role of the German army lay in Europe, and there it was to pursue limited though unquestionably

[12] Schlieffen, *Gesammelte Werke*, 1:17. See also Gerhard Ritter, *Der Schlieffenplan: Kritik eines Mythos* (Munich, 1956; Eng. trans. London, 1958).

expansionist objectives.[13] The world belonged to industry and patriotic pressure groups—or perhaps to the navy, but none of these greatly concerned the chief of staff of the imperial German army.

These principles of war rested foremost on a "government of experts," which demanded autonomy and promised success without jeopardy for the bourgeoisie and industry. Its enemy was not civilian society, but society's demand to participate in the process of determining strategy, which became a key problem with the concurrent rise of mass participation in national politics and mass armies. It remained a major challenge to professional strategy and all those who pleaded for elite rule. Schlieffen's strategy, of course, needed the "masses" and industry as means of war, but not as subjects in their own right. In this respect he was less an aristocratic-"feudal" officer than a "bureaucratic" one who insisted on the primacy of institutional rationality.

Schlieffen's strategy aimed at a quick decision that developed from the "right" operational approach. What matters is not the *idée fixe* of Cannae, but the limitation of war by military means. Operations reigned supreme; politics had no say. But the imperial army failed to create the crushing dynamics that Schlieffen envisioned; it failed to establish control and command; and it failed to create the conditions for a short war. Although the principles of limited war were compelling, their practice had to be rebuilt from scratch.

The two years following August 1914 were characterized by a general lack of purpose in military operations, which were punctuated by continuous action with an ever-higher intensity of destruction. Armies ceased to express an overarching professional rationale and became, instead, conduits through which societies poured their mobilized resources as well as their hatred and prejudice. Once decisive victory was precluded, military planners were at a loss how to use the massed manpower and the material means of destruction that had been placed at their disposal. Strategy as a unified and directional guidance of war fell apart. Without the guidance of any particular strategy the war moved on as micropolitics and microstrategies, an extension of the internal and external antagonisms unleashed by the decision to go to war.

The failure to achieve a quick victory had far-reaching repercussions.[14] In 1915 we see the high point of the consolidation of power

---

[13] On war aims see Fritz Fischer, *Griff nach der Weltmacht*, 3d ed. (Düsseldorf, 1964) and idem, *Krieg der Illusionen* (Düsseldorf, 1969); and from a power-politics perspective, Andreas Hillgruber, *Kontinuität und Diskontinuität in der deutschen Aussenpolitik von Bismarck bis Hitler* (Düsseldorf, 1971).

[14] Walter Elze, *Das deutsche Heer von 1914: Der strategische Aufbau des Weltkrieges 1914-1918*, vol. 16 of Bibliotheca rerum Militarium (Osnabrück, 1968), 57-77.

blocs that had begun to shape European affairs in the 1890s, and with this came genuinely new forms of international behavior. In lieu of diplomacy, we increasingly find the hostile projection of ideological images against the other camp and a military strategy that relied more on mobilizing the sources of economic and social power against the other bloc than on the limited and limiting "play" of nineteenth-century power politics. It is as if the age of imperialism had finally come to maturity and had begun to transform Europe.[15] It destroyed Schlieffen's professional strategy. At home, the seeds of the 1890s were harvested as well. The more intense the war effort became, the more it necessitated a mobilization of society which, in turn, led to demands for participation in the political decision-making process over war and peace. It became a direct challenge to the domestic order of the Central Powers and to the autonomy of the military profession.

It is in this perspective that the strategy and politics of the chief of the general staff in the (Second) Supreme Command, Erich von Falkenhayn, and the imperial chancellor, Theobald von Bethmann Hollweg, should be seen. At the political end of an increasingly tenuous elite consensus we find a chancellor who had been able in 1914 to establish a basic agreement that war should be left to the specialists in government, the military and diplomats. For these professionals, *Burgfrieden* meant, that they could proceed to fight their war unhindered. This policy was already in jeopardy by the end of 1914 mainly because of the demands for a public war-aims debate. Bethmann Hollweg tried to stem the tide. But for that purpose he needed a military victory, and he was inclined to side with anyone who would promise it.[16] In 1915 this was the Second Supreme Command under Falkenhayn.

Falkenhayn concluded quite bluntly at the end of 1915 that no direct approach could overthrow Germany's main and most enduring enemy, Great Britain, and that the German army, given the state of its resources, was unable to fight a decisive breakthrough battle on the western front without undue hazard. Nor did he expect decisive military victories in the East. Instead he proposed an operation that aimed at breaking the stranglehold of Great Britain over its Continental allies by indirect means. He suggested deterring France from continuing war by "opening the eyes of her people to the fact that in a military sense they have nothing more to hope for."[17] He contemplated an operation against Verdun that aimed

[15] George Kennan, *The Fateful Alliance: France, Russia, and the Coming of the First World War* (New York, 1984).

[16] Karl-Heinz Janssen, *Der Kanzler und der General* (Göttingen, 1967); Konrad Jarausch, *The Enigmatic Chancellor* (New Haven and London, 1973).

[17] Erich von Falkenhayn, *The German General Staff and Its Decisions, 1914-1916* (New York, 1920), 249.

at the "morale" of France by pounding away on its army. The destruction of national determination took the place of military victory over enemy forces.

Bethmann Hollweg and Falkenhayn sketched out an alternative to the *Vernichtungsschlacht* within the confines of elite strategy. They stretched the limits of professionalism to preserve the autonomy of the military and the state. Its key operational variable consisted in convincing the Allies of the futility of continuing to fight and, by doing so, achieving one's own hegemonic but limited goals. This has been likened to a strategy of attrition, but Falkenhayn's strategy more resembled a conventional deterrence strategy insofar as it played off clearly circumscribed interests against the threat of social calamity.[18] The difference is quite revealing. Attritional warfare as discussed by Wilhelmine thinkers like Delbrück assumed a joint interest of the opposing sides in the social control of war. Falkenhayn's strategy, on the other hand, hoped for the collapse of elite control in the enemy's camp by "bleeding its forces to death," which would set free social pressures for peace.[19] If peace negotiations could be achieved quickly enough, the necessity of involving one's own society in the decisions over war and peace could be forestalled. This was an elite response to the collapse of professional control over the war and, at the same time, a means to control mass involvement in military matters. It was an attempt to turn the domestic flank of France, so that it could not turn one's own by continuing the war.

Falkenhayn's concept led to the disaster of Verdun.[20] It began with the miscalculation that the Allies were near the breaking point and thus could be coaxed to the bargaining table. They were not. Mismanagement of the operation compounded strategic miscalculations. German operational planning and German tactics were geared to all-out offensives, and found it difficult to shift to a war of calculated and one-sided attrition. Falkenhayn's own operational designs, moreover, were not entirely consistent with his strategic outlook. In operational terms he wanted to knock hard on Verdun, in order to shake loose an Allied counteroffensive elsewhere that, in turn, could initiate a counterassault against the enemy flanks. Perhaps he could snatch the prestige, if not of overall victory at

[18] A somewhat different argument is presented in John J. Mearsheimer, *Conventional Deterrence* (Ithaca and London, 1983).

[19] Falkenhayn, *German General Staff*, 249; Lancelot L. Farrar, Jr., "Peace through Exhaustion: German Diplomatic Motivation for the Verdun Campaign," *Revue internationale d'histoire militaire* 32 (1972-75), 477-94; Michael Salewski, "Verdun und die Folgen: Eine militärische und geistesgeschichtliche Betrachtung," *Wehrwissenschaftliche Rundschau* 25 (1976), 89-96.

[20] The best and only reliable analysis still is Hans Wendt, *Verdun 1916* (Berlin, 1931); on a more popular level see Alistair Horne, *The Price of Glory: Verdun 1916* (London, 1962).

least of some specific victories from the commanders in the East—Erich Ludendorff and Paul von Hindenburg.

Instead, the controlled war against enemy morale turned into an uncontrolled slugging match without decision or purpose that produced staggering losses on both sides. The questionable strategy of pounding the enemy to the negotiation table was matched with operational plans that did not fit the strategic goal, and was executed with tactics that were self-defeating. The battle was fought in the most traditional manner of nineteenth-century offensive land warfare at a point of attack where the old guard of professional strategists would have avoided battle at all costs. It failed as a deterrence strategy because it was flawed in one crucial respect. Falkenhayn did not send machines against human beings, but men against a fortified region. More than any other battle, Verdun showed the military impasse of World War I, the complete disjuncture between strategy, battle design, and tactics, and the inability to use the modern means of war. But most of all, it showed, at horrendous costs, the impasse of professional strategies.

The same basic experience characterized the main defensive battle of 1916, the battle at the Somme. This debacle not only showed that the strategic estimates of the Supreme Command were wrong, but made it evident that the German army had not adapted its internal structure to defense under the new conditions of industrial war. Manuals and officers alike emphasized stationary defense in which the first line was held. They had difficulties with flexible tactics that adapted to local conditions. The German defenses were organized to block off an attack like a solid wall, only now they began to introduce a second and third wall behind the first, just in case the enemy broke through.[21]

Why this stubborn insistence on such rigid methods of warfare? Operations and tactics reflected the same elitist-conservative approach that informed the turn to Bethmann Hollweg's *Burgfrieden* politics and a war of one-sided attrition. Subordination to the chain of command, with its "modern Alexander" at the top, strict control of action and movement, and hence limitation of collective initiatives "from the bottom up," seems to be the key to the political and social meaning of the disaster at Verdun and the extraordinarily high costs of the battle at the Somme. Rather than solving the riddle of the trenches after the demise of the *Vernichtungsschlacht*, Falkenhayn and Bethmann Hollweg had compounded the disaster. If war was to be continued beyond 1916, a remedy had to be found for all aspects of the *Gesamtschlacht* and a new balance

---

[21] Reichsarchiv, ed., *Die Operationen des Jahres 1916 bis zum Wechsel der Obersten Heeresleitung*, vol. 10 of *Der Weltkrieg 1914-1918* (Berlin, 1936), 338-88, 674-76; Ernst Kabisch, *Somme 1916* (Berlin, 1937).

had to be sought between strategy, operations, and tactics. Strategy had to link military campaigns to goals and means once again. Individual battles at multiple fronts had to be integrated into an operational design that added movement to the direction of the overarching strategy. The battle itself had to be rebuilt, that is, the use of force, tactics, and organization had to be integrated in a new way. This task, however, meant nothing less than to change the very fabric of military institutions and military-political affairs; if war was to be fought on the basis of the mobilization of society and industry, both had to find a place in the making of strategy.

II

A new (Third) Supreme Command did all three with a vengeance. It modernized the German army to a point at which little was left of the old Wilhelmine army. With Hindenburg and Ludendorff, military brilliance and recklessness of leadership avoided a continuation of disaster, but led to defeat and revolution as a result of their innovative measures.

Their promotion signalled a new age of strategy. To begin with, the institutional relations between the commander in chief and the general staff took on a new dimension.[22] Hindenburg was hailed as the savior of East Prussia by broad segments of German society and Ludendorff became the Faustian genius of war who engineered it all. At the eastern front a younger general staff officer, Colonel Max Hoffmann, already stood behind the two, a configuration that proved to be more enduring and consequential than anyone at the time might have envisioned. Strategy became a composite, reflecting and expressing public sentiments on the one hand and the craft of operations on the other, both being welded together by the organizational talents of a supreme engineer. This triangle became the institutional aspect of strategy in the machine age.

Hindenburg and Ludendorff made a strong impact on the German public. They were revered not so much for a single battle, as for their ability to do the right things or, at least, appearing to do so. Their ability to shape events also gave them the allegiance of fellow officers. What counted was activity; it mattered remarkably little whether or not the actions made strategic sense. With Ludendorff and Hindenburg an age began in which strategic thinking declined and strategic expectations grew as long as something happened. This is the second theme of strategy in the machine age.

[22] Karl-Heinz Janssen, "Der Wechsel der OHL 1916," *Vierteljahrshefte für Zeitgeschichte* 7 (1954), 337-71; Max Hoffmann, *War Diaries and Other Papers* (London, 1929), 2:242-343; Erich Ludendorff, *Meine Kriegserinnerungen, 1914-1918* (Berlin, 1919), 203-227.

Ludendorff has been called a combination of genius and madman.[23] It would be more accurate to think of him as a military fanatic. Yet his fanaticism was different from that of Napoleon and Cromwell, to whom he is sometimes compared. He possessed a striking ability to delegate tasks, and did not hesitate to delegate them to very junior officers or to experienced front-line officers. The corporate practice that Ludendorff introduced combined function with efficiency instead of hierarchy and fused the military with society in the pursuit of excellence. Ludendorff paid respect to the senior generals who commanded the armies, but he preferred to be with those who "worked for war."[24] Fanaticism, as part of military work routines, was a third element embedded in the new conduct of war.

Ludendorff expected the same efficiency-oriented outlook in politics without ever showing politicians the same deference that he gave to military commanders. He became an advocate of "what may be called a technical dictatorship for purposes of the conduct of mass warfare" or what we more commonly call technocratic rule.[25] Ludendorff's politics cannot be understood as a mere expression of political naïveté from an otherwise splendid strategist nor as a radicalization of a Prussian tradition that was otherwise sound.[26] "Working for war" was, in Ludendorff's mind, an all-encompassing undertaking in which nothing short of total dedication and commitment as well as maximum performance counted for both the military and society. Military work and politics became inseparable in the machine age.

It was the combination of military charisma, fanaticism, and quest for efficiency that singled out the two years in which Hindenburg and Ludendorff shaped strategy and, increasingly, politics as well. Contemporaries likened their ascendance and their politics to the rise of total war. The war took over and engulfed all of society in an ever-expanding machine of violence. The more the war effort ground down societies and took hold of every aspect of life, the more war was portrayed as a metaphysical or, in any case, superhuman state.[27] It is true that the war

---

[23] Norman Stone, "Ludendorff," in *The War Lords: Military Commanders of the Twentieth Century*, ed. Michael Carver (London, 1976), 13-74; P. Neame, *German Strategy in the Great War* (London, 1923), 120; Wolfgang Foerster, *Der Feldherr Ludendorff im Unglück: Eine Studie über seine seelische Haltung in der Endphase des Ersten Weltkrieges* (Wiesbaden, 1952).

[24] Ludendorff, *Kriegserinnerungen*, 419.

[25] Hans Speier, "Ludendorff: The German Concept of Total War," *Makers of Modern Strategy*, ed. Edward Mead Earle (Princeton, 1943), 308.

[26] Gerhard Ritter, *The Sword and the Scepter: The Problem of Militarism in Germany*, 4 vols. (Coral Gables, Fla., 1969-73).

[27] This notion is most clearly expressed in Friedrich G. Jünger, *Die Perfektion der Technik*, Appendix: Die Weltkriege, 5th ed. (Frankfurt, 1968), 180-97; as counterpoint see Raymond

became ever more encompassing. But rather than becoming metaphysical, war was linked to the social dynamics of nations. The main effort of the Third Supreme Command centered around channeling these social forces into the pursuit of victory. This was strategy in the machine age. Like all good strategists, they did not follow the lead of war, in this case "total war," but they made total war happen.

Hindenburg's and Ludendorff's insistence on victory at any price, rather than any particular strategic or operational insight, had propelled them into their elevated position. Both had clearly misjudged the situation, but rather than contemplating a negotiated end to the war, they threw themselves into activity.[28] It is typical of their approach that a strategic outlook emerged only slowly. Their main concern was how to fight the battles ahead. A promised offensive to decide the war was quickly buried. Merely to continue, German defenses had to be reorganized so that the disastrous losses at the Somme did not recur. Drastic measures were taken almost immediately to "improve the fighting power of the army."[29] Within six months tactics, organization, and training for defensive warfare were completely revamped. The new measures helped the German army to withstand the 1917 campaign and, in fact, brought France close to the breaking point. Then another round of innovations was introduced to prepare the army for a major offensive thrust in 1918 which, according to the standard histories of that campaign, came so close to success that only a single operational mistake prevented victory. This doubtful hyperbole reflects the awe with which friend and foe alike evaluated the reforms of the Third Supreme Command.[30]

Front-line and general staff officers as well as reserve officers who had experimented with new tactics and organization were called upon to discuss and formulate new directions.[31] An intense debate produced the "Principles of Field Construction" of November 1916, which were employed to construct the Hindenburg line, and the famous "Principles

---

Aron, *The Century of Total War* (Garden City, N.Y., 1954). See also Tony Ashworth, *Trench Warfare 1914-1918: The Live and Let Live System* (London, 1980); Eric J. Leed, *No Man's Land: Combat and Identity in World War I* (New York, 1981).

[28] Ludendorff, *Kriegserinnerungen*, 208-216, 240-57; Generalfeldmarschall Paul von Hindenburg, *Aus meinem Leben* (Leipzig, 1934), pp. 159-60, 176-78.

[29] Ludendorff, *Kriegserinnerungen*, 349.

[30] Trevor N. Dupuy, *The Military Lives of Hindenburg and Ludendorff of Imperial Germany* (New York, 1979); Donald Goodspeed, *Ludendorff: Genius of World War I* (Boston, 1966); G. C. Wynne, *If Germany Attacks: The Battle in Depth in the West* (London, 1940).

[31] Among others, Cols. Bauer and Lossberg, Majs. Wetzell and Bruchmüller, and Capts. Geyer, Reddemann, and Rohr; see Wilhelm Balck, *Entwicklung der Taktik im Weltkrieg*, 2d ed. (Berlin, 1922); Eugène Carrias, *La pensée militaire allemande* (Paris, 1948), 335-43.

of Command in the Defensive Battle in Position Warfare" of December 1916. The major aspects of the new approach to defensive warfare can be summarized as follows:

> [The Principles] proposed to thin the [German] front line, and to create the main line of resistance and a line of reserve trenches further back. The attack would therefore be filtered by a line of outposts, and then would be drawn deeper into the position and away from its [artillery] support to be smashed between the main line of resistance and the line of reserve trenches. Counter-attacks would be launched by local reserves before the enemy could consolidate gains. If a counterattack could not be made immediately, it would be postponed until it could be launched with full deliberation. Ideally the German line should be sited behind the crest of a slope, so that it lay out of British or French artillery observation but within German view. The observers themselves were to be back from the line so as to be able to direct German fire with coolness and circumspection.[32]

This was an admirable concept of elastic in-depth warfare, which favored independent action and granted an unusual amount of flexibility within the wider context of operational decisions. With it came organizational changes, which were combined with a far-reaching reform of training outlined in the "Orders Concerning the Training of Infantry during the Current War" of January 1917.[33] Individual and small-group training was strengthened, and exercises with automatic weapons were emphasized. Mechanical drill, for over two centuries the mainstay of military training, was largely abolished. Even the command to "present arms" and the goose step were cut from the training program. Military socialization turned into battle-oriented, on-the-job training that stressed fitness as well as coordination and cooperation within and between military units.[34]

Although the military value of the German defense-in-depth is well understood, its essence and consequences are little appreciated.[35] The German staff system and its openness to debate and innovation, the

---

[32] Hew Strachan, *European Armies and the Conduct of War* (London, 1983), 140.

[33] Timothy T. Lupfer, *The Dynamics of Doctrine: The Changes in German Tactical Doctrine during the First World War* (Ford Leavenworth, Kans., 1981); for a contemporary account see Friedrich Lossberg, *Meine Tätigkeit im Weltkriege 1914-1918* (Berlin, 1939).

[34] Hans-Ludger Borgert, "Grundzüge der Landkriegführung von Schlieffen bis Guderian," *Deutsche Militärgeschichte 1648-1939*, ed. Militärgeschichtliches Forschungsamt (repr. Herrsching, 1983), 9:517-18.

[35] Friedrich Seesselberg, *Der Stellungskrieg 1914-1918* (Berlin, 1926); L. Loizeau, *Succès stratégiques, succès tactiques* (Paris, 1931); P. Lucas, *L'évolution des idées tactiques* (Paris, 1923); S. Pagano, *Evoluzione della tattica durante la grande guerra* (Torino, 1929); Neame, *German Strategy*.

radical reorganization of the chain of command with its emphasis on commanders in the battle zone and on the infantry division as the basic tactical unit, the independence of the infantry combat group with its eight to eleven men led by a noncommissioned officer—all were important and admirable.[36] But it is a different matter to appreciate the social and institutional meaning of what happened when discipline and military socialization were rebuilt around weapons skills and performance; when formal hierarchies were dissolved in favor of functional commands in the battle zone; and when captains wrote manuals for generals. What happened?

The restructuring effort for defensive warfare implied nothing less than the displacement of the well-tried hierarchical control of men over men in favor of a functional organization of violence. In the newly emerging field army the optimal use of weapons alone shaped command and deployment. The use of weapons even organized the coordination and cooperation among units. The Supreme Command's reforms amounted to a comprehensive effort to "rationalize" warfare much in the same way that German industry "rationalized" production. The substitution of machines for men forced the adaptation of the army to the handling of "war machines." The shift from hierarchical structures to functional ones was a drastic, even revolutionary step, because it shed more than a century of military traditions within half a year. The Supreme Command began to approach operations in terms of "tasks" and available "resources," assessing units according to their weapons capabilities. Battle plans were drawn up accordingly, stressing the capabilities of the assembled weaponry rather than specific principles of strategy. The optimal use of weapons, instead of the "art" or "science" of military leadership, was seen as guaranteeing military victory. *Material* won out over *Geist* as the contemporary debate put it—or more precisely: technical and instrumental rationality replaced the remnants of a holistic approach to the conduct of war. Operational planning and strategy became a matter of the management of arms. It is this system that made Ludendorff and the Third Supreme Command into the most radical exponents of machine-culture in the military.[37]

In view of the predilection for technological arguments in military writing ever since World War I, it may be useful to discuss briefly the differences between the German, French, and British war experience. All three, of course, engaged in a war of matériel. In fact, after overcoming

---

[36] Helmuth Gruss, *Die deutschen Sturmbataillone im Weltkrieg: Aufbau und Verwendung* (Berlin, 1939); Balck, *Entwicklung der Taktik*; Seesselberg, *Stellungskrieg*, with detailed discussions; see also Lupfer, *Dynamics of Doctrine*, for a summary statement.

[37] See Ludendorff's own assessment in *Kriegserinnerungen*, 214.

the initial munitions crisis, the two Allies gained and retained a distinct edge over Germany in this respect. They were able to pour more matériel into battle than Germany. However, we are not concerned here with the number and the quality of weapons and the stockpiles of ammunition that each nation was able to send to the front. The main difference consisted in the way these means of industrial warfare were used. The French and the British leadership resisted the development of new forms of tactics and organization of forces. They fought industrial war in the tradition of European land warfare and put a premium on maintaining this tradition—at a very high price for their soldiers and their nations. The German leadership, on the other hand, actively engaged in a search for new ways to use force that was calibrated to the means of industrial war.

On a more speculative plane one might venture an explanation of these differences. It appears first of all that the Allies continued through-out the war to fight a war of "abundance," even if that abundance was increasingly borrowed from overseas—not just from the United States, but from the Commonwealth and the colonies as well. Germany, on the other hand, fought a war of increasing "scarcity" after the initial attempt at Verdun to outproduce and outkill the enemy had failed. Ludendorff's answer to this situation was the optimization of the available means. Efficiency was achieved in a social, rather than a technical, reorganization of the use of force; that is, an army reform rather than a procurement revolution. This, it might be added, is quite a curious choice, considering the tremendous advances of German industry over the previous decades. It points to the fact that "scarcity" and "abundance" alone do not suffice to explain the German and Allied responses to the war of matériel. It seems that the German military was locked into a procurement system, centered around heavy industry, that was hostile to new weapons systems like tanks and their producers, the "new" capital goods industries. It proved to be easier to change the army than to crack open the system of weapons procurement. The British took exactly the opposite course. It appears that they used technological innovation, tank warfare, in order to bypass a reform of the structure and use of the main bulk of the fighting forces and to preserve the existing hierarchies within the army. Both choices, in other words, indicate "frictions" in warfare that were no longer limited to the armed forces but pertained to the whole nation in arms.

In no country, however, was the military leadership greatly con-cerned with what troubled their nations most. The terrible carnage of the Great War obsessed its survivors and the popular mind in general. This sparked protest during the war and nourished pacifist sentiments in the interwar years. Not a single book in the genre of war literature failed to address this issue, and the national responses accurately reflected the kinds of armies nations had sent to their deaths. The French mourned the exhaustion of their *pays*, the loss of life in rural and provincial France; the Germans remembered their "men of steel," the increasingly proletarian and urban armies that fought and died between 1917 and 1918; and the British commemorated the "lost generation" of young men of the middle- and upper-classes. During the war military leaders were less concerned with the carnage than with the operationally useless waste of soldiers. More discipline and order to counter the cataclysmic aspects of industrial war were the French and the British answers to the search for a better use of their human material—perhaps appropriate to the kind of recruits they sent into battle. A more machine-oriented behavior was the German response, and it fit the kind of soldier whom the German army increasingly conscripted. None of these changes dramatically reduced casualties, but all of them gave death and destruction a more purposeful appearance. Verdun and the Somme were not repeated, but the subsequent battles are not memorable for being more humane. They were simply more directed and purpose-oriented on all levels. Thus the devaluation of life was a universal phenomenon; the difference lay in what life was deflated to. French and British soldiers became human sacrifices on the altar of the nation or tragic losses in the rebuilding of civilian life. In Germany soldiers became appendices to anonymous machines of war (Remarque and Renn) or conversely their skilled and proud craftsmen (E. Jünger). The war of matériel affected nations differently, because the practice of war—its sociology and political economy—reflected different national modes of mobilizing society and economy and of organizing the use of force. This was the "friction" of war underneath the surface of a universal expansion of force and violence.

The German transition to a military machine-culture, which by 1945 was accepted by all armies, brought to an end a century of land warfare. The formation of a military machine-culture and the instrumental organization of units undermined the very essence of the Prusso-German military institution and profession, traditionally based on uniformity, hierarchy, and subordination. It altered the way battles were fought and armies were organized, and created a new kind of military leader, who developed the laws of operations from the available means rather than deriving them from eternal and scientific laws of operational knowledge about war and leadership. The "strategist" became the supreme organizer of weapons—or, to use the role model of the time, he turned into an engineer.

The Third Supreme Command recognized that its reforms had far-reaching consequences for the relations between army and society and were, indeed, only made possible by the reshaping of these relations. Machine warfare forced the loose nexus between military organization and operation on the one hand and industrial and popular mobilization on the other into a tight and functional linkage. Machine warfare was only possible with the systematic organization of economic resources and national manpower reserves. "The more the army demanded, the more the home front had to give, the greater was the task of the government and of the war ministry."[38] Plans for a dictatorship were discussed in political, military, and industrial circles for a long time, but the Third Supreme Command's growing role in politics, its "silent dictatorship," was only indirectly linked to them.[39] The former aimed at the protection of the elite status of aristocracy, industry, and agriculture against popular insurgence; the latter aimed at the total organization of society and economy for the purpose of war. As Ludendorff stated after the war, the producers and organizers of weapons ruled this kind of warfare state as the supreme managers of power and domination.[40] The army reforms of 1916 dovetailed with the demand for rule by the experts of production and destruction that now encompassed the whole nation.

The Supreme Command was especially aware of the intramilitary consequences that the organizational reform implied. The new Principles and their application gave unprecedented freedom of action to soldiers and noncommissioned officers, and an extraordinary independence to the lower echelons of front officers. "Tactics became ever more individualized. It was a risky undertaking to demand higher standards from the lower officers down to the last man, especially if one considers the decline in training of officers, NCOs, and soldiers and the concomitant lowering of discipline."[41] The Principles could be "dangerous," if applied at the wrong place; only those troops who were imbued with "complete dedication and true discipline" could fulfill the demand.[42] Here another nexus, the one between popular and army morale, became a tight linkage. The new practice of war depended more than ever on high army morale, which in turn depended on popular sentiments. Consequently the Third Supreme Command stepped up its propaganda efforts inside and outside of the army, and intensified censorship and criminal proceedings under

[38] Ibid., 215.

[39] Martin Kitchen, *The Silent Dictatorship: The Politics of the German High Command under Hindenburg and Ludendorff, 1916-1918* (London and New York, 1976).

[40] This is the main message of Erich Ludendorff, *Kriegführung und Politik* (Berlin, 1922) and idem, *Der totale Krieg* (Munich, 1935).

[41] Ludendorff, *Kriegserinnerungen*, 307.

[42] Ibid.

the law of siege.[43] Machine warfare was fought best by soldiers fortified by propaganda and backed up by an ideologically unified nation. The propagandistic mobilization of society as well as indoctrination in the army facilitated efficiency-oriented war.[44] In the eyes of the Supreme Command, machine war and ideological mobilization complemented each other.

In retrospect we might conclude that there was no necessary or automatic linkage between national mobilization and technocratic dictatorship—in any case, a technocratic military dictatorship—just as there is very little proof that ideological commitment, especially of the right-radical and nationalist type that was propagated by the Supreme Command, improved unit cohesion. But that is not the main point. Rather the efficiency-oriented program of the Third Supreme Command, in facilitating a more optimal use of force, dissolved traditional forms of control and, with them, the professional autonomy of the military. This was reason enough for serious concern; machine warfare reshaped the tenuous balance between domination and subordination within the military, and national mobilization restructured the relations between classes, between city and countryside, and between regions in Germany.[45] It made military leadership more vulnerable and authority more uncertain. Most of all, it brought an end to the government of military notables. The military leadership had to come to terms with mass involvement in war, not only because more and more people were sucked into the war machine, but also because control over the use of force no longer lay exclusively with military command and control. Soldiers fought their own war within general guidelines, industry produced weapons according to its own rationale, and social mobilization for war was fraught with all the class and regional tensions that characterized Germany during the Wilhelmine period.[46] Strategy mediated between these elements and gave them purpose and direction; it extended both inward to the nation and outward against the enemy. It became a political act, and since it was denied any organized political expression, it surfaced as the ideology of mobilization and the technocratic use of force. Both were forms of strat-

[43] Wilhelm Deist, comp., *Militär und Innenpolitik im Weltkrieg 1914-1918* (Düsseldorf, 1970), vol. 2, esp. 7, doc. #328, 331.

[44] Erich Ludendorff, ed., *The General Staff and Its Problems* (New York, 1927), 2:385-400. Hans-Dieter Fischer, ed., *Pressekonzentration und Zensurpraxis im Ersten Weltkrieg* (Berlin, 1973).

[45] Gerald D. Feldman, *Army, Industry, and Labor in Germany, 1914-1918* (Princeton, 1966); H. Schäffer, *Regionale Wirtschaftspolitik in der Kriegswirtschaft: Staat, Industrie und Verbände in Baden* (Stuttgart, 1981).

[46] David Blackbourne and Geoffrey Eley, *The Peculiarities of German History: Bourgeois Society and Politics in 19th-Century Germany* (Oxford and New York, 1984); Hans-Ulrich Wehler, *Krisenherde des Kaiserreichs 1871-1918* (Göttingen, 1970).

egy that did not acknowledge its political aspects and reserved the control of war for military managers.

During its preparations for the defensive battles in 1917 the Supreme Command began to realize that it had miscalculated Germany's military situation.[47] Hindenburg and Ludendorff could see no way of knocking France out and had to acknowledge that time favored the Allies. Britain and the Atlantic harbors of France continued to be the major conduits for matériel from overseas and Russia threatened to mobilize yet another mass army, perhaps better armed with Allied help while Germany's forces were depleted in the defensive struggles at the western front. Of course, Hindenburg and Ludendorff could have chosen to join the Reichstag in new efforts to bring about peace, but they rejected this option and clung more tightly to the notion of victory at any price. The first casualty of this insistence was strategy as the principled analysis of war.

In rejecting strategy in this sense, the Supreme Command proceeded along two paths. On the one hand, it diversified and expanded the understanding of what constituted a decision-oriented use of force by introducing indirect means of warfare against the morale and the social fabric of Allied nations. On the other hand, it dissolved the instrumental nexus between means and ends that had guided "idealist" strategy and the utilitarian approach to limiting warfare in the nineteenth century. The new "strategy" expanded war beyond the confines of the military institution and provided a rationale for national mobilization. Strategy lost its instrumental character and became an explanation and legitimation for total war. The Supreme Command ended up with reinterpreting power politics in terms of racial or *völkisch* antagonisms. War became truly total once it was seen as an ideological and cultural clash (*Kulturkrieg*) between mobilized nations whose goal was national-racial survival through the subordination of other nations.[48]

Let us turn to the expansion of warfare first. While the Supreme Command modernized and reconcentrated the war effort of the German army on the western front against France, the major Continental rival, it stepped up efforts against Great Britain and Russia as well. Both remained largely invulnerable to direct attack. Yet they formed the backbone of the Continental fighting power of the Allies as seemingly inexhaustible suppliers of men and matériel, and in this respect reflected the changing conditions of international relations. Against Britain and Russia novel means of warfare had to be employed. The indirect approach

[47] Ludendorff, *Kriegserinnerungen*, 240-57.

[48] H. Kellermann, ed., *Der Krieg der Geister* (Dresden, 1915); Cincinnatus, *Der Krieg der Worte* (Stuttgart, 1916); Klaus Schwabe, *Wissenschaft und Kriegsmoral: Die deutschen Hochschullehrer und die politischen Grundfragen des Ersten Weltkrieges* (Göttingen, 1969).

against Britain entailed unrestricted submarine warfare with the goal of cutting Britain off from world markets, its empire, and the United States. This was pressed upon a hesitant Bethmann Hollweg as the only means to defeat Britain, and with its introduction into the ensemble of forces the era of battle- and decision-oriented land warfare came to an end.[49] Equally important was the attempt to step up the war against Russia by fomenting domestic unrest aimed at limiting the Russian capacity to mobilize and support troops. This approach was not planned or executed in systematic fashion or on a grand scale, but it is worth noting both because the element of social war was to grow in importance throughout the twentieth century, and because it effectively ended the era of institutionally contained warfare between armed forces.[50] The dimensions of European warfare were significantly expanded.

The calculus of using force underwent drastic changes with this shift. Operations were now guided by the sense that "more is better," the belief that the optimal and unrestricted use of all possible means of warfare was now necessary to break the enemy—an essentially opportunistic view, based on the hope that more and more force would eventually somehow create a situation that could be exploited for a final and annihilating blow. An expansive and escalating use of force, rather than its concentration and limitation, would ensure victory, according to the Supreme Command's strategic logic. It is at this point that managerial organization of violence and unlimited warfare came together.[51] War was now fought by deliberately intensifying the use of force—an approach whose solution differed from nation to nation.[52] Germany's answer throughout the next thirty years lay in producing more of its best weapons and mobilizing more of its skilled manpower resources rather than in

---

[49] Karl Birnbaum, *Peace Moves and U-Boat Warfare* (Stockholm, 1958); Bernhard Kaulisch, *Die Auseinandersetzungen um den uneingeschränkten U-Boot-Krieg innerhalb der herrschenden Klasse Deutschlands während des Ersten Weltkrieges* (diss., Humboldt University, Berlin/GDR, 1970); Lancelot L. Farrar, Jr., *Divide and Conquer: German Efforts to Conclude a Separate Peace, 1914-1918* (New York, 1978), 72-84.

[50] Fritz Fischer, "Deutsche Kriegsziele, Revolutionierung und Separatfrieden im Osten 1914-1918," *Historische Zeitschrift* 188 (1959), 249-310.

[51] I will call this process the "strategy of escalatory warfare" as opposed to the "professional" strategy of limiting war. See in this context the discussion of Erich Marcks, *Angriff und Verteidigung im Grossen Kriege* (Berlin, 1923).

[52] Keith Robbins, *The First World War* (Oxford and New York, 1984), 82-103; Strachan, *European Armies*, 130-50. A scholarly analysis of the German choice is missing. Most of the secondary literature is based on Max Schwarte, *Die Technik im Weltkrieg* (Berlin, 1920) and Karl Justrow, *Feldherr und Kriegstechnik* (Oldenburg, 1933). For Great Britain see the detailed study of Shelford Bidwell and Dominick Graham, *Fire Power: British Army Weapons and Theories of War, 1904-1945* (London, 1982). None of these or a host of similar studies considers the political-economic aspects of the change in procurement decisions.

developing new weapons. Strategy turned from an operational calculus of limiting and concentrating the war effort into a rationale for expanding and escalating the use of force.

Escalation of force as the new strategic principle necessitated an intensification of the war effort at home. The Supreme Command quickly instituted an expanded munitions program (*Hindenburg Program*), an economic agency (*Kriegsamt*), which was to coordinate the total mobilization of industry and manpower, and the mobilization of German society for war work (Auxiliary Service Law).[53] Politics became a means to improve "the effectiveness (*Kraft*) of the people through permanent activity."[54] Politics followed strategy as the purpose and meaning of strategy changed. It no longer calculated instrumentally, but sought to inspire and direct people in an unlimited war effort. Propaganda became its principal tool, looming ever larger in the minds of Ludendorff and his coterie in the Supreme Command. Speier has pointed to this fact:

> The most original contribution General Ludendorff made to the theory of war [lay] in the realm of what is often inadequately called "psychological warfare." Ludendorff is almost excessively concerned with the problem of the "cohesion" of the people. . . . He despised and regarded as ineffective, any attempt to achieve social unity by force or drill. Such methods he called "mechanical" or "external." An external unity of the people, achieved by compulsion . . . is not a unity which people and army need in war, but a mechanical phantom dangerous to the government and the state.[55]

Ludendorff condensed the consequence and the meaning of the new approach to strategy in the famous non sequitur: "All theories of Clausewitz have to be thrown overboard. War and politics not only serve the survival of the people, but war is the highest expression of the racial will of life."[56] Escalatory strategy thrived on ideology rather than on instrumental rationality, its aim being to mobilize the nation for unlimited war.

Strategy as a form of social mobilization adjusted goals to means in a peculiar way. Let us recall that idealistic strategy established goals in an intramilitary or civil-military elite discourse.[57] The role of the military staffs consisted in evaluating the availability of means and the costs of achieving these goals. Ideally means were subordinated to goals, in that

[53] See Feldman, *Army, Industry, and Labor* for the most detailed analysis.

[54] Ludendorff, *Kriegserinnerungen*, 349.

[55] Speier, "Ludendorff," 316.

[56] Ludendorff, *Der totale Krieg*, 10; see also idem, *Kriegführung und Politik*, 23.

[57] On the inverse relation between goals and means in escalatory warfare, see Ludendorff, *Kriegführung und Politik*, 10-23; Andreas Hillgruber, *Deutschlands Rolle in der Vorgeschichte der beiden Weltkriege* (Göttingen, 1967), 58-67.

general staffs ascertained the marginal utility of each new increment of violence and established a balance between goals (expected benefits of an operation or campaign) and means (the resources necessary to achieve the goal). Strategy as a form of social mobilization (and soon as a form of technical mobilizaton of industrial forces of destruction, which has reached its high point in the nuclear age) proceeded to turn this calculus on its head. The mobilization of means began to determine the goals of war in a more complex and—in view of idealistic strategy—perverse equation. At its core was the technical (and soon economic) calculation of the marginal utility of weapons. The availability of weapons and resources, however, was no longer determined in a debate over goals, but by the ability of the military and political leadership to mobilize the nation, that is, society and industry. The limits of this process, which now became the process of strategic planning, were defined by social resistance—how much can society take?—and by the industrial apparatus—how much can industry produce without endangering reproduction? Goals were adjusted to the degree of mobilization. The more society and industry were mobilized, the more encompassing became the goals. Total mobilization, as Ludendorff put it in his postwar writing, required total goals, that is, a war à outrance. This was not just a more intensely fought war, but a war that could end only with the *Niederwerfung* of the enemy nation as a whole, the actual subjugation of enemy societies and their complete and unconditional surrender to the will of the victorious nation(s) in arms. Gone were the days of princely and mercantilistic aggrandizement and of the balance-of-power considerations in which territories and people were the bargaining chips in an all-European power game. Total war and its strategy of social mobilization only knew antagonism and the murderous clash of armed camps—the unconditional antagonism between *Freund* and *Feind*, as the self-acclaimed theoretician of a postaristocratic and postbourgeois totalitarian age, Carl Schmitt, elaborated in the interwar years.

The ramifications of this strategy of social mobilization can be detected in the evolution of the war-aims debate in Germany during the First World War. Not only did the radical pan-German war aims gain new adherents, who transformed pan-German splinter groups into the quickest-growing mass movement of the war, centered in the Vaterlandspartei and the Kyffhäusser-Bund; the more intense the effort of mobilization and its concomitant political struggles, the more elaborate and encompassing—the more "total"—became the objectives of the German war effort. In 1918 the debate had reached an all-time high with goals far more expansionist and total—demanding the subjugation of nations rather than the "mere" acquisition of territory and resources—than in

1914, coupled with equally far-reaching ideas about social and national purification. These war aims stood in sharp contrast to a deteriorating military situation. In fact, the more precarious the military situation, the more radical and encompassing the war aims.

This paradox was unthinkable to idealistic strategy, with its marginal-utility calculus of violence. Idealistic strategy would have counseled the limitation and scaling down of goals in an increasingly desperate military situation. Escalatory strategy, however, discarded this central calculus of limited and professional war. It subordinated goals to the mobilization of means, independent of the actual military use-value of each new increment of force. "Strategy" thus thrived on the escalatory mobilization and use of force and, in this process, lost its instrumental significance. This strategy, no doubt, was "rational" and "logical" in its own right, in that it put the capability and degree of social mobilization at the center of its strategic calculus, but it differed radically from what had been considered the "art" and "science" of military leadership in the post-Napoleonic era. It escalated rather than limited war in a military effort that concentrated on the management of weapons and demanded unlimited disposal over the resources of nations.

The new measures of defensive warfare helped to blunt the Allied offensives of 1917, but the costs of tactical and operational opportunism and technocratic mobilization grew faster than the benefits. The use of unrestricted submarine warfare drew the United States into the war, thus expanding the resources of the Allies rather than diminishing them. At the same time, social war against Russia was successful only on the surface. The October revolution freed units in the east and for the first time gave the German army an advantage on the western front. However, the Third Supreme Command was now also forced to cope with a revolutionary government in Russia that was radically opposed to all the Supreme Command stood for and made no bones about intervening with demands for immediate peace. At the same time the political costs of the escalating war effort rose quickly. Economic and social mobilization polarized Germany to an unprecedented degree. In the defensive battles of 1917 the performance of the new army was paid for by the whittling away of the very foundations on which it had been built.

This deterioration of the overall military situation while the performance of the field army and the output in weapons were improving somehow had to be explained to the German people. How was it possible that the more the nation invested in the war effort the less it achieved? The Third Supreme Command found an answer in blaming workers, the bourgeoisie, women, intellectuals, universities, homosexuals, and youth, and increasingly turned its own lack of comprehension of what was happening into venomous attacks against a "Jewish conspiracy" eating away at the vitals of the German army.[58] Radical nationalists lost interest in even the most ambitious territorial goals as the war became for them a struggle for the liberation of the German race from evil. Germany began to cross over into apocalyptic war.[59]

It is not by chance that Colonel Max Bauer, one of the coolest of the technocrats and the Supreme Headquarters' most effective link with industry, was one of the most insistent and poisonous of these ideologues.[60] The efficiency-oriented officers of the Third Supreme Command knew no limits in their quest for the optimal use of force. They escalated the national war effort in their search for victory, always conceived to be as absolute as the war effort itself. The escalatory strategy guided a war that was shaped in equal measure by rational organization (*Planmässigkeit*) and by the general lack of ideas (*Ideenlosigkeit*).[61] This was the basis for military paranoia in the machine age.

Although the Third Supreme Command could not explain and never tried to understand the deterioration of the military situation, the leading officers recognized that the odds had turned against them. Aware that the German army was incapable of holding out for another year under the pressures of defensive warfare, and that a negotiated peace would have a politically dangerous effect on public opinion indoctrinated in the certainty of total victory, Ludendorff chose the only viable alternative, a "quick decision" on the western front. This assault, the "most difficult operation in world history," would make or break imperial Germany.[62] It began as a gamble and ended by, in Friedrich Engels's words, "Throwing power into the street."

As earlier in defensive warfare, the tactical and operational ideas for a breakthrough accumulated slowly. They all reaffirmed the efficiency of machine-based warfare with its many independent bases of fire. The various elements were brought together in new guidelines, a manual called "Attack in Position Warfare," which emphasized surprise combined with searching out the weakest points of the enemy, the use of speed and deep

[58] Abraham J. Peck, *Radicals and Reactionaries: The Crisis of Conservatism in Wilhelmine Germany* (Washington, D.C., 1978), 215.

[59] Once again it should be noted that apocalyptic wars are not necessarily wars of total destruction, but wars that "follow technical [or instrumental] rationality without following any [substantive] rational goal" (Jünger, *Perfektion der Technik*, 189).

[60] Martin Kitchen, "Militarism and the Development of Fascist Ideology: The Political Ideas of Colonel Max Bauer, 1916-1918," *Central European History* 8 (1975), 199-220; Adolf Vogt, *Oberst Max Bauer: Generalstabsoffizier im Zwielicht, 1869-1929* (Osnabrück, 1974).

[61] Jünger, *Perfektion der Technik*, 184.

[62] Ludendorff, *Kriegserinnerungen*, p. 434, 435; Reichsarchiv, ed., *Die Kriegführung im Frühjahr 1917*, vol. 12 of *Der Weltkrieg 1914-1918* (Berlin, 1939), 560-89.

penetration, and the tactical exploitation of advantages. The military practitioners began to take a serious look at ways to escape the rigidity of trench warfare.[63]

Yet these innovative techniques were largely invalidated by the inability to define a purpose for the campaign. Various offensive plans were discussed, but there is no indication of a debate on any objective except that of a breakthrough.[64] After the war, this led to two kinds of criticism: that Ludendorff did not escape attrition warfare after all, or that he was somehow overwhelmed by the task. Neither is very convincing, because both arguments overlook the state of "strategy" in 1917-18. Calculated operations were the victim of the discrepancy between ideologized strategic intent and the performance-oriented use of force, and this made clear formulation of an objective impossible. Here we see the operational costs of escalatory warfare in glaring light. The Supreme Command was unable to define the purpose of action except in tactical terms, and thus did not provide direction or leadership. Ludendorff's angry words about this issue can serve both as an epithet for the 1918 campaign as well as a reminder for generations of military technocrats to follow. "I do not want to hear the word operation. We hack a hole [into the front]. The rest comes on its own."[65]

The offensive operations at the western front were merely the core of a sequence of events that neither ended nor started there.[66] The prerequisite for an attack in the West was the collapse of the Russian front and the subsequent expansionist peace in the East. The winter of 1917-18 not only showed the wear and tear of four years of war, but was also the high point of social and ideological mobilization and an expansionist strategy.[67] Never before in war had so many troops been concentrated for a single operation; never before had so much firepower been amassed; and although German society was more polarized than ever, the *Siegfrieden* faction was in control, sweeping the moderates in parliament and

---

[63] Summaries in Lupfer, *Dynamics of Doctrine*, 37-54; Messenger, *Art of Blitzkrieg*, 9-29. See also Balck, *Taktik*; Gruss, *Die deutschen Sturmbataillone*; Georg Bruchmüller, *Die Artillerie beim Angriff im Stellungskrieg* (Berlin, 1926).

[64] K. Krafft von Delmensingen, *Der Durchbruch: Studie an Hand der Vorgänge des Weltkrieges 1914-1918* (Hamburg, 1937), 132-85; Wallach, *Dogma der Vernichtungsschlacht*, 271-88.

[65] Rupprecht von Bayern, *Mein Kriegstagebuch* (Berlin, 1929), 2:372; Hindenburg, *Aus meinem Leben*, 233-44; C. Barnett, *The Swordbearers: Studies in Supreme Command* (London, 1963), 282.

[66] Martin Middlebrook, *The Kaiser's Battle* (London, 1978); Reichsarchiv, ed., *Die Kriegführung an der Westfront im Jahre 1918*, vol. 14 of *Der Weltkrieg 1914-1918* (1944 [Berlin, 1956]).

[67] Peck, *Radicals and Reactionaries*, 203-221; Jürgen Kocka, *Klassengesellschaft im Kriege: Deutsche Sozialgeschichte 1914-1918* (Göttingen, 1973).

containing opposition in increasingly militant fashion. There were premonitions of a revolution, but there were equally strong signs of a right-radical dictatorship with a mass basis. The vision of prosperity and surplus coming from the occupied East was mixed with an explosive anti-Bolshevism and anti-Semitism.

When defeat in the west brought these hopes crashing down, the militant movements created by the war did not stop dead on November 11, 1918. Rather militant mobilization turned both inward and outward. While German troops began their retreat on the western front in the summer of 1918, they advanced in Russia in a move that eventually led them to the Caucasus. This movement outlasted the armistice with the Allies and extended into 1919. The troops in the East, cut off from defeated Germany, transformed themselves into armed bands that lived off the land.[68] Thus in its last stages, the war turned into a crusade in which German troops fought for land and at the same time waged an ideological and racist campaign against Russians and Bolsheviks. In 1919-20 they carried their militant ideology and their *völkisch* practice of war back to Germany.[69]

Meanwhile bitterness on the home front turned into revolt against the war and revolution against its leaders. The year 1919 saw a sweeping militarization of social relations in Germany. It was not just the army, the free corps, and workers who armed. The whole nation—civil authorities of all kinds, city halls, social groups, gangs—acquired weapons. The military monopoly of violence was shattered. What was left of the army—essentially the superstructure of the general staff—was embroiled in the same kind of protective armaments.[70] Wilhelm Groener, the successor of Ludendorff in the last months of the war, was a *Feldherr* without troops; Friedrich Ebert, the new chancellor, a political leader without authority. The war-induced social movements had successfully eroded and paralyzed the militant state and its military institutions. The power of the state all but collapsed.

Both outward thrust and inward convulsion bore little similarity to

---

[68] Dominique Venner, *Baltikum: Dans le Reich de la défaite: Le combat du Corps-Francs, 1918-1923* (Paris, 1974); Rüdiger von der Goltz, *Als politischer General im Osten*, 2d ed. (Leipzig, 1936). Kurt Fischer, *Deutsche Truppen und Entente-Intervention in Südrussland 1918/19* (Boppard, 1973).

[69] James Diehl, *Paramilitary Politics in Weimar Germany* (Bloomington, 1977), 75-116. Bernhard Thoss, *Der Ludendorff-Kreis 1919-1923: München als Zentrum der mitteleuropäischen Gegenrevolution zwischen Revolution und Hitler-Putsch* (Munich, 1978).

[70] Erwin Könnemann, *Einwohnerwehren und Zeitfreiwilligenverbände: Ihre Funktion beim Aufbau eines neuen imperialistischen Militärsystems 1918-1920* (Berlin/GDR, 1971); Michael Geyer, "Military Work, Civil Order, Militant Politics: The German Military Experience 1914-1945" Woodrow Wilson Center, ISSP Working Paper no. 39 (Washington, D.C., 1982), 34-36.

organized military campaigns, even though the military leadership played an important role in both. And yet they were part of the war effort. These two movements reflected and expressed the polar mobilization of German society in the Third Supreme Command's quest for victory and the national and ideological mobilization of the European people against each other. Mobilization for and against war petered out due to sheer exhaustion rather than turning into domestic stability.

Domestic developments were paralleled on the international level where armistices and peace were eventually concluded, but eastern Europe and the Near East never quieted down. The war led into the postwar wars—on a smaller scale in the ambushes along the German and Austrian borders, on a larger scale in the Russo-Polish war with its revolutionary and counterrevolutionary overtones, and on an apocalyptic level in the massacres in Turkey. Indeed, it was only when the Soviet Union's efforts wore thin because of internal chaos and when the counterrevolutionary thrust was brought under control in Germany—eastern European and Turkish ambitions being frustrated by social and economic difficulties— that the war of militant social movements, the last stage of World War I, died down. After some years of calm, it regained national and international momentum and linked up with the renewed social mobilization of the 1930s.

III

The primary concern of German military planners in the interwar years was to limit war in order to make it, once again, a purposeful and instrumental use of force on the basis of elite control of strategy.

The planners labored under a particularly restrictive set of conditions. Germany was disarmed and much weaker than any of its potential enemies.[71] At the same time, the planners insisted that they alone were capable of organizing national defense and ensuring German security— a prerequisite for restoring Germany's status in Europe. This problem proved intractable because the international stability of the Continent as a whole and the compromises governing the role of each nation's armed forces depended on Germany being disarmed. Because Europe's affairs were closely linked and national and international politics tended to dovetail, every effort to resolve or control internal dissension in order to fight wars led to renegotiation of all domestic and international arrange-

---

[71] Michael Salewski, *Entwaffnung und Militärkontrolle in Deutschland 1919 bis 1927* (Munich, 1966); Jürgen Heideking, "Vom Versailler Vertrag zur Genfer Abrüstungskonferenz: Das Scheitern der alliierten Militärkontrollpolitik gegenüber Deutschland nach dem Ersten Weltkrieg," *Militärgeschichtliche Mitteilungen* 28 (1980), 45-68.

ments, just as every change in international conditions opened new possibilities and set new limits for the German military effort.

The opportunity that Germany had, in the years 1918-1920, to rethink the role of force in domestic and international relations was never exploited and for the most part was not even recognized. Those who argued in favor of civil defense and organized passive resistance were not heard, even though their arguments were plausible in view of Germany's defenselessness.[72] The officer corps and the civilian leadership of the Weimar Republic emerged from defeat and revolutionary and counter-revolutionary violence with the conviction that military force was necessary, even vital for the survival of the nation.

It was up to the general staff to rebuild the army. This effort was closely associated with Hans von Seeckt, the first *Chef der Heeresleitung* (chief of the Army Command).[73] He sought to reestablish formal authority and discipline in a hierarchical, though expansive and "modernizing," military organization. Discipline and clear lines of command, control and subordination of the too-independent senior commanders, and thorough, skill-oriented training coupled with paternalistic welfare measures for the mass of soldiers became the hallmark of Seeckt's tenure. At the same time, he revived theoretical and practical training in grand strategy and in tactics for a large army. He generally favored modernization and mechanization, but subordinated these elements to a professional approach in the German military tradition.

Seeckt had to cope with two minority factions within the army leadership. One of them pleaded for the preparation of a nationalist war of liberation, reviving and mythologizing the Prussian tradition of rising against Napoleon, and, like the army reformers of that period, throwing the army wide open to popular forces.[74] This faction, led by Joachim von Stülpnagel and Werner von Blomberg, depreciated the primacy of institutionalized warfare and was willing to rethink all aspects of war. It focused on harnessing the powers of society, the "will" of the nation, and all of its productive forces. The other faction was very small and relied on its leverage over the politics of the Reichswehr. Its leader became

[72] Wolfgang Sternstein, "Der Ruhrkampf," in *Gewaltloser Widerstand gegen Aggressoren*, ed. A. Roberts (Göttingen, 1971), pp. 50-86; see also the memorandum of State Secretary Hamm of May 14-15, in Karl-Heinz Harbeck, comp., *Das Kabinett Cuno, 22 November 1922-12 August 1923* (Boppard, 1968), 260-61; Hermann Oncken, *Über das politische Motiv der deutschen Sicherheit in der europäischen Geschichte* (Berlin, 1926); and the little pamphlet by Carl Mertens, *Reichswehr oder Landesverteidigung* (Wiesbaden, 1926).

[73] Hans Meier-Welcker, *Seeckt* (Frankfurt, 1967); F. von Rabenau, *Seeckt: Aus seinem Leben* (Leipzig, 1940).

[74] Helm Speidel, *1813/1814: Eine militärpolitische Untersuchung* (Diss. phil., University of Tübingen, 1924).

Kurt von Schleicher, though its basic outlook was developed by Wilhelm Groener. This group insisted that a new army could only be rebuilt on the basis of a solid economic recovery that forged a new unity and a new cohesion of the nation. Schleicher and Groener increasingly shifted to an internationalist position and by 1924 had concluded that a military recovery of Germany—the reconstruction of a German army as well as of a German strategy—depended on American financial initiative.[75] As opposed to the military populists who emphasized operational and organizational reforms, they stressed the need to rethink strategy in the light of an expanding notion of power politics.

Seeckt's own concepts captivated the great majority of the military. His ideas also conformed to the insistence of German political and industrial elites that violence had to be monopolized and institutionalized in the state, and that social relations had to be demilitarized in order to overcome the revolutionary and counterrevolutionary insurgence from Left and Right. But Seeckt's strategic thinking never conformed to European realities. His operational doctrines posited an army that did not exist, and his hope of reconstituting an orthodox army was always chimerical. Despite efforts at modernization, rigidity and inflexibility characterized the internal practice of the Reichswehr. A gerontocracy ran its main offices. To quote an opponent of this regime, the army leadership produced "beautifully written" manuals, ideal for "training the leaders for a new war with the means of 1914," but these means were gone.[76] Seeckt envisioned an alliance with the Soviet Union against an all-European coalition, which was plausible in the thinking of power politics, but unrealistic in postwar Europe. In short, Seeckt moved to the very fringes of domestic and international affairs in order to reconstitute the autonomy and unequivocal identity of the army.[77]

It was a gamble that he lost. When French and Belgian forces occupied the Ruhr area in 1923, the army's ties with the Soviet Union proved ineffective, political and military unrest mounted, and French superiority made the concepts of grand strategy worthless. Worst of all, serious planning for mobilization in 1923 very quickly showed that

[75] Dorothea Fensch and Olaf Gröhler, "Imperialistische Ökonomie und militärische Strategie: Eine Denkschrift Wilhelm Groeners," *Zeitschrift für Geschichtswissenschaft* 19 (1971), 1167-77.

[76] Michael Geyer, *Aufrüstung oder Sicherheit: Reichswehr in der Krise der Machtpolitik 1924-1936* (Wiesbaden, 1980), 81.

[77] Hans Gatzke, *Stresemann and the Rearmament of Germany* (Baltimore, 1954); Heinz Hürten, comp., *Das Krisenjahr 1923: Militär und Innenpolitik 1923-1924* (Düsseldorf, 1980). The point here is that significant groups within German society supported Seeckt, but the option of "national recovery" through alliance warfare neither fit the national nor the international conditions.

Seeckt's own plans and concepts were based on unsound assumptions and inflated estimates. His belief that the Reichswehr could control social unrest without jeopardizing its own standards and discipline, could shape politics without getting involved in the contradictions of political affairs, and could induce German industry and conservatives to forsake Western capital in favor of an uncertain military future all proved to be mistaken. The very assumptions on which this army had been rebuilt and its strategy formulated were unrealistic. It was impossible to construct an autonomous army outside of domestic and international affairs. Seeckt had hoped to use the national and international forces that were opposed to the postwar status quo only to discover that the army could not control them.

Still, Seeckt's program remained compelling, even though it solved none of Germany's military problems, because military orthodoxy promised autonomy for the military caste, formulated an impressive body of "strategic" knowledge that gave the military exclusive control over warfare, and guaranteed limitation and control of war through decisive military action. Its evident appeal survived Seeckt himself, because as much as Reichswehr officers wanted to be able to wage war, most of them first and foremost wanted to fight it on their own terms.

It was only after a series of very tense internal and political conflicts that the Reichswehr began to turn away from the mirage of military power politics and to pursue a radically different course of planning for present contingencies and future war. Operational planning and strategic thinking made a quantum leap, first by embracing the possibilities of a people's war (*Volkskrieg*) as well as mobile warfare with tanks and subsequently by developing notions of strategic deterrence. Alternative operational practices replaced Seecktian notions of an autonomous army and traditional power politics and a strategy developed that had little in common with the old designs. Although the proponents of these new ideas never challenged the principles of war and continued to emphasize expert control over strategy, they suggested a radical and creative "retranslation" of these principles under current and future conditions of warfare.[78]

Officers in the operational section of the Truppenamt, the general staff, under Stülpnagel, were the main instigators of the first wave of reforms, centering around *Volkskrieg* and mobile war. People's war was a "desperate means . . . in a desperate situation," which virtually extinguished the difference between civilians and soldiers and turned "all

---

[78] Geyer, *Aufrüstung oder Sicherheit*, 85.

people and all means . . . into tools of war."[79] German planners counted on weakening and splintering the main thrust of enemy forces by drawing them into "area warfare with extremely deep zones" to a point at which the concentrated and surprising use of even a small counterattacking main force, if appropriately modernized, could make a major difference.[80] It was to be a most brutal kind of warfare that knew no rules and employed terroristic means of execution-style attacks (against enemy commanders as much as against the population), poison gas, kidnapping, flooding, and general destruction of infrastructure—in short, a mixture of terrorism and scorched-earth tactics combined with conventional operations.[81] The enemy thus would be forced "to eat slowly through" Germany.[82] It was a war that, even if it ended in victory, doomed much of the country.

Concurrently and in close connection with efforts to prepare a people's war, the Reichswehr modernized its main force. Mechanization of the army was part of a more encompassing program, and the creation of tank formations was initially a subordinate element in improving overall mobility. But tank warfare became increasingly important, and by 1929, formed the main thrust of army modernization.[83] The organ-

[79] Ibid.; the literature on *Volkskrieg* is still inadequate. Arthur Ehrhardt, *Kleinkrieg: Geschichtliche Erfahrungen und künftige Möglichkeiten* (Potsdam, 1935) is a summary.

[80] Geyer, *Aufrüstung oder Sicherheit*, 86.

[81] The reference to colonial warfare is explicit and frequent. On the formation of exterminist warfare in Germany see Helmut Bley, *Kolonialherrschaft und Sozialstruktur in Deutsch-Südwestafrika 1894-1914* (Hamburg, 1968).

[82] Geyer, *Aufrüstung oder Sicherheit*, 86-87.

[83] On army modernization see the theses of Heinz Sperling, *Die Tätigkeit und Wirksamkeit des Heereswaffenamtes der Reichswehr für die materiell-technische Ausstattung eines 21 Divisionen Heeres 1924-1934* (diss., Pädagogische Hochschule Potsdam, 1980); Manfred Lachmann, *Zum Problem der Bewaffnung des imperialistischen deutschen Heeres 1919-1939* (diss. phil., Leipzig, 1965); R. Barthel, *Theorie und Praxis der Heeresmotorisierung im faschistischen Deutschland bis 1939* (diss. phil., Leipzig, 1967). The problem is to come to terms with the adulation of Guderian in the English literature. Guderian is, at this point, just another general staff officer who supported and, in his special function as officer in the transport section, helped to flesh out a new doctrine of mobile (tank) warfare as a means to overcome the impasse of the *Vernichtungsgedanke* in World War I. Despite Karl J. Walde, *Guderian* (Frankfurt, 1967), Kenneth Macksey, *Guderian: Panzer General* (London, 1975), Dermot Bradley, *Generaloberst Heinz Guderian und die Entstehungsgeschichte des modernen Blitzkrieges* (Osnabrück, 1978), and Walther Nehring, *Die Geschichte der deutschen Panzerwaffe 1916-1945* (Berlin, 1969) there exists no sufficiently empirical study of the development of the tank weapon. The available literature, to the extent that it studies at least some of the available documents, is either embroiled in German intramilitary conflicts, dating back mostly to the discussion over missed chances in World War II rather than to the controversies in 1935-36, or in British debates over the missed chances of army modernization in France and Great Britain. It should be noted that the argument here consists of two parts: (a) the available literature skews the relation between proponents and opponents of tank forces; (b) the concentration on a technological escape from the impasse of World War I reflects an impoverishment of strategic thinking. It shifts from a principled study of war to doctrines concerning the practice of war.

izational and operational outlook for the incipient tank forces was initially shaped by French experience and led to the assessment that "the main purpose of the tank consist[s] in the direct support of the infantry advance."[84] This conclusion quickly changed with the evaluation of English maneuvers with armored forces. By late 1926 a directive set forth that tank units could be separated from a "slowly moving infantry" and that tanks could be best used either in conjunction with "mobile [*schnell bewegliche*] troops or as independent units."[85] This concept of turning either motorized infantry or tank units into the main assault troops of the army was grist to the mill of the operational planners. An army that set a premium on using the few soldiers it had in fighting units abhorred the idea of motorized units as part of the supply train. The turning point came in January 1927, when the operations section under Werner von Fritsch concluded that the principles of tank warfare had to be rethought. "Armored, quickly moving tanks most probably will become the operationally decisive offensive weapon [*schlachtentscheidende Angriffswaffe*]. From an operational perspective this weapon will be most effective, if concentrated in independent units like tank brigades."[86] By 1929 the training section of the Truppenamt under Werner von Blomberg had worked out training schedules for operationally independent tank regiments. The general staff, led by the "Young Turks" around Stülpnagel and Blomberg and supported by specialists like Bockelberg (procurement, weapons development) as well as Heinz Guderian (weapons inspectorate) wholeheartedly embraced the concept of decision-oriented, operationally independent tank warfare.[87]

The state of the art was best summarized in a book-length study on "operational mobility under conditions of material-intensive warfare" by Major von Rabenau.[88] He sought to combine a people's war—what he called the *Krieg der Nadelstiche*—with a highly mobile, mechanized and armored force in a new synthesis. Rabenau still favored a mostly counterforce-oriented attack, but this study, written by the future biog-

[84] See the directive RWM HL IV Nr. 601.26 geh. In6 (K), 10 November 1926; in the Bundesarchiv-Militärarchiv (hereafter cited as BA-MA) RH 39/v.115. [In6 (K) is the weapons inspectorate for motorized troops.]

[85] Ibid.

[86] T1 [Operations Section] 762/27 g. Kdos. II, 5 December 1927 [signed Fritsch]; BA-MA II H 539. In the same document the operations section argues in favor of a step-by-step conversion of motorized units from transportation to fighting units.

[87] The order of batle for (planned) tank regiment is in Chef H1 659/29 geh. T4II, 1 September 1929 [signed Blomberg; T4 is the Training Section]; BA-MA II H 540. The decision in favor of a conversion of motorized troops into fighting units came with the all-important organizational war game of 1928, which tested the needs of the army for the armaments phase in 1928-1933; see the briefing of the senior officers of the 7th (Bavarian) motorized unit, 6 January 1929; BA-MA RH 39/v.294.

[88] Geyer, *Aufrüstung oder Sicherheit*, 93-94.

rapher of Seeckt, shows how far the imagination could stretch in the mid-1920s even among more traditionally inclined officers. The book emphasized the dissolution of front lines as well as the transformation of the offensive thrust into a system of independently operating, continuously moving and shifting units that no longer followed set operational patterns but was characterized by mobility and movement in conjunction with firepower, and by the exploitation of tactical and operational opportunities. In this system of freely moving parts, command and authority began to take a different shape. The main task became coordination through communication rather than actual deployment and direct control of movement.

People's war and mobile, armored attacks were the response of the Young Turks to the discovery that Germany could not act as though nothing had changed since 1914. Yet all came to naught, although not for reasons of institutional sluggishness. The new designs were incompatible with the domestic conditions in Germany. The proposed *levée en masse* and short-term training assumed a cohesion of the nation that did not exist. The class divisions of German society imposed limits on all efforts to create a military *Volksgemeinschaft*.[89] Tank development ran into similar problems. In an army that expected roughly 700 million Reichsmarks but could spend only 450 million for procurement between 1928 and 1932, large-scale mechanization was out of reach. Ideally the weapons inspectorate had planned for six thousand vehicles and eight hundred to one thousand tanks at an initial cost of 3.6 million Reichsmarks for the first preparatory stage, 235 million for the second, and over one billion for the third.[90] The Weimar Republic could not possibly pay for this mechanized army without creating budgetary havoc.

The Young Turks had learned the lesson of 1923 that one had to rely on the existing structure of the Weimar Republic; the republican leaders proved to be accommodating, even eager to embrace what the soldiers had planned.[91] But people's war and army mechanization quickly ran afoul of the obstacles created by pluralist political compromises in a divided society. In order to pursue their goals, the military planners

[89] Michael Geyer, "Der zur Organisation erhobene Burgfrieden," in *Militär und Militarismus in der Weimarer Republik*, ed. Klaus-Jürgen Müller and Eckhard Opitz (Düsseldorf, 1978), 15-100.

[90] Calculations according to the data sheet in HWaA [Army Procurement Office] 588/28 geh. Kdos "z" WiStb, no date [1928]; BA-MA RH8/v.892; concluding remarks of Wehramt 767/30 g. Kdos "z" Wehramt, 23 July 1930; BA-MA RH8/v.906, which slashed procurement to field kitchens and transport vehicles.

[91] Ernst W. Hansen, *Reichswehr und Industrie* (Boppard, 1978); Karl Nuss, *Militär und Wiederaufrüstung in der Weimarer Republik: Zur politischen Rolle und Entwicklung der Reichswehr* (Berlin/GDR, 1977).

had to attack these compromises. In short, military security for Germany was incompatible with the political stability of the Weimar Republic.

The military security of Germany and the maintenance of the country's national and international status quo were mutually exclusive. This was the main lesson of the two major experiments of the 1920s—the traditional approach by Seeckt and the radical departure by Stülpnagel and his associates—in controlling war (always, of course, with the intent to fight it). Once again, this incompatibilty raised the issue whether the purely military path to national security and potential revision of the postwar order was not the wrong approach in the first place. It seemed that German power politics had reached an impasse, and indeed all efforts by Weimar politicians to overcome the status quo within the context of the postwar order were frustrated.[92]

Against growing odds, and faced with the first signs of an incipient economic crisis, a last attempt was made to come to grips with both the German military tradition and the strategic conditions of the postwar world. Groener, known as one of the staunchest supporters of the Schlieffen tradition, proposed a new look at German strategy.[93] His assessment was brief and blunt. Germany possessed neither the society, nor the economy, nor the logistics to contemplate a long, attritional defensive war. In case of war, it had to act quickly and decisively in order to bring the conflict to an end almost before it had started. The Reichswehr could not fight a "real," that is to say, a European war.[94]

The conclusions that Groener and his staff in the Ministeramt, the political office of the Reichswehr, reached were startling. Because there were situations in which Weimar Germany simply could not wage war, it was necessary to avoid them. Such a suggestion could be accepted only because the Young Turks around Stülpnagel in the general staff had hit rock bottom with their own designs. Serious officers that they were, they had put their plans to the test of two war games. The results were devastating. The attacking armies annihilated the German forces in a two-front war, and even a concentrated Polish attack proved to be beyond German capabilities.[95] Although Stülpnagel and Blomberg remained un-

[92] Jon Jacobson, *Locarno Diplomacy: Germany and the West, 1925-1929* (Princeton, 1972). See also Karl H. Pohl, *Weimars Wirtschaft und die Aussenpolitik der Republik 1924-1926* (Düsseldorf, 1979); Martin Enssle, *Stresemann's Territorial Revisionism* (Wiesbaden, 1980).

[93] Wilhelm Groener, *Der Weltkrieg und seine Probleme: Rückschau und Ausblick* (Berlin, 1930); idem, *Das Testament des Grafen Schlieffen* (Berlin, 1927); see the summary in Wallach, *Dogma der Vernichtungsschlacht*, 305-323.

[94] Session of the Mittwochsgesellschaft, 5 November 1930: W. Groener, Die Kriegführung der Zukunft, Bundesarchiv, Kl. Erw. 179-1.

[95] Geyer, *Aufrüstung oder Sicherheit*, 191-95; Gaines Post, Jr., *The Civil-Military Fabric of Weimar Foreign Policy* (Princeton, 1973), 203-238; TA [Truppenamt/General Staff]

convinced by these results, Groener and his political staff concluded that nothing could stave off defeat in a two-front war, and that it was not up to the military profession to propose suicidal operations; the survival of the nation was more important than military predilections.[96] Both Blomberg and Stülpnagel accused Groener of not understanding the nature of power politics, in which each nation had the "duty" to defend itself against "military rape."[97] The Ministeramt countered that these officers neither understood the nature of international affairs in the 1920s, nor German interests, nor the processes of German recovery.

In the Ministeramt's view, there was little chance for war between Germany and France as long as both depended financially on the United States.[98] Among economically strong nations credit was more important than nationalism. Economic recovery under American tutelage, moreover, could become the prerequisite for rearmament without politically disastrous struggles for budgetary redistribution in Germany. Things were quite different with Poland, which in the Ministeramt's view was less well integrated into international networks, more prone to national outbursts, and also formed a more legitimate target for a German attack. A Polish war was the one war that Groener was ready to fight, but to fight it successfully the war had to be scaled down to German capabilities.[99] In the case of Polish border incursions, speed was the decisive element. To this end, a "partly reinforced Reichswehr" needed to be mobilized in 48 hours in order to annihilate the Polish forces in a quick and decisive sweep in the border area.[100] A major attack was a more difficult matter. The preparations for this case, *Fall Pilsudski*, covered both a Polish invasion and an attack by Germany on Poland, "if a favorable political situation should arise"—that is, an internal Polish collapse.[101] Given German inferiority in the face of a direct Polish assault, a straightforward operational response would not suffice, as the war games had shown. Groener argued instead for an expedient in the spirit of Schlieffen, but applied to the conditions of the 1920s. A scenario for conventional deterrence thus emerged.

284/29 g. Kdos., 26 March 1929: "Conclusions from the studies of the general staff in winter 1927/29 and 1928/29"; BA-MA II H 597.

[96] Geyer, *Aufrüstung oder Sicherheit*, 208-209.

[97] TA 284/29 g. Kdos, see ft. 107.

[98] M.A. [Ministeramt] 221/29 W, 22 April 1929; BA-MA II H 597.

[99] Geyer, *Aufrüstung oder Sicherheit*, 209-213; Post, *Civil-Military Fabric*, 101-108.

[100] Post, *Civil-Military Fabric*, 197-98.

[101] "Case Pilsudski" was the fourth "scenario" according to the basic document for mobilization planning of the Reichswehr, RWM 147.30 WIIA [indicates that the document originated in the "political" Ministeramt rather than in the general staff or Truppenamt], 16 April 1930: "Tasks of the Wehrmacht"; BA-MA M16/34072; discussed extensively in Post, *Civil-Military Fabric*, 231-37.

The deployment of the armed forces in an immediate counterstrike [*Gegenschlag*] is meant to keep an initial encounter from developing into a full-scale war, insofar as this counterassault shows that Germany is not willing to accept a violation of its sovereignty; insofar as it also prevents a fait accompli by the occupation of German territory; finally, insofar as our demonstrated capacity for self-defense deters other nations from intervening against us and encourages interested nations to use their influence in our favor on the basis of contractual responsibilities towards us.[102]

Success depended on three factors. First, a Polish main-force assault had to be slowed down by a defensive retreat, which was the task of the combined main army and militia forces. Second, a counterstrike had to be prepared, which, however, could not aim at the annihilation of the enemy forces. Instead, the counterassault had the purpose of alerting the international community. To that end, the one element in which Germany was superior to Poland, the navy, was employed. Naval planners were ordered to prepare a naval attack against Gdynia. This immediate assault was intended to draw sufficient international attention to the violation of German sovereignty and the potential dangers to European stability, thus generating the pressure needed to end the conflict. The stage for the third phase of the conflict would then be the League of Nations. The Ministeramt as well as the Foreign Office expected a negotiated peace in favor of the economically stronger nation—Germany.[103]

Groener's approach broke with German strategic thinking by returning to the essentials of Schlieffen's notion of a short war. Groener implied that—at least for the forseeable future—Germany was unable to fight autonomous wars with its limited resources, and he was highly skeptical of traditional coalition warfare for which Germany was not prepared in any case. New "alliances" should be of a different kind to exploit the expanding web of transnational interactions. He saw advantages and a partial identity of interests in German and American economic power.[104] Although he doubted the potential of economic means to revise the Versailles settlement, he considered them to be a limiting and constraining force that could be exploited by the militarily weak. If this advantage was properly used, Germany could slip away from the Treaty of Versailles and begin an active process of renewal in which military force would, once again, reassert itself.[105] He never favored peaceful

[102] Geyer, *Aufrüstung oder Sicherheit*, 221.
[103] Post, *Civil-Military Fabric*, 204-214, 234-38.
[104] Geyer, *Aufrüstung oder Sicherheit*, 182-83.
[105] Heinrich Brüning, *Memoiren 1918-1934* (Stuttgart, 1970), 552-54.

relations above all else, but he saw more than one way to wage war. His deterrence doctrine, combining conventional military operations with nonmilitary means, suggested that the nineteenth-century tradition could be maintained only by politicizing strategy and hence by abandoning the military control of war.

The strategic "new look" found little sympathy outside of its small circle of exponents. The German officer corps at large was not ready to share military control, which is perhaps the strongest indication of the political mood in the officer corps at the time. The majority of officers was not particularly conservative, but they were orthodox soldiers whose main concern was the autonomy of the military, the formation of a specific military identity, and the preservation of the special skills of planning and fighting war under rapidly changing conditions of warfare. In the emotional climate of 1933, the creation of a modernized yet autonomous military institution and the return to an operation-centered strategy still seemed feasible.

Military nostalgia replaced realistic efforts to come to grips with the postwar situation. The return to war as an exclusively military domain coincided with the breakup of domestic and international stability caused by the world economic crisis, which destroyed the political basis for Groener's "new look." While the international crisis opened up new possibilities for reordering national and international society, in Germany it strengthened the militant and authoritarian parts of society. These shaped the German response in favor of military revisionism. It was as if the military had given up trying to solve the Weimar dilemma. Instead they reverted to a better past and became, at the same time, more combative in demanding from society, government, and the economy the means that would allow them to close the gap between fantasy and reality. Military leaders had experimented with various expedients to overcome German weakness, only to discover that not "strategy," but more arms and more soldiers was the surest way to reach the point at which wars could be fought again. The Truppenamt entered the Third Reich with the firm intent of restoring the past in order to fight the wars of the future.[106] Rearmament, and little else, became the major issue of the following years.

Military nostalgia was given an additional aggressive edge with the National Socialist rise to power. The marriage of convenience between Reichswehr and National Socialist leadership occurred, first, because Hitler promised to fulfill the military dream of a "large army." Most of

[106] Edward W. Bennett, *German Rearmament and the West, 1932-1933* (Princeton, 1979), 235-41, 338-55.

564

the senior officers did not particularly like Hitler's populism or, for that matter, the self-confidence of the paramilitary (SA) leaders and the rowdy style of their rank and file, but Hitler guaranteed rearmament and the new government immediately began to fulfill this promise. Little more was required to convince the officers that the new government was good for them and thus good for Germany.[107] For a brief moment the military lived in the best of all worlds. An initially subordinate and docile National Socialist leadership—who had ever heard of a German chancellor attending an assembly of officers to convince them of the benefits of his government?[108]—provided the financial, material, and personal resources needed by repressing everything that stood in the way of military recovery, even including its own paramilitary mass-following. The officer corps also gained a degree of autonomy unheard of in German, which allowed officers to use all their skills in rebuilding the army. After a short period of insecurity in the first six months following the seizure of power, the general staff became the exclusive source of rearmament plans, operational concepts, and strategic visions during these early years.[109]

But from the beginning soldiers and National Socialists thought differently about war. Their conflict cannot simply be defined as a clash between conservative and National Socialist world views, of military revisionism opposed to the more radical ambitions of the National Socialist leadership, such as Hitler's dream of establishing a racist empire by conquering and exploiting "living space" in the East. More fundamental was the fact that, while the Party stressed the militant dynamics of the regime as a political system geared to conquest and domination, the army emphasized the institutional control of violence.

The National Socialists were prepared to provide the resources for military action, but they were never ready to accept complete subordination to the imperatives of a war planned by the military. They followed a different model, which subordinated the military use of force to the mobilization of the nation, thus creating a new and distinct rationale for war. For the military, fighting war was a matter of skillfully preparing and using the "raw material" provided by a unified and otherwise silent

[107] Michael Geyer, "National Socialism and the Military in the Weimar Republic," in *The Nazi Machtergreifung*, ed. Peter Stachura (London, 1983), 101-123; a more cautious assessment is in Andreas Hillgruber, "Die Reichswehr und das Scheitern der Weimarer Republik," in *Weimar, Selbstpreisgabe einer Demokratie: Eine Bilanz heute*, ed. Karl-Dietrich Erdmann and Hagen Schulze (Düsseldorf, 1980), 177-92.

[108] Thilo Vogelsang, "Neue Dokumente zur Geschichte der Reichswehr 1930-1933," *Vierteljahrshefte für Zeitgeschichte* 2 (1954), 397-436.

[109] Klaus-Jürgen Müller, *Das Heer und Hitler: Armee und Nationalsozialistisches Regime 1933-1940* (Stuttgart, 1969); Robert J. O'Neill, *The German Army and the Nazi Party, 1933-1939* (London, 1966) is still the best English treatment of the subject.

society; for the National Socialists war was a way of life. For them military action was only one specific task in a more encompassing strategy of conquest. The destruction of the armed power of potential enemies was merely the first step in creating a new German master race.

This racist militancy grew out of the ideology and practice of "total mobilization" in World War I.[110] Yet it also became the vehicle with which the National Socialist leadership emancipated itself from the technocratic military dictatorship, exemplified by Ludendorff. Their insistence upon autonomy for a militant society marked the difference between technocratic elite rule and militant populist insurgence. Thus, National Socialist war was radically different from the elite traditions of European land warfare. National Socialist war was war for the sake of social reconstruction through the destruction of conquered societies. Total discretionary power over subjugated people was to maintain and guarantee the social life and organization of the Germans. A terrorist racism became the essence of National Socialist politics as its leaders strove toward war. In their mind, it was the foundation on which the war-making capabilities of the Third Reich rested, just as its expansion was the major goal that the war would achieve.[111]

Although National Socialist and military conceptions of war, each emerging from the experience of total war, differed radically, they depended on each other. As much as National Socialists and the military were kept apart in their struggle over the control of war, they were held together by the effort of making war feasible. If the military needed national mobilization to wage war, the Nazis needed the military instrument to secure racist rule. The dependence of National Socialist leaders on the military instrument gave the military leadership an advantage that they preserved as long as they could maintain their monopoly over operational planning, the rise of National Socialist military forces like the SS notwithstanding. Such a monopoly depended, however, on the general staff's ability to assess accurately Germany's capability to fight war. This was the tenuous balance that shaped the relations between the National Socialist leadership and the military. Only when leading officers began to question whether war was feasible at all could the National Socialists begin to put into practice their goals of national purification through conquest or, as we have called it, apocalyptic war.

[110] Ludolf Herbst, *Der totale Krieg und die Ordnung der Wirtschaft: Die Kriegswirtschaft im Spannungsfeld von Politik, Ideologie und Propaganda 1939-1945* (Stuttgart, 1982), 42-61, 82-92; Hans-Adolf Jacobsen, "Krieg in Weltanschauung und Praxis des Nationalsozialismus 1919-1945," in *Hitlerwelle und historische Fakten*, ed. A. Manzmann (Königstein/Ts., 1979), 71-80.

[111] Andreas Hillgruber, *Hitlers Strategie: Politik und Kriegführung 1940-1941*, 2d ed. (Munich, 1982); idem, *Deutschlands Rolle in der Vorgeschichte der beiden Weltkriege*.

Paradoxically, the establishment of firm professional control over the army as the main military service was the most important outcome of the first year of Nazi rule.[112] For such control the Reichswehr was well prepared. Under Ludwig Beck's tenure as chief of the general staff between 1933 and 1938, the army published yet another incisive manual, *Truppenführung*, which guided military planning and the preparation for war.[113] It returned to the classical doctrines of a war of movement without neglecting changing technological conditions. It emphasized artillery and infantry, but paid attention to tank forces as well. Indeed, it referred to tanks as the leading (*tonangebend*) weapon in the battle zone. In assessing the strategic situation of Germany and the wars most likely to be fought, it provided an unusually balanced view of the merits of offense and defense. Most of all, however, the manual stressed a systematic approach to operations on all levels of planning and execution that demanded a "penetrating intellectual effort that covers all potentialities of war." Only this effort made planning and execution of operations into a truly professional exercise, that is, "the free and creative undertaking that rests on a scientific basis." *Truppenführung* distilled the essence of professional strategy as creative yet rigorously controlled, an artistic yet scientifically based undertaking. It was one of the clearest examples of the revival of German strategic idealism.

The manual also shaped the outlook of the general staff on a potential war. Almost as a matter of principle, the general staff insisted on the planning and command unity of the European theater of war. The coherence of the European system formed the premise for an integrated military approach to power politics and, as such, should not be confused with "worst-case scenarios" of operational managers.[114] *Truppenführung* provided an analysis of warfare based on principle rather than an option-oriented assessment of military doctrines and actions. War in Europe would always be an all-European war and, due to the mobilization potentials of European nations, a multifront war would tend to be a long war. In this respect, the authors of *Truppenführung* distanced themselves from Schlieffen's notion of an integral *Gesamtschlacht* with all the operational implications that followed from it. Contrary to Schlieffen, they concluded that the mobility of modern defense and the interrelatedness of European affairs did not bode well for an integral battle that evolved out of deployment. They explicitly cautioned against the omnipotence

[112] Klaus-Jürgen Müller, "The Army in the Third Reich: An Historical Interpretation," *Journal of Strategic Studies* 2 (1979), 123-52.

[113] *Truppenführung (T.F.)* (Berlin, 1936).

[114] Williamson Murray, *The Change in the European Balance of Power, 1938-1939: The Path to Ruin* (Princeton, 1984), 174.

of operations, probably in response to Ludendorff's 1918 offensives, not so much because they did not believe in the possible success of any one operation, but because each had to be seen in the overall context of winning a war, which was now defined much more comprehensively as annihilating the enemy's main forces and controlling his mobilization capabilities. The authors of *Truppenführung* wrote in full awareness of Germany's strategic position in central Europe, and of the gravity of multifront war that necessitated a comprehensive, systematic, and holistic approach, if one wanted to do more than to win a few battles. Their ideas were certainly not adventurous, but neither did the German situation nor the professionalism of the military craft invite taking great risks.

The German general staff approached rearmament as a prerequisite for operational planning in the same systematic fashion. It established professional control and authority, which in turn hinged on the capability of the army to wage a controlled war once the rebuilding program was completed. This also formed the basis for relations with the National Socialist leaders.[115]

By 1935, the army had taken the first hurdle on the path of leading the Third Reich out of the "risk zone" of military defenselessness.[116] At this point the general staff had already paid a certain price for its desire to move ahead as quickly as possible by accepting an acceleration of rearmament that did not quite fit its ideas of an internationally "neutral" rearmament, but it preserved its authority while impressing on National Socialist leaders the necessity to abstain from domestic and international adventures.[117]

In the summer of 1935, the general staff began comprehensive preparations for war, which coincided with the "creation of a mobilized army with the highest possible operational capability (*Operationsfähigkeit*) and offensive potential (*Angriffskraft*)" and a further acceleration of rearmament originating in the general staff.[118] The intraservice friction over the independence of tank forces, the economic consequences of this effort, the Four Year Plan, and the international drama of the introduction of

[115] Herrman Rahne, *Die militärische Mobilmachungsplanung und -technik in Preussen und im Deutschen Reich* (diss., Leipzig, 1972).

[116] Hans-Jürgen Rautenberg, *Deutsche Rüstungspolitik vom Beginn der Genfer Abrüstungskonferenz bis zur Wiedereinführung der Allgemeinen Wehrpflicht 1932-1935* (diss. phil., Bonn, 1973), 302-319.

[117] Klaus-Jürgen Müller, *General Ludwig Beck: Studien und Dokumente zur politisch-militärischen Vorstellungswelt und Tätigkeit des Generalstabschefs des deutschen Heeres 1933-1938* (Boppard, 1980), 163-84.

[118] Michael Geyer, "Militär, Rüstung und Aussenpolitik: Aspekte militärischer Revisionspolitik in der Zwischenkriegszeit," in *Hitler, Deutschland und die Mächte*, 2d ed., ed. Manfred Funke (Düsseldorf, 1978), 239-68.

conscription and the militarization of the Rhineland have all been emphasized by historians, but it has often been overlooked that deployment planning formed the focal point for organizing and preparing an army with offensive capabilities, and became the basis for the operational planning of future war.[119]

The army's plans for a two-front war, which were summed up in "directives" from 1936 on, were linked to the progress of rearmament, particularly to a new four-year plan for offensive armament, which was put into effect in August 1936.[120] The structure of the deployment plans remained essentially the same from year to year, while military capabilities grew with every yearly increment of rearmament. The general staff was prepared to accept the challenge of defensive war throughout this period, but believed that offensive operations should wait on the completion of the rearmament plan, ideally in 1940.[121] At that time the political leadership could rationally decide to fight a war in central Europe. When in 1938—two years short of the ideal target date, which had been delayed due to bottlenecks in rearmament—Beck spoke of the irresponsibility of the political leadership, he had in mind the deployment plan and its strategic and operational calculus of a two-front war.

This very peculiar kind of deployment planning misled the judges in Nuremberg and has misled historians ever since, because it was growth-oriented and teleological. It assumed a strategic defense in a European war with potential offensive actions on secondary fronts during the growth phase. Upon completion of rearmament, however, it was turned inside out into a plan for offensive warfare, a "deliberate strategic attack, planned and prepared in peacetime."[122] More important, these deployment plans were not contingency plans but, insofar as they prescribed action according to the stages of German military preparedness rather than in response to the intentions of potential enemies, formed a comprehensive calculus for war. Last, they assured the general staff complete control over war in the transition from strategic defense to strategic offense, because this transition was exclusively defined in terms of military

[119] Wilhelm Deist et al., *Ursachen und Voraussetzungen der deutschen Kriegspolitik* (Stuttgart, 1979).

[120] A detailed and scholarly study of German deployment planning between 1935 and 1939 does not exist. The following is based on Rahne, *Mobilmachungsplanung*; Burkhart Müller-Hildebrand, *Das Heer 1933-1945*, 3 vols. (Darmstadt and Frankfurt, 1954-59) and unpublished material by Donald Shearer, "Initial Military Preparations, Peacetime Activation, Mobilization, Deployment, and Transportation Planning" (ms.). See also Wilhelm Deist, *The Wehrmacht and German Rearmament* (London and Basingstoke, 1981), 36-53.

[121] Geyer, *Aufrüstung oder Sicherheit*, 446-49.

[122] RKM u. ObdW 55/37 geh. Kdos., Chef Sache LIa, 24 June 1937, "Directives 1937/38," in: *IMT* 34, Doc. #175-C, pp. 733-47.

preparedness as specified by the general staff's assessments of the shifting balance of power. These plans show the military's readiness to wage offensive war just as much as their insistence on control over decisions concerning war and peace. Germany would be ready for war when the general staff decided that it was.

Deployment and its rationale of professional warfare depended on the ability of the nation to provide the necessary military means at the appropriate time. The general staff relentlessly pushed for more armaments.[123] But despite all efforts, German strengths could not match those of a combination of other European nations. This increasingly became an issue as tensions spread outward from Central Europe in response to German rearmament. At the very moment when deployment plans were introduced in 1935, Hitler and the German military leadership had already begun to question whether the army would every gain the superiority necessary for fighting war according to standards of professional expertise. They were haunted by the fear that Germany "may be well armed . . . , but otherwise incapable of either defense or offense."[124]

This is the origin of the first assault, in 1935, on the operational prerogatives of the general staff, launched by the political office of the Armed Forces Command, which had been excluded from operational planning. The political office began to explore alternative approaches to warfare along more unconventional and, ultimately, "unprofessional" lines, beginning with the debate on a potential surprise attack against Czechoslovakia (code-named *Schulung*). *Schulung* was a curious exercise—it was never a contingency plan—that the general staff opposed, even though general staff officers eventually prepared it. *Schulung* was the forerunner of a whole series of plans that were named *Sonderfälle*, special deployment plans. They aimed at the exploitation of fortuitous political circumstances that would allow the "premature" use of force.[125] It is often overlooked that these *Sonderfälle* were never meant to be full-fledged contingency plans; their preparation was "ordered in each specific case according to the political situation."[126] It is quite evident that these plans radically contradicted everything the general staff stood for.

[123] See Beck's "Observations on the military-political situation in May 1938," 5 May 1938, in Müller, *Beck*, 502-511, and Michael Geyer, "Rüstungsbeschleunigung und Inflation: Zur Inflationsdenkschrift des Oberkommandos der Wehrmacht vom November 1938," *Militärgeschichtliche Mitteilungen* 30 (1981), 121-86.

[124] Müller, *Beck*, 182-83.

[125] Geyer, *Aufrüstung oder Sicherheit*, 419-28, 429-32.

[126] See appendix #2 to ObdW 94/37 geh. Kdos., Chef Sache LIa, 7 December 1937 [First supplement to directives, 1937/38]; BA-MA Case 1197/33306c. It should be noted that these *Sonderfälle* were never supposed to be planned in advance. They were to be "thought through" (*durchdenken*). Hence, the ad hoc planning for the operation against Austria fit the directives, even though it ran counter to the demands of the "professionals" around Beck.

The debate over these plans continued until 1937 and was closely intertwined with the power struggles between Armed Forces Command (Blomberg) and Army Command (Fritsch).[127] It came to a sudden and surprising head, though the moment was exceptionally appropriate, on November 5, 1937, when Hitler challenged the whole system of military planning.[128] The Führer questioned whether the military would ever be ready for war, and made it clear that he was prepared, for a number of domestic and international reasons, to skip the carefully crafted deployment plans in favor of politically and militarily improvised warfare. He threatened moreover to replace the underlying military rationale of deployment planning with a mix of political and ideological considerations. This was the most serious challenge, so far, to the military control of operational planning.

Beck, as chief of staff, disagreed with the attempt to tear the decision over war and peace from its "meaningful (*sinngebend*) context."[129] He was less concerned with Hitler's vision of living space in the East—and not simply because he misinterpreted Hitler's rambling elaborations. Most of all Beck feared the loss of military control over strategy, and he began strenuously to counter Hitler's efforts to introduce an opportunistic approach. But, in opposing Hitler, he too began to realize that the German army might never be ready for war. While trying to prove that war could not be fought in Hitler's way, Beck began to indicate more and more forcefully that fighting a major war in a professional manner was beyond the army's capacity. In fact, his arguments spoke more effectively against professional strategy than against Hitler's adventurist intentions. All of Beck's arguments pointed to the conclusion that systematic operational planning and concomitant rearmament had led to a dead end as far as a calculated and instrumental use of force was concerned.[130]

The dilemmas that Beck described in great detail indicated a fundamental challenge to professional war as outlined in *Truppenführung*. If Beck was right, the army's autonomy was in jeopardy. If it had to rely on extramilitary factors that it did not control and whose evaluation it had to share with others, the general staff's ability to control the military and war evaporated. In other words, the actual strategic problem in 1937-38, whether or not one could fight an isolated war against Czechoslovakia, was the agenda for one of the basic power struggles in the Third Reich. It was fought as a struggle over the nature of strategy.

[127] Müller, *Beck*, 225-72.
[128] Niederschrift über die Besprechung in der Reichskanzlei am 5. November 1937, in: *IMT* 25, Doc. #386-PS, 402-413.
[129] This was most clearly expressed in his opposition to preparations for a military attack against Austria (Memorandum of 20 May 1937, in Müller, *Beck*, 493-97).
[130] Ibid., 503-50.

At this point, however, Beck was already isolated in the army. He was sidelined by a younger generation of officers, who not only were more reckless, but displayed a profoundly different operational style. Beck repeatedly criticized them during exercises for "simply" maximizing the use of weapons. He complained that they had never learned to evaluate operations within the context of a coherent strategy and that they lightheartedly followed the orders of their superiors instead of questioning whether these orders were at all feasible given the strategic situation, the state of the craft, and the readiness and availability of weapons. They were technocrats rather than strategists.[131] But it was these officers who now became the proponents of blitzkrieg, which was neither an outgrowth of military technology nor of the German doctrine of mobile offense, but operational management devouring professional strategy, in short, a manifestation of the strategic bankruptcy of professional strategy.

The collapse of a coherent military strategy also opened up the possibility of introducing ideology as a surrogate for deficient strategic planning. To be sure, military technocrats with their functional outlook and National Socialists with their goal of ideological war remained apart and often were at cross purposes, but they complemented each other and, in crucial moments, when the Third Reich turned from preparing to fighting war, achieved a symbiosis.

IV

After the turmoil of the preceding twenty years, the Second World War brought German strategy to an apocalyptic climax. National and international order had rested on uncertain grounds. The semblance of order that had existed for a few years gave way to a period in which nations sought recovery from the world economic crisis by means of highly competitive economic diplomacy, each trying to ensure its own well-being by using any means at hand. Great Britain and France exploited their empires; National Socialist Germany turned first to the Balkans, but harbored far more ambitious plans. Only two powers turned inward: under Stalin's rule, the Soviet Union concentrated on the effort to implement socialism and industrialization, and the United States strove to make capitalism safe for its own people. The world as a whole seemed to drift away from integration toward segregated economic and social blocs.

In this tumultuous setting, "strategy" in the Third Reich likewise drifted between a variety of options after the collapse of professional

[131] Ibid., 266-70.

572

strategy in 1938.[132] Although German leaders pursued ambitious goals, they were uncertain how to achieve them. Only when Germany and Japan decided to attack—for different reasons, to be sure, but with similar global consequences—was the world brought back together, in military antagonism. Their attack was ultimately directed against those nations, the Soviet Union and the United States, that had emerged from the 1930s as integrated political and economic blocs, relying on their own national resources in formulating and executing a counterstrategy. Germany's and Japan's decisions to attack were the critical acts of the time. They fused disparate campaigns into a global war, and laid the basis for the world to come. Although the reactions of the United States and the Soviet Union, like those of Germany and Japan, were based on particular national reasons and were in no way symmetrical,[133] the strategies of all these powers, taken together, reflected a new kind of war. It was a war fought to reorder the world rather than to preserve or adjust existing structures of international relations. This radical objective distinguished the major protagonists from minor powers like France, Great Britain, or Italy, whatever the exertions of any particular nation. Thus, Great Britain undoubtedly fought a more "total" war than any other nation except, perhaps, the Soviet Union, but Britain fought this war for limited goals— to stave off a threat to its existence and to reestablish a status quo. The far-reaching and, in many ways, Napoleonic, goals of the major combatants involved establishing a new national and international order by destroying or subordinating the enemy. With such unlimited goals, the use of force turned into a cataclysmic war between irreconcilable ideologies. Warfare could not be contained by the instrumental and professional rationality of European land warfare nor by its traditional calculus of limiting force and damage. But Germany alone went beyond these extreme goals, fighting a war that was truly apocalyptic.

We have observed the rise of apocalyptic sentiments in Germany; that is, the mixture of a technocratic use of force coexisting with the concept of war as a process of national purification. In the Third Reich the apocalyptic vision was organized into a strategic calculus. National Socialist leaders fought their war both in an expansionist outward thrust against Soviet armed forces and as a war of annihilation whose twin goals were the enslavement of the eastern European populations and an

---

[132] See the survey of Manfred Messerschmidt, "La stratégie allemande 1939-1945," *Revue d'histoire de la deuxième guerre mondiale* 25 (1975), 1-26 and of Andreas Hillgruber, *Der Zweite Weltkrieg 1939-1945: Kriegsziele und Strategie der grossen Mächte*, 2d ed. (Stuttgart, 1982).

[133] Hans-Adolf Jacobsen, *Zur Konzeption einer Geschichte des Zweiten Weltkrieges 1939-1945: Disposition mit kritisch ausgewähltem Schrifttum* (Frankfurt, 1964) and idem, *Deutsche Kriegführung 1939-1945* (Hanover, 1961).

Armageddon for the Jewish minorities of occupied Europe. The logic of escalatory war, which only came to a halt when whole societies were subordinated, combined with the terrorist logic of national regeneration, which could end only when a purified German society had established its hegemony in Europe.

Seen in this way, German strategy reached its "zenith"[134] with the Barbarossa campaign against the Soviet Union, where conquest, racist domination, and the reforging of German society into a master race were brought together, linking in a grand concentric movement all the previously disconnected and nascent dynamics of the state against a single target. The Russo-German war encompassed not just the battlefronts, but also the battle zones and the rear areas. It was fought in swift envelopments and cauldron battles and in the murderous and premeditated pogroms in Poland and Russia. It was fought in the ghettos and in the concentration and annihilation camps. And it was fought in the German core of the expanded Reich with the matériel and human resources of occupied Europe. Between 1941 and 1943, the apocalyptic vision of war became strategic reality in the East.[135]

Apocalyptic war was carried on by different organizations that, more often than not, were at odds with each other. Historians should not be misled by their competition and bickering. Just as the *Gesamtschlacht* at Königgrätz succeeded in 1866 despite the jealousies of German army commanders, so an integral, apocalyptic campaign was waged in the East and extended back into the West, even though it unfolded in many parts, often in tension or conflict with one another. The diverse operations at the front, in the rear, and at home combined into a single war directed by a single strategy that was concerned less with military operations than with establishing a new national and international order through subjugation and extermination.

Although the tide of war turned against Germany in 1942-43, destruction and extermination did not reach a peak until near the end of 1943-44. When control over the war passed to the Allies, Hitler and his closest associates responded by concentrating and rationalizing their efforts toward a single elemental aim: behind a slow and grinding retreat to destroy those whom it perceived to be its mortal enemies. Even though the outcome of the war had been decided by 1944, the Third Reich clung to is original concept of apocalyptic war, and the German people at home

[134] Andreas Hillgruber, *Der Zenit des Zweiten Weltkrieges, Juli 1941* (Wiesbaden, 1977).
[135] Andreas Hillgruber, "Die 'Endlösung' und das deutsche Ostimperium als Kernstück des rassenideologischen Programms des Nationalsozialismus," in *Hitler, Deutschland und die Mächte*, 2d ed., ed. Mandred Funke (Düsseldorf, 1978), 94-114.

and in the field, disillusioned and wary of their leaders, fought on in the fear of the retribution that they knew defeat would surely bring.

The course of German strategy during the Third Reich was not determined by a set of rationally formulated grand objectives. Instead it was shaped by a series of gambles—gambles on the army's ability to obtain adequate support from the country's limited economic base, which was made more difficult by the regime's unwillingness to compromise its goal of domestic pacification and purification, and on the government's ability to allay concern over its growing domination of Europe and to prevent the formation of effective anti-German alliances. The constraints on strategy shaped its choices. Although conquest would enhance the economic base and strategic perimeters of the Third Reich, it would, at the same time, increase the potential of coalitions against Germany. Every operational success, for military commanders rewarding and a goal in itself, raised the odds for the strategist. It was an escalatory ladder in which the use of force maintained the ability to fight future wars, but also strengthened the countervailing forces. The major strategic and operational problem—to escape this trap—prompted a penchant for taking audacious risks.

The race to conquer living space reached its first threshold in 1938. The still incomplete rearmament drive had exhausted existing resources and was outgrowing German economic and financial potentials. As a result, the distance between the National Socialist regime—though not Hitler—and the German people began to widen. Added to the economic and political strain was the fear that the probable opponents of the Third Reich, especially Great Britain, would tilt the European balance either by rearming themselves or by being reinforced by the United States. The narrow confines of central Europe had to be left behind as quicky as possible, before containing forces could be mobilized. These concerns conditioned the first swift and militarily "premature" actions of 1938 and 1939—the *Anschluss* of Austria, the Munich agreement to partition Czechoslovakia, and the German occupation of Prague.

Strategic success in 1938-39 depended on two conditions: the continued fragmentation of continental Europe into isolated and competing states, and the indifference of the great European "rim" powers to central European affairs. Both conditions—a heritage of the world economic crisis—came to an end with this first phase of German expansion. The British guarantee of Poland undermined Germany's attempt to build a Continental empire on a predominantly domestic timetable and raised the specter of a general European war. Moreover, both the Soviet Union and the United States began to reconsider their policies in light of this potential war, drawing America closer to the point of commitment and setting the Soviet Union on a course of heightening and possibly exploiting the contradictions within the "capitalist-imperialist" camp.[136] The strategic choices of 1939 were made with the probability of global war in Central Europe clearly in view.[137] While France and Britain attempted to create the conditions for a regionalized European war with global dimensions, the Third Reich struggled to maintain its freedom of action and to preserve through preemptive war the overall direction of basic National Socialist strategy.[138]

The essence of the strategic duel of 1939-1940 was belied by appearances. Despite their public declarations, the French and British governments were really seeking to peripheralize the conflict and to draw Germany into a long war, fought on the backs of the small nations of Europe. This kind of war would stretch German resources and reduce the German ability for a decision-seeking strategy against them. While the central front—to be established along the Rhine rather than on French soil—was frozen, military-political envelopment would force Germany ever deeper into sideshows in the east (Poland), the north (Scandinavia), and in the Mediterranean.[139] The novelty in this indirect strategy of 1939-1940, contrasted with the direct strategy of World War I, lay in two aspects. First, it was an expedient of the French and British governments which were neither ready nor willing to fight a general war and had only a limited ability to support their "proxies" in northern, southern, and eastern Europe, either by supplying weapons or sending expeditionary forces, or by the indirect means of putting pressure on the frozen central front. Second, this indirect strategy was always incomplete in that it never included the Soviet Union. Thus, a gap opened that was instantly exploited by the Third Reich. The Allied peripheral strategy collapsed under the counterpressure of the Nazi-Soviet pact, which effectively ended cold war envelopment and devalued the key feature of a protracted war—the naval blockade. Allied strategy was unmasked by the reluctance to chal-

[136] Gerhard L. Weinberg, *Germany and the Soviet Union, 1939-1941*, 2d ed. (Leiden, 1972); B. Peitrow, *Deutschland in der Konzeption der sowjetischen Aussenpolitik 1933-1941* (diss. rer. pol., Kassel, 1981).

[137] Karl Rohe, ed., *Die Westmächte und das Dritte Reich 1933-1939* (Paderborn, 1982); Andreas Hillgruber, "Der Faktor Amerika in Hitler's Strategie 1938-1941," *Deutsche Grossmachtpolitik im 19. und 20. Jahrhundert* (Düsseldorf, 1977), 197-222.

[138] See Gerhard L. Weinberg, *The Foreign Policy of Hitler's Germany: Starting World War II, 1937-1939* (Chicago, 1982), chs. 12-14, who emphasizes the diplomatic aspects and Murray, *Change in the Balance of Power*, who stresses the domestic constraints.

[139] See Klaus A. Maier et al., *Die Errichtung der Hegemonie auf dem europäischen Kontinent* (Stuttgart, 1979), a straightforward operational survey of these campaigns; Walther Hubatsch, '*Weserübung': Die deutsche Besetzung von Dänemark und Norwegen, nach amtlichen Unterlagen dargestellt*, 2d ed. (Göttingen, 1960); Gerhard Schreiber, "Der Mittelmeerraum in Hitlers Strategie 1940: 'Programm' und militärische Planung," *Militärgeschichtliche Mitteilungen* 28 (1980), 69-99.

lenge Germany on the main front. The Third Reich thus gained the opportunity to sweep through one sideshow after another—a process that began with the war against Poland (September 1939), continued with the occupation of Norway (March-April 1940), and ended with the thrust into Greece. These campaigns brought spectacular military victories for the Third Reich, but their strategic value consisted merely in holding the course against diversions.

As ineffective as the Allied indirect strategy proved to be, and as ruthlessly and quickly as these peripheral dangers were nipped in the bud by the German army, the fact that the war continued after September 1939 posed a critical strategic problem. After all, even the *drôle de guerre* diminished Germany's chances of achieving its strategic objective in the East. The Allied blockade, reinforced by growing American support, pushed the Third Reich into dependence on the Soviet Union, away from its goal of apocalyptic war. A war with Great Britain over hegemony in Europe, fought prior to the expansion and racial purification of Germany was, from a military perspective, not feasible and from Hitler's perspective, pointless.[140]

This vexation shaped the preparations for Operation Yellow and the attendant, and perplexing, stop-and-go decision making that continued for months before May 1940.[141] The contentious nature of operational planning and the adventurous character of the final scheme have obscured the ambivalence of the strategic intent. No doubt France had to be "neutralized" as a prerequisite of the great campaign for living space. Operationally this was difficult, but the strategic problem was posed less by France than by Great Britain. The main strategic objective was to gain British consent for a German Continental empire by stripping Britain of its European allies,[142] and from this perspective the campaign that ended the first phase of the war, however spectacular, was a strategic failure. Though France, together with the Benelux countries was partly occupied and partly neutralized, and though continental Europe fell under the hegemony of the Third Reich, Britain, helped by the Commonwealth and the United States, fought off a direct military attack in the battle of Britain and resisted German peace feelers.[143]

---

[140] Williamson Murray, "The Strategy of the 'Phoney War': A Re-Evaluation," *Military Affairs* 45 (1981), 13-17; Gerhart Haas, "Der 'seltsame Krieg' vom September 1939 bis zum Frühjahr 1940," *Militärgeschichte* 18 (1979), 271-80; Josef Hencke, *England in Hitlers politischem Kalkül 1935-1939* (Boppard, 1973).

[141] Hans-Adolf Jacobsen, *Fall Gelb: Der Kampf um den deutschen Operationsplan zur Westoffensive* (Wiesbaden, 1957). On early plans see Charles B. Burdick "German Military Planning and France, 1930-1938," *World Affairs Quarterly* (1959-60), 299-313.

[142] Bernd Martin, *Friedensinitiativen und Machtpolitik im Zweiten Weltkrieg 1939-1942*, 2d ed. (Düsseldorf, 1976).

[143] Martin Gilbert, *Winston Churchill: Finest Hour, 1939-1941* (Boston, 1983); François

In fact, by engaging the United States ever more deeply in the British effort after Dunkirk, Britain took the first step in reversing the overall balance of the war. It was Great Britain, as against Napoleon, that began to draw together the "world" against a Europe under German hegemony. By denying strategic success to Germany, Britain set the stage for the global war to come. While Germany celebrated its victories, its people as well as its military and industrial elites showing almost unlimited trust in Hitler's capacities as leader and strategist, the strategic odds once again began to outrun operational successes. Germany was simply not prepared for global war, and time was against it. The trap of escalatory war began to close again, as it had in 1916-1918. Japan, it may be said, found itself in an almost identical predicament at almost the same time. However successful the first two years of the war, the Third Reich never came close to escaping the dilemma posed by the fact that the political and military-strategic costs of expansion continuously outran the benefits of a newly gained hegemonic position.

At the height of its power, Germany was falling behind. In fact, Germany's strategic position in 1940 was more tenuous than at any time in the interwar years. This may seem surprising in view of Germany's self-acclaimed defenselessness until 1935 and its extraordinary military feats between 1938 and 1940. However, in the past military weaknesses had always been balanced by economic strength, even dominance, and by the tacit support of either the Soviet Union, the United States, or both. By 1940 Germany had achieved hegemony in Europe, but faced Great Britain, the United States, and the Soviet Union in what was now a global conflict. Hitler was one of the few to see these new conditions clearly. He argued that the old core of Europe was too small and too vulnerable to sustain global conflict.[144] A much larger base than the "old" Europe

---

Bédarida, *La stratégie secrète de la drôle de guerre: Le Conseil Suprême Interallié, septembre 1939-avril 1940* (Paris, 1979); Corelli Barnett, *The Collapse of British Power* (New York, 1972); N. Fieldhouse, "The Anglo-German War 1939-1942: Some Movements to End It by Negotiated Peace," *Transactions of the Royal Society of Canada* 9 (1971).

[144] Generaloberst Franz Halder, *Kriegstagebuch*, ed. Hans-Adolf Jacobsen (Stuttgart, 1962), 1:374-75; Hillgruber, *Hitlers Strategie*, 144-91; Hans-Adolf Jacobsen and Arthur L. Smith, eds., *World War II, Policy and Strategy: Selected Documents with Commentary* (Santa Barbara, 1979), ch. 5. On the strategic situation in 1940, after the failure of a direct attack against Great Britain, see Ronald Wheatley, *Operation Sea Lion* (Oxford, 1958); on the battle of Britain see the remarkably judicious account of Telford Taylor, *The Breaking Wave* (New York, 1967), which illuminates the German attempt to maintain the strategic initiative; that is, to prevent a long drawn-out "economic" war from the Central European pivot. This choice reflects both domestic considerations (war of national purification) as well as the acknowledgement of Germany's dependence on world markets, which is discussed by Murray, *Change in the European Balance*, 326-34. On the short-war option see also Gerhard Förster, *Totaler Krieg und Blitzkrieg* (Berlin, 1967) with the standard "instrumental" interpretation that explains blitzkrieg as an attempt to balance means and

and a much more intensive use of the means of destruction were necessary to project force on a global scale.

The basic strategic decision for the Third Reich was how to rise to this challenge. One option—to consolidate its hegemony over the European core—was unacceptable because it would make Germany a leading regional power, but one with limited global liabilities between a Eurasian continental bloc, dominated by the Soviet Union, and an Atlantic-American bloc, dominated by the Unied States.[145] A second option, an alliance of the principal Eurasian powers—Germany with its junior partner Italy, the Soviet Union as the major land power on the Continent, and Japan as the East Asian pillar—against the Anglo-American seapowers with their continental center in the Americas, was at least temporarily contemplated in 1940-41, although it ran counter to Hitler's ideological goal of conquering living space in the East.[146] The third option fit the long-held visions of an apocalyptic war for the conquest of living space and the purification of the German race. It was chosen with Directive 21, Operation Barbarossa, in December 1940.[147]

The war against the Soviet Union now acquired a new meaning and a new significance. When Directive 21 was issued, it became a race to establish new, intercontinental strategic perimeters. This novel dimension of the war was most clearly expressed in Directive 32, "Preparation for the Time after Barbarossa," of June 11, 1941, eleven days before the invasion of the Soviet Union began. Directive 32, together with orders to the navy, outlined three basic goals:[148] (1) the organization and ex-

---

ends. Following General Thomas, Alan Milward, *The German Economy at War* (London, 1965) interprets these campaigns on the background of the internal German dispute between "armaments in depth" (Thomas) and "armaments in breadth" (Hitler).

[145] This option reflects the old elite goals of 1914. See Wolfgang Schumann and Dietrich Eichholtz, eds., *Anatomie des Krieges: Neue Dokumente über die Rolle des deutschen Monopolkapitals bei der Vorbereitung und Durchführung des Zweiten Weltkrieges* (Berlin, 1969); Gerhard Hass and Wolfgang Schumann, *Anatomie der Aggression: Neue Dokumente zu den Kriegszielen des faschistischen Imperialismus im Zweiten Weltkrieg* (Berlin/GDR, 1972); Dietrich Eichholtz, *Geschichte der Kriegswirtschaft 1939-1945* (Berlin/GDR, 1969).

[146] Wolfgang Michalka, *Ribbentrop und die deutsche Weltpolitik 1933-1940: Aussenpolitische Konzeptionen und Entscheidungsprozess im Dritten Reich* (Munich, 1980).

[147] Hillgruber, *Der Zweite Weltkrieg*, 129-34; Walther Hubatsch, ed., *Hitlers Weisungen für die Kriegführung 1939-1945: Dokumente des Oberkommandos der Wehrmacht* (Frankfurt, 1962), 84-88; *Auf anti-sowjetischem Kriegskurs: Studien zur militärischen Vorbereitung des deutschen Imperialismus auf die Aggression gegen die UdSSR 1933-1941* (Berlin/GDR, 1970). See also Peter Krüger, "Das Jahr 1941 in der deutschen Kriegs- und Aussenpolitik," in *Das Jahr 1941 in der europäischen Politik*, ed. Karl Bosl (Munich, 1972), 7-38. On the Balkan interlude see Martin Van Creveld, *Hitler's Strategy 1940-41: The Balkan Clue* (Cambridge, 1973).

[148] Hubatsch, *Hitlers Weisungen*, 129-34; Michael Salewski, ed., *Die deutsche Seekriegsleitung 1935-1945* (Frankfurt, 1973), 3:189-214; Gerhard Wagner, ed., *Lagevorträge des Oberbefehlshabers der Kriegsmarine vor Hitler 1939 bis 1945* (Munich, 1972); Karl Klee,

ploitation of the Soviet resource base as a prerequisite for fighting intercontinental war; (2) the destruction of the British hold over the imperial periphery with a thrust in the direction of Iran and Afghanistan, though this would remain a secondary front;[149] and (3) the establishment of new Atlantic "defense" perimeters, reaching from France to North and West Africa. Behind an Atlantic wall and with the resources of the occupied territories, the Third Reich, as the only remaining Continental power, hoped to prepare its navy and air force for a highly technological and intercontinental confrontation with the Anglo-American world.[150] But Germany never reached the point at which its intercontinental strategy could unfold. The Red Army denied the prerequisites for such strategy in the defensive battles of 1941 and in the counteroffensives of the winter of 1941-42. Also, the United States, provoked by Japan, entered the war sooner and with greater strength than the German leaders had anticipated. The ability of the Soviet Union and the United States to achieve rapid mobilization made the decisive difference after 1941.

At this point the strategic initiative shifted to the Allied side, even if it was not yet certain that the war against Germany could actually be won.[151] However, German strategy, which had been so successful in the previous years, collapsed. Its place was taken by two distinct developments. The Third Reich escalated its war effort in the faint hope of splitting the Allies through limited operational successes. Militarily, it turned to a course of attrition, punctuated by selective counteroffensives. The events in North Africa, the great tank battles in the East, and the battle of the Bulge all fall into this category. More important, the army in the East and the navy in the Atlantic became a shield behind which the Third Reich stepped up its campaign against what the National Socialist leaders perceived as their most bitter enemy. The Third Reich rationalized and industrialized mass annihilation.[152]

"Der Entwurf zur Führerweisung Nr. 32 vom 11. Juni 1941: Eine quellenkritische Untersuchung," *Wehrwissenschaftliche Rundschau* 6 (1976), 127-41.

[149] Milan Hauner, *India in Axis Strategy: Germany, Japan, and Indian Nationalists in the Second World War* (Stuttgart, 1981), 133-92.

[150] Saul Friedländer, *Auftakt zum Untergang: Hitler und die Vereinigten Staaten von Amerika 1939-1941* (Stuttgart, 1965); Richard J. Overy, "From 'Uralbomber' to 'Amerikabomber': The Luftwaffe and Strategic Bombing," *Journal of Strategic Studies* 1 (1978), 154-78; James V. Compton, *The Swastika and the Eagle: Hitler, the United States, and the Origins of World War II* (Boston, 1967).

[151] There is no comprehensive study on the overall *strategic* development between 1941 and 1943, that is, the phase that began with the end of the blitzkrieg before Moscow and ended with Stalingrad and the loss of North Africa, the defeat in the Atlantic, and the collapse of the German air defense. Hans-Adolf Jacobsen and Jürgen Rohwer, eds., *Decisive Battles of World War II: The German View* (New York, 1965), 180-313; Hillgruber, *Zweite Weltkrieg*, 88-105; Jacobsen and Smith, *World War II*, ch. 4, outline the major strategic and operational decisions on the German side.

[152] The most recent summary is *Albert Seaton, The Fall of Fortress Europe 1943-1945*

For a second time, with new approaches, Germany had tried to escape from the constrictions of central Europe by means of force. Although it was remarkably successful for three long years, ultimately it failed once again. The European theater could indeed be fractured under the peculiar conditions of the 1930s, but the world could not be separated from Europe. Rather, European and global dynamics were increasingly intertwined by the Third Reich's desperate dash to escape these conditions. There was no escape—at least no military escape. The use of force, however cunningly it was engineered, involved Germany in a ladder of escalating violence in which, as a result of the expansion of the theater of war, countervailing forces outmatched German capabilities. Traditional professional strategy could not ultimately succeed in the context of modern Europe; the expedients after 1938 ran aground in the ensuing intercontinental confrontation.

Even before this long drawn-out phase of the war began, an era of German warfare had come to an end. German operational planners had claimed control over strategy, because they thought they had found military means to limit war and thus had discovered a way of using force instrumentally. However, time and again, the German use of force was countered by expanding the theater of war to a point at which Germany was no longer able to match the resources of its enemies. In the Second World War, the intensification of destruction through new weapons created an added dimension. German strategists did not find an answer to either of these problems, and it might be assumed that there was no military solution for them. Once this threshold was passed, war became self-destructive for Germany. Unable to meet its enemies on equal terms, German leaders preyed on their internal foes.

The dissolution of a professional approach to strategy was evident after 1938. While it contributed to the German victories before 1941 and released new energies, it also contained the seeds of disaster. The very means of achieving victory rendered German military and political leaders unable to gauge the limits of success. Indeed, they were pulled into ever more hazardous undertakings.

Two distinct developments allowed Germany to escape momentarily from its European confinement and to exploit the weaknesses of a still-fractured European order. Both were major steps in the formulation of a new German practice of war—a strategy in a new sense of the word. The military leadership broke with its traditional professional assessments of the European military situation and increasingly inclined toward

(London, 1981); see Raul Hilberg, *The Destruction of the European Jews* (New York, 1961) for the development of the annihilation campaign.

Hitler's political and ideological interpretations of the dynamics of national and international affairs.[153] At the same time, it discarded the comprehensive nature of deployment planning and turned to an ad hoc and opportunistic use of force as its main operational "doctrine." These changes occurred gradually and against initial internal resistance, but by 1940 they had replaced the heritage of Schlieffen and military professionalism. After France was defeated in 1940 (and despite the blemish of the battle of Britain, which thoroughly devalued the role of the *Luftwaffe* as a strategic weapon[154]) they fused and formed a new military practice that transformed the political and military end of strategy.

Let us turn first to the far more treacherous part of this innovative surge, the rise of political-ideological strategy. Hitler's strategy—steeped as it was in racist beliefs mediated by political experience—rejected the traditional analyses of the military strengths of the opposing sides in favor of assessing the domestic and international contradictions of each "people" and "race." Hitler cracked open the closed world of military deployment planning by substituting for the eternal concepts of strategy the equally eternal and pseudoscientific laws of race. This was a very feeble basis for strategy. But as derogatory as he could be about any "race" when it pleased his political temperament or his rhetorical style, this substitution also allowed Hitler to employ his experience as political organizer and tactician, producing cunning and, at times, clever assessments of national and international "politics."[155] Whereas the military counted and compared the military strengths and war potentials of nations, Hitler insisted that the politics of mobilizing and concentrating resources for military purposes shaped the ability (and willingness) to fight war. The actual ability and especially the willingness to fight war was more limited than the gross potential of a nation would indicate. In other words, Hitler acknowledged the problem of friction in war, while seeking to overcome it ideologically with assertions of will.

[153] Most clearly shown by Andreas Hillgruber, "Das Russlandbild der führenden deutschen Militärs vor Beginn des Angriffs auf die Sowjetunion," in *Russland—Deutschland—Amerika*, Festschrift für F. Epstein (Wiesbaden, 1980), 296-310; Gerhard L. Weinberg, "Hitler's Image of the United States," *American Historical Review* 69 (1964), 1006-1021. See also the provocative piece by Manfred Messerschmidt, "Das Verhältnis von Wehrmacht und NS-Staat und die Frage der Traditionsbildung," *Aus Politik und Zeitgeschichte* B 17/81 (25 April 1981), 11-23.

[154] Williamson Murray, *Strategy for Defeat: The Luftwaffe, 1933-1945* (Maxwell Air Force Base, Ala., 1983); Richard J. Overy, *The Air War 1939-1945* (New York, 1981).

[155] Percy E. Schramm, *Hitler: The Man and Military Leader* (Chicago, 1971); Martin Van Creveld, "War Lord Hitler: Some Points Reconsidered," *European Studies Review* 4 (1974), 57-79; Murray, *Change in the European Balance of Power*, passim. The Literature on Hitler as Feldherr is endless. The most comprehensive and, at the same time, most idiosyncratic and biased study is by David Irving, *Hitler's War* (New York, 1977).

Hitler replaced the notion of military readiness by an assessment of the cohesion of particular nations and of the international system. This never provided a systematic alternative to the instrumental or, for that matter, idealist calculus of professional strategy. Nor could it, for Hitler's gifts were intuitive rather than systematic. It is true that in shifting the focus of planning and decision making from operations to the political assessment of national and international conflict, Hitler developed strategic ideas that surpassed the most sophisticated military analyses. Even so, his ideological and racist strategy, based upon inspiration rather than upon logic, required a leap of faith from its followers, rather than acceptance based on rational conviction.[156] The only measure for this strategy was success, for as strategy it was nothing more than the promise to create fortuitous political circumstances that would allow the military to wage war.

Strategy thus degenerated into one of its permanent components: cunning. Hitler became celebrated as strategist and *Feldherr*, simply because for a time he was successful, not for any particular quality of his approach to strategy. No single method and no principle of strategy guided his policies. Strategic planning, once the hallmark of the principled and holistic approach to war by the German general staff, had become the captive of militant politics. It was expressed in continuous jockeying for position, testing the ground, exploring alternatives and options.[157] This kind of strategy—as distinct from the professional approach—was not guided by an inherent sense of national and international order. What guidance and direction it possessed, were shaped by the vision of a new order to be created by war which would secure the dominance of German society and the permanence of National Socialist rule. As long as this priority was maintained, strategy could be no more than an ad hoc enterprise.

The implications of this combination of flexibility and direction were far-reaching. If, in the old professional school, war was an instrumental exercise of elite politics, periodically regulating and adjusting the disorders of national life by military means, National Socialist war estab-

---

[156] Winfried Baumgart, "Zur Ansprache Hitlers vor den Führern der Wehrmacht am 22. August 1939," *Vierteljahrshefte für Zeitgeschichte* 16 (1968), 120-49; Gordon A. Craig, "Totalitarian Approaches to Diplomatic Negotiations," *Studies in Diplomatic History and Historiography in Honor of G. P. Gooch*, ed. A. O. Sarkissian (London, 1961), 107-135; see also Jacobsen, *Fall Gelb*, 59-64 and Jan Kershaw, *Der Hitler-Mythos: Volksmeinung und Propaganda im Dritten Reich* (Stuttgart, 1980).

[157] As in strategy, ideological direction and tactical opportunism went together in diplomacy; see Gerhard L. Weinberg, *The Foreign Policy of Hitler's Germany*; Klaus Hildebrand, *Deutsche Aussenpolitik 1933-1945: Kalkül oder Dogma?* (Stuttgart, 1971) tends to set them apart in a long tradition of studies that try to distinguish ideological (dogmatic) and pragmatic (power-political or opportunistic) considerations in Hitler's approach.

lished and maintained order in a limitless expansion of violence. War became the very basis of national and international relations. As a result, strategy was no longer a rational means of achieving specific goals, nor was it guided, in this process, by rational concepts of the use of force. Rather strategy became the main approach for shaping a world whose basic interrelations were based on struggle and conflict. Strategy was no longer instrumental but was ideological in its direction and opportunist in its methods.

The generals were never able to counter this approach, partly because they directly benefited from it and partly because they were unwilling to acknowledge what their own limited, narrow, and "professional" analysis discovered: that under the prevailing national and international conditions, the future of Germany did not lie with the professional military. Instead, they sided with the Führer, because against all odds he promised action and success.[158] Most officers remained dubious about the ideological bases of Hitler's strategy, but they did not have the intellectual strength or integrity to challenge or replace them, for that would have meant to limit the use of force in international politics and, perhaps, to forsake war. Instead they concentrated their efforts and brilliance on just one aspect of strategy: operational planning. In this way technocratic thinking and ideological strategy joined forces again after twenty years of unsuccessful attempts by the military to reconstruct strategy and regain control of war.

The flight into military fancy that had begun in 1916 continued in 1938 after all alternatives of providing an instrumentally rational military calculus for war either were rejected or collapsed. However, the balance between ideology and technocracy had changed since the dictatorship of the Third Supreme Command in the First World War. In 1916-17, ideological mobilization was subordinated to technocratic planning and only gained the upper hand for a brief moment, when technocratic planning and the state fell apart in defeat. Now, ideological mobilization for the creation of a new national and international order increasingly defined the perimeters of technocratic planning, which consumed itself in maximizing the use of weapons and abandoned its old traditions.

It would be wrong to synthesize Hitler's strategy into a coherent

---

[158] The role of action and success is demonstrated in Hitler's mobilization strategy before 1933 (Albrecht Tyrell, *Vom Trommler zum Führer: Der Wandel von Hitlers Selbstverständnis zwischen 1919 und 1924 und die Entstehung der NSDAP* [Munich, 1975]). Both continue to play a major role throughout his career and are outlined most succinctly in his late speeches; see Hans-Heinrich Wilhelm, ed., "Hitlers Ansprache vor Generalen und Offizieren am 26. Mai 1944," *Militärgeschichtliche Mitteilungen* 20 (1976), 123-70. For the role of "success" in the collapse of the military opposition see Harold C. Deutsch, *The Conspiracy against Hitler in the Twilight War* (Minneapolis, 1958).

and unified doctrine; it is equally misleading to condense the operational practices of the military into new principles of war. It is easy enough to highlight the morsels of old and new experience with mechanized warfare that furnished the elements of success and consisted of "a particular kind of mechanized warfare—cooperation of tanks, aircraft, dive bombers, and mobilized infantry and artillery—[which produced] a revolutionary change in military operations."[159] Much has been made of the combination of these elements, which have been summarized under the label of blitzkrieg.

> The Blitzkrieg advocates . . . stressed mobility and speed over firepower, although in the form of the tank, the dive bomber, and high-velocity anti-tank or anti-aircraft gun it aimed for great firepower at decisive points. Blitzkrieg welcomed encounter battles. It employed concentrated air power offensively and defensively, to prepare the way for advancing armor. Like German doctrine at the end of World War I, Blitzkrieg stressed infiltration tactics and flanking movements for both infantry and armor. As in the classic pre-World War I German doctrine, the new doctrine sought single and double envelopments. Unlike the earlier doctrine, it aimed as much at the disorientation and dislocation of the enemy command system as it did at the annihilation of enemy forces. This was to be achieved by deep penetrations into the rear areas of an enemy army. It was believed that if dislocation could be achieved, the battle of annihilation might be avoided, or at least easier.[160]

Blitzkrieg was all this, but as such it was not new—we may recall Rabenau—and even if all elements were put together in a "mission of paralysis"[161]—that is, a countercommand rather than a counterforce "strategy"—they did not make the crucial difference. The core of these operations did not consist in any particular use of the new means of warfare, but in a kind of operational opportunism that knew no pre-set and standardized methods, only the fullest possible exploitation of success with all available means in the pursuit of the ultimate goal of overthrowing the enemy by breaking the will of its leadership. Blitzkrieg lived off the destruction of a systematic approach to military command decisions. It was the opposite of a doctrine. Blitzkrieg operations consisted of an avalanche of actions that were sorted out less by design than by success.

---

[159] Murray, *Change in the European Balance*, 37.

[160] Barry R. Posen, *The Sources of Military Doctrine: France, Britain, and Germany between the World Wars* (Ithaca and London, 1984), 86.

[161] Matthew Cooper, *The German Army 1933-1945: Its Political and Military Failures* (New York, 1978), 149.

This kind of operation befitted a generation of exceedingly ambitious German commanders who were set free by the Third Reich and who emulated, in the military field, the mobilizing strategy of Hitler. Not that any of them was a committed National Socialist, but they fitted well into a system that honored success in the pursuit of conquest. In hindsight—and with some help from Liddell Hart—this torrent of action was squeezed into something it never was: an operational design.[162] Such as it was, this rested on the belief that technology (Guderian) or superior command performance (von Manstein) would make the difference in war. This, in turn, has attracted a host of pocket strategists who have given up thinking about war in favor of displaying their knowledge of weapons.

The cost of these impromptu operations is conveniently overlooked. What made them possible was the replacement a unified body of professional knowledge by competitive planning. Rather than enhancing cooperation and creating a smooth-functioning machine for mechanized warfare, Blitzkrieg pitted staffs and commanders against each other in the quest for optimal performance in the planning and conduct of war.[163] It created competing operational bases and very often left undecided which one would capture the initiative.[164] Indeed, the general condition that shaped Blitzkrieg strategy was the conjuncture of two elements: the emphasis on the optimal use of weapons and competitive military leadership. What was truly novel, however, was the dissolution of the corporate professional unity of the military leadership. This was the dominant force behind the successes of blitzkrieg operations, but also one of the major reasons for the permanent frictions and quarrels that became integral elements of competitive military planning.

The German military reached this point more by default than by design in the wake of the National Socialist coup against the "professional" military in 1938. This coup initiated the last phase of the long transformation of the German army and was a prerequisite for the transformation of its operational planning. Technocratically organized armed forces and soldiers trained in skill-oriented programs were placed under military commanders who had long renounced, and were mostly incapable of, comprehensive operational thinking and who knew no other

[162] Basil H. Liddell Hart, *The Other Side of the Hill*, 2d ed. (London, 1951); Brian Bond, "Liddell Hart and the German Generals," *Military Affairs* 41 (1977), 16-20.

[163] Once again, Operation Yellow is the best example; see Hans-Adolf Jacobsen, ed., *Dokumente zur Vorgeschichte des Westfeldzuges 1939-1940* (Göttingen, 1956).

[164] Hans-Adolf Jacobsen, ed., *Dokumente zum Westfeldzug 1940* (Göttingen, 1960); see also Macksey, *Guderian*, 80-90, and Guderian's self-portrait, Heinz Guderian, *Erinnerungen eines Soldaten*, 9th ed. (Neckargemünd, 1976); in addition see Erwin Rommel, *The Rommel Papers*, ed. B. H. Liddell Hart (London, 1953).

principle of war than the optimization of force at any cost. Hitler, of course, favored this kind of leadership and contributed to its rise in the reorganization of the armed forces in 1938. The National Socialist regime gave it legitimacy by underscoring the leadership principle grounded in a racial theory that also facilitated competition in the pursuit of conquest. Thus the two essential elements of National Socialist warfare—technocracy and ideology—were combined into strategy.[165]

The military response to the process of opening up their closed professional world changed over time. At first, strong groups within the military—in fact, the overwhelming majority of the commanding officers—rejected this development. They insisted on the cohesiveness, unity, and the autonomous and self-contained nature of military planning even after the framework of professional strategy had collapsed. Rather than principles of war, we find under Franz Halder the principles of bureaucratic rationality and hierarchy holding together operational planning. Intramilitary competition and National Socialist activism were temporarily blunted by bureaucratic routine.[166] But the pull of competition among military leaders was too strong. The early political and military successes of the Third Reich had their own momentum. If in 1938 the military was driven into competitive "strategy" by default, by 1940 they were thriving on competition. The grander the goal, the more its achievement highlighted the quality of the military performance. The technocracy of military planning and ideology began to fuse in a dynamic interplay. One could not exist without the other.

More than any other campaign, Barbarossa showed the fusion of technocracy and ideology in the context of competitive military planning. Much has been made of the ideological conditioning for this campaign. Certainly, the shared anti-Bolshevism of the military and of Hitler played an important role. But crucial was the fact that both expected instant

---

[165] Manfred Messerschmidt, *Die Wehrmacht im NS-Staat: Zeit der Indoktrination* (Hamburg, 1969) has the most detailed analysis. The role of competition and success becomes most evident in new forms of advancement and privilege; on dotations: Olaf Groehler, "Die Güter der Generäle: Dotationen im Zweiten Weltkrieg," *Zeitschrift für Geschichtswissenschaft* 19 (1971), 655-63; on promotion: Reinhard Stumpf, *Die Wehrmacht Elite: Rang- und Herkunfts-Struktur der deutschen Generale und Admirale 1933-1945* (Boppard, 1982).

[166] See Halder, *Kriegstagebuch*, passim, on the bureaucratic nature of decision making as well as Eduard Wagner, *Der Generalquartiermeister: Briefe und Tagebuchaufzeichnungen des Generalquartiermeisters des Heeres, General der Artillerie Eduard Wagner* (Munich, 1963). The outlook of the OKW was altogether less bureaucratic and more efficiency-oriented: Walther Warlimont, *Im Hauptquartier der deutschen Wehrmacht 1939-1945* (Frankfurt, 1962). One may contrast these two styles with the personalized infighting at the top; see Nicolaus von Below, *Als Hitlers Adjutant 1937-1945* (Mainz, 1980) and Hildegard von Kotze, ed., *Heeresadjutant bei Hitler 1938-1943: Aufzeichnungen des Majors Engel* (Stuttgart, 1974).

rewards from fighting a war against the Soviet Union. The military, with a very few exceptions, hoped to display their professional skills and looked forward to tangible returns in the form of prestige, promotions, and remuneration.[167] They acted throughout the planning phase and the first months of the campaign much as managers do, assuming that their value as individuals and as a collective would rise dramatically with the victorious completion of the campaign. Hence, everything that served the purpose of the campaign was good for them. Hitler considered the Soviet Union his object of conquest, the capstone of his efforts to establish the Third Reich as a racist Continental empire. These expectations together formed the basis for an almost universal eagerness to have a hand in the defeat of the Soviet Union that overrode any hesitation and caution. The planning for Barbarossa was a display of unlimited greed.

It was indicative of the nature of competitive strategy that, despite countless studies, the actual objectives and even the operational approaches of the campaign were never clearly defined. Instead we see competing objectives and competing approaches, and everyone hedged his bets in the expectation that the campaign would sooner or later swing in his direction. No doubt serious substantive differences did exist over the manner in which to fight the Soviet Union, but questions of substance arose in the context of a pervasive competitiveness among the senior commanders. Thus, the Army Command under Halder hoped to establish its predominant role by betting on Moscow as the decisive target of the campaign (and hoped to keep its reputation by dropping it in December 1941); individual commanders hoped to make their mark with one or another operational approach that would guarantee victory. In fact, the only point of view based on principle was the ideological one that came from Hitler, and his view was shaped by race and conquest.[168] Hitler's ideological aims, while consistent, were not much guidance in operational decisions.

The variance of operational opinions—Moscow versus Leningrad and the Ukraine—reflected differing assumptions about the outcome of the campaign and the role Hitler and the military played in it. Halder aimed at the destruction of the Soviet state with a resultant dissolution of national resistance, while Hitler thought in terms of conquering the country's centers of economic and social power. However, if we look

[167] Barry Leach, *German Strategy against Russia 1939-1941* (Oxford, 1973), 87-123. E. Moritz, ed., *Fall Barbarossa: Dokumente zur Vorbereitung der faschistischen Wehrmacht auf die Aggression gegen die Sowjetunion 1940/41* (Berlin/GDR, 1970).

[168] See a somewhat different emphasis in Horst Boog et al., *Der Angriff auf die Sowjetunion* (Stuttgart, 1983), 202-276, which is the most complete study on Operation Barbarossa so far. It is also the only study that highlights the apocalyptic dimensions of the operation as part of the military conduct of war.

carefully at the actual plans, neither Hitler nor Halder actually expected that the campaign would be decided by conquering any of these objectives. Their different approaches merely reflected hidden ambitions and latent antagonism. Simply put, the victory would be a military one if the goal was Moscow and the destruction or paralysis of the Soviet state; the victory would be National Socialist if the Ukraine was conquered. The conflict over operational priorities thus became a symbolic one, and neither side cared to clarify what would be achieved by attaining one or the other goal.[169] In any case, these choices became important only in the second stage of the campaign, after July 1941, when military and militant expectations had to be changed.

According to the final directive for Operation Barbarossa, the planners hoped to defeat the Soviet army by the second stage of the campaign and thus to render the nation defenseless, making further military progress only a matter of exploiting the defeat. The final plan for Barbarossa only specified the first, and what was considered to be the decisive, stage of the advance, whose main task was "to defeat Soviet Russia in a quick campaign." This was to be achieved by large-scale pincer movements, that is, "swift and deep thrusts . . . to tear open the front of the mass of the Russian army which, it is anticipated, will be in western Russia. The enemy groups separated by these penetrations will then be destroyed" in cauldron battles that were to take place west of the rivers Dnjepr and Dvina. This was the main and only truly operational goal of the campaign, because it was assumed that the decisive first blows would ensure "the freedom of movement for further tasks."[170]

This plan did not satisfy all staff officers and army commanders. It kept them on a short leash and under the tight control of the Army Command. They aimed at a greater and more independent role in operations and after the war claimed that undue restrictions "from above" had been the main flaw in a campaign that otherwise might have been successful. Thus the more daring emphasized "the importance of keeping the Russians on the run and allowing them no time to rally." Guderian "wanted to drive straight on to Moscow, and was convinced that he could get there if no time was wasted. Russia's resistance might be paralyzed by the thrust at the center of Stalin's power." As such these plans were not necessarily better or more adequate than the actual operations

[169] Ibid., 233-47. Frans Pieter ten Kate, *De Duitse aanval of de Sovjet-Unie en 1941*, 2 vols. (Groningen, 1968). The most detailed discussion is A. Beer, *Der Fall Barbarossa: Untersuchungen zur Geschichte der Vorbereitungen des deutschen Feldzuges gegen die UdSSR* (diss. phil., Münster, 1978).

[170] Boog, *Angriff auf die Sowjetunion*, 242-48 (final deployment plan of 8 June 1941) and 238-42 (Directive #21).

though they were and still are heartwarming for advocates of tank forces.[171] However, they were primarily a reflection of the competitive nature of operational planning in Germany as it reached a climax in a campaign characterized more by its disagreements than by any particular doctrine.

Yet these debates miss the decisive issue altogether. The outcome of the war against the Soviet Union was neither a matter of armor versus operations with combined weapons (the intramilitary conflict) nor a matter of Moscow versus the Ukraine (a conflict between military and ideological politics). It was rather the product of an escalatory and competitive use of force. The Third Reich faced the consequences of a strategy and a process of operational planning grounded in the competitive optimization of force and terror. These limits were already evident in July–August 1941.

The first stage of the campaign was a success beyond anyone's expectations. Everybody agreed that the war was virtually won, and so it was, at least in the eyes of almost all—and not just German—observers. This assumption was more than reasonable if we consider the fact that the main forces of the Soviet Union were annihilated or captured in the first weeks and that Stalin's rule was thrown into disarray. However, it soon became obvious that the Soviet Union was not defeated. The freedom of movement that the German side expected to gain was never achieved. The Soviet leadership continued the war desperately and with tremendous brutality against its own people as well as against the German enemy. The Soviet Union would not surrender; if it was to be defeated it would have to be occupied. Only at this point did space and time truly begin to matter, not because there was a mud season with a winter to follow, but because every square mile had to be taken from a defiant enemy and held against the resistance of the occupied.[172]

To be sure, with appropriate action, it might have been possible to advance on Moscow much faster and perhaps to arrive there before the rain and mud season, paralyzing the Soviet capital and, possibly, capturing even more troops in another major cauldron battle (which even-

[171] Quoted in Cooper, *German Army*, 272; see also Hermann Hoth, *Panzer-Operationen: Die Heeresgruppe 3 und der operative Gedanke der deutschen Fahrung im Sommer 1941* (Heidelberg, 1956). See the critical evaluation of these concepts in Brian Fugate, *Thunder on the Dneiper: The End of the Blitzkrieg Era, Summer 1941* (Ph.D. diss., University of Texas, Austin, 1976). On confusion and conflict in the German leadership, see Earl F. Ziemke, "Franz Halder and Orsha: The German General Staff Seeks a Consensus," *Military Affairs* 39 (1975), 173-76.

[172] Albert Seaton, *The Russo-German War, 1941-1945* (London, 1971); Klaus Reinhardt, *Die Wende vor Moskau: Das Scheitern der Strategie Hitlers im Winter 1941/42* (Stuttgart, 1972).

tually did take place, though with rising German costs and too late to reach Moscow). But these were the dreams of ambitious commanders who were increasingly at odds with each other and had long lost any idea how, after all, the Soviet Union could be defeated—that is, how the will of the nation and its leadership could be broken. Hitler, pondering the experience of the first six weeks of the war, concluded "that one cannot beat the Russian with operational successes . . . , because he simply does not acknowledge defeat."[173] Hitler's exasperation reflected the true issue. What more could be done than to defeat major parts of the Russian army? How could one break the will of a nation that would not surrender, but recuperated again and again, while German forces became weaker and weaker? More battles could be won, perhaps at Leningrad, at Moscow, or in the Ukraine, but obviously one could win battles and lose the war. This was the main operational problem after August 1941. It was the insoluble operational problem for an army and a political leadership that had come to believe that the mere accumulation of success would ensure victory. This is a prime example of strategic decadence, but by no means the last of its kind. All show one common characteristic: the understanding of war is displaced by the competitive management of military action.

It is often argued that the German leadership underestimated the Soviet war potential and thus engaged in a campaign that was poorly planned from the start and doomed to failure. This view misses the crucial point. German forces found their limits not in the industrial capacity of the Soviet Union, but in the ability of the Soviet leadership not only to keep factories going but also to send wave upon wave of recruits into battle. The Soviet military cadres continued to lead their troops into battle, perhaps not as elegantly, but every bit as effectively as their British and German counterparts. Russia's ability to mobilize and fight made possible the decisive turn of the war that came with the defeat of the frontal attack against Moscow and the beginning of massive Soviet counterattacks in December 1941.[174]

We know next to nothing about what motivated the Soviet leadership in the months between June and December and what enabled them to mobilize manpower and resources even in those areas of Soviet Asia and the southern Soviet Union that it had barely pacified and brought under control, because Soviet historians believe the Soviet victory was predes-

---

[173] Halder, *Kriegstagebuch*, 3:123.
[174] Reinhardt, *Wende vor Moskau*, 197-254; Boog, *Angriff auf die Sowjetunion*, 600-51; Alexander Werth, *Russia at War, 1941-1945* (New York, 1964), 225-74; Albert Seaton, *The Battle for Moscow, 1941-1942* (London, 1971). See also John Erickson, *The Road to Stalingrad* (New York, 1975).

tined just as some German historians believe in a predestined defeat. But we do know this much: Soviet resistance and determination, wavering at first and leading to massive defections, stiffened with the growing awareness of German policy and terror. The more the German army advanced, the more they defeated and captured enemy forces, and the more brutal Germany's efforts were to subdue an enemy that did not recognize defeat, the tougher and more desperate Soviet resistance became and the higher rose the costs on the German side.

The German defeat had many sources, and it is not enough to regard only the military ones. Others were the concept of hegemonic order that the Third Reich began to impose and the way in which the war was fought. It was a war of terrorist subjugation and of what was called, in National Socialist jargon, "special treatment" (*Sonderbehandlung*) of whole societies. It was a war of ruthless starvation and decimation of all "Slavic" peoples, fought with utter disregard for the basic human rights of captured soldiers and officers. And it was a war of plunder and exploitation of the people in eastern Europe that freely calculated the death of "many millions."[175] The strategy of racist war permeated every aspect of the struggle in the East, strengthening the resolve of the Soviet people and, in fact, making it possible to unite them under an all-Russian banner.

What made German "strategists" pursue this counterproductive course? One might point to ideology, but ideology followed a distinct logic rather than being a metahistorical force that intruded into an otherwise "traditionalist" or professional military. On the front this war was fought with utter brutality from the very beginning, because victory had to be achieved quickly.[176] Thus destruction became an end in itself in the hope that unleashing violence would eventually destroy the enemy. The military had little choice in this matter. If it wanted to win, it had to act quickly. If it wanted to do so against a defiant enemy, it had to escalate the use of force. If victory was not forthcoming, it could only resort to further escalation. In the end, however, this undermined the very basis of success. However ambivalent the military might be about ideological terrorism, its course led inexorably from the use of war as a means of attaining a rational end to its use as a means of extermination.

This escalatory practice guided not only the military effort, but also

---

[175] Boog, *Angriff auf die Sowjetunion*, 150. See the detailed analysis of the ideological, racist, and economic war in the same volume.

[176] Boog, *Angriff auf die Sowjetunion*, 242-58, 470-97, 959-1021; Hans Hohn, "Zur Entwicklung der Einsatzgrundsätze der Infanterie der deutschen Wehrmacht im Zweiten Weltkrieg," *Zeitschrift für Militärgeschichte* 9 (1970), 554-66. Jürgen Förster, "Zur Rolle der Wehrmacht im Krieg gegen die Sowjetunion," *Aus Politik und Zeitgeschichte* B 45/80 (8 November 1980), 3-15; Seaton, *Russo-German War*; Omar Bartov, *The Eastern Front 1941-45: German Troops and the Barbarisation of Warfare* (Basingstoke, 1985).

that of the rear formations (*Sicherheits Divisionen*) of the Wehrmacht and of the *Einsatzgruppen*, the SS, and the host of other civilian and military organizations in the rear. Force was the only means of establishing and maintaining German hegemony over Europe. Military victory, the paralysis of the enemy's ability to concentrate and project force, was its decisive prerequisite; terror was its main consequence. Together these formed the essence of National Socialist war making. One fed the other, and subsequent analysis should not seek to separate them. Together they turned war on the eastern front into a struggle for survival because ideological goals were at the center of operations, but even more because the unshackling of plain violence was the only "principle" that guided the conduct of war.

Escalatory warfare—foreshadowed in the First World War, but held back by a growing opposition to the war—evolved unhindered after 1939. However skillfully individual battles and campaigns were fought, it was a war in which the expanding torrent of destruction became the main operational and tactical rationale. Its main and only operational goal was to inflict damage and destruction, to destroy the enemy state and to batter enemy societies and their armed forces into submission. In this process the very basis of professional warfare evaporated.

What, then, was the operational challenge of World War II? Perhaps in part, the question of how to employ armor effectively—an arm that was not, in fact, used in the best possible way, since the "high" tactics of combining counterforce and countercommand practices were never properly developed. But the real challenge of the world war consisted less in the technical methods of using force than in its limitation—that is, in combining the use of the resources and manpower of a mobilized nation to ensure maximum efficiency in destroying enemy concentrations and paralyzing enemy command, while using no more destructive force than was needed for that purpose. The challenge of total war was to calibrate the increase of violence to the decline of the enemy's resolve. The unpremeditated outcome of the German practice of war was to escalate force and terror to the point that it stiffened the resistance of old enemies and created new ones.

This most vital issue of the practice of war was rarely raised in Germany. Its consideration suited neither the militant strategy of conquest nor the operational opportunism and the competitive character of the German military. As far as the German army was concerned, the very methods that helped to overcome the stalemate of the First World War produced the escalatory ladder to apocalyptic war. There was no return to a holistic approach to strategy in the German tradition, but the way forward led into disaster. It was the disaster of a military that was, at times, brilliant in its use of force, but unable and unwilling to limit this use because the limitation of force would have raised the issue of whether war was still feasible for Germany.

V

If the history of the German army from the 1930s to the middle years of the Second World War had indeed been "essentially the record of the unresolved conflicts between protagonists of a new strategy founded on the revolutionary use of armoured, motorized, and air forces engaged in a mission of paralysis, and the adherents of the traditional strategy based on infantry armies . . . ,"[177] we might as well forget about thirty years of turmoil in the making of German strategy. How, why, and with what consequences German strategy became a matter of maximizing weapons, this essay has tried to analyze. In conclusion, strategy beyond military technocracy and operational opportunism must be reemphasized. What exactly were Germany's strategic options in the first half of the twentieth-century, and which strategic choices were made?

Germany's development after unification rested on the twin pillars of its economy and its intellectual life, not on arms. But these sources of strength were also sources of German vulnerability. In a narrow military sense, these consisted in Germany's geopolitical situation in the center of Europe, which was exacerbated by the growing reach and destructiveness of weapons, and by Germany's dependence on markets and food stuffs beyond its control. In a wider social and political sense these weaknesses consisted in a loss of autonomy of the new nation-state in an increasingly internationalized economy and in the dependence of society's well-being on global market conditions. German strategy was shaped by the way in which Germans—and not just German elites—and Germany's neighbors dealt with Germany's rise to a position of economic and scientific predominance in Europe, the advantages that this position brought and the challenges that it created. It was the outcome of choices within constraints.

German politics could and did, at times, choose to capitalize on its economic strength and to scale down the military consequences of unification. This option appeared, in its "strong" version, for the first time in the late 1880s and the early 1890s with the attempt to freeze the military situation in Europe so that industry—supported by the navy—could expand unhindered. This choice is most commonly linked to the brief chancellorship of Leo von Caprivi (1890-1894), but it was also the

---

[177] Cooper, *German Army*, 149.

594

basis of Schlieffen's strategy.[178] It was a solution that promised neither peace nor war, but produced a fragile balance in Europe based upon opposing military blocs and a diplomacy that was largely preoccupied with armaments. As such, this choice was inherently unstable. It depended on the international system's ability to maintain the balance in Europe and, at the domestic level, on the government's ability to check both pacifism and socialist internationalism, and the demands of economic interests for more supportive and militant policies. In the end the strategy collapsed under the pressures of imperial rivalries and of populist politics. It is worth noting that European elites, entering the twentieth century, increasingly lost their ability to establish international consensus and to impose it on their societies. This was the most important precondition for the eventual collapse of "professional" strategy, which depended on the ability to limit wars and to maintain military autonomy at home.

A "weak" version of this choice also existed, which looked promising for a moment, but quickly faded. This option was based on the disarmament of Germany and on the attempt in the 1920s to rebuild national and international stability on the foundation of a revitalized and internationalized economy. But the weak version failed almost as soon as it was conceived—though it produced some brilliant operational concepts—mainly for two reasons that repay careful scrutiny. Even the radical, unilateral disarmament of Germany to a point of defenselessness could not calm the general tendency to distrust a nation that remained the strongest economic power in continental Europe and retained all the potential for threatening the European status quo. At the same time, economic stabilization could not reconcile large segments of the German population to Germany's diminished international status, but rather nurtured a reaction: increasingly rampant militant nationalism. Once stabilization proved to be a mirage, this combination of foreign distrust and militant nationalism at home congealed into an explosive mixture that set Europe ablaze. However much we must emphasize the collapse of the economic world order as a destabilizing factor and however much we must stress German revisionism and nationalism in this context,[179] we can also conclude that Europe as a whole failed. It could not rise to the challenge of attempting to order its affairs on the basis of a militarily "weak" version of national and international stabilization.

The alternative German choice consisted in reinforcing economic power by military might. Because of the nature of an expansive and

[178] Michael Geyer, *Deutsche Rüstungspolitik, 1860-1980* (Frankfurt, 1984), 61-63.

[179] Josef Becker and Klaus Hildebrand, eds., *Internationale Beziehungen in der Weltwirtschaftskrise 1929-1933* (Munich, 1980).

595

internationalized economy, this was necessarily a hegemonic approach.[180] This choice, once again, came in a "weak" and a "strong" version. The "weak" version has been considered the main source of the German problem in this century. This was fuelled by the quest for military autonomy, by the search for strategically secure borders as well as industrial control of principal markets and resources, and by the fear of left-wing politics. Its primary motivation was domestic: the preservation of elite rule, which may be glimpsed both in the operational and organizational details of the preparation and use of force. Bethmann Hollweg, Falkenhayn, and Seeckt are the best representatives of this course between 1914 and 1945. Rearmament and the resurgence of professional strategy in the 1930s reflected the same basic outlook. It was an extension of elite rule both inward into German politics and outward into international economic and political affairs. However, all these concepts failed before the wars in this century moved into their decisive stage. The imperial army's operational designs unravelled at the Marne and again at Verdun; Seeckt's army was never able to engage in combat, and Beck's and Fritsch's deployment plans ran into a dead end. The plans were beautifully conceived, but useless. The German wars in the twentieth century began in a serious way when, in search for expedients, national society was mobilized.

Goals of mass war began to shape the options in 1916 and 1938. These formed the "strong" version of the hegemonic choice that underwent a significant transformation from the First to the Second World War. In demanding the functional subordination of all of German society—Ludendorff's technocratic solution—in favor of a more efficient organization of production and destruction, industry and the military attempted to accommodate mass politics by promising to share the spoils of efficiency in due course; that is, they inflated war goals and opened the floodgates for a war of national purification. The National Socialists were no less totalitarian in their claims for organizing society. However, they aimed at a reconstruction of German society and of the German state on the basis of conquest, annihilation, and subjugation. At last, German society was to be autonomous, free from the vagaries of the market,[181] and secure behind its extended imperial borders. The National Socialist answer to the challenge of mass participation in politics and war and their response to the economic and social crisis of the interwar years consisted in a populist and militant form of hegemony. The resulting

[180] Fischer, *Griff nach der Weltmacht.*
[181] See the Niederschrift über die Besprechung in der Reichskanzlei am 5. November 1937 (see note 128).

ideological strategy fused with the operational opportunism of the German military.

The brutality and inhumanity of this choice seems to transcend historical explanation, and yet it is only comprehensible on the basis of strategic choices made to deal with Germany's position of economic predominance in Europe and its dependence upon world markets, on the one hand, and to come to terms with the domestic conflict between the challenge of mass participation and the defense of elite rule, on the other.

This solution was not formulated by the military. It was first of all the German intelligentsia who expressed this fateful strategic choice for Germany in the twentieth century. Germany, they argued, could only survive if it controlled its own destiny. German sovereignty and social and cultural integrity depended on expansion to a point at which it covered all the bases of its dependence.[182] The combination of expansive, "scientific" arrogance and cultural despair gave twentieth-century German wars their ideological agenda, which were then endlessly multiplied and vulgarized through the increasing power of propaganda. It also created an insoluble operational problem, for Germany never possessed enough military power to control its own destiny, which instead was shaped by global economic processes.

These doctrines only mushroomed when they were taken up by pivotal segments of German society and when visions of apocalyptic war began to shape domestic and international affairs. Visions of hegemony and national regeneration were able to overcome even the most deep-seated fears of destruction and death. More than any particular technology, they determined the destructive scope of the Second World War. The war was unleashed by a nation strong enough to challenge the world, but unable, at any time in the first half of the twentieth century, to cope with its vulnerabilities, themselves the results of its extraordinary rise. The source of German strategic hubris—and the root for the operational opportunism of Ludendorff, Halder, Guderian, Rommel, Manstein, and their peers—was the conviction that Germans could rule others in lieu of governing themselves and that Germany must either rule or perish as a nation.

[182] Rüdiger vom Bruch, *Wissenschaft, Politik und öffentliche Meinung: Gelehrtenpolitik im wilhelminischen Deutschland 1890-1914* (Husum, 1980); Schwabe, *Wissenschaft und Kriegsmoral.*

20. Liddell Hart and De Gaulle: The Doctrines of Limited Liability and Mobile Defense

BRIAN BOND AND MARTIN ALEXANDER

D ESPITE THE clear-cut defeat of Germany in 1918 and the severe restrictions placed on its armed forces and armaments by the Treaty of Versailles, Germany's inevitable revival and determination to overthrow these humiliations constituted the focal point for French military thinkers throughout the interwar period.

The First World War cost France over 1,300,000 military casualties and the occupation of ten of its economically richest departments. No other combatant power suffered such proportionate losses. France emerged nominally among the victors but in reality had not so much won as survived. In the aftermath its security policies and doctrines naturally became defensive, and the 1920s witnessed a return to the traditional military credo of the Third Republic: faith in the trinity of a fortified eastern border, foreign alliances, and universal conscription.

Concurrently with this self-imposed defensive retrenchment the military authorities believed that if a European war ever recurred it would probably again assume attritional form. Memories of the exhaustion and mutinies in the French army in 1917 were as fresh as the example of the importance of American forces in defeating Germany in 1918. Victory in a new conflict would require another multinational coalition enjoying economic resilience and immense potential armed strength. For France the latter lay partly in legions of mobilizable reservists, partly in its military industries, and partly in diversionary actions by its central and eastern European allies. Much, nevertheless, depended on the development and organization of motorization and mechanization, the tools presented to the generals in 1917-1918 as possible decisive war winners, if these underlying strengths were to be harnessed to keep the French army in the front rank.

In contrast, Britain in the 1920s perceived no obvious enemy in the near future and the contingency plans—if they can be dignified with such a term—made against France, the Soviet Union, and the United States now have an air of unreality. Under acute financial pressure and in a state of war weariness, Britain demobilized its huge armies at a breakneck pace. In November 1918 over 3.5 million men were in uniform (excluding those paid for by the Government of India); two years later they had been reduced to 370,000. Thereafter, despite the onerous new imperial and European commitments undertaken in the post-1918 treaties, annual defense budgets and establishments were steadily reduced until 1932. Not only were expenditures and numbers drastically cut: most of the armaments firms were closed or converted to nonmilitary production; the higher military formations above divisional level disappeared; and no systematic effort was made to record the main lessons of the unprecedented national war effort of 1914-1918. The report of the single War Office Committee that recommended preserving at least the organization for raising an army of forty-one divisions in a future national emergency, was stillborn.[1] Although occupation forces were retained in various parts of Europe until 1930, the British army became fully extended in its traditional role of imperial policing. This priority was justified by the stipulation of the Ten Year Rule, a Cabinet directive originally issued to the service ministries in 1919 for the coming financial year, but later placed on a moving basis (so that the end of the ten years never became any nearer) and retained until 1932. The directive stated: "It should be assumed, for framing revised Estimates, that the British Empire will not be engaged in any great war during the next ten years, and that no Expeditionary Force is required for this purpose."[2] There was much to be said in favor of such a broad directive, which in effect embodied the financial and strategic realities of 1920, but it was far less relevant by the end of that decade. The effects of the Ten Year Rule have been debated, but there can be little doubt that it put a damper on radical thinking and experiment within the services.

Given these restrictions and the growing public disillusionment with the aftermath of the First World War, it was perhaps surprising that in the 1920s Britain produced some outstanding military thinkers and also led the way in field trials with experimental mechanical forces. How can we explain this phenomenon? Britain's leading theorists had experienced the incompetence and waste of First World War operations, mostly as junior officers. Convinced that there would soon be another great war

---

[1] W. O. Paper A2277 of 1919, Committee on the Organisation of the After War Army, Public Record Office, London (hereafter PRO). For further details on the British sources used in this essay see Brian Bond, *Liddell Hart: A Study of His Military Thought* (London, 1977) and Brian Bond, *British Military Policy between the Two World Wars* (Oxford, 1980).

[2] Cab 23/15, 15 August 1919, PRO. See Bond, *British Military Policy*, 23-26, 94-97.

and reposing little faith in international treaties or the League of Nations, they were obsessed with learning the "correct lessons" from the First World War, overhauling the structure of the army, and restoring mobility to operations. It seems probable that both tactical and strategic ideas flourished in Britain in the 1920s for two main reasons: there was considerable public impetus behind the writers' concern to analyze and profit from the painful experience of 1914-1918; and the absence of an immediate obvious enemy provided a comparatively relaxed atmosphere in which theories could be developed in a quasiscientific way. A marked contrast existed between the unspecific "Redland versus Blueland" exercises of the 1920s and the practical realities that became all too apparent when likely enemies appeared after 1933. We shall later examine in some detail the difficulties that one distinguished writer, Basil H. Liddell Hart, experienced in making the transition from discussing general theories of mechanization and armored warfare to formulating a specific national strategy.

Before this crisis occurred, however, the ferment of ideas and wide scope for experiment in Britain, particularly on the issue of mechanization, was envied by the French, who regarded J. F. C. Fuller and Liddell Hart as the outstanding pioneers.[3] As this essay will suggest, Fuller, Liddell Hart and their closest counterpart in France, Charles de Gaulle, were not "makers of modern strategy" in the sense that they decisively influenced their own nations' defense policies. But they certainly merit inclusion in this distinguished company for their wide-ranging and original contributions to military theory and the conduct of war both in the interwar period and later.

This is not meant to imply that the years between the wars were characterized by a heroic but vain struggle of a handful of brilliant iconoclasts, who were later proved right, against a compact majority of antediluvian cavalry-loving diehards. Closer inspection of the records and service journals in both Britain and France shows that the reality was more complex. The progressives or radicals did not agree with each other on all points and in some respects their predictions proved mistaken or inadequate. Moreover, although diehards or reactionaries certainly existed, the majority of officers whose views can be traced could be described as cautious or moderate progressives; that is, they recognized that machines such as tanks would play an increasingly important part

___

[3] See Lieut.-Col. Gemeau, "Les tanks dans l'Armée Brittanique: Passé, présent, avenir," *Revue d'infanterie*, no. 63 (April 1923), 520-35; Emile Alléhaut, "Motorisation et conceptions militaires britanniques," *Revue d'infanterie*, no. 81 (October-November 1927), 418-631; report by Col. R. Voruz, French military attaché London, no. 124, 1930, and by Major Cuny, assistant military attaché, London, 23 January 1932, cartons 7N2798 and 7N2800, Service Historique de l'Armée de Terre, Vincennes (hereafter SHAT).

in future war, but they tended to stress the numerous problems and uncertainties. How, for example, would armored forces be supplied and repaired when far from base? Would they not soon be countered by antitank guns? And above all, what part would armored units play in military organization as a whole, given the shortage of funds and equipment, and traditional interservice rivalries?[4]

I

Within the complex environment of military thinking, between the two world wars, the leading tank pioneers—and most particularly Colonel J. F. C. Fuller—blazed the trail with impressive self-confidence and panache. Fuller had already made his name as the author of the revolutionary "Plan 1919," which envisaged employing about five thousand heavy and medium tanks with close air support for a thrust some twenty miles deep that would paralyze the German command system. Throughout the 1920s, in a variety of unorthodox and controversial publications, Fuller continued to be the chief spokesman of the radical advocates of mechanization. In a prize-winning essay in 1919, for example, he asserted that the tank could completely replace the infantry and cavalry, and that artillery, in order to survive, would have to develop into a kind of tank. He estimated that it would take five years to convert the army into mechanized divisions and another five to overcome prejudices and vested interests. In this forecast he was much too sanguine.[5] Liddell Hart, seventeen years younger than Fuller and a far less experienced soldier, was the junior partner on the mechanization issue until the late 1920s. In frequent meetings and a voluminous correspondence the two helped each other to refine and develop their ideas. Fuller was the bolder, more dynamic, and original thinker; Liddell Hart was more balanced, tactful, and less extravagant as a military polemicist. Two main differences between the pioneers' thinking on mechanization may be discerned at this stage. First, Liddell Hart advanced more detailed and realistic plans for the gradual conversion, in four stages, to a "New Model" army though he did not completely allow for the rigid restrictions imposed by the Treasury. Second, though giving precedence to the tank, he always stressed the need for infantry (or "tank marines") as an integral part of the mechanized force, whereas for the most part Fuller relegated infantry

[4] Bond, *British Military Policy*, 127-33. The best analysis of British officers' views on mechanization is H. R. Winton, "General Sir John Burnett-Stuart and British Military Reform, 1927-1938" (Ph.D. diss., Stanford University, 1977).

[5] "Plan 1919" is published as an appendix in J. F. C. Fuller, *Memoirs of an Unconventional Soldier* (London, 1936). See also Jay Luvaas, *The Education of an Army* (London, 1964), 335-75 and A. J. Trythall, *'Boney' Fuller: The Intellectual General* (London, 1977).

to a strictly subordinate role of protecting lines of communication and fixed bases.[6]

Although he became unjustly associated with the notion of "all tank" armies, Fuller's interest in mechanization was from the early 1920s only part of a wider concern with the impact of science and technology on warfare. He believed that the future lay with small professional armies. He also developed the image of a land battle analogous to naval operations between mechanized forces. He predicted, accurately, that when tank armor became penetrable this would lead not to obsolescence but to a greater emphasis on firepower and mobility at the expense of protection. Throughout this period his main concern was to secure armies that could achieve victory at the least cost, or even prevent or deter war altogether. Unfortunately, as his biographer stresses, temperament and professional frustrations caused Fuller to adopt an increasingly strident, hectoring tone. He suggested that since war was a matter of racial survival and since democracies were unwilling to carry out essential military reforms, a more authoritarian system might be necessary. It was not therefore surprising that, soon after retiring in 1933 with the rank of major-general, he threw in his lot with Sir Oswald Mosley and the Fascist Movement in Britain.[7]

By the mid-1920s Liddell Hart, who after leaving the army quickly became a well-known writer on military affairs, had evolved the notion of a "New Model" army to operate independently of roads and railways and to advance one hundred miles in a day. In his little book *Paris* he distilled his ideas about the future of warfare and sketched exciting prospects for mechanized armies:

> Once appreciate that tanks are not an extra arm or a mere aid to infantry but the modern form of heavy cavalry and their true military use is obvious—to be concentrated and used in as large masses as possible for a decisive blow against the Achilles' heel of the enemy army, the communications and command centres which form its nerve system. Then not only may we see the rescue of mobility from the toils of trench-warfare, but with it the revival of generalship and the art of war, in contrast to its mere mechanics.[8]

France also made considerable progress in the 1920s in the study and development of mechanization. Encouraged by an innovative chief

---

[6] Trythall, *'Boney' Fuller*, 92-93. Bond, *Liddell Hart*, 27-30 and Bond, *British Military Policy*, 137.

[7] Trythall, *'Boney' Fuller*, 99, 146.

[8] B. H. Liddell Hart, *Paris, or the Future of War* (New York, 1925), 79-85. For Liddell Hart's perceptive comments on French and German military doctrines in the 1920s, see his *The Remaking of Modern Armies* (Boston, 1927), 250, 276.

of staff from 1920-1923, General Edmond Buat, French officers explored the potential of the new weapons of mobility: motor transport, infantry carriers, armored cars, and tanks. Motorization flourished under visionaries like Colonels Emile Alléhaut, Charles Chedeville, and Joseph Doumenc. The army was equipped from the wartime military output of a burgeoning motor industry, led by Renault and Citroën who, with the military, benefited from long-distance supply and exploration ventures in French Africa. Simultaneously Doumenc, building on his experience of organizing the motor columns along the *voie sacrée* to relieve the supply crisis at Verdun during the 1916 siege, experimented with structures for large motorized units.

Mechanization prospered similarly. France had rapidly evolved an armored force after 1915-1916, possessing by the end of the war three thousand Renault FT-17 light tanks, and heavier Schneiders and St. Chamonds. General Jean-Baptiste Estienne, "father" of this tank arm, remained responsible for mechanized experimentation in the first years of peace. With Buat, he preached the cause of tactical mobility and the utility of armor's striking power both offensively and in counterattack. A prophetic and unconventional officer of a type characteristically thrown up by tank corps in succeeding decades, Estienne believed that "the tank is undeniably the most powerful weapon of surprise and therefore of victory." He urged that armor be an independent branch, distinguished from the infantry to which it was "not in the least analogous" by its armament, modes of combat, and logistical organization. He deemed it "essential . . . that tanks remain in general reserve under the commander-in-chief who assigns them temporarily to an attacking army or to a mission formerly performed by cavalry"; it was "neither rational nor practicable to assign tanks organically to an infantry division whose task is to resist, come what may, by firepower and fortification." A motorized corps of only twenty thousand men would be mobile, "thereby possessing a formidable advantage over the cumbersome armies of the recent past."[9]

Thus inspired, younger officers like Colonels Jean Perré, Joseph Molinié, and Pol-Maurice Velpry studied the doctrine and practical em-

[9] Jean-Baptiste Estienne, preface of 9 April 1931 to G. Murray Wilson, *Les chars d'assaut au combat, 1916-1919*, trans. A. Thomazi (Paris, 1931), 14-15. See also Estienne's "Conférence faite le 15 février 1920 sur les chars d'assaut: Histoire technique, histoire tactique, vues d'avenir" (Paris, 1920), reprinted in *Bulletin trimestriel de l'Association des Amis de l'Ecole de Guerre* 14 (October 1961), 22-30. Cf. Pierre-André Bourget, *Le général Estienne: Penseur, ingénieur, soldat* (Paris, 1956); Emile Alléhaut, *Etre prêts: Puissance aérienne, forces de terre* (Paris, 1935); Charles Chedeville, "Etude sur l'emploi des chars de combat," *Revue d'infanterie*, no. 59 (December 1921), 35-61, 174-88, 290-305, 395-405, 529-42, 650-75; Joseph E. A. Doumenc, "Les transports automobiles dans la guerre de mouvement," *Revue militaire française*, no. 6 (October-November 1922), 61-76, 191-210 and ibid., "Puissance et mobilité," *Revue militaire française*, nos. 8, 9 (June-July, August 1923), 342-65, 44-45.

ployment of the mechanized formations of the future. The conference chambers of the Ecole de Guerre and the training grounds of Coetquidan, Mailly, and Mourmelin were alive in the 1920s to the sound of the theory and practice of mobile experimentation. As the decade wore on, however, stultification replaced innovation. Experimentation diminished as technologically advanced and thus costly activities fell prey to the reductions in military budgets that went with the postwar climate of peace. Franco-German rapprochement in 1925 strengthened political optimism about a more peaceful European order. Mechanization and motorization, appearing more suitable for "offensive" or "aggressive" military action, were criticized politically in France as inappropriate to an avowedly defensive strategy.

Finally, the decade culminated in the ascendancy of Marshal Philippe Pétain and General Eugène Debeney over military policy and thought. The former, the "savior of Verdun," and the latter, who became chief of the general staff when Buat died in 1923, influenced the officer corps by their advocacy of the dogma of static prepared defenses. Estienne, his Tank Inspectorate already subordinated since 1920 to the infantry, was blocked as a major-general and forced to retire in 1927. Reduced, somewhat like Fuller in Britain, to be an outside observer, he could only privately advocate projects, which were most often simply ignored. Before he died in 1936, France's independent heavy mechanized forces would be threatened with extinction.

The years from 1927 to 1930, dominated by Pétain and Debeney, saw the systematic suppression of tactical initiative in favor of centralized command control. Maneuver around fortified regions and strong points with some emphasis on mobile counterattack, prescribed by the previous regime of Marshal Foch and Buat, ceded primacy to "continuous prepared battlefields" on the frontiers, and massed defensive artillery. Pétain's watchword, *Le feu tue* (firepower kills), became the slogan of an army whose military thought froze in a temporary ice age of the mind.[10]

Systematizing and symbolizing the new mode were the fixed fortifications from Switzerland to Luxembourg. This was the line decided on

[10] See Maurice Gamelin, *Servir*, vol. 2, *Le prologue du drame (1930-août 1939)* (Paris, 1946), 10, 120-30; Henri-Philippe Pétain, *La bataille de Verdun* (Paris, 1941), 143-54; Victor Bourret, *La tragédie de l'Armée Française* (Paris, 1947), 56-61; Marie-Eugène Debeney, *Sur la securité militaire de la France* (Paris, 1930) and ibid., *La guerre et les hommes: Réflexions d'après-guerre* (Paris, 1937), 44-106, 127-45, 163-71, 194-200, 263-308; Richard Griffiths, *Marshal Pétain* (London, 1970), 3-75, 97-103, 127-39, 156-57. Cf. Jean Perré, "Essai sur la défense contre les chars," *Revue militaire française*, no. 12 (April-May 1924), 119-34, 235-55; Pol-Maurice Velpry, "Emploi des chars dans la bataille," *Revue d'infanterie*, no. 61 (July-August 1922), 41-55, 183-212. Cf. also Velpry's articles on armor in *Revue militaire française*, no. 9 (August 1923), 205-230; no. 12 (April 1924), 92-118; no. 17 (July 1925), 52-71; no. 18 (December 1927), 305-328.

by military commissions between 1922 and 1927, but always attributed to the war minister, André Maginot, who piloted the laws for its finance through parliament. Permanently garrisoned, the line was politically un-contentious by virtue of appearing strictly defensive. It was a prudent investment, for it afforded not only security to vulnerable industrial re-gions only recently recoverd from Germany but also protection for the two-week process of mobilization and concentration of the army's re-serves. Notwithstanding this rationale, the system and the institution of twelve-month service meant that France henceforth did little to develop greater operational mobility.

II

By the late 1920s the War Office and the general staff were becoming increasingly worried about the British army's deterioration in numbers and equipment and its inability to meet possible commitments. The planned expeditionary force for extra-European commitments was much smaller and less ready to take the field than its pre-1914 equivalent. It was in these unpropitious conditions that the remarkable experimental trials with mechanized and mixed units took place between 1927 and 1931. Although these exercises were on a comparatively small scale and proved to be a false dawn, they aroused considerable foreign interest and admiration at the time.

The so-called mechanized force that carried out the first serious exercises on Salisbury Plain in August 1927 comprised an ill-assorted miscellany of armored cars, light and medium tanks, horsed cavalry, tractor-drawn artillery, and infantry transported on trucks and half-tracked carriers. The brigade commander, Colonel Jack Collins, distrib-uted the brigade into "fast," "medium," and "slow" groups according to their vehicles' road speed, but this did not coincide with their cross-country capability. The result, as Liddell Hart reported in the *Daily Telegraph*, was a serpentine column that coiled over a distance of thirty-two miles and frequently became congested at bottlenecks. The lack of radio communications and of effective antitank guns (represented by colored flags) were just two of the serious deficiencies, but even so the exercises demonstrated the superiority of mechanized units over tradi-tional infantry and cavalry units.

For its exercises in 1928 the renamed "Armoured Force" had the advantage of 150 wireless sets, but there was still a chronic shortage of suitable tanks and vehicles. Only sixteen light tanks were available, which lacked turrets and were armed only with machine guns. Admirable re-placements were designed for the obsolescent Vickers Medium tank but lack of money prevented their development. The infantry's motor transport did not enable it to keep up with tanks across the country. The most successful aspect of the 1928 exercises was the well-rehearsed set-piece maneuvers designed to impress senior officers, visiting dignitaries, and members of Parliament.

The culmination of this experimental phase occurred in 1931 with the exercises of the 1st Brigade Royal Tank Regiment. Unlike its predecessors, this force was composed entirely of tracked vehicles. Another significant feature was that each company of the tank battalions comprised a section of medium and a section of light tanks, proving that the two could work together. Using a combination of radios and colored flags for communication between the tanks, Brigadier Charles Broad evolved a drill that enabled the whole brigade of some 180 tanks to maneuver as a unit in response to his orders. Broad brought the exercises to a triumphant conclusion by moving the brigade several miles across Salisbury Plain in a thick fog to emerge on time and to parade past the Army Council "with an almost inhuman precision."

At least as important as these early field exercises was the publication in 1929 of the first official manual on mechanized warfare. This was Broad's booklet *Mechanised and Armoured Formations*, popularly known from the color of its covers as the "Purple Primer." The manual exerted an important influence on British armored doctrine in the 1930s and was carefully studied in Germany. At the core of Broad's thinking lay the belief that tanks should be used primarily to exploit their firepower and shock action in attack and that they should ideally be employed in independent formations. Despite understandable caution, Broad's sketch of armored forces used independently to break through an enemy's front lines, sever his communications, and create chaos in the rear areas was truly visionary in the light of existing tank capabilities and organization.[11]

After this brief invigorating period of experiment there was a marked loss of impetus and inspiration from the army's leaders, explained in part by Sir George Milne's increasing caution as chief of the Imperial General Staff. When he eventually retired in 1933 there were still only four established tank battalions compared to 136 infantry battalions; and only two out of twenty cavalry regiments had converted from horses to armored cars. As well as traditional military conservatism, the 1931 financial crisis put a severe limit on expenditure and greatly discouraged further innovation and experiment.

In France in the early 1930s the struggle for army reform was dominated by Generals Maxime Weygand and Maurice Gamelin and Colonel

---

[11] Bond, *British Military Policy*, 141-58. Liddell Hart, *Memoirs* (London, 1965), 1:86-136. Kenneth Macksey, *The Tank Pioneers* (London, 1981), pt. 3.

Charles de Gaulle. All three played decisive parts in the form and degree of the French conversion to mobility and in the drama of 1940. Weygand, an officer of great energy, outstanding ability, and much experience, a cavalryman and chief of staff to Marshal Foch throughout the First World War, succeeded Debeney in 1930 as chief of the general staff. Gamelin, an infantryman and former aide to Marshal Joffre, was simultaneously appointed deputy chief. A year later they rose together to the summit, Weygand replacing Pétain as army inspector-general and Gamelin becoming chief of the general staff before, with Weygand's retirement in 1935, combining the two functions until the Second World War. Both generals were committed to harnessing the revolutionary hitting power and mobility of mechanical weapons and transport in pursuit of a more cost-effective, highly trained, and combat-ready army.

This resurgence of encouragement for "modernity" by the highest commanders reflected concern over three nascent threats to France: first, the growing evidence of clandestine German military stockpiling under the Weimar Republic, in contravention of the Versailles treaty; second, the rise and accession to power in January 1933 of National Socialism, with its avowedly aggressive and revisionist foreign ambitions; and finally, the diminishing prospect of verifiable arms control issuing from the Geneva Disarmament Conference, which deadlocked rapidly over the issue of German "equality of rights." Aggravating these difficulties for France were its emergent financial and demographic weaknesses. Not only did the French defense effort feel the chill wind of the world's post-1929 economic depression, but it was also buffeted by the onset of the "lean years" for the conscript contingents, two decades after the halving of France's birthrate during World War I. "French public opinion," the British Foreign Office noted in 1933, "is ... very apprehensive about the level of effectives during the *années creuses*, 1936, 1937, 1938."[12]

Weygand, sustained politically by Maginot, had initiated a program of military modernization, including the motorization of seven of the twenty active peacetime infantry divisions in June 1930. Counterbalanc-

[12] M. J. Creswell, minute on 28 December 1933 despatch from Col. T. G. G. Heywood, British military attaché, Paris, FO 371, 17652, C85/85/17, PRO. Cf. Jeffrey A. Gunsburg, *Divided and Conquered: The French High Command and the Defeat of the West, 1940* (Westport, Conn., 1979), 13-17; Henri-Philippe Pétain, "La sécurité de la France au cours des années creuses," *Revue des deux mondes*, per. 8, vol. 26, 1 March 1935, pp. i-xx; Georges Castellan, *Le réarmement clandestin du Reich, 1930-35, vu par le 2e Bureau Français* (Paris, 1954); Edward W. Bennett, *German Rearmament and the West, 1932-1933* (Princeton, 1979); Maurice Vaïsse, *Sécurité d'abord: La politique française en matière de désarmement, 9 décembre 1930-17 avril 1934* (Paris, 1918); Judith M. Hughes, *To the Maginot Line: The Politics of French Military Preparation in the 1920s* (Cambridge, Mass., 1971); Paul-Emile Tournoux, *Défense des frontières: Haut commandement, gouvernement, 1919-39* (Paris, 1960).

ing this, however, was France's premature evacuation in the same month of the Rhineland, in accordance with the Briand-Stresemann agreements. Moreover, the defensive benefits from the Maginot line began to be enjoyed only from 1934, owing to the complexities and scale of the construction work involved. Weygand's invigorating spirit was observed immediately; September 1930 witnessed the first corps-scale maneuvers since the end of the First World War. They marked, according to the previously critical British military attaché, "the transition of French military mentality from an undue tenacity to the methods of trench warfare as practised in 1918 to a more vigorous policy ... especially directed towards solving the problems connected with a war of movement." Although the units involved were hampered by the absence of undelivered half-tracks, the British attaché was impressed "by the improved methods of movement and concealment of tanks which had hitherto usually been puerile." He concluded that the French had "really woken up" to modern warfare's transformation through mobility.[13]

The early 1930s were rich in technical and doctrinal reflection and experiment in France, both officially and semiprivately. The maneuvers of 1932 at Mailly Camp tested an experimental mechanized cavalry brigade. Its success encouraged Weygand to establish a new "Type 32" Light Cavalry Division. This comprised a mechanized brigade of armored cars and half-tracks, motorized dragoons, and artillery, but also still two mounted brigades. The division continued to require 5,600 horses, which did not integrate easily with the vehicles. Four of the army's five cavalry divisions were thus modified, and three remained in this form when war came in 1939.

Heartened, Weygand secured the approval of the new war minister, Edouard Daladier, for the experimental mechanization of the 4th Cavalry Division based at Rheims. By decree of May 30, 1933, this became the first light mechanized division (DLM). It embodied the army's most progressive ideas, being equipped with 240 armored combat vehicles, supported by four motorized dragoon battalions, plus integral motorized engineer, artillery, communication, and logistic units. Established permanently in December 1933, substantially ahead of Germany's first Panzer division, this DLM was commanded by Jean Flavigny, the experienced orthodox exponent of mechanization. The new unit was in "everything but name ... the 1934 version of an armoured division." According to

[13] Henry Needham, report on Lorraine manoeuvres, 8 September 1930, FO 371, 14902, W9268/38/17, PRO. Cf. Maxime Weygand, *Mémoires*, vol. 2, *Mirages et réalité* (Paris, 1957), 313, 340-60; Gamelin, *Servir*, 2:11-53; François-André Paoli, *L'Armée Française de 1919 à 1939*, vol. 3, *Le temps des compromis, 1924-30* (Vincennes, 1974), 155-69, 188-92.

the army's overall doctrinal manual, the Provisional Instructions on the Tactical Employment of Large Units of August 1936, the DLM had three missions: security, exploitation, and direct intervention in the main battle.[14]

Weygand's patronage of mobility was sustained and significant. He formed a Technical Cabinet to advise the inspector-general directly on equipment procurement, and a Tank Study Commission to examine organizations for large armored formations. Not least, he preserved the allocations for equipment against enormous pressure for economies from the Leftist governments of 1932 to 1934, which sought to extricate France from the economic depression through a deflation of costs and prices and a balanced budget. Finally, eager to compare France's military reforms with the most modern developments among its old allies, Weygand visited Britain in the summers of 1933 and 1934, inspecting the applicability of Vickers Carden-Lloyd infantry carriers, watching tank maneuvers at Sandhurst and Tidworth, and departing doubly sure of the importance of his promotion of mobility. In short, Weygand worked to furnish France with a capability of rapid intervention in defense of vital interests—perhaps to succor its military partner in Belgium or to reoccupy the demilitarized Rhineland to "administer what he termed a *fessée* to the Germans to stop their rearming.[15]

Less encouraging were the setbacks of this period. Chief among these were the continued division of France's mobile forces into "infantry" and "cavalry" types, each dependent on their parent branch's particular interests in mechanized weaponry. Trials at Mailly in 1932, with a "mechanized combat detachment," failed to offer indisputable evidence of the need for large autonomous tank formations. Indeed this force's unsatisfactory performance, admittedly under artificially unfavorable conditions, prompted such severe criticism from the infantry inspector-general, Joseph Dufieux, that Weygand and Gamelin were forced to disband the unit. Progress toward permanent establishment of independent heavy

---

[14] France, Ministère de la Défense Nationale et de la Guerre—Etat Major de l'Armée (hereafter MDNG-EMA), *Instruction provisoire sur l'emploi tactique des grandes unités*, 12 August 1936 (published Paris, 1940), arts. 204-205. Cf. Jeffrey Johnstone Clarke *Military Technology in Republican France: The Evolution of the French Armored Force, 1917-1940* (Ann Arbor, 1970, microfilm), pp. 109-118; François-André Paoli, *L'Armée Française de 1919 à 1939*, vol. 4, *La fin des illusions, 1930-35* (Vincennes, 1977), 78-83.

[15] Col. Heywood, report of 25 October 1933, enclosure in *Documents on British Foreign Policy* (hereafter *DBFP*), ed. Sir E. L. Woodward and Rohan Butler (London, 1946ff), 2d ser. v, doc, no. 508, p. 737. Cf. report by Ronald H. Campbell, counsellor, Paris Embassy, on a talk with Weygand, 30 April 1934, in ibid., VI, doc. no. 415, pp. 681-82; Weygand, *Memoires*, 2:407-25; Griffiths, *Marshal Pétain*, 151-54; Philip C. F. Bankwitz, *Maxime Weygand and Civil-Military Relations in Modern France* (Cambridge, Mass., 1967), 86-89, 99-115.

armored divisions was gravely retarded; another experimental unit was not created until November 1936, under Gamelin's insistence that France acquire a "tool more powerful than the Panzer Division." Development of the heavy Char B battle tank almost ceased; the three prototypes used in 1932 had increased to only fifteen of the tanks in army hands four years later. Similarly, production of the D1 medium tank ended after delivery of only 160 machines. Output of its improved successor, the D2, reached only 45 vehicles before being halted to divert manufacturing capacity to cavalry tanks in 1937.

Meanwhile the general staff's operations section recognized the idea of husbanding armor in an autonomous strategic reserve under the supreme commander's hand, but withheld approval. "This concept," it noted in 1935, "offers advantages of a rational use of tanks . . . permitting the Command to engage divisions with tank support appropriate to their maneuver and in conformity with the principle of economy of force." However, this was only a "poor man's solution," since it required only fifteen to twenty battalions of modern tanks; it was to be displaced, when industrial productivity permitted, by dispersion of one armored battalion to each infantry division. General Maurin, formerly inspector of motorization, now war minister, informed the Army Committee of the Chamber of Deputies of the rationale for this: "small close-support tanks are indispensable because it is now impossible to launch an infantry unit into attack if it is not preceded by armor."[16] These, then, were some of the difficulties of resources and attitudes facing orthodox exponents of mobility from within the army's own ranks.

III

The advent of power in Germany of Hitler in 1933 also led to a thorough review of Britain's armed forces in relation to possible commitments, but the notion of a spearhead of powerful armored divisions did not find favor. Instead, in the mid-1930s, the War Office opted for the gradual mechanization of the traditional arms (including the conversion of the cavalry to armored cars or light tanks) instead of expanding the Royal Tank Corps. Fervent advocates of the latter course and of armored divisions generally, such as Charles Broad, Pile, Martel, Percy

---

[16] Commission de l'Armée de la Chambre des Députés (hereafter CACD), 15th Legislature, 1932-36, session of 5 December 1934: "Audience de M. le Général Maurin, Ministre de la Guerre," pp. 8-10, carton XV/739/48 bis, Archives de l'Assemblée Nationale, Paris (hereafter AAN). Gamelin's view occurs in *Conseil supérieur de la guerre*: study meeting, 14 October 1936, "Soir—La division cuirassée,"Gamelin Papers, carton 1K224/8, SHAT. The staff's standpoint is in EMA: Bureau des Opérations Militaires et Instruction Générale de l'Armée, "Note concernant l'emploi des chars modernes," 8 January 1935, Jean Fabry Papers, carton 1K93/2, SHAT. Cf. Gamelin, *Servir*, 2:81-83, 186-90, 244-45, 289-94.

Hobart, and above all Liddell Hart, tended to see the frustration of their dreams as the result of a deliberate conspiracy by a reactionary general staff. The success of German blitzkrieg operations in 1939 and 1940 added weight to their indictment, since the Wehrmacht had adopted the armored warfare philosophy at precisely the time when the British army was rejecting it. A longer perspective, however, enables us to understand why Britain's pioneering efforts before 1931 were not developed to more effect thereafter. First, the government decided in 1934 that Germany was the most dangerous potential enemy and that defense expenditure over the next five years should be primarily distributed to counter the German threat. In theory this decision should have assisted the army, particularly as the need for a Continental expeditionary force was now accepted in principle. In practice, however, such a role for the army was politically unpopular and financially hard to reconcile with proposed expenditure on the other two services. After protracted ministerial discussions, the army's already meager allocation of £40 million over five years to remedy its worst deficiencies was cut to £19 million. Little was done to prepare an expeditionary force for a European war.

Second, when every allowance has been made for lack of funds and political prestige, it must be said that the army's leadership in the mid-1930s was unimaginative. Montgomery-Massingberd (Chief of the Imperial General Staff, 1933-1936) was certainly not a keen supporter of tanks and armored warfare; indeed he detested Fuller and also blocked the advance of other progressive senior officers. Moreover the general staff gave little thought to what role an expeditionary force would play if it was sent to the Continent. Critics could argue, with some justification, that the army seemed bent on repeating the experience of 1914, only this time with the light tanks of former cavalry regiments performing the reconnaissance role of the former cavalry division.

Third, and perhaps most serious, the leading military thinkers and generals were themselves opposed to a European role for a variety of reasons. In 1936 Fuller, now in retirement, expressed the view shared by serving officers such as Ironside, Burnett-Stuart, Pile, and Bernard Montgomery when he wrote to Liddell Hart, "I fully agree that *in no circumstances* should we use it [the army] in a continental war, because, if we do, it will prove nothing short of a suicide club." Officers serving on the general staff such as Gort (CIGS, 1937-1939) and Henry Pownall (Director of Military Operations, 1938-1939) recognized that whatever was said in peacetime, the expeditionary force would almost certainly be sent to France on the outbreak of war; but they remained anxious and despondent, lacking confidence equally in the French army and their own politicians. The one senior officer who unequivocally declared that the

611

European commitment was vital, and demanded powerful armored forces for the counterattack role was Major-General Sir Percy Hobart, but he allegedly was reprimanded for these subversive views and shortly afterwards posted to Egypt.[17]

Liddell Hart's opposition to a Continental commitment for the British army fundamentally reflected his interpretation of Britain's part in the First World War. The British army's pathetic unpreparedness for any kind of war by the mid-1930s certainly added weight to this viewpoint, but Liddell Hart's aversion to the role preceded both the advent of Hitler and the certainty of Britain's lack of armored divisions. Liddell Hart was the outstanding advocate of what became known as the policy of "limited liability" (the commitment of the fewest possible troops and ideally none at all to a European alliance), but he articulated the fears of a vast number of people in all walks of life.[18]

A major theme in Liddell Hart's publications on this issue is that the defense is markedly superior to the attack in modern land warfare and that weapon developments actually increase this superiority. In his book *Europe in Arms* he disputed the view that mechanized divisions would be able to pierce the defenses in the early days of a war unless the enemy was taken by surprise and his own forces were unmechanized. Nor did he believe that air power could tip the scales in favor of the attacker. His comforting deduction was that victims of aggression were unlikely to be beaten provided they refrained from foolish indulgence in attacks. Fuller, in his excellent final word on mechanization, *Lectures on Field Service Regulations*, also suggested that an antidote would be found to tank offensives and armies would again be faced by siege warfare. In contrast to the static linear defense of the First World War resulting from the employment of "horde" armies, Fuller anticipated that stalemate between mechanized forces would be transformed into the mobile defense of large areas. From these secure areas or zones air attacks would then be launched on the enemy and his people.[19]

A curious aspect of Liddell Hart's thinking about a British commitment to France was his belief that the French were bent on repeating

[17] Bond, *British Military Policy*, 162-63, 172-75, 189-90. Bond, *Liddell Hart*, 78, 106-107. Hobart's seven-page memorandum, "AFV's and the Field Force," was enclosed in a letter to Liddell Hart on 21 October 1937, Liddell Hart Papers, Centre for Military Archives, King's College, London. On Hobart see also Kenneth Macksey, *Armoured Crusader* (London, 1967). For the views of Major-General Henry Pownall, an able but conservative staff officer, see Brian Bond, ed., *Chief of Staff*, vol. 1 (London, 1972).

[18] Bond, *Liddell Hart*, 91-97. See also Michael Howard, *The Causes of Wars* (Cambridge, Mass., 1983), 198-208.

[19] Bond, *Liddell Hart*, 97-98. J. F. C. Fuller, *Lectures on Field Service Regulations III*, 106-107, 118.

an all-out initial offensive like that of 1914, and that if the British Ex-peditionary Force arrived in time it would be fatally drawn in. This was a strange interpretation of French strategic thinking in the light of the profound impact of First World War losses and devastation; the con-struction of the costly Maginot line; reliance on a short-service conscript army; and the lack of powerful offensive armored forces. Liddell Hart's intelligence about current French military doctrine was evidently defective and unreliable, but it must be noted that he held a similar delusion that the British general staff was wedded to an offensive doctrine when he was well placed to check on the facts. The government's adoption of Liddell Hart's limited liability policy in 1937 actually resulted in a re-duction in the orders for tanks.[20]

France's closest equivalent to Liddell Hart in the 1930s was Charles de Gaulle, who had served on Pétain's staff in the 1920s and belonged to the Secretariat of the Superior Council of National Defense from 1931 to 1937. As with the British journalist's polemics on current British military issues, de Gaulle's campaign for an autonomous, professionally manned, mechanized corps (his *armée de métier*) was politically conten-tious. He first publicized his vision for the transformation of the army in his book *Le fil de l'épée* in 1932. A year later this was followed by an article in the *Revue politique et parlementaire*, "Vers l'armée de métier" (Toward the professional army), itself extended into a book of the same title in 1934. These works elaborated de Gaulle's anxiety that concern over the "lean years" had become so consuming as to obscure from those politically responsible for French defense the need for a thorough analysis of the army's qualitative and doctrinal, as well as merely numerical, inadequacies. He pointed to what he regarded as the decay of French institutions and of the country's cohesion and vitality, and demanded fundamental reforms of the army.

His first recommendation, resembling Weygand's scheme in prog-ress, was for massive expansion of mobile automotive forces with their permanent peacetime organization and training as a homogenous shock formation. The second was the constitution of an entirely professional corps to man this mechanized and motorized force. De Gaulle urged that there be six mechanized infantry divisions, a lighter reconnaissance di-vision, and reserves comprising an assault armor brigade, a heavy artillery brigade, and an air observation group. The force would have entirely tracked vehicles and would require 100,000 specialist career soldiers.

[20] Bond, *Liddell Hart*, 98-99. Bond, *British Military Policy*, 176-77. When the Cabinet endorsed the limited liability policy in December 1937, it was estimated that the reduced expenditure on tank production would exceed all other army economies added together. In 1937 the army actually underspent its allowance for warlike stores by nearly £6 million.

Like a stone cast into a mill pond this proposal sent shock waves rippling through the usually placid backwaters of the general staff.

The latter judged the *métier*-mechanization marriage to be unnatural, unnecessary, and unworkable. To preclude further discussion of what was perceived as a disreputable liaison, General Louis Colson, chief of army staff, acted to block dissemination of the scheme in army circles. In December 1934 he refused to publish in the official *Revue militaire française* an article by de Gaulle on the means of creating a professional army. Colson reasoned that such a piece might risk "setting a professional army in conflict with the national army in officers' minds" when the ministry "unequivocally rejected any such separate distinction."[21] Balked, de Gaulle turned that month to Paul Reynaud, an independent right-wing parliamentarian and former minister, who was a reputed exponent of strengthening French defenses against Germany. After the colonel learned in January 1935 of the formation of Germany's first Panzer divisions, Reynaud was recruited as political propagandist for de Gaulle's reform project.

On March 15, 1935, the scheme was advocated for the first time on a national platform, when the Chamber of Deputies debated the application of emergency articles in the 1928 military recruitment law, in order to restore two-year conscription to combat the manpower shortfall of the "lean years." Reynaud contended that the general staff sought "only the greatest possible number of identically organized units." He asserted the "need, as in the navy and airforce, for specialization in the motorized portion of our land forces."[22] The first accusation was tendentiously inaccurate; it disregarded the establishment by Weygand and Gamelin of specialized motorized infantry, mechanized cavalry, and fortress divisions. Supported only by a dissident Socialist, Philippe Serre, and the independent Jean Le Cour Grandmaison, Reynaud failed to shake the governing majority. He therefore reiterated his charges in a privately tabled parliamentary amendment that also recommended concentration of mobile elements into only seven divisions. It restated that "technological development demands specialization of our military . . . and hence demands technical, consequently professional, manpower for the mechanical part of our forces."[23]

[21] Colson, letter to de Gaulle, 17 December 1934, Paul Reynaud Papers, carton 74 AP.12, Archives Nationales de France, Paris (hereafter AN). See also Charles de Gaulle, *Vers l'armée de métier* (Paris, 1934), 87-92.

[22] *Journal Officiel de la République Française: Chambre des Députés* (hereafter *JOC*): *Debats*, Paris, 16 March 1935, p. 1042. Cf. Charles de Gaulle, *Lettres, notes et carnets*, vol. 2, *1919-juin 1940* (Paris, 1980), 376-81; ibid., *Mémoires de Guerre*, vol. 1, *L'Appel*, 1940-42 (Paris, 1954), 18-25; Paul Reynaud, *La France a sauvé l'Europe* (Paris, 1947), 1:308-321.

[23] *Amendement par M. Paul Reynaud, Député, au Projet de Loi portant modification à*

De Gaulle's writings omitted acknowledgment to earlier and contemporary serving pioneers of mobility like Estienne, Doumenc, and Velpry. Nevertheless the antipathy that he evoked within France's military leaders was far from inevitable. Weygand and Gamelin had a declared interest in mobile warfare. Indeed there might have been widespread support if de Gaulle and Reynaud had trumpeted a straightforward clarion call for urgent rearmament centered on the primacy of armored and motorized equipment. Instead they provocatively claimed that mechanization and professionalization were synonymous prerequisites for military modernization. De Gaulle's vagueness over the means of creating his new military structures aroused the scorn of senior officers. Gamelin could not ignore the fact that a seven-division force overlooked the complex defense requirements of the territorial expanses of metropolitan France, North Africa, and the Levant for which the army was responsible. Most decisively, de Gaulle's colorful romanticism rekindled political distrust of supposedly "aggressive" armored forces. "At bottom," Gamelin subsequently stressed, "it was the conjunction made between the issue of large armored units and the issue of the professional army that was detrimental in parliament and within a section of military opinion to the creation of tank divisions."[24]

The paradox of de Gaulle's intervention was that it produced an effect precisely opposite to that intended. By activating political and doctrinal brakes on developments in mobility in the crucial years 1935 to 1937 he hindered the army's reequipment. Prophecies of mobile offensives undeniably merited closer attention than they received, since they addressed the key issue of an early rupture of the French defenses. That this was a peril of exceptional gravity had been perceived by Maginot himself and reiterated as late as 1934 by Colonel André Laffargue, a senior aide to Weygand. Reynaud too underlined in early 1937, "Our industrial riches are concentrated chiefly along our frontiers and . . . alas our capital is neither at Bourges nor at Clermont-Ferrand."[25] A rapid

la Loi du 31 mars 1928 sur le recrutement de l'armée, Paris, 28 March 1935, p. 5. See also Reynaud, *La France*, 1:322-24; de Gaulle, *Lettres, notes et carnets* 2:382-86; Evelyne Demey, *Paul Reynaud, mon père* (Paris, 1980), 287-91.

[24] Maurice Gamelin, testimony of 2 December 1947, in France: *Commission chargée d'Enquêter sur les Evènements survenus en France de 1933 à 1945. Annexes: Dépositions de témoignages et documents recueillis par la Commission d'Enquête Parlementaire*, Paris, 1951-52, vol. 2, p. 385. Cf. Marie-Eugène Debeney, "Encore l'armée de métier," *Revue de deux mondes*, per. 8, vol. 28, 15 July 1935, pp. 279-95, and ibid., "La motorisation des armées modernes," ibid., per. 8, vol. 32, 15 March 1936, pp. 273-91.

[25] *JOC: Débats*, Paris, 27 January 1937, p. 169. Cf. Demey, *Paul Reynaud*, 310 (de Gaulle, letter to Reynaud, 28 January 1937); Reynaud, *La France*, 1:401-415; interview of Maginot by Louis Béraud in *Le journal*, 16 August 1930, enclosure in FO 371, 14902, W8604/38/17, PRO; André Laffargue, *Fantassin de Gascogne: De mon jardin à la Marne*

breakthrough could negate, at a stroke, every painstaking preparation for the protracted coalition conflict that alone seemed to promise success against Germany.

However, these warnings were rendered inaudible by the shrill controversy generated by de Gaulle's and Reynaud's indiscriminate attack on the competence of the army's training, the intentions of the command, and the politically sacrosanct nation-in-arms. Thus rhetorical weapons were gratuitously proffered to generals, like the cavalry inspector Robert Altmayer, who were either hostile or at best apathetic about large-scale mechanization.

Central to the army's difficulties were shortages of men and material. Senior officers, from renowned skeptics like Debeney and Colson to enthusiasts like Flavigny, rejected the call for an all-professional corps on military grounds. They argued that professionalization should be limited to those needing special skills, such as mechanics and wireless operators. The military staff of War Minister Daladier explained, "The army reflects the nation technically as well as socially; with over one million automobiles in the country it should not be . . . difficult to recruit and train drivers. . . . Surely in even the most modern tank only the commander and driver need be career soldiers?"[26] Staff studies revealed, furthermore, that without implausibly heavy extra expenditure to improve pay and conditions, France had a "recruitment ceiling" too low to make an all-professional force feasible in addition to the 106,000 career soldiers needed for the Maginot line and infantry cadres. In 1936 70 percent of time-served professionals were not re-enlisting; consequently, the bulk of recruitment served only to maintain, not expand, the existing cadres. Yet down to 1937 de Gaulle and Reynaud persistently made light of these pay and recruitment difficulties, suggesting obtaining their corps from the ranks of the unemployed and diverting a disproportionate amount of general-staff energy into a running battle of memoranda over structures and statistics.

Equally detrimental to mechanization was the political suspicion aroused by heavy tanks. Perceptions of them as "aggressive" weapons,

et au Danube (Paris, 1962), 179-87; Henry Lémery, D'une république à l'autre: Souvenirs de la mêlée politique, 1894-1944 (Paris, 1964), 165-66; Bankwitz, Maxime Weygand, 121-31.

[26] MDNG, Cabinet du Ministre: "Analyse d'interpellation de M. Reynaud sur la politique militaire du gouvernement," Daladier Papers, 4DA3/Dr.4/sdr.b, Fondation Nationale de Sciences Politiques, Paris (hereafter FNSP). See also "Note complémentaire au sujet des difficultés de recrutement d'une armée de métier," 21 July 1936, ibid.; de Gaulle, Lettres, notes et carnets, 2:387-91, 401-407; Gamelin, Servir, 2:153, 186, 217, and vol. 3, La Guerre (septembre 1939-19 mai 1940) (Paris, 1947), 516-27; Maxime Weygand, En lisant les mémoires de guerre du Général de Gaulle (Paris, 1955), 13.

inappropriate to the defensive pretensions of democratic France, transcended normal party boundaries. Across the political spectrum, from the conservative war minister Jean Fabry in 1935 to the Radical Daladier the following year, pressure was applied to Gamelin to abandon the Char B program. Heavy tanks, moreover, when associated with career soldiers, had *coup d'état* connotations.[27]

Certainly the political stance of many officers was ambiguous, despite Gamelin's attempts to preserve an "apolitical army" in the *grande muette* tradition. Unavoidably, during the ferment of the Popular Front era, French leaders were troubled by contingency planning for civil unrest and the general staff was drawn into discussion with an "apprehensive" Roger Langeron, Paris prefect of police, during the unprecedented leftist *Rassemblement Populaire* on Bastille Day in 1935. Fabry, responsible as war minister for the Champs Elysées military pageant earlier that day, reflected ruefully that "Paris, patriotic in the morning, was singing the *Internationale* by the afternoon." In May 1936, when workers' factory occupations followed the Left's election victory, there was further consultation of General Colson by the prefect and Albert Sarraut, the outgoing prime minister. De Gaulle himself thought in 1935 that France's slide into generalized crisis was "little by little raising the issue of public order to the forefront of concerns." He wondered "how, in the growing tumult of the Popular Front and right-wing Leagues, to prevent anarchy, even civil war . . . ?"[28]

But with Germany at that moment introducing two-year conscription and the "Goering plan" for a war economy, Gamelin sought the adoption of a four-year rearmament program unimpeded by political controversy over military modernization. The command's conviction was shared by the dominant political groups. Roger Salengro, the Socialist interior minister, stressed that although France could not remain passive in the face of Germany's remilitarization, an equilibrium "would be reestablished not by keeping young Frenchmen away from their families

[27] See Griffiths, *Pétain*, 139-40; Pertinax [André Géraud], *Les fossoyeurs: Défaite militaire de la France, armistice, contre-révolution* (New York, 1943), 1:49; Jean Fabry, *Journal*, 11-20 September, 3-4 October 1935, carton 5N581, dr. 2, SHAT; "Memento" of 4 July 1936, General Victor-Henri Schweisguth Papers, carton 351 AP3/1SC2/dr. 9, AN; CACD, 16th Legislature, 1936-40, session of 1 December 1937: "Audience de M. Daladier, MDNG," pp. 15-16, carton xv, dr. "1937," AAN; Clarke, *Military Technology*, 189; Gamelin, *Servir*, 1:263-64.
[28] De Gaulle, *Lettres, notes et carnets*, 2:393, 404-405, 411-12; "Mementos," 16 July 1935, 28 May 1936, Schweisguth Papers, cartons 351 AP2/1SC2/dr. 5 and 351 AP3/1SC2/ dr. 9, AN; Jean Fabry, *De la Place de la Concorde au Cours de l'Intendance, février 1934-juin 1940* (Paris, 1942), 62-65. Cf. Griffiths, *Marshal Pétain*, 161-65, 169, 175-88, 195-96, 207-11 and Jacques Nobécourt, *Une histoire politique de l'armée*, vol. 1, *De Pétain à Pétain, 1919-1942* (Paris, 1967), 226-48.

even longer, but through a prodigious effort to motorize the French army." Daladier, for the Radicals, confirmed in the Chamber in February 1937 that he "was unable to agree with those ... who demanded a professional army or those who advocated a specialist corps of armored divisions" because it was "essential to preserve a proper balance and proportion between the various component parts of the army."[29]

The summer of 1937 witnessed the final incarnation of the de Gaulle-Reynaud projects in the latter's book *Le problème militaire français*. Reaction reflected officialdom's espousal of mobility by this time. General Duchêne, in a review in *L'echo de Paris*, trumpeted that "a defensive army is an army for defeat" and urged the "unequivocal rejection of the simplistic system of a Great Wall of China"; Gamelin confidentially informed Reynaud that "for a long time now we have been laboring to establish a larger number than even you propose of motorized, light mechanized, and armored divisions."[30]

IV

By the mid-1930s political indecision about the army's priorities in event of war, aided and abetted by the general staff's conservatism, caused Britain to forfeit the opportunity to produce an elite armored force for the counterattack role that theorists like Fuller and practical soldiers like Hobart had advocated. By the end of 1936 the great majority of existing tanks were light models suitable only for colonial warfare. The War Office prepared a "shopping list" of light cavalry tanks, medium models, and heavy infantry assault tanks, but throughout 1937 and 1938 little was done to produce new types. The single Mobile Division that existed on the outbreak of war was little more than a conglomeration of units without a clear role. In May 1940 the British Expeditionary Force in France contained only two battalions of the Royal Tank Regiment and the divisional light cavalry regiments. The 1st Armoured Division was still assembling on Salisbury Plain and arrived piecemeal in France too late to participate in the events that led to Dunkirk.[31]

In retrospect there is an element of irony in the fact that the chiefs

---

[29] Statement reported in Sir George Clerk, British ambassador, Paris, to the Foreign Office, 24 February 1937, FO 371, 20693, C1597/122/17, PRO. Salengro's assurance came in a speech at Denain reported in Clerk's 7 September 1936 despatch, ibid., 19859, C6327/1/17. Cf. Maxime Weygand, "L'état militaire de la France," *Revue de deux mondes*, per. 8, vol. 35, 15 October 1936, pp. 721-36, and ibid., "L'armée d'aujourd'hui," ibid., per. 8, vol. 45, 15 May 1938, pp. 325-36.

[30] Maurice Gamelin, letter of 1 June 1937 in Reynaud Papers, carton 74 AP. 12, AN. Duchêne's press notice, dated 17 June 1937, is in ibid. Cf. Reynaud, *La France*, 1:419-28; Gamelin, *Servir*, 1:257-62.

[31] Bond, *British Military Policy*, 172-78, 186-88, 255-57.

of staff, and even more the general staff, were sound in their assumptions that Britain still had vital interests in western Europe that could not be adequately ensured by a policy of limited liability but were conservative as regards mechanization and vague about what the expeditionary force would do after arriving in France. Liddell Hart, in contrast, had progressive ideas on the need for mechanization and the kind of mobile operations to which it could lead, but tended to deny the need for a Continental commitment that could have justified higher expenditure in the Army to create a thoroughly equipped Field Force capable of taking part in operations against a first-class European power.[32]

From today's perspective it is easier for historians to appreciate the limitations of critics such as Liddell Hart and de Gaulle and to have some sympathy for the British and French high commands. Ironically it was only when de Gaulle was posted to one of Gamelin's creations, the heavy armored experimental group in Lorraine in mid-1937, that he realized the many practical problems inherent in developing mobile forces and doctrine. Letters from the period he commanded the 507th Tank Regiment at Metz betray how great a revelation to him were the technical inadequacies, incompatibilities of equipment, and basic shortages confronting orthodox soldiers. These mundane but major obstacles were what he and Reynaud had underplayed or ignored in their politicized and tendentious *armée de métier* campaign.

For Gamelin the period from 1935 to 1938 was characterized by continual delays in the completion schedules of a succession of reequipment programs. At root the problems lay in an insufficiency of appropriate productive capacity among France's munitions manufacturers; expansion after 1936 was first disrupted by industrial unrest and reform under the Popular Front and later cramped by discoveries of shortages of skilled labor in the essential armaments, engineering, and steel trades. The result was to deprive the army throughout 1937 and 1938 of its anticipated levels of reequipment. Shortages were severe enough in armored vehicles to compel cancellation of the mechanized maneuvers of 1937 and to delay the availability of the second light mechanized division, approved in April 1936, until autumn 1938.

In these circumstances the unacceptability of de Gaulle's scheme meant that its reemergence in January and February 1937, through Reynaud, imposed additional political burdens on those like Gamelin, Doumenc, Flavigny, and Velpry who were striving for discreet but nonetheless effective development and expansion of armored forces. The manner in which the Gaullist case was presented left it open to denunciation as

[32] Bond, *Liddell Hart*, 98-99.

619

militarily impracticable, strategically dangerous, and politically provocative to the point of perversity. Of cardinal importance was the militarily
irrelevant conjunction given in 1935 to tanks and professional soldiery.
Here de Gaulle was not merely on factually dubious ground in his own
propagandizing (as over the doubtful availability of recruits), but Reynaud, by agitating suspicious parliamentarians, materially worsened conditions for orthodox pro-mechanization advocates at work inside the
civil-military establishment.

De Gaulle's prescriptions harbored a final critical flaw through their
apparent casting of mechanization as an *alternative* to total industrialized
war of the 1914-1918 kind. Quality was envisaged as superseding quantity. Fuller too had contended, in his *Lectures on F.S.R. III*, that armies
would grow smaller as mechanization widened the gulf between the truly
fighting forces and those that do the occupying.[33] With a professional
mobile group of six or seven divisions it was implicit that the remaining
French national forces would be relegated to semi-militias fit only for
second-line or fortress duties. Not until 1937 did Reynaud dispose of
this unacceptable corollary through a remolding of his ideas to stress a
large, elite, mobile force *with* the conventional reserve army. Gamelin's
attitude was also ambiguous, although this was perhaps understandable
in view of the uncertain nature of future warfare. He insisted that France
develop a unit more powerful than a Panzer division, but also suggested
that improvements in antitank weapons would considerably restrict the
role of armor on the battlefield. Despite Gamelin's equivocal stance, the
French army was preparing for both offensive and defensive operations.
Thus the general staff was justified in protesting against the charge that
it had "consigned the army to an attitude of unvaryingly passive
defense."[34]

Nevertheless, de Gaulle neglected to volunteer any form of "new
model" structure for the full panoply of the nation's armed strength,
despite his reflections at the Ecole de Guerre and Superior Council of
National Defense on economic warfare and national mobilization. Gamelin's achievement lay in modernizing the French army while attending
to those complexities of overall defense planning and the probable characteristics of future conflict so unsatisfactorily ignored in de Gaulle's

[33] Fuller, *Lectures on F.S.R. III*, 8, 29, 38.

[34] EMA, "Note au sujet de l'armée de métier," June 1936, Daladier Papers, 4DA3/Dr.4/
Sdr.b, FNSP. See also Gamelin memorandum of 17 April 1936 in ibid., 1DA7/Dr.4/Sdr.b;
Conseil supérieur de la guerre, minutes, 29 April 1936, 15 December 1937, 2 December
1938, carton 1N22, vol. 17, pp. 86, 100-103, 120-29, 133-34, SHAT; Bourret, *La tragédie*,
53-55; de Gaulle, *Memoires*, 1:27-34, and ibid., *Lettres, notes et carnets*, 2:452-61. Cf.
Laffargue, *Fantassin de Gascogne*, 122-32; Georges Loustaunau-Lacau, *Mémoires d'un
français rebelle, 1914-1948* (Paris, 1948), 54-58.

partial analysis. The command, decisively, was "more comprehensive and rational" than de Gaulle, whose "*Vers l'armée de métier* . . . never once deals with the possibility that his mechanized corps might be halted," enthusiastically envisaging "only ever-victorious offensives."[35]

By the outbreak of war, despite the digressions of the *métier* controversy and the shortcomings of industry, French mobile units were forming rapidly. There were six armored divisions, plus de Gaulle's own 4th *Division Cuirassée de Réserve* setting up to make a seventh, on May 10, 1940—together with seven motorized infantry divisions and the motorized British Expeditionary Force. Against them Germany moved a largely unmotorized infantry army spearheaded by just ten Panzer divisions. Perhaps influenced by the notion that at least a three-to-one superiority in attack is usually necessary to ensure success, this equilibrium has underlain more and more interpretations of the 1940 campaign in which questions of the location, coordination, and command of these "quality" Allied forces assume paramountcy.[36]

But if the available mobile formations might have seen the German bid for victory checked, no less essential for ultimate Allied triumph was the arming in depth that Britain and France *were* preparing in 1939-1940. Given their acute consciousness of short-term unpreparedness in face of rapid German rearmament—and the real prospect of a global conflict against Germany, Italy, and Japan—it was understandable that the British and French governments should rely on deterrence through the Royal Air Force, the Maginot line, and the large French army in being, while they mobilized manpower and material resources on a vast scale for the long haul.

V

This essay challenges the attractive but greatly oversimplified thesis that contrasts the unimaginative and obsessively defense-oriented British and French military establishments with the brilliant "outsiders" Fuller, Liddell Hart, and de Gaulle, whose concepts of blitzkrieg were rejected

[35] Richard D. Challener, "The Military Defeat of 1940 in Retrospect," in *Modern France: Problems of the Third and Fourth Republics*, ed. Edward Mead Earle (Princeton, 1951), 417n. See also de Gaulle, *Lettres, notes et carnets*, 2:363-65, 370-72, 415-38.

[36] See R. H. S. Stolfi, "Equipment for Victory in France in 1940," *History* 55, no. 183 (February 1970), 1-20; Gunsberg, *Divided and Conquered*; Robert J. Young, *In Command of France: French Foreign Policy and Military Planning, 1933-1940* (Cambridge, Mass., and London, 1978); Paul Huard, *Le Colonel de Gaulle et ses blindés: Laon, 15-20 mai 1940* (Paris, 1980); Pierre Le Goyet, *Le mystère Gamelin* (Paris, 1975); Donald W. Alexander, "Repercussions of the Breda Variant," *French Historical Studies* 8, no. 3 (Spring 1974), 459-88; John C. Cairns, "Along the Road back to France 1940," *American Historical Review* 64, no. 3 (April 1959), 583-603; and ibid., "Some Recent Historians and the 'Strange Defeat' of 1940," *Journal of Modern History* 46 (1974), 60-81.

by their own countries but eagerly adopted by Germany. Though certainly open to criticisms for their handling of rearmament, the British and French high commands in reality were understandably preoccupied in 1939 by the possibility of a shock defeat at the very outset of the war. Despite flaws in the Allies' strategic plans, notably the provision for a risky advance into the Low Countries and the failure to create a central armored reserve for the counterattack role, the forces assembled should have sufficed to check the initial German offensive. It is possible, even probable, that they would have done so had not the German plan of attack been drastically altered in the early weeks of 1940.[37]

As regards the proponents of mechanized forces and armored warfare, the rejection of their ideas was due to more complex reasons than the reactionary mentality of the British and French military establishments. The type of armies and the strategic concepts the champions of armor advocated were politically unacceptable, while in military terms they did not take account, or were simply ignorant of, many of the financial, material, and manpower problems confronting the British and French general staffs. Ironically, as we have seen, the well-intentioned polemics of Liddell Hart and de Gaulle actually hindered the modernization of their respective armies.

Above all, it should not be assumed that the critics' vision of future warfare was wholly borne out by the early campaigns of the Second World War. In revulsion against the static trench deadlock of 1914-1918, they sought to restore mobility, minimize casualties, and secure a speedy victory by means of small, elite, professional mechanized armies. Even Fuller, who envisaged the likelihood of stalemate when both sides were thoroughly mechanized, suggested that five hundred tanks would constitute a very large force. With tank forces on this scale it would still be possible to turn the enemy's flank and attack him in the rear: generalship would again be decisive and battles would be "works of art and not merely daubs of blood."[38] Even in the campaigns of 1939-1941, for example, large nonmechanized forces played a more important part than the armored theorists had anticipated.

This is not to dispute the valuable role that theorists can play as "gadflies" or catalysts. Indeed, in a study with wider scope, it could be argued that iconoclasts such as Fuller, Liddell Hart, and de Gaulle were

[37] For an excellent analysis of the evolution of German planning for an offensive in the West between October 1939 and May 1940, see John J. Mearsheimer, *Conventional Deterrence* (Ithaca, 1983), 99-133.

[38] Fuller, *Lectures on F.S.R. III*, 8, 29, 38. General von Blomberg epitomized this outlook when he remarked to Liddell Hart that he favored disarmament (in 1932) because it would "by restoring small and handy armies, bring back art, leadership, 'gentlemanliness', and the real warrior spirit into warfare." See Bond, *Liddell Hart*, 79-80.

immensely beneficial in their educative influence on the general public as well as on the armed forces. The general conclusions suggested by this essay are that in practice "outsiders" can seldom exert a direct influence on military reform because they lack full knowledge of the difficulties and of the options available. Liddell Hart, for example, eventually had to accept that "limited liability" was not a realistic strategy for Britain vis-à-vis France. On the other hand, the responsible military authorities tend to be all too well aware of the problems and to accept that only piecemeal or compromise measures are feasible. An example would be the weakness of Britain's armored forces and their lack of a clear doctrine at the outbreak of war. Most important of all, the interwar period bears out the Clausewitzian perception that political attitudes, priorities, and constraints exert a dominating influence on the development of armed forces and strategic doctrines.

21. Voices from the Central Blue: The Air Power Theorists

DAVID MacIsaac

SEVENTY-FIVE years have now elapsed since the advent of manned aircraft resulted in the extension of traditional forms of surface warfare into the skies above—and indeed beyond—armies and navies. Air power, the generic term widely adopted to identify this phenomenon, has nonetheless yet to find a clearly defined or unchallenged place in the history of military or strategic theory. There has been no lack of theorists, but they have had only limited influence in a field where the effects of technology and the deeds of practitioners have from the beginning played greater roles than have ideas. For the historian of ideas further difficulties arise from the confusion and controversy that have resulted from differing viewpoints regarding the multiple means of employing air forces: whether, for example, they are best used in cooperation with surface forces or in operations conducted independently of armies and navies. For these and other reasons the approach adopted for this essay divides it into five parts of unequal length.

The first part offers some reflections on the topic of air power in general and the problems it has posed for historians, among them its vocabulary, mystique, and remoteness from the day-to-day experience of most scholars. A second part addresses an earlier essay on this topic, whose widespread acceptance among writers and teachers has given it a special prominence. A third part deals primarily with the role played by air power in World War II, a topic of seemingly endless controversy. Finally, and altogether more tentatively, the last two sections address the most difficult period of all—the decades since then during which basic concepts at length conceived and tested had to be adapted to atomic weapons, transatmospheric (or space) flight, and the revolution in electronics.

NOTE: For their comments and suggestions, the author acknowledges the innocence of several colleagues: James B. Smith, Theodore Ropp, John Schlight, Kenneth J. Alnwick, Donald R. Baucom, R. A. Mason, Robert F. Futrell, David R. Mets, John F. Shiner, Alan L. Gropman, Dennis M. Drew, Ronald R. Fogleman, Dennis G. Hall, Timothy E. Kline, Thomas A. Fabyanic, Donald D. Stevens, Jack Neufeld, Bernard Nalty, and Herman S. Wolk.

624

I

Clausewitz began his innovative chapter "The People in Arms" with the observation that war by means of popular uprisings was a phenomenon of the nineteenth century. If we substitute air power for peoples' wars, we can begin by borrowing his observation that "any nation that uses it intelligently will, as a rule, gain some superiority over those who disdain its use. If this is so, the question only remains whether mankind at large will gain by this further expansion of the element of war; a question to which the answer should be the same as to the question of war itself. We shall leave both to the philosophers. . . . [and proceed to a discussion that is] less an objective analysis than a groping for the truth."[1]

When we consider how poorly Western nations—in particular the United States—have come to understand peoples' wars, despite two hundred years of fitful attempts to deal with them, we should not be surprised that "air power," the twentieth century's peculiar contribution to warfare, continues to defy our attempts at analysis. Even the first step in such an analysis—the discovery of an accepted vocabulary—continues to confound our efforts. Common terms like strategic bombing, interdiction, and air superiority mean different things to different writers—and on occasion different things to the same writers at different times. Among other terms that frequently engender confusion are the following: air supremacy, command of the air, and a whole raft of unwieldy but seemingly necessary neologisms like electronic counter-countermeasures. These shall be dealt with as they arise, but the reader should understand from the beginning that the air element of modern strategy is not yet a topic possessing an agreed vocabulary "from which on the basis of observed usage the grammar of air power may eventually be compiled."[2] Many reasons account for this condition.

The idea of flight, whose expression can be traced back to Greek mythology, had to contend from the very beginning with the feeling that it was somehow presumptuous of mankind to toy with the prerogatives of the gods—and later, angels. By the nineteenth century, nonetheless, two distinct visions arose as to the likely effect of man's conquering the heavens. One view, stressing images of death and destruction raining from the skies, was that the nature of warfare would be directly and vastly changed, often with the implication that armies and navies would be rendered impotent. Another view, reflecting the first yet altogether

---

[1] *On War*, ed. and trans. Michael Howard and Peter Paret, rev. ed. (Princeton, 1984), 479, 483.

[2] Noble Frankland, *The Bombing Offensive against Germany: Outlines and Perspectives* (London, 1965), 16-17.

more sanguine, held that "the ultimate effect will be to diminish greatly the frequency of wars and to substitute more rational methods of settling international misunderstandings. This may come to pass not only because of the additional horrors which will result in battle, but because no part of the field will be safe, no matter how distant from the actual scene of conflict."[3] Thus, even before the first aircraft flew, elements of controversy involving feeling and passion were present.

Once the Wright brothers and others unlocked the secrets of powered flight, aviation became predominantly a young man's game, one that by its very nature attracted adventurous souls who had to be physically adept, mentally alert, and pragmatically rather than philosophically inclined. Insofar as such people talked or wrote of their experiences, it was usually of the air as a new environment of endeavor, utterly untrammeled or impeded by the usages or customs of the past. Passionately committed to flying and the general advancement of aviation, the writers who emerged from among the aviation pioneers were rarely analytical and never dispassionate. Their vision of the role air power could play in warfare invariably outran the reality of the moment, provoking disappointment among the converted and derision from the unbelievers. Also in this respect, the fact that the aviators often deemed themselves a breed apart, possessors in Tom Wolfe's phrase of "the right stuff," discouraged many outside their limited circle from attempting to fathom the hidden secrets of the inner priesthood of flyers.

Yet another factor driving the contemplative or philosophical away from military aviation—whether as practitioners, historians, or analysts—has been a certain uneasiness about what seemed a callous assumption among airmen that the kind of future war of which they spoke could somehow provide quick, clean, mechanical, and impersonal solutions to problems with which others had struggled for centuries.[4] One result of these impressions has been a reluctance on the part of outsiders, especially academic historians, to specialize in the field of military aviation, thereby leaving the field for many years to a combination of the official historians of the various air services, and those who style themselves simply aviation writers, a group ranging from excited but inex-

---

[3] The words are those of Octave Chanute writing in 1894, quoted in Charles H. Gibbs-Smith, *Aviation: An Historical Survey from Its Origins to the End of World War II* (London, 1970), 221. In 1864 Victor Hugo had written in joyful phrases to the French balloonist, Nadar, that the invention of aircraft would mean the end of warfare. Out of science would come peace, since aircraft would bring about the immediate, absolute, instantaneous, universal, and perpetual abolition of frontiers. Most prophecy was less sanguine.

[4] Paraphrased from Robin Higham, *Air Power: A Concise History* (New York, 1972), 233. As those familiar with the work of the late Bernard Brodie will note, this problem would only be exacerbated in the age of atomic and later nuclear weapons.

perienced buffs to veterans now taken to reliving their glory days on paper. These reflections on the nature of air power as a subject for serious analytical study, however incomplete or unwarranted they may seem, must be voiced at the beginning of our discussion. Their implications are not always apparent to those new to the field, who are often discouraged too early in their efforts.[5]

The term air power itself[6] can be traced back at least as far as H. G. Wells's *War in the Air* (1908); other elements of the still-emerging vocabulary are of even greater antiquity. For example, the notion that the airplane would require governments to be prepared for a lightning war, one in which sea and land warfare would be possible only when a nation has "command of the air," was first set forth before a conference of military experts at Chicago's World Columbian Exposition of 1893 by Major J. D. Fullerton of the British Royal Engineers. Ten years before the flight of the Wright brothers, Fullerton spoke of a "revolution in the art of war" that would require changes in the design of naval ships, dispersion of armies on battlefields, and new standards for the construction of fortresses. In any case, "the chief work will be done in the air, and the arrival of the aerial fleet over the enemy's capital will probably conclude the campaign."[7] Most such far-seeing predictions, however, received little notice outside a small circle of aeronautical visionaries.

Even two decades later, on the eve of World War I, the first flimsy aircraft—constructed primarily of wood, canvas, and baling wire—sim-

---

[5] Even today, most of the important work in this field is being done by official historians, most of them government civil servants but including, especially in the United States and the Federal Republic of Germany, some exceptional contributions by military officers. When the International Committee for the History of the Second World War announced (in its News Bulletin #19, December 1983) a French plan for a conference in late 1984 on aviation in the interwar years, it added succinctly, "The problem is to find civilian historians." For an informed discussion on airmen in their relation to historians, see Dennis E. Showalter, "Two Different Worlds: The Military Historian and the U.S. Air Force," *Air University Review* 31, no. 4 (May-June 1980), 30-37.

[6] The term air power is variously used. Logically, it should be reserved for discussions of the full potential of a nation's air capability, in peace as well as war, in civilian as well as military pursuits. Such usage, however, is rare, Higham's *Air Power: A Concise History* being a notable exception. In this essay, the term will be used to denote specifically military applications. Airpower as a single word, a form that seems to connote a sense almost of incantation, may have been invented by Major Alford Joseph Williams in his *Airpower* (New York, 1940). It was later taken up by Major General Orvil A. Anderson, USAF, who adopted it in Pacific Report #71A of the U.S. Strategic Bombing Survey (1947) and later, in July 1959, changed the title of *The Air Power Historian* to *The Airpower Historian* (now *Aerospace Historian*, a change dating from October 1965). It remains the editorial usage of *Air Force Magazine* and is now enshrined in the Airpower Research Institute (ARI) of the Air University's Center for Aerospace Doctrine, Research, and Education (CADRE) at Maxwell Air Force Base in Alabama.

[7] On Fullerton, see Alfred F. Hurley, *Billy Mitchell: Crusader for Air Power*, new ed. (Bloomington, 1975), 141-42, 175 n. 2.

ply were not taken seriously by most officers, who were having trouble enough trying to figure out what to do about machine guns, the possibilities for motorized ground transport, and the concurrent revolutions in naval armor and armament. At most, they reasoned, the new aircraft might eventually become a modest addition to the traditional means of war. Existing limitations of range, speed, lifting capacity, and even safety would be overcome more quickly than anyone could then visualize. As World War I dawned, however, the only probable use for aircraft was deemed to be as extensions of the eyes of the ground commanders, just as balloons had been used on occasion since the French Revolution.

The great mobility and range of powered aircraft, as compared to tethered balloons, led to their use in reconnaissance—then called observation—from the beginning of the war. Soon artillery spotter planes became a serious threat to troops on the ground. Since artillery specifically designed for use against aircraft had not been developed before the war, the only way to drive off interlopers intent on reconnoitering one's positions was to attempt to shoot them down with weapons—at first handguns and rifles, later machine guns—mounted on one's own aircraft. Thus the reconnaissance and pursuit roles were the first to emerge clearly. Others quickly followed.

One innovation was the tactical support of engaged forces in which aircraft guns and bombs would be directed against troop positions on the ground, with the aim either of assisting the advance of one's own troops or of thwarting the advances of the enemy. Used in this manner, usually referred to as the attack role, the aircraft operated either close in to the troops or at short distances in the enemy's rear—against rallying points, supply dumps, key intersections, military headquarters, railheads, and the like. (Today we describe these as close air support and interdiction.) By the end of the war, spurred on largely by the German raids over England, yet another vision arose—that of aircraft operating independently of armies and navies. The task of such forces would be to attack targets far removed from the battle lines, with the aim of destroying essential elements of the enemy's capability to wage war by bombing his factories, transportation hubs, and centers of government. The Smuts Memorandum of August 1917, the paper that led directly to the creation of the Royal Air Force, discussed air warfare in these terms:

> As far as can at present be foreseen there is absolutely no limit to its future independent war use. And the day may not be far off when aerial operations with their devastation of enemy lands and destruction of industrial and populous centres on a vast scale may become

628

the principal operations of war, to which the older forms of military and naval operations may become secondary and subordinate.[8]

When the war ended in November 1918, however, air power had achieved no such primacy. As an instrument of warfare it was still in its infancy, having played an occasionally spectacular, increasingly important, but nonetheless largely unessential part in the outcome. Greater than the impact of air power upon the war was the influence of the war itself on the subsequent development of air power. This is particularly true in the sense that during the course of the fighting virtually every theory, attitude, ideal, hope, dream, and debate that would mark the course of air warfare a quarter century later had been foreshadowed.

II

"It is only in a very limited sense that one can speak with literal accuracy of theories of air power." So began Edward Warner's 1943 essay, "Douhet, Mitchell, Seversky: Theories of Air Warfare," whose widespread use in military schools ever since has endowed it with a special significance.[9] Warner's opening point was that the early theorists, glibly switching tenses from the future to the present after 1919, never properly acknowledged that the debates of the interwar period were concerned less with choices among various theories for the employment of air forces than with the acceptance or rejection of a fundamental doctrine: "that the airplane possesses such ubiquity, and such advantages of speed and elevation, as to possess the power of destroying all surface installations and instruments, ashore or afloat, while remaining comparatively safe from any effective reprisal from the ground."[10] Looked at in this light, Warner argued, what they were really writing about was a theory of warfare, one that postulated the fundamental power of a particular weapon—the aircraft—as the predominant instrument of war.

From this starting point, Warner moved on to an analysis of the published works of Guilio Douhet (1869-1930), William Mitchell (1879-1936), and Alexander de Seversky (1894-1974), devoting nine pages to the first, five to the second, and only two to the third. To this task Warner brought his skills as an aeronautical engineer along with his experience in high-level government posts and as a former professor at the Mas-

---

[8] For the Smuts Memorandum, see Walter Raleigh and H. A. Jones, *The War in the Air*, 7 vols. (London, 1932-37), 7:8-14 and Frankland, *Bombing Offensive against Germany*, 21-46.

[9] Warner's essay appeared in *Makers of Modern Strategy*, ed. Edward Mead Earle (Princeton, 1943), 485-503, and has been reprinted countless times in books of readings at the military academies, staff colleges, and war colleges.

[10] Ibid., 485.

sachusetts Institute of Technology (where one of his doctoral students during 1923-1925 had been a young Air Service lieutenant named James H. Doolittle). His background uniquely qualified him to analyze the theoretical and practical limitations applicable to the existing tools of war in the air.[11]

With perhaps one exception, Warner's pages on Douhet remain today both valid and helpful. As he outlined it, Douhet's theory of war broke down into a few key points that might be abbreviated as follows: (1) modern warfare allows for no distinction between combatants and noncombatants; (2) successful offensives by surface forces are no longer possible; (3) the advantages of speed and elevation in the three-dimensional arena of aerial warfare have made it impossible to take defensive measures against an offensive aerial strategy; (4) therefore, a nation must be prepared at the outset to launch massive bombing attacks against the enemy centers of population, government, and industry—hit first and hit hard to shatter enemy civilian morale, leaving the enemy government no option but to sue for peace; (5) to do this an independent air force armed with long-range bombardment aircraft, maintained in a constant state of readiness, is the primary requirement.[12]

Warner correctly acknowledged that Douhet's theory reflected Italy's geographic position to an extent greater than many had noticed; also that Douhet's inability to foresee radar led him to underestimate the possibilities for defense against air attack. Speaking to the events of 1940-1943, however, Warner may have chided Douhet unfairly in one instance. I refer to what he called Douhet's overestimation of the destructive and disruptive effect of bombing on civilian morale. Here Warner and other writers who have followed him[13] seem to have failed to take fully into account Douhet's assumption that attacks against population and industrial centers would employ three types of bombs—explosive, incendiary, and poison gas—each used, he tells us without explaining himself, "in the correct proportions." The refusal of the antagonists in World War II to employ chemical bombs—from fear of retaliation—should not, in a strictly logical sense, be ignored when criticizing the predictions of a writer who explicitly presumed they would be used.

Warner's pages on "Billy" Mitchell have not stood the test of time

---

[11] Warner was serving as vice-chairman of the Civil Aeronautics Board when his essay appeared. Earlier, he had served as assistant secretary of the navy for aeronautics and as editor of *Aviation*. For his career, see *Current Biography*, 1949, pp. 620-22, and the obituary in the *New York Times*, July 13, 1958.

[12] For Douhet's writings see the bibliographical note at the end of this volume.

[13] For a surprising example, see Bernard Brodie, *Strategy in the Missile Age* (Princeton, 1959), 88-90. Brodie's chapter "The Heritage of Douhet," pp. 71-106, is helpful but not up to his usual standards.

as well as his analysis of Douhet. In part this may be owing to Warner's tendency to emphasize, with Mitchell and Seversky as much as with Douhet, the degree to which each writer stressed the enemy industrial base and economic structure as the preferred target for bombardment operations. This aspect of Mitchell's writing did not become important until quite late; emphasizing it has the effect of drawing attention away from his many other contributions as leader, innovator, advocate, and symbol for all the means by which air power could dominate surface warfare. Whereas Douhet had looked on aircraft other than bombers as ancillary—nice to have, perhaps, but not absolutely necessary—Mitchell could argue the case for all types. The important thing for him was not strategic bombing, but rather the centralized coordination of all air assets under the control of an autonomous air force command, freed from its dependency on the army. If that goal could be achieved, he felt, everything else would fall into its proper place.

One further point: when Warner refers to Mitchell as "an originator," this should not be taken to mean original thinker, a fact that did not become widely understood until the publication of Alfred F. Hurley's *Billy Mitchell: Crusader for Air Power*.[14] Although Hurley's subtitle highlights Mitchell's main significance as a crusader, it tends to hide the volume's true topic, which is the aeronautical ideas of America's foremost military aviator. Hurley concludes that Mitchell's achievements did not lie in the realm of original thought; rather, "he borrowed his ideas largely from an international community of airmen which he joined during World War I."[15] (This conclusion could be applied almost as well to Douhet, whose significance, much like that of Alfred Thayer Mahan, resides less in his originality than in his being the first to pull together, in one place and in a structured order, ideas widely shared at the time.)[16]

Warner's inclusion of some remarks on Alexander de Seversky's *Victory Through Air Power* (1942) was indeed topical at the time, but has had the effect over the years of leading beginning students to assume a greater place for Seversky as a theorist than is warranted. As a promoter of a generalized thesis favoring air power over all other means of warfare, however, his popular influence was greater than anyone born much after 1935 can probably imagine—deriving as it did from a wartime propaganda film produced by Walt Disney.[17]

---

[14] Hurley's biography derives from his Princeton Ph.D. dissertation, "The Aeronautical Ideas of General William Mitchell," 1961. It was first published in 1964 (New York). References here are to the new edition (Bloomington, 1975).

[15] Ibid., 139.

[16] See Brodie, *Strategy in the Missile Age*, 71-72.

[17] The 65-minute animated Disney film, released in July 1943 while *Makers of Modern Strategy* was in press, combined a cartoon "history of aviation" with a fearsomely animated

When one looks back now on the interwar years and widens Warner's focus (1) from air power in general to specific theories for the employment of aircraft in battle, and (2) from individual to corporate contributions, several important developments deserve at least brief mention.[18]

Certainly ranking high on such a list would be the work of J. F. C. Fuller and Basil H. Liddell Hart in establishing the theoretical framework for the air-land team in armored warfare. Blitzkrieg warfare as employed by Germany owed much to their ideas and, contrary to popular assumptions, involved aircraft at a level equally important with tanks and motorized infantry. Its employment in France and Russia in 1940 and 1941 depended heavily on coordinated—in fact leading—air attacks applying aircraft in a manner that Mitchell would have understood well but Douhet and Seversky would have thought inefficient.[19]

Important at the same time in the United States and Japan were theoretical and technological developments affecting carrier-borne naval aviation, in which Mitchell, with his sinking of the *Ostfriesland* in 1921 and his early prophecies—in 1912 and again in 1924—of impending war with Japan, played the role of unwitting catalyst. At first, the U.S. Navy took the view that carrier-borne aircraft would be useful principally in scouting for the main battle fleet. A few renegade thinkers had more expansive ideas of what is now called a power-projection role against targets ashore, but no one had much success talking about carrier aircraft sinking capital ships in an engagement between fleets. Japan, less committed to traditional ships of the line and more concerned with power projection than with pure defense, proved its tactical readiness at Pearl Harbor in December 1941.

In Great Britain following World War I, the Royal Air Force, created in 1918 from the air arms of the older services, began a twenty-year struggle to retain its status as a separate entity. In December 1919 Win-

---

version of *Victory Through Air Power* (from which the entire production took its title). The film had a considerable—if now unmeasurable—effect on the public, suggesting a quick, clean, efficient victory over the Axis powers by means of enormous air fleets knocking out the means of production in Japan, Italy, and Germany. *Life* was uncritical ("good history and fine entertainment"), but some reviewers were rattled by the implications of it all, several noting that although the film illustrated the impending destruction of three nations it managed to do so without showing anyone on either side being killed or maimed. Seversky's promotional work continued after World War II (as in his *Air Power: Key to Survival* [New York, 1950]) and he remained a close confidant of senior American air officers until his death in 1974.

[18] After Douhet, Mitchell, and Trenchard in the 1920s and early 1930s, the development of air power theory and doctrine became a product of corporate rather than individual effort.

[19] On Liddell Hart and Fuller, refer to essay 20, above.

ston Churchill, then minister for war and air, declared that "the first duty of the RAF is to garrison the British Empire." Air Chief Marshal Sir Hugh Trenchard (chief of air staff from 1919 to 1929) had first suggested, with regard to Somaliland, that aircraft could be adapted to the policing functions of the empire. In 1920 Churchill asked that a practical scheme for "air control" be worked out for Mesopotamia (Iraq) as well. First employed in 1922, emphasizing presence, coercion, and minimum application of force, the substitution of air for ground forces in the Middle East had by 1923 lopped £750,000 from the annual costs of maintaining order. By the mid-1930s, a thoroughgoing doctrine for employment had been worked out and was being taught at the RAF Staff College and the Imperial Defence College.[20]

The other principal theme of RAF development between the wars centered on the future, and stressed independent air operations against an enemy's material and moral resources. A repetition of the slaughter in the First World War had to be avoided at all costs, a view widely shared in Britain and distinctly amenable to the RAF staff. Air attacks aimed at the sources as opposed to the manifestations of an enemy's strength, it was argued, would both restore decisiveness to warfare and produce a much swifter and hence in the end more humane decision. Here as well Trenchard took the lead, coming more and more to emphasize the decisiveness of an attack aimed at the enemy's morale. The necessary presumed enemy throughout the 1920s, for Trenchard if not for the government, was France, replaced by Germany only after the rise of Hitler. Trenchard's ethnocentric views shielded him from worrying about a two-way air war; the French, he was convinced, would "squeal first." Not until 1936-1937 would cooler heads in the government, principally in the Treasury, overcome the RAF's insistence on committing the majority of its resources to Bomber Command. The decision to switch the emphasis to air defense, and Fighter Command, came just in time and did not reflect the views of the majority of the air staff.

In the United States, the translation of Douhet's and Mitchell's broad concepts into an elaborated doctrine of employment for operations against the enemy industrial web was the work of the U.S. Army's Air Corps Tactical School. From its beginning in 1920, the Tactical School's curriculum treated all aspects of aerial tactics and strategy. But beginning around 1926, the strategic role of bombardment aircraft operating independently of surface forces emerged as an important theme, and after 1932 it became dominant. Perhaps because they found it impossible to

[20] See Lt. Colonel David J. Dean, USAF, "Air Power in Small Wars: The British Air Control Experience," *Air University Review* 34, no. 5 (July-August 1983), pp. 24-31 and the sources cited therein.

envisage bomber fleets of the size implied by Douhet, some of the instructors began to wonder whether it might be possible, through careful, scientific study of a nation's industry, to single out particular targets whose destruction would of itself bring to a halt an entire industry or series of industries. If a number of such "bottleneck" targets could be identified and destroyed, it might be possible, with a relatively small force, to bring an enemy's war production to a halt with almost surgical precision, thereby rendering the enemy incapable of further resistance. Accordingly, case studies were devised using the United States as a test case, to determine the degree of industrial concentration, the component parts of various industries, the relative importance of the parts, and the vulnerability to air attack of what appeared to be the most critical targets.

Identifying targets was one thing; hitting them from the air was something else. Yet technology, at least for the optimists, seemed to be keeping pace. The new B-17 had the range, speed, altitude, and bomb-carrying capacity deemed necessary. And when orders were placed for improved models of the Sperry bombsight and the new Norden Mark XV bombsight in 1933, it appeared possible that the day might not be far off when a fleet of perhaps 100 B-17s could take off from some friendly base (perhaps in England), fly at high altitudes (perhaps 25,000 feet, the purpose being to get above the effective height of enemy anti-aircraft guns and defensive fighters) for several hundred miles. There, grouped together in a large formation to multiply both the amount of force delivered on the target and the defensive firepower of the bombers' guns, they would carefully sight in the target with the new bombsights, trigger their bomb loads, and then return several hundred miles to their base. Behind them they would leave a badly crippled, if not devastated, industry (actually only one factory, perhaps, but so chosen that its destruction must inevitably cripple an entire industry). It was decided that such attacks should take place in daylight because accuracy could be expected to be better. The question whether the bomber fleet should be escorted to the target by fighter aircraft was decided in the negative, primarily because no such aircraft of sufficient range yet existed.[21]

Such, in rough outline, was the theory of "daylight, high altitude, precision bombardment of selected targets" that the U.S. Army Air Forces

[21] For a participant's account of the work of the Tactical School and its influence on American air strategy in World War II, see Major General Haywood S. Hansell, Jr., *The Air Plan That Defeated Hitler* (Atlanta, 1972); a brief treatment can be found in the present writer's *Strategic Bombing in World War II: The Story of the U.S. Strategic Bombing Survey* (New York and London, 1976), pp. 4-12, from which this and the preceding paragraph are drawn.

carried with them into the Second World War. Subsequent events would reveal many shortcomings in the theory, among which would have to be included: (1) the unstated assumption that precise intelligence regarding enemy targets would be available; (2) a prevailing tendency to magnify expected capabilities derived from designs still on the drawing boards, at the same time minimizing the likely effects of limiting factors—not the least of which would prove to be the impact of weather conditions on flying operations; (3) a pattern of looking at the parts of the problem at the expense of the whole, a form of reductionism surely not limited to air theorists, but one leading to a concentration on means rather than ends, running parallel with a tendency to confuse destruction with control, and at the same time reducing strategy to a targeting problem; and (4) a gross over-estimate of the self-defending capacity of bomber aircraft against a daring and dedicated defending air force. From the standpoint of theory, however, it should be clear that the initial American concept, with its overriding emphasis on economy of force artfully applied, cannot be dismissed as a Douhetan fantasy.

In the years between the world wars, the differing approaches to air warfare by the various theorists and among the major powers of the world were not derived from commonly accepted principles of air power. Despite the efforts of Douhet and Mitchell, neither proved to be a Mahan or a Jomini from whom the air power enthusiasts could draw the secrets of the third dimension in warfare. Rather, the airplane's application was a product of separate choice within each major nation, reflecting an effort to integrate the unique capabilities of aircraft in support of land and sea forces, or in independent operations, in a manner that was both affordable and attuned to the achievement of national objectives. A secondary driving force, especially in the United States, was the effort to create an independent air arm, one that would owe its establishment to its ability to perform a unique mission that could not be achieved by any of the other services.

III

Within two years after the publication of Edward Warner's essay in *Makers of Modern Strategy*, the Allied powers brought the war to an end. "Air power," as Bernard Brodie would later write, "had a mighty vindication in World War II. But it was Mitchell's conception of it— anything that flies—rather than Douhet's that was vindicated. It was in tactical employment that success was most spectacular and that the air forces won the unqualified respect and admiration of the older services. By contrast, the purely strategic successes, however far-reaching in particular circumstances, were never completely convincing to uncommitted observers."[22]

The mass of data that quickly became available to theorists and critics alike was unmatched in extent in the earlier history of warfare. The air activities of every major participant save Russia were laid bare: for Germany and Japan because they were not offered a choice; for Italy and France because there wasn't much to tell; and for the United States because its government, senior airmen, and public felt secure behind their new-found "atomic shield." In the United Kingdom, the government exercised its traditional restraint, but not to the extent of holding in check the outspoken assessment of its senior air commander, Air Chief Marshal Sir Arthur Harris.[23]

Brodie's interpretation of what had happened to the theories of Douhet and Mitchell was that of a critic of the strategic air campaigns conducted against Germany and Japan; indeed, of a critic who by the mid-1950s had come to view those campaigns as having derived inexorably from a tendency among the industrialized nations of the nineteenth and twentieth centuries to employ force beyond reason. Furthermore, he believed the campaigns pointed the way to an even more devastating future. But although colored by his fears for a future armed with atomic and thermonuclear weapons, Brodie's criticism was nonetheless restrained and limited to the evidence as he saw it. The same could be said for many others, for whom Noble Frankland's memorable comment—people have preferred to feel rather than to know about strategic bombing—is more appropriate. Although this is not the place to summarize the unending debate about the effectiveness of strategic bombing in World War II, a few principal themes should be mentioned.[24]

With regard to the war in Western Europe, controversy has centered on (1) the ineffectiveness and inhumanity of RAF Bomber Command's avowed policy of area bombing directed against German civilian morale, (2) the long-delayed effectiveness of U.S. precision bombing efforts, (3)

---

[22] Brodie, *Strategy in the Missile Age*, 107. This is a view not calculated to inspire universal assent. One committed observer, Lt. General Ira C. Eaker, wartime commander of the U.S. Eighth Air Force, described this paragraph in 1977 as " a slanted, prejudiced view wholly unrelated to the facts."

[23] Arthur Harris, *Bomber Offensive* (London and New York, 1947).

[24] In the United States a presidential commission (the United States Strategic Bombing Survey, or USSBS) published a total of 321 reports between 1945 and 1947: 212 on the war in Europe and 109 on the war in the Pacific. The story of the USSBS is told in MacIsaac, *Strategic Bombing in World War II*, which also includes a capsule account of its lesser counterpart, the British Bombing Survey Unit (or BBSU). See also the general introduction to Garland Publishing's *The U.S. Strategic Bombing Survey: Selected Reports in Ten Volumes* (New York and London, 1976), 1:vii–xxix, which summarizes, through 1975, the still on-going controversies about the effectiveness of strategic bombing in World War II.

636

the drift of the U.S. attacks by early 1945 towards a bombing effort more clublike than swordlike, and (4) given that victory through air power alone proved unattainable in the prevailing circumstances, whether the immense material and human resources devoted to the bombing campaigns might have been better employed in other ways. With regard to Japan, controversy has centered on the atomic bomb decision. Effectiveness, given that surrender was induced without the dreaded invasion, became a moot point. The U.S. adoption in March 1945 of new tactics resulting in the incineration of Japanese cities has received far less criticism over the years than might have been expected. Pearl Harbor and subsequent Japanese atrocities against prisoners of war seemed to justify almost anything in response and in any case, the atomic bomb issue quickly devoured all others.

Although the American and British strategic bombing campaigns of World War II have received widespread attention, and indeed formed the basis for most postwar planning in both countries, at least equally important—more so when measured in terms of effort expended and tactical success in every theater—were some of the non-Douhetan aspects of the air war.

Despite its technical status as a separate service, the *Luftwaffe* from beginning to end remained firmly under the control of the High Command so far as its doctrinal development and equipment were concerned. The roles of its fighting aircraft, its airborne parachutists, and its air transport forces were all designed to support the operations of the *Wehrmacht*. The German capability to conduct long-range air operations of the sort that had any hope of producing decisions independently of surface forces was nil throughout the war. This is not to suggest that it was easy for the RAF to win the battle of Britain—yet another "nearest run thing you ever saw in your life"—but German equipment, employment doctrine, and leadership deprived the *Luftwaffe* of any real chance of success, just as they later did in the airlift operations at Stalingrad. It is true that German "Douhetists" of sorts had appeared now and then in the thirties—General Walter Wever being the most prominent until his death in 1936—but had proved out of place. Hitler himself, until at least 1943 it must be remembered, had visions of conquests that would not be useless rubble but that could add to Germany's economic and military strength.

Japan's army and navy each had an air contingent, but only the naval air arm developed a long-range striking force of formidable proportions. Within four months of its success at Pearl Harbor, the Halsey-Doolittle raid launched from the carrier *Hornet* (from Shangri-La, said President Roosevelt) against Tokyo in April 1942 signaled a new vulnerability not taken into account by Japanese planners. In May the battle of the Coral Sea became the first naval engagement where the opposing fleets were never in sight of one another. And at Midway in June 1942, the sinking of four Japanese carriers by a combination of courage and luck made it apparent to all that naval warfare had entered a new age.

The contributions of the Soviet Union's air forces to final victory remain clouded in an obscurity best revealed by its initial postwar de-emphasis on the kind of air force developed in the United States in the years immediately following 1945. Then as now, the Soviet air forces were composed primarily, but not exclusively, of aircraft designed to support surface forces, during World War II primarily ground forces but now also including naval units. The nonexistent bomber gap of the fifties, like the similarly nonexistent missile gap of the early sixties, was, not unlike the *Luftwaffe*'s psychological superiority of 1936-1940, more a product of the beholders' minds than of the forces in question.

An aspect of air power theory of great significance to the U.S. Air Force after 1945, which has been largely neglected by historians, concerns what is now called tactical air power—in particular, its command and control when employed in support of ground forces. At the Air Corps Tactical School in the 1930s, attack aviation (as it was then called) was assigned three functions. First, with the assistance when necessary of pursuit aviation, was the attainment of air superiority in the theater of operations. Establishing dominance (supremacy if possible) over the enemy air force was seen as in and of itself the single greatest contribution an air force could make to friendly surface forces. Next in order of priority would come efforts to isolate the battlefield by striking enemy forces and supplies that lay beyond the effective range of artillery—what is now called battlefield interdiction. Third, and last, would come attacks directly against enemy troops on the battlefield—or close air support.

Experiences in North Africa in late 1942 and early 1943 seemed to confirm this arrangement of priorities, at least to the airmen. Ground commanders remained skeptical until the end of the Tunisian campaign in May 1943, in part because they resented the efforts of the air commanders to establish centralized control over all air assets—and thereby to enhance flexibility of employment against the decisive points as seen by the overall theater commander. The airmen managed a coup of sorts with the publication by the War Department in July 1943 of Field Manual 100-20, *Command and Employment of Air Power*, a document prepared by the Army Air Forces without the assistance of the Army Ground Forces. It opened by asserting, in capital letters: Land power and air power are co-equal and independent forces: neither is an auxiliary of the other.

The manual went on to spell out that "inherent flexibility" was to be seen as the single greatest asset of an air force; that such flexibility could be exploited effectively only if command were in the hands of an airman responsible exclusively to the overall theater commander. There could be no more frittering away of air power's latent decisiveness by parcelling out air assets to subordinate division-or-corps-level commanders. Also, the manual spelled out an explicit hierarchy of priorities for the tactical air forces: (1) air superiority, (2) interdiction, and (3) close air support. In Europe after the June 1944 landings in Normandy the abundance of available aircraft and crews (against an already staggering *Luftwaffe*) made it unnecessary for the airmen to wave FM 100-20 in the faces of their ground forces partners; timing and circumstances had provided enough in the way of air forces to do everything desired and such debates as occurred were related to specific operations rather than doctrinal differences, although the latter retained a lively relevance for doctrinaires on both sides.

For present purposes, two aspects of the maturation of air power theory as applied to tactical air forces are important to keep in mind: in the immediate postwar period, with the emphasis attached to developing long-range forces for "the new Air Atomic Age," tactical air forces and doctrine were neglected, and by the mid-1960s in Indochina the battle of 1943 over centralized control would have to be fought out all over again, not with ground forces but with three other air forces—those of the navy, army, and marine corps.[25]

IV

Decades have now passed since two atomic bombs were dropped on Japan in August 1945. In the interim, theorizing about air—and now space—warfare has become almost an industry unto itself, one heavily populated with game theorists, statistically oriented behavioral scientists, economists, and other social scientists—many of whom seem addicted to a jargon that may be subconsciously aimed at making the unthinkable appear rational. Although the topic of strategy as it relates to nuclear weapons falls outside the realm of this discussion, it so closely impinges on air power after 1945 that a few observations are unavoidable here.

The roster of participants in the field of nuclear strategy whose ideas have had striking if sometimes only momentary impact is a long one.[26] In their different ways, most of these writers have addressed the question

[25] See William W. Momyer, *Air Power in Three Wars* (Washington, D.C., 1978) and Thomas A. Cardwell III, *Command Structure for Theater Warfare: The Quest for Unity of Command* (Maxwell Air Force Base, Ala., 1984).

[26] My own "short list" would include: Bernard Brodie, Herman Kahn, Henry A. Kissinger, Albert J. Wohlstetter, Thomas C. Schelling, Oskar Morgenstern, P. M. S. Blackett, André Beaufre, Alistair Buchan, Pierre Gallois, Robert E. Osgood, William W. Kaufman, Maxwell Taylor, V. D. Sokolovskii, Basil H. Liddell Hart, James M. Gavin, Michael Howard, Sir John Slessor, and Raymond Aron.

of *war* in the nuclear age, rather than *air* warfare specifically or exclusively—in this respect paralleling the aviation enthusiasts of the early twentieth century. Most of the important writings date from the mid-1950s to the late 1960s, and collectively the group makes up the core of the so-called strategy intellectuals. A patient examination of their collective efforts is not something one can expect from pilots. This is probably just as well, since their innate skepticism of the theoretical would leave them wondering what all the fuss is about. For those who do make the effort, one of two results is regularly predictable: either they become enmeshed in the conceptual intricacies separating various "schools," or they come to the stark and not very confidence-inspiring conclusion that the number of truly new ideas that have surfaced since the fall of 1945 is disconcertingly small.

Bernard Brodie's November 1945 paper "The Atomic Bomb and American Security," later included in expanded form as two chapters of *The Absolute Weapon*, staked out deterrence as the dominant concept of nuclear strategy. "Thus far the chief purpose of our military establishment has been to win wars. From now on its chief purpose must be to avert them. It can have almost no other purpose."[27] For the next two decades Brodie set the pace among thinkers in the field. His *Strategy in the Missile Age* remains even today the only true classic we have yet seen on the essential questions of force structure (how much is enough?) and force postures (offensive, defensive, retaliatory, preemptive, etc.). Unlike some early writers on the atomic question, Brodie faced up to the fact that there was probably no way to turn back the clock, and that the imperative question would become how to regulate the new weapons so as to minimize both the chances of their use and the levels of devastation that would result if they were used. His imposing realism separated him from certain other theorists—not the least of whom was Edward Mead Earle—who launched a more despairing line of argument that saw no answer other than the outlawing of war, a now regrettably but inevitably discredited theme whose active pursuers can be found among those who make up the arms control and disarmament school of contemporary strategic thought.[28]

---

[27] Bernard Brodie, *The Absolute Weapon* (New York, 1946), 76. In March 1946, Arthur C. Clarke, than a young RAF flight lieutenant with no knowledge of Brodie's work, reached essentially the same conclusion: "The only defense against the weapons of the future is to prevent them ever being used. In other words, the problem is political and not military at all. *A country's armed forces can no longer defend it; the most they can promise is the destruction of the attacker.*" (Emphasis in original.) See his "The Rocket and the Future of Warfare," *Royal Air Force Quarterly* 17, no. 2 (March 1946), 61-69.

[28] Earle's *Yale Review* article of June 1946, "The Influence of Air Power upon History," concluded with the thought that "it is no longer mere rhetoric to assert that unless we

Initially, theorizing about air warfare between 1945 and 1953 took a back seat to the more urgent problems of postwar recovery and the hardening Cold War between the United States and the Soviet Union. Demobilization to the point of disintegration of American military forces quickly led the government toward a policy of deterrence through the threat of atomic, later nuclear, retaliation, a posture that over the years has gone through innumerable convolutions of form and detail but none of conceptual substance.[29] At first America's "atomic monopoly" consisted of a handful of weapons that could be delivered only by very large bombers and required elaborate and time-consuming assembly processes, for which at one time in the late forties no more than six qualified assembly teams were available. By the mid-1950s, however, a combination of technical breakthroughs and the unleashing of the purse strings, brought on by the war in Korea, opened an era of "nuclear plenty" that was reflected in the "doctrine" of massive retaliation.

The conceptual origins of massive retaliation via nuclear weapons can be seen in testimony by Generals Henry H. Arnold and Carl A. Spaatz before the U.S. Congress as early as the fall of 1945.[30] The military capability to carry it out was born of budget and force-structure decisions made in the summer of 1951. And its announcement in early 1954, following the new Eisenhower administration's year-long review of defense policy, was driven by the frustrations of the Korean experience and Eisenhower's fears relating to the future vulnerability of the American economy. Essentially, it was an economic rather than a strategic decision, one that sought "more bang for the buck over the long haul."

Theorists immediately questioned the credibility of massive retaliation in instances other than a final face-off between the United States and the Soviet Union. Others questioned the sanity of introducing an "age of overkill,"[31] arguing that the ability to deliver with certainty a relatively few nuclear weapons would be sufficient for the needs of de-

---

destroy war, war will ultimately destroy us." (Since most readers who come across Earle's essay do so via the excerpted version in Eugene Emme, *Impact of Air Power* [New York, 1959], I should note that Emme's ellipses thoroughly mask the dismal tone of Earle's conclusions, omitting for example the conclusion quoted in this note.)

[29] For the best short statement of the view I advance in the text, see Bernard Brodie's final comment on these matters in "The Development of Nuclear Strategy," *International Security* 2, no. 4 (Spring 1978), 65-83.

[30] See my "The Air Force and Strategic Thought, 1945-51," International Security Studies Program Working Paper #8, The Wilson Center, Washington, D.C., June 1979; Samuel F. Wells, Jr., "The Origins of Massive Retaliation," *Political Science Quarterly* 96, no. 1 (Spring 1981), 31-52; and D. MacIsaac and S. F. Wells, Jr., "A Minuteman Tradition," *The Wilson Quarterly* 3, no. 2 (Spring 1979), 109-24.

[31] The title is Max Lerner's (New York, 1962), but the theme is that of Ralph E. Lapp (e.g., *Kill and Overkill* [New York, 1962]) and his fellow contributors over the years to *The Bulletin of the Atomic Scientists*.

terrence. The "finite deterrence" school, despite a strong effort by the U.S. Navy in 1957, never really got off the ground in the United States; in Europe, particularly in France but also to some extent in the United Kingdom, it was adopted out of necessity. Under Eisenhower, the threat of massive retaliation was muted over time and steps were taken to improve conventional (non-nuclear-armed) military forces for use in less than mortal confrontations. This trend was accelerated under the Kennedy administration ("flexible response"), but another decision made at the same time was to build up the strategic nuclear forces to previously undreamt-of levels, primarily by switching the emphasis from bombers to sea- and land-launched ballistic missiles of intercontinental range, consisting of 1,000 Minuteman and 54 Titan ICBMs and a fleet of 41 Polaris-type submarines armed with 16 SLBMs each.

Future historians may come to see the Kennedy/McNamara decisions of 1961 as true watersheds, the improved flexible response capability contributing to a willingness, if not simply an itch, to try it out in Vietnam, and the strategic force buildup, cold-bloodedly flaunted during the Cuban missile crisis of October 1962, leading to a Soviet decision never again to be faced down by vastly superior strategic forces in American hands. Such a thesis—not widely accepted among Sovietologists—will have to survive accusations that it represents no more than a *post hoc, ergo propter hoc* argument; it will have to demonstrate that the Russian buildup of the 1970s derived from a "never again" syndrome rather than from a desire to create forces capable of either a disarming first strike or "nuclear blackmail" based on U.S. perceptions of the vulnerability of its own forces and their allied command-and-control mechanisms.[32]

Air and space warfare involving nuclear weapons, along with theorizing on the subject, is therefore now in limbo, an excessively high "noise level" in the early 1980s to the contrary notwithstanding. Neither superpower seems able to overcome the momentum of internal constituencies bent on improving deterrence by making the costs of its failure mutually suicidal. Like virtually every other initiative since the Eisenhower years to restore sanity to the nuclear arms buildup, the SALT II proposals of 1978-1979 foundered on the twin problems of presidential politics and international crises. Future analysts and historians would do well to keep in mind at least one unwelcome fact: the effort to untangle developments in the theory of nuclear-armed air warfare from changes in defense postures arising from Cold War initiatives is a virtually impossible task.

[32] For a review of the 1979-1983 literature on the "window of vulnerability" and other myths, see my "The Nuclear Weapons Debate and American Society," *Air University Review* 35, no. 4 (May-June 1984), 81-96.

V

Conventional air warfare in the years since 1945 has attracted far less attention from theorists, despite its having occurred frequently—most notably in Korea (1950-1953), the Arab-Israeli Wars (1967 and 1973), and Indochina (1960-75). Improvements in range, speed, payload, and weapons-delivery accuracy have been phenomenal, but have only rarely exerted decisive effect on the course of war on land, notably over Egypt in 1967 and arguably over Hanoi in December 1972.

The prevailing circumstances in the opening months of the war in Korea demanded instant employment of the few available aircraft in direct support of ground forces. The low priority given to tactical aircraft between 1945 and 1950 was matched in the field of doctrine as well, leading General O. P. Weyland, commander of the U.S. Far East Air Forces, to comment for years afterward to the effect that what was remembered from World War II was not written down, or if written down was not disseminated, or if disseminated was not read or understood. Except for the northern reaches of North Korea following the Chinese intervention, air superiority was not much of a problem, and the greatest level of effort by the air forces was devoted to interdiction of enemy supplies and reinforcements. Here the lesson of northern Italy in 1944 and 1945 had to be learned all over again: for air interdiction to be effective, the surface forces had to be in control of the tactical initiative. Operating by themselves without pressure being applied on the enemy by cooperating ground forces, aircraft could harass the enemy and delay the movement of supplies, but could not carry the day by themselves.[33]

Following Korea, the American tactical air forces went into decline once again. Overwhelming emphasis was placed on the buildup of the Strategic Air Command. The Korean experience was looked on as an aberration, unlikely to be repeated in the future. In 1955 Thomas K. Finletter, who had been secretary of the air force during the Korean War, wrote that the war had been "a special case, and air power can learn little from there about its future role in United States foreign policy in the East." The final report of the Far East Air Forces agreed, stating that "certainly any attempt to build an air force from the model of the Korean requirements could be fatal to the United States.[34] Although these views

[33] See M. J. Armitage and R. A. Mason, *Air Power in the Nuclear Age* (Champaign, Ill., 1983), ch. 2. The official history is Robert F. Futrell, *The United States Air Force in Korea, 1950-1953* (New York, 1961; rev. ed. Washington, D.C., 1983). A valuable retrospective by four senior air commanders is provided in *Air Superiority in World War II and Korea,* ed. Richard H. Kohn and Joseph P. Harahan (Washington, D.C., 1983).
[34] Quoted in Armitage and Mason, *Air Power in the Nuclear Age,* 44.

prevailed in the end, other military thinkers tried to stem the overriding emphasis being devoted to the Strategic Air Command.

Returning from the Far East in 1954 to take over the Tactical Air Command, General Weyland began an unsuccessful five-year struggle to gain an equal place for the tactical air forces. Most of his effort, however, was directed toward creating a nuclear capability for fighter-bombers. (Throughout the last half of the 1950s it was accepted as given that "tactical" nuclear weapons would be used in "the next war.") Consequently, aircraft designed strictly for the air-to-air (or air superiority) role were neglected and the development of conventional munitions was brought to a halt. This occurred despite Weyland's view, expressed in 1956, that "the most likely conflict in the immediate future will be the peripheral type. In this event it will be primarily a tactical air war."[35] In Great Britain, Air Chief Marshal Sir John Slessor went further: "We must expect to be faced with other Koreas. . . . The idea that superior air power can in some way be a substitute for hard slogging and professional skill on the ground in this sort of war is beguiling but illusory; . . . all this is cold comfort for anyone who hopes that air power will provide some kind of short cut to victory."[36]

In the colonial wars after World War II (for example, Indochina, 1945-1954; Malaya, 1948-1960; and Algeria, 1954-1962), air power functioned almost entirely in a supporting mode. The few analysts who studied these events generally concluded that air power's most effective use was in its non-firepower roles—reconnaissance, transport, liaison, and in general providing increased mobility for other arms. Such conclusions attracted little notice in the United States. The cry of "No more Koreas!" sounded out other considerations and virtually all preparatory thought centered on preparing for large-scale warfare, most likely with the Soviet Union and probably in Europe. When the Israeli air force "Pearl Harbored" the Egyptian air force in 1967 in the Six Day War, American airmen, by then thoroughly frustrated by the restraints imposed in Indochina, saw in the Israeli planning and execution the kind of air war they understood.

When viewed from the standpoint of air power theory and doctrine, the United States efforts in Indochina from 1965 through 1972 present several problems. The command-and-control arrangements that evolved over time, driven by a combination of external diplomatic concerns and

[35] Ibid., 44-45.

[36] Ibid., 45. This statement comes from his October 1954 *Foreign Affairs* article, "Air Power and World Strategy." A few years later in *The Great Deterrent* (New York, 1958) he was arguing that even the airmen had best turn their attention to countering "the tactics of the termite—subversion, infiltration, and the exploitation of factors like immature nationalism." There were few takers.

institutional imperatives internal to the U.S. military services, created a situation in which it appeared that five separate air wars were under way simultaneously: one in South Vietnam, involving by far the greatest level of effort and military success; another over North Vietnam; two others, mostly secret at the time, over northern Laos and Cambodia; and a fifth in southern Laos along the Ho Chi Minh trail. Most public attention centered on the air wars over North Vietnam.

The initial goals for that campaign were (1) to pressure the government in Hanoi to withdraw support from the insurgents in the South, (2) to interrupt the flow of supplies and men to the South, and (3) to strengthen the morale of progovernment forces in South Vietnam by demonstrating the U.S. commitment to the struggle. The decisions regarding how this was to be accomplished were rigidly controlled by the government in Washington, which dictated the timing, pace, target priorities (down to individual targets), and even sortie rates. From the beginning strict "rules of engagement" limited the options open to commanders on the scene and even prohibited the necessary steps to achieve air superiority by preventing, for example, attacks against surface-to-air (SAM) missile sites under construction and even enemy airfields (for fear of killing Russian and Chinese advisors at those locations, leading to possible escalation of tensions between the superpowers). If the government's concern over the possibilities for unintended escalation were warranted, the same cannot be said of its decision nonetheless to commit its air forces (including naval and marine corps air) to a half-hearted effort of "controlled, gradual escalation of limited pressure." No precedent existed for using air power to attain limited, essentially psychological, goals—let alone in a jungle campaign directed from a headquarters ten thousand miles away.

The airmen chafed under these restrictions, but did not rebel. Instead they performed as best they could in the prevailing circumstances, hoping that their leaders in government would come to see the light. Frequently in South Vietnam, for example at the seige of Khe Sanh in 1968, and on occasion in North Vietnam, as for example during the Linebacker operations in 1972, air power proved individually decisive in the limited circumstances of the moment. On the whole, however, the Indochina experience, for all the experimentation with new tactics and weapons (such as air-sea rescue techniques, helicopter and fixed-wing gunships, defoliation, precision-guided munitions) proved disappointing to theorists and practitioners alike. Except, of course, when we remind ourselves that success or failure is not the yardstick by which to measure heroism, the record of which in Indochina can never be sullied.

Israel's success in 1967 could not be repeated in 1973 owing both to the surprise achieved by the Egyptians and to the great improvements in surface-based antiaircraft defenses (both surface-to-air missiles and radar-directed, rapid-firing antiaircraft artillery). The Americans in Indochina had faced an earlier generation of SAMs, and given a relatively permissive air environment over most (but not all) land targets, had proved able to cope. Technological advances over the past decade alone, however, especially those deriving from all but daily advances in microelectronics, have thrown the whole offense versus defense question into doubt.

This is nowhere more evident than in Europe, where with Indochina behind them the Americans have fostered a large buildup of NATO air power as a counter to the Warsaw Pact's superiority in the accouterments of mechanized land warfare (as well as an alarming buildup of Soviet Frontal and Long Range Aviation). With both conventional and nuclear capabilities, NATO fighter and fighter-bomber aircraft have first and foremost a deterrent function. If called into action, however, no one on either side is very sure what will happen, given what is likely to be the busiest air space ever encountered and the uncertainties of electronic warfare techniques and of rapidly emerging SAM technology.

The only thing certain about the current pell-mell pace of technology in conventional air warfare is its spiraling costs, which are driving the price of individual aircraft up into the tens of millions of dollars. Since these cost increases must inevitably have the effect of reducing the numbers that will be made available, if not indeed the willingness to commit them to combat, some airmen—usually lonely renegades—have begun to call for a retreat to greater numbers of slightly less capable aircraft. Should that happen, a true watershed would be at hand, since never yet in the history of air warfare have the pilots who fly and fight been willing to surrender in advance a technological advantage. Nonetheless, the increased vulnerability of aircraft to antiair defenses, along with high unit costs, may combine to force a reevaluation of traditional priorities.

One possible switch of emphasis would be from the weapons platform—that is, the aircraft—to the weapons themselves, in particular precision-guided munitions, or PGMs. It is only natural that airmen have tended to concentrate on the platform itself, especially with regard to improvements in speed, range, agility, and other performance characteristics. It is similarly only natural that airmen have proved reluctant to foster rapid advances in the field of remotely piloted vehicles, or RPVs. However much the official spokesmen of the air services may deny it, RPVs are not considered an appropriate topic for discussion by most pilots, among whom it is an article of faith that a manned aircraft can perform any mission better than an unmanned aircraft.

Two senior British airmen have recently speculated about the im-

646

plications for the future of some of the problems air forces now face, ranging from political restraints to questions of vulnerabilities and costs. They conclude that the answer to present dilemmas must be found in improved tactical precision. If the new technology can be harnessed to the achievement of such a goal, they argue, political leaders may be less reluctant to look on air power as a ubiquitous arm of the first hour, rather than as a weapon of last resort. With regard to the vulnerability and cost factors, they write, this will mean "that the number of attacking aircraft put at risk must be reduced while at the same time more ground targets are engaged. The solution to that dilemma must lie in tactics that hold aircraft outside the most effective defences yet permit the use of multiple, highly accurate, and flexible weapons. A change from the past emphasis on platform performance and on to weapon performance therefore seems not only inevitable but imperative."[37]

Whether any significant changes in emphasis are close at hand remains an open question. One important inhibiting factor is the relative paucity of experience in air warfare over the past decade. Not only have the samples been small—not once large enough to be considered definitive—but they have been transitory. In addition, any answer to what these limited experiences have "proved" has been muddied by the limited nature of the objectives sought. Another problem is how well existing bureaucracies, interests, and fiefdoms can adapt to change. In the United States, for just one example, although remotely piloted vehicles are presently under development by both the army and the air force, each service has problems within its own constituencies regarding even the organizational implications of incorporating RPVs.

Nothing in the field of air warfare is more uncertain at this writing than its future course. As stated at the outset, the effects of technology and the actions of practitioners have from the beginning played greater roles than have ideas. It is even possible that we have arrived at a threshold of technological advance that may markedly change the identity of air power. Electronic combat, new satellite capabilities, precision-guided munitions, and pilotless aircraft suggest a new era in aviation—just as they have already begun to create a new vocabulary. Indeed, the advances in space travel, the space shuttle, and the "star wars" technologies of laser beams and directed energy weapons presage vastly new horizons for the airman. One might conclude, with some distress, that technology itself may be today's primary air power theorist; that invention may, for the moment, be the mother of application.

[37] For both the quotation and the preceding paragraph, see Armitage and Mason, *Air Power in the Nuclear Age*, 256-57. Chapter 9, "Challenge and Opportunities," is an excellent summary of its topic.

22. The Making of Soviet Strategy

CONDOLEEZZA RICE

FEW SECULAR philosophies are as holistic as Marxism. Explaining and predicting all of human history in terms of enduring class struggle, Marxism explicitly rejects compartmentalization of the human experience. Narrow definitions of military strategy that neatly separate war and peace or the army and society were foreign to the Bolsheviks. Lenin and his cohorts were impressed with Clausewitz's systematic analysis of the permanent interaction of politics and war. When the Soviets seized power in the war-ravaged Russian Empire in October 1917, there was no doubt in their minds that war, revolution, politics, and society were inseparable.

Ideological predilection and historical experience suggested that conflict, sometimes violent, was a locomotive for historical progress. But although Marxism provided a framework, it did not provide a blueprint. The Bolsheviks tried to take seriously Engels's promise that "freeing the proletariat will create its special and entirely new military method."[1] The revolution and the creation of the new socialist society, however, took place in complex and fluid circumstances. The victory, so recently won, was threatened by internal and external enemies and at times it seemed that the Bolshevik experiment would last but a matter of months. Facing first the war with Germany and then civil war, Soviet leaders fought to protect the embryonic socialist society while "correctly" divining the relationship of armed force to socialist progress. The few clues that they received from their ideological heritage often clashed with the reality of their circumstances. To harmonize ideological expectation with cold reality is a fundamental task facing new societies. It was never more critical than in revolutionary Russia, where necessity, more often than not, dictated the direction taken.

I

The initial clash between expectation and reality concerned the significance of the Russian Revolution itself. As Marxists, the Bolsheviks expected worldwide revolution to follow the victory of the proletariat in

[1] Karl Marx and Friedrich Engels, *Sochineniia* (Moscow, 1960), 8:460.

648

Russia. Workers in the advanced capitalist states would rise up, over-throw their rulers, and construct socialism without regard to national boundaries. The Bolsheviks had devoted most of their energy to starting the chain of events. Now in power, they disagreed over how long it would be before the workers of the world rose up to join the workers of Russia. This was hardly idle debate. The Bolsheviks, in no position to fight Germany, could not wait very long.

Radicals like Bukharin on the Left believed that Germany could be defeated from within, by fomenting revolution. Seriously overestimating both the solidarity of the workers and the weakness of Germany, they assumed that victory could be achieved by armed insurrection. Some, flushed with the victory of October, wished to fight a "bare-handed" revolutionary war against Germany. More moderate ideas were put forth by Lev Trotsky, who wished to threaten Germany with a dictum of "no war, no peace," in which the Soviets would refuse to make war while allowing internal instability to halt the German advance. The more con-servative Lenin argued that peace had to be secured immediately and at any cost in order to provide a respite for the embattled Russian state. Trotsky won the debate, and delivered his terms to the German nego-tiators; Germany responded with a massive offensive against the new Soviet state. When the enemy was less than two weeks from Moscow, Lenin delivered a now-famous ultimatum to his fellow Central Committee members. There was no choice but to declare peace, he said. The revo-lution in Germany was inevitable, but there was no way to gauge when it would occur. "We may have two weeks," Lenin is reported as saying. "Is there anyone who can guarantee that the workers will rise up in two weeks?"[2] Lenin threatened to resign if the Treaty of Brest-Litovsk was not signed, and won the argument. The Bolsheviks ratified a humiliating peace in which one-third of Russia's population and 60 percent of its European territory were lost.

The significance of Lenin's victory cannot be overstated. Not only may it have saved the Revolution, it set the path of future Soviet devel-opment. Major political decisions are not made in a vacuum, but in relationship to others made before. Once launched on a particular course, other decisions follow and the cumulative effect is to push a society along one path, while virtually eliminating parallel ones. The decision to protect the existing gains of socialism within Russia, rather than reaching for worldwide revolution, was the single most important decision that the early Bolsheviks made. One of its effects was to set the character of the

[2] Cited in Adam Ulam, *Expansion and Coexistence* (Cambridge, Mass., 1967), 72.

first armed forces, placing the Soviet Union on a path of military development from which it has never diverged.

Although the Treaty of Brest-Litovsk provided a respite, the Bolsheviks did not have sufficient armed strength either to guarantee the peace with Germany or to withstand the onslaught of internal enemies ready to launch a civil war. Military councils (soviets) were created before the Revolution, but their primary function was to direct disruptive activities and sow discord among the imperial forces. They were well suited to that task, but lacked the discipline and skill to defend the Revolution against former imperial generals like Kolchak and Denikin. The "White Forces" were soon joined by external enemies of the regime, troops from Japan, France, Britain, the United States, and units of former Czechoslovak soldiers in the Austrian army. At the same time, Polish forces engaged the Bolsheviks in battle on the western front, threatening to push the frontiers of the young Soviet state even further east. In this desperate situation, the Bolsheviks needed an army able to protect their revolution.

They faced a difficult choice. Centralized, disciplined, and trained forces were critical for victory, but sounded to some like the resurrection of the standing army that they had recently helped to destroy. There were those who worried that the army's form at birth would dictate its character once the internal enemies of the revolution were defeated. Nevertheless, Trotsky, the people's commissar for war, succeeded in replacing decentralized workers' formations with a tightly disciplined army under a unified command.[3]

The Bolsheviks made significant compromises in the creation of the Red Army. There were not enough workers and sympathizers to fill the ranks of a volunteer army. After appeals for volunteers fell short, the Bolsheviks turned to the more traditional means of forced mobilization of citizens and impressment of prisoners of war. On April 8, 1918, standardized Military Commissariats were organized to administer new centralized directives, and ideologically motivated notions like "elective command" (where the men elected and recalled their commanders at will) were revoked.[4]

The decision to entrust the leadership of the armed forces to "military specialists," a euphemism for former czarist officers, was however far more controversial and its effects were more long-lasting. By December 1918, 22,315 former imperial officers served in the Red Army and by

---

[3] L. D. Trotsky, *Kak voorazhalas' revoliutsiia* (How the revolution was armed), 3 vols. (Moscow, 1925), vol. 1. This basic work, first cited by John Erickson in *The Soviet High Command* (New York and London, 1962), describes the building of the army during the civil war.

[4] Trotsky, *Kak voorazhalas' revoliutsiia*, vol. 1.

August 1920 that number had grown to 48,409.[5] At the highest levels, the recruitment brought in future luminaries like General A. A. Svechin, who had been a senior imperial officer. Younger men, like Mikhail Tukhachevsky, previously a junior lieutenant in the imperial army, were also recruited. (Tukhachevsky, who became a legendary figure, was thoroughly committed to the communist cause and held, throughout his life, a curious mixture of military ideas from both the imperial and Bolshevik legacies.) Because of their superior educational background and their numbers, these men dominated the Red Army Command. The Bolsheviks also worked to create a cadre of "Red Commanders." Young workers were put through hastily developed military training academics and by the end of the Civil War, there were significant numbers of them as well. But former imperial officers remained powerful and the troubled Bolsheviks took great care to make certain that political loyalty could be forged and maintained.

The very creation of a standing army was a distasteful compromise for the young Soviet state. Such a force was thought to be a reflection of a prior epoch, when the ruling classes needed coercion, internally and externally, to maintain their power. Lenin, Engels, and Marx all declared the militia (the concept of a citizen's volunteer army—the armed working class) to be the appropriate form in the socialist era. Engels stated categorically, "In the communist society, no one will think of a regular army."[6] Moreover, based on their reading of the Revolution of 1848 in France, they believed that standing armies were easily subverted and used as a force of counterrevolution. An unflattering term, "Bonapartism," is still in the Soviet lexicon to describe the union of military officers with remnants of hostile classes to crush infant revolutions. The Bolsheviks, watching their own civil war, doubtless found their fears confirmed by the alliance of Alexander Kerensky, czarist generals, and the foreign capitalist powers. If the ideological question of the need for regular armed forces was receding, concern for the potential danger they constituted was growing.

As a substitute for the kind of army that they preferred, the Bolsheviks worked to politicize and control the one that they had, of necessity, created. The military commissar system that exists in name to the present day was developed for this purpose. If the Red Army could not be, for the time being, a voluntary association of armed workers committed to the cause, political officers would make certain that those who filled the ranks would fight loyally for it. But the political officers

---

[5] Cited in Erickson, *The Soviet High Command*, 33.
[6] Friedrich Engels, *Izbrannye voennye proizvedeniia* (Moscow, 1957), xiv.

often showed an interest in military command and the system did not operate smoothly. The struggle between the commissar and the commander for the authority to direct military operations was constant. More often than not, the military hierarchy under Trotsky favored the commanders' expertise and insisted on unified command. This only exacerbated tensions between commissars and commanders and complicated the already difficult task of defeating Russia's enemies. Not until many years later, when officers both communist and technically competent were in command, did these tensions subside.[7]

In spite of overwhelming odds, the Bolsheviks and the newly created Red Army survived the threats to their power. Many Bolsheviks were never completely satisfied with Trotsky's Red Army, however. It was created as a temporary device in 1918, to be demobilized and replaced by the militia as quickly as possible after the Civil War. Moreover, even though the Red Army proved equal to its task, it did not escape criticism. A body of political opposition grew up at the Eighth Party Congress in March 1918 that criticized Trotsky, his commanders, and the Red Army. The war commissar survived the attacks of Stalin, Dzerzhinski, and others who accused him of mimicking the imperial army and failing to rely at all on the special nature of proletarian warfare. Ultimately, Trotsky's best defense was the Red Army's success, but the opposition that would later challenge him more successfully began to crystallize long before the Civil War was won.

These tensions reflected divisions within the Red Army command between "military specialists" and the "Red Commanders," self-taught Bolsheviks whose military training had occurred on the battlefields of the Civil War. The "specialists" were assailed for reactionary thinking, but the Red Commanders were not without flaws either. The most important mistake was made by the influential Tukhachevsky, who insisted in the later stages of the war on launching an ill-conceived offensive against Warsaw. This could be relegated to the annals of Soviet military history were it not for the significant political statement Tukhachevsky sought to make with it—that "revolution" could be exported by bayonet. Arguing for an assault on Warsaw in spite of seriously overextended supply lines and insufficient reserves, he may have placed too much weight on the expectation that the working class would rise up to greet the Soviet forces. He held radical ideas, even for his day, going so far as to propose an international proletarian army. The army would not be a militia, but a regular, socialist army whose mission would be the export of revolution.

---

[7] Timothy Colton, *Commissars, Commanders and Civilian Authority* (Cambridge, Mass., 1979) provides an excellent discussion of the development of the Main Political Administration and the changing role of the political commissar.

Poland was the first chance to seize the political as well as the military offensive.

Tukhachevsky failed to attend to military details. The Red Army, lacking the necessary reserves, communications, and transport to carry out his complicated strategy, fell victim to determined attacks on the rear. It was forced to retreat, and just managed to stop the Poles short of Russian territory. Although Tukhachevsky justified the offensive and blamed its failure on "technical errors in staff coordination," the defeat haunted the Red Commanders throughout their military careers. Deputy Chief of Staff V. Triandifilov and Chief of Staff Boris Shaposhnikov later produced assessments that stated bluntly that the Red Army was simply not strong enough to undertake the offensive, and cautioned that the "military" factor had been underestimated.[8] Just how prominently the workers figured in Tukhachevsky's plan is unclear. Certainly, he defended the campaign on military grounds. Whatever the case, calls for exporting revolution were not completely silenced; but after the sobering experience of Poland, those who wished to concentrate on securing Russia's frontiers and subduing unrest in the East prevailed. Ultimately, the most important lesson of Poland was that revolutionary fervor and expectation were no substitute for military preparation.

II

As the Civil War drew to a close, debate about the future of the Red Army intensified. With their rule stabilized at last, the Bolsheviks were ready to address the fundamental issues of military strategy: the character of the next war, the form of the Red Army, and the nature of the "new military method" under socialist rule. As in 1918, Trotsky stood on one side, confronting the Red Commanders on the other, now led by S. I. Gusev and M. V. Frunze. The stakes were high; political and personal divisions pervaded the debate and made its outcome a matter of political survival for the rivals. The Frunze-Trotsky debates therefore loom large not only in the military history of the Soviet Union, but in its political development as well.

The opening salvo was fired in March 1921 with the presentation of a set of theses to the Tenth Party Congress by Gusev.[9] The theses

---

[8] The debate concerning the Polish campaign is discussed briefly but usefully in several essays in a recent Soviet historiographic volume, *Istoriia sovetskoi voennoi mysli* (History of Soviet military thought), ed. I. A. Korotkov (Moscow, 1980). There is wider disagreement about the failure of the campaign in earlier Soviet commentary. See, for example, N. E. Kakurin and V. A. Melikov, *Voina s belopolyakhami* (The war with the White Poles) (Moscow, 1925) for one view.

[9] The theses, primarily written by Gusev, can be found in S. I. Gusev, *Grazhdanskaia voina i krasnaia armiia* (Moscow, 1958), 216-21.

called for a "unified military doctrine" (*edinaia voennaia doktrina*) but failed miserably in trying to explain what this meant. Rather, the authors attacked the existing army, and put forward only vague suggestions of their own. Stating a fairly safe assumption, the theses declared that there would definitely be a protracted and difficult war in the future. The Civil War had been merely a first stage in a general war because the imperialists would counterattack. The imperialist armies would be technically superior and the Revolution would suffer certain defeat if the Red Army was not prepared to minimize its weaknesses. Its only hope was to become a "unified organism," welded together by political ideology and trained on the basis of the experiences of the first proletarian victory—the Civil War. Maneuver and offensive operations had won the Civil War and would win future wars; the Red Army could draw on its moral strength and superior tactics to neutralize the imperialists' technical expertise. The concept of a territorial militia, which was already being created, was attacked as unworkable. Socialism needed a regular army, drawn from the masses.

Trotsky launched a vigorous attack against these arguments, calling them incorrect in theory and sterile in practice. He rejected the notion of a unified military doctrine and thought training based on the special experience of the Civil War an even less defensible idea.[10] The delegates to the congress apparently agreed and Frunze and Gusev withdrew their theses; Frunze acknowledged that they had a "certain vagueness and lack of understanding in formulation."[11] Following this rebuff, it fell to Frunze to salvage the ideas so dearly held by the Red Commanders. In an article in July 1921 called "A Unified Military Doctrine and the Red Army," he revised his ideas, noting that a unified doctrine was important to all countries; it reflected the system of life and the class character of the state. Germany, England, and France all had unified doctrines, but Russia did not, owing to the pathetic state of military affairs under the czar. "It was not even possible to have discussion about any broad scientific work."[12] Here Frunze tried to put his "unified military doctrine" into perspective. Soviet, proletarian doctrine would be different—but the need for doctrine was not peculiar to the revolutionary state. Interestingly, the desirability of a unified military doctrine was an old theme in Russian military thought and had been an issue hotly debated by the imperial

[10] Trotsky, *Kak vooruzhalas' revoliutsiia*, 2:242.

[11] Frunze's formulation of the concept of unified military doctrine can be found in M. V. Frunze, *Edinaia voennaia doktrina i Krasnaia armii* (Moscow, 1921).

[12] Ibid. The article from which a monograph was later produced appeared in *Armiia i revoliutsiia*, a journal for distribution to troops in the Ukraine and in *Voennaia nauka i revoliutsiia*, a central theoretical journal. See a volume by Walter Darnell Jacobs, *Frunze: The Soviet Clausewitz: 1885-1925* (The Hague, 1969).

staff from the end of the Russo-Japanese War until the outbreak of World War I. Frunze did not rule out the role that the military specialist could play in formulating doctrine, but he did note that only those capable of moving beyond the "spirit of Philistine stupidity and dullness of czarist thought should engage in the debate."[13]

This new formulation was also much clearer on the character of the Red Army and the nature of its military strategy. Frunze argued for mass warfare—the total mobilization of the state. Believing that the small, professional army characteristic of bourgeois states could not win the future war, he predicted that every single member of the population would have to be "inducted" into the war effort. Here, ideological tenets clearly played a role. The theory of mass warfare had been developed by Engels, who suggested that only the socialist society dared fight mass warfare. The bourgeoisie would be too fearful of the working class to rely on it for a mass army.

At the same time, though, Frunze argued that the Red Army should be a cadre army and not a militia. There were still too many peasants in Russia, he claimed, who were not reliable, and not enough workers in Russia to create sufficient militia strength. Moreover, pointing to the experience of the Civil War, Frunze once again emphasized the primacy of the offensive and the centrality of maneuver in warfare. The Civil War had been won on the strength of the most mobile arm, the cavalry, and on the basis of skillful maneuver warfare. The peasant, Frunze argued, was defense-minded; proletarians were naturally gifted for the offensive. Consequently, it was both dangerous to rely on peasants in territorial militia formations and an ineffective way to prepare for the next war. Although he suggested that other forms of warfare, including partisan (peasant) warfare, should be studied, Frunze declared that the offensive was the appropriate strategy. It could only be carried out by a well-trained cadre army.

Frunze's rejection of the militia system was an important departure for the Bolsheviks. Under an order of March 1920, the transition to a militia had already begun. But the influence of the Red Commanders, who did not relish being exiled in territorial militia formations, began to be felt. They sought ideological justification for a regular, but socialist army. Tukhachevsky put forth an elaborate ideological justification that ignored Engels's admonition and claimed that the ideal of the militia was a legacy of the erroneous conclusions of the Second International. In a very strange twist, Trotsky, who out of respect for bourgeois methods of waging war had brought military specialists into the Red Army, found

---

[13] Frunze, *Edinaia voennaia doktrina*, 18.

himself defending the militia system in 1920. In reality, though, the militia had few proponents. By decree of the Central Committee a mixed military system was established. Again the compromise was one of necessity, for the cadre army that Frunze wanted was too expensive for the young Soviet state. For about ten years, the militia remained a significant portion of Soviet military strength. The cadre army was the center of attention, however, and steadily eclipsed the militia.

Quite apart from the fate of the militia, there was an important contradiction in Frunze's simultaneous defense of the cadre army and mass warfare. While paying significant attention to the concept of the "mass army," Frunze admitted that technology would play an increasingly important, even decisive, role in the next war. Although he almost glorified the technological inferiority and moral superiority of the socialist army, Frunze presented a program to transform the technical level of the Red Army rapidly. The pursuit of technical competence and purposeful training put it just one step away from the specialized elite army he despised, yet the mass army could not fight the "technological" war. This unresolved issue of the place of expert and elite forces haunted Soviet military planners long after Frunze's death.

Trotsky answered Frunze's revised theses a few months later in an article entitled "Military Doctrine or Pseudo-Military Doctrinairism." The Red Army, he said, was nothing but an army created out of "the historical material available . . . for the self-preservation of the workers' state." The Civil War had been "overwhelmingly a war of defense and retreat," as had been the French Revolution in its first stages. Attacking the idea of the special character of maneuver, Trotsky reminded Frunze that this was characteristic of civil wars in general. It was necessary to attack sometimes, retreat sometimes, and mix the two at other times. He summoned the ghost of Brest-Litovsk, undeniably defensive in nature, to support his cause. Throughout, he attacked the formulation of doctrine as premature, stating that in a period of great upheaval the only doctrine needed was "Be on the alert and keep your eyes open."[14]

Frunze, seemingly always reeling from Trotsky's attacks, recast his ideas once again. He admitted that military doctrine should not become formalized as dogma, but should be a guide. Trotsky was not pacified: "The proponents of a new unified military doctrine not only improperly formulate general goals, strategy, and tactics . . . but divert attention from most practical and vital tasks."[15] The Civil War had demonstrated only the "enthusiasm and selflessness" of the working class; to elevate

[14] Trotsky, *Kak vooruzhalas' revoliutsiia*, 2:202.
[15] Ibid., 2:206.

these experiences to doctrine was propaganda. He warned, as his supporter A. A. Svechin, a former imperial officer, noted, that doctrine would rigidify planning and stop debate. Maneuver, for example, was "taught to us by our enemies." Finally, Trotsky asked rhetorically why the principles expounded by Frunze were to be found in the writings of the great Russian general Suvorov, who had emphasized maneuver and the offense. This last point should have been quite embarrassing for Frunze, a well-known devotee of Suvorov, who had, of course, commanded armies composed of serfs. Nevertheless, Frunze, while apologizing for vagueness ("these things must be worked out practically"), doggedly restated his position. Ultimately, Frunze, not Trotsky, triumphed.

On the surface, Trotsky's cogent and stinging critique would seem irresistible to those charged with deciding the military future of the Soviet Union. But Trotsky's essentially negative campaign and admonitions to deal with mundane matters like "how to grease boots" didn't offer definitive answers, while Frunze, though clearly lacking Trotsky's flair, did not emerge as an ignorant and utopian communist. At times Trotsky seized upon the imprecise nature of Frunze's theses to simplify and trivialize important concepts. The primacy of the offensive is a case in point. Frunze never made it clear whether the "offensive" was the governing political precept or should merely determine strategy after the outbreak of war. There were indeed those among the Red Commanders, most notably Tukhachevsky, who believed in seizing the offensive and forcefully starting revolutionary wars in far-off lands. The Polish campaign had been one such disastrous attempt. Frunze seemed to separate himself from this extreme position in his condemnation of recklessness in selecting the time for offensive action.

If Frunze was referring to the primacy of the offense once the war had begun, he was engaging in a central military debate of his time. In 1914 all major power favored or felt compelled to go on the offensive. But the experience of the First World War, in which the tyranny of the offensive had led to disaster, was reverberating throughout the international military community. Defensive preparation and war of position were thought by many to have won the war. But clearly the notion of "defensive" operations was foreign to communist thinkers; Marxism as a dynamic theory of historical progress saw defense only as a temporary condition until the offensive could be seized. But this ideological concern masked a serious military debate, in which such soldiers as Tukhachevsky, Svechin, and Shaposhnikov took part. Trotsky, influenced primarily by military specialists, like Svechin, whom he brought into the army, found the worship of the offensive repugnant, drawing his conclusions from the world war. Frunze never succeeded in clarifying whether the political offensive or the military strategy of the offensive was at the core of his argument. But the debate survived both Frunze and Trotsky. A version of this unresolved dichotomy lingers in Soviet thought today. Soviet political doctrine is explicitly defensive, but Soviet military strategy is undeniably offensive, even preemptive in character. There is a peculiar wedding of a defensive political doctrine and an offensive military strategy that would seek to gain the upper hand by initiating attack.

In spite of his stinging critique, Trotsky failed to produce a satisfactory and politically acceptable program of his own. It did not help that his attack took the form of ridiculing his opponents and that he displayed an arrogance that, although an effective debating posture, won him few allies. Trotsky failed to comprehend how desperately the Red Commanders, flushed with victory, longed to discover a unity of ideas and practice in the Civil War. He made light of their efforts and left open to them only one line of attack: that he was a reactionary, who did not understand the historic significance of the Bolshevik revolution and the Civil War.

Modern Soviet historiographers have accused the young Red Commanders of arrogantly misinterpreting the experience of the Civil War and of underestimating the importance of the lessons of the First World War.[16] But in the early 1920s the Civil War was the one experience on which the Red Command could draw. The "military specialists," brought into the Red Army command precisely because of their knowledge of standard military theory and practice, had every reason to deny the Civil War's importance. Although Trotsky and his followers could not rightly be accused of ignoring the impact of the October Revolution, they were willing to diminish its value.

As Trotsky weakened politically, Frunze began to take control of the War Commissariat, first as Trotsky's deputy, and a few months later as war commissar. The principle of maneuver and the primacy of the offensive became enshrined in Soviet thinking. The need for the much-debated "unified military doctrine" was accepted. But high doctrinal debates quickly receded into the background, and with the reforms of 1924-1925 Frunze found himself consumed by the overwhelming and rather mundane problems of the Red Army.

Trotsky has been glorified as the father of the Red Army by some

---

[16] Virtually all essays in the volume edited by I. A. Korotkov, *Istoriia sovetskoi voennoi mysli*, present this view, but criticism of the worship of the Civil War experience began much earlier. See, for example, M. V. Tukhachevsky, "On the New Field Regulations of the RKKA," *Bol'shevik*, no. 9 (May 1937), 46-47.

and vilified as the Bonapartist who almost destroyed it by others.[17] Neither designation is completely deserved. But clearly, while as commissar of war Trotsky debated the future of military strategy, the Red Army was disintegrating. Some of Trotsky's wilder schemes for the army, including its use in labor brigades, were complete failures and detracted from the training of qualified personnel. Even more serious problems were caused simply by neglect. In 1924 Frunze said, "The situation in the army is extremely serious and we cannot consider the army fit for combat."[18] The Military Commission that met in January 1924 supported this assessment. Some members wished to discredit Trotsky for political reasons and their evaluation must be seen in that light. But reports of neutral observers, like the German High Command, support the idea that the Red Army was in shambles.[19] Post-demobilization planning had been haphazard. There was tremendous instability in the middle and junior officer ranks; a third were without combat experience and 12 percent lacked any formal military education. Virtually no attention had been paid to ordnance and weapons development. Frunze's task was undeniably difficult. The creation of regular forces numbering 1.5 million for which he had hoped was not financially feasible, and the level of the regular Red Army was eventually set at 562,000.[20] The territorial militia had to play, for the time being, a major role in Soviet military organization, accounting for over 50 percent of the infantry strength of the army.[21] The mixed-territorial system, in which a core of regular forces was augmented by territorial formations in industrial centers, was the organizational form of the Soviet armed forces for almost two decades, but the militia was insufficiently trained for combat.

Not all of this was Trotsky's fault. Economic difficulties and the protracted debates played a part. But when Frunze took over, he acted quickly to devote whatever resources he could find to the fledgling cadre army. Frunze was convinced of the importance of technology, and predicted that machines would play an ever-increasing role in modern warfare. Technology by itself was "lifeless," he said, but "the outcome of the future war might depend more on the people of pure science than

[17] Trotsky's reputation has, of course, never been rehabilitated in the Soviet Union. See, for example, the vilification of Trotsky in Korotkov's introduction to *Istoriia sovetskoi voennoi mysli*. Western assessments of his role vary but are certainly more charitable. John Erickson's in *The Soviet High Command* is one favorable assessment.

[18] The criticisms of the Red Army are detailed in I. B. Berkhin, *Voennaia reforma vSSSR* (Moscow, 1958), 57-59.

[19] Erickson, *The Soviet High Command*, discusses the problems that Frunze faced, pp. 173-213.

[20] Berkhin, *Voennaia reforma vSSSR*, 46.

[21] Ibid.

on the commander."[22] The war commissar therefore devoted considerable attention to acquiring foreign technology while simultaneously laying the foundation of an indigenous base. It is also to Frunze that the Soviet Union owes the legacy of a whole country prepared for war, a garrison state. He argued for the militarization of key industries and the centralization of authority in military decision making.

Frunze entrusted the creation of the intellectual capital on which the Red Army would run to an expert military staff. He had nothing but contempt for the weak and sloppy staffing arrangements of the Civil War, which had often led to defeat. When he created the Red Army staff, he was determined that it would be both excellent and respected, to lend it credibility he himself held the post of chief for a short time. The focus of Soviet military thought for the next decade therefore shifted from the drama of high politics to the Red Army staff, the brain of the army. Men like Mikhail Tukhachevsky, Boris Shaposhnikov, and A. A. Svechin made the staff the elite body of the Red Army. This was not perhaps as Frunze wanted it; he warned that the staff should not close itself off and that political workers should be included. But he took it as a matter of fact that sound military planning was the key to future victory, and he did not allow ideological considerations to hinder the development of the general staff. Frunze did not live to see the Red Army transformed. He died in 1925, following an unnecessary medical operation reputedly ordered by Stalin. But the machinery that he left functioned between 1927 and 1937 to lay the foundation for the new Red Army.

III

The Red Army staff's task was made easier by the clarification of the political mission of the Soviet armed forces. The temporary solutions of the past, a regular army and the spirit of Brest-Litovsk, became permanent in Soviet politics. Once again the Soviets branched in the direction of statehood and away from immediate revolution. In this regard, the victory of Josef Stalin and his dictum of "socialism in one country" is singularly important.

Socialism in one country firmly set the priority of the Soviet state: to protect the Soviet revolution. In debates with his opposition over the future of the country, Stalin sought to lay to rest, once and for all, the idea that the Soviet Union could not survive without immediate world revolution. Trotsky and others argued that to build the Soviet state in the absence of world revolution would require a degree of coercion and militarization that would create dictatorship. The Soviet Union would

[22] M. V. Frunze, *Sobranie sochinenii*, ed. A. S. Bubnov (Moscow, 1929), 1:254.

have to be an armed camp, encircled by hostile powers and so fearful of internal enemies that it would be brutally repressive. So many compromises would have to be made to hostile classes that right-wing capitalist restoration would follow.

Stalin argued that the revolutionary tides, which ebbed dramatically in 1923 with the failure of revolutionary movements in Germany, had not reappeared. Citing Lenin's Treaty of Brest-Litovsk and his policy of peaceful coexistence, he argued that the Soviet Union had no choice but to become as strong as possible, arm, and await the next war. The only problem with Lenin's policy had been that the Soviet Union was too weak and suffered needlessly in its period of retreat. In memorable language Stalin declared, "The Soviet Union must never be toothless and groveling before the West again."[23] It would only be a matter of time before the capitalists attacked. As a permanent solution, he admitted, "socialism in one country" might endanger the revolution. The Soviet Union would never be safe until there was a "ring of brother states." But a strong Soviet Union could aid revolution while a weak one would simply be overcome. Stalin thereby reversed the notion that what was good for the proletarian revolution was good for the Soviet Union. Now, proletarian internationalism would serve the Soviet state. By political maneuvering and the logic of his argument, Stalin won. The proponents of "permanent revolution" could point to few arguments in their favor and by 1926 "socialism in one country" seemed to be the Soviets' only choice. Trotsky's warnings were, in part, borne out by the subsequent development of the Soviet state. But at great cost, under the fist of Stalin, the dictatorship of the proletariat was secured.

"Socialism in one country" provided the ideal political rationale for the precept put forth by Frunze in 1920, the preparation of the whole country for total and decisive war. Following in the footsteps of Frunze and with the approval of Stalin, Soviet military men began to advocate the mobilization of the entire economy to support the military and the role of diplomacy in positioning the Red Army for military success. Led by Chief of Staff Boris Shaposhnikov and former Chief of Staff Tukhachevsky, men who were themselves often at odds, the military staff enjoyed remarkable freedom in addressing these issues so fundamental to the development of Soviet state.

Although very different personalities, Tukhachevsky and Shaposhnikov shared many ideas. Shaposhnikov was the consummate military professional; at the time of his appointment he did not even belong to

[23] J. V. Stalin, *On the Opposition* (Peking, 1974), 325. Stalin's defense of socialism in one country on both ideological and practical grounds can be found in this volume.

the Communist Party. He was, however, an astute observer of politics and capable of adapting his position to the climate of the times. In his work *Mozg armii* (Brain of the army), Shaposhnikov argued, like Frunze, that future wars would be on a vast scale. No single agency was capable of protecting the state; complete coordination was indispensable. The general staff should participate in the formulation of military and political objectives, since war was the continuation of politics by other means.[24]

Shaposhnikov's rather cautious formulation was in many ways similar to one put forth by Tukhachevsky. But this committed communist was much bolder, suggesting a still greater role for integrated policy. Perhaps reversing priorities a bit, Tukhachevsky developed theses on how the economy and diplomacy could serve military objectives.[25] Diplomacy could fashion relations with the capitalist world so that the most dangerous capitalist countries would be isolated. An "economic blockade" of the Soviet Union, a prevalent fear at that time, could be forestalled by encouraging some portion of the capitalist world to apply its economic strength to aiding the USSR.

Tukhachevsky went on to suggest that to be really secure, industrial plans and war plans had to be coordinated. Among the problems to be attacked were underdeveloped chemical industries (reflecting his growing interest in chemical warfare) and defects in transport and communication. He noted that in spite of its weaknesses, the Soviet Union was a vast country, which allowed strategic dispersal of industry.

Planning and management of the war economy required a union of political and military expertise according to both Shaposhnikov and Tukhachevsky. It was not possible, they thought, to undertake the coordination of diplomatic, economic, and military policy on the basis of specialized knowledge. Tukhachevsky, however, did suggest that military science was an area where political interference or sensitivity to the current political line could be damaging. In spite of his political beliefs and faith in proletarian military doctrine, he was a soldier who wished to guard the integrity of military planning and preparation. He was known, for example, to have little respect for the military expertise of Klementi Voroshilov, Frunze's successor and ardent follower of Stalin. The two clashed repeatedly and on significant military matters Tukhachevsky often won. Voroshilov played an important role, but lacking the talent of men like Tukhachevsky, he confined his activities to the administration of the economic buildup. Tukhachevsky fell out of favor at the end of 1927 and was banished to command of the Leningrad Military District.

---

[24] B. M. Shaposhnikov, *Mozg armii* (Brain of the army) (Moscow, 1927), 1:14.
[25] M. N. Tukhachevsky, "Voina kak problema vooruzhennoi bor'by," in *Boevoi put' Sovestskikh vooruzhennykh sil* (Moscow, 1960).

Four years later, however, he was brought back as chief of armaments to oversee the program to equip the Red Army. He was a man of considerable talents and at that time the Red Army could not do without him.

Tukhachevsky and Shaposhnikov believed in the need for total effort in war. Because war was just another step on the continuum (and a vital one for the infant Bolshevik state), they held that all the economic resources of the Soviet Union had to be mobilized to support the effort in the coming war. The industrialization drive that was launched was, however, geared primarily to the development of heavy industry. War industry certainly benefited but in 1929 was administratively separated from heavy industry. The goal was to give the Soviet Union a solid industrial base and the ability to mobilize civilian industries rapidly in the event of war. The rate of procurement of military hardware increased considerably between 1927 and 1929, then slowed, and began to increase again in 1932. The Soviet Union was now launched on the path of military industrialization and the preparation for war as the basis for the protection of "socialism in one country."

In the years since the Civil War an extensive and in some respects unique Soviet military doctrine had developed. The lessons of the Civil War were enshrined in the preparation to fight an offensive war of maneuver. Defensive measures were secondary, but growing attention was paid to fortification of the rear and to transport and communication. The most important concept that had come down to the Soviet military leadership was the preparation of the whole country for war. Investment in heavy industry and in indigenous arms production for the Red Army was undertaken. The population was prepared, too, with a new martial spirit in premilitary training for children and the paramilitary organization of the whole population. The territorial militia was further developed, but increasingly the cadre army was emphasized as the backbone of Soviet strength. It is difficult in retrospect to say what influenced these formative years most. Political struggles between personalities like Trotsky and Frunze were important. The heritage of imperial Russia's general staff as well as the impact of the fluid state of worldwide military debate after the disasters of World War I were certainly felt. On balance these early years seem to have been dominated by a series of answers to questions dictated by military necessity and tempered by ideology, rather than the other way around.

IV

Soviet military strategy has two parts: the political-military side, which attempts to define the purpose and character of military power, and the military-technical side, which determines how Soviet military

663

forces will operate in the field. Until 1927 the Bolsheviks were preoc-cupied with the former. Those issues settled, greater attention was given to strategic and operational issues. One of the outstanding characteristics of the late twenties and early thirties was the freedom of debate in the Red Army. The breadth and intensity of the debate is in marked contrast to the period a few years later, when Stalinist military science and the infallibility of Stalin himself crippled Soviet military thought.

The exchange of ideas took place in a period in which the battlefield was changing rapidly. Soviet strategists regarded themselves as a part of the international community of military thinkers. The significance of the Russian Revolution was naturally upheld, but emphasis on the special character of proletarian warfare began to give way to hard analysis of the requirements of the new battlefield.

European soldiers were haunted by the costly trench warfare of the First World War, and new technologies, particularly the tank, were thought to provide potential answers to the problem. But the effective use of armor was not self-evident. Early solutions envisioned simply the incorporation of armor into existing battlefield arrangements, using tanks in support of infantry to break through enemy lines, for example. Slowly, the potential for revolutionary new forms of warfare was recognized, one of the more novel of which developed during this period in the Soviet Union.

The first treatise on this new type of warfare was written around 1928 by the head of the operations administration of the Red Army staff, V. Triandifilov.[26] Triandifilov laid out a case for "successive operations" in battle. He argued that decisive victory could only be achieved if the enemy did not have an opportunity to regroup. He devoted considerable attention, therefore, not just to breaking through the enemy lines, but to exploiting the penetration to deliver a decisive and annihilating blow. This theory of "successive operations" recognized the potential that ar-mor, with increased mobility and speed, held for deep operations. In the First World War battle had usually been linear, concentrating on pene-trating enemy lines. Triandifilov's formulation recognized the importance of operating in depth against the enemy's supporting units and lines of communication.

These ideas were further developed by Tukhachevsky, Berzin, Ni-kovov, and others. Although they believed Triandifilov too optimistic about the current potential for encircling and crushing the enemy, they developed theories that would enable the Red Army, in time, to carry

[26] Col. R. Savushkin, "K voprosu o zarozhdenii teorii posledovatel'nykh nastupatel'nykh operatsii," *Voennoe istoricheskii zhurnal* (May 1983) 77-83.

out such operations for breakthrough, encirclement, and decisive victory.[27] Tukhachevsky envisioned the combined use of motorized rifle units, self-propelled artillery, and aviation to achieve breakthrough. Bombers were to be used to interdict enemy reserves and a new type of force, paratroopers, was to be used to seize targets and block the enemy's retreat, allowing a crushing blow to be delivered by the second echelon of forces.

The Soviets also recognized the potential of mechanized formations to incorporate various forms of armor that could move at the same speed. The Soviets denounced "one-weapon" theories, rejecting the idea of specialized, elite units in favor of mass armies. Nevertheless, armored formations also required specialized training and the Soviets tacitly accepted the need for elite, well-trained units, pushing them one step further away from mass armies and toward the elite units that they rejected on ideological grounds.

This view of the new battlefield won adherents in the Soviet military hierarchy, and plans for equipping and training the Red Army were increasingly formulated on the basis of combined-arms operations in depth. The attractiveness of this form of warfare doubtless lay in the concept of decisive and total victory and in its compatibility with the primacy of the offense. Tukhachevsky's ideological justification probably further increased the attractiveness of the option. He argued that victory in the next war would depend on an offensive blow that would shock the weakened capitalist countries suffering from deep class divisions. The decisive blow leading to ultimate annihilation could then be delivered. But the role of ideology must not be overstated. Operations in depth were above all a way to exploit the potential of new technologies. The concept bore some resemblance to the thought of Guderian and others in the German army, another service convinced, in spite of the First World War, of the importance of the offense.

This line of thought was, however, strongly opposed. A strange alliance between Voroshilov and the former imperial officer Svechin promoted the opposing view, which was convinced of the fallacy of operations in depth to achieve decisive victory. Svechin had argued in *Strategiia* that the next war would be of attrition in which the "productive forces" of the country would be decisive.[28] Total victory could not be achieved rapidly and the war would be long and protracted; defensive operations were also considered to be key to victory. The critics disagreed

[27] Benjamin Miller, in an unpublished dissertation, has documented thoroughly the evolution of Soviet thought on the uses of armor. Benjamin Miller, "The Development of Soviet Armor" (Ph.D. diss., Cornell University, 1984).

[28] A. A. Svechin, *Strategiia* (Moscow, 1927).

as well with Tukhachevsky and the Red Army staff on the use of armor. They believed that armor should reinforce the infantry and artillery units. Possibly the feeling of infantry and cavalry officers that the new technologies threatened their status played a role in the debate. In the end Tukhachevsky's line triumphed and the concept of operations in depth governed Soviet thinking. An operations faculty was created at the military staff academy after 1931 to work out the details of operations in depth with combined arms. Tukhachevsky's victory was not total, however. Some of the expensive new tanks were diverted to infantry and cavalry support. According to students of armor development, there is no evidence that Tukhachevsky opposed the use of armor in this way, but the decision proved to be a critical mistake in the first two years of the Second World War.[29]

The development of Tukhachevsky's doctrine did not take place in a vacuum. Foreign military thought was studied by the Soviets and played an important role in the formulation of these concepts. One conduit was the collaboration with Germany. This marriage of convenience existed since the Treaty of Rapallo in 1922. The Germans needed a place to rearm out of view of the signatories to the Treaty of Versailles and the Soviets needed foreign military assistance. The collaboration helped the Soviets through joint production of military equipment and through German instructors sent to the Soviet Union who taught tactics and training. The Soviets are virtually silent on how extensive the collaboration was, but its most important period seems to have been in the mid-1920s. Agreements were reached on the manufacture of German aircraft (at an annual rate of three hundred, with the Soviets receiving sixty).[30] The plant was run by German technicians with Russian raw materials and laborers. By 1923-1924, cooperation had extended to include German technical courses for Soviet airmen and to the service of German officers on the Red Army staff.

These policies later met with some resistance as the need for indigenous production was recognized, and there were always problems of coordination, but the cooperation continued for years. One arrangement that might have had an impact on the development of Soviet military thought was the creation of training programs to test new weapons and technologies, and to exchange and evaluate information.

The impact on Soviet thought of the collaboration with the German army must not be overestimated, however. Soviet soldiers in any case

[29] See Miller, "Development of Soviet Armor," and Arthur J. Alexander, *Armor Development in the Soviet Union and the United States* (Santa Monica, Calif., 1976).

[30] Erickson, *The Soviet High Command*, 257. Erickson's discussion of the collaboration with Germany is most useful (pp. 247-82).

666

took care to read the foreign literature on new military developments. Fuller's work on tanks, for instance, was translated into Russian in 1923, three years after its publication. A student of Soviet armor development contends that the Soviets arrived at an answer for the deployment of tanks that shared features with other thought, particularly German, but actually antedated other solutions.[31] The Soviets' strategic thought appears to have been primarily an indigenous solution to the problems that were peculiar to their country.[32]

In the 1930s the cadre army, able to incorporate the new technologies and to defend the Soviet Union from other powers, slowly eclipsed the militia, which was shrinking. By 1936, 77 percent of the Red Army's strength was in the cadre force.[33] The Red Army moved rapidly into line with other European armies. In September, 1935, the Red Army staff was renamed the General Staff of the Workers' and Peasants' Red Army. A decree also created formal distinctions of rank in the army. The transformation was complete.

The new Red Army faced dangers rising in both East and West. A two-front war was regarded as a real possibility; in 1928, this fear had already produced a suggestion that the massive Soviet territory be split into halves. The decision was taken between 1928 and 1930 to make the Soviet Far East economically and administratively independent of the European half of the country.

Japan's designs on Siberia and the weakness of Soviet Far Eastern defenses were causes for concern. The Japanese had, of course, developed plans for war against the Soviet Union, but it was their actions against Manchuria in September 1931 that called attention to the Japanese threat. Although the Soviets maintained strict neutrality, Soviet forces were placed on alert and moved toward the Soviet-Manchurian border. Fears grew as the Japanese occupied Shanghai. In reaction to Japanese activity in the area, the Soviets began a buildup of forces, including the creation of the Soviet Pacific Fleet and investment in transport facilities. From 1933 to 1936 relations between the Soviets and the Japanese were strained. Skirmishes actually occurred between forces of the two sides. But eventually skillful diplomacy and the deterrent effect of the Soviet buildup prevented the war with Japan that some expected. The Kwantung

---

[31] There is considerable disagreement about the originality of Soviet thought. Miller, "Development of Soviet Armor," looks comparatively at French, German, and British development, and contends that the thought was very original. Arthur Alexander, although suggesting that there were some unique solutions, contends that the Soviets relied heavily on foreign ideas (Alexander, *Armor Development in the Soviet Union and the United States*).

[32] Alexander, *Armor Development in the Soviet Union and the United States*, 22-23.

[33] Erickson, *The Soviet High Command*, 763.

Army turned south, instead, toward Indochina and Southeast Asia. The preparations taken in the Far East thus gave the Soviets excess capacity for the war with Germany, capacity that was protected, far away from the decimated western front.

Trends in Europe were equally disturbing with Hitler's rise to power. Some, among them most members of the High Command, were convinced that the threat lay primarily to the West. Preparatory steps were taken there as well, with the shifting of Soviet forces to the European theater of operations, the construction of supply facilities, and the hurried mobilization and training of reserves.

In spite of their concern about the German danger, Soviet commanders continued their contacts with their former collaborators and some began to question the anti-German front forming in the West. Stalin, engaged in delicately balanced diplomatic maneuvers, was apparently troubled by the tendency of some of his officers, among them the independent Tukhachevsky, to depart from strictly military concerns. In 1937, the secret police (NKVD) moved quickly and massively against the Red Army Command. Stalin seems to have believed, in spite of overwhelming evidence to the contrary, that many generals were pro-German and politically unreliable. The consequences of his decision to purge the military were immense. Roughly 60 percent of officers at the level of division commander or above fell victim to the purge; the officer corps as a whole was depleted by 20 to 35 percent.[34] A few commanders survived, Shaposhnikov, for instance, who would become chief of staff. But many of the Soviet Union's best military minds, among them Tukhachevsky, Uborevitch, Yakir, and Yegorov, were executed. Those who were not, like Isserson, were silenced.

The purges could not have come at a more inopportune time for the development of Soviet military thought. The theory of combined-arms operations in depth was maturing in 1936. In fact, Tukhachevsky, his concept of offensive operations victorious, was now turning to questions of defense in depth. Slavish worship of the Civil War was under attack. The principle of maneuver is a case in point; the theory of "special" maneuver was challenged in 1937. Decrying the idolization of the Civil War of which he himself had once been guilty, Tukhachevsky noted that "special maneuver [was a] theory based not on the study and appraisal of the new armaments of our potential enemies, . . . but only on some lessons of the Civil War . . . based more on ideas suggested by the heroic sentiments than on . . . present conditions."[35] Defensive operations and

[34] Ibid.
[35] M. V. Tukhachevsky, Commentary on Field Regulations of 1936, "On the New Field Regulations of the RKKA," Bol'shevik, no. 9 (May, 1937), 46-47.

the war of position were discussed as methods of warfare that should be understood and mastered, though avoided if at all possible.

The purges cut this process short and threw Soviet military thought into chaos. Elaboration of the principles of operations in depth, associated with Tukhachevsky and other liquidated commanders, stopped immediately. According to Petro Grigorenko, then a student at the General Staff Academy, it was forbidden to even speak of operations in depth.[36] Texts based on these principles were destroyed and for a while there was absolute confusion on what Soviet offensive strategy actually was. In this atmosphere, freedom to discuss new ideas to replace those discredited was severely compromised by the High Command's understandable timidity.

V

With the Tukhachevsky doctrine of deep penetration silenced, Voroshilov and the proponents of positional warfare, a strategy dependent on defensive fortification and maintenance of territorial position, began to reformulate strategy.[37] Operating in the chaotic environment, however, they did not have time to change the course of Soviet thought and training. As a result, the Soviets were caught between preparation for the war of maneuver and the war of position, and were not ready for either. Evidence of the confusion that reigned in the Red Army was abundant in the disasters of the Winter War against Finland in 1939-1940. Soviet forces sought to fight an offensive war with deep operations, but troops were badly trained, and the heralded cooperation of arms too often broke down. Paratroopers were hardly used at all and the policy of employing tanks with infantry turned out to be faulty as the infantry, unable to withstand enemy fire, took cover and exposed armored vehicles to artillery barrage.[38] Only an eleventh-hour reorganization and reinforcement of Soviet forces saved the Red Army from defeat.

The experiences of the Finnish war led the Red Army command to make some changes. Stalin "promoted" his lieutenant Voroshilov and entrusted real responsibility for the Red Army to S. Timoshenko. Ti-

---

[36] Petro Grigorenko, *Memoirs* (New York, 1982), 92. According to Grigorenko, who was a student in Isserson's class on operations, Isserson continued to teach on the basis of the theory of operations in depth. He did so, however, never calling the theory by name.

[37] The proponents of positional warfare would soon find confirmation of their views in the Spanish Civil War of 1936. There, the ability of Franco's forces to fight a war of attrition was the key to victory. Men returning from this experience apparently made a major impact on the teaching of operations in officer training (Grigorenko, *Memoirs*, 92). Grigorenko also argues that positional warfare was favored by key political-military leaders like Voroshilov because it did not expose the technological backwardness of the Soviet forces.

[38] Erickson, *The Soviet High Command*, 405.

moshenko launched an intensive training program and succeeded in re-establishing the primacy of the military commanders over the commissars, who had, as in the Civil War, begun to take initiatives in the field. Mobilization of industry to replenish matériel and an emphasis on training began to reverse the dislocation caused by the purges. There was not enough time, however, to finish the job.

Stalin's willingness to launch extensive purges in the midst of a war scare is difficult to understand. Certainly, the chief architect of "socialism in one country" did not intend to have the Soviet Union commit suicide. Perhaps Stalin the Marxist believed that history makes men, and under-estimated individual genius—his own excepted, of course. He may have assumed that given time the new officers would learn their art. The fact that there was far less time than he expected almost proved fatal for the Soviet Union.

The purges were but one mistake that Stalin made in the critical years prior to the German attack. With the better military minds silenced, Stalin was left to assume unquestioned responsibility for the conduct of military preparation. He was convinced that the coming war would have two phases. The first would involve the capitalist powers, with the Soviet Union neutral in the conflict. The key task for Stalin, then, was to prolong the first phase as long as possible. He trusted in the infallibility of his personal diplomatic skill to postponing the war and this became the prism through which all decisions were taken. He was so fearful of provoking war with Germany that he refused to allow the High Command to undertake precautionary mobilization of the forces, even when irrefutable evidence of German troop movements was available. His own expectations so blinded Stalin that he refused to accept warnings. Undeniably, the industrial mobilization of the country continued at a frantic pace, and Stalin strove to acquire every inch of territory between the Soviet Union and the West in Finland and Poland. The Nazi-Soviet Pact of 1939 must be understood in this light. War with the capitalist states he regarded as inevitable, but the contradictions inherent in capitalism would lead them to war with each other first. If a temporary alliance with one warring faction could buy more time, a pact with Nazi Germany was justified. In fact, it made sense to come to an agreement with Hitler because Britain and France would be far less likely to attack the Soviet Union. His diplomatic maneuvering did buy the Soviet Union a few months and some valuable territory. But it did not postpone the war quite long enough. When it came on June 22, 1941, the Soviet state was not fully prepared. As in 1918, the Germans were only a few hundred kilometers short of destroying socialism in Russia.

In retrospect, the fact that the German advance fell short is in itself

670

a remarkable occurrence, the result of Russian tenacity and of German strategic and operational errors. In the early days Soviet forces fought so poorly that Western intelligence estimated the fall of Moscow in four weeks. The Soviet were in a state of utter confusion. One-fourth of Soviet armor was lost in the first few weeks because of faulty equipment and faultier tactics. There was virtual chaos in the Soviet command, captured by the words of a beleaguered Soviet officer that have become famous: "We are being fired upon—what shall we do?"[39]

Russia's victory in World War II was in many ways a victory for the concept of the whole country mobilized for war. Effective resistance by the population, now fully aware of the behavior of the Nazis toward the Slavs, buttressed the effort of the Soviet Union's forces at the front. Partisan warfare, which had been little understood by the makers of Soviet strategy, triumphed in urban and rural areas. An underestimated contribution to the Soviet effort was made through massive industrial relocations. Tukhachevsky and many others had argued that Russia's strength lay in its vast territory and potential for strategic dispersal of industry. Remarkably, during the German advance, large portions of Soviet industry were moved, sometimes brick by brick, out of reach of the Germans. In seeking the support of the population, Stalin dropped distinctions between proletarian and peasant, communist and nationalist. Stirred by the heroic music of the finest Soviet composers that was written expressly for the war effort, the battle against the Germans became a struggle for Mother Russia, a struggle that had been waged many times in Russian history.

The ability of the Soviet command to reverse the catastrophic events of the 1941-1942 period at the front was hailed as a victory for the genius of Stalin until Khrushchev began the de-Stalinization campaign.[40] Since 1956, the defeat of the German invasion has been hailed as a victory for the Soviet people and its system.[41] Modern Soviet thought has found a position between these extremes and through it, it is finally possible to reconstruct the factors that reversed the tides of the war.

First, the war proved to be an excellent judge of talent, and the leadership of the Red Army improved as commanders who lacked ability failed to survive. Moreover, in these dire circumstances, there was no room for political favoritism and Stalin brought many of his political

[39] Ibid.

[40] The worship of Stalin can be seen in any early postwar history. For a particularly good example, see Klement Voroshilov, *A Commander of Genius of the Great Patriotic War* (Moscow, 1950).

[41] A party history makes such a claim about the war and Stalin's mistakes (Ministertstva Oborony Soyuza SSR, *Istoriya velikoi otechestvennoi voiny sovetskovo soyuza 1941-45*, editorial commission headed by P. N. Pospelov (Moscow, 1960).

favorites, such as Budenny and Voroshilov, back from the field and replaced them with more capable commanders.

More importantly, Soviet performance improved in the course of the fighting; through initiative and flexibility in the field, and through better planning, preparation, and coordination at the center. The former is characteristic of most wars—ingenious commanders learn to adopt tactics suited to the conditions of the particular conflict. The failure to achieve the latter has been the downfall of many campaigns. In the Soviet case, it was an especially remarkable feat, because major adjustments had to be undertaken.

The most important alteration occurred in the area of defensive strategy and tactics. In the early stages of the war, Soviet soldiers did not know how to maneuver defensively and, according to German observers, stubbornly held their positions well beyond the point at which retreat would have been advisable.[42] When they did retreat, they found it difficult to maintain order. The need for strategic withdrawals had been recognized, but little effort had been devoted to train commanders and troops. The most successful part of the Soviet retreat, the scorched-earth policy, was learned through experience, often out of frustration and anger rather than by central direction facilities were denied to the Germans.

The lack of attention to defense was reversed with the Field Regulations of 1942.[43] Defense was finally discussed explicitly as a "normal form of combat," although offense was hailed as the "fundamental aspect of combat action for the Red Army." The Soviets went to great lengths to encourage their forces to defend in depth and to use active, flexible tactics. Defense did not have to be static. In fact, those who had fought according to static, "linear" principles of defense in the early days were assailed by Stalin himself, who said, "Tens of thousands of Red Army commanders have become expert military leaders . . . they have thrown out the stupid and pernicious linear tactics and have finally adopted the tactic of mobile warfare."[44]

Eventually, the improvement in defensive operations gave the Soviets the opportunity to return to the much-admired offensive. Counterattacks were used successfully in conjunction with defense after 1942, but the decisive phase of the war really arrived in the fall of 1942 at Stalingrad, the battle hailed by the Soviets as the turning point of the war. There,

[42] Raymond Garthoff, *Soviet Military Doctrine* (Santa Monica, Calif., 1953), 76.

[43] *Uremennyi polevoi ustav RKKA*, 1936 (The provisional field regulations of the RKKA), cited in Garthoff, *Soviet Military Doctrine*, 74.

[44] J. V. Stalin, *On The Great Patriotic War* (Moscow, 1950), 373. Translated from the collected wartime addresses of Stalin.

the Soviets finally fought the war of maneuver for which they had prepared. When in February 1943 the Sixth Army, west of Stalingrad, succeeded in encircling and crushing the German forces, the Red Army's counteroffensive began. Subsequent histories describe the whole of the war effort until Stalingrad as the struggle to seize the initiative that had been lost in June 1941. At Stalingrad and later at the decisive battle of Kursk, the Soviets relied on surprise, maneuver, overwhelming quantitative superiority, and aimed at the absolute annihilation of the enemy. The use of armor for operations in depth was finally achieved. These experiences became enshrined in Soviet thinking after the war. Although the "Great Patriotic War" taught them never again to ignore defensive preparation, the counteroffensives launched at Stalingrad and Kursk vindicated the primacy of the offense on which Soviet military thought was founded.

Stalin once asked army general S. M. Shtemenko, "Why did we win the war?" Before Shtemenko could answer, Stalin, ever modest, said, "Because I prepared the country for war."[45] The Second World War was indeed a victory for the total preparation of the society for war for which Frunze had lobbied in 1924. It was also a victory for Soviet strategy and operations, belatedly adjusted to meet the new contingencies. But the war was above all one of attrition, just as Svechin had imagined. The ability to mobilize industry to support a protracted war was decisive. The determination of the Soviet soldier and the ability of the command to mobilize, train, and commit a never-ending supply of manpower triumphed. German forces, overextended and stretched thinly into hostile territory, were ultimately no match for the vastness of Mother Russia fully prepared for war.

Little mention is made in Soviet history of the contribution of the Western allies to the Soviet victory. The tremendous war matériel provided through Lend-Lease and other programs was simply written out of history during the Cold War. In truth, though, the Red Army did face the brunt of the German invasion alone. The issue of the second front lies outside the scope of this essay. But when it was finally launched in 1944, after numerous delays, the battles of Stalingrad and Kursk had already been won. The political ramifications of both the timing and the direction of the second front were immense. Stalin ultimately won the greatest battles of the war at the conference table. If ever the inextricable link between politics and war was made clear, it was at Teheran, Yalta, and Potsdam. At great cost, the Red Army fulfilled the promise that men like Tukhachevsky had claimed for it, delivering, at bayonet point, the

---

[45] S. M. Shtemenko, *Generalnni stab v gody voiny*, 2 vols. (Moscow, 1973), 2:447.

workers' revolution to states well outside the boundaries of the old Russian Empire. Together with the victory over Germany, Stalin finally got the ring of brother states that vindicated his insistence that "socialism in one country" would eventually lead to socialist victories abroad. As if to remind all that protection of the first socialist state was still the mission of the Red Army, in 1946 Stalin changed the name of the Workers' and Peasants' Red Army to the Armed Forces of the Soviet Union. The union of "socialist progress" and Soviet state power was now complete.

VI

Soviet military thought, as it evolved from the uncertain days of 1917 to the victory over Germany in 1945, is the basis on which Soviet military power as we know it today is built. At the end of the Second World War the Soviet Union's attainment of military power of global significance was still more than two decades away. New challenges, most importantly the challenge of nuclear weapons, would face the makers of Soviet strategy.

But in spite of the technological revolution of the nuclear age, a great deal remains in Soviet thinking that can be traced to its formative period. Combined-arms doctrine still pervades Soviet thinking and the offensive is still the preferred method of warfare. In fact, emphasis on combined arms has led to a disturbing tendency to discuss nuclear weapons as a method of waging warfare, almost indistinguishable from conventional weaponry. Maneuver and surprise continue to be worshipped. The dictum of surprise, indelibly etched on Soviet thinking by June 22, 1941, has led to further contradictions in the nuclear age. Surprise, the offensive, and acceptance of the necessity of preemption form a doctrine that is inherently contradictory with Soviet political pronouncements that they would use weapons (especially nuclear weapons) only in response to provocation. Statements that are difficult to define abound, like the notions that the Soviets will use their forces "when war becomes inevitable" and that their forces will not sit and wait to be attacked.[46] Soviet political doctrine is undeniably defensive, speaking of war only in the context of an "imperialist" attack, but its military strategy is undeniably offensive. The tension between political activity and the military offensive has remained largely unresolved since Frunze. Modern-day Soviet strategy attempts to make a distinction between military-political doctrine, which is supreme and essentially defensive, and military-technical doctrine (similar to strategy), which upholds the primacy of the offense and

---

[46] For an excellent discussion of the development of Soviet military doctrine in the nuclear age see David Holloway, *The Soviet Union and the Arms Race* (New Haven, 1983).

the need for surprise and initiative. This is a distinction that fails to remove the confusion, and the Soviets themselves elaborate no further.

These contradictions remind us that Soviet military strategy is created on two levels, one political and the other military-technical. The political side is said to be superior. But either considered alone is likely to lead to a failure to understand the complexity of Soviet military thought. The formative years for Soviet strategy must be understood not only as the work of Lenin, Trotsky, and Stalin, but of soldiers like Tukhachevsky, Triandifilov, and Svechin. The two levels have not always coexisted easily. The right to direct the course of Soviet military development theoretically rests with the Party. The expertise to deal with the science of contemporary warfare is found in the professional military officer, however. Much of the history of the development of Soviet doctrine is made up of efforts to find a balance between the two worlds. The parallel development of military-political and military-technical doctrine continues in Soviet thought today.

The greatest legacy bequeathed to modern Soviet strategists, though, is the concept of the preparation of the whole society for continuous struggle. The inevitability of war was dropped as a tenet of Soviet political doctrine in 1956. It has been replaced by the concept of "peaceful competition and coexistence" with the hostile capitalist camp and the expectation that socialism will, in the long term, win. Since the Soviets accept that there would be "no winners" in a nuclear war (though they would try to survive it), they now believe that only a fatal mistake by the socialist world—perhaps leading to global annihilation—will abort the final communist victory. But the Soviets do not believe that the fundamental hostility of the capitalist world to socialism has been undone by the nuclear age. Consequently, the preparation of the country for war, even if it is to be avoided, is essential. The Soviets are locked into the hostile relationship for the long term. Today, on the basis of Soviet power, the leadership can play an active role in the international system that it once pathologically feared. The relaxation of tensions and search for areas of cooperation with the capitalist world, characteristic of recent Soviet policy, is predicated on the belief that the Soviet Union is strong enough to make Western adventurism a remote possibility. The conclusion is that the stronger the Soviet Union, the more secure the peace. Only from a secure base at home, and now from a broader socialist community as well, can the Soviets hope to move forward. This approach, which protects the gains of socialism first and seeks other gains cautiously, is the legacy of Lenin and the decisions of 1918.

Certainly, military might is not the only factor in the equation that the Soviets call the correlation of forces, a kind of measurement of how

675

history is progressing. Hard choices have to be made to ensure moral, political, and above all, economic growth as well. Just as before, Marxism-Leninism does not provide a blueprint for balancing the factors and preparing the socialist state for the long term. It provides only the underlying premise: the concept of continuous struggle and extraordinary vigilance. Reliance on the military power of the state, acquired at great cost and organized like that of military powers of the past, was handed down to the Soviets by historical experience. It is this experience that gives the Soviet version of permanent struggle a decidedly martial ring.

23. Allied Strategy in Europe, 1939-1945

MAURICE MATLOFF

SCARCELY HAD THE fighting ended in the Second World War when a great debate broke out in the Western world over the way the war had been planned, fought, and concluded.[1] Amid the frustrations and crises of the Cold War and the suspicions and strains between the Soviet Union and its former partners in the Grand Alliance, that debate, transferred from secret wartime councils to public forums, was fed by a flood of writing dealing with the controversial issues and decisions of the conflict. Critics on both sides of the Atlantic charged that the peace was lost as a result of political and strategic mistakes made by the Western Allies. Especially heavy criticism was leveled at the American strategy for the war in Europe. Winston Churchill lashed out at what he termed the American "large-scale mass-production style of thought."[2] J. F. C. Fuller, the British analyst, characterized this type of strategy as "ironmongering."[3] Out of the popular writing of Chester Wilmot, an Australian journalist, emerged a sharp contrast—a naive Roosevelt versus a prescient Churchill, a politically oriented British strategy versus a narrow doctrinaire American military strategy. In Wilmot's portrait, the Americans put their strategic faith in fashioning a gigantic "military steamroller" in their training camps and factories that they propelled across the Atlantic to crush the Germans by a massive frontal assault without much thought for the political consequences.[4] Such criticisms shaped the stereotypes and images of the American and British approach

[1] This essay is in large measure an outgrowth of the author's research and writing on Allied strategy in World War II incorporated in *Strategic Planning for Coalition Warfare, 1941-1942*, with Edwin M. Snell (Washington, D.C., 1953), and *Strategic Planning for Coalition Warfare, 1943-1944* (Washington, D.C., 1959), volumes in the official U.S. Army in World War II series, and in various published essays and articles indicated in the footnotes and the bibliographical note.

[2] Winston S. Churchill, *The Second World War: Closing the Ring* (Boston, 1951), 426.

[3] J. F. C. Fuller, *The Second World War, 1939-1945* (New York, 1949), 250, 266, 385.

[4] Chester Wilmot, *The Struggle for Europe* (New York, 1952), esp. pp. 11, 12, 109, 128, 138, 338, 448. For an analysis of Wilmot's thesis see Maurice Matloff, "Wilmot Revisited: Myth and Reality in Anglo-American Strategy for the Second Front," an essay published by the Eisenhower Foundation in *D-Day: The Normandy Invasion in Retrospect* (Lawrence, Kans., 1971).

to Second World War strategy that became imbedded in the postwar literature and still enjoy considerable popular currency.

In the light of the lingering controversy and the lengthened perspective of the years that have elapsed since 1945, those stereotypes need to be reexamined. It becomes all the more important to take stock of the strategy developed by the Allies in the Second World War—to consider how it came about, what influences shaped it, what forms it assumed, and in what sense it succeeded or failed. This essay will focus on strategic ideas with which the Allies fought, particularly as they bore on the area of their greatest common effort, the war in Europe. It will deal with the strategy fashioned by coalition planning in the Allied capitals, in and out of the great international conferences, and with special emphasis on the Anglo-American experience in that planning.

I

The story of Allied strategy for the defeat of Germany is, simply put, the search for common denominators among three sovereign partners—the United Kingdom, the Soviet Union, and the United States—faced with a common enemy. That strategy was the product of many minds on both sides of the Atlantic, and of changing pressures and circumstances in the global war. It was the result of an evolutionary process and a series of compromises, and of a constant struggle to adjust ends and means. Above all, it was fashioned by powers with diverse national interests. If the national objectives sought by each of the participating powers in the war against Germany were consistently held, the means and methods used by each to achieve them varied from time to time. In the process of planning and waging the war against Germany, moreover, the foundations of the Grand Alliance shifted and the relationships among the powers changed. These shifts are an integral part of the strategic history of the war.

What was the nature of the Grand Alliance and what did each partner bring to it? It is important to recognize that the Grand Alliance was forged in war and for purposes of war; it was a war marriage, a marriage of expediency. A common bond of danger brought the three partners together in 1941, but their alliance was composed of different levels of relationships. The United States and the United Kingdom formed the inner web of the Grand Alliance and represented an alliance within an alliance. Relations between these two powers were as close as their relationship with the Soviet Union was formal and distant. Indeed, the two Western leaders, Prime Minister Winston Churchill and President Franklin Roosevelt, were often more in agreement with each other on the conduct of the war than they were with their own military staffs.

678

Each power in the Grand Alliance fought the war for its own objectives; each had its own politico-military system in which its strategy was produced. Each had to compromise as a result of its membership in the coalition and changing fortunes in the war. Because of their varying traditions, interests, policies, geography, and resources, the three partners looked at the European war through different spectacles.

Great Britain, an island empire, first to enter the war against Germany, had been for a whole year after the fall of France in June 1940 the only major power directly opposing the German threat. For centuries it had put its faith in the balance of power. Experienced in war, diplomacy, and coalitions, its historic policy in European war was to utilize what Liddell Hart called "the indirect approach"—to make use of its economic resources and its navy, and to shore up Continental allies against any major power threatening the balance in Europe. The lifeline to its empire in the Far East lay through the Mediterranean, and Britain could be expected to intervene actively there and in the Middle East, another area of special political and economic interest. Dependent upon the sea lanes for its very existence, Great Britain was not self-sufficient. The Atlantic had to be kept open for supplies from America if Britain was to stay in the war. Its economy, although highly industrialized, was small-scale in comparison with that of the United States. In a global war its resources would be stretched thin. Keenly sensitive to its huge manpower losses in the First World War, it put its faith in its navy, air force, and in what might be called a peripheral strategy to hit Germany around the edges of the Continent, gradually to weaken it, to support the occupied countries by arms and subversion against Germany, and eventually to strike at the heart of Germany. For the short run it wanted the occupied countries to rise and revolt; in the long run it wanted to return to the *status quo ante bellum*. Churchill was determined not to preside over the liquidation of the British Empire. British soldiers were accustomed to work closely with their political leadership and Britain's policy in war could be expected to give political matters a primary place.

Like Great Britain, the United States in World War II became involved in its second major coalition war in the twentieth century. Rich in resources, and highly industrialized, the United States made the transition by stages from major supplier of Britain to full military collaborator. As a result, when Japan attacked Pearl Harbor, American entry into the war was a natural step for which the two partners were more or less prepared.

To Americans war was an aberration, a disturber of normalcy. War and peace were viewed as distinct and separate episodes, and American tradition in war had been first to declare, then to prepare. Traditionally

679

opposed to becoming involved in European quarrels, the United States, nevertheless, had strong cultural bonds with Europe. Based on its experience in the First World War, the American approach to European war was to hold off as long as possible, enter only long enough to thrash the bully or bullies who started it, get the boys home, and then try to remain as uninvolved in European affairs as before. Entering late in the First World War, it had been an associate power, a junior partner in the alliance, and had fought the war in accord with the basic strategy set by the European partners. In the era of disillusionment after the war, popular beliefs that the United States should neither enter into military alliances nor maintain military forces capable of offensive action deeply influenced national policy.

From the Munich settlement in 1938 onward, American leaders gradually became alert to threats to the Western democracies and began to mobilize. Laying aside their earlier academic planning exercises, the strategic planners in Washington began to think in terms of global and coalition warfare. In the uneasy transition between war and peace, little was known about Russian capabilities and intentions—a condition that continued throughout the war. In the months after the German attack on the Soviet Union the American military staff seriously doubted the ability of the Soviets to continue as an active participant against Germany. But by the time of Pearl Harbor American planners had begun to brush up against British strategic theory and concepts and to gear their plans for a world at war. For the first time the United States entered a war considerably advanced in its strategic thinking on how to fight it.

Despite Roosevelt's bold leadership between 1939 and 1941, the country was still largely divided until Pearl Harbor. The British and Soviet political-military systems were much more tightly knit than was the American. Gradually Roosevelt drew the military staff closer to him and in his somewhat informal and unsystematic way developed a close relationship with it. Terming the Second World War "the war for survival," from 1939 onward he became an active commander in chief and reserved his independent voice in strategic matters, even if his methods appeared loose and disjointed.

In the Second World War the United States was confronted for the first time with the demands of a truly worldwide war, even more so than its major partners, as it turned out. From the beginning American interests and lines of communication in the war were global. Possessed of a strong sympathy for the Chinese, the United States was brought into the war by an attack on a Pacific possession, and in the Anglo-American division of strategic tasks soon after Pearl Harbor, it was given the main responsibility for the war against Japan. Throughout the war President Roosevelt and his military staff could never forget the war in the Pacific and Far East. To many Americans Japan rather than Germany appeared to be the natural enemy. This fixation was to play an important part in the relations among the three partners and in the evolution of the strategy for the defeat of Germany. Under the pressures of domestic politics and the Japanese, the United States simply could not fight a long war in Europe. As General George C. Marshall, the army chief of staff, later succinctly put it, "a democracy cannot fight a Seven Years War."[5]

The Soviet Union, the third partner, dedicated to a different political and economic ideology, represented an enigma. Lacking air and naval traditions, it was essentially a land power with interior lines of communication. It possessed an enormous population and great resources, but its industrial program was incomplete. Unlike the United Kingdom and the United States, the Soviets were to be at war with only one enemy at a time, staying out of the war against Japan until the closing days of the Second World War. In this sense its strategic problem, next to that of the United States and the United Kingdom, was comparatively simple. Of course, in the defensive phase of its struggle with Germany, it had to ensure its survival and it relied on geography, the endurance of its people, and the army. Whether by design or by force of circumstances, it resorted to the historic policy of yielding territory and even lives to gain time.

For all its Communist trimmings and ideological connotations, Soviet foreign policy resembled in certain respects that of the czars. Its defensive struggle against Germany was merely a pause in its twin drives for security and expansion. These drives appeared to have motivated the Soviet Union in its war with Finland and to have been at work even during the period of its pact with Hitler. One of the main reasons for Hitler's break with the Soviet Union was the latter's aggressive action in pushing westward into Poland and the Balkans, which Hitler, confronted with a stubborn Britain in the West, regarded as too dangerous. The German invasion of the Soviet Union in June 1941 reinforced the Soviet desire to strengthen its position in eastern Europe, an objective deeply rooted in Russian history. Although Soviet political and territorial ambitions were not absent during the first two years after the Nazi invasion, military considerations of necessity became paramount in the desperate struggle for survival. Still fearful of capitalist encirclement, suspicious of friend and foe alike, the Soviet Union remained throughout the Second World War an uneasy ally in the partnership that General John R. Deane,

[5] Interview, Dr. Sidney Mathews, Major Roy Lamson, and Major David Hamilton with General Marshall, 25 July 1949, Office Chief of Military History Files, quoted in Matloff, *Strategic Planning for Coalition Warfare, 1943-1944,* 5.

head ot the wartime U.S. Military Mission in Moscow, later termed "the strange alliance."[6]

These, then, were the three sovereign powers who gradually came together under the pressure of war. From the beginning the close ties between the United States and Great Britain formed the bedrock of the Grand Alliance. The Soviet Union's role in developing and directing the combined strategy of the war was to be relatively small. There were at least two reasons for this disparity. Partly it resulted from the diverse nature of the struggles in which the partners were involved—the Soviet concentration on the eastern front in continental Europe against Germany, the British and American involvement in worldwide demands and widely scattered fronts in the struggle with the Axis partners. Partly the difference reflected the legacy of suspicion inherited by the partners. From the beginning the Soviet relationship with the United States and Great Britain consisted of demanding pressure on the enemy and asking for and receiving material aid. But collaboration, even in these fields, was to prove difficult. The strategic decisions of the United States and Great Britain were normally transmitted in general terms to the Soviets. But they remained outside the Anglo-American Combined Chiefs system and took formal part in decisions only at the international conferences at Moscow, Teheran, Yalta, and Potsdam. With their forces far apart, for most of the war the western and eastern wings of the alliance operated at long range from each other. From the start, the troubled relations of the past and the lack of free interchange made genuine understanding difficult. A curious "arms-length" war partnership came into being. The long debate over strategy in Western circles led to a delicate relationship and became a bone of contention with the Soviet Union. From the beginning the Soviets, locked in a death struggle on the eastern front, had no doubts about the proper Western strategy. They wanted a second front; they wanted it soon; and they wanted it in the West. Each Anglo-American postponement of this second front added fuel to the fire.

The basis for the close military association between the Western powers began with the dispatch of American navy and army observers to Great Britain in 1940. Out of the Anglo-American meeting in Washington directly after Pearl Harbor (the Arcadia Conference) came the establishment of the Combined Chiefs of Staff (CCS) system—the machinery for the day-to-day coordination of the war and for hammering out the Western strategy. Over the CCS were the prime minister and the President, whose association became as close and warm as their rela-

---

[6] For a first-hand account of relations with the Soviet Union in World War II as seen from Moscow, consult John R. Deane, *The Strange Alliance* (New York, 1947).

tionship with Stalin remained reserved and remote. Each of the two Western leaders wore two hats—one military, the other political. The work of the CCS went on in and out of the big conferences with the President and prime minister. The summit meetings occurred when planners were ready for top-level decisions on major items of Allied strategy and policy.

II

Of the three main phases in the development of the Allied partnership and strategy, 1941-1942 represents the formative era. This period witnessed the emergence of the Grand Alliance and the beginning of the pattern of arms-length collaboration between the Soviet Union and the West—a pattern that essentially was to obtain for the remainder of the war. For the Allies this was also the period of defensive strategy. Their basic fear was of defeat; their great concern, the survival of the Soviet Union. For the Western partners it marked the earliest of their important strategic decisions—the "Europe First" (or "Germany First") decision, and the first stage in the search for a strategic plan against Germany.

In the evolution of Allied strategy, the early adoption of the principle of defeating Germany first was the most significant and controlling decision in Anglo-American polices of the Second World War. The groundwork for that basic strategic decision was laid early in 1941—almost a year before Pearl Harbor—at the so-called ABC Conference in Washington. Out of these exploratory British and American staff talks emerged the principle that if the United States entered the war, the Allies would seek first to defeat Germany.[7] On the basis of the belief that Germany would be the predominant member of the hostile coalition, the main Anglo-American effort was to be made in the Atlantic and European area. If Japan entered the war, military strategy in the Far Pacific would be defensive until the Allies could assemble enough strength to take the offensive. When war did come to the United States, despite initial Japanese successes and the critical situation in the Pacific following the attack on Pearl Harbor, the basic decision was confirmed during the meetings with Churchill and his staff at the Arcadia Conference in Washington.[8]

During the postwar debate over Allied strategy, some questioned the wisdom of the Europe-first decision. But in the critical early period of

[7] For accounts of the ABC Conference see Mark S. Watson, *Chief of Staff: Prewar Plans and Preparations* (Washington, D.C., 1950), ch. 12; Matloff and Snell, *Strategic Planning for Coalition Warfare, 1941-1942*, ch. 3; and Louis Morton, "Germany First: The Basic Concept of Allied Strategy in World War II" in *Command Decisions*, ed. Kent R. Greenfield (Washington, D.C., 1960).

[8] The Arcadia Conference is discussed at length in Matloff and Snell, *Strategic Planning for Coalition Warfare, 1941-1942*, ch. 5.

the war considerations of political expediency combined with logistics to reinforce the decision. For political, military, geographic, and economic reasons, the three Allies could agree. The immediate threat to two of the Allies was in Europe; there immediate action might be taken, and all were formally and publicly agreed on the enemy. The Soviet Union and Great Britain simply could not wait for a decisive ending of the war with Japan. Substantial Allied forces were already at hand and would not have to be moved, as they would have had to be against Japan. It followed, therefore, that the defeat of Germany should be the first major objective.

Although that basic decision held throughout the war, the question of how it was to be interpreted and applied arose early in the conflict and continued to the end. One of the most persistent questions concerned the proportion in which available resources should be divided between the war in Europe and the war against Japan. This reflected a divergence of political as well as military factors in Anglo-American strategy. For Britain, given its predominant interests in the Mediterranean, the Middle East, and on the Continent, the war against Japan tended to be a side-show. But for the United States, early given the major responsibility for the war against Japan, Japan was in many ways the politically preferable primary objective. As a result, differences arose from time to time between the United States and Great Britain over the distribution of resources.

As close together as the United States and the United Kingdom had been drawn by Pearl Harbor, and as agreed as they were on the need to defeat Germany first, they still had no mutually acceptable plan of how to go about it. The British concept of how to defeat Germany early became apparent. Essentially, they proposed relying on blockade, bombing, subversive activities, and propaganda to weaken the will and ability of Germany to resist. The emphasis would be on mobile, hard-hitting armored forces operating on the periphery of German-controlled territory rather than on large-scale ground action in confrontation with the full power of the German military machine. No vast armies of infantry as in the First World War would be needed. This whole approach was in accord with the Churchillian theory of waging war on the Continent with a peripheral strategy, a concept he had developed after the searing British experience between 1914 and 1918. Although the Mediterranean or "soft underbelly" part of the peripheral thesis has received great attention in the postwar debate, Norway was also always a favorite objective of the prime minister in the Second World War. From the beginning the British leadership envisaged a cross-Channel operation in force only as the last blow against a Germany already in process of collapse. These two ideas of the British—emphasis on the Mediterranean, and the cross-Channel operation as a final blow—continued down to the Normandy invasion.

684

The British concept was a compound of military, political, and economic factors, of caution resulting from the experience of the First World War and Dunkirk, and of the prime minister's predilections. It was tailored to suit scattered interests, a small-scale economy, and limited manpower for ground armies.

The American ideas were quite different. As far back as November 1940, the chief of naval operations, Admiral Harold R. Stark, had decided that large-scale land operations would be needed to beat Germany.[9] In the summer of 1941 the army's strategic planners concluded that sooner or later "we must prepare to fight Germany by actually coming to grips with and defeating her ground forces and definitely breaking her will to combat."[10] Vague as they were about preliminary preparations, they were already disposed to think in terms of meeting the German army head-on. They believed an American army of approximately 215 divisions was needed to win. Here was the core of the American theory of a war of mass and concentration. It reflected American optimism, confidence in its industrial machine to produce the military hardware, and the faith of its military in its ability to raise, equip, and train a large citizen army for offensive purposes.

The divergent approaches to the European war were most clearly reflected in 1942 in the struggle over Operation Bolero versus Operation Torch. The Bolero plan was the brainchild of the American army. Secretary of War Stimson, General Marshall, and the army planners became disturbed over the theatened dispersion of troops, ships, and supplies after Pearl Harbor, to meet immediate crises in non-European parts of the globe—the Pacific, Middle East, Far East, and Africa. The concept of invading Europe in force from the United Kingdom—the so-called Bolero plan—was adopted by the American Joint Chiefs as the solution. This plan was designed to assemble forces for a major cross-Channel invasion in force in the spring of 1943 (called Roundup). A subsidiary plan (termed Sledgehammer) provided for an emergency small-scale return in the autumn of 1942 to the Continent in either of two contingencies—the threatened collapse of Germany or the threatened collapse of Russia. Although the British approved Bolero "in principle" in April 1942, the agreement lasted less than three months.

To the American staff, Bolero was especially desirable for a number of reasons. It would meet the Russian demand for a second front. It

<hr>

[9] For a discussion of Admiral Stark's Plan Dog Memorandum, see ibid., 25-28; Watson, *Chief of Staff: Prewar Plans and Preparations*, ch. 4; and Samuel E. Morison, *The Battle of the Atlantic, September 1939-May 1943* (Boston, 1947), 271-72.

[10] Quoted in Matloff and Snell, *Strategic Planning for Coalition Warfare, 1941-1942*, 61.

would furnish a definite long-range strategic goal for industrial and man-power mobilization. Above all, it promised decisive action by early 1943 and offered a long-range plan that would fulfill the principle of concentration. For a while plans went ahead for the second front. On June 24, 1942, General Eisenhower arrived in England, assumed command in the European theater of operations (ETO), and considerable American forces began to arrive.

But the tide soon turned against the army's plan. In June the prime minister came to Washington and urged a North African operation. So stirred up was the American military staff over the evident British intention to scuttle Bolero that in July the Joint Chiefs even considered threatening the British with going all-out in the Pacific—a threat the President refused to allow. Out of further discussions in London in July came the decision to launch a North African attack in the autumn of 1942. Torch (the invasion of North Africa) replaced Bolero. The American staff had lost out; the President had overruled them.

The Torch decision resulted from two basic factors—Roosevelt's insistence on action for American ground forces against Germany in 1942, and the categoric refusal of Churchill and his staff to accept the notion of a 1942 cross-Channel operation. Both sides recognized that Torch, if successful, could produce some positive advantages. Allied shipping was extremely tight. Savings of over two hundred ships per month could be made if convoy routes to the Middle East and India could go through the Mediterranean instead of around the Cape of Good Hope. Serious questions concerning the feasibility of a cross-Channel operation in 1942 also arose. Practical considerations played an important part: resources existed for Torch; those for the cross-Channel undertaking were more doubtful.

To Marshall and Stimson the Torch decision was a bitter disappointment. To them it meant the adoption of a strategy of encirclement, of periphery-pecking, and of what a top Pentagon planner termed "scatterization." It also meant the inevitable postponement of a definitely scheduled direct thrust against Germany. This delay further complicated relations with the hard-pressed Soviets, and fed their suspicions about Western intentions. When Torch won out, Churchill felt the full weight of Stalin's disapproval in a stormy interview in Moscow.

In retrospect Bolero seems to have been premature. Neither the British nor the forces and means to cross the Channel appeared to be ready. But, as the American military planners learned, forces in being have a way of generating a strategy of their own and the impatience and pressure of political leaders for action may override the strategy of the military, however sound. There were enough forces and means to do Torch; the Western Allies did Torch.

The launching of the Torch operation ended the first stage in the search for an Anglo-American strategic plan against Germany. From 1941 to 1942, a period of defensive strategy, was also the era of a strategy of scarcity for the Western partners. Their two approaches to war had conflicted, and British opportunism or peripheral strategy had won the first round. But the issue was not yet squarely joined. That British notions of strategy had tended to prevail was not surprising. Their forces had been mobilized earlier and were in the European theater of operations in greater numbers than the Americans. Their position in North Africa and the Middle East was desperate. The British were also more experienced in military diplomacy than the Americans, and Churchill found a sympathetic ear in Roosevelt. It had taken the better part of the year after Pearl Harbor for American forces to have any appreciable impact in the theaters. American strategic planning, limited by critical shortages in shipping and munitions, had been largely short-run. Troops had been parceled out piecemeal to meet immediate threats and crises. New to the art of military diplomacy and negotiation, the Americans were still thinking in either-or terms, of this operation or that. The one plan in which they had placed their faith, to put Allied planning on an orderly, long-range basis and observe the principles of mass and concentration, had failed. Fearful of the continued dissipation of their forces and matériel in what they regarded as secondary ventures, they had to start over and find new formulas.

The Torch decision also complicated Western relations with their Soviet partner. In 1942 the Americans and the British justified their respective strategic approaches toward the European war in terms of relieving pressure on the embattled Soviet Union. For each the geography and manpower of the Soviet Union early became the key to victory. Although the plans of the Western Allies were tied to the outcome of the struggle on the eastern front, the West had still not agreed on strategy against Germany and its plans had not been coordinated with those of the Soviet Union. The West could expect no real improvement in military relations with the USSR except where such collaboration would clearly contribute to their one common interest—the early defeat of Germany. The expectation of the Soviet Union for a second front had not been met.

III

In 1943 the debate over European strategy entered a second stage. This phase, covering the midwar period down to the landings in Normandy, was one of more plentiful means and of the offensive phase of coalition warfare. The power to determine strategy and choose the time and place to do battle passed from the Axis powers to the Allied coalition. The full impact of American mobilization and production began to be felt not only in the theaters but also in Allied strategy councils. Standing fast before Stalingrad, the Soviets demonstrated their ability to survive the German onslaught, and Soviet ideas on Allied strategy also carried more weight. But as the tide of the war turned, the strategy of waging coalition warfare began to appear far more complex than the Americans originally envisaged.

The decision for Torch opened a great debate on European strategy between the Americans and the British that endured to the summer of 1944. North Africa led to Sicily; Sicily, to the invasion of Italy. Always Churchill urged ever onward in the Mediterranean—Sicily, landing in Italy, to Rome, then to the Pisa-Rimini line, then "north and northeast"—advances that to a considerable extent Roosevelt, himself fascinated by the Mediterranean, seconded, but that the American Joint Chiefs only reluctantly accepted. The skillful and resourceful arguments of the British leader always stressed the need to continue the momentum of the softening-up process and the immediate advantages, the "great prizes" to be picked up in the Mediterranean, while the Allies waited for the right opportunity to invade the Continent across the Channel. The existence of sizeable Allied forces and the immediate chance to weaken the enemy in the Mediterranean were telling arguments. But at the same time the Americans, with General Marshall as their foremost spokesman, gradually made progress toward limiting the Mediterranean advance, pointing it to the west rather than the east, linking it directly with a definite cross-Channel operation (Overlord), and winning their way back to the notion of waging a war of mass and concentration on the Continent. Part of their task was securing agreement with the President, part with the British, and eventually with the Soviets. The series of decisions reached at the international conferences of 1943, from Casablanca in January to Teheran in November, reflected the compromises of the Americans and British between the principle of opportunism and long-range commitments, between a war of attrition and a war of mass and concentration.

In the course of debate and negotiation, the planning techniques and methods of the Americans in midwar became more nearly like those of their British ally, even if their strategic ideas still differed. The Americans became more skilled in the art of military diplomacy, of quid pro quo, or what might be termed the tactics of strategic planning. At the same time their strategic thinking became more sophisticated. They began to broaden the scope of their thinking from this *or* that operation to terms of this *and* that—what one American planner fittingly called "permutations and combinations." The outstanding strategic questions were no longer to be phrased in terms of either a Mediterranean operation or a cross-Channel invasion, but in terms of defining the precise relations between those undertakings and the combined bomber offensive, on which all were agreed.

In the debate, the American Joint Chiefs countered British demands for more emphasis upon the Mediterranean, particularly the eastern Mediterranean, by threatening further development of Pacific offensives. Holding open the "Pacific alternative" carried with it the threat of no cross-Channel operation at all, which was contrary to British wishes. The war in the Pacific thereby offered the U.S. staff a signficant lever for keeping the Mediterranean issue under control. At the same time General Marshall recognized that the Mediterranean offensive could not be stopped completely with North Africa or Sicily and that definite advantages would accrue from knocking out Italy, opening the Mediterranean further for Allied shipping, and widening the air offensive against Germany.

Teheran was the decisive conference for European strategy. There, for the first time in the war, Roosevelt, Churchill, and their staffs met with Stalin and his staff. Churchill made eloquent appeals for operations in Italy, the Aegean, and the eastern Mediterranean, even at the expense of a delay in Overlord. But the Soviet Union, for reasons of its own, unequivocally put its weight behind the American concept of European strategy. Confident of its capabilities, it asserted its full power as an equal member of the coalition. Stalin came out strongly in favor of Overlord and limiting further operations in the Mediterranean solely to the one undertaking, an invasion of southern France, that directly assisted Overlord. In turn, the Soviets promised to launch an all-out offensive on the eastern front to go with them. Stalin's stand put the capstone on Anglo-American European strategy, and in a real sense, therefore, he fixed Western strategy. The Anglo-American chiefs agreed to launch Overlord in the spring of 1944, in conjunction with a southern France operation, and to consider these the supreme operations for that year. The final blueprint for Allied victory in Europe had taken shape. Germany was to be crushed by a great pincers—an Anglo-American drive in the West and a Soviet drive from the East. General Eisenhower was appointed the supreme commander for Overlord, and preparations for the big blow began.

The last lingering element in the long drawn out Anglo-American debate was not fully settled until the summer of 1944. In the months following Teheran, the southern France operation came perilously close to being abandoned in favor of the British desire for further exploitation in Italy and possibly the Balkans. But General Marshall and the American staff remained adamant and Roosevelt held firm. Final agreement was not reached until August 1944—two months after the cross-Channel attack, and just a few days before the southern France operation was actually launched, when Churchill reluctantly yielded. The war had already entered a new era and this last attempt represented peripheral strategy with a new twist and in a starker political form. Churchill was already looking at the European continent with one eye on the retreating Germans, and the other on the advancing Soviets.

At stake in the midwar debate was not whether there should be a cross-Channel operation. Rather the question was: should that operation be the full-bodied drive launched with the highest priority on a definite target date that the Americans desired, or a final blow to an enemy critically weakened in a war of attrition that the British wanted? In other words, was it to be a "power drive" or a "mop up"? It is a mistake to assume that the British did not from the first want a cross-Channel operation. The evidence points the other way. Anglo-American differences revolved essentially around timing and the extent and direction of preparatory operations. It is also a mistake to believe that the Americans remained opposed to all Mediterranean operations. In fact, a considerable part of their planning labors in 1943 was spent in reconciling those operations with the cross-Channel attack and weaving both with the combined bomber offensive.

The controversy that has arisen over the question of the Balkan operation demands some attention. Would it not have been wiser to have invaded the Continent through the Balkans, thereby forestalling Soviet domination of Eastern Europe? It must be emphasized that this is a postwar debate. The Balkan invasion was never proposed by any responsible leader in Allied strategy councils as an alternative to Overlord and no Allied debate or combined planning occurred with it in mind. The evidence is clear on this matter. Churchill steadfastly denied in his postwar writings that he wanted a Balkan invasion and the evidence, on the whole, seems to bear him out.[11] But there were ambiguities in his position that remain to be explained. Clearly, he was in favor of raids, assistance for native populations, and throwing in a few armored divisions in the Balkans, but nowhere in his wartime or postwar writing did he face up to the question that so frightened the American staff: the ultimate costs and requirements of an operation in the Balkans, an area

[11] For an examination in the official British series of Churchill's position on the Balkans in 1943, see John Ehrman, *Grand Strategy*, vol. 5, August 1943-September 1944 (London, 1956), 112-13 and appendix, 554-56.

of difficult terrain and poor communications. This factor becomes all the more important in the light of the experience with Mediterranean operations, a striking demonstration of how great the costs of a war of attrition can be. In any event, neither the American President nor his military staff wanted to get involved in the thorny politics of the Balkan area.

Most of the criticisms that have been raised in the postwar era on the conduct of the war in Europe have centered on the American strategy of the "big blow." The American approach was attacked, particularly by British critics, as too shortsighted, too direct and blunt, too intent on military victory, too forgetful of the larger objectives of war. Such criticism begs the question of whether the Churchillian approach—the peripheral approach—however suitable to British manpower, economy, traditions, and objectives, was suited to American experience, capacities, and traditions. As Gordon Harrison, author of *Cross-Channel Attack*, a volume in the official American Army series on the Second World War, put it: "To accuse Americans of mass-production thinking is only to accuse them of having a mass-production economy and of recognizing the military advantage of such an economy. The Americans were power-minded."[12] From the beginning they thought in terms of taking on the main German armies and beating them. To launch a major cross-Channel attack on a definite target date represented to them the best hope of ending the war quickly and with the fewest casualties. That target date in their view was sacrosanct since it was the pivot about which their other plans and programs for the global war revolved. In back of the American staff's opposition to attritional and peripheral warfare against Germany lay their continued anxiety over its ultimate costs in men, money, and time, a concern heightened by their responsibility for the war against Japan. Basic in their thought was a growing realization of the ultimate limits of American manpower available for war purposes.[13] This factor and the anxiety about the effects of a long-term mobilization confirmed their doctrine of military concentration, and made them suspicious of British stress on Mediterranean operations, of what they regarded as a penchant for Balkan operations, and of the delays in definitely setting the cross-Channel attack.

In any event, the final strategy against Germany was a compromise

---

[12] Gordon A. Harrison, "Operation Overlord," transcript of an address delivered at the Army War College, November 1951, Office Chief of Military History Files, quoted in Matloff, "The Anvil Decision: Crossroads of Strategy," in *Command Decisions*, ed. Greenfield.

[13] This theme is developed in an essay by Maurice Matloff, "The 90-Division Gamble," in *Command Decisions*, ed. Greenfield.

691

of American and British views—of British peripheral strategy and the American principle of concentration. To the extent that the cross-Channel operation was delayed a year later than Americans wished in order to advance in the Mediterranean and continue the softening-up process, the British prevailed. The British also set the conditions for Overlord, notably, the maximum enemy strength to be expected in the West. But the American views triumphed in determining the nature, timing, and priority of the cross-Channel attack. Overlord became the overriding operation in force with a fixed target date. It was given the highest priority and all efforts were concentrated on making it successful. It was given the maximum force to drive directly at the heart of German power.

Behind the Anglo-American midwar debate, significant changes had taken place in the balance of military power within the coalition—developments that had as important implications for the determination of war strategy as for the future relations among the partners in the wartime coalition. At the close of 1943, the Americans, with their mighty industrial and military machine in high gear, had with Soviet help made the British yield to their notions of Continental strategy. The growing flow of American military strength and supplies to the European theater ensured the triumph of the American staff concept of a concentrated, decisive military war, a concept reinforced by the addition, from the Casablanca Conference in January 1943 onward, of Roosevelt's insistence on Germany's unconditional surrender. The Soviet Union, steadily gathering strength and confidence after Stalingrad, had been able to make its weight felt on the strategic scales at a critical point in Allied councils. Britain had practically completed its mobilization at the end of 1943, and strains had begun to show in its economy. The Americans in midwar drew up to and threatened to overtake the British in deployed strength in the European theater. Britain's military power, along with its notions of fighting the war, was being outstripped. By way of the military doctrine of concentration, the strategists of the Kremlin and the Pentagon had found common ground. The foundations of the alliance were changing.

IV

The third and final phase of the Allied strategy against Germany marked the last nine months of the European conflict—the period of the pursuit of victory and the unfolding of the strategy in practice. In this period the problems of winning the war began to come up against the problems of winning the peace, as the course of the war began to shape the conditions of the peace. After the successful landings on Normandy on June 6, 1944, the Western Allied forces broke out of their beachheads and advanced across the Continent, intent on the pursuit of the main

German armies, while the Russians, driving westward, picked up capital after capital in eastern and central Europe, beating the Western forces to Berlin, Vienna, and Prague, and pouring into the Balkans to fill the vacuum left by the retreating Germans. The direction of the Soviet drives suggests that the flow of their power against key political and strategic positions was more than merely coincidental. In this period, which has aroused much controversy in the postwar debate over Allied strategy, the curtain began to lift on the divergent national objectives and war aims of the Allies.

By the summer of 1944 the pattern of Allied strategy against Germany was complete and in the process of realization. But the full impact of American concepts was to be felt even more strongly in the subsequent months down to the surrender of Germany in May 1945. Once the Allied forces became firmly ensconced on the European continent, the war became for General Marshall and his staff essentially a matter of logistics and tactics, with General Eisenhower, the Supreme Allied Commander in Europe, to take over and make his decisions as military circumstances in the field dictated. But to Churchill, warily watching the swift Soviet advance into Poland and the Balkans, the war had become more than ever a contest for great political stakes and he wished Western Allied strength diverted to fill the vacuum left by the retreating Germans and thereby to forestall the Soviet surge. As the strategy unrolled in the field, the two approaches to the war boiled down to a question of military tactics versus political maneuvers.

Had the President joined with the prime minister as he often had in the past, the American military staff's concentration on bringing the war against Germany to a swift military conclusion might still have been tempered and the war steered into more direct political channels. But Roosevelt would not, and Churchill by himself could not. By 1944-1945 the American President was caught in a political dilemma. He was not unconcerned about the unilateral efforts of the Soviet Union to put its imprint on the shape of postwar Europe, notably in the dispute over the reconstruction of the Polish government. But from the viewpoint of domestic political considerations he had to fight a quick and decisive war that would justify American entry and the dispatch of American troops abroad. He wanted to wind up the war against Germany and get on with the war against Japan. He had educated the American public about the need for active participation in the European conflict, but whether he could have led it in a prolonged war or occupation that might have resulted from the more active American role in southeastern Europe desired by the prime minister is more doubtful. Besides, Roosevelt's policy for peace seemed to lie in the same direction as Woodrow Wilson's—

national self-determination and an international organization to maintain the peace, rather than a reliance on the balance of power. To achieve this aim he had to take the calculated risk of being able to handle Stalin and winning and maintaining the friendship of the Soviet Union. Although Churchill appeared willing to go a long way in the same direction, he seemed to want to hedge more toward traditional balance-of-power theory. In any event, American national policy in the final year placed no obstacle in the way of a decisive ending of the European conflict.

By the summer of 1944 the signs of things to come were already apparent. Once on the Continent, General Eisenhower was given more and more responsibility for political decisions, or fell heir to them by default. Lacking clear and consistent guidance from Washington, he made decisions on the basis of military considerations, and fell back on the American staff notions of bringing the enemy to bay and ending the war quickly and decisively with the fewest casualties. This trend became even more marked later, in 1945, in his decision to stop at the Elbe and not to take Berlin or Prague ahead of the Soviets.[14] As usual, General Marshall and the American staff backed the decisions of the commander in the field.[15] Whatever the ultimate political implications, from the military viewpoint of decisively ending the war against Germany it made little difference whether the forces of the United States or those of the Soviet Union took Berlin or Prague.

The inability of Churchill in the last year of the war to reverse the trend reflected the changed relationship between the American and British military and the shifting bases of the Grand Alliance. If the military strength that the American staff had conserved for the major blow on the Continent offered a powerful weapon, American leadership did not choose to use it for political purpose; the prime minister, on the other hand, had the purpose but not the power. After the middle of 1944 British production came under increasing strain and the British fought the remainder of the war with a contracting economy. The greater capacity of the American economy and population to support a sustained large-scale Allied offensive effort showed up clearly in the last year of the European war. Through the huge stockpile of American production already built up and through control of the increasing U.S. military manpower on the Continent General Eisenhower, the Supreme Allied Commander, could put the imprint of American staff notions on winning the

---

[14] Forrest C. Pogue, *The Supreme Command* (Washington, D.C., 1954) chs. 23, 24; Forrest C. Pogue, "The Decision to Halt at the Elbe" in *Command Decisions*, ed. Greenfield; and Churchill, *Triumph and Tragedy* (Boston, 1953), chs. 8, 11.

[15] For General Marshall's position on Berlin and Prague, see Matloff, *Strategic Planning for Coalition Warfare, 1943-1944*, 534.

war. Whatever political orientation Churchill hoped to give the character of the Western Allied military effort had to yield. As the war against Germany lengthened out beyond the hoped-for conclusion in 1944, British influence in high Allied councils went into further decline. Between the growing power of the American military machine driving eastward, intent on the destruction of the German armies, and the Soviets making their weight felt in central and eastern Europe, the British were largely left to their own devices to salvage what they could of their European and Mediterranean policy. Clearly the last year of the war saw the foundations of the coalition in further transition; British influence was waning, and the United States and the Soviet Union were emerging as the two strongest military powers in Europe. With the Americans determined to withdraw from the Continent as quickly as possible after the defeat of Germany and the Russians showing increasing signs of entrenching themselves, Churchill began to be alarmed. To the prime minister the singleness of purpose of the Washington High Command, despite the growing political character of the war, was most frustrating. In his memoirs he lashed out: "In Washington especially longer and wider views should have prevailed."[16]

In the absence of political instructions to the contrary, the American military staff fell back upon the task of applying the given resources and manpower to get the disagreeable business over with as quickly as possible. Thus the war against Germany was to be concluded—on the Western side—as the American military chiefs had wished to wage it from the beginning, a conventional war of concentration, a technical military game. To the end the Soviet Union showed its determination to fight the war in its own way, and for its own objectives.

As the power balance in and out of the Grand Alliance shifted in the last year of the war on the Continent, the three Allied partners stood considerably apart on European issues. American policy, intent on withdrawing American troops within two years after the end of the fighting, remained opposed to recognizing territorial settlements before a peace conference and the establishment of a new international organization. The British were more amenable to accepting moderate Soviet demands and even to entering into temporary expedients with the Soviet Union, applying the sphere-of-influence principle to the Balkans. The Soviet Union began to make its political claims more openly and strongly. What it could not obtain by negotiation, it sought through unilateral action. From that standpoint, the Yalta Conference—about which controversy

[16] Churchill, *Triumph and Tragedy*, 455.

still revolves—may be regarded as a symptom of Western divergence and disunity and increasing Soviet strength and influence.

V

What, then, may we conclude about the character of Allied strategy in the Second World War? The evidence suggests that neither the Americans nor the British started with a fully developed strategic blueprint. The patterns they fashioned for victory were molded by circumstances, necessity, trial and error, and compromises among themselves and with their allies in the changing context of the war. Each strategic case reflected national traditions, interests, geography, resources, and the predilections of its political and military leaders—an amalgam molded on the anvil of necessity. The relative position and influence of each power in the alliance changed as its national strength weakened or increased in the crucible of war.

In retrospect the impact of the First World War on national approaches to coalition strategy in the Second World War needs more emphasis. Each Allied power was to a considerable degree a captive of its own past, and in its strategic legacy the earlier conflict and its aftermath exerted a strong influence: after that drawn-out bloody struggle, a classic case of arrested strategy, no Allied power wanted another long war. The huge losses suffered by Britain in the great carnage of mass armies and ground battles in the First World War bred caution in its political and military leadership and a return, insofar as circumstances in the global coalition war permitted, to a more traditional "indirect approach" to counter and defeat the Nazi foe that had upset the European balance of power.

Entering late in 1917, the Americans had emerged relatively unbloodied and flushed with Pershing's victories in offensive warfare, as the long-stalemated conflict became a war of movement again. For the American military, the First World War confirmed the doctrines of concentration and of fighting for complete victory, and out of the battlefields of Europe came the foundations of strategic faith that military leaders like General George C. Marshall sought to apply in the multitheater context of the Second World War. The war against imperial Germany raised the American army in importance on the strategic scales, and participation in that conflict bred confidence and faith among the military in their ability to raise, deploy, support, and fight large citizen armies overseas in offensive warfare. That approach meshed neatly with Roosevelt's policy, after 1941, in studied contrast with that of President Wilson, to exact unconditional surrender from Germany this time, to defeat its forces thoroughly in the field, and to offer no "escape clauses" of another Fourteen Points.

696

Although participation in the First World War left a legacy of optimism to the Americans and caution to the British, Soviet experience in 1917 and the counterrevolutionary aftermath heightened its distrust of capitalistic powers and conditioned the approach of its leadership to the Second World War. Throughout that war the Soviet leadership, suspicious of both partner and enemy, was determined to recover the western borderlands it had lost in the Treaty of Brest-Litovsk and to strengthen its position in eastern Europe. These objectives remained fundamental in Soviet politico-military strategy in the Second World War. In many ways the Second World War, fought largely with the refined weapons of the First World War, may be regarded as its confirmation, and the strategic links between the two conflicts need further exploration.

Critics of the American case have charged that the American military were overly paranoid about British intentions, too suspicious of British imperialism—that the Balkan question became a specter that had little basis in fact. They argue that the British were more sophisticated in warfare and diplomacy and that had their advice been followed, the political results of the war would have been far different.

The question may well be raised: Was there a coherent British strategy for the war against Germany, and did it present a better alternative to the American strategy for war and postwar purposes? The writings of the official British historians on grand strategy indicate that the British strategy in the Second World War, like its American counterpart, grew essentially in response to changing opportunities and pressures and to compromises among the position of its leaders. There appears to have been not one but a number of British cases for the Mediterranean; the British chiefs and Churchill were not in total agreement over Balkan or Aegean operations. Michael Howard, who has contributed a volume on strategy to the British official history of the Second World War, has suggested that however opportunistically Mediterranean operations were supported by the British during most of 1943 and justified as paving the way for Overlord, by the end of that year the Mediterranean strategy appeared to be taking on a direction and rationale of its own. Denying that the British leaders in 1943 viewed Mediterranean operations "as a way of forestalling the Russians," or that their Mediterranean strategy was based on "prophetic insights," he concluded: "Increasingly they appear to have abandoned their own earlier arguments and to have regarded the Mediterranean theatre, not as subsidiary, but as an end in itself, the success of whose operations was its own justification."[17]

Whether Churchill really wanted to invade the Balkans is still being

[17] Michael Howard, *The Mediterranean Strategy in the Second World War* (New York, 1968), 69-70.

debated. Certainly the British were growing weaker even in 1943, when Churchillian notions were largely being followed and peripheral strategy was in its heyday. The "soft underbelly" turned out, in the case of Italy, to be a hard-shelled back. Each Mediterranean operation absorbed more troops and supplies than originally contemplated, as the Americans had feared. Balkan operations in any form, as noted above, aroused genuine anxieties among the Americans. Critics of the American case tend to minimize the U.S. planners' maturation as strategists, the global context of their planning, and the war of opportunism they fought in the Pacific, not unlike that advocated by the British for the Mediterranean. The same critics also tend to overestimate the coherence of the British case and to forget that the strategy the Americans espoused for direct, total solutions was born of European prewar doctrine to which they had fallen heir as well as of their own traditions. The American Joint Chiefs of Staff left politics to the President and never advanced a coherent politico-military strategy of their own. But postwar writers who have stressed the complete absence of political sophistication on the part of the U.S. military staff have overdrawn the case. It would appear in retrospect that, despite the alleged disparity in political and military sophistication, neither the British nor the Americans evolved and presented a fully developed politico-military strategy in the Second World War.

The war against Japan, predominantly an American affair, needs special attention in connection with its impact on coalition strategy. From the beginning the war against Japan threatened to overturn Anglo-American basic strategy and the pressures led to further compromises and adjustments in strategic theories and concepts. Despite the agreed primacy of Europe, the Japanese attack on Pearl Harbor and the need to stem the Japanese advance compromised the Germany-first concept from the outset. The Americans accepted the principle of fighting a strategically defensive war against Japan but had no doctrine on how to fight a limited war. Nor would American public opinion condone a completely defensive, limited war against Japan, pending the defeat of Germany. As U.S. military resources poured swiftly into the Pacific, American strategists learned that forces in that theater, as in the Mediterranean, had a way of generating their own strategy. Ground and air forces concentrated in Australia after the early advance of the Japanese through the Western Pacific could not be left idle. As American naval power in the Pacific recovered from the disaster at Pearl Harbor, American naval strategists pushed for the execution of the old Orange plan concept of a Central Pacific offensive. Meanwhile, the President's decision to bolster China led to a further drain on American military resources. The limited war would not stay limited. For two years after Pearl Harbor the requirements of the war against Japan almost equalled those of the war against the European axis. Despite the Germany-first principle, not until 1944 did the preponderance of American military strength shift to the task of defeating Germany.

While the U.S. Navy with its traditional interests in the Pacific carried the main burden in developing the offensive strategy for the area, naval plans for the Central Pacific had to be reconciled with General Douglas MacArthur's concept of advancing on Japan via the New Guinea-Mindanao axis. Thus, a two-pronged strategy replaced the original single-axis approach, and this wartime improvisation led to a strategy of opportunism, not unlike that urged by the British for the war in Europe. The critical question whether Japan could be defeated by bombardment and blockade alone or whether an invasion would be necessary, to which American prewar theory had not given a definitive answer, was debated until the Japanese surrender rendered the subject academic.

The successes and failures of British and American leadership in the Second World War, it may be argued, were a product of their systems and their ingrained approaches to war and peace. The relationship forged by the Americans under the stress of war empowered the military to secure the decisive victory Roosevelt wanted. It enabled them to apply the revolution in technology, tactics, and doctrine that had developed between the world wars to the war of mass and mobility that the Second World War turned out to be. American flexibility in terms of the military strategy they forged among themselves and with their allies has been underestimated. How far the American military had come in the quarter century since the First World War was reflected in the transformation of the United States from its role of junior partner in that war, fought in conformity with a strategy set by the European allies, to its large share in shaping European strategy and its preeminent role in directing the war in the Pacific in the Second World War.

American strategies came of age between 1941 and 1945. They had entered the war with a strategic framework fashioned out of a patchwork of European theory and American experience and innovation. No American master strategist emerged to issue a call for an American declaration of independence from European doctrine. But the principles Americans chose to stress in the common body of strategic thought they shared with Europeans were entirely in harmony with their own traditions and national policies. Throughout they showed a preference for quick, direct, total solutions. In accord with their national tradition, they regarded war as an aberration, an interruption to normality to be concluded as swiftly as possible. As American power flowed into the field in overwhelming strength, they gained confidence in Allied councils, imposed an American style and approach on global war and strategy, and forced the partners in their coalition to reckon with them. In effect the rising military power from the New World asserted its strategic independence from the old.

In the final analysis, the Second World War may appear from the Western standpoint to have been the climax of the joining of a moral crusade with massive power that let loose forces and expectations that neither their policy makers nor their strategists could by themselves control. Thorny problems of political and territorial adjustments emerged for which no solutions had been foreseen. The basic assumptions of presidential policy—the cooperation of the Soviet Union, the survival of Britain as a strong power, and China's elevation as a great power in the near future—came into question. In the end American leadership sanctioned the use of the atomic bomb, planning for which had grown up outside regular strategic channels, before a military theory or doctrine for it had been developed or its place in the future of warfare or international relations had been fully comprehended.

The United States emerged from the Second World War as a global power, stronger than ever, but with its leaders more conscious than ever of the limits of power. Even in waging the war they found that they could not launch a major cross-Channel attack as early as they wished. Nor could they support a large operation on the mainland of Asia along with establishing a second front in Europe. Through the Yalta Conference they called for Soviet help in pinning down Japanese forces on the Asiatic mainland before an invasion of Japan. In contrast to the 215 Army divisions the American planners had orginally projected in 1941, the United States was able to mobilize only ninety, all of which were deployed overseas at the end. Nor, despite its great industrial strength, could it completely overcome the shortages of shipping and landing craft that plagued Allied planning throughout.

Military theory and practice in the Second World War, as in so many previous wars, turned out not to be in full accord. Despite the claims of prewar British and American air enthusiasts, the ability of air power to defeat enemies was not proved. On the other hand, after Pearl Harbor aircraft carriers, not battleships, proved to be queens of the fleet. Events almost as often determined strategy as the reverse. Western Allied strategy was hammered out in a series of compromises at the international conferences marked by a constant struggle to adjust ends and means.

In many ways the Second World War was a series of wars within wars. Indeed, it may be argued that the Western powers fought their war and the Soviets theirs; that there never was an overall Allied strategy; that the two strategies—Anglo-American on the one hand, and Soviet on the other—just happened to be compatible; that on a military plane

700

their efforts proved successful but their national interests and political objectives were not really meshed; and that the Grand Alliance began to break up before the war was over, when the common bond of danger that had brought the Allies together in 1941 began to loosen.

To the end negotiations with the Soviets proved difficult. Despite the postwar criticism of American wartime leadership, it is doubtful whether, within the means available, any different strategy or policy would have produced a faster decisive victory over Germany and put the West in a fundamentally better position vis-à-vis the Soviet Union, or would have surmounted the legacy of mutual suspicion that the wartime partners had inherited from the outset—a legacy that remains, with added scars from the Second World War. From the Soviet standpoint, while the Allies postponed the second front, the Russians suffered twenty million casualties. The war ended with dilemmas piling up for the President and his military staff; political problems in Europe mounted for which neither the military strategy of victory nor the President's policy of postponing political decisions provided answers. Whatever virtue unconditional surrender had as a war slogan and war aim, it did not prove to be a good peace aim. It cloaked the divergence in national objectives and interests of the Allies and offered no basis for reconciling them.

The Second World War shed no certain light on the motivations and intentions of Soviet policy, problems that have also troubled postwar Western leadership. Roosevelt staked much on using the wartime partnership to bring the Soviet Union out of its prewar isolation. "The only way to have a friend," he once quoted Ralph Waldo Emerson, "is to be one."[18] But at the very end, wary of Russian intransigence over Poland, he advocated firmness in dealing with the Soviet Union—somewhat akin to General Marshall's urging in January 1945 that Eisenhower treat the Russians "in simple Main Street Abilene style."[19] At no point, however, did Roosevelt or his chief military advisors propose to use military power for direct and specific political purposes vis-à-vis the Soviet Union.

The events of 1945 demonstrated the capacity of the Allies to forge a strategy that was completely successful in a military sense. That strategy was a hybrid product—a composite of American directness, British caution, and Soviet bluntness. It found its common denominator in the defeat of Germany by a giant nutcracker squeeze on the Continent. But as the forces of the coalition partners came closer and the defeat of Germany more certain, their political differences became more apparent and the

[18] Samuel I. Rosenman, ed., *The Public Papers and Addresses of Franklin D. Roosevelt*, 1944-1945 volume (New York, 1950), 524.
[19] For Gen. Marshall's recommendation see Marshall to Eisenhower, January 17, 1945, Eisenhower personal file, quoted in Pogue, *Supreme Command*, 407.

cement that had held them together crumbled. What the Western and Eastern partners had set out to do in common was to defeat Germany and this goal they had successfully accomplished. By May 8, 1945, Germany surrendered. But in the eyes of the West, Germany was only half liberated and Poland and eastern Europe were already in the Soviet dictator's grip. Out of the wartime comradeship-in-arms a new rivalry for power was to emerge, with a firm peace still to be won.

In the end, it may be argued, the war outran the strategists and the statesmen. In the perspective of the intervening years, it is apparent that the Second World War represented a fundamental shift in the international balance of power, for which a coalition strategy fashioned for victory provided no real or grand solutions. Total war brought neither total peace nor total national security. In the final analysis, the Second World War may be viewed as part of the unfinished business of the first and the uneasy era after 1945 a carryover of the unfinished business of the war—a quest for the peace and security that had eluded military victory. The Second World War was total but incomplete.

24. American and Japanese Strategies in the Pacific War

D. CLAYTON JAMES

THE DEMISE and rebirth of China as an Asian power were central to the rivalry and eventual armed conflict between America and Japan in the first half of the twentieth century. America and Japan went to war in 1941 because their national strategies had become irreconcilable, particularly regarding China. Both nourished illusions about China and developed unrealistic policies toward it before and during the Second World War. Japan's pursuit of a continental military strategy, with much of its combat power channeled to China, and America's emphasis on a maritime strategy against Japan, with priority given to Central Pacific operations, shaped the course of the Far Eastern war. Important to the postwar reconciliation of America and Japan was their common concern over the advance of communism in Asia, especially in China.

The war of 1941-1945 posed challenges to earlier strategic thinking on both sides, requiring each to adapt priorities and plans to new, unforeseen situations. Thus the national and military strategies of Japan and America will be considered not only for the war years but also in the context of the preceding four decades. Our discussion will distinguish between national and military strategy. By the former we mean the utilization of all necessary resources—political, diplomatic, military, technological, economic, propagandistic, and others—in achieving the objectives of national policy. By military strategy we refer to the employment of armed services to secure the ends of national policy by force or the threat of force.

I

The complex elements underlying Japanese nationalism and modernization in the late nineteenth century combined to produce the first powerful Asian challenge to Western interests in that region. Concomitant with its impressive industrial and military growth, Japan set out on the path to empire. After obtaining the Ryukyus and the Kuriles in the 1870s, it resumed expansionism with vigor in 1894-1915: soundly defeated China and Russia in successive wars, acquiring Formosa, the Pescadores, Korea, and portions of Manchuria and Sakhalin; negotiated a defensive alliance with Great Britain; seized Germany's colonies in China and the Central Pacific; and carved economic inroads into China, nearly making that revolution-torn land a Japanese protectorate. In the wake of the First World War, Japan appeared set on a collision course with Western colonial powers, especially after the Versailles Conference's refusal to include a Japanese-sponsored declaration on racial equality in the League of Nations Covenant, an insult to national pride exacerbated by the American immigration law excluding Japanese.

But surprisingly, Japan retreated from confrontations with the West in the 1920s, and contributed to putting Wilsonian ideals of international harmony into practice. It became the only non-Western member of the League of Nations Council, Japanese judges served with distinction on the World Court, and its representatives on League committees and agencies were generally progressive in such matters as improving East-West cultural relations and promoting free international trade policies. Japanese economic diplomacy was governed increasingly by the principle of cooperation with the other major industrial nations in a framework of economic interdependence, integration, and mutual trade benefits. Turning away from aggressive expansionism, Japan returned the former German colony in Shantung to China; withdrew its troops from the Soviet Union's Far Eastern territory; joined the signatories of the Washington Conference treaties that provided for naval reductions, respect for China's political integrity, and settlement of differences between the Pacific powers by diplomacy; and became a party to the Kellogg-Briand Pact on the renunciation of war. Japanese domestic affairs in the 1920s were characterized by liberal, democratic trends, with the rise of political parties, trade unionism, and a much-broadened electorate, while militaristic, ultra-nationalistic interests appeared dormant. Externally and internally, Japan seemed to be moving in line with Western, especially Anglo-American, ideas of how to secure peace, attain domestic stability, and prosper.[1]

The onset of the Great Depression in 1929-1930, which soon struck capitalist economies all around the globe, brought a major change. Japan was beset by internal economic distress, by paralysis of its vital foreign trade, and by want of strong leadership among the liberal and moderate political elements that had emerged in the 1920s. After some futile efforts

[1] Ryusaku Tsunoda et al., comps., *Sources of the Japanese Tradition* (New York, 1958), 718-58; Akira Iriye, *After Imperialism: The Search for a New Order in the Far East, 1921-1933* (Cambridge, Mass., 1965), 17-22, 222-23, 300-303; Roger Dingman, *Power in the Pacific: the Origins of Naval Arms Limitation, 1914-1922* (Chicago, 1976), 63, 194-95, 218.

at international cooperation, the Western industrial nations turned to separate devices in coping with the depression. The United States, the world's foremost capitalist power and the Western country with whom Japan by then had its closest trade and diplomatic ties, led the way in adopting isolationist economic policies that worked to the detriment of its trading partners. Extreme nationalists again rose to the fore by exploiting the economic crisis, and Japan plunged into a new era of reaction against cooperation with the West and in favor of the old panacea of continental expansion. Spearheading the new aggressiveness was the army. Defying civilian authorities in Tokyo, it provoked a clash with China over Manchuria and then conquered the territory in 1932.

Five years later the government, now dominated by the army, led the nation into a fateful war for the greatest prize yet—the conquest of China. Reviving and revamping earlier justifications, the Japanese leaders maintained that control of China was essential to provide raw materials and markets for the ailing Japanese economy, resettlement areas for Japan's burgeoning population, security against potential Soviet armed incursion in China, and opportunities for propagating the superior Japanese culture and values. Moreover, in this great effort to take all of China, the Japanese people would experience a resurgence of national unity and pride that would eradicate the widespread discontent bred by the depression. It was also true that administrative centralization made necessary by the war would enable the new political leaders to solidify their power, while the industrial elite would reap enormous profits from war production—two aims discreetly not publicized. All these gains depended, however, on a relatively quick triumph in China.

Japanese armies soon captured the northern and coastal regions of China, including the principal population and economic centers, but the anticipated collapse of Chinese resistance did not occur. Deceived by the long, bitter struggles between the Chinese Nationalist, Communist, and warlord factions, the Japanese had greatly underestimated the Chinese people's will to resist and the ability of divided political groups to mount effective, if separate, mobilization and defense efforts. By late 1938, Japan found itself locked into a war of attrition with an alarmingly heavy drain on its military manpower and matériel and no decision in sight. A puppet regime in Nanking proved of little use in winning converts to Japan's cause among the Chinese, and Tokyo's attempts to negotiate peace on its own terms with the Chinese Nationalist and Communist regimes were unsuccessful.[2]

---

[2] Akira Iriye, *Power and Culture: The Japanese-American War, 1941-1945* (Cambridge, Mass., 1981), 2-16, 28, 34-39, 49; Saburo Ienaga, *The Pacific War: World War II and the Japanese, 1931-1945* (New York, 1978), 57-96.

As the logistical needs of the Japanese war effort neared critical levels with the stalemate in China, Tokyo began laying plans to gain control of the vast resources of Southeast Asia in oil, rubber, bauxite, tin, and other strategic materials and foodstuffs. Extending its appeal for pan-Asian unity against Western intervention and for an integrated regional economy to the Koreans, Manchurians, and Chinese, the Japanese government now proclaimed its commitment to creating a Greater East Asia Co-Prosperity Sphere, which was to encompass Southeast Asia. In early 1939, Japan made its first moves into the South China Sea, seizing Hainan and the Spratly Islands. With the fall of France the next summer, Japanese forces began establishing bases in northern French Indochina for possible future operations to the south. Japanese negotiations with Dutch authorities in the East Indies and with the American government to obtain the strategic materials needed to sustain operations in China were unavailing. To gain allies and protect its flanks during the conquest of Southeast Asia, which Tokyo saw as inevitably necessary but also likely to provoke war with both Britain and America, Japan joined Germany and Italy in the Axis Pact in September 1940 and concluded a neutrality treaty with the Soviet Union the next spring. Japanese troops occupied the southern portion of French Indochina in mid-1941, and that December the main operations to take what Tokyo called the Southern Resources Area were launched. In trying to refurbish its war effort in China and decide that conflict, Japan risked all by taking on the Anglo-American powers.[3]

In the evolution of Japanese military strategy since the 1880s, the army and navy had developed priorities and plans consonant with the objective of continental expansion that was implicit in national policy except during the 1920s. Although Japan bore a geopolitical similarity to Britain in its insular position near traditionally hostile continental nations, Japanese leaders from the Meiji Restoration of 1868 onward had envisioned their nation not as a leading maritime state but rather as the dominant continental power of East Asia. They saw the army as the primary instrument to achieve continental hegemony. The navy was to transport, supply, support, and protect the army and to provide security for its principal base of operations, the home islands. Although the navy won several victories at sea during the wars with China and Russia near the turn of the century, notably over the Russian Baltic Fleet at Tsushima

[3] Robert J. C. Butow, *Tojo and the Coming of the War* (Princeton, 1961), 133-63; Hilary Conroy, "Nomura Kichisaburo: The Diplomacy of Drama and Deception," in *Diplomats in Crisis: United States-Chinese-Japanese Relations, 1919-1941*, ed. Richard D. Burns and Edward M. Bennett (Santa Barbara, Calif., 1974), 297-316; Basil Collier, *The War in the Far East, 1941-1945: A Military History* (New York, 1969), 94-97.

Strait, Japanese naval strategists until 1941 planned in terms of the fleet's subordinate service role to ground operations. Large-scale offensive fleet actions far from home waters were not much studied. Since the fleet's primary mission was to assist the ground forces, there were no plans to risk the ships in major naval confrontations when that was avoidable. Japanese naval design between the world wars generally reflected the prevailing emphasis on speed and rapidity of fire rather than on armor. During this period the Japanese navy became a leader in undersea and naval air developments, but the submarine and the aircraft carrier were still viewed basically as supportive weapons for army actions, not as potent devices of offensive firepower.

Admiral Isoroku Yamamoto's plan to attack Pearl Harbor did not mark an aberration from the navy's traditional role, for the raid was to be a minimum-risk, hit-and-run mission with the attacking units immediately assigned thereafter to supporting ground operations in Southeast Asia. Japanese war plans in 1941 called for not only the capture of the Southern Resources Area but also the establishment of a defense perimeter through the Pacific islands on its eastern flank. One might have expected that Japanese naval leaders would anticipate Mahanian-style fleet engagements after the American navy recovered from the blow of Pearl Harbor and tried to interdict Japan's lines of communication to the south. But the Japanese calculated that a year or more would be needed for full American economic mobilization and that by the time new ship reinforcements were sent to the United States Pacific Fleet, the Japanese defense perimeter in the West Pacific would be strong enough to deter or repel any attempts at penetration.[4]

Although Japan won spectacular tactical victories for six months after Pearl Harbor, its early strategic blunders amounted to more than badly miscalculating America's capability to mobilize its industry. In the first place, Japan might well have gained the Southern Resources Area without provoking America into war if it had bypassed the Philippines, which had few economic resources Japan needed anyway. Moreover, although the long-range Japanese plan provided for a negotiated settlement with the Western adversaries after Southeast Asia was secured, the treacherous nature of the opening move at Pearl Harbor so inflamed the

[4] Alexander Kiralfy, "Japanese Naval Strategy," in *Makers of Modern Strategy*, ed. Edward Mead Earle (Princeton, 1943), 457-58, 462-64, 478, 480-84; Clark G. Reynolds, "The Continental Strategy of Imperial Japan" *U.S. Naval Institute Proceedings* 109 (August 1983), 65-70; Stephen E. Pelz, *Race to Pearl Harbor: The Failure of the Second London Naval Conference and the Onset of World War II* (Cambridge, Mass., 1974), 25-40; Asada Sadao, "The Japanese Navy and the United States," in *Pearl Harbor as History: Japanese-American Relations, 1931-1941*, ed. Dorothy Borg and Shumpei Okamoto (New York, 1973), 225-59.

American public that not only were later negotiations made impossible but British leaders feared that popular and political pressures at home might compel the United States government to abandon its commitment to the strategic priority of the war against Germany. Also, the Japanese intention was to fight only a limited war for Southeast Asia and Tokyo had prepared no alternative strategy; the nation lacked the resources to wage total war against the West if the plan went awry. By late 1941, Japanese strategy shifted from conquering China to seizing the Southern Resources Area and finally to engaging in combat the United States and its allies. This predicament was occasioned by what Admiral Kichisaburo Nomura, ambassador to the United States in 1941, later called "the principal cancer of Japan," namely, the independence of the military from civilian control. By the time Japan went to war against the West, its military strategy dominated but contradicted its national strategy.[5]

II

The end of the nineteenth century marked both the emergence of Japan as a modern power and of America as the newest imperialist contender in the Pacific. By 1898 the American flag flew over Alaska and the Aleutians at the northern end of the Pacific and over Guam, Wake, Midway, the Hawaiian Islands, and a number of small islands extending from Hawaii to Samoa in the Central and South Pacific. But it was the acquisition of the Philippines that brought American territorial and security interests to the periphery of Japanese imperialism. Refusing to station adequate defensive forces in the archipelago, the American government reluctantly acceded to Japanese expansionist moves on the continent in several bilateral agreements of the 1905-1917 period that, in return, provided Japanese pledges to respect the American position in the Philippines. In effect, the Philippines became a virtual hostage of Japan to gain American acquiescence to Japanese expansionism.

The main irritant in American-Japanese diplomatic relations was the Open Door policy, first enunciated by Secretary of State John Hay at the turn of the century. For the ensuing four decades its key principles constituted the linchpin of the Far Eastern policy of the United States: preservation of the independence, sovereignty, and territorial and administrative integrity of China; and establishment of equal opportunity for all nations engaged in commercial and industrial relations with China. The first strong diplomatic protest sent by Washington to Tokyo resulted

[5] Gordon W. Prange et al., *At Dawn We Slept: The Untold Story of Pearl Harbor* (New York, 1981), 547-50, 582-83; Pelz, *Race to Pearl Harbor*, 212-28; Louis Morton, "The Japanese Decision for War," *U.S. Naval Institute Proceedings* 80 (December 1954), 1325-35.

from Japan's attempt in 1915 to reduce China to a protectorate. The Open Door policy received multilateral endorsement in the Nine-Power Pact of 1922, but America continued to be the principal Western nation concerned with guarding China's integrity, although diplomatic pressure and moral suasion, rather than military or economic sanctions, were the only responses of the United States to Japanese moves against China until 1939. Upon Japan's invasion of Manchuria, America took the lead in refusing to recognize the seizure of that territory. When Japan subsequently undertook the conquest of China, American assistance to China by 1939-1941 was in the form of loans, relief aid, lend-lease supplies, and volunteer American combat aviators. The United States also abrogated its trade treaty with Japan and, in response both to Japan's continuing aggression in China and its moves into Indochina, inaugurated a graduated series of embargoes on oil, iron, steel, and other strategic exports to Japan. The diplomatic negotiations between Washington and Tokyo in 1941 repeatedly broke down over the fundamental issue of China. Secretary of State Cordell Hull would not compromise on the withdrawal of all Japanese forces from China as a prerequisite to the further resolution of American-Japanese differences.

The four basic aims of America's pre-1941 national strategy in the Far East were to prepare the Philippines for independence, to keep the China market open to American traders, to maintain the flow of raw materials from Southeast Asia important to American industry, and by means short of force to deter Japanese expansion in those areas. Although the administration of the Philippines had been more progressive than other colonial regimes in Asia, the archipelago sorely lacked political stability, economic self-sufficiency, and adequate defenses after gaining commonwealth status in 1935. The American obsession with the China market was at odds with reality, for the trade between the two countries was negligible, while export-import business between the United States and Asia's one developed capitalist nation, Japan, had grown steadily. Like the illusion of amity with the French people since the 1770s, Americans cultivated a misperception of special friendship with the Chinese nation—a strange idea that was not buttressed by empirical evidence but pervaded official Washington, too. During 1939-1941, President Roosevelt began entertaining another illusion which would greatly affect policy: that China was en route to big-power status again under the pro-American leadership of Chiang Kai-shek. In Southeast Asia native nationalists identified America with their European colonial overlords because, in order to preserve its access to the region's resources, the United States continued to acquiesce in the colonial exploitation of the natural wealth and native peoples. America's tendency to respond to aggressive moves by Japan unilaterally rather than through collective action and to rely upon moralistic diplomacy appeared increasingly ineffective in the 1930s. Until bombs began falling on American bases on Oahu and Luzon, Roosevelt and his advisors were uncertain whether the American public would support an armed commitment to stop Japanese aggression.[6]

America's pre-1941 military strategy developed in the early 1920s, when the war plans divisions of the War and Navy departments in Washington began revising the Color series of pre-1914 war plans covering certain hypothetical scenarios, in which a color was the code name for the strategic plan to be used if America were attacked by a particular nation, for example, red for Britain, green for Mexico, black for Germany, and orange for Japan. The plans were limited in scope, with only superficial attention to logistical aspects and with no provisions for coalitions or for conditions of total or global warfare. They were unrealistic about contemporary or future international alignments; War Plan Orange, which was viewed as the most likely to be used, was conceived in terms of a clash solely between the United States and Japan.

In their numerous revisions of Orange from 1924 to 1938, the Washington planners always assumed that it would be mainly a naval conflict. By the 1930s they envisaged a long, costly war in the Pacific with the early loss of the Philippines. In the joint planning sessions navy spokesmen wanted priority given to an advance spearheaded by navy and marine forces across the Central Pacific to capture the Japanese-mandated Marshall, Caroline, and Marianas islands, and to secure the line of communication between Pearl Harbor and Manila. Army planners argued that the current American strength in the Philippines, comprised of small army and army air units and the weak Asiatic Fleet, could not hold the islands against a sizable Japanese assault, that efforts to reinforce or retake the archipelago in the war's early stages would be costly and futile, and that therefore the American forces should be withdrawn to more defensible bases in Alaska, Hawaii, and Panama. But naval strategists, contemplating a preeminent role for the Pacific Fleet west of Hawaii, refused to concur in a military withdrawal from the Philippines.

After three years of stalemate, the army and navy planners compromised and produced the final major edition of the war plan in 1938. References to offensive operations and the early advance of the navy into the West Pacific were omitted in deference to the army planners, and

[6] Christopher Thorne, *Allies of a Kind: The United States, Britain, and the War against Japan, 1941-1945* (New York, 1978), 22-24, 40-45; Fred Greene, "The Military View of American National Policy, 1904-1940," *American Historical Review* 67 (January 1961), 354-77; Samuel E. Morison, *The Two-Ocean War: A Short History of the United States Navy in the Second World War* (Boston, 1963), 3-45. See also Dorothy Borg, *The United States and the Far Eastern Crisis of 1933-1938* (Cambridge, Mass., 1964).

presidential authorization for offensive missions west of Hawaii, long insisted upon by the War Department representatives, was deleted to the satisfaction of the navy. The revised Orange plan called for American-Filipino forces to hold the entrance to Manila Bay as long as possible but offered little hope of their immediate relief, with no stipulation on how long it would take the navy to reach the Philippines. Like the United States Congress, which wanted neither to abandon the archipelago nor to provide funds for its adequate defense, the planners of the War and Navy departments could not solve the dilemma of Philippine strategic security.[7]

When the Second World War erupted in Europe in 1939, the Washington planners were preparing five plans in the newly conceived Rainbow series, which provided for war situations involving various coalitions of belligerents engaged in several theaters of combat. The new plans were an improvement over the Color series in realistically projecting America's wartime role in the context of friendly and hostile coalitions of nations as well as in situations where the United States would be fighting without allies. Rainbow 5 most nearly approximated the coalitions and operational theaters as they actually evolved in the war; in the Pacific, it envisaged the quick loss of the Philippines and strategic defensive operations against Japan until major Anglo-American forces could be released from the higher-priority European theater following the defeat of Germany and Italy. In late 1940 Admiral Harold R. Stark's Plan Dog Memorandum, a strategic study by the chief of naval operations, also called for focusing on the war against the European members of the Axis Pact, as did the ABC-1 Report the next spring that resulted from several months of secret Anglo-American military staff sessions in Washington. Assuming that Germany was the most dangerous of the Axis powers, the ABC-1 drafters stressed the development of close Anglo-American coordination in planning and operations and called for priority commitment of Anglo-American military resources to the war against Germany. In May 1941 the Joint Army-Navy Board in Washington gave its approval to Rainbow 5 and ABC-1 and, though not formally endorsed by President Roosevelt prior to America's entry into the war, those plans became the basis for determining the main directions of Allied strategy for the next four years.[8]

[7] Louis Morton, *Strategy and Command: The First Two Years. United States Army in World War II [USAWW2 hereafter]: The War in the Pacific* (Washington, D.C., 1962), 21-44; Grace P. Hayes, *The History of the Joint Chiefs of Staff in World War II: The War against Japan* (Annapolis, 1982), 4-8; Waldo H. Heinrichs, Jr., "The Role of the United States Navy," in *Pearl Harbor as History*, ed. Borg and Okamoto, 197-223.

[8] Morton, *Strategy and Command*, 67-91; Hayes, *History of the Joint Chiefs*, 8-15;

Thus, although Japan had concentrated on a continental military strategy and American-Japanese diplomatic differences had originated primarily over China, American war planners had been in basic agreement from the 1920s on that the United States would pursue a maritime strategy in case of war with Japan, with the navy playing the principal role in a decisive Central Pacific offensive. The planners had differed mostly over the strategic place of the Philippines. Although their general concept of a Pacific naval war was clear enough and rather consistently held before Pearl Harbor, other factors would come into play once the war began that made the implementation of the Germany-first and Pacific-maritime strategies more difficult than envisaged.

III

Although Americans during the Second World War generally viewed Japan as a fascist, totalitarian state like its Axis partners, actually the differences between Japan's ideology and political system and those of Germany and Italy far exceeded the similarities. Japan was attracted to the Axis coalition, in part, because its members had in common disappointing earlier experiences with democratic politics, population pressures that kept alive the urge for *Lebensraum*, shocks to their economies during the Great Depression that were more far-reaching than those felt in most other nations, an acute sense of being have-not societies and of not being accepted on an equal level by the more mature industrial powers, and a strong fear of communism. By the end of the 1930s, Japan was in the grips of ultra-nationalism and militarism, but neither bore much resemblance to those phenomena under Nazism or Italian fascism; and no Japanese premier, even Hideki Tojo, possessed the dictatorial powers of Adolf Hitler or Benito Mussolini. In Axis relations, Japanese leaders found that their Berlin and Rome colleagues never grasped the nature of their imperial system, the unique values and heritage of Japanese culture, and their concept of pan-Asianism. Racism also contributed to the inability of the European and Asian members of the Axis Pact to establish close wartime communications.

Japanese interests were virtually ignored in Berlin and Rome where actions in China and the Pacific seemed to have little bearing on strategies for European and Mediterranean operations. In contrast to the close coordination of military planning between the Anglo-American leaders, there was little cooperation toward coalition strategy making between the Japanese war planners and those of the European Axis powers. Thus

Forrest C. Pogue, *George C. Marshall*, 3 vols. to date (New York, 1963-), 2:122-27; T. B. Kittredge, "United States Defense Policy and Strategy, 1941," *U.S. News and World Report*, December 3, 1954, 53-63, 110-39.

two of the early pivotal decisions of Axis strategy were made unilaterally and surprised the other pact members: the German invasion of the Soviet Union and the Japanese attack on Pearl Harbor. Coordinated strategic planning by Germany and Japan probably would have pointed up the mutual long-range assets in joint concentration on defeating the Soviet Union first, but neither government was willing to subordinate national interests in order to work toward common strategic objectives. The course of the war might have been quite different had Japan struck the Soviet Far East when Hitler's armies penetrated the European border of the USSR. The Axis failure to develop strategic planning at the alliance level, especially against the Soviets, was almost as important to the final outcome of World War II as the success of America and Britain in molding their coalition strategy.[9]

Unable to break the military deadlock on the mainland before going to war against the West, Japan became anxious to negotiate a settlement in China as the Americans mounted dual offensives across the Southwest and Central Pacific. In 1943, armistice overtures were made directly by Japanese authorities and indirectly through their puppet regime to the Nationalists in Chungking and the Communists in Yenan. Concessions proffered included withdrawal of Japanese troops, termination of Japanese economic spheres of influence, and assistance for rehabilitation programs in China, as well as proposed Sino-Japanese agreements on mutual respect for each other's territorial and political integrity, collaboration in regional economic development, and cooperation in maintaining peace and stability. The Chinese were to cease hostilities and sever their ties with the Anglo-American alliance. After its earlier objective of conquering China, combat exigencies now forced Japan to try appeasement and, in an appeal based on pan-Asianism, even to propose that China join the war against the Anglo-American powers. The drastic change in Japanese war aims was too much for the Chinese to accept on good faith; Chiang's Nationalist regime continued to solicit Western military assistance, while the Chinese Communists remained convinced of their eventual triumph over both the Japanese and the Kuomintang. Except for a Japanese offensive in South China that overran some American B-29 bases in 1944, the war in China dragged on in a desultory,

---

[9] Maruyama Masao, *Thought and Behavior in Modern Japanese Politics*, ed. Ivan Morris (London, 1963), 90-95; Carl Boyd, *The Extraordinary Envoy: General Hiroshi Oshima and Diplomacy in the Third Reich, 1934-1939* (Washington, D.C., 1980), passim; Frank W. Iklé, *German-Japanese Relations, 1936-1941* (New York, 1956), 111-18; Paul W. Schroeder, *The Axis Alliance and Japanese-American Relations, 1941* (Ithaca, 1958), 126-53.

inconclusive fashion, tying down large Japanese forces that were badly needed in the Pacific.[10]

Similarly, in Southeast Asia the Japanese largely failed to persuade the natives that they were sincerely dedicated to their slogan of "Asia for the Asiatics." The early Japanese military successes did much to dispel illusions among Southeast Asians regarding the white man's superiority, and Japanese propaganda in occupied areas continually reminded the people that Japan had liberated them from their white overlords, pointed out differences between the value systems of the Asians and their former colonial masters, and emphasized the blessings of belonging to Japan's Greater East Asia Co-Prosperity Sphere. But as the occupation wore on, growing numbers of Indonesians, Malays, Thais, Burmese, Vietnamese, and Filipinos were repelled by the oppressive, exploitative methods of the Japanese, who worked native laborers as brutally, seized raw materials and foodstuffs as rapaciously, and stifled dissent as ruthlessly as the worst of the white colonialists.

Belatedly, with the tide of battle having turned decisively in the Pacific, Japan tried to redefine its war aims in terms designed to elicit better cooperation from the occupied countries. At the Greater East Asia Conference in Tokyo in the autumn of 1943, attended by delegates from occupied China and the conquered Southeast Asian countries, Japanese officials sponsored a declaration of regional political, economic, and social cooperation and of mutual respect and amity that rivaled the Anglo-American Atlantic Charter of 1941 in espousing idealistic Wilsonian principles of national self-determination and fair, open international relations. Nevertheless, although desperately needing the Southeast Asian peoples' support against impending Allied assaults in the region, Japanese officials and troops in the occupied areas continued to reveal glaring discrepancies between the ideals enunciated at the Tokyo assembly and their conduct, the consequence being an increase in guerrilla forces and operations in all the Southeast Asian lands. Japan had succeeded in stimulating nascent nationalist movements but had gained little support for its occupation policies. Even before June of 1944, when Allied naval and air forces seriously interdicted Japan's supply lines from Southeast Asia and guerrilla activities were mounting, the Southern Resources Area had become more of a liability than an asset to Japan.[11]

---

[10] Iriye, *Power and Culture*, 47, 63, 90-97, 110-12, 223-25; Ienaga, *Pacific War*, 72-96, 130-42, 165-71. The most recent study is Dick Wilson, *When Tigers Fight: The Story of the Sino-Japanese War, 1937-1945* (New York, 1982).

[11] Iriye, *Power and Culture*, 64-66, 72, 118-21, 153-54; Ienaga, *Pacific War*, 153-80. See also Joyce C. Lebra, ed., *Japan's Greater East Asia Co-prosperity Sphere in World War II: Selected Readings and Documents* (New York, 1975); Harry J. Benda, *The Crescent and the Rising Sun: Indonesian Islam under the Japanese Occupation, 1942-1945* (The Hague, 1958).

714

By mid-1944 the Tojo ministry had failed in all its wartime objectives of national strategy: the Axis Pact had proved of little worth; a solution to the China problem had been obtainable neither by force nor by diplomacy; and access to the strategic resources of Southeast Asia had been interrupted, while Japanese forces there faced widespread popular discontent and threats of imminent Allied invasion. With the Japanese defeat that July in the Marianas, which provided base sites for B-29 raids on Honshu for the first time, the Tojo ministry collapsed and was succeeded by one headed by General Kuniaki Koiso. Instead of acknowledging the hopelessness of the war and initiating peace negotiations with America and its allies, as some senior Japanese statesmen secretly wanted but did not dare urge because they still feared the militarists, the Koiso cabinet, as well as the ministry of Admiral Kantaro Suzuki that followed in April 1945, set up quixotic goals of separating the Soviet Union from its alliance with the West and using Soviet intercession to obtain satisfactory peace terms with the Anglo-American powers. These exercises in diplomatic futility ended in August 1945 when the Soviet army launched a massive drive that swiftly routed Japanese forces in Manchuria and northern Korea. The scheme to use Moscow to salvage something from the war was the final and most foolish machination of the militarists before their ouster.[12]

Throughout the war the Japanese High Command manifested a lack of flexibility in adjusting to the changing circumstances of combat. Little heed was paid to the principle formulated by Carl von Clausewitz over a century earlier: "The first, the supreme, the most far-reaching act of judgment that the statesman and commander have to make is to establish ... the kind of war on which they are embarking; neither mistaking it for, nor trying to turn it into, something that is alien to its nature."[13] Having long planned within the framework of a continental strategy, the Japanese were slow to realize that this new war with the West would be shaped by the primarily maritime strategy employed by their most powerful enemy, the United States. Despite being forced on the defensive in the Pacific by mid-1942, Japan never committed the bulk of its military strength against the American offensives. Although the strong Kwangtung Army in Manchuria lost some of its best ground units by transfer to Pacific defenses, 1.8 million, or 56 percent, of the 3.2 million troops deployed outside the home islands were still stationed in China and Manchuria by early August 1945. During 1942-1945, Japanese ground and air forces on the China front were unnecessarily strong for the es-

[12] Robert J. C. Butow, *Japan's Decision to Surrender* (Stanford, Calif., 1954), 112-41; Iriye, *Power and Culture*, 86-89, 182-83, 235-36, 242-48.
[13] Carl von Clausewitz, *On War*, ed. and trans. Michael Howard and Peter Paret, rev. ed. (Princeton, 1984), 88.

sentially holding operations in which they were engaged, except for the South China offensive in 1944. By the time Tokyo decided to transfer forces from China and Manchuria to the Pacific in substantial numbers, American naval and air units had gained control of the skies and seas of the West Pacific, exacting a heavy toll of Japanese troop shipments southward and eventually thwarting such reinforcements altogether.[14]

Not only were Japanese military strategists late in setting a higher priority on the Pacific, but they also misjudged which of the American-led advances was the more menacing. General Douglas MacArthur's self-promotion helped to make him the first major American hero of the war, but his publicity campaign and his first successes in the field also led Tokyo to focus more on defensive measures against his Southwest Pacific advance than on countering the moves of Admiral Chester W. Nimitz's forces in the Central Pacific. Japanese attention on MacArthur's offensive was justified in part because of its proximity to the heart of the Southern Resources Area, though the Central Pacific operations actually posed the more direct threat to interdicting all supply lines from Southeast Asia to Japan. Moreover, the advantages that might have accrued to Japan from operating on interior lines in defense of the Southern Resources Area, such as a shorter distance from bases of operations to front sectors and superior mobility in shifting units to different areas without exposing the main lines of communication, were negated by the Americans' introduction of new long-range submarines, the ingenious at-sea resupply system of the Third Fleet that enabled it to range the West Pacific for long periods, and Admiral Marc A. Mitscher's fast carrier force that could launch over nine hundred aircraft—all of which operated under Nimitz, not MacArthur. Except off Midway in June 1942 and the Marianas in June 1944, both of which were severe defeats, the Japanese Combined Fleet did not venture forth into the path of Nimitz's forces in the Central Pacific, but instead serviced and supported Japanese ground operations against MacArthur's New Guinea-Philippines axis of advance and against Admiral William F. Halsey's forces in the Solomons. The four large engagements in October 1944 collectively called the battle for Leyte Gulf, which pitted the Japanese and American fleets against each other in the greatest naval action in history, actually resulted from the Japanese navy's attempt to function in its traditional role of supporting the army, this time against MacArthur's invasion of the central Philippines.[15]

[14] Charles A. Willoughby, ed., *Reports of General MacArthur*, 4 vols. (Washington, D.C., 1966), 1:458-60, 464, 2:64-65, 3:665.

[15] John B. Lundstrom, *The First South Pacific Campaign: Pacific Fleet Strategy, December 1941-June 1942* (Annapolis, 1976),195-205; Morton, *Strategy and Command*, 444-53, 534-47, 584-91; Reynolds, "Continental Strategy," 14-16; C. Vann Woodward, *The Battle*

Just as American strategic planning did not fully consider logistical requirements in devising war plans in the 1920s and 1930s, so neither before nor during the war of 1941-1945 did the Japanese give a high priority to logistics. Indeed, had they done so, they would probably have realized that in its Southeast Asian and Pacific conquests Japan had overextended itself and that its current and future capabilities were inadequate for producing and distributing equipment and supplies to forces on the continental and island fronts. Compared to the European theater, the conflict in the Pacific was, indeed, a war of distances. The sea route from Batavia, Java, to Tokyo was 4,100 miles. The width of the southern reaches of the Japanese Empire at its greatest extent was 6,400 miles. The empire's north-south extremities were 5,300 miles apart. The oceanic perimeter of the Japanese advance at its zenith was 14,200 miles in length—equivalent to well over half the earth's circumference. Such enormous distances placed premiums on shipping and long-range aircraft, but by 1943 Japanese ships were being sunk at a faster rate than new ones could be built, and Japan never possessed long-range planes comparable in quality or quantity to those of the United States. In the Pacific war, Japan was severely handicapped by its inability to maintain long logistical lines. In ground operations, this was offset somewhat by the lower logistical needs in some categories for its army units, whose degree of mechanization and standard of living were generally not as high as similar American units.

When Japanese forces pushed westward into Burma and southward into New Guinea and the Solomons, they encountered logistical nightmares: great distances from supply centers, inhospitable terrain and weather that exerted constant, adverse influences on matériel and men. Supplies and equipment rapidly deteriorated, and prodigious engineering feats were required to develop air fields, harbors, and other military installations. In technology and engineering skills needed to overcome these challenges, the Japanese were far behind their Western adversaries. Tokyo had not considered this aspect of logistics in plotting advances into Southeast Asia and the Southwest Pacific.

Perhaps more important, the Japanese had overlooked medical logistics as a vital adjunct of military strategy. As a consequence, the rugged living conditions found in much of the Southern Resources Area and its

for *Leyte Gulf* (New York, 1965), 7-12, 40-41, 232-35. Perceptive on strategy as well as operations are Clark G. Reynolds, *The Fast Carriers: The Forging of an Air Navy* (New York, 1968); and Clay Blair, *Silent Victory: The U.S. Submarine War against Japan* (Philadelphia, 1975). See also H. P. Willmott, *Empires in the Balance: Japanese and Allied Pacific Strategies to April 1942* (Annapolis, 1982); H. P. Willmott, *The Barrier and the Javelin: Japanese and Allied Pacific Strategies, February to June 1942* (Annapolis, 1983).

defense perimeter produced appalling troop losses to disease. Awaiting both sides were a host of diseases—malaria, dengue fever, bacillary and amoebic dysentery, scrub typhus, and yellow fever, to name a few. But Japanese medicine and public health were not nearly as advanced as those of the Western powers, and because Japanese lines of communication were interdicted with increasing frequency after the first year of combat, Japanese units at the front suffered from the scarcity or absence of medical facilities and supplies.

In the island warfare in the Pacific, the Japanese were superior to their American and Allied opponents in some categories: they proved more adept at night fighting both on the ground and at sea, utilized a higher proportion of their personnel in combat rather than in service and support roles, and generally demonstrated a stronger will to fight than did their adversaries when forces of similar size and firepower engaged each other. They also gradually learned that a more effective defense against landing assaults backed by overwhelming naval and air firepower was to develop interlocking positions rather than to expend their forces at the beaches. By the time of the Okinawa campaign they had mastered this defensive technique, but it was too late to affect the course of the war. Another aspect of island defensive strategy that belatedly received attention was the value of *Tokko*, or special-attack suicide operations by land, sea, and air. The *Kamikazes*, the only sizable *Tokko* forces used, first went into action in late 1944 and showed devastating potential, with American and British naval units never able to devise a sound defense against them, as was apparent off Luzon and Okinawa. If developed earlier, as the fortunes of war shifted against Japan in late 1942, the *Tokko*, in effect manned missiles, might conceivably have proven so costly to the Allies that a negotiated peace would have been possible.

On the other hand, the recurring piecemeal nature of Japanese ground, sea, and air defensive operations demonstrated a serious lack of coordination and cooperation between the army and navy commands (air units were integral parts of those two services) that made American interservice rivalries appear mild in contrast. In one of the most crucial command breakdowns, General Tomoyuki Yamashita's able leadership and judicious strategy for defending the Philippines were undone by Imperial General Headquarters in Tokyo, which disliked him and his plans, by the Southern Army commander in Saigon who insisted on an all-out battle for Leyte instead of concentrating forces to defend the strategically more valuable island of Luzon, and by the admiral in Manila who instead of obeying Yamashita's orders to evacuate committed his naval troops to a suicidal defense of the city. In numerous ground, naval, and air engagements, Japanese forces failed to achieve concentration

718

before battle, resulting in poorly timed, usually ineffective attacks in piecemeal fashion that reflected lack of joint planning far beyond the immediate combat area.

The Japanese, moreover, unrealistically decided to defend an island as though it were an isolated citadel, instead of a strongpoint in a defense-in-depth system of interlocking firepower. Instead of developing clusters of mutually supportive island bases around their Pacific perimeter, Japanese commanders were ordered to prepare concentrated defenses on single islands separated by large distances and with vulnerable lines of communication. Amphibious defense, like amphibious assault, demanded close coordination of ground, sea, and air units, but by the time of invasion the defending Japanese army garrison frequently was isolated from its naval and air support and supply. In short, Japan had no viable strategy of amphibious defensive warfare to counter American amphibious offensives.[16]

During the early part of the war, propaganda was primarily an instrument of Japanese national strategy. It proved of mixed value. In the later stage of the conflict propaganda was also used in the military realm with some decidedly negative results. At first Japanese propaganda had the purpose of inspiring the Japanese people to greater war efforts and of converting Asians to the benefits of the Co-Prosperity Sphere. By the fall of 1943, when Nimitz began to advance in the Central Pacific, the defenders of the Southern Resources Area had suffered a steady succession of defeats, starting with the naval setbacks in the Coral Sea and off Midway in May-June 1942. As customary, officers delivered exhortations to their men about loyalty to the Emperor and to *Bushido*, the hallowed *samurai* code, but Imperial General Headquarters also decided to boost morale through the use of propaganda and censorship in revising general war news relayed to field commands. Tokyo reported steady progress toward the final defeat of Japan's enemies, and field headquarters increasingly amended their after-action reports to present optimistic results to superior echelons. With the invasion of the Marianas in June 1944, there was a marked rise in the distortions of operational developments from Tokyo to the field forces and vice versa, creating a bizarre atmosphere of unreality that sometimes affected strategic and logistical considerations because it became difficult to separate myth from

[16] Willoughby, *Reports of General MacArthur*, 1:40-43, 2:54-58, 3:561-74; Morton, *Strategy and Command*, 235-36; Masatake Okumiya and Jiro Horikoshi, *Zero!* (New York, 1957), 239-54; U.S. Strategic Bombing Survey, *Interrogations of Japanese Officials*, 2 vols. (Washington, D.C., 1946), passim. See also Saburo Hayashi and Alvin D. Coox, *Kogun: The Japanese Army in the Pacific War* (Quantico, Va., 1959); Raymond J. O'Connor, ed., *The Japanese Navy in World War II* (Annapolis, 1970).

reality. When Japan surrendered, many of its fighting men in the field as well as most citizens of the home islands were in a state of shock and disbelief, having accepted the stories of glorious victories since 1943 despite the destructive air raids on their major cities.[17]

IV

The chief aims of America's national strategy in the Pacific war were to defeat Japan as soon as possible within the constraints imposed by the higher-priority European theater; to keep China in the war, while assisting its return to big-power status under the aegis of Chiang Kai-shek and reopening the door to American trade there; to restore American access to the rich resources of Southeast Asia, while prodding the British to set the pace among the European colonial powers in planning toward self-determination for their colonies, as the United States had pledged to the Philippines; to maintain the valuable wartime relationships with Australia and New Zealand; to encourage the Soviet Union to enter the conflict against Japan; and to preserve America's augmented role in Pacific affairs through dominance of planning in wartime military strategy and in arrangements for postwar administration and security in occupied Japan and the West Pacific.

Although the United States was committed to defeating Germany first in its grand strategy with Britain and by early 1945 had sent the preponderance of its strength in army ground and air forces to Europe, the balance in America's overseas deployment up to the autumn of 1943 was in favor of the Pacific theater. Through the first year of fighting American resources had been channeled mainly against Japan, though by mid-1943 the bulk of its overseas shipments began to go across the Atlantic. Nevertheless, as of December 31, 1943, American military resources remained about equally divided between the European and Pacific theaters: 1.8 million personnel (army, army air forces, navy, and marine), 17 army divisions, 8,800 army and navy aircraft, and 515 combat ships involved in the war against Germany compared to 1.9 million personnel, 16.5 army and marine divisions, 7,900 army, navy, and marine planes, and 713 warships committed to Pacific operations. The compromising of the Anglo-American agreement on a maximum effort against Germany first resulted from such unforeseen developments as the Allies' inability to stop Japanese offensives without greater firepower, the sustained intensity of the American public's interest in defeating Japan, and perhaps most important, the long delay of Anglo-American leaders in reaching

[17] L. D. Meo, *Japan's Radio War on Australia, 1941-1945* (Melbourne, 1968), 26-32; Woodward, *Battle for Leyte Gulf*, 18-20; Butow, *Tojo*, 411-16; Ienaga, *Pacific War*, 98-106.

an agreement on a specific plan and date for the massive cross-Channel invasion of France. As anticipated in prewar planning, the main American naval and marine strength was in the Pacific throughout the Second World War, but the drain of army ground and air units to the war with Japan during the first two years had not been expected. More significant in affecting strategic planning for the defeat of Germany was the logistical crisis created by the heavy absorption of shipping, landing craft, and service troops in Pacific operations.[18]

The fixation of President Roosevelt on the potential of China's wartime and postwar roles in East Asia led to deepening American involvement in Chinese political and military affairs after 1942 when, ironically, Japan was desperately trying to lessen its entanglements there. Although Stalin and Churchill disparaged China's worth to the Allied cause and the American Joint Chiefs often disagreed with their commander in chief's views on China's military value, Roosevelt endeavored to support Chinese defensive efforts, especially Chiang's forces, with American arms and advisors. But American assistance, because of the theater's low priority in Anglo-American strategic planning and the difficulty in supplying China via the Himalayan air route or the overland route across North Burma, was inadequate to alter the combat situation on the China front appreciably. A grandiose scheme to stage the main B-29 raids on Japan from Chinese bases proved disappointing. General Joseph W. Stilwell and other American commanders and diplomats stationed in wartime China generally failed to comprehend the intricacies of Chinese politics and to bring about Nationalist-Communist coordination for decisive offensive operations. Roosevelt persisted in viewing China as a major Allied power, but American efforts in that country were no more influential than those of Japan in their impact on Chinese military and political conditions. China seemed bent on working out its own destiny almost as if there had never been a Japanese or American presence there.[19]

America's access to other sources and to synthetics obviated its immediate need for Southeast Asia's strategic raw materials, and the only

[18] Kent R. Greenfield, *American Strategy in World War II: A Reconsideration* (Baltimore, 1963), 4-5, 7; Samuel E. Morison, *Strategy and Compromise* (Boston, 1958), 17-22; Maurice Matloff, *Strategic Planning for Coalition Warfare, 1943-1944. USAWW2: The War Department* (Washington, D.C., 1959), 395-401; Richard M. Leighton and Robert W. Coakley, *Global Logistics and Strategy, 1940-1943. USAWW2: The War Department* (Washington, D.C., 1955), 13-17, 662-68, 709-721, 732-35; Hayes, *History of the Joint Chiefs,* 104-120.

[19] Thorne, *Allies of a Kind,* 170-83, 322-27, 424-39, 563-80; Michael Schaller, *The U.S. Crusade in China, 1938-1945* (New York, 1979), 90-99, 122-23, 171-78; Herbert Feis, *The China Tangle: The American Effort in China from Pearl Harbor to the Marshall Mission* (New York, 1965), 3-13, 55-62, 290-303; Barbara W. Tuchman, *Stilwell and the American Experience in China, 1911-45* (New York, 1970), 237-38, 491-502.

thrust into the heart of the Southern Resources Area, the invasion of Borneo, did not come until the final months of the war in 1945. Otherwise, major Allied operations bypassed the region on eastern and northern envelopments, first hindering and then cutting its lines of communication to Japan. All through the war years Roosevelt and other American leaders voiced anticolonial rhetoric together with pious statements about Philippine independence that irritated the British and the French and Dutch governments in exile. But, despite its own revolutionary origins, the United States condoned and assisted in the restoration of the British, Dutch, and French colonial regimes in Southeast Asia upon Japan's capitulation, primarily to get American supplies of the area's natural resources flowing again and to ensure Western European support against possible postwar expansionist moves by the Soviet Union. The postwar nationalist upheavals in Southeast Asia found the United States basically in the same dilemma as during the war period, moralistically espousing anticolonialism but bound to the European colonial powers by economic and security ties. It has been suggested that temporary American occupation of the lands of the Southern Resources Area during the months of the immediate aftermath of Japan's surrender would have ameliorated the extreme anticolonial tendencies of the formative independence movements. But as China had, the Southeast Asian nations likely would have gone their ways regardless of American efforts, particularly since the United States' commitment to anticolonialism was largely theoretical. During the war years the American political and military leaders' assumption that in general all British positions on strategy in the war against Japan were colored by their desire to restore or even expand their imperial holdings in postwar Asia did much to exacerbate tensions in the Anglo-American alliance.[20]

Whereas compromise was the key ingredient in Anglo-American strategy making in the war against Germany and Italy, the strategic direction of the Allied war in the Pacific was carefully monopolized by the United States. Early in 1942 this concession was wrung from the British, and the Combined Chiefs of Staff delegated to the American Joint Chiefs the responsibility for conducting operations in the Pacific. In dealing with the Pacific theater commanders, the respective American service chiefs acted as the executive agents of the Joint Chiefs; thus Nimitz, commanding the Pacific Ocean Areas, received his directives and orders from Admiral Ernest J. King, chief of naval operations, and MacArthur got his from General George C. Marshall, army chief of staff.[21]

[20] Iriye, *Power and Culture*, 247-48; Thorne, *Allies of a Kind*, 224-28, 699-730.
[21] Hayes, *History of the Joint Chiefs*, 88-90; Morton, *Strategy and Command*, 240-44.

The American grip on strategy and policy in the war with Japan in the Pacific was seldom relaxed to permit contributions by the twelve other allied nations in that conflict, thereby provoking sometimes serious stresses in alliance relations not only with Britain but also with China, the Dutch and French exile governments, New Zealand, and Australia. While Nimitz's base of operations was Hawaii, MacArthur's was Australia—a country that was trying to lessen its ties with Britain as the war began. Australia became invaluable in supplying troops, war matériel, and reverse lend-lease assistance for the Southwest Pacific theater. Because of its generous and important contributions, Australia felt it deserved a voice in deciding the direction of the war with Japan. But except for setting up an innocuous Pacific War Council as a sounding board for the lesser allies, Roosevelt and his military chiefs consistently thwarted Australia's attempts to play a more prominent part in Pacific war and postwar planning. Bilateral differences over the nature of consultative machinery, command arrangements, logistical and strategic priorities, and MacArthur's authority as theater commander all were inevitably resolved in accordance with American objectives. A similar relationship evolved between the United States and New Zealand, although its leaders were less vociferous than Canberra in their protests. Throughout the conflict the United States treated the other nations at war against Japan as unequal allies. In view of its wartime coalition experience, it is not surprising that at the San Francisco Conference in the spring of 1945 Australia emerged as one of the chief advocates on behalf of the smaller nations' rights and powers in the United Nations organization. During the final half year of the war even Britain's position in the Pacific had become so weak that Royal Navy units were permitted to operate in those waters in support of the United States Navy only after lengthy negotiations; to the end, Admiral King was reluctant to allow British participation in the "American theater."[22]

If Japan's flirtation with the Soviet Union during the later stage of the war was quixotic, American interest in obtaining the help of the USSR in defeating Japan was unrealistic to say the least. By the early autumn of 1944, Nimitz, MacArthur, and their planning staffs, together with the Joint Chiefs and their planners, were generally agreed that aerial bombing and naval blockade would not suffice to force Japan's surrender and that immense invasions of Kyushu and Honshu would be needed. Tentatively setting the first operation for November 1945 and the second for early 1946, the Pentagon and the field commanders envisaged those assaults

[22] Roger J. Bell, *Unequal Allies: Australian-American Relations and the Pacific War* (Melbourne, 1977), 226-32; Hayes, *Allies of a Kind*, 630-38; Thorne, *History of the Joint Chiefs*, 252-67, 364-69, 479-87, 645-51; Morison, *Two-Ocean War*, 423-24.

as difficult and likely to produce high American casualties. Both groups favored a Soviet attack on Manchuria to prevent the sizable Japanese forces there and in North China from reinforcing the defenders of the home islands.

At Yalta in February 1945, Roosevelt, with his military advisors' backing, agreed to Stalin's price for Soviet intervention: the Kuriles, South Sakhalin, Outer Mongolia, Dairen, Port Arthur, and Manchuria's main railways. The deal, which contradicted territorial pledges to Chiang at Cairo in late 1943, hurt the prestige of the Nationalist regime and caused further deterioration in its relations with the Western Allies. By July, with the success of the atomic-bomb test and evidence that Japan's economy was collapsing fast, Pentagon planners began reevaluating the need for Soviet assistance. By then, however, the Kyushu assault preparations were developing their own momentum, with the operational plan undergoing final revision and huge forces assembling at staging bases from Okinawa and Luzon to Oahu. The invasion plan was not rescinded, so some rationale for Soviet help remained. The rush of events overcame further reconsiderations; in quick order America subjected Japan to the horror of atomic warfare and Soviet forces rapidly moved into Manchuria, Outer Mongolia, northern Korea, the Kuriles, and South Sakhalin. In retrospect, it seems that once the Kyushu assault plan was drafted, military strategy essentially became dominant, with American national strategy bound inflexibly to it in its acceptance of Soviet intervention.[23]

As early as 1943, the State, War, and Navy departments in Washington undertook studies on the administration of occupied Japan and on America's postwar security needs in the Pacific. By late 1944, when the State-War-Navy Coordinating Committee was established to formulate policy on matters common to all three departments, especially future occupations of Germany and Japan, American research on the postwar governance of Japan and the West Pacific was far in advance of that done by its allies. Well before the United Nations Charter was approved at San Francisco, Washington was preparing to secure strategic positions in the West Pacific through trusteeships over the Ryukyus, Bonins, Marianas, Marshalls, and Carolines, as well as through agreements on American bases in the Philippines after that nation's impending independence.

Specialists on Japan, such as Hugh Borton and Joseph C. Grew,

[23] Louis Morton, "The Soviet Intervention in the War with Japan," *Foreign Affairs* 40 (July 1962), 652-66; Schaller, *U.S. Crusade*, 209-212; Iriye, *Power and Culture*, 181-82, 220, 230-33, 241-47, 252; Peter W. Vigor and Christopher Donnelly, "The Manchurian Campaign and Its Relevance to Modern Strategy," *Comparative Strategy* 2 (1980), 163-65.

724

helped to mold an enlightened, moderate approach by the State-War-Navy Coordinating Committee to policy for the occupation of Japan. The American-controlled occupation machinery would work through the emperor and existing governmental structure to demilitarize and democratize Japan and to prepare it for readmittance into the framework of international relations and trade. The occupation directives drafted by the Coordinating Committee were based largely on liberal, democratic concepts and were harsh only regarding trials of war criminals and purges of militarists and ultra-nationalists. It was unfortunate that the Japanese government after Tojo's downfall did not know of the benevolent occupation planned, for moderates on both sides were ready to terminate the war and to reorient Japan toward its position in the 1920s of cooperative diplomatic and commercial ties with the West.[24]

The policy of unconditional surrender, proclaimed by Roosevelt at Casablanca in early 1943, was viewed by most Washington planners working on occupation guidelines as far more flexible than the Japanese imagined. The latter interpretations ranged from annihilation of their people to abolition of the imperial system and punishment of the emperor as a war criminal. Unfortunately for Japanese perceptions, the State-War-Navy planners were shaping postwar policies in an environment closed to public notice, while what was communicated openly by the American government and press was generally negative about Japan's prospects after its defeat. American public opinion, as reflected mainly in the press, was strongly influenced by racist, ethnocentric, and war-bred feelings that displayed little sympathy for the Japanese, and Washington officials, in part because they did not want to invite charges of appeasement toward the Japanese militarist leadership, made no move to disavow or revise the no-surrender policy. President Truman missed an opportunity to send a favorable signal to Japan when, on poor counsel from his close advisors, he omitted from the Potsdam Declaration in July 1945 any reference to the American government's intention to retain and use the emperor during the occupation. Since early 1943 American propaganda had portrayed the United States as irrevocably bound to the unconditional surrender of Japan, a development that, in fact, was not anticipated in the Coordinating Committee's deliberations and did not take place. But the continuing lip service paid to the policy by top American officials and propagandists was influential in keeping both sides from direct bilateral communications that might have terminated the war well before mid-August 1945.[25]

[24] Hugh Borton, *American Presurrender Planning for Postwar Japan* (New York, 1967), 3-37; Iriye, *Power and Culture*, 201-202, 208-213, 225-27.
[25] Kazuo Kawai, "Mokusatsu: Japan's Response to the Potsdam Declaration," *Pacific*

V

American military strategy in the Pacific was affected for three years by a Joint Chiefs' directive of March 1942 establishing two theaters of operations: the Southwest Pacific Area, to be headed by General MacArthur, and the Pacific Ocean Areas, to be commanded by Admiral Nimitz, who also was to head the Pacific Fleet and the Central Pacific subtheater. The Joint Chiefs violated the principle of unity of command primarily because of navy objections to selecting the senior officer in the region, MacArthur, as overall Pacific commander. Idealistically, the Joint Chiefs declared that as a body they would serve as the Supreme Command for Pacific planning and operations as a whole. But the Joint Chiefs had a chairman who lacked centralizing authority and functioned mainly as a moderator, and their system of working committees evolved into a complex and cumbersome arrangement. The consequences were that the Washington command post for the Pacific became diffused in its authority, entangled in interservice friction, and handicapped in quick decision making by debates and compromises on revising theater proposals and its own recommendations. No single authority in the Pacific was empowered to decide between conflicting plans and needs of the theaters or to coordinate their operations.[26] Most senior Pacific officers were critical of the system. MacArthur charged that "of all the faulty decisions of the war perhaps the most unexplainable one was the failure to unify the command in the Pacific. . . . It resulted in divided effort, the waste, diffusion, and duplication of force, and the consequent extension of the war with added casualties and cost."[27] He did not add, however, that he wanted unity of command only if he were the supreme commander or that naval leaders had some justification for not entrusting the Pacific Fleet to him and his American army-controlled headquarters.

War Plan Orange had called for a single American axis of advance by way of the Central Pacific, but the Joint Chiefs' directive of March 1942 set the stage for dual offensives through the Southwest and Central Pacific. If large Japanese forces had been redeployed from China to the Pacific, the strategy of dividing the American striking power on widely separated axes would have been unwise. But with the overwhelming

Historical Review 19 (November 1950), 409-414; Butow, *Japan's Decision*, 189-209; Hanson W. Baldwin, *Great Mistakes of the War* (New York, 1949), 14-25; Brian L. Villa, "The U.S. Army, Unconditional Surrender, and the Potsdam Declaration," *Journal of American History* 63 (June 1976), 66-92.

[26] Hayes, *History of the Joint Chiefs*, 93-103, 265-72; Willoughby, *Reports of General MacArthur*, 1:30-31; Morton, *Strategy and Command*, 244-63; Louis Morton, "Pacific Command: A Study in Interservice Relations," (Harmon Memorial Lecture, U.S. Air Force Academy, 1961), 6-29.

[27] Douglas MacArthur, *Reminiscences* (New York, 1964), 172-73.

strength of MacArthur's and Nimitz's commands by autumn 1943, the offensives in the Central and South Pacific were effective in keeping the Japanese off balance along their extensive cordon in the Pacific. The American operations from mid-1943 to mid-1944, for example, demonstrate that, despite its flaws, the divided-command arrangement had some assets, although often the commands' teamwork was more inadvertent than planned. During Operation Cartwheel, from summer 1943 to spring 1944, Southwest and South Pacific offensives on New Guinea, New Britain, the Admiralties, and the Solomons attracted enemy air power from Central Pacific bases, allowing Nimitz's units to seize the Gilberts and the Marshalls without serious air opposition. On the other hand, the Pacific Fleet's destructive raids from Truk to the Palaus forced the Japanese navy out of the waters north of New Guinea and permitted MacArthur's army to advance along the coast of Dutch New Guinea without strong naval protection. His assault on Biak, in turn, siphoned off Japanese air strength intended for the defense of the Marianas. The Central Pacific forces invaded Saipan in June 1944 just as the Japanese First Mobile Fleet was preparing to escort troopships from the Moluccas to northwestern New Guinea and to attack MacArthur's beachhead on Biak and the small supporting force of the American Seventh Fleet. Upon getting news of Nimitz's move against Saipan, the Japanese navy rushed northeastward, subsequently meeting disaster in the battle of the Philippine Sea while MacArthur's troops completed their conquest of Dutch New Guinea.[28]

The Pacific issue that absorbed the Joint Chiefs' attention by spring 1944 was whether Luzon or Formosa was the better invasion target prior to direct operations against Japan. King had long objected to any landings in the Philippines, and by May 1944 Marshall and General Henry H. Arnold, the army air chief, thought any advance by way of Luzon would be slower and more costly than one from the Marianas to Formosa. MacArthur asserted that humanitarian, political, and strategic considerations required Luzon's capture, and both President Roosevelt and Admiral William D. Leahy seemed favorable to his argument at Pearl Harbor that July. The Joint Chiefs continued to debate the alternatives until early October when King, Nimitz, and their planners concluded that a Formosa assault would not be logistically feasible in the near future. Thereupon the Joint Chiefs issued a directive authorizing the Luzon invasion. As feared by the plan's opponents, the Luzon campaign became the costliest of the Pacific war in American troops killed in action.

[28] E. B. Potter and Chester W. Nimitz, *Triumph in the Pacific: The Navy's Struggle against Japan* (Englewood Cliffs, N.J., 1963), 101-103.

Whether the conquest of Luzon was necessary would remain moot, but the question of necessity would be raised about other operations also, especially the invasion of the Palaus. In fact, the only island assaults whose necessity has not been questioned are the Marianas operations.[29]

In his 1943-1944 campaigns from Northeast New Guinea through Morotai, MacArthur brilliantly exploited relatively meager and unbalanced logistical support to the maximum and neutralized Japanese strongholds by shrewd envelopments. But from early 1945 onward, when he had strong forces and adequate supplies, he ordered operations south of Luzon that appear tangential. Although the U.S. Sixth Army needed reinforcements in its fight against Yamashita's formidable army on Luzon, MacArthur sent the American Eighth Army to assault bypassed enemy garrisons in the southern Philippines. Against the advice of Washington planners, he dispatched the Australian I Corps to Borneo where it sustained heavy losses in taking Tarakan, Brunei Bay, and Balikpapan. He also ordered the Australian First Army to annihilate the isolated enemy units on Bougainville, New Britain, and Northeast New Guinea with resultant high casualties. Had the Joint Chiefs expected MacArthur's operations south of Luzon, they probably would have concurred with King's demand to terminate the Southwest Pacific offensive after the conquest of Dutch New Guinea.[30]

In spite of the Joint Chiefs' establishment of a command structure for American forces in what was designated the China-Burma-India theater, the American contribution to military strategy for that region was minimal. Its logistical priority was always low, and there was no planning coordination between the two Pacific headquarters and General Stilwell's China-Burma-India Command. In early 1944 the Joint Chiefs considered a plan for an invasion of the South China coast by Nimitz's forces that would have involved collaboration with the China-Burma-India Command, but it was shelved when the Japanese mounted an offensive in the region that summer. The British Southeast Asia Command under Admiral Lord Mountbatten seldom enjoyed harmonious relations with Stilwell

[29] Robert R. Smith, "Luzon Versus Formosa," in *Command Decisions*, ed. Kent R. Greenfield (Washington, D.C., 1960), 461-77; Pogue, *George C. Marshall*, 3:451-54; Hayes, *Allies of a Kind*, 603-624; Clark G. Reynolds, "MacArthur as Maritime Strategist," *Naval War College Review* 32 (March-April 1980), 81-82; D. Clayton James, *The Years of MacArthur*, 3 vols. (Boston, 1970-85), 2:521-42.

[30] Robert R. Smith, *Triumph in the Philippines. USAWW2: The War in the Pacific* (Washington, D.C., 1963), 363-64, 389, 539, 584-85; Gavin Long, *The Final Campaigns. Australia in the War of 1939-1945*, series 1 (Canberra, 1963), 43-44, 389, 547, 609; Samuel E. Morison, *The Liberation of the Philippines: Luzon, Mindanao, the Visayas, 1944-1945. History of the United States Naval Operations in World War II*, vol. 13 (Boston, 1959), 214; D. Clayton James, "MacArthur's Lapses from an Envelopment Strategy in 1945," *Parameters* 10 (June 1980), 26-32.

and his staff, and neither group achieved good communications with Chiang's headquarters. All too often national prejudice and mutual distrust and resentment characterized relations between senior British, American, and Chinese commanders.

In the summer of 1945 the Anglo-American Combined Chiefs transferred the East Indies' operational jurisdiction from MacArthur to Mountbatten. The war ended before the Southeast Asia Command could launch its planned operations to retake Malaya and Singapore. Before the Dutch returned after Japan's capitulation, British forces moved into Java and Sumatra to oversee troop surrenders and to restore civil order, but caught the brunt of the early violence of the rising Indonesian nationalist movement. Some historians have lamented the lack of better cooperation among the British, American, and Chinese commands, but none has shown how a pooling of their few available military resources beyond higher-priority commitments could have significantly affected the military situation in the region. Each national group was too suspicious of the others' motives to coordinate efforts for a decisive joint venture. Their most notable endeavor together, the recapture of Burma in 1944-1945, was characterized by friction and half-hearted cooperation.[31]

Possessing great superiority in firepower, mobility, and material resources in 1943-1945, the Americans could afford some flaws in their strategy and command arrangements, particularly since they were privy to many of the Japanese plans, moves, unit strengths, and orders of battle. Long before the Pearl Harbor raid American code and cipher experts had penetrated diplomatic signals enciphered on Japan's Purple machine. This decrypting system of gathering intelligence data was known as Magic. Throughout the war Magic was a valuable Allied source of intelligence, though largely on nonmilitary matters because the signal intercepts were messages between the Japanese Foreign Office and its diplomats. Although Magic's existence has long been known, only in recent years have nonofficial researchers gained access to the large body of information derived by American cryptanalysts from Japan's wartime navy and army codes. At the time this data was officially termed Ultra intelligence, though it should not be confused with the better-known Ultra material acquired by breaking German messages enciphered on the Enigma device. The information obtained through Magic and especially Ultra intercepts was vital to the American fleet at Midway and other battles, to its submarines in their devastating campaign against Japan's merchant marine, and to Central and Southwest Pacific army ground and

[31] Hayes, *Allies of a Kind*, 437-38, 569-79, 588-90; Schaller, *U.S. Crusade*, 52-53, 102-110, 138, 144, 151-55, 164-75; Thorne, *History of the Joint Chiefs*, 333-39, 450-55, 586-92.

air forces in numerous operations. Ultra was responsible also for an incalculable loss to Japanese strategic leadership: the fatal aerial ambush of Admiral Yamamoto, Combined Fleet commander and a brilliant naval strategist, over Bougainville in April 1943. Undoubtedly much of what remains to be learned about the Pacific conflict will emerge from the formerly closed American signal intelligence records and, like post-1973 writings about the Ultra of the European war, will compel revisions of earlier evaluations of strategy, tactics, and command on both sides.[32]

In spite of the varied implications of the Pacific Ultra, scholars in the future may well conclude that the most important contribution of the Pacific war to the history of military strategy was the American system of amphibious warfare. The maritime strategy adopted by the American High Command would have amounted to little more than the unrealistic Color series of war plans had strategic and tactical doctrine not already been developed for assaulting enemy-held islands, especially strongly defended ones. In the early 1930s at Quantico, Virginia, Fleet Marine Force leaders began to work on the problems of conducting amphibious offensives, which they found required new combat techniques and a high degree of combined-arms coordination, as well as special landing craft and weapons. The Tarawa invasion of November 1943 showed that Nimitz's navy and marine forces still had much to learn, but by the time of their assaults on the Marianas the next summer they had mastered the intricacies of amphibious warfare. Meanwhile, in the more than eighty amphibious landings by Southwest Pacific units, army troops with strong land-based air and only moderate naval support demonstrated successful variations of amphibious attack.[33]

The Pacific war will always remain distinctive for the introduction of the atomic bomb, which, in turn, precipitated a postwar revolution in military strategy. President Truman and Secretary of War Stimson established the official rationale for its use, maintaining that it would end the war quickly and save many times the number of lives lost at Hiroshima and Nagasaki, particularly if the Kyushu and Honshu invasions had to be staged. Growing evidence since August 1945, however, has indicated that Japan, under the pressures of aerial destruction, naval

[32] Ronald Lewin, *The American Magic: Codes, Ciphers, and the Defeat of Japan* (New York, 1982), 14-16, 106, 223-25, 246-47, 293-95; W. J. Holmes, *Double-Edged Secrets: U.S. Naval Intelligence Operations in the Pacific during World War II* (Annapolis, 1979), 125-26.

[33] Jeter A. Isely and Philip A. Crowl, *The U.S. Marines and Amphibious War: Its Theory and Practice in the Pacific* (Princeton, 1951), 45-71, 580-90; Daniel E. Barbey, *MacArthur's Amphibious Navy: Seventh Amphibious Force Operations, 1943-1945* (Annapolis, 1969), 11-20, 43-49, 357-58. See also George C. Dyer, *The Amphibians Came to Conquer: The Story of Admiral Richmond Kelly Turner*, 2 vols. (Washington, D.C., 1972).

blockade, and the Soviet Union's entry into the war, may have surrendered shortly without the need for resorting to atomic warfare. Revisionist scholars, moreover, have argued that Washington's decision to use the atomic weapons may have been influenced by changing attitudes toward the Soviet Union in what later proved to be the formative stage of the Cold War.[34]

VI

This essay has portrayed no one on either side as playing a paramount role in the strategies of the war in the Pacific. On the whole, the strategies adopted by America and Japan had developed over many years before 1940 and involved the efforts of scores of civilians and soldiers. Indeed, the delineation of individual contributions in the realm of American military strategy from 1941 to 1945 not only is difficult but reveals no persons who truly stand out. The Joint Chiefs system favored strategy making by compromise and by committee, or group thinking. Although adulatory works on MacArthur claim he was one of the great strategists of the war, in truth his role usually was confined to implementing strategic directives from the Joint Chiefs—and in the subordinate theater of Pacific operations. Some biographers have declared, for example, that the decision to bypass the stronghold of Rabaul was made by MacArthur, but actually the Joint Chiefs ordered its envelopment after overruling his proposal for an assault on it. Conceivably, strong cases could be made for Admirals King and Yamamoto as the principal shapers of naval strategy. But King, in looking back, saw the formulation of the overall American military strategy of the war as a series of compromises in which he lost more arguments than he won. On the other hand, Yamamoto's death at the midpoint of the war relegates to conjecture all questions of how he might have adapted his strategy to the later developments of the conflict.[35]

The consequences of the Pacific war for the national strategies of Japan and the United States, despite considerable losses in human and material resources, were more favorable than for the former European

---

[34] Gregg Herken, *The Winning Weapon: The Atomic Bomb in the Cold War, 1945-1950* (New York, 1982), 4-42; Martin J. Sherwin, *A World Destroyed: The Atomic Bomb and the Grand Alliance* (New York, 1975), 61-63; Butow, *Japan's Decision*, 142-209; U.S. Strategic Bombing Survey, *Japan's Struggle to End the War* (Washington, D.C., 1946), 3-13; Louis Morton, "The Decision to Use the Atomic Bomb," *Foreign Affairs* 25 (January 1957), 334-53.

[35] On King and Yamashita, see Ernest J. King and Walter M. Whitehill, *Fleet Admiral King: A Naval Record* (New York, 1952); Thomas B. Buell, *Master of Sea Power: A Biography of Fleet Admiral Ernest J. King* (Boston, 1980); Hiroyuki Agawa, *The Reluctant Admiral: Yamamoto and the Imperial Navy* (New York, 1980).

imperialist powers in the Far East, who lost both their colonies and their lucrative economic dominance of much of that region. The Japanese expansionists' old aim of controlling China died in the morass of the Sino-Japanese war of 1937-1945 and was buried by the postwar emergence of the Chinese Communist state and the expanded Soviet presence in Northeast Asia. But the national objectives pursued by Japan's moderate and internationalist leaders of the 1920s were largely realized in the war's aftermath. Following the American-controlled occupation of 1945-1952, Japan began a phenomenal economic boom that propelled its gross national product to the third highest in the world and that gave it profitable economic penetrations into Southeast Asia and strongly competitive trade relations with the West. Far more beneficial than the Anglo-Japanese alliance of 1902, its 1951 security pact with the West's most powerful nation enabled Japan to rely primarily on American forces for its defense and thereby to devote most of its national budget to nonmilitary needs.

In the wake of the Second World War the United States firmly established its strategic control over much of the Central and West Pacific. More important, in lieu of Roosevelt's illusion of a strong pro-American China, the United States gained in Japan a strong ally that was committed to capitalism, anticommunism, and a uniquely Japanese version of democracy. While Britain, America's key partner against the Axis, declined steadily after the war in political and economic influence, the United States, for the first time in its history, found itself allied with a non-Western power that was perhaps its most valuable friend in the ongoing strategic maneuvering against the communist states and its virtual tutor in how to turn trade profits. Both Japan and America seemed to have returned to building the framework of international cooperation that was begun in the 1920s but interrupted by the Great Depression and militarism between 1931 and 1945.

PART FIVE

Since 1945

25. The First Two Generations of Nuclear Strategists

LAWRENCE FREEDMAN

IN JULY 1945, the first atomic bomb was tested in New Mexico. The next month the second and third weapons off the production line were dropped on Japan. Since then no atomic weapons have been used in anger, although tens of thousands have been accumulated by the major powers and their destructiveness and sophistication increased immensely. The study of nuclear strategy is therefore the study of the nonuse of these weapons. Suppositions about their actual employment in combat may influence their peacetime role, but historical experience provides minimal guidance.

The lack of actual campaigns involving nuclear weapons and the problems inherent in any attempt to make sense of how such a campaign might develop in the future has not inhibited the development of nuclear strategy. Indeed, the quest for a nuclear strategy that can serve definite political objectives without triggering a holocaust has occupied some of the best minds of our time. By and large the leaders in this field have been civilians rather than the military, because the issues involved relate more to the character of international politics and the nature of higher decision making in times of extreme crisis than to the employment of force along traditional lines for traditional purposes.

This essay will only consider nuclear weapons as a problem in strategy, that is, in terms of military means to be related to political ends, rather than as a problem in ethics or culture or disarmament although of course a rich literature exists in all of these areas. Second, it will focus on the dominant issue in Western nuclear strategy, which revolves around the dependence of the North Atlantic Treaty Organization (NATO) on the threat to use nuclear weapons first in an effort to contain a Soviet conventional invasion, despite the evident risk of a Soviet nuclear counterattack. The strategists and strategies examined are largely those of the United States, as these have been the most important and innovative over the past four decades. It is difficult enough in one essay to do justice to this central strategic debate; it would be impossible to cover the parallel debates in the Soviet Union, France, the United Kingdom, and China, let alone the relevance of nuclear weapons to security debates beyond the East-West conflict.[1]

I

The origins of nuclear strategy go back to well before the formal arrival of the nuclear age on August 6, 1945. The bombs that destroyed Hiroshima and Nagasaki clearly represented a dramatic leap in capabilities for mass destruction, but their implications could still be understood in terms of the prevailing theories of strategic air power.

The theorists of strategic bombardment of the 1920s and 1930s had established certain precepts that the experience of World War II qualified but did not completely overturn: in the air the advantages lay with the offense rather than the defense; relevant targets for an air offense could be the enemy's political and economic centers as much as his military forces; attacks on these targets could provide an independent and distinctive contribution to victory. It had been in overstating these precepts that the air power enthusiasts had been in error. The bomber could not always get through and civil populations were more resilient in the face of bombardment than the professional warriors had supposed. Air power was a devastating instrument of attrition, but not necessarily of decisive shock, and thus was incapable of bringing about victory on its own accord.

With the arrival of the atomic bomb it was argued that the enthusiasts had not been in error—merely premature. Nuclear weapons would still depend on aircraft for delivery and there might still be a battle before they reached their targets, but the leap in destructive power meant that one aircraft could now achieve the same impact as two hundred.[2] The experience of Japan, which had been forced to surrender after Hiroshima and Nagasaki had been destroyed, provided a grim reminder of the new bomb's power and strategic impact. The eventual marriage of nuclear fission with the sort of rocket technology exhibited in the German V-2s promised an unstoppable weapon. In prospect was a battering that not even the most cohesive and substantial society could withstand. In the face of the atomic bomb all other forms of military power would fade into the background.

The presumption that with the atomic bomb air power had come of age was somewhat premature; the lessons of Hiroshima were much more ambiguous than acknowledged at the time. By August 1945 the

[1] I have inevitably drawn on my *Evolution of Nuclear Strategy* (London, 1981) in writing this chapter.
[2] H. H. Arnold, "Air Force in the Atomic Age" in *One World or None*, ed. Dexter Masters and Katherine Way (New York, 1946), 26-27.

Japanese were already close to surrender and they were knocked off balance as much by the Soviet entry into the war as by the loss of the two cities. Moreover, an attack on an enemy that had minimal air defense and no ability to retaliate in any form was hardly a critical test of the new weapon's effectiveness.[3] The American stockpile was still relatively small, and although few outsiders could guess just how small it was the limitations of scarcity were recognized.[4] Effective intercontinental missiles were believed to be at least two decades away, and the air force, unwilling to contemplate the obsolescence of its pilots, was doing its best to make this prediction more accurate than it need have been.[5]

Because the weapons were scarce and could only be delivered to their targets if the planes carrying them were protected against enemy defenses by a large number of accompanying aircraft, their cost effectiveness was in practice severely qualified.[6] Furthermore, the enormity of their destructive power was still found distasteful, even after the hardening experience of the previous war. Before the weapons had been properly incorporated into military strategy, there was a serious but ultimately futile attempt to control them through the United Nations that floundered on the developing suspicions of the Cold War.[7]

It was the Cold War, and in particular the Berlin blockade of the summer of 1948, that eventually led to the incorporation of atomic bombs into American war plans.[8] This occurred despite clear unease on the part of President Harry S. Truman at the prospect of using them in combat.[9] When the Korean War broke out in 1950 no bombs were used. Furthermore, in the reappraisal of American strategy that followed the test

[3] Paul Kecskemeti, *Strategic Surrender: The Politics of Victory and Defeat* (New York, 1964), 202-204. See also interviews in the appendix of L. Giovannitti and F. Freed, *The Decision to Drop the Bomb* (London, 1967). This is an extremely useful history of the decision to attack Hiroshima. For a discussion of the more general strategic issues raised by the attack see Lawrence Freedman, "The Study of Hiroshima," *Journal of Strategic Studies* 1, no. 1 (May 1978).

[4] David Alan Rosenberg, "U.S. Nuclear Stockpile, 1945 to 1950," *Bulletin of the Atomic Scientists* 38 (May 1982). In 1946 Bernard Brodie guessed a figure of twenty bombs while recognizing that it might be smaller; it was actually nine (*The Absolute Weapon* [New York, 1946], 41). By July 1947 the stockpile had only reached thirteen.

[5] Edmund Beard, *Developing the ICBM: A Study in Bureaucratic Politics* (New York, 1976).

[6] Vannevar Bush, *Modern Arms and Free Men* (London, 1950), 96-97.

[7] Barton J. Bernstein, "The Quest for Security: American Foreign Policy and International Control of the Atomic Bomb, 1942-1946," *Journal of American History* 60 (March 1974).

[8] David Alan Rosenberg, "The Origins of Overkill: Nuclear Weapons and American Strategy, 1945-1960," *International Security* 7, no. 4 (Spring 1983), 12-13.

[9] Truman told David Lilienthal in 1947: "I don't think we ought to use this thing unless we absolutely have to. It is a terrible thing to order the use of something that is so terribly destructive beyond anything we have ever had" (*The Journals of David E. Lilienthal*, vol. 2, *The Atomic Energy Years, 1945-1950* [New York, 1964], 391).

of the first Soviet atomic device in 1949, it was presumed that the days in which the West could rely on nuclear weapons for its strategic advantage were numbered.

To be sure, one of the first decisions was to raise the nuclear stakes even higher by authorizing development of the hydrogen (thermonuclear) bomb in order to stay in the lead, although the prospect of eventual inferiority was starting to become as influential as the desire to maintain superiority.[10] The key document of the period, NSC-68, believed the hydrogen bomb would preserve the American nuclear advantage for much of the 1950s, but recognized that this advantage would diminish as the Soviet Union caught up in this area as it had already done with fission bombs. The advantage was therefore best used as a shield, providing cover while a process of conventional rearmament was set in motion.[11] The North Korean invasion of the South in 1950 provided the stimulus for the rearmament process, which might otherwise have been stillborn had the call been confined largely to NSC-68.

The legacy of the Truman administration to President Dwight D. Eisenhower in January 1953 was therefore mixed. On the one hand, by proceeding with the hydrogen bomb, the United States was carrying "much further than the atomic bomb itself the policy of exterminating civilian populations."[12] On the other hand, largely because this threat of extermination would eventually face the people of the West, moves had already been made to prepare for a defense of Western interests far less dependent on nuclear weapons.[13]

II

Taken together this legacy implied that the sole long-term role of nuclear weapons was to deter their use by the enemy. However, in practice the weapons never left center stage. This was in part because short-term developments obscured the implications of the Truman administration's policy, and in part because the incoming Eisenhower administration re-

[10] On the H-bomb decision see Herbert York, The Advisors: Oppenheimer, Teller and the Superbomb (San Francisco, 1976); Warner R. Schilling, "The H-Bomb Decision: How to Decide without Actually Choosing," Political Science Quarterly 76 (March 1961); David Alan Rosenberg, "American Atomic Strategy and the Hydrogen Bomb Decision," Journal of American History 66 (June 1979).

[11] National Security Council, NSC-68, A Report to the National Security Council by the Executive Secretary on United States Objectives and Programs for National Security, April 14, 1950. The main author was Paul Nitze.

[12] Report of the General Advisory Committee to the Atomic Energy Commission of October 30, 1949, repr. in York, The Advisors.

[13] The most important results of this shift were the assignment of American ground troops to Europe and the ambitious Force Goals adopted by NATO at Lisbon in February 1952.

versed the policy with alacrity and vigor. But the story of the decades of nuclear strategy that followed is of a gradual return to the simple view that, in conditions of nuclear stalemate, arsenals of these tremendously powerful weapons tend to cancel each other out.

In the early 1950s events were moving too fast for such an assessment to be sustained with confidence. The intensity of the Cold War had endowed the atomic bomb with an immediate relevance that it might not have developed had international relations been more relaxed. Furthermore, the most pronounced long-term trend was toward a plentiful supply of weapons of ever-increasing destructiveness. Mass production of the weapons was under way. With the hydrogen bomb, there were no limits on destructive power. Before, this power could be measured in the tens of thousands of tons of TNT equivalent (kilotons or KT) as with the 16KT of Hiroshima. Now the measure was of millions of tons of TNT equivalent (megatons or MT). It was possible to envisage individual "city-busters." Lastly, the arrival of a Soviet nuclear capability meant that decisions on the role of these weapons was no longer solely the prerogative of the United States. Against these profound developments, the tentative moves toward conventional rearmament, which were all presented as no more than temporary expedients, could not make a great impact.

In an age of nuclear plenty and from a starting point in which American nuclear superiority was already seen as a vital counter to Soviet advantages in mobilized manpower and geography, it was going to take an act of unusual self-restraint for any American administration to keep nuclear weapons on the strategic sidelines. Thus, although the Eisenhower administration accepted that nuclear superiority could not last forever, it was far less willing than its predecessor to forgo any immediate benefits that temporary superiority might afford. This position was determined by its extremely tough attitude toward the Soviet Union, the nature of the particular diplomatic problems of the time, and concern over the evident difficulties connected with a greater reliance on conventional forces.

The Korean War brought these difficulties into focus. The fighting itself was prolonged, disagreeable, inconclusive, and in consequence politically unpopular. One explanation for the limited success achieved by the United Nations' forces under American command was the political constraints under which they had been forced to operate—in particular the veto on the use of nuclear weapons and the respect for Soviet and Chinese territory as sanctuaries. In seeking to break the deadlock in 1953, the administration dropped hints that these constraints might well be removed. The consequent progress at the armistice talks appears to have

739

convinced the administration that America's nuclear superiority was, at least for the time being, a powerful diplomatic lever.[14]

A second problem with conventional forces was their cost. To the conservative governments of both Britain and the United States the rearmament programs that they had inherited involved enormous economic strain. The only way to reduce costs without reneging on commitments was to relax the inhibitions surrounding nuclear use and to substitute nuclear for conventional firepower. In 1952 the British government had already concluded that the best bet for the West in its confrontation with the East was to rely on nuclear deterrence.[15] Air Marshal Sir John Slessor, who was closely associated with this shift, became a major publicist for the "Great Deterrent."[16]

In January 1954, in one of the seminal speeches of the nuclear age, U.S. Secretary of State John Foster Dulles announced that the United States intended in the future to deter aggression by depending "primarily upon a great capacity to retaliate, instantly, by means and at places of our own choosing."[17] The policy became known as "massive retaliation," and was generally interpreted as a threat to devastate Soviet and Chinese economic and political centers in response to any aggression, no matter how limited. It was an interpretation that was not wholly fair but one that the administration failed to dispel.

One of the difficulties in explaining the policy was that it reflected two different objectives. The first was to produce more value for money (or a "bigger bang for a buck" as one secretary of defense put it). But the military did not know whether or not they would be authorized to use nuclear weapons as a matter of course. This means that far larger conventional forces were maintained than would have been necessary had there been confidence that nuclear release would be permitted. Given such confidence, the conventional forces could be cut, which would lead to substantial savings. This involved the new short-range tactical nuclear weapons, designed for battlefield use, as much as the more familiar stra-

[14] Barry Blechman and Robert Powell, "What in the Name of God is Strategic Superiority?" *Political Science Quarterly* 97, no. 4 (Winter 1982-83) suggest that the role of the nuclear hints in securing progress was exaggerated.

[15] Margaret Gowing, *Independence and Deterrence: Britain and Atomic Energy 1945-1952*, vol. 1, *Policy Making* (London, 1974), 441.

[16] Slessor described the "Great Deterrent" in terms very similar to those later used by Dulles. It was, he wrote, "the counter-threat to the vast armies and tactical air forces of our potential enemy. Moreover it gives us some degree, and an increasing degree, of initiative in the cold war, instead of always dancing to the enemy's tune" (John Slessor, "The Place of the Bomber in British Strategy," *International Affairs* 23, no. 3 [July 1953], 302-303). See also his *Strategy for the West* (London, 1954).

[17] John Foster Dulles, "The Evolution of Foreign Policy," Department of State Bulletin, vol. 30, January 25, 1954.

tegic weapons designed for use against the enemy homeland. The basis of this aspect of the policy, therefore, was to reduce force requirements by changing the rules of engagement for general war. It was approved as NSC-162/2 in October 1953. As Eisenhower noted at the time, nuclear superiority was unlikely to be available to support this policy for more than a few years. The Soviet Union was already mounting a substantial threat against America's allies. It would not be long before the continental United States would be at risk; already Soviet aircraft were capable of inflicting serious damage on the Eastern seaboard. The President added to the original paper that it would be necessary to reconsider the "emphasis on the capability of inflicting massive retaliatory damage" if this came to "work to the disadvantage of the United States."[18] This was therefore a short-term set of circumstances in which to set in motion a fundamental reorientation of American policy.

This contrast between long-term consequences and short-term rationales becomes even more pronounced when one considers the sense of immediate diplomatic opportunities arising out of the current superiority that Dulles brought to the policy. When he spoke in January 1954 he had in mind the previous year's success in using nuclear threats to unlock the Korean stalemate and the current crisis in Indochina, where the administration was debating if and how to aid the beleaguered French. Dulles was reflecting the Republican critique of the Truman administration's foreign policy, which was deemed to have been too restrained in allowing the Soviet Union to set the rules of engagement for the Cold War. Communists would try to expand their dominion by taking advantage of superior manpower in areas where the West was weak. They had to recognize that in such circumstances the Western nations would respond in a manner that suited them, and that could well include massive nuclear retaliation against the centers of Soviet power. Dulles was mainly interested in extracting political leverage from this threat while he could, rather than developing a long-term basis for American strategy. But this approach was valid only as long as the United States could make such threats with confidence.

The inevitable interpretation of the "massive retaliation" speech was provided by James Reston: "In the event of another proxy or bushfire war in Korea, Indochina, Iran or anywhere else, the United States might

[18] National Security Council NSC-162/2, *Review of Basic National Security Policy*, October 30, 1953. For background see John Lewis Gaddis, *Strategies of Containment: A Critical Appraisal of Postwar American National Security Policy* (New York, 1982), 127-163; Glenn Snyder, "The New Look of 1953" in *Politics and Defense Budgets*, ed. Warner R. Schilling et al. (New York, 1962); and Samuel Wells, Jr., "The Origins of Massive Retaliation," *Political Science Quarterly* 96 (Spring 1981).

retaliate instantly with atomic weapons against the USSR or Red China."[19] The thought that the United States was tending in this direction was widespread. For example, rather than leading America's allies to support the administration's Indochina policy, their suspicions probably encouraged them to keep their distance.[20] This interpretation was inviting though to some extent unfair. The basic idea was that the choice of response was not to be restricted, but it was never envisaged that the United States would immediately turn any small-scale confrontation into an all-out nuclear war. Nevertheless, even the assertion that the punishment meted out by the West would always fit the crime required confidence that the West would not be deterred by the threat of counterpunishment. Because the Soviet Union had already demonstrated its determination and ability to catch up with the United States it did not take great foresight to recognize that this policy was resting on shaky foundations.

The massive retaliation speech of John Foster Dulles served as a stimulus for American scholars to interest themselves in strategic matters. During the second half of the 1950s a series of books and articles explored the contradictions in the administration's policy. By and large the initial studies—certainly those that reached the public domain—were more political than military in nature. Although, as we shall see, there was consideration of such questions as the survivability of retaliatory forces or the utility of tactical nuclear weapons, the essential thrust of the critiques was that now that the United States itself faced a risk of nuclear destruction, its foreign policy could no longer be as uninhibited as it might have been with an effective monopoly.

Three basic points were hammered home: it would not now be possible either to pursue the confrontation with the Communist world to a decisive conclusion or to conduct wars with unlimited objectives using unlimited means, when the consequences for the United States were also likely to be unlimited. Therefore, unless the West could respond with appropriately limited means it could find itself in an awful dilemma in the event of a modest Soviet challenge somewhere on the periphery of the "free world." As William Kaufmann explained in one of the first academic critiques of massive retaliation: "If the Communists should challenge our security and they would have good reasons for daring to do so, we would either have to put up or shut up. If we put up, we would plunge into all the immeasurable horrors of atomic war. If we shut up,

[19] *New York Times*, January 16, 1954.
[20] For a discussion of the inability of nuclear deterrence to cope with the Indochina crisis, see chapter 8 of Alexander L. George and Richard Smoke, *Deterrence in American Foreign Policy: Theory and Practice* (New York, 1974).

742

we would suffer a serious loss of prestige and damage our capacity to establish deterrents against further Communist expansion."[21] According to the academics, unless the administration was prepared to be extremely reckless, it was unlikely to find that its nuclear superiority would serve as a source of great political muscle beyond the mid-1950s.

Once implemented, it was not going to be easy to retreat from a policy of massive retaliation. The political advantages of nuclear deterrence might turn out to be elusive, but the financial benefits were real enough. Any attempt to revert to a more conventional strategy would face the question of resources, and as long as the extra money could not be found, the logic of massive retaliation was being institutionalized. This was particularly true in NATO, which was then going through a profound reappraisal following its failure to agree on a European Defense Community and to meet the Lisbon Force Goals of 1952 while still intending to rearm West Germany. The administration's nuclear policy had a serious effect on the way in which American commitments to its allies were understood and appreciated.

It had been recognized in NSC-162/2 that garrisons might have to be maintained on allied territory to reassure them that the United States would remain committed to their security, even if prudence suggested a less generous policy. The original American commitment to Western Europe at the time of the 1949 North Atlantic Treaty was concerned less with the manner of America's promised intervention on behalf of its allies than with the fact of its existence. The presumption was that if there had been such a commitment in 1914 or 1939 the Kaiser or Hitler would not have wished to take on all the Western democracies at once and war would have been prevented.

It was only with the shock of the Korean War that NATO began to develop and coordinate its military capabilities. Although this led to a substantial increase in conventional forces it was not to the level that had been deemed necessary, so pessimism already existed about the al-

---

[21] William W. Kaufmann, ed., *Military Policy and National Security* (Princeton, 1956), 24-25. Kaufmann's views were initially circulated in a November 1954 memorandum entitled *The Requirements of Deterrence*, published by the Princeton Center of International Studies. The same point was made by many others, encouraged as much by awareness of the increases in destructive power of the new hydrogen bombs as by the massive retaliation speech. In Britain, for example, Liddell Hart warned in April 1954 that "to the extent that the H-bomb reduces the likelihood of full-scale war, it *increases* the possibilities of limited war pursued by widespread local aggression" (article reprinted in B. H. Liddell Hart, *Deterrent or Defence* [London, 1960], 23). Other important articles and books on limited war were: Robert Endicott Osgood, *Limited War: The Challenge to American Strategy* (Chicago, 1957); Henry Kissinger, *Nuclear Weapons and Foreign Policy* (New York, 1957); and Bernard Brodie, "Unlimited Weapons and Limited War," *The Reporter*, November 11, 1954.

liance's ability to cope with the Soviet military challenge in Europe. Alliance members were therefore receptive to any American ideas that might make it possible to deter Soviet aggression at a more manageable cost.

With the adoption of the 1954 New Look, the United States was not only increasing the reliance on the deterrent effect of U.S. nuclear power, but was also forcing its allies to associate themselves with U.S. nuclear strategy. It was of long-term significance that the switch in American policy was taking place at the same time as German rearmament. Under the plan for a European Defense Community, which was rejected by the French in 1954, German rearmament would have taken place as part of a European conventional force. And under the Paris Agreements of that year it was made plain the rearmament required a rejection of a "German bomb." But for its part, Germany insisted that its territory should not constitute a future European battleground, which meant that it had to be defended at its borders—forward defense. Because conventional means were now unlikely to achieve this, the early invocation of nuclear deterrence was required. Moreover, Germany also refused to be a second-class NATO power. As NATO planned to integrate nuclear weapons into its ground and air forces, so German forces were to operate with these weapons (albeit with the warheads controlled by the United States under a dual-key arrangement). So the timing of the New Look meant that it turned into a means not only for shifting the balance of American forces from the conventional to the nuclear but also for instituting a nuclear bias into the basic structure of NATO forces that thereafter became extremely difficult to dislodge.

Dulles had tied the commitment so closely to nuclear weapons that its credibility was seen to depend on the ability of the United States to take nuclear risks on its allies' behalf, which in turn depended on a substantial imbalance of terror in the West's favor. The development of a balance of terror would inevitably qualify the American nuclear commitment to Europe, even though it might also serve to reinforce the general sense of the risks of war. It should be added that this crisis in the extension of the American nuclear deterrent to Western Europe might have developed even had there never been a guarantee to use nuclear weapons in response to a conventional attack on Western Europe. Soviet nuclear capabilities posed a threat to Western Europe that could only be countered by American capabilities. A balance of terror put a question mark against any American move that could involve it in nuclear war. Nevertheless, it was the need to deter a conventional attack that was seen to be imposing a far larger burden on American nuclear forces than they could conceivably carry, apart from over the very short term.

744

Over the next few years administration officials recognized the problems posed by reliance on nuclear threats of diminishing credibility. The qualifications began almost at once. Following the furor caused by his January 1954 speech, Dulles acknowledged in an article that whatever the current dominance of the United States' "air striking power," this "may not have the same significance forever." In the long term, rather than rely on certain threats based on a confident superiority, it would be necessary to keep an aggressor guessing, although Dulles still was confident enough to reaffirm that the choice of response would be "ours and not his."[22]

By 1956 the administration was already forced to review its strategy. A "new new look" was agreed on, in which there was to be no attempt either to maintain nuclear superiority or to redress the conventional imbalance. Instead it was hoped that potential aggressors would remain sufficiently in awe of the prospect of nuclear war not to court disaster by testing American resolve. Certainly by 1956 key members of the administration were prepared to describe the situation in terms of a "balanced terror" and to cast doubt on the possibility of a useful nuclear superiority.[23] The implication of this balance of terror for American diplomacy was, as the academics were warning, that it was going to be increasingly difficult to extract political leverage from nuclear superiority. In an unguarded comment in 1956, Dulles revealed that he had already found it necessary to rely on his capacity to demonstrate resolve—even when on the brink of a catastrophic war—rather than on nuclear superiority.[24] Dulles's successor, in another unguarded moment, acknowledged officially for the first time that America's allies could not rely on the United States to invoke nuclear deterrence on their behalf. In April 1959 Secretary of State Christian Herter informed a Senate committee: "I cannot conceive of any President engaging in all-out nuclear war unless we were in danger of all-out devastation ourselves."[25]

[22] John Foster Dulles, "Policy for Security and Peace," *Foreign Affairs* 30 (April 1954). Dulles also repudiated the notion that the United States "intended to rely wholly on large-scale strategic bombing as the sole means to deter and counter aggression."

[23] Secretary of the Air Force Donald Quarles in August 1956: "Neither side can hope by a mere margin of superiority in airplanes or other means of delivery of atomic weapons to escape the catastrophe of such a war. Beyond a certain point, this prospect is not the result of *relative* strength of the two opposed forces. It is the *absolute* in the hands of each, and in the substantial invulnerability to interdiction" (quoted in Samuel P. Huntington, *The Common Defense* [New York, 1961], 101).

[24] Dulles observed: "The ability to get to the verge without getting into war is the necessary art. If you cannot master it, you inevitably get into war. If you try to run away from it, if you are scared to go to the brink, you are lost" (interview with James Shepley, *Life Magazine*, January 16, 1956).

[25] Quoted in Alfred Grosser, *The Western Alliance: European-American Relations since 1945* (London, 1980), 173.

III

The position seemed to be one in which the development of Soviet nuclear capability was progressively undermining the fundamental premise underlying the Eisenhower administration's policy, yet the policy itself remained essentially unchanged. Certainly no change was evident in the force structure. The natural response was to revert to the pre-1954 policy of building up conventional forces to compensate for the diminution in nuclear deterrence. As we have seen, whatever the logic behind such a shift, there were powerful economic and institutional reasons why it would be opposed. This became perfectly clear when the Kennedy administration later attempted to make a similar change. Instead, from the mid-1950s to the early 1960s attempts were made both inside and outside government to develop strategic formulations that would support American foreign policy and in particular its alliance commitments by drawing on what was still seen to be the West's advantage in nuclear weapons. These formulations became the foundation for efforts in subsequent decades to solve the basic dilemmas of nuclear strategy.

The first approach was based on the possibilities identified in the early 1950s for relatively small-yield and short-range tactical nuclear weapons. This followed the division of air forces into strategic and tactical wings, the former to attack vital targets in the enemy's heartland and the latter to support ground combat. Those promoting tactical nuclear weapons hoped that they could encourage a shift from strategies of mass destruction and bring, to quote Robert Oppenheimer, "battle back to the battlefield."[26] For the same reasons the Strategic Air Command of the U.S. Air Force, still imbued with the philosophy of strategic bombardment, opposed this development. As it became clear that NATO was unlikely to raise its conventional forces to the level deemed necessary to meet any Soviet challenge on its own terms, there was natural interest in the possibility of using tactical nuclear weapons to redress conventional deficiencies. This became seen not as an alternative line of development to strategic bombardment but as a supplement. In an age of nuclear plenty both could be developed.

The argument in favor of tactical nuclear weapons rested on three propositions: that these weapons would remain an area of Western advantage for some time to come; that their use would favor the defense; and that they could be used without exceptional damage to the sur-

---

[26] This was the view of those members of the general advisory committee of the Atomic Energy Commission who opposed the development of the hydrogen bomb. See York, *The Advisors.*

746

rounding civil communities.[27] The first of these propositions was inevitably short-lived; the Soviet Union developed its own tactical nuclear weapons during the 1950s. This would not have mattered so much had the other propositions been valid. The suggestion that tactical nuclear weapons would favor the defense assumed that the offense would have to mass its forces preparatory to an invasion and in doing so would provide lucrative targets for a nuclear attack. However, it was arguable that the offense might also use these weapons—in the manner of traditional artillery—to knock a hole in the defenses through which their ground forces might pour. There was evidence that the Soviet Union was indeed considering using its weapons in this manner.[28]

The main problems came with the third proposition. In December 1953 the chairman of the Joint Chiefs of Staff observed that "today atomic weapons have virtually achieved a conventional status within our armed forces," and his President commented in March 1955 that "where these things are used on strictly military targets and for strictly military purposes, I see no reason why they shouldn't be used just exactly as you would a bullet or anything else." It soon became clear, however, that nuclear weapons could not be used just as if they were conventional weapons. Their radius of destruction was too large and their aftereffects too pervasive to employ them in such a precise and discriminating fashion. Once the military began exercising with tactical nuclear weapons, the potentially dire consequences for the civilian population became clear.[29] Advocates had envisaged that somehow limited nuclear warfare would be akin to naval warfare with mobile and self-sufficient units maneuvering around each other, but the reality of large units operating in highly populated areas of Germany would be quite different.[30] As Bernard Brodie observed, "a people saved by us through our free use of nuclear

[27] One of the more notable examples of this approach is found in Kissinger, *Nuclear Weapons and Foreign Policy*. See also Anthony Buzzard, "Massive Retaliation and Graduated Deterrence," *World Politics* 8, no. 2 (January 1956). Dulles himself came to argue along these lines in an effort to sustain administration policy without a shift back to conventional forces (John Foster Dulles, "Challenge and Response in U.S. Foreign Policy," *Foreign Affairs* 36, no. 1 [October 1957]).

[28] See chapter 7 of Raymond Garthoff, *Soviet Strategy in the Nuclear Age* (New York, 1958).

[29] The most notorious such exercise was Carte Blanche, which took place in West Germany in 1955. In it tactical nuclear weapons were only "used" by the NATO side. Over two days 355 devices were "exploded," mostly over West German territory. Even without the effects of residual radiation, this would have left up to 1.7 million Germans dead and 3.5 million wounded.

[30] See the reviews of Kissinger's book by William Kaufmann, "The Crisis in Military Affairs," *World Politics* 10, no. 4 (July 1958) and by James King, *The New Republic*, July 8 and 15, 1957.

weapons over their territories would probably be the last that would ever ask us to help them."[31]

If nuclear weapons could not be used as if they were conventional ones, or if such action would involve strategic decisions that would belie the tactical description allotted these weapons, then the military calculations surrounding their use became even more complicated. Tactical nuclear weapons might be of some value while an enemy was concentrating his forces for an offensive on his side of the border, but if they could not be weapons of first resort then by the time authorization came through for their release the enemy forces would be dispersed over the territory being defended. In these circumstances the consequences for the civilian population would be even more dire and the likelihood of military success even more remote. The army, which had argued all along that the integration of nuclear weapons into its inventory would increase rather than decrease its troop requirements (on the grounds that limited nuclear warfare would turn into a campaign of attrition in which the side with the largest reserves was the most likely to prevail, found it increasingly difficult to develop nuclear tactics. Ground troops, noted one critic, "are not capable of existing, let alone operating, in the very nuclear environment to which our strategy has consigned them."[32]

It was not long before most academic and independent strategists lost their enthusiasm for concepts of limited nuclear warfare. To prevent a future war from leading to unrestricted violence, the best course was not to use nuclear weapons at all. The distinction between tactical and tactical strategic nuclear weapons was likely to prove impossible to sustain in practice, and all that would be achieved by their early employment on the battlefield would be an earlier transformation of the conflict into something more horrific and less controllable than would otherwise have been the case. By 1960 even Henry Kissinger was acknowledging that a limited nuclear strategy would be ill-advised.[33] Again reflecting the prevailing mood, he now argued for a shift toward conventional forces. However, even though the intellectual support for a strategy based on battlefield nuclear weapons[34] had been short-lived, the effects were long

[31] Bernard Brodie, "More about Limited War," *World Politics* 10, no. 1 (October 1957), 117.

[32] T. N. Dupuy, "Can America Fight a Limited Nuclear War," *Orbis* 5, no. 1 (Spring 1961).

[33] Henry A. Kissinger, "Limited War: Conventional or Nuclear?" *Daedalus* 89, no. 4 (1960). Reprinted in *Arms Control, Disarmament and National Security*, ed. Donald Brennan (New York, 1961).

[34] Terminology in this area is notoriously difficult. As it became clear that the notion of a *tactical* nuclear weapon was intellectually suspect, the term *theater* nuclear force was adopted, which classified the weapons by location rather than by role. It was then necessary to distinguish between the longer-range theater systems that would be used against targets

lasting because the weapons themselves had been produced, shipped, and introduced into the ground forces of a number of NATO countries as well as to the U.S. forces stationed in Europe. Taking them away would now be politically awkward. Furthermore, as the Soviet Union was also introducing weapons of this nature, there would always be the argument that they were now needed on the Western side if for no other reason than to deter Soviet use.

Because the weapons remained in Europe, integrated into ground forces, there was continual interest in modernizing them into instruments of sufficient precision to fulfill their early promise as effective defense against Soviet advances. Such thinking, for example, was behind the development of the "neutron bomb" or (as NATO preferred it to be called) the "enhanced radiation weapon" that became a source of great controversy in the late 1970s.[35] Supporters of such weapons might be persuasive in arguing that if nuclear weapons were to be kept available for battlefield use then they might as well be discriminating and threaten less collateral damage, but not in making a case for a strategy based on their early battlefield use. NATO studies consistently reached negative conclusions on the likely military value of widespread nuclear use.[36] As we shall see, if tactical nuclear weapons had any value it was as a peacetime symbol of the American commitment to Europe, and as a possible means of signaling resolve in the event of war.

---

well to the rear of the battlefield and the shorter-range intended for battlefield use. However, many Europeans noted that in all these cases, the comparisons were still being made with intercontinental *strategic* weapons, which implied that the use of weapons of similar yield against any allies of the two larger powers would be something less serious than "strategic." In an attempt to meet such objections the United States introduced the term *intermediate* nuclear forces in 1981. Although many commentators would have been happy to use that instead of what had hitherto been known as *long-range theater* forces as part of a classification based on range, NATO complicated matters by referring to the weapons originally known as *tactical* as *short-range intermediate*. Meanwhile, outside commentators were increasingly using the more revealing term *battlefield* to label these weapons. This tedious terminological confusion is relevant only because of the larger doctrinal confusion that it reveals.

[35] For a proposal based on the exploitation of new technologies see W. S. Bennett et al., "A Credible Nuclear-Emphasis Defense for NATO," *Orbis* (Summer 1973). For the views of the inventor of the "neutron bomb" see Sam Cohen, *The Truth about the Neutron Bomb* (New York, 1983). The controversy is described in Sherri L. Wasserman, *The Neutron Bomb Controversy: A Study in Alliance Politics*, (New York, 1983).

[36] For example, Michael Legge records how in studies of follow-on use of theater nuclear weapons for NATO's Nuclear Planning Group in the early 1970s, all suggested that although use "in the form of selective strikes could result in a short-term advantage in the area concerned, and quite possibly a pause in the conflict; . . . if the Warsaw Pact responded with a nuclear attack on a similar (or greater) scale, neither side would gain a significant military advantage as a direct consequence of using nuclear weapons" and that large-scale use "would also result in totally unacceptable levels of collateral damage, much of it on NATO territory" (J. Michael Legge, *Theater Nuclear Weapons and the NATO Strategy of Flexible Response* [Santa Monica, Calif., 1983], 26-27).

IV

The difficulty with the battlefield use of nuclear weapons was that once the first weapons had been unleashed, the success of the operation and the extent to which destruction could be contained were wholly dependent upon the character of the enemy's response. As long as the enemy had a capacity for a substantial riposte, first use by the West would involve terrible risks. A second way out of the nuclear dilemma depended on the possibility of removing the enemy's capacity for effective retaliation.

An early version of this—to indulge in a preventive war before the Soviet Union had built up its nuclear capability—need not detain us because it was only an option early in the 1950s and does not seem to have been seriously considered at that time.[37] More serious was the concept of a preemptive attack. The idea here would be to disarm the enemy of his nuclear capability by destroying it on the ground. This sort of approach was well within the traditions of air power. However, although it was very much assumed in the first set of reactions to the new atomic bombs that these weapons would be used in a surprise attack, it was also assumed that the targets would be civilians.[38] As soon as realization dawned that after the other side had a retaliatory capability it would be foolhardy to initiate nuclear hostilities, the presumption that the next war would inevitably start with a surprise nuclear onslaught faded.[39] The consensus view in the late 1940s was that the retaliatory forces would not themselves be suitable targets for a surprise attack because of the difficulties that were anticipated in finding the relevant targets.[40]

With the prospect of a nuclear stalemate with the Soviet Union, however, and also with major improvements in surveillance and targeting technologies, interest in this sort of approach grew notably, particularly in air force circles.[41] Indeed nuclear war plans by this time were already

[37] See Bernard Brodie, *Strategy in the Missile Age* (Princeton, 1959), 228-29. In the fall of 1954, the Basic National Security Policy paper stated, following some discussion of the problem, that "the United States and its allies must reject the concept of preventive war or acts intended to provoke war" (see Rosenberg, "Origins of Overkill," 34).

[38] For example, Edward Mead Earle wrote that the combination of atom bombs and rockets would "put an enormous premium on the surprise attack, planned in secrecy and waged *à outrance*" ("The Influence of Airpower upon History," *Yale Review* 35, no. 4 [June 1946]).

[39] One of the first to draw attention to this was Jacob Viner in a speech of November 1945 ("The Implications of the Atomic Bomb for International Relations," *Proceedings of the American Philosophical Society* 90, no. 1 [January 1946]).

[40] One exception was William Borden, *There Will Be No Time* (New York, 1946).

[41] For early examples see T. F. Walkowicz, "Counter-force Strategy: How We Can Exploit America's Atomic Advantage," *Air Force Magazine* (February 1951); Richard Leghorn, "No Need to Bomb Cities to Win War," *U.S. News & World Report*, January 28, 1955.

putting a great deal of effort into methods for seeking out and destroying the growing Soviet nuclear capability.[42] Given the strong nuclear bias in the U.S. strategic pronouncements of the 1950s and the commitments that had been made to allies, it was very hard to see how the logic of preemption could be avoided. As the 1950s progressed the influence of this logic grew, although in the administration itself counterforce targeting was criticized by those (including the army and navy) who felt that Strategic Air Command's inclusion of large numbers of military targets in the plans made it difficult to set limits on either the eventual scale of destruction or U.S. force requirements. The air force still maintained, to quote its chief of staff in 1959, that "U.S. policy must encompass the requirement for forces adequate to permit the U.S. to have initiative under all circumstances of war."[43]

Over the 1950s the question of whether one side might be able to disarm the other in a surprise attack impressed itself on U.S. policy makers from a different direction. A series of studies undertaken by a team at the Rand Corporation led by Albert Wohlstetter addressed the problem from a completely different angle. What would happen if the Soviet Union tried such a sneak attack on the bases of the U.S. Strategic Air Command? SAC, which had every intention of taking the initiative itself and therefore none at all of allowing its forces to be caught in such an attack, had not asked the Rand team to address this issue. The team was looking at the factors that might govern the choice of air bases—apparently a rather mundane matter—but it soon concluded that vulnerability to surprise attack was one of the most vital factors. Further investigation suggested that existing bases came out very badly when judged against this criterion, and Wohlstetter made a major effort to convince the air force and policy makers in general of the risks involved should the Soviet Union develop the requisite capabilities.[44]

This concern was picked up in other studies in the mid-1950s and by the end of the decade was very much part of the conventional wisdom, supported by the widespread belief that the Soviet Union was firmly in the lead in the development of intercontinental ballistic missiles.[45] This belief was rather recklessly encouraged by the Soviet leader Nikita Khru-

---

[42] The requirement in the plans for an attack on Soviet nuclear capability went back to the Truman administration (Rosenberg, "Origins of Overkill," 25).

[43] Ibid., 58.

[44] The original report was published as A. J. Wohlstetter, F. S. Hoffman, R. J. Lutz, and H. S. Rowen *Selection and Use of Strategic Air Bases*, RAND R-266, April 1, 1954. For background see Bruce L. R. Smith, *The RAND Corporation: Case Study of a Nonprofit Advisory Corporation* (Cambridge, Mass., 1966) and at a more anecdotal level, Kaplan, *Wizards of Armageddon: Strategists of the Nuclear Age* (New York, 1983).

[45] Lawrence Freedman, *U.S. Intelligence and the Soviet Strategic Threat* (London, 1977), ch. 40.

shchev, who had assumed prematurely that his country's head start in the development of ICBMs would be translated into a lead in deployed weapons.[46] After the Soviet Union succeeded in being the first to launch an artificial earth satellite—Sputnik I—in October 1957, there were many who felt that the United States was indeed falling behind in the arms race. Those concerned about the vulnerability of American bases could certainly point to dramatic changes in Soviet strategic thinking since the death of Stalin; it had moved from disparagement to celebration of the technical-military revolution (nuclear weapons plus long-range rockets) and the possible role of surprise in achieving a decisive victory.[47]

Wohlstetter made his own concerns public in a seminal article published early in 1959. He provided a technical assessment of the various problems connected with maintaining a retaliatory capability, including surviving an enemy attack, communicating a decision to retaliate, penetrating active air defenses, and overcoming passive civil defense. He concluded: "The notion that a carefully planned surprise attack can be checkmated almost effortlessly, that, in short, we may resume our deep pre-Sputnik sleep, is wrong and its nearly universal acceptance is terribly dangerous."[48] In fact by that time this particular notion was by no means universally accepted—at least outside of government—partly due to Wohlstetter's efforts. Most civilian specialists were expressing similar sentiments.[49] When the Kennedy administration took over in 1961 the vulnerability problem was taken seriously at the highest levels.[50]

What was distinctive was the style and method of Wohlstetter's article. A number of academics with backgrounds in political science or history had begun to command public attention during the 1950s, but less attention had been paid to the work of those with backgrounds in economics, engineering, and the natural sciences—largely because much

[46] Arnold Horelick and Myron Rush, *Strategic Power and Soviet Foreign Policy* (Chicago, 1966).

[47] One article that related developments in Soviet thinking to these concerns was Herbert S. Dinerstein, "The Revolution in Soviet Strategic Thinking," *Foreign Affairs* 36, no. 2 (January 1958).

[48] Albert Wohlstetter, "The Delicate Balance of Terror," *Foreign Affairs* 37, no. 2 (January 1959).

[49] For example, Bernard Brodie said, in a book published in the same year, "Our ability to retaliate in great force to a direct Soviet attack is taken far too much for granted by almost everybody, including our highest national policy-makers" *Strategy in the Missile Age*, 282, and Hennry Kissinger wrote, two years later, "A precondition of deterrence is an invulnerable retaliatory force" (*Necessity for Choice* [New York, 1961], 22).

[50] See Alain C. Enthoven and K. Wayne Smith, *How Much is Enough? Shaping the Defense Program 1961-1969* (New York, 1971). They also comment that the "vulnerability problem was not widely or well understood." Although the need to protect U.S. offensive weapons had been recognized, there was less awareness of the problems connected with the high-level command structure and communications networks (ibid., 166).

of this work had been conducted in secret.[51] The new style of strategic analysis revealed by Wohlstetter was much more systematic and sensitive to technological developments than previous analyses and had its own terminology and concepts. For example, Wohlstetter introduced the critical concepts of first strike and second strike. These concepts have been at the center of strategic debate ever since and are particularly relevant to the questions of preemption and vulnerability.

A first strike refers not simply to the first shots in a nuclear war but to an attack directed against the enemy's means of retaliation. A successful first strike would be one that either destroyed all the enemy's nuclear forces on the ground or else intercepted them en route before they could reach their targets. A second-strike capability represented the ability to absorb a first strike and still inflict a devastating retaliation on the enemy. Forces designed for a first strike had to be able to attack the military assets of the enemy, but it was not essential that they should be survivable themselves. The intention was not to wait for the other side to get its blow in first. Of course the more vulnerable these key forces were, the greater the pressures were to use them before the enemy could attack, however much responsible authorities might prefer to exercise restraint. The key requirement for a second-strike force was that it should be survivable.

The concern with the vulnerability of U.S. forces pushed the fundamental issue back from one of sustaining some form of meaningful strategic superiority to keep the expansive tendencies of the Soviet bloc in check to a worry that after some nuclear Pearl Harbor the United States would find itself defeated. Out of this developed a third concern that with both sides striving for a first-strike capability and fearful lest the other side get there first, crises could be even more tense and dangerous than would otherwise be the case. Both sides might wish to avoid war— especially nuclear war—yet still find themselves drawn into a terrible confrontation out of fear of what the other side was up to. Kissinger

[51] The major exception to this statement is the influence enjoyed by the atomic scientists immediately after the war. They founded the *Bulletin of the Atomic Scientists*, which for many years was the main nongovernmental publication for the discussion of the issues raised by nuclear weapons, and they provided an important lobby for international controls on nuclear developments. Their internal influence waned after their leaders, including Robert Oppenheimer, were defeated on the question of hydrogen bomb development. The community was split further when Edward Teller, who had promoted the hydrogen bomb, associated himself with the effort in 1954 to deny Oppenheimer a security clearance. After Sputnik, scientists returned to higher advisory positions but were less visible outside of government. See Robert Gilpin, *American Scientists and Nuclear Weapons Policy* (Princeton, 1962). For a discussion of the various approaches to strategic issues see the essays in *Scientists and National Policy-Making*, ed. Robert Gilpin and Christopher Wright (New York, 1964).

warned that the structure of the two sides' strategic forces might "contribute to instability regardless of the intentions of the two sides."[52] Thomas Schelling developed the concept of the "reciprocal fear of surprise attack," by which "a modest temptation on each side to sneak in a first blow" would become "compounded through a process of interacting expectations." There would be successive cycles of "he thinks we think he thinks we think . . . he thinks we think he'll attack; so he thinks we shall; so he will; so we must."[53]

By the turn of the decade the risk of sliding into an inadvertent nuclear war through an irresistible military logic, à la August 1914, was becoming a dominant theme. The quest was for "stability," meaning a situation in which neither side would feel compelled to take the military initiative in a crisis out of a desire either to exploit its own first-strike capability or to prevent the other side from exploiting its. Whether or not stability could be achieved would depend on the development of the respective force structures. "In order to create a nuclear stalemate under conditions of nuclear plenty it is necessary for *both* sides to possess invulnerable retaliatory forces."[54] Thus it was necessary not only to ensure that American forces would not be vulnerable to a Soviet surprise attack, but also to reassure the Soviet Union that its forces were not vulnerable to an American surprise attack. This novel idea of seeking to convince a potential enemy that there was no serious threat to his most precious strategic assets was not one that occurred naturally to the military (unless they were planning some grand deception) and they were not overly impressed when the idea was put forward by this new breed of civilian strategists. Nevertheless, a combination of a fear of nuclear war, the persistent crises over such questions as the status of West Berlin, the demonstration by the Soviet Union of impressive technical prowess with the launch of Sputnik, and the prevailing sensation of engaging in a technological arms race meant that there was a real concern that the situation could rapidly get out of control. Again responding to the concerns of the civilian strategists, the Kennedy administration accepted a need to encourage the development of a stable nuclear balance rather than one in which the United States was palpably superior, although its early actions and pronouncements appeared to be more consistent with a drive for superiority.[55]

[52] Henry Kissinger, "Arms Control, Inspection and Surprise Attack," *Foreign Affairs* 38, no. 3 (April 1960).
[53] Thomas B. Schelling, *The Strategy of Conflict* (New York, 1960), 207. For a critique of this concept see Glenn Snyder, *Deterrence and Defense* (Princeton, 1961), 108.
[54] Oskar Morgenstern, *The Question of National Defense* (New York, 1959), 74.
[55] Assistant Secretary of Defense John McNaughton, speaking in December 1962 at the University of Michigan, used Schelling's phrase "the reciprocal fear of surprise attack" and

For all sides of the nuclear debate—those who believed that the United States must enjoy strategic superiority, those concerned that the Soviet Union was on the verge of achieving such a superiority, and those convinced that the best situation would be one of unambiguous stalemate—the key question was whether or not forces would tend toward first- or second-strike capabilities. Bernard Brodie had stated the issue with his customary lucidity as early as 1954.

> If . . . we are living in a world where either side can make a surprise attack upon the other which destroys the latter's capability to make a meaningful retaliation (which is almost a minimum definition of "success" for the enterprise), then it makes sense to be trigger-happy with one's strategic air power. How could one afford under those circumstances to withhold one's SAC from its critical blunting mission while waiting to test other pressures and strategies? This would be the situation of the American gunfighter duel, Western frontier style. The one who leads on the draw and the aim achieves a good clean win. The other is dead. But if, on the other hand, the situation is such that neither side can hope to eliminate the retaliatory power of the other, that restraint which was suicidal in one situation now becomes prudence, and it is trigger-happiness that is suicidal.[56]

V

In the second half of the 1950s it seemed reasonable to suppose that the rapid pace of technological advance would be inherently destabilizing. Dramatic breakthroughs seemed the norm rather than the exception. The long-range bomber had been followed by the radar, and then the atom bomb, hydrogen bomb, earth satellite, ICBM, and so on. So long as massive resources were expended on research and development there seemed no reason to believe that the pace would slacken. Furthermore, there seemed to be a pattern behind the technological developments of an offense-defense duel. As new offensive means were found, prodigious efforts were made to develop countermeasures, which in turn stimulated innovations in the offense. Thus although both sides made major efforts to build up their defenses against long-range bombers during the 1950s, long-range missiles were proceeding through their final stages of devel-

---

stated, "We must, in every decision we make, concern ourselves with the factors of stability and of the dynamic effect on the arms race." For a full account of the doctrinal and weapons decision of the Kennedy years see Desmond Ball, *Policies and Force Levels: The Strategic Missile Program of the Kennedy Administration* (Berkeley, 1980).

[56] Bernard Brodie, "Unlimited Weapons and Limited War." The "blunting mission" referred to is equivalent to what would later be described as a counterforce attack.

opment. In anticipation of this new challenge, work was already well under way on antiballistic missiles.[57]

The extremely influential Gaither Report, which was presented to President Eisenhower just after the news had come through of the Soviet success with Sputnik, summed up these expectations. The report looked into the future and saw nothing but "a continuing race between the offense and the defense. Neither side can afford to lag or fail to match the other's efforts. There will be no end to the moves and countermoves." The situation was not tending towards stability but to an "extremely unstable equilibrium" in which either nation might come close to a decisive capability only for the other to turn the tables. For the moment, certainly without remedial action, "a surprise attack could determine the outcome of a clash between [the] two major powers."[58]

In 1959 Bernard Brodie, somewhat gloomily, answered his own question of five years before: "Today the supreme advantage of the initiative in launching an unrestricted thermonuclear war can hardly be contested, for the side possessing it can hope, reasonably under some circumstances, to obliterate the opponent's power to retaliate."[59] He based this assessment on the assumption that the tendencies evident in the air age were going to be as influential in the missile age. James King noted in a review of Brodie's book that this reflected the real dangers involved in the transition from the air to the missile age, while long-range missiles were being "appraised mainly in terms of the unprecedented threat they offer to bombers sitting on their bases." However, once two missile forces were facing each other, a surprise attack might well seem far less attractive because the missiles themselves could be more easily protected.[60] This point had in fact been made as early as 1954 by some scientists associated with the ICBM development program. Missiles would not be very good at fighting each other. They could be hidden, protected, or moved around to prevent them being caught on the ground, and they moved too fast to be caught in the air. "We may well expect that the conversion to intercontinental missiles will be followed shortly by strategies which are fundamentally deterrent."[61]

[57] For an example of the influence of expectations of regular technological advance see Herman Kahn, *On Thermonuclear War* (Princeton, 1960). Kahn predicted eight technological revolutions by the mid-1970s. For a skeptical account of the period's enthusiasms see Herbert York, *Race to Oblivion: A Participant's View of the Arms Race* (New York, 1971).
[58] Security Resources Panel of the Scientific Advisory Committee, *Deterrence and Survival in the Nuclear Age* (Washington, D.C., November 1957). For background see Morton Halperin, "The Gaither Committee and the Policy Process," *World Politics* 13, no. 3 (April 1961).
[59] Brodie, *Strategy in the Missile Age*, 176.
[60] James E. King, "Airpower in the Missile Gap," *World Politics* 12, no. 4 (July 1960).
[61] Warren Amster, "Design for Deterrence," *Bulletin of the Atomic Scientists* (May 1956),

This is exactly what happened, contrary to the prophets of the technological arms race. Missile forces were introduced with full awareness of the problems of vulnerability. By the early 1960s some were being placed in reinforced-concrete underground silos. More critically still, others were being placed on nuclear-powered submarines. Submarine-launched ballistic missiles (SLBMs) were celebrated as being positively stabilizing. Techniques of antisubmarine warfare had not (and still have not) progressed sufficiently to threaten seriously the survivability of a moderately sized submarine force, while the missiles themselves were somewhat inaccurate and therefore incapable of alarming the enemy by threatening his means of retaliation.[62] By 1964 two leading scientists, who had both recently held critical positions in government, could suggest that military technology had effectively reached a plateau in that any more decisive breakthroughs were unlikely. Populations could not be protected against attack but weapons could. They pointed to only one serious "potential destabilizing element in the present nuclear standoff," the development of "a successful antimissile defense," which represented the last opportunity for a true first-strike capability. The authors, however, did not think such a development was likely: the defenses would have to be absolutely watertight, able themselves to survive a concentrated attack, and could only be planned against the known qualities of the offense, which were likely to have been improved by the time that the defense came into service.[63] Thus the condition of stability based on invulnerable retaliatory forces appeared to have arrived.

Secretary of Defense Robert McNamara had come to office sympathetic to the idea that if nuclear war was to be fought every effort must be taken to limit the damage to civilians. As he became convinced, however, through the analysis of proposals for a large civil defense program, that all the advantages would still lie with the offense and that the attempt to develop effective defenses would most likely both fail and be provocative at the same time, he put his efforts into reinforcing stability.[64] The concept was recast as mutual assured destruction, which reflected his predisposition toward systematization and quantification. Assured destruction, entering the jargon in 1964, was defined as "the ability to deter a deliberate nuclear attack upon the United States or its allies by

165. In the same issue, see also C. W. Sherwin, "Securing Peace through Military Technology."

[62] Schelling, *The Strategy of Conflict*, 288.

[63] Herbert York and Jerome Wiesner, "National Security and the Nuclear Test Ban," *Scientific American*, October 1964.

[64] There had been a number of proposals for an elaborate civil defense network (including one in the Gaither Report). In July 1961 President Kennedy submitted a major program but by the mid-1960s it had been virtually abandoned. Calculations suggested that at each level of damage the defense had to spend three times as much as the offense.

maintaining at all times a clear and unmistakable ability to inflict an unacceptable degree of damage upon any aggressor, or combination of aggressors—even after absorbing a surprise first attack."[65] Unacceptable damage, calculated as much by reference to the law of diminishing marginal returns when applied to nuclear destructiveness as by any sense of the Soviet threshold of tolerance, was put at the loss of 20 to 25 percent of population and 50 percent of industrial capacity. There was little doubt that by the mid-1960s the United States could ensure destruction at levels much higher than this.

Mutual assured destruction enjoyed the unfortunate acronym MAD[66] and later was severely criticized as stating a preference for attacking civilian as opposed to military targets, and for threatening another's population rather than defending one's own. Such criticisms are unfair. McNamara was doing little more than describing an existing state of affairs. It seemed the best nuclear state available and the attempt to achieve any other would, McNamara believed, merely lead to instability. Assured destruction was more of an aid to force planning, a criterion against which new developments could be assessed, than a doctrine for nuclear war. If it was the latter then it implied that targeting would be wholly concentrated on cities. This was not actually the case.[67] It was not really a strategy at all and its critical weakness (to which we shall return) was that it contained no guidelines for the employment of strategic forces should deterrence fail. The presumption was that with both sides able to ensure destruction, the risks connected with aggressive action would be so great that deterrence simply would not fail.[68]

The main threat to assured destruction came from antiballistic missiles (ABMs). If the offense-defense duel was not to be given a new stimulus, then the powerful pressures building up in the United States behind development of such a system had to be resisted. In the event, the Soviet Union pushed ahead with its own ABMs and this undermined McNamara. In terms of the assured destruction theory the response to such a development would not be a comparable American effort in the same area but another move forward with the offense. McNamara took such a move in late 1966 when he authorized the development of multiple

[65] Enthoven and Smith, *How Much is Enough?*, 174.

[66] The acronym was first exploited by Donald Brennan in "Symposium on the SALT Agreements," *Survival* (September/October 1972).

[67] Desmond Ball, *Targeting for Strategic Deterrence*, Adelphi Paper 185 (London, 1983), 14-15.

[68] "No meaningful victory is even conceivable in a third unlimited world war, for no nation can possibly win a full-scale thermo-nuclear exchange. The two world powers that have now achieved a mutual assured-destruction capability fully realize that" (Robert S. McNamara, *The Essence of Security: Reflections in Office* [London, 1968], 159-60).

independently targetable re-entry vehicles (MIRVs). This involved splitting the front end of missiles into a number of individual warheads, thus multiplying the number of warheads with which the defense had to cope.[69] The fact that the Soviet Union was pushing ahead with ABMs, coupled with advances in radar technology, made the pressure for an American ABM deployment almost irresistible. McNamara bowed to the inevitable in September 1967, attempting to salvage what he could from the situation by somewhat unconvincingly diverting the American ABM program from being anti-Soviet to anti-Chinese, and by providing a powerful critique of the persistent dynamic behind the arms race. In an extraordinary speech for an American secretary of defense, which not surprisingly turned out to be a valedictory, he identified an action-reaction phenomenon at work: "Whatever their intentions or our intentions, actions—or even realistically potential actions—on either side relating to the build-up of nuclear forces necessarily trigger reactions on the other side." The offense-defense duel, apparently in check a few years ago, was on the verge of reasserting itself: "Were we to deploy a heavy ABM system through the United States, the Soviets would clearly be strongly motivated to so increase their offensive capability as to cancel out our defensive advantage."[70] The difference between McNamara's analysis of the duel to those of a decade earlier is that, sobered by his experience in government, he had come to recognize that the strategic assessments on which planning had to be based involved imperfect information, particularly with regard to the future capabilities of the other side, and so could be driven by institutionalized mistrust as much as rational analysis.

The "action-reaction" phenomenon and the concern with the institutional pressures behind the arms race became part of the staple fare of the strategic debate for the next few years.[71] The fear was of a "mad momentum" (another of McNamara's phrases) pushing an arms race to more dangerous levels just when things might have settled down into a stable condition of mutual assured destruction. Much of the analysis was bound up with the campaign to prevent deployment of an American ABM system. The Nixon administration, coming into power in 1969,

[69] Ted Greenwood, *Making the MIRV: A Study in Defense Decision-Making* (Cambridge, Mass., 1975).

[70] Robert S. McNamara, "The Dynamics of Nuclear Strategy," Department of State Bulletin, vol. 57, October 9, 1967.

[71] For example George Rathjens, "The Dynamics of the Arms Race," *Scientific Armerican*, April 1969. *Scientific American* published a number of articles on this general theme in the late 1960s and early 1970s, largely concerned with ABMs and MIRVs. They are collected in *Arms Control*, ed. Herbert York (San Francisco, 1973). The interest in the domestic sources of the arms race is very evident in the essays on arms control contained in a special issue of *Daedalus* 104, no. 3 (Summer 1975).

recast the anti-China program bequeathed by McNamara and turned it into one designed to protect American ICBM silos (but not cities) from a Soviet attack. The administration had some difficulty in demonstrating that this particular system, known as Safeguard, was suited to the task, but on the other hand the task itself could not be seen as a challenge to the Soviet assured-destruction capability.[72]

As things turned out, the offense-defense duel was not entering a new and more dangerous phase. The Soviet Union appears to have been sufficiently impressed by the revelation of the means by which the Americans proposed to penetrate its first generation ABMs, including MIRVs, that it virtually abandoned the project in 1968 and began to explore the next generation. The Nixon administration, finding it difficult to make a case for Safeguard on its merits, argued that it was necessary to continue to support the program as a bargaining chip for the new Strategic Arms Limitation Talks (SALT). In May 1972 the first SALT agreement was signed in Moscow. In this the two sides agreed to tight limitations on ABM deployments, thereby confirming the supremacy of the offense.[73]

The duel in practice was always one-sided. Taking the challenge of the defense more seriously than it deserved in the 1960s left a legacy in the form of the MIRV program which was to haunt the 1970s. Here there were no problems with feasibility. By the mid-1970s the United States had multiplied the numbers of available warheads on its ICBMs and SLBMs by a startling amount. The number of U.S. missiles was held constant at 1,750 from 1967. A decade later these missiles could carry well over 7,000 warheads. The Soviet Union's MIRV program began later and it lagged behind with its sea-based force. But the larger size of its ICBM force meant that it was able to multiply its numbers more rapidly, and that the yield of the individual warheads was much greater.

The implications of this proliferation of offensive warheads and the associated improvements in the accuracy of these warheads dominated strategic debate in the 1970s. We will consider this debate below. For the moment suffice it to note that the main consequence of this development was to improve counterforce options, and in particular to threaten the land-based forces of the other side. Although there have been attempts to demonstrate that submarines are also becoming increasingly vulnerable,[74] the consensus is that there are few signs of the relatively quiet strategic submarines with their long-range missiles being put at risk by any offensive measures currently in the offing.[75] Even if

[72] See Freedman, *US Intelligence and the Soviet Strategic Threat*, ch. 8.
[73] John Newhouse, *Cold Dawn: The Story of SALT* (New York, 1973).
[74] For example Roger Speed, *Strategic Deterrence in the 1980s* (Stanford, 1979), 56-64.
[75] Richard L. Garwin, "Will Strategic Submarines Be Vulnerable?" *International Security* 8, no. 2 (Fall 1983).

there were major breakthroughs in antisubmarine warfare, the problems in executing a coordinated attack with unproven systems against such a wide range of platforms, and with such a high penalty for a marginal failure, would be daunting and the uncertainties too great to warrant any cold-blooded preemption. The acknowledged vulnerability of ICBMs and bombers still fell far short of a true first-strike capability and the decisive strategic advantage that had been sought or the fundamental source of instability that had been feared since the 1950s.

The 1980s saw renewed interest in the possibility of a breakthrough on behalf of the defense. President Reagan enjoined the nation's scientists to develop a counter to "the awesome Soviet missile threat with measures that are defensive" in March 1983. He was looking to new possibilities of space-based systems employing directed energy for intercepts. The President claimed that he was not seeking "military superiority" through this project (although he might well feel that he had such superiority, should it succeed). He also admitted that success would be decades away.[76] Others doubted that it would ever be possible because of a series of technical, political, and resource problems.[77] There was certainly no evidence that there was a decisive shift from the offense to the defense under way. Indeed, the President's plan appeared to depend on some sort of negotiated restraints in offensive missiles to keep the threat down to manageable proportions. For the moment the safest assumption is that the search for a true first-strike capability is likely to prove as futile in the future as it has in the past.

VI

The attempts to develop ways to use nuclear weapons as if they were conventional or to develop an effective first-strike capability could be understood in terms of prenuclear theories of strategic and tactical air power. If neither of these avenues appeared promising then there would have to be a virtual revolution in thinking to match the revolution in technology.

Escalation was the basic concept around which many of the attempts to develop a compelling nuclear strategic revolved. The term is now understood to refer to a qualitative transformation in the character of a conflict in the direction of increasing scope and intensity. The concept took time to develop and has been used in a number of different ways.[78] There is now general agreement that it refers to something more than

[76] *New York Times*, March 24, 1983.
[77] On the state of the ABM debate in the 1980s, see Ashton B. Carter and David Schwartz, eds., *Ballistic Missile Defense* (Washington, D.C., 1984).
[78] See Freedman, *Evolution of Nuclear Strategy*, 210-211.

just an expansion of a conflict, to a movement across a limit that had been previously accepted by both sides. Examples of the sort of limits involved are those between military and civilian targets, between attacks on allied territory and on the superpowers themselves, and between the use of conventional and nuclear munitions. Although the process can be detected at work in many prenuclear conflicts,[79] there is a lack of experience available to serve as a guide to conflicts in the nuclear age. Fortunately, no superpower confrontation has progressed to a level beyond the showdown in October 1962 over the Soviet attempt to place missiles in Cuba.

This means that attempts to predict the course of a future war have always involved a high degree of guesswork. The nuclear threshold—the point at which restraints on nuclear employment are abandoned—could be clearly identified, but many of the most interesting questions revolved around the existence and sustainability of thresholds beyond these weapons' initial use. Herman Kahn, who did as much as anyone to develop the concept, was able to identify forty-four rungs on an "escalation ladder" with nuclear weapons first used on rung fifteen, although the nuclear threshold was not truly passed until rung twenty-two. Kahn did not claim that his ladder was predictive and he also recognized that the Soviet Union might be working on the basis of a completely different ladder. The point he was trying to get across, a consistent theme in all his work, was that control could be exercised by policy makers all the way to the final apocalyptic "spasm war."[80] How easily the most salient thresholds could be recognized was the first question, and the second was whether passage through these thresholds would be deliberate or involuntary. Much of the debate on nuclear strategy over the past two decades has revolved around the possibility of one side or the other being able to control a nuclear conflict to the extent of not being forced to suffer an unacceptable level of damage while still meeting strategic objectives.

We have already noted the problems of achieving this through either a first strike or the use of tactical nuclear weapons. The discussion of the possibilities of limited nuclear war is relevant to the question of escalation because it indicates declining confidence in the capacity to control the course of a nuclear conflict even at its earliest stages.

If nuclear weapons could not be used to achieve a straightforward military victory, then employment would have to be geared to political objectives. According to Kahn, "almost every analyst is now agreed that

[79] Richard Smoke, *War: Controlling Escalation* (Cambridge, Mass., 1977).
[80] Herman Kahn, *On Escalation: Metaphors and Scenarios* (New York, 1965).

the first use of nuclear weapons—even if against military targets—is likely to be less for the purpose of destroying the other's military forces or handicapping its operations, than for redress, warning, bargaining, punitive, fining or deterrence purposes."[81] Most of the attempts to develop a more "political" nuclear strategy did not progress much beyond the idea of a crude bargaining process or a "competition in resolve."[82] The difficulty with many of the proposed schemes was that implementation would be quite complicated and success would depend on a degree of mutual comprehension that was unlikely to be available in the presence of nuclear exchanges.

It was one thing to demonstrate the sort of reasons that might lie behind a rather tentative move toward early nuclear exchanges, and quite another to explain how these exchanges could eventually lead to a resolution of the conflict on satisfactory terms. If it was the case that the two sides were both operating according to some agreed rules, how could these rules allow for either to improve its overall position through individual strikes? If nuclear use could only be contemplated because of a failure at the conventional level, would it make sense to use the initial strike to make a political point rather than to retrieve the military position on the ground? Would it be the case that the bargain achieved at the end of the nuclear exchanges would be strikingly different from that which might have been achieved beforehand? How important would be factors other than nuclear exchanges, in particular the course of a land battle in Europe, in influencing the final settlement? To the extent that the nuclear strikes did achieve results, would this be because of the relative capacities to withstand punishment or because of the different stakes in the issue that had prompted the conflict in the first place?

Two basic approaches to the question of escalation eventually emerged. The first involved an attempt to prevail in a conflict by dominating at any particular level of escalation and putting the onus on the other side to move to a higher and more dangerous level. The second involved drawing on the uncertainties inherent in the escalation process to achieve deterrence by warning the other side that things could get out

[81] Ibid., 138.

[82] An early scheme for conducting nuclear exchanges without things getting completely out of hand was developed by Leo Szilard in "Disarmament and the Problem of Peace," *Bulletin of the Atomic Scientists* 11, no. 8 (October 1955). Morton Kaplan pursued this approach first in an article in which he advocated an American response to a sustained attack on Europe involving a "series of installment reprisals that eventually progress to reprisals double the value of Europe" ("The Calculus of Nuclear Deterrence," *World Politics* 10, no. 4 [July 1958]). Later he contributed to a collection of essays by a number of leading civilian strategists that sought to explore this approach (Klaus Knorr and Thornton Read, eds., *Limited Strategic War* [New York, 1962]).

of control. They can best be understood by considering the views of two outstanding theorists—Herman Kahn and Thomas Schelling.

As we have already noted, Kahn's basic assumption was that even a nuclear conflict could be conducted in a controlled, discriminating manner. There would be elements of irrationality present, but even these could be exploited for some rational purpose. If, to use one of the more familiar metaphors, a confrontation between the two superpowers represented the juvenile game of "chicken" in which two old cars speed toward each other with the chicken being the first to swerve, then there were advantages in feigning irresponsibility or recklessness. However, matters would only degenerate into a pure contest of resolve if there was a complete symmetry of capabilities, and most likely this would not be the case. At each stage of movement up the escalation ladder, one of the two sides would feel better equipped to fight. At a stage in which the enemy enjoyed the advantage a decision would have to be made whether to seek settlement on extremely damaging terms or to raise the stakes by moving to the next stage, which would be more violent and dangerous and perhaps less controllable but where the advantages might begin to flow in a more favorable direction.

This decision would be harder the farther up the escalation ladder it was necessary to go in order to have a reasonable chance of success. Thus even though the ultimate logic pointed towards a "spasm war" in which both sides would lose all, a sufficient asymmetry of capabilities at lower levels would ensure that an intolerable burden would be put on the side forced to raise the stakes. Kahn described such a condition as escalation dominance: "This is a capacity, other things being equal, to enable the side possessing it to enjoy marked advantages in a given region of the escalation ladder. . . . It depends on the jet effect of the competing capabilities on the rung being occupied, the estimate by each side of what would happen if the confrontation moved to these other rungs, and the means each side has to shift the confrontation to these other rungs."[83]

The major difficulty with this approach in operational terms was that the escalation ladder was unlikely to appear as clear in practice as in theory. Certain thresholds might be self-evident at the conventional level but they might be both more controversial and harder to recognize once the nuclear threshold had been passed. In particular it was an open question whether distinctions could be readily made between limited strikes against military targets and large strikes against cities (given the collateral damage likely to result from detonating even the smaller-yield weapons) or between attacks on allies and attacks on superpower ter-

---

[83] Kahn, *On Escalation*, 290.

ritory (given the proximity of Soviet territory to a European battle-ground). What would happen if one side tried a move that the other did not recognize as an orderly progression up the ladder or if a communications failure led to a substantial overestimation of the scale of the other side's activities? If there was no guarantee that the situation could be kept under control, an involuntary escalatory process could take over and the two sides could find themselves involved in massive exchanges of nuclear weapons against their better judgment. In practice, the critical threshold was likely to be the nuclear threshold. This was the conclusion to which the first theorists of limited nuclear war had been driven. In this case the most useful escalation dominance would be at the conventional level. To rely on a putative dominance in a certain type of nuclear capability when there was no way of protecting one's own society from the consequences of a miscalculation offered a thin reed on which to rely for deterrence purposes or as a means of strengthening one's hand at earlier stages of a conflict.

An alternative method of exploiting escalation sought to draw on the uncertainties inherent in the process. Schelling argued that even after deterrence had failed in its primary task to stop the outbreak of war there would still be a possibility of retrieving the situation. The important point was to remember that nuclear weapons gained their deterrent effect not through a capacity to redress a military imbalance but because of their capacity to hurt. This could still influence an adversary after hostilities had begun. It would only cease to influence adversary behavior once it had all been used up, and therefore it could only serve a deterrent purpose while it existed as a potential, as a threat. The threat would be most credible if either (a) it was not matched by a counterthreat, which was no longer possible, or (b) it would be implemented automatically by the adversary's misbehavior, although neither side was unlikely to put itself in such a position if (a) did not obtain. The threat thus risked being exposed as a bluff, especially if it had already not been implemented following enemy aggression.

But suppose there was an unavoidable element of risk that the hurt would be imposed whether or not either side thought this to be a particular rational step in the circumstances. Schelling did not expect escalation to develop as a result of deliberate steps taken by calculating governments fully aware of the consequences of their actions: "Violence, especially in war, is a confused and uncertain activity, highly unpredictable depending on decisions taken by fallible human beings organized into imperfect governments depending on fallible communications and warning systems and on the untested performance of people and equipment. It is furthermore a hot-headed activity, in which commitments and

765

reputations can develop a momentum of their own."[84] There was an unavoidable risk of things getting out of hand in the move from limited to general war, particularly once nuclear weapons were in use. The point was to exploit this risk through skillful tactics. By allowing the situation to begin to deteriorate, one would force the adversary to confront the possibility of matters getting completely out of hand and this might make him more accommodating. If deterrent threats in or out of war could not be credible so long as the threatener was in full control, then it would be necessary to relinquish some control in order to achieve credibility. Schelling called this "the threat that leaves something to chance." "The key to these threats," he explained, "is that, though one may or may not carry them out, *the final decision is not altogether under the threatener's control.*"[85]

The approach was to create a situation in which only the other's compliance could relieve the shared pain and remove the shared risk.[86] This, of course, assumed that the adversary was sufficiently in control to be able to comply. The dangers of handing over responsibility for the course of such a crucial conflict to the adversary were clearly enormous. It would involve the abdication of responsibility at the most critical time in a nation's history. Nevertheless, Schelling was clearly working with a much more realistic sense of the character of a future war than Kahn or others who believed that nuclear war could take the form of rather stylized signals, with slight regard for what would happen to those at the receiving end of the signals. To the extent that even preparing to fight a war of such an uncertain nature was in effect making a threat that left something to chance, Schelling was offering a real insight into how deterrence might operate in peacetime—as a function of the fear of the unknown rather than of the specific threats of the potential enemy. As a prescription for intrawar deterrence Schelling's work was less persuasive: it failed to explain the mechanisms by which putting the onus on the enemy to escalate to higher levels of violence would compel him not to settle for the status quo but to relinquish the gains he had already made. Here Schelling's indifference to the military situation on the ground was a substantial weakness.

VII

The concept of escalation dominance was much more appealing to most strategists than the threat that left something to chance. A certain

[84] Thomas Schelling, *Arms and Influence* (New Haven, 1966), 93.

[85] Schelling, *The Strategy of Conflict*, 188. Emphasis in the original.

[86] Ibid., 194. "Preferably one creates the shared risk by irreversible manoeuvres or commitments, so that only the enemy's withdrawal can tranquilize the situation; otherwise it may turn out to be a contest of nerves."

amount of work was undertaken at Rand in the late 1950s to develop nuclear tactics involving counterforce attacks with a capacity for attacks on urban-industrial targets held in reserve. The presumption was that as long as Soviet cities were not being attacked, the Soviet incentive would be to respond only in kind to American attacks on its military forces, even if it was not particularly well endowed at this level. Robert McNamara recruited many from Rand to work for him at the Pentagon in January 1961, and they brought with them their ideas for a flexible nuclear strategy. By the middle of 1962 these had been reflected in official policy.[87]

McNamara himself was drawn to the view that the central authorities should remain in control of the situation for as long as possible even after the outbreak of nuclear war. Early on he explained to a congressional committee that he wanted a strategic force "to be of a character which will permit us its use, in event of attack, in a cool and deliberate fashion and always under the complete control of the constituted authority."[88] In July 1962, in a public presentation of a classified speech that had already been given to NATO, he said:

> The U.S. has come to the conclusion that to the extent feasible basic military strategy in a possible general nuclear war should be approached in much the same way that more conventional military options have been approached in the past. That is to say, principal military objectives, in the event of a nuclear war stemming from a major attack on the Alliance, should be the destruction of the enemy's military forces, not of his civilian population.
>
> The very strength and nature of the Alliance forces makes it possible for us to retain, even in the face of a massive surprise attack, sufficient reserve striking power to destroy an enemy society if driven to it. In other words we are giving a possible opponent the strongest possible incentive to refrain from striking our own cities.[89]

Given that the strategy inherited by McNamara for general nuclear war involved a massive and undiscriminating attack on the peoples of the Soviet Union, China, and Eastern Europe, this more controlled and

[87] For background see Kaplan, *Wizards of Armageddon*, ch. 18. One of the most influential figures in the development of the concepts at Rand and their translation into official policy was William Kaufmann. While the various themes of the McNamara period at the Pentagon were still fresh and untarnished, Kaufmann provided an effective public exposition of them in *The McNamara Strategy* (New York, 1964).

[88] To the House Armed Services Committee, February 1961. Quoted in Kaufmann, *The McNamara Strategy*, 53.

[89] Robert S. McNamara, "Defense Arrangements of the North Atlantic Community," Department of State Bulletin, no. 47, July 9, 1962. McNamara's original briefing to NATO ministers on May 5, 1962, has now been declassified.

flexible approach was truly revolutionary. The difficulty was that it was subject to a variety of interpretations. In part this was because of the novelty of the concepts involved, but in part it was also a result of a lack of clarity over objectives and a failure to relate the doctrine to the state of international affairs in the early 1960s. The influence of the United States nuclear guarantee to Europe has to be remembered as a critical influence on the development of American strategic doctrine. The basic conundrum was generally recognized to be that a Soviet conventional attack on Western Europe could not be thwarted without resorting to nuclear threats but that the nuclear threats themselves lacked credibility because of the extent of the Soviet counterthreat.

McNamara's instinct was to deny the hopelessness of the conventional situation, and he tried hard during his tenure to persuade the allies of this view. Should it be valid, then logic led to removing NATO's dependence on the threat to use nuclear weapons. This idea tempted President Kennedy in 1961. He was held back by the fact that the major crisis of that year was over West Berlin, which was the only part of the alliance indefensible by conventional means. In the course of the conflict Kennedy was obliged to reaffirm the commitment to the first-use threat.

If the West was forced to escalate then the administration was promising to attack military targets and to avoid cities. The sort of targets many had in mind were not the Soviet Union's strategic nuclear assets but targets related to a land war in Europe, although the nuclear assets would eventually become targets. It would be very hard, however, for the Soviet Union not to interpret McNamara's speech—and the associated surge in America's missile capacity—as preparations for a first strike. This problem of interpretation was accentuated by the fact that the concepts informing the new strategy had been developed during a period when it was assumed that the Soviet Union was winning the nuclear arms race. By the time the administration began to outline the strategy publicly it was clear that the Soviet Union was not only well behind but, because of the arrival of reconnaissance satellites, the Kremlin knew that the Americans were aware of its weaknesses.[90]

Certainly the Soviet leaders reacted with alarm to the new American doctrine and weapons buildup. Premier Khrushchev had recently been proclaiming his country's growing strength in missilery and had made this the basis for a reorientation of Soviet strategy. He reacted with a number of expedients, including stressing the vulnerability of the Western Europeans and so making them hostages for American good behavior.

[90] See Freedman, *Evolution of Nuclear Strategy*, ch. 15; see also Ball, *Policies and Force Levels* for a slightly different interpretation of the motivations behind the new strategy.

In the fall of 1962 he took the greatest gamble of all and sought to redress the balance by surreptitiously placing missiles in Cuba, thereby triggering one of the most serious crises of the nuclear age. What he did not do was give any encouragement to the idea that the Soviet Union was interested in fighting the sort of controlled affair that McNamara had proposed. The Soviet Union could not have fought that way in the early 1960s even if it had wanted to. Instead there was a stress on the terroristic properties of the Soviet nuclear arsenal, including a massive 56-megaton atmospheric test in September 1961. It is also of note that during the Cuban missile crisis, President Kennedy did not act at all according to the new strategy: he denied the Soviet Union a counterforce option by dispersing U.S. military aircraft to civilian airfields and threatening a "full retaliatory stroke."

McNamara became concerned at the construction being put on the new strategy by the Soviet Union, and even more concerned at the apparent desire by the United States Air Force to confirm the Soviet Union's worst fears by preparing for a full first strike. The discussions within the administration during the Berlin and Cuban missile crises convinced those who participated that the use of nuclear weapons on any scale was unlikely to appear as a feasible option for the United States.[91] McNamara became far more concerned with ensuring that the nuclear threshold was not passed than with what could be done after the passage of this threshold. Almost as soon as the new strategy had been announced McNamara began to drift away from it, at first still maintaining some of its aspects by talking of the need to limit damage before deciding to stress the inescapable tragedy of nuclear war in the concentration on assured destruction.

In terms of the theory, McNamara was still operating within an "escalation dominance" framework, especially in terms of maintaining second-strike forces in reserve to warn the Soviet Union of the dangers of escalation to that level, but he had become disenchanted with the notion of recognizable thresholds above the nuclear. This determination that the nuclear threshold should not be passed brought him into conflict

[91] This came over most clearly in a celebrated article by McGeorge Bundy, who was Kennedy's special assistant for national security affairs. He wrote: "There is an enormous gulf between what political leaders really think about nuclear weapons and what is assumed in complex calculations of relative 'advantage' in simulated strategic warfare. Think Tank analysts can set levels of 'acceptable' damage well up in the tens of millions of lives. They can assume that the loss of dozens of great cities is somehow a real choice for some men. In the real world of real political leaders—whether here or in the Soviet Union—a decision that would bring even one hydrogen bomb on one city of one's own country would be recognized in advance as a catastrophic blunder; ten bombs on ten cities would be a disaster beyond history; and a hundred bombs on a hundred cities are unthinkable" ("To Cap the Volcano," *Foreign Affairs* 48, no. 1 [October 1969], 9-10).

with the Western Europeans. They of course were not anxious to pass the threshold, but were worried about the implications for deterrence of the American arguments.

The Europeans depended on the United States for their nuclear protection, but they understood only too well the element of irrationality that the Soviet retaliatory capability had introduced into the American nuclear guarantee. The more the Americans talked about the need to avoid "going nuclear" the more the Europeans suspected that the guarantee was in the process of being removed. The Americans were reducing the risks to themselves of a war in Europe but, by confirming the unlikelihood of escalation to the nuclear level, they were also reducing the risks of aggression for the Soviet Union. More robust conventional forces for NATO might deny the Soviet Union a victory but the cost of failure to the Kremlin would be slight; Soviet territory itself would remain unscathed. Once there was no need to worry about nuclear catastrophe, Soviet risk calculations would be dangerously simplified. To the Europeans all war and not just nuclear war had to be deterred and deterrence required at least some prospect of a resort to nuclear weapons.

There was a subsidiary issue in that McNamara was anxious to prevent the allies from forcing the United States into a nuclear conflict against its better judgment and so was especially concerned at the development of smaller nuclear arsenals among the Europeans. In the July 1962 speech in which he outlined the new strategy he castigated these small forces as being "dangerous, prone to obsolescence and lacking in credibility as a deterrent." The French in particular took grave exception to what they correctly saw as an attempt to force them out of the nuclear business. They did not share the American confidence that a conventional defense was feasible and therefore argued that deterrence now depended on the sheer uncertainty of a future war. Extra centers of decision making contributed to this uncertainty and so reinforced deterrence.[92]

The French critique of NATO was based partly on doubts about the credibility of the American guarantee and a preference for national means of deterrence, and partly on an assumption that alliance ties were

[92] The development of the French theory is beyond the scope of this essay. The most important theorist arguing in terms of the needs of NATO was André Beaufre, *Deterrence and Strategy* (London, 1965), originally published as *Dissuasion et Stratégie* (Paris, 1964). Pierre Gallois questioned whether true alliances were possible in the nuclear age and developed a concept for a national nuclear force in *The Balance of Terror: Strategy for the Nuclear Age*, trans. Richard Howard (Boston, 1961), originally published as *Stratégie de l'âge nucléaire* (Paris, 1960). The British response to this debate was somewhat more inhibited than the French in that Britain was both an established nuclear power and already somewhat dependent on American largesse for maintaining a credible force. See Andrew Pierre, *Nuclear Politics: The British Experience with an Independent Strategic Force, 1939-1970* (London, 1972).

loosening. This latter presumption was incorrect, and the alliance structure in Europe held together even when France left NATO's Integrated Military Command in 1966. Nor did other countries rush to follow France's example in developing independent nuclear arsenals. Here the most important country was West Germany. The Germans knew that alarm bells would be set ringing throughout Europe should they decide to move in this direction, and they preferred to use the slight possibility that they might as a source of influence over the United States.[93] The desire to maintain control over all nuclear decision making while at the same time attempting to satisfy European desires to participate in nuclear decision making led to some extremely contrived schemes, of which the most notorious was for a multilateral force.[94]

The main thrust of the European complaint was that the United States was attempting to withdraw its nuclear guarantee by its continual stress on the need to stay well clear of the nuclear threshold. In the end a compromise was reached. In 1967—with the uncompromising French now departed—NATO adopted the strategy of flexible response.[95] The new strategy was more a form of words than a carefully worked-out plan of action and was thus subject to a variety of interpretations, but this was inevitable because it was an attempt to reconcile opposing views.

The nod toward the American position was the acceptance of a lack of an automatic nuclear response to conventional aggression. The attempt was made to hold back the aggression with conventional means. Should that fail there would be a move to tactical nuclear weapons. If this did not terminate the conflict on satisfactory terms, there would be recourse to the U.S. strategic nuclear arsenal. This was no more than a restatement of the accepted and simplified view of the escalation ladder. The question was whether progression up this ladder would be deliberate or inadvertent, whether NATO was aiming for escalation dominance or merely relying on the threat that left something to chance.

For a number of reasons it was clear that it would be the second of these two approaches that would be adopted, if only by default. The

---

[93] Catherine McArdle Kelleher, *Germany and the Politics of Nuclear Weapons* (New York, 1975).

[94] The background to this dispute is found in John Steinbruner, *The Cybernetic Theory of Decision* (Princeton, 1974). For a discussion of the problems the nuclear sharing issue posed to U.S. doctrine see Albert Wohlstetter, "Nuclear Sharing: NATO and the N + 1 Country," *Foreign Affairs* 39, no. 3 (April 1961).

[95] "This concept . . . is based upon a flexible and balanced range of appropriate responses, conventional and nuclear, to all levels of aggression or threats of aggression. These responses, subject to appropriate political control, are designed, first to deter aggression and thus preserve peace; but, should aggression unhappily occur, to maintain the security of the North Atlantic Treaty area within the concept of forward defense" (communiqué, ministerial meeting of the North Atlantic Council, December 14, 1967).

Europeans were proving to be extremely resistant to the American pressures to convince them that a feasible conventional option was readily available.[96] One of the European conditions for adopting the new strategy was that they were not to be expected to spend any more on ground forces, and by this time the United States Army was bogged down in Vietnam and there was less interest on the American side in adding to the European commitment. There was thus little chance that NATO was going to feel able to dominate at the conventional level.

If there had been confidence that the tactical (battlefield) nuclear weapons could turn a land war in Europe in favor of the West, then dominance might be achieved at that level. But as we have seen, by this time there was only a slight belief in the possibility of fighting a limited nuclear war. To the Europeans the importance of these weapons was that they were nuclear and not that they might be used as if they were conventional. Their value was not as a means of preventing escalation to the strategic level but as a means of creating a risk of exactly that. According to the doctrine, these would couple the U.S. strategic arsenal to a land war in Europe so that the Soviet Union could not avoid the risk of all-out nuclear war should it contemplate localized conventional aggression. In the first studies to be undertaken within NATO's Nuclear Planning Group on the implementation of flexible response (exceptionally led by the Europeans), the emphasis was on initial use to signal political resolve to the Soviet leadership rather than to gain a military advantage.[97]

By the early 1970s the adoption of flexible response and assured destruction together demonstrated a lack of confidence in the possibility of establishing and sustaining distinctive thresholds once nuclear weapons were in use. As long as nuclear weapons were available and linked in some way to the defense of the United States and its allies, the risks facing an aggressor would be unacceptable. There was no need to delve too deeply into the awkward question of what would be done if deterrence failed, because there seemed to be little reason to believe that deterrence would fail. The early 1970s was a period of détente when the two superpowers appeared to be sorting out their differences. Even in those areas of conflict and crisis that remained, nuclear weapons seemed largely irrelevant. Neither side was practicing a nuclear diplomacy. The last crisis in which nuclear weapons had been clearly involved was the 1962 Cuban missile crisis. Toward the end of the October 1973 Arab-Israeli War, the alert status of American strategic forces was raised to warn the Soviet Union against intervening directly on behalf of Egypt. What is noteworthy

[96] The debate is described from an American perspective in Enthoven and Smith, *How Much is Enough?* ch. 4.

[97] Legge, *Theater Nuclear Weapons and the NATO Strategy of Flexible Response.*

772

about this incident is that the threat that the United States sought to convey was the risk of things getting out of hand—a threat that left something to chance.[98]

VII

During the 1970s a challenge began to be mounted to this dependence on such an unspecific threat. To rely on leaving things to chance, however realistic in terms of the actual fears and perceptions of political leaders and the difficulty of controlling the process of escalation once it was under way, seemed like the abandonment of strategy. It provided no guidelines for the design of forces or the preparation of targeting options.

Dissatisfaction with this position at first focused on the question of mutual assured destruction. Although American planners did not envisage an all-out attack on cities as the one and only option, the stress on assured destruction was widely taken to imply as much. For example, in his 1970 foreign policy report to Congress, President Nixon asked: "Should a President, in the event of a nuclear attack, be left with the single option of ordering the mass destruction of enemy civilians, in the face of the certainty that it would be followed by the mass slaughter of Americans?"[99] Not a lot was done within the bureaucracy to take up the President's challenge to develop more attractive options, but a number of outsiders picked up the theme of frustration with the existing state of affairs. Fred Iklé, for example, condemned the "current smug complacency regarding the soundness and stability of mutual deterrence" resting as it did "on a form of warfare universally condemned since the Dark Ages—the mass killing of hostages." The response was that however unpleasant it might be to rely on the threat of mutual destruction as a source of peace, it had seemed to work, and that in any case this state of affairs was a fact of life and almost beyond policy.[100]

Gradually the desire for change gathered pace and the effects were seen in official pronouncements. A number of factors explain this change. First, the deterioration in international relations made the question of

[98] According to two students of the episode, the message U.S. actions were designed to convey was: "If you persist in your current activity, if you actually go ahead and land forces in Egypt, you will initiate an interactive process between our armed forces whose end results are not clear, but which could be devastating" (Barry M. Blechman and Douglas M. Hart, "The Political Utility of Nuclear Weapons: The 1973 Middle East Crisis," *International Security* 7, no. 1 [Summer 1982], 146-47).

[99] Richard M. Nixon, *United States Foreign Policy for the 1970s* (Washington, D.C., February 18, 1970), 54-55.

[100] Fred Iklé, "Can Nuclear Deterrence Last Out the Century," *Foreign Affairs* 51, no. 2 (January 1973); Wolfgang Panofsky, "The Mutual Hostage Relationship between America and Russia," *Foreign Affairs* 52, no. 1 (October 1973).

what to do should deterrence fail seem more pertinent. Second, it was argued that although the United States might be relying on the over-bearing threat of mass destruction, the Soviet Union was moving forward in a much more sophisticated manner and developing a strategy for actually fighting a nuclear war. This would involve attacks on military forces to limit their ability to damage the Soviet Union and its strategic assets and perhaps even to prepare the ground for a traditional military victory. The fears that the Soviet Union was bent on obtaining a decisive strategic advantage were given added force by the Soviet military buildup, covering all types of military capabilities, that began in earnest in the mid-1960s. The worrisome parts of Soviet doctrine had been present for some time. What made them more serious was the apparent convergence between doctrine and capability.[101]

Developments in weapons technology also encouraged the view that more sophisticated nuclear tactics were becoming possible. The arrival of multiple warheads atop single missiles, the reduction of yield-to-weight ratios, the ability to tailor nuclear effects, the growing capacity of communications, command, control, and surveillance systems, and, most of all, the ability to hit quite small and protected targets with astonishing accuracy all contributed to a sense that nuclear weapons were increasingly becoming instruments that could be used with precision and discrimination.

A final factor in shaping perceptions of nuclear strategy in the 1970s that deserves mention is that of arms control. In formal terms much of the negotiating activity of the 1970s was bound up with establishing parity between the two superpowers. It was a moot point whether parity or the sort of asymmetries that did exist between the force structures of the two sides was of any relevance at all, given the enormous quantities of offensive nuclear power available to both sides. However, negotiations on this matter inevitably encouraged debate on the meaning of particular disparities.[102] It also encouraged a perception of distinct categories of

[101] The Soviet debate is unfortunately outside of the scope of this essay. The debate within the United States on Soviet strategy can be gleaned from two collections of essays: Derek Leebaert, ed., *Soviet Military Thinking* (Cambridge, Mass., and London, 1981) and John Baylis and Gerald Segal, eds., *Soviet Strategy* (London, 1981). The debate can be divided into two questions. The first was whether or not the Soviet Union had worked out a strategy for the conduct of nuclear war based on attacks on military targets and containing some elements of preemption. The evidence seemed to suggest that this was indeed the Soviet approach. The second question was whether this strategy gave them sufficient confidence to fight and win a nuclear war so that the integrity of Western deterrence had been dangerously compromised. Here the evidence suggested that Soviet leaders remained extremely aware of the risks of nuclear war.

[102] This prompted one of Secretary of State Henry Kissinger's more celebrated outbursts: "And one of the questions which we have to ask ourselves as a country is what in the

nuclear weapons—the "strategic," the "intermediate," the "short-range." One reason for this was the simple problem of dividing up the negotiations into manageable areas, but an important consequence was to reinforce a concept of a graded ladder of escalation.[103]

All these factors worked together during the 1970s to encourage a return to strategies based on the concept of escalation dominance. The process began in 1974 when Secretary of Defense James Schlesinger announced that a range of selective nuclear options would be developed to reduce dependence on threats of assured destruction. Schlesinger made it clear that it was neither feasible nor desirable to develop a true first-strike capability but that in the event of a major conflict, it would be necessary to use nuclear weapons as effectively as possible to impede the enemy's advance and to warn him against continuing with his aggression.[104]

The trend continued under the Carter administration. In 1980 Secretary of Defense Harold Brown unveiled a countervailing strategy, better known by the presidential directive—PD59—that brought it into force. This took the development of options further, including an investigation of the possibilities for fighting a protracted nuclear war and targeting key political and economic assets of the Soviet Union. However, as the name implied, the basic concept was that should the Soviet Union move up the escalation ladder the United States would be able to respond effectively at each level.[105]

---

name of God is strategic superiority? What is the significance of it, politically, militarily, operationally, at these levels of numbers. What do you do with it?" (press conference of July 3, 1974, reprinted in *Survival* [September/October 1974]).

[103] The course of arms control is also outside the scope of this essay, although questions of strategy increasingly became bound up with those of arms control, and discussion of the various proposals became an occasion for a broader debate about defense and foreign policy in general. I have discussed the relationship between broad strategic concepts and arms control in "Weapons, Doctrines and Arms Control," *The Washington Quarterly* (Spring 1984). For histories of the main strategic arms talks see John Newhouse, *Cold Dawn: The Story of SALT* (New York, 1973); Strobe Talbott, *Endgame: The Inside Story of SALT II* (New York, 1979) and *Deadly Gambits: The Reagan Administration and the Stalemate in Nuclear Arms Control* (New York, 1984).

[104] *Report of Secretary of Defense James Schlesinger to the Congress on the FY 1975 Defense Budget and FY 1975-79 Defense Program*, (Washington, D.C., March 4, 1974). Lynn Etheridge Davis, *Limited Nuclear Options: Deterrence and the New American Doctrine* (London, 1976).

[105] One of the officials responsible made clear the connection with the concept of escalation dominance: "the policy dictated that the United States must have *countervailing* strategic options such that at a variety of levels of exchange, aggression would either be defeated or would result in unacceptable costs that exceeded gains.... In general, the need to be prepared for large-scale but less than all-out exchanges, is most applicable to a situation in which a major war has already begun—and probably one in which tactical nuclear weapons have already been used. In such a context, it would be critical that the Soviet Union continue to believe that there is no intermediate level of escalation at which their use could be successful" (Walter Slocombe, "The Countervailing Strategy," *International Security* 5, no. 4 [Spring 1981], 21-22).

In 1981 the Reagan administration took the process a stage further. It claimed to be doing no more than developing the forces necessary to implement the doctrine of the previous administration. There was a definite change of tone, however. It was still argued that flexibility was necessary should the Soviet Union force the pace of escalation, but joined with it was the suggestion that Western security would be immeasurably strengthened should the United States feel able to force the pace.[106] This line of argument had been developed by a number of civilian strategists who had pointed out that because the United States had committed itself to initiating nuclear hostilities in support of its allies, it needed to have some idea of where these hostilities might lead.[107]

During the 1970s and 1980s, the possibilities for actually exercising dominance at different levels of the escalation ladder were discussed exhaustively. We have already noted the proposals for using improved battlefield nuclear weapons to turn the course of a land war in Europe. These found little favor with the Europeans. The next stage up became known as the intermediate level. Involved here were those American weapons based in Western Europe that could hit the Soviet Union or those Soviet weapons designed to threaten Western European countries. These weapons provided the focal point for an unusually intense public debate on the whole subject of nuclear weapons. The European critics of a NATO program agreed upon in 1979 to bring in new long-range missiles to Western Europe charged that this was part of an American plan to wage a limited nuclear war in Europe. The irony of this charge was that these weapons were wholly unsuited to such a strategy. They provided a link between strategic nuclear exchanges and a land war in Europe and in this way, to use the jargon, they were coupling. If the United States had desired to contain a future nuclear war then the need was to refrain from threatening Soviet territory. The criticisms of the program thus reflected a widespread recognition of the influence of concepts of escalation dominance (and an equally widespread distrust of the foreign policies of the Reagan administration), but in practice the program undermined any plans by either superpower to limit nuclear war to allied territory.[108]

[106] "A wartime strategy that confronts the enemy, were he to attack, with the risk of our counter-offensive against his vulnerable points strengthens deterrence and serves the defensive peacetime strategy" (Under Secretary of Defense Fred Iklé, "The Reagan Defense Program: A Focus on the Strategic Imperative," *Strategic Review* [Spring 1982], 15). For a discussion of the relationship between the Carter and Reagan programs see Jeffrey Richelson, "PD-59, NSDD-13 and the Reagan Strategic Modernization Program," *The Journal of Strategic Studies* 6, no. 2 (June 1983).

[107] Colin Gray and Keith Payne, "Victory is Possible," *Foreign Policy*, no. 39 (Summer 1980).

[108] Andrew Pierre, ed. *Nuclear Weapons in Europe* (New York, 1984).

776

The level of escalation that led to most debate within the United States concerned the possibility of an intercontinental attack against the land-based missiles of the United States. The argument was that the destruction of American ICBMs would leave the United States without the ability to respond in kind (the residual American systems being insufficiently accurate) and so would force escalation to the unacceptable level of counter-city exchanges. One writer was moved to suggest that this vulnerability of fixed land-based missiles was "an event so momentous that its anticipation should be the occasion for a fundamental review of strategic doctrine."[109]

It was difficult to explain why this vulnerability was so significant. For a Soviet planner the risks involved with mounting such an attack were legion: whatever the theoretical capabilities of his missiles, he could not be sure that they would perform as advertised; there was always the risk of the Americans launching on warning; and there could be no guarantee of a subdued American response, particularly as it became clear that this "limited" strike would lead to American casualties in the tens of millions.[110] The debate on this matter tended to revolve around a new missile—the MX or Missile Experimental—that was to have sufficient offensive capability to provide imposing counterforce options but also to be relatively invulnerable to a Soviet attack. The second of these two requirements proved to be virtually impossible to meet except at enormous expense and effort.[111] The search was eventually brought to a close by a bipartisan presidential commission that put the ICBM vulnerability into perspective.[112]

In each of these instances, the difficulties facing either superpower in any attempt to achieve and exploit escalation dominance tended to undermine suggestions that it might serve as the basis for an effective nuclear strategy. Other studies of the practicalities of conducting protracted nuclear operations of whatever sort tended to confirm this view.[113] The more the Reagan administration persisted with the suggestion that

---

[109] Colin Gray, *The Future of Land-Based Missile Force* (London, 1978). See also Paul Nitze, "Deterring Our Deterrent," *Foreign Policy*, no. 25 (Winter 1976-77).

[110] United States Congress, Office of Technology Assessment, *The Effect of Nuclear War* (Washington, D.C., 1979); John Steinbruner and Thomas Garwin, "Strategic Vulnerability: The Balance between Prudence and Paranoia," *International Security 50*, no. 1 (Summer 1976).

[111] John Edwards, *Super Weapon: The Making of MX* (New York, 1982).

[112] "Although the survivability of our ICBMs is today a matter of concern (especially when that problem is viewed in isolation) it would be far more serious if we did not have a force of ballistic missile submarines at sea and a bomber force" (*Report of the President's Commission on Strategic Forces* [Washington, D.C., April 1983], 7).

[113] Desmond Ball, *Can Nuclear War Be Controlled?* (London, 1981); Paul Bracken, *The Command and Control of Nuclear Forces* (New Haven, 1984).

such operations could be conducted effectively, the more skeptics reaffirmed that in the end the West was still relying for its security on the threat that leaves something to chance.[114]

By the mid-1980s, therefore, four decades after the destruction of Hiroshima and Nagasaki, the nuclear strategists had still failed to come up with any convincing methods of employing nuclear weapons should deterrence fail that did not wholly offend common sense, nor had they even reached a consensus on whether or not the discovery of such methods was essential if deterrence was to endure. The fundamental dilemma of nuclear strategy remained as intractable as ever. If there was any consensus, it was that the West's security problems would be eased substantially if only it were possible to have stronger conventional forces and so be less reliant on nuclear weapons!

[114] See for example Theodore Draper's exchanges with Secretary of Defense Caspar Weinberger in the *New York Review of Books*, reprinted in Draper's book *Present History: On Nuclear War, Detente and Other Controversies* (New York, 1983). Robert Jervis, *The Illogic of American Nuclear Strategy* (Ithaca, 1984), opposes escalation dominance and explicitly favors the threat that leaves something to chance.

26. Conventional Warfare in the Nuclear Age

MICHAEL CARVER

W HEN THE Second World War was abruptly brought to an
end by the explosion of two atom bombs on Japanese cities,
views varied about the effect these weapons would have on
the conduct of war. Some of those airmen who had been dedicated to
strategic bombing, but disappointed that it had not made other forms of
warfare obsolete as had been predicted, believed that the atom bomb
made their predictions possible. Others, who took a less extreme view
but believed in strategic bombing as a major contribution to victory, now
saw it as even more decisive than they had earlier claimed it to be. Others
still, including many sailors and soldiers, were more skeptical. The huge
effort involved in the production of two bombs meant, they believed,
that even the most powerful nation would only be able to afford a few.
The principal result, which they welcomed, would be that strategic bombing fleets could be significantly smaller and therefore would not absorb
as much of defense manpower and money as they had during the war.
Until the appearance of the hydrogen or fusion bomb in 1952, the victors
of the Second World War planned and trained their forces as if nothing
had fundamentally changed, envisaging lengthy major campaigns on
land, at sea, and in the air, conducted on the same lines as those they
had experienced between 1941 and 1945. Although standing forces, except in the case of the Soviet Union, were sharply reduced, mobilization
of reserves, both of manpower and matériel, was expected to provide
the means by which such wars would be fought. Britain and France also
faced the problem of maintaining or restoring their imperial authority in
Africa and Asia, a task that required armies organized and equipped on
lines more akin to those the British had employed in Burma in 1944 and
1945 than to those deployed in Europe. The need was for large numbers
of infantry, plentifully supported by air transport. The former was supplied partly by conscription and partly by recruitment of African and
Asian soldiers; the latter was slow in coming, as air forces preferred to
concentrate on fighters and bombers.

I

The North Korean invasion of the South in June 1950 posed the
first test of these ideas. One of the first casualties was the concept that

779

the atom bomb had made land warfare obsolete; another was that possession of the bomb conferred either immunity from attack or exceptional power. Using World War II methods, including a bold amphibious landing at Inchon, General Douglas MacArthur came to the rescue of Syngman Rhee's Republic of Korea and drove the North Koreans back to the Yalu River by the end of October. Up to that time, he had not had to worry much about North Korean air attacks, but the entry of the Chinese into the war then changed its nature. Their methods resembled those that the Japanese had used in their victories over the British in Malaya and Burma in 1942, avoiding the roads to which the American army and its allies were tied and moving large numbers of infantry, carrying their own supplies, across the roadless hills. At the same time MacArthur was denied the ability to extend the potential power of the U.S. Air Force's and Navy's air fleets to attack Chinese forces and bases beyond the Yalu, operating from which the North Korean air force, reequipped with more modern Soviet aircraft, now posed more of a threat.

The war was to be limited for major strategic reasons: in order to avoid either direct conflict with the Soviet Union or a drawn-out war with China. To his intense annoyance, MacArthur found his freedom of action restrained for what he saw as political reasons, a situation that ran counter to the U.S. Army's concept of how wars should be conducted. The fighting in the first half of 1951, which by the time General Matthew B. Ridgway had replaced MacArthur had stabilized the line around the 38th Parallel, was more reminiscent of the First World War than the second. This was even truer of the two years of stalemate that followed before the armistice was signed in July 1953. Before the front became fixed, both sides employed a series of major infantry attacks, supported by intense artillery bombardments and limited tank support. The Chinese and North Korean infantry suffered heavy casualties as they attacked in close formation. After stabilization, all the old tricks of static trench warfare had to be learned afresh, the mine, both antitank and antipersonnel, adding to the hazards. When Dwight D. Eisenhower succeeded Harry S. Truman as President in 1953, he was determined that the most powerful nation in the world should not again find itself suffering casualties in such an outdated form of warfare, in which its modern armed forces, liberally equipped with firepower, were unable to force a decision.

Several other factors caused all the major powers at this time to reconsider how their armed forces should be prepared to fight. Prominent among these were the threat posed by Soviet intransigence in Europe, backed by its still large army, which occupied Eastern Europe; Mao Tsetung's extension of his power over all of China; developments in the field of nuclear weapons, particularly the Soviet Union's first test, and the development both of the fusion bomb and of smaller, so-called tactical, weapons, with the prospect that it would not be long before nuclear weapons became plentiful on both sides of the ideological divide; and the increasing difficulties faced by Britain and France in maintaining their imperial authority.

In Europe the breakdown of talks on a peace treaty to settle the future of Germany, the absorption of Czechoslovakia into the Soviet bloc, and the Soviet blockade of Berlin had led to the formation of the North Atlantic Treaty Alliance and the conversion of British, American, and French forces in West Germany from occupation to operational armies. The plan to defend Western Europe from the threat of an attempt by the Soviet Union to extend its power beyond the demarcation line dividing its zone from those of the others was based on making the Rhine River the main line of resistance. Based on World War II standards, this would require nearly one hundred divisions, about the same number as the Allied forces under Eisenhower had deployed in Germany at the end of the war. To raise more than a fraction of these as standing forces was out of the question, but hope (though not much trust) was placed on mobilizing the majority in time of crisis. Many of those mobilized would be men who had served in the war and still had a reserve liability, and some of the equipment needed could be found from that left over from that conflict. But even if reliance could be placed on mobilized divisions, there would still be a large shortfall. German rearmament was a partial solution; exploitation of the nuclear weapon another. It was not until 1955 that West Germany was received into the North Atlantic Alliance and the revival of its armed forces was begun. By that time it had become clear that nuclear weapons were not going to be the rarity that many people, including B. H. Liddell Hart, had assumed five years earlier.

In his collection of essays entitled *Defence of the West*, published in 1950, Liddell Hart had argued both against assuming that nuclear weapons made other forms of weapons obsolete and against placing too great reliance on them. He suggested that the Soviet Union and its armed forces were less vulnerable to atomic attack than the countries of Western Europe and also that when both sides possessed nuclear weapons, this might deter them from their use. He argued against reliance on mobilizing large armies of the Second World War pattern, which would be expected to advance into Eastern Europe and occupy the bases from which Soviet aircraft could operate. At that time, although he envisaged the use of ballistic or cruise missiles to deliver chemical warheads, he seems to have assumed that they would not be capable of delivering nuclear ones. He pressed for regular armies consisting of fully armored and tracked mobile divisions, the action of which would be combined with airborne infantry divisions, both exploiting the possibilities of modern developments in chemical warfare. He recognized that total warfare, employing nuclear weapons and large conscript armies, would be disastrous. He had little faith in schemes designed to prevent war, and urged the importance of trying to limit it. Forces of the kind that he proposed would, he believed, be more effective for that purpose. He deprecated talk of victory and was highly critical of the picture of "World War III" painted by Field Marshal Montgomery, then NATO's deputy supreme commander for Europe, in a significant lecture at the Royal United Services Institute in London, in October 1954. "I want to make it absolutely clear," Montgomery said, "that we at SHAPE are basing all our operational plans on using atomic and thermonuclear weapons in our defence. With us it is no longer: 'They may possibly be used.' It is very definitely: 'They will be used, if we are attacked.' The reason for this action is that we cannot match the strength that could be brought against us unless we use nuclear weapons. . . . There are some who say that if war is joined, nuclear weapons will not be used; I would disagree with that. My opinion is that the fear of atomic and thermonuclear weapons is a powerful deterrent to war; but once a world hot war has started, *both* sides are likely to use them. We would certainly use them ourselves if we are attacked."

In that same year President Eisenhower told the U.S. chiefs of staff that they could plan to use nuclear armaments of all shapes and sizes in the future, wherever this would work to the advantage of the United States.[1] The U.S. Army had been pressing its allies to accept this concept since it had become clear that nuclear weapons could be produced that were not of the huge size of the original. Different ideas developed on how to combine their use with the action of other forces. The most widely accepted concept was to use a river line as the area in which to exploit their destructive effect. A mobile covering force would delay the enemy's advance, while an observation force, well protected against atomic attack, would be deployed overlooking the river, with a mobile armored striking force assembled further in the rear. Nuclear weapons would be used to strike at the concentration of enemy troops as they assembled to cross, on their crossing places and on any bridgeheads that, in spite of this, they might have established on the near side. The armored striking forces would then attack and eliminate the remnants.

An alternative concept, more sensitive to the vulnerability of NATO's forces to enemy nuclear attack, was to disperse the defending forces in a series of well-protected static positions in depth, each equipped with

[1] National Security Council document NSC-162/2, *Basic National Security Policy*, 30.10.1953.

its own tactical nuclear delivery system, with which it would strike the enemy forces that had penetrated into the empty areas between the positions, the *coup de grâce* against remnants being delivered by airborne forces. Control of the battle in this concept posed difficult problems, as did the fate of inhabitants in the so-called killing areas. It was hoped that they could be evacuated beforehand.

Both these were purely defensive concepts. A more ambitious one was to drop nuclear weapons on the cities and military bases of the Soviet Union itself, followed up by airborne landings that would occupy the area and, it was hoped, overthrow the discredited and ruined communist regime. The alternative to this unrealistic concept was that of "broken-backed" war. This assumed that the initial exchange of nuclear weapons would have exhausted the stocks of both sides, after which, among the ruins, they would both revert to a campaign characteristic of the pre-nuclear age. It was a concept popular with navies and reserve forces, which otherwise would have little justification for their existence. As the nuclear arsenals of both sides increased, the concept withered as far as NATO was concerned.

In the late 1950s NATO began to have reservations about relying on the use of nuclear weapons on the battlefield to compensate for its members' unwillingness to provide conventional forces to balance those of the Soviet Union, by then significantly augmented by those of its satellites in the Warsaw pact. The two principal reasons for these reservations were the entry of the Federal Republic of Germany into the alliance, and the development of the Soviet Union's capability to deliver nuclear attacks on American cities with intercontinental ballistic missiles armed with fusion warheads. Both the West Germans and the Americans were reluctant to assume that nuclear weapons would be used at the first breach of the iron curtain. In addition, the Germans were not prepared to accept defensive plans that surrendered a large area of their narrow country before attempts were made to stop the enemy's advance. The credibility of a strategy based on immediate nuclear retaliation had already been undermined elsewhere in the world, and now appeared to have been considerably weakened as far as European defense was concerned.

The Korean War had not been the only conflict in which possession of nuclear weapons had proved irrelevant to the issue. When the French faced humiliating defeat at the hands of General Vo Nguyen Giap at Dien Bien Phu in May 1954, the considerations that had led Truman to refuse to employ nuclear weapons in Korea persuaded Eisenhower to observe the same restraint in support of the French in Indochina. Both international and domestic political factors had restrained Britain not only from considering the use of its nuclear weapons, but also from employing conventional air attack on targets other than airfields in the Anglo-French Suez operation in 1956. Even air attacks on a small scale, such as those of the French against Sakiet in Tunisia in 1957, aroused international outcry.

The end of the 1950s therefore saw a general reexamination in the Western world of the employment of armed forces "as a continuation of policy by other means." The conclusions took two forms. Harold Macmillan's Conservative administration in Britain adopted the view that ponderous forces, based on conscription in peacetime, which could be mobilized in an emergency, with their deployment supported by overseas bases retained to meet World War II types of threat, were obsolete. In a speech welcoming General Lauris Norstad as the new supreme commander of Allied powers in Europe in 1957, Macmillan said: "Let us be under no illusion; military forces today are not designed to wage war; their purpose is to prevent it. There will be no campaigns like the old ones, with victory at the end of a long and balanced struggle; total war can only mean total destruction." In common with many others at that time, he sought means of limiting war. To some, like Henry Kissinger and André Beaufre, that meant finding ways by which their nation's military strength could be employed in support of policy. To others, like Liddell Hart, it meant trying to ensure that a war, if it could not be prevented by deterrence, could be kept limited, so that it did not result in total destruction. American and French experience in the Far East and British and French experience in the Middle and Near East had left these powers intensely frustrated. In spite of the large commitment of manpower and finance to defense by all three, the positions they had tried to defend in Indochina, the Middle East, and North Africa had been eroded by the action of nations or political movements whose military resources, except in manpower, were much inferior. International and domestic disapproval of any military action, other than that of "liberation movements," and the fear that it could lead to a nuclear war combined to make it appear that military operations of almost any kind could no longer be embarked upon by a major power. Minor powers and subversive movements, encouraged and supported with arms supplies and training teams by the Soviet Union and China, were undermining the Western capitalist-democratic world, which appeared helpless to prevent this process.

In the Western countries experts called a halt to concentrating attention and effort on how to fight wars with nuclear weapons, although Kissinger and others in the United States initially sought ways of employing limited nuclear wars. But General Maxwell Taylor, chief of staff of the U.S. Army, and the American writer Robert Osgood took the lead in demanding that reliance should no longer be placed on nuclear weapons. André Beaufre and Raymond Aron in France, unwilling to reject them entirely, sought a solution in terms of "very limited nuclear use." In Britain Liddell Hart was almost tempted to join the French, but his sense of how political and military leaders tended to be carried away by the strong emotions aroused in war persuaded him to take the line that Kissinger, on second thought, had taken: that the only possible forms of limiting war to avoid mutual suicide were either to limit the geographical area in which operations took place, which was hardly possible in Europe, or to refrain from using nuclear weapons—perhaps both.[2] In another collection of articles and lectures published in 1960, *Deterrent or Defence*, Liddell Hart concluded the chapter entitled "Are Small Atomic Weapons the Answer?" with the words:

> In theory, these small-yield weapons offer a better chance of confining nuclear action to the battle-zone, and thus limiting its scale and scope of destructiveness—to the benefit of humanity and the preservation of civilisation. But once any kind of nuclear weapon is actually used, it could all too easily spread by rapid degrees, and lead to all-out nuclear war. The lessons of experience about the emotional impulses of men at war are much less comforting than the theory—the tactical theory which has led to the development of these weapons.

He took the line that the provision of adequate conventional forces to defend the area between the Alps and the Baltic was not as hopeless a task as was commonly supposed. The forces needed should be related to the area to be defended rather than to the maximum strength that the Warsaw Pact could deploy if all the forces it could mobilize were taken into account. He advocated that at least half of the divisions of NATO's standing forces in the Central Region should not be committed to defensive positions, but should be held as a mobile reserve, and that the standing forces should be backed by a citizen militia, some of whom would man a deep network of defense posts in the forward zone while others, in the rear areas, would guard key points against airborne attack. The standing forces should consist of twenty-six divisions, part armored and fully tracked, with a high proportion of tanks, and part light infantry. He summed up his proposals in these words: "The prime need to-day is to reinforce the H-bomb deterrent, which has turned into a two-edged

[2] See Henry Kissinger, *The Necessity for Choice* (London, 1960).

785

threat, by developing a non-nuclear fireguard and fire-extinguisher—on the ground and ready for use without hesitation or delay."

American minds had been turning in the same direction for rather different reasons. They did not relish the idea that, for lack of an adequate conventional defense in Europe, they should be expected to resort immediately to the use of nuclear weapons, which now meant risking Soviet nuclear counter-attack. Their nuclear "umbrella" or "guarantee" to their European allies, particularly the Federal Republic of Germany, which had forsworn possession of them, could not be withdrawn; but at least it could be postponed in the hope that hostilities could somehow be arrested before they escalated into mutual suicide. In the early 1960s Robert S. McNamara, President John F. Kennedy's secretary of defense, pressed his European allies to increase the strength of their conventional forces in order to bring this about. He met considerable resistance. European governments found it politically difficult to accept higher defense expenditures and an increase in the length of conscript service, when they were trying to move in the opposite direction (the British abolishing conscription altogether). It was also suspected that McNamara's proposals implied a weakening of the American nuclear guarantee and could encourage a weakening also of its conventional forces in Europe. The prolonged discussion that McNamara provoked eventually resulted in the adoption of the policy known as flexible response. Under this concept, which also incorporated that of forward defense, NATO's forces would attempt to contain and bring to a halt a Soviet invasion by the use of conventional forces alone if possible, in the hope that the awful prospect of a nuclear exchange would persuade both sides to make peace. If it did not, NATO would then implement what would more correctly be defined as graduated nuclear response, described by Beaufre as "sublimited nuclear war." A small number of nuclear weapons—perhaps only one "demonstration shot"—would be used with the intention of persuading the Soviet Union that NATO was prepared to take the nuclear decision, and that therefore both should hang back. If that again failed, NATO would climb the ladder of escalation rung by rung until, one had to assume, the approach of mutual suicide persuaded one side or the other to call a halt. It was not clear why it should be the other side.

The conduct of operations by NATO's non-nuclear forces under this concept raised many difficult problems, apart from that imposed by forward defense, which forbade trading space for time. They had to be prepared for nuclear weapons to be used both by them and against them at any time, and had to convey that impression; but they had to try and prolong the conventional phase of fighting for as long as possible without giving much ground. In practical terms this required large conventional

786

forces, which NATO's politicians had intended to avoid. The difficulties were aggravated by France's withdrawal from the military organization in 1966 and America's diversion of effort and attention to Vietnam.

Although this was called flexible response, that was not what had been meant by the term when it was coined by Maxwell Taylor in his paper "A National Military Program," written in 1955. He believed that the nuclear arsenals of both sides cancelled each other out. Under cover of this "nuclear nullity," as Liddell Hart described it, the communist powers were encouraging subversive movements to challenge the West, which, having put so much effort into navies and air forces and their nuclear armaments, had no effective forces to oppose them. A policy of flexible response would mean that the United States, and it was to be hoped the West as a whole, would have the capability to employ whatever means was appropriate to the threat, from diplomatic, political, or economic action, through clandestine or "special" forces, to full-scale conventional campaigns anywhere in the world. The idea that conventional military action should be ruled out as a support of policy should be discarded, as should the idea that any war in which the United States engaged must be total and unlimited.

When Kennedy became President in 1961, he accepted Taylor's ideas with enthusiasm, recalling him from retirement and appointing him chairman of the Joint Chiefs of Staff in October 1962. Taylor was to have the unpleasant experience of seeing his theory turn sour in practice. The Vietnam War, like the Algerian, showed that keeping a war limited to the extent one desires depends on the willingness of the opponent to accept the limitations. Neither China nor the Soviet Union wanted to become directly involved, and the United States did not wish to involve them; but the North Vietnamese, under Ho Chi Minh and Giap, were prepared to go to any limits—of sacrifice, of manpower, of space and of time—which the United States was not. Forced to expend an effort far beyond what was envisaged when it first intervened to replace the French support of Ngo Dinh Diem's regime in South Vietnam, the American government eventually decided that the political disadvantages of continuing outweighed those of giving up and ceding victory to the other side, however masked that might be. Eleven years previously, Charles de Gaulle had faced the same situation and taken the same road in Algeria. The theorists who had assumed that limited war could be conducted like a game of chess, had been discredited, and had to think again. The answer of the prophet of limited war, Robert Osgood, was that the United States should be more selective in designating the areas of the world that it considered to merit the use of force to contain Soviet influence. "They should relate," he wrote, "to specific milieu goals of substantial intrinsic value from the standpoint of U.S. military and economic security."[3] On that basis, he would have approved of the refusal by Congress to see the United States involved in Angola. The application of his policy to intervention in Central America or the Persian Gulf would be less clear cut.

Beaufre attributed the disarray of the West, with the collapse of its strategies in Indochina, the Middle East, and North Africa, to a failure to develop a real strategy—to having been mesmerized by concentrating on equipment rather than on ideas. In his book *Introduction to Strategy*, he advocated that the West pursue what he called a "total" strategy, embracing every field of political, economic, and diplomatic activity, backed by the threat and, if necessary, the actual use of military force, similar to the strategy pursued by the Soviet Union.[4] He glossed over the difficulty, in a group of independent democratic and sovereign nations, of agreeing on both a strategy and its implementation, let alone actually putting it into effect. The most valuable point he made was that no one strategy is applicable to all situations: alternative strategies should be chosen according to the circumstances of the case. He distinguished between total strategy, a term he preferred to grand strategy, and overall strategy, the former governing the conduct of war at the governmental level, the latter applying to the particular field—military, political, economic, or diplomatic, each of which has its own overall strategy as part of the total strategy. In the military field this is converted into operational strategy, which must be based on the resources available, the geography of the theater, and the military capability of both one's own forces and those of the enemy.

Beaufre listed five choices for total strategy. First, the direct threat may be employed when one has ample resources and the objective is not of overwhelming importance. In theory this should be applicable to a major nuclear power facing a lesser non-nuclear one. In practice it cannot be used because of the international, and possibly also domestic, political implications of threatening to use that power. Beaufre maintained that this is the strategy on which deterrence is based—the threat that all one's resources would be applied directly to the enemy's territory—although in that case the objective would be of overriding importance. The second choice he called indirect pressure, applicable where the objective is of moderate importance, but the resources are not available to exert a decisive threat. This was the strategy used by Hitler much of the time and currently used by the Soviet Union. It consists of sustained political, diplomatic and economic pressure, backed by the threat of force. Beaufre

[3] Robert Osgood, *Limited War Revisited* (Boulder, 1979), 106.
[4] André Beaufre, *Introduction to Strategy* (London, 1965). Originally published in Paris in 1963.

788

suggested that this is a suitable strategy when there are limitations on one's freedom of action. His third choice was a series of successive actions, a nibbling process, suitable when one's resources are limited, but one is content to move slowly toward the ultimate goal. A variant of this is the *fait accompli*, or "single slice of salami," similar in execution to a series, but with the hope of achieving one's aim with one blow. The Israeli wars of 1956 and 1967 are good examples, and Egypt hoped that the 1973 October war would be as well. His fourth choice was a protracted struggle, waged at a low level of intensity. This is clearly suitable when military, but not manpower, resources are limited, and one is prepared to take a long time to achieve one's aim. Wars of liberation, including Mao Tse-tung's defeat of Chiang Kai-shek, were mostly won in this way. The protracted struggle is not suitable to Western industrial democracies, which do not as a rule have the patience to provide the resources, especially the manpower, required to fight on the enemy's terms. Finally the classic violent conflict aiming at military victory, involving either the destruction of the enemy's armed forces or the occupation of his territory or both, is applicable when one's military resources are clearly superior to those of the enemy and there are no limitations, such as political inhibitions or fear of escalation to nuclear war, which would restrict the application of one's military strength.

Within these five categories of choice, one would design one's overall and operational military strategy. Beaufre followed Foch in suggesting that the object of strategy at both these levels is to achieve and maintain one's freedom of action and to try and limit that of the enemy. Retaining the initiative is essential if one is to impose one's will on the other side, for that is what war is all about. Beaufre defined war as "the dialectic of two opposing wills, using force to resolve their dispute" and strategy as the art of that dialectic. He concluded that the future lay in the field of indirect strategy. "The further nuclear strategy develops," he wrote, "and the nearer it gets to establishing a balance, however precarious, of overall deterrence, the more will indirect strategy be used. Peace will become less and less peaceful and will get nearer and nearer to what in 1939 I called 'war in peacetime' and which we know as the Cold War. . . . The vital phase in indirect strategy takes place when the first symptoms appear. Anything later is too late. . . . The psychological factor . . . in indirect strategy becomes dominant [but] the availability and the use of force are just as necessary as in direct strategy. . . . force is required to exploit (or threaten to exploit) the situations created by psychological manoeuvre." His final words were: "We must master the art of indirect strategy."[5]

[5] Ibid., 127.

II

Theory aside, how have wars actually been conducted since the beginning of the nuclear age? There have been no nuclear wars, and none fought under the shadow of the possible use of nuclear weapons, although their existence may have influenced both the United States and the Soviet Union to limit their involvement in Korea, Vietnam, and the Middle East. Nuclear-age wars have therefore all been conventional in a sense, but the majority have been civil wars in which, in some cases, external influence and support have played a part. These insurgency and counter-insurgency operations are dealt with in the essay by John Shy and Thomas Collier below. Since the Korean War, which has been discussed, conventional wars have been few, the majority having been conflicts between the Arab nations and Israel and between India and Pakistan. The Anglo-French Suez operation was an appendage of one of the former, and India was also involved in a short war with China. Iran and Iraq are now engaged in a very conventional war, and a flash in the conventional pan was provided by Argentina's invasion of the Falkland Islands in 1982 and Britain's expedition to recapture them. Britain and Malaysia's "confrontation" with Indonesia in Borneo from 1962 to 1966 was a very limited form of conventional war, which had many of the characteristics of a counterinsurgency campaign. All these wars, which will be discussed below, have been limited in one way or another. One limitation common to them all has been to avoid bombing each other's cities when at all possible, both from fear of reprisal and from fear of a hostile domestic and international reaction to inflicting casualties on noncombatants.

Arab-Israeli Wars. The Arab-Israeli wars have differed from all the others in that Israel has been fighting for its very existence. The limits have been set, in Israel's case, by its resources, both human and material, and by the recognition that there are limits to the extent to which it can rely on the support of its principal ally, the United States. The limits on Arab action have been set by the degree to which they have been prepared to cooperate with each other, the effort they have been prepared to devote to the cause, and their ability to make good practical use of the considerable military resources that they have assembled at various times, 1973 representing the peak.

The first of the wars, which established Israel's existence in 1948, was an unsophisticated affair. The Israeli troops were provided by the unofficial military organizations that the Jews of Palestine had established under British rule, and on the Arab side the burden of the fighting was borne by Jordan's British-led Arab Legion. It was primarily an infantry war, fought with infantry weapons, in which the age-old military virtues of determination, endurance, ingenuity, boldness, and courage enabled the Israelis to prevent their infant state from being crushed or reduced to the three unviable segments into which the General Assembly of the United Nations had proposed to divide it. As was to be the case in future Arab-Israeli conflicts, the fighting took place against the background of international pressure for a cease-fire. The campaign therefore tended to consist of attempts both to secure what one already had and to seize rapidly something more to use as a bargaining chip when the cease-fire was agreed on or imposed.

Between May 1949, when Israel and Jordan were recognized by the United Nations as independent states on the basis of the frontiers resulting from the fighting that had ended a month before, and the outbreak of the Suez War in 1956, Israel's armed forces became highly professional, well trained and equipped, including a formidable air force. During these years its Arab neighbors and Palestinian refugees had carried out a continuous series of acts of terrorism and sabotage against Israeli settlements and individuals, to which Israel responded with retaliatory raids across its borders. When Moshe Dayan became Israel's chief of staff in 1953, the scale and ferocity of these raids intensified. The result was to strengthen the resistance, so that the raids became more expensive, and this cast doubt on their value. With the departure of the British from their Suez Canal base in 1955, it became clear that Egypt was preparing for military operations against Israel. Dayan wished to preempt them, and Britain and France's quarrel with Gamel Abdel Nasser, sparked by his nationalization of the Suez Canal, provided the opportunity for Israel to do this with some international support, which distracted Egypt's attention and diverted its forces.

Dayan's campaign in 1956 was a model of the cooperation between airborne and armored forces that Liddell Hart had advocated, although in his initial plan Dayan had relegated the armor to a secondary role on the grounds that it was too slow and cumbersome and required too much logistic support. It was to be used to support the infantry attacks on the Egyptian defenses in eastern Sinai, while unarmored, wheeled mobile troops would be used to join up with the airborne drops on the passes in western Sinai. But Dayan was unable to restrain the enthusiasm of the Israeli tank commanders. In their tactical methods they did not waste time on "indirect approaches," but hit hard at the key Egyptian defenses and were successful. Ariel Sharon's paratroopers were less successful in their attack on the Mitla Pass after their unopposed airdrop east of it. They failed to secure the pass and suffered 150 casualties, more than half the total in the campaign, which captured the whole of Sinai in six days at a cost of only 200 dead. It had been a highly successful example of *fait accompli* strategy, but the international opposition, led by the United States, to the Franco-British expedition that followed immediately and was linked to it, deprived Israel of the fruits of victory. By March 1957 its forces were back behind the frontier from which they had started, surrendering the Gaza Strip and Sharm el Sheikh, which Israel had hung onto since December, when the British and French had left Port Said.

Ten years later Nasser, his forces trained and equipped by the Soviets, felt strong enough to provoke a clash with Israel. He thought he could win and thereby enhance his somewhat tawdry image as leader of the Arab world, although he probably did not expect this to lead to a full-scale war. In May 1967 he demanded the withdrawal of the United Nations force that had helped to preserve peace on Israel's Sinai frontier, and declared a blockade of the Straits of Tiran, leading to Israel's Red Sea port of Eilat. Jordan's King Hussein reluctantly allied himself with Egypt and Syria, agreeing to the presence of an Iraqi division in his territory. Pressure on the Israeli prime minister, Levi Eshkol, to take decisive action led to the recall of Moshe Dayan as defense minister. He told his colleagues that he believed that Egyptian forces in Sinai could be defeated at a probable cost of a thousand dead and that a preemptive strike against the Arab air forces would knock them out and guarantee Israel against air attack. Arab provocation had been such that striking the first blow would not antagonize the United States, and he was confident that the Soviet Union would not intervene directly. Within the frontiers to which it was limited at that time, the Arabs occupying all of what is now known as the West Bank and Egypt all of Sinai, Israel could not afford to let its enemies strike first. Dayan's argument was accepted, and on the morning of June 5, at the time when the Egyptian air force's dawn patrols had stood down and the early morning mist in the Nile Delta had cleared, the Israeli air force struck in successive attacks lasting for nearly three hours, and thereafter switched its effort to attacks on other Arab air forces. By the end of the second day, its 250 combat aircraft, of which about 150 were modern fighters, in more than a thousand sorties had destroyed 309 (out of 340 serviceable and 450 total) Egyptian combat aircraft, including all their long-range bombers, and 60 Syrian, 29 Jordanian, 17 Iraqi, and 1 Lebanese aircraft, most of them on the ground, against a loss of 26 aircraft of their own, some of them in attacking army targets. They had also knocked out 23 Egyptian radar stations and several surface-to-air missile (SAM) sites, 16 of them in Sinai.

This crushing victory greatly eased the task of Gavrish's Southern Command, whose forces were formed into three groups. The northern group under Tal, with two armored brigades totalling three hundred tanks, and a parachute brigade, was to deal with the Egyptian defenses near the Mediterranean coast. In the center Sharon's group had one armored brigade of two hundred tanks and one infantry brigade to deal with the defensive complex around Abu Agheila; and Yoffe's group, of two armored brigades, each of one hundred tanks, was to operate between the two. One infantry and two armored brigades were in reserve. Dayan's strategy was to concentrate on a rapid advance as far as the Gidi and Mitla passes in western Sinai. He opposed an advance to the Suez Canal as likely to arouse international opposition and make it more difficult for Nasser to come to terms, and he was not prepared to consider switching efforts to Jerusalem and the West Bank until Sinai had been secured. He estimated that the campaign could be completed in three weeks. In the event, greatly helped by the overwhelming victory of the Israeli air force, things turned out more successfully and moved more rapidly than expected.

The seven Egyptian divisions in Sinai—five infantry, one armored and one light armored—under General Murtagi, greatly exceeded Gavrish's forces in numbers, but a high proportion was tied to static defensive positions. Tal was quickly successful in a direct assault on the defenses of the Gaza Strip. Sharon tried the same tactic at Um Katef and met with a rebuff, but rapidly readjusted his plan, flying in a parachute battalion by helicopter for a night attack from the rear of the position. Yoffe managed to slip between the two. Tal's continued success loosened up the entire position, and Murtagi decided to withdraw all his forces to the passes fifty miles east of the Suez Canal.

Dayan and Itzhak Rabin, the chief of staff, were cautious about immediately exploiting this opportunity because they were concerned about the situation around Jerusalem and to the north of it. They had hoped to persuade Jordan to keep out of the war, but the Egyptian general Riad, who had been accepted as overall commander of the Jordanian, Syrian, and Iraqi forces on the Jordan Valley front, succeeded in persuading Hussein that he must help Egypt in the desperate straits to which the Israeli air attacks had reduced it. However, Riad's incompetence, the blow that the Israeli air force delivered against the Iraqi brigade, and the fear of the Syrians that they would suffer the same fate if they invaded Galilee relieved Dayan and Rabin of their anxiety about the situation on that front. Gavrish was given the go-ahead, and Sinai became the scene of confused battles as Tal and Yoffe thrust their tanks through and behind Murtagi's forces and Sharon recovered from the muddle into which his force had gotten itself.

Tal's troops had reached the Canal when Nasser asked the United

Nations at 7:00 P.M. on June 8 to arrange a cease-fire. This spurred the Israelis on to occupy all the territory they could before it was implemented. Yoffee pushed his tanks through the Mitla Pass to reach the Canal early in the morning of June 9, three hours before the UN cease-fire was supposed to come into effect. By that time Israeli forces had also occupied the areas of Judaea and Samaria, known as the West Bank, from which the Jordanian forces had withdrawn. Dayan, determined that the Syrians should be evicted from the Golan Heights before a cease-fire became effective, ordered Elazar to attack them that morning, without consulting either Eshkol or Rabin. The Syrians put up a stiff resistance in spite of intense air attacks, but withdrew after twenty-four hours of fierce fighting.

Israel's victory was achieved at a cost of 778 military and 26 civilian dead, less than a tenth of the casualties suffered by the Egyptians alone. As we have seen, the air force made a very significant contribution. After its initial victory, it was able to switch its effort in support of the army rapidly from one target and one front to another, achieving an astonishingly high sortie rate. Victory, however, brought its problems, primarily the desire of humiliated opponents for revenge and the problem of the future of the territories Israel had occupied—Sinai, the Gaza Strip, the West Bank, and the Golan Heights. Without at least the last two, Israel's security could never be assured. While international efforts both inside and outside the United Nations were under way to find a political solution, Egypt reacted in two ways: by commando raids and artillery bombardment to interfere with Israel's construction of the Bar-Lev line to defend the east bank of the Suez Canal and, with Soviet help, by building up an effective antiaircraft defense, under cover of which it could eventually regain Sinai. When Nasser died in 1970, Anwar Sadat devoted himself to this task. Israel retaliated with air attacks on targets deep inside Egypt and with commando raids to capture and destroy elements of the increasingly effective Egyptian air defense system, which progressively reduced and eventually put an end to these attacks in what was known as the War of Attrition.

By September 1973, Israeli intelligence was aware that both Egypt and Syria were building up their forces in the forward areas, but assumed that Egypt would not go to war until its air force could neutralize that of Israel, and that Syria would not attack unless Egypt did. The threat of Arab terrorism on the international scene was considered to be more immediate. It was not until October 3, two days after Egypt had started large-scale maneuvers west of the Canal, that Dayan, still defense minister, and Elazar, now chief of staff, became seriously alarmed. By October 5 there could be no doubt that an attack was imminent, and both army and air force favored a preemptive strike as in 1967. But Golda Meir, the prime minister, and Dayan refused. Israel would be accused of starting the war, prejudicing American support. Israel's frontiers now being further from its centers of population, it was in a better position to accept the risk of facing a first strike, and, with the improvement in Egypt's air defenses, Israel's own first strike would not have the decisive effect that it had had in 1967. Intelligence became available early on October 6 that Egypt and Syria were going to start hostilities at 6:00 P.M. that evening, and their air forces actually struck four hours earlier, as the first Egyptian troops began to cross the Canal.

Israel's army was ill prepared to meet this blow, and the most immediate and dangerous threat was that of the Syrian army's 1,500 tanks to the Golan Heights. It was held by a combination of intensive air attack, in which the Israeli air force suffered most of its casualties in the campaign, skillful and courageous fighting by the two Israeli tank battalions stationed there, and the rapid deployment of mobilized reserves, fed into the battle with the determination and ingenuity that is a hallmark of the Israeli armed forces. At one stage Syrian tanks overlooked the Sea of Galilee.

In Sinai the Egyptians launched a methodical assault across the Suez Canal, defended by one reserve infantry brigade on its annual training. They had two armies, the Second, north of the center of the Great Bitter Lake, with three divisions, and the Third, south of it, with two. In reserve were three mobile and two armored divisions. Altogether the Egyptian army had 2,200 tanks, 2,300 pieces of artillery, and 150 surface-to-air missile batteries, backed by 550 first-line aircraft. The problem facing Gonen of Israel's Southern Command was whether to use his three divisions, each with one hundred tanks, to reinforce the threatened Bar-Lev line, or to base his initial defense further east and, if the latter, whether west or east of the Khatmia, Gidi, and Mitla passes. He could not count on air support, which was concentrated on the Golan Heights. Attempts to support the Bar-Lev line with tanks led to heavy casualties from Egyptian antitank missiles, and Dayan, visiting Gonen on October 7, advised withdrawing to the western edge of the mountains, east of the passes. Gonen and Elazar disagreed. They argued for a temporary defense west of the passes, from which counterattacks could be launched on October 8, and their view prevailed. The counterattacks were not well coordinated and failed, but had the effect of frustrating Egyptian plans to advance their bridgeheads beyond the fifteen miles to which they had been extended.

With both Egyptian and Syrian attacks held, Israel could now turn to the counteroffensive. Gonen and Bar Lev, who was attached to him as an advisor, resisted Sharon's ambitious proposal for an attempt to turn the tables by crossing the Canal at its junction with the Great Bitter Lake at Deversoir. They wished to preserve their strength for a decisive counterstroke when the Egyptians attacked again. Meanwhile Elazar argued for an immediate and decisive air force and army attack on the Syrian forces, which had been driven back to their start-line. He wanted to knock them out while Jordan remained inactive and before Iraqi reinforcements, already on their way, could arrive, so that he could thereafter concentrate all his effort against Egypt. Dayan hesitated, fearing that the defeat and humiliation of Syria would force the Soviet Union to intervene to save its protégé. Not for the first time Golda Meir overruled his caution. The attack was launched on October 11 and, in spite of Jordanian and Iraqi help, Syria gave up the struggle on October 20.

In Sinai Gonen had been won over to Sharon's plan, but could not begin to implement it until a major Egyptian attempt to break out of their bridgeheads, into which the armored divisions were on the point of being deployed, had been halted. Two days of fierce fighting, on October 13 and 14, in which two thousand tanks were involved—the largest number in a single engagement since the tank battle of Kursk in 1943—ended in defeat of the Egyptian Second Army, whose commander, General Mamoun, suffered a heart attack. Exploiting this, Sharon was ordered to cross the Canal on the night of October 15. This attempt ran into considerable difficulties, and exceptionally fierce fighting took place around "Chinese Farm" on the east bank during the next two days. The position of the troops who had crossed was precarious until bridges were completed on the nights of October 18 and 19, by the end of which Bren's and Mandler's divisions had joined Sharon's on the far side, pushing on until Bren was on the outskirts of Suez and Mandler had cut the road from there to Cairo, encircling the Egyptian Third Army. A ceasefire was called for by the UN Security Council, after Aleksei Kosygin had visited Cairo and Henry Kissinger had flown to Moscow to agree on the terms of a resolution with Leonid Brezhnev. Once more Israel held the bargaining chips, which were indirectly to lead, after prolonged negotiation, to a stable condition of security on its southern border. In summing up that war and the conflicts that had preceded it, I can only repeat what I have already written elsewhere:

"It had been one of the fiercest and most intense struggles in the history of warfare. Both sides had been equipped with the most modern weapons, although their inventory also included a considerable number of older ones. Egypt and Syria started with some 2,200 and 2,000 tanks respectively. Of these they lost about 2,000, most of them, in spite of the publicity given to anti-tank guided missiles, to the gunfire of Israel's

1,700 tanks, of which she lost about half. Egypt and Syria each lost about 250 aircraft out of their combined total of about 800, mostly in air-to-air combat, while Israel lost only 115 out of her 500, almost all from surface-to-air guns or missiles, a large proportion incurred on ground support missions. Egypt and Syria each lost about 8,000 men killed, Israel 2,500. In terms of population, even in the case of Israel, . . . which now reached three million, . . . [this] could not be called high; but an average of 115 men killed a day, it seemed so. It was the very high rate of expenditure of equipment and munitions on both sides, for which neither was prepared, that caused alarm to them both. The result was an urgent plea to their respective sponsors for immediate supply, to which both responded with massive airlifts, Russian and American transport aircraft carrying them, crossing each other's routes in the Eastern Mediterreanean from 15 October onwards. The rate of expenditure made logisticians on both sides of the Iron Curtain revise their estimates of their own requirements. If half one's inventory could be lost in less than three weeks, how was a long war to be sustained? The lessons of the war were studied with great care and interest as the first example of the use of many of the most sophisticated and modern weapons produced both by the Western powers and by Soviet Russia in action against each other. This applied particularly to the tank and anti-tank and the aricraft and anti-aircraft fields, although the latter had been tested in the Vietnam war, where the US Air Force had encountered the Russian Surface-to-Air Missiles, except the SAM6. An interesting feature of the war was the continuing importance of tank *versus* tank and air-to-air combat.

"Israeli victories in all three wars seemed to be a vindication of the theories of those apostles of mobility, Fuller and Liddell Hart. Liddell Hart himself regarded the Six-Day War as 'the best demonstration yet of the theory of the indirect approach'. They had shown that a small, highly trained and skilled army, equipped for mobile operations and commanded from the front by men of high intelligence and speed of thought, could defeat much larger armies, more ponderous in thought and action. They had also shown that the combination of speed and surprise produced its own momentum and that operations aimed to upset the enemy's equilibrium, psychologically as well as physically, were more fruitful than direct assaults. But, unlike Fuller and Liddell Hart, the Israelis never hesitated to engage in such assaults if they thought them necessary, often when they could have avoided them. They did not recognize any short cuts to victory by avoiding action, nor could they afford to play for time. At their backs, for both political and military reasons, they always heard time's winged chariot hovering near. Unlike their opponents, they knew that they were fighting for their very existence,

797

and this spurred them on. Although very sensitive about casualties, much more so than their opponents, they took risks which few other soldiers would have been prepared to face, and, although boldness did not always pay, more often than not it did.

"Their opponents, Jordanian, Egyptian, Syrian and Palestinian Arab, often fought with dogged determination and courage in defence, as they did also in advancing to attack; but their overall command was ponderous and hesitant in its reaction, as well as being disunited. Syria and Egypt received a poor return for the vast resources devoted by them and by their Russian supporters to their armed forces. Their resort to war has so far achieved nothing. Israel, by her own defence effort, with significant help from the United States and some others, has survived. To her there is no doubt that security comes first."[6]

Israel's latest war, the invasion of Lebanon in 1982, can hardly be called conventional warfare, as there was no conventional opponent, although all the armament at the disposal of both the Israeli air force and army has been used. This had elements about it of the *fait accompli* strategy, but it remains to be seen whether, as in previous conflicts, short-term military success establishes security in the long term.

India's Wars. India's wars have been less sophisticated than the later Arab-Israeli conflicts; for one thing, air forces have not played such a prominent part. Fundamentally, these wars revolved around the fears of Pakistan that India had never genuinely accepted that a separate Muslim state should exist on the subcontinent, and the fears of India that Pakistan would subvert the allegiance of the considerable number of Muslims remaining within Indian borders. The original British proposal had been that, on independence, states could choose to which nation they should adhere, and Kashmir, with its Hindu ruler and divided population (77 percent Muslim) became the symbol of the dangers this posed to Indian unity. The Maharajah had vacillated over which nation he wished to join, hoping to be able to remain independent of both. Fighting between the Indian and Pakistani armies, so recently members of the same British-controlled Indian army, began soon after an Indian battalion had been flown to Srinagar in October 1947 to support the ruler in suppressing a Muslim rebellion against him. Pakistan intervened on the side of the rebels, and both sides built up their forces until they amounted to the equivalent of two infantry divisions on each side. After the Indians had secured most of the eastern half of the state, the two sides engaged in

[6] Michael Carver, *War since 1945* (London, 1980; New York, 1981), 270-72. Footnote omitted.

798

some inconclusive mountain warfare against each other until a cease-fire line was agreed to in January 1949, observed by a small United Nations team. It has remained the de facto international frontier ever since.

India's next war was with China, caused in part by sensitivity over Kashmir. The conflict arose from a dispute about India's frontier with Tibet, west and east of Nepal, which had long been complicated by doubt about the status of Tibet itself. Prime Minister Jawaharlal Nehru had come under criticism from right-wing elements for accepting without protest Mao Tse-tung's extension of China's authority over Tibet, and he rejected a series of approaches by Chou En-lai to discuss the issue. Nothing happened until India discoverd in 1957 that the Chinese had built a road from Sinkiang to Lhasa in Tibet through the area known as the Aksai Chin, north of Kashmir, which both sides claimed as their territory, but which India had never occupied. India then insisted that China withdraw from the area, and refused to negotiate the disputed areas. China's response was to offer to agree to the McMahon line, which had been the de facto frontier east of Nepal since 1913, provided that India accepted that west of Nepal the border followed the line of the Karakoram Mountains, on the southern edge of the Aksai Chin, which the British had accepted from 1899 to 1927. If India refused, China would maintain its claim to the foothills of Assam as the frontier in the east.

Nehru, over-confident that the political support of both the United States and the Soviet Union would deter China from taking any action, and under criticism for not having done more to support the Tibetan rebellion against the Chinese, refused discussions and instituted a forward policy, sending a series of military patrols to support India's claims in these remote mountains. It was a foolish step, but generals who pointed out the military realities were replaced by subservient ones. Chou En-lai repeatedly warned Nehru of the dangers of his policy, which was interpreted as designed to detach Tibet from China, but his warnings were ignored, and the number and strength of military posts increased in 1961. Early in 1962 the Chinese began to take countermeasures, surrounding Indian posts with superior forces. In September they used this tactic at the Thag La Pass near the junction of the McMahon line with the frontier of Bhutan, and once more offered to negotiate. Nehru refused and ordered his army to drive the Chinese back.

This precipitated a counteroffensive in October by the Chinese, who could produce much superior forces in the area, as they could also in Ladakh, west of Nepal, where they attacked at the same time. The Indian forces in Assam, which had been built up to a strength of two divisions, were scattered about in positions that could not support each other and were easily outflanked. The lack of adequate logistic preparations ruled out more suitable dispositions. The higher commanders, drawn from Nehru's sycophants, handled an impossible situation with incompetence. Although many units fought gallantly, the Chinese had no difficulty in driving them out of the foothills and back to the plains by November 20. In Ladakh, General Daulat Singh, an able officer, concentrated his forces, which had been brought to the strength of one division, on the Karakoram range and by mid-November had the situation under firm control.

Panicking at the prospect of a wholesale Chinese invasion of India, Nehru abandoned his nonalignment and appealed to the United States, Britain, and the Soviet Union for help. The first two responded rapidly, offering arms and air support. Neither was needed as, on November 21, Chou En-lai announced that Chinese "frontier guards" would withdraw twenty kilometers behind "the line of actual control which existed between China and India on 7 November 1959" and would expect Indian armed forces to observe the same distance, although civilian police posts could come up to it. Prisoners could then be exchanged and negotiations could proceed. Nehru did not publicly accept the Chinese terms, but in practice conformed and let Chou En-lai know that he would.

It had been an old-fashioned infantry war, in which modern heavy weapons had played little part, and the ability to move over mountainous country and bring a superior force to bear from an unexpected direction had usually carried the day. The actions of air forces had been almost entirely limited to transport in the rear areas. Even had helicopters been present in any number, the altitude at which operations took place would have seriously restricted the use of the types then available. On the part of the Chinese, the campaign had been the perfect example of a limited war, limited in aim and execution to effect a clear political purpose, the means being economically adapted to the end. They had followed the tenets of Sun Tzu, who had written in the sixth century B.C. that one should seek victory in the shortest possible time, with the least possible effort, and at the least cost in casualties to one's enemy, remembering that one had to continue to live next door to him when the fighting was over. Nehru was foolish to ignore the military realities, and the Indian army was lucky that its casualties were not greater—1,383 killed, 1,696 missing, and 3,968 captured. It was also fortunate in that it led to the dismissal of the incompetent among the generals.

India's war with China had repercussions on its relations with Pakistan. The latter's forces had recently received significant quantities of new equipment, including tanks and aircraft, from the United States, as part of America's policy of building up the Central Treaty Organization

(CENTO) as a bulwark against Soviet influence in the Middle East. Pakistan had proceeded with friendly negotiations with China, agreeing on the line of their common frontier. President Mohammad Ayub Khan, who faced domestic political problems, saw an opportunity to win over the rest of Kashmir, where serious riots occurred in 1963 and 1964. Nehru wanted a settlement but died in May of that year, and his successor, Lal Bahadur Shastri, was not strong enough politically to make concessions. Ayub Khan organized a force of thirty thousand men, mostly irregulars, commanded by regular Pakistan army officers, headed by General Malik, to infiltrate across the Kashmir cease-fire line. Either as a distraction or to try and pin the blame for the opening of hostilities on India, he engineered a frontier incident in January 1965 in the Rann of Kutch, an almost uninhabited region east of the mouth of the Indus River, flooded in the summer monsoon. Tension mounted, and in August Malik's force crossed the line in Kashmir in four thrusts, to which India reacted promptly. Malik's men failed in their plan to rouse the populace in support and were soon confined to an area within ten miles of the line, taking little further part in the war, which evolved into one between the two regular armies, each of about eight divisions, including one armored. The first clashes took place at the southern end of the Kashmir line and gradually extended southwards into the Punjab, as each side developed thrusts to draw off the other's threats to targets on its side. On September 6 India launched an attack with three divisions towards Lahore, which led to four days of fierce fighting, drawing in Pakistan's armored division. The results were inconclusive. On September 11 India launched another thrust further north, aimed at Sialkot, using four divisions including their armored one. This led to a major battle lasting two weeks, in which four hundred tanks were involved; it also ended in stalemate.

Meanwhile, international pressure to bring about a cease-fire had continued, the most effective being the American and British decision to cut off arms supplies to both sides who, by September 22, had begun to realize that they could not afford to go on losing major equipment at the rate they had been experiencing. A cease-fire was accepted, although it was not until January 1966, at a meeting under the chairmanship of Brezhnev in Tashkent, that agreement was reached: they would both withdraw to the positions they had held on August 5, 1965. Shastri died of a heart attack on the day of signature, and was succeeded by Indira Gandhi. There was no agreement about the future of Kashmir. Casualty figures are unreliable, but appear to have been about the same on both sides—a total of twelve thousand, of whom about three thousand were killed. Both sides appear to have lost about 200 tanks each, with another

150 out of action but repairable, although Pakistan's losses may have been slightly higher. India lost about seventy aircraft and Pakistan twenty; their navies had hardly been engaged at all. In terms of their total populations, these losses were, of course, very small, the effect on their armored forces and on their stocks of ammunition and spare parts being the most significant.

Although the war had been inconclusive, it weakened Pakistan in relation to India and also internally. East Pakistan resented the West's obsession with Kashmir, and Yahia Khan, who succeeded Ayub in 1969, faced severe difficulties in both West and East. These came to a head in March 1971 when Yahia indefinitely postponed the opening of a newly elected National Assembly in which East Pakistan's Awami League had won a majority over Zulfikar Ali Bhutto's People's Party in the West. The military assumed control over East Pakistan and pursued a policy of repression against the Awami League and the educated Bengali classes generally, who were supported by India. This led to a major refugee problem in India's East Bengal. Having failed to persuade Yahia Khan to change his policy of repression, Mrs. Gandhi decided to bring the artificial link between East and West Pakistan to an end by military action.

The Indian army had about 825,000 men, organized into one armored, thirteen infantry, and ten mountain divisions and a number of independent brigades. Its tank strength had been increased since 1965 by the acquisition of 450 Soviet T-55 and T-56 tanks and the production of the Vickers Vijayanta tank, less thickly armored but mounting the same powerful 105-mm gun as their British Centurions. The air force had increased its combat strength to 625 aircraft, including seven squadrons of Soviet MIG-21s, the rest being Soviet Sukhoi-7s, British Canberras and Hunters, and Indian-produced Gnats. The navy had also been strengthened, built around the aircraft carrier *Vikrant*. Pakistan had two armored and twelve infantry divisions and one independent armored brigade, two other divisions being in the process of formation to replace those deployed in East Pakistan. Its air force had fourteen fighter and three bomber squadrons, but only one squadron of Sabre fighter-bombers was deployed to East Pakistan, as was one regiment of fifty tanks, all of them light. Pakistan's repressive policy led to the desertion of almost all its soldiers recruited in East Pakistan to the ranks of the subversive movement, the Mukti Bahini, which supported the Awami League, with the result that they had to be replaced by soldiers from the West. The administration of the country became more than ever a military regime imposed by the West, and the activity of the Mukti Bahini, supported from across the border by India, became more widespread.

Hostilities between India and Pakistan started on December 3, 1971, with an ineffective attack by the Pakistan air force on Indian air force airfields, to which the Indian air force replied to greater purpose. It was accompanied by equally ineffective attacks across the Kashmir cease-fire line by both regular and irregular forces. These developed into a series of battles on the borders of Kashmir and the Punjab, in which Indian tanks gained the upper hand. They had no effect on the major operation in East Pakistan under the command of General Aurora in Calcutta. His plan was an imaginative one. He had three corps, one of two divisions in East Bengal, another of the same strength on East Pakistan's northern border in Assam, and a third, with three divisions, in Tripura, east of the country. He overcame his principal problem, that of numerous water obstacles, large and small, by making his troops as independent of road movement as he could, while using all the army engineers that could be provided to construct bridges and ferries. Movement of matériel for the latter was the highest priority task for the Indian air force helicopters. This plan for a concentric attack exploited the weakness of the Pakistani general Niazi Khan's dispositions. In order to deal with the Mukti Bahini and keep the country under control, his forces were scattered, particularly near the frontiers; such strength as he could concentrate being held to secure communications between the capital, Dacca, and the main port of Chittagong in the extreme southeast.

All three Indian attacks met with rapid success. The forward troops, enthusiastically supported and guided by the populace, moved across country taking risks that would have been foolish in a more conventional setting, while the Indian air force, having established total air supremacy, was able to give unrestricted transport, strike, and reconnaissance support. As all three corps thrusts made progress, Aurora dropped a parachute battalion on December 11 to cut off the Pakistani force facing the attack from western Assam, east of the major river obstacles. This thrust from the north, under General Nagra, was approaching Dacca when Niazi asked for a cease-fire and was in the outskirts of the city when he surrendered all his forces in East Pakistan on December 16, ten days after Mrs. Gandhi had recognized the independence of Bangladesh, as the country was henceforth to be known. The campaign was a true blitzkrieg, following the lines of Liddell Hart's theory of "the expanding torrent," derived from the tactics that the German army had used in its March 1918 offensive on the western front. It involved exploiting any weakness in the enemy's position by infiltrating troops, bypassing opposition, on the pattern by which water finds its way around obstacles in a streambed. India's aim had been a limited one, which it achieved in full conformity with the principles of Sun Tzu.

Britain's Battles. Throughout all the years of the nuclear age, except 1968, Britain's army has been in action somewhere in the world. Most of its campaigns have been concerned with internal challenges to its government's authority in colonies, former colonies, and, since 1969, within the United Kingdom itself in Northern Ireland. Apart from these and its contribution in the Korean War, which has been described, Britain has been involved in three "conventional" actions—the Franco-British Suez expedition, the campaign with Malaysia against Indonesia in Borneo from 1962 to 1966, and the recapture of the Falkland Islands in 1982. The navy's marines and helicopters and the air force's aircraft of all types participated in almost all of the campaigns in which the army was engaged, although it was only in the Falkland Islands operation that they had to fight against enemy ships and aircraft.

In the Suez action, the Egyptian air force was put out of action on the ground by long-range bombing of its airfields before the airborne and amphibious assaults took place, and the Egyptian navy put up no effective resistance. One factor was common to both the Suez and the Falklands operations: no previous contingency plan had been prepared for either of them; they had therefore to be improvised. In 1956 Britain had neither the amphibious nor the air transport resources to deploy troops in any numbers by sea or air. It had bases in Cyprus and Malta, but the small ports of Cyprus were unsuitable for assembling or loading shipping and its two airfields were of limited capacity. Malta is 1,100 miles from Port Said, a long sea journey for slow-sailing craft. The Franco-British operation suffered from many changes of plan, as well as uncertainty about its aim. It was never entirely clear whether the operation was limited to securing the Canal itself, in order that it might continue to be operated by the Suez Canal Company on behalf of a Suez Canal Users' Association, or designed to achieve a more ambitious purpose, to topple Nasser from power in the hope, presumably, of replacing him with someone more favorably inclined toward Western interests. The original plan had been to land at Alexandria and thrust an armored column up the desert road to Cairo, from which columns would make for the Canal at Port Said, Ismailia, and Suez. It was optimistically assumed that this could be completed in eight days. For a number of reasons, including the limitations imposed by the paucity of amphibious craft, the plan was changed to an assault on Port Said, part airborne, part amphibious, preceded by a night-time air attack on the bases of the Egyptian air force. The limited capacity of Franco-British transport aircraft restricted the airdrop to 668 British and 487 French parachutists.

The eventual declared aim of the operation, carried out in collusion with Israel's attack, as has been described, was to separate the Egyptian and Israeli forces on the line of the Canal, although it is doubtful if anybody believed this. Israeli troops had already occupied Sinai by the time that the British and French parachutists landed at dawn on November 5 behind Port Said. Twenty-four hours later two British marine battalions landed from tracked amphibians, followed by one in helicopters and the rest of the British parachute brigade in landing craft. Fighting in Port Said was sporadic, and the commander, the British general H. C. Stockwell, to whom General Beaufre was deputy commander, planned that the French parachutists under General Jacques Massu should launch a combined air- and canal-borne attack on Ismailia, fifty miles south on the Canal, where the British parachute brigade, traveling by road, would join him. But international pressure, principally from the United States, brought about a cease-fire before this could be fully executed. Although larger forces were assembled for the operation, only three brigades actually took part, one of British and one of French parachutists, and one of British marines, of whom eleven British and ten French were killed, and ninety-two British and thirty-three French were wounded. It was an ill-conceived operation that, although it would have been militarily successful, had little if any chance of achieving a satisfactory and maintainable political solution. It was intensely frustrating for the members of the armed forces who took part.

British confrontation in Borneo, on the other hand, was successful in all respects. Its aim was to prevent Indonesia from subverting the government of Brunei, and from absorbing Brunei and its neighbors Sabah and Sarawak. These efforts began in December 1962 with an Indonesia-backed rebellion in the Sultanate of Brunei, a British protectorate, which was rapidly and effectively suppressed by three British battalions flown in from Singapore. In April 1963 Indonesia began to infiltrate armed men, ostensibly volunteers to assist the local rebels, into Sarawak and later into Sabah. These "volunteers" found few local rebels to help; those that may have existed in Brunei had all been detained, and the only potential rebels in Sarawak were part of the communist element in the population's Chinese minority, the more active of whom were also locked up. British reinforcements, many of whom were Gurkha battalions, were brought in, as were Malayan units when sovereignty and overall command was transferred to the new Federation of Malaysia in August.

A short cease-fire in January 1964, in which talks between Malaysia and Indonesia under UN chairmanship ended in deadlock, was followed by Indonesia's abandoning pretense and acknowledging that its troops were operating north of Kalimantan's frontier, which ran for eight hundred miles along mountain tops in thick jungle. They moved in companies of about one hundred men, intimidating the local natives and trying to establish a de facto extension of Indonesian authority. At first General Walter Walker, in command of the British forces, relied on the natives, supported by special forces, to provide information about the movement of the small groups that had made their way down rivers into the cultivated areas. But he could not let the Indonesians establish bases on the Malaysian side of the frontier and had to protect the natives from their incursions. He therefore set up company bases of his own near the frontier, supplied by air, from which patrols of platoon strength operated. If large bodies of Indonesian troops were encountered, reinforcements could be flown in by helicopter, often lowered through holes created in the jungle by felling trees. The ambush was the most effective tactic by which the British units, who included Australians and New Zealanders as well as Gurkhas, inflicted heavy casualties on the less-skilled and less well informed Indonesian soldiers. By the end of 1964 Walker had some fourteen thousand in his force, supported by sixty naval and air force troop-carrying helicopters and forty small army ones, organized in three brigades, increased in 1965 to four. In that year he obtained permission to operate secretly over the border into Kalimantan, making extensive use of intercepted Indonesian radio communications to provide targets for ambushes. These tactics paid off and, after a coup against Sukarno in October 1965 set off months of fighting between pro- and anticommunist factions in Indonesia, the "confrontation" virtually came to an end, although it was not finally concluded until August 1966, five months after General Suharto replaced Sukarno as the de facto ruler.

It had been a strictly limited war, and a cheap one for Britain and Malaysia, for which it achieved much. At its peak seventeen thousand servicemen of the British Commonwealth were deployed at one time in Borneo, with ten thousand more available in Malaya and Singapore. Casualties were 114 killed and 181 wounded, a high proportion Gurkha. There were also 36 civilians killed, 53 wounded, and 4 captured, almost all local inhabitants. It was estimated that 590 Indonesians were killed, 222 wounded, and 771 captured. The fighting lasted for nearly four years and clearly and decisively achieved its aim of preventing Indonesia, or any other outside influence from strangling Malaysia at birth. It had not been in the interests of either side to extend hostilities outside Borneo, although in August 1964 Indonesia had launched an amphibious raid of one hundred men and an airborne one of two hundred against the mainland of Malaya, both of which proved totally abortive. To have indulged in air attacks on military bases or other targets, or on naval or other ships at sea, would have incurred disadvantages greatly outweighing the marginal military effect that they might have produced. Both sides were wise to label the conflict a "confrontation" and to keep it within strict limits, which were never formally agreed to but were tacitly observed. At times the British were tempted to test the waters by sailing their warships through one of the straits separating the main Indonesian islands, but prudently refrained from doing so.

The Falkland Islands operation in 1982 was an altogether shorter and sharper affair. For many years Britain had been trying to find a political solution to the problem posed by its sovereignty over these sparsely inhabited and largely desolate islands off the tip of South America, from which the dependency of South Georgia, populated entirely by penguins, was administered. The fall in the world price of wool in real terms had threatened the economy, virtually a monopoly of the Falkland Islands Company, which invested little in the islands, and the population was dwindling, having fallen to about eighteen hundred, 95 percent of British origin. In an attempt both to improve social and economic conditions and to find a compromise over Argentina's claim to sovereignty, successive British governments had discussed the future status of the islands and persuaded Argentina to build an airfield and operate a scheduled air service to the mainland, to which the islanders could travel for education, medical treatment, and other purposes, including travel to other countries. Attempts to persuade the islanders to accept some form of association with Argentina, however, met with strong resistance, supported by the Company and the majority of both the main British political parties. Britain's negotiators had therefore nothing to offer the Argentines, who became increasingly frustrated at the lack of progress to meet their claim.

The Argentine invasion took place on April 2, 1982. Since the beginning of the year an Argentine scrap merchant had been dismantling an abandoned whaling station on South Georgia, which led to incidents over the expedition's failure to observe the procedures laid down by the British representative, and tension over this matter mounted in March. The movement of British naval forces toward the Falklands could also have been used by Argentina as a pretext for action by them. The garrison of the islands—sixty-eight marines—was double its normal strength because a relief was in progress, and it put up a gallant, if hopeless resistance to the Argentine marine battalion that landed at Port Stanley. Britain's reaction was swift. On April 5 a naval task force sailed from Britain, joined by some ships that had been exercising off Gibraltar. The task force was eventually to include forty-four warships, twenty-two naval logistic ships, and forty-five merchant ships, carrying a total of 28,000 men. They included four naval and one air force squadron of helicopters, one brigade of marines, and two parachute and three infantry battalions with their supporting arms. The U.S. Air Force base on the British-owned Ascension Island in the South Atlantic played an essential part as an air staging post. To make use of it, many of the aged British V-bombers were rapidly transformed into tanker aircraft, as some had been many years before.

As the fleet set off on its eight-thousand-mile voyage, the United States led in trying to establish the basis of a negotiated settlement. This was accompanied by warnings to Argentina that Britain meant business. On April 12 it had declared a maritime exclusion zone two hundred miles from the coast of the islands, later to be enforced as a total exclusion zone, and had said that any approach by Argentine warships or military aircraft that amounted to a threat to the task force, "would be dealt with appropriately." It was presumably on this basis that a nuclear-powered submarine sank the Argentine cruiser *General Belgrano* outside the exclusion zone on May 2, eliminating any chance of a negotiated settlement. Before that, on April 25, a detachment from the task force had recaptured South Georgia, and on May 1 the first air attacks had been made on airfields, notably that of Port Stanley, which had been used to fly in Argentine troops and their supplies. In response to the sinking of the *Belgrano*, two French Super-Etendards of the Argentine air force on May 4 hit the British destroyer *Sheffield* with an Exocet missile, forcing it to be abandoned and subsequently sunk.

Admiral Woodward, the task force commander, had to resolve a number of conflicting factors. Time was not on his side: the weather was deteriorating; he could not keep his soldiers and marines at sea in foul weather for too long; and Prime Minister Margaret Thatcher was anxious for quick results. He could not afford to establish a base too far from his principal objective, Port Stanley, because the means of transport for men and equipment on land were limited by the absence of roads and by the restricted capacity of the helicopters and other vehicles that could be landed. The main threat came from Argentine land-based aircraft, which were operating, however, at the limit of their range. Woodward could keep his principal ships outside this, except when the actual landings or bombardments were taking place. After the landings, his limited number of Harrier VSTOL aircraft would have to cope with the air defense of the fleet, the landing area, and the troops as they moved forward. They also would have to provide direct strike support to the troops, who would be inferior in numbers to their opponents. General Mario B. Menendez, the commander of the Argentine forces on the islands, did not know where the British would land and faced problems of land transport similar to theirs. Inevitably he concentrated on the defense of Port Stanley. As the British fleet approached at the beginning of May, reinforcement and supply flights from the mainland were limited to the hours of darkness.

On May 21 the British marine brigade landed unopposed in San Carlos Bay on the west coast of East Falkland, sixty miles from Port Stanley. Over the next few days, as the base and its antiaircraft defense were established ashore, the Argentine air force carried out repeated and gallant attacks on the ships and the disembarkation area. In doing so, they lost forty-nine aircraft and sank one destroyer and one frigate, crippling another, and a large container ship that carried the British air force's heavy-lift helicopter squadron. On May 28, as pressure from London grew for the forces on land to press on toward Port Stanley, one of the parachute battalions captured the airfield at Goose Green, twenty miles south of San Carlos, after a fierce battle, in which they had little fire support either from artillery or from the navy's ships or aircraft. For the loss of 17 killed, including their commanding officer, and 36 wounded, they killed 250 of their opponents and took 1,400 prisoners with a large quantity of weapons.

The loss of the heavy-lift helicopters was now keenly felt. General Jeremy Moore, the land-force commander, had been reinforced on June 1 by an infantry brigade with three more battalions, giving him eight in his total force of ten thousand men ashore; but the means of moving forward over the trackless hilly country toward Port Stanley were almost nonexistent. Most of the men marched the whole way in cold, wet, windy weather, priority for helicopter lift being given to artillery and ammunition to support them on arrival. The military and political need to hurry led to the decision to send the three battalions of the infantry brigade around the southern side of East Falkland to land at Fitzroy settlement and Bluff Cove, sixteen miles southwest of Port Stanley. As a result of a number of misunderstandings, two of the landing ships were off shore for several hours in daylight in full view of an Argentine post on June 8. They were attacked by Argentine aircraft and set on fire. Fifty men were killed and eighty-five wounded, most of them from one battalion. In spite of this setback, the attack on the Argentine positions in the hills around Stanley started on June 11, with all the battalions, except one that had been left behind to guard the San Carlos base, taking part.

On June 14 General Menendez surrendered with 9,000 men, bringing the total captured, including those at Goose Green and in West Falkland, to 11,400. Argentina gave its losses of men killed and missing as 672, 368 from the *Belgrano*. British losses were 255 dead and 777 wounded. The British had lost 6 ships sunk and 10 seriously damaged. Five of their Harrier aircraft were shot down by ground fire and 4 lost in accidents. They claimed to have destroyed 109 Argentine aircraft, 30 on the ground, 31 by Harriers, 19 by ships' missiles, and 9 by land-based missiles.

There is little doubt that the British had good luck. Several ships were hit by bombs that did not explode. Time was running out when Menendez surrendered. The British artillery ammunition supply was dwindling, the sortie rate of the navy's aircraft would have had to have been significantly reduced for mechanical reasons, and the weather was deteriorating. If the Argentine defenders of Stanley had put up a stouter resistance, the result might have been different. The British superiority in fighting at night, assisted by modern vision devices, was a factor in their success, but more significant was their recapture of the initiative and their greatly superior state of training and morale. On the Argentine side, only their air force pilots came out of the campaign with credit.

In general strategic terms, Britain had shown that the deployment and use of armed force to protect its interests overseas was not a thing of the past. The operation had been limited to the extent that no hostile action was taken against the territory of Argentina, or its shipping and aircraft outside the exclusion zone, apart from the attack on the *Belgrano*; nor did Argentina attack British ships or aircraft outside that zone, although it observed them. But there seemed no limits to the resources which Britain was prepared to devote to the liberation of the tiny population of these remote and, in economic and military terms, almost valueless islands. A principle was at stake, as well as honor and political reputations. Patriotism played a significant role.

It is doubtful whether the operation could have been mounted without Ascension Island. It certainly could not have been if, on withdrawal from east of Suez over a decade before, Britain had not retained the amphibious capability represented by its Marine Brigade and two assault and six logistic landing ships; had not retained an old aircraft carrier, converted into a commando ship; built a new type, intended primarily as an antisubmarine helicopter carrier; and developed the Sea Harrier that could operate from both. Ironically, Mrs. Thatcher's Conservative administration had decided to phase out most of these on the logical grounds that their role in support of NATO had little validity. Some analysts interpret the Falklands operation as a sign that resort to military action to protect one's interests and further one's policies worldwide is coming back into fashion; but there are also those who regard it as an anomalous occurrence, and find it difficult to imagine where else Britain might contemplate executing a similar operation.

Iran and Iraq. The other conventional war, in progress since 1980, has been that between Iran and Iraq. It has resembled the First World War more than the Second although the initial stage, when both sides maneuvered significant numbers of tanks, was reminiscent of the latter. On neither side has the operation of air forces been significant, and navies have hardly been involved. The initiator, Iraq, assumed that the disarray into which Iran had fallen after the successful coup against the Shah in 1979 provided an opportunity to assert its claim to both shores of the Shatt el Arab, its only channel to the open sea; and at first it looked as if that judgment was correct. But in spite of the removal of most of the senior officers of its armed forces, Iran was able to make use of the large arsenal of modern military equipment that the Shah had acquired. Iraqi forces were driven back, until a situation closely resembling that in France after 1914 was established. In the process the important refinery and oil-exporting terminal of Abadan was reduced to ruins. Casualties on both sides as far as can be ascertained have been heavy, Iran having been forced to employ "revolutionary guards," including boys in their early teens, as infantry, thrown into suicidal assaults against Iraqi entrenched positions. Battle wastage and inability to maintain and repair the original stock of heavy equipment on both sides has converted the war into one of infantry, artillery, and engineers. Neither side has the margin of superiority to force a decision. As in France in the First World War, both sides have launched offensives on sectors of the front in order to relieve pressure on other sectors, which have stalled after an initial success. Outside attempts to find the basis of a negotiated armistice have, up to the time of writing, failed. Although it is cold comfort to the participants, the world at large has been relieved that the rival great powers have carefully refrained from supporting either side; thus, although it has not been a limited war for Iraq and Iran, it has been limited from the point of view of the rest of the world.

III

The essential difference between the Soviet and the NATO view of conventional warfare in the nuclear age has been the Russian belief throughout that offense is the best form of defense. The ability and willingness to take the offensive, in order to preempt the enemy's offensive if possible, has been a consistent theme of their military thinking, training, and organization, applied equally to nuclear and conventional warfare, which, for most of the period, they have refused to regard as separate. They have seen overall superiority in all forms of military capability as essential to this strategy and as the best way of conferring freedom of action, which they would agree with Beaufre is the fundamental aim of strategy.

As long as Stalin was alive, the methods of the Great Patriotic War could not be challenged, and the nuclear weapon was seen, as it was by many in the West, as calling for no fundamental change. But 1953, the year of his death, also saw the development of the fusion weapon and the decision by the Soviet Union to select the ballistic missile as the method of delivery. In the following year the Soviet General Staff Academy initiated a major study of the effect that nuclear weapons could have on war. Its report was submitted in 1957 to their chief, Marshal Vasili Sokolovskiy, and two more years were spent in discussing it and revising military doctrine. The analysis came to the firm conclusion that all operations must be based on exploitation of the use of nuclear weapons and on the assumption that they would be used against their forces.

Nuclear weapons were not to be used merely as fire support to infantry and tanks. The action of all other arms was to be designed to exploit nuclear strikes, the use of which against selected targets would be the main feature of the operational plan. That would be based on nuclear attack in depth, accompanied by strikes against all elements of the enemy's nuclear delivery means as well as major headquarters. Airborne forces, tanks, and infantry in armored personnel carriers would follow up these strikes on a wide front, penetrating as deeply as possible, with the principal aim of disorganizing and throwing into confusion the enemy's whole military structure. The latter would also be achieved by both physical and electronic attack on the enemy's communication, warning, and target acquisition systems. Concentration of large bodies of vehicles and men offered too vulnerable a target to enemy nuclear strikes. Concentration of effort was therefore to be achieved by the use of nuclear weapons. The deep penetration by mobile troops on a wide front, to head which special formations known as Operational Maneuver Groups have been organized in recent years, differed in purpose and method from the pincer-like envelopments of the Great Patriotic War. This was very similar to the concept proposed by Fuller and Liddell Hart in the 1920s and 1930s, but with nuclear strikes taking the place of air attacks, including the use of chemical weapons. It was also not very different from concepts developed by the U.S. Army and favored by Liddell Hart at that time. The intermingling of the Soviet forces with those of the enemy in the course of such penetrations would provide the former with a degree of protection against nuclear attack by those enemy delivery systems that had escaped destruction.

There was nothing limited in this concept of war. Because it would be a conflict between two opposing political systems, it was assumed that, if it took place at all, it would be unrestrained. The ideal was to preempt the enemy's action, when it was realized that hostilities were planned. Once started, the destruction of the enemy's forces, particularly his nuclear forces, would take priority. Remaining on the defensive was dismissed, except as a temporary measure while preparing for an attack. One of the Soviet Union's most influential military writers, Savkin, said: "A side that only defends is inevitably doomed to defeat." To make this concept possible, the "correlation of forces" had to be appropriate. In other words, the Soviet forces had to be assured of sufficient superiority in every field to be able to launch their offensive with the least possible delay. This posed an inevitable dilemma between adequate preparation and the need to achieve surprise, to which the Soviets also attached great importance.

Although Soviet strategy rejects the concept of limited war in any form, the general staff has taken note of NATO's concept of flexible response, which assumes an initial phase of non-nuclear warfare. Some Soviet military writings accept that this may occur, and it has been reflected in military exercises; but discussion of it centers on the importance of choosing the correct moment for the Soviet armed forces to initiate the use of nuclear weapons. They see that such a non-nuclear phase could be exploited to complete their preparations. They do, however, accept that "local" wars can occur—their operations in Afghanistan are an example—and that it is important to ensure that they do not escalate into a nuclear exchange; but not that such wars could occur in Europe. One consistent theme permeates the great volume of Soviet military literature—the importance of superiority in the "correlation of forces." Not only is superiority essential to ensure that "the Socialist Camp" and the Soviet Union are preserved against the threat of "capitalist and imperialist aggression" that is constantly trying to undermine them, but it gives the Soviet Union the freedom of action to engage successfully in "military actions at lower levels" if necessary. The Soviet Union's development of armed forces designed to be superior in quantity and quality to all those that "the aggressive circles of capitalist imperialism" could deploy against them is entirely consistent with the military doctrine and strategy that the Soviet general staff has outlined in all the literature that pours out in a constant stream from its military academies. It bodes ill for those who place their hopes on persuading them to accept measures of arms control that do not preserve their superiority, whether the approach preferred is that of "negotiation from strength" or unilateral disarmament.

IV

Fortunately for the world, so far wars since the coming of the nuclear age have remained conventional and limited. Nobody has yet faced the daunting prospect of fighting a conventional war under the threat that nuclear weapons might be used at any time, and no nation possessing nuclear weapons has fought another that also possessed them. Under the

813

nuclear shadow, wars like the First and Second World Wars, in which groups of the major industrial nations struggled against each other until one side was exhausted, seem inconceivable. For such nations to embark upon war against each other could not possibly be regarded as continuing a rational policy by other means.

There are reasons, other than the existence of nuclear weapons, why such total wars seem inconceivable. One is the cost and the gestation time of modern weapons and their platforms. The rate of attrition of such weapons, when used against each other, is likely to be significantly more rapid than the rate at which they could be replaced, the 1973 Arab-Israeli War being the clearest indication of this. Conventional war between such powers would have to be severely limited in time and probably also in space, and therefore in aim. Considerable pressure from other powers and from the international community would be exerted to bring it to an end. Theories, like those propounded by Beaufre, which combine conventional operations with a "sublimited" use, or threat of use, of nuclear weapons seem less soundly based than the views of Liddell Hart, of Henry Kissinger after his change of mind, and of Maxwell Taylor and Robert Osgood, all of whom recognized that the first use of any type of nuclear weapon was a watershed that converted war into what Clausewitz described as "something pointless and devoid of sense."

War therefore, if it is to be a rational "other means" of the continuation of state policy, will have to be conventional and limited. If it is to be limited in its effects, it must, as Clausewitz recognized, be limited in its aim. Nations, however powerful, will have to accept limits and recognize, as Sun Tzu did, that after the fighting is over, one has to continue to live next door to one's opponent. As the Soviet Union's military doctrine emphasizes, it is superiority in the "correlation of forces" that gives a nation the freedom of action—that essential of strategy—to determine the limits. The weaker party, on the defensive, or the one who is not prepared to go as far as his opponent, has no choice.

It is in this climate that the two superpowers face each other. They cannot expect a war between them to observe limits. The Soviet Union certainly does not expect it to. It is therefore devoutly to be hoped that reason will prevail over other, stronger influences on both sides of the iron curtain: that it will continue to persuade the two great powers, the United States and the Soviet Union, that direct conflict between them must be avoided at all costs; and eventually convince both that the perpetual search for superiority over the other does not enhance the security of either, and that some other method of achieving a stable balance between the two rival political and economic systems is to be preferred.

814

27. Revolutionary War

JOHN SHY AND THOMAS W. COLLIER

IN 1941, when the Princeton seminar in military affairs began the work that led to the original *Makers of Modern Strategy*, the subject of this essay did not exist. Of course modern history was littered with revolutions, and most of those revolutions had involved some kind of warfare. At least since the seventeenth century, the phenomenon of revolution had aroused considerable intellectual interest, and that interest rose with each revolutionary epoch—1776, 1789, 1848, 1917. Evidence of the rising interest in revolution, and of the close connection between outbreaks of revolution and military theory, is scattered through the essays of the first *Makers of Modern Strategy*. But nowhere in that volume, not in the essays on Marx, Trotsky, or the strategists of French colonial warfare, do we find a systematic treatment of ideas for the use of armed force in effecting radical political and social change. The gap was not the fault of Professor Earle and his colleagues; rather, it reflects the fact that in 1941 no such body of theory existed; or, more correctly, that no such theory was seen to exist or, if it existed, to deserve space in a book surveying military thought from Machiavelli to Hitler.[1]

Why "revolutionary war," as an important branch of military thought, has emerged only in the last half century is a complex question. The correlative question—why the subject seemed neither important nor clearly defined as late as 1941—warns us against accepting easy or obvious answers. The Second World War triggered and catalyzed a large number of revolutionary outbreaks and upheavals, whose results and sequels continue to change the world. But equally important, in answering our questions, has been the rapid shift in perspective. Revolutionary warfare, as a problem for separate analysis and a set of techniques that have given rise to a set of countertechniques, now seems important, even urgent, in a way that it did not for, say, J. F. C. Fuller or Schlieffen or Jomini. Why?

[1] Sigmund Neumann, "Engels and Marx: Military Concepts of the Social Revolutionaries," Jean Gottmann, "Bugeaud, Galliéni, Lyautey: The Development of French Colonial Warfare," and Edward Mead Earle, "Lenin, Trotsky, Stalin: Soviet Concepts of War," are the relevant essays in the original edition of *Makers of Modern Strategy*, ed. Edward Mead Earle (Princeton, 1943), 155-71, 234-59, 322-64.

A satisfactory answer must consider the role of military theorizing in the history of the modern nation-state. The nation-state system as it took shape in Europe by the seventeenth century has been continually threatened as well as energized by revolutionary pressures. But the system has imposed its own priorities. Competition and conflict, often violent, between states has determined the fate of states themselves. Sweden and Spain fell behind, England and Prussia fought their way to the front, while Poland and the Austro-Hungarian monarchy disappeared. The behavior of successive coalitions formed to fight the French Revolution demonstrates how difficult nation-states found it, no matter how great the threat from revolutionary ideology and movements, to subordinate their own conflicting vital interests. For brief periods and for limited goals, nation-states have curbed their competitive instincts, to defeat Napoleon or Hitler, or to restore order after 1815 or 1918. But the primacy of international competition, the inherent conflict of vital national interests, soon reappeared. The successful nation-state, ultimately and perhaps by definition, is a war-fighting organism. Even the danger of internal revolution came to seem dependent on the outcome of international conflict; defeat excited rebellion, but victory submerged discontent in national pride. Military theorists and strategists treated revolution only incidentally because nation-states, whose interest they tried to serve, were overwhelmingly concerned by war with one another.

By the end of the last century, a handful of winners virtually dominated the world. The more successful European nations, joined by the United States and Japan, seemed irresistible. Constant competition had honed their skills, enhanced their power, whetted their appetites, and built enormous confidence in their capacity to expand through Asia, Africa, and (for the United States) the Western Hemisphere. Nothing except the countervailing power of their chief competitors could limit the scope of imperial ambitions. Then, in three decades, the system collapsed. Its confidence and economic base shaken by one world war and shattered by a second, the system may never have been as invincible as it looked. Its intensely competitive nature was the basic cause of its downfall, as the earlier Napoleonic experience might suggest. But clearly the sudden decline in power and prestige of the traditional nation-state system accounts not only for the global epidemic since 1941 of revolutionary attacks on the system, but also for the emergence of revolutionary war as a distinct branch of military thought. The crumbling of European empires under colonial and even domestic assault, and the rapid appearance amidst the imperial ruins of new successor states, often weak, are the main reasons why we see this new dimension of military theory where none was apparent in 1941.

816

I

"Revolutionary war" refers to the seizure of political power by the use of armed force. Not everyone would accept such a simple definition, and indeed the term has other connotations: that the seizure of power is by a popular or broad-based political movement, that the seizure entails a fairly long period of armed conflict, and that power is seized in order to carry out a well-advertised political or social program. The term also implies a high degree of consciousness about goals and methods, a consciousness that a "revolutionary" war is being fought.

There is persistent confusion between revolutionary war and guerrilla warfare. The confusion is understandable, because revolutionary war includes guerrilla warfare. But the guerrilla tactics of hit and run, avoiding costly pitched battles, eluding enemy pursuit by hiding in the hills, in forests, or among the populace, are simply one means of carrying on revolutionary war. Others range from nonviolent political mobilization of people, legal political action, strikes, agitation, and terrorism, to large-scale battles and conventional military operations. Guerrilla operations, in turn, may have no revolutionary aim, though their revolutionary political potential is never absent. Vital to any definition of revolutionary war, however, is the existence of a revolutionary objective; the specific means to be employed are a secondary matter.

Revolutionary war is also distinguished by what it is not. It is not "war" in the generally understood sense of the word, not international war or war between nations, with its usual (though not invariable) expectation that fighting will lead, sooner or later, to some negotiated settlement between the belligerent powers. In practice the sharp distinction between the two kinds of war may become hazy. Revolutionary wars occur *within* nations, and have as their aim the seizure of state power. But once the definition moves beyond this simple distinction between international "war" and "revolutionary war," clarity gives way to murkiness. More often than not, one or several "foreign" powers will intervene in a revolutionary war, changing its course and often its outcome. To take one example, the military Communist movement led by Tito against a dictatorial and feudalistic regime in Yugoslavia was better known as resistance against German invasion and occupation; it was also a Croatian struggle against Serbian domination, and was strongly affected by the concurrent Anglo-American-Soviet "war" against Germany. Yet Tito's war was surely revolutionary, as was the Arab revolt against Ottoman rule in 1916-1918, so closely linked with the name of T. E. Lawrence, who was a British agent employed in attacking Turkey, an ally of Ger-

817

many, the chief enemy of Britain in the First World War. Neat definitions break down quickly in the face of actual historical cases.

One school of thought argues that revolutionary war has flourished in the nuclear age precisely because new weapons have made war between great military powers impossible or too dangerous. Corollary arguments are that the great powers, ponderously armed for a big war, have left themselves vulnerable to the tactics of revolutionary war; and that the classic distinction between international war (regrettable but legitimate) and revolutionary war (a domestic phenomenon to which the safeguards of international law do not apply) is itself biased in favor of the great military and industrial powers. The value of these arguments recognized, we can still assert that in both theory and practice revolutionary war is fundamentally different from "war," as that word is understood in the other essays of this volume.

Beyond the problem of adequately defining terms, there is another, more subtle difficulty in posing the question for study. The difficulty lies in the historian's natural tendency to seek continuities in the past. The historian assumes that the subject, whether a person or a community or a state, has something like a memory, which gives meaning to the idea of historical continuity. Even "strategy," treated as an idea, has a continuous history in the publication of books and the world of general staffs; or at least the discovery of discontinuities is itself historically interesting. But revolutionary warfare, treated historically as a set of ideas, challenges this notion of continuity. Revolutionary wars themselves are episodes, with little to institutionalize them effectively as bodies of thought and experience, and much to suppress or distort them in terms of memory. If successful, the victor mythologizes the war to sustain the national or social identity of the victorious revolutionary cause, while the loser wants to forget a painful, often disastrous and humiliating, experience. If a revolutionary war fails, it becomes a "revolt" or a "rebellion," of interest largely as a lesson in "mistakes" for students of revolution. In any case, revolutions are carried on in an atmosphere of secrecy, betrayal, and deception. Archival records are few, and survivors who write memoirs can seldom be checked and are seldom trustworthy. Thirty years after its outbreak in 1954, we know little with confidence about the insurgent side of the Algerian revolution. Even where revolutionary strategists appear to have been influenced by previous revolutionary experience, as in the case of the Vietnamese following the Chinese example, the connection tends to be plausible rather than definitive, and is inevitably disputed by some of those best qualified to know. The scholar who writes the history of revolutionary "strategy" may impute a spurious reality to the temporal development of his subject, distorting it in a fundamental way.

Closely related to our tendency to seek historical connections where none may exist is a further difficulty. "Revolution" since 1776 and 1789 has projected a powerful, highly emotive image. Its emotional power to attract and to frighten has contributed to the frequency and intensity of revolutionary conflicts in modern history. To abstract from this phenomenon some more limited and technical, more intellectual and less emotional, "strategy" of "revolutionary warfare" may be to miss the most important part of the subject—the specific social, political, and psychological conditions that make a revolution possible. Without those conditions, strategic technique is meaningless; and any strategy of revolution that does not reflect and exploit them as they exist, in a specific time and place, will almost certainly fail, as the Chinese Communist attempts to conform to Marxist orthodoxy failed in the early 1930s. Strategic thinking and planning for international war have foundered, as in 1914, on the same problem of relating military technique to underlying conditions, but at least the modern state has developed a capacity to transform volatile and various social forces into more or less predictable and manageable military instruments. But not so revolutionary warfare; revolutions, by definition, are not made by states and their bureaucracies, but by raw social energies, directed by leaders who must improvise, adapt quickly, and often act before they have time to think, if they are to win or even survive. Revolutionary wars, as Mao said, are not dinner parties, nor are they general staff studies, nor essays in scholarly journals. There is, to a degree difficult for the nonrevolutionary writer and reader to grasp, a unique quality to each revolutionary war, leaving the student of its "strategy" struggling to find a reasonable perspective, much less to tell readers the truth.

There is a danger, especially in dealing with the contemporary importance of revolutionary wars, of giving undue emphasis to theory at the expense of actual experience. Theory permits a degree of simplification that is attractive when confronted with the frequency, complexity, and variety of armed struggles that are in some sense "revolutionary" or "counterrevolutionary." But the formalistic reduction of revolution to "stages," for example, or of counterrevolution to isolating rebels from the "people" by winning their "hearts and minds," distorts the real world of modern experience. At the same time, it needs to be recognized that "theory," even if simplistic or unsound, has played a central role in shaping that experience, and in the continuing debate over how, exactly, this experience should be interpreted. While being careful not to succumb to the seduction of theoretical simplism, we should accept the power and

819

appeal of theory as a major facet of the phenomenon of revolutionary/counterrevolutionary war.

Each side in these conflicts has struggled with a central doctrinal question, and the question for each side arises as the reciprocal of the question chronically troubling the other side. For revolutionaries, it has been the question of when and how to undertake military action; answers have ranged from those who see military action as little more than a final stage of intensive, protracted political preparation and action, to those like the exponents of "focoism" in Latin America who argue that violence can, in effect, replace and catalyze the political process of revolution. Again and again, revolutionary leadership has divided between those who advocate and those who want to postpone military action.

On the other side—the side of the counterrevolutionaries—the crucial question concerns the relative importance of violence and persuasion, in effect the choice between war and politics. How far is a revolutionary movement dependent on popular political support, and thus how vulnerable is it to political action designed to undermine popular support? This is the recurring question for the opponents of revolution. Repeatedly, as in the Vietnam Wars, "hawks" will insist that the enemy relies only on bullets and terror ruthlessly applied, while "doves" argue that deep popular discontent is the key—and the key weakness—of revolutionary war. Here, too, the question centers on the relative roles of political and military action.

The virtually inevitable debate on both sides is carried on at two levels: at the level of specific circumstances and urgent, concrete necessities; and at the level of theory, which leads readily to arguments about the structure of politics and society, and to the nature of human existence. Why do people behave as they do? Why are they willing to fight, and to suffer? No matter how pragmatic and hard-headed leaders on both sides of a revolutionary war may be, there seems to be no escape from arguing these questions at the level of theory. And in the theoretical debate, language itself becomes critically important.

On October 23, 1983, a large truck packed with high explosive was driven at high speed, through a guarded gate, directly into the concrete headquarters of a U.S. Marine battalion at Beirut airport, Lebanon. The explosion destroyed the headquarters, killed 231 Marines, and soon led to the withdrawal of the American "peacekeeping" force sent to stop the Lebanese civil war. Two months later, a special commission of the U.S. Department of Defense listed the reasons why the attack had succeeded: the Marine mission in Lebanon had been poorly understood, the Marine battalion had a faulty position, the military command structure (developed during the Second World War) was not suited to the conditions of a civil war, lack of unity between U.S. military services hampered quick action, and, from a mass of military intelligence dumped on it, the small battalion staff was unable to find the vital piece of intelligence—which trucks in its area were overparked. The report stressed mistakes that in future should be avoided, but offered no broader analysis of the new problem, except to urge the Pentagon to meet the challenge of a "new" kind of warfare. The report—as did the President—defined this new kind of warfare narrowly, as "state-supported terrorism," and not as a specific instance of what it actually is—the much older phenomenon of revolutionary war.

Words, ideas, and perceptions have played an exceptionally important role in revolutionary war, whose modern history began with the Napoleonic Wars. Violent efforts to overthrow governments, seize power, and even change society, using unorthodox military means, are by definition politically disruptive. Political unity and support are usually assumed rather than explicitly stated in classical theories of international war, but the language of revolutionary war is politically hyperbolic and hypersensitive. Revolutionary soldiers are often called "bandits," in effect denying them the legal status of combatants, and their supporters described as "criminals" or "traitors." Government forces become "enemies of the people" or "mercenaries," the government itself being "fascist," "corrupt," or a "puppet regime." "Terrorism" is the word for attacking nonmilitary targets, or for attacks—like that at Beirut—using surprise and unusual methods. In revolutionary war there can be no neutral, apolitical vocabulary; words themselves are weapons.

Describing acts of revolutionary war as "new," or as unprecedented in their cruelty (or claiming that revolutionary strategy is deeply rooted in ancient philosophy) further illustrates how language itself becomes a weapon of revolutionary warfare. Language is used to isolate and confuse enemies, rally and motivate friends, and enlist the support of wavering bystanders. But the same language directs—or misdirects—military effort; the rhetoric of political conflict becomes the reality of strategic theory. Adapting quickly to technological change comes readily to European and American armed forces. But learning to cope with a very different kind of warfare, in which words do more to mask or distort military reality than to reveal it, has proved far more difficult. The unwillingness of the American President and the Pentagon to admit that the Beirut disaster was an incident of revolutionary warfare is understandable. To use the more accurate term would concede the legitimacy of the attack. But to use less accurate, moralistic language may have created more difficulty for their own side than for the enemy. This dilemma has itself become a unique feature of modern revolutionary war, and thus a major problem in analyzing the subject as a set of ideas. So we cannot begin with any simple assumptions about the objective nature of theory, or even about the relationship of theory to practice; these are matters for inquiry.

Because so much of the language of revolutionary war is polemical and highly charged, a strictly analytical approach seems doomed to take a side, implicitly and perhaps inadvertently, in the continuing debate. Virtually all of the literature of the subject is concerned with either how to conduct or how to defeat revolutionary war. The purpose of this essay is to examine the subject with as much detachment as possible, identifying key questions and problems as yet unresolved, and especially not to offer yet another guide to policy and operations for revolutionary war. Approaching the subject historically is no escape from judgment, but at least it provides an opportunity to step back from the polemics, describing what has been said and done without pretending to state the operational, political, and ethical truth about revolutionary war. Writing the history of a subject still so alive in the present, and whose future defies even guesswork, is always perilous; even the historical approach may not achieve the requisite detachment. But at least that approach provides our best chance to separate the analytical "What happened?" from the judgmental "What should have happened?"

The historical, analytically neutral approach, despite its various difficulties, allows us to see the subject whole and in context. This approach also suggests that "revolutionary war" may itself be a historical—not a timeless—phenomenon, with a discernible beginning and an imaginable term. Emerging in the 1930s as a set of unique ideas about how to carry on armed revolution, ideas widely promulgated as much by their apparent success as by their intrinsic quality, "revolutionary war" as a formula for political and military victory may already show signs of faltering. Admittedly, this is no more than a guess, perhaps a mistaken one. But at least it calls attention to the vital link between "revolutionary war" as a set of ideas, or theory, and the specific historical conditions that have made such a theory practical.

II

Revolutionary warfare, as a fully developed concept, is a relatively recent phenomenon largely because it is so closely associated with two aspects of modernity—industrialism and imperialism. Marxists and other radical critics of the modern industrial, economic, and social order were among the first to analyze the problem of mobilizing and employing armed force to defeat the police and army of the capitalist and ruling classes. While radical revolutionaries by the later nineteenth century were

822

studying the problem in its European and North American industrial context, radical advocates of colonial resistance in Asia were beginning to deal with the not dissimilar problems of overthrowing imperial bureaucrats and soldiers along with their native collaborators. Of course violent popular protests and uprisings have dotted European history, just as resistance to imperialist intrusion is as old as imperialism itself, but only a century or so ago did the *idea* of revolutionary warfare, considered as a set of formidable problems with specific strategic solutions, begin to take shape and acquire momentum.

A brief look at the intellectual precursors of the modern concept of revolutionary warfare also suggests why it appears so late. Students of Asian cultures have argued that more than two millennia ago Sun Tzu, the Chinese military philosopher, formulated the strategic principles of revolutionary warfare—attack weakness, avoid strength, be patient.[2] They have also emphasized that in Chinese and Vietnamese history, the popular belief in the "mandate of heaven," by which regimes both gain and lose legitimacy, has for centuries been a critical element in recruiting popular support for revolution.[3] Getting people to join, fight, and even die for the revolutionary cause and using popular zeal in strategically effective ways have been—and still are—the key points in all serious thought on revolutionary warfare. Sun Tzu and the "mandate of heaven" are therefore more than curious intellectual artifacts; each deals with central issues. But what remains unclear is how important Sun Tzu and the "mandate of heaven" have been in any continuing non-Western approach to the problem of revolutionary warfare. On the contrary, there is evidence suggesting a marked "Westernization" of anti-imperialist revolutionary thinking in modern times, with a return to the ancient sources a very late phenomenon, perhaps more a form of cultural nationalism than a guide to revolutionary action.[4]

The classic Age of Revolution in the West also offers some interesting precursors. During the American War of Independence both sides made a serious effort to keep warfare within conventional forms and limits. American provincial leaders had seized power from British officials in

[2] Sun Tzu, *The Art of War*, trans. Samuel B. Griffith (Oxford, 1963).

[3] John T. McAlister, Jr., and Paul Mus, *The Vietnamese and Their Revolution* (New York, 1970), particularly pp. 55-69, is the most accessible version of the work of Mus, whose *Vietnam: Sociologie d'une guerre* (Paris, 1952), stresses the central importance of the mandate of heaven. Frances FitzGerald, *Fire in the Lake* (Boston, 1972), gave the idea its widest currency among Western readers.

[4] For example, Mao Tse-tung frequently used the concept of "interior" and "exterior" lines of operation, obviously borrowed from the Swiss military theorist and historian Jomini. On doubts about the importance of the "mandate of heaven," see Gérard Chaliand, *Revolution in the Third World* (New York, 1977; Penguin ed., 1978), 89ff.

most areas even before the outbreak of fighting, so the "revolutionary" nature of warfare was minimized, and only at the very outset, along the frontier zones, and again during the last years in the South, did violence take on the popular, irregular character of "revolutionary warfare." If the revolutionary character of the war was minimal, what may be described as a strategic theory of revolution was nearly nonexistent. And yet one American general, Charles Lee, a former British officer who had taken part in the Polish uprising of 1769, formulated a strategy for "people's war" that implicitly opposed the strategy adopted by Washington, who relied on long-service soldiers and campaigns of conventional maneuvers. Lee argued that American democracy, numbers, and enthusiasm were the correct basis for an American strategy of protracted, attritional warfare relying on local resistance. Although Lee soon lost any influence in the conduct of the war, and his ideas were never taken up by anyone, his argument in favor of integrating the political, social, and military aspects of strategy could only have arisen in a revolutionary situation, and it forecasts a principal feature of later ideas about revolutionary warfare.[5]

The French Revolution gave rise to "the people in arms," linking nationalism with military service in the first great step toward mass citizen armies; but the Revolution unfolded in a way that never led to "revolutionary war" in the full modern sense. The Wars of the French Revolution were mainly foreign wars, fought to defend France and to weaken its external enemies. A new boldness characterized French strategy and operations, but strategic aims, while often more ambitious, were not unlike the goals of warfare before 1789. Royal government in France had effectively collapsed before war began, so that armed resistance to the new government in Paris was by definition *counter*-revolutionary. Whether in the Vendée region of western France, in the mountains of Italy and Austria, or in Spain and Russia, guerrillas and partisans fought to expel the forces of the Revolution and to aid in the restoration of legitimate government by the conservative powers allied against France.

Only once, very briefly, did the Revolution approach something like the modern concept of revolutionary war. In 1793, during the Reign of Terror, extremist factions demanded the creation of *armées révolutionnaires*. These "revolutionary armies" were not intended to defend the frontiers against the invading coalition, but rather as armed bands of self-directed "people" to find and attack "traitors"—aristocrats, recalcitrant priests, profiteers, counterrevolutionary Frenchmen whoever and wherever they might be, some no doubt in high office. Originally pro-

---

[5] John Shy, *A People Numerous and Armed* (New York, 1976), 133-62.

posed by Robespierre, the idea of *les armées révolutionnaires* was turned against him and his colleagues on the Committee of Public Safety as they tried to centralize and control the war-torn French state. Carried through as conceived, *les armées révolutionnaires* might have seized power from the Committee of Public Safety and the National Assembly, and given it to the most radical elements in the French Revolution. In the event, the conservative coup of 1794, ending the Reign of Terror, reduced the *armées révolutionnaires* to a nightmarish moment in French history. But the idea itself, however abortive, of ordinary people armed to wage war *within* their own society, perhaps even against their own revolutionary regime, offers a fascinating glimpse of the distant future.[6]

After Waterloo, with the advent of repressive regimes throughout a Europe obsessed by the dangers of popular unrest, something like a conscious theory of revolutionary war actually emerged, only to fade away by midcentury. Based on their faith in the unifying and mobilizing effect of nationalism, Italian and Polish revolutionists argued that mass armies, however ill-trained and ill-equipped, could by their nationalist enthusiasm and their overwhelming numbers defeat any imaginable body of governmental troops. Analysis of the revolutionary potential of their own societies did not go far enough to expose the deep divisions between the liberal goals of the middle classes, the radical hopes of a growing proletariat, and the often conservative fears of artisans, shop-keepers, and peasants. Those divisions, together with the loyalty and skill of government forces, repeatedly stopped the revolutionary movements of the 1820s and 1830s, finally smashing them in 1848-1849. Any lingering doubts about the inadequacy of existing revolutionary theory were resolved by new technology: rifled weapons, electrical communications, and steam power—all of which gave governments after 1850 vastly increased means to deploy force against popular insurrection.[7]

This new weaponry, steadily improved and developed, also gave European states the means to make their remarkable penetration of Asia and Africa in the later nineteenth century seem relatively easy. Within Europe, revolutionists now guided by Marx, Engels, and others shifted the focus of revolutionary thought from warfare to politics. Organization, education, and agitation became the chief tasks of a less romantic, more realistic revolutionary movement. Violence might still take place—in strikes, small-scale terrorism, or political assassination—but only as a means to some specific political end. The delays of the spontaneous mass uprising seemed over. Excessive or premature violence was seen to be

[6] Richard Cobb, *Les armées révolutionnaires*, 2 vols. (Paris, 1961-63).
[7] Geoffrey Best, *War and Society in Revolutionary Europe, 1770-1870* (London, 1982), 257-95.

counterproductive, alerting the enemy to its danger and bringing the full force of armed repression down on the revolutionary organization— small, unarmed, and highly vulnerable. But there were also rare moments, notably the Paris Commune of 1871, when revolutionaries fought openly and died as heroes and martyrs. The memory of these heroic moments fired the imagination of European revolutionaries, and of colonial resistance leaders as well, keeping alive the hopes of those who worked patiently and often in great danger to prepare the revolutionary millennium.

In his remarkable pamphlet *The Civil War in France*, completed just as the last Communard resistance was being crushed by government forces in Paris, Karl Marx presented no strategic theory for revolutionary war, but rather a concise account of the conditions under which such wars are waged, and the goals for which they must be fought. As might be expected, the analysis is radical, and the tone bitter. Violence is not, Marx says, the specialty of the people, who are invariably its victims. War is the invention of monarchs, the sport of aristocrats, and the hallmark of imperialism. Two executions and the suppression of a single riot were all the violence committed by the Commune before it came under external, all-out government attack. The sheer volume of killing, much of it atrocious and some of it sadistic, done by the government when it smashed the Commune during the spring of 1871 had been foreshadowed by the violent governmental repression of June 1848.[8]

The lesson was clear. Once threatened by the people armed, ruling groups would stop at nothing to disarm them and to terrorize them into submission. No compromise was possible, except perhaps as a short-term tactic. The duplicity of the "radical" Government of National Defense, and of its representatives in Paris, proved that moderate measures and goals were a sham, designed to entrap and disarm the people. The apparatus of the state, and of its supporting structures in society, could not simply be taken over; they had to be destroyed and rebuilt on revolutionary principles.

One need not be a Marxist to recognize the power of this analysis. However selective Marx may have been in his evidence, there was ample recent experience of the most brutal kind, in 1871, in 1849-1849, and in numerous other revolutionary outbreaks and failures since 1815 to persuade his readers that history had taught a few painful lessons to strategists of popular revolution. Moderation was foolish; Engels in his introduction to the 1891 edition of *The Civil War in France* deplored

[8] Karl Marx, *The Civil War in France: The Paris Commune* (1891 ed., intro. by Friedrich Engels), reprinted with added commentary by Lenin (New York, 1940; 1968).

"the holy awe" with which the Commune "remained standing respect-
fully outside the gates of the Bank of France."[9] Disciplined organization
and planning was essential; the followers of Blanqui and Proudhon who
dominated Communard leadership had been deluded by fantasies of the
spontaneous rallying and rising of "free" people. Violence was a weapon,
but just one among many. There could be no flinching from violence,
but it was not to be romanticized, or its potential wasted in futile gestures.
Marx's pamphlet is characterized by a fusion of realism and passion that
made it a major step in the development of a conscious theory of revolutionary war.

Lenin, in various observations on the Commune and Marx's pamphlet, pointed and hardened the lessons. Unlike Plekhanov in the Russian
Revolution of 1905, Marx had foreseen that a popular insurrection in
1870 would be "folly," but after the event did not use its failure to
advertise his own wisdom, but analyzed it sympathetically and realistically. In that respect (as in others), Marx's capacity to assess both the
prospects and the consequences of violence without being swayed by
hopes, fears, or other emotions was a model for revolutionary leadership.
The great mistakes of the Commune, as Lenin saw them, expanding on
the commentary of Marx and Engels, were moderation and magnanimity.
Not to seize the banks, and to keep the old rules of "fair exchange," was
to be led astray by "dreams of establishing a higher justice" in a united
France. Not to destroy all enemies, in the hope of exerting "moral influence" on them, was to make the major error of underestimating "the
significance of direct military operations in civil war." In the end, those
enemies had joined government forces in crushing the Commune. But
the Commune was simply a lost battle, the courage of the vanquished a
constant inspiration to comrades who would, eventually, win the ultimate
victory. The Commune demonstrated how much could be done by revolutionary action, even without favorable conditions and adequate organization. In the future, to build the revolutionary organization, to wait
patiently, and to foster suitable conditions for revolutionary action would
be the proper tasks of revolutionary strategy. Again and again, Lenin
follows Marx in his insistence on the need to "break up," "smash," or
"crush" the "bourgeois state machine," beginning with its standing army,
and to replace it with an organization created by the "people armed."[10]

Trotsky, not Lenin, used the lessons of the Paris Commune and the
Russian Revolution of 1905 to seek a strategy for revolutionary war.
The inevitability of an armed clash with government forces was obvious.

[9] Ibid., 18.
[10] Ibid., 91-106.

Governments had learned the lesson of 1789, when the French monarchy had hesitated to use its army, allowing the people to arm and organize themselves and to subvert the military garrisons of Paris and other cities. As 1848, 1871, and 1905 had demonstrated, even a weak and inefficient regime could be counted on to strike hard before the revolutionary movement was ready for an armed clash. How to deal with this problem? Between 1905 and 1917 Trotsky, more than any other Russian revolutionary, attempted to answer this question.[11]

Two answers suggested themselves: strengthen the armed force of revolution, and weaken the government army. Attacking morale and discipline were obvious ways of weakening enemy troops, but what specific tactics would be effective? Conscripted peasants lacked political consciousness, and so were less susceptible to revolutionary political appeals. In Moscow during the 1905 revolution, guerrilla warfare had been used to maximize the military effect of limited revolutionary forces, but such hit-and-run tactics had also infuriated government troops and increased the energy of repression. Terrorism had its advocates; but others, like Plekhanov, argued that terror would never attract mass support. A general strike, paralyzing the rail and telegraph systems that gave government forces so much of their power against revolution, seemed promising but would probably not be decisive. A desperate alternative method of weakening the army was to resist it passively, to persuade people to confront government troops as fellow Russians, if necessary dying for their beliefs in the hope that their martyrdom would break the bonds of discipline that made soldiers shoot workers.[12] But none of these various tactics seemed more feasible or effective than any other in undermining the overwhelming armed force of the regime, and before 1917 all lacked much support in actual experience. Mutinies at Kronstadt and elsewhere within the imperial armed forces in 1906 were encouraging, but susceptible to conflicting interpretations by revolutionary theorists. Fighting between partisan bands and government forces in the countryside continued, but the line between popular resistance and simple banditry was not easily drawn. The debate after 1905 over military strategy was in effect a political debate, the sides polarized between those, like Lenin, who supported direct military action (which would arouse the masses, train revolutionary fighters, and break the morale of the imperial army), and those, like Plekhanov, who emphasized the need for mass support (and consequently feared the effects of "premature" armed insurrection). In this debate Trotsky played a creative, mediating role.

[11] What follows on Trotsky is drawn from Harold W. Nelson, *Leon Trotsky and the Art of Insurrection, 1905-1917* (Ann Arbor, 1978).
[12] Ibid., 26ff.

Unable to decide how best to weaken the armed forces of the regime, the revolutionaries naturally concentrated on strengthening their own military arm. Here there was less disagreement. Because many were skeptical of the rural partisans, whose operations tended to degenerate into banditry and uncontrolled terrorism, and many others were equally skeptical of the cautious, somewhat romantic concept of a "mass" revolution when conditions were "suitable," agreement could center on the need to organize, arm, and train the most highly motivated, politically conscious parts of the proletariat. In this way, the Party, unlike the Commune of 1871 or the revolutionaries of 1905, would be as ready as possible for the armed struggle, whenever and however it came. But the result of such agreement was to emphasize the urban, industrial, even technocratic aspect of revolutionary warfare, with battles conceived as brief, climactic encounters fought for control of the nerve centers of a modern society. In this respect, the theory of revolutionary warfare emergent after 1905 in Russia reflected a much older tradition of Western military thought.

Trotsky's experience as a journalist in the Balkan Wars reinforced his belief that only a well-armed, trained, and well-led revolutionary army could hope to defeat the army of the government, and that popular forces, relying on numbers and enthusiasm, were obsolete. Guerrilla bands, like the *Chetniks* operating in the Macedonian mountains, could at most play an auxiliary role in revolutionary war.

In the event, the extreme pressures generated by World War I did more than revolutionary theorizing and agitation to weaken the Russian imperial army as the chief barrier to revolution, and the defection of large parts of that army to the revolutionary cause secured Bolshevik victory. The Civil War, in which Trotsky gained fame as military leader of the Russian Revolution, was fought not with a uniquely "revolutionary" strategy but with "modern"—that is, conventional—military methods. The direct legacy of the Russian Revolution to military theory was, then, to reject the idea that a strategy for revolutionary war could be based on any principles other than those prevailing in the staff colleges of the capitalist powers. Warfare, in that sense, involved a set of largely technical demands that placed it beyond the revolutionary critique of bourgeois ideology.

Outside their own continent, the European powers looked on revolts and insurrections more as problems of imperial policing than as expressions of popular discontent. In their efforts to maintain peace and order, colonial governments tended to see "native" leaders not as patriots or political radicals, but as troublemakers and bandits. The military forces of the colonies also looked on their foes as different from the armies of Europe; they were restless tribes, *insurrectos, dacoits* rather than the

829

people armed. These attitudes are easy enough to understand; fighting through a well-laid ambush teaches a lot about the weapons and tactics of an opponent, but very little about his political goals, sense of justice, or cosmology. Furthermore, the imperial powers commonly used an organizational rather than a doctrinal approach to colonial wars. They organized specialized colonial armies, usually a high proportion of local troops led by Europeans, and let them worry about the practical, day-to-day problems of fighting and winning the little wars in distant places. Separate organization divided the colonial military experience from problems of European warfare, and helped to keep the thinkers of the national war colleges unconcerned with strategies for dealing with revolutions.

The colonial military view is well expressed by Major Charles E. Callwell, Royal Artillery, who wrote at the turn of the century.[13] In *Small Wars*, Callwell clearly distinguishes such wars from regular campaigns between organized armies. He then goes on to explain how to conduct "expeditions against savages and semi-civilized races." He does this thoroughly and well, and does not pretend that irregular warriors and guerrillas can be simply overawed. But he also makes it clear that he is talking about military operations that are of importance only in the colonies. And so the rich legacy of operational experience in the colonies was kept largely separated from the theory and practice of the home armies before World War II.

There were exceptions. Great Britain mobilized contingents from throughout its empire to fight the Boer War, and in Ireland fought a vicious war against guerrillas on its doorstep. In France, Marshal Lyautey published a widely read article on the colonial army.[14] America expanded its regular army and raised twenty-five volunteer regiments during the Philippine "Insurrection." But even these exceptions involved fighting guerrillas rather than working with them, and thus had little impact on military thinking at home. One further exception, however, was widely noticed. It involved waging, rather than countering, guerrilla warfare: the Arab Revolt of 1916-1918.

The experience of T. E. Lawrence with the Arab forces of Sherif Hussein and his sons produced both an example and a theory of warfare that became legendary. Lawrence was only a British advisor, never a commander, to the Arab rebels against Ottoman rule, but he coordinated

[13] Charles E. Callwell, *Small Wars—Their Principles and Practice* (London, 1896), as quoted in Robert B. Asprey, *War in the Shadows: The Guerrilla in History*, 2 vols. (Garden City, N.Y., 1975), 1:221.

[14] L. H. G. Lyautey, "Du rôle colonial de l'Armée," *Revue des Deux Mondes* 157 (February 15, 1900), 308-328, later republished as a booklet by Librairie Armand Colin, Paris.

their political goals and military operations to complement the far different goals and operations of the British. He also integrated the latest technology with the horses and camels of the Arabs: machine guns, mortars, light artillery, armored cars, aircraft for both reconnaissance and ground attack, and naval gunfire and logistical support. Although he never claimed that his little war was more than "a sideshow of a sideshow," he did provide valuable assistance to the main British forces at very little cost in British resources and Arab lives. It is significant that his many detractors included neither those who fought with him nor his British and Arab superiors.[15]

On the theoretical side, Lawrence set out a very different view of guerrilla warfare from that sketched by Callwell. Applying his considerable background in military history to the specific problems of the Arab Revolt, Lawrence developed a theoretical base that had a more general application than he claimed for it. He clearly defined the political objectives of the war, carefully analyzed the strengths and weaknesses of the opposing forces, recognized the importance of a strategy of "detachment" operating from a secure base ("desert-power"), of using the initiative to attack with hit-and-run tactics, of intelligence and counterintelligence, and of psychological warfare and propaganda. In brief, he wrote that "granted mobility, security . . . time, and doctrine," the insurgents would win.[16] Perhaps Lawrence's ultimate failure to prepare Great Britain for waging revolutionary war outside the Continent was a result of his own dramatic personality. His distracting public image obscured his ideas as well as his actual accomplishments. The darling of the literary world and the bane of the officers' mess, he was taken seriously as a military prophet by almost no one, and he died in 1935 just as France and Britain were beginning to face the prospect of another world war—not at all the kind of war that Lawrence had fought.

In fairness to European military thinkers and planners, there was more than enough to worry them in the late 1930s. The Italian *Regia Aeronautica* and the German *Luftwaffe*, plus the specter of gas warfare, made civil defense a dominant concern. Tank formations and bombing attacks had looked fearsome to observers of the Spanish Civil War, while torpedo attacks from aircraft, fast boats, and submarines worried the

---

[15] T. E. Lawrence, *Seven Pillars of Wisdom* (New York, 1935). See especially chapters 33 and 59. For a more concise statement on strategy and tactics, see Lawrence, "The Evolution of a Revolt," originally published in *Army Quarterly* 1 (October 1920), and reprinted in *Evolution of a Revolt: Early Postwar Writings of T. E. Lawrence*, ed. Stanley Weintraub and Rodelle Weintraub (University Park, Penn., 1968), 100-119. For a retrospective view, see Konrad Morsey, "T. E. Lawrence: Strategist" in *The T. E. Lawrence Puzzle*, ed. Stephen E. Tabachnick (Athens, Ga., 1984), 185-203.

[16] Weintraub and Weintraub, *Evolution of a Revolt*, 119.

naval staffs. Add to these problems the economic crises of the Depression
and the popular antiwar sentiments that the Great War had generated,
then top them with the natural belief that war plans are made to win
victories, not to compensate for defeats, and it would have been an
exceptionally wise person who would have prepared during the 1930s
for guerrilla operations.

With the exception of Mao Tse-tung, whose strategy is yet to be
discussed, neither victors nor victims anticipated the importance and scale
of the resistance movements that opposed the Axis forces in the Second
World War. In England, for example, no person or institution carried
on the study of guerrilla warfare that Lawrence had personified. Winston
Churchill had employed Lawrence in the Colonial Office from 1921 to
1922, had corresponded with him over the years, and had included him
in his book, *Great Contemporaries*.[17] Yet Churchill does not seem to
have considered the future usefulness of Lawrence's type of warfare
should Great Britain again face a strong Continental power. Similarly,
the military critic B. H. Liddell Hart had corresponded with Lawrence,
exchanged books with him, and saw him on weekends in the 1930s. But
Liddell Hart regarded Lawrence's guerrilla strategy more as validation
for his own strategy of the "indirect approach" than as applicable to the
immediate future.[18] Thus, when Great Britain began to prepare seriously
for war after the Munich Crisis of 1938, guerrilla warfare was "half-
forgotten; no organization for conducting it survived, and there was no
readily available corpus of lessons learned or of trained operators in this
field. T. E. Lawrence's exploits in Arabia, one of the last irregular British
armed offensives, had become a romantic legend. . . ."[19] It was not until
the summer of 1940, after all other means of striking back at the Germans
had failed, that the British, at Churchill's urging, created Special Operations Executive, "to coordinate all action, by way of subversion and
sabotage, against the enemy overseas." Present at the creation were
George C. L. Lloyd, the Colonial Secretary and an old friend of Lawrence's from the days of the Arab Bureau in Cairo, and J. C. F. Holland
of the War Office's vestigial MIR (Military Intelligence Research), who
had won a medal flying for Lawrence in Arabia. Their almost accidental

[17] Winston S. Churchill, *Great Contemporaries* (London, 1937), 129-140.
[18] Basil H. Liddell Hart, *Strategy: The Indirect Approach*, 3d ed. (London, 1967), 197-
98, 373-82. See also Liddell Hart, *Colonel Lawrence: The Man Behind the Legend*, 2d ed.
(New York, 1935), 380-84, and Arnold W. Lawrence, ed., *T. E. Lawrence by His Friends*
(Garden City, N.Y., 1937), 157-58.
[19] Michael R. D. Foot, *SOE in France: An Account of the Work of the British Special
Operations Executive in France, 1940-1944* (London, 1966), 1. The first chapter, pp. 1-
10, describes the creation of SOE. See also Foot, *Resistance: European Resistance to
Nazism, 1940-1945* (New York, 1977), 137-38.

presence merely highlighted the lack of continuity in strategy for revolutionary warfare.

A year later, soon after the German army invaded the Soviet Union, Stalin broadcast an appeal to his people: "Partisan units, mounted and on foot, must be formed; divisions and groups must be organized to combat enemy units, to foment partisan warfare everywhere. . . ."[20] The truth was that secret Soviet plans for partisan warfare had never been implemented and no organization for partisans existed. With a Panzer trap already encircling almost a quarter-million Soviet soldiers east of Minsk, and the German Army Groups North and South gaining momentum, it was too late for orderly planning; hence Stalin's direct appeal to the populace to get something, anything, started immediately.

In Yugoslavia, the entire German invasion required only eleven days. In Greece it lasted seventeen days, and in France forty-two. With such rapid collapses of the armies and the general absence of prewar planning, it is surprising how quickly national resistance movements sprang up across Europe. The Germans themselves deserve much of the credit for this, since it became clear everywhere—brutally and rapidly clear in the Slavic regions—that Nazi doctrines of *Lebensraum* and race meant exploitation at best and extermination at worst for conquered populations. Under the twin shocks of the collapse of familiar government and the installation of an alien and antagonistic regime, many citizens of the defeated nations were shaken loose from their normal lives. Some turned to resistance as a way of expressing their new uncertainties, fears, and hopes, using whatever specific strategies became available in their particular part of Europe.

Two general strategies actually developed—one conservative, the other revolutionary. The Soviet Union provides the best example of a conservative strategy, in which the objective of resistance was to restore the former regime. Conservative strategy called for reestablishing communications with the government whether in the capital or in exile, accepting operational missions ordered by government officials, receiving whatever help could be spared, and building toward the eventual linkup with a national army and the reinstitution of the national political system. Revolutionary strategy, by contrast, developed most clearly in Yugoslavia, where Tito's partisans fought to take power from the exiled regime. Tito's partisans were fighting General Draja Mihailovitch's *Chetnik* guerrillas, as well as the Germans, only seven months after the invasion ended. Although Mihailovitch was officially appointed minister of war, commander in chief of the army, and sole receiver of Allied support, Tito

---

[20] Joseph Stalin, *The Great Patriotic War of the Soviet Union* (New York, 1945), 9.

remained independent and hostile. He organized a People's Liberation Anti-Fascist Front in 1942, and in 1943 the Front's council declared itself the government of Yugoslavia, with Tito as premier and commander in chief. In spite of his continuing conflict with the *Chetniks*, Tito's desperate combat against the Germans eventually won Allied support; Britain sent a mission in 1943, and the Soviet Union and the United States did so in early 1944. By September 1944 the Soviet Red Army was approaching Belgrade and the Allied Mediterranean Air Force was pounding the German lines of communication throughout the Balkans; by the end of October, Tito was in Belgrade at the head of his People's Liberation government. For Yugoslavia, a revolutionary objective had focused the efforts of the resistance from beginning to end.[21]

Elsewhere in Europe, resistance strategies where less clearly defined than in the Soviet Union and Yugoslavia. Although all of them sought a restoration of their national government, the political complexions of those governments were a matter of contention. Resistance movements were to a greater or lesser degree a coalition of competing political groups, and in many occupied countries the Communist Party was among the strongest and hardest fighting. All generally accepted coordination by the exiled government in order to receive support from the Allies and to expedite the defeat of the Germans, but they all also kept an eye on the postwar politics of their nations. In some cases, such as the Yugoslavian *Chetniks*, this led them to avoid combat with the Germans and to conserve their resources for the internal struggle. In others, such as the French Communist Party, it caused them to establish a record against the Germans that would strengthen their position after the war. Regardless of specific strategies, it is clear that one of the greatest consequences of the "Resistance" was in postwar national politics. For years after the war, those who had collaborated with the Germans tended to fare poorly and Resistance heroes well, regardless of the national effectiveness of the Resistance itself. As Lawrence might have predicted, the political and psychological consequences of the Resistance turned out to weigh more heavily over a longer time than did its direct military results.[22]

Southeast Asian resistance movements revealed one striking difference from those in Europe: the Japanese invaders were Asians, while the defeated governments were European or American—the legatees of ear-

---

[21] D. M. Condit, Bert H. Cooper et al., eds., *Challenge and Response in Internal Conflict*, vol. 2 (Washington, D.C., 1967) concisely describes eighteen insurgencies in Europe and the Middle East. For Yugoslavia, see Earl Ziemke, "Yugoslavia (1940-1944)," in ibid., 321-51.
[22] Condit et al., *Challenge and Response*, vol. 2.

lier invasions.[23] This gave the Japanese a great advantage, which they intended to exploit. The "Greater East Asia Co-Prosperity Sphere" was a concept that many Japanese believed in enthusiastically and sincerely, and to many other Asians it appeared to be a reasonable alternative to Western imperialism. The Japanese had been a source of pride and secret hope for Asians since their defeat of Russia in 1905, and their sudden and unexpected victories in 1942 made the slogan "Asia for the Asians!" a reality almost overnight. The underlying reality, however, was that Japan had overextended itself in a desperate war, and its sole hope of winning was the rapid exploitation of the resources of the newly liberated lands. Japan not only was determined to make war pay in 1942, but had staked its national future on continuing to make war pay in a struggle against the richest nations and empires of the world.

Added to this need for resources was the ethnocentric Japanese view of the rest of the world. Japan had a singularly proud record of never having been conquered or invaded, and in the preceding forty years had handily defeated its giant neighbors, China and Russia. It is fair to say that the Japanese, particularly the soldiers of the imperial army, did not see the Asian people that they had liberated as their equals. This sense of superiority made the Japanese difficult to love and accept, although they could easily be feared and even respected.

The former colonial powers were not well loved either, and so the populations properly based their choices on self-interest, guided by the performances and promises of the warring sides. Important exceptions were the local Communist parties, which supported the side that the Soviets were on; Chinese minorities, which supported the side that China was on; and many military and civil officials of the displaced colonial regimes, who continued to support their former employers loyally. In this complex mixture of loyalty and self-interest, there was by early 1942 a possibility of anti-Japanese resistance movements, and the likelihood increased with time, partly because the Japanese increased their economic demands and their insults, partly because of a concurrent increase in the credibility of Allied victory.

More than in Europe, resistance strategies in Asia had a variety of objectives. In Burma, for example, most ethnic Burmans initially saw no need for resistance at all. Thirty young Burmese patriots, the "Thirty Heroes" who had left Burma when under British rule, returned with the

---

[23] For a summary of revolutionary warfare in Southeast Asia during and immediately after World War II, see David Joel Steinberg, ed., *In Search of Southeast Asia* (New York, 1971), 337-342, and also Condit et al., *Challenge and Response*, vol. 1. Joyce Lebra details the Japanese role in *Japanese-Trained Armies in Southeast Asia: Independence and Volunteer Armies in World War II* (New York, 1977).

Japanese army in 1942. They recruited a Burmese Independence Army, set up an autonomous government in Rangoon, and were granted independence by the Japanese in 1943. Eventually disillusioned with the Japanese, however, they formed a secret opposition party and a guerrilla resistance force in late 1944, and cooperated with the British army that retook Burma from the Japanese in 1945. Using the political and military power-base gained by collaboration with—and then resistance to—the Japanese, the Burmese negotiated independence in the postwar period. In an unfortunate but not uncommon legacy of the Resistance, the several hill tribes that had been armed against the Japanese, as well as two different Communist groups, continued guerrilla war against the Rangoon government for years afterward.[24]

The Philippine Commonwealth had a different experience. With a new Philippine army under training in 1941 and a date set for independence within five years, the Filipinos fought beside the Americans until their defeat on the Bataan Peninsula in April 1942. After that, many of the Manila politicians agreed to serve in the Japanese-sponsored Philippine Republic, while thousands of ordinary Filipinos continued to fight with and support the Filipino-American guerrillas. The very destructive fighting of 1944-1945, when American forces returned, and the split—exacerbated by the war—between the political elite and the masses, left the Philippines with an uncertain future when independence was granted.[25]

Both Malayans and Vietnamese resisted the Japanese, but in very different ways. The Malayan Peoples' Anti-Japanese Army was ethnically Chinese—not Malay—and built around the Malayan Communist Party; it was willing to accept British aid. It disbanded in 1945, but reappeared as the Malayan Races Liberation Army soon after the war to fight the British for twelve years before acknowledging defeat.[26] The Vietnamese leader Ho Chi Minh founded the Vietminh party in 1941 at a meeting in China of the exiled Indochina Community Party. More than three years passed as Ho gradually formed an army and a political organization in northern Vietnam. By August 1945, when the Japanese handed power to Emperor Bao Dai, the Vietminh was the only working political organization in the country, and Bao Dai abdicated, relinquishing his authority to it. In September 1945 the independent Democratic Republic

[24] Lebra, *Japanese-Trained Armies*, 39-74, 157-65.

[25] Steinberg, *In Search of Southeast Asia*, 372-377, and Asprey, *War in the Shadows*, 1:562-78.

[26] F. Spencer Chapman, *The Jungle is Neutral* (London, 1949) is a personal account of World War II in Malaya. See also Steinberg, *In Search of Southeast Asia*, 364-70.

of Vietnam was proclaimed in Hanoi, but it would have to fight for thirty years before becoming unified and independent.[27]

In Indonesia and Thailand there were no significant resistance movements. Thailand was independent, and chose to collaborate with the Japanese while maintaining undercover contacts with the Americans and British. Indonesia was too important strategically and economically to be granted independenece, so the Japanese army took over the Dutch administrative system and ran the country until August 1945. Their rule was firm, but encouraged pro-Japanese nationalism with support from Sukarno and Mohammed Hatta. They also trained an Indonesian army of about 65,000. Two days after the abrupt Japanese surrender in August 1945, Sukarno and Hatta announced the independence of Indonesia, but it took five more years of civil wars and wars against the British and Dutch before Indonesia was unified and independent.[28]

Resistance movements during the Second World War were so diverse that all generalization is hazardous; but one common feature, seldom noted, was technological. It is commonplace to say that guerrillas fight against technologically more advanced enemies, and are often able to exploit weaknesses that dependence on advanced technology creates. But it is also true that modern technology has facilitated guerrilla warfare; the wartime Resistance in both Europe and Asia owed its victories as well as its survival in large measure to two new tools of war—the radio and the airplane. The radio made Resistance fighters strategically relevant and tactically effective, while aircraft supplied and often protected them. Without radios, control from London, Moscow, or elsewhere would have been impossible. At the same time, many of the guerrilla operations depended on rapid communications. Intelligence reporting would have been too slow without the radio, and airdrops, pickups of downed airmen, and coordinated ground action would have been much more difficult. The development of small, long-range radios and the training of radio operators were important functions of headquarters such as Special Operations Executive, while the Germans and Japanese worked on direction-finding equipment, code-breaking, jamming, and deceptive techniques in their war against this key link in the Resistance. Aircraft for support of guerrillas needed adequate ranges and payloads, and the ability either to drop people and bundles by parachute, or to take off and land from short fields, or both. Obsolescent bombers, such as the British

[27] Jean Lacouture, *Ho Chi Minh: A Political Biography* (Paris, 1967) and Vo Nguyen Giap, *Unforgettable Months and Years* (Ithaca, N.Y., 1975). See also Steinberg, *In Search of Southeast Asia*, 356-64.
[28] Lebra, *Japanese-Trained Armies*, 75-112, 146-56, and Steinberg, *In Search of Southeast Asia*, 347-51, 377-84.

Wellington, worked well, as did the American C-46 and C-47 transports. For lighter work, the venerable Soviet PO-2 (or U-2) two-seat biplane could land a commissar in any small field, and then take off with two wounded partisans strapped to its wings. Aircrew training for these missions was important, and crews without special night-flying and navigation abilities had little success. Allied air forces developed squadrons specifically trained and equipped for these missions. Although the technological details may now seem unimportant, the experience itself created a set of skills, and to some extent a collection of hardware, that in the postwar period would become part of a new consciousness that "revolutionary war" could no longer be regarded as of minor significance.[29]

III

It is possible to look back and see the phenomenon of revolutionary war emerging in the eighteenth century from the first wave of modern revolutions in America and France. Catalyzed by the Napoleonic Wars, demands for national independence, for democratic rights, and for social justice fused in the nineteenth century to provide a powerful impetus to armed revolution. By the early years of the present century, the specific problem of revolutionary military struggle was receiving considerable attention, and the Russian Revolution of 1917 would see the culmination of a long historic process. But this plausible perspective is mistaken; the vital fusion of ideas and actual conditions, of theory and practice, never took place, not even in the 1917 revolution. The real story, until the 1940s, is one of false starts, dead ends, at most brief flashes of the future— not at all the anticipated emergence of a radically new kind of warfare, whose aim and methods diverged sharply from the long tradition of Western warfare. Not even in 1941 was this new kind of war, considered either as a class of military events or as a body of strategic thinking, perceptible. Since then, awareness has risen sharply. The victory of the Chinese Communists in 1949, with the attendant publicity for the writings on revolutionary war of their leader, Mao Tse-tung, the more or less violent dismantling of the great European empires in Asia and Africa, and the Cold War have all combined to give the subject an unprecedented salience in contemporary Western military thought. What is new is not the phenomenon itself, but our perception of it.

However much we may seek it elsewhere, the basic text for ideas

---

[29] Aerospace Studies Institute, *The Role of Airpower in Guerrilla Warfare* (Maxwell Air Force Base, Ala., 1962) is a comprehensive account of the subject. Harris Warren, "Air Support for the Underground" in *The Army Air Forces in World War II*, ed. Wesley F. Craven and James L. Cate, 7 vols. (Chicago, 1948-58), 3:493-524 describes operations in Europe.

about revolutionary war is in the writings of Mao Tse-tung. When the Chinese Communist revolutionary movement realized that the Marxist model of proletarian revolution did not apply to China, an agrarian society with a weak industrial sector, it turned away from the cities and workers to the countryside and the peasantry as the main support for revolution. In their violent struggle with the Nationalist government, and still more in their fight against the Japanese after 1937, Mao and the Chinese built a new doctrine for revolution around the tactics and techniques of waging a peasant-based guerrilla war. Guerrillas, weaker than their enemy, could not be effective or even survive without strong, well-organized popular support. Mobilizing that support was a political rather than a military task, and the primacy of political over military concerns became a hallmark of Mao's theorizing about warfare. In this respect he diverged markedly from traditional Western military thought, with its fairly rigid distinctions between war and peace, and between political and military affairs.

Mao diverged in other important respects as well, especially in the values given to time and space. In the Western tradition, epitomized by Napoleon, military victory was to be achieved quickly, and the seizure or defense of territory was central to the very purpose of warfare. For Mao, long without the means either to seize and hold territory or to win quick victory, space and time became weapons rather than goals. "Protracted struggle" promised to exhaust the enemy, if not militarily then at least politically, as he failed to achieve the quick victory demanded by the Western tradition. Similarly, trying to hold territory could be suicidal for guerrilla forces, but by operating in vast or difficult terrain, better known to them than to their enemy, they could entice, mislead, and wear him down, creating chances for damaging surprise attacks. These were key Maoist ideas centering on politics, time, and space. His great victory in 1949 ensured that these ideas, so divergent from the military concepts that presumably underlay European military predominance in the world, would be widely publicized, attracting enormous attention from revolutionaries and counterrevolutionaries alike.[30]

The problem in analyzing Mao's thought on revolutionary war lies in keeping what he said distinct from what he was generally understood

---

[30] The principal form in which Mao's ideas have been transmitted to the English-reading world is the four-volume *Selected Works of Mao Tse-tung* (London and New York, 1954-56). *Selected Military Writings of Mao Tse-tung* (Peking, 1963) brings together relevant essays from the earlier publications. *Mao*, in the "What They *Really* Said" series, ed. Philippe Devillers (London, 1969), is also useful. Best known by far is the "little red book"—*Chairman Mao Tse-tung on People's War* (Peking, 1967)—millions of which were published and circulated. Quotations below are from this little "Red Book" wherever possible, with citation to the *Selected Works* or other source also given.

to have said. As with other influential military theorists, like Jomini, Clausewitz, and Mahan, admirers as well as enemies have taken Mao's ideas out of the context in which they were developed, expressed, and meant to be understood. It is well to remember that the ideas themselves were worked out in the midst of great danger and hardship: the ferocious civil war against the Nationalists and the equally desperate resistance to Japanese invasion.

Resorting to guerrilla warfare was, initially, a pragmatic recognition that the Nationalists, like the Japanese, were stronger militarily. As early as 1930, Mao wrote:

> Ours are guerrilla tactics. . . . Divide our forces to arouse the masses, concentrate our forces to deal with the enemy.
>
> The enemy advances, we retreat; the enemy camps, we harass; the enemy tires, we attack; the enemy retreats, we pursue. . . .
>
> Arouse the largest numbers of the masses in the shortest possible time and by the best possible methods.[31]

At about the same time, in a message called "On Correcting Mistaken Ideas in the Party," he expanded on his order to arouse the masses: "The Red Army fights not merely for the sake of fighting but in order to conduct propaganda among the masses, organize them, arm them, and help them to establish revolutionary political power. Without these objectives, fighting loses its meaning and the Red Army loses the reason for its existence."[32] Here he was obviously refuting an opinion in his own camp that called for a division of labor between military and political tasks. That his own opinion was more pragmatic than ideological is indicated by an earlier passage in the same essay: "*Especially at present*, the Red Army should certainly not confine itself to fighting. . . ."[33]

By the later 1930s, after the Long March and the Japanese invasion, pragmatism was becoming party orthodoxy. In a 1937 interview with a British journalist, he spoke in terms of "principles" guiding the political work of the Eighth Route Army. The second of three principles was that of "unity between the army and the people, which means maintaining a discipline that forbids the slightest violation of the people's interests, conducting propaganda among the masses, organizing and arming them, lightening their economic burdens and suppressing the traitors and collaborators who do harm to the army and the people—as a result of which

[31] "Red Book," 32; "A Single Spark Can Start a Prairie Fire," *Selected Works*, 1:124.
[32] "Red Book," 25; *Selected Works*, 1:106, where the translation differs slightly.
[33] "Red Book," 24; *Selected Works*, 1:106, where the translation differs. Emphasis added.

the army is closely united with the people and *welcomed everywhere.*" Elsewhere he wrote of the "laws of revolutionary war."[34]

Not only did the emphasis in his pronouncements shift from the pragmatic to the dogmatic (in part, no doubt, because in Marxist-Leninist terms Mao was preaching heterodoxy), but emphasis also shifted from the army's role in *politicizing* people to the army's *reliance* on the people. The cities, where the revolutionary proletariat lived, were occupied by reactionaries and imperialists, so the revolution must "turn the backward villages into advanced, consolidated base areas." And again: "Without such strategic bases, there will be nothing to depend on in carrying out any of our strategic tasks or achieving the aim of the war."[35] That other Chinese Communist leaders (Chou En-lai) saw matters differently is apparent: "The protracted revolutionary struggle in the revolutionary base areas consists mainly in peasant guerrilla warfare led by the Chinese Communist Party. Therefore *it is wrong* to ignore the necessity of using rural districts as revolutionary base areas, to neglect painstaking work among the peasants, and to neglect guerrilla warfare."[36] Throughout, Mao attacks those who would shift away from the villages to the cities, from regional forces to the main army, from human motivation to military technique, and from warfare to political action. "Political power," he repeats, "grows out of the barrel of a gun."[37]

All of these statements on revolutionary war are taken from Mao's *Selected Works*, translated into many languages and circulated throughout the world. They are also found in the little red book on "People's War," published in 1967 when Lin Piao was ascendant.[38] The little red book is, among other things, a carefully arranged set of quotations, with interpolation by Lin himself, to buttress the controversial policy of pitting Chinese ideology against American technology, and to defend Mao's unleashing of the Cultural Revolution in 1966. Although the quotations add up to an essentially accurate picture of Mao's thinking on revolutionary war, all nuances, qualifications, and contextual references are lost, and chronology is ignored; instead, Mao's ideas are allowed to float free, as universally valid, at least for countries like China, "semi-colonial and semi-feudal."[39] It was in this highly condensed, abstract form that

[34] "Red Book," 26, 38; *Selected Works*, 2:96, 175, with slight difference in translation. Emphasis added.

[35] "Red Book," 19-20; *Selected Works*, 3:85; 2:135.

[36] "Red Book," 21; *Selected Works*, 3:85-86, where "incorrect" was used instead of "wrong" to describe the "errors." Emphasis added.

[37] "Red Book," 4; *Selected Works*, 2:272.

[38] Yao Ming-le, *The Conspiracy and Death of Lin Biao*, with an introduction by Stanley Karnow (New York, 1983), xv.

[39] "Red Book," 38; *Selected Works*, 1:175.

Mao's thought on revolutionary war impressed itself on those caught up in comparable struggles.

The most serious distortion caused by this elevation of Mao's writing from operational memoranda of the 1930s to the biblical text for revolutionary war is the loss or muting of his emphasis on the need to make correct strategic assessments. If read in one way, his various treatises on revolutionary strategy are filled with what have become clichés: military and political action are closely interdependent; guerrillas depend on popular support, which they get by bringing the benefits of revolution to the masses; revolutionary fighters are fish, the people are the sea in which they swim. These treatises are also filled with ponderous polemics, attacks left and right on those who reject, doubt, or misunderstand Mao's strategy; "flightism," "desperadoism," "opportunism," and "guerillaism" are among the many heresies denounced by Mao, and readers may be tempted to regard these attacks as simply reflecting the political struggles of the Chinese Revolution at the time Mao wrote.

But if read in another way, as a fundamental means of addressing the problem of strategy manifesting itself in a variety of specific strategic situations, then these polemical sections, together with other parts of his writing ostensibly unrelated to military matters, become very interesting and important, the more so because many who have looked to Mao as the seminal theorist of revolutionary warfare have neglected this part of his theory. Mao was obsessed by the problem of knowledge, and his polemical attacks on heretical views, while directed against personal and political targets, deal with failures of systematic learning and thinking. In the stressful and emotional realm of revolutionary action, leaders were easily carried away by their feelings—intoxicated by victory, downcast by defeat, confused by the unexpected. The social structure of revolution compounded the difficulty: intellectuals knew only what they got from books and talk, peasants trusted only their five senses and personal experience. Even revolutionary action did little more than harden preconceptions. Bitter factionalism, gross blunders, and revolutionary failure were the predictable fruits of this deeply rooted ailment, this failure to grasp revolutionary reality.

Mao wrote as if only he, with his enormous strength and vision, had the capacity to recognize the problem of superficial knowledge and impulsive decision and to cope with it. In these long essays, many written under the most difficult physical circumstances, with little food or sleep, he reiterates that every situation must be totally understood and rigorously analyzed before action is taken. The language, length, and frequency of these passages remove all suspicion that he was merely indulging in some obligatory Marxist-Leninist incantation; these passages reveal, as

842

clearly as is possible in cold translated print, the passion of the revolutionary evangelist trying to confront the original sin of lazy, subjective thinking. The clichés of his now-famous strategic doctrine were, for him, no more than simple guidelines that could set the right direction for revolutionary strategy and warn against the worst kinds of strategic blunders. But only realistic application, which required the utmost intellectual effort, could turn these strategic formulae into actual victory. It is this vital aspect of Maoist strategy that is lost from view in much of the subsequent discussion.[40]

Classic Western theorists of strategy, notably Jomini and Clausewitz, addressed the same problem—how to close the gap between theory and its application. For Clausewitz, the key was to keep theory close to its empirical roots, not letting the language, logic, and polemics of theoretical discourse break away from the untidy, multifarious reality of actual warfare. His chief fear—his contemporary Bülow being the bad example to avoid—was to create a military theory that had no value in the real world of military action, a theory that was only a sterile intellectual exercise. Like Clausewitz, Jomini accepted the dichotomy between theory and practice, but Jomini had no hesitation in pushing theory toward its most abstract, simplified form. For Jomini, closing the gap between theory and practice was the commander's problem, and he regularly warned his readers that however true the scientific maxims of strategy might be, the key lay in their correct application.

Mao, in this respect, seems closer to Jomini than to Clausewitz. Mao, like Jomini, seems untroubled by the problem of "theory" as such; the existence and nature of a true theory of strategy worried Clausewitz, but not Jomini and Mao. Their concern, once theory was understood, was in applying it. For Jomini, strategic theory could be grasped by any intelligent and receptive person, but only "genius" could apply it consistently in the real world of warfare. Mao offered, at least by implication, a similar answer: the revolutionary leader must fuse knowledge, intellect, passion, and discipline into a single, directed purpose; only human frailty created the gap between theory and practice, between thinking and acting. Properly understood, no gap existed between theory and practice; theorizing about revolutionary strategy is itself part of revolution, not—like this essay—a misguided attempt at detached observation. The main difference between Jomini and Mao on this point was that, for Mao, "genius" was himself, and others could not do better than listen and follow where he led.

---

[40] Devillers, *Mao*, 71-152, is especially helpful in bringing Mao's ideas on military theory and its application into sharp focus.

Readers in the West and elsewhere have persistently given great weight to Mao's maxims of revolutionary strategy, but little to his ideas about how they should be applied. His reiterated message that strategic theory has meaning only in terms of the concrete political, social, and international circumstances at the moment in which theory is being elucidated seems to have fallen on deaf ears. Lack of expert knowledge about China in the 1930s, when all his major treatises were written, partly explains this chronic selectivity of perception. But the enduring, pervasive influence of Jominian categories on Western strategic thinking must also explain a good deal. Superficially, Mao looks like an Asian Jomini: we find similar maxims, repetitions, and exhortations; there is the same deliberate compounding of analysis and prescription, the same didactic drive, the same invocation of the "genius"—a romanticized Napoleon for Jomini, and himself for Mao—who can turn strategic theory into victory.[41]

It is at the point where Mao tries to explain exactly *how* victory grows out of theory—a question that fascinated Clausewitz but did not attract Jomini—that Western readers seem to stop listening. They are unable or unwilling to give up the comfortable assumptions that dichotomize strategy; just as they persist in separating military and political matters, they compartmentalize theory and practice. "Theory," in this view, exists apart from practice; more important, "theory"—if it is not defective—contains all possible intellectual elements that can inform its application, which is seen as a secondary process, dependent mainly on the soundness of the informing theory. Mao does not reverse this relationship, but he changes it fundamentally, first by denying the dichotomy of theory and practice, and then (for the incorrigible non-Marxist Westerner) by effectively integrating theory and practice, treating the two things as one, on the same plane, often rapping the knuckles of his blinkered, Westernized colleagues. The difficulty for later readers lies in losing the specific context of his argument and in being unable to relinquish their own view of theory. The Western concept of theory, derived from natural science and simply incorporated by Jomini into his own influential work on strategy, assigns to theory the main intellectual effort, leaving to practice such quite different qualities as care, courage, intuition, and luck. Mao, by contrast, assigns equal or greater *intellectual* effort to the *application* of theory. Studying, listening, learning, thinking, eval-

---

[41] For example, the famous series of lectures, "On Protracted War," given in 1938 (*Selected Works*, 2:157-243), has a number of Jominian passages like the following: "In this stage, our war will be no longer one of strategic defensive, but one of strategic counteroffensive in the form of strategic offensive and we shall no longer operate on strategically interior lines, but shift to strategically exterior lines" (p. 188).

uating, and reevaluating—these are the Maoist keys to victory. His monumental arrogance lay, partly, in his absolute confidence that he did these things better than any of his rivals. But the point, somehow, has been lost on most of his avowed disciples.

IV

The fall of the Chinese Nationalist regime in 1949 to the Communists led by Mao, more than any other event, created a new Western consciousness of how protracted armed conflict, using guerrilla tactics and guided by a heterodox version of Marxism-Leninism, might achieve decisive revolutionary victory. Other events prepared the way for this new consciousness, and still others strengthened its influence. The armed resistance to German and Japanese occupation during the Second World War had quickly become part of the collective memory of that struggle. Philippine guerrillas, Yugoslav partisans, and French *maquis* were among those groups who had played heroic roles—sometimes exaggerated for political purposes—in the "liberation" of their "people" from tyrannical, foreign rule. Before the war had ended, some of these Resistance movements became revolutionary in aim—to seize power, to destroy feudalism or capitalism or colonialism, to build a new society. During the postwar decade European empires confronted armed liberation movements that were almost indistinguishable in doctrine, tactics, and often in personnel from the admired wartime Resistance. Mao's ideas and, more important, Mao's great victory played into these wartime and postwar events, linking them all in a shocking new sense that the world was being changed by an unorthodox military technique coupled to a radical political program.

While the Chinese were fighting their civil war, revolutionary wars—real and imagined—were breaking out elsewhere in a decolonizing world. The Jewish organizations in Palestine levered the British out by 1948 in a bold and skillful campaign of terror, a strategy that would be used again by the Greek Cypriots a few years later. In Greece, a revolutionary civil war was decided largely on the basis of foreign support. Yugoslav support for the Greek Communist rebels was suspect because of the Yugoslav-Greek dispute over Macedonia; that support stopped abruptly in 1949, just as Field Marshal Alexandros Papagos was bringing the full weight of his American-equipped army to bear on the major base area of the rebels.[42]

Southeast Asia, however, was the center of gravity for revolutionary wars after 1945, facilitated by the disruption of the Japanese conquest,

[42] Condit et al., *Challenge and Response*, vol. 2 describes operations in Palestine, Cyprus, and Greece.

and inspired by the theory and example of Mao and the Chinese People's Liberation Army. A rash of revolts broke out in Burma along the mountainous arc of its northern borders. In the East Indies, wars flared up, died, and flared up again as British, Dutch, and Indonesian factions fought among themselves. Communist-led popular-front parties in Malaya and the Philippines reactivated wartime guerrilla forces to threaten the central governments. Only by dint of well-conceived and coordinated civil and military programs carried out over many years did the British regime in Malaya and the American-backed Philippine government defeat the insurgents. In many of these campaigns, Mao's ideas appeared piecemeal in strategy, in organization, and in priority given to revolutionary political indoctrination; in all of them, his victorious example sustained guerrilla morale, just as it worried the incumbent governments and their international supporters.[43] But the fullest development of what may be called Maoism took place in Indochina, where the Vietnamese waged a revolutionary struggle against the French from 1941 to 1954. That struggle deserves careful examination.

The exploits of the Chinese Communist guerrillas and even Mao's own writings were well known, particularly in East and Southeast Asia.[44] The Vietnamese leader, Ho Chi Minh, had not only read about Mao but had visited Yenan in 1938, and later instructed Chinese Nationalist troops in Mao's guerrilla tactics.[45] Vo Nguyen Giap, future military chief of the Vietnamese Revolution, first met Ho in Kunming in 1940; together in southern China they planned a response to the fall of France and the Japanese occupation of Tonkin, the northern region of Vietnam. Giap recruited a platoon of Vietnamese refugees, his first command, and trained them in guerrilla tactics in preparation for recrossing the border.[46] In early 1941 Ho proclaimed the first "liberated zone" in the rugged mountains on the Vietnamese side of the frontier, and there founded the League for Vietnamese Independence, or Vietminh, pledged to overthrow the Japanese and the French. For the rest of the year, Ho wrote pamphlets on the guerrilla war and trained cadres, while Giap organized propaganda teams and wrote articles for the party newspaper. By the end of 1941, they had moved their headquarters deeper into the country and expanded their training programs as the news of the Vietminh fight against the

[43] Ibid., vol. 1 describes nineteen insurgencies in Asia.

[44] Mao's *Yu Chi Chan* (Guerrilla warfare) was published in 1937 and was then widely sold throughout "Free China" for ten cents a copy, according to Samuel B. Griffith, *Mao Tse-tung on Guerrilla Warfare* (New York, 1961), 37. Mao's strategy and tactics are described by Edgar Snow, *Red Star Over China* (New York, 1938) and Evans F. Carlson, *Twin Stars Over China* and *The Chinese Army* (both New York, 1940).

[45] Lacouture, *Ho Chi Minh*, 69-70.

[46] Robert J. O'Neill, *General Giap: Politician and Strategist* (New York, 1969), 20-23.

Japanese-sanctioned French regime generated recruits. Ho spent the next two years in Chinese jails, while Giap continued to expand operations slowly southward, meeting increasing resistance from the French garrisons, and responding to it with ambushes against French forces, reprisals against their Vietnamese collaborators, and propaganda for the villagers. By the summer of 1944 Giap was ready to extend his guerrilla system throughout Vietnam. When Ho returned in late 1944, however, he changed these plans on the ground that a more thorough political preparation was needed before further military expansion.[47] Ho's decision was only the first of several critical points when Vietnamese revolutionary policy bore out Mao's stress on the need for care and caution in putting revolutionary theory into practice.

After the Japanese seizure of direct control in Indochina, disarming French forces in March 1945, Vietminh headquarters moved closer to the northern capital city of Hanoi, and political operations increased throughout Vietnam in anticipation of an imminent Japanese surrender. When surrender came in August 1945, Ho quickly effected a *coup d'état* and the Japanese-supported emperor Bao Dai abdicated, giving up his authority to the Vietminh. Giap led his troops into Hanoi and took over the public buildings; banners and leaflets proclaimed a general uprising, and Ho Chi Minh was sworn in as president of the Democratic Republic of Vietnam. This swift change from protracted war to revolutionary *coup* indicates that Ho was a master—not a slave—of Maoist doctrine.

For the next year Ho worked among the several forces at play in Vietnam: the powerful occupation armies of the British in the South and the Nationalist Chinese in the North, the edgy and well-armed returning French troops, and the aroused passion for independence of the Vietnamese, peasants and leaders alike. With ultimate independence as the objective, Ho refused to be diverted by the pleasures of denouncing French colonialists or the pressures for a premature war. While long and difficult negotiations with the French failed to produce the desired result, Ho consolidated his political base, expanded Giap's army, sped the Japanese, the British, and especially the Chinese armies on their way, and tried without success to interest other nations in the plight of Vietnam. His most difficult task was to gauge French political and military intentions and capacities, and to respond effectively to them. Little evidence on this troubled period is available, but it appears that Giap was pressing for the use of force against both domestic and foreign enemies, while Ho sought the broadest possible political appeal based simply on the goal

[47] Vo Nguyen Giap, "Origins of the People's Army" in *The Military Art of People's War: Selected Writings of Vo Nguyen Giap*, ed. Russell Stetler (New York, 1970), p. 66.

of independence. Arguing with French negotiators seemed preferable to attacking the French army.

As talks dragged on, evident bad faith on both sides and sporadic violence led to a serious incident in November, a cease-fire, a French ultimatum, and finally the French bombardment in December of the port city of Haiphong. The French cleared the coastal cities of their enemies in a few days of fighting, while Giap ordered his forces back to the old bases in northern Tonkin. After fifteen months of negotiation, both sides prepared for all-out war.[48]

Ho and Giap had a firm grasp by this time of the costs as well as the potential of revolutionary guerrilla warfare. Their great strength lay in the political appeal of Vietnamese independence, a point on which the French could not compete. The war was long and hard fought; a correct political position did not guarantee victory. Within the Maoist doctrine of revolutionary war, the recurrent key questions, addressed continually, concerned the relative strength of the two sides, and the best strategy for any particular moment. For example, in December 1946 the Vietminh attacked French-held cities, not to win military victory, but to symbolize the end of negotiation and the onset of war, and to show both French and Vietnamese that it had the will and the means to fight. After a period of small-scale but nationwide guerrilla operations, the Vietminh met a French offensive in late 1947 against its base areas by withdrawal, minor counterattacks, and local guerrilla actions elsewhere in Vietnam.

Fighting in 1948 and 1949 continued at low intensity, training Vietminh troops and building their morale, weakening the French as opportunity offered, and consolidating the revolutionary position. The balance of forces shifted in 1949 when the Chinese Red Army appeared on the northern frontier. New weapons and safe training areas allowed Giap to organize larger, division-sized units. Vietminh divisions in 1950 struck French posts on the Chinese border, capturing large amounts of equipment and securing Vietminh links with China.

Encouraged by these successes in 1950, Ho and Giap appear to have erred in their application of Maoist theory. They decided to launch an offensive against French posititons in the Red River Delta. In three major battles, the Vietminh suffered heavy losses, Ho and Giap lost the strategic initiative, and their battered forces withdrew to the northern bases. But the strength of Maoist strategy and the Vietnamese grasp of its principles were demonstrated in the sequel. Using Chinese supplies, a strong political base, and widespread guerrilla organization to rebuild his forces in 1951,

---

[48] O'Neill, *General Giap*, 38-49, and Lacouture, *Ho Chi Minh*, 109-171. The description of the First Indochina War that follows is based on Bernard B. Fall, *Street Without Joy* (New York, 1957), 21-55.

Giap left the next move to the French commander, Marshal de Lattre de Tassigny. De Lattre was under pressure to exploit his recent success; both the French Assembly and the U.S. Congress were then debating military budgets for the Indochina War, and his own reputation for dash and élan demanded further victories, not a return to defensive warfare.

At Hoa Binh, twenty-five miles beyond his delta defenses, de Lattre established in November 1951 a large garrison intended to draw the Vietminh into a decisive battle. After a month in which Giap planned, reconnoitered, and carefully deployed his forces, the Vietminh struck— not at Hoa Binh, but at its supply line along the Black River. In two months of fighting costly to both sides, the French garrison of Hoa Binh slowly strangled. A major French counterattack in February 1952 finally reopened the Black River line, but only long enough to withdraw the garrison to the delta from which it had advanced four months earlier. Hoa Binh set the pattern: French mobility and firepower could take them almost anywhere in Vietnam, but they could not stay, and could show only wasted resources and time for their efforts. Time, to the French, was a dwindling resource as patience ran out in Paris. To the Vietnamese, time built confidence, and allowed the transformation of popular support for independence into more tangible kinds of strength: training, supplies, and troop strength. Mistaken judgments by Ho and Giap could still be costly, as they had been in 1950, but a correct application of Maoist theory made recovery possible. Changing the tempo and locus of operations, shifting tactics and weapons, taking full advantage of opportunities, Giap wore down the French and their American supporters in the next years until impatience and pressure produced the decisive battle at Dienbienphu in 1954. The same methods, informed by Maoist theory, would serve equally well for the next twenty years, in the Second Indochina War.

If Mao and Giap are the chief theorists of revolutionary war, Ernesto "Che" Guevara ranks high among their disciples. Guevara served as lieutenant to Fidel Castro in the Cuban Revolution, and soon became known as the strategist of that remarkably successful revolutionary war. While Castro consolidated his revolution in Cuba, Guevara continued the revolutionary struggle elsewhere. He joined the Bolivian insurrection, which was quickly smashed and where he was killed. But before he died, Guevara wrote a short book on revolutionary war, and his ideas were further developed by his comrade in Bolivia, Régis Debray.[49]

The Guevara-Debray variant of Maoism has had important conse-

[49] Che Guevara, *Guerrilla Warfare* (New York, 1961); Régis Debray, *Revolution in the Revolution?* (New York, 1967).

quences in Latin America, and perhaps elsewhere in the Third World. According to Mao and Giap, the first phase of revolutionary war must be political mobilization—the lengthy, painstaking process of recruiting and organizing popular support, building a dedicated and disciplined revolutionary cadre at the village level. During this first phase, only the most limited and selective use of violence is permissible; overt military action is better avoided altogether because it risks awakening the government to its peril and bringing armed repression down on an unready revolutionary organization.

But no such "first-phase" preparation had taken place in Cuba. Instead, Castro's small guerrilla band had established itself in the remote eastern region of the island, and had gathered support as it moved toward Havana. The Batista regime was very unpopular with all classes of Cubans; it collapsed as Castro's growing force approached the Cuban capital. This spectacular result was almost certainly the result of unique conditions, but it became the basis for a deviation from Maoist orthodoxy as great as Mao's own departure from Marxist-Leninist doctrine. The Cuban variant is known as *focoism.*[50]

"Foco" refers to the "mobile point of insurrection"; the concept, generalizing the peculiar Cuban experience, is that lengthy political preparation at the village level, as prescribed by Mao and Giap, is not essential. A small revolutionary force, by using violence, can mobilize popular support much more quickly; instead of political mobilization leading eventually to violence, violence transforms the political situation. Awakened and excited by foco attacks, angered and encouraged by the brutality and ineptitude of governmental response, alienated if the government seeks help from a foreign power, people will be mobilized for revolution in a process in which violence itself is the catalyst.

Experience so far indicates that focoism, however plausible, is not effective; results have been, from the revolutionary point of view, disastrous.[51] Mao and Giap might have told Guevara and Debray that foco violence, rather than catalyzing revolution, would instead expose the revolutionary movement at its weakest moment to a crushing counterattack, as happened in Bolivia. The people who might have been recruited for revolutionary war are instead frightened and discouraged by focoist failure. Perhaps the most serious flaw of focoism is that it ignores the

[50] Chaliand, *Revolution in the Third World,* 43ff.

[51] A brief but incisive account of why focoism has failed is Eldon Kenworthy, "Latin American Revolutionary Theory: Is It Back to the Paris Commune?" *Journal of International Affairs* 25 (1971), 164-70. The entire issue of this journal is devoted to "Revolutionary War: Western Response," and its chief articles (though not the short essays by Kenworthy and others) were republished in book form under the same title, edited by David S. Sullivan and Martin J. Sattler (New York, 1971).

reciprocal nature of the orthodox first phase of revolutionary war: the long hard work of political preparation not only organizes the peasantry and proletariat, but it also teaches the revolutionary activists—usually young urbanized intellectuals—about the people, the villages, the attitudes and grievances, even the physical terrain, on which revolutionary war must be based. Sheer ignorance of local conditions played a major part in the Bolivian fiasco. Critics have suggested that the focoist heresy reflects both the impatience characteristic of Latin American culture (in contrast to sinicized East Asia) and the characteristic arrogance of young intellectuals. Moved to action by what they have learned through reading and talking, they enter the countryside—not unlike the old imperialists— eager to change the lives of the oppressed masses but insensitive to whatever in those lies may not fit preconceived abstractions.

Mao himself, writing in 1930, anticipated and rejected the heresy later—and elsewhere—known as focoism:

> Some comrades in our Party still do not know how to appraise the situation correctly and how to settle the attendant question of what action to take. Though they believe that a revolutionary high tide is inevitable, they do not believe it to be imminent. . . . at the same time, as they do not have a deep understanding of what it means to establish Red political power in the guerrilla areas, they do not have a real understanding of the idea of accelerating the nation-wide revolutionary high tide through the consolidation and expansion of Red political power. They seem to think that, since the revolutionary high tide is still remote, it will be labour lost to attempt to establish political power by hard work. Instead, they want to extend our political influence through the easier method of roving guerrilla actions, and, once the masses throughout the country have been won over, or more or less won over, they want to launch a nation-wide armed insurrection which, with the participation of the Red Army, would become a nation-wide revolution. Their theory that we must first win over the masses on a country-wide scale and in all regions and then establish political power does not accord with the actual state of the Chinese revolution. . . . The establishment and expansion of the Red army the guerrilla forces and the Red areas is the highest form of peasant struggle. . . . The policy which merely calls for roving guerrilla actions cannot accomplish the task of accelerating this nation-wide revolutionary high tide. . . ."[52]

[52] Devillers, *Mao*, 85-86, from "A Single Spark Can Start a Prairie Fire," with substantial differences in translation from *Selected Works*, 1:116ff.

His criticism of what would become the Guevara-Debray variant of Maoist strategy leads directly back to his neglected emphasis on getting the fullest and most accurate picture of the strategic situation, and then thinking through, as dispassionately as possible, the strategic problem. Not only did Mao bring astonishing energy and force to his leadership of the Chinese Revolution, he also knew that his mind worked harder and better than those around him on the intellectual problems of revolutionary strategy.

Western awareness of revolutionary war as a strategic problem began with the Cold War, reaching its earliest clear expression within the French military. Indochina, where the French military was determined to avenge its humiliation of 1940, and where the Vietnamese people provided an exceptionally strong basis for revolutionary war, became the caldron from which emerged the counterrevolutionary theory known as *guerre révolutionnaire*. With the Soviet Union and, after 1949, China supporting the Vietnamese revolutionaries, and the United States increasingly behind the French effort to "contain Communism," war had lasted eight years. Despite American aid and exhortation, the French government in 1954 decided that the war could not be won, and gave up its claim to rule Indochina. But within the French officer corps, faced with yet another defeat, there arose an obsessive concern with learning the lessons of the Indochina war so that future revolutionary wars, already imminent elsewhere in the French Empire, might be won.[53]

Guerre révolutionnaire was more than the French phrase for revolutionary war; it described a diagnosis and a prescription for what an influential group of French career soldiers saw as the chief illness of the modern world—Western failure to meet the challenge of atheistic Communist subversion. Politically very conservative, they drew on a mystical Catholicism and an unshaken faith in the civilizing mission of French colonialism to argue, with Cartesian logic, that the Third World War had already begun. While the United States and its allies were mesmerized by the prospect of nuclear warfare, Communism was outflanking Western defenses from the South, and if not stopped would ultimately destroy Western civilization. Communism, from its base in the Soviet Union, had won its first victory in China, its second in Indochina, and was winning its other battles in Asia. The war had reached North Africa, where Nasser's coup in Egypt was seen as yet another Communist victory, and the outbreak of war in French Algeria in 1954 as another Communist of-

---

[53] Peter Paret, *French Revolutionary Warfare from Indochina to Algeria* (New York, 1964) is the best analysis. Claude Delmas, *La guerre révolutionnaire* (Paris, 1959), no. 826 in the popular series *Que sais-je?*, is an adherent's brief account of the revolutionary threat to which the doctrine was the "correct" response.

fensive. With sub-Saharan Africa and Latin America obvious future targets, Western Europe and the United States would soon be isolated, their powerful armaments never employed in a global war already lost.

The prescription offered by *guerre révolutionnaire* mirrored the diagnosis; both reflected this French military vision of Communism in the contemporary world. Communism was seen as a secular religion, filling the void left by the declining hold of traditional religion on the masses. The faith and discipline of Communism was admired, even while it was opposed as totally dedicated to Evil. Nationalism, anticolonialism, and demands for social justice were regarded as no more than limited, superficial attitudes that Communism was exploiting in order to bring all non-Western, underdeveloped areas into a global, Communist-led coalition against the Christian West. Offering hope for a better future to the poor and ignorant masses, Communists used all means, however cruel, to reach their goals; no legal or ethical barrier stopped them. The West, its religious faith long in decline, its confidence shaken by two world wars, its range of governmental—and military—action severely limited by its liberal democratic structure, had as yet found no effective response to Communist revolutionary war. In effect, fighting fire with fire was the only answer. No admirer of Mao and Ho did more to present revolutionary war as virtually invincible than did the French theorists of *guerre révolutionnaire*.

Their detailed prescription mirrored what they took to be revolutionary doctrine at every point. First, renewed faith in the counter-Crusade against Communism (and Evil) was essential; Christian revival would necessarily be at the heart of this faith—liberal humanism, like nationalism, was too soft and divisive when unity and courage were needed above all. An expanded program of psychological warfare to promulgate the renewed faith and to expose the evil of Communism was the next step. A parallel program of social and economic action must also deal vigorously with problems like education, public health, and poverty that created conditions ripe for Communist exploitation. Reorganizing and reorienting armed forces, some into mobile antiguerrilla units and others into quasi-governmental garrison forces, was the military part of the prescription, which in effect shifted administrative power from civilian to military hands. Only on one point did the theorists of *guerre révolutionnaire* disagree—on the use of terror and torture. Some rejected it on moral grounds; others argued that it was counterproductive for a government to terrorize its own subjects; more than a few were ready to follow the logic of *guerre révolutionnaire* to its grisly end—in the final confrontation between Good and Evil, all means were justified.

The most extreme versions of *guerre révolutionnaire* readily lend themselves to being categorized as paranoid, totalitarian, and fascist. Applied to some extent in the Algerian war, the methods of *guerre ré-volutionnaire* were not ineffective, in the countryside as well as in the notorious battle of Algiers. But they also led to deep division in France itself, to the coup of May 1958, and to the *Organisation Armée Secrète*, which for several years waged a terrorist campaign against de Gaulle's Fifth Republic. In the end it was de Gaulle, brought back to power by the 1958 coup, who decided that the Algerian war should be ended by granting independence to this former "department" of France. Even now, the theorists of *guerre révolutionnaire* insist that the Algerian revolutionary movement had lost the war when de Gaulle gave it victory.[54]

The British, unlike the French, faced Maoist revolutionary warfare only once, on a small scale in Malaya, although the tactics used against them in Palestine, Cyprus, and Kenya bore certain similarities. The British response had none of the ideological fervor of *guerre révolutionnaire*, but was instead more like that of their colonial tradition at its best: tight integration of civil and military authority, minimum force with police instead of army used when possible, good intelligence of the kind produced by "Special Branch" operatives, administrative tidiness on such matters as the resettlement of civilians in habitable, sanitary camps, and a general readiness to negotiate for something less than total victory. On the military side, British colonial experience showed again its capacity to train effective local forces, a patient view of the time required for success, and a preference for the employment of small, highly skilled troops in well-planned operations rather than massive use of large numbers and heavy firepower. Exploiting ethnic divisions to mobilize Malays against Chinese rebels, the British still required more than a decade to put down the Malayan rebellion. Whether their flexibile, patient methods would have succeeded against a more powerful revolutionary movement must remain a question.[55]

The American response to revolutionary war will be forever linked to Vietnam, and to the experience of painful defeat. A fairly successful effort in suport of the Philippine government against the Huk rebellion had created a measure of confidence among American civilian and military leaders that such wars could be won by the correct attitudes and tactics. Disdain for the French performance in Indochina, where the

---

[54] Typical is the memoir of a chief architect of *guerre révolutionnaire*, Colonel Roger Trinquier, *Le temps perdu* (Paris, 1978), 349: "De Gaulle asked us to pacify Algeria; he gave us the means to do it. We had done it."

[55] Julian Paget, *Counter-Insurgency Campaigning* (London, 1967), 43-79, 155-79. Two comparative studies of Malaya and Vietnam are Richard L. Clutterbuck, *The Long, Long War* (New York 1966) and Robert Thompson, *Defeating Communist Insurgency* (London, 1966).

Americans had also provided considerable material assistance, was widely expressed, notably in the popular novel and film, *The Ugly American.*[56] After the French agreement to partition Vietnam in 1954, the United States continued to support an anti-Communist government of South Vietnam against the new regime of Ho Chi Minh in Hanoi and against his supporters in the South.

In the event, American confidence proved to be misplaced. Neither the U.S. Department of State nor various agencies (USOM, JUSPAO, CORDS, and others) showed sufficient capacity to deal with fundamental political problems; the Americans had no civilian organization comparable to the British and French colonial services, much less comparable to the disciplined, vanguard Communist party of Vietnam. The American civilians gathered information and submitted reports, but had neither the training nor the tradition needed to operate directly against a revolutionary movement. In that sense, the American "counterinsurgency" effort in Vietnam was not unlike Latin American "focoism"—earnest, naive, and impatient; incapable of meeting the Maoist demand that operations be based on closely reasoned political and social analysis; doomed romantics in the brutal world of revolutionary war, not unlike the central figure in another popular novel of the period, Graham Greene's *The Quiet American.*[57]

On the military side, the Americans showed similar deficiencies. In 1962 President Kennedy encouraged a brief flirtation with "Special Warfare," but the organizational base of the Army's elite Special Forces was never strong, and was further weakened by rapid expansion. The U.S. Army establishment mistrusted a group trained for irregular operations, and the final estrangement came when Special Forces units began to work closely with the U.S. Central Intelligence Agency. The arrest and imprisonment by Army authorities of the officer commanding Special Forces in Vietnam indicates the degree to which even the American military could not unify its counterrevolutionary strategy. American technicians and military advisors with the South Vietnamese armed forces accepted their mission in good conscience, but assumed that political matters—

[56] Eugene Burdick and William J. Lederer, *The Ugly American* (New York, 1958) was one of the most widely discussed books of the period, and its title added a phrase to political discourse. The film version of 1963, starring Marlon Brando, grossly distorted the argument of the novel without altering its strongly anti-Communist, counterrevolutionary tone. Here and in notes 57 and 59 popular novels and films have been cited to indicate the important role played by American public opinion in developing ideas about the nature and importance of contemporary revolutionary war.

[57] Graham Greene, *The Quiet American* (London, 1955). American reviews attacked the author's critical view of the United States, and questioned his relationship to the Communist Party. The film version of 1958 blunted the political message of the book by transforming it into a murder mystery.

the heart of revolutionary war—were not their responsibility. Although the fighting effectiveness of the South Vietnamese improved markedly with American tutelage and support, nothing was done to confront the political appeal of Ho's national stature, the problems of South Vietnamese society, and the taint of a regime dependent on foreign assistance.

Sustained aerial attack on North Vietnam and the shipment of large American combat forces to the South were symptoms in 1965 of strategic bankruptcy. Whether an Americanized war could have been won, short of destroying the country and its population, continues to be a debated question. But surely massive American military intervention exacerbated the basic political, social, and economic conditions that gave revolutionary war, in Vietnam and elsewhere, its impetus. And Americanizing the war made it almost impossible for the vital political effort, necessarily a civilian effort, to deal with whatever made so many Vietnamese ready to wage or support a revolutionary war. Instead, U.S. Army divisions, usually with poor intelligence but with great mobility, firepower, and determination, sought to find and destroy comparable enemy formations. The senior American military commanders never took seriously the idea that the political effort, presumably going on behind the security screen provided by large-scale combat operations, should have equal or greater priority.

American "counterinsurgency," as it came to be known, was very costly, both to the Vietnamese and to the Americans themselves.[58] Intellectually, it was shallow, lacking either the fusion of mysticism and rationalism of *guerre révolutionnaire*, or the phlegmatic pragmatism of British civil-military coordination. It was almost a purely military approach, like the Normandy landings or the liberation of Luzon in 1944, targeted on an enemy presumed to be the mirror image of American combat units, the peasants (like the grateful Italians of yet another popular novel, John Hersey's *A Bell for Adano*) waiting passively for the blessings attendant on American liberation.[59] American strategy severely challenged Ho and Giap, but in the end it failed to defeat them, in large part because it never grasped the kind of war being fought nor the particular Vietnamese conditions that gave the war its revolutionary character.

[58] Douglas S. Blaufarb, *The Counterinsurgency Era: U.S. Doctrine and Performance* (New York, 1977) is the basic account, but debate has continued, and the judgment expressed in the text of this essay is unacceptable to many who argue that the United States came close to winning its war in Vietnam. Another view is expressed in Harry G. Summers, Jr., *On Strategy* (Novato, Calif., 1982).

[59] John Hersey, *A Bell for Adano* (New York, 1944). This slight, sentimental story of the "liberation" and democratization of an Italian village in World War II won the Pulitzer Prize, and in 1945—like *The Ugly American*—became a popular film.

V

The theory of revolutionary war is often discussed, by revolutionaries and counterrevolutionaries alike, as if it were a doctrine of universal applicability. Of course the discussion routinely includes mention of the need for flexibility, adapting the doctrine to specific political, social, geographical, and international conditions. But only recently has the possibility been raised that the doctrine, at least in its classic Maoist formulation, is valid only in a limited range of circumstances. Gerard Chaliand, whose wide experience of revolutionary wars in the 1960s and 1970s, along with his professed sympathy for most revolutionary movements, gives weight to his cautionary views on the subject, has expressed serious doubts about the global validity of the doctrine.[60] He notes that with the peculiar exception of Cuba (and perhaps now Iran), revolutionary war has been successful only in the Sinicized parts of Asia—China and Vietnam. National identity and social cohesion are much weaker in the rest of Asia, Africa, and Latin America, probably too weak to endure the terrific, prolonged strain of waging revolutionary war. Elsewhere, revolutionary wars have collapsed in the face of determined repression, or split into ethnic, regional, or tribal factions whose hostility to one another seems stronger than the common revolutionary goal. Not even Algeria can claim to have won its revolutionary war. Chaliand is far from dogmatic in his view, but he raises a vital question.

Asking what has led to victory or defeat in the dozens of revolutionary wars fought since 1945 is a way of bringing the question of doctrinal validity into sharper focus. Rebel victory has been most likely against foreign occupation or a colonial regime, where national and sometimes racial feelings are mustered against a government of outsiders and their collaborators. The chances of victory are also good against a regime that is unpopular, corrupt, and weak, like Batista's in Cuba or the Shah's in Iran, where even government forces soon lose heart and join the rebellion. But beyond these fairly clear points of reference, the answer to the question becomes uncertain. The doctrine of revolutionary war developed in societies of rice-growing peasants, with their powerful tradition of family solidarity and communal cooperation. Guerrilla warfare, which has been the central military method of revolutionary war, is necessarily based on such peasants. But peasants are basically conservative, more disposed to suffer than risk their hard-earned all. They are no more receptive to rebel agitators, usually educated and urbanized outsiders, than they are to agents of a distant and mistrusted central

[60] These doubts are expressed both in his *Revolution in the Third World* (New York, 1977) and in the introduction to his anthology, *Guerrilla Strategies* (Berkeley, 1982).

government. In fact, almost all of the post-Mao theorizing about revolutionary war has come from just such intellectuals, whose inability to understand the peasant world is notorious. In that sense, the doctrine of revolutionary war becomes mythological, giving hope to a small revolutionary vanguard when actual chances for victory may be remote.

It appears that peasants can be mobilized for revolutionary war only when their lives have deteriorated so rapidly and radically that they feel desperate. In part to escape this dilemma of an unrevolutionary peasantry, "urban guerrilla warfare" has received a certain amount of attention, its chief weapon being acts usually called "terrorist." But terrorism has yet to win a victory anywhere, and urban guerrillas have found physical survival as difficult as Maoist theory indicated they would.[61]

Turning from the theoretical debate to the specifics of actual experience since 1945, the international situation often appears to be the crucial factor in explaining the outcome of revolutionary war. The victory of the Chinese Communists in 1949, which owed little or nothing to the Soviet Union (popular legends to the contrary notwithstanding), is the great and misleading exception. The Lebanese civil war, which U.S. Marines and other "peace-keeping" forces failed to stop in 1983, is an extreme case in the opposite sense. Lebanon became a battleground between Israel and Syria, the Palestinians, and "volunteers" from Iran. It is also possible to argue that Lebanon was a "proxy war" between the United States and the Soviet Union, who supplied the respective sides. In any case, the intertwined revolutionary wars, of the Palestinians to recover their homeland from the Israelis, and of the Muslim majority of Lebanon to take power from the Christians, were utterly dependent on the clash between stronger powers.

Other civil upheavals, from Ireland to Sri Lanka, where revolutionary movements depend more heavily on support from outside than on a broad base of mobilized internal support, suggest that there is often no more than a loose, rhetorical relationship between the realities of rebellion and the theory of revolutionary war. And wherever urgent circumstances have forced the operational realities to diverge very far from classical Maoist theory, the chances for revolutionary victory—barring some major "external" event, the revolutionary equivalent of an act of God—appear to be slim.

In a famous speech, the Chinese leader Lin Piao described the capitalist powers as the "cities" of the world and Asia, Africa, and Latin

---

[61] Eric R. Wolf, *Peasant Wars of the Twentieth Century* (New York, 1969) is valuable on peasants and revolution. Johan Niezing, ed., *Urban Guerilla* (Rotterdam, 1974) documents the growing interest in its subject.

America as the "countryside."[62] Revolutionary guerrilla movements in this global countryside, led by China, would organize, mobilize, and fight a protracted war, as Mao had done, until cities, no more than isolated bastions of reaction in a revolutionized world, would collapse, starved for vital resources that only the countryside could supply. This prophecy, in its grandiosity so like the extreme visions of the French proponents of *guerre révolutionnaire*, alarmed many "city-dwellers" throughout the world, and itself was an important factor in the rapid rise of Western interest in the theory and doctrine of revolutionary war. But not long after Lin Piao's death, the world hardly matched his alarming prophecy. In every Southeast Asian state, nearest to the font of revolutionary leadership and support in China, there were guerrilla movements attempting to overthrow non-Communist, often conservative governments. Yet these movements received at most token support from China. Chinese relations with the associated governments of Southeast Asia (ASEAN) were clearly more important to Chinese leaders than their commitment to globalized revolutionary war, and the Communist-influenced guerrilla movements in Southeast Asia more an embarrassment to Peking than a weapon in its armory.[63]

Historians, perhaps better than anyone, should understand the hazards of prophecy. But a concluding attempt to place the idea of revolutionary warfare historically entails an estimate of the future as well as an explanation of the past. In 1941 Edward Mead Earle and his Princeton seminar were not impressed by the importance of revolutionary war. Compared to the impact of one world war and the outbreak of another, armed uprisings to overthrow governments seemed a peripheral aspect of strategy. Three decades later all had changed; except for airborne nuclear explosives too destructive to consider using, the most urgent and puzzling problem for contemporary strategy was the remarkable ubiquity and success of revolutionary wars.

We have already suggested some of the explanation for this rapid shift in strategic perception. The Western European empires, weakened by world war, crumbled rapidly after 1945. If the process in any particular colony involved violence, it naturally pitted guerrillas and terrorists against government forces. After decolonization, successor regimes often governed with difficulty, troubled by inadequate resources and by the internal divisions of artificially defined state boundaries. Against these postcolonial regimes, armed resistance movements, similar to those or-

[62] *Long Live the Victory of People's War* (Peking, 1965), extracted in Walter Laquer, *The Guerrilla Reader* (Philadelphia, 1977), 197-202.
[63] This development can be traced through the annual report, *Southeast Asian Affairs*, published since 1974 by the Institute of Southeast Asian Studies, Singapore.

ganized earlier against the European colonial powers, often formed. And behind the continuing turmoil in the former colonial regions of the world, including Latin America, was the division of the predominantly northern, industrialized nations into two mutually hostile armed camps, each afraid to risk nuclear war, but both almost too ready to confront one another indirectly, on the battlefields of the "Third World."

If this picture of the recent past is essentially accurate, then it points toward some possibilities for the future of revolutionary war. The old European empires are virtually gone, and with them the intense xenophobic nationalism and its vulnerable targets that gave revolutionary warfare so much of its energy. The post-colonial regimes continue to be troubled, but it may be that after a period of violent conflict, full-scale revolutionary war will become a less frequent manifestation of trouble in those parts of the world. And, finally, the superpowers have not gained much from their involvement in these expensive, protracted, often unmanageable struggles. The Vietnam War was a disaster for the United States, and the Soviet Union has little to show for its frequent intervention in anticolonial and revolutionary conflicts. If current Soviet operations against guerrilla resistance in neighboring Afghanistan and comparable American maneuvers in Central America and the Caribbean are no more than what they seem—limited military ventures to secure the sensitive border areas of acknowledged spheres of influence, clumsy perhaps but not surprising—then even the apparently endless Cold War does not promise that revolutionary warfare will continue to be as important as it was in the 1950s and 1960s.

A generation of costly experiences may have had a sobering effect on enthusiasts—in the military centers of Washington and Moscow as well as in the jungles and mountains of the Third World—for the revolutionary strategy of Giap and Mao. The careers and writing of both men, studied closely, suggest that revolutionary warfare, waged against any but the most feeble regime, is hardly a magic prescription for military and political victory. In China and Vietnam, revolutionary war meant millions dead and a generation of suffering for millions more; the brutal discipline required for revolutionary endurance stretches the powers of comprehension. As Mao himself put it, "a revolution is not a dinner party, or writing an essay, or painting a picture, or doing embroidery; it cannot be so refined, so leisurely and gentle, so temperate, kind, courteous, restrained and magnanimous. A revolution is an insurrection, an act of violence. . . ."[64] There has been, inevitably, a superficial, romantic

[64] Devillers, Mao 59, quoting "Report of an Investigation into the Peasant Movement in Hunan"; with slight differences in translation from Selected Works, 1:27.

element in the rise of revolutionary war to international prominence. This romanticism is visible in the deification of Mao himself, in the more extreme statements of French and American "experts" on *guerre révolutionnaire* and counterinsurgency, and in the views of some who support revolutionary causes from the relative security of London, Paris, or New York. This romanticism, itself a historical fact however transitory, may be simply noted and assigned a place in the larger phenomenon.

A last question must raise some doubt about our estimate of a declining role for revolutionary warfare. The regions known as the Third World have been, and in all likelihood will remain, the locus of revolutionary warfare, whatever importance this kind of military action may have in the future. A few basic facts and trends pertaining to those regions ought to be noted: the economic gap between the Third World and the industrialized nations continues to increase. At the same time, population in most of these regions has been growing at a rate that, even by the most optimistic estimates, will mean that within a few decades vastly larger numbers of people cannot possibly be supported by already scarce resources. If the political systems of these regions were generally stable and effective, and their social systems fairly equitable, a concerted effort by ruling groups to avert economic and demographic catastrophe might be expected. But the political and social realities in the Third World do not encourage any such expectation, nor does the behavior of the richest nations offer much hope for salvation from that quarter.

To quote from a recent description of conditions characteristic of certain parts of Latin America:

> The seizure of the vast majority of the wealth by an oligarchy of owners bereft of social consciousness, the practical absence or the shortcomings of a rule of law, military dictators making a mockery of elementary human rights, the corruption of certain powerful officials, the savage practices of some foreign capital interests constitute factors which nourish a passion for revolt among those who thus consider themselves the powerless victims of a new colonialism in the technological, financial, monetary or economic order.

This passage is not from a revolutionary tract, or a liberal denunciation of neocolonial exploitation, but an official papal statement, warning Catholic clergy against becoming involved in Third World revolutionary movements.[65] The papal pronouncement, despite its conservative aim, concedes the widespread existence of the conditions described, which,

---

[65] Excerpts from the Vatican statement on "Liberation Theology," *New York Times*, September 4, 1984.

861

suitably amended, apply to much of the Third World beyond Latin America as well. Present trends give no reason to believe that any form of gradual, evolutionary process will change these conditions.

Mao, in 1927, described the appalling conditions of the poor Chinese peasants in Hunan province. Taking issue with the orthodox line that peasants had, at most, limited revolutionary potential, Mao insisted that conditions were so bad in Hunan, and elsewhere in rural China, that revolution could be based on the desperate Chinese peasantry. These people, unlike the European peasantry of the nineteenth century, had nothing left to lose. A decade later, after bitter battles within the Chinese Communisty Party, Mao had won the argument, and was undisputed leader of the revolutionary movement. No one, not even Mao himself, believed in 1937 that within twelve years the Chinese revolutionary war would be won. As we survey the world, its prospects, the likely role of violence in those prospects, and especially the strategic ideas guiding the use of armed force, Mao's experience is suggestive. We can only ask whether large numbers of people, in large parts of the world, will sink to the level of Hunan peasantry in 1927, creating a vast explosive potential for revolutionary war.

862

28. Reflections on Strategy in the Present and Future

GORDON A. CRAIG AND FELIX GILBERT

AT THE END of a book that has dealt with the evolution of military thought and practice from Machiavelli's time to the Second World War and the nuclear age, it is necessary to return to the question raised in its first pages, namely, that of relevance. Has the experience of the past any real bearing upon the problems that confront us in the nuclear age, or are we living, as some military writers have claimed, in an age without useful precedents, a situation that is most pronounced in the field of strategy?

It is easy enough, when one considers the dangerously bipolar nature of world politics, the preoccupation of the superpowers with nuclear weapons, and the intensity of the arms race between them, to incline to the latter view and to conclude that the present age is not congenial to the kind of strategical principles elaborated by the masters of the past. When Clausewitz, for instance, wrote his famous sentence "War is the continuation of politics by other means," he was, while emphasizing the links between war and peace, probably assuming a clearer distinction between them than we can today, when it is, indeed, questionable whether the two conditions are separable in any real sense. The collapse in 1914 of the international system that had preserved peace during most of the nineteenth century and the subsequent failure of all attempts to find an effective substitute for it, the paramount influence of ideology upon international relations since 1917 and—despite the definitive defeat of Fascism and National Socialism by a coalition that transcended the ideological divisions among its members—its increased intensity after 1945, the hypernationalism of countries that freed themselves from colonial status in the wake of the second world conflict, and—particularly in the Middle East—the emergence of militant religious zealotry have made the years since 1945 a period of almost unremitting conflict on many levels. If the greatest of the Great Powers have avoided open war against each other, their involvement in regional disputes on behalf of client states has on occasion brought them dangerously close to it, and their normal attitude toward each other between such crises has been of such fixed hostility that the years from 1949 to 1969 are referred to in the history books as the years of the Cold War, and those since 1980 have seemed to many observers to betoken a return to that condition.

In these circumstances it is perhaps not surprising that public opinion polls should report that an ever larger number of ordinary people in Europe and America no longer believe in the durability of peace between the superpowers and that some specialists—like the scientists, military experts, and peace researchers who met in Groningen in the Netherlands in April 1981—are inclined to believe that it cannot survive the end of the decade. Such views were, indeed, already having their effects upon personal behavior, on the one hand, in a growing fatalism, a frustrated distrust of political leaders and a withdrawal from political participation, a new focus on regional and environmental problems, and an internalization of life at the expense of the *polis*[1] and, on the other hand, in participation in grass-roots, direct-action movements that demand immediate and total solutions for complicated political and military problems, often with scant regard for the technical, diplomatic, and strategical factors that are involved.

Notable also in some countries is an ambivalence of mood that permits fear of war to exist side by side both with an exalted state of national feeling that is capable of belligerent expression and with a high degree of profitable involvement in preparation for war. Richard Barnet has written of this last activity that "the war economy provides comfortable niches for tens of thousands of bureaucrats in and out of military uniform who go to the office every day to build nuclear weapons or to plan nuclear war; millions of workers whose jobs depend upon the system of nuclear terrorism; scientists and engineers hired to look for that final 'technological breakthrough' that can provide total security; contractors unwilling to give up easy profits; warrior intellectuals who sell threats and bless wars."[2]

An age in which such tendencies exist cannot be described as a time of peace without straining the meaning of the word, and a pessimist might be inclined to believe that it resembles more closely that transitional state that the East German novelist Christa Wolf calls *der Vorkrieg*, the prelude to war.[3]

Modern technology may require some adjustment to another assumption by Clausewitz, namely that in time of both peace and war the responsible political leadership will usually be able to make all significant

---

[1] See, *inter alia*, Fritz J. Raddatz, "Die Aufklärung entlässt ihre Kinder," and "Unser Verhängnis als unsere Verantwortung," *Die Zeit*, 6, 13 July 1984.

[2] Richard J. Barnet, *Real Security* (New York, 1981), 97.

[3] Christa Wolf, *Kassandra: Erzählung* (Darmstadt, 1984), 76f.

policy decisions. The actions that will be taken in future crises promise, indeed, to be predetermined and automatic in nature. One can argue plausibly that the autonomy of the political leadership begins to shrink from the moment that it authorizes the expenditure of national resources on this or that kind of weapons research or the production of this or that kind of bomber, missile, or submarine. Because of the lead time required for the realization of such projects, the decision made today inevitably determines or circumscribes policy at a later date, thus pre-judging situations that have not been foreseen and limiting one's capa-bilities for contingencies that have not yet arisen.

Concurrent with this inclination to rely on weapons ordered and manufactured according to notions of efficiency formed in drafting rooms, arms production tends to assume its own momentum and to create pressures and anxieties that statesmen find difficult to withstand. The general role that armament plays in the economy of a country—increasing industrial earnings and reducing unemployment—makes it almost im-possible to resist forces driving toward an arms race, and this tendency is encouraged by the apprehensions engendered by the nature of the response (or the imagined response) of potential antagonists to one's own efforts. As the competition to produce weapons becomes more frenetic, the restraints upon their use may loosen or dissolve. In 1914, it was the German High Command's fear that military superiority would shift de-finitively to the side of the Entente powers within the next three years that determined its decision to push for war, and in the final crisis the political leaders were overborne by technical arguments about the ad-vantages to be gained in mobilization time by immediate declaration of war—arguments in short, to use modern parlance, about the advantage of a first-strike strategy. The dangers of this process repeating itself are infinitely greater in the nuclear arms race, as is illustrated by the way in which the superpowers' competition to achieve what is called counter-force capability has led to a heightened preoccupation with timing and to advocacy of "preemptive strike" and "launch-under-attack" doctrines. Fred C. Iklé, former head of the United States Arms Control and Dis-armament Agency, has pointed out that such systems put "incredible responsibilities on some tech sergeant in the innards of the system. The more quick and automatic it is, the more you're turning over decisions—the most fateful decisions in the nation's history—to people far removed from the President and the Joint Chiefs."[4]

When strategy is freed from effective political control, it becomes mindless and heedless, and it is then that war assumes that absolute form

[4] Cited in Barnet, *Real Security*, 30.

that Clausewitz dreaded. There is a well-known story of a report reaching the German Imperial Headquarters at the height of the August crisis of 1914, indicating that the British would not enter the pending war provided that the Germans refrained from attacking France. The Emperor is said to have told Generaloberst Helmuth von Moltke, the chief of the general staff, that if this were true Germany should shift the focus of its offensive to the East. Moltke answered that this was impossible, because the army had only one war plan, which could not now be changed. "Your uncle would have given me a different answer," William II grumbled, but this peevish if reasonable retort did not stop the fateful westward movement of the German columns.[5] It is not difficult to think of a similar scenario in our times, with the computer taking the role of the intractable war plan. No one who has suffered the irritation of having his personal records hopelessly tangled by the erratic behavior of bank and corporation computer systems will deny the justice of a recent Marxist description of superpower reliance upon mechanized warning systems as "the lunatic error of making security dependent upon a machine rather than upon the analysis of the historical situation, which only people with historical understanding (and that means also with an understanding of the historical situation of the other side) are capable of."[6]

In this connection, it is worth remarking that contemporary nuclear strategy, in addition to being characterized by a hair-trigger methodology of implementation and a reliance upon mechanical techniques that greatly weakens political control, is guided by an intelligence system that can hardly be described as being adequate to the needs of uniquely dangerous times. In a recent study of intelligence assessment before the two world wars, Ernest R. May has written that, in judging the capabilities of other powers, the governments of our time may be worse off than those before the First World War. "They can count missiles, bombers, carriers, submarines, and armored divisions at least as precisely as governments before 1914 could count guns, horses, and dreadnoughts; but now, as then, no one can be confident what the totals signify." Moreover, since none of the new weapons has been tested in warfare between major powers, "intelligence analysts, staff officers, and decision-makers have to rely on imagination rather than experience to assess capabilities."[7]

[5] Gordon A. Craig, *The Politics of the Prussian Army, 1640-1945* (New York, 1964), 294.
[6] Christa Wolf, *Voraussetzungen einer Erzählung: Frankfurter Poetik-Vorlesungen* (Darmstadt, 1983), 87.
[7] Ernest R. May, "Capabilities and Proclivities," in *Knowing One's Enemies: Intelligence Assessment before the Two World Wars* (Princeton, 1984), 530. On the predetermined nature of current strategy and the problematical character of intelligence, see also Paul Bracken, *The Command and Control of Nuclear Forces* (New Haven, 1984).

With respect to the proclivities of other powers, they are probably as much in the dark as they were in the 1930s, a time not blessed by the gifts of accurate prediction. Governments have in recent years become more and more complex and consequently less foreseeable in their behavior. It is now sometimes difficult to discover in the foreign policy of the Great Powers the coherence and continuity that in earlier times were considered to be the prerequisites of a successful conduct of foreign affairs. In these circumstances, an objective assessment of the intentions of the other side is always difficult, and the danger always exists that arguments based on little more than ideological zeal will be given as much weight as those that are based strictly on available evidence but are, because of its contradictory nature, cautious and tentative. Thus, in the nuclear competition, war-winning strategies have been advanced on the basis of assessments of the proclivities of the potential antagonist that find no corroboration in its history, psychology, or recent behavior and that show a reckless optimism with respect to the relative capabilities of the two sides.

Having said all this, however, one must note that it is not inevitable that the tendencies we have discussed will continue to be as dominant as they now appear to be. If we live in a nuclear age, we do not yet live in any age of nuclear war. None of the interstate conflicts that have taken place since 1945 has seen the employment of nuclear weapons, and all have been waged, with varying degrees of efficiency, in accordance with strategical concepts inherited from the past. Moreover, modern technology, which created the bombs that were dropped on Hiroshima and Nagasaki and the more sophisticated ones that have in the years since 1945 aroused visions of a conflict between the superpowers that would end in mutual annihilation, is now, in its restless energy, creating new kinds of weapons that may in time make nuclear war obsolete and re-create the conditions in which the principles of classical strategy were formulated.

In his interesting study *Weapons and Hope*, Freeman Dyson has written of the vigorous and rapidly advancing area of military technology known as precision-guided missiles or PGM, non-nuclear in nature, small enough to be fired by individual soldiers or from armored cars or helicopters, and already tested with effect against Israeli armor in the 1973 war. Since that time, PGM technology has been pushed further, and Dyson writes:

> It seems likely that the rapid development of microcomputer and sensor technology will result in a growing proliferation of sophisticated non-nuclear weapons [that] will cause armies to take a step

867

back into an older, more professional style of warfare. The new weapons need elite, highly trained soldiers to use them effectively. They do not need the mass armies that provided the cannon fodder of the two world wars. The Falklands campaign of 1982 provides some additional evidence that the winds of change are blowing in this direction. The Argentine air force, a small elite force using precise weapons with daring and skill, did great damage to the invading forces, while the Argentine army, a mass army of conscripts, was crushingly defeated. It seems that modern technology is taking us back toward the eighteenth century, toward the era when small professional armies fought small professional wars.[8]

Such considerations are strengthened by growing doubts about the credibility of a NATO strategy that has been based upon the doctrine of first use of nuclear weapons in the event of an overwhelming conventional attack from the East. Of late there has been lively discussion of the possibility of strengthening conventional deterrence by adding to it a retaliatory capability that would not involve the use of nuclear weapons and thus would not risk escalation; and this has centered around the feasibility of countering a Soviet attack by means of a conventional offensive thrust against the Soviet flanks and deep into the heart of Eastern Europe.[9]

Advocates of this kind of strategy are not deterred by critics who point to NATO's inferiority to the Warsaw Pact in conventional strength. On the contrary, they argue that history is filled with examples of successful offensive action by forces that were faced by superior numbers: Grant's Vicksburg campaign, the German drive into France in 1940, the United States Third Army's end run in 1944, the United States offensive in Korea in 1951, and the Israeli Sinai campaign in 1967. In addition, they point out that a conventional offensive into Eastern Europe by NATO would threaten the Soviet Union where it is politically weak by providing opportunities to exploit the political unreliability of its East European allies, an argument strikingly similar to that in Moltke's war

[8] Freeman Dyson, *Weapons and Hope* (New York, 1984), 55. On PGM, see also Horst Afheldt, *Verteidigung und Frieden* (Munich, 1976).

[9] Criticisms of NATO strategy are to be found in Emil Spannocchi and Guy Brossolet, *Verteidigung ohne Schlacht* (Munich, 1976) and Carl Friedrich von Weizsäcker, *Wege in der Gefahr* (Munich, 1976). On alternatives, see, *inter alia*, General Bernard W. Rogers, "Greater Flexibility for NATO's Flexible Response," *Strategic Review* (Spring 1983), and "Prescription for a Difficult Decade: The Atlantic Alliance in the 80's," *Foreign Affairs* 60 (1981-82), 1145-56. It might also be noted that in the past frequently, almost regularly, new aggressive weapons would appear to be irresistible, but gradually, some time after their introduction, defensive counterweapons were invented and produced so that strategical considerations regained their traditional role.

plan of 1879, which called for an offensive in Russia's western provinces that would be combined with a systematic attempt to encourage insurrection among such subject peoples as the Poles.[10] It would, in addition, they believe, "confront the Soviets with just exactly the situation their doctrine and strategy attempt to avoid: one in which they do not have control of developments and in which they face a high probability of uncertainty and surprise."[11]

These examples are perhaps enough to show that the strategical experience of the past is by no means irrelevant to our current thinking about battlefield problems and that, if Dyson's predictions come true, it will become even more pertinent. Even in the present situation, knowledge of past mistakes should indicate the advisability of bringing military planning and armament under firmer political control and should make it evident that the entanglement of planning with economics and technology requires an overall organization in which the role of the military is subject to prudent limitation.

That, of course, is not the whole story. Strategy is not merely the art of preparing for the armed conflicts in which a nation may become involved and planning the use of its resources and the deployment of its forces in such a way as to bring a successful issue. It is also, in a broader sense, the modern equivalent of what was, in the seventeenth and eighteenth centuries, called *ragione di stato* or *raison d'état*. It is the rational determination of a nation's vital interests, the things that are essential to its security, its fundamental purposes in its relations with other nations, and its priorities with respect to goals. This broader form of strategy should animate and guide the narrower strategy of war planning and war fighting, and Clausewitz implied as much in the famous statement cited at the outset of these observations.

Historical examples of the effective formulation and execution of strategy in the broader sense are not hard to find. One thinks of the series of methodical analyses of national interest made at the beginning of our nation's history in such works as *The Federalist* and George Washington's *Farewell Address*. The salient characteristic of these is their economical and objective presentation of the basic premises of national existence in a dangerously competitive world, as in John Jay's *Federalist No. 3* with its almost matter-of-fact statement of first principles: "Among the many objects to which a wise and free people find it necessary to direct their attention, that of providing for their safety seems to be the first. . . . But

[10] Graf Moltke, *Die deutschen Aufmarschpläne 1871-1890*, ed. Ferdinand von Schmerzfeld (*Forschungen und Darstellungen aus dem Reichsarchiv*, Heft 7) (Berlin, 1929), 80.
[11] Samuel P. Huntington, "Conventional Deterrence and Conventional Retaliation in Europe," *International Security* (Winter 1983-84), 43.

the safety of the people of America against dangers from foreign force depends not only upon their forbearing to give just causes of war to other nations, but also on their placing and continuing themselves in such a situation as not to invite hostility and insult."[12]

The political testaments of the Founding Fathers—for that is what these state papers amounted to—formulated the guiding principles of the Republic's policy in its first years, declaring that its vital interests were its political freedom and its economic strength and arguing that the prerequisites of security were domestic union (that is, freedom from internecine brawls and divisions), an appropriate military establishment (meaning one that, under the guise of protecting the nation, would threaten neither its republican form of government nor its economic health), and a wise foreign policy, which, for extraordinary emergencies, would rely upon temporary alliances with foreign powers. This was the theoretical underpinning of the military strategy that carried the fledgling American nation through the storms of the Napoleonic Wars, not, to be sure, without mishap, but in the end without significant hurt to American security and sovereignty.[13]

A second example of strategy in the broader sense, and this time one that was aggressive in nature, was that followed by the Kingdom of Prussia in the years from 1862 to 1866, which had its basic formulation in a series of incisive dispatches written by Otto von Bismarck when he was ambassador to the Frankfurt Diet in the 1850s. These delineated Prussian interests and opportunities in the context of the confusion and ineffectiveness of the international system after the Crimean War, analyzed the capabilities of its chief rival Austria, and advocated a course of policy that found its implementation, after Bismarck had assumed direction of Prussian affairs, in the policy that led to Königgrätz and hegemony over northern Germany—all in all, a strategy that has been regarded as a classic illustration of the effective coordination of force and statecraft for the attainment of political aims.[14]

Finally, a more recent example of a systematic and carefully coordinated national strategy can be found in the way in which the Truman administration responded to the challenge of the years 1947-1950 by a shrewd determination of the nature of American interests in the postwar world, by the effective mobilization of public support for its European

[12] *The Federalist*, ed. Edward Mead Earle (New York, 1937), 13, 18.
[13] Felix Gilbert, *To the Farewell Address: Ideas of Early American Foreign Policy* (Princeton, 1961), chs. 4, 5.
[14] Lothar Gall, *Bismarck, der weisse Revolutionär* (Frankfurt a.M., 1980), 127-173; Otto Pflanze, *Bismarck and the Development of Germany: The Period of Unification, 1815-1871* (Princeton, 1963), 87ff; Craig, *Politics of the Prussian Army*, ch. 5.

commitments and the skillful use of economic resources to gain its objectives, and, finally, when hostilities broke out in Korea, by the imposition upon its military operations there of limitations determined by political considerations—all in all, an exercise in strategy that would almost certainly have won Clausewitz's approbation.

Common to these strategies was their complete rationality in formulation and, in their implementation, a realistic appraisal of the international context in which they were to be pursued, an accurate view of the capabilities and proclivities of potential opponents, an underlying assumption that the accumulation and employment of military force must be justified by demonstrable political advantage and must not impose too heavy a burden upon national resources, and a determination that the use of force should end with the attainment of the political objective.

How relevant are such historical examples to our present situation? At the very least, they provide those who are charged with decisions affecting national security with cases for study and reflection and models against which to measure present practice. At a time when the ongoing arms race threatens to create its own pattern of compulsions, to engross both congressional and public attention, and, by doing so, to make logical and systematic thought about the realities and the requirements of our situation all but impossible,[15] it is surely worthwhile to be reminded, for example, that the key to the successes won by Germany's most distinguished political strategist was his refusal to submit to the pressures created by the rush of events and his unremitting search for those elements in the *rebus sic stantibus* that were compatible with the interests of his country.

The introduction to this volume referred to the stubborn refusal of the past to yield direct lessons to the present. History can never tell us how to act, but is prolific in case studies from which we can draw ideas and cautionary prescriptions. The cases that we have cited are both models and admonitions. They remind us that, regardless of temporal context, effective strategy is always a calculated employment of force and statecraft for a political end. Indeed, the history of war and diplomacy, which makes up such a large part of history in general, is little more than the record of the readiness or refusal of nations to base their policies upon that truth.

[15] See George F. Kennan, "A Plea for Diplomacy," speech, November 1983, reprinted in part in *Harper's*, April 1984, p. 20.

Contributors

MARTIN ALEXANDER, Lecturer in Modern British and European History at Southampton University, wrote his dissertation on "Maurice Gamelin and the Defence of France."

BRIAN BOND is Reader in War Studies, King's College, University of London. He has written extensively on the history of war. Among his books are *France and Belgium, 1939-1940; Liddell Hart: A Study of His Military Thought; British Military Policy between the Two World Wars*; and *War and Society in Europe, 1870-1970*.

MICHAEL CARVER, Field Marshal, British Army, is the author of many works on the history of war and defense policy, among them *War since 1945, The Apostles of Mobility, A Policy for Peace*, and *The Seven Ages of the British Army*.

THOMAS W. COLLIER is a former U.S. Army officer who served in the Vietnam War during 1962-1967. He has taught military history at West Point, and currently is completing graduate study in history at the University of Michigan.

GORDON A. CRAIG is J. E. Wallace Sterling Professor of Humanities Emeritus at Stanford University. Among his books are *The Politics of the Prussian Army, 1640-1945; The Battle of Königgrätz; Germany, 1866-1945*; and *The Germans*. With Alexander L. George he wrote *Force and Statecraft*, and with Felix Gilbert he edited *The Diplomats, 1919-1939*.

PHILIP A. CROWL is Ernest J. King Professor of Maritime History Emeritus at the Naval War College. Among his books are *Maryland During and After the Revolution* and *Campaign in the Marianas*. With Jeter A. Isely he wrote *The U.S. Marines and Amphibious War*, and with E. G. Love he wrote *Seizure of the Gilberts and Marshalls*.

EDWARD MEAD EARLE, the editor of the original *Makers of Modern Strategy*, was Professor at the Institute for Advanced Study in Princeton. Among his other works are *Against This Torrent* and *Modern France*.

LAWRENCE FREEDMAN is Professor of War Studies, King's College, London. He is the author of *US Intelligence and the Soviet Strategic Threat, Britain and Nuclear Weapons*, and *The Evolution of Nuclear Strategy*, and the editor of *The Troubled Alliance*.

MICHAEL GEYER is Associate Professor of History at the University of Chicago. He is the author of a monograph on the Reichswehr, *Aufrüstung oder Sicherheit*, and of *Deutsche Rüstungspolitik, 1860-1980*.

873

FELIX GILBERT is Professor Emeritus in the School of Historical Studies, Institute for Advanced Study, Princeton. Among his books on European and world history are *Hitler Directs His War; To the Farewell Address; Machiavelli and Guicciardini; The Pope, His Banker and Venice*; and a collection of essays, *History: Choice and Commitment*. With Gordon A. Craig he edited *The Diplomats, 1919-1939.*

HENRY GUERLAC was Professor of the History of Science, Cornell University. He wrote *Lavoisier, The Crucial Year; Lavoisier, Chemist and Revolutionary; Newton on the Continent*; and *Essays and Papers in the History of Modern Science.*

MARK VON HAGEN is Assistant Professor of History at Columbia University. He wrote his dissertation on "School of the Revolution: Bolsheviks and Peasants in the Red Army, 1918-1928."

HAJO HOLBORN was Sterling Professor of History at Yale University. Among his works are *A History of Modern Germany* in three volumes, *American Military Government, The Political Collapse of Europe*, and a collection of essays, *Germany and Europe.*

MICHAEL HOWARD is Regius Professor of Modern History at the University of Oxford. Among his many books on the history and theory of war are Volume IV of the Grand Strategy series of the United Kingdom official history of the Second World War, *The Franco-Prussian War, War and the Liberal Conscience*, and two collections of essays, *Studies in War and Peace* and *The Causes of War*. With Peter Paret he translated and edited Clausewitz's *On War.*

D. CLAYTON JAMES, Distinguished Professor of History, Mississippi State University, is the author of *The Years of MacArthur* in three volumes. He also edited *South to Bataan, North to Mukden: The Prison Diary of Brigadier General W. E. Brougher.*

DAVID MACISAAC, Lieutenant Colonel, USAF, Ret., was Senior Research Fellow at the Center for Aerospace Doctrine, Research, and Education, Air University, when he wrote the essay on air power for this volume. He is the author of *Strategic Bombing in World War II.*

MAURICE MATLOFF, formerly Chief Historian, Center of Military History, Department of the Army, is the author of *Strategic Planning for Coalition Warfare, 1943-1944* in the official history of the United States Army in World War II, and coauthor of the preceding volume in the series, *Strategic Planning for Coalition Warfare, 1941-1942*. He has also edited *American Military History.*

SIGMUND NEUMANN was Professor of Government at Wesleyan University. He wrote *Permanent Revolution* and *Germany: Promise and Perils.*

R. R. PALMER is Professor of History Emeritus, Yale University. Among his many books are *Catholics and Unbelievers in Eighteenth Century France, Twelve Who Ruled*, and *The Age of the Democratic Revolution.*

874

PETER PARET is Andrew W. Mellon Professor in the Humanities, Institute for Advanced Study, Princeton. With John Shy he wrote *Guerrillas in the 1960s*. Among his other books are *French Revolutionary Warfare from Indochina to Algeria, Yorck and the Era of Prussian Reform*, and *Clausewitz and the State*. With Michael Howard he translated and edited Clausewitz's *On War*.

WALTER PINTNER, Professor of History, Cornell University, is the author of *Russian Economic Policy under Nicholas I*. With Don Karl Rowney he has edited *Russian Officialdom*.

DOUGLAS PORCH is Mark W. Clark Professor of History at the Citadel. Among his works on French military history are *Army and Revolution: France 1815-1848, The March to the Marne*, and *The Conquest of Morocco*.

CONDOLEEZZA RICE is Assistant Professor of Political Science, Stanford University. She is the author of *The Soviet Union and the Czechoslovak Army*.

GUNTHER E. ROTHENBERG is Professor of History at Purdue University. Among his many works on the history of war are two monographs on the Austrian military border in Croatia, as well as *The Army of Francis Joseph* and *The Anatomy of the Israeli Army*.

JOHN SHY is Professor of History at the University of Michigan. He wrote *Guerrillas in the 1960s* with Peter Paret and is also the author of *Toward Lexington* and of a collection of essays, *A People Numerous and Armed*.

RUSSELL F. WEIGLEY is Professor of History at Temple University. Among his numerous works on American military history are *Towards an American Army; A History of the United States Army, The Partisan War, The American Way of War*, and *Eisenhower's Lieutenants*.

Bibliographical Notes

INTRODUCTION

The vast literature on war does not contain a comprehensive analytical history of strategic thought. Probably the best general account of the development of strategy in Europe from antiquity to the age of Napoleon and Clausewitz can be found in the first four volumes of Hans Delbrück's *Geschichte der Kriegskunst im Rahmen der politischen Geschichte*, reprinted with an important introduction by Otto Haintz (Berlin, 1962). Delbrück integrates his analysis of strategy with much else: the history of battles, campaigns, and social, technological, and political change. An English translation in progress by Walter J. Renfroe, Jr., *History of the Art of War within the Framework of Political History* (Westport, Conn., 1975-) is adequate but unscholarly; no attempt has been made to update the bibliographies or to discuss Delbrück's interpretations in light of research since the work's original appearance between 1900 and 1920.

Accounts of the history of strategy of a particular society such as Eugène Carrias, *La pensée militaire allemande* (Paris, 1948), and the same author's *La pensée militaire française* (Paris, 1960), tend to be introductory surveys. More sophisticated analyses of the strategic thought of an individual or a generation may be found in the monographic literature, in biographies, or in studies of particular wars or campaigns, some of which are listed in the footnotes and bibliographical notes of this volume.

The original *Makers of Modern Strategy* (Princeton, 1943) brought together essays on a number of important theorists, which are still worth reading. Werner Hahlweg edited a similar work in German, *Klassiker der Kriegskunst* (Darmstadt, 1960), which includes brief excerpts from the writings of the men discussed. Valuable comments on the development of strategy in the Western world may be found in two recent, general accounts: Michael Howard's excellent *War in European History* (Oxford and New York, 1976) and Hew Strachan's equally fine *European Armies and the Conduct of War* (London and Boston, 1983), which covers less ground than Howard does—beginning with the eighteenth century rather than with the Middle Ages—but goes into greater detail.

Containing little on strategy as such, but of fundamental importance to the historical study of military institutions and of war, is Otto Hintze's essay "Staatsverfassung und Heeresverfassung," written in 1906, which is included in the English edition of Hintze's selected papers, *The Historical Essays of Otto Hintze*, ed.

The BIBLIOGRAPHICAL NOTES have been prepared by the authors of the essays unless otherwise indicated.

Felix Gilbert (New York, 1975). On the place of the history of war in historical studies today, see Peter Paret, "The History of War," *Daedalus* 100 (Spring 1971), and Walter Emil Kaegi, Jr., "The Crisis in Military Historiography," *Armed Forces and Society* 7, no. 2 (Winter 1981), which also offers stimulating observations on the relationship between the historical study of strategic thought, the history of ideas, and the development of current strategic thinking.

1. MACHIAVELLI: THE RENAISSANCE OF THE ART OF WAR

The critical edition of Machiavelli's works in the Biblioteca di Classici Italiani of the publishing house Feltrinelli, edited by Sergio Bertelli and Francesco Gaeta in eight volumes (Milan, 1960-64), contains valuable introductions explaining the origin of individual works and the scholarly discussion they aroused. Convenient to use also is the large (1,282 pages) one-volume edition edited by Mario Martelli for the Sansoni publishing house (Florence, 1971). The relevant material regarding Machiavelli's activities in the Florentine Chancellery is published and analyzed in Jean-Jacques Marchand, *Niccolò Machiavelli; I primi scritti politici (1499-1512)* (Padua, 1975).

Machiavelli's *Chief Works* have been translated in three volumes by Allan Gilbert (Durham, 1965). Machiavelli's *Art of War* was translated into English in the eighteenth century and a version of this translation, slightly modified and modernized by Neal Wood, has been published by Bobbs Merrill in its Library of Liberal Arts (Indianapolis, 1965); Wood's long introduction to this volume gives an excellent analysis of the importance and the influence of this work. The intellectual origins of Machiavelli's ideas on military affairs and war have been studied in Charles Calvert Bayley, *War and Society in Renaissance Florence: The De Militia of Leonardo Bruni* (Toronto, 1961).

The bibliographical essay in the 1984 paperback edition of my *Machiavelli and Guicciardini* (New York: W. W. Norton & Co.) can serve as an introduction to recent Machiavelli scholarship.

The role of war and military affairs in the European policy of this period is outlined in J. R. Hale, *War and Society in Renaissance Europe 1450-1620*, Fontana History of European War and Society (London, 1985), and details about the military events of Machiavelli's time in Italy can be found in Piero Pieri, *Il Rinascimento e la crisi militare italiana* (Torino, 1952). The early stages of the development and the influence of gunpowder are outlined in Fernand Braudel, *Capitalism and Material Life 1400-1800*, trans. M. Kochan (London, 1973), pp. 285-95, and M. E. Mallett and J. R. Hale, *The Military Organization of a Renaissance State: Venice circa 1400-1617* (Cambridge, 1984), although concerned with Venice and not with Florence, throws light on the military practice of the time: the procedures involved in hiring a condottiere and mercenaries, the impact of military expenses on the city finances, and the relation between military commanders and the governments.

878

2. Maurice of Nassau, Gustavus Adolphus, Raimondo Montecuccoli, and the "Military Revolution" of the Seventeenth Century

Beginning with the Revolt of the Netherlands, continuing through the Thirty Years' War, and ending with the Dutch War of Louis XIV, the "military revolution" analyzed in this essay spans over one century. At the same time, Europeans continued to wage war against the Turks, fought in numerous conflicts against each other, and everywhere began to lay the foundations for standing armies. An enormous primary and secondary literature exists on these developments. But when we turn to the three exponents of military revolution discussed in this essay, Maurice, Gustavus, and Montecuccoli, we find that the literature is abundant only in Dutch, Spanish, Swedish, German, French, and Italian.

For a general background on this period, turn to Oliver L. Spaulding, Hoffman Nickerson, and John W. Wright, *Warfare: A Study of Military Methods from the Earliest Times* (Washington, D.C., 1937), which, despite its title, concentrates heavily on the early modern period and contains a useful bibliography. Also still valuable are the relevant volumes of Hans Delbrück, *Geschichte der Kriegskunst im Rahmen der politischen Geschichte*, 4 vols., new ed. (Berlin, 1962-64). An English translation is now in progress by Walter J. Renfroe, Jr., *History of the Art of War within the Framework of Political History* (Westport, Conn., 1975-). Useful, if tendentious, is Eugen von Frauenholz, *Entwicklungsgeschichte des deutschen Heerwesens*, 5 vols. (Munich, 1935-41). Georges Livet, *Guerre et paix de Machiavel à Hobbes* (Paris, 1972) addresses the philosophical background. There is interesting material in the chapters by Piero Pieri, Jan W. Wijn, and Werner Gembruch in *Klassiker der Kriegskunst*, ed. Werner Hahlweg (Darmstadt, 1960) and in the interpretive essay by Victor G. Kiernan, "Foreign Mercenaries and Absolute Monarchy," in *Crisis in Europe 1560-1660*, ed. Trevor H. Aston (London and New York, 1965).

Nothing covering the long and tortuous course of the campaigns in the Low Countries is available in English. An overview is provided by I. L. Uiterschout, *Geknopt overzicht van de belangrijkste gebeurtenissen uit de nederlandsche krijgsgeschiedenis van 1568 tot heden* (The Hague, 1937), supplementing the work of F. J. G. ten Raa and François de Bas in *Het Staatsche Leger 1568-1795* (Breda, 1913). For the early campaigns of Maurice, the standard account remains T. Fruin, *Tien jaren uit den 80 jarigen oorlog 1588-1598* (Leiden, 1857). A detailed source on the Orangist reforms is the diary of a high civil servant, *Journaal van Anthonis Duyck, advokaat-fiskaal van den Raad van Staate*, ed. Lodewijk Mulder, 3 vols. (The Hague, 1862-86). No full-scale military biography exists for Maurice, but his cousin William Louis is discussed in Lutzen H. Wagenaar, *Het leven van Willem Lodewijk* (Amsterdam, 1904), a somewhat too patriotic work. On the campaigns in Friesland see Gerrit Overdiep, *De Groningen schansenkrijg: De strategie van graaf Willem Lodewijk* (Groningen, 1970). For the political-administrative side there is P. F. M. Fontaine, *De Raad van Staat: Zijn taak, organisatie en werkzaamheden in de jaren 1588-1590* (Groningen, 1970). An excellent discussion of the tactical reforms and shoulder arms is contained in the introduction by J. B. Kist to the facsimile edition of Jacob de Gheyn, *The exercise of armes for calivers, muskettes, and pikes after the Order of his Excellence Maurits Prince of Orange, Counte of Nassau* (The Hague, 1607; repr. New York, 1971). In addition, there are two important biographies. The first is Jan den Tex, *Oldenbarneveldt*, 5 vols. (Haarlem-Groningen, 1960-72), happily available in an abridged English edition (2 vols., Cambridge, 1973). The Spanish view and much more is discussed in Léon van der Essen, *Alexandre Farnèse, prince de Parme, gouverneur-général des Pays Bas, 1545-1592*, 5 vols. (Brussels, 1933-37). Finally, recent writings are covered in the paper by J. W. Smit, "The Present Position of Studies regarding the Revolt of the Netherlands," in *Britain and the Netherlands*, ed. John S. Bromley and Ernst H. Kossmann (London, 1960), 1:11-28.

Gustavus Adolphus has been well served by his English biographer, Michael Roberts, who also translated Nils Ahlund, *Gustav Adolf the Great* (Princeton, 1940) from the Swedish. The standard reference for the wars of Gustavus Adolphus is Generalstaben, *Sveriges Krig 1611-1632*, 5 vols. and 2 supp. vols. (Stockholm, 1936-38). A short treatment of the Swedish army is found in Claude Nordmann, "L'armée suédoise au XVIIᵉ siècle," *Revue du Nord* 54 (1972), 133-47. The king's major adversaries also have had good biographers. Tilly is discussed in Georg Gilardone, *Tilly, der Heilige im Harnisch* (Munich, 1932), a rather too favorable study, but based on the Bavarian archives. For Wallenstein the most recent biography is Hellmut Diwald, *Wallenstein* (Munich-Esslingen, 1969), and his operational skills are assessed in the essay by Hans Schmidt, "Wallenstein als Feldherr," *Mitteilungen des Oberösterreichischen Landesarchivs* 14 (1984), 241-60. Material on the fighting in Germany can be found in G. Benedecke, *Germany in the Thirty Years' War* (London, 1978). On the influence of Swedish fighting methods on the British army, see Charles H. Firth, *Cromwell's Army*, 3rd. ed. (London, 1921), which also contains useful information on the Swedish army. For the early development of the French army the most useful works remain Louis André, *Michel Le Tellier et l'organisation de l'armée monarchique* (Paris, 1906; repr. Geneva, 1980) and Léon Mention, *L'armée française de l'Ancien Régime* (Paris, 1900). Camille F. A. Rousset, *Histoire de Louvois et de son administration politique et militaire*, 4 vols. (Paris, 1862-64) also remains a valuable source.

On Montecuccoli, Cesare Campori, *Raimondo Montecuccoli, la sua famiglia e i suoi tempi* (Florence, 1876) is still the best biography. The work by Tommaso Sandonnini, *Il Generale Raimondo Montecuccoli e la sua famiglia*, 2 vols. (Modena, 1914) is marred by a chauvinistic Italian interpretation. For Montecuccoli's intellectual development, in addition to the studies cited to the notes, there is Piero Pieri, "La formazione dottrinale di Raimondo Montecuccoli," *Revue internationale d'histoire militaire*, no. 10 (1951), 92-115. His most famous battle is ably discussed in Kurt Peball, *Die Schlacht bei St. Gotthard-Mogersdorf 1664*, no. 1 of *Militärhistorische Schriftenreihe* (Vienna, 1964). A discussion of his logistic problems and strategic system is presented by Géza Perjés, "Army Provisioning, Logistics, and Strategy in the Second Half of the 17th Century," *Acta*

Historica Academiae Scientiarium Hungaricae 16 (1970), 1-51. The older study by Ernst Heischmann, *Die Anfänge des stehenden Heeres in Österrich* (Vienna, 1925), should be supplemented by the detailed data in Philipp Hoyos, "Die kaiserliche Armee 1648-1650," *Schriftenreihe des Heeresgeschichtlichen Museums (Militärwissenschaftliches Institut) in Wien* 7 (1976), 169-232. For the formation of frontier defenses against the Turks see Gunther E. Rothenberg, *The Austrian Military Border in Croatia, 1522-1747* (Urbana, 1960) and for the state of siege and defense technology consult Walter Hummelberger, "Bemerkungen zur Taktik und Bewaffnung der Verteidiger Wiens 1683," *Studia Austro-Polonica* 3 (1983), 81-110.

Mutual aid between the Hapsburg courts is discussed in Bogdan Chudoba, *Spain and the Empire* (Chicago, 1952). For the development of the German armies associated with the Hapsburgs see the first volume of Curt Jany, *Geschichte der königlich-preussischen Armee*, 4 vols. (Berlin, 1928-33) and F. A. Francke, *Geschichte der sächsischen Armee*, 3 vols. (Leipzig, 1885). An overview of the state of the armies and the art of war at the close of the military revolution is provided by David G. Chandler, *The Art of Warfare in the Age of Marlborough* (London, 1976).

3. VAUBAN: THE IMPACT OF SCIENCE ON WAR*

A still indispensable older study of French military institutions in the seventeenth century is Louis André, *Michel Le Tellier et l'organisation de l'armée monarchique* (Paris, 1906; repr. Geneva, 1980). A companion volume by the same author is *Michel Le Tellier et Louvois* (Paris, 1942). André Corvisier's *Armies and Societies in Europe, 1494-1789* (Bloomington, 1979) is a useful introductory survey, better on France than on the rest of Europe. An interesting discussion of Vauban's efforts at reforming French military institutions is Werner Gembruch, "Zur Kritik an der Heeresreform und Wehrpolitik von Le Tellier und Louvois in der Spätzeit der Herrschaft Ludwig XIV," *Militärgeschichtliche Mitteilungen* 12 (1972). See also Gembruch's earlier writings on Vauban: "Vauban, zu seinem 325. Geburtstag am 15 Mai 1958," *Wehrwissenschaftliche Rundschau* 8, no. 5 (1958); "Gedanken Vaubans über den Seekrieg," *Marine Rundschau* 56, no. 2 (1959); "Vauban," in *Klassiker der Kriegskunst*, ed. Werner Hahlweg (Darmstadt, 1960); and "Zwei Denkschriften Vaubans zur Kolonialpolitik und Aussenpolitik Frankreichs aus den Jahren 1699 und 1700," *Historische Zeitschrift* 195, no. 2 (1962).

Christopher Duffy has written two good surveys of the history of fortification: *Fire and Stone: The Science of Fortress Warfare, 1660-1860* (Newton Abbot, 1975), and *Siege Warfare: The Fortress in the Early Modern World, 1494-1660* (London, 1979), which provide the historical context of Vauban's work. Perhaps best known of Vauban's writings is his *Traité de l'attaque et de la défense des places* (The Hague, 1737), which has been reprinted several times. Vauban's *Mémoire pour servir d'instruction dans la conduite des sièges et dans*

* Prepared by Donald Abenheim.

la défense des places (Leiden, 1740), has been translated and edited by George Rothrock with an excellent introduction and a useful annotated bibliography: Sébastien Le Prestre de Vauban, *A Manual on Siegecraft and Fortification* (Ann Arbor, 1968). Also important are Vauban's memoirs—the so-called *Oisivetés*—the first four volumes of which were published by Antoine Augoyat, and, brought out by the same editor, his *Abrégé des services du maréchal de Vauban, fait par lui en 1703* (Paris, 1839).

Like his fortifications, Vauban's writings were varied and numerous, their subjects ranging from military architecture to systems of taxation to the most efficient way of raising pigs. Few of his nonmilitary works have been translated into English. Perhaps his politically most controversial work was his *Projet d'une dixme royale* (n.p., n.d.). One of many reprints is *Projet d'une dixme royale, suivi de deux écrits financiers par Vauban,* ed. E. Coornaert (Paris, 1933). An interesting account of the circumstances in which Vauban wrote his treatise on taxation, and of the political effects of its publication, is contained in a two-part article by F. J. Hebbert and George Rothrock, "Marshal Vauban, Writer and Critic," *History Today* 24, nos. 3, 4 (1974).

A very good if in many respects outdated biography of Vauban is Albert de Rochas d'Aiglun, *Vauban, sa famille et ses écrits, ses oisivetés, et sa correspondance,* 2 vols. (Paris, 1910), which incorporates extracts from Vauban's memoirs and his frequently quoted correspondence with Louvois. Also useful is the published dissertation by Pierre Elizier Lazard, *Vauban* (Paris, 1934). Reginald Blomfield, an architect, drew heavily on Lazard's work for his *Sébastien Le Prestre de Vauban, 1633-1707* (London, 1938), which concentrates on Vauban's fortifications and engineering projects. Since the Second World War several biographies for the general reader have appeared: George Toudoze, *Monsieur de Vauban* (Paris, 1954); Alfred Rebelliau, *Vauban* (Paris, 1962); Michel Parent and Jacques Verroust, *Vauban* (Paris, 1971); and Michel Parent, *Vauban, un encyclopédiste avant la lettre* (Paris, 1982). Among recent studies in English, see the article by Hebbert and Rothrock mentioned above and Henry Guerlac's important, brief article, "Sébastien Le Prestre de Vauban," in the *Dictionary of Scientific Biography* (New York, 1976), with a useful, wide-ranging bibliography.

Finally, two monographs on special aspects of Vauban's life are Jacques Guttin, *Vauban et le corps des ingénieurs militaires* (Paris, 1957); and Walter Bräuer, *Frankreichs Wirtschaftliche und Soziale Lage um 1700* (Marburg, 1968), which contains an extensive bibliography of Vauban's writings and works on him, with an emphasis on economic issues.

4. FREDERICK THE GREAT, GUIBERT, BÜLOW: FROM DYNASTIC TO NATIONAL WAR*

Far too much has been written on eighteenth-century strategy without an understanding of its basic components—manpower policies, army organization, methods of supply, and tactical doctrine. Among works on these subjects that

* Prepared by Peter Paret.

are especially enlightening because they draw extensively on contemporary sources, are, for France: Louis Bacquet, *L'infanterie au XVIIIᵉ siècle: L'orga- nisation* (Paris, 1907), Jean Colin, *L'infanterie au XVIIIᵉ siècle: La tactique* (Paris, 1907), Edouard Desbrière, *La cavalerie de 1740 à 1789* (Paris, 1906), Edouard Desbrière and Maurice Sautai, *La cavalerie pendant la Révolution*, 2 vols. (Paris, 1907-1908), and Ernest Picard and Louis Jouan, *L'artillerie française au XVIIIᵉ siècle* (Paris, 1906); for Germany and Austria: Eugen von Frauenholz, *Das Heer- wesen in der Zeit des Absolutismus*, vol. 4 of his *Entwicklungsgeschichte des deutschen Heerwesens* (Munich, 1940), and Rainer Wohlfeil, *Vom Stehenden Heer des Absolutismus zur Allgemeinen Wehrpflicht* (Frankfurt a.M., 1964) and Jürgen Zimmermann, *Militärverwaltung und Heeresaufbringung in Österreich bis 1806* (Frankfurt a.M., 1965), which are volumes 2 and 3 of *Handbuch zur deutschen Militärgeschichte*, both with good annotated bibliographies. The most extensive analysis of the contemporary literature is still contained in the second and third volumes of Max Jähns, *Geschichte der Kriegswissenschaften vor- nehmlich in Deutschland*, 3 vols. (Munich and Leipzig, 1889-91), the last volume of which includes good discussions of Frederick, Guibert, and Bülow. A brilliant reconstruction of an eighteenth-century campaign, derived from profound knowl- edge of the realities of war at the time, is Piers Mackesy, *The Coward of Minden* (London, 1978).

Most of Frederick the Great's official and unofficial military writings are printed in volumes 28-30 of *Oeuvres de Frédéric le Grand*, ed. Johann Dietrich Erdmann Preuss, 30 vols. (Berlin, 1846-56), and in *Die Werke Friedrichs des Grossen*, ed. Gustav Berthold Volz, 10 vols. (Berlin, 1912-14). The texts in these editions are not always accurate, and better versions of some of the pieces have been published separately, e.g., *Die Instruktion Friedrichs des Grossen für seine Generale von 1747*, ed. Richard Fester (Berlin, 1936). Jay Luvaas has edited a selection of Frederick's writings in English, *Frederick the Great on the Art of War* (New York, 1966).

The basic history of Frederick's campaigns is *Die Kriege Friedrichs des Grossen*, published by the historical section of the Great General Staff, 24 vols. (Berlin, 1890-1913). This detailed work with excellent maps is supplemented by many studies on special subjects by the historical section, e.g., *Die taktische Schulung der Preussischen Armee*, nos. 28-30 of *Kriegsgeschichtliche Einzel- schriften* (Berlin, 1900). The earlier literature on the debate of Frederician strategy that was initiated by Hans Delbrück is analyzed in Otto Hintze's article "Del- brück, Clausewitz und die Strategie Friedrichs des Grossen," *Forschungen zur Brandenburgisch-Preussischen Geschichte* 33 (1920). Notable among more re- cent studies are Eberhard Kessel's articles, for instance, "Friedrich der Grosse im Wandel der Kriegsgeschichtlichen Überlieferung," *Wissen und Wehr* 17 (1936). Concise analyses of Frederician strategy and tactics are contained in Peter Paret, *Yorck and the Era of Prussian Reform* (Princeton, 1966), and Gerhard Ritter, *Frederick the Great*, rev. ed., ed. and trans. Peter Paret (Berkeley and Los Angeles, 1974). A good overview for the general reader is Christopher Duffy, *The Army of Frederick the Great* (New York, 1974). The most recent biography of Frederick, Theodor Schieder, *Friedrich der Grosse* (Berlin, 1983) has nothing new to say about Frederick as strategist and commander.

Guibert's military writings were collected by his widow in *Oeuvres militaires du comte de Guibert*, 5 vols. (Paris, 1803). Two modern editions are: a selection, edited by General Ménard, Jacques-Antoine-Hippolyte, comte de Guibert, *Ecrits militaires* (Paris, 1977), and the more substantial *Oeuvres militaires*, ed. Jean-Paul Charnay and Martine Burgos (Paris, 1977). Lucien Poirier's brief monograph *Guibert (1743-1790)* (Paris, 1977) is interesting and thought-provoking, but a thorough analysis of the development of Guibert's thought in the context of the late Enlightenment and the military issues of the last years of the French monarchy remains to be written.

None of Bülow's sixteen books has yet been reissued in a modern edition, and scholars are dependent on the originals, which are reasonably accessible in major research libraries in Europe and the United States. A valuable selection, *Militärische und vermischte Schriften von Heinrich Dietrich von Bülow* (Leipzig, 1853) was edited by Eduard Bülow and Wilhelm Rüstow, with interesting biographical and analytic introductions. Reinhold Höhn discusses Bülow extensively in his *Revolution—Heer—Kriegsbild* (Darmstadt, 1944). The much-abbreviated revised edition that appeared under the title *Scharnhorsts Vermächtnis* (Frankfurt a.M., 1952 and 1972) contains little on Bülow. Both works suffer from Höhn's primitive and unreliable methodology. Some aspects of Bülow's thought are discussed in Peter Paret, *Clausewitz and the State* (New York and London, 1976; repr. Princeton, 1985), and in the same author's "Revolutions in Warfare: An Earlier Generation of Interpreters," *National Security and International Stability*, ed. Bernard Brodie, Michael Intriligator, and Roman Kolkowicz (Cambridge, Mass., 1983), and "Napoleon as Enemy," in *Proceedings of the Thirteenth Consortium on Revolutionary Europe*, ed. Clarence B. Davis (Athens, Ga., 1985), but there is great need for further research. Bülow, like Guibert, still awaits his modern interpreter.

5. NAPOLEON AND THE REVOLUTION IN WAR

The basic source for Napoleon's ideas on war and for his practice of warfare is the edition of his letters, orders, and other writings, *Correspondance de Napoléon Ier*, 32 vols. (Paris, 1857-70). Since its appearance, the work has been supplemented by numerous publications of additional letters and documents, and of corrections of errors and falsifications in the original edition. A second body of sources, almost immeasurable in extent, is formed by the correspondence, diaries, and memoirs of Napoleon's generals and soldiers, as well as of his opponents. A good example is the edition by the historical section of the French general staff of Davout's official papers in the War of 1806, *Opérations du 3e corps, 1806-1807: Rapport du Maréchal Davout* (Paris, 1896).

Unfortunately few Napoleonic campaigns have been the subject of detailed and comprehensive documentary accounts based on the holdings of the French archives. An exception is the carefully prepared work by E. Buat, *1809: De*

Ratisbonne à Znaim, 2 vols. (Paris, 1909). The major project by G. Fabry, *Campagne de Russie (1812)*, 5 vols. (Paris, 1900-1903), supplemented by the same editor's two-volume *Campagne de 1812* (Paris, 1912), remains incomplete. Particular operations and battles have, however, been comprehensively documented and analyzed; see, for instance, the archival studies by P. J. Foucart, *Bautzen* (Paris, 1897) and Capitaine Alombert, *Combat de Dürrenstein* (Paris, 1897). A series of excellent maps, illustrating Napoleon's campaigns from 1796 to 1815, forms the core of Vincent J. Esposito and John Robert Elting, *A Military History and Atlas of the Napoleonic Wars* (New York, 1964), which also contains a useful if idiosyncratic annotated bibliography. Less comprehensive but worth consulting is the similar work by J.-C. Quennevat, *Atlas de la grande armée* (Paris and Brussels, 1966).

For a general account of Napoleon's campaigns it is still useful to consult Jomini, in particular his *Histoire critique et militaire des guerres de la révolution*, 15 vols. (Paris 1820-24), and his *Vie politique et militaire de Napoléon*, 4 vols. (Paris, 1827), a translation of which by Henry W. Halleck, *Life of Napoleon*, appeared in London in 1864 and has been reprinted several times. Clausewitz did not write a similarly comprehensive work; but his studies of the campaigns of 1796, 1799, 1812, 1813, 1814, and 1815 in volumes 4 to 8 of his *Hinterlassene Werke*, 10 vols. (Berlin, 1832-37) cover much of the period and contain some of his most important historical analyses. *On War* is, of course, full of references to Napoleon and Napoleonic war.

The modern interpretation of Napoleon as strategist and commander was largely shaped by officers belonging to, or associated with, the *section historique* of the French general staff. Here we need to note only the numerous works of Hubert Camon, among them *La guerre napoléonienne*, 3 vols. (Paris, 1903-1910), reprinted in a seventh enlarged edition in 1925; *La fortification dans la guerre napoléonienne* (Paris, 1914); *Le système de guerre de Napoléon* (Paris, 1923); and *Génie et métier chez Napoléon* (Paris, 1930). Equally convinced that Napoleon was the great teacher of modern war was General Henri Bonnal, whose many writings—among them *De Rosbach à Ulm* (Paris, 1903) and *La manoeuvre de Landshut* (Paris, 1905)—began as texts for the Ecole Superieure de Guerre. Much better in their specificity and historical sensitivity are the books of another officer, the future general Jean Colin. His studies of war during the French Revolution, his more general work *The Transformations of War* (London, 1912), and especially his *L'éducation militaire de Napoléon* (Paris, 1900) set a standard of excellence that later authors have only rarely approached.

The most original analysis of Napoleonic strategy by a scholar who is not French remains that of Hans Delbrück in the fourth volume of his *Geschichte der Kriegskunst*, new ed. (Berlin, 1962). The interpretations by Hugo von Freytag-Loringhoven, Count Yorck von Wartenburg, and others that Delbrück rejected are today only of antiquarian interest. On the other hand, the analyses of French methods in the German general staff histories of the War of 1806 and of the Wars of Liberation retain much of their value—especially in the areas of command structure, supply, operations, and tactics.

The standard general account in English is David G. Chandler, *The Campaigns of Napoleon* (New York, 1966), which the author characterizes as merely a " 'curtain raiser' to the more detailed and authoritative military studies now available." A knowledgeable introductory survey is Gunther E. Rothenberg, *The Art of Warfare in the Age of Napoleon* (London, 1978). Far less satisfactory is the comprehensive but unanalytic work by Henri Lachouque, *Napoléon: Vingt ans de campagnes* (Paris, 1964). Lachouque's nearly two dozen books on Napoleonic war are characteristic of much of the vast modern literature in the field. They offer a colorful, enthusiastic treatment of personalities and events, without ever raising let alone answering the many hard questions that remain to be asked. Finally, the best modern analysis of Napoleon's generalship seems to me to be James Marshall-Cornwall, *Napoleon as Military Commander* (London, 1967).

6. JOMINI

Jomini's most important works are *Traité des grandes opérations militaires*, 2d ed., 4 vols. (Paris, 1811), and *Précis de l'art de la guerre*, 2 vols. (Paris, 1838). The first edition of the *Traité*, parts I and II, was published as *Traité de grande tactique* (Paris, 1805), and Part V in 1806 under the same title; the remaining two parts, III and IV, were published in 1807 and 1809 respectively. Both the *Traite* and *Précis* were republished and translated in various editions. The indispensable guide to the complexities of Jomini's bibliography is John I. Alger, *Antoine-Henri Jomini: A Bibliographical Survey* (West Point, N.Y., 1975). The most recent edition of the *Précis* in English is *Jomini and His Summary of the Art of War: A Condensed Version*, edited by J. D. Hittle (Harrisburg, Penn., 1947), and the definitive 1855 edition of the *Précis* has been republished in Osnabrück (1973), with an introduction in German by H. R. Kurz.

Other important works by Jomini include *Histoire critique et militaire des guerres de la révolution*, 15 vols. (Paris, 1820-24), which had first begun to appear in 1811 as a continuation of the *Traité*; *Vie politique et militaire de Napoléon*, 4 vols. (Paris, 1827), originally published anonymously; *Précis politique et militaire de la campagne de 1815* (Paris, 1839), which Jomini claimed was the "lost" section on the Waterloo campaign of his life of Napoleon; and *Tableau analytique des principales combinaisons de la guerre* (Paris, 1830), which was his first book-length elaboration of the "principles of war." All of these works have later editions and have been translated into English and other languages.

The basic biography remains that of Ferdinand Lecomte, *Le général Jomini, sa vie et ses écrits* (Paris, 1860; 3d ed., Lausanne, 1888). Lecomte was a Swiss officer, a close friend and disciple of Jomini; his biography is a primary source of information. An important review of Lecomte's *Jomini* by Georges Gilbert appeared in *La nouvelle revue* (December 1, 1888), 674-85. C. A. Sainte-Beuve added to Jomini's fame without adding new information in *Le général Jomini* (Paris, 1869). Xavier de Courville, Jomini's great-grandson, drew on papers in his possession for *Jomini, ou le devin de Napoléon* (Paris, 1935), but adds disappointingly little to Lecomte. Two large excerpts from Jomini's unpublished memoirs are *Guerre d'Espagne* (Paris, 1892) and *Précis politiques et militaire des campagnes de 1812 à 1814* (Paris, 1886), both published by Lecomte after Jomini's death. The most accessible portion of Jomini's unpublished papers is in the British Library (Egerton Manuscripts 3166-3168, 3198, and 3217), part of a larger collection acquired in 1940 from Mme. Nathalie Onu; these deal only with his last years in Paris. Especially valuable, both for its subject and its brief account of other unpublished material, is Daniel Reichel, "La position du général Jomini en tant qu'expert militaire à la cour de Russie," *Actes du symposium 1982*, Service historique, Travaux d'histoire militaire et de polémologie, vol. 1 Service historique, (Lausanne, 1982), 51-75. On the anniversary of Jomini's death appeared a series of biographical essays, *Le général Antoine-Henri Jomini (1779-1869): Contributions à sa biographie*, Bibliothèque Historique Vaudoise, no. 41 (Lausanne, 1969), as well as the catalogue of an exhibit, *Général Antoine-Henri Jomini, 1779-1869* (Payerne, 1969), published by the Comité du Centenaire du Général Jomini. Both are valuable.

The essay on Jomini by Brinton, Craig, and Gilbert in the 1943 edition of *Makers of Modern Strategy* is the benchmark for all other work. Earlier appraisals of Jomini's theories include Edouard Guillon, *Nos écrivains militaires*, 2 vols. (Paris, 1898-99), and Rudolph von Caemmerer, *The Development of Strategical Science during the Nineteenth Century* (London, 1905). Michael Howard, "Jomini and the Classical Tradition," in *The Theory and Practice of War*, ed. Michael Howard (London and New York, 1965), 5-20, first explored the influence of Lloyd, and is a notably sympathetic account of Jomini. Bernard Brodie, among contemporary writers on strategy, dealt more harshly with Jomini and his influence, particularly in *Strategy in the Missile Age* (Princeton, 1959), 3-39. Other modern accounts include Gustav Däniker in *Klassiker der Kriegskunst*, ed. Werner Hahlweg (Darmstadt, 1960), 267-84; Jehuda L. Wallach, *Kriegstheorien: Ihre Entwicklung im 19. und 20. Jahrhundert* (Frankfurt am Main, 1972), 11-27; and Hew Strachan, *European Armies and the Conduct of War* (London and Boston, 1983), 60-75. Controversy continues over the degree to which Jomini influenced strategy in the American Civil War; Thomas L. Connelly and Archer Jones, *The Politics of Command: Factions and Ideas in Confederate Strategy* (Baton Rouge, 1973), 3-30, 174-176, and 226-229, is a full introduction but not the last word.

7. CLAUSEWITZ

A complete edition of Clausewitz's writings does not exist. Soon after his death, an extensive selection of his manuscripts was published: *Hinterlassene Werke des Generals Carl von Clausewitz über Krieg und Kriegführung*, 10 vols. (Berlin, 1832-37). Additional manuscripts have been published since then, often in editions that partly duplicate each other. The most important are: "Über das Leben und den Charakter von Scharnhorst," *Historisch-Politische Zeitschrift* 1 (1832); *Nachrichten über Preussen in seiner grossen Katastrophe*, vol. 10 of

Kriegsgeschichtliche Einzelschriften (Berlin, 1888) and reprinted several times; *Politische Schriften und Briefe,* ed. Hans Rothfels (Munich, 1922; new ed. Bonn, 1980); *Strategie aus dem Jahr 1804, mit Zusätzen von 1808 und 1809,* ed. Eberhard Kessel (Hamburg, 1937); *Zwei Briefe des Generals von Clausewitz: Gedanken zur Abwehr,* special issue of the *Militärwissenschaftliche Rundschau* 2 (1937), recently published in English as *Two Letters on Strategy,* ed. and trans. Peter Paret and Daniel Moran (Carlisle, Penn., 1984). Despite its frequently absurd commentary, a National-Socialist collection of Clausewitz's writings, *Geist und Tat,* ed. Walther Malmsten Schering (Stuttgart, 1941), should be noted because it includes some shorter pieces by Clausewitz that had not been previously published and now seem to be lost. Clausewitz's analysis of the campaign of 1806, which appeared anonymously in 1807, has been reprinted with a useful introduction by Joachim Niemeyer, *Historische Briefe über die grossen Kriegsereignisse im Oktober 1806* (Bonn, 1977).

The dean of Clausewitz editors and bibliographers, Werner Hahlweg, has brought out an exhaustively annotated edition of some of Clausewitz's manuscripts and letters, many of which are printed for the first time: Carl von Clausewitz, *Schriften-Aufsätze-Studien-Briefe,* 2 vols. (Göttingen, 1966, 1986). A collection by the same editor, Carl von Clausewitz, *Verstreute kleine Schriften* (Osnabrück, 1979), is designed for the general reader. Professor Hahlweg is also the editor of the most scholarly text of *Vom Kriege* (Bonn, 1980). The most recent English translation of Clausewitz's major theoretical work is by Michael Howard and Peter Paret, *On War* (Princeton, 1976; rev. ed. 1984), with essays and commentary by Peter Paret, Michael Howard, and Bernard Brodie.

The correspondence between Clausewitz and his wife, a biographical and historical source of great importance, has been edited by Karl Linnebach, *Karl u. Marie v. Clausewitz* (Berlin, 1917).

The best survey of the secondary literature is found in Werner Hahlweg's 1980 edition of *Vom Kriege,* which lists several hundred books and articles. To be noted here are the two-volume life and letters by Karl Schwartz, *Leben des Generals Carl von Clausewitz und der Frau Marie von Clausewitz geb. Gräfin von Brühl* (Berlin, 1878); the important though somewhat romantic study by Hans Rothfels, *Carl von Clausewitz: Politik und Krieg* (Berlin, 1920); and two brief, valuable studies: Rudolf von Caemmerer, *Clausewitz* (Berlin, 1905), and Werner Hahlweg, *Clausewitz* (Göttingen, 1957). Peter Paret, *Clausewitz and the State* (Oxford and New York, 1976; repr. Princeton, 1985) combines biography and the history of ideas (see the review by Raymond Aron in *Annales* 32, no. 6 [1977]). Raymond Aron's two-volume study *Penser la guerre: Clausewitz* (Paris, 1976) is an important discussion of Clausewitz's theories linked with a highly speculative effort to expand and adapt them to the present (see the review by Peter Paret in the *Journal of Interdisciplinary History* 8, no. 2 [1977]). The English edition of Aron's work, *Clausewitz: Philosopher of War* (London, 1984), does not contain the full text of the original, is badly edited, and marred by numerous errors (see the review by Hew Strachan in *The Times Higher Education Supple-*

ment, June 1, 1984). Michael Howard has written a brief discussion of Clausewitz's theories, *Clausewitz* (Oxford and New York, 1983).

Most efforts by political scientists and strategic analysts to bring Clausewitz to bear on current problems of strategy and war have been relatively unproductive. An exception is the responsible and stimulating essay by Harry G. Summers, Jr., *On Strategy* (Novato, Calif., 1982). John E. Tashjean has written several brief, imaginative articles on the significance of Clausewitz today, for instance "The Cannon in the Swimming Pool: Clausewitzian Studies and Strategic Ethnocentrism," *Journal of the Royal United Services Institute* (June 1983). Two German colloquia that have had some success in linking the study of Clausewitz with contemporary strategic analysis are *Freiheit ohne Krieg*, ed. Ulrich de Maizière (Bonn, 1980) and the proceedings of the International Clausewitz Conference, 1980, in *Wehrwissenschaftliche Rundschau* 29, no. 3 (1980).

8. Adam Smith, Alexander Hamilton, Friedrich List: The Economic Foundations of Military Power[*]

On mercantilism, see the still valuable work of Eli F. Heckscher, *Merkantilismen* (Stockholm, 1931), translated into English by M. Shapiro, *Mercantilism*, 2 vols. (London, 1935); Gustav Schmoller, *The Mercantile System and Its Historical Significance*, trans. W. J. Ashely (London, 1896); C. W. Cole, *Colbert and a Century of French Mercantilism* (New York, 1939).

Originally published in 1776. Adam Smith's *An Inquiry into the Nature and Causes of the Wealth of Nations* has often been reprinted. Outstanding is the edition by R. H. Campbell, A. S. Skinner, and W. B. Todd (Oxford, 1976), part of the invaluable multivolume Glasgow Edition of the Works and Correspondence of Adam Smith that appeared in the 1970s. John Rae, *Life of Adam Smith* (New York, 1895) has been republished with a commentary by Jacob Viner (New York, 1965). For a biography by two editors of Smith's collected works, see R. H. Campbell and A. S. Skinner, *Adam Smith* (London, 1982). Also of note are several volumes of essays from the 1970s commemorating Adam Smith: Andrew Skinner and Thomas Wilson, eds., *Essays on Adam Smith* (Oxford, 1975); Fred Glahe, ed., *Adam Smith and the Wealth of Nations 1776-1976: Bicentennial Essays* (Boulder, 1978); Gerald P. O'Driscoll, Jr., ed., *Adam Smith and Modern Political Economy: Bicentennial Essays on the Wealth of Nations* (Ames, 1979).

The best source on Alexander Hamilton is *The Papers of Alexander Hamilton*, ed. Harold C. Syrett and Jacob E. Cooke, 26 vols. (New York, 1961-79). Among the many biographies of Hamilton, see Broadus Mitchell, *Alexander Hamilton*, 2 vols. (New York, 1957, 1962; repr. 1976), and John C. Miller, *Alexander Hamilton: Portrait in Paradox* (New York, 1959). Two more works by Mitchell appeared in the 1970s: *Alexander Hamilton: The Revolutionary Years* (New York, 1970), which includes an account of Hamilton's military career, and *Alexander Hamilton: A Concise Biography* (New York, 1976). Jacob

---

[*] Prepared by Donald Abenheim.

Ernest Cooke, *Alexander Hamilton* (New York, 1982) is a biography written by an editor of Hamilton's papers.

Still indispensable is the collection of Friedrich List's works published by the Friedrich List Gesellschaft, *Schriften, Reden, Briefe*, 10 vols. (Berlin, 1927-35). *The National System of Political Economy* (New York, 1966) is a reprint of the 1885 translation by Sampson S. Lloyd of List's *Das Nationale System der politischen Ökonomie* (Stuttgart, 1841). Of special interest is *The Natural System of Political Economy*, trans. and ed. W. O. Henderson (London, 1983). Among the many biographies of List, see Friedrich Lenz, *Friedrich List: Der Mann und das Werk* (Munich and Berlin, 1936); Hans Gehrig, *Friedrich List und Deutschlands politisch ökonomische Einheit* (Leipzig, 1956); Paul Gehring, *Friedrich List: Jugend und Reifejahre, 1789-1825* (Tübingen, 1964). An attractive illustrated volume on List is Eugen Wendler, *Friedrich List: Leben und Wirken in Dokumenten* (Reutlingen, 1976). The number of specialized studies on List is great. Of note are: Georg Weippert, *Der Späte List: Ein Beitrag zur Grundlegung der Wissenschaft von der Politik und zur politischen Ökonomie als Gestaltungslehre der Wirtschaft* (Erlangen, 1956); Werner Strosslin, *Friedrich Lists Lehre von der wirtschaftlichen Entwicklung: Zur Geschichte von Entwicklungstheorie und -politik* (Basel, 1968); Harald Randak, *Friedrich List und die wissenschaftliche Wirtschaftspolitik* (Tübingen, 1972).

9. Engels and Marx on Revolution, War, and the Army in Society*

In 1975 the first volume of the *Marx-Engels Gesamtausgabe* (MEGA) appeared in East Berlin, the product of a collaboration between the Institutes of Marxism-Leninism affiliated with the Central Committees of the Communist Party of the Soviet Union and the German Socialist Unity Party (SED). When complete, this authoritative all-original-language edition will supersede all previous editions. The best English *Collected Works* also began publication in 1975 and represents a joint effort between Progress Publishers in Moscow, the C.P.S.U.'s Institute of Marxism-Leninism, and the Communist Parties of the U.S.A. and Britain (London). Until these two editions are complete, scholars will find the handiest and most nearly complete edition to be the *Karl Marx-Friedrich Engels Werke*, 41 vols. plus supp. vols. (East Berlin, 1960-74). All three editions include published works, correspondence, and a large number of hitherto unpublished manuscript materials.

W. H. Chaloner and W. O. Henderson have edited a collection of Engels's articles in English, reprinted from the *Volunteer Journal* and the *Manchester Guardian* of the 1860s, entitled *Engels as Military Critic* (Manchester, 1959). Engels's military writings have been translated and published in both Russian and German: F. Engel's, *Izbrannye voennye proizvedeniia* (Moscow, 1957); F. Engels, *Ausgewählte militärische Schriften*, 2 vols. (Berlin, 1958-64); and with Lenin's military writings, in F. Engels and V. I. Lenin, *Militärpolitische Schriften*, ed. Erich Wollenberg (Offenbach a.M., 1952). Engels's *New American Cyclo-*

* Prepared by Mark von Hagen.

paedia entries on the army, infantry, attack, and battle have been published separately: *Die Armee* (Berlin, 1956); *Die Infantrie, Der Angriff, Die Schlacht* (Berlin, 1956). One of the earliest collections, and still a valuable one, is the Russian edition of 1924, Fridrikh Engel's, *Stat'i i pis'ma po voennym voprosam* (Moscow).

Modern biographies include: Gerhard Zirke, *Der General: Friedrich Engels, der erste Militärtheoretiker der Arbeiterklasse* (Leipzig, 1957); Grace Carlton, *Friedrich Engels: The Shadow Prophet* (London, 1965; W. O. Henderson, *Life of Friedrich Engels*, 2 vols. (London, 1976). Among earlier works, the classic remains Gustav Mayer, *Friedrich Engels: Eine Biographie* (The Hague, 1934). For Engels's military activities in the late 1840s, see a recent German study: Heinz Helmert, *Friedrich Engels: Adjutant der Revolution, 1848-49* (Leipzig, 1973). The best modern biography of Karl Marx, albeit hagiographic in places, is David McLellan, *Karl Marx: His Life and Thought* (New York, 1973). Other helpful works include: Jerrold Seigel, *Marx's Fate: The Shape of a Life* (Princeton, 1978); Fritz J. Raddatz, *Karl Marx: A Political Biography*, trans. Richard Barry (Boston, 1978); Arnold Kuenzli, *Karl Marx: Eine Psychobiographie* (Vienna, 1966). Also to be noted are the classic biographies of Franz Mehring, *Karl Marx: Geschichte seines Lebens* (Leipzig, 1918); and D. Ryazanov, *Karl Marx and Friedrich Engels* (New York, 1927).

In the past twenty years, works in German, Russian, and English have signaled a new interest in the military aspects of Engels's writings. In German, Jehuda L. Wallach offers an outline of Engels's major ideas on war and armies in *Die Kriegslehre von Friedrich Engels* (Frankfurt a.M., 1968). Wolfram Wette, in *Kriegstheorien deutscher Sozialisten* (Stuttgart, 1971), argues that Marx and Engels laid the foundations for a socialist contribution to the peace and disarmament movements. Hans Pelger has edited the proceedings of a 1970 conference on Engels, *Friedrich Engels 1820-1970: Referate—Diskussionen—Dokumente* (Hanover, 1971). Several articles in the *Zeitschrift für Militärgeschichte* also discuss Engels's military writings. The pioneering works in German are those of August Happich, *Friedrich Engels als Soldat der Revolution* (Hessische Beiträge zur Staat und Wirtschaftskunde, 1931) and Ernst Drahn, *Friedrich Engels als Kriegswissenschaftler* (*Kultur und Fortschritt*, nos. 524, 525). The Soviet specialist on Engels's military thought is A. I. Babin. See his *Formirovanie i razvitie voenno-teoreticheskikh vzgliadov F. Engel'sa* (Moscow, 1975) and an earlier study *F. Engel's: Vydaiushchiisia voennyi teoretik rabochego klassa* (Moscow, 1970). Babin's latest work includes an extensive bibliography of articles and books published in Russian. The Soviet Institute of Military History convened two conferences dedicated to the 150th anniversaries of the births of Marx and Engels. The articles presented at the conferences were published in two editions, which include annotated indices to the military writings of the two revolutionaries: *Karl Marks i voennaia istoriia* (Moscow, 1969), and *Fridrikh Engel's i voennaia istoriia* (Moscow, 1972). Until recently no major monograph on the military thinking of Marx and Engels existed in English. This gap has been filled with an interesting book by Martin Berger, *Engels, Armies, and Revolution* (Hamden, Conn., 1977). Berger includes a useful bibliography of works in German and English. W. B. Gallie includes an insightful essay on Marx and Engels in his book, *Philosophers of Peace and War* (Cambridge, 1978), which, however, suffers from a tendency that can be noted in much of the writing about Marx and Engels; at the outset Gallie describes Marx and Engels as rigorously dogmatic theorists, only to devote most of his essay to faulting them for failing to live up to his claims on their behalf. Finally, Bernard Semmel discusses Marx and Engels in his collection, *Marxism and the Science of War* (Oxford, 1981).

10. The Prusso-German School: Moltke and the Rise of the General Staff*

The literature on the general history of the Prussian army during the nineteenth century is too large to be enumerated here. Any historical study of Prussian military legislation still has to start with the classics on the military reforms after 1806: Max Lehmann, *Scharnhorst* (Leipzig, 1886-87); Hans Delbrück, *Gneisenau*, 3d ed. (Berlin, 1908); Friedrich Meinecke, *Boyen* (Stuttgart, 1896-99). Among more recent works, see Peter Paret, *Yorck and the Era of Prussian Reform* (Princeton, 1966); and the same author's *Clausewitz and the State* (New York and London, 1976; repr. Princeton, 1985). For the general military history of the period, Colmar Frh. von der Goltz, *Kriegsgeschichte Deutschlands im 19. Jahrhundert* (Berlin, 1914), should be consulted as well as volume 5 of Hans Delbrück, *Geschichte der Kriegskunst* (Berlin, 1928). Although this volume, written by Emil Daniels, does not reach the level of Delbrück's earlier four volumes, it constitutes a useful compilation. The best introduction to the specialized study of nineteenth-century strategy continues to be Rudolf von Caemmerer, *Entwicklung der strategischen Wissenschaft im 19. Jahrhundert* (Berlin, 1904). An English translation appeared in London in 1905. A more recent essay on modern strategy may be found in the article "Kriegskunst" by T. von Schaefer in the military dictionary *Handbuch der neuzeitlichen Wehrwissenschaften* (1936), 1:180-227.

The writings of Moltke were collected after his death in two large editions: Helmuth von Moltke, *Gesammelte Schriften und Denkwürdigkeiten*, 8 vols. (Berlin, 1891-93); and *Militärische Werke*, edited by the German general staff, 13 vols. (Berlin, 1892-1912). These editions do not contain his memoranda on the problems of a two-front war during 1871-1890. They were edited by Ferdinand von Schmerfeld: H. Graf von Moltke, *Die deutschen Aufmarschpläne 1971-1890: Forschungen und Darstellungen aus dem Reichsarchiv*, vol. 7 (Berlin, 1928). (A brief analysis and description will be found in Peter Rassow, *Der Plan des Feldmarschalls Grafen Moltke für den Zweifronten-Krieg, 1871-1890* [Breslau, 1936].) Additional material on Moltke's thought about the two-front war is to be found in volume 6 of the German publication on the origins of the First World War, *Die grosse Politik der europäischen Kabinette, 1871-1914*. Of some documentary value is the study prepared by the historical section of the German general staff, *Moltke in der Vorbereitung und Durchführung der Operationen*, no. 37 of *Kriegsgeschichtliche Einzelschriften* (Berlin, 1905).

* Hajo Holborn's original note has been revised by Donald Abenheim, and some of it has been incorporated into the bibliographical note for essay 11.

For the study of Moltke's strategy the military histories of the wars of 1866 and 1870-1871 should be consulted. Among the general historical works most useful for the understanding of Moltke's strategy are Heinrich Friedjung, *Der Kampf um die Vorherrschaft Deutschlands* (1st ed., Stuttgart, 1896; 10th ed., 1916), and Oscar von Lettow-Vorbeck, *Geschichte des Krieges von 1866 in Deutschland* (Berlin, 1896-1902).

The monographic studies of Moltke's strategy are even more important. First place should be given to General Sigismund von Schlichting's monograph *Moltke und Benedek* (1900), one of the classics of the history of modern strategy. Schlichting's study was written as a critique of the military chapters of Friedjung's historical work and, through its historical understanding of the military and strategic problems, arrived at a fairer historical judgment of both victors and vanquished of 1866. A long debate developed, which is summed up in later editions of Friedjung. In the literature the following books and articles should be noted: Alfred Krauss, *Moltke, Benedek und Napoleon* (Vienna, 1901); Hans Delbrück, "Moltke," *Erinnerungen, Aufsätze und Reden* (Berlin, 1902); A. von Boguslawski, *Strategische Erörterungen* (1901); Hugo von Freytag-Loringhoven, *Die Heerführung Napoleons in ihrer Bedeutung für unsere Zeit* (Berlin, 1910). Of particular interest is, of course, Schlieffen's treatment of Moltke's strategy in his *Cannae* articles. See bibliographical note for essay 11, below.

The impact of railroad building on modern strategy is treated by E. A. Pratt, *The Rise of Rail-Power in War and Conquest, 1833-1914* (London, 1915) and Dennis Showalter, *Railroads and Rifles* (Hamden, Conn., 1975). For the history of the German railroads as means of warfare see H. von Staabs, *Aufmarsch nach zwei Fronten, auf Grund der Operationspläne von 1871-1914* (1925). His successor as chief of the railroad section of the German general staff, Wilhelm Groener, contributed an article on the railroad mobilization in 1914 to the work *Die deutschen Eisenbahnen der Gegenwart*, ed. Prussian Ministry of Public Works (new ed. 1923). Since then the subject has received a full treatment in the official German history of the First World War: Reichsarchiv, *Der Weltkrieg: Das deutsche Feldeisenbahnwesen*, vol. 1, *Die Eisenbahnen zu Kriegsbeginn* (Berlin, 1928).

A good many studies deal with the relationship between politics and strategy. The following may be mentioned: Wilhelm von Blume, "Politik und Strategie: Bismarck und Moltke," *Preussische Jahrbücher* 111 (1903); Wilhelm Busch, *Bismarck und Moltke* (1916); Hans von Haeften, "Bismarck und Moltke," *Preussische Jahrbücher* 177 (1919); Paul Schmitthenner, *Politik und Kriegsführung in der neuesten Geschichte* (Hamburg, 1937).

11. MOLTKE, SCHLIEFFEN, AND THE DOCTRINE OF STRATEGIC ENVELOPMENT*

Hajo Holborn's bibliographical note surveyed the extensive literature on the Prusso-German school of land warfare published up to the early 1940s. Since

* Prepared by the author, with additions from the bibliographical note for Hajo Holborn's original essay.

then a considerable number of additional works have appeared. While there has been no new documentary material on Moltke the Elder, the text of Schlieffen's famous December 1905 memorandum, together with earlier drafts and later revisions, was published in Gerhard Ritter, *The Schlieffen Plan* (London, 1958). In addition, Eberhard Kessel edited a collection of Schlieffen's *Briefe* (Göttingen, 1958) with an important introduction by the editor, and selections from Moltke's and Schlieffen's official writing can be found in the chapters by Gerhard Papke and Hans Meier-Welker in *Klassiker der Kriegskunst*, ed. Werner Hahlweg (Darmstadt, 1960).

Shortly after Schlieffen's death his published articles and public speeches were collected under the title: Graf Alfred von Schlieffen, *Gesammelte Schriften*, 2 vols. (Berlin, 1913). An abbreviated edition of these collected writings appeared in 1925 under the title *Cannae*. The bulk of both editions is formed by the series of studies that Schlieffen devoted to the encirclement battles from Cannae to Sedan. An abbreviated English translation of the Cannae articles was published in 1931 at Fort Leavenworth, Kansas. The most important addition to the writings of Schlieffen is contained in the luxurious edition of his official writings started by the German general staff in 1937: *Dienstschriften des Chefs des Generalstabes der Armee, Generalfeldmarschall Graf von Schlieffen*. The best historical sources for the Schlieffen plan today are still Hans von Kuhl, *Der deutsche Generalstab in Vorbereitung und Durchführung des Weltkrieges*, 2d ed. (Berlin, 1920); Wolfgang Foerster, *Graf Schlieffen und der Weltkrieg* (Berlin, 1921); the official German history of the First World War: Reichsarchiv, *Der Weltkrieg 1914-1918*, 14 vols. (Berlin, 1925-44); Rüdt von Collenberg, "Graf Schlieffen und die deutsche Mobilmachung," *Wissen und Wehr* (1927); Wolfgang Foerster, *Aus der Gedankenwerkstatt des deutschen Generalstabes* (Berlin, 1931).

The discussion of Schlieffen's strategic ideas runs like a red thread through all modern German books on strategy. It plays the greatest part in the German critique of the operations of the First World War. In addition to the above-mentioned studies by Hans von Kuhl and Wolfgang Foerster and the official German history of the First World War, which was written chiefly under the direction of General Hans von Haeften, the outstanding work came from the pen of General Wilhelm Groener, who was chief of the railroad section of the general staff in 1914, and succeeded Ludendorff in the fall of 1918. As minister of war under the Republic he became one of the chief fathers of the modern German army and its strategy. His *Das Testament des Grafen Schlieffen* (Berlin, 1927) is the most distinguished and profound study of Schlieffen. Groener supplemented it later with his *Der Feldherr wider Willen* (Berlin, 1931), a study of the strategy of the younger Moltke. The veneration enjoyed by Schlieffen in German military circles is almost general. A good expression of it is found in a special issue of the *Militärwissenschaftliche Rundschau* in 1938: Lieutenant General von Zoellner, *Schlieffens Vermächtnis*. The chief opponent of Schlieffen before 1914, General Friedrich von Bernhardi, failed to attract many followers. However, there has been a school of military thought that placed Moltke the Elder above Schlieffen, criticizing either the rigidity of Schlieffen's operational schemes or recommending Moltke's idea of an offensive in the east as the better solution of the two-front war. The best representative of this school is probably General E. Buchfinck. See his article "Moltke und Schlieffen," *Historische Zeitschrift* 158 (1938). Ludendorff himself defended the change of the Schlieffen plan by the younger Moltke in an article in *Deutsche Wehr* (1930).

J. V. Bredt, *Die belgische Neutralität und der Schlieffensche Feldzugplan* (1929), is the chief source for the treatment of the Belgian question in German military and political circles before 1914. Special volumes of the official German history of the First World War show the influence of Schlieffen's concept of modern war upon the economic and financial preparations in Germany: Reichsarchiv, *Der Weltkrieg, Kriegsrüstung und Kriegswirtschaft*, vol. 1 and vol. 1, Annexes.

Much interest has been shown in the relations between the soldiers and the state, especially between the chief of the general staff and the political authorities. Major works include Rudolf Stadelmann, *Moltke und der Staat* (Krefeld, 1950); Gerhard Ritter, *The Sword and the Scepter*, 4 vols. (Coral Gables, Fla., 1969-73), and Gordon A. Craig, *The Politics of the Prussian Army 1640-1945* (New York, 1964). Some useful information can be found in Jacques Benoist-Mechin, *Histoire de l'armée allemagne*, 10 vols. (Paris, 1938-64), though the overall analysis is flawed by the author's extreme right-wing perceptions. There now exist a number of special studies of the Prussian general staff. These include Walter Goerlitz, *History of the German General Staff* (New York, 1953), though the translation omits sections of the original, *Der deutsche Generalstab* (Frankfurt a.M., 1951). Wiegand Schmidt-Richberg, *Die Generalstäbe in Deutschland 1871-1945* (Stuttgart, 1962), is more specialized and limited in coverage. Examinations of Schlieffen's work are provided by Herbert Rosinski, "Scharnhorst to Schlieffen: The Rise and Decline of German Military Thought," *U.S. Naval War College Review* 29 (1976), 83-103; Helmut Otto, *Schlieffen und der Generalstab* (E. Berlin, 1966), and N. T. Tsarev, *Ot Schlieffen do Gindenburga* (Moscow, 1946). The latter two works display a strong ideological bent. The only new publication on Waldersee is the important article by Eberhard Kessel, "Die Tätigkeit des Grafen Waldersee als Quartiermeister und Chef des Generalstabes der Armes," *Die Welt als Geschichte* 15 (1954), 181-210. The most recent American study, dealing with personalities as well as operational doctrine, is Trevor N. Dupuy, *A Genius for War: The German Army and General Staff, 1807-1945* (Englewood Cliffs, N.J., 1977). It is not based on new research and reflects the somewhat uncritical admiration of German methods and dogma common in U.S. Army staff schools for many years.

On the operational side, the *Grundzüge der militärischen Kriegsführung*, Vol. 9 of Militärgeschichtliches Forschungsamt, *Handbuch zur deutschen Militärgeschichte* (Munich, 1979), is indispensable. The continuing influence of the battle of annihilation doctrine can be studied in Jehuda L. Wallach, *Das Dogma der Vernichtungsschlacht* (Frankfurt a.M., 1967), and in Edgar Röhricht, *Probleme der Kesselschlacht dargestellt durch Einkreisungsoperationen im zweiten Weltkrieg* (Karlsruhe, 1958). Specialized topics are addressed by Eberhard Kessel,

"Zur Genesis der modernen Kriegslehre," *Wehrwissenschaftliche Rundschau* 3 (1952), 405-23; E. v. Kiliani, "Die Operationslehre des Grafen Schlieffen und ihre deutschen Gegner," *Wehrkunde* 2 (1961), 71-76; and E. Kaulbach, "Schlieffen—Zur Frage der Bedeutung und Wirkung Seiner Arbeit," *Wehrwissenschaftliche Rundschau* 13 (1963), 137-49. Often-neglected logistical aspects are treated in Larry H. Addington, *The Blitzkrieg Era and the German General Staff 1865-1941* (New Brunswick, N.J., 1971) and in the relevant chapers of Martin Van Creveld, *Supplying War: Logistics from Wallenstein to Patton* (Cambridge, 1977).

Strategic-political issues are raised among others by Hans-Ulrich Wehler, " 'Absoluter' und 'totaler' Krieg von Clausewitz zu Ludendorff," *Politische Vierteljahreszeitschrift* 10 (1969), 220-48; Klaus E. Knorr, "Strategic Surprise in Four European Wars," in *Strategic Military Surprise*, ed. Klaus E. Knorr and Patrick Morgan (Brunswick, N.J., 1983), 41-75; Lancelot L. Farrar, Jr., *The Short-War Illusion* (Santa Barbara, 1973); and in Robert E. Harkavy, *Preemption in a Two-Front Conventional War: A Comparison of the 1967 Israeli Strategy with the Pre-World War I German Schlieffen Plan* (Jerusalem, 1977). Prewar planning is discussed in several notable essays in *The War Plans of the Great Powers, 1880-1914*, ed. Paul M. Kennedy (London, 1979); Dennis Showalter, "The Eastern Front and German Military Planning, 1871-1914: Some Observations," *East European Quarterly* 15 (1981), 163-80; and Norman Stone, "Moltke-Conrad: Relations between the Austro-Hungarian and German General Staffs, 1909-1914," *The Historical Journal* 9 (1966), 201-28.

Although somewhat hagiographic, Eberhard Kessel, *Moltke* (Stuttgart, 1957), is a work of great sophistication and now the standard biography. There still is no full biography of Schlieffen. Friedrich v. Boetticher, *Schlieffen* (Göttingen, 1957), is brief, but informative. See also Eugen Bircher and Walter Bode, *Schlieffen: Mann und Idee* (Zurich, 1937). Moltke the Younger remains almost completely neglected. The long chapter, "The Tragic Delusion: Colonel General Helmuth Johannes Ludwig von Moltke," in Correlli Barnett, *The Sword Bearers* (New York, 1963), is well written but contains little that is new. Both Gordon A. Craig, *The Battle of Königgrätz* (Philadelphia, 1964) and Michael Howard, *The Franco-Prussian War* (New York, 1961) are reinterpretations of the elder Moltke's two major triumphs.

12. DELBRÜCK: THE MILITARY HISTORIAN

Delbrück's first major work was *Das Leben des Feldmarschalls Grafen Neidhardt von Gneisenau* (Berlin, 1882). This work, which has gone through four editions since its initial publication, remains the standard biography of the Prussian general. In *Die Perserkriege und die Burgunderkriege: Zwei kombinierte kriegsgeschichtliche Studien* (Berlin, 1887), Delbrück first clearly outlined his method of approaching military history and his conception of the importance of reconstructing single battles. Early full-scale presentations of his strategical theories will be found in *Die Strategie des Perikles erläutert durch die Strategie*

Friedrichs des Grossen: Mit einem Anhang über Thucydides und Kleon (Berlin, 1890); and *Friedrich, Napoleon, Moltke* (Berlin, 1892).

The first volume of the *Geschichte der Kriegskunst im Rahmen der politischen Geschichte* appeared in 1900; the second in 1902; and the third and fourth in 1907 and 1920 respectively. A second edition of the first two volumes (Berlin, 1908) and a third edition of the first volume (Berlin, 1920) contain additional notes and answers to critics but are otherwise unchanged. The fourth volume of the *Geschichte*, the last that Delbrück wrote, ends with an account of the wars of Liberation. The work was continued by Emil Daniels; the fifth and sixth volumes, covering the period between the Crimean and Franco-Prussian wars, appearing in 1928 and 1932. In 1936, a seventh volume, which discusses the American Civil War and the Boer and Russo-Japanese wars, was published under the joint authorship of Daniels and Otto Haintz.

Hans Delbrück, *Numbers in History* (London, 1913) is a reprint of two lectures delivered by the historian at the University of London in 1913. This volume, in brief compass and in Delbrück's own words, surveys the first three volumes of the *Geschichte der Kriegskunst* and outlines the main themes.

Delbrück's shorter military writings are scattered through the pages of the *Preussische Jahrbücher* and other publications. There are, however, four collections of the articles that Delbrück himself considered most important. *Historische und politische Aufsätze* (Berlin, 1886; 2d ed., 1907) contains an important essay, "Über die Verschiedenheit der Strategie Friedrichs und Napoleons." *Erinnerungen, Aufsätze und Reden* (Berlin, 1902; 3d ed., 1905) includes an article on the work of the general staff in the Danish War of 1864, in addition to a notable essay on Moltke. Delbrück's First World War writings have been collected in the three volumes of *Krieg und Politik* (Berlin, 1917-19). A final collection appeared in 1926 under the title *Vor und nach dem Weltkrieg* and includes Delbrück's most important articles for the periods 1902-1914 and 1919-1925.

For Delbrück's position during the First World War, see the collections cited above, and also the pamphlet *Bismarcks Erbe* (Berlin, 1915), which is perhaps his most impassioned plea for a negotiated peace with the Allies. Delbrück's masterly critique of Ludendorff's strategy in 1918 is printed in *Das Werk des Untersuchungsausschusses der Deutschen Verfassunggebenden Nationalversammlung und des Deutschen Reichstages 1919-1926: Die Ursachen des Deutschen Zusammenbruchs im Jahre 1918* (Vierte Reihe im Werk des Untersuchungsausschusses) (Berlin, 1925), 3:239-373. Selections from Delbrück's testimony will be found also in *The Causes of the German Collapse in 1918*, ed. R. H. Lutz, Hoover War Library Publications, no. 4 (Stanford, 1934).

Many of Delbrück's afterthoughts on the war exist only in pamphlet form. See, for example, *Ludendorff, Tirpitz, Falkenhayn* (Berlin, 1920); *Ludendorffs Selbstporträt* (Berlin, 1922), an answer to Ludendorff's *Kriegführung und Politik* (Berlin, 1922); *Kautsky und Harden* (Berlin, 1920); and *Der Stand der Kriegsschuldfrage* (Berlin, 1925). The last two works are largely concerned with the question of war guilt.

Even an incomplete listing of Delbrück's works must also include his *Re-*

gierung und Volkswille (Berlin, 1914), a series of lectures on the imperial government and constitution; and his five-volume *Weltgeschichte* (Berlin, 1924-28). The former work has been translated into English by Roy S. MacElwee under the title *Government and the Will of the People* (New York, 1923).

No full-scale biography of Delbrück has yet been written. For biographical details, consult the introductions to volumes 1 and 4 of the *Geschichte der Kriegskunst* and the epilogue to *Krieg und Politik*; and see also Johannes Ziekursch in *Deutsches biographisches Jahrbuch* (Berlin, 1929) and Friedrich Meinecke in *Historische Zeitschrift* 140 (1929), 703. Richard H. Bauer's article in *Some Historians of Modern Europe*, ed. Bernadotte Schmitt (Chicago, 1942), 100-127, is a careful account of Delbrück's life and work although Delbrück's military writings are treated only in a general manner. F. J. Schmidt, Konrad Molinski, and Siegfried Mette in *Hans Delbrück: Der Historiker und Politiker* (Berlin, 1928) discuss the philosophical basis of Delbrück's writings and his importance as a historian and a politician. The historian's political and military ideas are also treated fully in *Am Webstuhl der Zeit: Eine Erinnerungsgabe Hans Delbrück dem Achtzigjährigen von Freunden und Schülern dargebracht* (Berlin, 1928), a collection of essays by Emil Daniels, Paul Rohrbach, Generals Groener and Buchfinck, and others. See also Arthur Rosenberg, "Hans Delbrück, der Kritiker der Kriegsgeschichte," *Die Gesellschaft* (1921), 245; Franz Mehring, "Eine Geschichte der Kriegskunst," *Die Neue Zeit*, Ergänzungsheft, no. 4 (October 16, 1908); and V. Marcu, *Men and Forces of Our Time*, trans. Eden and Cedar Paul (New York, 1931), 201ff.

Delbrück's strategical theories gave rise to a flood of controversial literature. The most important articles appearing before 1920 are listed in *Geschichte der Kriegskunst*, 4:439-44. The most thorough appraisal of Delbrück's strategical concepts during the Weimar period was Otto Hintze, "Delbrück, Clausewitz und die Strategie Friedrichs des Grossen," *Forschungen zur brandenburgischen und preussischen Geschichte* 33 (1920), 131-77.

After 1945, there was renewed interest in Delbrück's strategical and political writings. The fourth volume of the *Kriegskunst* was reprinted in Berlin in 1962 and the first three in 1964. An English translation by Walter J. Renfroe, Jr., is under way: *History of the Art of War within the Framework of Political History*, (Westport, Conn., 1975-   ). On Delbrück's political activities, the following are worth consulting: A. Harnack, "Hans Delbrück als Historiker und Politiker," *Neue Rundschau* 63 (1952), 408-26; Peter Rassow, "Hans Delbrück als Historiker und Politiker," *Die Sammlung* 4 (1949), 134-44; Anneliese Thimme, *Hans Delbrück als Kritiker der wilhelminischen Epoche* (Düsseldorf, 1955), which is the best work on this subject. Delbrück's political activities also receive appropriate attention in K. Schwabe, *Wissenschaft und Kriegsmoral: Die deutschen Hochschullehrer und die politischen Grundfragen des Ersten Weltkrieges* (Göttingen, 1965). A good appraisal of his stature as a historian is Andreas Hillgruber's essay in *Deutsche Historiker*, ed. Hans-Ulrich Wehler, IV (Göttingen, 1972), 40-52. Arden Bucholz, *Hans Delbrück and the German Military Establishment* (Iowa City, 1985) describes the conflict between Delbrück's views of war and those of the general staff historians and how it was influenced by events in the real world.

13. RUSSIAN MILITARY THOUGHT: THE WESTERN MODEL AND THE SHADOW OF SUVOROV

Imperial Russian military history in general has received very little attention in modern Western scholarship and not a great deal more in the Soviet Union. The interested researcher must therefore rely primarily on the very extensive prerevolutionary Russian literature on current military problems and on the history of war. Unfortunately most of these works are available if at all in only a few major Western libraries and, of course, are in Russian.

Among the small number of Western studies dealing with Russian military affairs almost none is primarily devoted to military doctrine. The only general study of Russian military thought in a Western language is the excellent, but unfortunately unpublished Ph.D. dissertation by Peter H. C. Von Wahlde, "Military Thought in Imperial Russia" (Indiana University, 1966). Not much more is available in Russian. G. P. Meshcheriakov, *Russkaia voennaia mysl' v XIX v.* (Russian military thought in the 19th century) (Moscow 1973) is relatively brief, highly ideological, and discusses nothing published after 1899. The most prolific of Soviet military writers, L. G. Beskrovnyi, has published little on theoretical matters. His useful collection of source material, *Russkaia voenno-teoreticheskaia mysl' XIX i nachala XX vekov* (Russian military-theoretical thought of the 19th and the beginning of the 20th centuries) (Moscow, 1960), has an introductory essay. In *Ocherki po istochnikovedeniiu voennoi istorii Rossii* (Essays on the sources for the military history of Russia) (Moscow 1957), Beskrovnyi includes relatively brief sections on theoretical matters.

The works of the chief military thinkers are conveniently listed in the bibliographies of Von Wahlde and, to 1900, in Meshcheriakov. Christopher Duffy, *Russia's Military Way to the West: Origins and Nature of Russian Military Power, 1700-1800* (London 1981) provides an excellent survey of both the institutions and the major campaigns of the eighteenth century, although its scope necessarily means that the treatment is summary. There is no similar general work for the nineteenth century as a whole. John Shelton Curtiss, *The Russian Army under Nicholas I, 1825-1855* (Durham, 1965) is useful although it has almost nothing on military thought. Of the great Russian commanders, only Suvorov has been the subject of a satisfactory English study, Philip Longworth, *The Art of Victory: The Life and Achievements of Generalissimo Suvorov, 1729-1800* (New York, 1965). Kutuzov and Barclay de Tolly have received much less satisfactory treatment in Michael and Diana Josselson, *The Commander: A Life of Barclay de Tolly* (Oxford, 1980) and Roger Parkinson's very superficial *The Fox of the North: The Life of Kutuzov, General of War and Peace* (London, 1976). The Soviet literature on Suvorov and Kutuzov is extensive. On Dmitrii Miliutin the great reformer, see Forrestt A. Miller, *Dmitrii Miliutin and the Reform Era in Russia* (Nashville, 1968) and Robert F. Baumann, "The Debate over Universal Military Service in Russia, 1870-1874" (Ph.D. dissertation, Yale University, 1982).

In recent years several Western scholars have turned their attention to Russian military history, although not primarily to theory, notably Dietrich Beyrau, John L. H. Keep, Jacob Kipp, and Bruce Menning. Beyrau, Keep, and Menning have written on the army and Kipp on the navy. Their articles through 1980 are discussed in the bibliographical essay by Walter M. Pintner, "The Russian Military (1700-1917): Social and Economic Aspects," *Trends in History* 2, no. 2 (Winter 1981). Consult also Menning's more recent "Russia and the West: The Problem of 18th Century Military Models" in *Russia and the West in the Eighteenth Century* ed. A. G. Cross Newtonville, Mass., 1983); "G. A. Potemkin: Soldier Statesman of the Age of the Enlightenment," International Commission on Military History, *ACTA*, no. 7 (Washington, D.C., 1982); and "Russian Military Innovation in the 18th Century," *War and Society* 2, no. 1 (1984). See also Walter M. Pintner, "Russia's Military Style, Russian Society, and Russian Power in the Eighteenth Century," in *Russia and the West in the Eighteenth Century*. In addition to John L. H. Keep's forthcoming book, *Soldiers of the Tsar*, see his "The Military Style of the Romanov Rulers," *War and Society* 1, no. 2 (1983). Dietrich Beyrau's work, *Militär und Gesellschaft im Vorrevolutionären Russland* (Cologne, 1984) was not available when this essay was in preparation.

The last fifty years of the old regime almost until World War I are less well covered in the modern literature than are earlier periods. The most useful Soviet works are L. G. Beskrovnyi, *Russkaia armiia i flot v XIX veke: Voenno-ekonomicheskii potentsial Rossii* (The Russian army and Navy in the 19th century: The military-economic potential of Russia) (Moscow, 1973) and P. A. Zaionchkovskii, *Samoderzhavie i russkaia armiia na rubezhe XIX-XX stoletii, 1881-1903* (The autocracy and the Russian army at the turn of the 19th-20th centuries, 1881-1903) (Moscow, 1973). Neither deals significantly with military thought. On the Russian army on the eve of the First World War see Allan K. Wildman, *The End of the Russian Imperial Army: The Old Army and the Soldier's Revolt (March-April, 1917)* (New York, 1975). On strategic plans and international relations, see A. M. Zaionchkovskii, *Podgotovka Rossii k imperialisticheskoi voine* (Moscow, 1926); Jack Snyder, *The Cult of the Offensive in European War Planning, 1870-1914* (Ithaca, 1984); Norman Stone, *The Eastern Front, 1914-1917* (London and New York, 1975); and D. C. B. Lieven, *Russia and the Origins of the First World War* (New York, 1983).

14. Bugeaud, Galliéni, Lyautey: The Development of French Colonial Warfare

Of France's three major colonial soldiers, only Bugeaud has acquired an objective biographer. Anthony Thrall Sullivan's *Thomas-Robert Bugeaud* (Hamden, Conn., 1983) concentrates rather more on the evolution of the marshal's attitudes toward the France of the July Monarchy than on his Algerian experiences

900

as such. However, the book is important in pointing up the alienation felt by the *armée d'Afrique* almost from the beginning of the Algerian conquest. Galliéni and Lyautey have been more the object of hero worship than objective study. No good biography of Galliéni exists. He appears with some frequency in A. S. Kanya-Forstner, *Conquest of the Western Sudan* (Cambridge, 1963) and, for his Indochinese policies, in the article by Kim Munholland, " 'Collaboration Strategy' and the French Pacification of Tonkin, 1885-1897," *The Historical Journal* 24, no. 3 (1981), 629-50. Lyautey has attracted a number of biographers including André Maurois, *Lyautey* (1931) and André le Révérend, *Lyautey* (Paris, 1983). Lyautey was a charming and plausible propagandist for French imperialism, and these authors look at the world very much through his eyes. Lyautey's own "Du rôle colonial de l'Armée" in the *Revue des deux mondes* of January 15, 1900, is an imaginative and idealized description of French methods in Tonkin, which was written to coincide with the debates on the colonial army bill of that year. For a corrective on the efficiency of Lyautey's methods in Morocco, see my own *The Conquest of Morocco* (New York, 1983).

No equivalent of C. E. Callwell's *Small Wars* (London, 1896), which forms the basis of Hew Strachan's chapter on colonial warfare in *European Armies and the Conduct of War* (London and Boston, 1983), exists for France. Kanya-Forstner is excellent for the Western Sudan. He concentrates on civil-military friction and upon the headstrong and ambitious character of colonial soldiers rather than on the methods of campaigning per se. My own books, *The Conquest of Morocco* and *The Conquest of the Sahara* (New York, 1984) examine the politico-military problems of conquest in two other regions. Ross E. Dunn, *Resistance in the Desert* (London, 1977) is a partly anthropological and partly historical study of the tribes on the Algero-Moroccan frontier at the time of conquest. It assesses the impact of French penetration on tribal cohesion and their ability to resist. Kenneth J. Perkins, *Quaids, Captains, and Colons* (New York, 1981) looks at the differing methods of military administration of the native populations in North Africa. Although it makes interesting points on the different approaches followed by officers in Tunisia, Algeria, and Morocco, it is somewhat sweeping in its generalization and can be challenged in detail. Marc Michel, *L'appel à l'Afrique* (Paris, 1982) is written in the exhaustive and magisterial tradition of a French *thèse d'état*. He not only examines how colonial troops were recruited and employed during the Great War but reveals many interesting attitudes held by colonial officers toward their troops and their value in combat.

15. American Strategy from Its Beginnings through the First World War

American strategic thought to the time of World War II expressed itself less in written and spoken form than in action, in the conduct of war. The thought behind American military actions must usually be extracted from scattered references in the reports, correspondence, and memoirs of American military leaders, or simply inferred from the actions themselves. Partly because there was thus a dearth of systematic American strategic writing before 1945 and partly because with such writing having developed only recently, historical interest in its background has naturally been only recent, the exploration of the history of American strategic thought is only beginning.

John Shy, "The American Military Experience: History and Learning," *The Journal of Interdisciplinary History* 1 (Winter 1971), 205-228, offers an excellent brief introduction to the history of American attitudes toward war and implicitly toward strategic thought. The essay is reprinted along with various of Shy's essays on the American Revolution, some of them also touching on strategy, in John Shy, *A People Numerous and Armed: Reflections on the Military Struggle for American Independence* (New York, 1976), 225-54. Russell F. Weigley, *The American Way of War: A History of United States Military Strategy and Policy* (New York and London, 1973), a volume of The Macmillan Wars of the United States, Louis Morton, general editor, is a more comprehensive effort than Shy's but still in many ways a preliminary exploration.

Such systematic strategic writing as there was in the United States in the nineteenth century exists mainly in three books: Henry Wager Halleck, *Elements of Military Art and Science* ... (New York and Philadelphia, 1846), which appeared in a third edition, with critical notes on the Mexican and Crimean Wars (New York and London, 1862); Dennis Hart Mahan, *An Elementary Treatise on Advanced-Guard, Out-Post, and Detachment Service of Troops* ... (New York, 1847; rev. ed., New York, 1864), which offers brief considerations of strategy despite the heavily tactical emphasis implied by the title; and Captain John Bigelow, *The Principles of Strategy Illustrated Mainly from American Campaigns* (New York and London, 1891; 2d ed., rev. and enl., Philadelphia, 1894; repr. New York, 1968). Among military memoirs before World War II, those most articulately developing their authors' strategic conceptions are not surprisingly those of Generals Ulysses S. Grant and William Tecumseh Sherman: *Personal Memoirs of U.S. Grant*, 2 vols. (New York, 1885-86), and *Memoirs of General William T. Sherman by Himself*, foreword by B. H. Liddell Hart, 2 vols. (New York, 1875; repr., 2 vols. in 1, Bloomington, 1957).

Historians' views of the evolution of American strategic thought have to be drawn largely from histories of particular wars; again, the emphasis has been on strategy in action. Only recently have American writers' histories of wars diverged from a preoccupation with tactics and operations to include considerations in depth of strategy and the conceptions shaping it. Dave Richard Palmer, *The Way of the Fox: American Strategy in the War for America, 1775-1783*, Contributions in Military History, no. 8 (Westport, Conn., and London, 1975) remains an almost unique effort to assess the history of an American war primarily from a strategic perspective. Indispensable on the strategy of the War of Independence although not mainly directed toward strategy is Douglas Southall Freeman, *George Washington: A Biography*, vol. 6, *Patriot and President*, and vol. 7, *First in Peace*, by John Alexander Carroll and Mary Wells Ashworth (New York, 1948-57).

Freeman's studies of Confederate leadership in the American Civil War also pioneered in raising American war history from tactical and operational details to strategic considerations, although Freeman often blurred strategy with other levels of the military art: Douglas Southall Freeman, *R. E. Lee: A Biography*, 4 vols. (New York, 1934) and *Lee's Lieutenants: A Study in Command*, 3 vols. (New York, 1942-44). The closest approximation to Freeman's command studies on the Union side is Kenneth P. Williams, *Lincoln Finds a General: A Military Study of the Civil War*, 5 vols. (New York, 1950-59). Except for Freeman's *Lee*, no biography of a Civil War military leader written by an American can rival in concern for the subject's strategic conceptions the British colonel George F. R. Henderson's *Stonewall Jackson and the American Civil War*, introduction by Field-Marshal [Garnet] Viscount Wolseley, 2 vols. (London and New York, 1898; 2 vols. in 1, New York, 1936).

Among innumerable histories of the Civil War, it is significant that the one devoting most attention to the strategy of the war is among the most recent: Herman Hattaway and Archer Jones, *How the North Won: A Military History of the Civil War* (Urbana, Chicago, and London, 1983). Archer Jones, outstanding among military historians of the United States for his knowledge of the entire history of armies and war, also contributed to a work that includes the best available study of the influence of European strategic thought on the military leaders of the Confederacy: Thomas Lawrence Connelly and Archer Jones, *The Politics of Command: Factions and Ideas in Confederate Strategy* (Baton Rouge, 1973).

A major reason for the paucity of American strategic studies in the nineteenth century was the need for American soldiers to concern themselves largely with their duties on the western frontier, which involved more peace-keeping constabulary work than war making. Therefore the Indian frontier diverted attention from strategy. To the extent that the Indian wars did pose strategic problems, a tendency of American soldiers to regard strategy as inseparable from the European tradition of warfare often strangely blinded them to the strategic dimensions of the issues before them. The best considerations of the relationship between the Indian frontier and American military thought are to be found in two of the works of Robert M. Utley: *Frontier Regulars: The United States Army and the Indian, 1866-1891* (New York and London, 1973), in The Macmillan Wars of the United States, Louis Morton, general editor; and "The Contribution of the Frontier to the American Military Tradition," in *The American Military on the Frontier: The Proceedings of the 7th Military History Symposium, United States Air Force Academy, 30 September-1 October 1976*, ed. James P. Tate (Washington, D.C., 1978), pp. 3-13.

On land, in contrast to the blossoming of American naval strategy, the emergence of the United States as a world power at the turn of the century did little to change the neglect of strategic study. The military element in the first projections of American power overseas was, naturally, for the most part an exertion of sea power, and the army played a comparatively minor role, largely an extension of its constabulary duties. Even the American experience of European land warfare in 1917-1918 did little immediately to stimulate a more vigorous American strategic thought, largely because national policy through the 1920s and much of the 1930s disavowed the prospect of any second large-scale military intervention in Europe. Nevertheless, by the third and fourth decades of the twentieth century a foreshadowing of the maturation of American strategic thought to come can be perceived in the curricular archives and in a few military writings. Particularly worth mentioning are Lieutenant Commander Holloway H. Frost's "National Strategy," United States Naval Institute *Proceedings*, 51 (August 1925), 1343-90, a remarkably wide-ranging and prescient essay by no means exclusively naval, and Colonel Oliver Prescott Robinson, *The Fundamentals of National Strategy* (Washington, D.C., 1928).

16. ALFRED THAYER MAHAN: THE NAVAL HISTORIAN

Mahan's published works fall conveniently into the following categories:

Naval histories: *The Gulf and Inland Waters* (New York, 1885); *The Influence of Sea Power upon History, 1660-1783* (Boston, 1890); *The Influence of Sea Power upon the French Revolution and Empire*, 2 vols. (Boston, 1892); *Sea Power in Its Relations to the War of 1812*, 2 vols. (Boston, 1905); and *The Major Operations of the Navies in the War of Independence* (Boston, 1913).

Current histories: *The Story of War in South Africa, 1899-1900* (London, 1900); and *The War in South Africa* (New York, 1900).

Biographical studies: *Admiral Farragut* (New York, 1897); *The Life of Nelson: The Embodiment of the Sea Power of Great Britain*, 2 vols. (Boston, 1897); and *Types of Naval Officers Drawn from the History of the British Navy* (Boston, 1901).

Autobiography: *From Sail to Steam: Recollections of Naval Life* (New York and London, 1907).

Devotional: *The Harvest Within: Thoughts on the Life of a Christian* (Boston, 1909).

Collections of essays and lectures: *The Interest of America in Sea Power, Present and Future* (Boston, 1897); *Lessons of the War with Spain and Other Articles* (Boston, 1899); *The Problem of Asia and Its Effects upon International Policies* (Boston, 1900); *Retrospect and Prospect: Studies in International Relations, Naval and Political* (Boston, 1902); *Some Neglected Aspects of War* (Boston, 1907); *Naval Administration and Warfare, Some General Principles with Other Essays* (Boston, 1908); *Naval Strategy, Compared with the Principles of Military Operations on Land* (Boston, 1911); and *Armaments and Arbitration, or the Place of Force in the International Relations of States* (New York and London, 1912).

A wealth of biographic and other pertinent data is to be found in Robert Seager II and Doris D. Maguire, eds., *Letters and Papers of Alfred Thayer Mahan*, 3 vols. (Annapolis, 1975). The full-length biographic studies of Mahan are, in order of publication, Charles Carlisle Taylor, *The Life of Admiral Mahan* (New York 1920); William D. Puleston, *Mahan: The Life and Work of Captain Alfred*

Thayer Mahan, USN (New Haven, 1939); Robert Seager II, *Alfred Thayer Mahan: The Man and His Letters* (Annapolis, 1977); and William E. Livezey, *Mahan on Sea Power* (Norman, Okla., 1981, rev. ed.). The first two are adulatory; the third critical and generally unsympathetic; the fourth favorable with reservations.

Essays and articles on the subject of Mahan and his work abound. The most useful are: James A. Field, "Admiral Mahan Speaks for Himself," *Naval War College Review* (Fall 1976); Kenneth J. Hagan, "Alfred Thayer Mahan: Turning America Back to the Sea," in *Makers of American Diplomacy*, ed. Frank J. Merli and Theodore A. Wilson, 2 vols. (New York, 1974), vol. 1, ch. 11; Julius W. Pratt, "Alfred Thayer Mahan," in *The Marcus W. Jernegan Essays in American Historiography*, ed. William T. Hutchinson (Chicago, 1937), ch. 11; William Reitzel, "Mahan on the Use of the Sea," *Naval War College Review* (May-June, 1973); and Margaret T. Sprout, "Mahan: Evangelist of Sea Power," *Makers of Modern Strategy*, ed. Edward Mead Earle (Princeton, 1943).

The founding and early years of the Naval War College are well covered in Ronald Spector, *Professors of War: The Naval War College and the Development of the Naval Profession* (Newport, R.I., 1977). Mahan's analysis of the role of sea power in the history of the British Empire is critically examined in Gerald S. Graham, *The Politics of Naval Supremacy: Studies in British Maritime Ascendancy* (Cambridge, 1965); and Paul M. Kennedy, *The Rise and Fall of British Naval Mastery* (New York, 1976). The influence of Mahan on American imperialism is treated, and overstated, in Julius Pratt, *Expansionists of 1898* (Baltimore, 1936); and Walter LaFeber, *The New Empire: An Interpretation of American Expansion, 1860-1898* (Ithaca and London, 1963). His role as navalist is thoroughly examined in Peter Karsten, *The Naval Aristocracy: The Golden Age of Annapolis and the Emergence of Modern Amerian Navalism* (New York, 1972).

17. THE POLITICAL LEADER AS STRATEGIST*

Defined in the wider sense, the issues of civil-military relations take up much of the literature of modern history. On the general problem of civilian leadership in wartime, Harvey A. DeWeerd's essay, "Churchill, Lloyd George, Clemenceau: The Emergence of the Civilian," in the original *Makers of Modern Strategy*, is still valuable. DeWeerd drew on such general works as Lewis Mumford, *Technics and Civilization* (New York, 1934) and Jesse D. Clarkson and Thomas C. Cochran, eds., *War as a Social Institution* (New York, 1941), a collection of essays that includes a discussion of civilian and modern war. Also of interest remains J. F. C. Fuller, *War and Western Civilization: A Study of War as a Political Instrument and the Expression of Mass Democracy* (London, 1932).

Since World War II, the number of studies on civil-military relations has grown enormously. Samuel P. Huntington's *The Soldier and the State: The Theory and Politics of Civil-Military Relations* (Cambridge, Mass., 1957) is a standard work. A recent book by Gordon A. Craig and Alexander L. George, *Force and*

* Prepared by Donald Abenheim.

Statecraft: The Diplomatic Revolution of Our Time (New York, 1982), contains a discussion of wartime leadership and civilians.

The Vietnam War produced many works on the subject, the best of which, despite its tendentiousness and lack of citation of sources, is David Halberstam, *The Best and the Brightest* (New York, 1972). Henry Kissinger's two volumes of memoirs, *White House Years* (Boston, 1979) and *Years of Upheaval* (Boston, 1982), should be consulted, as well as Seymour Hersh's answer to the secretary of state, *The Price of Power* (New York, 1983). A work with a military perspective on recent U.S. civilian leadership in war is the noteworthy study by Harry G. Summers, Jr., *On Strategy: A Critical Analysis of the Vietnam War* (Novato, Calif., 1982).

The literature on politics and strategy in the First World War is compendious, especially for Germany. For a general treatment of the problem of Theobald von Bethmann Hollweg and the military, see Gordon A. Craig, *The Politics of the Prussian Army* (New York, 1964). Indispensable are the works of Gerhard Ritter: *Der Schlieffenplan: Kritik eines Mythos* (Munich, 1956; Eng. trans. London, 1958), and volumes 3 and 4 of his major study, *Staatskunst und Kriegshandwerk* (Munich, 1954ff). Fritz Fischer, *Germany's Aims in the First World War* (New York, 1967) has had far-reaching effect. Konrad Jarausch has written a workmanlike biography of Bethmann, *The Enigmatic Chancellor: Bethmann-Hollweg and the Hubris of Imperial Germany* (New Haven, 1973). For a study of relations between Bethmann and the military, see Karl-Heinz Janssen, *Der Kanzler und der General: Die Führungskrise von Bethmann Hollweg and Falkenhayn* (Göttingen, 1967). Among the many memoirs of participants should be noted Erich von Falkenhayn, *Die Oberste Heeresleitung, 1914-1916* (Berlin, 1920).

Among the general studies on the British in the First World War are Ernest Llewellyn Woodward, *Great Britain and the War of 1914-1918* (New York, 1967); A. J. P. Taylor, *Politics in Wartime* (New York, 1965); and Peter Stansky, ed., *The Left and the War: The British Labor Party and World War One* (New York, 1969). For biographies of the principal wartime leadership, the following works should be consulted: J. A. Spender and Cyril Asquith, *The Life of Herbert Henry Asquith, Lord Oxford of Asquith* (London, 1932); Roy Jenkins, *Asquith* (London, 1978), which is the updated version of Jenkins's 1964 work, regarded as the best biography of Asquith; Magnus Philip, *Kitchener: Portrait of an Imperialist* (New York, 1959); Harold Nicolson, *George V, His Life and Times* (London, 1953); David Lloyd George, *War Memoirs* (London, 1933-37), now supplemented critically by Martin Gilbert, *Lloyd George* (Englewood Cliffs, N.J., 1968) and David R. Woodward, *Lloyd George and the Generals* (London, 1984). Martin Gilbert's works on Winston Churchill are of great value: *Winston Churchill: The Challenge of War* (Boston, 1971), the third volume of the biography supplemented by a companion volume of papers in two parts *Winston Churchill: Companion Volume III* (Boston, 1973). See also Lord Beaverbrook, *Politicians and the War* (London, 1968).

Of primary importance among the many accounts of French civilian leadership in the First World War is Georges Clemenceau, *Grandeurs et misères d'une victoire* (Paris, 1930). Pierre Renouvin, *The Forms of War Government in France*

(New Haven, 1927) and Geoffrey Bruun's short biography, *Clemenceau* (Cambridge, 1943) are still useful. Other works on Clemenceau include: Jere Clemens King, *Foch versus Clemenceau* (Cambridge, 1960); David Robins Watson, *Clemenceau—A Political Biography* (London, 1974); and Edgar Holt, *The Tiger* (London, 1976).

The literature on the problem of unified command and political leadership in the Second World War is too voluminous to allow more than a citation of some of the most useful books. For a general introduction to the German experience, see the appropriate chapters in Gordon A. Craig, *Germany, 1866-1945* (Oxford and New York, 1978). Almost every German general who attained authority and later wrote his memoirs had something to say about Adolf Hitler as a military leader. Among the most noteworthy are: Heinz Guderian, *Erinnerungen eines Soldaten* (Heidelberg, 1951); Franz Halder, *Kriegstagebuch: Tägliche Aufzeichnungen des Chefs des Generalstabs des Heeres, 1939-1942*, ed. Hans-Adolf Jacobsen, 3 vols. (Stuttgart, 1962-64); Adolf Heusinger, *Befehl im Widerstreit* (Tübingen, 1950); Erich von Manstein, *Verlorene Siege* (Bonn, 1955); Walter Warlimont, *Im Hauptquartier der deutschen Wehrmacht, 1939-45* (Frankfurt a.M., 1962). Also worth consulting are the war diaries of the German Supreme Command: *Kriegstagebücher des Oberkommandos der Wehrmacht*, ed. Percy E. Schramm, 4 vols. (Frankfurt a.M., 1961ff). Such general biographies of Hitler as Allan Bullock, *Hitler: A Study in Tyranny* (New York, 1964) and Joachim Fest, *Hitler: Eine Biographie* (Frankfurt a.M., 1973) contain much material. David Irving's controversial *Hitler's War* (New York, 1977) shows events from what might have been Hitler's perspective. Special studies on Hitler and the military abound and include such important books as Andreas Hillgruber, *Hitlers Strategie: Politik und Kriegführung, 1940-1941*, 2d ed. (Munich, 1982); Klaus-Jürgen Müller, *Das Heer und Hitler: Armee und NS Regime* (Stuttgart, 1969); Barry A. Leach, *German Strategy against Russia, 1939-1941* (Oxford, 1973) and *Das Deutsche Reich und der Zweite Weltkrieg*, ed. Militärgeschichtliches Forschungsamt (Stuttgart, 1979-   ).

On Churchill as a military leader, the volumes of his Second World War memoirs continue to be of value, especially: Winston S. Churchill, *The Grand Alliance* (Boston, 1950). Martin Gilbert, *Winston Churchill: Finest Hour, 1939-1941* (Boston, 1983) is indispensable. Other recent books on Churchill include: Ronald Lewin, *Churchill as Warlord* (New York, 1973) and R. W. Thompson, *Generalissimo Churchill* (New York, 1973). Excellent accounts of two leading British military figures are to be found in John Connell, *Wavell: Soldier and Statesman* (London, 1964) and David Fraser, *Alanbrooke* (London, 1982). The British official work, *History of the Second World War: United Kingdom Military Series*, ed. J. R. M. Butler (London, various dates) includes six volumes on strategy, of which J. R. M. Butler, *Grand Strategy, vol. 2, September 1939-June 1941* (London, 1957) is representaive.

American and British coalition warfare is the subject of a wide literature. For a fine example see Herbert Feis, *Churchill, Roosevelt, Stalin: The War They Waged and the Peace They Sought* (Princeton, 1957). Also excellent is *Roosevelt and Churchill: Their Secret Wartime Correspondence*, ed. Francis L. Loewenheim,

Harold D. Langley, and Manfred Jonas (New York, 1975). Subsequent efforts have not improved on this work. Robert Dallek, *Franklin D. Roosevelt and American Foreign Policy, 1932-1945* (New York, 1979) should also be consulted. There is unfortunately no definitive account of Roosevelt's accomplishments as a military leader. Nonetheless, see James MacGregor Burns, *Roosevelt: The Lion and the Fox* (New York, 1956) and his *Roosevelt: Soldier of Freedom* (New York, 1971).

The U.S. Army's official history of the war contains several outstanding volumes: Mark S. Watson, *Chief of Staff: Prewar Plans and Preparations* (Washington, D.C., 1950); Maurice Matloff and Edwin S. Snell, *Strategic Planning for Coalition Warfare, 1941-1942* (Washington, D.C., 1953); Maurice Matloff, *Strategic Planning for Coalition Warfare, 1943-44* (Washington, D.C., 1959); and Ray S. Cline, *Washington Command Post: The Operations Division* (Washington, D.C., 1951). Several of the memoirs and biographies of leading U.S. officials are important: Henry L. Stimson and McGeorge Bundy, *On Active Service in Peace and War* (New York, 1948); Forrest C. Pogue, *George C. Marshall: Organizer of Victory, 1943-1945* (New York, 1973); Stephen Ambrose, *The Supreme Commander: The War Years of Dwight David Eisenhower* (Baltimore, 1970). Also indispensable are *The Papers of Dwight David Eisenhower: The War Years*, ed. Alfred Chandler, Jr., 5 vols. (Baltimore, 1970).

18. MEN AGAINST FIRE: THE DOCTRINE OF THE OFFENSIVE IN 1914

The best and most easily available source for the evolution of tactical doctrine before 1914 is *The Journal of the Royal United Services Institution* (London, 1855–), which not only publishes the main contributions to the debate within the British army but summarizes the principal articles that appear in Continental periodicals and carries reviews of the literature, foreign as well as British. Wilhelm Balck, *Taktik* (Berlin, 1892) went through four editions, of which the last was translated into English (Fort Leavenworth, Kans., 1911). The changes in the successive editions reflect the development in tactical thinking during the critical period of the pre-1914 era, not only in the German but in all the principal European armies. Balck also gives details of the changing armament and equipment of these armies. Further such details, for the turn of the century, will be found in Jean de Bloch, *La guerre future*, 6 vols. (Paris, 1898). There are also Russian and German editions of this massive work, but a project for an English edition collapsed, and only the final volume, summarizing the arguments of the work, has been translated. It was published under the titles *Is War Now Impossible?* (London 1899) and *The Future of War* (Boston, 1899). The unabridged editions, however, contain many technical details not easily available elsewhere.

In the German army, Balck's work needs to be supplemented by the brilliant and heterodox works of Friedrich von Bernhardi, especially *Vom heutigen Kriege*, translated as *On War Today* (London, 1912). This is an interesting attempt to bring Clausewitz up to date to the twentieth century, and in addition to its many pertinent criticisms of Schlieffen and his teachings, it contains a great deal of shrewd tactical analysis. The most recent general account of the Germany army during this period is B. F. Schulte, *Die deutsche Armee 1900-1914: Zwischen Beharren und Veränderen* (Düsseldorf, 1977).

The confused state of theory and practice in the French army is well described by Douglas Porch, *The March to the Marne* (Cambridge and London, 1981) and Henri Contamine, *La revanche 1871-1914* (Paris, 1957). These put the lectures of Ferdinand Foch, *Des principes de la guerre* (Paris, 1903), translated as *The Principles of War* (New York, 1918), and of de Grandmaison, *Deux conférences faites aux officiers de l'état major de l'armée* (Paris, 1911) in perspective. Charles Ardent du Picq's *Études sur le combat* was posthumously published (Paris, 1903) and has been frequently reprinted. An English translation, *Battle Studies*, was published by the U.S. Army War College (Harrisburg, Penn., 1920; repr. 1946). The work has been well described by J. N. Cru as "l'oeuvre la plus forte, la plus vraie, la plus scientifique qui soit jamais venue d'une plume militaire française" (*Témoins* [Paris, 1929], 52). There is also a valuable article by Joseph C. Arnold, "French Tactical Doctrine 1870-1914" in *Military Affairs* 42, no. 2 (April 1978).

For the British army the best starting point is the seminal article by T. H. E. Travers, "Technology Tactics and Morale: Jean de Bloch, the Boer War and British Military Theory 1900-1914," *Journal of Modern History* 51, no. 2 (June 1979). G. F. R. Henderson, *The Science of War* (London, 1905) contains the main tactical studies by this writer between 1892 and 1905 and illustrates the impact made on the British army by the South African War of 1899-1902. E. A. Altham, *The Principles of War Historically Illustrated* (London, 1914) gives a clear account of the strategic and tactical thinking of the British general staff on the eve of the First World War. The polemic over national service between Earl Roberts, *A Nation in Arms* (London, 1907) and Sir Ian Hamilton, *Compulsory Service* (London, 1911) also provides good insight into professional military thought in Edwardian England. Robert Blake, ed., *The Private Papers of Sir Douglas Haig, 1914-1919* (London, 1952) carries the story into the war years. A Russian writer whose work may have had some influence was General Dragomirov. His *Course on Tactics* (1879) was translated both into French and German.

A recent study bearing directly on the topic of this essay is Jack Snyder, *The Cult of the Offensive in European War Planning, 1870-1914* (Ithaca, 1984).

The broader intellectual background to these ideas should also be studied, and there are excellent general surveys by Robert Wohl, *The Generation of 1914* (Cambridge, Mass., 1979) and Roland N. Stromberg, *Redemption by War: The Intellectuals and 1914* (Lawrence, Kans., 1982). For Britain in particular see Caroline Playne, *The Pre-War Mind in Britain* (London, 1928).

19. German Strategy in the Age of Machine Warfare, 1914-1945

The state of the literature on the German use of force during World War I is remarkably underdeveloped. Although the number of books and articles has been steadily increasing over the years, actual research has declined to near zero.

A notable exception is Helmut Otto, *Zur Militärstrategie des deutschen Imperialismus vor und während des ersten imperialistischen Weltkrieges* (Diss. B., Potsdam, 1977). Sober introductions, on the basis of the available literature, are provided by Peter Graf v. Kielmansegg, *Deutschland und der Erste Weltkrieg*, 2d ed. (Stuttgart, 1980) and by Helmut Otto and K. Schmiedel, *Der erste Weltkrieg: Militärhistorischer Abriss*, 4th ed., (Berlin/GDR, 1983), from a West and East German perspective respectively. A brief study on the strategic character of World War I by Walter Elze, *Das deutsche Heer von 1914 [and] Der strategische Aufbau des Weltkrieges 1914-1918* (repr. Osnabrück, 1968) is valuable, though biased. Keith Robbins, *The First World War* (Oxford and New York, 1984) is the latest attempt by an English author to write yet another book on the battles of World War I without any reference to German sources. One is well advised to forget this kind of study and to concentrate on B. H. Liddell Hart, *History of the First World War* (Boston, 1964), and J. F. C. Fuller, *The Conduct of War 1789-1961* (London, 1961) and his *Machine Warfare* (London, 1942), instead. Donald J. Goodspeed, *The German Wars 1914-1945* (Boston, 1977) and Trevor N. Dupuy, *A Genius for War: The German Army and General Staff, 1807-1945* (Englewood Cliffs, N.J., 1977) are examples of the widespread tendency to romanticize the German military experience.

The debate on grand strategy is still shaped by Fritz Fischer, *Griff nach der Weltmacht*, 3d ed. (Düsseldorf, 1964) which is discussed by John A. Moses, *The Politics of Illusion: The Fischer Controversy in German Historiography* (London, 1975). Lancelot L. Farrar, Jr., *Divide and Conquer: German Efforts to Conclude a Separate Peace, 1914-1918* (New York, 1978) sheds new light on the conduct of operations. Falkenhayn is discussed by Karl-Heinz Janssen, *Der Kanzler und der General* (Göttingen, 1967), but Ludendorff still awaits a professional biography despite a host of studies. Ludendorff's concept of war was put in perspective most recently by Hans-Ulrich Wehler, " 'Absoluter' und 'totaler' Krieg: Von Clausewitz zu Ludendorff," *Politische Vierteljahreszeitschrift* 10 (1969), 220-48. There is little on the German senior commanders, and it remains necessary to rely heavily on their memoirs. Isabel Hull, *The Entourage of Kaiser Wilhelm II, 1888-1918* (Cambridge, 1982) integrates biography with political and military history.

A good operational study is Norman Stone, *The Eastern Front, 1914-1917* (London and New York, 1975). Surprisingly, there is no similarly comprehensive analysis of any of the other fronts of the war. As a result one is forced to rely on the cumbersome *Der Weltkrieg 1914-1918: Die militärischen Operationen zu Lande*, ed. Reichsarchiv, 14 vols. (Berlin, 1925-44) and *Schlachten des Weltkrieges in Einzeldarstellungen*, ed. Reichsarchiv, 37 vols. (Oldenburg, 1921-1930), the German official histories with all the advantages and disadvantages of general staff historiography. The occasional paper by Michael Salewski, "Verdun und die Folgen: Eine militärische und geistesgeschichtliche Betrachtung," *Wehrwissenschaftliche Rundschau* 25 (1976), 89-96, is noteworthy. Tactics are analyzed by Timothy Lupfer, *The Dynamics of Doctrine: The Changes in German Tactical Doctrine during the First World War* (Fort Leavenworth, Kans., 1981).

910

Outstanding are Tony Ashworth, *Trench Warfare 1914-1918: The Live and Let Live System* (London, 1980) and Eric J. Leed, *No Man's Land: Combat and Identity in World War I* (New York, 1981). The most valuable study on offense and defense in World War I is still Erich Marcks, *Angriff und Verteidigung im Grossen Krieg* (Berlin, 1923).

The grand military-political treatments of the subject are Gerhard Ritter, *The Sword and the Scepter: The Problem of Militarism in Germany*, 4 vols. (Coral Gables, Fla., 1969-73), especially vol. 4, *The Reign of German Militarism and the Disaster of 1918*, and F. Klein et al., *Deutschland im Ersten Weltkrieg*, 3 vols. (Berlin, 1968-69). More limited is Martin Kitchen, *The Silent Dictatorship: The Politics of the German High Command under Hindenburg and Ludendorff, 1916-1918* (London and New York, 1976). The monumental compilation of documents by Wilhelm Deist, *Militär und Innenpolitik im Weltkrieg 1914-1918*, 2 vols. (Düsseldorf, 1970) is indispensable for any student of the period. On the peace movement during the war see Francis L. Carsten, *War against War: British and German Radical Movements in the First World War* (London, 1982).

Anyone who wants to study the nature of World War I will have to consult the seductive and tendentious essay "Die Weltkriege" in Friedrich G. Jünger, *Die Perfektion der Technik*, 5th ed. (Frankfurt, 1968) as well as Raymond Aron, *The Century of Total War* (Garden City, N.Y., 1954), and the sober assessment by Geoffrey Best, *Humanity in Warfare* (New York, 1980).

A study of the Reichswehr's problems must begin with Francis Carsten, *Reichswehr and Politics* (Oxford, 1966) and Harold J. Gordon, *The Reichswehr and the German Republic* (Princeton, 1957), who discuss Reichswehr politics from a liberal and a professional perspective respectively. Among German contributions are Rainer Wohlfeil and Hans Dollinger, eds., *Die deutsche Reichswehr: Bilder, Dokumente, Texte* (Frankfurt, 1972); Thilo Vogelsang, *Reichswehr, Staat und NSDAP* (Stuttgart, 1962); and Karl Nuss, *Militär und Wiederaufrüstung in der Weimarer Republick: Zur politischen Rolle und Entwicklung der Reichswehr* (Berlin/GDR, 1977), as well as the collections of documents edited by Heinz Hürten: *Die Anfänge der Ära Seeckt* (Düsseldorf, 1979), *Zwischen Revolution und Kapp-Putsch* (Düsseldorf, 1977), and *Das Krisenjahr 1923* (Düsseldorf, 1980). The essay by Hans Herzfeld, "Politik, Heer und Rüstung in der Zwischenkriegszeit: Ein Versuch," *Ausgewählte Aufsätze* (Berlin, 1962) should not be overlooked.

Hans Meier-Welcker, *Seeckt* (Frankfurt, 1967) is a monumental tribute to the first *Chef der Heeresleitung*. Peter Hayes, "A Question Mark with Epaulettes? Kurt v. Schleicher und Weimar Politics," *Journal of Modern History* 52 (1980) is the best study on Schleicher. There is no good biography on the most interesting figure, Wilhelm Groener. Dorothea Groener-Geyer, *General Groener: Soldat und Staatsmann* (Frankfurt, 1955) is a poor substitute. Wilhelm Deist, *The Wehrmacht and German Rearmament* (London, 1981) contains the best brief assessment. The group of "Young Turks" in the army is briefly discussed in Michael Geyer, *Aufrüstung oder Sicherheit: Reichswehr in der Krise der Machtpolitik 1924-1936* (Wiesbaden, 1980).

On operational and strategic problems consult Geyer, *Aufrüstung oder Sicherheit*, and especially Gaines Post, Jr., *The Civil-Military Fabric of Weimar Foreign Policy* (Princeton, 1973). On the political-economic context of strategy see Dorothea Fensch and Olaf Groehler, eds., "Imperialistische Ökonomie und militärische Strategie: Eine Denkschrift Wilhelm Groeners," *Zeitschrift für Geschichtswissenschaft* 19 (1971), 1167-77. On the navy see the definitive interpretations by Werner Rahn, *Reichsmarine und Landesverteidigung 1919-1928: Konzeption und Führung der Marine in der Weimarer Republik* (Munich, 1976) and Jost Dülffer, *Weimar, Hitler und die Marine: Reichspolitik und Flottenbau* (Düsseldorf, 1972), as well as A. Gemzell, *Organization, Conflict, and Innovation: A Study of German Naval Strategic Planning, 1888-1940* (Stockholm, 1973).

On security and disarmament/rearmament, see Michael Salewski, *Entwaffnung und Militärkontrolle in Deutschland 1919 bis 1927* (Munich, 1966); idem, "Zur deutschen Sicherheitspolitik in der Spätphase der Weimarer Republik," *Vierteljahrshefte für Zeitgeschichte* 21 (1974), 121-47; Marshall M. Lee, "Disarmament and Security: The German Security Proposals in the League of Nations, 1926-1930: A Study of Revisionist Aims in an International Organization," *Militärgeschichtliche Mitteilungen* 25 (1979), 7-34; and especially Edward W. Bennett, *German Rearmament and the West, 1932-1933* (Princeton, 1979). Alternative approaches to German security (as opposed to German diplomacy, which is discussed by Jon Jacobson, *Locarno Diplomacy: Germany and the West, 1925-1929* [Princeton, 1972]) still need careful exploration. A useful start is Karl Holl and Wolfram Wette, eds., *Pazifismus in der Weimarer Republik: Beiträge zur historischen Friedensforschung* (Paderborn, 1981), but Leo Gross, *Pazifismus und Imperialismus: Eine kritische Untersuchung ihrer theoretischen Begründung* (Leipzig, 1931) remains the magnum opus. On the debates and options of the German government see Josef Becker and Klaus Hildebrand, eds., *Internationale Beziehungen in der Weltwirtschaftskrise 1929-1933* (Munich, 1980).

Strategy and operations during the Second World War are a very wide field indeed. It is useful to begin with Gordon Wright, *The Ordeal of Total War* (New York, 1968) and the two excellent German surveys, *Das Deutsche Reich und der Zweite Weltkrieg*, ed. Militärgeschichtliches Forschungsamt, 10 vols. (Stuttgart, 1979ff) and *Deutschland im Zweiten Weltkrieg*, ed. Gerhart Haas et al., 6 vols. (Berlin/GDR, 1974ff), which combine encyclopedic treatment with painstaking research. Hans-Adolf Jacobsen, *Zur Konzeption einer Geschichte des Zweiten Weltkrieges 1939-1945* (Frankfurt, 1964) and idem, *Der Zweite Weltkrieg: Grundzüge der Politik und Strategie in Dokumenten* (Frankfurt, 1965), as well as idem and Arthur L. Smith, eds., *World War II, Policy and Strategy: Selected Documents with Commentary* (Santa Barbara, 1979) place German strategy in the context of world political developments. Andreas Hillgruber, *Hitlers Strategie: Politik und Kriegführung 1940-1941*, 2d ed. (Munich, 1982) is by far the most incisive study of German strategy. His *Der Zweite Weltkrieg*, 2d ed. (Stuttgart, 1982) is a useful survey and his "Die 'Endlösung' und das deutsche Ostimperium als Kernstück des rassenideologischen Programms des

912

Nationalsozialismus," in *Hitler, Deutschland und die Mächte*, 2d ed., ed. M. Funke (Düsseldorf, 1978), 94-115, is a seminal essay on the combination of military and ideological war. A useful chronology is provided by Andreas Hillgruber and Gerhard Hümmelchen, *Chronik des Zweiten Weltkrieges*, rev. ed. (Königstein/Ts., 1978). Of the older literature Walter Görlitz, *Der Zweite Weltkrieg*, 2 vols. (Stuttgart, 1951-52) and Kurt von Tippelskirch, *Geschichte des Zweiten Weltkrieges* (Bonn, 1954) are worth mentioning.

The most important studies on war aims are Norman Rich, *Hitler's War Aims*, 2 vols. (New York, 1973-74) and the challenging recent work of Ludolf Herbst, *Der totale Krieg und die Ordnung der Wirtschaft: Die Kriegswirtschaft im Spannungsfeld von Politik, Ideologie und Propaganda 1939-1945* (Stuttgart, 1982). Wolfgang Schumann and Dietrich Eichholtz, eds., *Anatomie des Krieges: Neue Dokumente über die Rolle des deutschen Monopolkapitals bei der Vorbereitung und Durchführung des Zweiten Weltkrieges* (Berlin/GDR, 1969) and Gerhart Hass and Wolfgang Schumann, *Anatomie der Aggression: Neue Dokumente zu den Kriegszielen des faschistischen Imperialismus im Zweiten Weltkrieg* (Berlin/GDR, 1972) outline the same problem from an orthodox Marxist perspective. Eberhard Jäckel, *Hitler's World View* (Cambridge, Mass., 1981) outlines Hitler's perspectives on the war. Klaus Hildebrand, *Deutsche Aussenpolitik: Kalkül oder Dogma* (Stuttgart, 1971) is the best short summary on diplomacy between 1933 and 1945.

Blitzkrieg has received inordinate attention. The basic studies are by Alan S. Milward, *The German Economy at War* (London, 1965); Gerhard Förster, *Totaler Krieg und Blitzkrieg* (Berlin/GDR, 1967); Charles Messenger, *The Art of Blitzkrieg* (London, 1967); and as a corrective Matthew Cooper, *The German Army 1933-1945: Its Political and Military Failures* (London, 1978).

Among the indispensable documents for the study of the war are the *Kriegstagebücher des Oberkommandos der Wehrmacht*, ed. Percy E. Schramm et al., 4 vols. (Frankfurt, 1969); Franz Halder, *Tägliche Aufzeichnungen des Chefs des Generalstabs des Heeres 1939-1942* [Kriegstagebuch], ed. Arbeitskreis für Wehrforschung, 3 vols. (Stuttgart, 1962-64); and Walther Hubatsch, ed., *Hitlers Weisungen für die Kriegführung* (Frankfurt, 1962). For the navy see Michael Salewski, *Die deutsche Seekriegsleitung 1935-1945*, 3 vols. (Frankfurt, 1970-75), especially vol. 3, and Gerhard Wagner, ed., *Lagevorträge des Oberbefehlshabers der Kriegsmarine vor Hitler 1939 bis 1945* (Munich, 1972).

The abundance of operational studies on any conceivable aspect of the war contrasts with the lack of studies on the overall character of World War II. Basic treatments are Hans-Adolf Jacobsen and Jürgen Rohwer, eds., *Decisive Battles of World War II: The German View* (New York, 1965), Larry H. Addington, *The Blitzkrieg Era and the German General Staff, 1865-1941* (New Brunswick, N.J., 1971), and Cooper, *The German Army*, despite Cooper's fascination with armored warfare.

For the campaigns between 1938 and 1940 see Williamson Murray, *The Change in the European Balance of Power, 1938-1939: The Path to Ruin* (Princeton, 1984). More specific studies are Robert M. Kennedy, *The German Campaign in Poland* (Washington, D.C., 1956); Hans-Adolf Jacobsen, *Fall Gelb: Der Kampf um den deutschen Operationsplan bis zur Westoffensive 1940* (Wiesbaden, 1957); idem, *Dokumente zur Vorgeschichte des Westfeldzuges 1939-1940* (Göttingen, 1956); idem, *Dokumente zum Westfeldzug 1940* (Göttingen, 1960); and R. H. S. Stolfi, "Reality and Myth: French and German Preparations for War, 1933-1940" (Ph.D. diss., Stanford Univ., 1966). For the campaign against Great Britain, see Ronald Wheatley, *Operation Sea Lion* (Oxford, 1958); K. Klee, *Das Unternehmen 'Seelöwe.' Die geplante deutsche Landung in England* (Göttingen, 1958); idem, *Dokumente zum Unternehmen 'Seelöwe'* (Göttingen, 1953); Walter Ansel, *Hitler Confronts England* (Durham, N.C., 1960); Telford Taylor, *The March of Conquest* (New York, 1958); and idem, *The Breaking Wave* (New York, 1967).

The events in the Balkan theater are discussed by Martin Van Creveld, *Hitler's Strategy 1940-1941: The Balkan Clue* (Cambridge, 1974); Klaus Olshausen, *Zwischenspiel auf dem Balkan: Die deutsche Politik gegenüber Jugoslawien und Griechenland vom Mai bis Juli 1941* (Stuttgart, 1973); and Paul N. Hehn, *The German Struggle against Yugoslav Guerrillas in World War II: German Counterinsurgency in Yugoslavaia 1941-1943* (New York, 1979). For the Mediterranean, see Gerhard Schreiber, "Der Mittelmeeraum in Hitlers Strategie: 'Programm' und militärische Planung," *Militärgeschichtliche Mitteilungen* 28 (1980), 69-99, the third volume of *Das Deutsche Reich und der Zweite Weltkrieg*, and Josef Schröder, *Italiens Kriegsaustritt 1943* (Göttingen, 1969). For the North African theater, see Charles B. Burdick, *Unternehmen Sonnenblume: Der Entschluss zum Afrika-Feldzug* (Vowickel, 1972); Waldis Greiselis, *Das Ringen um den Brückenkopf Tunesien 1942/43* (Frankfurt, 1976); and the small operational study by A. von Taysen, *Tobruk 1941* (Freiburg, 1976).

It is altogether appropriate that the war against the Soviet Union has attracted the most attention. Albert Seaton, *The Russo-German War 1941-1945* (London, 1971), Alexander Werth, *Russia at War, 1941-1945* (New York, 1964), and Earl F. Ziemke, *Stalingrad to Berlin: The German Defeat in the East* (Washington, D.C., 1968) are excellent introductions. In addition the fourth volume of *Das Deutsche Reich und der Zweite Weltkrieg, Der Angriff auf die Sowjetunion*, ed. Horst Boog et al. (Stuttgart, 1983) is indispensable. Among the more specialized studies, one may want to consult A. Beer, *Der Fall Barbarossa* (Diss. phil., Münster, 1978); F. P. ten Korte, *De Duitse aanval of de Sovjet-Unie en 1941*, 2 vols. (Groningen, 1968); Barry Leach, *German Strategy against Russia, 1939-1941* (Oxford, 1973); Klaus Reinhardt, *Die Wende vor Moskau: Das Scheitern der Strategie Hitlers im Winter 1941/42* (Stuttgart, 1972); Albert Seaton, *The Battle for Moscow, 1941-1942* (London, 1971); Earl F. Ziemke, *The German Northern Theater of Operations, 1940-1945* (Washington, D.C., 1959); Manfred Kehrig, *Stalingrat* (Stuttgart, 1974); Ernst Klink, *Das Gesetz des Handelns: Die Operation 'Zitadelle,' 1943* (Stuttgart, 1966); Wolfgang Wünsche, *Die Entschlussfassung der obersten politischen und militärischen Führung des faschistischen Deutschland für die Sommeroffensive der Wehrmacht an der sowjetischdeutschen Front 1943* (Diss. A., Dresden, 1975); Hans Meier-Welcker, ed., *Ab-*

914

wehrkämpfe am Nordflügel der Ostfront 1944-45 (Stuttgart, 1963); and Heinz Magenheimer, *Abwehrschlact an der Weichsel 1945* (Freiburg, 1976).

Albert Seaton, *The Fall of Fortress Europe, 1943-1945* (London, 1981) provides a comprehensive picture of the last two years of the war. He also covers the western theater of war, which is less well studied than the eastern. Basic studies are Hans Speidel, *Invasion 1944* (Tübingen, 1944); Alan Wilt, *The Atlantic Wall: Hitler's Defenses in the West 1941-1945* (Ames, 1971); John Keegan, *Six Armies in Normandy: From D-Day to the Liberation of Paris, June 6th-August 25th, 1944* (London, 1964); and Hermann Jung, *Die Ardennen-Offensive 1944/45* (Göttingen, 1971).

Lavish attention has been given to tank warfare, but it suffices to point to Walther Nehring, *Die Geschichte der deutscher Panzerwaffe 1916 bis 1945* (Berlin, 1968) and Friedrich Wilhelm von Mellenthin, *Panzer Battles* (London, 1955). For the *Luftwaffe* and navy consult Williamson Murray, *Strategy for Defeat: The Luftwaffe, 1933-1945* (Maxwell Air Force Base, Ala., 1983); Richard J. Overy, *The Air War, 1939-1945* (New York, 1981); Michael Salewski, *Die deutsche Seekriegsleitung 1935-1945*, 3 vols. (Frankfurt, 1970-75); and Friedrich Ruge, *Der Seekrieg 1939 bis 1945*, 3d ed. (Stuttgart, 1962). On the Waffen SS, see George H. Stein, *The Waffen-SS: Hitler's Elite Guard at War, 1939-1945* (Ithaca, N.Y., 1966); B. Wegner, *Hitlers politische Soldaten: Die Waffen-SS 1933-1945* (Paderborn, 1982); and Richard Koehl, *The Black Corps: The Structure and Power Struggles of the Nazi SS* (Madison, 1983).

On military-political relations, Manfred Messerschmidt, *Die Wehrmacht im NS-Staat: Zeit der Indoktrination* (Hamburg, 1969), Klaus-Jürgen Müller, *Das Heer und Hitler: Armee und nationalsozialistisches Regime 1933-1940* (Stuttgart, 1969), and Robert J. O'Neill, *The German Army and the Nazi Party, 1933-1939* (London, 1966) set very high standards. A comprehensive treatment of the relations between the army and the National Socialist regime during the war has yet to be written.

Surveying the whole period once more one may want to go back to Gordon A. Craig, *The Politics of the Prussian Army* (New York, 1964) and Herbert Rosinski, *The German Army* (New York, 1966).

20. LIDDELL HART AND DE GAULLE: THE DOCTRINES OF LIMITED LIABILITY AND MOBILE DEFENSE

The most comprehensive account of the evolution of British strategy between the world wars is Norman Gibbs' official history, *Grand Strategy*, vol. 1 (London, 1976). Michael Howard provides a scintillating survey of Britain's strategic dilemmas in the twentieth century in *The Continental Commitment* (London, 1972). Basil H. Liddell Hart's *Memoirs*, 2 vols. (London, 1965) must be read with caution because of their pervasive tone of self-justification and their excessively critical view of Britain's military leaders, but they nevertheless excel in conveying the character of the army between the wars. Brian Bond, *Liddell Hart: A Study of His Military Thought* (London and New Brunswick, N.J., 1977), the only full-length account of its subject to date, devotes three chapters to a critical analysis of Liddell Hart's ideas in the 1920s and 1930s. The obituary essay on Liddell Hart reprinted in Michael Howard, *The Causes of Wars* (London, 1983; 2d ed. Cambridge, Mass., 1984), points out the confusion in his thinking about the Continental commitment. Jay Luvaas's chapters on Fuller and Liddell Hart in *The Education of an Army* (London, 1965) still constitute a stimulating introduction to both writers, though whether either succeeded in "educating the army" remains open to question. Anthony Trythall, *'Boney' Fuller* (London, 1977) is a sound biography based on its subject's surviving papers, which unfortunately are sparse in comparison with Liddell Hart's. A lively account of Fuller and other British advocates of mechanization is Kenneth Macksey, *The Tank Pioneers* (London, 1981). An excellent summary of the literature on German military planning in 1939-1940 is contained in John J. Mearsheimer, *Conventional Deterrence* (Ithaca, 1983). Among the more important military memoirs and military biographies are Brian Bond, ed., *Chief of Staff: The Diaries of Lt. Gen. Sir Henry Pownall*, vol. 1 (London, 1972); Roderick Macleod and Denis Kelly, eds., *The Ironside Diaries, 1937-1940* (London, 1962); R. J. Minney, *The Private Papers of Hore-Belisha* (London, 1960); and John Colville, *Man of Valour: Field Marshal Lord Gort VC* (London, 1972). Two other books that deserve mention for the light they throw on the making of British military policy are Peter Dennis, *Decision By Default* (London, 1972), and George Peden, *British Rearmament and the Treasury, 1932-1939* (Edinburgh, 1978).

No single volume yet documents the interwar development of French strategy. Jere King, *Foch versus Clemenceau: France and German Dismemberment 1918-1919* (Cambridge, Mass., 1960) outlines the origins of the dilemmas of the 1920s and early 1930s. The issues are more closely explored in Judith M. Hughes, *To the Maginot Line: The Politics of French Military Preparation in the 1920s* (Cambridge, Mass., 1971), and Paul-Emile Tournoux, *Défense des frontières: Haut commandement, gouvernement, 1919-1939* (Paris, 1960). Relations between the officers and civilian authorities are illuminated by Philip C. F. Bankwitz, *Maxime Weygand and Civil-Military Relations in Modern France* (Cambridge, Mass., 1967) and are investigated further in Paul-Marie de la Gorce, *La République et son armée* (Paris, 1963), and in Jacques Nobécourt's *Une histoire politique de l'armée, vol. 1, De Pétain à Pétain, 1919-1942* (Paris, 1967). The French army's technical evolution in these years is best examined through François-André Paoli, *L'Armée Française de 1919 à 1939*, 4 vols. (Vincennes, 1970-77), completed by Henry Dutailly, *Les problèmes de l'armée de terre française, 1935-1939* (Vincennes, 1981). Conflicts over mechanization and doctrine are clearly analyzed and set in perspective by Jeffrey Clarke, *Military Technology in Republican France: The Evolution of the French Armored Force, 1917-1940* (Ann Arbor, 1970), and Ladislas Mysyrowicz, *Autopsie d'une défaite* (Lausanne, 1973). De Gaulle's own recommendations emerge from the first volume of his *Mémoires de guerre* (Paris, 1954), but may be best consulted in their original form through his *Le fil de l'epée, Vers l'armée de métier, La France et son armée*, and *Trois études*, the last incorporating his prophetic "Mémorandum du 26

916

janvier 1940," (Paris, 1932, 1934, 1938, and 1945, respectively). Additional significant evidence about his thinking appears in his collected *Lettres, notes et carnets, vol. 2, 1919-juin 1940* (Paris, 1980), and in his correspondence with Reynaud in the 1930s published as appendices in Evelyne Demey, *Paul Reynaud, mon père* (Paris, 1980). Reynaud's *Le problème militaire français* (Paris, 1937) is another important source, but his subsequent memoir, *La France a sauvé l'Europe* (Paris, 1947), contains an over-dramatized and tendentious account of his and de Gaulle's disputes with the military establishment and should be read with caution. Studies of the formulation and reception of de Gaulle's ideas extend from Lucien Nachin's almost hagiographical *Charles de Gaulle: Général de France* (Paris, 1944), to the more investigative Arthur Robertson, *La doctrine de guerre du Général de Gaulle*, Jean-Raymond Tournoux, *Pétain et De Gaulle* and Paul Huard's *Le Colonel de Gaulle et ses blindés* (Paris, 1959, 1964, 1980 respectively). De Gaulle's biographers also consider his influence on military thought. Examples include Brian Crozier, *De Gaulle: The Warrior* (London, 1967); Bernard Ledwidge, *De Gaulle* (London, 1982); and Don Cook, *Charles de Gaulle* (London, 1984). Further light is shed in recollections by junior officers who knew the young de Gaulle at the Ecole de Guerre, such as André Laffargue, *Fantassin de Gascogne* (Paris, 1962) and Georges Loustaunau-Lacau, *Mémoires d'un français rebelle, 1914-1948* (Paris, 1948). Orthodox soldiers' views may be gauged through the principal memoirs and biographies, notably Maxime Weygand, *Mémoires*, 3 vols. (Paris, 1950-57); Maurice Gamelin, *Servir*, 3 vols. (Paris, 1946-47); Alfred Conquet, *Auprès du Maréchal Pétain: Le chef, le politique, l'homme* (Paris, 1970); Marie-Eugène Debeney, *La guerre et les hommes* (Paris, 1937); Richard Griffiths, *Marshal Pétain* (London, 1970); Herbert Lottman, *Pétain* (New York, 1983); and Pierre Le Goyet, *Le mystère Gamelin* (Paris, 1975). The rationales for careful modernization rather than wholesale and disruptive change also emerge from J. Duval, *Les leçons de la guerre d'Espagne* (Paris, 1938); Jeffery Gunsburg, *Divided and Conquered: The French High Command and the Defeat of the West, 1940* (Westport, Conn., 1979); and from essays by Gunsburg, Jean Delmas, and Gilbert Bodinier in the *Revue Historique des Armées*, no. 4 (1979). Finally, the diplomatic and economic context of the debate over de Gaulle's proposals may be understood through Jean-Baptiste Duroselle, *La décadence, 1932-1939* (Paris, 1979); Robert Frrankenstein's *Le prix du réarmement français, 1935-1939* (Paris, 1982); and Robert Young, *In Command of France: French Foreign Policy and Military Planning, 1933-1940* (Cambridge, Mass., 1978).

21. VOICES FROM THE CENTRAL BLUE: THE AIR POWER THEORISTS

Among general works treating the history of military aviation are the following: Robin Higham, *Air Power: A Concise History* (New York, 1972); Basil Collier, *A History of Air Power* (New York, 1974); Charles H. Gibbs-Smith, *Aviation: An Historical Survey from Its Origins to the End of World War II*

(London, 1970) and *Flight Through the Ages* (New York, 1974); Alfred F. Hurley and Robert C. Ehrhart, eds., *Air Power and Warfare* (Washington, D.C., 1979); Eugene M. Emme, ed., *The Impact of Air Power* (New York, 1959) and *Two Hundred Years of Flight in America* (San Diego, 1977); Howard S. Wolko, *In the Cause of Flight: Technologists of Aeronautics and Astronautics* (Washington, D.C., 1981); John W. R. Taylor and Kenneth Munson, *History of Aviation* (New York, 1978); Roger E. Bilstein, *Flight in America, 1900-1983: From the Wright Brothers to the Astronauts* (Baltimore, 1984); and Robert F. Futrell, *Ideas, Concepts, Doctrine: A History of Basic Thinking in the United States Air Force, 1907-1964* (Maxwell Air Force Base, Ala., 1971). At this writing, Professor Futrell has completed the first draft of his follow-on volume covering the years 1965 through 1980. An excellent recent bibliography is Richard P. Hallion, *The Literature of Aeronautics, Astronautics, and Air Power* (Washington, D.C., 1984). For a valuable set of thirteen bibliographical essays treating "Aviation History: The State of the Art," see the thirtieth anniversary issue of *Aerospace Historian* 31, no. 1 (March 1984).

For the prehistory of manned flight, see Beril Becker, *Dreams and Realities of the Conquest of the Skies* (New York, 1967) and Clive Hart, *The Dream of Flight: Aeronautics from Classical Times to the Renaissance* (New York, 1972). Shorter accounts appear in the opening chapters of M. J. Bernard Davy, *Air Power and Civilization* (London, 1941) and Collier, *History of Air Power*. For nineteenth- and early twentieth-century developments prior to World War I, see the sources cited on pages 10-12 of Hallion's bibliography.

The basic history of British military aviation in World War I is Walter Raleigh and H. A. Jones, *The War in the Air*, 7 vols. (London, 1922-37). For the German bombing raids against England, see Raymond H. Fredette, *The Sky on Fire* (New York, 1966). For the operations of the Independent Force, see Raleigh and Jones, *The War in the Air*, 6:118-74, and Alan Morris, *First of the Many: The Story of the Independent Force, RAF* (London, 1968). Also helpful are Neville Jones, *The Origins of Strategic Bombing* (London, 1973) and Lee Kennett, *A History of Strategic Bombing* (New York, 1982). Other important works treating aviation in World War I include: M. Maurer, ed., *The U. S. Air Service in World War I*, 4 vols. (Washington, D.C., 1978-79); I. B. Holley, Jr., *Ideas and Weapons* (New Haven, 1953; repr. Hamden, Conn., 1971, and Washington, D.C., 1983); James J. Hudson, *Hostile Skies* (Syracuse, 1968); Aaron Norman, *The Great Air War* (New York, 1968); Alan Clark, *Aces High: The War in the Air over the Western Front* (New York, 1973); John R. Cuneo, *The Air Weapon, 1914-1916* (Harrisburg, 1947); John H. Morrow, Jr., *German Air Power in World War I* (Lincoln, Nebr., 1982); George van Deurs, *Wings for the Fleet: A Narrative of Naval Aviation's Early Development, 1910-1916* (Annapolis, 1966); Douglas Robinson, *The Zeppelin in Combat: A History of the German Naval Airship Division, 1912-1918* (Seattle, 1980); Richard P. Hallion, *Rise of the Fighters: Air Combat in World War I* (Annapolis, 1984); Denis Winter, *The First of the Few: Fighter Pilots of the First World War* (Athens, Ga., 1983); Pierre Lissarague and Charles Christienne, eds., *Histoire de l'aviation militaire française* (Paris, 1980; English

918

translation forthcoming from the Smithsonian Institution Press); and Sydney F. Wise, *Canadian Airmen in the First World War* (Toronto, 1980). For other sources in various languages see the essays in *Aerospace Historian* 31, no. 1 (March 1984) and in Kennett, *History of Strategic Bombing*, 204-205. For a thorough compilation of English-language sources, see Myron J. Smith, Jr., *World War I in the Air: A Bibliography and Chronology* (Metuchen, N.J., 1977).

For the best sources on aviation developments between the wars, see pp. 16-24 of Richard Hallion's bibliography cited above. The Italian and French sources for Douhet are listed in *Makers of Modern Strategy*, ed. Edward Mead Earle (Princeton, 1943), 546. The standard English translation is by Dino Ferrari, *The Command of the Air* (New York, 1942; repr. Washington, D.C., 1983). This volume includes *The Command of the Air* (c. 1921; rev. ed. 1927); a 1928 monograph; a 1929 article from *Revista Aeronautica*; and Douhet's long essay on "The War of 19—," which originally appeared in *Revista Aeronautica* (March 1930), 409-502. Other English language sources on Douhet are cited in the notes to Bernard Brodie's chapter on "The Heritage of Douhet," in his *Strategy in the Missile Age* (Princeton, 1959) and in the notes to the editors' introduction to the 1983 reprinting of *Command of the Air*. To these should be added Frank J. Cappeluti, "The Life and Thought of Guilio Douhet" (Ph.D. diss., Rutgers University, 1967).

Mitchell's most important published writings were probably his numerous magazine articles, most of which are listed in Library of Congress, *A List of References on Brigadier General William Mitchell 1879-1936* (Washington, D.C., 1942). His books included *Our Air Force: The Keystone of National Defense* (New York, 1921), *Winged Defense: The Development and Possibilities of Modern Air Power—Economic and Military* (New York, 1925), and *Skyways* (London and Philadelphia, 1930). The only reliable biography of Mitchell is Alfred F. Hurley, *Billy Mitchell: Crusader for Air Power* (New York, 1964; new ed., Bloomington, 1975), which concentrates on his ideas rather than his exploits. On Trenchard, whose personality counted for more than his ideas, see Andrew Boyle, *Trenchard* (London, 1962). For this period Noble Frankland, *The Bombing Offensive against Germany: Outlines and Perspectives* (London, 1965) says much in few words. The most relevant contemporary book on the RAF stance was John Slessor, *Air Power and Armies* (London, 1936). Slessor remained until the 1960s the RAF's most eloquent theorist; see, for examples, his *Strategy for the West* (New York, 1954), *The Central Blue* (London, 1956), and *The Great Deterrent* (London, 1957). On bombers and politics, see Uri Bialer, *The Shadow of the Bomber: The Fear of Air Attack and British Politics, 1932-1939* (London, 1980).

Important sources for theoretical developments in the United States between the wars include: Futrell, *Ideas, Concepts, Doctrine;* Haywood S. Hansell, Jr., *The Air Plan That Defeated Hitler* (Atlanta, 1972); Robert T. Finney, *History of the Air Corps Tactical School, 1920-1940*, and Thomas H. Greer, *The Development of Air Doctrine in the Army Air Arm, 1917-1941* (both Maxwell Air Force Base, Ala., 1955); Charles M. Melhorn, *Two Block Fox: The Rise of the*

Aircraft Carrier, 1911-1929 (Annapolis, 1974); John F. Shiner, *Foulois and the U.S. Army Air Corps, 1931-1935* (Washington, D.C., 1983); and DeWitt S. Copp, *A Few Great Captains: The Men and Events That Shaped the Development of U. S. Air Power* (Garden City, N.Y., 1980).

For a recent critique of both British and American prewar theory and doctrine, see Williamson Murray, "The Prewar Development of British and American Air Power Doctrine," appendix 1 to his *Strategy for Defeat: The Luftwaffe, 1933-1945* (Maxwell Air Force Base, Ala., 1983), 321-39. For the American portion, Murray leans heavily on the perceptive insights of Thomas A. Fabyanic, "A Critique of U.S. Air War Planning, 1941-1944" (Ph.D. diss., St. Louis University, 1973). For Japan between the wars, see Alvin D. Coox, "The Rise and Fall of the Imperial Japanese Air Forces," in *Air Power and Modern Warfare*, ed. A. F. Hurley and R. C. Ehrhart, pp. 84-97 and the sources cited therein; also, Roger Pineau, "Admiral Isoroku Yamamoto," in *The War Lords*, ed. Michael Carver (Boston, 1976), 390-403. For naval aviation in general, with emphasis on the United States, see Clark G. Reynolds, "Writing on Naval Flying," *Aerospace Historian* 31, no. 1 (March 1984), 21-29. For the *Luftwaffe*, see Horst Boog, "Germanic Air Forces and the Historiography of the Air War," *Aerospace Historian* 31, no. 1 (March 1984), 38-42, and his "Higher Command and Leadership in the German Luftwaffe, 1935-1945," *Air Power and Modern Warfare*, ed. Hurley and Ehrhart. Cf. Murray, *Strategy for Defeat*; Edward L. Homze, *Arming the Luftwaffe* (Lincoln, Nebr., 1976); and Raymond L. Proctor, *Hitler's Luftwaffe in the Spanish Civil War* (Westport, Conn., 1983). A model study of a long-neglected topic, crucial to understanding air capabilities on the eve of World War II, is Monte Duane Wright, *Most Probable Position: A History of Aerial Navigation to 1941* (Lawrence, Kans., 1972).

The literature on air power in World War II is so extensive that the most thorough bibliography yet attempted, of English-language sources alone, runs to five thick volumes; see Myron J. Smith, Jr., *Air War Bibliography, 1939-1945*, 5 vols. (Manhattan, Kans., 1977-82). Basic starting points are the official histories: for the U.S. Army Air Forces as a whole, Wesley Frank Craven and James Lea Cate, eds., *The Army Air Forces in World War II*, 7 vols. (Chicago, 1948-58); for RAF Bomber Command, Sir Charles Webster and Noble Frankland, *The Strategic Air Offensive against Germany*, 4 vols. (London, 1961). For important works published up to 1975, see the bibliography and notes to my *Strategic Bombing in World War II* (New York and London, 1976). Among the most important contributions since then that have not yet been cited in this note are: Thomas M. Coffey, *Decision over Schweinfurt: The U.S. 8th Air Force Battle for Daylight Bombing* (New York, 1977); Max Hastings, *Bomber Command: The Myths and Realities of the Strategic Bombing Offensive, 1939-1945* (London and New York, 1979); Wilbur H. Morrison, *Point of No Return* (New York, 1979) and *Fortress Without a Roof* (New York, 1982); Haywood S. Hansell, Jr., *Strategic Air War against Japan* (Maxwell Air Force Base, Ala., 1980); Richard J. Overy, *The Air War, 1939-1945* (New York, 1981), which is unquestionably the most comprehensive single-volume history of the air war as a whole; W. W.

Rostow, *Pre-invasion Bombing Strategy* (Austin, 1981); De Witt S. Copp, *Forged in Fire* (New York, 1982); James C. Gaston, *Planning the American Air War* (Washington, D.C., 1982); and Richard H. Kohn and Joseph P. Harahan, eds., *Air Superiority in World War II and Korea* (Washington, D.C., 1983).

Clark G. Reynolds, *The Fast Carriers* (New York, 1968) remains the best treatment of its topic, but see also William J. Armstrong and Clarke Van Fleet, *United States Naval Aviation, 1910-1980*, 3d ed. (Washington, D.C., 1981) and Robert L. Sherrod, *History of United States Marine Corps Aviation in World War II*, new ed. (San Rafael, Calif., 1980). Among the best first-person accounts that have appeared in recent years are: Edwards Park, *Nanette* (New York, 1977); Philip Ardery, *Bomber Pilot* (Lexington, Ky., 1978); Elmer Bendiner, *The Fall of Fortresses* (New York, 1980); and James A. Goodson, *Tumult in the Clouds* (New York, 1984).

On the dismal topic of the massive bombing of cities, three short essays are instructive: Robert C. Batchelder, "The Evolution of Mass Bombing," in his *The Irreversible Decision, 1939-1950* (Boston, 1962), 170-89; Michael Sherry, "The Slide to Total Air War," *The New Republic*, December 16, 1981, 20-25; and Earl R. Beck, "The Allied Bombing of Germany, 1942-1945, and the German Response: Dilemmas of Judgment," *German Studies Review* 5, no. 3 (October 1982), 325-37. For a brief review of prewar efforts to outlaw the bombing of cities, see Major Richard H. Wyman, USA, "The First Rules of Air Warfare," *Air University Review* 35, no. 3 (March-April 1984), 94-102.

Tactical aviation in World War II still awaits its historian. Helpful starting points are: William A. Jacobs, "Tactical Air Doctrine and AAF Close Air Support in the European Theater, 1944-1945," *Aerospace Historian* 27, no. 1 (March 1980), 35-49, which treats more than its title implies; Kent Roberts Greenfield, *Army Ground Forces and the Air-Ground Battle Team*, Historical Study No. 35, Army Ground Forces, 1948; Futrell, *Ideas, Concepts, Doctrine*; and Kohn and Harahan, *Air Superiority in World War II and Korea*.

Standard works on Soviet air power published since 1950 include: Asher Lee, *The Soviet Air Force* (New York, 1950); Robert A. Kilmarx, *A History of the Soviet Air Force* (New York, 1962); Robert Jackson, *The Red Falcons* (New York, 1970); Ray Wagner, ed., and Leland Fetzer, trans., *The Soviet Air Force in World War II: The Official History* (New York, 1973); Kenneth R. Whiting, *Soviet Air Power, 1917-1978* (Maxwell Air Force Base, Ala., 1979) and "Soviet Air Power in World War II," in *Air Power and Modern Warfare*, ed. Hurley and Ehrhart, 98-127; Alexander Boyd, *The Soviet Air Force since 1918* (New York, 1977); Robin Higham and Jacob W. Kipp, eds., *Soviet Aviation and Air Power* (Boulder, 1977); Robert P. Berman, *Soviet Air Power in Transition* (Washington, D.C., 1978); Von Hardesty, *Red Phoenix: The Rise of Soviet Air Power, 1941-1945* (Washington, D.C., 1982); Paul J. Murphy, ed., *The Soviet Air Forces* (Jefferson, N.C., 1984); and Joshua M. Epstein, *Measuring Military Power: The Soviet Air Threat to Europe* (Princeton, 1984). Compare Jacob W. Kipp, "Studies in Soviet Aviation and Air Power," *Aerospace Historian* 31, no. 1 (March 1984), 43-50, and Myron J. Smith, Jr., *The Soviet Air and Strategic Rocket Forces,*

1939-1980: A Guide to Sources in English (Santa Barbara, Calif., 1981). Each year, the March issue of *Air Force Magazine* is devoted to a full-scale updating on what is known of the Soviet air forces.

For the literature regarding air power in relation to nuclear weapons, see the bibliographical note for Lawrence Freedman's essay in this volume. For the best summary accounts of conventional air power between 1950 and 1982, see M. J. Armitage and R. A. Mason, *Air Power in the Nuclear Age* (Champaign, Ill., 1983) and the sources cited therein. The longest and by far the most extensive air power "laboratory" to date, the American experience in Indochina from 1960 through 1975, awaits its historian, whose efforts even a decade later are severely restricted owing to the failure of the U.S. government to pursue an aggressive program of declassifying the surviving documentary evidence. For English-language sources published through December 1977, see Myron J. Smith, Jr., *Air War Southeast Asia, 1961-1973* (Metuchen, N.J., 1979). A helpful supplement to Smith's bibliography is Richard Dean Burns and Milton Leitenberg, *The Wars in Vietnam, Cambodia, and Laos, 1945-1982: A Bibliographic Guide* (Santa Barbara, Calif., 1984); see especially chapter 7. Momyer, *Air Power in Three Wars*, provides the views of the senior American air commander. Armitage and Mason, *Air Power in the Nuclear Age*, has a valuable introductory chapter. Raphael Littauer and Norman Uphoff, eds., *The Air War In Indochina* (Boston, 1972) is highly critical but nonetheless balanced. The USAF Office of Air Force History has published at least six volumes of its series entitled, *The United States Air Force in Southeast Asia*; these are listed, along with other sources, in Michael Gorn and Charles J. Gross, "Published Air Force History: Still on the Runway," *Aerospace Historian* 31, no. 1 (March 1984), 30-37. Occasional insights on Indochina can be found as well in Kohn and Harahan, *Air Superiority in World War II and Korea*, such as retired Lt. General Elwood R. Quesada's characterization of the air effort in Vietnam as "a little bit of what I used to refer to as operational masturbation" (pp. 69-70). For naval air power in Vietnam, see Naval Historical Center, *A Select Bibliography of the United States Navy and the Southeast Asian Conflict, 1950-1975*, rev. ed. (Washington, D.C., November 1983).

Finally, although it is not yet the province of the historian, the emerging trends in the technology of airpower, especially in electronics, can be glimpsed in R. A. Mason, *Readings in Air Power* (Bracknell, England, 1980), one chapter of which presents a brief survey of contemporary developments in technology and their possible implications for the future application of air power. Mason (with Armitage) develops these points further in chapter 9 of *Air Power in the Nuclear Age*. Two provocative essays on the potential for remotely-piloted vehicles are: John S. Sanders, "World Without Man," *Defense and Foreign Affairs*, Paris Air Show edition (1981); and Michael C. Dunn, "Bringing 'em Back Alive," *Defense and Foreign Affairs* (May 1984), 25-27.

22. THE MAKING OF SOVIET STRATEGY

An abundance of material is available to the student of the evolution of Soviet strategy; there are a number of excellent works in English, and the Soviets have produced a voluminous literature on the subject. The Soviet sources must be used with a clear understanding of the prevailing political conditions at any given time. For instance, in order to achieve a balanced view of the role of Josef Stalin, one must not rely on either pre-1956 works, which slavishly worship him, or works written during Khrushchev's reign, which vilify him. With such caveats in mind, one finds Soviet historiography useful on a wide-ranging set of issues.

Background on the history of foreign and domestic policy in the Soviet Union can be acquired through Adam Ulam's excellent *Expansion and Coexistence*, 2d ed. (Cambridge, Mass., 1974). The history of the Soviet Communist Party is chronicled by Leonard Shapiro in *The Communist Party of the Soviet Union*. The thought of Karl Marx and Friedrich Engels on the military is scattered among their collected works. The most useful include Friedrich Engels on the role of force in history in *Anti-Dühring*, trans. Emile Burns and ed. C. P. Dutt (New York, 1939) and Engels, *Izbrannye voennye proizvedeniia* (Moscow, 1957). General points about the problem of the counterrevolutinary nature of the armed forces can be understood through a reading of "The Eighteenth Brumaire of Louis Bonaparte" in Karl Marx and Friedrich Engels, *Selected Works* (New York, 1974).

The best single source on the creation of the Red Army is John Erickson, *The Soviet High Command* (New York and London, 1962). Soviet sources on this period include L. D. Trotsky, *Kak voorazhalas' revoliutsiia*, 3 vols. (Moscow, 1925) and a more dispassionate account by N. I. Shatagin, *Organizatsiya i stroitel'stvo sovetskoi armii v period inostrannoi interventsii i grazhdanskoi voiny* (Moscow, 1954). The Polish campaign is examined in an excellent Soviet study by N. E. Kakurin and V. A. Melikov, *Voina s belopolyakhami* (Moscow, 1925). A number of older works on the Red Army are still valuable. These include Max Werner, *The Military Strength of the Powers* (New York, 1939) and D. Feodotoff-White, *The Growth of the Red Army* (Princeton, 1943).

The most valuable study of the evolution of Soviet military thought is Raymond Garthoff, *Soviet Military Doctrine* (Santa Monica, Calif., 1954). English language sources specifically on the impact of the civil war on Soviet thought are sparse; John Erickson's book is the most useful. The Soviets, however, have written extensively on this subject. One particularly interesting book is S. I. Aralov, *V. I. Lenin i krasnaia armiia* (Moscow, 1958). The primary sources on the Trotsky-Frunze debates include Frunze's collected works, *Sobranie sochinenii*, ed. A. S. Bubnov (Moscow, 1927) and the numerous editions of the selected works, *Izbrannye proizvedeniia* (Moscow, 1934, 1950, 1957, 1965). A useful English-language source on the thought of Mikhail Frunze and the debates is Walter Darnell Jacob, *Frunze: The Soviet Clausewitz: 1885-1925* (The Hague, 1969). See also V. Triandafilov, *The Character of Operations of Modern Armies* (Moscow, 1929); Mikhail Tukhachevsky, "War as a Problem of Military Struggle," in the *Great Soviet Encyclopedia*, vol. 12 (1934); Boris Shaposhnikov, *Mogz armii* (Moscow, 1927); and A. A. Svechin, *Strategiia* (Moscow, 1927).

The period of the late 1920s until the purges is chronicled in some of the richest Soviet historiographic material available. See for instance, a recent collection of brief essays edited by I. A. Korotkov, *Istoriia sovetskoi voennoi mysli:*

Kratki ocherk 1917 iyun-1941 (Moscow, 1980). I. Tyushkevich, *Stroitel'stvo vooruzhenniykh sil'* (Moscow, 1980) is also detailed, current, and dispassionate. *Voprosy strategii i operativnogo iskusstva v sovetskikh voennykh trudakh 1917-1940*, edited by A. B. Kadishev, is excellent if somewhat more technical (Moscow, 1965). The biographical literature from this period is also useful; especially informative is Lev Nikulin, *Tukhachevskii: biograficheskii ocherk* (Moscow, 1964).

The Second World War is the dominant experience in Soviet military history and as such is the subject of an enormous and growing literature. The six-volume *Istoriya velikoi otechestvennoi voiny Sovetskogo Soyuza* (Moscow, 1955) is the official history. The general staff has also produced a number of histories that are less polemical, including *Vtoraya mirovaya voina 1939-1945*, edited by Lt. General S. P. Platonov and Col. I. V. Parotkhin (Moscow, 1960). There is also a rich, if diffuse, memoir literature. S. M. Shtemenko's two-volume *Generalnii stab v gody voiny* (Moscow, 1973) is a fine example. It is available in English as *The General Staff in the Years of the War* (New York, 1976). The best English-language sources include John Erickson's epic works *The Road to Stalingrad* (New York, 1975) and *The Road to Berlin* (New York, 1983).

The evolution and development of the Soviet military commissar system has been brilliantly researched by Timothy Colton in *Commissars, Commanders, and Civilian Authority: The Structure of Soviet Military Politics* (Cambridge, Mass., 1979), which covers all periods in Soviet military history.

23. ALLIED STRATEGY IN EUROPE, 1939-1945

Literature dealing with Allied strategy in the Second World War is voluminous, varied, and scattered in official and unofficial sources. Among the most valuable of the secondary sources are the multivolume officially sponsored historical series, based on the massive collections of primary records in the national archives of Great Britain and the United States, and produced by the official historical offices of those countries after the war. Particularly useful on the British side are the volumes in the Grand Strategy subseries of the History of the Second World War, United Kingdom Military Series, edited by J. R. M. Butler. Pertinent works on American strategy as it evolved in Washington, the overseas theaters, and in international meetings are in the U.S. Army in World War II series, edited by Kent R. Greenfield, in the History of U.S. Naval Operations in World War II series, produced by Samuel E. Morison, and in the Army Air Forces in World War II series, edited by Wesley F. Craven and James L. Cate.

Biographies and memoirs of the leading British and American political and military leaders contain valuable information but naturally vary in quality. On the British side, the masterful volumes by Winston S. Churchill in his series, *The Second World War*, based on primary material as well as his recollections, are of enormous value for the study of war strategy and statesmanship. Unfortunately, President Franklin D. Roosevelt did not leave memoirs. The correspondence of Churchill and Roosevelt has been collected in *Churchill and Roosevelt, The*

Complete Correspondence, ed. Warren F. Kimball, 3 vols. (Princeton, 1984). Secondary literature on Roosevelt's war leadership continues to grow. Robert E. Sherwood, *Roosevelt and Hopkins: An Intimate History*, rev. ed. (New York, 1950), a vivid, often firsthand account, remains one of the most useful published volumes on wartime strategy and policy. For an analysis of Roosevelt's wartime role and policies see Maurice Matloff, "Mr. Roosevelt's Three Wars: FDR as War Leader," Harmon Memorial Lecture in Military History, no. 6, United States Air Force Academy (Colorado, 1964) and the same author's essay, "Franklin Roosevelt as War Leader," in *Total War and Cold War*, ed. Harry L. Coles (Columbus, 1962). For an appraisal of American leadership in the Second World War, including the relations of the President and his military advisors, and their successes and failures, see the essay by Maurice Matloff, "The Limits of Tradition: American Leadership in World War II Reconsidered," in *The Second World War as a National Experience*, ed. Sidney Aster (Ottawa, 1981). A valuable treatment of American strategy and policy, as viewed by the secretary of war, is contained in the account by Henry L. Stimson and McGeorge Bundy, *On Active Service in Peace and War* (New York, 1948). John R. Deane, *The Strange Alliance* (New York, 1947) remains an accurate and illuminating eyewitness account of Anglo-American and Soviet wartime collaboration. Useful accounts by the wartime members of the Joint Chiefs of Staff are the memoirs of General Henry H. Arnold, Admiral Ernest J. King, and Admiral William D. Leahy. General George C. Marshall, the army chief of staff, did not leave memoirs of his wartime service but Forrest C. Pogue's multivolume biography, based on a careful appraisal of the primary and secondary sources and numerous interviews with him, supplies an important part of the story.

For a fuller discussion of American strategic planning before 1941 see Mark S. Watson, *Chief of Staff: Prewar Plans and Preparations* (Washington, D.C., 1950), especially chapters 1-5, 10, in the official U.S. Army in World War II series; Maurice Matloff and Edwin M. Snell, *Strategic Planning for Coalition Warfare, 1941-1942* (Washington, D.C., 1953), chapters 1-3; Maurice Matloff, "The American Approach to War, 1919-1945," in *The Theory and Practice of War*, ed. Michael Howard (London, 1965); and Maurice Matloff, "Prewar Military Plans and Preparations, 1939-1941," *United States Naval Institute Proceedings* 79 (July 1953).

On the development of the Bolero plan and the decision for Torch, see Matloff and Snell, *Strategic Planning for Coalition Warfare, 1941-1942*, chapters 8, 12, 13; Sherwood, *Roosevelt and Hopkins*, chapters 23, 25; Stimson and Bundy, *On Active Service in Peace and War*, chapter 17; and Winston S. Churchill, *The Hinge of Fate* (Boston, 1950), book 1, chapters 18, 22 and book 2, chapter 2.

The midwar debate over Anglo-American strategy is treated in detail in Maurice Matloff, *Strategic Planning for Coalition Warfare, 1943-1944* (Washington, D.C., 1953); Michael Howard, *Grand Strategy*, vol. 4, August 1942-September 1943 (London, 1972); John Ehrman, *Grand Strategy*, vol. 5, August 1943-September 1944 (London, 1956); Churchill, *The Hinge of Fate* and *Closing the Ring* (Boston, 1951). The volumes by Michael Howard and John Ehrman are part of the History of the Second World War, United Kingdom Military Series.

Details of the discussion on the Teheran Conference may be found in Churchill, *Closing the Ring*, chapters 4, 5, 6; Sherwood, *Roosevelt and Hopkins*, chapter 23; Matloff, *Strategic Planning for Coalition Warfare, 1943-1944*, chapter 16; and Ehrman, *Grand Strategy*, vol. 5, chapter 4. See also U.S. Department of State, *The Conferences at Cairo and Tehran, 1943* (Washington, D.C., 1961).

Details of the Anglo-American debate in the early months of 1944 are traced in Matloff, *Strategic Planning for Coalition Warfare, 1943-1944*, chapters 18, 21; Gordon A. Harrison, *Cross-Channel Attack* (Washington, D.C., 1951), chapter 5, and Forrest C. Pogue, *The Supreme Command* (Washington, D.C., 1954), chapters 6, 12, both volumes in the official U.S. Army in World War II series; Ehrman, *Grand Strategy*, vol. 5, chapters 6, 7, 9; Churchill, *Closing the Ring*, chapter 11, and *Triumph and Tragedy* (Boston, 1953), chapter 4. For an analysis of the last phase of the debate over European strategy see Maurice Matloff, "The Anvil Decision: Crossroads of Strategy," in *Command Decisions*, ed. Kent R. Greenfield (Washington, D.C., 1960).

For the detailed story of American strategy and planning for the war in the Pacific, see particularly Louis Morton, *Strategy and Command, The First Two Years* (Washington, D.C., 1961); Philip A. Crowl, *Campaign in the Marianas* (Washington, D.C., 1959); and Robert Ross Smith, *Triumph in the Philippines* (Washington, D.C., 1963), all volumes in the U.S. Army in World War II series; Samuel E. Morison, *Aleutians, Gilberts and Marshalls, New Guinea and the Marianas*, and *Victory in the Pacific*, vols. 7, 8, and 14 (Boston, 1951-60) in the History of U.S. Naval Operations in World War II series; and Greenfield, *Command Decisions*, chapters 11, 21.

Particularly useful for American wartime policies and relations with the Soviet Union are the contemporary sources incorporated in two official documentaries, *The Entry of the Soviet Union into the War against Japan: Military Plans 1941-1945*, Department of Defense Press Release, September, 1955; and U.S. Department of State, *The Conferences at Malta and Yalta, 1945* (Washington, D.C., 1955). For summary analyses of American politico-military relations with the Soviet Union in the war against Japan and Germany respectively, see Ernest R. May, "The United States, the Soviet Union, and the Far Eastern War, 1941-1945," *Pacific Historical Review* 24 (May 1955); and Maurice Matloff, "The Soviet Union and the War in the West," *United States Naval Institute Proceedings* 82 (March 1956).

24. AMERICAN AND JAPANESE STRATEGIES IN THE PACIFIC WAR

In general, the English-language literature on American and Japanese strategies preceding and during the war of 1941-1945 has been characterized by emphasis on the prewar period, especially the diplomatic and naval strategic aspects; and by the nearly total lack of translation of important studies by Japanese scholars (nor are there plans yet for an English edition of the Japan Self-Defense Agency's ongoing multivolume history of the war).

For the era from the First World War to Pearl Harbor, the best books are Roger Dingman, *Power in the Pacific: The Origins of Naval Arms Limitation, 1914-1922* (Chicago, 1976); Akira Iriye, *After Imperialism: The Search for a New Order in the Far East, 1921-1933* (Cambridge, Mass., 1965); Dorothy Borg, *The United States and the Far Eastern Crisis of 1933-1938* (Cambridge, Mass., 1964); Stephen E. Pelz, *Race to Pearl Harbor: The Failure of the Second London Naval Conference and the Onset of World War II* (Cambridge, Mass., 1974); Dorothy Borg and Shumpei Okamoto, eds., *Pearl Harbor as History: Japanese-American Relations, 1931-1941* (New York, 1973); Robert J. C. Butow, *Tojo and the Coming of the War* (Princeton, 1961); and Gordon W. Prange et al., *At Dawn We Slept: The Untold Story of Pearl Harbor* (New York, 1981).

Three recent works stand out as the most thoughtful and sound on American and Japanese national strategies during the Second World War: Akira Iriye, *Power and Culture: The Japanese-American War, 1941-1945* (Cambridge, Mass., 1981), the starting point for any serious student; Christopher Thorne, *Allies of a Kind: The United States, Britain, and the War against Japan, 1941-1945* (New York, 1978), a searching and disturbing analysis; and Michael Schaller, *The U.S. Crusade in China, 1938-1945* (New York, 1979), a provocative reexamination of a subject about which much has been written.

There is no single volume on Japanese and American, or Allied, national and military strategies in the Pacific war. Perceptive but brief studies on overall Anglo-American military strategy are Kent R. Greenfield, *American Strategy in World War II: A Reconsideration* (Baltimore, 1963); and Samuel E. Morison, *Strategy and Compromise* (Boston, 1958).

The American, British, Australian, New Zealand, and Indian official histories of the Second World War all contain volumes on the war with Japan, some of which devote valuable sections to strategy. For the most part, however, the emphasis is on operations. The United Kingdom series includes a volume on British foreign policy and three on grand strategy that contain much data about American strategy making for the Pacific. Two volumes that are indispensable on American military strategy in the war against Japan are Louis Morton, *Strategy and Command: The First Two Years*, United States Army in World War II: The War in the Pacific (Washington, D.C., 1962); and Grace P. Hayes, *The History of the Joint Chiefs of Staff in World War II: The War against Japan* (Annapolis, 1982), which actually was completed in 1953. Additional volumes in the United States Army in World War II series that have a great deal of information on the evolution of United States military strategy in the Pacific conflict are Maurice Matloff and Edwin M. Snell, *Strategic Planning for Coalition Warfare, 1941-1942* (Washington, D.C., 1953); Maurice Matloff, *Strategic Planning for Coalition Warfare, 1943-1944* (Washington, D.C., 1959); Richard M. Leighton and Robert W. Coakley, *Global Logistics and Strategy, 1940-1943* (Washington, D.C., 1955); and Robert W. Coakley and Richard M. Leighton, *Global Logistics and Strategy, 1943-1945* (Washington, D.C., 1968). The first three volumes of

927

Charles A. Willoughby, ed., *Reports of General MacArthur*, 4 vols. (Washington, D.C., 1966), cover both American and Japanese strategy and tactics in Southwest Pacific operations.

25. THE FIRST TWO GENERATIONS OF NUCLEAR STRATEGISTS

In addition to my *Evolution of Nuclear Strategy* (London, 1981), there are a number of general histories of nuclear strategy. Donald Snow, *Nuclear Strategy in a Dynamic World* (University, Ala., 1981) provides a broad overview. Michael Mandelbaum's *The Nuclear Question* (Cambridge and New York, 1979) is a not wholly satisfactory history, concentrating too much on the Kennedy period; by contrast, his *The Nuclear Revolution* (Cambridge and New York, 1981) is far more substantial and contains many interesting insights on the changes to the international system resulting from the advent of nuclear weapons. Fred Kaplan's *The Wizards of Armageddon: Strategists of the Nuclear Age* (New York, 1983) is anecdoctal and lacking in breadth, but it contains much of interest on the nuclear strategists themselves, especially those involved with the Rand Corporation. From a completely different perspective, Colin Gray's *Strategic Studies and Public Policy* (Lexington, Ky., 1982) provides a critical assessment of the performance of the American strategic studies community. The most impressive detailed research on the development of U.S. strategic policy has been conducted by David Alan Rosenberg. His "The Origins of Overkill: Nuclear Weapons and American Strategy, 1945-1960," *International Security* 7, no. 4 (Spring 1983) is particularly important.

The first major academic work on nuclear strategy was edited by Bernard Brodie, *The Absolute Weapon* (New York, 1946). His *Strategy in the Missile Age* (Princeton, 1959) was the first textbook on the subject and remains an extremely valuable introduction. Brodie became more and more disenchanted with developments in strategic thinking. This is reflected in his *Escalation and the Nuclear Option* (Princeton, 1966) and in a collection of essays, *War and Politics* (London, 1973).

The public image of nuclear strategists came to be dominated by the formidable figure of Herman Kahn. His first book, based on a famous lecture series, was *On Thermonuclear War* (Princeton, 1960). The second, titled in response to criticism of the first, was *Thinking about the Unthinkable* (New York, 1962). His third, and possibly his best, was *On Escalation: Metaphors and Scenarios* (New York, 1965).

Thomas Schelling has probably had a more lasting influence in terms of the conceptual framework within which nuclear issues are commonly understood, and his writing is imaginative and rich in insight. His two best-known books are *The Strategy of Conflict* (New York, 1960) and *Arms and Influence* (New Haven, 1966). Less well known but a useful exposition of his basic approach is a pamphlet published by the Institute for Strategic Studies in London in June 1965, *Controlled Response and Strategic Warfare: Strategy and Arms Control* (New York, 1962), writtten in collaboration with Morton Halperin, which provides an early discussion of the concept of arms control.

Albert Wohlstetter has exercised a considerable influence on the development of contemporary strategic thinking, especially in its relationship to policy making. He has not written any full-length books but has contributed a number of significant articles. The most important of these is "The Delicate Balance of Terror," *Foreign Affairs* 37, no. 2 (January 1959). Two articles published in successive issues of *Foreign Policy*, "Is There a Strategic Arms Race?" and "Rivals but No Race" (Summer and Fall 1974), had a major impact on the public debate.

These writers all made their names during the "golden age" of contemporary strategic studies, which lasted from the mid-1950s to the mid-1960s. The other seminal works of this period were William Kaufmann, ed., *Military Policy and National Security* (Princeton, 1956), Robert Endicott Osgood, *Limited War: The Challenge to American Strategy* (Chicago, 1957), and Henry Kissinger, *Nuclear Weapons and Foreign Policy* (New York, 1957). These were all written in response to what were seen to be the deficiencies in the policy of "massive retaliation." Another important book of this period was Glenn Snyder, *Deterrence and Defense* (Princeton, 1961).

After this period the most important analyses of nuclear strategic issues tended to come from American secretaries of defense. Robert McNamara in particular set the terms of the debate for many years, both during his tenure at the Pentagon from 1961 to 1968 and after. His basic ideas are contained in essays derived from his annual statements to Congress but published after his resignation: *The Essence of Security: Reflections in Office* (London, 1968). James Schlesinger was the first strategist actually to become secretary of defense. His presentations to Congress of early 1974 and 1975 convey his attempt to reorient U.S. strategy away from the approach laid down by McNamara. This attempt continued in the late 1970s under the Carter administration. See for example Walter Slocombe "The Countervailing Strategy," *International Security* 5, no. 4 (Spring 1981).

Among academic strategists attempting to push U.S. policy even further away from the McNamara approach, Colin Gray has been particularly active. An article that gained considerable attention was written with Keith Payne, "Victory is Possible," *Foreign Policy*, no. 39 (Summer 1980). An example of the reaction to this sort of argument, and one based firmly in the concepts of the "golden age" is Robert Jervis, *The Illogic of American Nuclear Strategy* (Ithaca, 1984).

26. CONVENTIONAL WARFARE IN THE NUCLEAR AGE

Literature discussing the theory of how wars might or should be conducted with conventional forces in the nuclear age is sparse. The minds of those who have thought and written about war since 1945 have naturally been dominated by the problems raised by nuclear weapons. There is a vast field of literature on that subject, within which conventional operations are generally considered as a phase in or adjunct to ones including nuclear weapons, and little attention is given to how they are conducted. There was a tendency, particularly in the late 1950s and early 1960s to think that the only form of conventional war likely to occur under the shadow of nuclear weapons was some form of guerrilla or so-called brush-fire war.

Basil H. Liddell Hart was an exception. His *Defence of the West* (London, 1950) and *Deterrent or Defence* (London, 1960) are important books, both collections of essays or lectures dealing with the form wars might take and how forces should be organized to fight them. The need to escape from being mesmerized by nuclear weapons and to have armed forces capable of fighting limited wars without them was also emphasized by Robert E. Osgood in his important book *Limited War* (Chicago, 1957) and by General Maxwell D. Taylor, the author of flexible response, in his *The Uncertain Trumpet* (New York, 1959). Other important contributions to the discussion at that time were Morton H. Halperin, *Limited War in the Nuclear Age* (New York and London, 1963) and his later *Contemporary Military Strategy* (Boston, 1967). Henry Kissinger, *The Necessity for Choice* (London, 1960) is important in recording the change in his views about limited war from those given in his *Nuclear Weapons and Foreign Policy* (New York, 1957).

A typical wide-ranging British military view of the time is given in E. J. Kingston-McCloughry, *Global Strategy* (London, 1957). A more theoretical one from the French is contained in Raymond Aron, *The Great Debate* (New York, 1965) and General André Beaufre's important books, *An Introduction to Strategy* (Paris, 1963; London, 1965) and *Strategy of Action* (Paris, 1966; London, 1967). Valuable collections of essays, some of which deal with the theoretical aspects of conventional war in the nuclear age, are to be found in *Problems of Modern Strategy*, edited by Alastair Buchan for the International Institute of Strategic Studies (London, 1980); *Arms and Stability in Europe*, edited by Alastair Buchan and Philip Windsor for the same institute in conjunction with Le Centre d'Etudes de Politique Etrangère and Die Deutsche Gesellschaft für Auswärtige Politik (London, 1963); *La securité de l'Europe dans les années 80*, edited by Pierre Lellouche for the Institut Français des Rélations Internationaux (Paris, 1980); and *New Directions in Strategic Thinking*, edited by Robert O'Neill and D. M. Horner (London, 1981). Robert Osgood, *Limited War Revisited* (Boulder, 1979) adjusted his views in the light of the end of the Vietnam War, and both Shelford Bidwell, *Modern Warfare* (London, 1973) and Julian Lider, *Military Theory* (New York, 1983) review warfare with a broad brush.

The author's own *War since 1945* (London, 1980; New York, 1981) describes and comments on the conventional conflicts referred to in the essay and contains a full bibliography covering them.

The particular problem of the conventional defense of Western Europe is covered by a number of pamphlets, articles, and books, of which some of the most valuable are: "A Conventional Strategy for the Central Front in NATO," report of a seminar at the Royal United Services Institute, London, 1975; Robert Komer, "Needed—Preparation for Coalition War," Rand Paper, August, 1976; Ulrich de Maizière, "Armed Forces in the NATO Alliance," Georgetown University, 1976; "The Wrong Force for the Right Mission," edited by Goebel, Queen's University, Ontario, 1981; "Central Region: Forward Defense," by Freeman, U.S. National Defense University, 1981; Ian Bellany et al., "Conventional Forces and the European Balance," Lancaster University, 1981; and General Ferdinand von Senger u. Etterlin, "Defence of Central Europe—the Challenge of the 1980s," *Fifteen Nations*, special issue no. 2 (1981). *Strengthening Conventional Deterrence in Europe*, a report of the European Security Study (London and New York, 1983), provides a recent assessment and incorporates valuable papers by experts in different aspects of the issue. *Not Over by Christmas*, by P. Griffith and E. Dinter (Chichester, 1983), puts forward a less orthodox view.

There is a plethora of literature on the Soviet perspective. Those who wish to wade through the turgid prose of the original material can read Marshal Vasili Sokolovskiy, *Soviet Military Strategy* (New York, 1975); *Selected Readings from Soviet Military Thought, 1963-1973*, edited by Joseph Douglas and Amoretta Hoeber (Arlington, Va., 1980); or Harriet F. Scott and William F. Scott, *The Soviet Art of War* (Boulder, 1982). A series of essays is to be found in *Soviet Military Thinking*, edited by Derek Leebaert (Cambridge, Mass., and London, 1981); *Soviet Military Power and Performance*, edited by John Erickson and E. J. Feuchtwanger (London, 1979); and *Soviet Strategy*, edited by John Baylis and Gerald Segal (London, 1981). Christopher Donnelly's articles on various aspects of the subject in the *International Defense Review* (vol. 11, no. 9, 1978; vol. 12, no. 7, 1979; vol. 14, no. 9, 1981; vol. 15, no. 9, 1982) are of high quality, as is the contribution of Donnelly and others to part 2 of *Strengthening Conventional Deterrence in Europe*. The best and most readable volume covering the whole subject is Joseph D. Douglass, *Soviet Military Strategy in Europe* (New York, 1980).

27. REVOLUTIONARY WAR

The literature of the subject is enormous and virtually unmanageable; even bibliographies relevant to revolutionary war are of overwhelming length. Recent examples are Myron J. Smith, Jr., *The Secret Wars: A Guide to the Sources*, 3 vols. (Santa Barbara, Calif., and Oxford, 1980), which deals only with 1939-1980; Robert Blackey, *Modern Revolutions and Revolutionists* (Santa Barbara, Calif., 1976); Edward F. Mickolus, *The Literature of Terrorism: A Selected Annotated Bibliography* (Westport, Conn., 1980); and Christopher L. Sugnet et al., *Vietnam War Bibliography* (Lexington, Mass., and Toronto, 1983).

Comprehensive general works include Robert Asprey, *War in the Shadows: The Guerilla in History*, 2 vols. (Garden City, N.Y., 1975), and the trilogy of Walter Laquer: *Guerrilla* (Boston, 1976), *The Guerrilla Reader: A Historical Anthology* (Philadelphia, 1977), and *Terrorism* (Boston, 1977). Fifty-seven historical cases are treated in D. M. Condit, Bert H. Cooper, Jr. et al., eds., *Challenge and Response in Internal Conflict*, 3 vols. (Washington, D.C., 1967). An early effort to treat the subject broadly and systematically is Harry Eckstein, ed., *Internal War, Problems and Approaches* (New York, 1964).

The writings of Mao Tse-tung are of central importance. The four-volume *Selected Works* (London and New York, 1954-56) is basic, while the *Selected Military Writings* (Peking, 1963) usefully collects essays from the larger work. His ideas are analyzed in Samuel B. Griffith, *Mao Tse-tung on Guerrilla Warfare* (New York, 1961), which includes a translation of the 1937 essay Yu Chi Chan (Guerrilla Warfare). The most widely read version is *Chairman Mao Tse-tung on People's War* (Peking, 1967), compiled by Lin Piao, and generally known as the "little red book." Of the various compilations, that by Philippe Devillers, *Mao* (London, 1969), has been most useful.

Among contemporary students of revolutionary war, Gérard Chaliand is one of the most incisive. *Revolution in the Third World* (New York, 1977) brings together the results of both research and direct involvement in several revolutionary movements, and is complemented by his compilation, *Guerrilla Strategies: An Historical Anthology from the Long March to Afghanistan* (Berkeley, 1982). Peter Paret explored counterrevolutionary theory in *French Revolutionary Warfare from Indochina to Algeria* (New York, 1964), and with John Shy wrote an early introduction to revolutionary warfare, *Guerrillas in the 1960s*, 2d ed. (New York, 1962). Many American readers first encountered Maoist theory in Edward L. Katzenbach and Gene Z. Hanrahan, "The Revolutionary Strategy of Mao Tse-tung," *Political Science Quarterly* 70 (1955), 321-40, and first learned about the Vietnamese revolution from Bernard Fall, *Street Without Joy* (New York, 1957). Notable among the many "experts" on counterrevolutionary war are Roger Trinquier, *Modern Warfare: A French View of Counterinsurgency* (New York, 1964), and Robert Thompson, *Revolutionary War in World Strategy, 1945-1969* (New York, 1970). Of special interest for its heroic and controversial effort to apply classical Western theory to a revolutionary war is Harry G. Summers, Jr., *On Strategy: The Vietnam War in Context* (Novato, Calif., 1982).

Index

933

II. Chronological List of the More Important Wars and Campaigns